IMPORTANT

HERE IS YOUR REGISTRATION CODE TO ACCESS MCGRAW-HILL PREMIUM CONTENT AND MCGRAW-HILL ONLINE RESOURCES

For key premium online resources you need THIS CODE to gain access. Once the code is entered, you will be able to use the web resources for the length of your course.

Access is provided only if you have purchased a new book.

If the registration code is missing from this book, the registration screen on our website, and within your WebCT or Blackboard course will tell you how to obtain your new code. Your registration code can be used only once to establish access. It is not transferable.

To gain access to these online resources

1. **USE** your web browser to go to: **www.mhhe.com/franzoi4**

2. **CLICK** on "First Time User"

3. **ENTER** the Registration Code printed on the tear-off bookmark on the right

4. After you have entered your registration code, click on "Register"

5. **FOLLOW** the instructions to setup your personal UserID and Password

6. **WRITE** your UserID and Password down for future reference. Keep it in a safe place.

If your course is using WebCT or Blackboard, you'll be able to use this code to access the McGraw-Hill content within your instructor's online course.

To gain access to the McGraw-Hill content in your instructor's WebCT or Blackboard course simply log into the course with the user ID and Password provided by your instructor. Enter the registration code exactly as it appears to the right when prompted by the system. You will only need to use this code the first time you click on McGraw-Hill content.

These instructions are specifically for student access. Instructors are not required to register via the above instructions.

The McGraw-Hill Companies
Mc Graw Hill **Higher Education**

Thank you, and welcome to your McGraw-Hill Online Resources.

ISBN-13: 978-0-07-313735-3
ISBN-10: 0-07-313735-9 t/a
Franzoi
Social Psychology, 4/e

SOCIAL PSYCHOLOGY

Fourth Edition

SOCIAL PSYCHOLOGY

Stephen L. Franzoi

Marquette University

Boston   Burr Ridge, IL   Dubuque, IA   Madison, WI   New York   San Francisco   St. Louis
Bangkok   Bogotá   Caracas   Kuala Lumpur   Lisbon   London   Madrid   Mexico City
Milan   Montreal   New Delhi   Santiago   Seoul   Singapore   Sydney   Taipei   Toronto

Higher Education

SOCIAL PSYCHOLOGY

Published by McGraw-Hill, a business unit of The McGraw-Hill Companies, Inc., 1221 Avenue of the Americas, New York, NY, 10020. Copyright © 2006, 2003, 2000, 1996 by The McGraw-Hill Companies, Inc. All rights reserved. No part of this publication may be reproduced or distributed in any form or by any means, or stored in a database or retrieval system, without the prior written consent of The McGraw-Hill Companies, Inc., including, but not limited to, in any network or other electronic storage or transmission, or broadcast for distance learning.

Some ancillaries, including electronic and print components, may not be available to customers outside the United States.
This book is printed on acid-free paper.

2 3 4 5 6 7 8 9 0 VNH/VNH 0 9 8 7 6

ISBN-13: 978-0-07-296747-0
ISBN-10: 0-07-296747-1

Editor in Chief: *Emily Barrosse*
Executive Editor: *Mike Sugarman*
Marketing Manager: *Melissa Caughlin*
Director of Development: *Judith Kromm*
Editorial Coordinator: *Kate Russillo*
Managing Editor: *Jean Dal Porto*
Project Manager: *Ruth Smith*
Senior Production Supervisor: *Richard DeVitto*
Associate Designer: *Srdjan Savanovic*
Cover Designer: *Joan Greenfield*
Art Editor: *Katherine McNab*
Photo Research Coordinator: *Nora Agbayani*
Photo Researcher: *Judy Mason*
Cover Credit: *Background photo: © Superstock; Interracial couple: © Stockbyte; Black man: © Creatas*
Media Project Manager: *Alex Rohrs*
Senior Media Producer: *Stephanie George*
Permissions Editor: *Marty Granahan*
Typeface: *10/12 Times Roman*
Compositor: *Carlisle Communications, Ltd.*
Printer: *Von Hoffmann Press*

Credits: The credits section for this book begins on page C-1 and is considered an extension of the copyright page.

Library of Congress Cataloging-in-Publication Data

Franzoi, Stephen L.
    Social psychology / Stephen L. Franzoi.—4th ed.
        p. cm.
    Includes bibliographical references and index.
    ISBN 0-07-296747-1 (alk. paper)
    1. Social psychology. I. Title.
  HM1033.F73 2006
                            2004061074

The Internet addresses listed in the text were accurate at the time of publication. The inclusion of a Web site does not indicate an endorsement by the authors of McGraw-Hill, and McGraw-Hill does not guarantee the accuracy of the information presented at these sites.

www.mhhe.com

ABOUT THE AUTHOR

Stephen L. Franzoi is a professor of psychology at Marquette University in Milwaukee, Wisconsin. Born and raised in Iron Mountain, Michigan, he received his B.S. in both psychology and sociology from Western Michigan University and his Ph.D. in Psychology from the University of California at Davis. He also was a post-doctoral fellow in the NIMH-sponsored Self Program at Indiana University and served as assistant editor of *Social Psychology Quarterly.* At Marquette University, Professor Franzoi teaches both undergraduate and graduate courses in social psychology. He is the author of the textbook *Psychology: A Journey of Discovery* (third edition), is an active researcher in the areas of body esteem and self-awareness, and is currently the associate editor of *Social Problems.* Over the years, Dr. Franzoi has discussed his research in such media outlets as the *New York Times, USA Today,* National Public Radio, and the *Oprah Winfrey Show.* Because of his desire to apply social psychological knowledge to real-world problems, Dr. Franzoi regularly provides gender equity and multicultural workshops to schools and organizations, including NAACP-sponsored programs. He and Cheryl Figg are the proud parents of Amelia, and Lillian.

BRIEF CONTENTS

C O N T E N T S

CHAPTER 7

Persuasion   211

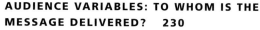

CHAPTER 8

Prejudice and Discrimination 251

PART THREE

UNDERSTANDING OUR PLACE WITHIN THE GROUP   307

CHAPTER 9

Social Influence   309

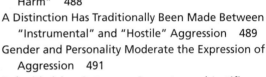

CHAPTER **14**

Prosocial Behavior: Helping Others   531

$\mathcal{T}$ hese are exciting times for social psychologists! In the past few years, world events have kept many concepts from social psychology in the headlines. We read about children in New York raising money for the victims of the tsunami that devastated parts of South Asia in 2004 and applaud their altruistic act. We hear about the abuse of prisoners by military guards and interrogators and wonder why no one did anything to prevent it. And in the policy arena, some officials ask whether the emphasis in the public schools on developing self-esteem has left too many young adults unable to read and write well enough to get a decent job. These stories are inherently captivating, but they also hint at other great stories, stories about social psychology research on altruism, on self-awareness, and on the possible negative effects of high self-esteem.

One of the most important lessons I have learned as a teacher is that you should always have a good story to tell. Fortunately, social psychology is a dynamic science consisting of many fascinating stories. These "scientific stories" form the basis of this text, and my goal as an instructor and a textbook author is to emphasize the process of research in social psychology: to engage students in an exploration of how what we know about social psychology has evolved, to put students in the mind-set of the social psychologists who have left their mark on the field. Together, we explore the stories behind these classic and contemporary studies.

As a textbook author, I've learned that the text, too, must have its own story—one that resonates with students and instructors alike and helps tie all of the various theories and concepts together. In this fourth edition, I continue to emphasize a central theme—one that has worked well for me and my students—that I believe is essential to how we think about social psychology, and one that will encourage students to think about their own stories as they explore the concepts in this course.

THE SELF: AN INTEGRATED THEME

Social psychology is sometimes described as a scientific discipline consisting of loosely connected research topics with no "grand theory" to connect everything. Although we have no single theory that neatly packages social psychology for our students, I end the analysis of the topic areas in each chapter with a discussion of how these particular theories and studies "fit" into our overall understanding of social behavior. Throughout the text I emphasize a core concept in social psychology: *the self*. Social psychology is the study of how the individual, as a self, interacts with the social world. As selves we become active agents in our social world, not only defining reality but also anticipating the future and often changing our behavior to be in line with the anticipated reality. This essential fact of social living has always been at the heart of this book, and it reflects the orientation of social psychology in the twenty-first century.

To that end, the theme of the self is reflected in this text through the following:

- In Chapter 1, a section titled "The self is shaped by—and shapes—the social environment" introduces this central theme.

- The central theme of the self is integrated through the discussion of key concepts, including the following examples: Chapter 4's discussion of self-serving attributions that enhance and protect self-esteem; Chapter 5's analysis of the motivated-tactician model; Chapter 6's self-perception theory and attitudes; Chapter 7's look at the role of the self in persuasion; Chapter 8's analysis of self-regulation and prejudice reduction; Chapter 9's discussion of compliance and self-consistency; Chapter 10's coverage of reduced self-awareness and deindividuation; Chapter 11's research on gender differences in the relational self; Chapter 12's analysis of the self-inclusionary process of intimacy; Chapter 13's look at the self-regulation of aggressive thoughts; and Chapter 14's research on how giving and receiving help can affect self-esteem.

- Beginning with Chapter 3's analysis of *The Self,* each chapter concludes with a "Big Picture" summary. These summaries discuss how we, as self-reflective creatures, can use the social psychological knowledge covered in the chapter to understand and actively shape our social world.

EMPHASIZING SOCIAL PSYCHOLOGY'S RESEARCH BASIS

Often I hear from instructors that students enter the course assuming that social psychology is "just plain common sense." It's a common goal among most social psychology instructors to emphasize that social psychology is research based and relies heavily on the experimental method.

With this common goal in mind, I emphasize research methods throughout the book in the following ways:

- **Chapter 2,** "Research Methods in Social Psychology," expands on the introductory chapter's distinction between the scientific process and everyday thinking. This chapter explores the process of conducting research, diverse scientific methods and research strategies, emerging new scientific methodologies and measuring instruments, and includes comprehensive coverage of survey construction, meta-analysis, and ethical issues.

- Each chapter contains new **neuroscience research** on social behavior.

- **Featured Study** sections at the end of every chapter summarize the purpose, method, and results of a recently published scientific article that is relevant to the chapter content. These studies are presented in the general format and style of a journal article, although they are much shorter and do not contain the statistical analyses.

- **Applications** sections at the end of Chapters 3-14 demonstrate how the theories and research in a particular area of social psychology can be applied to real-world settings and to your life.

- The **Social Sense Student CD-ROM** that accompanies this text features **video-integrated reviews of research methods and concepts** addressed in Chapter 2, as well as other video-based exercises. In many of the video segments, prominent social psychology researchers are featured. Following the videos, students are asked to answer a series of questions that test their ability to understand how these researchers designed, conducted, and concluded the experiments they discuss. All of the video segments on the CD-ROM are keyed in the text with verbal references and marginal icons directing students to them.

ORGANIZATION

The book opens with a chapter that introduces the discipline of social psychology and discusses its history and organizing principles. This chapter also makes a distinction between scientific analysis and everyday thinking.

Chapter 2 expands on this discussion by describing the research process and the scientific methods that social psychologists employ. The chapter also examines ethical issues in conducting research and the effect of values on scientific inquiry and on the application of scientific knowledge. The purpose of these two chapters is to provide the background knowledge necessary for students to critically analyze the social psychological topics covered in the chapters that follow.

The remainder of the book is divided into **four major sections:**

- **Part One** examines the scientific analysis of perceiving people and events and contains chapters on the self, self-presentation and social perception, and social cognition.

- **Part Two** evaluates our social world and includes chapters on attitudes, persuasion, and prejudice.

- **Part Three** seeks to understand our place within the group in chapters on social influence and group behavior.

- **Part Four** focuses on our interactions with others and contains chapters on interpersonal attraction, intimate relationships, aggression, and prosocial behavior.

HALLMARKS AND NEW FEATURES OF THE FOURTH EDITION

Revising a textbook is like renovating a building. The goal is to retain those designs and features that are essential in maintaining the integrity and attractiveness of the original product, while enhancing and updating the contents so that it will continue to serve a useful function. Just as successful architects base their renovations on the feedback of those who actually live in the buildings being restored, I have substantially based my "renovations" of this fourth edition on the opinions expressed by professors and students who used the third edition. For those of you who "inhabited" previous editions, I think you will find many familiar features among the new additions. The primary goal of this updating process was to make the fourth edition of *Social Psychology* an even better structure for teaching and learning.

The fourth edition offers the following *familiar features:*

- **More than twenty self-report questionnaires** directly ask students to consider how the specific text material relates to their own lives. The self-report questionnaires are those currently used by researchers, and the results of studies employing them are part of the text material. Thus, as students learn about various social psychological theories and relevant research findings, they also learn something about themselves.

- **Critical thinking questions** encourage students to **examine their own social surroundings** while they simultaneously digest social psychological theories and research. These questions often invite students to guess a study's hypotheses, results, or alternative interpretation of findings. The questions, many of which are new, are either inserted in the captions of figures, tables, photos, and cartoons, or are displayed in prominent critical thinking sidebars. Answers to the former can be found on the same text page; while the end-of-book appendix offers a possible answer to the latter.

- **Coverage of diversity and cultural analysis** is fully integrated in each chapter, rather than treated as a separate boxed insert or separate chapter. As in previous editions, I seek to foster a sense of inclusion for all readers. For example, in the discussion of social behavior in a cross-cultural context, the particular aspect of culture highlighted is individualism versus collectivism. Why? Throughout the history of American social psychology, the concept of individualism has been an influential, yet unexamined, force directing our analysis of social life. All too often American social psychologists have generalized their findings about social life in this country to all the inhabitants of the planet. Now, with the emerging influence of social psychology in Europe and in developing countries, some of the basic assumptions of the relationship of the individual to the group have been questioned. This text discusses how people from individualist and collectivist cultures respond to similar social situations, helping students to understand the richness and flexibility of social life.

- **The evolutionary perspective** illuminates how a universal pattern of social behavior might have developed. One of the benefits of cross-cultural research is that it not only allows us to identify those aspects of social behavior that vary from one culture to the next, but it also allows us to identify social behaviors that are not culturally constrained. When a universal social behavior is identified, discussion turns to how this pattern of behavior may have evolved. Throughout the text I examine how evolutionary forces might have left us with certain behavioral capacities, while also recognizing that current social and environmental forces encourage or discourage the actual development and use of these capacities.

- **Bulleted end-of-section summaries** provide a concise presentation to better facilitate students' studying. The bulleted summaries in the third edition were well received and have been retained in the new edition.

- **Appendix: The Profession of Social Psychology** For students who are interested in learning more about how one becomes a social psychologist, this appendix offers an overview of the profession as a career option, highlighting the process of graduate school education and career opportunities. This guide also discusses the discipline's possible future interconnections with other disciplines. Other *new features* of the fourth edition are as follows:

- **Updated research and theories**

  450 new citations, studies, theories, and examples

- **Approximately 50 new figures and tables** describe and illustrate new theories and research

- **New neuroscience research and theories**

  New discussion in each chapter of neuroscientific studies employing the latest cutting-edge technology

CHAPTER-BY-CHAPTER CHANGES

Chapter 1: Introducing Social Psychology

- New chapter-opening story
- Expanded section on the social cognitive perspective
- Expanded section on the evolutionary perspective
- Expanded section on the social neuroscience perspective

Chapter 2: Research Methods in Social Psychology

- Expanded coverage of the steps in the research process
- Expanded coverage of survey research
- New section on emerging technologies, including virtual environments, the Internet, and brain imaging

Chapter 3: The Self

- Completely rewritten and reorganized chapter
- New chapter-opening story
- New sections on the neurological basis of self-awareness and self-regulation
- Expanded coverage of private self-consciousness effects

- New research and expanded coverage on how culture shapes self-concept
- Expanded coverage of how bicultural individuals negotiate competing cultural expectations
- New section on self-esteem development and stability
- New section on how self-esteem affects responses to positive and negative events
- New discussion of implicit versus explicit self-esteem
- New Featured Study on adaptive self-regulation

Chapter 4: Self-Presentation and Person Perception

- New chapter-opening story
- New discussion on automatic versus consciously controlled self-presentations
- New section on nonconscious mimicry
- New section on how culture, gender, and personality factors shape expression and perception of nonverbal behavior
- Revamped section on personality impressions
- Inclusion of Gustav Ichheiser's early contributions to attribution theory
- New section on effortful versus effortless attributions and pragmatic accuracy in person perception
- New Featured Study on the multiple audience problem in maintaining lies

Chapter 5: Thinking About Our Social World

- Completely rewritten and reorganized chapter
- New section on serial versus sequential information processing
- New section on implicit versus explicit cognition
- New section on thought suppression
- New sections on how schemas shape social thinking
- Expanded discussion of heuristics
- Expanded discussion of the confirmation bias and the just-world belief
- Expanded Applications discussion of how we explain negative events in our lives

Chapter 6: Attitudes

- Expanded discussion of implicit attitudes
- New theory and research on how values shape attitudes and behavior
- New research on the neurological basis of attitudes
- New research on how body movements may unconsciously shape attitudes
- New Featured Study on group membership and assumed attitude similarity

Chapter 7: Persuasion

- New chapter-opening story
- New research on the sleeper effect
- New research on how fear and humor affect persuasion
- New research on age and life-stage effects on persuasion
- New section on attempting to resist persuasion
- New Featured Study on subliminal priming and persuasion
- Expanded Applications discussion of new research on subliminal persuasion

Chapter 8: Prejudice And Discrimination

- Completely rewritten and reorganized chapter
- New chapter-opening story
- Updated definition of prejudice and new section on three basic forms of prejudice
- New research on the neurological correlates of prejudice
- New section on stigma and prejudice
- New section on weight prejudice
- Completely revised sections on stereotyping and prejudice
- New research on race-based cues and prejudice
- New research on authoritarianism and prejudice
- New section on a dual process model of personality-influenced prejudice
- New research on sexual harrassment
- New research on the contact hypothesis
- New Featured Study on intergroup contact, friendship, and prejudice reduction
- Expanded Applications discussion of reducing intergroup conflict and promoting academic achievement in schools

Chapter 9: Social Influence

- New chapter-opening story
- New section on social power
- New section on the automatic activation of social norms
- New research on the neurological correlates with conformity
- New research on minority influence

Chapter 10: Group Behavior

- New discussion of brain evolution and optimum group size
- Expanded discussion of the temporal model of group membership
- Expanded discussion of social loafing
- New research on Internet use and deindividuation
- Expanded discussion of social dilemmas, including the prisoner's dilemma
- New Featured Study on group decision rules in civil juries

Chapter 11: Interpersonal Attraction

- New chapter-opening story
- Expanded coverage of evolutionary and neurological explanations for affiliation desires
- Expanded coverage of culture and affiliation desires
- New research on Internet use and the mere exposure effect
- New section on anxiety and affiliation in the aftermath of a national disaster
- New research on the physical attractiveness stereotype
- New research on physical attractiveness standards and body esteem effects
- New research on possible cultural shifts in physical attractiveness standards in mate selection
- New Featured Study on the alleviation of speech anxiety

Chapter 12: Intimate Relationships

- Updated and expanded coverage of attachment styles and intimacy
- New research on gender differences in friendships
- New research on the neurological correlates of romantic love
- Expanded discussion of evolutionary and sociocultural explanations of romantic love
- New section on how self-esteem influences romantic love
- New section on how romantic partners "read" each other
- New Featured Study on mate poaching
- Expanded Applications discussion on coping with jealousy

Chapter 13: Aggression

- New research on personality and aggression
- Expanded coverage of collective aggression
- Expanded coverage of the evolutionary and biological influences on aggression
- New research on the weapons effect
- New discussion of the influence of violent muic videos and video games on aggression
- New Featured Study on sexually aggressive men's cognitive associations about women, sex, hostility, and power

Chapter 14: Prosocial Behavior

- New research on culture and helping
- New research on diffusion of responsibility and helping on the Internet
- New Featured Study on how imagining the presence of others can induce the bystander effect

ACKNOWLEDGMENTS

Many people have provided invaluable assistance and understanding while I was revising this text. I first want to thank my family for not only supporting my writing efforts and forgiving my memory lapses during this time, but also providing me with wonderful examples of social psychological principles that I used throughout the text. I apologize to my daughters, Amelia and Lillian, for any future embarrassment I may cause them by retelling some of their life experiences in the book!

I also wish to thank the students in my social psychology courses at Marquette University, who are the first to be exposed to my new stories of the social psychological enterprise. In addition, I thank those students using my book at other colleges and universities who wrote me letters and e-mail concerning their reactions to what they read. The encouragement, enthusiasm, and criticism of all these students have made revising the book much easier.

My appreciation also goes to the many Internet-user members of the Society of Personality and Social Psychology (SPSP) who graciously responded to my requests for reprints and preprints of recent scientific articles describing recent advances in our understanding of social behavior. Their responses greatly aided me in preparing a fourth edition *Social Psychology* that includes exciting new research and theoretical developments.

Listed below are some of these individuals:

David Amodio *University of Wisconsin*

Bilge Ataca *Bogazioi University*

Mahzarin Banaji *Harvard University*

Bruce Bartholow *University of North Carolina, Chapel Hill*

Veronica Benet-Martinez *University of California-Riverside*

Andreas Birgegard *Uppsala University*

Irene Blair *University of Colorado, Boulder*

Stephen Blumberg *Centers for Disease Control & Prevention*

Galen Bodenhausen *Northwestern University*

Laura Bogart *RAND Corporation*

Gerd Bohner *Universtat Bielefeld*

Jennifer Bosson *University of Texas, Austin*

Gary Brase *University of Missouri, Columbia*

C. Miguel Brendl *INSEAD*

James Cameron *University of Queensland*

Tamlin Conner *Boston College*

Gabriel Cook *University of Georgia*

Philip Cozzolino *University of Minnesota*

Alex Czopp *University of Toledo*

Stéphane Dandeneau *McGill University*

Chris Davis *Carleton University*

Ed Diener *University of Illinois, Urbana*

Roger Drake *Western State College of Colorado*

Naomi Eisenberger *University of California, Los Angeles*

Steven Elias *Western Carolina University*

Anja Eller *University of Kent at Canterbury*

Christian End *University of Missouri, Rolla*

Julie Exline *Case Western Reserve University*

Susan Fiske *Princeton University*

Gordon Forbes *Millikin University*

Thomas Ford *Western Michigan University*

Josh Foster *University of Georgia*

Renae Franiuk *University of Wisconsin, Stevens Point*

Cynthia Frantz *Oberlin College*

James Friedrich *Williamette University*

Lowell Gaertner *University of Delaware*

Faby Gagne *Wellesley College*

Bertram Gawronski *Northwestern University*

Rosanna Guadagno *University of California, Santa Barbara*

Stephen Guastello *Marquette University*

Michael Gill *Lehigh University*

Jack Glaser *University of California, Berkeley*

Sam Gosling *University of Texas, Austin*

Jamin Halberstadt *University of Otago*

Christine Harris *University of California, San Diego*

Kathi Heffner *University of Nevada, Reno*

Rolf Holtz *Ohio State University, Lima*

Crystal Hoyt *University of St. Thomas*

Eric Igou *Universiteit van Tilburg*

Mary Inman *Hope College*

Michael Inzlicht *Wilfrid Laurier University*

William Jellison *University of Southern California*

Jeff Joireman *Washington State University*

Cheryl Kaiser *Michigan State University*

Martin Kaplan *Northern Illinois University*

Henry Kaplowitz *Kean University*

Do-Yeong Kim *University of California, Santa Barbara*

Eric Knowles *University of Arkansas*

Joachim Krueger *Brown University*

Brian Lakey *Wayne State University*

Jessica Lakin *Drew University*

Benjamin Le *Haverford College*

Robert Levine *Ohio State University*

Matthew Lieberman *University of California, Los Angeles*

Stanley Lieberman *Harvard University*

Geoff MacDonald *University of Queensland*

William Marelich *California State University, Fullerton*

Keith Markman *Ohio University*

Marianne Schmid Mast *Northeastern University*

Rodolfo Mendoza-Denton *Columbia University*

Arthur Miller *Miami University*

Karin S. Moser *University of Zurich*

Michelle Nario-Redmond *Reed College*

Clayton Neighbors *University of Washington*

Matthew Newman *University of Texas, Austin*

Franz Neyer *Humboldt Universitat*

Brian Nosek *University of Virginia*

Kimberly O'Farrell *Tulane University*

Debra Oswald *Marquette University*

Daphna Oyserman *University of Michigan*

Emil Posavac *Loyola University*

Susannah Paletz *NASA Ames Research Center*

Keith Payne *Ohio State University*

Richard Petty *Ohio State University*

Mark Pezzo *University of South Florida*

Emily Pronin *Princeton University*

Bertram Raven *University of California, Los Angeles*
Glenn D. Reeder *Illinois State University*
Harry T. Reis *University of Rochester*
Janet Riggs *Gettysburg College*
Paul Rose *Union College*
Angela Rowe *University of Bristol*
Steven Samuels *U.S. Air Force Academy*
Michael Sargent *Bates College*
Dory Ann Schachner *University of California, Davis*
David Schmitt *Bradley University*
Howard Schuman *University of Michigan*
Norbert Schwarz *University of Michigan*
Paul Silvia *University of North Carolina, Greensboro*
Linda Skitka *University of Illinois at Chicago*
Charles Stangor *University of Maryland*
Jeffrey Stone *University of Arizona*

Jeroen Stouten *Maastricht University*
Fritz Strack *University of Würzburg*
John Tauer *University of St. Thomas*
Geoff Thomas *Cardiff University*
Kendell Thornton *Dowling College*
Jean Twenge *San Diego State University*
Robert Vallerand *University of Quebec at Montreal*
Bas Verplanken *University of Tromso*
Terri Vescio *Pennsylvania State University*
Kathleen Vohs *University of British Columbia*
Gregory Walton *Yale University*
Mark Whatley *Valdosta State University*
Timothy Wilson *University of Virginia*
Piotr Winkielman *University of California, San Diego*
Toshio Yanagishi *Hokkaido University*
Ilan Yaniv *Hebrew University of Jerusalem*

The writing of this book was helped tremendously by the input of numerous reviewers who obviously care very much about the field of social psychology and about the art and craft of teaching. I would like to thank the following individuals, among others, for their input on this edition of *Social Psychology:*

Deletha Hardin, *University of Tampa*
Richard D. Harvey, *St. Louis University*
Myrna Nicollette, *Charleston Southern University*
Shana Pack, *Western Kentucky University—Glasgow*
Neal Roese, *University of Illinois—Urbana/Champaign*

Darla Silverman, *Sussess County Community College*
Katrina L. Steers-Wentzell, *University of Pittsburgh*
Kendell Thornton, *Dowling College*

In addition, the following colleagues reviewed the manuscript for previous editions of the book. Their contributions have also influenced the development of subsequent revisions, including this one.

Michele Acker, *Otterbein College*
Lisa M. Bohon, *California State University at Sacramento*
Jack A. Cohen, *Camden County College*
Jack Croxton, *State University of New York at Fredonia*
Casimir J. Danielski, *Community College of Vermont*
Dorothee Dietrich, *Hamline University*
Evelyn M. Finney, *Southeast Missouri State University*
William Rick Fry, *Youngstown State University*
Ann Fuehrer, *Miami University of Ohio*

Stella Hargett, *Morgan State University at Baltimore*
Linda M. Isbell, *University of Massachusetts at Amherst*
Julia Rae Jacks, *University of North Carolina at Greensboro*
J. R. Jones, *Cuyamaca College*
G. Daniel Lassiter, *Ohio University*
Wendy Micham, *Chapman University*
Jeffrey Ratliff-Crain, *University of Minnesota*
Steve R. Riskin, *California State University at Dominquez Hills*

Vann B. Scott, Jr., *Armstrong Atlantic State University*

Kimberly Smirles, *Emmanuel College*

Charles Stagor, *University of Maryland at College Park*

Janice Steil, *Derner Institute at Adelphi University*

David Trafimow, *New Mexico State University*

Matthew P. Winslow, *Eastern Kentucky University*

Finally, I would like to thank selected members of editorial staffs who have worked with me over the years. Were it not for Michael Lange, Steven Yetter, and Ed Laube at the old Brown & Benchmark, I would not have undertaken this project thirteen years ago. At McGraw-Hill, Executive Editor Mike Sugarman provided unwavering support and advice during all phases of this current revision process. Thanks Mike! I was also extremely fortunate to work with Project Manager Ruth Smith, who kept everything on schedule. I had fun working with Photo Research Coordinator Nora Agbayani and copyeditor Laurie Mc Gee. Designer Srdj Savanovic and Art Editor Katherine McNab made sure the book has the right "look" and that it would be pleasing to the reader's eye.

Supplements

Social Psychology, fourth edition, is accompanied by a comprehensive and fully integrated array of supplemental materials, both print and electronic, written specifically for instructors and students of social psychology. Please contact your McGraw-Hill representative for details concerning policies, prices, and availability as some restrictions may apply.

FOR THE INSTRUCTOR

The Social Connection Video Modules—VHS Tapes or CD-ROM

McGraw-Hill has teamed up with Frank Vattano and Colorado State University's Office of Instructional Services to produce an all-new series of video modules, *The Social Connection.* This two-hour video series consists of one-on-one interviews with some of the leading social psychology researchers today discussing their work and its relevance to the course. The modules also incorporate footage from classic research studies and new reenactments of social psychology studies. Among the researchers included in the video are John Darley, Phil Zimbardo, Anthony Pratkanis, Elizabeth Loftus, Elliot Aronson, just to name a few. A video guide tailored to the organization of Franzoi's *Social Psychology,* fourth edition, is also available.

Instructor's Manual

By Jeffrey Ratliff-Crain, University of Minnesota, Morris

This highly useful resource has been fully updated to reflect the major changes in the fourth edition of the text, including the new material on social cognition and the increased neuroscience coverage. It also continues to include a lot of cross-cultural and gender-related topics. Each chapter contains the innovative Total Teaching Package Outline, which correlates McGraw-Hill resources to the key concepts in each chapter; learning objectives (referenced explicitly in the Test Bank); discussion questions; and classroom activities and demonstrations. The Instructor's Manual is available on the password-protected instructor's side of the text Web site (*www.mhhe.com/franzoi4*) and on the Instructor's Resource CD-ROM.

Test Bank

By Kimberly Eretzian Smirles, Emmanuel College

Available on the Instructor's Resource CD-ROM, this comprehensive Test Bank has been extensively revised and expanded to include a wide range of multiple-choice, fill-in-the-blank, critical thinking, and short essay questions for each of the text's fourteen chapters. Each item is designated as factual, conceptual, and applied for ease of instructor use and is explicitly linked to the appropriate learning objective in the Instructor's Manual. This CD-ROM provides all of the questions in both Word files and a computerized format with a fully functioning editing feature that enables instructors to integrate their own questions, scramble items, and modify questions. The CD-ROM can be used with both Macintosh and Windows operating systems.

Instructor's Resource CD-ROM

This resourceful tool offers instructors the opportunity to customize McGraw-Hill materials to create their lecture presentations. Resources for instructors include the Instructor's Manual Test Bank and Computerized Test Bank, PowerPoint presentation slides by Chrisanne Christensen of Southern Arkansas University, and the Image Database for Social Psychology.

The McGraw-Hill Social Psychology Image Database

This set of 200 full-color images represents the best selection of our social psychology art and tables and is available on both the Instructor's Resource CD-ROM and online at www.mhhe.com/franzoi4

Online Learning Center (OLC)

This extensive Web site, designed specifically to accompany Franzoi's *Social Psychology,* fourth edition, offers an array of resources for students and instructors. The password-protected instructor's side of the site contains the Instructors Manual, PowerPoint Presentations, Web links, and other teaching resources. Visit the OLC at www.mhhe.com/franzoi4

PageOut™ Build your own course Web site in less than an hour

You don't have to be a *computer whiz* to create a Web site—especially with an exclusive McGraw-Hill product called **PageOut**™. It requires no prior knowledge of HTML, no long hours of coding, and no design skills on your part. To learn more, visit www.pageout.net

FOR THE STUDENT

SocialSense CD-ROM to accompany **Social Psychology,** Fourth Edition

This interactive tool, packaged at no additional charge with each new copy of the textbook, is designed to help students learn and review important concepts in the course. A key feature of this CD is the inclusion of video-based activities that extend the text coverage and challenge students to apply what they have learned. Also included on the CD are multiple-choice, test preparation questions written by Marcus Patterson (Boston University and the University of Massachusetts, Boston) and keyed to each chapter of the text. Feedback accompanies each question.

Online Learning Center (OLC)

This extensive Web site, designed specifically to accompany **Social Psychology,** Fourth Edition, offers an array of resources for students, including practice quizzes (by Marcus Patterson of Boston University and the University of Massachusetts, Boston), Internet exercises, and an innovative polling feature that allows students to participate in a real-time survey. Visit the OLC at www.mhhe.com/franzoi4

A SPECIAL NOTE TO INSTRUCTORS AND STUDENTS

Whenever I teach a course in psychology, I learn a lot from my students and fellow instructors about how to make the course better. I would like to have a similar opportunity to learn from you how I can improve this textbook. Your feedback about what you like or do not like about the book is important to me. To make it easy for you to provide this feedback, my school address, telephone number, and e-mail address are listed below. I will personally respond to all comments and questions.

Professor Stephen L. Franzoi
Department of Psychology
Marquette University
P.O. Box 1881
Milwaukee, WI 53201-1881
Telephone: (414)288-1650
E-mail: Stephen.Franzoi@marquette.edu

SOCIAL PSYCHOLOGY

CHAPTER **1**

Introducing Social Psychology

Do you ever catch yourself watching and being fascinated by a slice of life playing out in front of you? That is, while observing others going about their normal daily routines, do you ever stop and think to yourself, "Isn't this interesting. I'm watching people living!"?

The first time I remember identifying myself as a "people watcher" was when I was a teenager working as a bagger at a grocery store in my hometown. It was about nine at night, near closing time. I had just carried an armload of grocery bags out to a customer's car in the parking lot and turned back toward the store when I paused to take in the scene before me. It was dark outside and the illuminated interior of the store made the people inside—behind the windows—appear like actors projected onto a movie screen in a darkened theater. The scene was so mundane that I'm sure no one else took any notice: friends, coworkers, and strangers interacting and moving about as they unwittingly became the stars in my silent movie. For a few seconds I stood transfixed by this flow of life, yet at the same time feeling detached, an observer.

I was reminded of this past event while waiting tonight for my older daughter, Amelia, to finish her dance class. Once again I was outside in the dark, sitting in my car looking into the illuminated interior of the studio while the young dancers inside conversed as they put on coats and prepared to leave. At that moment the thought occurred to me that I have spent a good portion of my life as an observer, both personally and professionally.

My life as an observer of people is far from unique. We are all actors and spectators on the social stage. It just so happens that I am actually paid a salary to observe and analyze people and events. What a great deal! I get paid to do what everybody else does for free! That is a typical comment that new acquaintances make when they learn that I am a

We are all observers of social life. What distinguishes the observations made by social psychologists from those made by the casual observer?

social psychologist. Yet is the salary that I receive the only distinction between my observations as a social psychologist and those made by the typical layperson? Occasionally, a brave soul will press the point and ask what many others are undoubtedly thinking: "Isn't social psychology just warmed-over common sense?"

WHAT IS SOCIAL PSYCHOLOGY?

Before addressing the question of whether social psychologists are simply repackaging common folk wisdom, let us first identify what they study. You, the new student in social psychology, will likely feel a natural affinity to this subject matter because it directly addresses aspects of your daily experience in the social world.

Social Psychology Studies How We Are Influenced by Others

Gordon Allport, one of the influential figures in social psychology, provided a definition of the field that captures its essence. He stated that **social psychology** is a discipline that uses scientific methods in "an attempt to understand and explain how the thought, feeling, and behavior of individuals are influenced by the actual, imagined, or implied presence of others" (1985, p. 3).

> **Social Psychology**
>
> The scientific discipline that attempts to understand and explain how the thoughts, feelings, and behavior of individuals are influenced by the actual, imagined, or implied presence of others.

To better understand this definition, let us consider a few examples. First, how might the actual presence of others influence someone's thoughts, feelings, and behavior? Consider the response that basketball players have to the actions of the opposing team's fans as they prepare to shoot a free throw. Fans from the opposing team often attempt to influence the shooting accuracy of the players by making loud noises and gesturing wildly in the hope of diverting the player's attention from the task at hand. Another example of how the presence of others can influence the individual occurs when a member of a group discovers that she holds a different opinion than others on some important issue. Faced with the raised eyebrows and hushed comments, she may abandon her dissent and join the majority.

Regarding how the imagined presence of others might influence thoughts, feelings, and behavior, think about past incidents when you were considering doing something that ran counter to your parents' wishes. Although they may not have actually been present, did their imagined presence influence your behavior? Imaginal figures can guide our actions by shaping our interpretation of events just as surely as do those who are physically present (Honeycutt, 2003; Shaw, 2003). In stressful situations, imagining the presence of others can actually lower your anxiety and provide you with an emotional security blanket (Andersen & Glassman, 1996; McGowan, 2002). These imaginal individuals may even be purely fictional characters (Caughey, 1984). When my younger daughter, Lillian, told me a few years ago that she wanted to be as brave as Hermione and Harry, two young wizards in J. K. Rowling's Harry Potter book series, we have a perfect illustration of the power of pure imaginal figures.

Finally, how can the implied presence of others influence an individual? Have you ever had the experience of driving on the freeway, going well beyond the speed limit, only to pass a sign with a little helicopter painted on it with the words "We're watching you" printed below? Did the implied presence of a police helicopter circling overhead influence your thoughts and feelings, as well as your pressure on the gas pedal?

Based on this discussion of the definition of social psychology, you should better understand the type of topics we will analyze in this book. Shelley Taylor (2004) recently commented that although social psychology once was a relatively small field of scholars talking primarily to one another, there now are many opportunities to collaborate with the other sciences. Today, social psychology draws on the insights of sociology, anthropology, neurology, political science, economics, and biology to gain a better understanding of how the individual fits into the larger social system. Capitalizing on this movement toward an "integrative science," in this text we will periodically analyze how sociologists, neuroscientists, anthropologists, ethologists, and biologists explain various aspects of social behavior.

Imaginal figures can influence our thoughts, feelings, and actions. For example, seeing that the lead fictional characters in J. K. Rowling's Harry Potter book series overcome immense obstacles to protect themselves and the wizard world from evil wizards may inspire young viewers to persevere when they themselves face life challenges. What imaginal figures inspired you when you were a child? What imaginal figures—either real or fictional—influence you today?

Social Psychology Is More Than Common Sense

As suggested by my opening story, one reason some people think of social psychology as simply rephrasing what we already know is because its subject matter is so personal and familiar: we all informally think about our own thoughts, feelings, and actions and those of others. Why would such informally attained knowledge be appreciably different from what social psychologists achieve through scientific observations? In many ways, this is true. For example, consider the following findings from social psychology that confirm what many of us already know:

- Attending to people's faces leads to the greatest success in detecting their lies. (chapter 4)
- People are less likely to blame accident victims for their injuries if they are similar to them. (chapter 5)
- People who are paid a great deal of money to perform a boring task enjoy it more than those who are paid very little. (chapter 6)
- Men express more hostile attitudes toward women than women do toward men. (chapter 8)
- People think that physically attractive individuals are less intelligent than those who are physically unattractive. (chapter 11)
- Playing violent video games or engaging in contact sports allows people to "blow off steam," making them less likely to behave aggressively in other areas of their lives. (chapter 13)
- Accident victims are most likely to be helped when there are many bystanders nearby. (chapter 14)

All these findings make sense, and you can probably think of examples from your own life that coincide with them. However, the problem is that I lied: social psychological research actually informs us that all these statements are generally false and the exact opposite is true. Of course, social psychology often confirms many commonsense notions about social behavior, but you will find many instances in this text where the scientific findings challenge your current social beliefs.

In most cases, our social world beliefs are best characterized as being embedded within a *naive psychology*. That is, instead of being based on careful scientific analysis, they often develop from everyday experiences and uncritical acceptance of other people's views and opinions. Although these commonsense psychological beliefs often result in good decision making, they can also produce distorted and contradictory judgments (Cacioppo, 2004).

Now that I've proposed that our everyday thinking can lead to faulty judgments, a natural question is whether social psychologists have developed a special formula to eliminate these biases and errors when conducting their research. The answer is no. There is no magic formula to erase these mental quirks and glitches so that our minds run with computer-like precision. Even if there were such a formula, who would be so foolhardy to "cure" themselves in this manner? Although it is true that social psychologists are not immune to error-prone thinking, they do rely on special methods to *minimize* these problems when conducting research. These *scientific methods* will be the topic of discussion in chapter 2.

Social Psychology Is Studied in Both Psychology and Sociology

You might be surprised to learn that there actually are two scientific disciplines known as social psychology, one in psychology and the other in sociology. As Edward Jones (1998) points out in the *Handbook of Social Psychology,* the larger of the two is the psychological branch. Although both disciplines study social behavior, they do so from different perspectives.

The central focus of *psychological social psychology* tends to be individuals and how they respond to social stimuli. Variations in behavior are believed to be due to people's interpretation of social stimuli or differences in their personalities and temperament. Even when psychological social psychologists study group dynamics, they generally emphasize the processes that occur at the individual level (Quiñones-Vidal et al., 2004). The definition of social psychology in this text reflects the psychological perspective.

In contrast, *sociological social psychology* downplays the importance of individual differences and the effects of immediate social stimuli on behavior. Instead, the focus is on larger group or societal variables, such as people's socioeconomic status, their social roles, and cultural norms (Stryker, 1997). The role these larger group variables play in determining social behavior is of much keener interest to this discipline than to its psychological "cousin." Therefore, sociological social psychologists are more interested in providing explanations for such societal-based problems as poverty, crime, and deviance. Table 1.1 contrasts the two branches of social psychology.

T A B L E   1 . 1

Two Social Psychologies

Differences Between Psychological and Sociological Social Psychology

Psychological Social Psychology	Sociological Social Psychology
The central focus is on the *individual.*	The central focus is on the *group or society.*
Researchers attempt to understand social behavior by analyzing *immediate stimuli of psychological states,* and *personality traits.*	Researchers attempt to understand social behavior by analyzing *societal variables,* such as social status, social roles, and social norms.
Experimentation is the primary research method, followed by correlational studies, and then observational studies.	Observational and correlational studies are the primary research methods, followed by experimentation.
The main scientific journal in the field is the *Journal of Personality and Social Psychology.*	The main scientific journal in the field is *Social Psychology Quarterly.*

Although there have been calls to merge the two branches into a single field (Backman, 1983)—and even a joint psychology-sociology doctoral program at the University of Michigan from 1946 to 1967—their different orientations make it doubtful that this will transpire in the foreseeable future. Despite the likelihood that an interdisciplinary social psychology will never materialize, the two fields do influence each other. The recent interest of psychological social psychologists in the impact of culture on social behavior is partly due to the importance it is given in the sociological discipline. Similarly, sociological social psychologists' increased attention to individual differences reflects an appreciation of the insights derived from the psychological approach. Yet, regardless of the cross-pollination that has occurred over the years, the two disciplines will continue to provide important, yet differing, perspectives on social behavior.

The History of Social Psychology Reveals Its American Roots

As a scientific discipline, social psychology is only a bit older than one hundred years, with most of the growth occurring during the past five decades (McGarty & Haslam, 1997). By most standards, social psychology is a relatively young science.

THE EARLY YEARS: 1885–1934

An American psychologist at Indiana University, Norman Triplett, is generally credited with having conducted the first empirical social psychological study. In 1895 Triplett asked the following question: "How does a person's performance of a task change when other people are present?" The question was prompted by Triplett noticing that a bicycle racer's speed was faster when he was paced by other cyclists than when he raced alone. Being a racing enthusiast and desiring to learn what caused these different race times, he devised the first social scientific experiment.

In this study, he asked children to quickly wind line on a fishing reel either alone or in the presence of other children performing the same task. As he had predicted, the children wound the line faster when in the presence of other children. Published in 1897, this study is credited with introducing the experimental method into the social sciences. Despite the significance of this study, it took a full generation for researchers to understand the social psychological dynamics underlying Triplett's findings (see the chapter 10 discussion of *social facilitation*).

Although Triplett is given credit for conducting the first social psychological study, he did nothing to establish social psychology as a distinct subfield of psychology. Credit for this achievement goes to the first authors of textbooks bearing that title, namely, English psychologist William McDougall and American sociologist Edward Ross, who each published separate texts in 1908. Consistent with the contemporary perspective in psychological social psychology, McDougall considered the individual to be the principal unit of analysis in this new science, while Ross, true to the contemporary sociological social psychology perspective, highlighted groups.

Despite the inauguration of this new subfield within psychology and sociology, social psychology still lacked a distinct identity. How was it different from the other subdisciplines within the two larger disciplines? What were its methods of inquiry? In 1924 a third social psychology text, published by Floyd Allport (older brother of Gordon Allport), went a long way in answering these questions for psychological social psychology. Reading his words today, you can see the emerging perspective that would one day permeate the psychological branch of the field:

> I believe that only within the individual can we find the behavior mechanisms and consciousness which are fundamental in the interactions between individuals. . . . There is no psychology of groups which is not essentially and entirely a psychology of individuals. . . . Psychology in all its branches is a science of the individual. (Allport, 1924, p. 4)

In contrast to the more philosophical approach that both Ross and McDougall had taken sixteen years earlier, Allport's text emphasized experimental studies in such areas as

In 1924, Floyd H. Allport published *Social Psychology*, a book that demonstrated how carefully conducted research could provide valuable insights into a wide range of social behaviors.

conformity, nonverbal communication, and social facilitation. The pursuit of social psychological knowledge through carefully controlled experimental procedures would increasingly characterize the field in the coming years.

THE COMING OF AGE: 1935–1945

During the first three decades of the twentieth century, social psychologists primarily strove to generate basic concepts and sound research methods. By the mid-1930s, the vessel of social psychology was ready to be filled with new ideas and theories. The two events that had the greatest impact on social psychology at this critical juncture in its history were the Great Depression in the United States and the social and political upheaval in Europe generated by World War II.

Following the stock market crash of 1929, many young psychologists were unable to find or hold jobs. Experiencing firsthand the impact of societal forces, many of them adopted the liberal ideals of the Roosevelt "New Dealers" or the more radical left-wing political views of the socialist and communist parties. In 1936 these social scientists formed an organization dedicated to the scientific study of important social issues and the support for progressive social action (Stagner, 1986). This organization, known as the *Society for the Psychological Study of Social Issues* (SPSSI), contained many social psychologists who were interested in applying their newly developed theories and political activism to real-world problems. One of the important contributions of SPSSI to social psychology was, and continues to be, the infusion of ethics and values into the discussion of social life.

At the same time, the rise of fascism in Germany, Spain, and Italy created a strong anti-intellectual and anti-Semitic atmosphere in many of Europe's educational institutions. To escape this persecution, many of Europe's leading social scientists, such as Fritz Heider, Kurt Lewin, and Theodor Adorno, immigrated to America. When the United States entered the war, many social psychologists—both American and European—applied their knowledge of human behavior in a wide variety of wartime programs, including the selection of officers for the Office of Strategic Services (the forerunner of the Central Intelligence Agency) and the undermining of enemy morale (Hoffman, 1992). The constructive work resulting from this collaboration demonstrated the practical usefulness of social psychology.

During this time of global strife, one of the most influential social psychologists was Kurt Lewin, a Jewish refugee from Nazi Germany.[1] Lewin was instrumental in founding SPSSI and served as its president in 1941. He firmly believed that social psychology did not have to make a choice between being either a pure science or an applied science. His oft-repeated maxim, "No research without action, and no action without research" continues to influence social psychologists interested in applying their knowledge to current social problems (Ash, 1992). By the time of his death in 1947 at the age of 57, Lewin had provided many of social psychology's defining characteristics (Lewin, 1936; Lewin et al., 1939).

With the end of the war, prospects were bright for social psychology in North America. Based on their heightened stature in the scientific community, social psychologists established new research facilities, secured government grants, and, most important, trained graduate students. These future social psychologists were predominantly white, male, and middle class. Many of their mentors were the European scholars who had fled their native countries and then remained in America following the war. Yet, while social psychology was flourishing in this country, the devastating effects of the world war virtually destroyed the discipline overseas. In this postwar period, the United States emerged as the unchallenged world power, and just as it exported its material goods to other countries, it exported its social psychology as well. This brand of social psychology reflected

Kurt Lewin (1890–1947), a Jewish refugee from Nazi Germany, was instrumental in establishing social psychology as a respected field of scientific inquiry.

CRITICAL *thinking*

Why do you think that some social psychologists have named Adolf Hitler as the one person who had the greatest impact on the development of social psychology?

---

[1]Nobody is quite sure how to properly pronounce Kurt Lewin's name. When he first arrived in the United States from Germany, he used the German pronunciation, "La-veen." However, due to his children's embarrassment of having to explain this pronunciation to their new American friends (Marrow, 1969), Lewin began referring to himself as "Loo-in."

the political ideology of American society and the social problems encountered within its boundaries (Farr, 1996).

RAPID EXPANSION: 1946–1969

With its infusion of European intellectuals and the recently trained young American social psychologists, the maturing science of social psychology expanded its theoretical and research base. To understand how a civilized society like Germany could fall under the influence of a ruthless demagogue like Adolf Hitler, Theodor Adorno and his colleagues (Adorno et al., 1950) studied the psychological parameters of the *authoritarian personality*. Some years later, Stanley Milgram (1963) extended this line of research in his now famous obedience experiments, which examined the conditions that make people more likely to obey destructive authority figures. Social psychologists also focused their attention on the influence that the group had on the individual (Asch, 1956) and of the power of persuasive communication (Hovland et al., 1949). Arguably the most significant line of research and theorizing during this period was Leon Festinger's theory of cognitive dissonance (Festinger, 1957). This theory asserted that people's thoughts and actions were motivated by a desire to maintain cognitive consistency. The simplicity of the theory and its often surprising findings generated interest and enthusiasm both inside and outside of social psychology for many years.

The decade of the 1960s was a time of turmoil in the United States, with the country caught in the grip of political assassinations, urban violence, social protests, and the Vietnam War. People were searching for constructive ways to change society for the better. Following this lead, social psychologists devoted more research time to such topics as aggression, helping, attraction, and love. The groundbreaking research of Elaine Hatfield and Ellen Berscheid (Berscheid & Hatfield, 1969; Hatfield et al., 1966) on interpersonal and romantic attraction, for example, was not only important in widening the scope of social psychological inquiry, but it also generated considerable controversy outside the field. A number of public officials and ordinary citizens thought social scientists should not try to understand the mysteries of romance.

Despite the wariness of some, during the 1960s the federal government expanded its attempts to cure societal ills with the guidance of social scientists. Within this cultural context, the number of social psychologists rose dramatically. Among these new social scientists were an increasing number of women and, to a lesser degree, minority members. Whole new lines of inquiry into social behavior commenced, with an increasing interest in the interaction of the social situation with personality factors. The multitude and diversity of these lines of research would continue into the following decades (Pion et al., 1996).

CRISIS AND REASSESSMENT: 1970–1984

When social psychology first emerged from World War II and embarked on its rapid expansion, one of the pioneers in the field, Theodore Newcomb (1951), expressed concern that expectations were greater than anything that could be delivered in the near future. By the 1970s, when solutions to societal problems were no closer to being solved, and as the usefulness and ethics of experimental research came under increased scrutiny, a "crisis of confidence" emerged (Elms, 1975). When this disappointment and criticism was followed by accusations from women and minorities that past research and theory reflected the biases of a white, male-dominated view of reality, many began to reassess the field's basic premises.

Fortunately, out of this crisis emerged a more vital and inclusive field of social psychology. More rigorous ethical standards were established, and although experiments remained the method of choice, researchers began conducting more correlational studies, as well as employing other methods. Regarding accusations of racial and gender bias, social psychology began moving toward more responsible positions, but such biases have yet to be eliminated from the discipline (Graham, 1992; Tesser & Bau, 2002).

One final important development during this time period was the importing of ideas from cognitive psychology in explaining social behavior. This "cognitive revolution" (see p. 14) greatly enhanced theory and research in all areas of social psychology, and its impact persists today.

AN EXPANDING GLOBAL VIEW OF SOCIAL PSYCHOLOGY: 1985–PRESENT

In the 1970s, both European and Latin American social psychological associations had been founded. The social psychology that developed overseas placed more emphasis on intergroup and societal variables in explaining social behavior than did its American cousin. In the mid-1980s, this overseas influence began to reshape the discipline, as social psychologists throughout the world actively exchanged ideas and collaborated on multinational studies (Fiske et al., 1998; Vala et al., 1996). One of the principal questions generated by this exchange of information concerns which aspects of human behavior are *culture specific*—due to conditions existing within a particular culture—and which ones are due to our shared *evolutionary* heritage. Although social psychology's "professional center of gravity" still resides in the United States, European and Third World social psychology offers the entire field opportunities to escape what some consider the limitations of this "gravitational pull" to perceive new worlds of social reality (Shinha, 2003; Tam et al., 2003). This multicultural perspective will continue to guide research in the coming years.

Contemporary social psychologists have also continued the legacy of Kurt Lewin and SPSSI by applying their knowledge to a wide arena of everyday life, such as law, health, education, politics, sports, and business (Ellsworth & Mauro, 1998; Kinder, 1998; Salovey et al., 1998). This interest in applying the principles and findings of social psychology is a natural outgrowth of the search for understanding.

In this quest for scientific insight, some social psychologists contend that the discipline has focused too much attention on negative social behavior and the flaws in human nature (Krueger & Funder, 2004). There are those in the profession who disagree with this critique (Regan & Gilovich, 2004), but others reply that focusing on the problems we have as social beings will have more long-term benefits than focusing on our human strengths (Dunning, 2004; Epley et al., 2004). Regardless of the merits of these arguments, in this text we will examine both constructive and destructive social behavior, as well as discuss how people sometimes find themselves in very difficult predicaments where they contend with powerful situational forces.

In concluding this historical overview, if the life of a scientific discipline is analogous to a person's life, then contemporary social psychology is best thought of as a "young adult" in the social sciences. Compared with some of the more established sciences, social psychology is "barely dry behind the ears" and still subject to growing pains (Rozin, 2001). Indeed, some social psychologists have suggested that the discipline's failure to develop a "grand theory" that explains all aspects of social behavior may be a sign that it has not yet fully matured (Abrams & Hogg, 2004; Brewer, 2004; Kruglanski, 2001). Whether or not a grand theory is the hallmark of a science's maturity is open to debate (Fiedler, 2004; Simonton, 2001). Yet even as a young science, social psychology reveals important insights into how we function as social creatures. Some of the milestones of the field are listed in table 1.2.

SECTION SUMMARY

- Social psychology uses scientific methods to study how the thought, feeling, and behavior of individuals are influenced by the actual, imagined, or implied presence of others
- Social psychology has both psychological and sociological branches
- Social psychology bears a distinctive American imprint
- Social psychology has become more international in its focus

Some Milestones in the Field of Social Psychology

The Early Years

1897: Norman Triplett publishes the first scientific study of social behavior, on a topic that was later called social facilitation. (See chapter 10.)

1908: Psychologist William McDougall and sociologist Edward Ross separately publish social psychology textbooks.

1920: Willy Hellpach founds the first Institute for Social Psychology in Germany. Hitler's rise to power leads to the institute's demise in 1933.

1924: Floyd Allport publishes the third social psychology text, clearly identifying the focus for the psychological branch of the discipline and covering many topics that are still studied today.

1925: Edward Bogardus develops the social distance scale to measure attitudes toward ethnic groups. Shortly, Louis Thurstone (1928) and Rensis Likert (1932) further advance attitude scale development. (See chapter 6.)

1934: George Herbert Mead's book Mind, Self, and Society is published, stressing the interaction between the self and others. (See chapter 3.)

The Coming-of-Age Years

1936: The Society for the Psychological Study of Social Issues is founded. Muzafir Sherif publishes The Psychology of Social Norms, describing research on norm formation. (See chapter 9.)

1939: John Dollard and his colleagues introduce the frustration-aggression hypothesis. (See chapter 13.)

1941–1945: Social psychologists are recruited by the U.S. government for the war effort.

Rapid Expansion Years

1949: Carl Hovland and his colleagues publish their first experiments on attitude change and persuasion. (See chapter 7.)

1950: Theodor Adorno and his colleagues publish The Authoritarian Personality, which examines how extreme prejudice can be shaped by personality conflicts in childhood. (See chapter 8.)

1951: Solomon Asch demonstrates conformity to false majority judgments. (See chapter 9.)

1954: Gordon Allport publishes The Nature of Prejudice, which provides the framework for much of the future research on prejudice. Social psychologists provide key testimony in the U.S. Supreme Court desegregation case, Brown v. Board of Education. (See chapter 8.)

1957: Leon Festinger publishes A Theory of Cognitive Dissonance, emphasizing the need for consistency between cognition and behavior. (See chapter 6.)

1958: Fritz Heider publishes The Psychology of Interpersonal Relations, laying the groundwork for attribution theory. (See chapter 4.)

1963: Stanley Milgram publishes his obedience research, demonstrating under what conditions people are likely to obey destructive authority figures. (See chapter 9.)

1965: The Society of Experimental Social Psychology is founded. Edward Jones and Kenneth Davis publish their ideas on social perception, stimulating attribution and social cognition research. (See chapters 4 and 5.)

ORGANIZING PRINCIPLES OF EXPLANATION IN SOCIAL PSYCHOLOGY

I have already mentioned that the focus of mainstream social psychology is the individual and her or his interpretation of social situations. Although social psychology has no grand theory that explains all aspects of social behavior, social psychologists use some important organizing principles and perspectives in understanding social interaction. Let us briefly examine these central concepts and theoretical perspectives.

The Self Is Shaped by—and Shapes—the Social Environment

Because of the way in which human beings are biologically and socially put together, the way they interpret social situations is quite complex. The **self**—meaning a symbol-using social being who can reflect on his or her own behavior—was one of the first areas of inquiry by social psychologists during the first third of the twentieth century. In the 1980s, the self reemerged as perhaps the single most important concept in understanding social behavior.

Self

A symbol-using social being who can reflect on his or her own behavior.

Rapid Expansion Years

1966: The European Association of Experimental Social Psychology is founded. Elaine (Walster) Hatfield and her colleagues publish the first studies of romantic attraction. (See chapters 11 and 12.)

1968: John Darley and Bibb Latané present the bystander intervention model, explaining why people often do not help in emergencies. (See chapter 14.)

Crisis and Reassessment Years

1972: *Attribution: Perceiving the Causes of Behavior,* written by six influential attribution theorists, is published. (See chapter 4.) Robert Wicklund and Shelley Duval publish *Objective Self-Awareness Theory,* describing how self-awareness influences cognition and behavior. (See chapter 3.)

1974: The Society for Personality and Social Psychology (SPSP) is founded. Sandra Bem develops the Bem Sex Role Inventory and Janet Spence and Robert Helmreich develop the Personal Attributes Questionnaire, both of which measure gender roles. (See chapters 3 and 5.)

1981: Alice Eagly and her colleagues begin conducting meta-analyses of gender comparisons in social behavior, reopening the debate on gender differences. (See relevant chapters.)

1984: Susan Fiske and Shelly Taylor publish *Social Cognition,* summarizing theory and research on the social cognitive perspective in social psychology. (See chapter 5.)

The Expanding Global View Years

1986: Richard Petty and John Cacioppo publish *Communication and Persuasion: Central and Peripheral Routes,* describing a dual-process model of persuasion. (See chapter 7.)

1989: Jennifer Crocker and Brenda Major publish their *Psychological Review* article on "Social Stigma and Self-Esteem," examining how people respond to being the targets of discrimination. (See chapter 8.)

1991: Hazel Markus and Shinobu Kitayama publish their *Psychological Review* article on how culture shapes the self. (See chapter 3.)

1995: Claude Steele and Joshua Aronson publish "Stereotype Threat and the Intellectual Test Performance of African Americans" in *Journal of Personality and Social Psychology,* presenting their research on how negative stereotypes can shape intellectual identity and performance. (See chapter 8.)

1996: David Buss and Neal Malamuth publish *Sex, Power, Conflict,* an edited text offering evolutionary and feminist perspectives on sex and gender interactions. A growing number of social psychologists attempt to integrate these previously divergent perspectives. (See relevant chapters.)

(Because the passage of time ultimately determines what events significantly shape a field, I will wait a few years before adding any more milestones to this list.)

As selves, we not only have the ability to communicate with others through the use of symbols, but we also reflect on our thoughts and actions (Mead, 1934). Because of these abilities, we can define social reality, anticipate the future, and change our behavior to be in line with the anticipated reality. For example, suppose Jack has been working long hours at the office and, as a result, has ignored his wife and children. One day, it dawns on Jack that if he continues in this pattern of "all work and no play," he will not only be dull, but also divorced and depressed. Based on this anticipation, he revises his work schedule to enjoy the company of his family. In other words, Jack consciously changes his behavior to avoid what he perceives to be a host of unpleasant future consequences. This ability to analyze ourselves, our surroundings, and possible future realities allows us to actively create and re-create ourselves and our social world.

In this process of being active agents in changing our environment, social psychology has empirically demonstrated that on some occasions we pay more attention to social cues, while on other occasions we act more in line with our own personal standards (Silvia & Duval, 2001a; Snyder, 1987). These shifts in attention to private aspects of the self versus public self-aspects can significantly alter our behavior.

In addition to our focus of attention, the way we think of ourselves (our *self-concept*) also influences social behavior (Baumeister, 1998). Self-concept, however, does not develop in a social vacuum—it is based on group membership as well as on more unique personal qualities (Turner, 1985). Numerous studies have found that when self-concept is manipulated by others so that we think of ourselves a certain way, we tend to act consistent with this externally derived definition (Rosenthal, 1991). As you study the various areas of social psychological inquiry in this book, you will realize that something as personal, and often as private, as our self-beliefs are often molded by forces outside us.

Social psychology's renewed emphasis on the self represents a reaffirmation of Kurt Lewin's belief that both person and situational factors influence social behavior. Lewin's perspective, later called **interactionism** (Blass, 1984; Seeman, 1997), combines personality psychology (which stresses differences among people) with traditional social psychology (which stresses differences among situations). In keeping with Lewin's legacy, throughout this text we will examine how these two factors contribute to the social interaction equation, and we will use the self as the primary "person" variable.

Social Cognition Involves Multiple Cognitive Strategies Shaped by People's Motives and Desires

Throughout the history of social psychology there has been a running debate concerning the nature of human behavior. One perspective is that people are moved to act due to their needs, desires, and emotions (also known as *affect*). Social psychologists subscribing to this "hot" approach argue that cool, calculated planning of behavior is secondary to heated action that fulfills desires (Zajonc, 1984). The alternative viewpoint is that people's actions are principally influenced by the rational analysis of choices facing them in particular situations. Followers of this "cold" approach assert that how people think will ultimately determine what they want and how they feel (Lazarus, 1984).

In the 1950s and 1960s, the hot perspective was most influential, but by the 1980s the cold perspective dominated the thinking within social psychology. One reason for this shift was the advent of the computer age, which resulted in people's everyday lives being saturated with the terminology and thinking of this new "technoscience." Reflecting this new view of reality, many social psychologists borrowed concepts from cognitive psychology (Robins et al., 1999). Using the computer as a model for human thought, they developed theories outlining how behavior was determined by rational and methodical cognitive programs that were part of a larger central processing system. These theories of **social cognition** have provided numerous insights into how we interpret, analyze, remember, and use information about our social world. Throughout the textbook, you will recognize the influence that the "cold" perspective has had on how we understand social behavior, especially in the numerous social cognitive theories that we will examine.

Even though many in the field enthusiastically embraced the social cognitive perspective, others expressed concern that the person was in danger of being lost in this new information-processing approach (Koch, 1981). They argued that to think of motives and affect as merely end products in a central processing system was to dehumanize social psychology. In the early 1990s, a number of social psychologists sought to establish a more balanced view of human nature by blending the traditional hot and cold perspectives into what some have termed the *Warm Look* (Sorrentino, 2003; Sorrentino & Higgins, 1986). Reflecting this warm perspective, most contemporary social cognitive theories discuss how people employ multiple cognitive strategies based on their current goals, motives, and needs (Dunning, 1999; Strack & Deutsch, in press). In such discussions, theorists typically propose **dual-process models of cognition,** meaning that our social thinking and behavior is determined by two different ways of understanding and responding to social stimuli (Gilovich & Griffin, 2002; Petty, 2004). One mode of information processing—related to the cold perspective legacy in social psychology—is based on effortful, reflective thinking, in which no action is taken until its potential consequences are properly weighed and evaluated. The alternative mode of processing information—related to the hot perspective legacy in social psychology—is based on minimal cognitive effort, in which behavior is often impulsively and unintentionally activated by emotions, habits, or biological drives. Which of the two avenues of informa-

---

Interactionism

An important perspective in social psychology that emphasizes the combined effects of both the person and the situation on human behavior.

General laws and individual differences are merely two aspects of one problem; they are mutually dependent on each other and the study of the one cannot proceed without the study of the other.

Kurt Lewin, German-born social psychologist, 1890–1947

Social Cognition

The way in which we interpret, analyze, remember, and use information about our social world.

Dual-Process Models of Social Cognition

Theories of social cognition which propose that people employ two broad cognitive strategies to understand and respond to social stimuli, one involving effortless thinking and the other involving effortful thinking.

tion processing people take at any given time is the subject of ongoing research that we will examine throughout this text.

When social psychologists discuss effortful and effortless thinking they also often discuss two related concepts: explicit cognition and implicit cognition. *Explicit cognition* involves deliberate judgments or decisions of which we are consciously aware, while *implicit cognition* involves judgments or decisions that are under the control of automatically activated evaluations occurring without our awareness (Dorfman et al., 1996). How does implicit and explicit cognition relate to effortful and effortless information processing? By definition, implicit cognition is effortless and unintentionally activated, but explicit cognition involves both effortful and relatively effortless thinking.

How might implicit cognition affect social interaction? Feeling uneasy and irritable around a new acquaintance because she unconsciously reminds you of a disagreeable person from your past is an example of how unconscious, automatically activated evaluations can shape your social judgments. For many years, social psychologists primarily studied and discussed the conscious decision making that shapes social interaction, but recently there has been a great deal of interest in how thinking below the "radar" of conscious awareness can influence social judgments and behavior (Karpinski, 2004). Throughout the text, we will discuss how both explicit and implicit cognitive processes shape our social world.

In fact, I cannot totally grasp all that I am. Thus, the mind is not large enough to contain itself; but where can that part of it be which it does not contain?

St. Augustine, Christian theologian, A.D. 354–434

Culture Shapes Social Behavior

In defining social psychology, I have stated that the main focus is the person's interpretation of social reality. Yet in attempting to understand how people interpret and respond to social reality, we must remember that people view the world through cultural lenses. By **culture,** I mean the total lifestyle of a people, including all the ideas, symbols, preferences, and material objects that they share. This cultural experience shapes their view of reality, and thus, significantly influences their social behavior (Markus et al., 1996; Valsiner, 2000).

IDEOLOGY

The values and beliefs of any culture are subsumed under a larger social construction called an ideology. An **ideology** is a set of beliefs and values held by the members of a social group, which explains its culture both to itself and to other groups. These beliefs and values produce a psychological reality that promotes a particular way of life within the culture (Giddens, 1981). Put more simply, an ideology is the theory that a social group has about itself. Thus, just as we have a theory about ourselves (self-concept) that guides our behavior, so too does a society (ideology).

Although homogeneous societies have only one ideology, societies containing diverse cultures contain multiple ideologies. In Canada, for example, there is the culture of the English-speaking provinces, as well as the cultures of French-speaking Quebec and the Native American tribes. Although the dominant ideology within a multicultural society will be that of the most powerful social group (in Canada's case, it is that of the English-speaking culture), the other cultures' views of reality will also significantly influence social life within the society. In the United States, social scientists have investigated how African American, Asian American, European American, Hispanic American, and Native American ideologies are similar to and different from one another (Delgado-Gaitan, 1994; Tharp, 1994). Throughout this text, we will periodically examine how the differing ideologies permeating a multicultural society can lead to different patterns of social behavior.

INDIVIDUALISM AND COLLECTIVISM

Directly related to our understanding of social behavior are the cultural belief systems concerning how individuals relate to their group, namely *individualism* and *collectivism* (Adamopoulos, 1999; Miller & Prentice, 1994). **Individualism** is a preference for a loosely knit social framework in society in which individuals are supposed to take care of themselves and their immediate families only. This belief system asserts that society is a collection of unique individuals who pursue their own goals and interests and strive to be relatively free from the influence of others (Bhargava, 1992).

Culture

The total lifestyle of a people, including all the ideas, symbols, preferences, and material objects that they share.

Ideology

A set of beliefs and values held by the members of a social group, which explains its culture both to itself and to other groups.

Individualism

A philosophy of life stressing the priority of individual needs over group needs, a preference for loosely knit social relationships, and a desire to be relatively autonomous of others' influence.

Canada is an example of a society with diverse cultures, such as the French-speaking province of Quebec. Think about your own upbringing. Do different cultural ideologies influence your own view of the world?

The union is only perfect when all the individuals are isolated.

Ralph Waldo Emerson, U.S. philosopher/poet, 1803–1882

Human beings draw close to one another by their common nature, but habits and customs keep them apart.

Confucius, Chinese sage, 551–479 B.C.

Collectivism

A philosophy of life stressing the priority of group needs over individual needs, a preference for tightly knit social relationships, and a willingness to submit to the influence of one's group.

As a philosophy of life, traces of individualism can be seen in early Greek and Roman writings and in the values and ideas of the medieval Anglo-Saxon poets of England (Harbus, 2002). However, it did not make a significant appearance on the world stage until the sixteenth century, when people became more geographically mobile and, thus, more likely to come into contact with radically different cultures (Kim, 1994). Exposed to different social norms and practices, people began to entertain the possibility of having goals separate from those of their group (Kashima & Foddy, 2002). In the arts, characters in novels and plays began to be portrayed as having individual states of emotion and as struggling with the distinction between their true self and the social roles assigned to them by their family and community (Stone, 1977). During the late 1800s and early 1900s—the age of industrialization and urbanization in Western societies—social roles became increasingly complex and compartmentalized. Now it was common practice to "find" or "create" one's own personal identity rather than to be given an identity by one's group. This belief also holds true today in our contemporary society. Self-discipline, self-sufficiency, personal accountability, and autonomy are highly valued characteristics in a person (Kâğitcibaşi, 1994).

Examples of this individualist orientation can be seen throughout U.S. history. In the 1700s, Thomas Jefferson's penning of the Declaration of Independence was essentially a bold assertion that individual rights were more important than group rights. In the 1800s, poet/philosopher Ralph Waldo Emerson believed that individualism was the route that, if truly traveled, would result in a spontaneous social order of self-determined, self-reliant, and fully developed citizens. In contemporary America, one can see the striving for individualism in the most mundane of everyday activities. For example, households strive to be self-sufficient units by accumulating all the necessary appliances for daily tasks. There is seldom communal ownership of lawnmowers, washing machines, or personal computers, despite the fact that these items could be shared by neighbors, thereby saving money for all. Yet such sharing would reduce one's freedom to use the products whenever one wished, and thus, it runs counter to our individualist mind-set.

In contrast to individualism, there is an alternative perspective known as **collectivism,** which represents a preference for a tightly knit social framework in which individuals can expect their relatives or other members of their social group to look after them in exchange for unquestioning loyalty. This cultural belief system asserts that people become human only when they are integrated into a group, not isolated from it. Although individualists give priority to personal goals, collectivists often make no distinctions between personal and group goals. When they do make such distinctions, collectivists subordinate their personal goals to the collective good (Abrams et al., 1998; Oyserman et al., 2002). Due to the greater importance given to group aspirations over individual desires, collectivist cultures tend to value similarity and conformity, rather than uniqueness and independence. (See chapter 9 for a more detailed discussion.)

How does this different perspective on the relationship between the individual and the group influence thought and behavior? Consider a modern, industrialized society with a collectivist orientation: Japan. The Japanese, like other people living in a collectivist society, view group inclusion and allegiance to be one of the primary goals in life. Indeed, in Japan the expression for individualist, *kojin-shugi,* is considered a socially undesirable characteristic, suggesting selfishness rather than personal responsibility (Ishii-Kuntz, 1989). Persons who defy the group's wishes, often considered heroes in an individualist culture, would bring shame upon themselves and their families (and their ancestors) in Japan. In North American society, to stand above the crowd, to be recognized as unique and special, is highly valued. In Japan, such attention detracts from the group. The different perspectives these cultures have about the individual standing out from the group is illustrated in contrasting proverbs or mottos. In North America, "The squeaky wheel gets the grease" and "Do your own thing" are commonly heard phrases, while the Japanese credo is "The nail that sticks up shall be hammered down." View social psychologist Hazel Markus's comments on these cultural differences and how they influence athletes' reactions to success in their sports on your Social Sense CD-ROM.

It may surprise you to know that approximately 70 percent of the world's population lives in cultures with a collectivist orientation (Singelis et al., 1995). Indeed, the collectivist perspective is a much older view of the relationship between the individual and the group than is the individualist orientation. For most of human history, the group was the basic unit of society. Whether you were born into a clan or a tribe, you would generally live in one geographic region your entire life and would, upon maturing, assume the same social role as your parents. You did not have to "search" for your identity; it was given to you by your group. Political scientist Ronald Inglehart and social psychologist Daphna Oyserman contend that collectivism is the older of the two philosophies because it focuses on the type of thinking and behavior that affords the most protection for people who live in threatening environments where survival needs are extremely salient. This is exactly the type of environment that has historically confronted all human groups until fairly recently. In contrast, individualism is a much more recent philosophy of life because it develops among people who inhabit relatively safe environments where their survival is less dependent on maintaining strong group ties. This liberation from immediate physical threats reduces the importance of survival-focused values and gives higher priority to freedom of choice (Inglehart & Oyserman, in press).

Table 1.3 lists some of the differences between these two cultural ideologies. Currently, individualism and collectivism are considered by the majority of cross-cultural researchers to be two ends of a continuum, with the United States, Canada, Australia, and Western European societies located more toward the individualist end, and Asian, African, and Latin and South American nations situated near the collectivist end. Within both individualist and collectivist cultures, individualist tendencies tend to be stronger in large urban settings—where people are less dependent on group ties—while collectivist tendencies are more pronounced in small regional cities and rural settings—where social relationships are more interdependent (Kashima et al., 2004; Ma & Schoeneman, 1997).

Which perspective is better? Your answer depends on what values you have internalized (Sampson, 1988). As previously mentioned, although individualism and collectivism are seen by many theorists as two ends of a continuum, this doesn't mean that individualist tendencies do not influence people living in collectivist cultures, nor that collectivist yearnings do not shape individualists (Göregenli, 1997). Indeed, a growing number of theorists think of these differing ideologies as reflecting two seemingly universal and common human needs: the *need for autonomy* and the *need for communion* (Aaker et al., 2001; Schwartz, 2003). Thus, although all humans have both a need for autonomy and communion, individualist cultures place greater value on autonomy, while collectivist cultures place greater value on communion. Because one of the goals of social psychology is to understand how the past

An individual has not started living until he can rise above the narrow confines of his individualistic concerns to the broader concerns of all humanity.

Martin Luther King, Jr., U.S. civil rights leader, 1929–1968

Social Sense

View an interview with social psychologist Hazel Markus.

TABLE 1.3

Differences Between Collectivist and Individualist Cultures

Collectivist	Individualist
Identity is based in the social system and given by one's group.	Identity is based in the individual and achieved by one's own striving.
People are socialized to be emotionally dependent on organizations and institutions.	People are socialized to be emotionally independent of organizations and institutions.
Personal and group goals are generally consistent; and when inconsistent, group goals get priority.	Personal and group goals are often inconsistent, and when inconsistent, personal goals get priority.
People explain others' social behavior as being more determined by social norms and roles than by personal attitudes.	People explain others' social behavior as being more determined by personal attitudes than by social norms and roles.
Emphasis is on belonging to organizations, and membership is the ideal.	Emphasis is on individual initiative, individual achievement, and leadership is the ideal.
Trust is placed in group decisions.	Trust is placed in individual decisions.

experiences and present conditions of others influence their interpretation of reality, these two contrasting perspectives will periodically figure in our chapter discussions. Spend a few minutes completing the "Values Hierarchy Exercise" in table 1.4 to better understand the relative importance of these two cultural orientations in your own life.

A few additional points bear mentioning regarding these two cultural orientations. As already suggested, individualism and collectivism are not permanent, unchanging characteristics of given societies (Park et al., 2003). Individualism is closely linked with socioeconomic development (Welzel et al., 2003). When collectivist cultures become industrialized and experience economic development, they often experience a shift toward some of the cultural beliefs associated with individualism and away from some of the cultural beliefs associated with collectivism. This is at least partly so because the increased prosperity brought on by economic development minimizes the type of concerns for survival that prompt people to strongly identify with—and unquestionably submit to—their social group (Inglehart & Baker, 2000; Oyserman et al., 2002). When economic conditions shift in this manner, many collectivists begin developing an interest in individual freedom-focused rights and privileges. The transition to democracy, which stresses individual rights over the rights of the state, is currently taking place in such collectivist countries as Turkey, the Philippines, South Africa, Taiwan, and Slovenia. Both China and Vietnam are experiencing rapid economic growth, which should lead to increased individualist desires among their citizenry as well.

Evolution Shapes Universal Patterns of Social Behavior

One of the added benefits of cross-cultural research is that it not only allows us to identify those aspects of social behavior that vary from one culture to the next, but it also allows us to identify social behaviors that are not culturally constrained. When a universal social behavior is identified, discussion naturally turns to how this pattern of behavior may have evolved. **Evolutionary psychology** may provide useful insights here (Barrett et al., 2002; Kenrick & Maner, 2004).

Evolutionary Psychology

An approach to psychology based on the principle of natural selection.

Many social scientists contend that individualist and collectivist tendencies can and do coexist within a person. The conflict that can often result from striving for personal goals that may hinder group health and harmony is often depicted in popular television shows and Hollywood movies. For example, in the classic 1947 Christmas movie, It's a Wonderful Life, Jimmy Stewart's character, George Bailey, is continually faced with life decisions that pit his own personal desires against his feelings of obligation toward his community. Although he is an individualist, George Bailey repeatedly puts aside his own desires and serves his community. This movie has a clear collectivist message: the self is affirmed by fulfilling the needs of the group. Why do you think this movie's message is so warmly received in North America's individualist culture? Does this message appeal to you? Would you put aside your own personal desires and ambitions in order to serve your community?

TABLE 1.4

Individualist-Collectivist Values Hierarchy Exercise

Directions

Listed below are twelve values. Please rank them in their order of importance to you with "1" being the "most important" and "12" being the "least important."

Pleasure (Gratification of Desires)

Honor of Parents and Elders (Showing Respect)

Creativity (Uniqueness, Imagination)

Social Order (Stability of Society)

A Varied Life (Filled with Challenge, Novelty, and Change)

National Security (Protection of My Nation from Enemies)

Being Daring (Seeking Adventure, Risk)

Self-discipline (Self-restraint, Resistance to Temptation)

Freedom (Freedom of Action and Thought)

Politeness (Courtesy, Good Manners)

Independence (Self-reliance, Choice of Own Goals)

Obedience (Fulfilling Duties, Meeting Obligations)

Scoring

The individualist and collectivist values are listed in alternating order, with the first (Pleasure) being an individualist value and the second (Honor of Parents and Elders) being a collectivist value. People from individualist cultures such as the United States, Canada, England, or Australia tend to have more individualist values than collectivist values in the upper half of their values hierarchy. This order tends to be reversed for those from collectivist cultures such as Mexico, Japan, Korea, or China. Which of the two cultural belief systems is predominant in your own values hierarchy? If you know someone from another culture, how do they rank these values?

Genes

The biochemical units of inheritance for all living organisms.

Natural Selection

The process by which organisms with inherited traits best suited to the environment reproduce more successfully than less well adapted organisms over a number of generations. Natural selection leads to evolutionary changes.

Evolution

The genetic changes that occur in a species over generations due to natural selection.

It may metaphorically be said that natural selection is daily and hourly scrutinizing . . . the slightest variations; rejecting those that are bad, preserving and adding up all that are good. . . . We see nothing of these slow changes in progress, . . . we see only that the forms of life are now different from what they formerly were.

Charles Darwin, 1859, *On the Origin of Species by Natural Selection,* pp. 90–91

The evolutionary perspective is partly based on the writings of biologist Charles Darwin (1809–1882), who theorized that genetic changes in the population of a species occur over many generations due to the interaction of environmental and biological variables. **Genes** are the biochemical units of inheritance for all living organisms, and the human species has about 30,000 different genes. According to Darwin (1859, 1871), all living organisms struggle for survival, and within each species a great deal of competition and genetic variation occurs between individuals. Those members of a species with genetic traits best adapted for survival in their present environment will produce more offspring, and, as a result, their numbers will increase in the population. As the environment changes, however, other members within the species possessing traits better suited to the new conditions will flourish, a process called **natural selection.** In this way, the environment selects which genes of a species will be passed onto future generations. As this process of natural selection continues, and as the features best suited for survival change, the result is **evolution,** a term that refers to the gradual genetic changes that occur in a species over generations. *Reproduction* is central to the natural selection process, and the essence of natural selection is that the characteristics of some individuals allow them to produce more offspring than others.

An example of social behavior from another species that may be the product of natural selection is water splashing by male gorillas. Males regularly create massive water plumes by leaping into pools or by slapping the water with their powerful hands. Why is it that female gorillas do not engage in this behavior nearly to the same degree, and what precipitates male splashing? Evolutionary theorists hypothesized that male gorillas engage in water splashing to intimidate other males and keep them away from their females. To test this hypothesis, researchers observed the splashing displays of lowland gorillas in the Congo over a three-year period (Parnell & Buchanan-Smith, 2001). They found that more than 70 percent of the splashing was carried out by dominant males in the presence of males not from their social group, with more than half the displays occurring when no females were present. These findings suggested to the researchers that the splashing was being directed at strange males who might challenge the dominant male's control of his group. They speculated that over the course of gorilla evolution, males who engaged in intimidating behavior like water splashing were more successful in preventing strange males from stealing females from their group than those who did not water splash. Thus, acting tough by literally making a big splash when other males were present resulted in greater reproductive success, and that is why this social behavior persists in the male gorilla population today.

Social psychologists who adopt the evolutionary approach apply a similar type of logic to understanding humans. Many social behaviors extensively studied by social psychologists, such as aggression, helping, interpersonal attraction, romantic love, and stereotyping, are thought to be shaped by inherited traits (Buss & Kenrick, 1998; Gangestad & Simpson, 2002). If this is true, then attempts to understand human social behavior should consider how these inherited traits might have given our ancestors a competitive advantage in their environment, thus maximizing their ability to survive and reproduce.

There are two important points to keep in mind when considering the process of evolution. First, individual organisms don't evolve, populations evolve. The role that individuals play in evolution is their interaction with the environment and their genes being screened by natural selection. Thus, individuals contribute to a change in their species' population by their own successes or failures in reproducing. Over many generations, the accumulated effects of literally thousands or even millions of individuals' reproductive successes and failures leads to evolution of the species. The second point to remember is that evolution does not necessarily result in species being transformed into more complex forms of life (Smith & Szathmáry, 1995). Instead, the key feature of the evolutionary process has to do with the degree to which an organism's inborn genetic traits help it adapt to its current environment. Thus, just as a trait that was once highly adaptive can become maladaptive if the environmental conditions change, the reverse is also true: a maladaptive trait can become extremely adaptive.

Despite the importance of adding the evolutionary perspective to our explanation of social behavior, many social scientists are cautious in applying these principles to contemporary human behavior (Conway & Schaller, 2002; Scher & Rauscher, 2003). The grounds for such caution rest on the fact that when biologists study an animal, they tend to examine it in terms of how it has adapted to its environment so that it can reproduce and pass on its genes. But as British ethologists Mark Ridley and Richard Dawkins (1981) point out, when a species changes environments—or when its environment changes—an unavoidable period of time exists in which its biological makeup is not in tune with its surroundings. They contend that all species are probably slightly "behind" their environment, but this is especially so for human beings. We are the youngest primate species on earth, but our brains and bodies are biologically no different than they were 150,000 years ago when our ancestors lived on the Pleistocene plains of East Africa. How we behave today in the modern world of city congestion and space-age technology may bear some relation to the roles for which our brains and bodies were originally selected, but the connection is probably weaker than we might think and needs to be interpreted with a great deal of care. In this text, we will approach evolutionary explanations with this sort of justifiable caution—that is, acknowledging that ancient evolutionary forces may have left us with capacities (such as the capacity to behave helpfully), but recognizing that current social and environmental forces encourage or discourage the actual development and use of those capacities.

Brain Activity Affects and Is Affected by Social Behavior

Beyond the organizing principles currently shaping theory and research, social psychologists are constantly exploring new connections with other disciplines, both within and outside the social and behavioral sciences. Like the evolutionary perspective, one new connection that comes from the field of biology is the subfield of **social neuroscience,** which studies the relationship between neural processes of the brain and social processes (Harmon-Jones & Devine, 2003; Ochsner & Lieberman, 2001). This analysis not only emphasizes how the brain influences social interaction, but also how social interaction can influence the brain.

Social Neuroscience

The study of the relationship between neural processes of the brain and social processes.

The increased collaboration between social psychology and neuroscience is largely due to the development of more accurate measures of physiological changes, especially those involving *brain-imaging techniques* that provide pictures—or scans—of this body organ (Cacioppo et al., 2004). These techniques generate "maps" of the brains of living people by examining their electrical activity, structure, blood flow, and chemistry (Cunningham et al., 2003; Ito & Urland, 2003). For example, *functional magnetic resonance imaging (fMRI)* measures the brain's metabolic activity in different regions, revealing which parts of the brain are most active in such social tasks as talking or listening to others, watching social interactions, and thinking about oneself (Iacoboni et al., 2004; Lieberman & Pfeifer, in press). Researchers using fMRI technology have found that when love-struck research participants look at photos of their romantic partners, specific brain regions (the *caudate nucleus*) that play key roles in motivation and rewards—including feelings of elation and passion—exhibit heightened activation (Fisher, 2004). Such research offers the potential for another layer of insight into the dynamic process of social interaction.

Although it is still in its early formative stages, the application of biological theories to traditional social psychological topics may play an instrumental role in reshaping existing theories (Cacioppo et al., 2003; Wood, 2004). Indeed, the U.S. federal government's National Institute of Mental Health—which has an annual budget of 1.3 billion dollars—has recently given priority to research grants that combine social psychology and neuroscience (Willingham & Dunn, 2003). In this text, we discuss some of the findings in this new area of research. For example, when discussing self-awareness and self-regulation (chapter 3), we examine how specific brain regions facilitate the monitoring and controlling of intentional behavior and focused problem solving. Similarly, when discussing attitude formation and change (chapter 6), we analyze how one brain region engages in an immediate primitive "good-bad" emotional assessment that may be followed by higher-order processing conducted in the brain's cerebral cortex. This neuroscientific analysis will provide another layer of knowledge in our understanding of social interaction.

As you can see, social psychology continues to expand its areas of inquiry, developing more sophisticated methods and theories that will provide greater insights into the social process. The remaining chapters in this text will provide you with some fascinating insights into your social world, and yourself. That is the beauty of social psychology. The more you learn about the psychology of social interaction, the more you will learn about how you can more effectively fit into—and actively shape—your own social surroundings. Let us now begin that inquiry.

SECTION SUMMARY

- The self is a central and organizing concept in social psychology
- Interactionism studies the combined effects of both the situation and the person on human behavior
- Many contemporary social cognitive theories attempt to reconcile the "hot" and the "cold" perspectives of human nature into a more inclusive Warm Look
- Social psychologists have become more attentive to cultural influences on social behavior
- The cultural variables of individualism and collectivism are particularly helpful in understanding cultural differences
- Evolutionary theory is increasingly used to explain social behavior
- Integrating ideas from neuroscience and social psychology are becoming more a part of social psychological research and theory

 WEB SITES
accessed through **http://www.mhhe.com/franzoi4**

Social Psychology Network

This is the largest social psychology database on the Internet, with more than 5,000 links to psychology-related resources.

Society for Personality and Social Psychology Home Page

This is the Web site for the largest organization of social and personality psychologists in the world. This organization was founded in 1974.

Evolutionary Psychology for the Common Person

This Web site provides an introduction to evolutionary psychology and provides links to other related web resources.

Michael's garden   Hyacinth Manning

CHAPTER 2

Research Methods in Social Psychology

CHAPTER OUTLINE

*I*n the early 1960s, Leonard Eron was conducting research at an elementary school in the hope of gaining a better understanding of aggression in children. One aspect of the study involved administering a survey to parents, asking them a series of questions about their children. Included in the survey were a few items covering children's TV-viewing habits. Eron inserted these TV queries solely as interesting "ice-breakers," hoping to provide parents with a brief diversion from the central research questions. However, when he analyzed his data, Eron was surprised by what he found. The one thing that was most associated with children's aggression was how much violent television they watched. "What was going on here?" wondered Eron.

Scientific discovery is essentially a form of human problem solving (Klahr & Simon, 1999). The type of problem solving that occurs in scientific enterprises is highly valued because it enhances our ability to understand, predict, and control the forces that shape our physical and social world. The question that Eron asked after analyzing his initial aggression study set him on a scientific exploration that spanned three decades. His work also inspired other social scientists to conduct their own studies of TV violence. Together, their findings have prompted concerned parents, educators, and politicians to lobby the television industry to modify the content of its programs. In this chapter we examine the scientific methods that social psychologists use in their research, and in so doing, we review some of the influential studies that examined the relationship between TV violence and aggression.

CONDUCTING RESEARCH IN SOCIAL PSYCHOLOGY

Basic Research

Research designed to increase knowledge about social behavior.

Applied Research

Research designed to increase the understanding of and solutions to real-world problems by using current social psychological knowledge.

Social psychologists conduct both *basic* and *applied research.* The goal in **basic research** is to simply increase knowledge about social behavior, knowledge for knowledge's sake (Fiske, 2004). No attempt is made to solve a specific social or psychological problem. In contrast, **applied research** is designed to increase the understanding of and solutions to real-world problems by using current social psychological knowledge (Maruyama, 2004). Although many social psychologists label themselves as either basic or applied researchers, the efforts of one group often influence those of the other. As in other sciences, the knowledge gained through the work of basic researchers provides applied researchers with a better understanding of how to solve specific social problems. Likewise, when applied researchers cannot solve problems by employing basic research findings, such failure often suggests to basic researchers that they need to refine their theories to better reflect how the social world operates.

Our discussion in each chapter of this text will begin with an analysis of the findings of basic research, for as Kurt Lewin (1951) argued, it is essential to have a good understanding of psychological processes *before* trying to solve difficult social problems. Yet, in keeping with Lewin's maxim of "No research without action, and no action without research," throughout the text we will also examine how basic research is applied to important social problems. In addition, each chapter (beginning with chapter 3) will conclude with an Application section in which you can learn how the content of that chapter sheds light on a specific social or personal issue.

The Research Process Involves a Series of Sequential Steps

Remember when you were a child and decided to build a model airplane, make clothes for your dolls, or undertake some other project? Perhaps you were so excited about completing that final product displayed on the outside of the model box or on the front of the clothes pattern envelope that you threw aside the directions and slapped your project together as fast as your little fingers could handle the assorted parts. Unfortunately, using such a slap-dash method often led to a final product that bore little resemblance to the picture displayed on the box or envelope. Hopefully you learned, through such experiences, the importance of designing a plan of action in undertaking projects. This basic lesson of childhood is exactly what the remainder of this chapter is all about.

For social psychologists to effectively study social behavior—be it basic or applied research—they must carefully plan and execute their research projects (Sansone et al., 2004). In doing so, social psychologists employ the **scientific method,** which consists of a set of procedures used to gather, analyze, and interpret information in a way that reduces error and leads to dependable generalizations. This entire process of scientific inquiry unfolds in six basic steps, which are summarized in table 2.1.

STEP 1: SELECT A TOPIC AND REVIEW PAST RESEARCH

Research ideas do not develop in a vacuum. In selecting a topic to study, inspiration could come from someone else's research, from an incident in the daily news, or from some personal experience in the researcher's own life. As stated in chapter 1 (pp. 9–10), it is not a coincidence that the research topics chosen by American social psychologists have the greatest meaning to Americans. Social psychologists generally investigate topics that have relevance to their own lives and culture.

There is nothing so practical as a good theory.

Kurt Lewin, German-born social psychologist, 1890–1947

Scientific Method

A set of procedures used to gather, analyze, and interpret information in a way that reduces error and leads to dependable generalizations.

T A B L E   2 . 1

Steps in the Process of Social Psychological Research

Step 1: Select a topic and review past research. *Ideas come from a variety of sources, including existing theories, past research, current social events, and personal experiences. Social psychologists must also become knowledgeable about past research findings in their area of interest and keep abreast of recently published studies and those reported at scientific meetings.*

Step 2: Develop a theory and hypotheses. *Once the research literature has been digested, a theory and/or hypotheses that can be empirically tested must then be developed.*

Step 3: Select a scientific method and obtain approval to conduct the study. *Research can be conducted in the laboratory or in the field, and the social psychologist can either employ observational, correlational, or experimental methodology.*

Step 4: Collect the data. *Social psychologists use both qualitative and quantitative data. The three basic techniques of data collection are self-reports, direct observations, and archival information.*

Step 5: Analyze the data and reevaluate the theory. *Data can be analyzed using either descriptive or inferential statistics, with the latter mathematical analysis being the more valuable because it allows researchers to generalize their findings to the population of interest. If the results from these analyses do not support the study's hypotheses, the theory from which the hypotheses were derived needs to be reconsidered and perhaps revised.*

Step 6: Report the results. *Just because a social psychologist conducts a study does not mean it will be published and make its way into the social psychological literature. In most cases, a scientific journal will not publish a submitted article if there are problems with the hypotheses or methods, or flaws in the data analysis. In addition, articles are often rejected for publication because reviewers decide the research is not very important. Due to these factors, the top journals in social psychology (Journal of Personality and Social Psychology, Personality and Social Psychology Bulletin) regularly publish less than 10 percent of the submitted research articles.*

Once a topic has been chosen, the researcher must search the scientific literature to determine whether prior investigations of the topic exist. The findings from these previous studies generally shape the course of the current investigation. Today, literature searches can be vastly accelerated by using a number of computer-based searching programs that catalog even the most recently published studies. In addition, social psychologists can often instantly obtain unpublished articles from researchers at other universities either through computer networks or fax machines. This means that access to others' scholarly contributions is often literally at one's fingertips.

STEP 2: DEVELOP A THEORY AND HYPOTHESES

As previously noted, the basic motivation underlying research is the desire to answer questions. The questions of interest usually revolve around whether some phenomenon can be explained by a particular principle or theory. A **theory** is an organized system of ideas that seeks to explain why two or more events are related. Put simply, a theory provides a particular picture of reality concerning some phenomenon. What makes a good theory depends on a number of factors, some of which are listed in table 2.2 (Higgins, 2004; Nowak, 2004).

The most salient factor to the working scientist is the *predictive accuracy* of the theory: can it reliably predict behavior? A second necessary factor is *internal coherence*—there should not be any logical inconsistencies or unexplained coincidences among any of the theoretical ideas. A third characteristic of a good theory is that it should be *economical,* meaning that it only contains the principles or concepts necessary to explain the phenomenon in question and no more. Finally, a fourth and very important quality in a good theory is *fertility*—the ability to fire the imagination of other scientists so that the ideas in the theory are tested and extended to a wide variety of social behavior.

The way that scientists determine the predictive accuracy of a theory is by formulating hypotheses. **Hypotheses** are specific propositions or expectations about the nature of things derived from a theory—they are the logical implications of the theory. The researcher asks, "If the theory is true, what observations would we expect to make in our investigation?" For example, during the course of his work, Leonard Eron developed the idea that exposure to a lot of TV violence was detrimental to children's social development. This theory led him to formulate the hypothesis that individuals who watch a great deal of TV violence during childhood will be more physically aggressive in adulthood than individuals who watch little TV violence.

STEP 3: SELECT A SCIENTIFIC METHOD AND OBTAIN APPROVAL TO CONDUCT THE STUDY

After developing a theory and hypotheses, researchers must next select a scientific method that allows the hypotheses to be tested in a way that minimizes error and leads to dependable generalizations. The three primary scientific methods used by social psychologists are *observational, correlational,* and *experimental.* Whereas observational research describes

Theory
An organized system of ideas that seeks to explain why two or more events are related.

Hypotheses
Specific propositions or expectations about the nature of things derived from a theory.

TABLE 2.2

What Makes a Good Theory?

Predictive Accuracy: Can it reliably predict behavior?

Internal Coherence: Are there any logical inconsistencies between any of the theoretical ideas?

Economy: Does it only contain what is necessary to explain the phenomenon in question?

Fertility: Does it generate research and can it be used to explain a wide variety of social behavior?

behavior, the correlational and experimental methods study the relationships among variables. Of the three, experimentation is much more widely used by social psychologists in psychology, observational studies are more often conducted by sociological social psychologists, and correlational methods enjoy roughly equal popularity in both disciplines (Morrill & Fine, 1997; Sherman et al., 1999). We will discuss these three methods in the next section of the chapter.

In all scientific methods, social psychologists seek to determine the nature of the relationship between two or more factors, called **variables** because they are things that can be measured and that can vary. When scientists describe their variables, they do so by using **operational definitions,** which are very precise descriptions of how the variables have been quantified so that they can be measured. For example, social psychologists studying TV violence and aggression among children may operationally define aggression as any behavior that appears to have the goal of causing physical harm or physical discomfort to another person. This concrete definition of aggression would help other social psychologists know what was measured in the study, and it would also allow them to repeat the study if they desired.

To ensure the health and safety of participants in social psychological studies, all research-oriented institutions have **institutional review boards (IRBs)** to monitor and evaluate research proposals involving both human and animal subjects. IRBs consist of a panel of both scientists and nonscientists who ensure the protection and welfare of research participants by formally reviewing the methodologies and procedures of proposed studies prior to the commencement of data collection (more on this later).

STEP 4: COLLECT THE DATA

When the IRB has granted approval, it is time to collect data from your sample. A **sample** is a group of people who are selected to participate in a given study. The people who are selected to participate in the study come from a **population,** which consists of all the members of an identifiable group from which a sample is drawn. The closer a sample is in representing the population, the greater confidence researchers have in generalizing their findings beyond the sample.

Regarding the data collected from your sample of participants, there are two broad categories: *qualitative* and *quantitative.* Qualitative data exists in a nonnumeric form, such as a scientist's narrative report of a conversation between two people. In contrast, quantitative data is numerical. A scientist collecting this type of data, when studying the same two people conversing, might rate each person's level of physical attractiveness with a numerical scale in which "1" indicates "very unattractive" and "5" indicates "very attractive." As this example suggests, researchers often collect both qualitative and quantitative data in the same study.

Besides data categories, there are three basic techniques of data collection: (1) *self-reports,* (2) *direct observations,* and (3) *archival information.* Collecting data using self-reports allows researchers to measure important subjective states, such as people's perceptions, emotions, or attitudes. The disadvantage of self-report data, however, is that it relies on people accurately describing these internal states—something they are not always willing or able to do (Greenwald et al., 1998; Holden et al., 2001; Schwarz, 2003). Because of this drawback, many researchers prefer to directly observe people's behavior, recording its quantity and direction of change over time. This technique is widely employed in observational and experimental studies. Finally, researchers sometimes examine existing documents, or archives, to gather information. These accumulated records come from a wide variety of sources (for example, census information, court records, and newspaper articles) and can provide researchers with a great deal of valuable information (Simonton, 1998). These three ways of collecting information are not always mutually exclusive. For example, the personal memoirs of historical figures represent both self-report and archived data.

STEP 5: ANALYZE THE DATA AND REEVALUATE THE THEORY

Once the data have been collected, the first part of the fifth step is to conduct data analysis, which usually requires extensive knowledge of statistical procedures and computer software packages. The two basic kinds of statistics are descriptive and inferential. *Descriptive*

Variables

In scientific research, things that can be measured and that can vary.

Operational Definition

A scientist's precise description of how a variable has been quantified so that it can be measured.

Institutional Review Boards (IRBs)

A panel of scientists and nonscientists who ensure the protection and welfare of research participants by formally reviewing researchers' methodologies and procedures prior to data collection.

CRITICAL *thinking*

Prior to conducting research, what precautions do you think social psychologists should take to ensure that the people who participate in their research will not be harmed? Should social psychologists be allowed to study people without their consent?

Science has to be understood in its broadest sense, as a method for comprehending all observable reality, and not merely as an instrument for acquiring specialized knowledge.

Alexis Carrel, French-American surgeon and Nobel Prize winner for medicine, 1873–1944

Sample

A group of people who are selected to participate in a research study.

Population

All the members of an identifiable group from which a sample is drawn.

FIGURE 2.1

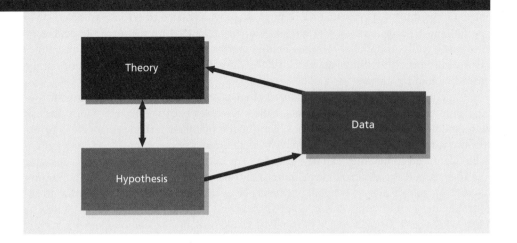

The Cyclical Nature of the Theory-Hypothesis Relationship

The data from a study provides the evidence to support or disconfirm the hypothesis. If the hypothesis is supported, the validity of the theory is also supported, generating new hypotheses to test in future research. If the hypothesis is not supported, the validity of the theory is questioned, prompting researchers to revise the theory to reflect the insights gained from their investigation. This revised theory is then used to develop new hypotheses that are then tested in another round of research. Research results that disconfirm a study's hypotheses not only reveal flaws in a scientist's theory, they also provide clues to greater scientific truths. Scientists who can think "outside the box" of their own theories and regularly entertain alternative explanations for their hypotheses are best equipped to advance scientific knowledge.

Imagine that you are the leader of a team of researchers studying social psychological topics at a university. Under your tutelage, students are learning about the research process while working on your team. Besides instructing them on the proper scientific methods, statistical procedures, and ethical standards to adopt when conducting research, what advice would you give them concerning how they should approach scientific problems in their work?

statistics merely summarize and describe the behavior or characteristics of a particular sample of participants in a study, whereas *inferential statistics* move beyond mere description to make inferences about the larger population from which the sample was drawn. Inferential statistics are used to estimate the likelihood that a difference found in the people studied would also be found if everyone in the population participated in the study. Social psychologists generally accept a difference as *statistically significant* if the likelihood of it having occurred by mere chance is less than one in twenty; that is, a probability of less than 5 percent (Krueger, 2001; Nickerson, 2000). Because one of the main objectives of social psychological research is to generalize research findings to the population of interest, inferential statistics are the more valued type of statistic in the discipline.

After data analysis determines whether the hypotheses successfully predicted the outcome of the study, researchers next reevaluate the theory. Were the research hypotheses supported by the data, which thereby supports the validity of the theory? If the data do not support the study's hypotheses, or if only some of the hypotheses were supported, the theory probably needs revising. Although results that do not support stated hypotheses are often greeted with disappointment by researchers, many also realize that great discoveries often follow such disappointment. In this regard, social psychologist William McGuire (1999) asserts that the task of science is "not the dull and easy job of showing that a fixed hypothesis is right or wrong in a given context. . . . Science has the more exciting task of discovering in what senses the hypotheses and its theoretical explanations are true and in what senses false" (p. 407). From this perspective, failure to find support for a research hypothesis provides the opportunity for future discovery (Banaji, 2004; McGuire, 2004). Figure 2.1 illustrates the cyclical nature of the relationship between a theory and a testable hypothesis.

STEP 6: REPORT THE RESULTS

As in any scholarly pursuit, for advancements to be made researchers must share their knowledge with others in the field. Researchers disseminate their findings by either publishing articles in scientific journals, making presentations at professional meetings, or by personally informing other researchers. Through the dissemination of these findings, researchers build upon and refine one another's work, and our understanding of social behavior is enriched.

This final step in the research process is a very important one for the advancement of the discipline. However, others do not uncritically accept these findings. At scientific conventions, where research is often first reported, all steps in the research process are scrutinized and the study's strengths and weaknesses are illuminated.

When a written report of the study is later submitted to a scientific journal, it is reviewed to determine whether it should be published. So throughout this process of scientific inquiry, there are numerous checks and balances that ultimately determine whether a research project will make its way into the discipline's body of knowledge. One of the most important factors in this determination is a study's scientific procedure for collecting, analyzing, and interpreting information. Let us now examine the primary scientific methods employed by social psychologists.

Description Is the Goal of Observational Research

To understand behavior so that it can be predicted, controlled, or explained, a scientist must first describe it accurately. **Observational research** is a scientific method involving systematic qualitative and/or quantitative descriptions of behavior. In collecting this data, the scientific observer would not try to manipulate (that is, change) the behavior under study but would simply record it. Description is the primary goal here. Three common types of observational methods employed by social psychologists are *naturalistic observation, participant observation,* and *archival research.*

NATURALISTIC OBSERVATION
Naturalistic observation is a form of observational method that investigates behavior in its natural environment (Lofland & Lofland, 1995). Settings for such social psychological research could take place at sporting events, where the interactions between opposing fans might be recorded, or in neighborhood shopping malls, where the courtship behavior of adolescents might be documented. In such naturalistic studies, observers usually remain as unobtrusive as possible, so that their presence does not influence the behavior under study. In some observational studies, researchers are not present at all during data collection— hidden video cameras record the events. Later, researchers analyze the behaviors being investigated (Pomerantz et al., 2004). Besides employing naturalistic observation as a primary scientific method, researchers often use it during the initial stages of a project to generate ideas and to gather descriptive data.

PARTICIPANT OBSERVATION
Another type of observational method is **participant observation.** Here, as in naturalistic observation, a researcher records behavior as it occurs in its natural environment but does so as a participant of the group being studied (Whyte, 1994). One of the chief benefits of this research strategy is that it allows investigators to get closer to what they are studying than any other method.

A classic example of participant observation research in social psychology was Leon Festinger's study of a Chicago-based doomsday cult in the 1950s (Festinger et al., 1956). The leader of the cult, Mrs. Keetch, claimed she was in contact with aliens from outer space who had told her the world was going to end on a specific date, December 21. She told reporters that the only survivors of this catastrophe would be members of her group. When Festinger and his coworkers learned of Mrs. Keetch, they became interested in documenting how the cult members would react when the doomsday passed with the world still intact. Acting quickly, these researchers infiltrated the cult as participant observers and described the interactions of the members and its leader. This descriptive study was one of the first tests of Festinger's (1957) *cognitive dissonance theory* (see chapter 6, pp. 195–200). The rich narrative accounts emerging from this participant observation method proved invaluable in demonstrating how some of the basic principles of cognitive dissonance operate in a specific—albeit unusual—situation.

Listed below are four advantages of both naturalistic and participant observation research (Hong & Duff, 2002; Weick, 1985):

1. Allow researchers the opportunity to watch behavior in its "wholeness," providing the full context in which to understand it.

Observation, not old age, brings wisdom.

Publilius Syrus, ca. 42 B.C.

Observational Research

A scientific method involving systematic qualitative and/or quantitative descriptions of behavior.

Naturalistic Observation

A descriptive scientific method that investigates behavior in its usual natural environment.

Participant Observation

A descriptive scientific method where a group is studied from within by a researcher who records behavior as it occurs in its usual natural environment.

The goal of observational research is to systematically describe behavior, such as the deliberations of this work group in a large corporation. Using this scientific method, social psychologists do not manipulate events, but instead, allow them to unfold on their own. What are some of the strengths and weaknesses of this method?

2. Provide researchers the opportunity to record rare events that may never occur in a controlled laboratory environment.

3. Allow researchers the opportunity to systematically record events that were previously seen only by nonscientists.

4. Allow researchers to observe events that would be too risky, dangerous, or unethical to create in the laboratory.

Despite numerous benefits in using naturalistic and participant observation methods, some problems also bear mentioning. First, due to the absence of control that researchers have in such studies, conclusions must be drawn very cautiously. For example, if you observe that shoppers are more likely to donate money after walking out of a store rather than when walking in, do you know for certain what is causing this difference in behavior? Perhaps shoppers have more spare change after making purchases, or perhaps something in the store puts them in a giving mood. Because observational research does not manipulate events to determine their effect on outcomes, researchers must be careful in concluding how events are related to one another.

Observer Bias

Occurs when preconceived ideas held by the researcher affect the nature of the observations made.

A second problem is **observer bias,** which occurs when scientists' preconceived ideas about what they are studying affect the nature of their observations. For instance, if you are investigating aggression and believe ahead of time that men are more aggressive than women, you might more likely perceive an ambiguous shove as a nonaggressive nudge when delivered by a woman rather than by a man. Such biasing can be minimized if the behaviors observed are carefully defined and more than one observer is trained in identifying them. If these trained observers, working independently, exhibit a high level of agreement in identifying the behaviors, you have high *interobserver reliability.* With modern technology, researchers often videotape events for later reliability checks.

A third potential problem facing you in naturalistic and participant observation research is that your presence can significantly alter the behavior of those being studied and thus taint the data. This is especially troublesome in participant observation research, where the observer is often actively involved in the observed events. Although observational researchers assume that after a period of time those who are being observed will become accustomed to their presence, it is difficult to evaluate to what degree this actually occurs.

Every journey into the past is complicated by delusions, false memories, false namings of real events.

Adrienne Rich, U.S. poet, b. 1929

Finally, one last problem posed by these types of observational methods is that, more than any other scientific methods, they pose the most ethical problems involving invasion of others' privacy. In a later chapter section we will discuss some of the ethical guidelines that all researchers follow to minimize any potential harm to those they are studying.

ARCHIVAL RESEARCH

The third observational method that we will discuss is **archival research,** which examines the already-existing records of an individual, group, or culture. Examples of archival material include diaries, music lyrics, television programs, census information, novels, and newspapers. Archival research is often employed as one component in a larger research effort that includes other scientific methods. For example, in studying friendship networks in high school, a researcher might use information found in the yearbook to evaluate students' physical attractiveness and involvement in school activities. This archival information might be combined with self-reports from students and teachers using survey research and then analyzed together.

A popular procedure for evaluating information in archives is *content analysis,* a technique in which two or more people (called judges), working independently, count words, sentences, ideas, or whatever other category of information is of interest. As with all scientific inquiry, it is important to clearly define the research variables before beginning a content analysis. It is also important that the judges are carefully trained so that they consistently follow the same guidelines when coding information (Hoyt, 2000). If each category of information is clearly defined and if the judges are adequately trained, *interjudge reliability*—which means the same thing as interobserver reliability—should be sufficiently high to ensure that the observations are not the result of observer bias.

Archival research is often used to examine the beliefs, values, and interests of a culture. As mentioned in the chapter-opening story, television has been identified as a potentially powerful socializing agent, and TV violence has been the subject of social psychological study for decades. From 1994 to 1997, over eighty researchers at four universities assessed television violence as part of the National Television Violence Study, with one component of their work involving archival research (Federman, 1998). Each year, these researchers conducted content analysis of about 2,700 randomly selected programs broadcast between 6:00 A.M. and 11:00 P.M., representing more than 2,000 hours of television. Their analysis covered many areas, including how characters reacted when violence occurred, how violence was presented in the context of the overall program, and whether violent interactions showed pain, realistic injury, and long-term negative consequences. For the study, violence was defined as any depiction of physical force, or the credible threat of such force, intended to harm an animate being or group of beings.

Their results indicated that violence was a popular theme in TV programs over the three-year period of the study. More than 60 percent of all TV shows contained some violence, with premium cable channels having the highest rate (85 percent) and public broadcasting having the lowest (18 percent). Regarding how violence was depicted, most incidents were sanitized—they showed no pain and little harm for victims, and there were seldom any long-term negative effects. Only 4 percent of violent programs emphasized an antiviolence theme. Instead, violence was often glamorized. More than one of every three violent incidents involved attractive perpetrators, who were likely role models for children, using violence to solve problems. Equally alarming were the findings that children's programs were the least likely to show the long-term negative effects of violence, and they frequently portrayed violence in a humorous context (67 percent of the time). The researchers contended that the message conveyed to young viewers in these programs is that violence is a successful and an appropriate method for good people to solve problems, and that it rarely results in any serious harm to victims or their families.

As this study illustrates, archival research can provide us with valuable information about a culture. The high level of violence in television programming, and the manner in which it is portrayed, suggests that many people enjoy this form of entertainment (Hamilton, 1998). Does watching violent programs cause people to become more violent themselves? Or does observing such violent events have a purging effect on viewers, reducing their aggressive impulses? Archival research cannot answer these questions. Given the purely descriptive nature of all observational research, we must look to other scientific methods to answer questions about how variables are related to one another.

Correlational Research Assesses the Direction and Strength of the Relationship Between Variables

Besides describing behavior, social psychologists are also interested in learning whether two or more variables are related, and if so, how strongly. When changes in one variable relate to changes in another variable, we say that they *correlate*. **Correlational research** assesses the nature of the relationship between two or more variables that are not controlled by the researcher. In studying the relationship between children's TV viewing habits and their aggressive behavior, researchers using the correlational method do not try to influence how much time any of the children in the study actually spend viewing violent shows. Instead, they merely gather information on the amount of time the children spend watching such programs and their degree of aggressive behavior, and then determine how these two variables correlate.

SURVEYS

Although studying the relationships among variables can be done by directly observing behavior or examining archived information, it is often accomplished by asking people carefully constructed questions. **Surveys** are structured sets of questions or statements given to a group of people to measure their attitudes, beliefs, values, or behavioral tendencies (Lavrakas, 1993; Schuman, 2002).

The four major survey techniques are *face-to-face surveys, written surveys, phone surveys,* and *computer surveys.* The face-to-face format provides highly detailed information and allows researchers the best opportunity to clarify any unclear questions. However, it is costly and there is always the possibility that people's responses might be influenced by the interviewer's presence. Written, phone, and computer surveys eliminate such interviewer bias and are much less expensive. Although obtaining information using surveys is generally relatively easy, the main disadvantage in all three techniques is that they rely on self-report data. As previously mentioned, self-reports suffer from respondents' faulty memories, wishful thinking, and outright deception.

An important consideration in constructing surveys involves how questions are asked. Survey questions usually are either open-ended or closed-ended. An *open-ended question* requires a response that must have more than just a yes or no answer—research participants provide a narrative response. A *closed-ended question,* in contrast, is answered with a yes or no, or by choosing a single response from several alternatives. To illustrate this difference, consider how these two formats might be used to study people's TV-viewing preferences:

Closed-ended: Do you enjoy watching violent TV shows?

Response: Yes_____ No_____

Open-ended: Why do you enjoy (or not enjoy) watching violent TV shows?

*Response:*_____

Each question format has advantages and disadvantages. Closed-ended questions are the quickest and easiest to score. In contrast, open-ended questions may provide information from respondents that might be missed with closed-ended questions. However, open-ended responses require coding by carefully trained judges (see previous discussion of interjudge reliability, p. 33), and this is a time-consuming process.

Attempting to capitalize on the strengths of both types of questions, survey researchers sometimes provide a set of response alternatives and then invite participants to write down a response of their own choosing if they wish. Despite the increased freedom of this type of response format, most respondents are reluctant to go outside the frame of reference provided by the fixed answers. For example, in one study examining this blended format, Howard Schuman and Jacqueline Scott (1987) asked a national sample of Americans to name the most important problem facing the country. From these responses, they identified four problems that had been mentioned by fewer than 3 percent of the respondents. Next, Schuman and Scott asked a second sample of Americans a parallel question, but provided as choices the four infrequently chosen problems identified in the previous sample. The question also invited participants to

TABLE 2.3

Does Adding an Open-Ended Response Choice Correct the Problem with Closed-Ended Survey Questions?

Open-Ended Question	Closed-Ended Question
What do you think is the most important problem facing this country today?	Which of the following do you think is the most important problem facing this country today? If you prefer, you may name a different problem as most important. 1. Energy shortage 2. Quality of public schools 3. Legalized abortion 4. Pollution 5. _____

When a national sample of Americans were asked to identify the most important problem facing the country, fewer than 3 percent named the energy shortage, the quality of public schools, legalized abortion, or pollution. However, when these infrequently chosen problems were placed on a second questionnaire and given to another national sample of Americans, 60 percent of the respondents picked one of these items as the most important national problem, despite being told that they could write in a different problem of their own choosing (Schuman & Scott, 1987). What do these findings suggest about the effects of adding an open-ended response format to a closed-format question?

Adapted from H. Schuman and J. Scott, "Problems in the Use of Survey Questions to Measure Public Opinion," *Science, 236,* pp. 957–959, May 22, 1987.

substitute a different problem of their own choosing if they desired (see table 2.3). Despite this invitation, the majority of the respondents (60 percent) picked one of the rare problems. Were these respondents too cognitively lazy to sift through their own beliefs about the nation's problems? Did the listing of the four problems elevate their importance in the respondents' minds? Whatever the reason, these results suggest that the form of a question often conveys the "rules of the game" for respondents, and researchers must keep this in mind when interpreting survey findings (Schuman, 2002). Most of the surveys that you will be asked to complete in this textbook include closed-ended questions (for example, see chapter 3, p. 63 and p. 77).

As previously noted (p. 29), one of the most important considerations in conducting surveys—as well as when using other methods—is getting responses from people who represent the population as a whole. This *representative sample* is often obtained through **random selection,** which is a procedure in which everyone in the population has an equal chance of being selected for the sample. As long as a sample is selected randomly, you are reasonably assured that the data will represent the overall population. However, when samples are not randomly selected, drawing conclusions from the data can lead to serious errors. For example, in 1936, a large survey conducted by the magazine *Literary Digest* indicated that Republican Alf Landon would soundly defeat then-president Franklin Roosevelt in the upcoming election. In fact, Roosevelt won by a landslide. The problem with the magazine's survey was that it did not randomly select voters from the population—the sample was obtained from telephone books and automobile registration listings. Because telephones and cars were luxury items during the Depression of the 1930s, most of the people in the sample were affluent Republicans who represented a minority of eligible voters.

Today, major polling organizations typically are very careful in securing representative samples in order to avoid errors in generalizing their findings to the population. However, many surveys that you find in popular magazines or on the Internet asking you to report your opinions on various personal and social issues have limited generalizability.

Random Selection

A procedure for selecting a sample of people to study in which everyone in the population has an equal chance of being chosen.

Why? Because the results are based on only those people who read the magazine or go to the website and are sufficiently motivated to send in their opinions. The results of such non-representative surveys may not provide an accurate portrayal of societal opinions.

Finally, one last problem in conducting survey research is **social desirability bias,** which occurs when people respond to survey questions by trying to portray themselves in a favorable light rather than responding in an accurate and truthful manner. Over the years, researchers have discovered that people exaggerate their tendency to engage in such socially desirable behaviors as attending religious services and voting, while underreporting their socially undesirable actions, such as taking illegal drugs or evading taxes (Hadaway et al., 1993; Krosnick, 1999). On the more positive side, recent studies indicate that even when survey participants have a desire to "look good" in the researchers' eyes, they also often have a concern with the accuracy of their responses (Holtgraves, 2004). In the final analysis, as with all research methods, the results of survey research have to be interpreted with its strengths and weaknesses in mind, and increased confidence in its conclusions will occur when other methods provide converging results.

THE CORRELATION COEFFICIENT

Whether information for studying the relationships among variables is obtained from surveys or some other data-gathering procedure, the primary benefit of conducting correlational research is *prediction*. This method allows researchers to predict a change in one variable by knowing the value of another variable. More specifically, it provides information on the *direction* and *strength* of the relationship between variables. The direction of the relationship between variable A and variable B tells *how* they are related (positively or negatively). The strength of the relationship can be thought of as the degree of accuracy with which you can predict the value of one variable by knowing the value of the other variable. The direction and strength of the relationship between two variables are described by the statistical measure known as the **correlation coefficient** (*r*). This correlation coefficient can range from -1.00 to $+1.00$.

Returning to the previous example of television viewing and aggression, a correlation at or very near zero indicates the absence of a *linear relationship* between these two variables. This zero correlation may mean one of two things: (1) viewing television violence has no association with children's aggressive behavior, or (2) there is a *curvilinear relationship* between television viewing and aggression. One can easily determine the meaning of a zero correlation by plotting the pairing of these two variables on a graph, as is illustrated in figure 2.2. A correlation close to "0.00" would have dots scattered all around the graph, while a correlation near $+1.00$ would have dots lining up on an imaginary straight line running between the X and Y axes of the graph. The farther the dots on the graph fall from the imaginary straight line, the lower is the correlation.

In marked contrast to a zero correlation, one that is near -1.00 would suggest that children who watch a lot of violent television are less aggressive than those who watch little violence on television. In contrast, a correlation near $+1.00$ indicates that children who watch a lot of violent television are more aggressive than those who watch little violence.

Regarding the strength of a relationship, researchers seldom find a perfect or near perfect ($r = +1.00$ or $r = -1.00$) correlation between variables. In Leonard Eron's (1963) initial study, he examined the relationship between the viewing of violent television shows by 8- and 9-year-old children and their aggressiveness (as rated by their classmates and teachers). For boys, he found a correlation of $+.21$ between viewing television violence and aggression, whereas for girls, the correlation was $+.02$. Thus in this sample, if you knew that a particular boy watched a lot of violent television, you would predict that he may be rather aggressive (due to the direction of the relationship), but you would not be confident in your prediction (due to its low strength). For girls, because the correlation is virtually nonexistent, you would be wise not to make any predictions.

Although the boys' correlation of $+.21$ might seem small, social science correlations rarely exceed .60. The reason for this is that many factors determine human behavior. What variables besides television viewing might influence aggression in children? Personality,

Social Desirability Bias

A type of response bias in surveys in which people respond to a question by trying to portray themselves in a favorable light rather than responding in an accurate and truthful manner.

Correlation Coefficient

A statistical measure of the direction and strength of the linear relationship between two variables, which can range from -1.00 to $+1.00$.

FIGURE 2.2

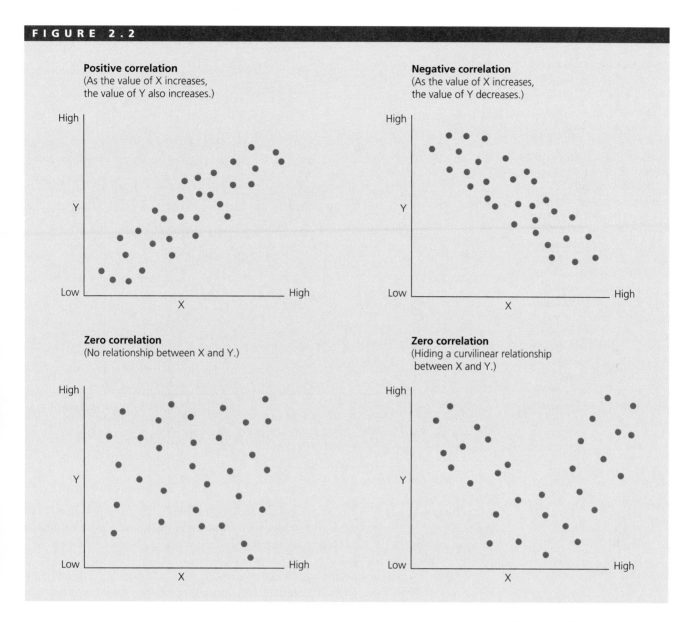

Positive correlation
(As the value of X increases, the value of Y also increases.)

Negative correlation
(As the value of X increases, the value of Y decreases.)

Zero correlation
(No relationship between X and Y.)

Zero correlation
(Hiding a curvilinear relationship between X and Y.)

Plotting the Relationship Between Variable X and Variable Y on a Graph

Each point on the graphs represents a pairing of variable X with variable Y for each participant in the study. Examine the curvilinear relationship graph. The zero correlation is hiding a meaningful relationship, where both high and low levels of X are associated with high levels of Y, but moderate levels of X are associated with low levels of Y. What sort of social variables might have a curvilinear relationship?

mood, social class, and parental attitudes certainly influence aggressive tendencies. Furthermore, even if we could identify all relevant variables influencing aggression, because of the nature of our subject—humans with self-reflective abilities and minds of their own—we would not be able to perfectly predict people's actions.

The major disadvantage of the correlational study is that it cannot definitively determine the *cause* of the relationship between two variables. That is, besides knowing the strength and direction of a relationship, it is extremely valuable to know which variable caused a change in the other. Does watching violent shows make boys more aggressive, or are aggressive boys more likely to watch violent shows? This methodological disadvantage can result in the *reverse-causality problem,* which occurs whenever either of the two variables correlated with each other could just as plausibly be the cause or the effect. Thus, you might falsely conclude that watching violence on television causes increased aggressiveness in boys when, in fact, aggressive boys are simply more likely to choose to watch violent television shows.

Sometimes when you have a significant correlation between two variables, there is only one possible causal direction. For example, a number of studies have found a strong correlation between being the victim of physical abuse as a child and being the perpetrator

FIGURE 2.3

A Cross-Lagged Panel Correlation Study of Violent TV and Male Aggression

The important correlations in Eron et al.'s (1972) cross-lagged panel correlation study are on the diagonals. The correlation between the amount of TV violence watched by the male children at age 9 and aggression ten years later was much larger than the correlation between male aggression at age 9 and TV watching ten years later. What do these different correlations suggest about which variable is causing a change in the other? Although this study's findings make us more confident that TV violence causes increased aggression in boys, strictly speaking, we can never definitely infer causality from correlational data.

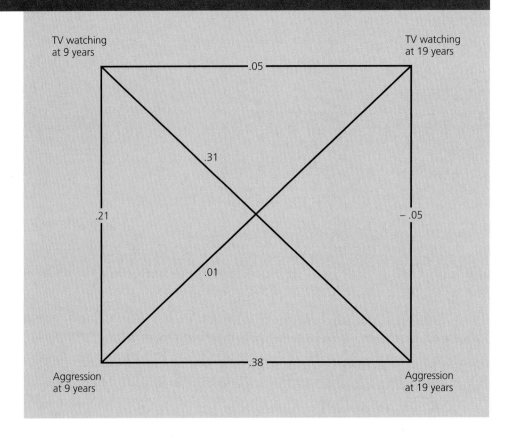

of family violence as an adult (Straus et al., 1980; Widom, 1989). Because a past event cannot be caused by a future event, researchers conducting these studies were more confident in asserting that the physical abuse suffered in childhood was a likely cause of the victimization of others in adulthood.

Another way to address the problem of reverse-causality is to measure your variables twice. In such a *cross-lagged panel correlation study,* the two variables are measured at two different times, and correlations between the variables across time are examined. For example, in Eron's study of the relationship between childhood television-viewing preferences and aggressive behavior, he recontacted the children ten years later and obtained new information on these two variables (Eron et al., 1972). As you can see in figure 2.3, when the across-time correlations were examined, the researchers found that the amount of violent television the males had watched as children was positively correlated ($r = .31$) with their current aggressive behavior at age 19. On the other hand, no relationship was found between their childhood aggression and their current preferences for violent television shows ($r = .01$). Again, as before, no relationship was found for females. Based on these findings, the researchers felt more confident in concluding that the single most plausible causal hypothesis was that a preference for watching violent television during childhood contributes to the aggressive habits in males.

A second problem resulting from the inability to confidently determine causality is that it is possible that a third, unspecified variable causes differences in both variables under study. This is known as the *third-variable problem.* In the Eron study, the positive correlation between television violence and boys' aggression may be due to a third variable not measured by the researcher. Therefore, what looks like an actual relationship between these two variables is really an illusion. The third variable could be the beliefs that the children's parents have toward violence as a force in childrearing and society. That is, parents who use

Over the years, social psychologists have studied the effect that television violence has on people's aggression, especially children's antisocial behavior. Both experimental and correlational methods have been employed to better understand this issue. Of the two methods, which is susceptible to the third-variable problem?

Reprinted by permission of Copley News Service.

physical punishment in discipline may also prefer violent television shows because they seem more realistic and familiar. As a result of this mind-set toward violence, these children are taught to be aggressive and are also exposed to many violent television programs through their parents' own viewing habits. Can you think of other possible variables that might also explain the relationship between TV violence and children's aggression? For further examples of third-variable problems, look at the video *Understanding Correlation* on your Social Sense CD-ROM.

Social Sense

View excerpts from *Understanding Correlation*

Experimental Research Can Determine Cause-Effect Relationships

Because correlational studies cannot definitively tell us why variables are related to one another, social psychologists use **experimental methods** to examine cause-effect relationships. In an experiment, the scientist manipulates one variable by exposing research participants to it at contrasting levels (for example, high, medium, low, no exposure), and then observes what effect this manipulation has on the other variable that has not been manipulated. The variable that is manipulated is called the **independent variable,** and it is the one the experimenter is testing as the possible cause of any changes that might occur in the other variable. The variable whose changes are considered to be the effect of the manipulated changes in the independent variable is called the **dependent variable.** The dependent variable is the response measure of an experiment that is *dependent* on the participant's response to the experimenter's manipulation of the setting (the independent variable). Once the participants in the study have been exposed to the independent variable, their behavior is carefully monitored to determine whether it varies in the predicted fashion with different levels of the independent variable. If it does, the experimenter can tentatively conclude that the independent variable is the cause of the changes in the dependent variable.

Experimental Methods

Research designed to examine cause-effect relationships between variables.

Independent Variable

The experimental variable that the researcher manipulates.

Dependent Variable

The experimental variable that is measured because it is believed to depend on the manipulated changes in the independent variable.

Let's return to the question of whether watching violent entertainment programs leads to increased aggressiveness in children. A number of experimental studies have explored this topic. For example, Jacques-Philippe Leyens and his colleagues (1975) conducted an experiment in a Belgian private institution for secondary-school boys. The independent variable in this study was exposure to violent films. In two cottages at the school, boys were shown a violent film every night for one week (for example, *Bonnie and Clyde, The Dirty Dozen*). The boys in two other cottages were shown the same number of nonviolent films during the same period of time (for example, *Lily, Daddy's Fiancée*). Thus, the experimenters created two levels of the independent variable—one group of boys (the *treatment group*) were exposed to the phenomenon believed to cause aggressiveness (violent films); the other group of boys (the *control group*) were not exposed to it. The experimenters then observed and recorded the children's aggressive behavior (the dependent variable) outside of the film-viewing settings. Significant differences were found between the two groups of boys, with the treatment group exhibiting higher levels of aggression both toward other boys and toward inanimate objects. Based on these findings, the social psychologists concluded that exposure to violent films had indeed caused increased aggressiveness.

FIELD EXPERIMENTS

The study just described is a special type of experiment called a *field experiment,* which is similar to the more common *laboratory experiment,* except that it is run in a natural setting, and participants often do not realize they are being studied. Because of this more natural atmosphere, participants tend to be less suspicious of what they are experiencing than in laboratory studies, and thus, their responses tend to be more spontaneous. This greater realism increases the study's **external validity,** which is the extent to which its findings can be generalized to people beyond those in the study itself.

Unfortunately, one drawback to field experiments is that researchers have less control over what is happening to each participant during the study because they are in a setting where many variables are uncontrollable (such as boys being called away from their cottages during a movie by a phone call from their parents). Another drawback is that experimenters have less control over precisely measuring the dependent variable because participants often move outside an area of easy observation (such as boys fighting in the bathroom or during "lights out"). These problems of control decrease the study's **internal validity,** which is the extent to which cause-and-effect conclusions can validly be made (Cook & Shadish, 1994). There is often a trade-off between internal and external validity, meaning that if you strengthen one you tend to weaken the other. By conducting his experiment in the children's normal social environment, Leyens was maximizing his external validity, making him reasonably confident that his findings would provide insights into how similar children respond to media violence. But did the "realness" of the research setting seriously compromise the study's internal validity? That is the risk often taken in field experiments.

LABORATORY EXPERIMENTS

By far, most social psychology experiments are conducted in laboratories. As an illustration, consider the following experiment investigating the effects that two independent variables, television violence and anger, have on boys' aggressive behavior. In this study, Donald Hartmann (1969) randomly assigned teenage boys to different levels of the two independent variables. At the beginning of the experiment, the boys' anger was manipulated by either having a **confederate** of the experimenter—who was posing as a fellow participant—insult him or treat him in a neutral fashion. Following the anger manipulation, the boys were assigned to one of three film conditions lasting two minutes. The first minute of each film showed two boys shooting baskets on a basketball court. For the remaining minute, the boys in the control group film merely played basketball, while in the two treatment-group films one of the boys began beating the other following an argument. In one of these violent films, the camera focused on the pain experienced by the boy who was being beaten. In the other, the camera focused on the aggressor's actions and facial expressions during the beating.

After viewing the film, each boy participated in a seemingly unrelated learning study. As the "teacher" in the study, the participant was instructed to administer an electrical shock to a "learner" whenever the learner made a mistake on the learning task. The learner was the confederate who had either insulted the participant or treated him neutrally. The intensity of the shock chosen by the boys was the dependent variable. In reality, no shocks were ever delivered, but the boys were not aware of this until the end of the experiment. As predicted, boys exposed to a violent film and boys previously angered tried to deliver stronger shocks to the learner than did boys in the control conditions. Further, boys who had been both angered and exposed to a violent film chose the strongest shock levels of the six groups of boys. No significant differences were found, however, between the two types of aggressive films. Thus, the combination of being exposed to a violent film while angry caused the greatest amount of aggression. This latter finding, in which the combined effects of the two

External Validity

The extent to which a study's findings can be generalized to people beyond those in the study itself.

Internal Validity

The extent to which cause-and-effect conclusions can validly be made in a study.

Confederate

An accomplice of an experimenter whom research participants assume is a fellow participant or bystander.

THE FAR SIDE® By GARY LARSON

Very few laboratory experiments ever come close to achieving the type of realism Eddie is experiencing here.

independent variables have different effects on the dependent variable than when alone, is known as an **interaction effect.**

As previously mentioned, the main advantage of a lab experiment like Hartmann's is that variables can be well controlled, thus increasing internal validity. An important component of this control is that participants can be randomly assigned to the different levels of the independent variable. In **random assignment,** the experimenter, by some random procedure, decides which participants are exposed to which level of the independent variable. Due to this random assignment, the experimenter can be reasonably confident that there are no preexisting average differences between the participants who are in the different experimental conditions. Often in a field study, groupings of participants already exist (as in the Belgian aggression study). In such cases, the researcher must collect additional data to determine if any preexisting differences between the groups might account for different variations of the dependent variable. If such assurances can be obtained, or preexisting conditions can be controlled when the data are analyzed, then failure to obtain random assignment is less of a threat to the study's internal validity.

Unfortunately, because of the researcher's desire to control as much of the experimental situation as possible in order to properly assign causality, an air of artificiality may exist in the lab (Gosling, 2004; Rozin, 2001). In the Hartmann lab study, for instance, the boys believed that delivering shocks was part of a learning study, and therefore whatever "aggression" they exhibited could be thought of as socially sanctioned by the experimenter. Because there was no possibility of retaliation or punishment surrounding this experimental aggression, some social psychologists have argued that it is difficult to generalize these types of findings to real-world aggression (Freedman, 1984). Despite the potential problem of external validity in some lab experiments, a recent analysis of many aggression studies conducted inside and outside the laboratory found that the results in both types of settings

Interaction Effect

An experimental result that occurs when two independent variables in combination have different effects on the dependent variable than when alone.

Random Assignment

Placement of research participants into experimental conditions in a manner that guarantees that all have an equal chance of being exposed to each level of the independent variable.

What are some similarities and some differences between "random assignment" and "random selection"?

Replication

Repeating a study using different participants in an attempt to duplicate previous findings.

Meta-analysis

The use of statistical techniques to sum up a body of similar studies in order to objectively estimate the reliability and overall size of the effect.

were very similar (Anderson & Bushman, 1997). These findings suggest that lab experiments on aggression generally appear to have adequate external validity, and that field experiments appear to have adequate internal validity.

Based on this overview of observational, correlational, and experimental research, you can see that there is no one best method in all research settings. In each investigation, social psychologists must decide what method provides the best opportunity of meeting the study's goals. Given the ability of the observational method to capture the richness of social behavior as it happens, many social psychologists believe that this approach is best suited for *theory building* (Fine & Elsbach, 2000). In contrast, because the experimental method can determine the cause of events, it is generally considered the method best suited for *theory testing*. The best overall strategy in developing theories of social behavior that are valid and useful is to take a *multimethod* approach—employing different methods to study the same topic, thereby capitalizing on each method's strengths and controlling for their weaknesses.

Meta-analysis Is a Statistical Procedure Used to Understand the Outcomes of Many Studies

The findings from a single study are far less convincing than the findings from a series of related studies. This is why researchers are so interested in **replication,** which involves repeating a study using different participants in an attempt to duplicate previous findings. The issue often faced in replications is that of contradictory findings from one study to the next. If, for example, seven studies find that boys are more aggressive than girls and three studies find no differences, what conclusions should be drawn? In the past, researchers used the "majority rules" approach to resolve such controversies. That is, they merely counted up the number of studies that found or did not find a particular effect and then concluded that the effect existed if it occurred in the majority of studies.

To rely on more sophisticated comparison procedures when dealing with contradictory findings from replication studies, researchers now use techniques called meta-analysis (Hall & Brannick, 2002). **Meta-analysis** is the use of statistical techniques to sum up a body of similar studies in order to objectively estimate the reliability and overall size of the effect (Rothstein et al., 2002; Stamps, 2002). Because many studies may find small differences between groups that do not reach statistical levels of significance, meta-analysis can determine whether these small effects are indeed "real" or merely measurement error. Throughout this text, you will see how meta-analysis helps us better understand social psychological findings.

Social Psychologists Are Increasingly Using Emerging Technologies in Their Research

In addition to using more powerful statistical techniques, an increasing number of social psychologists are employing new technologies in their study of social interaction. Three of the more prominent cutting-edge technologies currently being used in research are virtual environment devices, the Internet, and brain-imaging techniques.

VIRTUAL ENVIRONMENT TECHNOLOGY

As previously discussed, the high degree of control that a researcher can obtain in laboratory experiments often has a price: the danger of artificiality. In contrast, the realism in a field experiment is accompanied by the researcher having less control over variables that may markedly influence participants' thoughts and actions. Recently, some social psychologists believe they have found a possible remedy to the dilemma of choosing between greater control and greater realism in experiments (Blascovich, 2003). They recommend using *virtual environment technology,* in which they create a virtual research environment using a computer. Once this simulated reality is created, participants wearing virtual reality equipment are "immersed" in the setting. A commonly used piece of virtual reality equipment is a head-mounted or binocular-style device that allows an individual to view 3-D images and to "walk" through the virtual environment. Despite the fact that this type of simulated environment is completely

Some social psychologists are beginning to employ virtual environment technology, in which they create a virtual research environment using a computer. How might this new technology provide a possible solution to the dilemma of choosing between greater control and greater realism in experiments?

controlled by the experimenter—even more than the traditional laboratory setting—it has a very "real-world" feel to it, similar to that of a field experiment.

Early studies employing virtual environment technology suggest that participants behave relatively naturally in such settings (Blascovich, 2002; Waller et al., 2002). Although still in its infancy, virtual environment technology is currently being used to study such topics as conformity, eyewitness testimony, and violent video games. As this technology improves, psychologists hope to involve senses beyond sight and hearing, as well as to improve the ways people can interact with the virtual creations they encounter. This technology is not meant to replace traditional field and laboratory studies, but instead to provide another research vehicle that social psychologists can use in their work.

THE INTERNET

The Internet is a relatively new medium for communication, and many social psychologists are employing it as an avenue to collect data. One of the biggest advantages in using the Internet is that researchers can recruit participants from the entire world and test them remotely (Birnbaum, 2004). This technology has greatly facilitated the ability of social psychologists to conduct cross-cultural research. For example, in a series of Internet experiments on social exclusion, Kipling Williams and his colleagues (2000) collected data from more than 1,500 participants from over sixty countries. Other advantages of the Internet as a data collection site are that studies can be run without the presence of a researcher, without the need for large laboratories, without expensive equipment (except access to a computer and an Internet connection), and without limitations on the time of day in which the data are collected. These advantages can yield huge data sets. Over a four-year period, one research team studying attitudes collected a data set of over 1.5 million completed responses (Nosek et al., 2002a)! The advantages of Internet research do not end with merely obtaining participants and collecting data. Once researchers have programmed the computer, data can be automatically coded and stored by an Internet server, saving researchers great amounts of tedious labor. Together, these advantages add up to low-cost studies with large sample sizes, and the ability to do in weeks what previously took months or years to accomplish.

Web-based studies are not without limitations. In the United States, Internet users are more likely to be White, to be young, and to have children than the general population (U.S. Department of Commerce, 2002). Thus, obtaining a representative sample is one of the primary concerns with Internet studies. Further, even when researchers intentionally target certain groups on the Internet, they cannot control completely the nature of the sample obtained. For example, if researchers use the Internet to survey young adults about their alcohol use, webmasters who manage websites for self-help groups for alcoholics may establish links for their web users to the study's website. The consequence of this link between the self-help sites and the study site could be that the survey results

The Internet is becoming a popular avenue by which social psychologists collect data. What are the advantages and limitations of such web-based studies?

are not an accurate representation of alcohol use among young adults. Currently, there is no effective way in which Internet researchers can guarantee obtaining a representative sample (Kraut et al., in press).

Another limitation of the Internet is that researchers cannot guarantee that someone hasn't sent multiple copies of the same data to them masquerading as different participants. Although such multiple submissions would jeopardize the validity of a study's findings, studies that have examined the possibility of such abuse by respondents suggest that it does not appear to be a serious problem (Musch & Reips, 2000). Because of the advantages of using the Internet for research, it is highly likely that web-based social psychological studies will dramatically increase in the coming years.

BRAIN-IMAGING TECHNIQUES

In the last decade, new technologies have permitted us to peer deep into the living brain, providing researchers with a unique opportunity to understand how social thinking and behavior are associated with neural activity. The most commonly used brain-imaging techniques are the *electroencephalograph (EEG), computerized axial tomography (CAT), magnetic resonance imaging (MRI), positron-emission tomography (PET),* and *functional magnetic resonance imaging (fMRI).*

The EEG records "waves" of electrical activity in the brain using many metal electrodes placed on a person's scalp. In contrast, CAT and MRI scans document the brain's structure. The CAT scan accomplishes this task by taking thousands of X-ray photos of the brain, while the MRI produces three-dimensional images of the brain's soft tissues by detecting magnetic activity from nuclear particles in brain molecules (Senior et al., 2002). Instead of recording the brain's electrical activity or mapping its structure, the PET scan and fMRI measure the brain's metabolic activity in different regions. The PET scan accomplishes this by showing each region's consumption of glucose, the sugar that is the brain's chemical fuel (Nyberg et al., 2002). The disadvantage of this technique is that the pictures of brain activity that PET scans provide are an average of the activity that occurs over several minutes. Another disadvantage is that it exposes people to small amounts of radioactivity, making extensive scanning somewhat risky. The newer technology of fMRI does not have these drawbacks (Georgopoulos et al., 2001). First, fMRI can produce a picture of neural activity averaged over seconds, not minutes. Second, like a standard MRI, it uses magnetism to measure fluctuations in naturally occurring blood oxygen levels, not fluctuations in ingested radioactive glucose. The images produced by fMRI scans are also much sharper, and thus they can be used to identify much smaller brain structures than those of PET scans.

Brain-imaging techniques are becoming so good at detecting the ebb and flow of neural activity that it is not far-fetched to predict that this technology will one day be able to literally "read" people's minds, determining such things as their degree of racial prejudice or their truthfulness when answering specific questions (Cacioppo et al., 2004). For example, research by Tatia Lee and her colleagues (2002) indicates that certain areas of the brain are more active when people lie. These researchers are now trying to determine whether this knowledge can be used to produce an effective lie detector that would outperform the conventional polygraph machine. Such possibilities raise ethical concerns among many scientists and social commentators (Illes & Raffin, 2002; Kulynych, 2002). "If you were to ask me what the ethical hot potato of this coming century is," remarked Arthur Caplan, director of the University of Pennsylvania's Center for Bioethics, "I'd say it's new knowledge of the brain, its structure and function" (Goldberg, 2003).

SECTION SUMMARY

- Social psychologists conduct both basic and applied research
- The research process unfolds in sequential steps involving theory building and theory testing
- *Observational* research involves systematic qualitative and/or quantitative descriptions of behavior

    Primary advantage: Provide opportunity to study behavior in its wholeness

    Primary disadvantage: Cannot determine how variables are related to one another
- *Correlational* research provides information on the direction and strength of the relationship between variables

    Primary advantage: Prediction

    Primary disadvantage: Cannot establish causality
- *Experimental* research manipulates one or more variables to determine what effect this has on nonmanipulated variables

    Primary advantage: Can determine causality

    Primary disadvantage: High control can make generalizability difficult
- *Meta-analysis* is a statistical technique to determine whether specific variables have important effects across many studies
- Virtual environment technology creates a virtual research environment using a computer; the Internet allows researchers to conduct low-cost studies with many participants from the entire world and test them remotely; brain-imaging techniques provide researchers with measures of participants' neural activity while they engage in various tasks

ETHICS IN SOCIAL PSYCHOLOGY

Ethical concerns regarding new brain-imaging technology is just the latest issue confronting social psychology in its quest to gain knowledge without endangering the health and welfare of its research participants. Although careful attention to a study's methodology is essential in any scientific investigation, even more important is the safety and psychological security of the research participants. Let us review the ethical factors social psychologists consider before conducting any study.

All Proposed Social Psychological Studies Must Submit to Ethical Evaluation

Motivation toward ethical regulation often follows in the wake of either ethical misconduct or the reporting of studies involving questionable treatment of research participants (Kimmel, 2004; Kuschel, 1998). In the 1960s and 1970s, the issue of research ethics was uppermost in the minds of social psychologists because of a few controversial studies that appeared to put participants at risk for psychological harm (Milgram, 1963; Zimbardo, 1972). The most controversial of these studies were Stanley Milgram's obedience experiments, in which volunteers agreed to act as teachers in a learning experiment that in actuality was a study of obedience. During the course of the experiment, teachers were ordered to deliver seemingly painful electrical shocks to a person merely because he was not performing well on a memory task. Even when the victim screamed in agony and demanded to be released, the experimenter insisted that the teacher continue delivering the shocks. In reality, no shocks were ever delivered—the victim was a confederate and only pretended to be in pain—but the stress experienced by the participants in their role as teacher/torturer was indeed real. Although this study and others of its kind asked important questions about social behavior, serious concerns were raised about whether the significance of the research topics justified exposing participants to potentially harmful psychological consequences (Baumrind, 1964; Savin, 1973). To further explore ethical issues in conducting research, view excerpts from a social psychological study on prison life on your Social Sense CD-ROM.

The psychological harm that could occur in such studies may take many forms. For example, to conduct his obedience studies Milgram had to use **deception,** a technique in which the researcher consciously deceives participants about the true nature of what they are experiencing (Ortmann & Hertwig, 1997). Such deception could lead to a loss of trust in social scientists by those participating if they believe the researcher had abused them in the course of the investigation. Beyond the possible loss of trust, placing participants in situations where they are encouraged or coerced to engage in antisocial activity may induce feelings of guilt, shame, or inferiority.

Although this type of reaction is possible, little empirical evidence indicates this is the case. In Milgram's (1963) obedience research, for example, only 1.3 percent of those who participated reported any negative feelings about their experiences, and 84 percent were glad to have participated. Other studies employing deception have found that the vast majority of participants are not bothered by subterfuge (Epley & Huff, 1998; Smith & Berard, 1982). Yet, even though the incidence of negative consequences due to research participation appears to be quite low, social psychologists must be sensitive to the effects such studies may have on individuals' views of themselves and the discipline of social psychology. Ignoring these potentially negative effects may lead to a "participant beware" atmosphere surrounding social psychological research, a development harmful to all concerned (Elms, 1994).

Spurred by the debate surrounding these issues, in 1974 the U.S. government developed regulations requiring all institutions seeking federal funding to establish *institu-*

Social Sense

View video clips on role playing. (See chapter 9, pages 339–345 about Milgrams obedience research.)

Deception

A research technique that provides false information to persons participating in a study.

In Stanley Milgram's famous experiments, research participants continued to obey the destructive commands of an authority figure and delivered what they thought were painful shocks to a restrained individual (who was actually a Milgram confederate), despite his demands to be released. If you were a member of an institutional review board overseeing this study, would you recommend that Milgram be allowed to conduct this obedience research? What factors would you consider in arriving at your decision?

tional review boards (IRBs) for research involving human participants (there are comparable IRBs for studies using nonhuman subjects). These reviewing bodies, which are composed of scientists, medical professionals, clergy, and other community members, make sure that the welfare of human participants is protected (Hayes, 2003). In 1982, the American Psychological Association attempted to facilitate this review process by publishing detailed guidelines on the conduct of research with human participants (American Psychological Association, 1982). These guidelines focus on the *risk/benefit ratio*, which weighs the potential risks to those participating in a study against the benefits that the study may have for advancing knowledge about humanity. In assessing proposed studies, priority is always given to the welfare of the participants over any potential benefits of the research (Colombo, 1995). However, unlike risks in medical research, which are often established and quantified, the risks in psychological studies are often speculative and unquantified (Follette et al., 2003). This results in more guesswork by IRBs in assessing the risks involved in psychological studies.

In addition to assessing risks and benefits, the guidelines for conducting research with human participants also urge scientists to:

1. Provide adequate information about the research to potential participants so they can freely decide whether they want to take part. This procedure is known as **informed consent.**

2. Be truthful whenever possible. *Deception* should be used only when absolutely necessary and when adequate debriefing is provided.

3. Allow participants the *right to decline* to be a part of the study or to discontinue their participation at any point without this decision resulting in any negative consequences (for example, not receiving full payment for their participation).

4. *Protect participants* from both physical and psychological harm.

5. Ensure that any information provided by individual participants is kept *confidential.*

6. **Debrief** individuals once they have completed their participation. Explain all aspects of the research, attempt to answer all questions and resolve any negative feelings, and make sure they realize that their participation contributes to better scientific understanding.

7. Provide participants information on the results of the research if they request it.

As it now stands, participating in social psychological research is a very low risk activity, despite the fact that deception often is incorporated into research designs (Kemmelmeier et al., 2003). When treated with respect and dignity, individuals generally come away from the research experience feeling enriched, even if they were initially deceived about its true nature (Christensen, 1988). In the final analysis, the ethical treatment of research participants must be of primary concern to social psychologists, because it is a reflection of the discipline's view of their species as a whole. If social psychologists treat those who participate in their studies as objects rather than individuals, any knowledge gained in such an exercise will have limited value in our understanding of humankind.

A Recurring Debate Is Whether Social Psychology Should Be a Value-Free Science

Beyond the ethics of conducting research, what about the ethics of the field of social psychology in general? How should social psychological knowledge be used? For example, as you will see in chapters 7 and 9, basic social psychological research has taught us a great deal about the conditions under which people become susceptible to persuasion and influence. Social influence theories could be utilized to help the tobacco industry persuade consumers to purchase their products, which are known to cause serious, long-term health problems. These same theories could also be used to design television, radio, and magazine

Informed Consent

A procedure by which people freely choose to participate in a study only after they are told about the activities they will perform.

Debriefing

A procedure at the conclusion of a research session in which participants are given full information about the nature and hypotheses of the study.

CRITICAL *thinking*

If you were a member of your college's institutional review board and a research proposal similar to the Milgram obedience study was submitted for approval, what questions would you ask to determine its risk/benefit ratio? Based on your assessment, would you approve the study?

ads to convince people not to use tobacco products. Although most of us would have few qualms about social psychological theory being used to prevent people from consuming products known to cause serious health problems, grave reservations would be expressed about using these theories to encourage such consumption.

These very concerns have stirred considerable debate about the proper role that social psychologists should play in applying their knowledge in the world. One point of view is that the discoveries of any science should be used for whatever purposes interested parties consider important. In such endeavors, scientists should be neutral truth seekers and should not be concerned about how their discoveries are utilized (Kimble, 1989). Followers of this *value-free* perspective believe that social psychologists who use the facts of their science to influence social policy decisions undermine the scientific basis of the discipline (Hammond, 2004). A second point of view, first proposed by Kurt Lewin in the 1940s, is that social science and social action should not be separated. Contemporary followers of this *value-laden* perspective believe that merely studying society and its problems without a commitment to changing society for the better is irresponsible (Álvarez, 2001; Fox, 1985).

A commonly accepted belief within the philosophy of science today is that no science is untouched by values and the politics of the culture in which it is practiced (Harris, 1999). In social psychology, the things studied matter a great deal to people, including those who do the investigating. Social psychologists are human beings, and their own values often determine what sort of research and application they are most interested in undertaking, as well as influencing the theories they develop to explain the social facts (Redding, 2001). Yet when there is a clash of social psychological theories based on different value orientations, science does not grind to a halt. Instead, scientific inquiry persists, studies are conducted and published, and new social facts are discovered. In some instances, the adversaries in a scientific dispute even work together to resolve their differences (Mellers et al., 2001). By relying on the scientific method, social psychology will continue to contribute to our understanding of human behavior, and many of those within the discipline will also use this knowledge to make changes in their social world (refer to table 2.4).

TABLE 2.4

Values and Social Commitment in the Field of Social Psychology

Social psychologist Dalmas Taylor expresses the problem faced by scientists who study aspects of social behavior directly related to contemporary social issues:

The problem is that when you are involved in studying something, it requires a certain amount of objectivity and detachment. When you are involved in pursuing a remedy, there is less objectivity and a great deal of attachment. So you essentially end up wearing two hats, playing two different roles. I think that can be done, but it's very difficult. So occasionally I have advocated that the practitioners of social psychology not be the same people who generate the data or the findings. But I've modified that over the years, consistent with the discipline itself recognizing that the very selection of hypotheses and the paradigms that we use contain values either covertly or overtly, and at any point along the line there's a certain amount of subjectivity. What we have is a series of methodological strategies that mitigate against our biases, and I think they perform a sufficient check and balance to let us play this dual role with less concern and less error (Aron & Aron, 1986, pp. 125–126).

Social psychologist Dalmas Taylor.

- The American Psychological Association established strict guidelines to ensure the protection of research participants
- The value-free perspective contends that scientific discoveries should be used for whatever purposes people consider important
- The value-laden perspective asserts that scientists should be concerned about how their discoveries are utilized

WEB SITES
accessed through http://www.mhhe.com/franzoi4

Web sites for this chapter contain the main scientific journals in both psychological and sociological social psychology, information on recent theory and research, as well as a Web page containing social psychological studies currently being conducted on the Web, many of which you can participate in.

Journal of Personality and Social Psychology Web Site

Check out the Web site for the main scientific journal in psychological social psychology. Here you will find current abstracts of journal articles. The journal publishes theoretical and empirical papers on attitudes and social cognition, interpersonal relations and group processes, and personality processes and individual differences.

Social Psychology Quarterly Web Site

Explore the Web site for the main scientific journal in sociological social psychology, where you will find information on current journal articles. The journal publishes theoretical and empirical papers on the link between the individual and society.

International Association for Cross-Cultural Psychology

This is the Web site for an organization devoted to facilitating communication among persons interested in a diverse range of issues involving the intersection of culture and psychology.

Wesleyan's Social Psychology Network

This Web site contains social psychological studies that are currently being conducted on the Internet, many of which you can participate in.

Psychological Tests for Student Use

This Web site at Atkinson College of York University in Canada contains psychological tests and measures that are used by social psychologists in their research. Examples of some of the measures listed on this site are the Attitudes Toward Women Scale, Authoritarianism-Rebellion Scale, Body Esteem Scale, Personal Attributes Questionnaire, and Rosenberg Self-Esteem Scale.

UNDERSTANDING THE PERSON AND LIFE EVENTS

The guiding principle in social psychology is that person and situational variables interact in shaping social behavior. This *interactionist* approach takes into account such things as people's attitudes and beliefs about themselves and the social world, their personality and genetic tendencies (person variables), as well as who and what is present in the social settings, and what is expected of them as social actors (situational variables). Throughout this text, we analyze how this interaction of person and situational factors contributes to the social interaction equation, and we use the *self* as the primary person variable.

In this first book section (Part I), we examine *how we understand the person and life events*. Chapter 3 analyzes how we attend to and understand a very important person in our lives, namely, ourselves. How does self-awareness influence our social behavior? How are we shaped by our surroundings? How do we balance our need to have positive self-beliefs with our need to have accurate self-beliefs?

Chapter 4 looks at how the psychology of social interaction is similar to a theatrical performance. As actors, how do we try to manage others' impressions of us? Likewise, as the audience, how do we form first impressions and how do we explain the causes of other people's behavior?

Finally, chapter 5 explores how we interpret, analyze, remember, and use information about the social world. Are we careful or lazy social thinkers? What cognitive traps are we prone to fall into? Later book sections unfold around the themes of *how we evaluate our social world* (Part II), *how we understand our place within the group* (Part III), and *how we interact with others* (Part IV).

CHAPTER 3

The Self

CHAPTER OUTLINE

*A*t the pivotal age of 16, I was ready to surmount one of the most important adolescent hurdles: the driver's test. My mother had driven me to the license bureau, but I was sure I would be driving home. The small testing room was filled with would-be drivers. After a thirty-minute wait, the "testing" man motioned me to come behind the counter. As I complied, he first pointed to an eye chart, then pointed at a line on the floor some twenty feet from the chart, and said, "Touch your toes to the line."

For some reason, I placed the most significance on the first three words in this sentence—"Touch your toes"—and guessed this was a coordination test before the eye and driving exams. So first I placed the tips of my shoes on the line. Then, with stiffened knees, I bent down and touched my toes! Because his instructions mentioned nothing about the duration of this "coordination test," I remained in this contorted position and awaited further instructions. As the blood rushed to my head, I happened to glance at my mother sitting on the other side of the room and noticed her shocked expression as she tried to fathom what her son was doing making a spectacle of himself in front of a room full of strangers. Now realizing that something was amiss, I suddenly understood the true meaning of the tester's words and stood bolt upright. Even though my head was no longer south of my knees, the blood now seemed to be rushing to my face ten times faster. The tester and the other exam takers didn't laugh at me outright, but I was so flustered by my social gaffe that I actually failed the eye exam!

I'm sure you can relate to the embarrassment I felt on that day so long ago. Yet, why do we often become red-faced when our social behavior is out of step with the situation? Why do we sometimes misinterpret the meaning of others' words and gestures? Why do success and failure mean so much to us? For an answer to these questions, we must examine a central concept in social psychological theory and research: the self.

NATURE OF THE SELF

Who are you? As an exercise to open this chapter, spend a few minutes answering the "Who Am I?" question. Take out a sheet of paper and write the numbers 1 to 20 down the left column of the page. Then, beginning each sentence with the statement "I am," list up to twenty different responses to that question. Respond as if you were giving the answers to yourself, not to someone else. Later in this chapter, I will tell you how social psychologists have used this "Twenty Statements Test" (TST) to understand how we develop a sense of our own identity. At that time, you will not only discover something about the psychology of self-development, but I guarantee you will learn something fascinating about yourself.

The Self Is a Symbol-Using, Self-Reflective, Social Being

Self

A symbol-using social being who can reflect on his or her own behavior.

The **self** is both a simple and a complex concept. It is not a mental construct located inside your head—it is you, a social being with the ability to engage in symbolic communication and self-awareness. The reason I use *social being* to define the self is because selves do not develop in isolation, but only do so within a social context (Baumeister & Twenge, 2003; Hardin, 2004). Likewise, the reason the cognitive processes of *symbol usage* and *self-awareness* are so important in this definition is that both are essential for us to mutually engage in planned, coordinated activities in which we can regulate our behavior and anticipate the actions of others (Gecas, 2001; Harré, 1984). In other words, they allow us to actively create and re-create ourselves and our social world. This definition of the self excludes those who cannot communicate symbolically and who cannot take themselves as objects of attention, such as young infants and some people with severe brain damage. It also rules out the notion of the self being a "thing" separate from the person. We do not *possess* a self or *have* a self, but we *become* a self through maturation and socialization (Elliott, 2001).

Self-awareness and symbol usage—and thus, the self—may have evolved in our ancestors as a means to better deal with an increasingly complex social environment (Oda, 2001; Sedikides & Skowronski, 1997). For instance, self-awareness not only provided our ancestors with knowledge about their own behavior, but they could also use this inner experience to anticipate how rivals might behave in the future—perhaps in war or in social bargaining—thus giving them an advantage in these activities. Similarly, the development of language not only allowed our ancestors to better coordinate group activities, but they could also use this symbolic communication to discuss things not physically present, such as a herd of antelope or a band of hostile warriors (Dunbar, 1993). According to this evolutionary view, these two defining features of the self became the means by which our ancestors developed an adaptive advantage in their environment, thus increasing their chances of surviving and reproducing.

In contemplating the adaptive advantages of selfhood in our evolutionary history, numerous social scientists have asserted that these advantages were accompanied by the ability of our ancestors to now ponder their existence and mortality: Why are we here? What happens when we die? The artwork and elaborate burial sites created by our ancestors during the Upper Paleolithic period 40,000 years ago provide compelling evidence that the modern human mind—and the self—was emerging (Mellars, 1996; Rossano, 2003). Social psychologist M. Brewster Smith (2002), among others, contends that this new search for ultimate meaning led to the development of myth, ritual, and religion, which affirmed to each social group its value as "The People." Beyond seeking meaning and value in group life, our ancestors also used self-awareness to size up their own self-worth. As you will discover throughout this text, this search for meaning and value in ourselves and in our groups profoundly shapes social interactions.

What brain area accounts for these remarkable cognitive abilities? Neuroscientists have identified the *frontal lobes* of the cerebral cortex as the primary source (Heatherton et al., 2004). The **cerebral cortex** is the wrinkled-looking outer layer of brain tissue that coordinates and integrates all other brain areas into a fully functioning unit. As you can see in figure 3.1, the cerebral cortex in humans has a great number of *convolutions* (folds), allowing a greater volume of it to fit into the skull cavity. Indeed, if you were able to unfold the cortex, it would cover four sheets of typing paper! In comparison, a chimpanzee's flattened cortex would cover only one sheet, a monkey's would cover a postcard, and a rat's would cover a postage stamp

The Self is the honey of all beings, and all beings are the honey of this Self.

The Upanishads, sacred texts of Hinduism, 800-500 B.C.

Nothing is greater than one's self.

Walt Whitman, U.S. poet, 1819–1892

Self-awareness is, then, one of the most fundamental, possibly the most fundamental, characteristic of the human species. . . . Self-awareness has, however, brought in its train somber companions—fear, anxiety, and death-awareness . . . A being who knows that he will die arose from ancestors who did not know.

Theodosius Dobzhansky, Russian-born geneticist, 1900–1975

Cerebral Cortex

The wrinkled-looking outer layer of the brain that coordinates and integrates all other brain areas into a fully functioning unit. This is the brain's "thinking" center, and it is much larger in humans than in other animals.

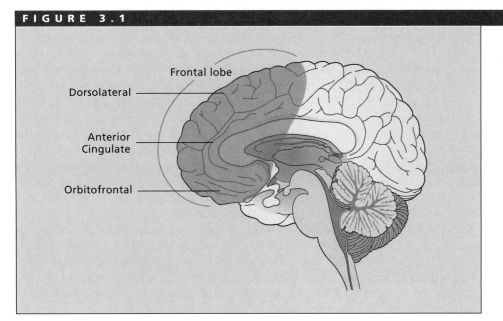

FIGURE 3.1

Frontal lobe
Dorsolateral
Anterior Cingulate
Orbitofrontal

Major Brain Regions in the Frontal Lobes Associated with Self-Awareness and Self-Regulation

The primary neural source for self-awareness is the frontal lobe of the cerebral cortex, which is the wrinkled-looking front outer layer of the brain. The frontal lobe is involved in the coordination of movement and higher mental processes, such as planning, social skills, and abstract thinking. A region in the frontal lobe, the anterior cingulate, is especially active when people are self-aware.

(Calvin, 1996). The relative sizes of the cerebral cortex and brain stem of species with different evolutionary ages indicates that most of the growth has occurred in the cerebral cortex (Parker et al., 2000). Not only do humans have a larger cerebral cortex than other species, but a human's cerebral cortex also has a great many more convolutions. About 90 percent of our cerebral cortex is of relatively recent evolution, and the frontal lobes are its largest regions. The **frontal lobes** are involved in the coordination of movement and higher mental processes, such as planning, social skills, and abstract thinking (Goldberg, 2001; Poldrack & Wagner, 2004). Later in the chapter we discuss the role that the frontal lobes play in self-awareness and self-regulation.

Contemporary Self Theories Are Based on the Insights of George Herbert Mead and William James

Arguably, the most influential contributors to our understanding of the self were two early social theorists, psychologist William James and sociologist George Herbert Mead. In both James's and Mead's theories, the self is described as having two separate aspects, the self as knower (the *I*) and the self as known (the *me*). The "I" is the active perceiver, initiator, and regulator of action; the "me" is the knowledge one has about oneself. One way to think of these two discriminated self-aspects is that, no matter what you are conscious of, you—in the form of the "I"—are always the *subject* of awareness (the subjective self). Whenever consciousness becomes self-reflexive, you—in the form of the "me"—become the *object* of awareness (the objective self). To keep these two aspects of the self straight in your mind, repeat this phrase: Whenever I think about something, "I" am always the subject of consciousness, and one of the things I may be consciously attending to is "me."

MEAD AND THE DEVELOPMENT OF THE SELF

Mead asserted that a human infant is not born a self, but rather, a self *emerges* through social interaction and role taking. Regarding social interaction, a critical ingredient in developing a self is learning to use symbols. *Symbols* are arbitrary signs of objects that stand in the place of those objects. Spoken or printed words are symbols—their symbolic nature is confirmed by the fact that the groupings of letters on this page are meaningful to you. A hand gesture can also be a symbol. We interpret others' gestures and act on the basis of this interpreted meaning. If we misinterpret, social interaction can become awkward, as illustrated by what happened to me at the license bureau.

The exact meaning assigned to each gesture is substantially determined by the social context in which it takes place. Raising your index finger in North American culture, for example, may mean that you are asking for permission to speak to an assembled group, or that your sports team is "Number One," or that you would like others to look up in the air. Sometimes, if a gesture is repeatedly associated with a particular meaning, you may be less attentive to the situational context in which it is used. This may explain my misinterpretation at the license bureau. Being active in sports as a teenager, the phrase "touch your toes" had a specific meaning for me. *Cultural context* can also significantly alter the meaning of a gesture, as is illustrated in figure 3.2 (p. 57) and in the video clip on your Social Sense CD-ROM.

In this symbolic interaction, participants must continually consider one another's ongoing acts and reorganize or adjust their own intentions in terms of the others' intentions. To ascertain others' intentions, Mead argued that we must engage in *role taking,* which is imaginatively assuming the point of view of others and observing our own behavior (the "me") from this other perspective. Mead believed that through such symbolic interaction humans cease to merely be passive responders to their social environment and, instead, become coactors in creating (and re-creating) their social reality.

According to Mead, the self develops as children acquire language and start taking the role of the other in their play activities. The roles they adopt in this *play stage* are those of specific others, such as parents and siblings, but Mead believed children at this stage could only adopt one role at a time. An example of role taking here would be a boy adopting the perspective of "Daddy" and reprimanding himself for disobeying a family rule. Through role taking children develop beliefs about themselves, which are largely a

The "V" sign is the symbol of the unconquerable will of the occupied territories, and a portent of the fate awaiting the Nazi tyranny.

Winston Churchill, British prime minister during World War II, 1874–1965, message to the people of Europe on launching the "V" for Victory propaganda campaign, July 20, 1941

Social Sense

According to George Herbert Mead, the self develops as children learn to engage in symbolic interaction and role taking.

FIGURE 3.2

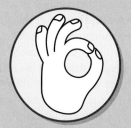

Thumb extended up with closed fingers

Index finger at ear and rotated in a circle

Thumb and index finger forming a circle

Hand pushed out toward another person

In North America, Russia, France, and Arab countries, it normally means "Good job!" or "Excellent!"

In Nigeria it is a rude gesture, expressing strong disapproval.

In Japan, it is used in counting and means "five."

In Australia using this gesture with a slight jerk upward means "Up yours!"

In Argentina it means that someone is wanted on the telephone—probably a vestige of the old, hand-cranked phones.

In North America, Russia, Japan, France, and Germany, it means "Something is wrong with his (or her) head" or "They're crazy."

In Laos and France it means "Bad," "Zero," or "Worthless."

In Japan it means "money."

In North America and Russia it means "That's good!"

In Latin America it means "You asshole!"

In Arab states (accompanied by a baring of the teeth) it expresses extreme hostility.

In North America, it normally means "Stop!"

In Greece it is an insulting gesture.

In West Africa this gesture means "You could have any one of five Fathers!" which is another way of calling a person a bastard.

Gestures and Their Meaning Around the World

reflection of how they believe others evaluate them. This *reflected appraisal* is an important determinant of self-beliefs (Cast et al., 1999). As children mature, Mead stated that they learn to take the role of many others simultaneously and, as a result, the self becomes more cognitively complex. In this *game stage,* they can engage in complex activities (often in the form of games) involving the interaction of many roles. An example of such role taking would be you playing baseball. To play effectively, you must understand how all the players on the field are related to one another, and you must be able to cognitively adopt these multiple roles simultaneously. Early in the game stage, Mead believed the multiple role taking involves mostly those who are physically present. However, as the self becomes increasingly complex, he stated that children begin to respond to themselves from the point of view of not just a number of discrete others, but from the perspective of society as a whole. By internalizing the attitudes and expectations commonly held by the larger society— what Mead called the *generalized other*—the person becomes a fully formed self.

JAMES AND THE SELF AS A PROCESS OF IDENTIFICATION

While Mead focused on cognitive factors and explained how the self develops, James focused on the mature self and its affective or emotional aspects. Things become part of the "me," James argued, through our *emotional identification* with them. Your body, your feelings, your beliefs and values are all part of your "me." But because what is part of the "me" is determined by emotional identification, your parents, siblings, friends, and lovers are also likely to be incorporated into your "me" (Mashek et al., 2003; E. Smith et al., 1999). Indeed, your clothes,

An important aspect of William James's theory of the self was that things became a part of the "me" through our emotional identification with them.

your stereo system, your major area of study in college, and perhaps even your fuzzy little teddy bear could be elements in your "me" (Crocker et al., 2003). In this regard, the "me" includes not just that which is inside your body, but anything that symbolizes and affirms who and what you are. This belief that the objective self can extend beyond the person is noteworthy, for it represents a break with the traditional assumption that people are separate, encapsulated egos.

James's notion of the identification process also illustrates his belief in the ever changing nature of the self. He contended that due to the evolving nature of life as reflected in our social relationships and material possessions, and the fallibility and reconstructive nature of our own memories, the objective self is not stable like a diamond, but rather, it is constantly changing—"we are dealing with a fluctuating material." The implication here is that our self of today is different, even if only subtly, from our self of yesterday.

SHADOWS OF OUR PAST IN CONTEMPORARY RESEARCH

Both James's and Mead's theories of the self have profoundly influenced social psychology, with James's writings reflecting the affective or "hot" perspective on the nature of human behavior, and Mead's writings reflecting the cognitive or "cold" approach (see chapter 1). Despite these different orientations, both theorists' contributions revolve around a common theme: as social beings, we are aware of our self-aspirations and how our appearance and behavior are seen and judged by others. Through their work, James and Mead provided the path by which later theorists would explore central issues of social life, such as willpower and self-regulation (Baumeister & Vohs, 2004), self-awareness and self-discrepancy (Higgins, 1987), social identity (Tajfel, 1982), and self-presentation (Schlenker, 1980). Mead's idea that people creatively shape reality through social interaction forms the cornerstone for **symbolic interaction theory** in sociological social psychology (Altheide, 2000; Musolf, 2003) and is echoed in the *social constructionist* perspective seen in the social sciences as a whole (Harré, 1999; Holstein & Miller, 2000). Contemporary social psychologists have also borrowed James's notion of self-expansion in their analysis of love (Aron et al., 2001) and group affiliation (Smith & Henry, 1996). Table 3.1 summarizes some of the similarities and differences between James's, Mead's, and contemporary self theories.

Symbolic Interaction Theory

A contemporary sociological theory, inspired by Mead's insights and based on the premise that people, as selves, creatively shape reality through social interaction.

TABLE 3.1

Aspects of the Self

William James's Self Theory	George Herbert Mead's Self Theory	Contemporary Theories
Outlined the dimensions of the mature self, and contended that things become part of the self through *emotional identification*	Outlined how the self develops and contended that it was largely a *cognitive process*, brought about through symbolic interaction and role taking	Have expanded on the insights of these two past theorists
Term Used to Describe the Subjective Self	**Term Used to Describe the Subjective Self**	**Term Used to Describe the Subjective Self**
The "I": the self as active perceiver and initiator of action	The "I": the self as active perceiver and initiator of action	"Executive function": all cognitive and affective processes that initiate and regulate behavior
Term Used to Describe the Objective Self	**Term Used to Describe the Objective Self**	**Term Used to Describe the Objective Self**
The "me": the self as anything that symbolizes and affirms who, and what one is	The "me": the self as seen from the imagined perspective of others	"Self-concept": the sum total of a person's thoughts and feelings that define the self as an object

In the upcoming discussion of contemporary self theories, we analyze the subjective self and the objective self, previously identified by James and Mead as the "I" and "me." Essentially the "I" is the self's *executive function:* it makes decisions, initiates behavior, and exerts control over the self and the environment. Our analysis of this executive function focuses on how we regulate our behavior through self-awareness, and how we process and evaluate self-relevant information.

Regarding James's and Mead's "me," this aspect of the self is discussed using the term "self-concept" (Snodgrass & Thompson, 1997). **Self-concept** is the sum total of a person's thoughts and feelings that defines the self as an object. Put another way, self-concept is a "theory" of our personal behavior, abilities, and social relationships that we construct through social interaction (Epstein, 1973; Oyserman & Packer, 1996). Consistent with James's thinking, self-concept has no precise location or boundaries, but rather, is framed through identification (Burris & Rempel, 2004). Thus, my two precious daughters, Amelia and Lillian, are very much a part of my self-concept. The bike that carried me on a 3,000-mile, cross-country trek in 1977 was once encompassed within my self-concept. Yet years later, this same bike, collecting dust in the garage, is not something with which I strongly identify. It is now on the periphery of my self-concept.

Self-Concept

The sum total of a person's thoughts and feelings that defines the self as an object.

Self-concepts are like grand self-portraits we paint and repaint throughout our lives—a little change here, a small alteration there, most of the time so insignificant that no one notices, least of all us. Sometimes as we paint, those who are important to us guide our hands, shaping the alterations. At other times, those who view the changed portrait express disapproval and we restore the old image. If we become sufficiently dissatisfied with the portrait and feel that we can no longer reliably paint, we may consult a master painter who will help us create a more accurate and pleasing visage. In rare instances, as a result of dramatic life changes, we may scrap the entire portrait and paint a new, very different self-concept. The ability to define ourselves and the ability to consciously strive to become what we desire involve two essential human characteristics: *self-awareness* and *self-regulation.* Let us now examine how social psychologists have studied these complementary psychological processes.

SECTION SUMMARY

- The self is a social being, a symbol-user, and a person who reflects on her or his own behavior
- The self may have evolved because it provided our ancestors with an adaptive advantage in an increasingly complex social environment
- The frontal lobe of the cerebral cortex is the primary neurological source of the self
- Both William James and George Herbert Mead identified the *self* as having two separate aspects: the self as knower (the "*I*"); the self as known (the "*me*" or *self-concept*)
- *Self-concept* is our theory of our personal behavior, abilities, and social relationship constructed with the help of others

THE SELF AS BOTH TARGET OF ATTENTION AND ACTIVE AGENT

The self as the "I" is the initiator and regulator of behavior, yet, in the form of the "me," it is also the object of the "I"'s attention. Let us explore the interplay between the "I" and the "me" in the process of self-awareness and self-regulation.

Self-Awareness Is a Temporary Psychological State

Stop for a moment and think about your current mood. If you followed my suggestion, you just engaged in **self-awareness,** which is a psychological state in which you take yourself as an object of attention. To have a self-concept, you must be able to engage in self-awareness. Recent brain-imaging studies find that a region in the frontal lobe of the cerebral cortex, called the *anterior cingulate* (refer back to figure 3.1), is especially active when people are self-aware (Kjaer et al., 2002; Lieberman et al., in press). The anterior cingulate contains large, specialized brain cells or neurons, called *spindle cells,* which collect information from one region of the brain and send it on to other regions. Although other brain areas undoubtedly play a role in self-awareness, some neuroscientists think that the anterior cingulate with its spindle cells acts as an executive attention system that facilitates the monitoring and controlling of intentional behavior and focused problem solving (Stuphorn et al., 2003; Weissman et al., 2003).

Two different types of self-awareness have been identified. *Private self-awareness* is the temporary state of being aware of hidden, private self-aspects, whereas *public self-awareness* is the temporary state of being aware of public self-aspects. Feeling sad or content, seeing your face in a small mirror, or feeling the hunger pangs of your stomach will likely cause you to become privately self-aware. Being watched by others, having your picture taken, or seeing your entire body in a full-length mirror can induce public self-awareness (Buss, 1980; Green & Sedikides, 1999).

SELF-AWARENESS DEVELOPMENT

You might be surprised to know that we are not born with self-awareness ability, but rather, we develop it. Psychologists discovered this fact by placing a spot of rouge on babies' noses and then placing them in front of a mirror (Lewis & Brooks, 1978). They reasoned that in order for the infants to recognize their mirror image as their own they must have an internalized identity that permits them to recognize this external representation of themselves. Infants between the ages of 9 and 12 months treated their mirror image as if it was another child, showing no interest in the unusual rouge spot: they literally were not able to take themselves as an object of awareness. Yet those around 18 months of age exhibited self-recognition—and thus, self-awareness ability—by staring in the mirror and touching the mysterious spot on their noses. Recognizing the image in the mirror as their own, they realized that they looked different. Based on such studies, it appears that self-awareness develops at about 18 months of age (Amsterdam, 1972; Butterworth, 1992). Perhaps not coincidentally, the development of self-awareness occurs at the same time as children's brains' are experiencing a rapid growth of spindle cells—which are not present at birth—in the frontal lobe of the cerebral cortex (Allman & Hasenstaub, 1999).

SELF-AWARENESS IN OTHER PRIMATES

The only other animals known to have spindle cells in the brain are the great apes, our closest relatives (Allman, 1998; Nimchinsky et al., 1999). Do these animals also possess self-awareness? In one telling study, comparative psychologist Gordon Gallup (1977) painted an odorless red dye on one eyebrow and one ear of anesthetized chimpanzees. When the chimps later looked into a mirror they immediately began to touch the red dye marks on their bodies, indicating that they recognized the mirror image as their own. Subsequent research further supported the hypothesis that our great ape cousins (chimpanzees, bonobos, orangutans, and gorillas) do indeed possess self-awareness (Boysen & Himes, 1999; Hyatt & Hopkins, 1994; Patterson & Cohen, 1994). In contrast, most monkey species do not recognize their image in the mirror (Mitchell & Anderson, 1993). Do the findings of our great ape cousins having self-awareness ability suggest that these animals also possess self-concepts? As yet, we do not know, but contrary to previous scientific beliefs, humans may not have a monopoly on the self-concept.

PRIVATE AND PUBLIC SELF-AWARENESS EFFECTS

There are a number of consequences of inducing private and public self-awareness (Silvia & O'Brien, 2004). One effect of private self-awareness is *intensification of affect,* meaning that any positive or negative feelings experienced when privately self-aware will be exaggerated (Lyubomirsky et al., 1998; Scheier & Carver, 1977). Thus, if you are happy and become privately self-aware, your happiness is intensified. Likewise, if angered, private self-awareness causes more anger. A second consequence, *clarification of knowledge,* means that private events become clearer and more distinct, thus increasing your ability to accurately report on them (Gibbons et al., 1979). A third consequence of private self-awareness is *greater adherence to personal standards of behavior* (Froming et al., 1998). Thus, when privately self-aware, you are more likely to act in line with your personal beliefs than to conform to social pressures.

Regarding public self-awareness, one likely effect is *evaluation apprehension* when you realize you are the object of others' attention (Culos-Reed et al., 2002). This is because you have learned through experience that public scrutiny often results in either positive or negative outcomes. Evaluation apprehension is the reason you get butterflies in your stomach before making an important class presentation or calling that special person for a date. A second effect is a *temporary loss of self-esteem* due to realizing that there is a discrepancy between your ideal and actual public self. This explains why you feel badly after a failed presentation or date request. Finally, a third consequence of public self-awareness is *greater adherence to social standards of behavior,* meaning a heightened degree of conformity (Duval & Wicklund, 1972).

If you look at the consequences for both private and public self-awareness in table 3.2, do you notice something interesting? Whether behavior is more influenced by personal or social standards is at least partially determined by what aspect of the self is salient (private or public). This proposition is an important one to consider, for social scientists have long debated the importance of personal versus social standards. Some theorists have assumed that people are motivated primarily by a desire to meet personal goals and are responsive

The type of self-awareness typically induced by a full-length mirror can cause a temporary loss of self-esteem if you notice a discrepancy between your ideal appearance and actual appearance. Is this private or public self-awareness?

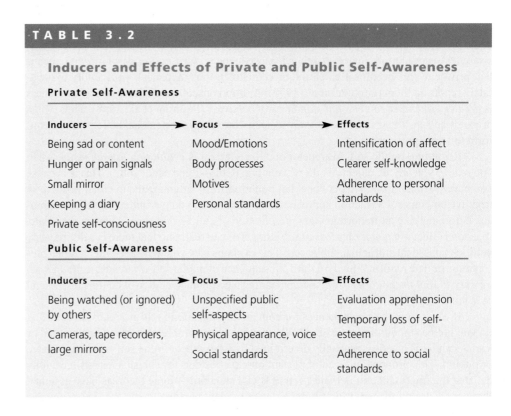

TABLE 3.2

Inducers and Effects of Private and Public Self-Awareness

Private Self-Awareness

Inducers ➞	Focus ➞	Effects
Being sad or content	Mood/Emotions	Intensification of affect
Hunger or pain signals	Body processes	Clearer self-knowledge
Small mirror	Motives	Adherence to personal standards
Keeping a diary	Personal standards	
Private self-consciousness		

Public Self-Awareness

Inducers ➞	Focus ➞	Effects
Being watched (or ignored) by others	Unspecified public self-aspects	Evaluation apprehension
Cameras, tape recorders, large mirrors	Physical appearance, voice	Temporary loss of self-esteem
	Social standards	Adherence to social standards

largely to their own attitudes and feelings (Maslow, 1970; Rogers, 1947). Others have argued that we are largely a reflected image of our social group and that prior to acting, we consider how we will be judged by others (Cooley, 1902; Goffman, 1959). As in most such debates, both perspectives are true in their own limited fashion. When privately self-aware, we tend to act in line with our personal standards, but social standards are more influential when we are publicly self-aware (Franzoi & Davis, 2005; Froming et al., 1982).

Self-Consciousness Is a Personality Trait

As adults, we all have the ability to engage in either private or public self-awareness. However, when some stimulus induces self-awareness, that focus is only temporary. Besides becoming self-aware due to external stimuli, researchers have also determined that some people spend more time self-reflecting than others. This habitual tendency to engage in self-awareness is known as the personality trait of **self-consciousness.**

Just as there are two types of self-awareness, there are also two types of self-consciousness. In 1975, Allan Fenigstein, Michael Scheier, and Arnold Buss developed the Self-Consciousness Scale to measure these two traits (see table 3.3). *Private self-consciousness* is the tendency to be aware of the private aspects of the self, while *public self-consciousness* is the tendency to be aware of publicly displayed self-aspects. These traits are two distinct tendencies; therefore, a person could either be very attentive to both sides of the self, attentive to one but inattentive to another, or relatively inattentive to both. Spend a few minutes completing the items in table 3.3 to learn more about your own levels of private and public self-consciousness.

PRIVATE SELF-CONSCIOUSNESS EFFECTS

Many private self-attention effects are the same whether they result from the psychological state of private self-awareness or the personality trait of private self-consciousness (Kemmelmeier, 2001; Scheier & Carver, 1980). Therefore, individuals high in private self-consciousness tend to experience greater intensification of affect, greater clarification of knowledge, and greater attention and adherence to personal standards of behav-

Self-Consciousness

The habitual tendency to engage in self-awareness.

There are three things extremely hard. Steel, a diamond, and to know one's self.

Benjamin Franklin, U.S. statesman and scientist, 1706–1790

Know thyself? If I knew myself, I'd run away.

Johann Wolfgang von Goethe, German intellectual, writer, and composer, 1749–1832

TABLE 3.3

Measuring Private and Public Self-Consciousness

The personality traits of private and public self-consciousness are measured by items on the Self-Consciousness Scale (SCS: Fenigstein et al., 1975). To take the SCS, read each item below and then indicate how well each statement describes you using the following scale:

0 = extremely uncharacteristic (not at all like me)

1 = uncharacteristic (somewhat unlike me)

2 = neither characteristic nor uncharacteristic

3 = characteristic (somewhat like me)

4 = extremely characteristic (very much like me)

_____ 1. I'm always trying to figure myself out.

_____ 2. I'm concerned about my style of doing things.

_____ 3. Generally, I'm not very aware of myself.*

_____ 4. I reflect about myself a lot.

_____ 5. I'm concerned about the way I present myself.

_____ 6. I'm often the subject of my own fantasies.

_____ 7. I never scrutinize myself.*

_____ 8. I'm self-conscious about the way I look.

_____ 9. I'm generally attentive to my inner feelings.

_____ 10. I usually worry about making a good impression.

_____ 11. I'm constantly examining my motives.

_____ 12. One of the last things I do before I leave my house is look in the mirror.

_____ 13. I sometimes have the feeling that I'm off somewhere watching myself.

_____ 14. I'm concerned about what other people think of me.

_____ 15. I'm alert to changes in my mood.

_____ 16. I'm usually aware of my appearance.

_____ 17. I'm aware of the way my mind works when I work through a problem.

Directions for Scoring

Several of the SCS items are reverse-scored; that is, for these items a lower rating actually indicates a higher level of self-consciousness. Before summing the items, recode those with an asterisk ("") so that 0 = 4, 1 = 3, 3 = 1, and 4 = 0.*

Private self-consciousness. To calculate your private self-consciousness score, add up your responses to the following items: 1, 3, 4, 6, 7*, 9, 11, 13, 15, and 17.*

Public self-consciousness. To calculate your public self-consciousness score, add up your responses to the following items: 2, 5, 8, 10, 12, 14, and 16.

When Fenigstein, Scheier, and Buss developed the SCS in 1975, the mean college score for college students on private self-consciousness was about 26, whereas the average score of public self-consciousness was about 19. The higher your score is above one of these values, the more of this type of self-consciousness you probably possess. The lower your score is below one of these values, the less of this type of self-consciousness you probably possess.

ior than do their less self-conscious counterparts. A number of studies have also found that the self-concepts of those high in private self-consciousness are not only more accurate reflections of their actual behavior than those low in private self-consciousness, but they are also more complex and more in line with others' perceptions of them (Davies, 1994). Based on these findings, you might be wondering whether it is better to be high or low in private self-consciousness. Is it true that the more we learn about ourselves the better persons we become? Or are those people correct who sometimes warn us not to analyze our thoughts and feelings so much ("It will drive you crazy! You will make yourself depressed!")?

On the plus side, those high in private self-consciousness are more likely to reveal private self-aspects to their friends and romantic partners, and this self-disclosure in turn reduces loneliness and increases relationship satisfaction (Davis & Franzoi, 1986). In addition, the physical health of persons high in private self-consciousness is less likely to be adversely affected by stressful life events than is the health of low self-conscious persons (Mullen & Suls, 1982; Suls & Fletcher, 1985). One explanation for this finding is that people who regularly pay attention to their physiological states (an aspect of the private self) are more likely to notice early warning signs of illness-inducing stress, and thus are more likely to take precautionary steps to avoid the onset of illness. On the negative side, habitual attention to private self-aspects can contribute to depression and neuroticism, which is essentially the trait of chronic unhappiness (Ingram, 1990; Trapnell & Campbell, 1999). Why might heightened private self-focus be associated with depression and unhappiness? One possible reason is that greater attention to private self-aspects intensifies people's current emotional states. When people's experiences fall short of their expectations, the resulting disappointment would be heightened by prolonging private self-attention. Thus, the *trait* of private self-consciousness or the *state* of private self-awareness might encourage the sort of destructive self-critical analysis associated with depression and chronic unhappiness (Hull et al., 1990; Silvia & O'Brien, 2004). Indeed, a number of studies suggest that reducing self-awareness by engaging in distracting activities that shift attention away from the self—such as watching television—can improve well-being (Moskalenko & Heine, 2003; Nix et al., 1995).

Taking these studies into account, it appears that attending to our private self has both benefits and drawbacks. For persons high in private self-consciousness, there is not only a greater likelihood of understanding themselves better and sharing this knowledge with loved ones, but their greater self-attentiveness appears to provide them with a better early warning system for physical illness. On the other hand, self-attentiveness can also make one more susceptible to negative emotional states such as depression because of a greater focus on negative outcomes, and a susceptibility to entering destructive self-attention cycles (Ward et al., 2003). The insights gained from this research can perhaps help you gauge how your own life might benefit from or be harmed by the amount of attention you devote to your private self (refer again to table 3.3).

PUBLIC SELF-CONSCIOUSNESS EFFECTS

As with situationally induced public self-awareness, persons high in public self-consciousness are more concerned about how others judge them (Fenigstein & Vanable, 1992; MacDonald & Nail, in press), are more conforming to group norms (Chang et al., 2001), and are more likely to withdraw from embarrassing situations (Froming et al., 1990) than those low in this trait. This tendency to comply with external standards encompasses physical appearance as well. High public self-conscious individuals are more concerned about their physical appearance and are more likely to judge others based on their looks (Ryckman et al., 1991; Striegel-Moore et al., 1993).

A good deal of the research investigating public self-consciousness has also explored private self-consciousness. How do these two traits interact in a public setting? As you might expect, people high on private self-consciousness and low on public self-consciousness are the ones most likely to act according to their true attitudes. On the other hand, people high on public self-consciousness, regardless of their level of private self-consciousness, are much less likely to publicly act according to their true attitudes (Scheier, 1980). Therefore, even when people have an accurate understanding of their own attitudes as a result of their habitual private self-focus, being simultaneously high in public self-consciousness can lead to behavior that runs counter to those attitudes.

The one self-knowledge worth having is to know one's own mind.

F. H. Bradley, English philosopher, 1846–1924

He who knows others is clever; He who knows himself has discernment.

Lao-Tzu, Chinese philosopher and founder of Taoism, sixth century B.C.

Self-Regulation Is the Self's Most Important Function

Have you ever driven your car somewhere and were so absorbed in your thoughts that you barely noticed your surroundings? You obeyed all traffic rules, negotiated all turns, and maintained a safe distance from nearby cars while thinking about other matters. During the course of our everyday life, there are countless activities that are so well learned that we carry them out automatically, without conscious thought. These *habits* are very beneficial because they allow us to perform actions without expending much cognitive effort (Bargh & Chartrand, 1999). However, there are other times when we must consciously control and direct our behavior, expending a great deal of cognitive effort in the process (Hull, 2002). How is this process of **self-regulation** related to self-awareness?

Simply put, you must be self-aware to engage in self-regulation (Baumeister & Vohs, 2002; Lieberman, 2003). Indeed, self-regulation involves activation of the same brain region—the anterior cingulate—as in self-awareness, as well as activation of areas in the prefrontal lobe regions (refer back to figure 3.1) associated with selecting and initiating actions (*dorsolateral*) and planning and coordinating behavior designed to achieve goals (*orbitofrontal*). Brain-imaging studies find significant activation of these brain regions when people are performing difficult tasks requiring considerable cognitive effort and attention, but not during simple memory recall tasks (Amodio et al., 2004b; Schacter & Buckner, 1998). Case studies of people with brain damage in these areas find that while they have intact intelligence and comprehension, they have great difficulty maintaining their interest and focus on tasks (Damasio & Anderson, 2003; Knight & Grabowecky, 1995). In this regard, one of the important functions of self-regulation is that it provides us with the capacity to forgo the immediate gratification of small rewards to later attain larger rewards (Mischel et al., 1996). Anyone who has ever turned down a party invitation to study for an exam understands this particular benefit of the self-regulatory process. People who learn how to delay gratification early in childhood are better adjusted later in life—both academically and socially—than low self-regulators (Oyserman et al., in press; Shoda et al., 1990).

In Charles Carver and Michael Scheier's (1981, 1998) **control theory of self-regulation,** they contend that self-awareness allows us to assess how we are doing in meeting our goals and ideals. The core idea in control theory is a cognitive feedback loop (see figure 3.3), summarized by the acronym TOTE, which stands for the steps taken in self-regulation: Test-Operate-Test-Exit. In self-regulation, engaging in self-awareness allows us to compare how we are doing against some standard. This is the first test phase. When privately self-aware we compare ourselves against a *private* standard (for example, our own values), but when publicly self-aware we compare ourselves against a *public* standard (for example, our beliefs about what other people value). In the test phase, if we discover that we are falling short of the standard (for example, not studying enough), then we operate to change ourselves (we study harder). Soon, we self-reflect again—the second test phase—to see whether we are closer to reaching our standard. This test and operate cycle repeats itself until there is no difference between our behavior and the standard. When we meet the standard, the control process ends, we feel happy, and we exit the feedback loop. If repeated attempts to move closer to the standard fail, we feel bad and eventually exit the loop (Silvia & Duval, 2001a).

What happens to us emotionally when self-regulation does not lead to us meeting our standards? That is, how do we react when a discrepancy exists between our self-concept and how we would ideally like to be or believe others think we should be? Tory Higgins (1987) suggests that these **self-discrepancies** produce strong emotions. When we realize there is a discrepancy between our actual self and our *ideal self* (for example, "I wish I was more physically attractive"), we experience *dejection-related emotions,* such as disappointment, frustration, and depression. On the other hand, when we notice a discrepancy between our actual self and what we think we ought to possess (*ought self*) to meet our obligations and responsibilities (for example, "I should be helping my family out more financially"), we are vulnerable to *agitation-related emotions,* such as anxiety and guilt (Higgins et al., 1986). A number of studies have found that people with considerable self-discrepancies not only experience negative emotions but are often indecisive in their

Self-Regulation

The ways in which people control and direct their own actions.

Control Theory of Self-Regulation

A theory contending that, through self-awareness, people compare their behavior to a standard, and if there is a discrepancy, they work to reduce it.

Self-Discrepancies

Discrepancies between our self-concept and how we would ideally like to be (ideal self) or believe others think we should be (ought self).

FIGURE 3.3

Control Theory of Self-Regulation

According to the control theory of self-regulation, self-awareness provides the means by which we assess how successful we are in meeting our standards. When we become self-aware, we enter the first "test" phase. If we notice a difference between our actual behavior and our standards, we next enter the "operate" phase in which we try to change our behavior to match the standard. Soon, we again self-reflect—the second "test" phase—to discover whether we have reduced or eliminated the discrepancy. When there is no longer a difference between our behavior and the standard, we exit this control process.

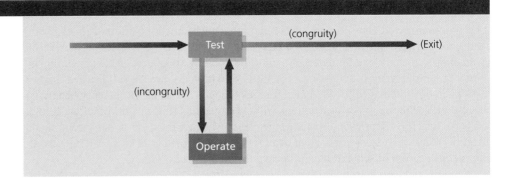

It is not enough to understand what we ought to be, unless we know what we are; and we do not understand what we are, unless we know what we ought to be.

T. S. Eliot, American poet, 1888–1965

behavior, have unclear self-concepts, and experience a loss of self-esteem (Dana et al., 1997). The more important these self-discrepant attributes are to the self-concept, the greater are the negative emotions experienced (Boldero & Francis, 2000).

In most instances, negative emotions hinder the type of self-regulation necessary for achieving longer-term goals (Tice et al., 2001). When people become upset, they tend to give in to their immediate impulses to make themselves feel better. For example, if you are trying to stop smoking, you are likely to grab for a cigarette after having an argument with someone. This "weakness" on your part amounts to giving short-term emotion regulation priority over your longer-term self-regulatory goal of being smoke-free.

Although a high capacity for self-regulation appears to improve your chances for success in life, self-regulating on one task makes it harder to immediately self-regulate on unrelated tasks (Baumeister et al., 1998). For example, Mark Muraven and his colleagues (1998) instructed some research participants to exercise self-control by suppressing their emotional reactions to an upsetting movie on environmental disasters. In contrast, other participants were either given no emotional control instructions or were told to increase their emotional responses by "really getting into the film." In this study, self-regulation was measured by determining how long participants would persist at a difficult physical task, namely squeezing a hand grip as long as possible. Such squeezing requires self-control to resist giving up and releasing the grip. Participants squeezed the grip both be-fore (*pretest*) and after (*posttest*) watching the movie, and the difference between the pre- and posttest was the dependent measure of self-regulation depletion. Consistent with the hypothesis that self-regulation strength is weakened following the exercise of self-control, those who were told to control their emotions while watching the upsetting film exhibited self-regulation depletion as measured by the hand grip test. No such depletion was found in the other participants. Because complex tasks require greater self-regulation than sim-ple tasks, prior self-regulation is most likely to harm people's subsequent activities when these later activities require higher-order cognitive processing (Schmeichel et al., 2003).

In explaining such findings, Roy Baumeister and his coworkers (1994) propose that controlling or regulating our behavior is best understood in terms of the following princi-ples from a *strength model* of self-regulation:

1. At any given time, we only have a limited amount of energy available to self-regulate.
2. Each exercise of self-regulation depletes this limited resource for a period of time.
3. Right after exercising self-regulation in one activity, we will find it harder to regulate our behavior in an unrelated activity.

According to this self-regulation model, if Tameeka is cramming for final exams and forces herself to study instead of going to a party (self-regulation success), she should be less able to control her anger later that evening (self-regulation failure) when her freeload-ing roommate eats the dessert Tameeka was saving for a late-night snack.

Although numerous studies have found that exertion of self-control causes a subse-quent decline in self-control performance on other tasks, it is unclear whether this decline is due to an actual decrease in people's ability to self-regulate—as proposed by the strength model—or instead is caused by a decrease in people's *motivation* to exert self-control (Muraven & Slessareva, 2003). In other words, after exercising self-control in one activity, are people less *able* to exercise self-control in a subsequent task, or is it that they are less *willing* to exercise this control? We do know that when people engage in a difficult self-regulatory task they have a subjective experience of time slowing down ("When will it end?!"), and this perception makes them less likely to continue self-regulating (Vohs & Schmeichel, 2003). It is possible that such an "extended now" not only reduces people's desire to continue in the present activity but also to exercise self-control in any activities immediately following the "never-ending" one. The Applications section at the end of the chapter discusses some social problems associated with self-regulation failure.

CRITICAL *thinking*

Spend a few minutes considering how self-regulation failure contributes to domestic violence. According to the strength model of self-regulation, when would a parent or a spouse be most likely to harm someone due to losing control of their emotions?

SECTION SUMMARY

- Self-awareness is necessary for self-concept development

  Humans develop self-awareness at around 18 months

  The great apes appear to have self-awareness ability

- Private self-awareness is a temporary state of being aware of hidden, private self-aspects

  Effects: affect intensification; knowledge clarification; adherence to personal standards

- Public self-awareness is a temporary state of being aware of observable, public self-aspects

  Effects: social uneasiness; temporary self-esteem loss; adherence to social standards

- The tendencies to habitually engage in private and public self-awareness are known as the personality traits of private self-consciousness and public self-consciousness

- Self-regulation involves the ways in which we control and direct our actions

- The control theory of self-regulation contends that we compare our behavior to a standard, and if there is a discrepancy, we try to reduce it

- Exerting self-control either depletes self-regulatory resources or reduces motivation to self-regulate

THE SELF AS A KNOWLEDGE STRUCTURE

Self-awareness allows us to analyze our thoughts and feelings, as well as anticipate how others might respond to us interpersonally. Through self-awareness, we develop a self-concept, which helps us regulate our behavior and adapt to our surroundings (Higgins, 1996). Yet how is this self-information organized in memory?

Self-Schemas Are the Ingredients of Self-Concept

Social psychologists have expended considerable effort to better understand how information about the self is stored and categorized in memory. In describing this process, the computer has often been used as a metaphor: the subjective self (the "I") consists of program components, and the objective self (the self-concept or the "me") is the data aspect of the computer (Greenwald & Pratkanis, 1984). To describe how self-knowledge is cognitively stored, investigators have borrowed the term "schemas" from cognitive psychology (Markus et al., 1985). A *schema* is a cognitive structure that represents knowledge about some stimulus, which is built up from experience

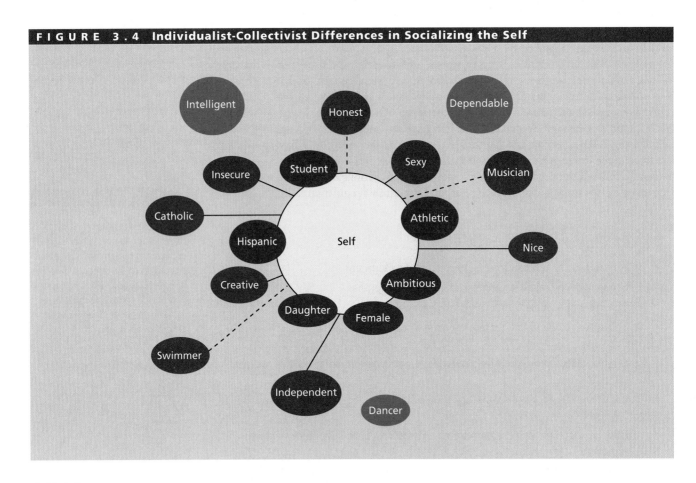

Self-Schemas

This is a simplified representation of one person's self-schemas. The length of lines connecting self-schemas to the self represents their importance to the person's self-concept, with highly important self-schemas embedded into the self. For this person, she is highly self-schematic for the descriptors of *daughter, Hispanic, student, athletic, ambitious,* and *female,* she is somewhat less self-schematic for such descriptors as *Catholic, insecure, sexy, nice, independent,* and *creative,* she is even less self-schematic for the descriptors of *honest, musician,* and *swimmer,* and she is aschematic for the descriptors of *dancer, intelligent,* and *dependable.* How do you know whether you possess a self-schema for a particular trait or social role?

Self-Schema

A cognitive structure that represents how you think about yourself in a particular domain and how you organize your experiences in that domain.

and which selectively guides the processing of new information. A schema directs our attention to relevant information, giving us a framework for assessing it. You can have schemas about people, things, and events (see chapter 5, pp. 141-145).

One of the most important types of schema is the **self-schema.** Some social psychologists use the term "self-schema" as equivalent to "self-concept," while others employ a more restrictive definition. This more restrictive definition is used in this text, and it refers to a cognitive structure that represents how you think about yourself in a particular domain and how you organize your experiences in that domain. Just as self-concept has been previously described as a theory that you have about yourself, self-schemas can be thought of as the hypotheses of this self-theory. Any particular self-schema is a generalization about the self established through life experiences. It helps you perceive, organize, interpret, and use information about yourself in a particular area of your life (see figure 3.4). For example, if you possess a self-schema of "sexiness," you consider this quality to be personally relevant and most likely have well-developed self-conceptions of this quality. How do you know if you possess such a self-schema? Markus (1977) states that people are self-schematic for qualities that are important to them, on which they think of themselves as *extreme* (high or low), and on which they are certain the *opposite* does not hold. In contrast, if people are not self-schematic for a particular quality, they are not invested in or concerned about it; it is not relevant to their self-concepts (they are *aschematic*). I would be willing to bet that actor Brad Pitt has a self-schema for sexiness, but Pope John Paul II is aschematic on this dimension.

Markus (1977) tested the effects of self-schemas on information processing by having college students rate themselves in terms of their independence/dependence. Those who rated themselves as decidedly independent (*independent schematics*) or decidedly dependent (*dependent schematics*), as well as those who did not consider themselves possessing either quality (*aschematics*), later participated in a seemingly unrelated study. Markus reasoned that possessing a schema would make it easier for people to process and recall from memory any information relevant to the schema. She therefore predicted that schematics would be able to decide faster whether adjectives relevant to their self-schema were descriptive of them than would aschematics, and that they would be able to recall more behavioral incidents from their past that were indicative of the self-schema.

In the study, trait adjectives associated with independence (for example, assertive) and dependence (for example, obliging) were projected on a screen one at a time, and participants were told to press a "me" button if the word was self-descriptive or a "not me" button if the word was not self-descriptive. As expected, independent schematics made faster judgments about words related to independence, and dependent schematics made faster judgments about words related to dependence. Aschematics' judgments about dependent- or independent-related adjectives did not differ at all. Schematics also recalled more incidents from their pasts in which they acted in line with their schema. This and other research supports the idea that self-schemas play a crucial role in explaining how potentially self-relevant information is processed, stored, and later recalled from memory.

If self-schemas influence information processing and memory recall, what determines which one of our self-schemas or which combination of them will be most influential at any given moment? For example, if you think of yourself as fun-loving, young, single, and intelligent, which, if any, of these self-schemas will affect how you process information at 8 P.M. on Saturday? Research by William McGuire and his colleagues (1978) indicates that *context* is a major determinant in activating certain self-schemas. The aspect of the self-concept that becomes salient and activated in a particular setting is called the *spontaneous self-concept*. If at 8 o'clock on Saturday night you find yourself at a very dull college party, you are more likely to think of yourself as the fun-loving one rather than the intelligent, single, or young one. Likewise, if you are at a festive party celebrating the fiftieth wedding anniversary of two senior citizens, you may not think about the fact that you are fun-loving or intelligent, but you may be quite aware that you are young and single. Existing research suggests that when one aspect of our self-concept is spontaneously activated, potentially conflicting self-schemas are more likely to be inhibited from being simultaneously activated (Hugenberg & Bodenhausen, 2004).

Whether or not a specific personal quality leads to a self-schema that is central to your self-concept often depends on the degree to which it "stands out" in everyday interactions. This is often the experience of people who have qualities that run counter to the stereotype of their social group. For example, White Americans are stereotypically perceived to be inferior to African Americans in athletic endeavors, while African Americans are typically perceived to be inferior to Americans in academic pursuits (see chapter 8, pp. 271–274). Research by William von Hippel and his colleagues (2001) suggests that when members of one of these groups behave counter to these stereotypes, their performances are more likely to be noticed and commented upon than are the stereotype-consistent performances of the other group members. Such unexpected behaviors not only grab observers' attention, but through reflected appraisal (refer back to p. 57), the performers themselves are more likely to think of their behaviors as distinctive. As a result, they are more likely to develop self-schemas around these abilities than are members of the other group who perform at the same level but for whom the performances are not considered unusual for their group. In other words, Black students who excel academically are more likely to be noticed and to form "academically gifted" self-schemas than are academically similar White students. Likewise, White athletes who excel in sports are more likely to form "athletically gifted" self-schemas than are Black students with similar athletic skills.

Consider self-schemas in the context of William James's hypothesis that the content of self-concept fluctuates over time. How would you design a study, using Markus's "me"/"not me" response format, to document the disappearance of a specific self-schema—say "sexiness"—from people's self-concept? Would this be a longitudinal study in which you would repeatedly test the same people over many years? Or would you instead test people of different age groups?

What you think of yourself is much more important than what others think of you.

Seneca, Roman playwright, 4 B.C.–A.D. 64

Gender Identity and Gender Schemas Are Important Aspects of Self-Concept

One evening as we ate dinner, Amelia, who was 3 years old at the time, surveyed the table, then looked at me and announced, "Daddy? I'm a girl, and Mommy's a girl, and Lillian's a girl, but you're not a girl. You're a boy." Then, glancing over at our dog, Yocker, who was sleeping on the floor near my feet, she added, "And Yocker's a boy, too." Ignoring the possibility that my daughter had recognized some characteristics other than sex that helped her in categorizing me with the family dog (perhaps a tendency to stare off in space or to pant at the sight of food), I complimented Amelia on her ability to distinguish males from females.

GENDER IDENTITY

Gender Identity

The knowledge that one is a male or a female and the internalization of this fact into one's self-concept.

This "Amelia story" describes an identification process that all children experience at approximately this age. This self-labeling, known as **gender identity,** is the identification of oneself as a male or a female and the internalization of this fact into one's self-concept. Knowing that "I am a girl" or "I am a boy" is one of the core building blocks in a child's developing self-theory (Bussey & Bandura, 1999). Shortly after self-awareness develops—by the age of 2—children begin to acquire an understanding of gender (Katz, 1986). Two-year-olds can reliably sort photographs into female and male categories, but they cannot consistently name their own sex (Fagot, 1985). By age 3 or 4, they can correctly label themselves as male or female (gender identity), but they are still unaware that their biological sex is unchangeable (Coker, 1984). What Amelia demonstrated at the dinner table was that she could successfully categorize herself and others based on gender cues. Once gender identity fully develops—around the age of 6 or 7—little if anything can change it (Money & Ehrhardt, 1972).

GENDER SCHEMA

Gender Schema

A cognitive structure for processing information based on its perceived female or male qualities.

When children develop gender identity they strive to act in ways consistent with this identity. According to Sandra Bem (1981), if a culture emphasizes distinctions between women and men, then children growing up in that culture learn to process information about themselves, other people, and even things and events according to their perceived gender associations. In other words, they develop a **gender schema,** which is a cognitive structure for processing information based on its perceived female or male qualities. Adults in the child's

Gender identity is fully developed by age 6 or 7, and then, many children use this identity when deciding which behaviors and activities are most appropriate for them. If my daughters are typical of girls their age, which of the two photographs do you think they most strongly identify with? Would it be that unusual if they identified more strongly with the shorts and caps than with the dresses? What if they were boys? Why would their identification with the "dresses" photo raise alarm bells among many adults? What do these different reactions suggest to you about gender socialization?

world help shape this developing gender schema by associating different objects and activities with one sex rather than the other (Klinger et al., 2001). For example, in North American culture, personal characteristics such as physical attractiveness, cooperation and empathy, activities such as skipping rope and cooking, or even animals such as cats and birds come to be perceived as having a female connotation. On the other hand, physical strength, independence and aggressiveness, football, woodworking, dogs, and bears are perceived as having a male connotation.

Bem believes that the self-concepts of children become assimilated into this culturally derived gender schema as they learn which attributes are associated with their own sex and, hence, with themselves. At the same time children's self-concepts become linked to the gender schema, they also learn to evaluate their adequacy as a person in terms of how well their own personal attributes match the standards of the gender schema. Thus, boys are more likely to evaluate themselves in terms of their physical strength and competitiveness, while girls are more likely to evaluate themselves according to their physical attractiveness and ability to get along with others. As adults, many of us continue to define ourselves through these same gender-filtered lenses, regulating our behavior so it conforms to the culture's definition of maleness and femaleness. The fact that, in most cultures, masculine activities are more highly valued than feminine activities may largely explain why men score slightly higher than women on standard measures of global self-esteem (Kling et al., 1999).

Are you *gender schematic?* That is, do you habitually organize things in your mind according to gender categories? Do you try to keep your own behavior consistent with traditional gender standards? Actually, in most Western societies today, rigid gender attitudes and beliefs are increasingly being challenged, especially by college-educated adults and their children (Lottes & Kuriloff, 1994). One effect is that some people can be characterized as being relatively *gender aschematic:* they do not cognitively divide the world into female-male qualities, and gender is not of primary relevance to either their self-concepts or their perceptions of others (Bem, 1993). As you will discover in future chapters, unlike gender schematics who try to keep their own behavior consistent with stereotypical gender standards, gender aschematics exhibit a great deal more flexibility.

Culture Shapes the Structure of Self-Concept

At the beginning of this chapter I asked you to contemplate who you are by describing yourself twenty times. Sociologists Manford Kuhn and Thomas McPartland devised this Twenty Statements Test (TST) in 1954 to measure self-concept. A common technique used to analyze TST responses (see Hartley, 1970) is to code each response into one of four categories: *physical self-descriptions* identify self in terms of physical qualities that do not imply social interaction ("I am a male"; "I am a brunette"; "I am overweight"); *social self-descriptions* identify self in terms of social roles, institutional memberships, or other socially defined statuses ("I am a student"; "I am a daughter"; "I am a Jew"); *attributive self-descriptions* identify self in terms of psychological or physiological states or traits ("I am intelligent"; "I am assertive"; "I am tired"); *global self-descriptions* identify self so comprehensively or vaguely that it does not distinguish one from any other person ("I am a human being"; "I am alive"; "I am me"). Return to your own TST responses and code each into one of these four categories. Which category occurs most frequently for you?

POSSIBLE HISTORICAL EFFECTS

Using this classification scheme, Louis Zurcher (1977) found that while American college students in the 1950s and early 1960s tended to describe themselves in terms of social roles, college students in the 1970s identified themselves in terms of psychological attributes. This self-concept trend has continued (Trafimow et al., 1991) and coincides with a rise in individualistic attitudes among Americans (Roberts & Helson, 1997). Do your own self-responses fit this pattern?

Zurcher suggests that these self-concept and attitudinal changes are due to widespread cultural changes beginning in the 1950s (Wood & Zurcher, 1988). For many Americans, the end of World War II brought increased economic prosperity and an accompanying willingness to move away from their extended families and hometowns to pursue personal and career goals. In the following decades, the social unrest caused by the Vietnam War and the Watergate scandal created a distrust of political institutions. Likewise, the recessions of the 1970s and early 1980s eroded people's faith that economic institutions could provide good-paying, secure jobs. The increasing divorce rate and weakening of the family unit, as well as the growing problems in the educational system created similar disaffection for these societal institutions. In reaction to this dissatisfaction, Zurcher asserted that college students' identification with personal qualities rather than institutional affiliations was an attempt to achieve a greater feeling of personal control over their lives.

INDIVIDUALIST-COLLECTIVIST COMPARISONS

In addition to investigating changes in the structure of self-concept over time, researchers have also conducted cross-cultural comparisons (Cross & Gore, 2002; Markus & Kitayama, 1991). As stated in chapter 1, most of the world's population resides in collectivist cultures. It is not surprising, then, that numerous studies have found cross-cultural differences in TST responses. In general, American, Canadian, and European self-concepts are composed of predominantly attributive self-descriptions, indicating that these individualist cultures foster the development of an **independent self** for their members. In contrast, people from collectivist cultures such as China, Mexico, Japan, India, and Kenya have more social self-descriptions, indicating a fostering of an **interdependent self** (Kanagawa et al., 2001; Ma & Schoeneman, 1997). Spend a few minutes viewing the interview with Hazel Markus and Shinovu Kitayama on your Social Sense CD-ROM, concerning how self-conceptions differ cross-culturally. Within the United States, European Americans, African Americans, and Latino Americans tend to have highly independent selves, despite the latter two ethnic groups having collectivist heritages (Oyserman et al., 2002). Latino Americans with interdependent selves are much more likely to be recent immigrants to the country than those with independent selves (Castro, 2003).

This differing view of the individual due to a culture's collectivist or individualist orientation not only shapes the structure of self-concept, it also determines beliefs about how self-development should proceed (Greenfield, 1994). Within collectivist societies, childrearing practices emphasize conformity, cooperation, dependence, and knowing one's proper place, whereas within more individualist societies, independence, self-reliance, and personal success are stressed. One consequence of these differing views is that in an individualist society, people develop a belief in their own uniqueness and diversity (Miller, 1988). This sense of individuality is nurtured and fostered within the educational system (see table 3.4), and its manifestation is considered a sign of maturity (Pratt, 1991). On the other hand, in a collectivist society, uniqueness and individual differences are often seen as impediments to proper self-growth (Kim & Choi, 1994). Instead, the self becomes most meaningful and complete when it is closely identified with—not independent of—the group (DeVos, 1985). In collectivist China, for example, one consequence of this group focus is that educational theories and practices emphasize shaping children's personalities to meet societal needs and goals (Pye, 1996). To employ the previous analogy of self-concept being a grand portrait, in individualist cultures people are given primary responsibility to paint their own image, while in collectivist cultures each person's self-portrait is expected to truly reflect a group effort.

As you see, conceiving the self as either independent or interdependent has important implications for how people think, feel, and interact in their social world. The ideas and activities of a culture promote a way of life that provides a constant reminder to its members of what type of self is valued. Immersed within these social environments, the dominant mode of thinking will be that which is compatible with either an independent self or an interdependent self. However, within these cultures there will be times when people enter settings that trigger the alternative sense of self. For example, people who live in an individualist culture may watch the movie *It's a Wonderful Life* (see chapter 1, p. 19) and be reminded how their own lives are deeply intertwined with their family, friends, and community. This setting triggers a spontaneous interdependent self, increasing the likelihood

Independent Self

A way of conceiving the self in terms of unique, personal attributes and as a being that is separate and autonomous from the group.

Interdependent Self

A way of conceiving the self in terms of social roles and as a being that is embedded in and dependent on the group.

Social Sense

View the video *Self and Culture.*

TABLE 3.4

Individualist-Collective Differences in Socializing the Self

"I Am Special"	"A Letter To Children"
No one looks	I wish you from your early age
The way I do.	to be obedient to father and mother;
I have noticed	respect teachers;
That it's true.	to have good thoughts and good moral character.
No one walks	All in all, I wish you to be like uncle Lei Feng (a national
The way I walk.	hero), to grow up healthy.
No one talks	To grow up to be successors of revolution;
The way I talk.	well rounded in morality, intelligence, physically, and beauty.
No one plays	
The way I play.	Zhongyang, J. K. Y. (Ed.). (1984). *Song Qingling lun*
No one says	*shaonian ertong jiaouyu (Song Qingling's essays on*
The things I say.	*education for youth and children)*. Beijing: Jiaoyu chubanshe.
I am special,	
I am me.	
There's no one else	
I'd rather be.	

Author Unknown

The poem on the left, posted at the hallway entrance to my daughters' elementary school, is a good illustration of how individualist cultures socialize children to think of themselves as being unique and "one of a kind." Next to the poem was a cutout of a snowflake and the accompanying words, "You're UNIQUE!" In marked contrast, the poem on the right, addressed to the children of China by the national leader of child and youth welfare, stresses obedience and respect as important values. As such, it reflects the time-honored Confucian ideal of the person as an insignificant self submitting to a significant larger (Chinese) collectivity. Which of these two poems best reflects the spirit of your own upbringing?

that people will at least temporarily set aside selfish interests, act cooperatively, and attend to others' needs (Gardner et al., 1999). In other words, cultures do not create people with rigidly independent or interdependent selves. Situational factors can trigger spontaneous self-concepts in people that run counter to the independent self or interdependent self fostered by their culture (Kühnen al., 2001; Kühnen & Oyserman, 2002).

CULTURAL VERSUS GENDER DISTINCTIONS

Gender socialization in North American culture has been described as fostering the construction of an *independent* self-concept among males and a *relational* self-concept among females (Cross & Madson, 1997; Cross & Morris, 2003). To what degree are these gender differences in self-concept similar to the cultural differences we have just reviewed? That is, are American women's self-concepts similar to the self-concepts of people from collectivist cultures?

Actually, it appears that the similarities are more superficial than substantive. A five-culture study by Yoshihisa Kashima and his colleagues (1995) indicates that American and Australian women's self-concepts are not like Asians' self-concepts. Instead, these researchers found that while individualist-collectivist cultural differences are captured mostly by the extent to which people see themselves as acting as independent agents in relation to the group, gender differences are best summarized by the extent to which people regard themselves as *emotionally related* to other individuals. This suggests that gender socialization has much more to do with encouraging girls to pay attention to the emotional "pulse" of their social relationships while discouraging boys from doing so, than it does in encouraging boys to be independent of the group and girls to be dependent on the group. In

CRITICAL *thinking*

If you were to tell someone to "just be yourself," what would that mean to them depending on whether they were from an individualist or a collectivist culture?

other words, individualist-collectivist socialization has decidedly different effects on the nature of self-concept than male-female socialization.

WHAT ABOUT BICULTURALISTS?

Although cultures can be characterized as being more oriented toward individualism or collectivism, not everyone living within a particular culture will have the same individualist-collectivist leanings (Ayyash-Abdo, 2001). For example, if you are a Native American, Indian American, or Asian American, your cultural heritage may still encourage you to seek collectivist goals (Gaines, 1995). The same is true of Jews and Arabs who live in Israel, where a Western individualist ideological system often conflicts with traditional Arab and Jewish collectivist cultures. Numerous studies indicate that individuals with such a *bicultural* background view themselves and the world through both individualist and collectivist lenses (Hong et al., 2001; Oyserman, 1993). Although we tend to cognitively suppress the simultaneous activation of competing social identities (Hugenberg & Bodenhausen, 2004), such suppression is not always successful. When biculturalists' dual views of themselves and their worlds collide, this can lead to internal conflict as they attempt to reconcile individualist strivings with collectivist yearnings (Sussman, 2000). As one 19-year-old second-generation Indian American explained these competing demands:

> Being "bicultural" makes me feel special and confused. Special because it adds to my identity: I enjoy my Indian culture, I feel that it is rich in tradition, morality, and beauty; Confused because I have been in many situations where I feel being both cultures is not an option. My cultures have very different views on things like dating and marriage. I feel like you have to choose one or the other. (Haritatos & Benet-Martínez, 2002)

How is this conflict best resolved? Based on studies of Pueblo, Navajo, Latino, Iranian American, Indian American, and Asia American/Canadian children and adults, neither abandoning one's ancestral collectivist culture nor isolating oneself from the dominant individualist culture is good for mental health (Benet-Martínez & Karakitapoglu-Aygun, 2003; Joe, 1994). Instead, successful biculturalism entails retaining ancestral values and practices while incorporating new values and practices from the dominant culture (see the section "Ethnic Identity of Minority Groups," pp. 83–84). This acknowledgment and acceptance that the two cultural identities are not fully compatible or overlapping results in a self-concept that is both more inclusive and more complex (Roccas & Brewer, 2002). Peo-

"I have a very valuable parrot," declared the pet store owner. "It speaks both Spanish and English! If you pull the left leg he speaks English, and if you pull the right leg he speaks Spanish." "What happens if you pull both legs at once?" asked the customer. "Will he speak Tex-Mex?" "Noooo," answered the parrot. "I will fall on my ass."

Mexican American folk tale, adapted from West (1988)

U.S. Senator Ben Nighthorse Campbell from Colorado is a testament to how a person with a bicultural background can successfully reconcile individualist strivings with collectivist yearnings. As a member of the Northern Cheyenne Indian Tribe, Senator Campbell is not only the lone American Indian in Congress, he is also a three-time U.S. judo champion and was captain of the 1964 U.S. Olympic judo team.

FIGURE 3.5

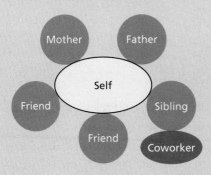

Individualist View: Independent Self

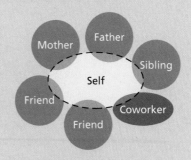

Collectivist View: Interdependent Self

The self should be independent of the group.

Self-concept is primarily defined by internal attributes.

People are socialized to be unique, to validate their internal attributes, to promote their own goals, and to "speak their minds."

Self-esteem is based on the ability to engage in self-expression and the ability to validate internal attributes.

The self should be dependent on the group.

Self-concept is primarily defined by social roles and relationships.

People are socialized to belong, to occupy their proper place, to engage in appropriate behavior, and to "read others' minds."

Self-esteem is based on one's ability to adjust to the group, restrain his or her own desires, and maintain social harmony.

How Is the Self Construed in Collectivist and Individualist Cultures?

Individualist cultures foster the development of the independent self characterized by independence, uniqueness, self-expression, and the validation of internal attributes. In contrast, collectivist cultures foster the development of the interdependent self characterized by dependence, conformity, and adjustment of one's social roles to accommodate group goals. How might these two different views of the self lead to personal conflicts between individualists and collectivists when they interact with one another?

ple who possess dual cultural identities engage in **cultural frame switching,** in which they move between the two different cultural belief systems in response to situational cues and demands (Benet-Martínez et al., 2002; Haritatos & Benet-Martínez, 2002). One Native American woman explained how she successfully attained her PhD while still maintaining her strong tribal ties:

> My family and I talked about the "I" and the "we," all the pressure there was when I was going to school to be this "I," to climb the old ladder, claw your way up to success. . . . I'm part of a "we" and I've never lost sight of that . . . Because of the "we," this community and my family, I can do all of this. (Stratham & Rhoades, 2001, p. 275)

By having access to their two different cultural belief systems, biculturalists can engage in culturally appropriate behaviors depending on the social context. This melding of the collectivist and individualist orientation not only benefits the health of biculturalists, it can also provide long-term benefits to society by infusing it with individuals who understand the value of both autonomy and social obligation (Oyserman et al., 1998).

Figure 3.5 outlines how cultural differences regarding individualism-collectivism may influence the structure of self-concept. The degree to which individualists and collectivists differ in the way they conceive of themselves is just beginning to be understood. Further, the self as a research topic has primarily been of interest to social scientists from individualist cultures, in which issues such as personal identity and self-

Cultural Frame Switching

The process by which biculturalists switch between different culturally appropriate behaviors depending on the context.

boundaries are woven into the fabric of socialization. Because of this relative lack of understanding of cultural effects on the self, as you read the remaining sections in this chapter, keep in mind that these findings are most confidently generalizable to cultures with an individualist orientation.

<table>
<tr><td colspan="2">S E C T I O N   S U M M A R Y</td></tr>
</table>

- *Self-schemas* help us process, store, and recall self-relevant information
- *Gender identity* is our awareness of being female or male
- The interdependent self identifies with societal institutions and is more common in collectivist cultures
- The independent self identifies with personal attributes and is more common in individualist cultures
- Biculturalists engage in cultural frame switching due to situational cues and demands

EVALUATING THE SELF

Self-Esteem

A person's evaluation of his or her self-concept.

So far we have seen how self-concept is constituted and how attention to private and public self-aspects can affect thinking, feelings, and action. Yet in discussing self-concept, we must understand that it is not a dispassionate self theory. It consists of numerous evaluations of self as being good, bad, or mediocre. This evaluative aspect of the "me" is called **self-esteem** (Brown & Marshall, 2001; Vohs & Heatherton, 2001; Watson et al., 2002). Mark Leary and his colleagues (1995) assert that during the course of human evolution, self-esteem emerged as an internal "meter" (Leary calls it our *sociometer*) of our sense of exclusion and inclusion in our social groups. For most of human evolution, individuals who belonged to social groups were more likely to survive and reproduce than those who were excluded and forced to survive on their own. According to Leary, when people behave in ways that decrease the likelihood they will be rejected, they experience an increase in self-esteem.

A review of self-esteem studies finds that the vast majority of people who are identified as having low self-esteem generally do not see themselves as worthless, incompetent losers (Baumeister et al., 1989). Instead, they are people who evaluate themselves more *neutrally* than either very positively or very negatively. In most cases, it is only in comparison to the very positive evaluations of people with high self-esteem that these individuals can be described as having "low" self-esteem (Baumeister, 1993). Yet this difference in evaluating the self has important consequences for people's lives. Individuals with low self-esteem are generally more unhappy and pessimistic (DeNeve & Cooper, 1998; Shepperd et al., 1996), less willing to take risks to benefit themselves (Josephs et al., 1992), more likely to encounter academic and financial problems (Crocker & Luhtanen, 2003), less likely to have successful careers (Judge & Bono, 2001), and less likely to be physically healthy (Vingilis et al., 1998) than high self-esteem individuals. Let us explore how social scientists have studied this important personal quality. However, before reading further, complete the self-esteem questionnaire in table 3.5.

Self-Esteem Develops During Middle Childhood and Is Most Stable During Young Adulthood

Feelings of self-worth gradually develop during childhood, with parents playing a critical role in determining its evaluative direction. Although young children do not have a recognizable sense of self-esteem, during middle childhood, their increasing cognitive maturity allows them to integrate others' evaluations of them and their own self-assessments into a global sense of

TABLE 3.5

Self-Esteem Scale

Instructions

Read each item below and then indicate how well each statement describes you using the following response scale:

0 = extremely uncharacteristic (not at all like me)

1 = uncharacteristic (somewhat unlike me)

2 = neither characteristic nor uncharacteristic

3 = characteristic (somewhat like me)

4 = extremely characteristic (very much like me)

_____ 1. On the whole, I am satisfied with myself.

_____ 2. At times I think I am no good at all.*

_____ 3. I feel that I have a number of good qualities.

_____ 4. I am able to do things as well as most other people.

_____ 5. I feel I do not have much to be proud of.*

_____ 6. I certainly feel useless at times.*

_____ 7. I feel that I'm a person of worth, at least on an equal plane with others.

_____ 8. I wish I could have more respect for myself.*

_____ 9. All in all, I am inclined to feel that I am a failure.*

_____ 10. I take a positive attitude toward myself.

Directions for Scoring

Half of the self-esteem items are reverse-scored; that is, for these items a lower rating actually indicates a higher level of self-esteem. Before summing all ten items to find out your total self-esteem score, recode those with an asterisk ("") so that 0 = 4, 1 = 3, 3 = 1, and 4 = 0. Your total self-esteem score can range from 0 to 40, with a higher score indicating a higher level of self-esteem. Scores greater than 20 indicate generally positive attitudes toward the self; those below 20 indicate generally negative self-attitudes.*

self-esteem (Marsh et al., 1991). Research conducted in more than 200 cultures indicates that children with high self-esteem usually have *authoritative parents*—parents who exert control not merely by imposing rules and consistently enforcing them, but also by allowing their children a fair amount of freedom within the rules and by discussing the rationale behind their decisions (Querido et al., 2002; Steinberg & Morris, 2001). This research indicates that children need love combined with a set of boundaries to structure their behavior. In contrast, parents who impose many rules and expect strict obedience (*authoritarian parents*) and those who make few demands and submit to their children's desires (*permissive parents*) tend to raise children who are less confident in their abilities and have lower self-esteem (Baumrind, 1996).

Among American children, the detrimental effect of authoritarian parenting is most apparent in Caucasian American families, where this parental style is often used to "break the child's will." However, there is also evidence that many ethnic-minority families place greater value on authoritarian parenting as a positive socialization tool (Lynch, 1994; Parke & Buriel, 1998). For example, Chinese American parents use authoritarian discipline to "train" (*chiao shun*) and "govern" (*guan*) children so that they will know what is expected of them. In such a cultural context, authoritarian parenting is not associated with lower self-esteem (Rao et al., 2003; Steinberg et al., 1992).

How stable is self-esteem across the life span? To answer this question, Kali Trzesniewski and her colleagues (2003) conducted a meta-analysis of fifty self-esteem studies involving almost 30,000 participants in the United States and other countries. Test-retest correlations of self-esteem measures across at least a one-year interval were obtained from

FIGURE 3.6

Stability of Self-Esteem Across the Life Span

A meta-analysis of 50 self-esteem studies involving almost 30,000 participants (ages 6 to 82 years) examined test-retest correlations of self-esteem measures across at least a 1-year interval (Trzesniewski et al., 2003). There were no gender or nationality differences in self-esteem stability, but stability was relatively low during childhood, it increased throughout adolescence and young adulthood, and then it declined during midlife and old age. What are some possible explanations for these age-related differences in self-esteem stability?

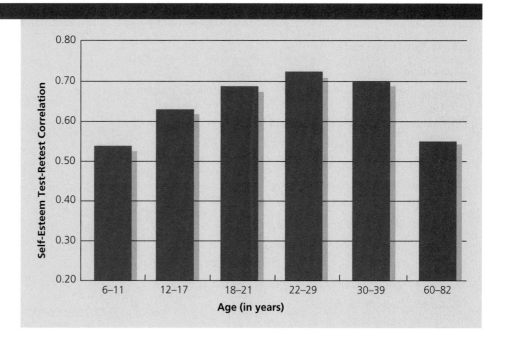

CRITICAL *thinking*

Based on Trzesniewski and her coworkers' (2003) research on the stability of self-esteem across the life span, during what stage in life (besides early childhood) would you likely be most successful in changing self-esteem?

samples involving people from age 6 to age 83. As you can see from figure 3.6, the researchers found that self-esteem stability is relatively low during childhood, increases throughout adolescence and young adulthood, and declines during midlife and old age. There was no evidence for gender or nationality differences in self-esteem stability, but White Americans had higher stability levels ($r = .68$) than Asian Americans ($r = .61$), African Americans ($r = .60$), Latino Americans ($r = .54$), and Native Americans ($r = .54$).

Trzesniewski and her coworkers suggest that the low stability levels during childhood may be caused by young children being unable to form abstract conceptions of themselves as good or bad, but it also may be due to young children not understanding the self-esteem questions posed to them by researchers. The increasing stability of self-esteem during adolescence and young adulthood may be caused by people achieving a sense of personal identity and gradually obtaining the psychological resources needed to properly adjust to life changes. Finally, the researchers speculated that the decline in self-esteem stability in later adulthood and old age may be due to the dramatic life changes (for example, retirement, death of loved ones, declining health) that are more likely to characterize this life stage than the others. These events may threaten some people's self-concepts, resulting in fluctuations in self-esteem levels that reduce the stability of self-esteem.

Self-Esteem Differences Shape Responses to Positive and Negative Events

One assumption about human beings is that they are motivated to feel good, to create and maintain pleasant or positive states of mind (Larsen, 2000). Yet is it true that everyone is motivated to maintain such pleasurable feelings to the same degree? Recent studies suggest that people who differ in self-esteem also differ in their emotional reactions to positive and negative daily events.

SELF-ESTEEM AND EMOTIONAL SELF-REGULATION

When experiencing positive emotions following some desirable outcome, high self-esteem individuals tend to savor their feelings, while low self-esteem individuals tend to dampen these emotions (Wood et al., 2003). In contrast, while negative events generally dampen people's daily moods regardless of their level of self-esteem, low self-esteem people are more adversely affected. In a ten-week study of college students' daily moods, John Nezlek and Rebecca Plesko (2003) found that individual differences in self-esteem had a significant impact on emotional reactions to daily events. Twice a week, these students reported their daily experiences, including how positive they felt about themselves that day. Results indicated that daily fluctuations in feelings of self-worth were affected by positive and negative events, but negative events were much more damaging to the daily feelings of self-worth among the low self-esteem students than among those with high self-esteem. These findings are consistent with other studies indicating that low self-esteem people are more adversely affected by hassles and personal setbacks in their everyday lives than high self-esteem people (Brown & Dutton, 1995). It appears that high self-esteem people self-regulate in a manner that helps to sustain their highly positive self-regard, whereas low self-esteem people regulate their emotions in a way that maintains their relatively low self-regard.

What is it about the emotional self-regulation of high and low self-esteem people that contributes to these differences? Recent studies suggest that low self-esteem persons are more adversely affected by negative events because they appear to be less motivated to repair their negative moods (Heimpel et al., 2002). One reason for this lack of motivation to engage in self-regulation may be that low self-esteem people are simply more accustomed to negative moods, and hence they come to accept them more readily than high self-esteem persons. Another possibility is that, for low self-esteem persons, negative emotions are accompanied by two experiences that are especially harmful to their motivation to self-regulate. First, the negative event depletes their self-regulatory resources (see pp. 65–67). Second, this depletion may be particularly harmful to them because engaging in mood regulation may require more energy than it does for high self-esteem persons, who have more experience with positive moods. This greater experience requires high self-esteem persons to expend less energy to repair their negative moods. Thus, a "double whammy" exists for low self-esteem persons, which has the effect of undermining their motivation to take any action to repair negative moods.

SELF-ENHANCEMENT AND SELF-VERIFICATION MOTIVES

The greater difficulty that low self-esteem people have in experiencing positive feelings may also be partly caused by conflicting self-enhancement and self-verification motives. Over the years there has been an ongoing debate regarding self-evaluation and self-concept that is related to the hot and cold perspectives discussed in chapter 1. The **self-enhancement** perspective embodies the emotional, or hot, viewpoint of human nature and is based on the notion that people are primarily motivated to maintain high self-esteem ((Beach & Tesser, 2000; Dunning et al., 1995). According to this view, the need for self-enhancement will increase as one's negative self-evaluations increase. In contrast, the **self-verification** perspective (more generally known as the *self-consistency view*) reflects the cognitive, or cold, viewpoint. According to this view, people are motivated to maintain consistent beliefs about themselves, even when these self-beliefs are negative (Swann, 1997). By verifying firmly held self-beliefs, people feel more secure that their social world is predictable and controllable.

For those with high self-esteem, there is no conflict between these two motives because receiving positive feedback verifies positive self-beliefs. However, for individuals with low self-esteem, these two motives often conflict: the need for self-enhancement causes those with low self-esteem to seek positive feedback, but that action conflicts with their desire to verify existing negative self-beliefs (Brown, 1993). Self-enhancement theorists contend that people with low self-esteem will seek out positive social feedback because it will bolster their self-esteem. In contrast, self-verification theorists argue that this positive feedback will create the fear in people with low self-esteem that they may not know themselves after all, and therefore, they will reject it. Which of these perspectives is correct?

J. Sidney Shrauger (1975) proposes that *both* the need for self-enhancement and the need for self-verification operate simultaneously, but the first operates in response to a person's feelings, while the second operates in response to a person's thoughts. That is, when judging social feedback about themselves, people's emotional reactions ("Do I like it?") are based on whether the feedback bolsters their self-esteem (self-enhancement need), and their

Self-Enhancement

The process of seeking out and interpreting situations so as to attain a positive view of oneself.

Self-Verification

The process of seeking out and interpreting situations so as to confirm one's self-concept.

Self-esteem and self-contempt have specific odors; they can be smelled.

Eric Hoffer, U.S. social philosopher, 1902–1983

FIGURE 3.7

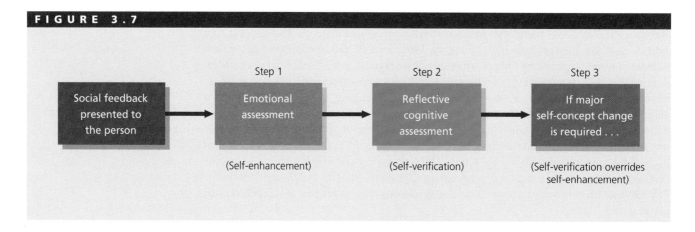

	Step 1	Step 2	Step 3
Social feedback presented to the person	Emotional assessment	Reflective cognitive assessment	If major self-concept change is required . . .
	(Self-enhancement)	(Self-verification)	(Self-verification overrides self-enhancement)

The Interplay Between Self-Enhancement and Self-Verification Motives

When confronted with positive feedback that contradicts a negative self-concept, how do people with low self-esteem resolve the conflict between self-enhancement and self-verification needs? Research suggests that people follow a three-step process in resolving this conflict (Swann, 1990). In step 1, the initial reaction is to self-enhance. This is especially true when people are distracted or aroused. However, with more time to critically analyze the feedback (step 2), self-verification dominates thinking. In step 3, if internalizing this positive feedback will necessitate a major reassessment of their self-concept, the need for self-verification tends to override self-enhancement needs and people reject the feedback. Generally low self-esteem people try to strike a balance in satisfying these two motives (Epstein & Morling, 1995). They prefer to associate with people who make them feel better about themselves without seriously calling into question their current self-concepts (Morling & Epstein, 1997). Why wouldn't people with high self-esteem have this same dilemma when given feedback from others?

cognitive reactions ("Is it correct?") are based on whether it is consistent with their self-concepts (self-verification need). Thus, negative feedback that is expected will be considered more accurate, but self-enhancing feedback will be more satisfying. A number of studies support Shrauger's hypothesis that cognitive reactions to social feedback conform to self-verification needs and affective reactions conform to self-enhancement needs (Jussim et al., 1995; Swann et al., 1987). In these studies, people were presented with either favorable or unfavorable feedback about themselves. Although people felt better after receiving positive feedback than after receiving negative feedback (as predicted by the self-enhancement view), they accepted more responsibility for feedback consistent with their self-concepts than inconsistent feedback (as predicted by the self-verification view).

So which of these motives is the strongest, the need for self-enhancement or the need for self-verification? Based on a host of studies, some with contradictory findings (Bernichon et al., 2003), the best current answer to this question is that it depends. As depicted in figure 3.7, self-enhancement appears to be the automatic and initially strongest response to favorable feedback (Sedikides & Strube, 1997), but self-verification is the slower, more deliberate, and perhaps more lasting response (Baumeister, 1998). When people first receive favorable evaluations, or when they are distracted or aroused, they tend to automatically self-enhance (Paulhus & Levitt, 1987), but when they have time to critically analyze the feedback, or are instructed to do so, they tend to self-verify (Krueger, 1998; Swann, 1990). To the casual observer who witnesses the person's initial delight in receiving praise from others, the need to self-enhance may seem the stronger of the two motives. However, later, once the warm emotional glow of the praise wears off, extra cognitive processing often results in self-verification overriding self-enhancement. For example, if you have low self-esteem and someone says you are absolutely wonderful, your initial reaction may be to accept this positive feedback and thereby increase your self-esteem. However, if you engage in more complex cognitive analysis, you may realize that internalizing this positive feedback will require a major reassessment of your self-concept, a task you may feel ill-equipped to accomplish. Faced with the possible upheaval caused by such a major self-reconstruction, you may well abandon self-enhancement and instead seek self-verification. Therefore, you reject the feedback and retain your original self-concept. If you had not analyzed the implications of the positive feedback, this incident probably would have ended with simple self-enhancement (step 1 in figure 3.7). Self-verification overrode self-enhancement only because of the later extra cognitive processing (step 2).

One of the curious things about how low self-esteem people respond to positive feedback about themselves is that they are more reluctant to accept it when it comes from themselves rather than from others (Josephs et al., 2003). In other words, low self-esteem people are their own harshest critics. Unlike most people who view self-administered "pats on the back" ("I look great!" "I'm smart!") as credible, those with low self-esteem reject such thoughts as untrue, perhaps because they view the source as not very credible (see chapter 7, pp. 216–217). One implication of these findings is that the advice given to low self-esteem people in many popular self-help books is misguided: Regularly making positive self-statements ("I *do* look great!" "I *am* smart!") is unlikely to raise self-esteem over the long haul.

In the final analysis, the need for self-enhancement and the need for self-verification appear to act as checks and balances on each other, and it is only in cases of maladjustment that one need rampantly dominates the other (Epstein & Morling, 1995). For example, individuals with delusions of grandeur require self-enhancement to lord over self-verification to maintain their grand, yet faulty, self-beliefs. On the other hand, chronic depressives continually avoid self-enhancement so that they can verify their negative self-beliefs. Most regular folk, however, seek *compromises* between these two motives. Epstein and Morling's research suggests that when low self-esteem individuals receive positive or negative feedback from others, they automatically compare it with their own self-beliefs and prefer to associate with people who make them feel better about themselves without seriously disconfirming their current self-concepts (Morling & Epstein, 1997).

There Is a Dark Side to High Self-Esteem

Thus far we have discussed research that generally extols the virtues of high self-esteem. One thing to keep in mind, however, is that individualist cultures are much more likely than collectivist cultures to believe that high self-esteem is essential for mental health and life satisfaction (Oishi et al., 1999; Spencer-Rodgers et al., 2004; Twenge & Campbell, 2001). Perhaps due to this cultural belief, American social psychologists have been slow to study any possible negative effects of people wanting to feel good about themselves. Fortunately, that trend is reversing.

Several studies have found evidence that there can be a hidden cost to trying to achieve or maintain high self-esteem: certain individuals with high self-esteem tend to react with aggression when someone challenges their favorable self-assessments (Baumeister et al., 1996; Blaine & Crocker, 1993). The source of this aggressive response appears to be a defensive reaction to avoid having to make any downward revision of self-esteem (Tangney et al., 1992).

What type of high self-esteem person is most likely to react in this aggressive manner? Michael Kernis (in press) asserts that it is the *stability* of high self-esteem that determines whether threats to self-esteem lead to aggression. He states that people with *unstable* high self-esteem are the ones who become angry and hostile when their self-worth is challenged, and they have trouble controlling these emotions (Kernis & Paradise, 2002; Kernis et al., 2000). It appears that those with unstable high self-esteem are not confident about that which they value so highly—namely, their own self-worth. As a result, they are much more dependent on having their self-worth regularly validated by others. When such validation is denied by social criticism, these unstable high self-esteem people react by attacking their critics (Bushman & Baumeister, 1998). In contrast, *stable* high self-esteem individuals are no more aggressive in such circumstances than low self-esteem people. Their general desire to enhance their self-esteem is not fed by a narcissistic defensiveness, but instead, is a sign of mental health (Taylor et al., 2003).

The intriguing possibility underlying unstable high self-esteem is that people who fit into this category may actually have two conflicting types of self-esteem. Their **explicit self-esteem,** which is their conscious and deliberate self-evaluation, is quite high, whereas their **implicit self-esteem,** which is their unconscious and unintentional self-evaluation, is quite low (Bosson et al., 2003; Farnham et al., 1999). Explicit self-esteem is what people report when they are asked directly how they feel about themselves on self-report measures.

CRITICAL *thinking*

If low self-esteem people are likely to reject your attempts to increase their feelings of self-worth, what strategy might you use to feed their self-enhancement needs without triggering their need for self-verification?

Explicit Self-Esteem

A person's conscious and deliberate evaluation of his or her self-concept.

Implicit Self-Esteem

A person's unconscious and unintentional evaluation of his or her self-concept.

Implicit Association Test (IAT)

A technique for measuring implicit attitudes and beliefs based on the idea that people will give faster responses to presented concepts that are more strongly associated in memory.

One way to assess implicit self-esteem is to use the computer-administered **Implicit Association Test (IAT)** measure of self-esteem (Greenwald et al., 2003; Karpinski, 2004). One version of this test measures the automatic associations between a person's self-concept and positive and negative affect. In one measurement stage, participants categorize pleasant words and self-related words on the same computer key and unpleasant and other-related words on another computer key (self + pleasant/other + unpleasant). In a later stage, the tasks are reversed and participants categorize unpleasant words and self-related words and other-related words on another computer key (self + unpleasant/other + pleasant). An overall IAT score is computed by taking the difference between the average response times to the two test stages. The assumption is that participants with high implicit self-esteem have many positive associations and few negative associations with the self. As a result, the self + pleasant task will be very easy for them and they will have fast response times, but the self + unpleasant task will be more difficult and they will have slow response times. In contrast, it is assumed that participants with low implicit self-esteem have many negative associations and few positive associations with the self. Therefore, they will have faster response times for self + unpleasant associations than self + pleasant associations. If you would like to take an implicit self-esteem test, check out the web site at the end of the chapter.

In a series of studies, Christian Jordan and his coworkers (2003) have found initial support for the hypothesis that unstable high self-esteem individuals have two conflicting types of self-esteem, one consciously positive and the other unconsciously negative. Their results indicate that among individuals with high explicit self-esteem, those with relatively low implicit self-esteem—compared with those with high implicit self-esteem—have feelings of self-worth that depend more on such shifting and unstable domains as social approval, physical appearance, and performance on competitive tasks. Further, after failing at a task, high explicit/low implicit self-esteem individuals are likely to quit, while the high explicit/high implicit self-esteem persons are likely to persist in the face of failure. Finally, and of particular interest, the researchers found that high explicit/low implicit self-esteem is associated with high levels of *narcissism,* a personality trait characterized by insecurity, the need for constant reassurance, and the tendency to respond to negative feedback with anger and aggression. As you can see in figure 3.8, while high explicit/low implicit self-esteem individuals score very high on narcissism, high explicit self-esteem persons who also have high implicit self-esteem score very low on narcissism.

In viewing this research from a cultural perspective, one could argue that the emphasis in individualist cultures on feeling good about oneself has resulted in some people being so desirous of self-esteem that they consciously construct a high sense of self-worth that is inconsistent with their life experiences. The result is they have two conflicting types of self-esteem, with the consciously positive form requiring constant bolstering and defense in order for it to survive. When others do not comply with this need and, instead, threaten their self-esteem through social criticism, these unstable high self-esteem people are likely to respond by engaging in antisocial self-enhancement strategies. This is the dark side of high self-esteem.

People with low implicit self-esteem don't like themselves but are not typically consciously aware of this negative self-regard. If you were a therapist, how might you use classical conditioning techniques to unconsciously increase a person's low implicit self-esteem?

SECTION SUMMARY

- Self-esteem is most stable in late adolescence and young adulthood
- *Self-enhancement* and *self-verification* are two principal self-motivators
- Low self-esteem persons take fewer risks than high self-esteem persons
- Unstable high self-esteem persons become angry and hostile when their self-worth is challenged

THE SELF AS A SOCIAL BEING

Having examined the self as an object of attention and evaluation, and having explored some of the primary self-motives that impel us to action, it is now time to analyze how the self operates as a social being (Taylor, 1998). We will examine how our social identities

FIGURE 3.8

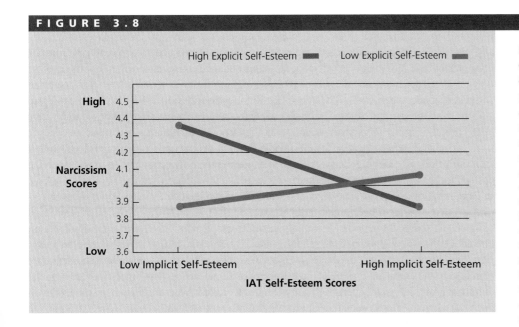

Narcissism is a personality trait characterized by insecurity, the need for constant reassurance, and the tendency to respond to negative feedback with anger and aggression. Jordan and his colleagues (2003) found that explicit self-esteem interacts with implicit self-esteem to create either high or low levels of narcissism. People who are high in explicit self-esteem but low in implicit self-esteem show the highest levels of narcissism. In contrast, those high in both explicit and implicit self-esteem show levels of narcissism no higher than people who are low in both implicit and explicit self-esteem. Why might this unstable form of self-esteem (high explicit/low implicit) be more prevalent in individualist cultures than in collectivist cultures?

constitute a very important aspect of our self-concepts, and how we protect our self-esteem in social relationships.

Social Identities Establish "What" and "Where" We Are as Social Beings

From our own personal experiences we all know that identification with a specific social group can have a great deal of importance for our self-concepts. This social aspect of the self was clearly and powerfully illustrated following the terrorist attacks of September 11, 2001. In the aftermath of the carnage, millions of Americans experienced a renewed sense of national unity. In explaining this process of group identification, Henri Tajfel (1982) and John Turner (1985) have taken William James's notion of the social "me" and developed it into the concept of social identity. **Social identities** are those aspects of our self-concepts based on our group memberships (Hogg & Abrams, 1988). They establish *what* and *where* we are in social terms. By having social identities, we feel situated within clearly defined groups (Cameron, in press; Mussweiler & Bodenhausen, 2002).

Social Identities

Aspects of a person's self-concept based on his or her group memberships.

ETHNIC IDENTITY OF MINORITY GROUPS

One of the consequences of group identification is an internalization of the group's view of social reality. Social identities provide members with a shared set of values, beliefs, and goals about themselves and their social world. As Mead might describe it, to have a social identity is to internalize the group within the individual, which in turn serves to regulate and coordinate the attitudes and behavior of the separate group members. However, if social identities are a representation of the group within the mind of the individual, what happens when we live in a society where our group is devalued by the larger culture? Don't we run the very serious risk of falling victim to a negative self-fulfilling prophecy?

This is the dilemma faced by members of social groups who have been subjected to prejudice, discrimination, and negative stereotypes (Crocker et al., 1994). One way minority groups have coped with this intolerance is by rediscovering their own ethnic heritage and actively rejecting the negative stereotypes in the larger culture (Kelman, 1998). **Ethnic identity,** which is a type of social identity, is an individual's sense of personal identification with a particular ethnic group (Hutnik, 1991). In a very real sense, ethnic identity is a state of mind, and acquiring it often requires considerable effort.

Most theories of ethnic identity formation describe an age-related progression from the unawareness of ethnic membership to the habitual use of an ethnic category to describe the self

Ethnic Identity

An individual's sense of personal identification with a particular ethnic group.

(Castro, 2003). For example, Jean Phinney (1991, 1993) has proposed a three-stage model (see table 3.6). In stage 1, the *unexamined ethnic identity* stage, individuals often have not personally examined ethnic identity issues and may have incorporated negative stereotypes from the dominant culture into their own self-concepts. One negative consequence of internalizing these derogatory social beliefs into the self-concept is that people may experience low self-esteem and feelings of inadequacy (Clark & Clark, 1939; Phinney & Kohatsu, 1997). In contrast to those who are ignorant of ethnicity issues, some people in stage 1 may have been exposed to positive ethnic attitudes from others but have simply not incorporated them into their self-concepts.

In stage 2, *ethnic identity search,* people have an experience that temporarily dislodges their old worldview, making them receptive to exploring their own ethnicity. In many cases, the catalyst for this exploration is a personal experience with prejudice (Sanders Thompson, 1991). In other instances, a person's more general search for personal identity in early adolescence kindles an interest in her or his ethnicity (Roberts et al., 1999). Whatever the initial spark, this stage often entails an intense period of searching, in which people passionately consume ethnic literature and participate in cultural events. During stage 2, some individuals may also develop an *oppositional identity,* in which they actively reject the values of the dominant culture and denigrate members of the dominant group. While in this oppositional stance, anything associated with the dominant group is typically perceived as evil and/or worthless, whereas anything associated with one's own ethnic group is declared superior and highly valued (Carter, 2003; Cross, 1991).

The third stage and culmination of this process is a deeper understanding and appreciation of one's ethnicity—what Phinney labels *achieved ethnic identity.* Confidence and security in a newfound ethnic identity allow people to feel a deep sense of ethnic pride along with a new understanding of their own place in the dominant culture. They are able to identify and internalize those aspects of the dominant culture that are acceptable (for example, financial security, independence, pursuit of academics) and stand against those that are oppressive (for example, racism, sexism). In this manner, the development of a positive ethnic identity not only functions to protect members of disparaged groups from continuing intolerance, but also allows them to use this positive social identity to pursue mainstream goals and participate in mainstream life.

A number of studies support Phinney's view of the mental health benefits of ethnic identity development, among them being high self-esteem and having a stable self-concept (Brookins et al., 1996; Phinney et al., 1997).[1] These findings indicate that it is our commitment and attitudes toward our ethnic group, rather than the evaluations of our group by the larger society, that influence our self-esteem. Such positive social identities can short-circuit the negative effects that prejudice can inflict on self-esteem (Branscombe et al., 1999; McCoy & Major, in press).

GROUP PERFORMANCE AND SOCIAL IDENTIFICATION

We not only categorize ourselves as members of certain groups, we also categorize others as either members of these same groups or as members of other groups (Deaux, 1996). An **ingroup** is a group to which we belong and that forms a part of our social identity. An

A race of people is like an individual man; until it uses its own talent, takes pride in its own history, expresses its own culture, affirms its own selfhood, it can never fulfill itself.

Malcolm X, U.S. Muslim and Black nationalist, 1925–1965

One cannot be "an Indian." One is a Comanche, an Oneida, a Hopi. . . . We progress as communities, not as individuals. We want to maintain ourselves as communities, according to our group identity, not just as mere individuals or as amorphous "Indians."

La Donna Harris, Comanche writer, 1988

Ingroup

A group to which we belong and that forms a part of our social identity.

TABLE 3.6

Stages in Ethnic Identity Formation

Stage 1: Unexamined ethnic identity. Lack of exploration of ethnicity, due to lack of interest or due to having merely adopted other people's opinions of ethnicity

Stage 2: Ethnic identity search. Involvement in exploring and seeking to understand the meaning of ethnicity for oneself, often sparked by some incident that focused attention on one's minority status in the dominant culture

Stage 3: Achieved ethnic identity. Clear and confident sense of one's own ethnicity; able to identify and internalize those aspects of the dominant culture that are acceptable and stand against those that are oppressive

---

[1]This process of identity development in oppressed ethnic groups has parallels in other social groups that have historically been discriminated against, such as women, lesbians and gay men, and the disabled.

outgroup is any group with which we do not share membership. In the course of daily activities, just as we compare our performance on a given task with the performance of others (see pp. 86–88 on self-evaluation maintenance), we also compare the performance of ingroup and outgroup members. When our ingroup members succeed, we respond with pride and satisfaction. Robert Cialdini has labeled this identification with and embracing of ingroup members' success as *basking in reflected glory (BIRGing)* and believes it is common in a variety of social arenas. Examples are fan reaction to their sports teams' victories, the pride ethnic group members have for other members' accomplishments, or the satisfaction that citizens express for their nation's military and political successes. When such successes occur, ingroup members often describe the success as "our victory." This process of reflected glory enhances individual self-esteem because people's social identity in this domain constitutes an integral part of their self-concept (End et al., 2004; Smith & Henry, 1996).

Although we readily share ingroup members' successes, what happens when they fail? Do we embrace the defeat as readily as the victory? Hardly. We tend to make excuses for ingroup members ("Our team was hurt!"), while devaluing the qualities in outgroup members that contributed to their success ("I'm glad our team isn't that vicious!"). By defending ingroup members, we are defending our own self-esteem (Hastorf & Cantril, 1954; Schmader & Major, 1999).

A different reaction to ingroup member failure is psychological distancing (Stapel et al., 1999), often referred to as *cutting off reflected failure (CORFing)*. In one study, Cialdini and his colleagues (1976) phoned students a few weeks after their college team had played a football game and asked them to describe the outcome. When the team won, students commonly used the pronoun "we" in describing the victory, but this pronoun was rarely used when describing a defeat. Instead, following a loss, students commonly used the pronoun "they," as in "They blew the game." This embracing of success and psychological distancing from failure—which is exactly the type of identification that William James contended was typical of the self—was clearly expressed by one student who exclaimed, "*They* threw away *our* chance for a national championship!"

Although fair-weather fans can CORF to their hearts' content, what about those of us whose sports teams truly are an integral part of our self-concepts? Research by Edward Hirt and his coworkers (1992) suggests that a team's poor performance can significantly lower a fan's own self-evaluations. In one of their studies, college students who were avid fans of their school's men's basketball team watched live televised games in which their team either won or lost. Not only were the moods of these zealous fans lower following defeat, but their immediate

Outgroup

Any group with which we do not share membership.

CRITICAL *thinking*

Does your ethnic heritage have relevance to who you are? If so, at what stage are you in Phinney's model? Is this an accurate portrayal of your own ethnic identity development? Are there aspects of the model that do not correspond to your own personal experiences?

Born into the skin of yellow women we are born into the armor of warriors.

Kitty Tsui, Chinese American poet, 1989 from Chinatown Talking Story, in *Making Waves: An Anthology of Writings By and About Asian American Women, ed.* Asian Women United of California, Boston: Beacon Press, 1989, p. 132

We treat our favorite sporting team's successes as if they are our own, and we suffer their defeats as well. What psychological term is used to describe what these hockey fans are experiencing while celebrating their team's victory?

self-esteem and feelings of competence were also depressed. These and other findings suggest that forming a strong allegiance to a team is a risky venture. Because true fans generally do not CORF, each season they subject themselves to an emotional roller coaster that must be ridden out, regardless of how exhilarating or nauseating the ride (Wann & Branscombe, 1990). CORFing would certainly provide psychological relief following a crushing defeat. Adopting a successful team would make life even easier for the long-suffering fan. But the true fans could no sooner change teams than they could change their names—for better or worse, their team affiliation is an important social identity (Bristow & Sebastian, 2001).

In Social Relationships, Self-Esteem Is Maintained Through Social Reflection and Social Comparison

Thus far we have examined how our own moods and self-evaluations are influenced by the successes and failures of ingroup members. This link between the quest for self-esteem and social relationships has been further elaborated in Abraham Tesser's (1988) **self-evaluation maintenance model.** This theory primarily explains how we draw closer to or draw away from successful people we have a relationship with due to our desire to maintain self-esteem.

Self-Evaluation Maintenance Model

A theory predicting under what conditions people are likely to react to the success of others with either pride or jealousy.

According to Tesser, in personal relationships, self-esteem is maintained by two social psychological processes: *social reflection* and *social comparison.* Social reflection, previously identified as BIRGing (see p. 85), is a process in which self-esteem is reinforced by identifying ourselves with the outstanding accomplishments of those close to us. In our daily conversations, we hear this reflection process when people tell us proudly about "My son, the banker" or "My best friend, who was on the David Letterman Show." Social comparison, on the other hand, is a process in which our accomplishments are evaluated by comparing them with those close to us, and our self-esteem suffers if we are outperformed (Festinger, 1954; Mussweiler & Rüter, 2003). As you can see, reflection and comparison produce opposite self-esteem results when others excel at some task: your self-esteem increases if you engage in reflection, but it decreases if you engage in comparison. The stronger the emotional bond between you and the successful person, the stronger the self-esteem effects for both reflection and comparison (Zuckerman & Jost, 2001). Thus, you gain (or lose) more self-esteem if your best friend accomplishes some great task than if your former third-grade classmate does.

What determines whether you engage in reflection or comparison following someone else's success? One important factor is the *relevance* of the task to your self-concept (Morf & Rhodewalt, 1993). If your sister wins first prize in the state chess tournament, your self-esteem may increase due to reflection, but only if chess is not highly relevant to your own self-concept. If you also entered the contest and did poorly, it's likely that your sister's success will lower your self-esteem because it makes you look that much worse by comparison.

Another significant factor that influences whether you engage in reflection or comparison following someone else's success is your *certainty* about your abilities in the domain under question. A series of studies conducted by Brett Pelham and Jeff Wachsmuth (1995) found that when people hold uncertain beliefs about their abilities in an important domain, they are motivated to reduce this uncertainty by carefully comparing their abilities with those of close relationship partners. For example, if my wife wins great praise for her cooking and I am uncertain about how good of a cook I am, I may experience a loss of self-esteem in this area of my life due to social comparison. In contrast, once people develop very certain beliefs about their abilities in a given domain, Pelham and Wachsmuth found that they tend not to engage in social comparison. Instead, they tend to engage in the less effortful process of social reflection, in which the strengths and weaknesses of their close relationship partners reflect directly (rather than comparatively) on themselves. Returning to my previous example, if I am certain I am a good (or bad) cook, when my wife wins great praise for her cooking, I am more likely to bask in the reflected glory of this praise rather than use it as a basis for comparison. As a result, I experience a boost in my own self-esteem.

What about those instances when social comparison makes you look bad? How can you try to recover lost self-esteem? One way is to exaggerate the ability of those who outperform you (Alicke et al., 1997). By seeing your victor as truly outstanding, you can still perceive yourself as well above average. Another way to recover self-esteem is to compare yourself with those who are even less capable, a process known as *downward comparison* (Gibbons et al., 2002; Lockwood, 2002). Although high and low self-esteem people both engage in downward social comparison, they respond differently to it. When self-esteem is threatened by comparison with superior others, persons with low self-esteem benefit from downward comparison: they not only feel better, but they also perceive their less capable comparison targets as more similar to them and more likable than persons with high self-esteem. In contrast, downward comparison does not improve the mood of those with high self-esteem. Instead, they react negatively to the self-esteem threat by being more critical of the downward comparison targets (Gibbons & McCoy, 1991). Thus, engaging in downward comparison only makes people with low self-esteem feel better. Perhaps simply realizing that there are others worse off than them may be sufficient to improve the mood of those who generally do not have a very favorable opinion of themselves.

Besides engaging in downward comparison, a second way to reduce self-esteem threat after comparing yourself with someone who has outperformed you is to reduce your closeness to this person (O'Mahen et al., 2000; Pleban & Tesser, 1981). Salvaging self-esteem through such emotional distancing, however, usually exacts a high price on the relationship—it often ends. A third method of protecting self-esteem—and one that also preserves your relationship—is to change your beliefs so that the task is no longer important to your self-concept (Pilkington & Smith, 2000). Now, instead of comparing yourself with this superior person, you simply bask in his or her reflected glory. This sort of emotional "disidentification" with the task is precisely the psychological process outlined by William James more than 100 years ago (refer back to p. 57). Let's return to your hypothetical sister, the budding chess master. Instead of her accomplishments making you feel bad and straining your relationship, by making chess a less defining aspect of your self-concept you can (through reflection) elevate your self-esteem. In this way, a decidedly different outcome is achieved: family ties and self-esteem prevail.

Despite the negative effect that comparing ourselves to superior others can have on our self-esteem, we sometimes consciously and repeatedly engage in these upward comparisons. Can you guess under what circumstances we are likely to do so? Often, when striving to improve ourselves in some important area of our lives we compare our performance with others who are doing much better (Collins, 1996; Wheeler et al., 1982). For example, an aspiring high-school golfer may try to improve her game by carefully studying the golf swing of superstar, Tiger Woods. Although such upward comparison may

CRITICAL *thinking*

Our self-esteem will often be threatened when we compare ourselves with those superior to us on some task. However, a review of the literature indicates that upward comparison can sometimes lead to higher self-esteem (Collins, 1996). How do you think this particular self-enhancement effect might occur?

In the TV show *Everybody Loves Raymond*, Ray's successes threaten his older brother's self-esteem due to the social comparison process. What social psychological process could boost his brother's self-esteem if used in place of social comparison?

TABLE 3.7

Self Terms and Their Relation to One Another

The "I"

Self-Awareness

This is awareness directed toward oneself, and it can be focused on private self-aspects (e.g., emotions, motives, personal standards) or public self-aspects (e.g., physical appearance, self-presentations). The tendency to engage in this self-aware state is known as self-consciousness, and it too is described in private and public terms.

Self-Regulation

These are the ways in which we control and direct our own actions. You must be self-aware to engage in self-regulation.

The "Me"

Self-Concept

Due to self-awareness, we develop a theory about ourselves.

Gender identity: the knowledge that one is a male or a female.

Self-schemas: the "hypotheses" that make up self-concept.

Spontaneous self-concept: the aspect of the self-concept that is salient and activated in a particular setting.

Social identities: the aspects of the self-concept based on group membership.

Self-Esteem

We not only develop a theory of ourselves, but we also develop an evaluation of this theory. The need to enhance self-esteem is a primary motive but may not be as strong as the need to verify the self-concept. In social relationships, we can enhance self-esteem by basking in others' reflected glory or by comparing ourselves with those we outperform. High self-esteem people tend to know themselves better, are higher risk-takers, and can recover from failure better than those low in self-esteem.

temporarily lower self-esteem ("I'm terrible compared to him!"), it can also motivate the less accomplished golfer to reduce the discrepancy between her current performance level and that of her role model (Tiger Woods). However, it is also possible that this aspiring golfer's self-esteem can be enhanced if she focuses on her social identity as a "Tiger Woods" fan (Wänke et al., 2001). By engaging in social reflection toward her role model, she can bask in reflected glory whenever Tiger Woods wins a tournament. Thus, role models may be in a unique position to temporarily both diminish our self-esteem through social comparison and heighten it through social reflection.

SECTION SUMMARY

- *Social identities* situate us within clearly defined groups
- *Ethnic identities* can insulate us from the negative effects that prejudice inflicts on self-esteem
- *Self-evaluation maintenance model* contends self-esteem is maintained by *social reflection* and *social comparison*

   In social reflection self-esteem enhanced by association with others' success

   In social comparison self-esteem enhanced by outperforming comparison others
- In table 3.7, review how the self terms are related to one another

FEATURED STUDY

ADAPTIVE SELF-REGULATION OF UNATTAINABLE GOALS

Wrosch, C., Scheier, M. F., Miller, G. E., Schulz, R., & Carver, C. S. (2003). Adaptive self-regulation of unattainable goals: Goal disengagement, goal reengagement, and subjective well-being. *Personality and Social Psychology Bulletin, 29,* 1494–1508.

An important part of adaptive self-regulation is knowing when to abandon personal goals that are unattainable and reengaging in valued alternative goals. The present study examined the relationship between goal disengagement, goal reengagement, and subjective well-being in three separate experiments. In this featured article, Experiment 3 will be described, which consisted of a sample of parents of children with cancer and parents of medically healthy children. Compared with parents of healthy children, parents of children with cancer were expected to have a number of important goal-directed activities challenged by the situation they were confronting (for example, being able to continue normal daily routines or pursue career plans). When confronted with this stressful, unexpected, and prolonged event, these parents are likely to face unattainable goals. How do they deal with these unattainable goals? Do they find it hard or easy to disengage from unattainable goals and reengage with new goals? It was hypothesized that goal disengagement and goal reengagement would be associated with ratings of high subjective well-being. It was further hypothesized that goal disengagement and goal reengagement would be more strongly related to low levels of depression in parents with cancer as compared with parents of healthy children.

Method

Participants were forty-five adults, twenty of whom were parents of children undergoing active treatment for cancer, with the remaining twenty-five parents having medically healthy children. Only one parent from each family was allowed to participate. If both parents were interested in participating, one parent was randomly chosen. Parents of medically healthy children were chosen to match parents of children with cancer in terms of age, gender, ethnicity, and marital status. Questionnaires measuring goal disengagement (sample item: "It's easy for me to reduce my effort toward the goal"), goal reengagement (sample item: "I convince myself that I have other meaningful goals to pursue"), and symptoms of depression were administered to all participants.

Results and Discussion

Participants' gender, race, age, and marital status were not significantly related to depression, but there was a significant negative correlation between education and depression ($r = -.42$). In other words, participants with a higher education reported lower levels of depression than participants with less education. Consistent with the research hypotheses, there was a significant interaction effect between goal reengagement and subject group and a marginally significant interaction effect between goal disengagement and subject group. That is, parents who tended to be able to disengage from unattainable goals and to reengage in other new goals showed lower levels of depressive symptoms than parents who reported difficulties disengaging from unattainable goals and reengaging in other new goals. Further, these effects were particularly strong among parents of children with cancer. However, parents of children with cancer did not have an easier time disengaging from unattainable goals and reengaging in new goals than did parents of healthy children. Results also indicated that goal disengagement and goal reengagement were not significantly correlated.

What do these results tell us? Past research indicates that the successful control and direction of behavior is essential in attaining goals. People with a high capacity for self-regulation are more successful in achieving their goals than those who have a lower capacity. Yet what happens when sought-after goals cannot be attained? The present findings suggest that goal disengagement and goal reengagement are important factors when people face challenging and unexpected life circumstances that might require them to adjust important life goals. People who find it hard to either disengage from unattainable goals or reengage in other goals are at risk for developing low subjective well-being. On the other hand, those who can successfully adapt to these challenges are likely to achieve relative happiness. However, people who can easily disengage from unattainable goals do not necessarily have an easy time finding new goals to pursue. On the positive side, it also appears that if people can reengage in new goals, their subjective well-being will likely improve, regardless of how difficult it was for them to abandon their unattainable goals. Taken together, these findings suggest that the capacity to find, commit to, and pursue new goals is a protective factor that helps people manage unattainable goals.

APPLICATIONS

DO YOU ENGAGE IN BINGE DRINKING OR EATING TO ESCAPE FROM YOURSELF?

As you have learned from reading this chapter, we all have the ability to engage in self-awareness. When we experience failure or a significant personal loss, we generally spend some time afterward in focused self-awareness as a means to better understand what happened. Although this self-focused answer seeking can be quite helpful, most of us soon disengage from intense introspection and return to our normal states of awareness. However, what happens when our failure or loss is very great, such that we can find no ready solution? In such instances, we may become depressed, which increases self-focus, which increases depression, and so forth (Pyszczynski & Greenberg, 1992). Thus, intense self-awareness can be thought of as both resulting from depression as well as contributing to it.

Unfortunately, one way depressed individuals sometimes try to break out of this negative self-aware state is by engaging in self-destructive behaviors that have the side benefit of temporarily reducing self-awareness, thereby temporarily reducing depression (Neighbors et al., in press). Binge eating and drinking are two activities that can be motivated by a desire to escape from self-awareness. They also are two of the most serious social problems faced by college students today (Vandereycken, 1994; Wechsler et al., 2000).

Regarding alcohol abuse, Jay Hull (1981) not only found evidence that alcohol reduces self-awareness, but that individuals high in private self-consciousness are more likely to use it to deal with negative information about themselves. In one study, undergraduate participants were given intelligence-related tests and were then randomly given either success or failure feedback (Hull & Young, 1983). Immediately following this feedback, they participated in a seemingly unrelated wine-tasting study. Although the amount of wine consumed by those low in private self-consciousness was not influenced by their previous success or failure, those high in private self-consciousness drank more wine after receiving failure feedback than after success feedback. In effect, consuming alcohol following failure temporarily caused the high private self-conscious individuals to act like low private self-conscious individuals—their degree of self-awareness was reduced, and they were then not as attentive to their failure. Similar results have been found in adolescent alcohol abuse: following academic failure, high private self-conscious students drink more than low self-conscious students (Hull et al., 1986). These studies suggest that some people—especially high private self-conscious individuals—may use alcohol as a "psychological crutch" to avoid the chronic attention to their own private thoughts and feelings that causes emotional pain.

While alcohol seems to reduce self-awareness by physically interfering with cognitive functioning, other techniques can accomplish the same result by simply focusing attention narrowly on concrete, unemotional stimuli. By paying attention to simple, here-and-now movements and sensations, a person can divert attention away from troubling self-aspects (Steele & Josephs, 1990). This shift from self-awareness to "other-awareness" effectively allows the person to avoid the type of self-reflective activities that evoke unpleasant emotion (Baumeister, 1991). *Binge eating,* which involves episodes of huge amounts of food consumption, may serve this function for some people. That is, by redirecting attentional focus from the self to the simple acts of chewing, tasting, and swallowing, binge eaters may temporarily find relief from depression (Heatherton & Baumeister, 1991). Or, as one binger expressed it, "Eating can help me bury my emotions when I don't want to feel them" (Smith et al., 1989).

Ironically, although some people may engage in binge behavior to escape negative self-awareness, self-regulation theory contends that they must actually consciously engage in self-awareness if they desire to gain control over their self-destructive actions. The following four suggestions, derived from self-regulation theory, indicate how binge drinkers and eaters can work to change their behavior by employing self-reflective thought and a special kind of behavioral intention:

1. *Focus your awareness beyond the immediate situation.* An important mechanism in effective self-regulation of negative behavior is keeping attention focused beyond the immediate situation to more distant, long-range goals (Baumeister & Heatherton, 1996). This sort of situational *transcendence* is clearly an important factor in effective food or alcohol management, because it requires you to forgo the temporary relief of bingeing so that you will achieve your long-term goal of learning to eat and drink responsibly. By focusing on your long-range goal, the more-immediate goal of bingeing on cheesecake or beer becomes cognitively *reframed:* it becomes an obstacle to your long-term goal rather than an appealing treat.

2. *Pay attention to cues that trigger undesirable behavior.* Certain stimuli in your social environment can serve as signals that you may be "sliding" down a path that leads to your undesirable behavior. The sooner you identify signals of impending undesirable behavior, the better chance you have of controlling your impulse to engage in that behavior (Wegner, 1994). Thus, if you know that arguments with family members have triggered binge behavior in the past, pay attention to your feelings when conversing with these people and try to defuse arguments before they get out of hand.

3. *Recognize when your resolve is weak.* As suggested by the *strength model of self-regulation* (p. 66), at any given time, you only have a limited amount of energy available to self-regulate. With

this knowledge, be aware that you are going to find it hardest to keep yourself from bingeing with food or alcohol right after exercising a great deal of control in some other unrelated activity.

4. When you realize that your past self-control has been weak, or if you expect to have a limited amount of energy available to self-regulate in a particular situation, a number of studies indicate that establishing an *implementation intention* is effective in steering yourself away from the problematic behavior (Sheeran, 2002). Implementation intentions are statements to yourself that as soon as a particular situation occurs you will automatically initiate goal-directed behavior. For example, if you wanted to avoid engaging in binge drinking at a party you might make the following implementation intention beforehand: "As soon as people start drinking shots of liquor I will switch to drinking soda." It appears that forming implementation intentions can cognitively bypass the need for normal self-control (Webb & Sheeran, 2003). In effect, by specifying ahead of time when and how you will act, this strategy passes control of behavior to anticipated environmental cues (Gollwitzer & Schaal, 1998). Evidence suggests that implementation intentions are particularly beneficial for people with low motivation (Brandstëtter et al., 2001).

THE BIG PICTURE

As stated at the beginning of the chapter, the self is both a simple and complex concept. It is not something "inside" you, but rather, it is you, a social being with the ability to communicate with others, analyze your past actions, regulate your present behavior, and anticipate the actions of others. In other words, being a self allows you to actively create and re-create your social world.

Your self-concept is significantly shaped by your culture and the groups to which you belong, and your social behavior is influenced by what aspect of your self-concept is most salient in a given situation. When you are attentive to your private self-aspects, you behave more in line with personal standards, while public standards exert greater influence when you are aware of your public self-aspects.

As a self, you sometimes struggle with conflicting desires. Should you seek out and interpret information to attain a more positive view of yourself, even if it contradicts your self-concept? There certainly are benefits to high self-esteem, especially in an individualist culture. However, the valuing of self-esteem is sometimes so strong that people with uncertain high self-regard react aggressively when others challenge it. This desire to maintain appropriately high levels of self-esteem also influences whether you react to the successes of those close to you with pride or jealousy. Throughout the remaining chapters, you will see how interpretations of social events are filtered through self-beliefs and self-desires.

WEB SITES
accessed through http://www.mhhe.com/franzoi4

Web sites for this chapter focus on the self, including cross-cultural research, an international society devoted to the study of the self, and information on the history of the self-concept in the social sciences.

Society for Cross-Cultural Psychology

This is the Web site for an organization pursuing cross-cultural research from a multidisciplinary perspective.

International Society for Self and Identity

This is the Web site for an interdisciplinary association of social and behavioral scientists dedicated to promoting the scientific study of the self. Users can find abstracts of unpublished articles and recent books.

Overview of Self-Concept Theories

This Web page investigates the history of the self-concept in the social sciences. It also includes ideas for people who aspire to be counselors.

American Psychological Association

The Web site for the American Psychological Association contains a Web page that discusses the possibility that high self-esteem narcissists tend to be aggressive when criticized.

Self-Presentation and Person Perception

CHAPTER OUTLINE

*R*eporter Stephen Glass was an ambitious young man. He exuded integrity, intelligence, and supreme confidence. In the mid-1990s, while serving as executive editor for the University of Pennsylvania's student-run newspaper, Glass wrote, "The role of *The Daily Pennsylvanian* is not to make allies and not to make enemies—it is to report the truth." As leader of the school's paper, Stephen was both charming and demanding. Holding court with fellow reporters, he enthralled them with vivid stories of his journalistic adventures, while simultaneously admonishing these budding journalists to check their facts before filing a story. One of those reporters recalled, "While fact-checking my writing, he once admonished me for inverting a quotation I had taken from a politician's speech. I had not changed the meaning of the speaker's words, but Steve insisted I quote the words in the order in which the speaker actually spoke them. At the time, I was impressed that Steve could be creative and also hold himself to such strict ethical standards" (Brus, 1998).

Following graduation, this likable, talented, and high-minded reporter soon became associate editor of *The New Republic,* and, at the age of 25, was a rising star in the world of journalism with his freelance reporting for such high-profile magazines as *George, Rolling Stone,* and *Harper's Magazine.* His articles about fundamentalist Christian nudists, the Union of Concerned Santas and Easter Bunnies, and his stint as a professional phone psychic were bold and goofy snapshots of contemporary American culture. Readers and fellow reporters loved his stories because they were so vivid and contained such lively quotes. But *The New Republic* readers were also drawn to Glass's stories because the people he wrote about conformed to cultural stereotypes: conservative Republicans who were secret sex maniacs; Wall Street brokers who were such workaholics that they kept deskside urinals; young African American men who were too lazy to drive a cab but not too lazy to rob the cab driver.

Then something happened. In May 1998, Glass wrote a story for *The New Republic* about a 15-year-old computer hacker who broke into the database of a software company and posted the salaries of its executives on its web site. Instead of prosecuting this wayward computer whiz, the executives wanted to hire him! During his salary negotiations, Glass reported

Sociologist Erving Goffman contended that social interaction is similar to a theatrical performance, with people playing prescribed roles like actors on stage. In observing both theatrical and everyday "performances," the audience generally does not question the validity of others' presented selves because this would disrupt the "play." When Stephen Glass's news stories were found to be fabrications, his particular performance as a principled reporter abruptly ended.

that the teenager shouted at the executives to "Show me the money!" One of the differences between this story and most of Glass's other stories was that he published the full name of the story's principal character and identified the company and its web site address. When a reporter at another magazine became curious and tried to contact the teenager, he could not locate him. In fact, the reporter could not confirm any of the facts in the Glass article. Soon everyone realized that the reason Stephen Glass's stories were so vivid and compelling was that he was fabricating almost all of the characters, quotes, and scenarios! As you might guess, Glass was fired and all his freelance employers dropped their contracts with him.

How was Stephen Glass able to fool so many people for so long? In 2003, Glass's escapades were depicted in the Hollywood movie *Shattered Glass.* Actor Peter Sarsgaard, who plays Glass's editor in the movie, offers the following opinion:

> I think what made all of this possible for him has more to do with the public than it does him. It's more interesting to think about why people believe people like that than why they lie. Why is our culture only interested in the hyperbolic, the entertaining, in journalism? (Rowe, 2003)

The Stephen Glass incident is unusual because it was played out on the national stage, but it is actually similar to events we face on a daily basis. That is, as *self-presenters,* we often consciously try to shape others' impressions, and we may sometimes rely on deception to achieve this end. In turn, as observers of others' self-presentations, we often try to explain their actions and gain insight into their motives and beliefs. The process by which we come to know about others' temporary states—such as their emotions, intentions, and desires—and enduring dispositions—such as their beliefs, traits, and abilities—is known as **person perception** (Gilbert, 1998). This type of perception is often not a single, instantaneous event, but rather comprises a number of ongoing processes, which can be roughly classified into two general areas: *impression formation* and *attribution.*

Impression formation is often based on rapid assessments of salient and observable qualities and behaviors in others. These judgments are obtained by attending to nonverbal cues, such as facial expressions and body posture, as well as incorporating more detailed and descriptive characteristics, such as traits, into an overall impression. What made Stephen Glass such an effective con artist was his adeptness at changing his self-presentation style to fit the mood and expectations of the situation. He could present himself to people in such a way that they wanted to not only be his friend but also believe anything he told them. As former colleague Charlie Ornstein recalled about his college days working with Glass at the college paper, "If you talk to anyone who was there at the same time as him, I don't think you'll find anyone at the paper who questioned his ethics at all." (Brus, 1998).

Impression formation is usually just the first step of person perception. Often, we also want to understand what causes people to act in a particular manner. This *attribution process* goes beyond discerning people's current moods and feelings and attempts instead to use their past actions to predict future behavior. For example, when deciding whether to vote for one political candidate over another, voters often examine the two individuals' past actions, both as private and public citizens. If they know what these politicians are like as individuals, voters believe they can better predict how they will act as elected officials. This chapter introduces you to these two areas of person perception.

Before examining how we judge others, let us first step into the shoes of those we are judging. As demonstrated in the chapter 3 discussion of the self, whenever we interact with others our self-esteem may be enhanced or diminished, and our self-concepts may be confirmed or cast in doubt. How does this social fact affect the way we present ourselves to others? And how do we—as social perceivers—use our knowledge as seasoned self-presenters to judge others' self-presentations?

Person Perception

The process by which we come to know about other people's temporary states and enduring dispositions (also called *social perception*).

SOCIAL INTERACTION AS "THEATER"

We often try to manage the impression we make on others by carefully constructing and monitoring our presented selves (Musolf, 2003; Schlenker & Wowra, 2003). Indeed, sociologist Erving Goffman (1959) suggests that social interaction is like a theatrical performance, with the interactants being the actors on stage playing prescribed roles. While "on stage," people act out "lines" and attempt to maintain competent and appropriate presented selves. In observing this performance, the audience generally accepts the presented selves at face value and treats them accordingly. The acceptance may not be genuine, but Goffman asserts that people have learned to keep their private opinions to themselves, unless the performers prove wholly incompetent. To do otherwise would disrupt the smooth flow of social interaction. Let us examine in more detail these everyday performances.

Self-Presentations Are Either Consciously or Automatically Constructed and Monitored

The process of constructing and presenting the self in order to shape other people's impressions and achieve ulterior goals is known as **strategic self-presentation** (Jones & Pittman, 1982; Nezlek & Leary, 2002). Because self-presenters sometimes worry about being judged incompetent, Goffman states that they often rehearse prior to the performance. They also rely on "props" and take care to "set the stage" in order to present a more believable self. In preparing for a romantic dinner date, for instance, you might purchase your date's favorite wine, splash on some enticing cologne, and bring along a romantic CD as a gift (the props) that will later be played at the right moment to properly set the stage for your romantic self-presentation. You might even practice your romantic gazes and postures in front of a mirror or rehearse a romantic speech beforehand. Such impression management is often stressful, and is associated with increases in heart rate and blood pressure (Hartley et al., 1999; Heffner et al., 2002).

If this description of social life sounds a bit too contrived, reflect on your early teenage memories a moment, especially those when you were preparing for your first social dance or date. Today, as the mature and knowledgeable social actor that you are (or at least think yourself to be), you may have forgotten how consciously manufactured and stilted some self-presentations can be when not well learned. The more skilled we become in particular self-presentations, the less effort is necessary in executing them. In fact, well-learned self-presentations are often automatically activated and guided without conscious monitoring. Such automatic self-presentations are efficient because they conserve cognitive resources that can then be devoted to other tasks (Pontari & Schlenker, 2000). This idea that self-presentation involves both automatic and deliberate cognitive processes reflects the *dual-process* approach to social cognition first introduced in chapter 1 (p. 14). According to this perspective, human beings employ two broad cognitive strategies to interact in their social world, one involving effortless thinking and the other involving effortful thinking.

The world's a stage and most of us are desperately unrehearsed.

Sean O'Casey, Irish playwright, 1880–1964

The concept of self-presentation often conjures up images of social gamesmanship and deception, as illustrated by Stephen Glass's life story. Like an actor on stage, Glass's self-presentations seemed to be carefully planned and executed, with the added element of dishonesty tossed in. At times Glass sought to present a competent, businesslike image, while at other times he presented himself as a bemused recorder of wacky and outrageous cultural events. After his fictional reporting was exposed and he was fired from his job, Glass wrote a book about these events, explaining his actions as caused by a desperate need to be liked and accepted by others. Many of his former coworkers viewed Glass's new presented self as just as false and contrived as his previous ones. Yet despite this example of habitual deceptive self-presentation, there is nothing necessarily unsavory about strategic self-presentations—we all employ them. A full range of motives can guide these self-presentations, some selfish and others seemingly altruistic (Schlenker, 2003; Schlenker & Britt, 2001). For example, if a friend is romantically interested in someone, you might act as a "go-between" who informs the romantic target of your friend's affections, while simultaneously extolling your friend's virtues. Your motives in this strategic self-presentation are based on a concern for your friend's welfare and happiness, not your own.

Do you think that people raised in collectivist cultures might sometimes have different self-presentation concerns than persons raised in individualist cultures?

Although we are most aware of employing strategic self-presentations when interacting with strangers or casual acquaintances (Leary et al., 1994; Tice et al., 1995), they also play important roles in our intimate relationships. Two common differences between most

When recalling instances in which you constructed and presented yourself in order to shape other people's impressions, what situations come to mind? Do you imagine interacting with strangers or casual acquaintances and not situations involving friends and family? According to some social psychologists, why might you be less likely to notice that you are employing strategic self-presentations with friends and family members?

of the self-presentations we construct in nonintimate and intimate relationships involve *evaluation concerns* and *cognitive effort.* When socializing with friends and loved ones, we are typically both less anxious about how we are being evaluated and more skilled with the self-presentations we typically employ. As a result, our intimate self-presentations are likely activated and guided with less conscious monitoring than when we are with strangers and casual acquaintances (Schlenker, 2003). In other words, they are operating below our level of awareness (implicit cognition), much like a computer program runs in the background without any obvious visual detection on the screen to remind us that it is active. Because these self-presentations are being activated and monitored nonconsciously, we think of them as "more genuine" than those that are more deliberately executed. However, we will consciously attend to and regulate our self-presentations on those occasions when our friends and family "get the wrong impression" of us.

SELF-PROMOTION

One common self-presentation strategy is *self-promotion,* which strives to convey positive information about the self either through one's behavior or by telling others about one's positive assets and accomplishments. People who use self-promotion want to be respected for their intelligence and competence, and thus, this strategy is commonly employed during job interviews (Ellis et al., 2002; Stevens & Kristof, 1995). Although often effective in conveying a positive social image, self-promotion does not always result in desired consequences. This is because in addition to evaluating competence, perceivers also judge such interpersonal dimensions as likability and humility. Therefore, while self-promoters may be seen as competent, they also may be judged to be less likable because they are perceived to be bragging (Godfrey et al., 1986; Inman et al., in press). To counter this social danger, astute self-promoters often acknowledge possessing certain minor flaws or shortcomings along with their many competencies (Baumeister & Jones, 1978). Boasting is considered to be a more masculine response following achievement, and thus, it is not surprising that men are more likely than women to employ self-promotion (Miller et al., 1992).

EXEMPLIFICATION

A strategy that has much in common with self-promotion is *exemplification,* which is a self-presentation designed to elicit perceptions of integrity and moral worthiness, at the same time that it arouses guilt and emulation in others (Leary, 1996). Exemplifiers often come across as being absorbed by devotion to some cause and suffering for the welfare of others. Workers who encourage fellow employees to go home while they sacrifice personal time for the "good of the company," religious leaders who profess to "walk with the Lord," or politicians who tell their constituents that they will be a "moral beacon" in government are all displaying this form of strategic self-presentation. The danger of taking on the saintlike role is that one runs the risk of being perceived as hypocritical if actions deviate from this moral high ground (Stone et al., 1997). Exemplifiers also run the risk of being socially shunned because some people experience guilt and shame while in their presence due to being reminded of their own shortcomings. Although there are dangers in using this strategy, skillful execution does bring benefits. Leaders who can effectively employ exemplification foster strong loyalty and group cohesion among their followers (Rozell & Gunderson, 2003).

MODESTY

A strategy that overcomes some of the self-presentational problems of self-promotion and exemplification is *modesty.* To be modest is to underrepresent one's positive traits, contributions, or accomplishments. Modesty can be extremely effective in increasing one's likability, even while it preserves high levels of perceived competence and honesty (Baumeister & Ilko, 1995). In contrast to self-promotion, modesty is considered a more feminine response following achievement (Miller et al., 1992), and thus, it is not surprising that women are not only more likely than men to employ it, but they also are more successful in using it (Wosinska et al., 1996). Despite the generally favorable response to modesty, you should only use it when others are aware of your successes and can recognize that an underrepresentation is taking place (Miller & Schlenker, 1985). For example, modesty will not be an effective strategy for talented students to employ when trying to secure strong letters of recommendation from professors who are unaware of their many accomplishments. Instead, self-promotion should be used.

Humility is something I've always prided myself on.

Bernie Kosar, former NFL quarterback

INTIMIDATION

When people want to coerce others into doing something, they might use *intimidation,* a self-presentation tactic of arousing fear and gaining power by convincing others that they are powerful and/or dangerous. This self-presentation strategy is the hallmark of schoolyard bullies and is also employed by athletes in such aggressive sports as football, hockey, and boxing (Jeffrey et al., 2001). Drivers who tailgate you on the highway are using this strategy to get what they want—a speedy unencumbered path (Bassett et al., 2002). In its more subtle forms, intimidation is also used by parents. A frown combined with a lowered tone of voice and a pointed index finger is often sufficient in securing compliance from a child.

SUPPLICATION

What if people lack the skills necessary for the preceding strategies? Under such circumstances, they may rely on *supplication.* In this technique, people advertise their weaknesses or their dependence on others, hoping to solicit help or sympathy out of a sense of social obligation. For example, an indigent alcoholic asking passersby for spare change relies on societal norms of empathy for those who are less fortunate (Dordick, 1997). A less extreme example is a student who repeatedly seeks help in completing class assignments, professing an inability to understand the material. This technique, while effective in many circumstances, is fraught with psychological land mines. One danger is that people tend to "blame the victim" (Lerner, 1980), often believing their suffering is self-inflicted. Another danger is that even though supplicators often receive help and support, they will be privately judged as poorly functioning individuals (Powers & Zuroff, 1988). Not surprisingly, the final toll of advertising one's incompetence is often a loss of self-esteem (Osborne, 2002).

SANDBAGGING

One sly self-presentation strategy that initially appears to be supplication is *sandbagging.* Here, people falsely claim or demonstrate to onlookers that they have poorer skills or abilities than they actually possess (Gibson & Sachau, 2000). Sandbagging is commonly used in competitive situations (Shepperd & Socherman, 1997). For example, a coach may publicly predict poor performance for her talented team, or a pool "shark" may deliberately lose a few billiard games to a less skilled competitor. This deception is meant to lull opponents into a false sense of security so that they exert less effort, allowing the sandbaggers to more easily defeat them with their superior skills. The downside to using this deceptive self-presentation strategy is that onlookers might explain the sandbaggers' success as being due to their competitors' reduced effort rather than to the sandbaggers' skills.

INGRATIATION

Last, and most important, people can also manipulate our impressions of them by flattering us. This self-presentation strategy, known as *ingratiation,* is used to describe behaviors that are motivated by a desire to be liked (Jones & Wortman, 1973). Because flattery does indeed increase recipients' self-esteem, and hence, increases their liking for the flatterer, Edward Jones (1990) calls ingratiation the most fundamental of all the strategies—"a pinch or two of ingratiation helps to leaven the other self-presentation strategies as well." A testament to the power of ingratiation is the finding from one study that managers in public and private organizations who regularly used this self-presentation strategy received the greatest salary increases and the most promotions over a five-year period (Orpen, 1996). Despite such potential rewards, ingratiation requires social skill, and like self-promotion, it is a double-edged sword (Vohra, 2000). A meta-analysis of sixty-nine ingratiation studies found that while the recipient of ingratiation is positively affected by flattery, bystanders who observe the ingratiating self-presentation are more likely to question the motives of the flatterer (Gordon, 1996). These findings suggest that such disparaging terms as *brownnoser* and *apple polisher* are more likely to be used by observers of ingratiation than recipients. Table 4.1 describes some common self-presentation strategies.

Make a list of the different self-presentation strategies that you employed today. Under what circumstances and with whom were they used? Which ones achieved the desired effect? Was there one strategy that you frequently employed? If you didn't use any, why was this the case?

Embarrassment and Excuse Making Commonly Follow Failed Self-Presentations

Despite our tendency to rehearse before important social interactions, we sometimes have self-presentation problems. For example, you could go into a job interview intending to convey intelligence and social skill, only to spill coffee all over yourself. Or you could act

TABLE 4.1

Common Self-Presentation Strategies

	Attributions Sought	Negative Attributions Risked	Emotions to Be Aroused	Typical Actions
Self-promotion	Competent	Conceited	Respect	Performance claims
Exemplification	Worthy	Hypocrite	Guilt	Self-denial
Modesty	Likable and competent	Nonassertive	Affection and respect	Understatement of achievements
Intimidation	Dangerous	Blowhard	Fear	Threats
Supplication	Helpless	Stigmatized	Nurturance	Self-deprecation
Sandbagging	Unskilled	Con artist	Complacency	Feigned inability
Ingratiation	Likable	Brownnoser	Affection	Compliments and favors

like an idiot while taking your driver's exam (see my story in chapter 3, p. 54). In such instances when we are unable to project an appropriate public image, we often feel embarrassed. **Embarrassment** is an unpleasant emotion experienced when we believe that others have good reason to think a flaw has been revealed in us (Sabini et al., 2001). Because friends and loved ones are often also part of our self-concepts, we can also experience embarrassment when their self-presentations are discredited (Thornton, 2003). However, like my mother at the license bureau, we might also laugh until we cry when others commit social blunders.

Embarrassment

An unpleasant emotion experienced when we believe that others have good reason to think a flaw has been revealed in us.

When embarrassed, we typically avert our gaze, lower our heads, touch our faces, and smile nervously (Keltner & Anderson, 2000). This is accompanied by an activation of the sympathetic nervous system, which is that part of our nervous system that prepares us to deal with threatening situations. The blushing, sweating, and heart pounding we experience during embarrassing incidents is our body's way of harnessing its energy to respond to the perceived threat (Gerlach et al., 2003).

How often does embarrassment occur? College students report being embarrassed at least once a week, while younger teenagers become embarrassed even more often (R. Miller, 1995). Answer the items in table 4.2 to assess your own susceptibility to embarrassment. Mark Knapp and his colleagues (1986) asked people to recall embarrassing moments in their lives. Perhaps you can relate to the following account of a woman's ill-fated attempt to impress the parents of her fiancé:

> I was invited to my fiancé's home for a special dinner. It was the first time I had met everyone and I was trying to impress them. As we sat down to eat, his father turned to me and said, "I hope you'll say grace." I was so unsettled by this request that I immediately bowed my head and said, "Now I lay me down to sleep. . . ." (p. 40)

One common way to recover from these self-presentation lapses is to provide excuses, which generally bolsters our mood, unless others do not buy the excuse (Mehlman & Snyder, 1985). The good news about embarrassment is that onlookers generally judge us less harshly for our social gaffes than we think they do (Savitsky et al., 2001). Further, embarrassing situations are also often unpleasant for onlookers, and thus, they typically help us recover our self-presentations (Marcus et al., 1996; Miller, 1987).

Sometimes people do not wait for a self-presentation to fail before providing an excuse. Instead, they take steps beforehand to sabotage their performance, thereby setting themselves up for failure. For example, the night before an important exam, Barry may go to a party instead of studying. By choosing to socialize, he is greatly decreasing his likelihood of success. An observer of Barry's actions might conclude that his decision not to study was self-defeating. But someone versed in social psychological theory might suggest that his actions serve a second purpose: to protect his self-esteem. Putting barriers in the way of your success not only provides you with an excuse for failure, but it also enhances your self-esteem if success is secured despite the handicap. Thus, creating obstacles to success can not only *protect* self-esteem, it can also *enhance* it. These are the two primary motives underlying **self-handicapping,** a self-presentation strategy in which a person creates obstacles to his or her own performance (Berglas & Jones, 1978). Self-handicapping is more likely to occur when people are being evaluated on skills or attributes central to their self-concepts rather than on unimportant characteristics (Ferrari & Tice, 2000).

Self-Handicapping

A self-presentation strategy in which a person creates obstacles to his or her own performance either to provide an excuse for failure or to enhance success.

Of the two motives underlying self-handicapping, which is dominant? A series of studies by Diane Tice (1991) indicates that it depends on a person's level of self-esteem. She found evidence that individuals with high self-esteem handicap themselves to enhance their success, and they are largely unconcerned about protecting themselves against failure. In contrast, low self-esteem persons self-handicap to protect themselves from the negative implications of failure. Thus, the desire to further enhance self-esteem appears to motivate high self-esteem people to self-handicap, but it is the desire to protect self-esteem that appears to motivate those low in self-esteem.

When people engage in self-handicapping they use two different forms. The milder form is *self-reported handicapping,* which simply involves people complaining about illness or stress-induced ailments before performing a task (Hirt et al., 1991). The beauty of

TABLE 4.2

Susceptibility to Embarrassment Scale

Instructions: *Listed below are a variety of statements. Please read each statement carefully and indicate to the left of each item the extent to which you feel it applies to you using the following scale:*

1	2	3	4	5	6	7
Not at all					Very much	
Like me					Like me	

____ 1. I feel unsure of myself.

____ 2. I don't feel comfortable in public unless my clothing, hair, etc. are just right.

____ 3. I feel uncomfortable in a group of people.

____ 4. I don't mind being the center of attention.*

____ 5. I probably care too much about how I come across to others.

____ 6. I feel inadequate when I am talking to someone I just met.

____ 7. I feel clumsy in social situations.

____ 8. I feel uncomfortable leaving the house when I don't look my best.

____ 9. Sometimes I just feel exposed.

____ 10. I feel humiliated if I make a mistake in front of a group.

____ 11. I get flustered when speaking in front of a group.

____ 12. I often feel emotionally exposed in public and with groups of people.

____ 13. It is unsettling to be the center of attention.

____ 14. I get tense just thinking about making a presentation by myself.

____ 15. I have felt mortified or humiliated over minor embarrassment.

____ 16. I am very much afraid of making mistakes in public.

____ 17. I don't like being in crowds.

____ 18. I do not blush easily.*

____ 19. I often worry about looking stupid.

____ 20. I feel so vulnerable.

____ 21. I am concerned about what others think of me.

____ 22. I'm afraid that things I say will sound stupid.

____ 23. I worry about making a fool out of myself.

____ 24. What other people think of me is very important.

____ 25. I am not easily embarrassed.*

Scoring instructions. *Before adding up your total score, ratings for the three "*" items should be reversed, so that 1=7, 2=6, 3=5, 4=4, 5=3, 6=2, and 7=1. The score range for the Susceptibility to Embarrassment Scale is 25 to 175. The mean score for college students is 92, with higher scores indicating higher degrees of embarrassability.*

self-reported handicapping is that it provides an excuse for failure without actually hampering performance. Further, employing self-reported handicapping can actually enhance performance! By providing plausible excuses for inadequate performance *prior* to actually performing the task, self-reported handicappers may sufficiently reduce their anxiety so that they perform better than they would normally (Sanna & Mark, 1995). In contrast to this rather benign self-handicapping, the more active and damaging form is *behavioral self-handicapping,* which involves people handicapping themselves either by not adequately

the neighborhood™ Jerry Van Amerongen

"Good Lord, Berlingham, any one of us could have mistaken this for a costume ball! . . ."

preparing for a task or by using drugs or alcohol beforehand to inhibit their performance (Higgins & Harris, 1988). Although both women and men equally use self-reported handicaps, numerous studies indicate that men are more likely to behaviorally self-handicap, especially when they are publicly self-aware (Hirt et al., 2000). Why might this be the case?

One possible explanation is that men are generally more competitive and driven by public standards in performance situations than women (Travis et al., 1988). When experiencing this heightened performance pressure and feeling uncertain concerning their own ability to succeed, men may seize upon behavioral self-handicapping as the best way for them to avoid self-esteem loss if they fail. However, when people behaviorally self-handicap they run the risk of being perceived as lazy and unmotivated (Luginbuhl & Palmer, 1991). Thus, the form of self-handicapping that men use more than women not only is more likely to guarantee failure, but it is also more likely to generate negative evaluations from observers. A series of studies conducted by Edward Hirt and his coworkers (2003) found that men are consistently less critical of behavioral self-handicappers than women. They are much less likely than women to question the motives of self-handicappers, and they are much less likely to perceive them as lazy. These results suggest that the people most likely to engage in behavioral self-handicapping (men) are also the people who are less likely to judge self-handicappers harshly.

High Self-Monitors Are Social Chameleons

We all use self-presentation strategies. However, some people are more likely than others to consciously construct self-presentations that best fit whatever social situations they encounter. According to Mark Snyder (1987), these differences are related to a personality trait called **self-monitoring,** which is the tendency to use cues from other people's self-presentations in controlling our own self-presentations. Those of us high in self-monitoring spend considerable time learning about other people and we tend to emphasize impression management in our social relationships (John et al., 1996; Renner et al., in press). In 1974, Snyder published a Self-Monitoring Scale to measure this personality trait, and it has been studied extensively since that time. To get an idea about your own level of self-monitoring, spend a few minutes completing the items in table 4.3.

Self-Monitoring

The tendency to use cues from other people's self-presentations in controlling one's own self-presentations.

The Self-Monitoring Scale

The personality trait of self-monitoring is measured by items on the Self-Monitoring Scale (Snyder, 1974; Snyder & Gangestad, 1982). To discover your level of self-monitoring, read each item below and then indicate whether each statement is true or false for you.

_____ 1. I find it hard to imitate the behavior of other people.

_____ 2. At parties and social gatherings, I do not attempt to do or say things that others will like.

_____ 3. I can only argue for ideas which I already believe.

_____ 4. I can make impromptu speeches even on topics about which I have almost no information.

_____ 5. I guess I put on a show to impress or entertain others.

_____ 6. I would probably make a good actor.

_____ 7. In a group of people I am rarely the center of attention.

_____ 8. In different situations and with different people, I often act like very different persons.

_____ 9. I am not particularly good at making other people like me.

_____ 10. I'm not always the person I appear to be.

_____ 11. I would not change my opinions (or the way I do things) to please someone or win their favor.

_____ 12. I have considered being an entertainer.

_____ 13. I have never been good at games like charades or improvisational acting.

_____ 14. I have trouble changing my behavior to suit different people and different situations.

_____ 15. At a party I let others keep the jokes and stories going.

_____ 16. I feel a bit awkward in company and do not show up quite as well as I should.

_____ 17. I can look anyone in the eye and tell a lie with a straight face (if for a right end).

_____ 18. I may deceive people by being friendly when I really dislike them.

Directions for scoring: Give yourself one point for answering "True" to each of the following items: 4, 5, 6, 8, 10, 12, 17, and 18. Also give yourself one point for answering "False" to each of the following items: 1, 2, 3, 7, 9, 11, 13, 14, 15, and 16. Next, add up your total number of points for your Self-Monitoring score.

The average self-monitoring score for North American college students is about 10 or 11. The higher your score is above these values, the more of this personality trait you probably possess. The lower your score is below these values, the less of this trait you probably possess.

Individuals who are high in self-monitoring are especially attuned to social cues concerning appropriate behavior in a given situation (Koestner et al., 1992). They are skilled impression managers who strive to perform whatever behavior projects a positive self-image, even if some degree of deception is required (see Applications section). In this regard, they tend to be extraverted, good actors, and willing to change their behavior to suit others (Chen et al., 1996; Leck & Simpson, 1999). For example, when trying to initiate a dating relationship, high self-monitoring men and women behave in a chameleon-like fashion, strategically and often deceptively changing their self-presentations in an attempt to appear more desirable (Rowatt et al., 1998). On the other hand, individuals low in self-monitoring are less attentive to situational cues, and their behavior is guided more by inner attitudes and beliefs. As a result, their behavior is more consistent across situations. They are also less interested than those high in self-monitoring in projecting a positive self-image that others will respect (Gonnerman et al., 2000).

Due to their greater attention to social cues, those high in self-monitoring are more socially skilled than those low in self-monitoring (Blakely et al., 2003). They are better able to communicate and discern the meaning of emotions and other nonverbal behaviors. They also learn more quickly how to behave in new situations and are more likely to initiate conversations (Gangestad & Snyder, 2000). When they employ impression management strategies, they favor those that are positive, and they are particularly more adept than low self-monitors at using ingratiation, self-promotion, and exemplification to achieve favorable impressions (Bolino & Turnley, 2003; Turnley & Bolino, 2001). On the negative side, people high in self-monitoring have less intimate and committed social relationships (Snyder & Simpson, 1984), and they tend to judge people more on superficial characteristics, such as physical appearance and social activities, rather than their attitudes and values (Jamieson et al., 1987).

Noting the differences between high and low self-monitoring, which orientation do you prefer? Perhaps you see high self-monitoring as being more socially adaptive because it allows one to better negotiate in an ever changing and complicated social world. Or maybe you view the chameleon-like nature of the high self-monitor as indicating a distasteful shallowness and instead prefer the principled consistency of someone low in self-monitoring. Yet what you see as principled consistency, others may interpret as inflexibility. The safest and perhaps wisest conclusion to draw is that neither high nor low self-monitoring is necessarily undesirable unless it is carried to the extreme. Fortunately, pure high and low self-monitoring is rare—most of us fall somewhere on a continuum of these two extremes (Miller & Thayer, 1989).

At this point, you may be wondering how self-monitoring differs from the personality trait of public self-consciousness discussed in chapter 3 (p. 64). Being high in self-monitoring is similar in some respects to being high in public self-consciousness—both have to do with a concern about and awareness of how others react to the self. They differ in that high self-monitoring, but not high public self-consciousness, describes individuals who are actively and effectively changing their behavior to adjust to the reactions and expectations of others. Individuals high in public self-consciousness may be aware of and concerned about themselves as social objects, but they are not necessarily sufficiently attentive to the subtle cues around them to structure their self-presentations in such a way as to manage the impressions others have of them (Vrij et al., 2001). In addition, although people high in public self-consciousness are motivated more by a concern to avoid presenting themselves negatively, high self-monitors strive to achieve a favorable self-presentation in others' minds. Do these two different motives sound familiar? They should, for the social motives of high public self-conscious individuals are similar to the motives of people with low self-esteem, while the social motives of high self-monitors are similar to those of people with high self-esteem (see chapter 3, pp. 76–82).

SECTION SUMMARY

- Self-presentations manage the impression we make on others
- Self-presentations involve both automatic and deliberate thinking, with well-learned self-presentations often operating on "autopilot"
- Common strategic self-presentations include self-promotion, exemplification, modesty, intimidation, supplication, sandbagging, and ingratiation
- Failed self-presentations cause embarrassment, which is associated with sympathetic nervous system arousal
- Self-handicapping creates performance obstacles to provide excuses for failure or enhanced success
- Behavioral self-handicapping is more destructive than self-reported handicapping
- Men use behavioral self-handicapping more than women
- High self-monitors are highly attuned to social cues

IMPRESSION FORMATION

Now that we have walked in the shoes of the self-presenter, let us next view the social stage from the perspective of the audience. **Impression formation** is the process by which observers integrate various sources of information about others' self-presentations into a unified and consistent judgment (Hamilton & Sherman, 1996; Ickes, 2003). The process of forming impressions is viewed by social psychologists as a dynamic one, with judgments being continually updated in response to new information. It is analogous to building a "working model" of a person and then using this as a guideline in our actions toward him or her. The model works if our mental representation of the person accurately predicts his or her behavior (Funder, 1999).

Impression formation is not only a dynamic process; it is also integrative. By this I mean that each bit of information about a person is interpreted within the context of all the other information we have about her or him. Each information "bit" takes its character from the other "bits" as a whole. As you will soon discover, however, not all bits of information are created equal. Some bits will carry more weight and even orchestrate all the other bits into a coherent whole (Kenny, 2004).

Impression Formation

The process by which one integrates various sources of information about another into an overall judgment.

Our Impressions of Others Are Shaped by Their Nonverbal Behavior

First impressions are often based on **nonverbal communication,** which is the sending and receiving of information using gestures, expressions, vocal cues, and body movements rather than words. Whether a person smiles when greeted by another, whether a person's walk is "bouncy" or "purposeful," or whether one's gestures are expansive or constricted can provide important information in developing a working model of those we meet on a daily basis. Two of the more important nonverbal channels of communication are facial expressions and body movements.

Nonverbal Communication

The sending and receiving of information using gestures, expressions, vocal cues, and body movements rather than words.

FACIAL EXPRESSIONS

More than two thousand years ago, the Roman orator Marcus Cicero wrote that the "face is the image of the soul." Centuries later, Charles Darwin (1872) proposed that *facial expressions* not only play an important role in communication, but that certain emotional expressions are inborn and thus are understood throughout the world. Studies conducted during the past thirty years provide support for Darwin's assertions: there is substantial cross-cultural agreement in both the experience and expression of emotions, although certain emotions are easier to distinguish than others (Ekman, 1994; Izard, 1994; Keating et al., 1981). For example, people from all cultures can easily tell the difference between happiness and anger, but it is harder for them to distinguish adoration from desire. The upshot of these findings is that most researchers have concluded that certain emotions are more basic, or *primary,* than others. Primary emotions are similar to primary colors in perception. Like primary colors, by combining primary emotions and altering their intensity, the full variety of other emotions can be derived. Most classification lists include the following seven primary emotions: *anger, disgust, fear, happiness, surprise, contempt,* and *sadness* (Ekman et al., 1987; Matsumoto, 1992). Other emotions that are considered basic by some theorists are *shame* and *guilt* (Bonanno et al., 2002; Reeve, 1992). The seven primary emotions are also the ones people around the world can accurately "read" by examining facial expressions.

When Darwin proposed that certain emotional expressions are universally understood, it was within the context of introducing evolutionary theory to the sciences. He believed that this ability to recognize emotion from the observation of facial expressions was genetically programmed into our species and had survival value for us. How might this ability aid survival? One possibility is that being able to read the emotions of others by attending to facial expressions allows us to not only better predict their behavioral intentions ("Do they mean to harm me?"), but also to understand how others are interpreting the world

("Why are they afraid? Are we all in danger in this situation?"). This "survival value" hypothesis would predict that we do not attend equally to all facial expressions, but rather exhibit the most sensitivity to those that would give us the best chances of survival. In other words, we should be most attentive to facial expressions that signal potential danger.

Research supports the survival value hypothesis. For instance, a number of studies have shown people pictures of crowds of faces to determine what facial expressions were most recognizable in such a clustered setting. As Darwin would have predicted, people spotted threatening faces (anger first, fear second) faster and more accurately than nonthreatening faces, even when the nonthreatening faces depicted negative emotions such as sadness (Hansen & Hansen, 1988; Lanzetta & Orr, 1986; Öhman et al., 2001). The threatening faces appeared to "pop out of the crowd," while the nonthreatening faces were often overlooked. Apparently, the threatening facial expressions function as general danger cues, evoking anxiety and preparing people for self-protective action.

BODY MOVEMENTS

Besides facial cues, the body as a whole can convey a wealth of information. For example, research indicates that people who walk with a good deal of hip sway, knee bending, loose jointedness, and body bounce are perceived to be younger and more powerful than those who walk with less pronounced gaits (Montepare & Zebrowitz-McArthur, 1988). Handshakes are also an important component in impression formation and may actually reveal something about people's personalities. William Chaplin and his coworkers (2000) have found evidence that in North American culture people with firm handshakes tend to be more extraverted, adventurous, and less neurotic and shy than those with weak handshakes. Recognizing the importance of this nonverbal behavior in forming favorable first impressions, many professional training seminars now teach attendees how to properly shake hands.

A series of studies by Joel Aronoff and his colleagues (1992) also suggest that people often infer underlying emotional states by reading the geometric patterns of bodies during social interaction. For example, in a creative analysis of dance characters in classical ballet, the researchers found that the body and arm displays of the threatening characters were more *diagonal* or *angular,* while those of the warm characters were more *rounded* (refer to figure 4.1). In subsequent studies, college students who were asked to evaluate various geometric shapes judged those with diagonal shapes to be more bad, powerful, and

You know about a person who deeply interests you more than you can be told. A look, a gesture, an act, which to everybody else is insignificant tells you more about that one than words can.

Henry David Thoreau, philosopher, author, naturalist, 1817–1862

Which of these two facial expressions do you think is most likely to "grab" people's attention? In all cultures, people can easily tell the difference between angry and happy facial expressions. Evolutionary theorists propose that our ability to recognize emotion from observing people's facial expressions was adaptive, helping our ancestors survive and reproduce. Yet according to this "survival value" hypothesis, we do not attend equally to all facial expressions, but rather are most attentive to those that signal potential danger.

Body display

Diagonal

Rounded

Arm display

Angled

Rounded

Rounded, Diagonal, and Angular Body Displays

Based on an analysis of classical ballet dance movement and people's judgments of simple geometric shapes, Aronoff and his colleagues (1992) contend that rounded body postures convey warmth and friendliness to an observer, while diagonal and angled body postures imply threat and danger. Using this information, try a little experiment on your friends. Act out some diagonal and angled body displays for them, as well as some that are rounded. In this variation of "charades," what sort of emotions do they believe underlie each of these body displays?

active than those that were rounded. These findings suggest that people analyze the *shape* of large-scale body movements to better determine another person's behavioral intentions. It appears then that body movements, in addition to facial gestures, convey a wide variety of information to others that may well have a significant impact on the impression formation process. Yet although there are commonly shared meanings of many physical gestures, it is also true that people from different cultures often assign different meanings to the same physical movements. Table 4.4 provides a brief sketch of how certain nonverbal cues are interpreted differently around the world.

NONCONSCIOUS MIMICRY

Beyond interpreting the meaning of specific nonverbal gestures, our impressions of others are also shaped by **nonconscious mimicry,** which is the tendency to adopt the behaviors, postures, or mannerisms of interaction partners without conscious awareness or intention (Chartrand et al., 2002). What are some examples of nonconscious mimicry? When conversing with others, we tend to mimic their speech tendencies and accents, we laugh and yawn when they do, and we adopt their body postures and gestures (DePaulo & Friedman, 1998; LaFrance & Broadbent, 1976). Mimicking others' facial expressions appears to be so inborn that 1-month-old infants have been shown to smile, stick out their tongues, and open their mouths when they see someone else doing the same (Metzlaff & Moore, 1989).

Evidence that mimicry is often nonconscious and unintentional comes from a number of studies (Lakin & Chartrand, 2003; van Baaren et al., 2003b), including an experiment by Tanya Chartrand and John Bargh (1999) where participants interacted with two unknown confederates. For half the participants, the first confederate rubbed her face and the second confederate shook her foot throughout their interaction. For the other participants, the confederates reversed roles. Results revealed that participants mimicked the gestures of the confederates—they rubbed their face more when they were with the face-rubber than the

Nonconscious Mimicry

The tendency to adopt the behaviors, postures, or mannerisms of interaction partners without conscious awareness or intention.

TABLE 4.4

Cultural Differences in Certain Nonverbal Cues, or, A North American's Brief Guide to Avoiding International Misunderstandings

Although a number of facial gestures appear to convey universal meaning, here are some nonverbal cues that are more culture-specific. To avoid misunderstandings when traveling overseas, or when hosting an international visitor, North Americans should duly note that everyday gestures and accepted interaction patterns in this culture are not universally shared.

Shaking hands: North Americans are taught to shake hands as a friendly sign of greeting. A firm, solid grip is thought to convey confidence and good character. Japanese prefer greeting one another by bowing, Southeast Asians press their own palms together in a praying motion, and when Middle Easterners and many Asians shake hands, they prefer a gentle grip, because a firm grip suggests aggressiveness.

Touching: North Americans and Asians are generally not touch-oriented, and hugging is almost never done among casual acquaintances. In contrast, Latin Americans and those in the Middle East often embrace and hold hands as a sign of friendship.

Space relationships: North Americans generally maintain a distance of about thirty inches during normal social interaction. Asians tend to stand farther apart, and Latin Americans and Middle Easterners stand very close, often brushing up against one another. In those cultures where space relationships are small, moving away is interpreted as a sign of unfriendliness.

Eye contact: North Americans are taught to look others directly in the eye when conversing. Avoiding eye contact is considered to be a sign of shyness, disinterest, or weakness. In Japan and Korea, people are taught to avert the eyes and avoid direct eye contact. There, engaging in eye contact is considered intimidating, or perhaps a signal of sexual interest.

foot-shaker, and they shook their foot more when they were with the foot-shaker than the face-rubber. When the experiment was over and participants were asked about the gestures of the confederates and about their own gestures, they did not report noticing either.

Insight into the biological basis for nonconscious mimicry comes from PET scans and EEG recordings of people's brains while they observe another person performing an action. These studies found that similar neural circuits are firing in the observers' brains as are firing in the brains of those who are carrying out the action. These specialized neural circuits located in the premotor cortex are called *mirror neurons* (Gallese & Goldman, 1998; Iacoboni et al., 1999). The firing of these mirror neurons probably does not directly cause imitative behavior, but they may serve as the basis of imitation learning, which is closely associated with mimicry (Rizzolatti et al., 2002).

How does mimicking affect impression formation? In a follow-up experiment to their face-rubbing/foot-shaking study, Chartrand and Bargh (1999) found evidence that mimicry increases liking for the imitator. The researchers instructed confederates to subtly imitate the mannerisms of people they were interacting with in a "get acquainted" session (for example, rubbing their face or tapping their foot when their partner did so). Their findings indicated that people whose gestures had been mimicked liked the confederates more than those who had not been mimicked. Similarly, in a field experiment (van Baaren et al., 2003a), waitresses who verbally mimicked their customers by repeating their orders were given bigger tips than those who replied to orders by saying "okay!" or "coming up!" Additional research indicates that as people interact with one another and establish rapport, they exhibit an increase in mimicking each other's gestures (Jefferis et al., 2003). This mimicry not only increases their prosocial behavior toward one another, but the latest findings suggest that the targets of mimickers also become more prosocial to others in the immediate vicinity (van Baaren et al., 2004). Together, these studies suggest that mimicry triggers positive reactions in people that lead to benefits to those who are present.

Why do we have this fascinating tendency to mimic? What function does it serve? As previously discussed in chapter 3 (p. 55 & p. 76), throughout evolution, individual survival and success at reproduction depended on our ancestors having successful social interactions. Individuals who were able to cooperate with others and maintain harmonious social ties were more likely to be included in group activities, thereby giving them an adaptive advantage over those who were ostracized from the group. Due to this process of natural selection, behaviors that fostered group cohesion eventually became widespread throughout the human population (Caporael, 2001). Over time, many of these behaviors became automatically activated without awareness. A number of social scientists believe that nonconscious mimicry is an example of this form of automatically activated behavior that creates affiliation and rapport among people, and thereby fosters safety in groups (Chartrand et al., in press; de Waal, 2002).

Culture and Personality Influence the Expression and Use of Nonverbal Cues

Research indicates that people recognize the important role that nonverbal behavior plays in impression formation and often consciously employ nonverbal cues in their self-presentation strategies (DePaulo, 1992). For example, have you ever forced yourself to smile at someone you did not like? Or have you ever deliberately fixed someone with a cold, angry stare to convey your displeasure or your feeling of social dominance?

INDIVIDUALISM AND COLLECTIVISM

Given the important role that emotions play in human interactions, it makes abundant sense that cultures would develop social rules for when and how different emotions are expressed (Mesquita & Frijda, 1992). For example, the cultural belief systems of individualism and collectivism have shaped norms related to acting in ways that might threaten group harmony. That is, collectivists are much more likely than individualists to monitor their behavior so that it does not disrupt the smooth functioning of the group. Regarding emotions, research suggests that although people from collectivist and individualist cultures do not differ in publicly displaying positive emotions, collectivists are much more uncomfortable about publicly expressing negative emotions (Stephan et al., 1996).

GENDER SOCIALIZATION

Within North American culture, whether you tend to use the forced smile over the cold stare may be associated with your gender socialization and the resulting social roles you learned. A **social role** is a cluster of socially defined expectations that individuals in a given situation are expected to fulfill. Social roles are (1) defined by society, (2) applied to all individuals in a particular social category, and (3) consist of well-learned responses by individuals. According to Alice Eagly's (1987, 1996) **social role theory,** the different social roles occupied by women and men lead to differences in the perception of women and men and in their behavior. In other words, because women and men typically operate in different domains within society—for example, women in the home and men in the world of paid employment—they engage in different patterns of behavior to properly play their roles.

Regarding the nonverbal expression of emotion, Stephanie Shields (2002) describes two contrasting emotional styles that are linked to gender socialization. Both are required of women and men, but each is expected more of one sex than the other. *Extravagant expressiveness* is an open style of experiencing and communicating emotion that is associated with femininity. It is evident in nurturing and is the form of emotion linked in our culture to intimacy. This is the kind of emotion we expect when we say, "Don't just tell me that you love me, say it like you really mean it!" The second emotional style telegraphs intense emotion under control, which Shields labels *manly emotion* because of its connection to a particular version of heterosexual masculinity. This is the kind of emotion we have come to expect from movie heroes—think of Tom Hanks in *Saving Private Ryan* or *Road to Perdition*.

Social Role

A cluster of socially defined expectations that individuals in a given situation are expected to fulfill.

Social Role Theory

A theory that explains gender differences as being due to the different social roles occupied by women and men in society.

These two emotional styles associated with female and male social roles convey different messages to people witnessing their expression. The strongly felt—yet controlled—manly emotion conveys the message that the person is independent: "I can control my emotion (and thereby, my *self*), and I can harness it to control the situation." The underlying message of extravagant expressiveness involves nurturance: "My emotion (and thereby, my *self*) is at your service." Shields contends that in North American culture manly emotion is ultimately considered more important than extravagant emotion because it is believed to express rational behavior. In contrast, although the feminine emotional standards underlying emotional expressiveness foster many socially desirable behaviors (such as tenderness and selflessness), they are culturally tainted because of their association with emotion out of control. According to Shields, *control* of emotion is more central to the masculine standards because control is associated with power and dominance. Being the historical holders of power in society, men are assumed to possess greater ability to control their emotions than women.

There is no scientific evidence of a gender difference in emotional control—and, of course, there is more than one way to define "control." Research indicates that boys are encouraged to express emotions—such as anger, contempt, and pride—that reflect a sense of entitlement to power in society and are discouraged from displaying vulnerable emotions. In contrast, this same research suggests that girls are encouraged to express emotions associated with satisfaction, powerlessness, and service to others, such as happiness, fear, and empathy (Buck, 1977; Saarni, 1999). Consistent with this encouragement, women are not only better nonverbal communicators of happiness than men, but they are also better at masking disappointment with a positive expression (Davis, 1995). In thinking about your own upbringing, are your skills at constructing fixed stares and forced smiles consistent with these gender socialization patterns?

Beyond the gender differences in using specific nonverbal cues, meta-analytic studies indicate that females are significantly more adept than males in *decoding* nonverbal communication. For example, in a review of seventy-five studies testing the ability of men and women to decode nonverbal behavior, Judith Hall (1978) found that 68 percent of the investigations reported superior female performance. Later meta-analyses found that this gender difference is greatest for decoding facial expressions, next largest for body cues, and smallest for correctly interpreting voice tone (Hall, 1984). The studies further suggest that this gender difference is not isolated in adult samples but can also be found in adolescents and children. Although these gender differences vary in size from study to study, females appear to be consistently better than males at decoding nonverbal cues (Brody & Hall, 1993).

As with emotional expression, social psychologists principally explain these gender differences in reading nonverbal cues by examining the different social roles played by females and males. According to social role theory, because the social roles played by women tend to have lower status relative to male roles, it is more important for women to learn to be accommodating and polite (Mast & Hall, in press). Thus, by being more skilled at nonverbal communication, females are better able to understand people's feelings and thus increase their interpersonal comfort. This explanation is consistent with research indicating that regardless of gender, those who have less powerful social roles are more sensitive to the feelings of their superiors than vice versa (Hecht & LaFrance, 1998).

INDIVIDUAL DIFFERENCES IN MONITORING NONVERBAL CUES

Besides cultural differences, one personality trait that identifies individuals who are more motivated to consciously use nonverbal cues in managing their social relationships is self-monitoring, which we discussed earlier in this chapter. In one study, Howard Friedman and Terry Miller-Herringer (1991) arranged for participants who were either high or low in self-monitoring to receive feedback indicating that they had done very well on a series of problem-solving tasks. In one condition, participants received this positive information in the presence of two other competitors who were told that they had not performed very well (these individuals were actually confederates). Because it is impolite to gloat in the company of those you have bettered, the researchers hypothesized that high

CRITICAL *thinking*

As previously discussed, evolutionary theory contends that the ability to recognize emotion from the observation of facial expressions is part of our evolutionary heritage. How might an evolutionary theorist explain the gender differences in decoding nonverbal communication? That is, from an evolutionary perspective, why would it be more beneficial for females than males to have good nonverbal skills?

self-monitors would be more successful in hiding their expressions of joy than would those low in self-monitoring. Judges, watching videotape of the participants' faces as they received the good news, rated that those high in self-monitoring did indeed exhibit fewer nonverbal signs of happiness than those low in self-monitoring. High self-monitors concealed their nonverbal expressions of joy by biting their lips or twisting their mouths to one side, presumably to prevent themselves from smiling. This study suggests that people high in self-monitoring are not only more attentive to their nonverbal behavior in social settings, but they are also better able to modify or suppress nonverbal gestures that might be considered socially inappropriate. In this respect, then, high self-monitors appear to be better at using their nonverbal behavior to convey a desired self-presentation to others.

We Form Personality Impressions with the Help of Traits

The initial phase of impression formation involves little cognitive effort and is based on easily recognizable physical characteristics, such as sex, age, and race (Fiske & Neuberg, 1990; Park, 1986). If the individuals are of no interest or the interaction is very brief, we will not bother to analyze them further. However, if we are motivated to learn more about these people, our thinking becomes more deliberate and effortful. This more conscious and controlled analysis results in our impressions becoming more abstract and less tied to superficial physical qualities (Sherman & Klein, 1994; Van Overwalle et al., 1999). Some of these more descriptive characteristics are *traits,* which are stable personal qualities such as "intelligent," "kind," and "unscrupulous." Because personality traits are commonly used in forming impressions (Fiske & Cox, 1979), one of the first questions asked by social psychologists was how traits are combined to form a meaningful picture of a person

CENTRAL TRAITS

In the 1940s, Solomon Asch was a social psychologist who worked within the German tradition of *Gestalt psychology,* which studied how the mind actively organizes stimuli into a coherent whole, or *gestalt.* In person perception, Asch hypothesized that our overall impression of others is not simply determined by adding up all their personality traits. Instead, certain traits exert a disproportionate influence on people's overall impressions, literally changing the meaning of other traits. In other words, not all traits are equally important in impression formation: the whole is more than the sum of its parts. He called the dominant traits **central traits.**

In his classic study, Asch (1946) told participants they would hear a list of discrete traits that belonged to a particular person and that they should try to form an impression based on this information. For some participants, the following traits were then presented: intelligent, skillful, industrious, warm, determined, practical, and cautious. For other participants, the trait *warm* was replaced with the trait *cold,* but otherwise everything else was identical. Those who had been told that the hypothetical person was warm rated him as significantly more *generous, humorous, sociable,* and *popular* than those who had been told that he was cold. In contrast to the effect of switching these two central traits, when Asch switched the traits *polite* and *blunt* from a similar list that people rated, the resulting impressions differed very little from one another. These less important traits Asch called *peripheral traits.*

Based on these results, Asch concluded that *warm* and *cold* are central traits that significantly influence overall impression formation. In a warm and caring individual, being industrious and determined would likely carry positive connotations, but in a cold and heartless individual these same peripheral traits carry very different, more negative, connotations. Thus, central traits can dramatically affect the meaning of the peripheral traits. In contrast to the influence of central traits, whether people are considered polite or blunt is much less likely to alter perceptions of their other traits.

In an elaboration of this research, Harold Kelley (1950) attempted to determine how these same traits might influence impression formation in a real-life situation. When students arrived at their college psychology class, they were greeted by a representative of the

Central Traits

Traits that exert a disproportionate influence on people's overall impressions, causing them to assume the presence of other traits.

instructor who told them they were to have a guest lecturer that day. The representative led some students to believe that the soon-to-arrive lecturer was a rather warm person, and other students were led to expect a rather cold individual. The lecturer then appeared and led the class in a twenty-minute discussion. Results indicated that those given the "warm" preinformation not only consistently rated the lecturer more favorably than those given the "cold" preinformation, but they also interacted with him more in class discussion. Thus, the "warm" and "cold" descriptors not only shaped the students' impressions of the guest lecturer but also their behavior toward him. Variations of this study have been conducted more recently, with results indicating similarly more positive impressions of the "warm" instructor compared with the "cold" instructor (Babad et al., 1999).

Since Asch's (1946) groundbreaking study, additional research found that as we become acquainted with others, we tend to form an overall impression by averaging all their traits together, but we give more weight to those we believe are most important (Anderson, 1968, 1981; Kashima & Kereckes, 1994). Further, the importance of specific traits may vary depending on the social context in which we make evaluations (Singh & Teoh, 2000). For example, the traits *intelligent* and *humorous* may have equal scale values, but *intelligent* would carry more weight for a psychology department's graduate school admissions committee when evaluating applicants, while *humorous* would have more of an impact on the owner of a comedy nightclub when looking for a new act. Finally, in keeping with Asch's original idea that we actively try to make sense of a person's traits as a coherent whole, a number of studies suggest that when we receive apparently conflicting information about someone, we often resolve the discrepancy by constructing a multidimensional impression (Asch & Zukier, 1984; Casselden & Hampson, 1990). For example, if Desmond is described to us as brilliant *and* foolish, instead of averaging these apparently opposite traits on an intelligent-unintelligent dimension, we are much more likely to perceive him as intellectually brilliant but foolish in a wordly sense. Therefore, although overall impressions tend to be the average of all traits, consistent with Asch's gestalt approach, we actively seek to make sense of traits in an integrated way, with some traits playing a more "central" role in this integration than others.

IMPLICIT PERSONALITY THEORY

When Stephen Glass was accused of fabricating his news stories, almost everybody who knew him or knew of him was shocked. Glass was the epitome of the young, hardworking, ambitious journalist. He just didn't seem like *the kind of person* who would do such a thing.

As suggested by research on central traits, our knowledge about people is structured by our prior set of beliefs about which traits go together, and the resulting personality judgments we make often defy the rules of cold logic. These assumptions or naive belief systems that we have about the associations among traits and behaviors are called an **implicit personality theory** (Bruner & Taguiri, 1954; Norenzayan et al., 2002). In these personality assumptions, we tend to assume that all good things occur together in persons and that all bad things do so as well, with little overlap between the two. Believing that an individual possesses one trait leads to the inference of other traits or behaviors assumed to be associated with the observed trait (Hosoda et al., 2003; Leyens, 1991). This is why many people initially believed that a respected, high-profile reporter like Stephen Glass could not possibly be making up his urban stories. This conclusion is arrived at because the alternative judgment ("Glass is a liar") is inconsistent with their assumptions about the relationships among traits and behaviors (Cook et al., 2003).

In an implicit personality theory, as in impression formation generally, there appears to be operating a principle of *evaluative consistency*—a tendency to view others in a way that is internally consistent. Even when contradictory information is made available, we still generally persist in viewing people as either consistently good or bad. In this effort toward consistency, we will often distort or explain away contradictory information.

Although implicit personality theories are commonly employed in making social judgments, some people rely on them more than others (Gervey et al., 1999). In studies conducted in both individualist and collectivist cultures, it appears that implicit theories are used more often by people who believe that personality consists of fixed, static traits than by those who believe that personality is dynamic and changing (Church et al., 2003; Werth & Foerster, 2002). These findings are important because they suggest that although implicit

Implicit Personality Theory

Assumptions or naive belief systems people make about which personality traits and behaviors go together.

personality theories may be used by people around the world, there is a good deal of *individual* variation in the extent to which they are used. Additionally, findings by Chi-yue Chiu and his colleagues (1997) point toward a possible *cultural* variation in the use of implicit personality theories. They found that more Americans than Chinese believe in fixed personality traits, which suggests that Americans use implicit personality theories more often.

Our Personality Judgments Are Most Influenced By Negative and Early-Presented Information

Besides evaluating people's personalities by making assumptions about which traits go with other traits, our person impressions are also influenced by what we naturally attend to and remember when we process and store information in memory. Two important characteristics that shape our personality judgments involve the evaluative quality of information and the order in which it is presented to us.

POSITIVITY BIAS AND NEGATIVITY EFFECT

A general evaluative bias operating in impression formation is to view people in a favorable light. Known as the **positivity bias,** it is the tendency for people to evaluate individual human beings more positively than groups or impersonal objects (Miller & Felicio, 1990). For example, in an analysis of more than 300,000 teacher evaluations, David Sears (1983) found that students rated 97 percent of their instructors as "above average," despite the negative experiences students often have in college classes. Why do we evaluate people so leniently? One possibility is that we feel better surrounded by good things, pleasant experiences, and nice people (Matlin & Stang, 1978) and therefore are motivated to see the world and others through "rose-colored glasses." A second possible explanation is that compared with groups or impersonal objects, people regard other human beings as relatively similar to themselves (Sears, 1983), and similarity heightens attraction (see chapter 11).

It may seem contradictory, but because people are biased toward perceiving others in a positive light, when they learn that someone has negative traits they place more weight on these unfavorable attributes in forming an impression of the person. This **negativity effect** is the tendency of people to give more weight to negative traits than positive traits in impression formation (Lupfer et al., 2000). Studies of voters' impression formation of political candidates (Peeters, 2003) suggest that voters seek positive information about candidates (positivity bias), but they are more likely to reject them after receiving negative information than they are to accept them after receiving positive information (negativity effect). In essence, what the positivity bias and negativity effect tell us about person perception is that we are motivated to view people favorably, but favorable impressions are more vulnerable to change than unfavorable impressions.

The common explanation for the negativity effect is that negative traits are more unusual and therefore more distinctive. People pay more attention to those negative qualities and give them more weight. This tendency to direct attention to negatively evaluated stimuli, like the tendency to notice fearful and angry faces in a crowd, is believed to have survival value for human beings (Rozin & Royzman, 2001). Indeed, the automatic nature of attending more quickly to negative information has been repeatedly demonstrated in brain-imaging studies and provides further evidence that evolution favored brain mechanisms that facilitate a rapid and intense response to aversive events (Carretie et al., 2003; Smith et al., 2003). Unfortunately, although this automatic vigilance may protect people from immediate harm, it may also contribute to harsher than warranted social judgments. The use of negative campaign ads in politics is testimony to the power of the negativity effect. Even though such mudslinging is criticized by political commentators, research indicates that public opinion is shaped more by negative news about candidates than by positive news (Ansolabehere & Iyengar, 1995).

PRIMACY AND RECENCY EFFECTS

One other simple and basic factor influences impression formation, and it is related to the *order* in which we learn bits of information about someone (Van Overwalle & Labiouse, 2004). Known as the **primacy effect,** it is the tendency for the first information received

Health experts have grown increasingly alarmed about AIDS among young adults because most of this population are not practicing safe sex by using condoms (Langer et al., 2001). How might young adults' implicit personality theories about safe-sex partners be shaping their decisions not to use condoms?

Positivity Bias

The tendency for people to evaluate individual human beings more positively than groups or impersonal objects.

Negativity Effect

The tendency for negative traits to be weighted more heavily than positive traits in impression formation.

Primacy Effect

The tendency for the first information received to carry more weight than later information on one's overall impression.

Research indicates that the first bits of information we learn about a person carry more weight in forming an overall impression than information learned later. Thus, if the woman in the photograph was described to you as intelligent, industrious, impulsive, critical, stubborn, and envious, your overall impression of her might be more favorable than if she was described as envious, stubborn, critical, impulsive, industrious, and intelligent. Although the information contained in these two descriptions is identical, Asch (1946) found that a hypothetical person described in the first manner was thought to be competent and ambitious, whereas a person described in the reverse order was considered overemotional and socially maladjusted.

Recency Effect
The tendency for the last information received to carry greater weight than earlier information.

to carry more weight in one's overall impression than later information. This effect was impressively demonstrated by Edward Jones and his colleagues (1968) when they had participants observe a confederate completing a thirty-item test of intellectual ability. As the confederate gave each answer, the experimenter publicly announced whether his response was correct. The confederate always answered fifteen questions correctly, but in one condition he would start off with many right answers and then end with many incorrect answers. In another condition, just the opposite would occur. At the end of the test, the participants predicted how well the confederate would do on the next thirty-item test, and to rate his intelligence. Even though the confederate always answered fifteen items correctly, he was rated as more intelligent and more likely to do well on the next test if he had started off with a number of correct responses rather than incorrect ones. See the accompanying photograph here for another example of how the primacy effect might operate in impression formation.

Why does early information figure more prominently than later information in our impression of others? One possible explanation is that the early bits of information we learn about another provide a cognitive *schema* or mental outline, which we then use to process later information. If the later information contradicts this schema, we are likely to ignore it (see chapter 5, pp. 141–145). Research suggests that the primacy effect is particularly strong when people are given little time to make judgments and are not under a great deal of pressure to be correct (Kruglanski & Freund, 1983). There is also evidence that some people are more likely than others to "seize" the early information they learn about people and "freeze" it into quick personality judgments (Kruglanski & Webster, 1996). Individuals who habitually make such snap judgments tend to have a high *need for closure*, which is the desire to reduce cognitive uncertainty. Their need for closure makes them impulsive in their judgments of others and also reluctant to revise their assessments when new information is offered.

Although the primacy effect regularly occurs in person perception, it can sometimes be reversed if people are warned against making hasty judgments or told that they will be asked to justify their impressions of a target person (Tetlock & Kim, 1987). In such circumstances, the last bits of information learned may be given greater weight than earlier information. This is known as the **recency effect.** Thus, if you have a shy friend whom you would like to introduce to a potential romantic partner, you might guard against the primacy effect in the following manner. You could inform this person that your friend is somewhat shy and that her true personality does not always shine through in first meetings. If this person takes your advice, he will ignore some of the early awkwardness and social fumbling and pay more attention to what he learns about her after she feels more comfortable with him.

SECTION SUMMARY

- First impressions are often based on nonverbal behavior
- We reliably identify seven primary emotions: anger, disgust, fear, happiness, surprise, contempt, and sadness
- Nonconscious mimicry is automatically activated and it fosters affiliation and rapport
- People differ in expressing and detecting emotional states
- Central traits exert more influence in personality impressions than peripheral traits
- Implicit personality theories operate on the principle of evaluative consistency
- The positivity bias is our tendency to view others positively while the negativity effect is our tendency to weigh negative traits more heavily when they come to light
- Early information generally has more influence (primacy effect) on impression formation than later information (recency effect)

MAKING ATTRIBUTIONS

A few years ago after a snowstorm, I arrived home from work and noticed that our garbage had not been picked up. When I phoned the company, an exasperated woman replied to my query by sarcastically stating, "Well sir, with all the snow we had yesterday I would have thought people wouldn't have been stupid enough to put out their garbage today." Now, despite the public perception of psychologists as detached observers, constantly analyzing other people's behavior and motivation, this psychologist's response was not quite so analytical. Later, however, I wondered what caused her to act so rudely. Was she simply an insensitive person, or was it just a bad day for her?

About a year later, my garbage was not picked up again and I had to contact this woman a second time. Now there was no snowstorm. As I dialed, I wondered if I was about to be chastised again for yet another mental failing. To my relief, she was very cordial and apologetic. Based on this second conversation, I concluded that her previous behavior was most likely not due to some stable personality trait such as rudeness, but rather to an external, uncontrollable, and unstable event—the situational stress she experienced on that snowy winter day. How did I arrive at this judgment, and how do people in general assign causal explanations for events?

We Rely upon Particular Information When Explaining People's Actions

In forming impressions of others, we attempt to determine what characteristics in each person explain their behavior and cause them to act the way they do. Yet in attempting to understand others, we do not solely focus on personality traits. We also consider the situational context, as well as the influence that others may have on them. Beyond trying to understand people as individuals, when we perceive events in general, we often are irresistibly drawn to understand *why* they unfold in the observed manner. This tendency is strongest when the events are the actions of other people and are unexpected, unusual, or distressing (Kanazawa, 1992). The process by which we use such information to make inferences about the causes of behavior or events is called **attribution.**

The two social psychologists who were the first to formally analyze how people attempt to understand the causes behind behavior were Gustav Ichheiser (1943) and Fritz Heider (1958). Both men were born in Austria and both were forced to flee Europe in the 1930s because of the rise of fascism. After settling in the United States, the careers of these two men sharply diverged. Whereas Heider became an influential theoretician whose work shaped the development of attribution theory, Ichheiser battled mental illness and his work slipped into obscurity (Rudmin, 1999). Only recently has a new generation of attribution theorists rediscovered Ichheiser's contributions (see p. 121).

Heider and Ichheiser both believed that everybody has a general theory of human behavior—what Heider called a *naive psychology*—and that they use it to search for explanations of social events. In seeking attributions, Heider believed people are motivated by two primary needs: the need to form a coherent view of the world, and the need to gain control of the environment. Being able to predict how people are going to behave goes a long way in satisfying both of these needs. If we can adequately explain and predict the actions of others, we will be much more likely to view the world as coherent and controllable than if we have no clue to their intentions and dispositions. In satisfying these two needs, Heider asserted that we act much like *naive scientists,* rationally and logically testing our hypotheses about the behavior of others.

LOCUS OF CAUSALITY

In making causal attributions, by far the most important judgment concerns the *locus of causality.* According to Heider, people broadly attribute a given action either to internal states or external factors. An **internal attribution** (also called *person attribution*) consists of any explanation that locates the cause as being internal to the person, such as

Attribution

The process by which people use information to make inferences about the causes of behavior or events.

Internal Attribution

An attribution that locates the cause of an event to factors internal to the person, such as personality traits, moods, attitudes, abilities, or effort.

personality traits, moods, attitudes, abilities, or effort. An **external attribution** (also called *situation attribution*) consists of any explanation that locates the cause as being external to the person under scrutiny, such as the actions of others, the nature of the situation, or luck. In my "garbage" example, I ultimately made an external attribution about the woman's actions, explaining it due to the stress of the job brought on by adverse weather. For Heider and other attribution theorists, whether my explanation is correct or not is not the issue. Their task is not to determine the *true* cause of events, but rather to explain how people *perceive* the causes.

STABILITY AND CONTROLLABILITY OF CAUSALITY

Besides making internal or external distinctions, people also attempt to answer other important attributional questions. Bernard Weiner and his colleagues expanded Heider's primary distinction between the internal and external locus of causality to include questions about stability and controllability (Weiner, 1986; Weiner et al., 1972). *Stable* causes are permanent and lasting, while *unstable* causes are temporary and fluctuating. This stable/unstable dimension is independent of the direction of causality. Some causes, called *dispositional,* are both internal and stable ("She insulted me because she is rude"). Other causes are considered to be internal but unstable ("She insulted me because she has a cold"). Likewise, some causes are seen as external and stable ("She insulted me because I, the external factor, rub people the wrong way"), while others are perceived as external and unstable ("She insulted me because the weather conditions that day made her job very difficult").

Although judgments of the locus and stability of causes are the most important in making attributions, a third dimension we often consider is the *controllability* of these causes. According to Weiner (1982), we think of some causes as being within people's control and others as being outside their control. The controllable/uncontrollable dimension is independent of either locus or stability. Weather is a good example of an uncontrollable factor.

Table 4.5 illustrates how these three dimensions might interact with one another in assigning causality to academic performance. For example, how much you generally study for exams would be considered an internal, stable, and controllable factor, while how much you *choose* to study for any particular exam would be an internal, unstable, and controllable factor. Sometimes a controllable factor like effort will only get you so far in academic achievement. Then we must consider internal factors that are seen as uncontrollable, such as innate intellectual ability (stable) and one's mood during exam time (unstable). External factors that are considered controllable might be rather stable, such as knowing that your teacher looks for specific definitions of terms and use of examples in test answers, or they might also be unstable, such as others deciding to help you prepare for an exam (this help is presumably under their control). Finally, the difficulty of tests given by the teacher would

TABLE 4.5

Possible Causes of Academic Achievement Due to Locus, Stability, and Controllability

| Controllability | Internal | | External | |
	Stable	Unstable	Stable	Unstable
Controllable	Typical effort	Temporary effort exerted for a particular exam	Some forms of teacher bias	Unusual help from others
Uncontrollable	Exerted ability	Mood	Exam difficulty	Luck

be perceived as being external, stable, and uncontrollable, while luck is an external, unstable factor typically perceived as uncontrollable.

The locus, stability, and controllability of causal attributions appear to be the primary dimensions employed when people explain events (Meyer & Koebl, 1982). For example, Weiner and his colleagues have demonstrated how people use these three dimensions to help them interpret requests for help, and how to view those who have stigmatizing diseases such as cancer and AIDS (Schmidt & Weiner, 1988). Cross-cultural studies have also demonstrated that these dimensions are not only employed in individualist countries but in collectivist ones as well (Hau & Salili, 1991; Schuster et al., 1989).

Following these initial formulations, other social psychologists expanded on their insights and developed formal attribution theories. The following pages focus on theories that have had the most influence on the field and also discuss recent refinements in our understanding of the attribution process. These discussions will refer to *actors,* meaning the persons whose behavior we are attempting to understand.

Correspondent Inference Theory Assumes That People Prefer Making Dispositional Attributions

When we observe others, we not only attend to their behavior, but we also are aware of the *consequences* of the behavior. In developing correspondent inference theory, Edward Jones and Keith Davis (1965) were particularly interested in how people infer the cause of a *single* instance of behavior (for example, why did the garbage woman act rudely?). According to them, people try to *infer* from an overt action whether it *corresponds* to a stable personal characteristic of the actor. Thus, a **correspondent inference** is an inference that the actor's action corresponds to, or is indicative of, a stable personal characteristic. For example, if Jane acts compassionately toward Bob, his correspondent inference would be that Jane is a compassionate person. But will Bob actually make a correspondent inference? Not always. If there are several plausible reasons why someone may have performed a certain act, correspondence is low, and therefore you cannot be confident about the cause of the act. However, if there is only one plausible reason to explain the act, correspondence is high and you will be confident in your attribution.

In explaining social events, Jones and Davis expanded on the earlier ideas of Gustav Ichheiser (1934, 1943) and argued that people have a preference for making dispositional attributions (that is, those that are internal and stable), and that external attributions are merely default options, made only when internal causes cannot be found. The reason for this preference is the belief that knowing the dispositional attributes of others will enable one to better understand and predict their behavior. The problem in confidently making these attributions, however, is that social behavior is often ambiguous and the causes are not always readily apparent to the observer. Therefore, to guide them in their attempts to infer personal characteristics from behavior, Jones and Davis stated that people use several logical rules of thumb.

One such rule deals with the *social desirability* of the behavior. That is, people are much more likely to make dispositional attributions about behavior that is socially undesirable than about behavior that is desirable. This is the case because socially desirable behavior is thought to tell us more about the cultural norms of the group than about the personality of the individuals within that group. Yet when people are willing to break from these norms to act in a certain way, such unexpected behavior demands an explanation. When such action is taken, people realize that the social costs incurred by the actor may be great, and they are much more confident that the behavior reflects a stable and internal disposition (Jones et al., 1961).

Imagine that you are watching several candidates for political office addressing a meeting of Mothers Against Drunk Drivers (MADD). Every candidate voices support for tougher laws against those who drive while intoxicated. How confident would you be in concluding that the candidates' words truly reflect an underlying personal conviction? Now let's imagine that one of the speakers stands up and denounces the actions of MADD as an infringement on a citizen's pursuit of happiness. It is likely that you would be more confident that this candidate's words reflect his or her true convictions because they run so counter to prevailing societal norms.

Correspondent Inference

An inference that the action of an actor corresponds to, or is indicative of, a stable personal characteristic.

Another rule people consider is the actor's degree of *choice*. Actions freely chosen are considered to be more indicative of an actor's true personal characteristics than those that are coerced. Support for the freedom of choice factor comes from a study in which college students read a speech, supposedly written by a fellow student who either supported or opposed Fidel Castro, the communist leader of Cuba (Jones & Harris, 1967). Some students were told that the student speechwriter had freely chosen her or his position, while others were told that the student was assigned the stated position by a professor. When asked to estimate what the student speechwriter's true attitudes were toward Castro, those who believed that the speechwriter had freely chosen her or his position were more likely to assume there was a correspondence between the student's essay (behavior) and her or his true attitudes.

According to Jones and Davis, we not only observe the social desirability of behaviors and the degree of choice of the actors, but we also analyze the actor's chosen behavior in the context of other potential behaviors. We then ask, "Is there some effect or outcome unique to the chosen behavior?" By comparing the consequences of the chosen behavior with the consequences of other actions not taken, people can often infer the strength of the underlying intention by looking for unique or "noncommon" consequences. Thus, this third rule of inference has to do with actions that produce *noncommon effects*—outcomes that could not be produced by any other action.

Research indicates that behaviors with unique noncommon effects result in stronger inferences about an actor's dispositions than behaviors with common effects (Ajzen & Holmes, 1976). For example, let's imagine Zoua is looking to buy a used car. She is considering a 1999 Honda Civic, a 2000 Buick Century, and a 1995 Chevy Corvette. As illustrated in figure 4.2, some effects are common to any of these cars (comfortable ride, good road handling, and respectable fuel economy). However, only one of these cars will attract a lot of attention to whoever is driving it. If Zoua chooses the Corvette as her new car, observers may likely conclude that she is an attention seeker. In drawing this conclusion, they are using the unique noncommon effect of Zoua's behavioral decision to infer her personality traits.

Taking these three rules into account, according to Jones and Davis's theory, people are most likely to conclude that other people's actions reflect underlying dispositional traits (that

CRITICAL *thinking*

Why might someone argue that correspondent inference theory would not have been developed in a collectivist culture? Put another way, what individualist assumption is at the core of this theory?

FIGURE 4.2

Why Did Zoua Buy the Chevy Corvette? Looking for Noncommon Effects

When there are a number of common effects for a given action, it is difficult to tell why people do what they do. However, when people engage in a behavior that has a noncommon effect—as is the case with Zoua's decision to buy the Chevy Corvette—it is much easier to make a correspondent inference: Zoua is an attention seeker.

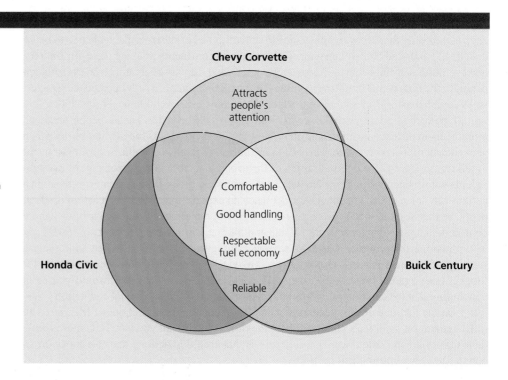

is, they are likely to make correspondent inferences) when the actions are perceived to (1) be low in social desirability, (2) be freely chosen, and (3) result in unique, noncommon effects.

The Covariation Model Explains Attributions Derived from Multiple Observation Points

The theory of correspondent inferences describes how we use certain rules of thumb in an attempt to infer dispositional (internal and stable) causes of behavior. However, the theory is generally applied only to single observations of behavior and only details the cognitive processes for making dispositional attributions. Yet it is quite clearly the case that many of our causal explanations are derived from an extended analysis of others and often result in attributions of causality *external* to the actor.

One theory that specifically attempts to explain attributions derived from multiple observational points and details the processes for making external, as well as internal, attributions is Harold Kelley's (1967) covariation model. Kelley agreed with Heider that human beings are rational and logical observers, acting much like naive scientists in the manner in which they tested their hypotheses about the behavior of others. Just as a scientist arrives at a judgment of causality by noticing that a particular variable is associated with a particular effect across a number of different conditions, Kelley believed that people make causal judgments about everyday events.

According to Kelley, people make attributions by using the **covariation principle.** This principle states that for something to be the cause of a particular behavior, it must be present when the behavior occurs and absent when it does not occur—the presumed cause and observed effect must "covary." If your boyfriend or girlfriend becomes cold and irritable only when you spend extended time with others, that is high covariation. If he or she is only occasionally cold and irritable when you spend extended time with others, that is low covariation. In attempting to assign a cause to the cold and irritable behavior, you would observe its covariation with as many potential causes as possible and attribute the effect to the cause with which it has the greatest covariance.

Our confidence in assigning a cause to some effect will be adversely affected if we cannot distinguish significant differences in the covariation between the effect we are interested in explaining and a number of possible causes (Fiedler et al., 1999). Kelley (1972) called this cognitive "fact" the **discounting principle.** Whenever a particular event has several possible causal explanations, we tend to be much less likely to attribute the effect to any particular cause (Morris & Larrick, 1995).

In describing the locus of causality, Kelley elaborated on the internal/external dimension by further delineating external attributions into the *entity* and *circumstances*. The *entity* is the object toward which the actor's behavior is directed and can be another person or a thing. *Circumstances* are simply the conditions in which actions or events occur.

In assessing covariation, Kelley stated that people rely on three kinds of information. *Consensus* information deals with the extent to which others react the same way to some stimulus or entity as the person whose actions we are attempting to explain. *Consistency* information concerns the extent to which the person reacts to this stimulus or entity in the same way on other occasions. Finally, *distinctiveness* information refers to the extent to which the person reacts the same way to other, different stimuli or entities. Kelley's theory predicts that people are most likely to attribute another person's behavior to internal and stable (dispositional) causes when consensus and distinctiveness are low but consistency is high. On the other hand, circumstance attributions are most likely when consensus and consistency are low and distinctiveness is high. When all three kinds of information are high, people are likely to make entity attributions.

How might the covariation model explain people's process of making attributions in the Stephen Glass scandal? In May of 1998 when another reporter could not verify Glass's *New Republic* story about a 15-year-old computer hacker, many journalists began wondering why this story contained so many unverified sources. Did Glass make some uncharacteristically bad decisions due to deadline pressures (circumstance attribution)? Was Glass a lying and deceitful reporter (dispositional attribution)? Was there something about the social norms and management style at *The New Republic* that caused bad reporting (entity attribution)?

Covariation Principle

A principle of attribution theory stating that for something to be the cause of a particular behavior, it must be present when the behavior occurs and absent when it does not occur.

Discounting Principle

A principle of attribution theory stating that whenever there are several possible causal explanations for a particular event, people tend to be much less likely to attribute the effect to any particular cause.

TABLE 4.6

Why Did Stephen Glass's Story Contain Unverified Sources?

Available Information

Condition	Consensus	Consistency	Distinctiveness	Most Common Attribution
1	Low—No other journalists at *The New Republic* are having problems with unverified sources	High—A number of Stephen Glass's previous *New Republic* stories also contain unverified sources	Low—Stephen Glass's stories for other magazines also contain unverified sources	Dispositional: Stephen is a lying and deceitful reporter
2	High—Many journalists at *The New Republic* have problems with unverified sources	High—A number of Stephen Glass's previous *New Republic* stories also contain unverified sources	High—Stephen Glass's stories for other magazines do not contain unverified sources	Entity: There is something about *The New Republic* management that causes bad reporting
3	Low—No other journalists at *The New Republic* have problems with unverified sources	Low—None of Stephen Glass's previous *New Republic* stories contain unverified sources	High—Stephen Glass's stories for other magazines do not contain unverified sources	Circumstance: Due to deadline pressures, or illness, Stephen Glass was unable to verify all the facts in his story

Table 4.6 outlines how Kelley's theory might predict specific attributions about this behavior. The covariation model predicts that people would seek an attribution by gathering consensus, consistency, and distinctiveness information. For consensus, they would look at the behavior of journalists at *The New Republic:* Are other journalists having problems with fact checking? For consistency, they would examine Glass's past *New Republic* stories. Did any of his previous *New Republic* stories contain unverified sources? For distinctiveness, they would gather information about Glass's stories for other magazines. Did he write any stories for other magazines that contained unverified sources?

For a dispositional attribution (Condition 1: Stephen Glass is a lying and deceitful reporter), there must be evidence for low consensus and distinctiveness and high consistency. This would be likely if none of the other *New Republic* reporters are found to have problems with fact checking, many other Glass articles for *The New Republic* are found to contain unverified sources, and it is discovered that Glass's stories for other magazines display a similar problem with fact checking. For an entity attribution (Condition 2: There is something about *The New Republic* management that causes bad reporting), there must be evidence of high consensus, distinctiveness, and consistency. This attribution is likely if many *New Republic* reporters are found to have fact-checking problems, and none of Glass's stories for other magazines contain unverified sources, even though many of his other *New Republic* stories do. A circumstance attribution is likely if consensus and consistency are low but distinctiveness is high (Condition 3). So if no one else at *The New Republic* is having problems with fact checking and Glass never had any problems before with any of his stories at *The New Republic* or elsewhere, some unusual circumstance must have caused this incident. Perhaps Glass was simply unable to check all his facts because of deadline pressure or because he was not feeling well. In the Glass scandal, the available information resulted in almost all observers making a dispositional attribution, concluding that Stephen Glass was a lying and deceitful reporter.

How accurate is the covariation model in explaining the attribution process? Empirical studies have generally supported the model, yet the three types of information do not appear to be equally influential (Chen et al., 1988). Of the three, consensus information has the weakest effect on attributions (Windschild & Wells, 1997). What this suggests is that, when trying to understand an actor's actions, we appear to primarily focus on information that can be obtained solely by attending to the actor (Was his or her behavior distinctive or consistent?), and we pay less attention to information that requires us to also attend to other actors' actions (consensus information).

Both correspondent inference theory and the covariation model have significantly advanced the original insights of Fritz Heider and Gustav Ichheiser by attempting to better understand how we make inferences about the causes of behavior. In its original form, correspondent inference theory dealt primarily with assigning meaning to *single instances* of behavior, whereas the covariation model was designed to explicitly explain how meaning is assigned to a *sequence* of behavior over time. Both theories assume that people are rational and logical observers, acting like naive scientists by testing hypotheses about the location of causality for social events. Yet how logical are we really in our daily attributions?

SECTION SUMMARY

- Locus of causality (internal or external) is the most important judgment in making attributions
- Correspondent inference theory states we use rules when inferring whether target person's action corresponds to a stable personal characteristic
    Rules: social desirability, choice, noncommon effects
- The covariation model explains attributions derived from multiple observations
- The information used in assessing covariation involves consensus, consistency, and distinctiveness

---

BIASES IN ATTRIBUTION

Based on the discussion thus far, the attribution process appears to be highly rational. Yet is it really? If people do follow logical principles in assigning causality to events, this cognitive process—likened by some to a computer program—has some interesting and all-too-illogical human "bugs."

The Fundamental Attribution Error Is the Tendency to Make Dispositional Attributions for Others' Actions

As discussed in chapter 1, behavior is generally caused by an interaction of an individual's internal characteristics and external factors. However, in explaining other people's actions, we tend to locate the cause in terms of their dispositional characteristics rather than to what might be more appropriate situational factors. In the 1940s, well before attribution theory developed as an area of research in social psychology, Gustav Ichheiser wrote about these "misattributions" in the following manner:

> The persisting pattern which permeates everyday life of interpreting individual behavior in light of personal factors (traits) rather than in the light of situational factors must be considered one of the fundamental sources of misunderstanding personality in our time. (Ichheiser, 1943)

More than thirty years later, Lee Ross (1977) officially named this tendency to overestimate the impact of dispositional causes and underestimate the impact of situational causes on other people's behavior the **fundamental attribution error.** In one of the more important studies to investigate this cognitive bias, Ross and his colleagues (1977a) devised a simulated TV quiz game in which students were randomly assigned to serve the role of

Fundamental Attribution Error

The tendency to overestimate the impact of dispositional causes and underestimate the impact of situational causes on other people's behavior.

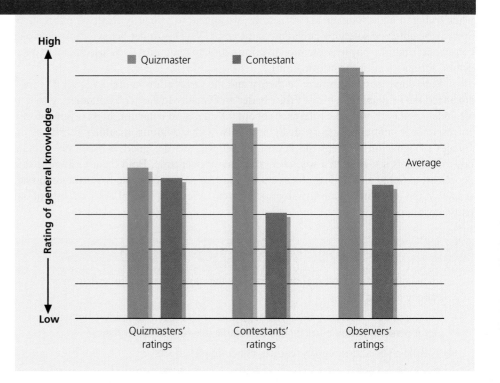

FIGURE 4.3

Fundamental Attribution Error and the TV Quiz Game

Even though students playing the role of quizmaster held a decided advantage over contestants, the contestants failed to discount or take this external factor into account in assigning a causal explanation for the quiz show's results. Like the observers, the contestants judged the quizmasters as more knowledgeable than themselves. What might explain this fundamental attribution error?

"quizmaster" or "contestant." The quizmasters were told to think up ten challenging but fair questions, and the contestants were told to answer as many as possible. Under such conditions, the quizmasters were able to devise some rather tough questions and, on average, the contestants answered only four of the ten questions correctly. Despite the fact that the quizmaster role gave students playing that part a decided advantage, the contestants failed to discount or take this external factor into account in assigning a causal explanation for the quiz show's results. As you can see in figure 4.3, contestants saw the quizmasters as far more knowledgeable than themselves. Observers who watched the game, but were not directly involved in the outcome, also rated the quizmasters as more knowledgeable than the contestants.

THE ROLE OF PREDICTABILITY NEED AND PERCEPTUAL SALIENCE

Why do we tend to engage in this sort of systematic bias? One possibility was already mentioned when discussing correspondent inference theory (see p. 117). We prefer making dispositional attributions because locating the cause of people's behavior in their attitudes and personalities gives us greater confidence that we can accurately predict their future behavior. Thus, our desire for predictability may make us more susceptible to the fundamental attribution error.

A second possibility has to do with what is most noticeable to us as social perceivers. When we observe a person in a social setting, what is often most *perceptually salient* is that particular person: their dynamic movements, their distinctive voice, and their overall physical presence. In comparison, the relatively static situational forces that may actually cause those behaviors are often less salient and therefore less likely to be factored into the attribution equation.

Shelley Taylor and Susan Fiske (1975) tested this hypothesis by varying the seating arrangements of six people who observed two actors engaging in a carefully staged, five-minute conversation. In each session, observers were seated so they faced either actor A, actor B, or both. This seating arrangement is illustrated in figure 4.4. Following the conversation, the observers were asked questions about the two actors to determine whom they

Perceptual Salience and the Fundamental Attribution Error

This is the seating arrangement for the two actors and six observers in the perceptual salience study. Taylor and Fiske found that observers rated the actor they could see most clearly as being the dominant contributor to the conversation. How do these findings help explain the fundamental attribution error?

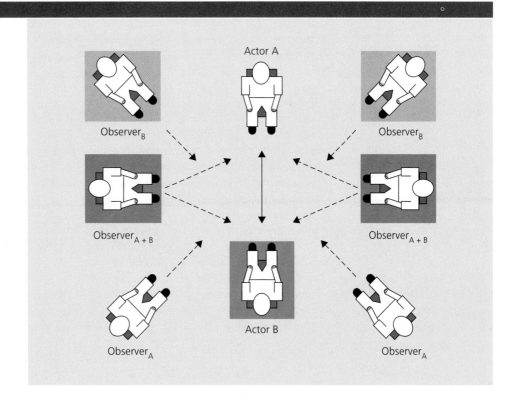

thought had the most impact on the conversation. Results indicated that whichever actor they faced was the one the observers judged as the more dominant member of the dyad. Further research has confirmed perceptual salience as a contributing factor to the fundamental attribution error (Krull & Dill, 1996).

CULTURAL DIFFERENCES

For many years social psychologists believed that the fundamental attribution error was exhibited equally by people throughout the world. Yet, as more research was conducted in non-Western cultures, it became clear that this particular attribution error was less common in collectivist cultures than in those that were individualist (Leung & Chan, 1999; Norenzayan & Nisbett, 2000). For example, Joan Miller (1984) found that Hindu Indians made more situational attributions when explaining people's everyday behavior, whereas Americans were much more likely to make dispositional attributions. Faced with such findings, social psychologists began wondering *why* culture affects the fundamental attribution error. Is it because collectivists are less attentive than individualists to how attitudes and personality traits (dispositions) can shape behavior? Or is it due to individualists being less attentive than collectivists to how situational forces can influence behavior?

Subsequent research found that collectivists are just as likely as individualists to take into account people's dispositions when explaining their behavior (Krull et al., 1999; Miyamoto & Kitayama, 2002). Where they differ is in their awareness of the situation's power. Collectivists are more attentive to how situational factors may influence people's behavior, and that is apparently why they are less susceptible to the fundamental attribution error (Choi & Nisbett, 1998; Choi et al., 1999).

This cultural difference in person perception is rooted in different views of the self. As stated in chapter 3, individualists view the self as internally driven and relatively uninfluenced by situational forces (the independent self). In contrast, collectivists view the self as dependent on the group and strongly influenced by social obligations (the interdependent self). It appears that the interdependent self fosters a greater appreciation of how personal and situational factors interact in shaping behavior, which is essentially how social psychology understands social behavior. Based on these findings, some social psychologists are raising the possibility that the type of naive psychology that members of collectivist cultures develop leads to more accurate attributions than that typically developed in individualist cultures (Choi et al., 1999).

However, as you recall from our discussion in chapter 3 (pp. 72-73), cultures do not create people with rigidly independent or interdependent selves. Situational factors can trigger spontaneous self-concepts in people that run counter to the independent self or interdependent self fostered by their culture (Kühnen & Oyserman, 2002). When this occurs in people whose typical self-views are independent, their situationally induced interdependent self will likely foster a greater awareness of how the interaction of dispositional and situational factors influences others' behaviors. Likewise, when collectivists' thoughts are temporarily shifted to an independent self-view, their social judgments are more likely to suffer from the fundamental attribution error (Hong et al., 2000, 2003). Before continuing, watch the interview with Lee Ross, the social psychologist who coined the term "fundamental attribution error," on your Social Sense CD-ROM.

Whether perceptual salience, individualism, or a combination of these and other factors explain the fundamental attribution error, this particular bias can have significant social consequences. Attributing the behavior of others to internal factors allows social perceivers to block actors' attempts to deny responsibility for negative events with which they are associated (Inman et al., 1993). For example, the tendency to disregard situational forces in explaining the plight of victims within our society (rape victims, street people, disadvantaged minorities, etc.) can result in less sympathy, because we hold these people responsible for their condition due to "bad" dispositions.

Even if our response is one of sympathetic caring for unfortunate others, the assignment of dispositional blame will influence the type of solutions we as a society implement for these people (Leung & Chan, 1999). That is, if we attribute the difficulties of unfortunate others to personal defects rather than to their circumstances, treatment programs will likely focus on changing individuals and not on improving their social environment. Yet if many of the individuals in these programs are members of social groups whose difficulties often stem from societal discrimination rather than personal defects (like ethnic minorities and women), our attempted interventions may prove to be psychologically damaging.

Actors Give More Weight to External Factors Than Do Observers

When explaining the actions of others, we are especially likely to commit the fundamental attribution error. But when explaining our own behavior, we tend to give more weight to external (or situational) factors. This tendency to attribute our own behavior to external causes but that of others to internal factors is known as the **actor-observer effect** (Jones & Nisbett, 1972; Karasawa, 1995). For example, if Charisse is talking with an attractive male stranger and her boyfriend, Singh, sees them from a distance, they may well arrive at different explanations for this social interaction. Although Charisse may attribute it to an external factor (the stranger was asking for directions), Singh may assign an internal cause (Charisse is infatuated with this guy).

Michael Storms (1973) created such conversational setups (minus the jealousy component) to test for the actor-observer effect. Employing a design similar to the previously discussed Taylor and Fiske (1975) study, Storms had four unacquainted research participants—two playing the role of observers and two playing the role of conversational actors—arranged in a seating pattern similar to the one shown in figure 4.5. The two actors were instructed to engage in a five-minute conversation, and the two observers were told to focus their attention on the actor they were facing. Two video cameras also separately recorded the facial expressions of the actors as they conversed. Immediately afterward, both the actors and the observers rated the actors' behavior along a number of dimensions, and then they were asked to indicate the degree to which the actors' behavior was determined by their personal characteristics and by the situation. Consistent with the actor-observer effect, the observers placed greater importance on *dis-*

Social Sense

View the video on *The Fundamental Attribution Error.*

CRITICAL *thinking*

Based on your understanding of correspondent inference theory, why do you think the fundamental attribution error is also known as the *correspondence bias?*

Actor-Observer Effect

The tendency for people to attribute their own behavior to external causes but that of others to internal factors.

FIGURE 4.5

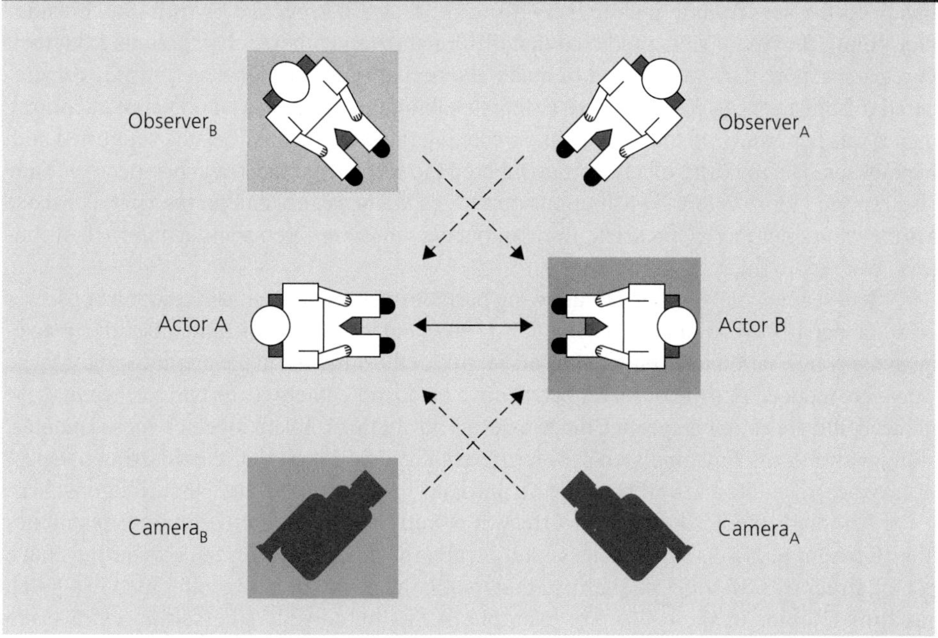

Perceptual Salience and the Actor-Observer Effect

This is the seating arrangement for the two actors and two observers in Storms's (1973) perceptual salience study. Why would two actors who watched themselves on videotape following the conversation with the other actor make more dispositional attributions about each other's behavior?

positional factors when explaining the actions of the actor they were watching, whereas the actors emphasized *situational* factors when explaining their own behavior.

Why does the actor-observer effect occur? As with the fundamental attribution error, a likely possibility is perceptual salience. While engaged in a particular activity, the actor's attention is typically turned outward toward the situation, but the observer's attention is likely focused on the actor. Thus, what is salient for the actor (the situation) and what is salient for the observer (the actor) differs due to their perspectives in viewing the event.

If perceptual salience is important in the attribution process, what would happen if you manipulated this salience *after* the event had transpired but *prior* to observers and actors making any formal attributions? In another condition of Storms's study, he showed the videotapes to the participants before they made their attributions. Instead of seeing on tape what they had experienced live, however, some of them watched the *opposite* visual perspective. Thus, actors A and B saw their own faces, observer A saw actor B, and observer B saw actor A. What do you think resulted from this perceptual flip-flop?

In contrast to participants who saw on tape what they had experienced live, these *reversed-perspective* viewers no longer exhibited the typical actor-observer effect. Instead, the actors who had seen themselves made more dispositional attributions, and the observers made more situational attributions about the actor they had previously faced. These findings, along with others, not only demonstrate the power of perceptual salience in the attribution process, but they also demonstrate that if we manipulate the attention of the actors so that they become *self-aware,* they tend to place more importance on internal factors when explaining their own actions, and the actor-observer effect disappears (Fejfar & Hoyle, 2000). In a very real psychological sense, when the actors engaged in self-awareness, they became observers of their own actions.

Keeping in mind how differing psychological perspectives—self-focused versus situation-focused—can influence perceptual salience, let us consider an extension of Storms's (1973) study by Mark Frank and Thomas Gilovich (1989). In their investigation, male and female college students engaged in a brief "get-acquainted" conversation with a stranger of their own sex. Immediately following this interaction, they rated their own behavior along similar dimensions used by Storms, and also assigned causality to these actions. Three weeks later, they returned and were asked to recall the previous conversation and to rate their behavior once again. This time they were also asked to indicate how they imagined the scene while recalling it—from their own perspective or from an "outside" viewpoint. The researchers predicted that if the actors remembered their actions from their own perspective, they would tend to make external attributions. However, if they remembered it from an "outside" perspective (that is, taking themselves as an object of attention), then it was hypothesized that they would make internal attributions. Results supported both hypotheses. The majority of actors remembered the scene from their own perspective. They also reported more external attributions on the second occasion than on the first. For those actors who remembered the scene from an outside observer's perspective, internal attributions were more likely.

In a second study, instead of allowing participants to spontaneously adopt an observer or actor perspective, Frank and Gilovich (1989) induced them to remember the get-acquainted conversation from either one perspective or the other. As in the previous study, those who were induced into the observer perspective made more internal attributions, while those induced into the actor perspective made external attributions. Taken together, these findings, along with Storms's manipulated self-awareness results, suggest that the differing perspectives typical of actors and observers are a significant cause of this particular attributional bias.

Although the actor-observer effect is a well-documented attributional phenomenon (Krueger et al., 1996), it is less likely when the actors making the attributions have personalities or self-concept qualities that match the behavior being explained in a given situation (Robins et al., 1996). For example, if Shalini considers herself an extraverted person (a dispositional attribution) and acts very outgoing when introduced to a group of people, she is as likely to explain her behavior in dispositional terms ("I am talking a lot because I'm an extraverted person") as are those who are observing her behavior. Thus, despite the general tendency for the actor-observer effect to operate, personality and self-concept differences among individuals help explain why it does not occur in certain situations.

Self-Serving Attributions Enhance and Protect Self-Esteem

Perhaps the best evidence that we are not coldly rational information processors is found in situations in which our own performance results in either success or failure. When such events transpire, where do you think we tend to assign the locus of causality? I probably do not need to cite numerous studies to convince you that the nature of the attribution process is decidedly self-protective in failure situations and self-enhancing in success situations. That is, we tend to take credit for positive behaviors or outcomes but to blame negative behaviors or outcomes on external causes (Campbell & Sedikides, 1999; McCall & Nattrass, 2001). For example, when students receive a good grade on an exam, they are likely to attribute it either to their intelligence (an uncontrollable, yet stable, internal factor), their strong work ethic (a controllable, stable, internal factor), or a combination of the two. However, if they receive a poor grade on this exam, they tend to attribute it to an unreasonable professor (a stable, yet uncontrollable, external factor) or pure bad luck (an unstable, uncontrollable, external factor). In those instances when we blame others for failure, our targets tend to be people we dislike (Silvia & Duval, 2001b). Overall, this tendency to assign an internal locus of causality for our positive outcomes and an external locus for our negative outcomes is known as the **self-serving bias.** Given our discussion in chapter 3 concerning the high value placed on self-esteem in individualist cultures, it should not be surprising to learn that individualists are more likely to exhibit the self-serving bias than collectivists (Boven et al., 2003; Heine & Lehman, 1999).

The most agreed-upon explanation for the self-serving bias is that it allows us to enhance and protect self-esteem. If we feel personally responsible for successes or positive events in our lives but do not feel blameworthy for failures or other negative events, our self-worth is likely to be bolstered. This self-enhancement explanation emphasizes the role of motivation in our self-serving biases and is appealing in that it can also provide insight

Self-Serving Bias

The tendency to assign an internal locus of causality for our positive outcomes and an external locus for our negative outcomes.

into how self-serving biases extend beyond ourselves to include our explanations of individuals or groups with which we identify (S. A. Miller, 1995; Mullen & Riordan, 1988). As discussed in chapter 3, self-esteem can be reinforced by associating ourselves with the success of others. In a psychological sense, those others with whom we strongly identify are part of our self-concept. When we observe their actions, we tend to ascribe their positive behaviors to internal factors and their negative behaviors to external factors. In so doing, we can "bask in the reflected glory" of their accomplishments and experience our own self-esteem benefits (Cialdini et al., 1976). This tendency to see the actions of ingroup members through the same "rose-colored glasses" as we view our own is a variation of the self-serving bias, known as the *ingroup bias.* As we will discuss more fully in chapter 8, ingroup biasing contributes to a host of social ills, such as sex and race discrimination.

In addition to the self-enhancement explanation, a second and more recent proposition claims that what is called the self-serving bias is actually a very rational information-processing outcome. These so-called self-serving attributions stem from our expectations for success in given situations (Taylor & Riess, 1989). The basic argument here is that people generally expect to succeed and therefore are more willing to accept responsibility when it occurs. Based on Kelley's covariation model, this explanation contends that when people do succeed, the success is low in distinctiveness and high in consistency; therefore, people will make an internal attribution. However, when people meet with failure, this event is considered unusual (high in distinctiveness and low in consistency), and they are therefore likely to make an external attribution. If others also fail on the same task, such high consensus will only strengthen an external attribution.

Whatever the ultimate cause, and despite the fact that they provide us with a less-than-accurate view of ourselves, self-serving attributional biases may be "functionally efficient" because they often boost our self-confidence. For example, attributing any current successes to enduring internal characteristics creates an expectation of future success in related tasks, increasing the likelihood that we will attempt new challenges (Taylor & Brown, 1988). Similarly, attributing repeated failures to external factors may well serve to maintain an optimistic belief in the possibility of future success, resulting in task persistence. Wilmar Schaufeli (1988), for instance, has found that unemployed workers seeking reemployment in the labor market have more success if they exhibit the self-serving bias in their job search (that is, not being hired for a particular job is attributed to external factors and not to internal ones such as incompetence). Although these are tangible benefits, self-serving attributions can create problems if they allow us to repeatedly overlook our own shortcomings in situations where a more realistic appraisal would generate useful corrective steps (Kruger & Dunning, 1999; Robins & Beer, 2001). Further, in group settings, the tendency to take credit for success and deny blame for failure can quickly lead to conflict and dissension among members. For example, the more the members of groups overestimate their individual contributions to group accomplishments, the less they want to work with each other in the future (Banaji et al., 2003; Caruso et al., 2004). Certainly with the self-serving bias, you can have too much of a good thing.

MAKING ATTRIBUTIONS OFTEN INVOLVES BOTH EFFORTLESS AND EFFORTFUL THINKING

So where are we in understanding the process of making attributions about people's behavior? The early attribution theorists conceived of human beings as *naive scientists,* who are highly rational and logical information processors, heavily relying on explicit cognition. This approach to understanding social perception reflects the classic "cold" perspective in social psychology (see chapter 1, p. 14). Those who developed correspondent inference theory and the covariation model assumed that people survey all the evidence and then decide on either an internal or an external attribution. However, many social psychologists now believe that the attribution process involves two different kinds of thinking, one that is automatic and simple, and the other that is deliberate and effortful. Further, they believe that the automatic and simple attributional assessment occurs first and is then followed by the

FIGURE 4.6

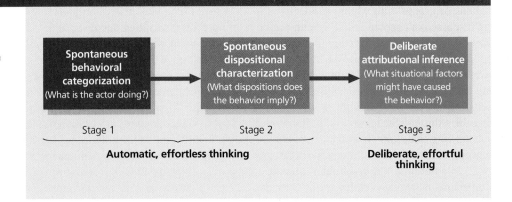

The Characterization-
Correction Model: A
Three-Stage Explanation
of the Attribution
Process

Early attribution theories assumed
that we are highly rational and
logical information processors,
heavily relying on explicit
cognition. The characterization-
correction model contends that
we initially automatically
characterize people's behavior as
being caused by dispositional
factors and then later consciously
correct this attribution to better
account for situational factors.
The first two stages in this model
involve automatic, effortless
thinking, while the third stage
entails deliberate effortful
thinking. Do we always get
through this final stage in the
attributional process? What might
short-circuit stage 3 thinking?

Characterization-
Correction Model

A dual-process model that
contends we initially automatically characterize people's
behavior as being caused by
dispositional factors and then
later correct attribution to better
account for situational factors.

deliberate and effortful analysis (Newman, 2001; Krull, 2001). Let us examine a prominent example of one of these *dual-process models* of the attribution process that reflects the newer Warm Look of social cognition in social psychology (again, see p. 14).

The Characterization-Correction Model

In developing their dual-process model, Daniel Gilbert and his colleagues (1988) suggest that when we observe others perform some action we first *characterize* this behavior as having a dispositional cause and then later may *correct* this initial judgment with situational information. As depicted in figure 4.6, this **characterization-correction model** occurs in three stages, with the first two stages involving spontaneous and relatively effortless thinking, and the third stage involving a deliberate and effortful adjustment of the spontaneous judgments made in the two previous stages. Our initial effortless thinking leads us to automatically make dispositional attributions because of our previously discussed desire for predictability and our perceptual bias of paying more attention to actors than situations.

As an example of how this process works, let's return to my "garbage lady" incident in which she responded to my phone inquiry about tardy garbage pickup by stating, "Well sir, with all the snow we had yesterday I would have thought people wouldn't have been stupid enough to put out their garbage today." What explains her behavior toward me? In the first stage of my attributional thinking, I would spontaneously categorize the garbage lady's behavior ("Whoa! That sounds like an insult directed at me!"). In the second stage, I would make an initial dispositional inference or characterization ("I think she is a rude person!"). Finally, in the third stage, I would consciously hesitate in going with my initial snap judgment and, instead, consider possible situational factors that might explain the garbage lady's response ("Maybe the weather stressed her out"; "Maybe my tone of voice sounded accusatory and this irritated her"; "Maybe this is the fiftieth call she received today and she's fed up").

Whereas the first and second stages in this process are automatic and relatively effortless, the third stage requires a good deal of cognitive effort. Because correcting the initial, spontaneous dispositional characterization of other people's behavior is cognitively demanding, when we are distracted, too busy, or unmotivated we may not complete the final stage. By not engaging in deliberate attributional inference, our explanations of other people's actions are likely to fall prey to the fundamental attribution error.

A good deal of evidence supports this sort of stage model in the attribution process. First, without realizing it, we do often make snap judgments of others after observing them behave, and these spontaneous judgments emphasize dispositional causes (Uleman, 1999). Second, this tendency to commit the fundamental attribution error is greatly reduced when we take the time to engage in more effortful thinking (Gawronski, 2003; Riggs & Gumbrecht, in press; Yost & Weary, 1996). Third, if stage 3 is not initiated or completed, we are unlikely to properly consider the situational factors that might explain others' actions (Trope, 1998).

One caveat to this theory is that some studies have found that the automatic, effortless thinking at the beginning of the attributional process can sometimes activate spontaneous situational inferences rather than spontaneous dispositional inferences (Ham & Vonk, 2003; Krull & Erickson, 1995). Spontaneously attending to situational causes of behavior may occur when the observer's motivation is to form an impression of the situation the actor is in (Krull & Dill, 1996). Based on our past discussion of culture and attribution, people living in individualist cultures will more likely be motivated to form impressions of actors in a situation rather than in forming impressions of the situation itself. Thus, the characterization-correction model may provide a more accurate explanation for how people tend to make attributions in individualist cultures than in collectivist cultures.

PRAGMATIC ACCURACY IN PERSON PERCEPTION?

Despite cultural and perceptual biases that increase our likelihood of making errors in person perception, we do acquire sufficiently accurate knowledge about those around us to often make sound social judgments (Funder, 1999). Although most of the research and theorizing in the area of person perception has assumed that we form inferences about people's broad personality traits and then use this information to explain and predict their behavior across an unlimited number of social settings, William Swann (1984) believes that our job as person perceivers is more modest. Instead of uncovering a trait or an array of traits that will explain a target person's behavior in many different situations, Swann contends that we try to acquire *pragmatic accuracy* about the target person (Gill & Swann, 2004; Swann et al., 2002). Pragmatic accuracy is the ability to understand how a target person will behave in a limited set of social settings and in terms of a limited number of behavioral dimensions.

For example, when we observe our new colleague Raymond speaking harshly to his wife on the phone and later berating a delivery person for some perceived slight, we probably will begin to deliberately formulate dispositional attributions about his behavior. These attributional inferences will likely be less focused on helping us explain how Raymond will behave at home, at church, or at the local health club but instead will be focused on explaining how he might behave at work when interacting with us. This smaller, more restricted understanding of Raymond may be what the person perception process is all about: helping us in "life's practical struggles."

SECTION SUMMARY

- The attribution process is characterized by cognitive biases that cause judgmental errors
- The fundamental attribution error is the tendency to make internal versus external attributions and is more common in individualist cultures that in collectivist cultures
- The actor-observer effect is the tendency to make external attributions for our own behavior but internal attributions for others
- The self-serving bias is the tendency to attribute our successes to internal factors and our failures to external factors
- The characterization-correction model describes how the attribution process involves both effortless and effortful thinking
- Despite cognitive biases, our person perceptions appear to be "functionally efficient"

FEATURED STUDY

MAINTAINING LIES: THE MULTIPLE-AUDIENCE PROBLEM

Bond, C. F., Jr., Thomas, B. J., & Paulson, R. M. (2004). Maintaining lies: The multiple-audience problem. *Journal of Experimental Social Psychology, 40,* 29–40.

Always tell the truth. Then you don't have to remember anything.

Mark Twain, American author and social satirist, 1835–1910

The research literature suggests that it is relatively easy to lie and fool others. However, deception may become more challenging over time. Successful liars run the risk of their deception being discovered at a later date and having their reputations compromised from this discovery. Due to this possibility, liars must be constantly on guard to prevent the disclosure of past deception. How does this challenge influence their self-presentations and social interactions? The present study examined this problem by confronting liars with a predicament. Students were asked to give a deceptive description of a teacher to one student, a truthful description of the same teacher to another student, and finally to describe the teacher to the same two students while they sat side by side. How does the liar handle this multiple-audience problem? The hypotheses in the present study were that deceivers would be successful in their initial deceptions, but would have a difficult time maintaining their lies when faced with this multiple-audience predicament. The first experiment in this study is described below.

Method

The researchers provided 244 psychology students with extra credit in their courses for participating in the study. After giving informed consent, 48 students (the *deceivers*) were videotaped while lying and telling the truth, and 196 students judged them for deception. Although some of the student judges (the *targets*) heard the actual true/false statements as they were presented by the deceivers, most student judges (the *observers*) evaluated the truthfulness of the statements after watching the videotapes. The deceivers were instructed to think of two teachers who had taught them prior to college—a teacher they liked and a teacher they disliked—and provide either a truthful or deceptive description of these teachers while in the presence of another college student (the *target*). As a control, some of the videotaped participants gave their teacher descriptions without a target being present. After this initial description, deceivers were instructed to describe the same teacher a second time to a different student, with those who had earlier told the truth instructed to lie and those who had earlier lied instructed to tell the truth. Finally, the deceivers were told to give a third description of the teacher described twice before while in the presence of two targets, with instructions to either lie or tell the truth. For some deceivers, the two targets had been present at the earlier teacher descriptions, while for other deceivers the two targets had not previously heard their teacher description. Throughout this procedure, the deceivers were not aware that when describing a teacher to a target they might later be required to describe that teacher again in an opposite fashion, or that this same target might be present at such a description.

Results and Discussion

Consistent with past research indicating that deception is often successful, there was no statistically significant difference between the one-member target audiences believing truthful or untruthful teacher descriptions (56 percent and 53 percent, respectively). What about the teacher description given to two targets simultaneously? The researchers had hypothesized that this multiple-audience predicament would undermine deceivers' ability to make targets believe their lies. However, the results found no significant difference in targets' impression of deceivers who lied in this multiple-audience predicament compared with those who lied with only one target present. Yet, while the multiple-audience predicament did not undermine deceivers' ability to successfully deceive, it did undermine their ability to convey the truth. When deceivers were told to tell the truth, they were much less successful about being believed in the multiple-audience predicament condition (50 percent believed) than in the one-member audience condition (83 percent believed).

The multiple-audience predicament forced half of the deceivers to describe a teacher to targets who had previously heard incompatible characterizations of that teacher. The researchers predicted that the deceiver would make a less honest impression on the target who had previously heard an inconsistent teacher characterization than on the target who had heard a consistent characterization. This expectation was not confirmed: half of the targets in both the consistent and inconsistent teacher characterization conditions judged the current description as dishonest.

Regarding the impressions the deceivers conveyed to the observers who watched their teacher descriptions on videotape, the researchers expected that in the multiple-audience predicament deceivers would appear dishonest only to people who had heard teacher characterizations that were discrepant from the one now being offered. Yet the results indicated that trying to maintain their deceptions under such difficult circumstances had a wider effect on the deceivers' self-presentation abilities. When describing a teacher to multiple audiences, deceivers appeared deceptive even to observers who earlier heard them give a description similar to the one now being offered. Further, they also appeared deceptive to observers who had never heard anything at all about the teacher.

In explaining the findings in this first experiment, the researchers suggest that deceivers in the multiple-audience predicament are forced to spend a lot of cognitive effort focusing on their stories in an attempt to reconcile lies they have told in the past. This extra cognitive effort placed on story construction causes them to be less attentive to how they look and sound while telling the stories. By not spending as much time monitoring their visible self-presentation, they leave themselves looking dishonest to those with whom they are directly interacting as well as to bystanders who are observing their self-presentation.

APPLICATIONS

HOW GOOD ARE YOU AT DETECTING LIES?

Do you believe that lying is common or uncommon for the average person? Would you be surprised to learn that research by Bella DePaulo and her colleagues indicates that, during an average week, people lie to about one-third of those with whom they interact? On average, people tell about ten lies per week, with the greatest lying committed by those who are more sociable, manipulative, and concerned about creating favorable self-presentations than others (DePaulo et al., 1996; Kashy & DePaulo, 1996). Most of the time, these untruths are told to benefit the liar (*self-centered lies*) rather than benefiting someone or something else (*other-oriented lies*).

When people lie to spare others' feelings, these "kind lies" are usually reserved for those they like (Bell & DePaulo, 1996). Further, people are most likely to be dishonest in providing unfavorable feedback when it involves something that is very important to the recipient's self-concept (DePaulo & Bell, 1996). Conformity to this *politeness norm* generally does not result in people raving about something they strongly dislike, but it usually prompts them to provide some degree of positive feedback.

Given that people sometimes try to conceal their true feelings and intentions from others, how do we—as social perceivers—respond to the possibility of such subterfuge? Erving Goffman (1959) contended that when we judge other people's self-presentations, we pay attention to two different types of social stimuli, which he called *expressions*. First, there are expressions that people freely "give" to others in what is typically thought of as their traditional communication patterns. These *expressions given* consist of the words and gestures that people are consciously trying to transmit to others. Besides these strategic gestures, there are also expressions that people "give off," which are mostly nonverbal in nature. *Expressions given off,* also known as *nonverbal leakage,* cover a wide range of behavior unintentionally transmitted and of which people are much less aware. The lack of gusto when chewing a host's poorly prepared meal and the tortured look behind your forced smile are examples of expressions given off.

Of the two types of expressions, those unintentionally "given off" by self-presenters are much better indicators of possible deception than those consciously "given." For example, in an analysis of accurate and inaccurate judges of deception, Paul Ekman and Maureen O'Sullivan (1991) found that the inaccurate judges (30 percent accuracy or worse) focused on verbal cues, while the accurate judges (80 percent accuracy or better) attended more to nonverbal cues. One factor determining which of these two types of expressions we pay most attention to when suspecting deception is how important the topic is to us. James Forrest and Robert Feldman (2000) found that when people were highly involved in a discussion topic, they paid more attention to speakers' verbal messages, and thus, they were more easily deceived than less involved people, who attended more to nonverbal behavior.

Although attending to nonverbal behavior can improve our ability to reveal the lie in others' self-presentations, not all nonverbal cues are equally instructive. One of the biggest mistakes we make is placing too much importance on the face to reveal deception. For example, we tend to believe that others do not smile when they lie, when in fact, smiling is a common device used by deceivers to hide their true feelings (Ekman et al., 1988). We also tend to be fooled by the *structure* of people's faces, falsely assuming that babyfaced individuals (large eyes and symmetrical facial features) and physically attractive persons are more honest than those with mature-looking and less attractive faces (Zebrowitz & Montepare, 1992; Zebrowitz et al., 1996).

Instead of focusing on the face, attending to other nonverbal cues appears to lead to more accurate person perception. For example, in one study, Ekman and Wallace Friesen (1974) showed a series of either pleasant or disgusting short films to a sample of female nurses and instructed them either to report their honest feelings about the film or to conceal their feelings. Hidden video cameras—some focused on the face and others focused on the body—recorded their behavioral expressions. These tapes were later viewed by participants acting as observers whose task it was to judge whether the nurses had been truthful or deceptive. Results indicated that observers who watched tapes focused on the face were not as accurate at detecting deception as were those who watched tapes focused on the body. Body movements that

significantly predicted deception were fidgeting of the hands and feet, and restless shifts in body posture. This and other research suggests that when trying to deceive others, people's facial expressions are more likely to be self-monitored and controlled (expressions given) than are their other bodily movements (expressions given off).

Although nonverbal behavior generally provides more useful information about lying than verbal behavior, it is sometimes possible to detect deception by attending to certain changes in a person's speech patterns—what is known as *paralanguage* (see table 4.7). Several studies indicate that when people lie, they tend to give shorter answers, the pitch in their voice often rises slightly, and their speech is slower and filled with many pauses ("ahs" and "uhms") and other sentence hesitations (DePaulo et al., 2003; Porter & Yuille, 1996). Liars also tend to use fewer first-person singular pronouns (*I, me, my*), which is thought to reflect their attempt to dissociate themselves from the lie (Campbell & Pennebaker, in press; Newman et al., 2003). Finally, liars also use negative emotion words at a higher rate than truthtellers, which may be caused by their feeling of guilt triggering negative emotions (Newman et al., 2003; Vrij, 2000).

A meta-analysis of seventeen studies involving almost 2800 participants found that our *confidence* in detecting deception does not predict our *accuracy* in distinguishing liars from nonliars (DePaulo et al., 1997). Even those who make these judgments for a living, such as judges, police officers, CIA polygraphers, and customs inspectors, generally do no better than chance (DePaulo & Pfeifer, 1986). Indeed, the best of the professional deception detectors, namely Secret Service agents, are successful only about 70 percent of the time (Ekman & O'Sullivan, 1991). These studies and others reveal that we are particularly bad at detecting deception from strangers (Anderson et al., 1999; DePaulo & Friedman, 1998). One important reason for this low level of accuracy among the unacquainted is that people often individually behave in distinctive ways when lying. However, when interacting with strangers you have no knowledge of their distinctive "lying signals." Fortunately, we do appear to gain insight into people's telltale lying signals as we become more familiar with their self-presentation strategies. In a longitudinal study of friendship development, researchers found that friends become more accurate in detecting each other's deception as their relationship progresses, improving from 47 percent accuracy early in the friendship to 61 percent accuracy after five months (Anderson et al., 2002). Of course, this accuracy level is still not up to the standards of Secret Service agents (who still have a 30 percent failure rate!), but

---

TABLE 4.7

What Are Some of the Verbal Symptoms of Lying?

Symptoms	Likely Causes
Shorter answers to questions	The cognitive burden of concealing the truth interferes with the generation of smooth conversation
Slower speech filled with pauses and other sentence hesitations	
Slight rise in voice pitch	Activation of the sympathetic nervous system
Less use of first-person singular pronouns	Psychological attempt to dissociate oneself from the lie
More use of negative emotion words	Feelings of guilt trigger negative emotions

it does provide some hope that we can improve our deception detection skills in important areas of our lives.

Taken as a whole, the research on deception tells us that despite the numerous deception signals available to us as person perceivers, we frequently make mistakes in judging whether others are being truthful. Deceivers succeed in duping us regardless of our sex, race, cultural background, socioeconomic status, or educational level, and they are most successful when we do not know them well and the issue is important to us. Perhaps the primary reason why we so often fail to detect deception is that, by and large, we tend to believe that oth-

ers are basically honest (Zuckerman et al., 1981). In the final analysis, there is no one verbal or nonverbal channel that can be thought of as a lie detector. If a deceiver is well prepared and exercises great self-control, even attention to body fidgeting, posture shifts, and voice pitch will not necessarily separate truths from lies. Yet one thing that works to our advantage when dealing with habitual liars is that while we may not detect their deception the first few times, we are more likely to do so as we observe them over time and become more familiar with their self-presentation strategies (Yamagishi et al., 2003).

THE BIG PICTURE

As social beings, we try to maintain competent and appropriate presented selves, and we often consciously try to manipulate people's impressions of us. We also realize that they are probably similarly interested in shaping our impressions of them. Thus, as both actors and audience members in this "social theater," we desire to win applause as we simultaneously attempt to explain the behavior of the other actors.

In judging social actors, we attend to both verbal and nonverbal behavior, and we try to create a working model of their personality. While watching them perform, we seek to learn the degree to which their actions are caused by their attitudes, personalities, moods, or by the situations in which they find themselves. Our preference—and our bias—is to explain their behavior in terms of attitudes and personality traits, because then we feel more confident that we can predict their future behavior. The better we can predict how others will act, the more successful we will be in our own social pursuits.

Of course, mixed into this person perception equation is the fact that we are trying to explain the actions of people who, like us, often have a vested interest in preventing others from discovering their true intentions. Together, these social facts set the stage for many compelling and memorable performances.

WEB SITES
accessed through http://www.mhhe.com/franzoi4

Web sites for this chapter focus on nonverbal communication and the history of attribution theory.

Dane Archer's Nonverbal Communication Web Page

Dane Archer's Web page will introduce you to the topic of nonverbal communication and give you a chance to try to guess the meaning of some real nonverbal communication.

Facial Analysis Web Site

This Web site highlights the work of many past and present researchers, including deBoulogne, Darwin, Ermiane, and Ekman.

Folk Explanations of Behavior

This Web page reviews the history of attribution theory and discusses how people act like naive scientists when trying to understand others' actions.

CHAPTER 5

Thinking About Our Social World

CHAPTER OUTLINE

*S*uppose you are visiting a city for the first time and have car trouble downtown in the dead of night. In desperation, you scan the faces of passing motorists, looking for someone who will help you out of this jam. How can you tell who will be your Good Samaritan? Can you seek help from the carload of teenagers who passed by twice in the past five minutes? Or should you try to flag down the neatly dressed and pleasant-looking young man driving the 1965 Chevy . . . who, on second glance, bears an uncanny resemblance to the character of Norman Bates in the movie *Psycho* that you just watched on television? Just as you are bemoaning the fact that you do not know anything about the people whom you are about to ask for help, something in the distance catches your eye. It is a white car with lettering and an emblem on the door, and a panel of light flashers on the roof. Inside are two people wearing blue uniforms and badges. Despite the fact that you are certain they are carrying loaded guns and wooden clubs, you immediately step out in the street and signal them to stop. Are you crazy? You have never seen these two people before in your life, yet you believe they will help you. Why?

Later, upon returning to your hotel room, you turn on the television to unwind. On the city news, there is a report about a local train crash in which two women were killed. You learn that while one of the women was a regular passenger on the train, the other woman was a first-time rider who had been on board only because the bus line she normally used was out on strike. While digesting this story, you realize that you feel sorrier for the first-time rider than for the regular commuter. Her death seems more tragic. Why?

Life is complicated. Nothing that you have learned thus far about the psychology of social interaction should argue against this statement. Faced with life's complications and thrust into the world as both actors and observers we try to make sense of it. Chapter 3 examined how we develop a theory of ourselves and chapter 4 examined how we form impressions of individuals and how we explain the causes of their behavior. As introduced in chapter 1 (p. 14), the theoretical perspective that examines how we actively interpret, analyze, remember, and use information about the social world is called **social cognition** (Kunda, 1999). Let us briefly review how psychology has "thought" about thinking before we continue our analysis of ourselves as social thinkers.

Social Cognition

The way in which we interpret, analyze, remember, and use information about the social world.

HOW DO WE THINK?

Up until the late 1950s, most psychologists viewed cognition as a single, simple system. This perspective was largely due to the influence of behaviorism, which considered learning simply a function of the strength of stimulus-response pairings. If a person or animal consistently responded in the same way to the same stimulus, this meant they had formed a strong memory for the response. According to behaviorists, this single conditioning process was the extent of thinking and memory. Unobservable events, such as cognition, were considered off-limits to the science of psychology. Then, psychologists' ideas about cognition dramatically changed due to technological advances outside the discipline and scientific discoveries within.

We Process Information Serially and "in Parallel"

As first mentioned in chapter 1, the event outside of psychology that served as a catalyst in changing psychologists' theories of cognition and memory was the advent of the computer age (Dodwell, 2000). As psychologists adopted the terms and concepts of computer scientists to explain human cognition, they viewed it as a kind of information-processing system.

Like a computer, they described people processing information in a fixed sequence, or *serially,* working on only one stream of data at a time. This does not mean that psychologists considered human thinking and computer "thinking" as identical, but they concluded that the two were similar enough for computer information processing to serve as a rough working model for human information processing (Searle, 1995).

The sequential computer model of thinking is useful in explaining many aspects of human cognition, especially how we sequentially execute certain mental operations or follow certain rules of logic when making some decisions. For instance, if a normally sociable person acts irritable just before taking his midterms, you may logically consider the available information and conclude that his irritability is caused by situational factors. Yet the computer model is less helpful in explaining other ways of thinking. The human brain is much more complex than a computer and performs many mental operations simultaneously, "in parallel" (Gabrieli, 1999). For example, why might a former soldier experience a panic attack while at a fireworks display? Here, a more useful model of cognition might conceive of information being represented in a weblike network of connections among thousands of interacting "processing units"—all active at once. For the former soldier, memories of war and loud explosions are stored in a neural network, in which activation of one part of the network leads to simultaneous activation of the rest of the network.

Although the computer may not be the last and best metaphor for the human mind, as of this writing it is still the most convenient and common one for organizing the major findings on cognition and memory (Tulving, 1997). Yet the neural network model with parallel processing is quickly gaining popularity. As we discuss social cognition, you will notice that some theories emphasize *serial processing* of information, while others stress *parallel processing.*

We Rely on Effortful and Effortless Thinking

Besides computers and neural webs serving as models for human information processing, social psychologists have adopted other metaphors when describing how we make social decisions. As noted in chapter 4, during the initial development of the social cognitive perspective, human beings were depicted as *naive scientists* who are highly rational and logical information processors. This idea reflects the traditional "cold" perspective in social psychology. Although these theorists acknowledged that our thinking has a number of glitches or "bugs," none suggested that people do not *try* to act logically and thoroughly in seeking social judgments.

As the social cognitive perspective matured, some theorists contended that people are better conceived of as lazy thinkers who often are governed by their emotions and habits. As social thinkers, instead of sparing no "cognitive expense," they described how people act like discount bargain shoppers who are always on the lookout for "blue-light specials." This view of social thinkers as *cognitive misers* stood in sharp contrast to the naive scientist conception. Today, an increasing number of theories in social psychology attempt to reconcile these two competing views of social cognition by proposing **dual-process models of social cognition** involving both effortful and effortless cognition (Stanovich, 2004). In essence, this dual-process view attempts to reconcile the hot and cold perspectives into what was described in chapter 1 as the Warm Look.

Some dual-process theories rely on the computer model of serial information processing, which assumes that people can only engage in one form of thinking at a time. According to this perspective, in human cognition there often is a conflict between an initial, reflexive evaluation and a more considered, rational assessment (Gilovich & Griffin, 2002). The only way you can resolve this conflict is by either engaging in effortful thinking or relatively effortless thinking. You can switch back and forth between the two forms of thinking, but you cannot do both simultaneously.

Besides this sequential "either-or" way of describing human thought, other dual-process theories describe two mental systems that operate simultaneously, or parallel to one another (Kahneman & Frederick, 2002). Social scientists who assume parallel-processing systems often make a distinction between *explicit cognition* and *implicit cognition.*

Dual-Process Models of Social Cognition

Theories of social cognition which propose that people employ two broad cognitive strategies to understand and respond to social stimuli, one involving effortless thinking and the other involving effortful thinking.

Explicit cognition involves deliberate judgments or decisions of which we are consciously aware. Although this type of cognition is intentional, it can sometimes be relatively effortless when the task is easy. However, a good deal of explicit thinking consumes considerable cognitive resources, but the upside is that it is flexible and can deal with new problems. Trying to understand this definition of explicit cognition is literally an example of this very thought process. In contrast, **implicit cognition** involves judgments or decisions that are under the control of automatically activated evaluations occurring without our awareness. This type of thinking is unintentional, it does not use up cognitive resources, and it operates quickly; but it is inflexible and often cannot deal with new problems. The unintentional and automatic qualities of implicit cognition are demonstrated by the fact that you cannot stop yourself from reading the words on this page when you see them. Your reading skills are automatically and effortlessly activated.

Although these two categories of dual-process theories differ in certain respects, they agree that there is an automatic, effortless way of thinking and a more controlled, effortful cognitive process. Many cognitive social psychologists believe that the joint insights from both categories of dual-process models provide us with the best understanding of social cognition (Sloman, 2002; Stanovich & West, 2002).

So how should we think of ourselves as social thinkers? Our overview should make it clear that social psychologists are not shy in generating metaphors to describe people as social thinkers. So, let me end this section with one final metaphor that attempts to include all the mental operations discussed by all the other models. Acknowledging the important role the self plays in human thought and action, Arie Kruglanski (1996) contends that whether we act like naive scientists or cognitive misers is often determined by what *motivates* us in a given situation. His **motivated-tactician model** proposes that we are flexible social thinkers who choose among multiple cognitive strategies based on our current goals, motives, and needs. If social judgment accuracy is the primary goal in a given situation, we will probably carefully assess information. However, if we need to make a quick decision and/or the issue is not important to us, we may take cognitive shortcuts (Ruscher et al., 2000; Schwarz, 1998). Thus, what directs the nature and quality of our social thinking is the self and its motives. Sometimes self-processes and motives involve a great deal of effortful, deliberate thinking, while other times they are automatically and effortlessly activated.

Suppressing Thoughts Can Sometimes Backfire

A good example of effortful and effortless cognition working in tandem is the successful execution of **thought suppression**—the attempt to prevent certain thoughts from entering consciousness. When studying for an exam, you engage in thought suppression by trying to not think about things that would distract you from learning the course material. Likewise, when dieting you avoid thinking about your favorite foods.

As these examples suggest, thought suppression plays an important role in self-regulation, which was a topic of discussion in chapter 3 (pp. 65–67). How does thought suppression work? According to Daniel Wegner (1994), keeping undesired thoughts out of consciousness requires two different cognitive processes, one that is relatively automatic and the other that is more deliberate. First, the automatic *monitoring process* acts like an "early warning system" by searching for evidence that the undesired thoughts are about to intrude into consciousness. When such evidence is found, the more controlled *operating process* is activated. This second cognitive process acts like an active prevention system, consciously distracting attention away from the unwanted thoughts by finding something else to think about.

When you are well rested and highly motivated, these two cognitive processes work pretty well together to keep unwanted thoughts from intruding into consciousness. However, as you know from personal experience, when you become tired or lose focus, your ability to suppress these thoughts declines rapidly. When studying for that test, you may find yourself thinking about your friends having fun at a party, despite your best efforts at concentration. When dieting, you may discover that the more you try to not consume your favorite foods, the more they seem to consume your thoughts ("They're calling to me!"). What appears to be happening here is that the automatic monitoring process continues its identification of unwanted thoughts, but the more controlled operating process no longer has sufficient cognitive resources to direct conscious awareness away from these thoughts. Faced with this breakdown, the unwanted thoughts come flooding into consciousness in what is called the *rebound effect* or *ironic reversal* (Wegner & Schneider, 2003).

Studies examining the neural correlates of thought suppression using functional magnetic resonance imaging (fMRI) have found a certain brain region more active when people are trying to suppress a particular thought than when they are thinking freely about any thought (Wyland et al., 2003). This region, the *anterior cingulate*, is in the frontal lobes of the cerebral cortex. As you recall from chapter 3 (p. 60 and p. 65), this same brain region plays a critical role in self-awareness and the general process of self-regulation. Neuroscientists believe that psychological disorders involving recurring, intrusive thoughts, such as depression and obsessive-compulsive disorder, may involve an underactive anterior cingulate.

Although thought suppression often plays a critical role in keeping us focused so that we can accomplish goals, there can be physical and emotional costs to this aspect of self-regulation. For instance, in one study, medical students were asked to write about a personal topic once a day for three days (Petrie et al., 1998). In the experimental condition, students were told to suppress all thoughts about what they had just written for five minutes, while in the control condition no such instructions were given. Results indicated that the students who engaged in thought suppression experienced a significant decrease in immune system functioning compared with those who had not suppressed thoughts. Similarly, Richard Wenzlaff and David Luxton (2003) identified people who had low levels of negative thoughts and depression but who differed in their habitual tendencies to engage in thought suppression. Ten weeks later, they found that high suppressors who had experienced relatively high levels of stress reported the greatest increase in negative thoughts and unhappiness compared with all other participants. Together, these studies suggest that thought suppression can take both a physical and mental toll on our health, especially during times of stress.

HOW DO WE ORGANIZE AND MAKE SENSE OF SOCIAL INFORMATION?

As much as you may desire to only respond to other people based on information you have personally learned about them as individuals—which was our topic of discussion in chapter 4—the complexity of your social environment often makes this an impractical task. In situations where you must make quick judgments about others based on minimal information, you generally do not have the luxury of engaging in detailed impression formation. Luckily, you come equipped with alternative social judgment strategies that rely on implicit cognition.

We Are Categorizing Creatures

A mental grouping of objects, ideas, or events that share common properties is called a **category** (also referred to as a *concept*). For example, the category *insect* stands for a class of animals that have three body divisions (head, thorax, abdomen), six legs, an external skeleton, and a rapid reproductive cycle. Categories are the building blocks of cognition (Markman, 1999; Woll, 2002). Like the heart that pumps life-giving blood throughout the body, or the lungs that replenish oxygen to this blood, the scientific consensus is that humans could not survive without categorizing things. Imagine, for example, how lost and bewildered you would be if you attended a college class without an appreciation of some key categories such as professor, student, lecture, chairs, or notes.

This automatic tendency to perceive and understand the world in categorical terms greatly expands our ability to deal with the huge amount of information constantly presented to us; it allows us to generalize from one experience to another, making it possible to assign meaning to novel stimuli. Thus, if someone tells you to meet them at the student

Category

A mental grouping of objects, ideas, or events that share common properties. Also known as *concept*.

union by the magnolia tree, you probably know what to look for even if you have never seen a magnolia tree. By understanding the general properties of the category *tree* you will probably seek out an object that is taller than yourself, with branches and leaves that provide shade from the sun. By relating new stimuli to familiar categories, you are much more efficient in understanding and making decisions in your environment.

We also naturally form categories about people based upon their common attributes. This process is called **social categorization** (Hampson, 1988). When categorizing people, we tend to initially rely on readily apparent physical features (Klauer et al., 2003; Stangor et al., 1992). Three of the most universally salient physical features are those based on sex, age, and race. In fact, these three physical features are considered so important in the social categorization process that various social psychologists have referred to them as *primary categories* for human beings (Schneider, 2004). These categories are believed to be special for both evolutionary and sociocultural reasons. Their evolutionary significance rests on the possibility that they provided our ancestors an easy way to distinguish people on the basis of reproductive potential (sex), accumulated wisdom and strength (age), and likelihood of belonging to one's own social group (race). From a sociocultural perspective, these three primary categories form the basis of dominance hierarchies in many cultures throughout the world. Because categorizing others by these key physical features is done so frequently, it becomes habitual and automatic, occurring without conscious thought or effort (Fiske & Neuberg, 1990). In fact, such categorization is so automatic that it probably is impossible to inhibit. Under normal circumstances can you meet someone and not notice whether the person is a she or he? Wouldn't it seem quite strange not to remember whether the person was young or old? Do you really believe it when people claim that they do not notice when they are interacting with someone of another race?

Exactly how do we mentally group things, including people, into categories? The classical view was that we form categories by identifying *defining features,* as in our insect example (Bruner et al., 1956). However, the problem with forming categories by definition is that many familiar categories have uncertain or *fuzzy* boundaries (Rosch, 1978). This fact makes categorizing some members of familiar concepts more difficult than others (Komatsu, 1992). Consider classifying someone based on race. How would you classify someone who has a combination of Caucasian and Afrocentric facial features? Do all Africans or all Caucasians have the same skin color? Research suggests that categorizing has less to do with the features that define all members of a category and has more to do

Social Categorization

The process of forming categories of people based on their common attributes.

We initially categorize people based on readily identifiable physical features. What features did you use to categorize the people in this photograph when you first looked at it? How many different social categories did you perceive?

with the features that characterize the typical member (McGarty, 1999). In the chapter-opening story, this is the reason I assumed you would quickly categorize the two uniformed and armed adults as police officers: they represent our culture's concept of people in this social category.

The most representative member of a category is known as a **prototype;** it is our mental model that stands for or symbolizes the category (Barsalou, 1991). Because a prototype is the member of a category that best represents it for you, members of that category will vary in how closely they match the prototype. Thus, although patrol officers and undercover officers both fit into our category of police officer, for most of us, patrol officers are more "coplike." Not surprisingly, we can more quickly categorize prototypical members than those who less closely match the prototype (Olson et al., 2004; Rosch & Mervis, 1975). Failing to correctly categorize people because they do not resemble the prototype often leads to errors in decision making. This is why female doctors are more often mistaken for nurses than are male doctors, while male nurses are more likely than female nurses to be miscategorized as doctors. In both cases, the mistaken judgments are due to our culturally derived prototypes for these two professions.

Prototype

The most representative member of a category.

Schemas Are Theories of How the Social World Operates

We not only mentally group objects, ideas, or events into categories, but we also develop theories about those categories. The theories we have about categories are called schemas. A **schema** is an organized structure of knowledge about a stimulus that is built up from experience and that contains causal relations; it is a theory about how the social world operates (Chen, 2001; Kunda, 1999). The stimulus could be a person, an object, a social group, a social role, or a common event. A student who observes her psychology professor conducting research will have a schema for the professor role, a schema for the research process, and schemas for various other relevant concepts that this particular professor fits (for example, female, middle-aged, and Pakistani). Without these schemas, the student would have great difficulty making sense of the professor and her actions. But with these schemas, the student can not only understand what is happening in the situation, but the student can also go beyond the presented information and anticipate the next set of events that might occur in this setting. Thus, schemas enrich our understanding of the world. Because they provide a theory about the category of interest, schemas also hasten the processing of information, and hence, decision making.

Schema

A schema is an organized structure of knowledge about a stimulus that is built up from experience and that contains causal relations; it is a theory about how the social world operates.

Some of our schemas are not well developed. For example, my computer schema is very limited. Sure, I can identify some major parts of the computer (I can proudly point to the central processing unit), but I lack the knowledge to accurately explain how the components work together to create the images that appear on the computer screen. People with well-developed schemas about some domain are often experts about that domain. A computer repairperson would have a highly developed computer schema and thus would be much more accurate than me in predicting how a computer will perform specific functions.

Culture shapes many schemas, such as *gender schema,* which is a cognitive structure for processing information based on its perceived female or male qualities. As discussed in chapter 3 (pp. 70–71), people with a well-developed gender schema habitually organize things in their minds according to gender categories. When information is filtered through a gender schema, social perceptions and judgments typically adhere to cultural gender standards. Thus, for example, if George and Laura have strong gender schemas, they may perceive such things as dogs, football, sports cars, math, assertiveness, meat and potatoes, and action movies as "guy-like," while labeling as "gal-like" things such as cats, aerobics, hybrid cars, the fine arts, empathy, salads, and romance movies. For George and Laura, their gender schemas will help them organize and make sense of their lives. If Laura's gender schema causes her to perceive math ability as a male quality, regardless of any inborn potential, Laura is now less likely to identify skill in math as an important personal quality (Nosek et al., 2002b). Due to this disidentification, she is unlikely to spend time developing her math skills, and she is unlikely to choose careers that emphasize math. In contrast, perceiving this same math = male association, George may develop positive attitudes toward math activities and may ultimately choose a career in a math-oriented occupation. This is just one example of how schemas can shape our social perceptions and thereby shape our own self-perceptions.

We also have schemas about common events. A **script** describes how a series of events is likely to occur in a well-known situation (Woll, 2002). The script is used as a guide for behavior and problem solving in the situation. We have numerous scripts, including those for attending class, eating dinner at a restaurant, going to the dentist, interacting with hired help, asking someone out on a date, and even breaking off a romantic relationship (Battaglia et al., 1998; Lan, 2003). Learning scripts is an important part of the socialization process, and children as young as three years of age have well-developed preconceptions about familiar routine events in their lives, such as having lunch at the day-care center or getting ready for bed at night (Nelson, 1986). Scripts often help us clear up ambiguities in social situations. For example, if you go over to someone's house for dinner and are later asked to "spend the night," your interpretation of this question will be shaped by the script that you have in mind. If this question is asked by a platonic friend, you are likely following a different script than if the questioner is a much-desired romantic partner. Embarrassment is likely if your host has a very different script in mind than your own.

When applied to members of a social group such as police officers, women, or the elderly, schemas are often called *stereotypes* (Banaji, in press; McGarty et al., 2002). Like other types of schemas, stereotypes significantly influence how we process and interpret information in our world, even when we are not consciously aware that the schema has been activated from memory (Kawakami & Dovidio, 2001; Schubert & Häfner, 2003). Once a stereotype is activated, we tend to see people within that social category as possessing the traits or characteristics associated with the stereotyped group (Krueger et al., 2003). For example, if a personnel director for a company thinks of elderly people as being frail, forgetful, and slow to grasp new skills, she may spend little time reviewing the employment histories of job applicants over a certain age. Likewise, her positive stereotypes of graduates from Ivy League schools may cause her to overlook glaring blemishes in another applicant's job history who is an Ivy Leaguer. In chapter 8 we will examine in detail how stereotypes are related to prejudice and discrimination.

Schemas Affect What Information We Notice and Later Remember

As you can see, once schemas are formed they can have a profound effect on our social thinking and behavior. Schemas will often determine what information in our surroundings we pay attention to and how quickly we process it, what information we form memories about, and what information we later recall when making decisions. In general, we tend to have better memories of past events and people when this information was originally processed through well-formed schemas (Hirt, 1990), but schemas can also cause us to "misremember" information. Why is this so?

Regarding attention and processing, a schema acts as a cognitive filter, often screening out information that is inconsistent with it (Dijksterhuis & Knippenberg, 1996; Sherman et al., 1998). How might this screening of information affect our impressions of people? According to the *characterization-correction model* described in chapter 4 (p. 128), we tend to make spontaneous dispositional inferences when attending to a person's behavior. For example, if you see someone assisting a handicapped person across the street, you typically spontaneously infer that the individual is empathic and helpful. However, what if this individual is a skinhead? Because empathy and helpfulness are qualities inconsistent with most people's skinhead schema, research indicates that in this situation you are much less likely to make these spontaneous dispositional inferences (Wigboldus et al., 2003). In other words, you automatically dismiss this behavioral information as not being useful in making inferences about the skinhead's personality. Instead, you may engage in more effortful, non-schematic-based thinking and consider what situational factors may be causing him to behave this way (perhaps this is a ploy to rob the handicapped person).

Script

A schema that describes how a series of events is likely to occur in a well-known situation, and which is used as a guide for behavior and problem solving.

Labels are devices for saving talkative persons the trouble of thinking.

John Morley, English statesman and author, 1838–1923

FIGURE 5.1

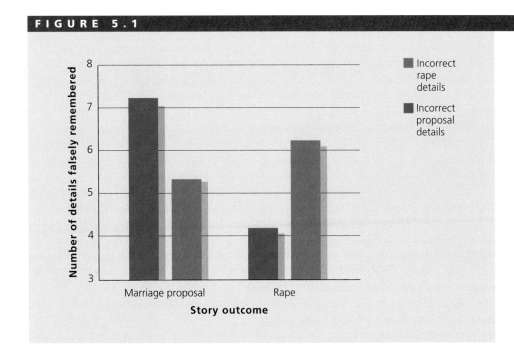

Schemas and Misremembering the Past

Linda Carli (1999) found evidence that people's schemas about a past event shaped their later recall of the event in a way that led them to falsely remember details that never occurred. Those who had read a story about a man raping his girlfriend were more likely to falsely remember details that were consistent with their rape schema, while those who read a story about a man proposing to his girlfriend were more likely to falsely remember details that were consistent with their proposal schema. What implications does this research have for the validity of witnesses' testimony in criminal trials?

Sometimes, however, information is so sharply inconsistent with an existing schema that we take great notice of it and store—or *encode*—it into a new, separate schema (Stangor & McMillan, 1992). With our skinhead, imagine that you learn that he volunteers at a homeless shelter and an AIDS center, and that he strongly believes in social justice and civil rights for all groups. This information may be so inconsistent with your skinhead schema that you spend time thinking about how he could have become a skinhead in the first place. This effortful thinking may result in you forming a new schema for "socially progressive skinheads," while still retaining your more general skinhead schema (see *stereotype subcategories* in chapter 8, p. 268).

Schemas also play an important role in what we remember. However, unlike photographs that freeze exact images of past events, scientific studies indicate that our memories are often sketchy reconstructions of the past. This characterization of memory was first proposed about seventy years ago by the English psychologist Sir Frederic Bartlett (1932). When testing people's memories of stories they had read, Bartlett found that accurate recollections by his participants were rare. Instead, participants seemed to reconstruct the material they had learned, shortening and lengthening different aspects, and changing details overall to better fit their own preexisting schemas. These memory distortions became more pronounced over time, yet Bartlett's participants were largely unaware that they had reconstructed the past. In fact, the reconstructed memories were often those aspects of the story that they most adamantly claimed to be true!

A more recent experiment demonstrating similar effects was conducted by Linda Carli (1999). In this study, college students read a story about a woman named Barbara and a man named Jack who had been dating awhile before going to a ski lodge for the weekend. In one condition of the experiment, Jack proposed marriage to Barbara at the end of the story, whereas in the other condition the story ended with Jack raping Barbara in their lodge room. Two weeks after reading their Jack-Barbara story, participants read several details about the two characters and were asked whether this information appeared in the original story or not. As depicted in figure 5.1, Carli found that in both conditions participants tended to misremember details that were consistent with their original schema for the Barbara and Jack event. Those in the *proposal* condition were likely to falsely remember that "Jack wanted Barbara to meet his parents" and "Jack gave Barbara a dozen roses." Similarly, participants in the *rape* condition were likely to misremember that "Jack was unpopular with women" and "Jack liked to drink."

Schemas Can Be Situationally or Chronically Activated

Schemas help us make sense out of our world, but what activates a schema from memory? Let's return to our chapter-opening story concerning who to seek help from when having car trouble in an unfamiliar city. In our scenario, you were about to flag down a neatly dressed and pleasant-looking young man driving a late-model Chevy, but then you hesitated. Why? Just having seen the movie *Psycho,* you were primed to perceive the world in terms of psychopaths, and this particular person reminded you of the main character in the film. **Priming** is the process by which recent exposure to certain stimuli or events increases the accessibility of certain memories, categories, or schemas. Priming is a good example of automatic thinking because it occurs spontaneously and nonconsciously.

In one priming experiment, Tory Higgins and his colleagues (1977) informed college student volunteers they would be participating in two different and unrelated studies. In the first "perception" study, the participants were asked to identify different colors while simultaneously memorizing a list of words. Some participants in the treatment condition were shown words designed to prime the positive schema of *adventurousness* (such as "brave" or "self-confident") while others were shown words designed to prime the negative schema of *recklessness* (such as "foolish" or "careless"). In the second "reading comprehension" study, the students read a story about a man named Donald who climbed mountains, shot rapids, piloted a jet-powered boat, and drove in a demolition derby. Donald was now planning on trying skydiving or crossing the Atlantic Ocean in a sailboat. What sort of impressions did the participants form of Donald? This was the dependent measure in the study.

Results indicated that it depended on what schemas had been primed. Those who previously memorized words associated with the schema of adventurousness tended to evaluate Donald positively, perceiving him as a likable person who enjoyed challenges. In contrast, those who had memorized words related to the schema of recklessness tended to evaluate Donald negatively, viewing him as a conceited person who took needless risks. In control conditions, when the researchers asked participants in the "perception" study to memorize positive or negative words that were not descriptive of Donald's actions, their later evaluations of him were not influenced by these words. These latter findings are important because they indicate that evaluations of Donald were not shaped by whether participants were first shown words that were simply positive or negative. To have an effect the words had to apply to Donald's actions. Stated differently, the words had to activate a schema that was related to the information about to be presented. Together, the results from this experiment demonstrate that situational cues can activate schemas, and these activated schemas will influence how we perceive new information in our surroundings if that information is relevant to the activated schemas.

Schema activation not only prompts us to think and evaluate others in terms of these organized structures of knowledge, they can also prompt us to physically behave in ways consistent with them. For example, in one experiment John Bargh and his coworkers (1996) asked participants to work on unscrambling word puzzles similar to the one depicted in figure 5.2. For some participants, the puzzles contained words related to the schema for *aging* (such as "elderly" and "slow"), while for others the puzzles included neutral words unrelated to the aging schema (such as "classroom" and "corn"). The researchers hypothesized that for those participants who worked on puzzles with embedded age-related cues, their culturally learned aging schema—a stereotype—would be automatically primed in such a way that it would shape their immediate behavior. Consistent with this prediction, when leaving the experiment, participants whose elderly schema had been primed walked more slowly down a hallway than those who had not been similarly primed.

In the studies discussed thus far, schemas were activated after people consciously focused their attention for a period of time on specific situational cues. Do you think we could activate schemas even if people do not consciously notice the relevant situational cues? What if the situational cue is presented *subliminally,* meaning that it is presented so fast or so faintly that it is just below the absolute threshold for conscious awareness? In another

Priming

The process by which recent exposure to certain stimuli or events increases the accessibility of certain memories, categories, or schemas.

How is the spontaneous self-concept discussed in chapter 3 related to schemas and priming effects?

d	e	g	d	y	i	t	n	d	c	e	f
e	a	g	e	d	a	l	w	m	t	l	t
c	m	e	c	k	n	p	g	a	a	d	s
r	w	j	e	n	c	r	j	e	f	e	e
e	o	p	i	a	i	y	a	u	r	r	n
p	l	d	d	e	e	c	h	y	n	l	i
i	s	w	r	i	n	k	l	e	d	y	l
t	y	p	f	j	t	e	u	g	v	p	e

Activated Schemas Can Effect Behavior: The Word Puzzle Study

How many words can you find in this word puzzle? When John Bargh and his colleagues (1996) asked people to engage in a similar word puzzle task, those who worked on puzzles with embedded aging-related words later walked more slowly down a hallway than people who worked on puzzles containing neutral words. How do these findings support the hypothesis that an aging schema was activated in those who saw the aging-related words?

"Donald" experiment, John Bargh and Paula Pietromonaco (1982) asked people to read a brief story on a computer screen about a salesman knocking on Donald's door and Donald responding by refusing to let the salesman in. The question of interest was how people would interpret Donald's behavior. Was this a hostile response or not? In the treatment group, hostile words such as "unkind" and "hostile" were subliminally flashed on the computer screen just prior to participants reading the story. In the control group, neutral words such as "water" and "between" were used as subliminal primes.

Consistent with the findings from the first "Donald" study, results indicated that participants who were presented with hostile words evaluated Donald as more hostile than those who were presented with neutral words—even though they did not know they had seen the words! These findings not only support the hypothesis that priming is an automatic, nonconscious process, but it also raises the possibility that our social judgments can be unconsciously manipulated. In chapter 7 we will examine in more detail the feasibility of using subliminal messages to substantially alter people's attitudes and behavior.

Thus far we have discussed how schemas can be situationally activated. Yet there are many examples in life where schemas are chronically accessible due to past experiences. For example, imagine observing a parent and child engaged in an animated and loud verbal exchange in a public setting. If you suffered from physical abuse as a child, you may habitually perceive such emotionally ambiguous scenes as signs of impending violence. However, if you grew up in a household where family members regularly expressed themselves in a raucous but loving manner you may expect such situations to end with hugs and smiles. The Applications section at the end of the chapter discusses how people with optimistic versus pessimistic outlooks on life habitually respond in different ways to similar life events. Their contrasting interpretations of positive and negative outcomes can be understood in terms of them having markedly different schemas chronically accessible.

Besides the existence of individual differences in *what* schemas are chronically activated, we may also differ in the *need* to create and use schemas to simplify our understanding of previous experiences. Those of us with a high need for structure or a low tolerance for ambiguity appear to employ more schemas to explain events than those of us who have a low need for structure and a high tolerance for ambiguity (Chiu et al., 2000; Neuberg et al., 1997).

- Sometimes mental operations occur in fixed sequences (serially) and other times they occur simultaneously ("in parallel")
- Dual-process models of social cognition explain how we engage in both automatic, effortless thinking and controlled, effortful thinking
- Social categorization entails classifying people into groups based on common attributes
- Schemas are organized knowledge structures that:

  provide theories about how the social world operates

  hasten information processing and decision making

  influence what information is remembered and later recalled

- Priming makes memories, categories, and schemas more accessible

WHAT SHORTCUTS STRETCH OUR COGNITIVE RESOURCES?

Imagine that you wanted to phone your friend John Smith but did not know his number. You could pull out the phone book and systematically dial every one of the thirty-seven John Smiths until you found the right one. This problem-solving strategy employs an *algorithm,* which involves following a specific step-by-step procedure until you inevitably produce the correct solution. In the dual-process model of cognition, employing algorithms is an example of high-intensity work. However, you could also try to solve this problem by relying on a simple rule of thumb: John is a student and most students live near campus and have a "288" phone prefix. You have just used a *heuristic* to reduce the number of John Smiths to seven. In the dual-process model, heuristics involve low-intensity work. As a problem-solving strategy they save time, but they may not work. What if your John Smith lives far away from campus or uses an unlisted cell phone?

As previously noted, when we adopt the strategy of a cognitive miser we are always on the lookout for time-saving mental shortcuts to help us make social judgments (Higgins, 2000). Amos Tversky and Daniel Kahneman (1974) called these shortcuts **heuristics.** Heuristics require very little thought; people merely take the shortcut and make the judgment. To be useful, heuristics must satisfy two requirements: (1) they must allow us to make quick social judgments, and (2) they must be reasonably accurate. Unfortunately, satisfying the first requirement often works against judgment accuracy (Ajzen, 1996). That is, you can make a quick judgment by ignoring a great deal of potentially relevant information in your environment, but what cost does this have on the accuracy of your judgment? Yet keep in mind that the second requirement of heuristics involves "reasonable" accuracy, not "high" accuracy. With that in mind, let us consider some commonly used mental shortcuts that social psychologists have identified and studied over the years.

Heuristics

Time-saving mental shortcuts that reduce complex judgments to simple rules of thumb.

The Representativeness Heuristic Helps Us Categorize

Representativeness Heuristic

The tendency to judge the category membership of things based on how closely they match the "typical" or "average" member of that category.

During my first few years as a professor, people often mistook me for a student. Why was this so? Well, to them I did not fit their image of what a university professor looked like. This judgment is an example of the **representativeness heuristic,** which is the tendency to judge the category membership of things based on how closely they match the prototype of that category (Gilovich & Savitsky, 2002; Kahneman & Tversky, 1973). Because I looked younger than my age, and because I dressed more casually than most professors, people guessed I was a student.

The representativeness heuristic helps people to quickly decide in what categories to place others. It is essentially stereotyping operating in reverse. That is, when we stereotype someone, we first place them in a particular social category and then infer that they possess the personal attributes associated with people in that category. When we rely on the representativeness heuristic, we merely reverse this cognitive process: because a person possesses attributes we associate with a particular social category, we infer that they must be a member of that category. The old saying "If it looks like a duck and if it quacks like a duck, then it probably is a duck" is an example of the representativeness heuristic.

Although this cognitive shortcut is a rapid method of identifying people, it does not consider other important qualifying information. The most important information relates to *base rates*—the frequency with which some event or pattern occurs in the general population. The tendency to overlook base-rate information was demonstrated in a study by Tversky and Kahneman (1973). Research participants were told that an imaginary person named Jack had been selected from a group of a hundred men. Some were told that thirty of the men were engineers (a base rate for engineers of 30 percent), and others were told that seventy were engineers (a base rate of 70 percent). Half the participants were given no other information, but the other half were given a description of Jack that either fit the common stereotype of engineers (for example, practical, likes to work with numbers) or did not. They were then asked to guess the probability that Jack was an engineer.

Results indicated that when participants received only information related to base rates, they were more likely to guess that Jack was an engineer when the base rate was 70 percent than when it was 30 percent. However, when they received information about Jack's personality and behavior, they tended to ignore the base-rate information and, instead, focus on whether Jack fit their image of an engineer. The tendency to ignore or underuse useful base-rate information and overuse personal descriptors of the individual being judged has been called the *base-rate fallacy*.

The Availability Heuristic Bases Judgment on Ease of Recall

I have a friend who was planning to purchase a new car, and I asked her if she was considering a particular brand that had received excellent reliability ratings in *Consumer Reports*. Her reply was no, because she knew a few people who had that type of car and were not satisfied with its reliability. In nixing this car from her list, my friend was basing her judgment on how easily she could recall those negative experiences of others. The **availability heuristic** is the tendency to judge the frequency or probability of an event in terms of how easy it is to think of examples of that event (Kunda, 1999; Tversky & Kahneman, 1973). Thus, in judging the reliability of this car model, my friend quickly sampled the information accessible in her memory to see how many examples came to mind. If the information in memory had been reasonably representative of the actual reliability of these cars, relying on the availability heuristic would have resulted in an accurate assessment. Unfortunately, this was not the case here.

In the use of the availability heuristic, the most important factor for people is not the *content* of their memory recall but the *ease* with which this content comes to mind (Higgins, 2000; Schwarz & Vaughn, 2002). For example, Norbert Schwarz and his colleagues (1991b) found that participants who were asked to recall twelve examples of their own assertive behaviors (a difficult cognitive task) subsequently rated themselves as less assertive than participants who were asked to recall only six examples (an easy cognitive task). Similar results were obtained for participants who were asked to recall examples of their unassertive behaviors (refer to figure 5.3). The implication here is that people pay attention to how easy or difficult it is for them to recall examples of a particular event or behavior in making attributions. They only rely on the content of their recall (for example, assertive behavior) if its implications are not called into question by the difficulty they experience in bringing the relevant material to mind. Thus, individuals would conclude that they must not be assertive if it is difficult to recall personal examples of assertive behavior in their past.

In general, availability is a fairly valid cue for the judgment of frequency, because frequent events are more likely than infrequent events to be stored in memory and later recalled. If a doctor is seeing patients during the height of the flu season, the fact that he

CRITICAL *thinking*

If the representativeness heuristic is stereotyping operating in reverse, does that mean that stereotyping is also a heuristic?

Availability Heuristic

The tendency to judge the frequency or probability of an event in terms of how easy it is to think of examples of that event.

FIGURE 5.3

People judged themselves to be more or less assertive based on how many examples of assertive or unassertive behaviors they were asked to recall from their past. For example, when asked to recall six examples of assertive behavior, they subsequently rated themselves as more assertive than when asked to recall twelve examples. The same pattern of findings occurred for unassertive behavior. How do these findings support the existence of the availability heuristic?

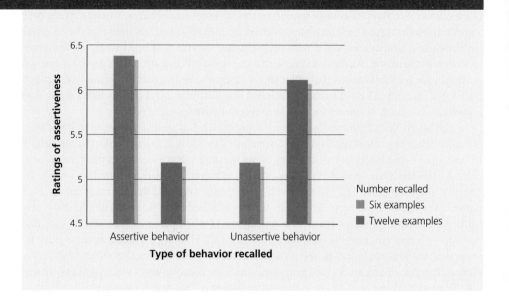

Anchoring and Adjustment Heuristic

A tendency to be biased toward the starting value or anchor in making quantitative judgments.

can easily bring the flu virus to mind will influence how many patients he diagnoses with this ailment. A busy doctor may quickly diagnose ailments as normal influenza and make correct judgments 99.9 percent of the time. But with "the flu" on his mind, he is also more likely to misdiagnose a far more serious ailment as simple influenza (Weber et al., 1993).

The Anchoring and Adjustment Heuristic Helps Us Make Estimations

Do you think the population of Cincinnati, Ohio, is more than 100,000? Yes is the correct answer. Now estimate Cincinnati's actual population, and then check on page 149 for the correct answer. If, instead of asking whether Cincinnati's population is *more than 100,000,* I had asked whether it is *less than 1,000,000,* your answer to the second question probably would have been higher. The reason this effect often happens is because we want to be correct in our judgments. In trying to meet this goal, our quantitative judgments are often biased toward an initial anchor point—in our example, this was the 100,000 figure. Later when making our estimate, we use this anchor as our starting point and, thus, usually insufficiently adjust toward the correct answer. This mental bias is known as the **anchoring and adjustment heuristic** (Epley & Gilovich, 2001; Tversky & Kahneman, 1974).

As demonstrated in a survey study Scott Plous (1989) conducted, the anchoring and adjustment heuristic can affect our social judgments. Respondents were first asked whether they thought there was greater than a 1 percent chance of a nuclear war occurring soon. Other respondents were asked whether nuclear war had less than a 90 percent chance of occurring soon. All respondents were then asked to estimate the likelihood of such a war occurring soon. Those who started from the 1 percent anchor guessed at a 10 percent risk factor, while those who started from the 90 percent anchor estimated the risk of nuclear war to be 25 percent.

Like other heuristics, anchoring and adjustment can help us make correct judgments. For example, imagine that you inherit an old painting from a distant relative and are trying to determine its value for resale. You notice that a local antique store is selling a similar old painting for $400, and that painting is in slightly better condition than your piece. In estimating a value for your painting you might start with that price, and then adjust downward slightly. In many instances, this would probably provide you with a quick and fairly accurate way to judge the painting's value. However, there are instances when people greatly overvalue their antiques because they think their pieces are similar to something they saw on Public Television's *Antiques Road Show* that was judged to be a masterpiece.

Why are we influenced by arbitrary numbers? In making a judgment, when we are given a number or value as a starting point, we appear to selectively recall information from memory that is consistent with this anchor (Chapman & Johnson, 1999; Mussweiler & Strack, 2000). Thus, after starting with the modest price of the antique store painting as the anchor value, you are likely to remember instances when other people sold antiques at a similar modest price. However, if your painting's anchor is the high price from the *Antiques Road Show,* you are likely to recall from memory stories of people discovering they had inherited masterpieces worth millions. In a very real sense, the anchor becomes a situational cue that triggers relevant memories, just as priming people with words can activate relevant schemas (refer back to the "Donald" experiments, pp. 144–145). In both instances, people's automatic, effortless thinking has an effect on the way they make judgments (Chapman & Johnson, 2002).

Heuristic Thinking Is Not (Generally) "Stupid Thinking"

Examining the research on heuristics may lead you to conclude that we are irrational decision makers, with distortions and errors being the most common end products of social thinking. In fact, John Kihlstrom (2004) half-jokingly suggests that social psychology has informally developed a new school of thought that he calls the "People Are Stupid" perspective. Similarly, other social psychologists assert that many experts within the field are too quick to conclude that our demonstrated cognitive biases reveal a fundamental flaw in social cognition (Krueger & Funder, 2004). Is "stupid thinking" the right descriptor for the relatively effortless process we engage in when using heuristics (and schemas)? Do we need to develop social programs to teach people how to set aside heuristics and think with effort and reason?

Although basing decisions on heuristics may lead to errors and may be motivated by lazy thinking, relying on them can actually be adaptive under conditions where we do not have the luxury of systematically analyzing all our options (Johnston et al., 1997; Klein, 1996). For example, reacting quickly in an emergency based only on information that is most accessible from memory (the availability heuristic) may often be the difference between life and death. Sure, heuristics can lead to sloppy decision making. But their time-saving quality may sometimes be a lifesaver. It is this quality that makes heuristics such valuable devices in the motivated-tactician's cognitive toolbox.

Cincinnati has a population of 364,000.

From an evolutionary perspective, human beings can be thought of as having evolved a large number of mental strategies to adapt to their surroundings. In this regard, heuristics and other effortless thinking have been very helpful to us because they yield reasonably accurate and adaptive results under most environmental conditions (Figueredo et al., 2004). If these heuristics were eliminated from human decision making, social judgment accuracy would get much worse, not better.

If the use of heuristics is considered to more often be a part of "useful thinking" rather than "stupid thinking," with what frequency do we pull these mental shortcuts out of our cognitive toolbox when making social judgments? Are we constantly cutting corners, or is it a rare occurrence? Common experience and social psychologists' best reasoned analysis suggest that we do not always rely on heuristics. Often we systematically analyze a situation using a variety of information. Research has identified the following conditions that are most likely to lead to the use of heuristics rather than more careful decision making (Macrae et al., 1993; Ruder & Bless, 2003):

1. We simply do not have *time* to engage in systematic analysis.

2. We are *overloaded with information* so that it is impossible to process all that is meaningful and relevant.

3. We consider the issues in question to be *not very important.*

4. We have *little other knowledge* or information to use in making a decision.

5. Something about the situation calls to mind a given heuristic, making it *cognitively available* (priming).

6. We are in a *positive mood,* signaling to us that everything is fine and no effortful thinking is necessary.

CRITICAL *thinking*

In the days and weeks following the suicide attacks at the Pentagon and World Trade Center by Arab terrorists, FBI offices around the country were flooded with calls from citizens reporting possible leads and suspects. Virtually every person who was perceived as being suspicious was of Arab descent. What cognitive heuristic was being used in making these social judgments? Why do you think people were relying on this heuristic?

- Heuristics allow quick judgments with minimal cognitive effort, but can cause biased and inaccurate judgments
- The representativeness heuristic *involves* judging the category membership of things based on how closely they match the prototype for that category
- The availability heuristic involves judging the probability of an event in terms of how easy it is to think of examples of it
- The anchoring and adjustment heuristic involves being biased toward the starting value or anchor in making quantitative judgments
- Using heuristics is adaptive, especially under conditions that hinder systematic analysis

WHAT ARE SOME WAYS OF THINKING ABOUT THE PAST?

In chapters 1 and 4 we discussed how imagining future events can help us construct effective self-presentations and anticipate possible outcomes. In chapter 3 we discussed how imagining our future self can motivate current behavior. Yet what about past events? We spend a lot of time "thinking about the past." For example, I recently discovered that this phrase yields 13,540 hits on the Internet. Earlier in this chapter we discussed how our recollection of past events is subject to alteration and reconstruction. What are some other ways that past events affect our thinking?

Simulating Past Events Can Alter Our Social Judgments

Our social judgments are sometimes shaped by our ability to actively imagine or *mentally simulate* events (Kahneman & Tversky, 1982). Throughout our lives, we invent imaginary scenarios of past, future, and alternative social realities. To imagine an event, we must temporarily assume that it is true. This fact sometimes causes the line between real and imagined events to become blurred in memory. As a result, the more often we imagine a particular scenario, the more likely we are to believe that it is possible (Heath et al., 1991). For example, you may have never feared that your romantic partner might be unfaithful until your best friend's lover is disloyal. This event may cause you to imagine how you would react in a similar scenario. Although your friend's betrayal does not involve you or your partner, simply imagining this event now leads to you more likely believing that your partner could be unfaithful.

Mental simulations play an important role in how jurors make decisions during courtroom trials. Beyond simply agreeing on the facts of the case, jurors must also agree on the *meaning* of those facts. Nancy Pennington and Reid Hastie (1992) believe that in attempting to impose this meaning on the presented evidence, individual jurors construct one or more plausible accounts or *stories* that explain the motives of the key players in the case. This *story model* of juror decision making hypothesizes that of the various stories jurors construct, the one that can organize the most evidence in the most cohesive fashion will be the one they use in rendering their final verdict. Research not only supports this hypothesis but also indicates that when evidence fits into a juror's cohesive story, that juror is more likely to consider it important, regardless of its actual strength or weakness (Pennington & Hastie, 1992).

Based on this evidence, you might think that all attorneys would emphasize storytelling in presenting their cases to juries. To an extent, this is true—both sides in a trial have a story to tell. However, the *way* evidence is presented in a court case may either highlight the story or highlight the witnesses. In the *story order* format, attorneys present witnesses in the sequence corresponding to the story they want jurors to believe. In the *witness order* format, lawyers present witnesses in the sequence meant to have the greatest impact, even if this means that evidence is presented out of sequence to the story they want jurors to believe. For example, imagine that Spencer is charged with embezzling $25,000 from a bank where he was a cashier. The crime took place on June 18. A prosecuting attorney using a story order would present his witnesses in the following manner:

1. Spencer's girlfriend testifies that she threatened to leave him on June 15 because he never had money to buy her gifts.

2. The bank janitor testifies that he saw a large sum of money in Spencer's gym bag at 3:00 P.M. on June 18.

3. The bank manager testifies that she noticed a $25,000 discrepancy in the bank books at 5:15 P.M. on June 18.

4. A local jeweler testifies that Spencer bought a $3,000 necklace at 6:30 P.M. on June 18, using cash in the transaction.

In contrast to this sequential presentation of the evidence, a prosecutor using a witness order might save his best witness, the bank janitor, for last, so that the trial ends with dramatic testimony. This sort of dramatic finish to a trial is the presentation style commonly depicted in TV criminal law series (that's why they call them "dramas"). Is one of these presentation styles more successful than the other? Not surprisingly, Pennington and Hastie believe that the story order will be more convincing to a jury than the witness order.

To test this hypothesis, they asked mock jurors to listen to a simulated trial in which the defense attorney and the prosecuting attorney varied the *way* in which they presented their cases (Pennington & Hastie, 1988). In one condition the attorneys both used the story order, in another condition they both used the witness order, and in the two remaining conditions they used opposing presentation orders. Results indicated that presenting evidence in the sequence that events occurred in one's desired story was the best strategy, especially when the opposing attorney relied on witness impact rather than story order. As you can see in table 5.1, when the defense used the story order and the prosecutor used the witness order, the jurors voted to convict only 31 percent of the time. When the tables were reversed so that the prosecutor used the story order and the defense employed the witness order, jurors convicted 78 percent of the time. These findings suggest that although dramatic testimony plays well in TV jury dramas, in real-life trials juries are more convinced by plausible stories.

The Hindsight Bias Is Fueled by Our Desire for Sense Making

When recalling past events we often believe that we "knew all along" how things would turn out. After learning that your friend's lover has been unfaithful, you might think, "I could see this coming for some time." Or after your favorite sports team defeats its archrival for the

---

TABLE 5.1

How Should Lawyers Present Their Evidence to the Jury?

Pennington and Hastie (1988) found that the best strategy for both prosecutors and defense attorneys was to present the evidence in the order that corresponds most closely to their desired story (story order), especially when the opposing attorney presented witnesses in the sequence meant to have the greatest impact (witness order).

Percentage of Jurors Voting to Convict Defendant

Prosecution Evidence	Defense Evidence	
	Story Order	Witness Order
Story order	59%	78%
Witness order	31%	63%

Based on what you have learned about the presentation of evidence during a jury trial, how should attorneys present witnesses? In the sequence corresponding to the story they want jurors to believe (story order), or in the sequence meant to have the greatest impact (witness order)?

Hindsight Bias

The tendency, once an event has occurred, to overestimate our ability to have foreseen the outcome.

I just knew I should have picked door number two.

Let's Make a Deal TV-show contestant

first time in years you exclaim, "All week long I could tell that my team would win!" In such instances, this after-the-fact overestimation of our ability to have foreseen the outcome is known as the **hindsight bias** (Blank et al., 2003; Hawkins & Hastie, 1990).

Cross-cultural studies indicate that the hindsight bias occurs throughout the world (Pohl et al., 2002). Why does it occur? It is our desire for *sense making* that fuels the hindsight bias, and we are most likely to rewrite our memory of a past event when the outcome is initially surprising (Pezzo, 2003). When thinking about a past event that had a surprising outcome, we appear to selectively recall information in constructing a plausible story that is consistent with the now-known outcome (Schwarz & Stahlberg, 2003). This "rewriting" of how events occurred allow us to insert the missing causal connections so that the story makes sense given the outcome. Claiming hindsight reassures us that we understand—and can anticipate—events in our world. Unfortunately, this confidence is false, and engaging in this sort of cognitive biasing can interfere with our ability to learn from the past.

Hindsight biasing can and does occur right after an event's outcome is known, but it tends to gain strength over time as we increasingly forget our earlier beliefs about what we thought would happen (Bryant & Guilbault, 2002). However, not all unexpected events produce the hindsight bias. It does not occur for events that are so unusual that you simply cannot think of any good reasons for why they would occur (Pezzo, 2003). For instance, few people showed much hindsight bias for the September 11, 2001, terrorist attacks or the 2000 Bush-Gore election results. These events were so bizarre that people could not easily reconstruct their memory of the prior events in a way that would allow them to think that they foresaw the final outcomes. The hindsight bias is also unlikely to occur if the sense making threatens self-esteem. For example, if you were among a group of employees laid off at work, do you think you would be more or less likely to claim that "there were many warning signals" than if you were merely an unaffected observer of these layoffs?

In one study that explored this question, people living near a factory were surveyed about their beliefs and opinions about recent factory layoffs (Mark & Mellor, 1991). Results indicated that townspeople who did not work at the factory and were not personally affected by the layoffs were most likely to claim that they knew the layoffs were coming (high hindsight bias). People who worked at the factory but kept their jobs were less likely to claim hindsight. Those who expressed the greatest surprise (no hindsight bias) were the workers who lost their jobs. These results and the findings from other studies suggest that, although we often engage in the hindsight bias when explaining past events, we are less likely to do so when those events affect us personally *and* are negative (Hoelzl et al., 2002; Mark et al., 2003). That is, we are less likely to claim hindsight for negative outcomes because claiming ignorance allows us to avoid blaming ourselves: "If I could not foresee being laid off, I cannot be blamed for not working harder or changing jobs."

Counterfactual Thinking Is Most Likely Following Negative and Unexpected Events

Besides our social judgments being shaped by simulating *actual* past events, they are also affected by the ease with which we can imagine *alternative* versions and outcomes of past events. Remember our chapter-opening imaginary scenario in which you learned about two people killed in a train crash, one a regular commuter and the other a first-time rider? Why did the first-time rider's death seem more tragic? As you ponder this question, imagine the following day at the ski slopes:

> Hector loves to snow ski but is cautious and never goes down the expert slope. Yesterday, however, he tried it and broke his leg. Martina also loves to ski and frequently goes down the expert slope. Yesterday she broke her leg going down this slope.

Research suggests that the majority of us believe that Hector will feel the greatest regret following his injury, and most of us will also express greater sympathy toward him than toward Martina, just as we will perceive the death of the first-time train rider as more tragic than that of the frequent rider (Roese et al., 1999). The reason for these different judgments is that we engage in **counterfactual thinking,** which is the tendency to evaluate events by imagining alternative versions or outcomes (Kahneman, 1995; Segura & McCloy, 2003). We are most likely to engage in counterfactual thinking following negative and unexpected events, and the thoughts that are generated usually deal with how the negative outcome might have been prevented (Mandel & Lehman, 1996; Sanna & Turley, 1996). Regarding Hector and Martina, it is easier for us to imagine that Hector would be uninjured if he had not deviated from his normal cautious skiing style than it is to imagine this altered outcome for Martina, given her tendency to take greater risks on the slopes. It is also easier to imagine that the first-time train rider would be alive if her regular form of transportation had been available than it is to imagine this altered outcome for the regular commuter. Because it is easier to undo Hector's broken leg and the first-time rider's death through counterfactual thinking ("If only they had stuck to their usual routines . . ."), we are more likely to feel sympathy for them. When our skiers engage in this same "What if . . . ?" thinking, Hector will experience greater regret over his injury than Martina, for the same reasons as do we.

Why do we engage in counterfactual thinking? Neal Roese (1997) suggests two possible functions served by these "What if . . . ?" thoughts. First, they may simply help us feel better following a negative outcome. Following a traffic accident in which your car is damaged, you may think, "At least I didn't get hurt." By imagining an even worse outcome, your accident seems less negative by contrast (Sanna et al., 2001). Besides helping us emotionally cope in the present, a second function of counterfactual thoughts may be to better prepare us for the future. By considering alternatives to past actions, we can better understand our mistakes and thereby improve our chances for future success (Galinsky & Moskowitz, 2000). For example, after doing poorly on an exam, you may mentally imagine alternative study strategies that you could have used, such as memorizing key terms or working through the study guide. If you implement these new strategies in preparing for your next exam, you may improve your grade.

Summarizing these two functions, then, we can say that imagining alternative versions or outcomes to what actually happened may not only help us emotionally cope with negative events, but it may also help us to achieve success in the future. Unfortunately, as discussed in chapter 3 (p. 65), the sustaining of negative affect is often necessary to motivate behavioral change. When counterfactual thinking is used to emotionally cope with a negative event, our improved mood can reduce our motivation to take corrective steps to avoid similar negative events in the future (McMullen & Markman, 2000).

Sometimes counterfactual thinking is not only ineffective in emotionally coping with negative events, it is downright counterproductive. This is most likely following traumatic

CRITICAL *thinking*

Why might a neuroscientist argue that the hindsight bias is triggered by some of the same neurological activity that creates the storyline of dreams?

*Oh God! That it were possible
To undo things done, to call back yesterday!
That Time could turn up his swift sandy glass,
To untell the days, and to redeem these hours.*

Thomas Heywood, English dramatist, 1574–1641

Counterfactual Thinking

The tendency to evaluate events by imagining alternative versions or outcomes to what actually happened.

For Better or For Worse®   **by Lynn Johnston**

life events when the reality is already the worst-case scenario. For instance, Christopher Davis and his coworkers (1995) interviewed people who had lost a spouse or a child in an accident. The more they imagined how the tragedy could have been averted by mentally undoing events preceding it, the more distress and guilt they felt. This tendency to engage in counterfactual thinking following traumatic life events also helps to explain why crime victims often blame themselves for their victimization (C. Davis et al., 1996). In trying to understand how their plight could have been avoided, victims tend to focus on trivial aspects of their own behavior rather than on the causally more significant behavior of the perpetrator. If they can imagine some plausible way in which they *could* have prevented the crime, they may come to believe that they *should* have prevented it. Although crime victims who engage in such counterfactual thinking may not blame themselves for being the cause of their injuries, they may blame themselves for not avoiding the situation that was the cause (Mandel, 2003; Miller & Turnbull, 1990).

SECTION SUMMARY

- Mentally simulating events can alter social thinking
- The hindsight bias involves overestimating our ability to have foreseen the outcome of an event
- Counterfactual thinking involves evaluating events by imagining alternative versions or outcomes

HOW DO EXPECTATIONS SHAPE OUR SOCIAL THINKING?

The beliefs we hold about how the social world operates shape many of our judgments and decisions. In this section, we examine our tendency to believe that others think and behave as we do (*false consensus*), our tendency to think and behave in ways that verify our beliefs (*confirmation bias* and *self-fulfilling prophecies*), our tendency to believe that the world is fair (*just-world belief*), and our tendency to stop trying after repeated failure (*learned helplessness*).

We Expect That Others Have Similar Views as Us

A man never discloses his own character so clearly as when he describes another's.

Johann Richter, German author, 1763–1825

If someone asked you to wear a sign around campus with a quirky message written on it like "Eat at Joe's," would you agree to do so? What percentage of your fellow students do you think would wear the sign? Although I don't know whether you would consent or refuse this hypothetical request, I am fairly confident that you think your peers would respond like you would. My confidence is based on the fact that we tend to perceive our own opinions as fairly typical. In many instances, however, this perception is wrong. The tendency to believe that our own attitudes, opinions, and beliefs are more common than they really are is known as the **false consensus effect** (Gross & Miller, 1997; Muller et al., 2002). This overestimation of the degree to which others endorse our views is most pronounced when the others are from our ingroup (Karasawa, 2003).

The first study to demonstrate the false consensus effect actually asked college students the question I asked you: Would you walk around campus for thirty minutes wearing a large sandwich board sign with the message, "Eat at Joe's" (Ross et al., 1977b)? Some students agreed and some refused. They were then asked to estimate the percentage of students who would make the same choice they made. Students who had agreed to wear the sign estimated that 62 percent of their peers would also agree, while those who had refused estimated that 67 percent of their peers would also refuse.

What explains the false consensus effect? One likely possibility is that false consensus is a product of the previously discussed availability heuristic. That is, we may often assume others share our attitudes and opinions because our own self-beliefs are easily recalled from memory. In a very real sense, then, our self-concept serves as the lens through which we view others (Alicke et al., 1996; Kulig, 2000).

Although the false consensus effect often occurs when we consider our attitudes and opinions, what happens when we judge the extent to which others possess our most prized and desirable traits and abilities? In such instances, we often underestimate the degree to which these desirable qualities are found in the population (Goethals et al., 1991). This tendency to believe that our desirable traits and abilities are less common than they really are is known as the **false uniqueness effect.** False uniqueness appears to be a product of the *self-serving bias* (see chapter 4, p. 126), which is the tendency to more often attribute positive than negative traits to ourselves. Together, these two different tendencies of personal exaggeration are a direct result of us filtering our social judgments through our self-concepts. When it comes to attitudes and opinions, we see ourselves more closely aligned with others than what is actually so (false consensus). However, when considering our socially valued traits and abilities, we are motivated to perceive them as less commonplace than they are (false uniqueness).

We Expect to Find Confirmation for Our Beliefs

When you think you have a solution to a problem, you may fall victim to the **confirmation bias,** which is the tendency to seek only information that verifies your beliefs (Frey & Schulz-Hardt, 2001; Jonas et al., 2001). Unfortunately, such selective attention inhibits problem solving when your solution is incorrect.

In one confirmation-bias study, college students were given the three-number sequence 2-4-6 and told to discover the rule used to generate it (Wason, 1960). Before announcing their beliefs about the rule (which is simply any three increasing numbers), students could make up their own number sequences, and the experimenter told them whether these sequences fit the rule. They were instructed to announce the rule only after receiving feedback from enough self-generated number sequences to feel certain that they knew the correct solution. True to the confirmation bias, 80 percent of the students convinced themselves of an incorrect rule. Typically, they would begin with a wrong hypothesis (for example, adding by twos) and then search only for confirming evidence (testing 8-10-12, 20-22-24, 19-21-23, etc.). Had they tried to disconfirm this hypothesis by testing other number sequences that simply increased in value (for example, 1-2-3 or 10-19-39), they would have realized their error. But their bias toward confirmation ruled out this important hypothesis-testing step.

How might this tendency to seek confirming information affect our social beliefs? In one experiment, Mark Snyder and William Swann (1978) asked research participants to find out whether the person they were about to interact with was an introvert, or an extravert, depending on the experimental condition. Consistent with the confirmation bias, the questions that participants asked their interaction partner were biased in the direction of the original question. For instance, if they had been asked to find out whether the person was an introvert, they asked questions such as, "What do you dislike about loud parties?" or "In what situations do you wish you could be more outgoing?" However, in the extravert condition,

they asked questions such as, "How do you liven things up at a party?" or "What kind of situations help you to meet new people?" Because most people can recall both introverted and extraverted incidents from their past, the interaction partners' answers provided confirmatory evidence for either personality trait. Experiments like this indicate that one barrier to accurate social judgments can be our tendency to search for information that will confirm our beliefs more energetically than we pursue information that might refute them (Edwards & Smith, 1996). Such confirmation-seeking not only leads to mistakes about individuals, but also perpetuates incorrect stereotypes about social groups (Yzerbyt et al., 1996).

We are more likely to engage in the confirmation bias when the situation we are analyzing is one in which we are personally invested and the possible solution is agreeable to us rather than threatening (Dawson et al., 2002). Faced with an agreeable possible solution, we are motivated to confirm it, and we ask ourselves, "*Can* I believe this?" In such situations our standards of judgment are rather permissive, paving the way for the confirmation bias. On the other hand, when the possible solution is threatening or disagreeable, we adopt a more stringent standard of judgment and instead ask "*Must* I believe this?" This latter question prompts more critical analysis, increasing the likelihood that any flaws or limitations in the available evidence will be discovered (Ditto et al., 1998).

Although the confirmation bias is traditionally thought of as being caused by people taking cognitive shortcuts in problem solving (the cognitive miser perspective), another view is that we may engage in the confirmation bias due to our desire to get along with others. Belgian social psychologists Jacques-Philippe Leyens and Benoit Dardenne argue that we sometimes adopt a confirmation-seeking strategy during getting-acquainted sessions to smooth the interaction and give others the impression that we understand them (Leyens, 1990; Leyens & Dardenne, 1994). For example, when a new acquaintance says that she prefers working alone and is shy, asking her *matching questions* (for example, "Do you prefer to spend your evenings reading a novel?") is more likely to result in a smooth and comfortable conversation than asking *nonmatching questions* (for example, "Do you like noisy and crowded parties?").

Research by Dardenne and Leyens (1995) indicates that such a matching strategy is more likely to be used by high self-monitoring individuals than those low in self-monitoring because high self-monitors know better what is appropriate to do with or say to others in specific social situations. This suggests that the interaction style adopted by socially skilled people is more likely to lead to a confirmation bias than the style adopted by those who are less socially skilled. Socially skilled individuals are more likely to use this flawed problem-solving strategy not necessarily because they are lazy thinkers, but rather, because they desire to be liked by those they are getting to know.

This alternative explanation of the confirmation bias makes sense from our motivated-tactician perspective. Instead of thinking of this bias as always being caused by flawed problem solving, we can also see it as sometimes being a by-product of exercising a social skill. As a motivated tactician, the socially skilled person sometimes adopts a flawed confirmation-seeking strategy because it helps them to better adjust to their immediate social surroundings: their desire to be liked supersedes their desire to be accurate. This does not necessarily mean that socially skilled people make more social judgment errors due to their interaction style. According to Dardenne and Leyens, what social psychologists from the cognitive miser perspective identify as social judgment errors may often be very practical and useful cognitive strategies that not only lead to "good-enough" social judgments, but also promote liking for those who employ them because they make others feel socially at ease.

Our Expectations Can Become Self-Fulfilling Prophecies

The confirmation bias highlights how our expectations often become the blueprint in defining social reality. In 1948, sociologist Robert Merton introduced the concept of the **self-fulfilling prophecy** to describe a situation in which someone's expectations about a person or group actually lead to the fulfillment of those expectations. As Merton described it:

> The self-fulfilling prophecy is, in the beginning, a *false* definition of the situation evoking a new behavior which makes the originally false conception come *true*. The specious validity

Self-Fulfilling Prophecy

The process by which someone's expectations about a person or group leads to the fulfillment of those expectations.

FIGURE 5.4

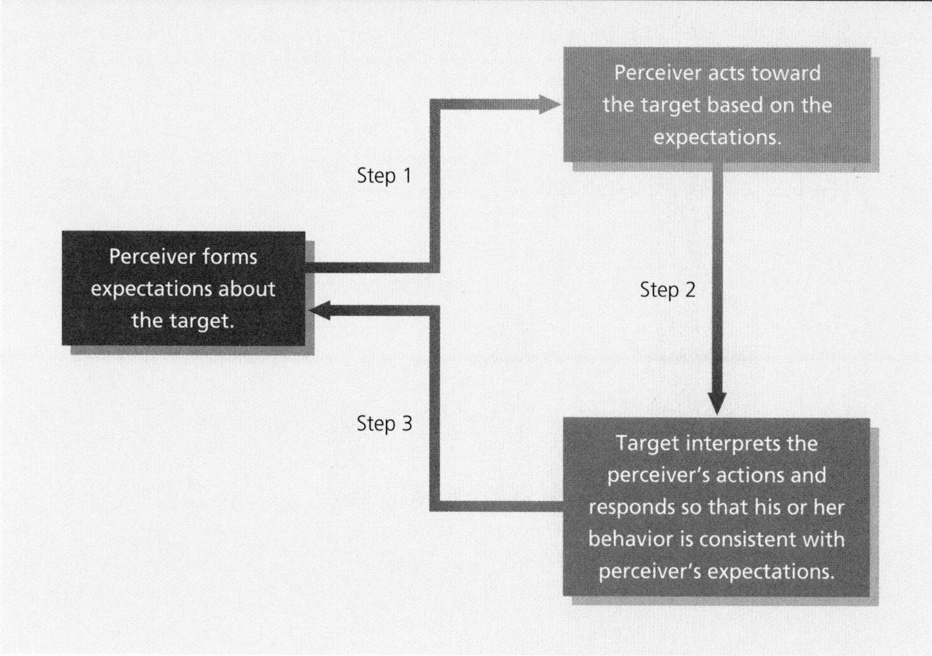

Step 1 — Perceiver forms expectations about the target. → Perceiver acts toward the target based on the expectations.

Step 2 — Target interprets the perceiver's actions and responds so that his or her behavior is consistent with perceiver's expectations.

Step 3

The Development of a Self-Fulfilling Prophecy

Self-fulfilling prophecies often develop as a three-step process. In step 1, the perceiver forms expectations about the target. In step 2, the perceiver behaves in a manner consistent with those expectations. In step 3, the target responds to the perceiver's actions in a manner that unwittingly confirms the perceiver's initial beliefs. The more interactions the target has with the perceiver, and the more this three-step process is repeated during those interactions, the more likely it is that the target will internalize the perceiver's expectations into his or her own self-concept. What personal qualities in a perceiver and in a target would make a self-fulfilling prophecy more or less likely?

of the self-fulfilling prophecy perpetuates a reign of error. For the prophet will cite the actual course of events as proof that he was right from the very beginning. (Merton, 1948, p. 195)

The self-fulfilling prophecy involves a three-step process (refer to figure 5.4). First, the perceiver (the "prophet") forms an impression of the target person. Second, the perceiver acts toward the target person in a manner consistent with this first impression. In response, the target person's behavior changes to correspond to the perceiver's actions (Diekmann et al., 2003; Reich, 2004). Research indicates that behavior changes due to self-fulfilling prophecies can be remarkably long-lasting (Smith et al., 1999).

The most famous empirical demonstration of the self-fulfilling prophecy was a study conducted by Robert Rosenthal and Lenore Jacobson (1968) in a South San Francisco elementary school. In this study, the researchers first gave IQ tests to children and then met with their teachers to share the results. At these information sessions, teachers were told that the tests identified certain students in their classroom as "potential bloomers" who should experience substantial IQ gains during the remaining school year. In reality, this information was merely part of the experimental manipulation. The children identified as potential bloomers had been randomly selected by the researchers and did not differ from their classmates in any systematic way. Although the potential-blooming label was fabricated for these children (approximately 20 percent of the class), Rosenthal and Jacobson hypothesized that the teachers' subsequent expectations would be sufficient to enhance the academic performance of these students. Eight months later, when the students were again tested, this hypothesis was confirmed. The potential bloomers not only exhibited improved schoolwork, they also showed higher gains on their IQ scores than those in the control group (see figure 5.5).

Follow-up studies indicated that students who are positively labeled in this manner tend to be treated differently by their teachers (Jussim, 1989; Rosenthal, 2002). First, teachers create a warmer *socioemotional climate* for these students than for those who are perceived less positively. Second, they provide these gifted students with more *feedback* on their academic performance than they do to their average students. Third, they *challenge* these positively labeled students with more difficult material than the rest of the class. Finally, they provide these students with a *greater opportunity to respond* to presented material in class. The positively labeled students are likely to assume either that the teacher especially likes them and has good judgment or that the teacher is a likable person. Whichever attribution is made, it is likely that the positively labeled students will work harder and begin thinking about themselves as high achievers. Through this behavioral and self-concept change, the prophecy is fulfilled.

FIGURE 5.5

Percentage of Schoolchildren Whose IQ Test Scores Improved Over the Course of the School Year Due to the Self-Fulfilling Prophecy

Those first- and second-grade students who were identified as "potential bloomers" showed a significant improvement in their IQ test scores during the course of the school year. In actuality, these students were randomly chosen for the "potential blooming" category—they did not differ from the other students in any way. Yet, their teachers' expectations that they were "gifted" resulted in those students being challenged more in class, which caused the bloomers to try harder and to learn more. The same social psychological mechanisms that result in beneficial self-fulfilling prophecies can also operate in reverse, causing normally capable children to believe that they are intellectually inferior to others. What types of schoolchildren are most likely to be categorized in this negative manner?

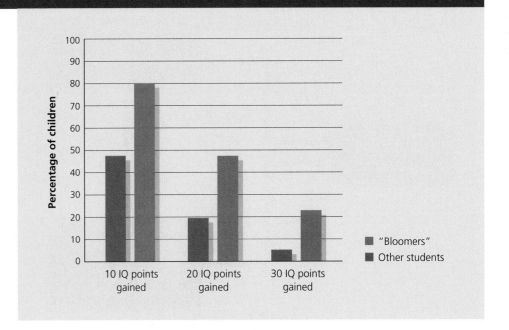

Imaginations which people have of one another are the solid facts of society.

Charles Horton Cooley, American sociologist, 1864–1929

If three people say you are an ass, put on a bridle.

Spanish proverb

Unfortunately, not all self-fulfilling prophecies are of the positive sort. Teachers and fellow students often treat children who are negatively labeled as "troubled" or "disruptive" in a way that reinforces the negative label so that it is more likely to be internalized (Rosenthal, 2003; Weinstein, 2002). To better understand this sort of negative self-concept change, Monica Harris and her colleagues (1992) studied the impact of *negative expectancies* on children's social interactions. In their research, sixty-eight pairs of unacquainted boys in third through sixth grade played together on two different tasks. The researchers designated one of the boys in the pairing as the *perceiver* and the other boy the *target.* Half the target boys had been previously diagnosed as being hyperactive, and the rest of the participants—the remaining targets and all the perceivers—had no history of behavioral problems. Prior to playing together, perceivers in the *hyperactive expectancy condition* were told—independently of their partner's actual behavior—that their partner had a special problem and may give them a hard time: he disrupted class a lot, talked when he shouldn't, didn't sit in his chair, and often acted silly. In the *control condition,* the perceivers were not given this information.

One of the activities the two boys mutually engaged in was an unstructured, cooperative task in which they planned and built a design with plastic blocks; the other task was more structured and competitive—separately coloring a dinosaur as quickly as possible using the same set of crayons. The boys' behavior on both tasks was videotaped and later rated by judges on a number of dimensions, such as friendliness, giving commands, and offering plans or suggestions. The boys also reported their own feelings and reactions to the tasks.

Results indicated that the target boys whose partners had been led to believe that they had a behavioral problem (the *hyperactive expectancy condition*) enjoyed the tasks less, rated their own performances as poorer, and took less credit for success than the boys whose partners were in the *control condition.* Likewise, the boys who held the negative expectancies about their partners enjoyed the tasks less themselves, worked less hard on them, talked less, and liked their partners less and were less friendly to them than those perceivers who were not provided with negative expectancies. These findings indicate that when people have negative expectations about others, they are more likely to treat these individuals in a negative manner, which often results in the targets of such negative treatment reacting in kind, thus confirming the initial negative expectations. For half of the boys in this study, the negative expectations were groundless, but this did not alter the outcome of the interaction. Unfortunately, this form of self-fulfilling prophecy is all too common, and, over time it leads to negative self-beliefs and low self-esteem.

Think of instances in your own life where negative expectations of others may have created undesirable self-fulfilling prophecies. If you can identify someone whom you've viewed and treated in a negative fashion, try a little exercise to reverse this process. The next time you interact with them, put aside your negative expectations, and instead, treat them as if they were your best friend. Based on the research we have reviewed here, by redefining them in your own eyes, you may create a new definition of social reality in theirs as well. People you thought were unfriendly, and even hostile, may respond to your redefinition by acting warm and friendly. If successful in redefining this particular social reality, you will have fulfilled one of my own prophecies of readers of this text—namely, that those who learn about social psychological principles will use this knowledge to improve the quality of their social relationships. Does this sound like an expectation worth internalizing?

Expecting a "Just World" Fosters Comfort and Blame

Do you believe the world is a "fair" place and that people get what they deserve in life? How do you react when you learn about tragedies that befall others? Sympathy and offers of help are common reactions, but so is blame. Before reading further, spend a few minutes answering the items in table 5.2.

In many cultures throughout the world, people are taught from early childhood that the world naturally operates out of a sense of justice (Bierhoff, 2002). Those who follow this **just-world belief** system perceive the world as a fair and equitable place. In a just world, hard work and clean living will be rewarded, while laziness and sinful living will be punished. According to Melvin Lerner (1980), this social belief system is simply a defensive reaction to the sometimes cruel twists of fate encountered in life, but it is comforting because most of us conceive ourselves to be good and decent people. By believing in a just world, we have the illusion that we have more control over our lives than we actually do.

Although an exaggerated sense of personal control could be dangerous if taken to extremes, in most instances, it is related to good psychological adjustment (Ormel & Schaufeli, 1991). This fact partly explains why people who believe in a just world tend to experience less depression and stress and greater life satisfaction than those who do not believe in a just world (Lipkus et al., 1996).

Another reason why this social belief system is related to psychosocial adjustment is due to its influence on the believers' approach to social relationships. Because they believe that

RITICAL *thinking*

Do you think that a judge's beliefs about the guilt or innocence of a defendant in a criminal trial could create a self-fulfilling prophecy among the jury, even if the judge does not voice her opinions?

Not everyone's life is what they make it. Some people's life is what other people make it.

Alice Walker, U.S. author, *You Can't Keep a Good Woman Down*, 1981, New York: Harcourt Brace Jovanovich

Just-World Belief

A belief system in which the world is perceived to be a fair and equitable place, with people getting what they deserve.

TABLE 5.2

Do You Believe in a Just World?

Instructions

Read the statements below and decide which of these you tend to agree with and with which you disagree.

1. Good deeds often go unnoticed.

2. When parents punish their children it is almost always for good reason.

3. Many people suffer through absolutely no fault of their own.

4. By and large, people deserve what they get.

5. The political candidate who sticks up for his principles rarely gets elected.

6. Although evil men may hold political power for a while, in the general course of history good wins out.

Scoring

The more of the even numbered statements you agreed with and the more of the odd numbered statements you disagreed with, the stronger is your belief in a just world. How does the belief in a just world influence both psychosocial well-being and willingness to help victims of unfortunate circumstances?

good deeds will be rewarded and bad deeds will be punished, just-world believers are more likely than nonbelievers to develop an accommodating interpersonal style (Lipkus, 1991; Zuckerman & Gerbasi, 1977). Accommodation typically involves putting aside your own immediate self-interests to satisfy other, long-term goals. When accommodation occurs in a social relationship, it is generally perceived by both the accommodator and the recipient as a positive deed that should be reciprocated. This greater willingness to accommodate may explain why just-world believers experience greater satisfaction in long-term romantic relationships than nonbelievers (Lipkus & Bissonnette, 1996). Simply put, their belief that relationship self-sacrifices will be rewarded motivates them to make concessions to their partners, which often are then reciprocated. This reciprocal accommodation, over time, promotes romantic happiness.

Although just-world believers often psychologically benefit from their positive illusions about how the world operates, this social belief can lead to some unfortunate social judgments, as illustrated by people's tendency to blame rape victims for their sexual assaults (Bell et al., 1994). Strong believers in a just world tend to make *defensive attributions* when explaining the plight of victims. In other words, they are prone to blame people for their misfortunes. Research demonstrates that this tendency to blame victims is strongest when people feel personally threatened by an apparent injustice (Hafer, 2000). Thus, accident victims are more likely blamed for their fate if they are similar to us on some relevant characteristic, or if their injuries are severe rather than mild (Burger, 1981). By disparaging the victim, we reassure ourselves that the world is not only just, but also that we are not likely to fall victim to similar circumstances ("Because I'm really not like *them*"). In chapter 14, we will explore in more detail the link between just-world beliefs and helping.

Finally, what happens when people who believe in a just world encounter overwhelming evidence that a bad thing has happened to a person or persons through no fault of their own? Further, what if they strongly identify with these victims? For most Americans, the September 11th terrorist attacks qualified as such an unjust event (Pyszczynski et al., 2003). The resulting fear, stress, anxiety, and vulnerability posed an extreme challenge to many people's just-world beliefs. In such instances where victim blaming is unlikely, people with strong just-world beliefs often respond to the negative event with a desire for revenge (McCullough et al., 2001). This is exactly what happened after September 11th. People who most strongly endorsed just-world beliefs prior to the terrorist attacks reported the most distress and were most likely to desire revenge (Kaiser et al., 2004). In such instances, the motivation for revenge is a means for those with strong just-world beliefs to restore a sense of justice in the world. Their reasoning is that although bad things happened to good people, if those responsible are punished, they will get what they deserve, which will restore justice.

Expecting Failure Breeds Helplessness

You have seen how a belief in a just world fosters a sense of personal control that can promote psychological health. Yet what happens when you repeatedly experience a lack of control in altering bad life circumstances? To help you envision this scenario, consider the present life of Desmond, a graduating college senior. During the past month, he was rejected from all twenty of the jobs for which he applied. With each rejection, Desmond felt his future slipping away. He now believes that he is not intellectually fit for any career success, and he envisions a life of endless failure and unhappiness. In such a state of mind, when Desmond is told about another job opportunity he thinks, "What's the use?"

When an unpleasant situation is perceived to be inescapable, humans and other animals develop the belief that they are helpless to alter their circumstances by means of any voluntary behaviors. Because of this *expectation* that one's behavior has no effect on outcome, the person or animal simply gives up trying to change the outcome. This psychological reaction, which is known as **learned helplessness,** was first discovered in animal research. Martin Seligman and Steven Maier found that when dogs were unable to escape electrical shocks, they simply gave up trying, even when escape was later possible (Seligman & Maier, 1967). In human studies, those exposed to uncontrollable bad events at first

Learned Helplessness

The passive resignation produced by repeated exposure to negative events that are perceived to be unavoidable.

feel angry and anxious that their goals are being blocked. However, as the extent of uncontrollable events increases and they begin to feel helpless, the previous anger and anxiety is replaced with depression (Peterson et al., 1993). Learned helplessness explains why, for example, many unemployed workers eventually give up trying after repeatedly being passed over for new jobs. Unfortunately, by concluding that there is nothing they can do to change their current situation, these individuals often overlook real possibilities for change.

Not everyone who is placed in an uncontrollable situation experiences learned helplessness. According to Lyn Abramson and her colleagues (1978), people's *attributions* about what caused the initial lack of control will ultimately determine whether an uncontrollable event leads to learned helplessness and depression. If people believe that the cause of an uncontrollable event is *stable* (it will not change over time) and *global* (it extends across many events), they are more likely to expect future events to also be uncontrollable. When those future events arrive, these expectations cause them to act passively and helplessly. If people further believe that their lack of control is caused by *internal* factors, such as personal characteristics and behaviors, they are further likely to experience a loss of self-esteem. This stable, global, and internal attributional set describes how Desmond interpreted his job rejections. The Applications section that follows examines an alternative attributional style that helps people weather these storms of failure.

SECTION SUMMARY

- The false consensus effect is the belief that our attitudes, opinions, and beliefs are more common than they are

- The false uniqueness effect involves underestimating how common our desirable traits and abilities are in the general population

- The confirmation bias occurs in problem solving when we seek information that verifies our beliefs, especially when:

    we are personally invested in the outcome

    the possible solution is agreeable to us

- The confirmation bias can lead to self-fulfilling prophecies

- People with a strong just-world belief perceive the world as a fair and equitable place, and such thinking fosters greater life satisfaction, but also victim-blaming

- Learned helplessness develops when an unpleasant situation is perceived to be inescapable

FEATURED STUDY

DOES UNREALISTIC OPTIMISM CHANGE FOLLOWING A NEGATIVE EXPERIENCE?

McKenna, F. P., & Albery, I. P. (2001). Does unrealistic optimism change following a negative experience? *Journal of Applied Social Psychology, 31,* 1146–1157.

Although numerous studies indicate that having an optimistic outlook on life is beneficial to one's health (see Applications), having an unrealistic optimism about one's ability to avoid harm can actually increase risk of injury (Klein & Weinstein, 1997). One area where individuals have demonstrated both a high estimate of their personal ability and a low estimate of their vulnerability to harm is in driving (McKenna et al., 1991). This study sought to determine whether personal experience with injury in a car accident would be related to a decrease in one's unrealistic optimism regarding risk perceptions in both driving and other domains.

Method

Participants in the sample included drivers who differed in their personal experience with car accidents. To obtain a group of accident-free drivers, a random sample of adults was approached in city parking lots. If they had a valid driver's license and had not been involved in a car accident, they were asked to complete a questionnaire at home and mail it back to the university. To obtain the accident-involved sample, names and addresses were picked from police accident reports. These drivers were then categorized as being (a) noninjured drivers involved in minor accidents in which no one required hospitalization, (b) noninjured drivers involved in accidents in which someone else required hospitalization, and (c) injured drivers taken to the hospital. Of the 910 drivers asked to participate in the study, a total of 468 (210 females and 258 males) agreed and completed the questionnaires (a 51 percent response rate).

In the questionnaire, drivers estimated, relative to the average driver, their driving skill and the likelihood that they would be involved in a car accident. They also indicated how likely, compared with the average person, they were to experience sunstroke, food poisoning, tooth decay, high blood pressure, skin cancer, and falling and breaking a bone sometime in the future.

Results and Discussion

All driving groups, regardless of accident incidents, rated themselves significantly more skilled than the average driver. However, drivers who had been involved in an accident in which someone was injured, rated themselves as less skilled and safe than did those who were accident free or who were involved in a minor accident. These findings are consistent with the hypothesis that personal experience with injury in a car accident decreases one's unrealistic optimism regarding risk perceptions in driving. There was no evidence, however, that this personal experience with injury increased drivers' risk perceptions in other areas of their lives. Overall, these findings suggest that people who have endured a serious negative experience in one area of their lives requiring a specific set of skills are less likely than other people to unrealistically overestimate their possession of these skills.

APPLICATIONS

HOW DO YOU EXPLAIN NEGATIVE EVENTS IN YOUR LIFE?

According to Lyn Abramson and her colleagues (1978), people differ in their attributional style, which can affect how they respond to uncontrollable life events. As previously discussed, reactions to uncontrollable events are determined by three types of attributions: *internal versus external, stable versus unstable,* and *global versus specific* (that is, whether the event extends to many spheres of life or is confined to one sphere). Those who make *internal* attributions for uncontrollable events tend to experience more negative self-esteem. Individuals who make *stable* and *global* attributions for uncontrollable events are more likely to feel helpless in future events. When all three types of negative attributions are habitually used to explain stressful events in one's life, this attributional tendency is called the **pessimistic explanatory style,** and people from cultures around the world who fit this pattern have been found to be at greater risk for depression (Lee et al., 2002; Nolen-Hoeksma et al., 1992; Sweeney et al., 1986). For them, an unfortunate event has an internal cause ("It's my fault"), a stable cause ("It will always be this way"), and a global cause ("It's this way in many different situations"). In contrast, when something positive happens to them, people with a pessimistic explanatory style tend to make external, unstable, and specific attributions.

Pessimistic Explanatory Style

A habitual tendency to attribute negative events to internal, stable, and global causes, and positive events to external, unstable, and specific causes.

An attributional style that contrasts sharply to the pessimistic style is the **optimistic explanatory style.** Optimists tend to explain negative events in terms of an external cause ("It's someone else's fault"), an unstable cause ("It won't happen again"), and a specific cause ("It's just in this one area"). On the other hand, when faced with positive events, optimists explain them by making internal, stable, and global attributions (Peterson & Steen, 2002; Seligman, 1991). Do you think you tend to have an optimistic or a pessimistic explanatory style of explaining the causes of good and bad events? Spend a few minutes answering the questions in table 5.3.

Christopher Peterson and Martin Seligman conducted a series of studies to better understand the relationship between explanatory style and illness. In one of their first studies, the researchers measured college students' attributional style and asked them to list all illnesses they had experienced during the previous month (Peterson & Seligman, 1987). Students also completed

Optimistic Explanatory Style

A habitual tendency to attribute negative events to external, unstable, and specific causes, and positive events to events to external, unstable, and specific causes.

The optimist sees the rose and not its thorns; the pessimist stares at the thorns, oblivious to the rose.

Kahlil Gibran, Lebanese poet, 1883–1931

TABLE 5.3

Do You Have a Pessimistic or an Optimistic Explanatory Style?

Directions

Imagine yourself in the two situations described below. Events often have many causes, but if these situations happened to you, what do you think would be the primary cause of each? Answer questions a-c about each situation by circling a number from 1 to 5 for each question.

Situation 1:

While eating at a restaurant, your dinner companion appears bored.

a. Is this outcome caused by you or by the other person or the circumstances?

| Completely caused by other people or circumstance | 1 | 2 | 3 | 4 | 5 | Completely caused by me |

b. Will this cause be present in the future?

| Will never be present again | 1 | 2 | 3 | 4 | 5 | Will always be present |

c. Is this cause unique to this situation, or does it also affect other areas of your life?

| Affects just this situation | 1 | 2 | 3 | 4 | 5 | Affects all situations in my life |

Situation 2:

You receive an award for a university or community project.

a. Is this outcome caused by you or by the other people or the circumstances?

| Completely caused by other people or circumstances | 1 | 2 | 3 | 4 | 5 | Completely caused by me |

b. Will this cause be present in the future?

| Will never be present again | 1 | 2 | 3 | 4 | 5 | Will always be present |

c. Is this cause unique to this situation, or does it also affect other areas of your life?

| Affects just this situation | 1 | 2 | 3 | 4 | 5 | Affects all situations in my life |

Scoring

For the negative outcome situation 1, high scores (4, 5) on questions a-c describe an internal, stable, and global attribution (pessimistic explanatory style). Low scores (1, 2) on these same questions describe an external, unstable, and specific attribution (optimistic explanatory style). For the positive outcome situation 2, high scores on questions a-c again describe an internal, stable, and global attribution, but now this indicates an optimistic explanatory style. Low scores indicate a pessimistic explanatory style.

this illness measure one year after the initial testing. Results indicated that even after controlling for the number of illnesses reported at the first session, students with an optimistic explanatory style reported fewer illnesses and fewer visits to a physician for diagnosis or treatment of an illness than did those with a pessimistic style.

In an archival investigation, the researchers used the responses that ninety-nine male college graduates gave in 1946 to an open-ended questionnaire about their wartime experiences to classify them in terms of their degree of pessimistic explanatory style (Peterson et al., 1988). Although style did not predict health in young adulthood—when nearly all the men were healthy—there was a link between explanatory style and illness by the age of 45, when health became more variable. After this age, the men who had a pessimistic explanatory style in their youth tended to have more health problems than those who had a more optimistic outlook. In a second archival study, Peterson and Seligman (1987) investigated the deceased members of the Baseball

Hall of Fame who played between 1900 and 1950. First, they searched the sports pages of old newspapers for the explanations these players gave of their successful and unsuccessful performances. Next, they had independent judges rate these quotes for internality, stability, and globality. Finally, they recorded the age at which each baseball player had died. Results indicated that players who made internal, stable, and global explanations for bad events died at a younger age, and those who explained positive events as being due to external, unstable, and specific factors died at a younger age.

One final archival study conducted by the researchers found that globality was a better predictor of early death than internality and stability (Peterson et al., 1998). When people habitually believed that a bad event in one specific life area would undermine everything else in their life, they were more likely to die at an early age. Globality was also a significantly better predictor of deaths by accident or violence than deaths by cardiovascular disease or cancer. The fact that globality best predicted deaths by accident or violence suggests that expecting bad

MISTER BOFFO

by Joe Martin

What type of explanatory style does Earl likely possess?

Copyright © 1997 Tribune Media Services. Reprinted with permission.

events to spread throughout one's life may lead to poor problem solving and risky decision making by pessimists.

Regarding deaths by disease, additional research indicates that optimists may have better immune systems than pessimists, making them less susceptible to diseases. For example, one study found that optimists have higher numbers of helper T cells that mediate immune reactions to infection than pessimists (Segerstrom et al., 1998). Combined with the previous results from the college sample and the first archival study, these findings suggest that pessimists may be more stress-prone than optimists. A central feature in this susceptibility to stress appears to be the beliefs that people develop about why both positive and negative events occur in their lives.

Fortunately, people with a pessimistic explanatory style can be taught to change their self-attributions through cognitive therapy (Hollon et al., 1991). Typically, this therapy involves keeping a diary of daily successes and failures, and identifying how you contributed to your successes and how external factors caused your failures. Essentially, it trains people

to do what most of us do naturally: engage in the self-serving bias. In one such intervention program among children in mainland China, David Yu and Martin Seligman (2002) found that children with a pessimistic explanatory style who were placed in an "optimistic child" intervention program showed significantly fewer depressive symptoms six months later compared with children in the control group. Because people in collectivist cultures are less likely to engage in the self-serving bias than are individualists, it is possible that these "optimistic" intervention programs might be particularly effective in such cultures. However, it is also possible that intervention programs to increase optimistic explanatory style may be short-lived in cultures where the overall approach to the self does not encourage the sort of self-esteem enhancement associated with self-optimism. The lesson to be learned from this research on explanatory style is one of the basic truths of social psychology: your interpretation of events will be shaped by those around you, and your subsequent social thinking will profoundly influence your emotions and actions.

THE BIG PICTURE

I trust that you now understand that social thinking involves many complex judgments that are fraught with potential errors and biases. Whether it is in first impressions, attributions, or beliefs about how our social world operates, problems can arise at many points in the social judgment process. Adding to this complexity is the fact that sometimes our judgments are under the control of automatically activated evaluation without our awareness. Because of these and other considerations, rational models are often inadequate in reliably describing the social judgmental process. Sometimes judgments must be made very quickly and do not allow for careful observation and logical analysis. At other times, information in our social world is so unreliable, biased, and incomplete that a rational analysis is not possible. In such situations, we typically rely on heuristics and other mental shortcuts as a means to judge our world.

You may be wondering how we survive in a complex and ever-changing world, given that we are predisposed to make such a wide variety of errors. One thing to keep in mind is that our social world is much more flexible and dynamic than the static and artificial laboratory conditions that often characterize social psychological research (Schliemann et al., 1997). In a laboratory study, once a research participant makes a judgmental error, it becomes a data point, frozen in time. But in the course of everyday life, people are constantly revising their social assessments due to feedback from the environment. As a result of this flexibility, many of the social judgment errors committed in the "real world" are corrected through normal interaction with others (Fiske & Haslam, 1996). For example, you may meet someone and, based on that limited encounter, form a certain impression. Another person, upon hearing of that impression, may provide new meaningful information that redefines your initial impression. This evolution of social reality is ongoing and can be extremely forgiving of individual judgmental errors, so that you can arrive at an "efficient definition" of others that can be used in the social world.

A second thing to keep in mind is how social cognitive theorists conceive of us as social thinkers. Whether we make careful and rational decisions or quick and sloppy ones is often determined by what motivates us in a given situation. The *motivated-tactician model* proposes that we are flexible social thinkers who choose among multiple cognitive strategies based on our current goals, motives, and needs. Central to the motivated-tactician model is the self. Unlike computers, we have an investment in our self-beliefs and our beliefs about others (Ames, 2004). This psychological fact makes motivational biases likely in social thinking. Through such biases we often can justify our self-concepts and our worldview, making it possible for us to more confidently engage in social interaction and meet daily challenges.

Anthony Greenwald (1980), in an analysis of how the self figures into the social cognition equation, makes this very point. He argues that cognitive biases serve very useful and self-protective functions. Likening the self to a totalitarian government, Greenwald states that both are designed to manage (and distort) information so as to maintain a stable and efficiently functioning system. The distortion of reality is functional for both the self and the dictatorship. If this biasing did not occur, the system—either self or governmental—would likely collapse.

In the final analysis, our social judgments should not be expected to be any more accurate or efficient than our self-judgments. Just as we have a need for consistency when assessing our self-beliefs, we also express that need in our social judgments. When we are faced with contradictory information, our inclination is to distort or explain away the contradictions. As proposed by Greenwald (1980), these distortions may well have functional value, allowing us to maintain a set of beliefs and perceptions of the world that have proven useful and efficient in making everyday decisions. And just as there are individual differences in accuracy of self-assessments, there are variations in people's ability to judge their social surroundings.

WEB SITES
accessed through http://www.mhhe.com/franzoi4

Web sites for this chapter focus on social cognition topics, including judgment and decision making, social categorization, stereotyping, and counterfactual thinking.

Social Cognition Paper Archive and Information Center

This Web page maintained at Purdue University archives various abstracts of social cognition articles in such areas as judgment and decision making, social categorization, stereotyping, and person memory.

Counterfactual Research News

How might your life have unfolded differently? This Web site contains a bibliography of counterfactual publications, in press articles, and cartoons.

EVALUATING OUR SOCIAL WORLD

*A*s a species, we not only have a desire to understand ourselves and others, but we also habitually evaluate our social world. Evaluation may seem like a simple and straightforward process, but how do we form our opinions? And how do we try to shape others' opinions?

Chapter 6 examines the nature of attitudes, including how they are formed and maintained. Does our behavior shape our attitudes, or do our attitudes shape our behavior? When do attitudes predict behavior? Can you have unconscious attitudes? Is cognitive consistency an important aspect of attitude formation and change?

In chapter 7 we analyze various theories on persuasion and attitude change. Specifically, how does the source of a persuasive message, its content, the manner of transmission, and the nature of the audience determine whether it will be effective? We examine persuasion not only from the "outside" but also from the "inside," meaning we explore the cognitive processes of the "persuadee."

Then, in chapter 8, we tackle an issue that has quite possibly plagued humankind since the dawn of our species, namely, prejudice and discrimination. How is stereotyping related to intergroup intolerance? What are the social causes of prejudice and discrimination? How do the victims of prejudice cope with and respond to stigmatization? Are there ways to combat these negative intergroup evaluations and behavior?

CHAPTER **6**

Attitudes

CHAPTER OUTLINE

*F*ew issues arouse more passion among so many people than abortion. As the debate is currently framed, two basic human values are often at loggerheads—life versus liberty. Pro-life activists claim that the issue boils down to the fetus's right to life. On the other hand, pro-choice activists state that the real issue revolves around the woman's right to choose. Most Americans support a woman's right to have an abortion during the early stages of pregnancy, when the embryo is a collection of cells with no discernible human features. Yet many of these same individuals express concerns about the more mature fetus, especially when it can survive outside the womb. Some people's attitudes, however, are not conflicted, and they feel so strongly that they publicly demonstrate their support for or against abortion rights. Two such individuals are Joan and Natasha, whom I interviewed outside a barricaded Milwaukee health clinic where abortions were performed.

Joan, a married woman in her midfifties, was active in the pro-life movement. Her reply to my question about why she held such strongly negative attitudes toward abortion was partly based on personal experience—she had an abortion forty years ago, when it was illegal:

> At the time I thought it was the right thing to do. Afterwards, I didn't think about it, I went on with my life. Much later I became a born-again Christian and began to rethink my action of forty years ago. Today, I believe I murdered my unborn child. Abortion is the killing of human life, done out of convenience. If I don't speak out against abortion now, young girls will also carry this burden the rest of their lives. I believe a woman has a choice before she gets pregnant, but not afterwards.

On the pro-choice side, Natasha, a single woman of 30, held a decidedly different attitude than Joan. Raised in Lebanon and Egypt during times of social conflict and war, she said these experiences shaped her current attitudes:

Strongly held attitudes can profoundly shape a person's actions and lifestyle choices. Are you the type of person who holds strong attitudes about many different things?

Having lived throughout the world and experienced war, I see a woman's choice over her body as a much broader issue than women in Milwaukee getting into a clinic. I'm pro-life in the sense that I want to raise the quality of life of those who are born. I've had firsthand experience with others interfering with a woman's right to choose. When I lived in Egypt I was raped and became pregnant. Abortion is illegal in Egypt. I had an unsafe and illegal abortion, and I had it during the second trimester of pregnancy due to all the obstacles I faced. I just cannot believe that people would work so hard to take rights away from women.

Listening to both women articulate their abortion attitudes, I was struck by a number of similarities imbedded within their sharply contrasting perspectives. First, their attitudes were based on a number of **beliefs.** Second, these attitudes were associated with a good deal of emotion, or *affect.* Finally, their attitudes were based on their past behavior.

Belief

An estimate of the probability that something is true.

THE NATURE OF ATTITUDES

Over the years, social psychologists have studied how attitudes influence behavior. In this chapter I guide you through this "theoretical maze" so that you more clearly understand how people like Joan and Natasha—and you yourself—are shaped by these psychological factors. As Dorothy from *The Wizard of Oz* was instructed by the Good Witch Glinda prior to setting out in search of the mysterious and powerful wizard, "It's always best to start at the beginning." With this in mind, let's start with first defining the attitude concept itself.

Attitudes Are Positive or Negative Evaluations of Objects

One of the earliest uses of the term *attitude* came from the theater and dates back to the 1800s, where it described a physical posture or body position. An actor onstage would assume a certain body posture (for example, drooping shoulders and head), to signify the mental state of the character (dejection or sadness). Later this term referred not to a body posture, but to a "posture of the mind." In 1935, in the *Handbook of Social Psychology,* Gordon Allport declared that attitude was social psychology's most indispensable concept:

> Without guiding attitudes the individual is confused and baffled. Some kind of preparation is essential before he can make a satisfactory observation, pass suitable judgment, or make any but the most primitive reflex type of response. Attitudes determine for each individual what he will see and hear, what he will think and what he will do. To borrow a phrase from William James, they "engender meaning upon the world"; they draw lines about and segregate an otherwise chaotic environment; they are our methods for finding our way about in an ambiguous universe. (Allport, 1935, p. 806)

The principal reason the attitude concept is so popular is that the aim of psychology is to study behavior, and attitudes are supposed to influence behavior. Any concept that is believed to have such power is bound to come under serious scrutiny by those who desire to unlock the mysteries of human functioning. Social psychologists are not alone in recognizing the importance of attitudes as a key to behavioral change. Most people believe that attitudes determine behavior, which explains why those who feel strongly about abortion, for example, voice their views in a public forum. They think that if they can influence people's attitudes, their behavior will follow.

Prior to the 1990s, attitudes were often defined in terms of three distinct components: beliefs, feelings, and behavioral intentions (Breckler, 1984). According to this multidimensional, or *tricomponent* view, attitudes are made up of our beliefs about an object, our feelings about the object, and our behavior toward the object. Although this definition is appealing because it so neatly carves up the attitude concept into three distinct categories, research indicates that not all three of these components need be in place for an attitude to exist (Eagly & Chaiken, 1993; Huskinson & Haddock, 2004). For example, you could develop a positive

FIGURE 6.1

Three Different Types of Attitude Antecedents

Attitudes are believed to be formed through affective, behavioral, and cognitive processes. The assumption that attitudes are formed on the basis of affective or emotional experiences is reflected in classical conditioning principles and the mere exposure hypothesis. The idea that evaluations are based on behavioral responses is reflected in operant conditioning principles, self-perception theory, and the facial feedback hypothesis. Finally, the claim that attitudes derive from a process of cognitive learning can be seen in a host of theories, including the theory of planned behavior and cognitive dissonance theory.

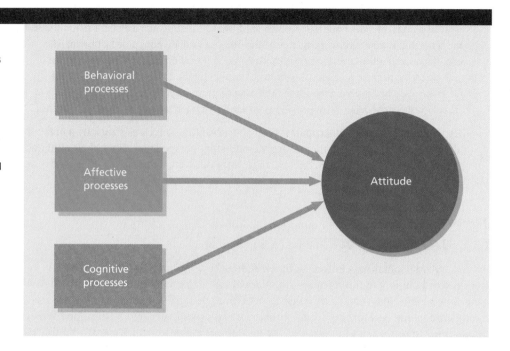

Attitude

A positive or negative evaluation of an object.

attitude toward a product you see on television without developing any beliefs about it or ever engaging in any behavior relevant to the product. As you will learn (see pp. 177–179), simply by repeatedly being exposed to the product, you can develop a positive attitude toward it.

Because the three aspects of the tricomponent definition are not always present in an attitude, many social psychologists have moved away from this elegant multidimensional view to an earlier, more basic unidimensional, or *single component,* definition in which *evaluation* is central. Here, **attitude** is simply defined as a positive or negative evaluation of an object (Schuman, 1995). "Objects" include people, things, events, and issues. When people use such words as *like, dislike, love, hate, good,* and *bad,* they are usually describing their attitudes. Social psychologists also use specialized terms to describe certain classes of attitudes. For example, an attitude toward the self is called *self-esteem* (chapter 3), certain attitudes toward groups are referred to as *prejudice* (chapter 8), and attitudes toward individuals are referred to as *interpersonal attraction* (chapter 11), *friendship,* and *love* (chapter 12). The movement away from the tricomponent attitude definition does not mean that social psychologists no longer consider beliefs, feelings, and behavior important in explaining attitudes. Instead, as illustrated in figure 6.1, these three sources of evaluative judgment—beliefs, feelings, and past behavior—are thought of as determining attitudes singly or in combination.

People Differ in Their Need to Evaluate

We appear to be automatic evaluators (Fazio, 2001; Ferguson & Bargh, 2004). Brain-imaging studies suggest that when encountering people, things, and events, the *amygdala* in the brain's limbic system engages in an immediate primitive "good-bad" emotional assessment that may be followed by higher-order processing by the cerebral cortex (Armony & LeDoux, 2000; Hamann et al., 2002). Greater amygdala activity occurs for initial negative assessments than for those that are positive, with much of this evaluative processing being nonconscious (Cunningham et al., 2003). It is the job of the cerebral cortex to analyze and interpret this initial emotional assessment into the subjective experience of various emotions, which often leads to consciously held positive or negative attitudes (LeDoux, 1998). However, just because we can evaluate with ease does not necessarily mean that we all place equal importance on the evaluative process: we differ in our need to evaluate (Jarvis & Petty,

TABLE 6.1

Measuring the Need to Evaluate

Instructions

The extent to which people chronically engage in evaluation is measured by items on the Need to Evaluate Scale (NES: Jarvis & Petty, 1996). To take the NES, read each item below and then indicate how well each statement describes you using the following scale:

1 = extremely uncharacteristic (very much unlike me)

2 = somewhat uncharacteristic (somewhat unlike me)

3 = uncertain

4 = somewhat characteristic (somewhat like me)

5 = extremely characteristic (very much like me)

_____ 1. I form opinions about everything.

_____ 2. I prefer to avoid taking extreme positions.*

_____ 3. It is very important to me to hold strong opinions.

_____ 4. I want to know exactly what is good and bad about everything.

_____ 5. I often prefer to remain neutral about complex issues.*

_____ 6. If something does not affect me, I do not usually determine if it is good or bad.*

_____ 7. I enjoy strongly liking and disliking new things.

_____ 8. There are many things for which I do not have a preference.*

_____ 9. It bothers me to remain neutral.

_____ 10. I like to have strong opinions even when I am not personally involved.

_____ 11. I have many more opinions than the average person.

_____ 12. I would rather have a strong opinion than no opinion at all.

_____ 13. I pay a lot of attention to whether things are good or bad.

_____ 14. I only form strong opinions when I have to.*

_____ 15. I like to decide that new things are really good or really bad.

_____ 16. I am pretty much indifferent to many important issues.*

Directions for Scoring

Several of the NTE items are reverse-scored; that is, for these items a lower rating actually indicates a higher level of evaluation need. Before summing the items, recode those with an asterisk ("") so that 1 = 5, 2 = 4, 4 = 2, and 5 = 1. To calculate your need to evaluate score, add up your responses to the sixteen items.*

When Jarvis and Petty developed the NTE in 1996, the mean score for college students was about 52. The higher your score is above this value, the greater is your motivation to evaluate objects and events. The lower your score is below this value, the less of this need to evaluate you probably possess.

1996; Tuten & Bosnjak, 2002). Spend a few minutes completing the *Need to Evaluate Scale* in table 6.1, which measures individual differences in the tendency to evaluate.

How do individuals with a high versus a low need to evaluate differ from one another? As would be expected, people with a high need to evaluate are more likely to hold attitudes toward issues they have previously encountered and are more likely to describe daily events in evaluative terms than those with a low need to evaluate (Jarvis & Petty, 1996). Further, the attitudes of high need to evaluate individuals are more accessible from memory and more extreme than those of low need to evaluate persons (Federico, 2004; Hermans et al., 2001). Individual differences in the need to evaluate are hypothesized to affect people's response to both positive and negative life events. For example, the impact that divorce or job loss might have on one's self-esteem or level of depression could be influenced by the degree to which one chronically evaluates these events. Insights into these possible relations await further research.

Implicit Attitudes May Underlie Explicit Attitudes

The Need to Evaluate Scale measures individual differences in the desire to engage in conscious evaluation. Besides such deliberate evaluation, an increasing number of social psychologists are studying attitude evaluations resulting from implicit cognitive processes (Betsch et al., 2001; Frings & Wentura, 2003). As discussed in chapter 5, *implicit cognition* involves judgments or decisions that occur automatically without our awareness (Schacter & Badgaiyan, 2001). Being a product of implicit cognition, an **implicit attitude** is an attitude that is activated automatically from memory, often without the person's awareness that she or he even possesses it (Dovidio et al., 2001). Feeling uneasy and irritable around new acquaintances because they unconsciously remind you of disagreeable persons from your past is an example of an implicit attitude. By comparison, an **explicit attitude** is consciously held.

Although the term "implicit attitude" is fairly new, a number of traditional attitude theories have discussed these hidden attitudes without giving them a specific name. Over forty years ago, attitude researchers who were inspired by Freud's psychoanalytic theory proposed the existence of unconsciously held attitudes, which they called *ego-defensive attitudes* (see pp. 186–187). For example, people might publicly express negative attitudes toward others they perceive as unintelligent in order to protect themselves from consciously acknowledging their own intellectual insecurities.

DUAL ATTITUDES

As this example suggests, a person may have two attitudes toward someone or something—one explicit and the other implicit. Yet what happens when a person's explicit and implicit attitudes are evaluatively opposite? This simultaneous possession of contradictory implicit and explicit attitudes toward the same object is known as **dual attitudes** (Wilson et al., 2000). In M. Kierstead's (1981) short story, "The Shetland Pony," a woman realizes while reminiscing about her beloved childhood pony—which regularly bit her—that she actually had an unconscious hatred of it as a child:

> It wasn't until Blake said it [that he hated the pony] that Kate realized that she too, had always hated Topper. For years they had been conned into loving him, because children love their pony, and their dog, and their parents, and picnics, and the ocean, and the lovely chocolate cake. (Kierstead, 1981, p. 48)

This literary example illustrates the idea that contradictory explicit and implicit attitudes can develop simultaneously, due to different situational factors (Wilson et al., 2000). For Kate, her positive explicit attitude toward Topper was shaped by other people's expectations that children should love their pets, while her negative implicit attitude developed because of Topper's unpleasant behavior. Here, the explicit attitude overrode the implicit attitude in young Kate's conscious evaluation of Topper.

MEASURING IMPLICIT ATTITUDES

In chapter 2 we discussed the most common means of measuring explicit attitudes, namely, self-reporting. In contrast to this relatively straightforward approach in measuring consciously held attitudes, determining a person's implicit attitudes requires less direct methods. Implicit attitude researchers believe that monitoring attitude holders' nonverbal behavior and physiological responses can reveal the existence of implicit attitudes that contradict explicit attitudes (Chen & Bargh, 1999; Cunningham et al., 2001). In our pony example, young Kate's tendency to flinch and frown when near Topper was a telltale sign that she possessed a negative implicit attitude toward her pet. Similarly, the dilation of your pupils and elevated blood pressure that occur whenever you are near your best friend's

Implicit Attitude

An attitude that is activated automatically from memory, often without the person's awareness that she or he possesses it.

Explicit Attitude

A consciously held attitude.

Dual Attitudes

The simultaneous possession of contradictory implicit and explicit attitudes toward the same object.

boyfriend or girlfriend may signify that you have an implicit romantic attitude of which you may be unaware.

Although implicit attitudes can be measured by attending to nonverbal responses and physiological arousal, the most popular technique employed by researchers is the Implicit Association Test (IAT), which was described in chapter 3 (p. 82). In assessing implicit attitudes, the IAT measures differences in memory associations between target categories (for example, *dog* or *cat*) and evaluative categories (such as *like* or *dislike*). This is accomplished by relying on a *response latency indicator* obtained by pairing target and evaluative categories. Using a computer, participants are asked to respond quickly with a right-hand key press to items representing one target category and one evaluative category (*dog* and *like*), and with a left-hand key press to items from the remaining two categories (*cat* and *dislike*). Participants then perform a second task in which the key assignments for one of the pairs is switched (*dog* and *dislike* share a response, likewise *cat* and *like*). If a person repeatedly responds to one of these pairings (for example, *dog* and *like*) faster than to the other pairing (for example, *dog* and *dislike*), this is interpreted as indicating that the person has a stronger tendency to automatically associate the category dog with positive evaluations.

Research suggests that dual attitudes will most likely develop for issues that are socially sensitive, such as people's attitudes toward pornography, racial and ethnic groups, or their friends' romantic partners (Wilson et al., 2000). Although much more research is needed before we understand how implicit attitudes operate and influence behavior, when describing traditional attitude theories in this chapter we will discuss how they might account for both explicit and implicit attitudes.

Values Can Shape Attitudes and Behavior

One psychological variable closely associated with attitudes is **values.** Although attitudes refer to evaluations of specific objects, values are enduring beliefs about important life goals that transcend specific situations (Rohan, 2000; Rokeach, 1973). "Pleasure," "freedom," "equality," and "obedience" are examples of values. Values constitute an important aspect of our self-concept: they convey what is important to us in our lives and serve as our guiding principles (Kristiansen & Hotte, 1996).

The importance that we attach to a particular value largely determines whether it will influence our attitudes and behavior. Values are organized into a hierarchy from most important to least important to the self (Ball-Rokeach et al., 1984). Where a specific value falls in this hierarchy will often determine its influence on our attitudes. Consider again the explanations the abortion activists gave about why they were either pro-choice or pro-life. To a considerable degree, these explanations hinged on where in their own values hierarchy the principles of "life," "liberty," and "quality of life" fell. When values of relatively equal importance (for example, life and liberty) conflict with one another on a particular issue, such as abortion, the person's subsequent attitudes tend to be not only complex but also ambivalent (Armitage & Conner, 2000). A person who has complex and ambivalent attitudes toward abortion is unlikely to demonstrate outside a medical clinic—on either side of the issue.

Research conducted by Shalom Schwartz (1994, 1997) in sixty-five different cultures has identified ten types of values that represent universal biological and social requirements of human existence. Some of these values are compatible while others are in conflict, and Schwartz represents these compatibilities and tensions in a circular value structure that is depicted in figure 6.2 (Schwartz & Bardi, 2001; Schwartz & Sagiv, 1995). In this structure, compatible values are located close to one another on the circle, while conflicting values are on opposing sides of the center. According to Schwartz, actions taken to foster social order (a security value) also are likely to promote politeness (a conformity value) and acceptance of conventional customs and ideas (a tradition value). However, these same actions are likely to conflict with independent thinking (a self-direction value) and behaviors focused on novelty and excitement (a stimulation value). A recent set of studies in twenty-three countries has provided further support for Schwartz's organization of values (Schwartz, 2003; Schwartz & Boehnke, 2002).

Values

Enduring beliefs about important life goals that transcend specific situations.

I happen to feel that the degree of a person's intelligence is directly reflected by the number of conflicting attitudes she can bring to bear on the same topic.

Lisa Alther, American novelist, 1976

FIGURE 6.2

Is There a Universal Structure of Values?

Schwartz's cross-cultural analysis of values suggests that there are ten types of values representing universal biological and social requirements of human existence. Some of these values are compatible with one another, while others are in conflict. Schultz depicts these values in a circular structure, with compatible values located close to one another on the value structure (for example, security, conformity, and tradition), while conflicting values are on opposing sides of the center (for example, conformity and stimulation). How might your decisions in college be influenced by whether you value stimulation and self-direction versus security, conformity, and tradition?

Schwartz, S. H. (1994). Are there universal aspects in the content and structure of values? *Journal of Social Issues, 50,* 19–45.

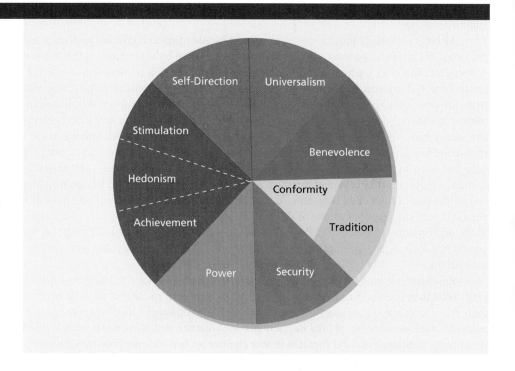

CRITICAL *thinking*

Refer back to the "Values Hierarchy" questionnaire in chapter 1 (p. 19). This questionnaire provides you with information about whether individualist or collectivist values are more important to your self-concept. If individualist values are more central to how you view yourself, they will have greater influence in shaping your attitudes, and thus, your behavior. Which were more important for you? Can you identify ways in which these values have influenced your attitudes and behavior?

Taking Schwartz's idea of contrasting and compatible values, how might young adults' values influence their decisions while in college? This was the question asked by Deborah Prentice and her coworkers in a study of more than 3,000 second-year students at four different East Coast universities (Prentice et al., 2001; Prentice, 2004). In their investigation, the researchers focused on Schwartz's contrasting values associated with "openness to change" (stimulation and self-direction values) and "conservatism" (security, tradition, and conformity values). These competing values were analyzed because they seemed to represent very different guidelines for deciding what to do with one's life. Prentice and her coworkers hypothesized that students who placed a high value on self-direction and freedom from constraints would approach college as an opportunity to "find themselves" and discover personally fulfilling goals. In contrast, they expected that students with conservative values would view their college years as a time to work toward already established goals that conformed to their family's wishes and desires.

Consistent with this thinking, results indicated that students whose values fell to the openness side of the values structure came to college with an open mind about their studies and an intention to "have fun" and explore a wide variety of activities and interests. These students tended to choose an academic major based on its perceived intellectual challenge. Their decisions to join extracurricular campus groups were based on such factors as the opportunity to learn a new skill, their level of interest in the group's activities, and their expected enjoyment in the group. What about those students whose values fell to the conservative side of the values structure? Prentice and her colleagues found that these students were much more likely to come to college with clear goals already established and follow a relatively straightforward path in pursuing their goals. These students tended to choose an academic major based on the advice of family members and friends, as well as practical considerations, such as the number of requirements for the major and the job prospects after graduation. Their decisions to join extracurricular groups were also influenced by family advice and considerations of how the groups might benefit their future goals.

This study and others demonstrate that values can shape attitudes and behavior (Bardi & Schwartz, 2003). However, attitudes and behavior are often determined by factors other than important life goals. Your attitudes toward abortion are probably shaped by your values, but your toothpaste preference is less likely influenced by such guiding principles. Attitudes formed mainly through the influence of long-standing values are called *symbolic attitudes* (Sears & Funk, 1991). They are symbolic because the attitude object is perceived not merely as it is, but rather as a symbol of something else. This type of attitude is likely associated with important ingroups, involves emotional intensity, and is relatively unresponsive to rational arguments (Abelson, 1982; Prentice, 1987). We will revisit symbolic attitudes later in the chapter (pp. 185–187).

SECTION SUMMARY

- Attitudes are positive or negative evaluations of objects
- Attitudes are determined by a number of factors, including past behavior, emotions, and cognitions
- High need to evaluate people are more likely to hold attitudes toward issues and describe daily events in evaluative terms
- Explicit attitudes are consciously held
- Implicit attitudes are activated automatically outside of conscious awareness and may conflict with explicit attitudes
- Values are enduring beliefs about important life goals that transcend situations and are important aspects of self-concept

---

HOW ARE ATTITUDES FORMED AND MAINTAINED?

You might think that forming attitudes is a fairly simple process. In some instances this is true. Yet remember that attitudes can develop from your beliefs, your feelings, and your behavior, singly or in combination. Due to the various ways in which attitudes form, social psychologists have generated or applied a number of theories to explain these various developmental processes. In this section of the chapter, we first examine theories that explain fairly simple attitudes formed through *mere exposure* and *classical conditioning*. These largely feeling or *affect-based* explanations are then followed by theories that involve more behavioral and/or cognitive sources (for example, *operant conditioning* and *self-perception theory*). We also examine one perspective on attitude formation and change, the *functional approach,* which describes how the three sources of attitudes—feeling, thinking, and behavior—might differently come into play due to a person's current psychological needs.

Mere Exposure Can Lead to Positive Attitudes

Larissa has developed a positive attitude toward an elderly man who lives in a nearby apartment. If you asked her why she likes this man, Larissa would be hard-pressed to give you a reason: she has never talked to the man and really knows nothing about him. The only way their lives intersect is that Larissa sees him every day on her way to and from work. With no actual contact, why did Larissa develop a liking for this man?

Larissa's positive attitude is best explained by a theory Robert Zajonc (pronounced like "science") first developed in 1968. Zajonc proposed that simply exposing people repeatedly to a particular object (such as an elderly man) causes them to develop a more positive attitude toward the object. This phenomenon, which he called the **mere exposure effect,** does not require any action toward the object, nor does it require the development of any beliefs about the object. Zajonc (1968) conducted several experiments in which increased exposure

Mere Exposure Effect

The tendency to develop more positive feelings toward objects and individuals the more we are exposed to them.

resulted in greater liking for previously neutral objects. In one study, college students were told that they were participating in an experiment on how people learn a foreign language. They were then shown ten Chinese-like characters for two seconds at a time, with instructions to pay close attention as they appeared on the screen. Two of the characters were presented only once, two others twice, two others five times, two others ten times, and a final two were presented twenty-five times. Besides these ten characters, Zajonc had two others that the participants did not see at all. Once the exposure trials were completed, participants were told that the characters were Chinese adjectives and they were now going to guess their meaning. The experimenter hastened to add that he realized it would be virtually impossible for them to guess the exact adjective; therefore, they should merely indicate whether each character meant something good or bad in Chinese. Participants then rated the characters—including the two they had not seen—using a seven-point good-bad scale. The results, shown in figure 6.3 indicated that the more often a character was repeated, the more favorable participants estimated its meaning. Zajonc obtained similar findings by using nonsense syllables and facial photographs taken from a college yearbook. Although there are some limitations and qualifications to repeated exposure (which will be discussed in chapter 7), more than 200 experiments confirm that the mere exposure effect leads to greater liking (Bornstein, 1989).

Theodore Mita and his coworkers (1977) conducted one of the more interesting mere exposure studies. They reasoned that people are more exposed to their mirrored facial images than they are to their true facial images, and thus, they should have more positive attitudes toward the former than the latter. To test this hypothesis, they photographed women students on campus and later showed each one her picture along with a mirror image print of it. When asked to indicate which of the two prints they "liked better," two-thirds of the women preferred the mirror print, while 61 percent of their close friends preferred the actual picture, a significant difference in preference. What is impressive about these findings is that the mirrored and true facial photographs were almost indistinguishable from one another, and no one suspected they were looking at altered images.

Overall, the significance of the mere exposure effect regarding our understanding of attitudes is that it illustrates how affect can become associated with an object independent

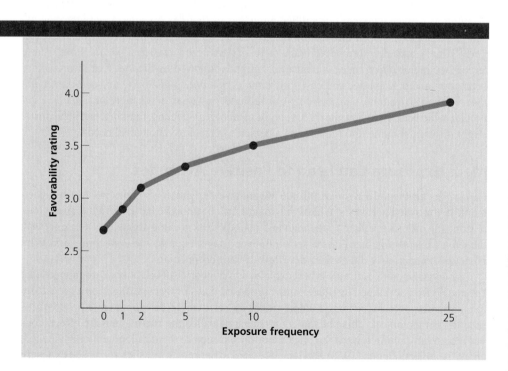

FIGURE 6.3

Frequency of Exposure and Liking

Research participants' attitudes toward Chinese-like characters became more positive as the frequency of their exposure to these stimuli increased. Can you think of how the mere exposure effect has influenced your own attitudes?

Source: Data from R. B. Zajonc, "Attitudinal Effects of Mere Exposure" in *Journal of Personality and Social Psychology Monograph Supplement,* 9 (2, part 2): 1–27, American Psychological Association, 1968.

of any knowledge about it (Lee, 2001; Murphy, 2001). These feeling-based attitudes develop outside the realm of rational thoughts and represent a very basic and powerful form of evaluation (Petty et al., 2001). In addition, many attitudes developed by mere exposure are implicit attitudes; they come into existence without the attitude holders' awareness and are automatically activated from memory. Yet even when an attitude formed by mere exposure is consciously held ("I like my mirror image better than my photo image"), the attitude holder is often unaware *why* they hold this attitude.

On a neurological level, scientists have hypothesized that different brain areas account for different kinds of mere exposure effects. This speculation is based on many years of research indicating that the right hemisphere of the brain tends to be superior to the left in identifying faces, while the left hemisphere is superior at language (Gazzaniga, 1967; McAuliffe & Knowlton, 2001). In a recent series of studies, Rebecca Compton and her colleagues (2002) asked participants to stare at a dot on a computer screen while either words or faces were flashed quickly across their visual field. In one condition the stimuli were presented to the left visual field of each eye (which is processed by the right hemisphere), while in another condition the stimuli were presented to the eyes' right visual field (which is processed by the left hemisphere). Later, participants were asked to rate their liking for the stimuli.

Results indicated that faces were liked better if they had previously been presented to the left visual field (right hemisphere processing), whereas words were liked better if they had previously been presented to the right visual field (left hemisphere processing). These findings suggest that the relationship between exposure and liking is primarily controlled by the right hemisphere for faces, while the left hemisphere shapes our liking for words and language. Taking these findings to a personal level, it may be that the right hemisphere of your brain played a larger role than the left hemisphere in shaping your preference for the face you see in the mirror each morning, while your left hemisphere may have been more active in shaping your positive response to seeing or hearing your name.

Beyond exploring the neurological basis for the mere exposure effect, perhaps a more important question is *why* does repeated exposure lead to positive attitudes? One possibility is that the mere exposure effect could have its roots in an evolutionarily adaptive tendency to be attracted toward those things that are familiar, because they are unlikely to pose a danger to our safety and health. That is, we may have evolved to view unfamiliar objects or situations with caution, hesitation, and even fear (Bornstein, 1989). Such caution in the presence of the unfamiliar enhances our biological fitness because we are better prepared for danger. Only through repeated exposure to that which is unfamiliar does our caution and hesitation subside—the unfamiliar and potentially dangerous becomes familiar and safe, and thus, our positive feelings increase.

Attitudes Can Form Through Classical Conditioning

Now let's consider another life situation. Andrew and Coretta are two young siblings who have developed extremely negative attitudes toward Muslims and Jews despite having no direct contact with anybody from these religions. How did they develop these hostile attitudes? Their hatred may have developed from listening to their parents and other adults use negatively evaluated words such as *greedy, dangerous, dishonest,* and *dirty* in referring to Muslims and Jews. Through such **classical conditioning,** a previously neutral attitude object (the conditioned stimulus) can come to evoke an attitude response (the conditioned response) simply by being paired with some other object (the unconditioned stimulus) that naturally evokes the attitude response (the unconditioned response).

Classical Conditioning

Learning through association, when a neutral stimulus (conditioned stimulus) is paired with a stimulus (unconditioned stimulus) that naturally produces an emotional response.

Arthur and Carolyn Staats were two of the first researchers to investigate the classical conditioning of attitudes. In one study (Staats et al., 1962), they repeatedly presented participants with meaningful words (for example, *large*) paired with aversive unconditioned stimuli (shocks or loud noises). Later, the conditioned words were presented alone and the participants were asked to evaluate them on a seven-point unpleasant-pleasant scale. As they completed this task, the participants' physiological arousal was measured by monitoring their galvanic skin response. Consistent with the classical conditioning hypothesis, participants showed increased arousal in response to the presentation of the conditioned words, but little arousal in response to control words. Additionally, in comparison to a control group who had not undergone the experimental treatment, the participants also expressed more extreme negative attitudes toward the classically conditioned words.

If classical conditioning only resulted in people disliking certain words, this research would have limited importance. Yet the Staatses demonstrated that people could also be conditioned to develop negative attitudes toward specific social groups. In another experiment (Staats & Staats, 1958), they asked participants to remember words paired with various nationality names, such as "German-table," "French-with," "Dutch-gift," and "Swedish-failure." For one group of participants, the target nationality "Dutch" was always followed by a word with a positive meaning, and the target nationality "Swedish" was always paired with negative words. This evaluative pairing was reversed for a second group of participants: "Dutch" was paired with negative words, and "Swedish" was followed by positive words. At the end of the experiment, participants rated how they actually felt about the various nationality groups using a seven-point pleasant-unpleasant scale. As figure 6.4 shows, the group that heard favorable word pairings with "Dutch" and negative pairings with "Swedish" had more positive attitudes toward the Dutch and less positive attitudes toward the Swedes. These ratings were reversed for the group that had opposite word pairings. Although the attitude shifts were not extreme (participants did not leave the lab hating one nationality and loving the other), the fact that these mild emotional stimuli produced significant attitude shifts caused attitude researchers to sit up and take notice. Classical conditioning could play a role in establishing some of the emotional components of attitudes and prejudice (Cacioppo & Berntson, 2001).

The Staats' research and other studies conditioned attitudes to familiar English words (Zanna et al., 1970). However, this effect is even stronger when the words are unfamiliar. John Cacioppo and his colleagues (1992) found stronger conditioning effects when electric

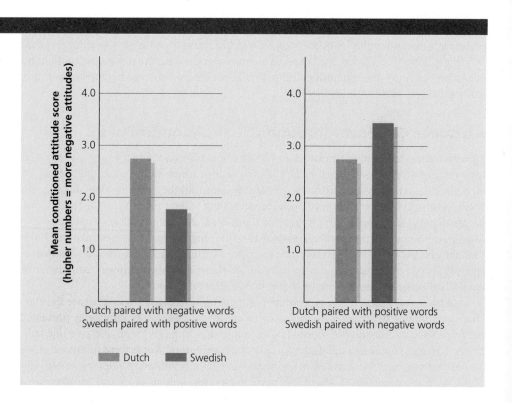

FIGURE 6.4

Classical Conditioning of Attitudes to Nationality Names

Research by Staats and Staats (1958) demonstrated that classical conditioning could play a role in establishing some of the emotional components of attitudes and prejudice. Participants who heard favorable word pairings with "Dutch" and negative pairings with "Swedish" subsequently had more positive attitudes toward the Dutch and less positive attitudes toward the Swedes. Those individuals who had opposite word pairings later had more favorable attitudes toward the Swedes. Can you think of instances in your own life in which certain attitudes toward other social groups have been similarly classically conditioned?

shock was paired with unfamiliar nonsense words (for example, *tasmer*) as compared with meaningful words (for example, *finger*). This study suggests that classical conditioning is a more powerful determinant of attitude formation when people possess little knowledge about the attitude object.

Having reviewed research on the conditioning of attitudes, let's return to our children, Andrew and Coretta. How might they have acquired negative attitudes toward Muslims and Jews by simply hearing their parents use a number of negative adjectives (dirty, dishonest, dangerous, greedy) in referring to these groups? As we have seen, the novel religious labels (like Muslims or Jews) were initially neutral stimuli to the children, because they had not previously been associated with either positive or negative adjectives. However, once the negative adjectives were introduced, repeated pairings of the religious labels with these negative adjectives caused Andrew and Coretta to acquire negative attitudes toward these people. They may never have met a Muslim or a Jew, but this attitude conditioning played a significant role in their aversion and hostility nonetheless.

Additional studies indicate that classical conditioning of attitudes can occur below the level of conscious awareness. In one such study, Jon Krosnick and his coworkers (1992) showed college students slide photos of a stranger going about her daily activities. These slides were preceded by very brief (13/1000 of a second) subliminal presentations of photos known to induce either positive emotions (for example, a bridal couple, people laughing, kittens) or negative emotions (for example, a skull, a werewolf, open-heart surgery). These pleasant and unpleasant photos were presented so quickly that the students did not consciously perceive them. However, despite not consciously perceiving these photos, they did affect the students' later attitudes toward the stranger. Those exposed to the positive photos reported more positive attitudes toward this unknown person than did those exposed to the negative photos. These findings suggest that attitudes can be formed through **subliminal conditioning,** which is classical conditioning that occurs in the absence of conscious awareness of the stimuli involved.

Subliminal Conditioning

Classical conditioning that occurs in the absence of conscious awareness of the stimuli involved.

Reinforcement and Punishment Can Shape Attitudes

Because classical conditioning and mere exposure influence emotions, they contribute most directly to shaping the *affective* component of attitudes (Petty et al., 2001). Yet one of the most powerful ways in which the *behavioral* component can shape attitudes is through **operant conditioning,** a form of learning extensively studied by such behavioral psychologists as Edward Thorndike (1911) and B. F. Skinner (1938). According to operant conditioning principles, when an action toward an object is rewarded or reinforced, it will probably be repeated in the future. On the other hand, if behavior is not rewarded or is punished, similar future actions are less likely. Learning theorists who study attitudes contend that accompanying this increase or decrease of behavior will be an attitude consistent with the behavior. For example, if a child's parents and teachers praise her for doing well in math, she may redouble her efforts and develop a positive attitude toward mathematics in general. However, if her academic accomplishments go unrewarded, her interest in math may diminish and eventually extinguish. She probably will also develop a negative attitude toward the subject matter.

Operant Conditioning

A type of learning in which behavior is strengthened if followed by reinforcement and weakened if followed by punishment.

Although attitudes can develop by being directly rewarded and punished when interacting with the attitude object, they can also develop through the indirect means of *observational learning* (Bandura, 1986). In such instances, attitudes are shaped by observing other people being reinforced or punished when interacting with the attitude object (Rowe et al., 1996). Thus, for example, you might develop a dislike for rock climbing after a friend is injured while climbing. Although your friend's newly formed dislike for rock climbing is due to operant conditioning, your negative attitude is a result of observational learning. In forming attitudes through observational learning, the people whom we observe and imitate are called *role models,* because they teach us how to play social roles. Observational learning helps children learn how to behave in their families and in their cultures, and it also help adults learn the attitudes and skills necessary for career success (Buunk & van der Laan, 2002; Rogoff et al., 2003).

Self-Perception Theory Contends That Behavior Causes Attitudes

Self-knowledge is best learned, not by contemplation, but action.

Johann Wolfgang von Goethe, German author, 1749–1832

Our lives teach us who we are.

Salman Rushdie, Indian-born British author, 1990

Another theory that emphasizes how behavior shapes attitudes is Daryl Bem's **self-perception theory.** Influenced by Skinner's behaviorist perspective, Bem (1965, 1972) downplays the importance of introspection and self-awareness in the development of attitudes. Instead, he argues that we often do not know what our attitudes are and, instead, simply infer them from our behavior and the circumstances under which the behavior occurs. Bem's theory is a radical explanation of the attitude concept, because it contends that, instead of attitudes causing behavior, it is *behavior* that *causes* attitudes.

If this notion that we do not automatically understand our own internal states sounds strange to you, consider the following story. A few years ago, I was asked to teach a research methods course and I reluctantly agreed. Whenever my colleagues asked why I was teaching this course, I replied that my arm had been twisted. I taught the course, without developing a clear liking or disliking for it. Then later while discussing with my colleagues how best to teach research methods, I suddenly realized that I was dominating the conversation. Why was I so enthusiastic about a course I had never placed high on my preferred teaching list? As I contemplated both my current behavior and my past actions in the course—involving numerous class projects—I literally thought, "Wow, maybe I do like teaching research methods!" According to self-perception theory, at that moment, I had formed an attitude by observing my behavior toward the attitude object.

This process of inferring attitudes based on observing behavior should sound familiar, because it describes the attribution principles introduced in chapter 4. Self-perception theory contends that when we form attitudes, we function like an observer, watching our behavior and then attributing it to either an external (the situation) or internal (attitude) source. Comparable to the *discounting principle* in Kelley's covariation model of attribution (p. 119), Bem argued that we are more likely to make attitude inferences when our behavior is *freely chosen* rather than coerced. In my case, Bem would assert that the reason I did not initially infer an attitude about teaching research methods was because I felt mildly coerced into teaching the course. I wasn't teaching research methods because I liked doing so (an internal attribution), but rather because I was yielding to someone's influence (an external attribution). At our faculty discussion, however, no one was forcing me to talk about this course, and thus my enthusiasm could not be easily attributed to an external source.

Shelly Chaiken and Mark Baldwin (1981) conducted an interesting empirical demonstration of how the self-perception process influences attitudes. First, they separated participants into two groups: those who held strong, consistent, proenvironmental attitudes and those who had weak, inconsistent attitudes on this issue. They then induced participants to endorse either relatively proenvironment or relatively antienvironment behavioral statements on a questionnaire. They were able to secure the desired behavioral endorsements by inserting either the word *frequently* or *occasionally* into the questions. For example, participants who were asked "Do you occasionally carpool?" were more likely to answer "Yes" and perceive themselves as proenvironment. In contrast, those asked "Do you frequently carpool?" were more likely to answer "No" and feel somewhat antienvironment. Figure 6.5 shows that participants who were induced into reporting proenvironmental behaviors later rated their attitude as more proenvironmental than those who were induced into reporting antienvironmental behaviors—but only if their initial environmental attitudes were weak and inconsistent. Among the participants whose prior attitudes were strong and consistently proenvironment, the manipulation of self-reported environmentalist behaviors had no significant impact on their attitudes.

Based on a number of such studies, it appears that Bem's self-perception theory provides an adequate explanation for how we can sometimes infer attitudes from behavior. If you have little prior experience with an attitude object, or your attitudes are vaguely defined, you may infer your attitudes by observing your behavior (Olson & Roese, 1995; Schnall et al., 2002; Schnall & Laird, 2003). However, when you possess well-defined attitudes on a particular topic, attending to your behavior is much less likely to influence any attitude change.

CRITICAL *thinking*

How do implicit and explicit attitudes relate to the self-perception process?

FIGURE 6.5

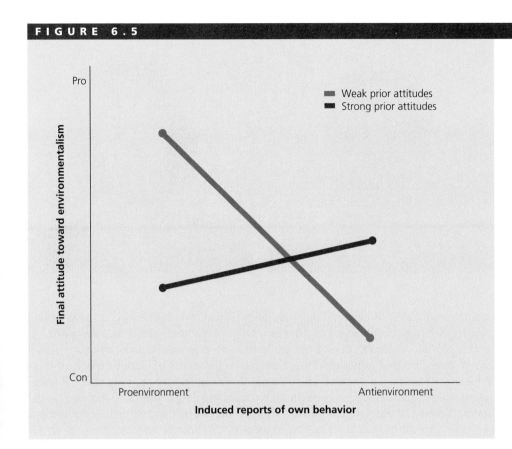

Self-Perception of Environmental Attitudes

In a study of environmental attitudes, Chaiken and Baldwin (1981) found that when people were induced into reporting past personal behavior that was either proenvironment or antienvironment, they came to view themselves in ways consistent with this behavior, but only if their prior environmental attitudes were weak and vaguely defined. What limits does this suggest about the self-perception process in attitude formation?

Attitudes Are Influenced by Changes in Facial Expression, Head Movement, and Body Posture

Related to self-perception theory is the view that people's emotions—and thus their attitudes—can be manipulated by changing their facial expressions, body posture, or other motor responses (Duclos et al., 1989). For example, in an innovative experiment, German psychologist Fritz Strack and his colleagues (1988) asked college students to hold a pen in their mouths while they were shown a series of amusing cartoons. Participants in the *lips condition* were instructed to hold the pen tightly with their lips, while those in the *teeth condition* were told to hold the pen with their front teeth (see photographs on p. 184). In a control condition, participants were told to hold the pen in their nondominant hand. After reading the cartoons, all students rated how funny they were using a ten-point scale. Results indicated that participants who held the pen between their teeth found the cartoons to be the most amusing, followed by those who held it in their hand. Students who held the pen in their lips gave the cartoons the lowest ratings of amusement. Why do you think this was the case?

Based on your understanding of self-perception theory, you know that people sometimes infer their attitudes based on their actions. You also can tell by looking at the photographs that holding a pen with the teeth causes a person to smile, while holding it with the lips prevents smiling. Could the participants have inferred their attitudes toward the cartoons based on their facial muscle movements? This is a possibility, referred to as the *facial feedback hypothesis,* and it would be consistent with self-perception theory. However, Robert Zajonc (1993) offers an alternative explanation, namely, the *vascular theory of emotion.* He contends that smiling causes facial muscles to increase the flow of air-cooled blood to the brain, which, in turn, produces a pleasant mood by lowering brain temperature. In contrast, frowning decreases blood flow, causing heightened brain temperature and

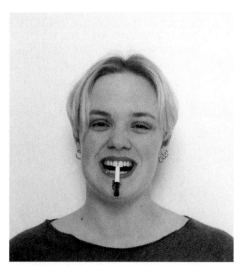

an unpleasant mood. Supporting this hypothesis, Zajonc and his coworkers (1989) found that simply having people repeat a series of vowel sounds twenty times each was sufficient to change their forehead temperature and their mood: sounds such as *ah* and *e,* which caused the speakers to mimic smiling, decreased temperature and elevated mood, whereas the *u* and the Germanic *ü* sound, which mimic frowning, had the opposite effect. Regardless of whether these findings are due to increased blood flow to the brain, this study is important because it indicates that even when people are not aware they are wearing a particular expression, movement of facial muscles can alter their mood. In other words, consciously recognized self-perception processes may not be necessary for facial feedback to work.

Besides facial expressions, other expressive behaviors also appear to influence feelings. For instance, when people feel proud, they assume an erect, upright posture, whereas when dejected, their posture becomes slumped. Using this knowledge, Sabine Stepper and Strack (1993) manipulated people's posture to determine what effect it would have on their feelings of pride following success on an achievement test. Posture was manipulated by having participants take a test and then learn about their results while either sitting upright at a normal-height table or sitting slumped over at a short-legged table. Those who sat upright felt prouder after succeeding than those who were slumped over. Similarly, Gary Wells and Richard Petty (1980) asked students to "test the sound quality of headphones" by moving their heads either vertically up and down (nodding) or horizontally side to side (shaking) while listening to a taped editorial. The head nodders later expressed more positive attitudes toward the editorial than did the head shakers. Finally, John Cacioppo and his colleagues (Cacioppo et al., 1993; Priester et al., 1996) found that when research participants were presented with neutral or meaningless words and symbols while gently pressing their arms upward against a table (mimicking an inviting "approach" gesture), they expressed greater liking for the words and symbols than participants who gently pressed their arms downward on a table (mimicking a rejecting "avoidance" gesture).

Because participants in all these studies did not perceive a connection between their motor responses and their attitudes, this suggests that these findings cannot be explained by self-perception. Likewise, Zajonc's vascular theory cannot account for these findings. Instead, what may best explain these effects is classical conditioning (refer back to pp. 179–181), where an upright posture, head nodding, and "approach" arm movements have become associated with and facilitate the generation of favorable thoughts, while the reverse is true for a slumped posture, head shaking, and "avoidant" arm movements (Alluisi & Warm, 1990; Förster & Strack, 1996).

Although classical conditioning may provide an adequate explanation for how these attitudes are formed, recent studies suggest that nonverbal actions can also shape people's attitudes by influencing their *confidence* in the thoughts they are having about the attitude object.

CRITICAL *thinking*

During childhood and early adolescence, did your parents periodically admonish you to straighten your posture and to avoid slouching? Based on what you have just learned about posture and attitudes, is there any wisdom in such admonishments? How might the manner in which parents try to correct slouching destroy these possible benefits?

In these studies, Pablo Brĭnol and Richard Petty (2003) induced people to either nod or to shake their heads while listening to persuasive messages. When the arguments in the persuasive messages were strong, thereby generating mostly favorable thoughts in listeners, head nodding produced more confidence in participants' resulting positive attitudes than head shaking. However, when the arguments were weak and generated mostly negative thoughts, participants' head shaking produced more confidence in the resulting negative attitudes than head nodding. These findings suggest that when people are already having positive or negative thoughts about an attitude object, their head movements can increase their confidence in these thoughts if they match the underlying feelings. Brĭnol and Petty contend that these findings are consistent with a *social validation* explanation, meaning that head nodding (or shaking) validates people's positive (or negative) thoughts, thereby increasing their confidence in the attitudes they are forming. Even here, however, classical conditioning is relevant, because we learn through conditioning to associate head nodding with approval and head shaking with disapproval.

Regardless of the ultimate explanation for how body movements affect attitudes, all these studies suggest that performing actions associated with happiness cause us not only to feel happier, but also to perceive other objects in our environment more favorably. Similarly, performing actions associated with sadness cause us to feel sadder and to perceive our world less favorably. So, smile and be happy!

The Functional Approach Asserts That Attitudes Are Formed to Satisfy Current Needs

The theories discussed thus far emphasize one attitude component over others in explaining attitude formation. For example, the mere exposure effect and classical conditioning highlight the affective component, while operant conditioning and self-perception theory largely focus on the behavioral component. In an attempt to understand when one attitude component will exercise greater influence than others in shaping a particular attitude, a number of theorists have argued that the purpose or *function* of attitudes needs to be examined. The crux of their argument is that people hold attitudes that fit their current psychological needs, and when those needs change, so will their attitudes. From this perspective, people could have similar attitudes toward an object, but for different reasons. In this process of attitude development and change, the **functional approach** views the individual as an active participant, changing attitudes to satisfy current needs (Maio & Olson, 2000). For example, I might like to drink "Figzoi" soda because all my friends like it and I want to do things to win their approval. You, on the other hand, might like Figzoi because the company making it is environmentally conscious (a *symbolic attitude*). Our attitudes may be the same, but they are based on different psychological needs.

Now, imagine that the makers of Figzoi are purchased by an environmentally irresponsible corporation that engages in strip mining and deforestation. Your attitude toward the soda is likely to change, because your support for the company's product is no longer in line with your desire to act in an environmentally responsible manner. I, on the other hand, am unlikely to change my attitude because it is based on a desire to gain acceptance and approval from my friends and not on a desire to act proenvironmentally. In the future, if my psychological needs change so that I no longer am so concerned about seeking others' approval, my attitudes toward Figzoi will more likely be based on the quality of the product itself, or perhaps, like you, on the way in which this product satisfies my socially conscious values. This belief that people are actively involved in developing and changing their own attitudes stands in sharp contrast to the previously discussed attitude theories, which view the person as rather passive in the attitude development process.

Early theorists, particularly Daniel Katz (1960) and M. Brewster Smith (Smith et al., 1956) proposed four psychological functions that attitudes may serve. These functions, listed in table 6.2, are closely associated with different theoretical perspectives in psychology and emphasize different components of attitudes.

Functional Approach

Attitude theories that emphasize that people develop and change their attitudes based on the degree to which they satisfy different psychological needs. To change an attitude, one must understand the underlying function that the attitude serves.

TABLE 6.2

Psychological Functions of Attitudes

Type of Attitude	Function Served by Attitude	Psychological Perspective
Utilitarian	Helps the person to achieve rewards and gain approval from others	Behaviorist
Knowledge	Helps the person to structure the world so that it makes sense	Cognitive
Ego Defense	Helps the person protect himself or herself from acknowledging basic self-truths	Psychoanalytic
Value-Expression	Helps the person express important aspects of the self-concept	Humanistic

UTILITARIAN FUNCTION

Sometimes we develop certain attitudes toward objects because we associate them with either positive or negative outcomes. Consistent with the previously discussed operant conditioning principles of behavioral psychology, the *utilitarian* function (also referred to as the *adjustment* function) presumes a basic need of self-interest—gaining rewards and avoiding punishments from the environment. Functional theorists contend that we develop positive attitudes toward those objects that are associated with rewards and develop negative attitudes toward those that are associated with punishment. Many children, for example, develop positive attitudes toward their parents because their mothers and fathers reward them much more than they punish them. In contrast, these same children develop negative attitudes toward the neighborhood "bullies" because the reinforcement contingencies are reversed. In both instances, the attitudes that the children develop *function* to satisfy their utilitarian needs, by drawing them toward those individuals who have rewarded them in the past (their parents) and avoiding those (the bullies) who have punished them.

KNOWLEDGE FUNCTION

Besides the need to achieve rewards and avoid punishments, functional theorists further contend that people need to attain a meaningful, stable, and organized view of the world. Inspired by the insight of cognitive psychology, Katz (1960) stated that attitudes satisfy this *knowledge* function when they provide a frame of reference for organizing the world so that it makes sense. In this way, attitudes can serve the same function as the cognitive schemas described in chapter 5—by organizing information and providing stability to people's experience. How might the knowledge function influence actual attitudes? Let's consider college students' attitudes toward professors. You might hold positive attitudes toward certain professors because their courses helped you to make sense out of a particular topic of interest. On the other hand, certain professors' lectures or course organization may have left you confused, and therefore they did not satisfy your need for knowledge. You likely have less positive attitudes toward them.

EGO-DEFENSIVE FUNCTION

Besides helping a person gain rewards and an organized view of the world, attitudes can also help a person cope with emotional conflicts and protect self-esteem. Consistent with the psychoanalytic principles of Freud, the *ego-defensive* function assumes that attitudes serve

Knowledge is happiness, because to have knowledge—broad, deep knowledge—is to know true ends from false, and lofty things from low.

Helen Keller, American author and humanitarian, 1880–1968

as defense mechanisms, shielding the self or ego from inner conflict and unpleasant truths (Kristiansen & Zanna, 1994). For example, Justin may not be performing well on the job and may unjustly blame his problems on fellow coworkers or supervisors. The function of holding these negative attitudes toward others is that it allows Justin the opportunity to avoid acknowledging the real source of the problem—himself. An ego-defensive attitude, by its very nature, is not grounded in a realistic perception of the attitude object, yet the theory assumes that the person holding such an attitude is largely unaware of its ego-defensive function. Thus, when Justin expresses his negative attitudes toward others on the job, he is believed to be generally oblivious to the fact that he is distorting reality to protect his own self-esteem. Underlying Justin's conscious favorable self-opinion resides an implicit negative self-directed attitude.

One can only face in others what one can face in oneself.

James Baldwin, American expatriate civil rights author, 1924–1987

VALUE-EXPRESSIVE FUNCTION

Although ego-defensive attitudes prevent people from acknowledging unpleasant truths about themselves, other attitudes help them to give a positive expression to their central values and core aspects of their self-concept. For example, Joe may have a positive attitude toward his volunteer work in building low-cost housing because this activity allows him to express his sense of social responsibility, a value that is central to his self-concept. Expressing such important attitudes is inherently satisfying to Joe, reinforcing a sense of self-realization and self-expression. In assuming the human need for positive expression of core values, the *value-expressive* function (previously referred to as *symbolic attitudes*) emphasizes principles consistent with humanistic theories in psychology.

CRITICAL *thinking*

In terms of Daniel Katz's four functions of attitudes, which functions do you think clothing attitudes serve for most people?

CONTEMPORARY CONCEPTIONS OF THE FUNCTIONAL APPROACH

The notion that people hold attitudes for different reasons has been an important contribution to the discussion of attitudes. For example, Jessie might have a negative attitude toward homosexual individuals because she once had an abrasive employer who was a lesbian. Jessie is hostile toward gay men and lesbians (a utilitarian function) because she generalizes her negative attitudes toward this person in her past to the entire gay and lesbian population. Another heterosexual, Gloria, might have antigay attitudes because her religion considers homosexuality to be immoral. The fact that she never had a bad experience with anyone who was gay or lesbian is irrelevant. Gloria's negative attitude satisfies her value-expressive function, allowing her to express an important value associated with her religious faith. Finally, Juan may be confused about his sexual orientation, and as a result, he may develop a hostile stance to those who are openly expressing a lifestyle that he unconsciously desires. This negative attitude fulfills the ego-defensive function because it protects Juan from acknowledging a basic truth about an important self-aspect.

According to attitude theorists who adhere to the functionalist perspective, a key factor in changing other people's attitudes is first determining what functions those attitudes serve for the targeted individuals (Gregory et al., 2002; Marsh & Julka, 2000). For example, to successfully change these people's anti-gay attitudes, different approaches would be needed (Herek & Capitanio, 1998). For Jessie, you would need to recondition her to the target group by perhaps having her experience positive social interactions with gay individuals. For Gloria, you might try to detach her from this particular religious group and attach her to a new religion with more tolerant attitudes. For Juan, you would need to create an accepting environment for him to resolve the confusion surrounding his own sexual orientation. These attitude-change strategies will not guarantee success, but functional theorists contend that they would certainly improve the probability of success over the use of one single persuasion strategy on all three individuals.

- Some attitudes form through simple emotional mechanisms

  In the mere exposure effect, we develop more positive feelings toward objects the more frequently we are exposed to them

  In classical conditioning, an attitude forms when a previously neutral attitude object (the conditioned stimulus) evokes an attitude response (the conditioned response) by being paired with some other object (the unconditioned stimulus) that naturally evokes the attitude response (the unconditioned response)

- Some attitudes form through performing behaviors

  In operant conditioning, we develop attitudes consistent with reinforced and punished behavior

  According to self-perception theory, we infer our attitudes based on observing our past behavior

  Attitudes can be influenced by our facial expressions, body posture, or other motor responses

- The functional approach contends that we hold attitudes that fit our needs, and when these needs change, so do the attitudes

  The four psychological functions that attitudes serve:

  utilitarian   knowledge   ego-defensive   value-expressive

Without doubt, it is a delightful harmony when doing and saying go together.

Michel de Montaigne, French writer, 1533–1592

WHEN DO ATTITUDES PREDICT BEHAVIOR?

One assumption underlying our discussion of attitudes has been that they do indeed influence behavior. To what extent is this true? How *strong* is the link between attitudes and behavior? During the 1970s, a "crisis of confidence" in the attitude concept developed because a number of studies had not found much of an association between attitudes and behavior (Wicker, 1969). Because attitudes failed to reliably predict behavior, many social scientists began to wonder whether attitudes still should be considered a central concept in social psychology (Abelson, 1972).

Several Factors Determine the Attitude-Behavior Relationship

The difficulty in predicting behavior from attitudes was first demonstrated in a classic study by sociologist Richard LaPiere in 1934. In the early 1930s, the majority of Americans held strongly negative attitudes toward Asians. Being aware of this racial prejudice, LaPiere, a White male, decided to use a three-month, cross-country automobile trip with a young Chinese couple to test how accurately attitudes would predict behavior. His question: Would restaurant and hotel managers act on their negative attitudes toward Asians and refuse service to the Chinese couple?

Surprisingly, only one of the 66 hotels they stopped at turned them away, and none of the 184 restaurants refused them service. Later, LaPiere sent a letter to each establishment asking whether they would accept Chinese as guests. Of the 128 proprietors who replied, more than 90 percent said they would not serve Chinese. Why were the proprietors' attitudes toward Chinese so unreliable in predicting their actual behavior toward this particular Chinese couple? Forty years later, the questions raised by LaPiere's findings and those of other studies led to some fruitful research to determine the conditions under which attitudes might better predict behavior.

CRITICAL *thinking*

Before reading further, what are some possible confounding variables in the LaPiere study? That is, how might the "true" association between attitudes and behavior have been tainted by the way LaPiere conducted his study?

LEVEL OF ATTITUDE-BEHAVIOR SPECIFICITY

One problem in predicting behavior from attitudes has been the *level of specificity* at which attitudes and behavior are measured. Too often in the past, researchers have used very general measures of attitudes to predict a very specific form of behavior. This was one of the problems with the LaPiere study. The attitude questionnaire mailed to proprietors asked about Chinese guests in general, but their behavioral decision was based on a specific Chinese couple, who were well dressed, well spoken, and accompanied by a White person. Later research indicated that specific attitudes are much better predictors of behavior than general attitudes (Newcomb et al., 1992; Weigel et al., 1974).

TIME FACTORS

Another variable that influences the success of attitudes in predicting behavior is *time*. The longer the time interval between measurements of attitude and behavior, the greater the probability that the person's attitude will change. As an example of how time influences attitudes, consider the electorate's opinions about political candidates. The accuracy of opinion polls (attitude and behavioral intention measures) one month before an election is lower than those taken one week before citizens cast their ballots (Fishbein & Coombs, 1974). Put simply, there is less time for attitudes to change during a week than during a month.

PRIVATE VERSUS PUBLIC SELF-AWARENESS

A third factor that influences the attitude-behavior association is *self-awareness*. As discussed in chapter 3 (pp. 60–62), people who are privately self-aware are more attentive to their personal standards of behavior, while those who are publicly self-aware are more attentive to public standards. In a two-stage experiment, William Froming and his colleagues (1982) demonstrated how attention to private versus public standards either strengthens or undermines the association between attitudes and behavior. First, the researchers pretested college students regarding their attitudes toward physical punishment. Next, they selected students from this group who had negative attitudes toward punishment but who also believed that most people approved of such behavior. Thus, these students had a private attitude that differed from what they perceived to be the public standard. Weeks later, these same students participated in a study that required them to administer electric shocks to someone (in reality, a confederate) as part of a "learning" study. Because the students could control the intensity of the shocks, the dependent variable was the average shock intensity chosen (although no shocks were actually delivered). Some students administered shocks while facing a small mirror (*private self-awareness condition*), others did so while a small audience observed and evaluated them as "effective teachers" (*public self-awareness condition*), and still others delivered shocks with neither a mirror nor an audience present (*control condition*). As seen in figure 6.6 (p. 190), participants who were made privately self-aware by the presence of a small mirror behaved more in line with their previously expressed attitudes than did those in the control group. In contrast, those facing the audience behaved more in accordance with their perception of the public standard than did the controls. These and other studies suggest that the *kind of self-awareness* people experience prior to engaging in an activity will significantly determine whether their behavior coincides with their privately held attitudes (Echabe & Garate, 1994).

ATTITUDE STRENGTH

Based on our previous discussion of abortion, it should come as no surprise to you that strongly held attitudes are most influential in determining behavior and most resistant to change (Judd & Brauer, 1995; Visser et al., 2003). But what makes an attitude "strong"? Research indicates that simply *acquiring more information* about an attitude object is often sufficient to strengthen people's attitudes (Chaiken et al., 1995; Wood et al., 1995). In one study, for instance, people were first questioned about their attitudes and knowledge about environmental issues and later were asked to participate in proenvironmental activities (Kallgren & Wood, 1986). Those who knew a lot about environmental issues showed more

FIGURE 6.6

Attitude-Behavior Consistency Due to Type of Self-Awareness

In the Froming et al. (1982) study, the researchers selected students to be in an experiment in which their task was to deliver electric shocks to another person as part of a "learning" study. These students had previously expressed negative attitudes toward physical punishment, even though they believed that most others favored such punishment. Those who delivered the shocks while privately self-aware chose the lowest shock levels, whereas those who were publicly self-aware chose the highest shock levels. Based on these findings, which of the two types of self-awareness promotes attitude-behavior consistency?

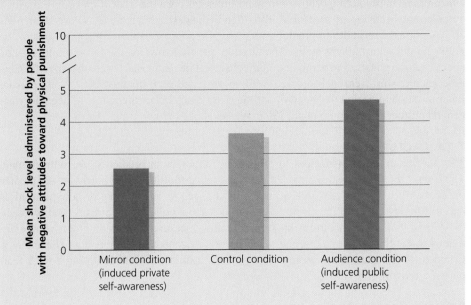

If you want to know the taste of a pear, you must change the pear by eating it yourself. . . . All genuine knowledge originates in direct experience.

Mao Zedong, Chinese communist revolutionary, 1893–1976

consistency between their environmental attitudes and their behavior than those who were less informed. The fact that thinking more about something often results in greater attitude-behavior consistency is an important finding, and we will discuss it more extensively in chapter 7 when we examine the *elaboration likelihood model* of persuasion (p. 214).

Another source of attitude strength is the amount of *personal involvement* an individual has with the attitude object (Crano, 1995; Liberman & Chaiken, 1996). For example, in 1978, a ballot initiative in Michigan proposed raising the legal drinking age from 18 to 21. To study the effects that personal involvement would have on attitude strength, John Sivacek and William Crano (1982) contacted college students and asked them to volunteer to help campaign against the proposed law. Although almost all the students opposed the ballot initiative, only some of them (those younger than 20) had a personal stake in the outcome. As expected, the younger students were much more likely to agree to campaign against the law than those who would be unaffected by its passage. In other words, the attitudes of the more personally involved individuals were stronger predictors of behavior than the attitudes of the less involved.

Related to personal involvement is the fact that attitudes formed through *direct experience* are stronger and, as a result, are better predictors of later behavior than attitudes formed without such experience (Millar & Millar, 1996). One possible reason that direct experience leads to stronger attitudes is that such encounters are more likely to engage all three attitude components: affective, behavioral, and cognitive (Zanna & Rempel, 1988). Remember Joan and Natasha? Their strong abortion attitudes were based not only on their past behavior surrounding this issue, but also on corresponding beliefs and emotions. This is certainly not meant to be an exhaustive list of the factors that contribute to attitude strength. The general point you should take from this discussion, however, is that the link between attitudes and behavior will be stronger when the attitude itself is strong.

ATTITUDE ACCESSIBILITY

One reason attitudes formed through direct experience have a powerful impact on behavior is that they tend to be highly *accessible;* that is, they are frequently thought about and come quickly to mind (Fazio, 1995; Smith et al., 1996). For example, during the 1984 presidential election campaign, Russ Fazio and Carol Williams (1986) measured the accessibility of people's attitudes toward then President Ronald Reagan. Attitude accessibility was measured by the *speed* with which respondents pressed buttons to answer Reagan questions: the quicker the response, the more accessible the attitude. Three months later, following the election, these people were recontacted and asked to reveal for whom they voted. Results indicated that those people with highly accessible attitudes toward Reagan showed a significantly stronger link between their attitudes and their voting behavior ($r = .89$) than those with low accessible attitudes ($r = .66$).

This notion of attitude accessibility is similar to the concept of the *availability heuristic* discussed in chapter 5 (p. 147). Recall that the availability heuristic is the tendency to judge the frequency or probability of an event in terms of how easy it is to recall examples of the event. Similarly, the ease with which relevant attitudes come to mind will partly determine our perceptions of an attitude object. In both instances, the more readily information is activated in memory, the greater impact it will have on subsequent behavior (Wänke et al., 1996). Additional research indicates that we are more likely to infer that highly accessible attitudes are strongly held attitudes (Holland et al., 2003). According to Fazio (1990), these more accessible attitudes can be spontaneously and automatically activated without our conscious awareness. In other words, attitudes can guide our behavior without us necessarily being aware of their influence.

The Theory of Planned Behavior Asserts That Attitudes Influence Behavior by Shaping Intentions

During the 1970s, one product of the debate about whether attitudes determine behavior was the development of a new attitude theory by Martin Fishbein and Icek Ajzen (1975) called the *theory of reasoned action.* Later, Ajzen (1991, 2001) further developed this theory and renamed it the **theory of planned behavior.** By using the term *reasoned action* in the original theory and *planned behavior* in the updated version, Ajzen and Fishbein convey their belief that people rationally think about the consequences of their behavior prior to acting. In other words, behavior is *intended* to achieve certain outcomes, and cognition is the primary process of attitude development. By discovering the intentions of others in a particular situation, they argued that you could predict their behavior.

According to this perspective, the most immediate cause of behavior is not attitudes, but rather *behavioral intentions,* which are conscious decisions to carry out specific actions. Thus, the theory argues that attitudes influence behavior by their influence on intentions (Sheeran et al., 1999). As you can see in figure 6.7, besides a person's attitude toward the behavior, behavioral intention is also determined by *subjective norms* and *perceived behavioral control.*

Theory of Planned Behavior

The theory that people's conscious decisions to engage in specific actions are determined by their attitudes toward the behavior in question, the relevant subjective norms, and their perceived behavioral control.

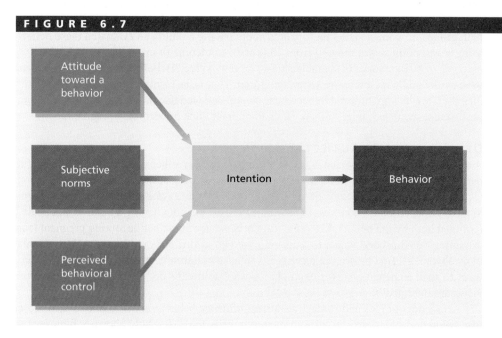

FIGURE 6.7

Theory of Planned Behavior

The theory of planned behavior hypothesizes that the most immediate cause of behavior is not attitudes, but rather, behavioral intentions. According to this theory, what factors combine with attitudes to determine these intentions?

TABLE 6.3

Attitudes of Women Intending and Not Intending to Have a Child Based on Their Mean Beliefs and Mean Evaluations

This table compares the attitude scores of women who intended and did not intend to have a child in the next three years. Their attitude scores are based on the product of their behavioral beliefs and evaluations of these beliefs, with higher (positive) values indicating more positive attitudes.

	Mean Belief × Evaluation Product	
	Intenders	Nonintenders
Having a child I could not afford	3.46	−2.57
Having a child while at a good age	7.13	2.95
Too much of an emotional strain	4.86	−0.97
A restriction on my freedom	0.22	−3.32
Stronger marriage	2.37	−3.62
Fulfillment of my family life	5.33	−1.41
An added responsibility	3.57	−4.14
Having less time for my own goals and plans	−0.56	−5.41

Source: Adapted from Fishbein, 1980.

DETERMINANTS OF ATTITUDES

The ancestor of every action is a thought.

Ralph Waldo Emerson, American philosopher/poet, 1803–1882

As you might expect, Fishbein and Ajzen believe that an attitude toward performing a particular behavior is formed according to a fairly rational process and is the product of two factors: (1) one's beliefs about the consequences of performing the particular behavior, and (2) one's evaluation of those possible consequences. Returning to our previous discussion of abortion, Fishbein and Ajzen would argue that a woman's attitude toward being pregnant could be predicted by learning what she believes the consequences of having a child would be, and by discovering her evaluations of these beliefs. Table 6.3 outlines the consequences that a sample of childless married women believed would follow from having a baby in the next three years (Fishbein, 1980). Some of these women wanted to have a child during this time, while others had no intention of becoming pregnant anytime soon. In a questionnaire, both groups of women stated their beliefs about having a child and evaluated these beliefs using seven-point scales ranging from 13 (positive outcome or evaluation) to 23 (negative outcome or evaluation). As the table shows, more positive "Belief × Evaluation" products were associated with intentions to have children. That is, as Fishbein and Ajzen would predict, the women who intended to become pregnant believed that this event would have more positive consequences than women who had no intentions of becoming pregnant.

DETERMINANTS OF SUBJECTIVE NORMS

A *subjective* norm is a person's judgment about whether other people will approve of a particular behavior. Like attitudes, subjective norms are also a product of two factors: (1) the perceived expectations of significant others, and (2) one's motivation to conform to those expectations. Thus, a woman's subjective norm about having a child would be determined both by the beliefs that significant others have about her becoming pregnant (for example, "My husband wants to wait until we can afford our own house"; "My parents think a woman's first priority in marriage is to have children"), and her motivation to conform to their expectations (for example, "I want to please my husband"; "My parents' views are outdated").

How do attitudes and subjective norms influence behavioral intentions? When these two different factors are carefully measured, results have generally shown a high correspondence between intention and behavior (Armitage & Conner, 1999). Research also indicates that, although behavioral intentions are generally more controlled by attitudes than by subjective norms, their individual contribution also depends on the particular attitude, setting, and population under study (Corby et al., 1996). For example, we have previously seen (p. 189) that situations that induce private self-awareness increase attitudes' influence on behavior, while situations that induce public self-awareness increase the influence of subjective norms. Further research indicates that whether people are more influenced by their attitudes or subjective norms is related to whether they have more of an individualist or collectivist orientation. The actions of individualists are more influenced by their attitudes, while collectivists' actions are more controlled by subjective norms (Trafimow & Finlay, 1996). Together, these studies demonstrate that even though attitudes and subjective norms determine behavioral intentions, their individual contributions to the intention equation can differ.

DETERMINANTS OF PERCEIVED CONTROL

In many instances, attitudes and subjective norms are adequate determinants of behavioral intention. Yet what about those cases in which people believe the behavior is difficult to control? Responding to this weakness in the original theory, Ajzen (1985, 1988) added the concept of *perceived behavioral control,* which is one's perception of how easy or difficult it is to perform the behavior. Ajzen argued that when people believe they have little control over performing a behavior because of a lack of ability or resources, then their behavioral intentions will be low regardless of their attitudes or subjective norms. For example, suppose that Lyle desires to quit his thirty-year smoking habit (positive attitude toward quitting smoking). In addition, he knows that his family and doctor approve of him quitting and he would like to please them (subjective norm). Over the course of time, however, after realizing how ingrained this habit is in his everyday activities, Lyle may lose confidence in his ability to become a nonsmoker (low perceived behavioral control). Thus, despite the proper attitude and subjective norm, Lyle is likely to change his intention to quit smoking.

Another example of perceived control thwarting intention was demonstrated by my daughter Lillian when she was 3 years old. We had been trying to get her to stop sucking her thumb and one day she said to me, "Dad, do you know . . . do you know . . . do you know why I don't like sucking my thumb anymore? Because . . . because . . . because I want to get big." I was pleased. Our little talks were finally paying off: she understood and wanted to conform to our household's "no thumbsucking" norm. Later that night, however, I saw Lillian vigorously sucking her thumb. When I reminded her about her previous pronouncement, she first claimed that she was not sucking it, but merely giving it a "good cleaning." Then, in the exasperated anger typical of 3-year-olds, she blurted out, "But I *have* to suck my thumb!" Despite Lillian's attitude and subjective norm both pointing toward the termination of thumbsucking, at the end of a hard day's play she just did not feel capable of keeping that thumb out of her mouth.

CRITICISMS OF THE THEORY OF PLANNED BEHAVIOR

Quite a few studies have tested the theory of planned behavior, and the general conclusion is that it does a good job of explaining behavior based on rational thinking and planning (Ajzene-tal, 2004; Albarra'cin et al., 2001; Reinecke et al., 1996). However, by placing intention after attitudes and before behavior, the theory ignores the possibility that attitudes sometimes result in spontaneous, *unintentional* behavior. For example, when I was 10 years old and at summer Bible camp, I developed a strong dislike for a tall, strong, and—as far as I was concerned—mean 11-year-old boy named Billy. One morning as he passed by me on the playgrounds, without provocation—and more important, without any deliberative thought—I pushed him. I distinctly remember this event because I was as surprised as anyone that I had instigated a physical confrontation with someone twice my size. Luckily, a camp counselor quickly intervened and prevented me from being rebaptized in the nearby lake at the hands of the irate "Pastor Billy." This example illustrates the fact that sometimes people act without thinking (refer back to *attitude accessibility,* pp. 190–191). By confining their theory to volitional and deliberate actions, Fishbein and Ajzen would be hard-pressed to explain my behavior at camp. Nor could they explain how a person's hatred or love for another sometimes elicits sudden, spontaneous violence or affection. Further, by focusing on explicit attitudes, this theory cannot account for actions prompted by implicit attitudes (Neumann et al., 2004).

Another class of behaviors that the planned behavior model cannot explain is well-established *habits* (Maddux & DuCharme, 1997; Verplanken & Orbell, 2003). With habits, there is no assessment of attitudes and norms prior to behaving. There is no real planning or conscious intention. Instead, the behavior is performed in a relatively unthinking fashion, with little self-regulation (Aarts & Dijksterhuis, 2000; Ajzen, 2001). Research indicates that habits shape many different kinds of behavior, including using condoms during sex (Maticka-Tyndalel & Herold, 1999), donating blood (Bagozzi, 1981), attending college classes (Fredricks & Dossett, 1983), voting for a particular political party (Echabe et al., 1988), and exercising (Bentler & Speckart, 1981). At one time, all of these behaviors were exclusively under conscious, self-regulatory control. However, through repetition, they may have slipped into a rather automatic mode and thus are now less influenced by conscious intentions. Under these circumstances, this relatively *mindless behavior* limits the likelihood that we will act rationally. Ask anyone who has ever tried to break a bad habit, such as eating fatty foods or tailgating fellow motorists on the highway. They will attest to the power that habitual behavior can have in overriding rational action.

When one begins to live by habit and by quotation, one has begun to stop living.

James Baldwin, American expatriate civil rights author, 1924–1987

SECTION SUMMARY

- Factors that determine the attitude-behavior relationship:

    level of attitude-behavior specificity

    time interval between attitude measurement and behavior

    type of self-awareness induced prior to behaving

    attitude strength

    attitude accessibility

- The theory of planned behavior contends that the most immediate cause of behavior is not your attitude, but rather your behavioral intention

    behavioral intentions are shaped by:

    attitudes   subjective norms   perceived behavioral control

- The theory of planned behavior is based on explicit attitudes and cannot explain unintentional or habitual behavior

---

IS COGNITIVE CONSISTENCY AN IMPORTANT ASPECT OF ATTITUDES?

Cognitive Consistency

The tendency to seek consistency in one's cognitions.

One of the most influential approaches in social psychology, especially in the study of attitudes, has been the notion that people are motivated to keep their own cognitions (beliefs, attitudes, self-perceptions) organized in a consistent and tension-free manner (refer to chapter 3, p. 79). This principle of **cognitive consistency** was first introduced by Fritz Heider (1946) and has its roots in the Gestalt belief that human beings not only expect and prefer their perceptions to be coherent and harmonious, but they are motivated to make them so (Koffka, 1935; Köhler, 1929). Consistency theories became popular in the late 1950s and shaped the study of attitudes for the following two decades. Even though this motivational approach toward understanding attitudes was eclipsed by the cognitive movement in the 1970s, it is still an influential perspective (Leippe & Eisenstadt, 1994).

Although the theory of planned behavior does a good job of predicting behavior based on people's behavioral intentions, what about those instances when people act spontaneously and unintentionally? Outbursts of violence—and affection—are often not planned, and are not adequately accounted for by this rational theory of attitudes.

Cognitive Dissonance Theory Asserts That Rationalization Shapes Attitudes

Over fifty years ago Leon Festinger (1957) developed the most influential consistency theory of attitudes. His *cognitive dissonance theory* proposed that although we may generally appear logical in our thinking and behavior, we often engage in irrational and maladaptive behavior to maintain cognitive consistency. It also describes and predicts how we spend much of our time *rationalizing* our behavior rather than actually engaging in rational action. Let's examine in some detail this prolific theory that has spawned so many experiments and countertheories.

INSUFFICIENT JUSTIFICATION AND DISSONANCE

Imagine that you volunteer to participate in an experiment and, upon arriving at the lab, are asked to perform two 30-minute tasks. The first task consists of emptying and refilling a tray with spools, and the second consists of repeatedly turning forty-eight wooden pegs on a board. As you work on these tasks, you silently curse their monotony. Finally, when your hour of boredom ends, the experimenter tells you that the real purpose of the study is to determine if a person's performance is influenced by whether he is told beforehand that it will be "very enjoyable" and "fun," or, like yourself, is told nothing. Then he tells you that his assistant is not able to help him with the next participant who will be in the "favorable information condition." The experimenter then asks if you would tell the participant that you had just completed the task—a true statement—and that you found it to be extremely enjoyable—a lie. You agree to become the assistant and tell your lie to the waiting participant. When the participant completes the tasks and departs, the experimenter sends you to an office where an interviewer asks how fun and interesting you in fact found the tasks to be. Do you think your attitude toward these tasks would be influenced by whether the experimenter

FIGURE 6.8

Effects of Payment on Attitudes Toward a Dull Task

Festinger and Carlsmith (1959) predicted that participants who were given insufficient monetary justification for lying (the $1 liars) would experience greater cognitive dissonance and, thus, would express more liking for the dull task than those who received sufficient monetary justification (the $20 liars). Why would insufficient justification create greater dissonance?

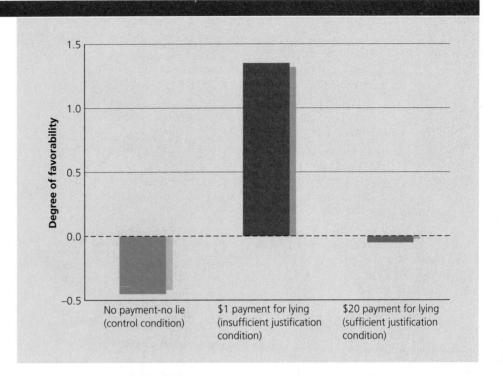

Cognitive Dissonance

A feeling of discomfort caused by performing an action that is inconsistent with one's attitudes.

Inconsistencies of opinion, arising from changes of circumstances, are often justifiable.

Daniel Webster, American statesman, 1782–1852

had promised you $1 versus $20 to tell your lie? If yes, which sum of money would lead to the greatest attitude shift?

This is the scenario of a classic cognitive dissonance experiment conducted by Festinger and J. Merrill Carlsmith (1959). As depicted in figure 6.8, participants who, for $1, told others (who were actually confederates) that the task was "very enjoyable" and "fun" came to believe that it was enjoyable to a far greater degree than those who said so for $20. These $1 liars also expressed greater enthusiasm for the task than a control group who were not asked to lie. Do these findings surprise you? They certainly surprised a lot of attitude researchers because it contradicted reward theories based on operant conditioning principles, which predicted that participants who were paid more to lie would exhibit greater attitude change than those who were paid less (see p. 181).

Although these findings seemed surprising to many, they are consistent with cognitive dissonance theory. The theory states that if you simultaneously hold two cognitions that are inconsistent ("This was a boring task" and "I told someone it was very enjoyable"), this will thwart your desire for cognitive consistency. Recognizing that you have acted inconsistently, you will experience a feeling of discomfort known as **cognitive dissonance.** Festinger believed dissonance was analogous to hunger in its aversiveness; that is, people are naturally motivated to reduce or eliminate the dissonance. How is this cognitive dissonance eliminated or reduced? Table 6.4 lists some ways to reduce dissonance.

In the Festinger and Carlsmith study, only two dissonance-reducing outlets were available to the liars: (1) they could add a third cognition to make their attitude-behavior inconsistency less inconsistent, or (2) they could change their attitude about the task. The reason the "$1 participants" showed more attitude change toward the boring task than the "$20 participants" was that they experienced a greater *amount* of cognitive dissonance. Festinger and Carlsmith reasoned that the $20 participants would not need to change their attitudes because they could justify their actions and, thus, reduce dissonance by adding a third cognition that makes the original cognition less inconsistent: their high payment was *sufficient justification* for their counterattitudinal behavior. Thus, the $20 participants had a reasonable justification for lying. The same could not be said for the $1 participants. They were only given $1 for their lie. This amount of payment provided *insufficient justification* for their counterattitudinal behavior. According to Festinger, when people engage in a counterattitudinal behavior without receiving a large reward, they should experience cognitive

TABLE 6.4

Ways to Reduce Cognitive Dissonance

There are a number of ways to reduce dissonance. For example, consider people who have quit smoking cigarettes because of the health risks, but then, resume the habit. How might they reduce the dissonance aroused by the discrepancy between their attitude ("I don't like smoking") and their behavior ("I'm smoking again")?

Common Strategies	Examples
Changing attitudes: People can simply change their attitudes to make them consistent with discrepant attitudes or prior behaviors.	"I don't really need to quit. I like smoking."
Adding cognitions: If two discrepant thoughts cause dissonance, people can add more consonant thoughts.	"Smoking relaxes me and keeps my weight down, which benefits my health."
Altering the importance of the discrepancy: People can alter the importance of the consonant and discrepant thoughts.	"It's more important to stay relaxed and slim than to worry about maybe getting cancer thirty years from now."
Reducing perceived choice: People can convince themselves that they are not freely choosing to engage in the discrepant behavior.	"I have no choice but to smoke. I have so much stress in my life now that smoking is one of the only ways to calm my nerves."
Changing behavior: People can change their behavior so it no longer conflicts with their attitudes.	"I'm going to stop smoking again."

dissonance. Faced with this dissonance, the $1 group strove to reduce the negative drive state. They could not deny that they lied, so instead they changed their attitude about the task: it was not so boring after all.

Just as the offer of a small reward is insufficient justification for engaging in counterattitudinal behavior, the threat of mild punishment is insufficient justification for *not* engaging in some desired action. In an experiment demonstrating this effect, 4-year-old children were prohibited by an adult from playing with a toy in a playroom (Aronson & Carlsmith, 1963). In one condition the prohibition was induced by a severe threat ("I don't want you to play with the toy on the table. If you play with it, I will be very angry. I will have to take all of my toys and go home!"). In another condition the threat was mild ("I don't want you to play with the toy on the table. If you play with it, I will be annoyed."). Even though all the children had previously stated that they liked this toy, all obeyed the adult's command.

Before reading further, based on your understanding of cognitive dissonance, how should these two groups of children have differed in their attitudes toward this toy after not playing with it? Remember, for both the mildly and severely threatened children, the attitude that "I like the toy on the table" was inconsistent with the realization that "I didn't play with the toy." Yet, for the children who received the severe threat, this was sufficient external justification for not engaging in the desired behavior, and therefore they should not have experienced much dissonance. However, the mildly threatened children had insufficient justification for not playing with the desired toy, and therefore they should have experienced greater dissonance. The only way for them to reduce their dissonance was to devalue the forbidden toy. This is exactly what they did. No similar attitude change was found in the severely threatened group, or in a control group of children who received no threats. Forty-five days after the initial testing, the children who had been mildly threatened still had more negative attitudes toward this toy than did those who had been severely threatened. A replication of this study found that the tendency to shun the highly attractive toy persisted up to nine weeks after the presentation of the mild threat (Freedman, 1965).

This notion of insufficient justification is so important in understanding how cognitive dissonance operates that it bears reviewing. As Festinger stated, if the reasons for engaging in counterattitudinal behavior are strong (for example, "I was paid $20 to lie" or "I was severely threatened not to play with the toy"), little or no dissonance will be generated. But if these reasons are weak ("I was paid only $1 to lie" or "I was only mildly threatened"), then people are confronted with the dissonant-producing thought that they had no strong or clear basis for acting inconsistently with their attitudes. In other words, cognitive dissonance theory demonstrates that the *weaker* the reasons for acting inconsistently with one's attitudes, the *greater* the pressures to change the attitudes in question.

FREEDOM OF CHOICE AND DISSONANCE

Another factor that can create cognitive dissonance is freely choosing to engage in a counterattitudinal behavior. For example, let's suppose young Jack tells his grade-school friends that he hates girls, but later they see him sitting next to Betty Lou on the bus. If the bus driver forced Jack to sit next to Betty Lou, he can legitimately explain his close proximity to her as being beyond his control. According to dissonance theory, due to Jack's lack of choice, he is unlikely to feel responsible for his actions, and therefore he will not experience cognitive dissonance. However, if no one forced Jack to sit next to Betty Lou, then his behavior would be seen as freely chosen; therefore, he should experience discomfort due to his dissonant thoughts ("I hate girls, but I sat next to a girl").

Darwyn Linder and his colleagues (1967) conducted an experiment that demonstrated the role that choice plays in dissonance arousal. College students were asked to write essays in favor of a law barring controversial individuals from speaking on campus. This law, in fact, was actually being discussed in the state legislature, and almost all students opposed its passage. Students were offered either $.50 or $2.50 for their essays. In the "free-choice" condition, the experimenter stressed the students' freedom to refuse to write the essay, while in the "no-choice" condition, no mention was made about the students' right to refuse. Instead, the experimenter acted as if by volunteering to participate in the study, the students had committed themselves to its requirements.

As predicted by cognitive dissonance theory, when students' free choice was stressed, the group that was paid $.50 changed their attitude toward the law so that it was more in line with the essay content, but the attitudes of the group paid $2.50 did not shift. In the "no-choice" condition, the exact opposite effects occurred: the larger amount of money produced greater attitude change (see figure 6.9). The attitude change in the "no-choice" condition does not conform to dissonance theory, but instead follows the principles of operant conditioning, in which external incentives shape attitudes. Thus, to experience dissonance, people must feel that they *freely chose* to behave in a counterattitudinal manner.

JUSTIFICATION OF EFFORT AND DISSONANCE

Although we have seen that using negative incentives—in the form of mild threats—can induce cognitive dissonance, which, in turn, results in less liking for the attitude object, negative incentives can also lead to *increased liking*. Recall the discussion in chapter 2 of Leon Festinger's study of doomsday cult members (Festinger et al., 1956). Here, people had given up their worldly possessions and had left loved ones to await the arrival of space aliens. As the evidence mounted that their leader's prophecy was false, many of the cult members increased their psychological commitment to the cult. Were they insane? Not according to cognitive dissonance theory. Dissonance theorists argue that when people have a bad experience with some group they have freely chosen to join, there is a natural tendency for them to try to transform the bad experience into a good one to reduce cognitive dissonance. In addition, the greater the sacrifice or hardship associated with the choice, the greater the level of dissonance people experience.

To better understand the actions of those who incur large costs in questionable ventures, let's look at an experiment carried out by Elliot Aronson and Judson Mills (1959) on

FIGURE 6.9

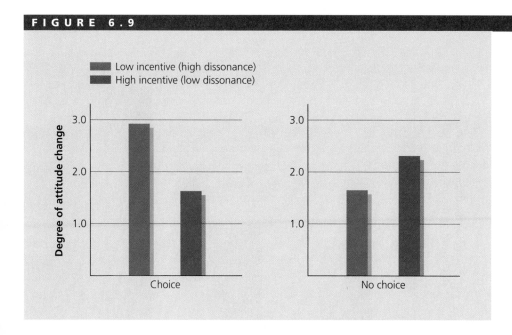

Low incentive (high dissonance)
High incentive (low dissonance)

Perceived Choice, Incentive, and Attitude Change

Linder, Cooper, and Jones (1967) manipulated participants' freedom of choice and incentive. Consistent with cognitive dissonance theory, in the "free-choice" condition, low-incentive students expressed greater attitude change than high-incentive students. However, in the "no-choice" condition, reward or incentive effects occurred: low-incentive students showed less attitude change than high-incentive students. What do these results tell you about the role that perceived freedom of choice plays in attitude change?

the effects of the *severity of initiation* on liking for a group. Participants were college women who volunteered to take part in discussions of the psychology of sex. It was their false understanding that these discussions would be analyzed to better understand group dynamics. Prior to being admitted into the discussion group, each woman, except those in the control condition, was told that she would have to take an "Embarrassment Test" to assure the researchers that she could talk frankly and freely about this intimate topic. The real purpose of this test was to make the participants pay a different "price" to get into the group. Those women in the *severe initiation* condition were required to read aloud to the male experimenter a list of obscene words, as well as some extremely graphic sexual scenes from contemporary novels. (Keep in mind that this was the 1950s, when uttering obscene and sexually graphic words to a university psychologist would make most undergraduates extremely uncomfortable.) In the *mild initiation* condition, women were asked to read aloud such mildly sex-related words as *prostitute, virgin,* and *petting.* This group, then, paid a lower initiation "price" than the severe group. Regardless of how embarrassed the women were or how haltingly they read the words in either condition, all were told they had passed the test and could join the group. The women were then given earphones and instructed to listen in on the group they would soon be joining. What they heard was a discussion that Aronson and Mills described in the following manner:

> The participants spoke dryly and haltingly on secondary sex behavior in the lower animals, contradicted themselves and one another, mumbled several non sequiturs, started sentences that they never finished, hemmed, hawed, and in general conducted one of the most worthless and uninteresting discussions imaginable. (Aronson & Mills, 1959)

After listening to this discussion, the women were asked to rate both the discussion and the group members on such evaluative scales as "dull-interesting" and "intelligent-unintelligent." According to dissonance theory, the women in the severe initiation group should have experienced a pair of dissonant thoughts: "I willingly went through a very embarrassing initiation in order to join this sex discussion group"; "These group discussions are dull and worthless." To reduce cognitive dissonance, these women had to alter one of these thoughts. Because they could not deny that they willingly paid a high price to join the group, the only thought they could reasonably alter was their group evaluation. In contrast, the women in the "mild" and "no initiation" groups had invested little,

Those who have free seats at a play hiss first.

Chinese proverb

That which costs little is less valued.

Miguel de Cervantes, Spanish writer, 1547–1616

FIGURE 6.10

Participants' attitudes toward the quality of the discussion in the Aronson and Mills (1959) experiment were significantly influenced by the "price" they had to pay to join the group. Based on cognitive dissonance theory, why did those women in the severe initiation condition express greater liking for the quality of the discussion?

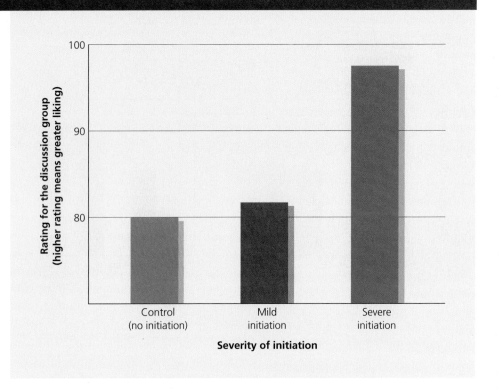

if anything, to join, and thus should not have experienced much dissonance. Consistent with this reasoning, the severe initiation group gave significantly more positive evaluations of the discussion than those who were in either the mild initiation or the control groups (see figure 6.10).

Replications of this experiment have demonstrated that this effect is strong: the more you pay for something, the more you like it (Axsom, 1989; Gerard & Mathewson, 1966). Is it any wonder that many of the members of Festinger's doomsday cult increased their allegiance when those outside the group were calling it a fraud and a sham? Agreeing with this judgment would have called into question all that they had suffered for. Faced with such a choice, they justified to themselves not only the actions of their group, but their own actions as well.

POSTDECISION DISSONANCE AND ALTERED PERCEPTIONS

A few years ago, a student in our department applied to several graduate programs in social psychology and was accepted into three of his top choices. Following a long process of weighing the strengths and weaknesses of each school, he made his choice. Shortly thereafter, I saw him on campus and asked if he had any regrets. "No, Dr. Franzoi," he said with genuine sincerity. "Since making my decision, I'm even more certain I made the right choice." Then, being the bright student that he was, he smiled and said, "Now I really understand the concept of postdecision dissonance."

What did this aspiring social psychologist mean by this last statement? He merely meant that he had firsthand experience with a phenomenon that Festinger first described in the 1950s. Festinger stated that making a decision often arouses dissonance. He explained that whenever we must decide between attractive alternatives, the final choice is to some extent inconsistent with some of our beliefs. That is, as soon as we *commit* ourselves to a particular course of action, the attractive aspects of the unchosen alternatives and the unattractive aspects of our choice are inconsistent with our decision. As the difficulty or importance of the decision increases, the amount of postdecision dissonance increases.

Because of our tendency to react to decisions in this manner, we often try to reduce dissonance by *altering our perceptions* of the choices we had entertained prior to making our final choice. We do this by improving our evaluation of the chosen alternative and lowering our evaluations of the unchosen alternatives (Frenkl & Doob, 1976).

Such after-the-fact, altered perceptions have been found in the behavior of consumers following product choices (Gilovich et al., 1995; Murphy & Miller, 1997), voters on election day (Regan & Kilduff, 1988), and even bettors at a racetrack (Brownstein et al., 2004; Knox & Inkster, 1968). Because votes, bets, and many product purchases cannot be changed once a decision has been made, once we commit ourselves we are motivated to reduce postdecision dissonance. Under these circumstances, the only way for us to accomplish this task is to convince ourselves that we made the right choice.

Cognitive Consistency Is Not a Universal Motive

In Festinger's theory, he assumed that everyone has an equal desire to engage in cognitively consistent actions. However, cross-cultural research later found that this desire is more descriptive of individualist cultures than those with a collectivist orientation (Heine & Lehman, 1997; Kashima, 1987; Kashima et al., 1992). Based on these findings, many cross-cultural researchers argued that the need for consistency is based on the premise that the person is an independent entity unaffected by the social context. Although this is the way people in individualist cultures are generally taught to think, people in collectivist cultures are socialized to develop interdependent selves, which are defined in relation to others, and thus, tend to be more flexible. This more flexible conception of the self encourages people from collectivist cultures to think in more holistic ways than individualists, making them more comfortable with contradiction and inconsistency (Choi & Nisbett, 2000; Heine & Lehman, 1997; Peng & Nisbett, 1999).

An illustration of the weaker attitude-behavior consistency need can be seen in the Japanese notion of the self. In Japanese culture, there are two important aspects to the self: "omote" (front) is presented to the public as a socially acceptable aspect of the self, whereas "ura" (back) is that aspect of the self that is hidden from the public (Bachnik, 1992). The Japanese value both self-aspects and teach their young how to appropriately use them. Thus, when presenting omote, not acting according to one's true attitudes is perfectly acceptable

The only completely consistent people are the dead.

Aldous Huxley, British novelist, 1894–1963

Consistency, madam, is the first of Christian duties.

Charlotte Brontë, American author, 1816–1855

Can you think of instances in your own life in which you convinced yourself that a bad experience was really a good and worthwhile one?

Dilbert reprinted by permission of United Feature Syndicate, Inc.

and would not cause dissonance. For example, in one study, Japanese and American students read episodes in which hypothetical characters had to choose between honestly expressing their attitudes or not doing so to maintain social appropriateness (Iwao, 1989). As expected, American students more likely favored attitude-consistent choices than their Japanese counterparts. For instance, in one hypothetical situation, a father privately disapproved of his daughter marrying someone of another race. Almost half of the American students (49 percent) stated that it would be wrong for the father to think to himself that he would never allow the marriage yet tell the couple that he favored it. On the contrary, less than 7 percent of the Japanese felt this sort of attitude-discrepant behavior was inappropriate. In summary, then, what many North Americans and other individualists consider to be discrepant and psychologically aversive—namely, believing one thing but saying something else—may not be as troubling to collectivists.

If you are from an individualistic culture, you might be thinking, "I don't often get upset with acting differently from my attitudes. What gives?" Beyond cultural considerations, research indicates that some people tolerate cognitive inconsistencies better than others. Spend a few minutes completing the *Preference for Consistency Scale* in table 6.5. Robert Cialdini and his colleagues (1995) have found that people who score high on this scale are highly motivated to keep their behavior consistent with their attitudes, as predicted by cognitive dissonance theory. In contrast, those who score low on this preference scale are much less bothered by inconsistent actions, and instead, appear open and oriented to flexibility in their behavior. Given these diverging motivational patterns, it is not surprising that those with a high preference for consistency are more likely to experience cognitive dissonance than those with a low consistency preference (Newby-Clark et al., 2002).

In the final analysis, when we consider the universality of the cognitive consistency motive, it appears that at least two factors can derail expected cognitive dissonance effects when otherwise they should be aroused: a person's cultural upbringing may make attitude-discrepant behavior an appropriate and valued option, and a person's underlying psychological needs may reduce the aversiveness of attitude-discrepant acts.

Several Theories Have Challenged Cognitive Dissonance Theory

In addition to questioning the universality of the cognitive consistency motive, a number of other researchers have challenged different aspects of cognitive dissonance theory and have offered various alterations or outright replacements of the original model (see Harmon-Jones & Mills, 1999).

SELF-PERCEPTION EXPLANATIONS

The first and most serious challenge to cognitive dissonance theory came from Bem's self-perception theory. As you recall from our previous discussion, this theory claims that we infer our attitudes by observing our own behavior and the context in which it occurs, much as we do when perceiving other people's actions. According to Bem, when people behave inconsistently, they first seek explanations outside themselves for their behavior, and when they cannot find a probable *external* cause for their behavior, they assume that there must be an internal cause, namely an attitude. This search for a cause of behavior is not fueled by a need to reduce an unpleasant psychological state—as is assumed in cognitive dissonance theory—but rather, it is based on calm rationality.

To test his hypothesis, Bem (1967) had people simply read a description of the Festinger and Carlsmith (1959) study, in which a person performs a dull task and then is paid either $1 or $20 to tell someone else that it was fun and interesting. Based on their observation of this study's procedures, Bem had readers guess the person's attitude toward the task. Despite the fact that these people experienced no cognitive dissonance, the pattern of results duplicated that found in the original study. As the readers perceived the situation, the person who was paid $20 to say the task was interesting really was lying—he did it for the money. However, the person who was paid $1 must have been sincere, because the small

TABLE 6.5

The Preference for Consistency Scale

Instructions

The extent to which people have a preference for consistency is measured by items on the Preference for Consistency Scale (PCS: Cialdini et al., 1995). To take the PCS, read each item below and then indicate how well each statement describes you using the following scale:

1 = Strongly disagree

2 = Disagree

3 = Somewhat disagree

4 = Slightly disagree

5 = Neither agree nor disagree

6 = Slightly agree

7 = Somewhat agree

8 = Agree

9 = Strongly agree

_____ 1. It is important to me that those who know me can predict what I will do.

_____ 2. I want to be described by others as a stable, predictable person.

_____ 3. The appearance of consistency is an important part of the image I present to the world.

_____ 4. An important requirement for any friend of mine is personal consistency.

_____ 5. I typically prefer to do things the same way.

_____ 6. I want my close friends to be predictable.

_____ 7. It is important to me that others view me as a stable person.

_____ 8. I make an effort to appear consistent to others.

_____ 9. It doesn't bother me much if my actions are inconsistent.

Directions for Scoring

The last PCS item (#9) is reverse-scored; that is, for this item a lower rating actually indicates a higher level of consistency preference. Before summing the items, recode item 9 so that 1 = 9, 2 = 8, 3 = 7, 4 = 6, 6 = 4, 7 = 3, 8 = 2, 9 = 1. To calculate your preference for consistency score, add up your responses to the 9 items.

When Cialdini and his colleagues developed the PCS in 1995, the mean score for college students was about 48. The higher your score is above this value, the greater is your preference for consistency. The lower your score is below this value, the less of this preference you probably possess.

amount of money certainly was not enough to justify lying. This study suggests that cognitive dissonance may not be necessary in explaining how behavioral inconsistencies can cause attitude change.

Which of these two competing theories is correct? Based on a number of studies, it appears that *both* are correct, but in different situations. People are most likely to experience dissonance, and respond in line with cognitive dissonance theory, when their behavior is sharply discrepant with their attitudes, when the behavior in question is central to the self, and when there is no external justification for the behavior (Aronson, 1969; Fazio et al., 1977). However, when the attitude-behavior inconsistency is only mild, these same people tend to behave in ways expected by self-perception theory. Thus, dissonance is likely if the attitude is important to the self or the discrepancy between attitude and behavior is substantial. When the issue is not important to the self or the attitude-behavior inconsistency is small, then self-perception processes are likely to operate.

TABLE 6.6

Cognitive Dissonance and Self-Perception Theories Compared

Cognitive Dissonance Theory	Self-Perception Theory
Attitudes directly known	Attitudes inferred from behavior
Attitudes in "dissonance groups" are distortions	Attitudes in "dissonance groups" are rationally inferred
Unpleasant affect necessary for attitude formation	No unpleasant affect or negative drive state involved in attitude formation

When Is Dissonance or Self-Perception of Attitudes Most Likely?

Cognitive Dissonance Theory	Self-Perception Theory
Dissonance is most likely when the attitude in question is important to the self or the attitude-discrepancy is large	Self-perception of attitudes is most likely when the attitude-behavior discrepancy is small

Table 6.6 compares the two theories. If you examine the conditions under which cognitive dissonance or self-perception most likely operate, do you see a pattern emerge? What type of attitude—explicit or implicit—do the two theories seem to account for? Hint: Recent studies indicate that arousing cognitive dissonance only causes changes in explicit attitudes, not implicit attitudes (Gawronski & Strack, 2004). In other words, cognitive dissonance theory only accounts for how our explicit attitudes are affected when we behave in a counterattitudinal manner. This makes sense, because dissonance only occurs when we become aware of an attitude-behavior inconsistency, and implicit attitudes by definition are attitudes of which we are unaware.

What about self-perception theory? It appears to best explain attitude change for small attitude-behavior inconsistencies or for unimportant issues. But perhaps more important, it may provide an explanation for how implicit attitudes become explicit attitudes. That is, according to this reinterpretation of self-perception theory, we may have an implicit attitude that is influencing our behavior, prompting us to consistently behave toward a target object in a particular way. This implicit attitude is influencing our actions but we have not yet formed an explicit attitude toward the target object. Then something happens to cause us to consider what our explicit attitude is toward this target object. We examine our past behavior, infer that we have an attitude that is consistent with our past actions, and articulate to ourselves an explicit attitude that is consistent with our already existing and long-operating implicit attitude. Thus, cognitive dissonance theory explains the conditions under which certain explicit attitudes are changed, while self-perception theory may explain how implicit attitudes prompt the development of evaluatively similar explicit attitudes. To date, no research has specifically tested this possible reinterpretation of self-perception theory, so it remains a speculative hunch.

SELF-AFFIRMATION EXPLANATIONS

Self-Affirmation Theory

A theory predicting that people will often cope with specific threats to the integrity of their self-concept by reminding themselves of other unrelated but cherished aspects of their self-concept.

Another interpretation of dissonance theory with a focus on the self is Claude Steele's **self-affirmation theory.** According to Steele (1988), when we act in a manner inconsistent with our sense of honesty or integrity, this threatens our self-concept. We ask ourselves, "If I acted this way, am I really who I think I am?" Steele contends that when our self-concept is threatened in this manner, we often can reduce or entirely avoid the negative affect that Festinger called cognitive dissonance by affirming our integrity in some other unrelated area of our lives. This self-affirmation can be achieved in many ways and does not necessarily have to resolve the specific dilemma that threatened the self in the first place. Thus, according to self-affirmation theory, we can reduce dissonance without resolving the self-inconsistency that originally caused it.

In one study supporting the self-affirmation perspective (Steele & Liu, 1981), researchers induced participants to write an essay opposing state funding for handicapped services. Before writing this essay, some participants were told that they would later be asked to help a blind student, while others were not given this expectation. Only those participants who were not given a chance to help the blind changed their attitudes to be more consistent with the essay. In other words, if people could reaffirm their sense of self-worth, they felt no need to resolve the inconsistency that initially threatened the self. This study and others suggest that inconsistency between our attitudes and our behavior may not be the motivating feature of cognitive dissonance (Aronson et al., 1995; Steele et al., 1993). Instead, *threats to the integrity of the self* may be the key motivator, and any response useful in restoring integrity reduces dissonance. Although research indicates that we often self-affirm when our self-concepts are threatened, it is also true that *level of self-esteem* affects our ability to engage in self-affirmation. That is, because people with high self-esteem have more positive aspects of their self-concept to affirm than those low in self-esteem, they find self-affirmation easier to engage in than people with low self-esteem (Dodgson & Wood, 1998; Holland et al., 2002).

As you can see, cognitive dissonance theory is an excellent example of a "fertile" theory (see chapter 1) that continues to generate novel ways of understanding attitudes (Harmon-Jones, 2000; Norton et al., 2003; Stone, 2003; Van Overwalle & Jordens, 2002). We now know that cognitive dissonance does not always result when we act in a counterattitudinal manner. Whether dissonance is aroused depends not only on how central the need for cognitive consistency is in our thinking, but also on whether the attitude-behavior discrepancy is important to the self and is substantial. And even when the attitude-behavior discrepancy is important and substantial, dissonance might still be avoided if we can redirect self-awareness to some other valued self-aspects.

SECTION SUMMARY

- Cognitive consistency is an important motive in many people's attitudes and behavior
- Cognitive dissonance theory contends that if people hold inconsistent cognitions, they experience an unpleasant emotion (cognitive dissonance), which they try to reduce
- Cognitive dissonance does not always occur when one acts inconsistently
- Cognitive dissonance is most likely when:
    the attitude is important to the self
    the inconsistency is substantial
- The need for cognitive consistency appears to be less in collectivist cultures
- Cognitive dissonance can be reduced through self-affirmation

FEATURED STUDY

GROUP MEMBERSHIP AND ASSUMED ATTITUDE SIMILARITY

Chen, F. F., & Kenrick, D. T. (2002). Repulsion or attraction? Group membership and assumed attitude similarity. *Journal of Personality and Social Psychology, 83,* 111–125.

We tend to like people who are similar to us and we also tend to like those with whom we share group membership. But what happens when a member of our group is discovered to disagree with our social and political attitudes or when a person who is a member of an outgroup is found to share our attitudes? In this article, the researchers investigated the possibility that the influence of attitude similarity and dissimilarity on attraction depends on whether the person being evaluated is regarded as an ingroup or as an outgroup member. Based on the belief that people assume that ingroup members are more similar to them than outgroup members, it was hypothesized that group membership would moderate the extent of the relationship between manipulated attitude similarity and attraction. Specifically, it was predicted that perceiving attitude similarity would produce a greater change in attraction toward an outgroup member than toward an ingroup member. In addition, it was also predicted that perceiving attitude dissimilarity would produce a greater change in repulsion toward an ingroup member than toward an outgroup member. The first experiment in this three-experiment study is described below.

Method

Participants were 389 psychology students, 228 women and 161 men, who were recruited for a study named "Interpersonal Judgment." Students participated in the study to partially fulfill an introductory psychology class requirement. Participants were run in small groups, ranging in size from 3 to 13. When they arrived at the testing site, participants first completed an attitude survey and then were informed that the target student whom they would be evaluating was their own age and sex and was a Democrat (or Republican). Participants then judged this person by completing an Interpersonal Judgment Scale designed to measure their initial attraction toward the target person. After completing the judgments, they were asked to guess at how the target person would respond to a series of attitude items. Researchers compared these responses to the participant's own attitude

responses to calculate a measure of assumed attitude similarity. After this intitial phase of the study, the experimenter asked participants to copy an article word for word while the experimenter was out of the room. This task was designed as a distraction to give the experimenter time to fabricate the target person's attitude responses. After ten minutes the experimenter gave participants the attitude survey supposedly completed by the target person and were told to examine it carefully because they would later be asked to recall the answers. Then they were asked to make another judgment of the target person. After completing this assessment, participants were handed a blank attitude survey and asked to recall how the target person had completed the survey. This was designed to check on the accuracy with which the participants perceived the attitude manipulation. Finally, participants were debriefed and thanked for their participation.

Results and Discussion

The attraction-repulsion effect was operationally defined by how far the final impression was from the baseline impression. As hypothesized, similar attitudes produced a stronger attraction effect for the outgroup target person than for the ingroup target person. Also as predicted, the lower the assumed similarity with the target person, the stronger the similarity-attraction effect toward him/her. Similarly, the higher the assumed similarity with the target person, the stronger the dissimilarity-repulsion effect toward him/her. In other words, because participants initially expected that the ingroup person would be more similar to them than would the outgroup person, similarity produced a greater change in attraction for the outgroup member.

All three experiments in this study provide evidence that after participants had been exposed to attitude information about the target person they were more attracted to similar than to dissimilar others, regardless of group membership. Moreover, political group membership was no longer important in determining liking. Membership in an outgroup still affected attraction, but compared with the effect of attitude similarity, the effect was much smaller. These findings are consistent with previous research indicating that similarity of beliefs and attitudes will override similarity of group membership as a determinant of who you will seek out for social interaction.

APPLICATIONS

HOW DO REFERENCE GROUPS SHAPE YOUR SOCIAL AND POLITICAL ATTITUDES?

*H*ave you ever observed pleasant dinner conversation change into bitter accusations and denunciations due to one person discovering that another held different attitudes about some political or social issue? Have you yourself been one of these dinner combatants?

Our values and many of our attitudes are often determined by the groups to which we seek membership or with which we identify. A **reference group** is a group to which people orient themselves, using its standards to judge themselves and the world. An important defining characteristic of a reference group is that people have an *emotional attachment* to it and refer to it for guidance, even if they are not actual members.[1] Reference groups can be large and inclusive, such as an entire nation or religion, but they can also be much smaller, such as one's family or friends.

Reference Group

A group to which people orient themselves, using its standards to judge themselves and the world.

One of the first and best studies investigating reference group influence on attitudes was the research of Theodore Newcomb in the 1930s documenting college students' shift from social and political conservatism when they entered college to liberalism when they graduated. Newcomb's research began in 1934 when he was hired as a young faculty member at the recently established Bennington College for women in Vermont. This new college was very exclusive, with almost all of the students coming from upper class, politically conservative New England families. In contrast, Newcomb and most of the other young faculty were very liberal in their social views. Thus, the first-year entering students were moving from one social context—a conservative family and social life—into a new context in which the authority figures and role models held exactly opposite social views.

Due to its small size (300 students and faculty) and its location in a relatively isolated area of rural Vermont, Bennington fostered a great deal of interaction between the faculty and the female student body. This unique convergence of circumstances prompted Newcomb to test a belief that he had about how people's attitudes are influenced by changes in their reference groups. To accomplish this task, Newcomb (1943) tested the social and political attitudes of the arriving first-year students, and he remeasured their attitudes each year until they graduated. His findings indicated that with each passing semester, the students' social and political attitudes became increasingly liberal. As one student explained

Political and social attitudes developed by many college students at Bennington College in the 1930s continued to influence their behavior throughout the rest of their lives.

her shift in attitudes over the course of time, "I simply got filled with new ideas here, and the only possible formulation of all of them was to adopt a radical approach" (Newcomb, 1958, p. 273). Another stated, "I'm easily influenced by people whom I respect, and the people who rescued me when I was down and out, intellectually, gave me a radical intellectual approach" (Newcomb, 1958, p. 273).

Newcomb believed that this attitude change was due to the students' disengagement from their conservative hometown reference group and their integration into a new, more liberal reference group at Bennington. Yet not all students experienced such a "radical" shift in their attitudes during their four years at Bennington. Indeed, some students maintained their conservative political perspective throughout their college years. How did these students differ from the rest of the Bennington population? Newcomb discovered that these students did not experience a shift in their reference groups. They spent their vacations with their parents and frequently traveled home on weekends and therefore did not blend into the Bennington culture.

How might the Bennington study relate to your own college experience? During your time at college, have your social and political attitudes changed from what they were in high school? To what degree have these attitudes been shaped by your college experiences?

The importance of reference groups in maintaining attitudes even when the person is no longer immersed within the group itself was demonstrated by Newcomb in two separate follow-up studies of the women who attended Bennington College in the late 1930s (Newcomb et al., 1967). The first

---

[1]Because emotional attachment and not membership itself is the key factor in defining reference groups, they are broader in scope than ingroups, which are discussed in chapters 3, 8, and 10.

follow-up interviews were conducted in the 1960s, twenty-five years after the original study. These Bennington alumnae were now in their 40s and 50s and were also in the top 1 percent of the population in socioeconomic status. Comparing them with non-Bennington-educated women of comparable wealth, age, religion, and geographic region, Newcomb found that the Bennington women's political attitudes and behavior were much more liberal. In addition, the Bennington women's selection of a spouse and friends was partly based on their liberal political preferences.

In the 1980s, Newcomb and his coworkers again recontacted the Bennington women, who were now in their 60s and 70s. Of the 527 women who participated in the original studies, 77 had died and 51 could not be located or contacted. Ultimately, 335 agreed to participate in this final study (Alwin et al., 1991). The results supported Newcomb's initial hypothesis about the strength of reference groups. The women's liberal reference groups, forged during their college days a half century ago, still significantly influenced their lives. As you can see in table 6.7, when compared with other college-educated women in their same age group, the Bennington graduates consistently preferred the more liberal candidate in each presidential election from 1952 to 1984. They also expressed greater interest in following government affairs and political events. Despite the fact that college-educated women of the 1930s generation were much more likely than noncollege-educated women to align themselves with the more conservative Republican Party throughout their lives, this was not the case for the Bennington women. In fact, their social and political attitudes were even more intensely liberal than most women of their generation.

The Bennington study highlights the important role that reference groups play in shaping life choices (Cohen & Alwin, 1993). Other studies, testing different social groups, have replicated Newcomb's overall findings (Marwell et al., 1987; McAdam, 1989). For example, female college students who enroll in women's studies courses tend to develop stronger feminist attitudes and beliefs than women who are

TABLE 6.7

Voting Preferences of Bennington Graduates in Presidential Elections

The liberal political attitudes that many Bennington students developed in the 1930s were maintained over the years and are reflected in their presidential preferences, where they consistently voted for the more liberal Democratic candidate in all elections studied. In contrast, women with similar educational background and age tended to prefer the more conservative Republican candidates. Where do you think your own university environment stacks up on the liberal-conservative dimension? Have your political attitudes shifted in the direction of this dominant campus view during your time in college?

Election Year	Conservative Candidate	Liberal Candidate
1952		
Bennington women	43%	57%
Comparable women	64%	36%
1960		
Bennington women	26%	74%
Comparable women	75%	25%
1968		
Bennington women	33%	67%
Comparable women	79%	19%
1976		
Bennington women	31%	69%
Comparable women	55%	45%
1984		
Bennington women	27%	72%
Comparable women	73%	26%

interested, but do not enroll, in these courses (Henderson-King & Stewart, 1999). Together, these findings illustrate the important role that reference groups play in shaping and maintaining social and political attitudes, as well as the role that these attitudes play in shaping the life course of those who hold them. To a substantial degree, when you select a college or a university to attend following high school graduation, you may also be inadvertently choosing a new social and political perspective. Sometimes, these newly adopted political and social attitudes become the "little surprises" that young adults spring upon their parents around the dinner table during semester breaks and summer holidays. If you have had such conversations with your parents, or believe you will have some in the not-too-distant future, now you can also describe the social psychological dynamics of your political transformation as well. Pleasant dining!

THE BIG PICTURE

My goal in this chapter was to guide you through the "theoretical attitude maze" so that you gained a greater understanding of how you and others evaluate your social world. As attitude holders, we differ in our need to evaluate the world, just as we differ in the need to keep our attitudes consistent with our behavior. Sometimes our attitudes are shaped by our self-concepts, and at other times, our self-beliefs and personal values have little impact on how we evaluate things in our world. We are sometimes active and at other times relatively passive in this process of attitude formation and change. Further, our attitudes can form, change, and guide our behavior with or without our conscious awareness.

Social psychologists' attempts to understand the attitude concept has been a journey in which different theoretical perspectives have taken turns trying to make sense of the diverse empirical findings that have accumulated over the years (Eagly, 1992). In the 1960s, cognitive dissonance theory and other motivation-based theories held everyone's interest. Beginning in the 1970s, the cognitive approach became the perspective of choice among most attitude researchers. Now, as we begin the twenty-first century, besides the continued development of various cognitive theories, there has been a new wave of interest in the motivational point of view, and a recognition that even unconsciously held attitudes can shape the direction of our social behavior. One of the more important issues attitude researchers are now exploring involves the conditions under which explicit versus implicit attitudes predict behavior. Accompanying this increased theoretical sophistication and diversity is a renewed confidence that attitudes can substantially predict future behavior. One of the most successful attempts at theoretical integration is the *elaboration likelihood model* of Richard Petty and John Cacioppo (1984, 1986), which we will closely examine in our chapter 7 analysis of persuasion.

WEB SITES
accessed through http://www.mhhe.com/franzoi4

Web sites for this chapter focus on attitude formation and change, including cognitive consistency theories and how consistency needs can be used to increase retail sales.

Theories of Cognitive Consistency

This Web page analyzes cognitive consistency theories and explores the question of whether cognitive consistency needs can be used to increase retail sales.

Steve's Primer of Practical Persuasion and Influence

This Web page discusses the elements of attitude theory, including vivid examples that demonstrate how attitudes function in daily living.

Persuasion

CHAPTER OUTLINE

PREVIEW   *Many factors determine whether a
persuasive message will be effective. To what degree are
subliminal messages an effective avenue of persuasion?*

THE BIG PICTURE

WEB SITES

*A*lcohol is very often a key ingredient at college parties. It is also the key contributing factor to an array of antisocial behaviors on college campuses, including fights, vandalism, rape, and drunk-driving accidents (Wechsler et al., 2002; Weitzman et al., 2003). An extensive three-year investigation by the Task Force on College Drinking, commissioned by the National Institute on Alcohol Abuse and Alcoholism, found that every year approximately 1,400 college students die from alcohol-related causes and another 150,000 students develop a health problem related to alcohol (NIAAA, 2002). In addition, each year more than 600,000 students are assaulted by other students who have been drinking.

Imagine for a minute that you are a college administrator trying to figure out how to deal with the problem of excess alcohol consumption on your campus. Further imagine that within the past year you have had the heartbreaking task of informing a mother and a father that their son had died of alcohol poisoning, and you regularly work with campus security and local law enforcement officials on incidents involving physical and sexual assaults in which alcohol was a contributing factor. How would you try to persuade students to change

Binge drinking is a serious problem on college campuses. What sort of persuasive messages might be effective in convincing young adults to drink responsibly?

their attitudes toward alcohol and excess drinking? Would you promote "Just Say No" or "Think Before You Drink" ad campaigns to convince students to drink less? Could social psychological theory and research help you develop an effective program to lower students' health and safety risks involving alcohol?

In this chapter, we examine the social psychological dynamics of **persuasion,** which is the process of consciously attempting to change attitudes through the transmission of some message. What I want you to understand from the outset is that it is not just college administrators and other authority figures who try to change attitudes. We all engage in this universal avocation. If you doubt this assertion, read on and I will attempt to change your mind.

HOW HAVE VIEWS OF PERSUASION CHANGED?

Attitudes can be changed in many different ways. Before exploring these avenues, let us examine how social psychologists' views of persuasion have changed over the years (Albarracín, 2002; Petty, 1997).

The Message-Learning Approach Identified What Strengthens and Weakens a Persuasive Message

One of the first and most influential research programs on attitude change was developed during and after World War II, under the direction of Carl Hovland at Yale University (McGuire, 1999). In this endeavor, Hovland collaborated with other prominent social psychologists such as Irving Janis, Harold Kelley, Herbert Kelman, and Muzafer Sherif (Hovland et al., 1949, 1953). Their *message-learning* approach to understanding persuasion, which William McGuire later elaborated and extended in the 1960s, employed basic principles of learning theory to explain the distinctions between effective and ineffective persuasive communications. According to this perspective, attitude change followed a series of stages. First, we must pay *attention* to the message; second, we must *comprehend* the message; and third, we must *accept* the message. Each stage in this process is dependent on the preceding stage. Comprehension cannot occur if we do not pay attention to the message. Likewise, a message will not be accepted if it is not understood. However, if we do attend to and understand the message, acceptance will occur if the rewards or incentives for the new attitudinal position outweigh those associated with the old attitude.

In their investigations of attitude change, the Yale researchers conducted experiments that focused on four factors that influence persuasion: (1) *source variables,* (2) *message variables,* (3) *medium* or *channel variables,* and (4) *target variables.* They attempted to explain how a person or group (the source) communicates a message through some medium or channel to change the attitudes of some target person or group. Put simply, they studied *who* says *what* by *what means* and to *whom.*

The Cognitive-Response Approach Seeks to Identify What Makes People Think About Persuasive Arguments

The message-learning approach is generally credited with providing a good deal of insight into *when* and *how* persuasion occurs. In contrast, the more recent *cognitive-response* approach has been helpful in better understanding *why* people change their attitudes in response to persuasive messages (Chaiken, 1987; Petty & Cacioppo, 1986). Further, whereas the message-learning approach took a relatively *passive* view of the recipient of persuasion, the cognitive-response approach conceives of people as being *active* participants in the persuasion process. That is, the thoughts that people generate in response to a message are believed to be the end result of information-processing activity (Chaiken & Trope, 1999). Social psychologists who adopt this perspective attempt to systematically analyze (1) what

Elaboration Likelihood Model

A theory that persuasive messages can cause attitude change in two ways, each differing in the amount of cognitive effort or elaboration it requires.

Central Route to Persuasion

Persuasion that occurs when people think carefully about a communication and are influenced by the strength of its arguments.

Peripheral Route to Persuasion

Persuasion that occurs when people do not think carefully about a communication and instead are influenced by cues that are irrelevant to the content or quality of the communication.

Profound thoughts arise only in debate, with a possibility of counterargument, only when there is a possibility of expressing not only correct ideas, but also dubious ideas.

Andrei Sakharov, Russian scientist and social critic, 1921–1989

Social Sense

View the video on the elaboration likelihood model

people attend to when they receive a persuasive communication, and (2) how their cognitive assessment of the appeal influences their current attitudes.

The most influential theory to develop out of the cognitive-response approach is Richard Petty and John Cacioppo's (1986) **elaboration likelihood model** (ELM), which assumes that people want to be correct in their attitudes. The term *elaboration likelihood* refers to the probability that the target of a persuasive message will elaborate (that is, carefully analyze and attempt to comprehend) the information contained in the message. According to the model, we either engage in high or low elaboration when attending to and processing persuasive messages.

When motivated and able to think carefully about the content of a message (high elaboration), we are influenced by the strength and quality of the arguments: Petty and Cacioppo say we have taken the **central route to persuasion.** Whether central-route processing leads to attitude change or not is determined by the proportion of thoughts we generate that are consistent with or counter to the persuasive message. If our elaboration of the message yields more thoughts consistent with the message arguments we are likely to be persuaded, but no attitude change occurs when we generate many counterarguments.

In contrast to this critical thinking, when unable or unwilling to analyze message content we take the **peripheral route to persuasion.** In peripheral-route processing, we pay attention to cues that are irrelevant to the content or quality of the communication (low elaboration), such as the attractiveness of the communicator or the sheer amount of information presented. By attending to these peripheral cues, we can evaluate a message without engaging in any extensive thinking about the actual issues under consideration. This means that it is not necessary for a person who takes the peripheral route to comprehend the content of a message: attitude change can occur without comprehension. This is one of the main differences between the cognitive-response approach and the message-learning approach.[1] Figure 7.1 depicts these two different persuasion routes.

Do these two different types of cognitive processes sound familiar? Think back to our discussion of social cognition in previous chapters. As flexible social thinkers, we sometimes carefully analyze all relevant factors and behave in a systematic and rational fashion, but at other times we try to save time by taking mental shortcuts. This "thoughtful" versus "lazy" way of thinking is essentially what comprises the two routes to persuasion. The assumption underlying this theory of persuasion is that at any given time we either engage in central-route processing of information or peripheral-route processing; we cannot do both simultaneously. A good deal of evidence suggests that we do indeed have to switch back and forth between these two different modes of thinking, but some social psychologists believe that it is possible to use both central-route and peripheral-route processing simultaneously. As it now stands, the research evidence provides most support for the separate dual modes approach to persuasion proposed by the elaboration likelihood model (Petty et al., 2004a; Wegener et al., 2004). Check out a description of the elaboration likelihood model by Richard Petty on your Social Sense CD-ROM.

According to the elaboration likelihood model and other cognitive-response theories, although attitude change can occur through either the thoughtful mode of central processing or the lazy mode of peripheral processing, attitudes formed by means of the lazy route are weaker, less resistant to counterarguments, and less predictive of actual

---

[1]Although the elaboration likelihood model is the most influential of the cognitive-response theories, a related theory that also adds to our understanding of persuasion is the heuristic-systematic model developed by Shelly Chaiken (1980). Like the ELM, this model asserts that people either attempt to carefully and intentionally judge the truth of a persuasive message (systematic processing) or use simple decision rules, called heuristics, to spontaneously and automatically estimate the validity of a persuasive message (heuristic processing). Because these two theories are similar in many important ways, for simplicity's sake, I use the ELM's terminology in describing the cognitive processing of persuasive messages.

FIGURE 7.1

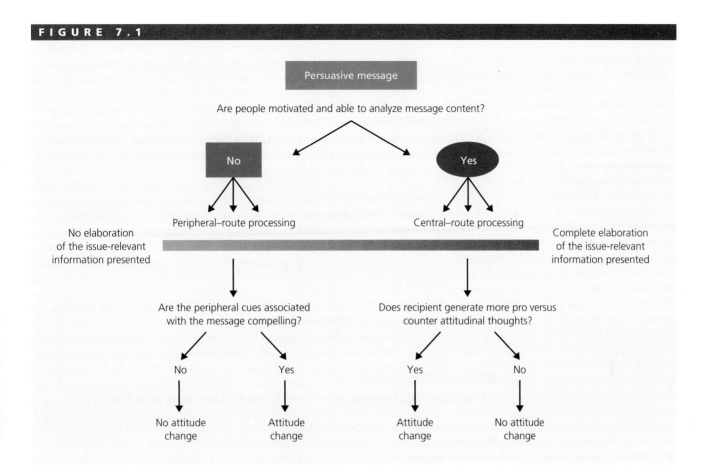

Two Routes to Persuasion

The elaboration likelihood model describes how people evaluate persuasive messages based on their ability and motivation to analyze its content. As the likelihood of thinking about the persuasive message increases, the processes specified by the central route become more likely determinants of attitudes, and those specified by the peripheral route become less likely determinants. This process is reversed as the likelihood of thinking about the persuasive message decreases. In central-route processing, message content is carefully scrutinized, and attitude change is likely if the message recipient generates a greater proportion of thoughts that are consistent with the message rather than counter to the message. However, in peripheral-route processing, evaluation of the message is based on a shallow analysis of incidental cues, such as the communicator's credibility, status, or likability. If these peripheral cues are compelling, the recipient's attitudes will change in line with the persuasive message, even if the recipient doesn't comprehend the message arguments. Of the two routes to persuasion, which do you think secures the most enduring attitude change?

behavior than those formed through the thoughtful route (Petty et al., 1995). An analogy might be that if attitudes are like houses, then attitudes formed by the peripheral route are like houses made from straw or sticks. They require little effort to develop and are extremely vulnerable to destruction. In contrast, attitudes formed by the central route are like houses made of bricks. They take a good deal of effort to construct and are strong and durable. As we know from both childhood fairy tales and our own life experiences, well-built houses and highly elaborated attitudes are the best insurance against the huffing and puffing of someone with either a strong set of lungs or a strong set of counterarguments.

To more fully understand how thoughtful or lazy processing can influence people's perspectives on an issue, and how other psychological processes figure into the persuasion equation, let's examine the four related factors first explored by the Yale Communication Research Program and later elaborated by the cognitive-response perspective: source variables, message variables, channel variables, and target variables.

SECTION SUMMARY

- Persuasion involves conscious attempts to change attitudes through the transmission of some message
- The early message-learning approach to understanding persuasion is credited with providing insight into when and how persuasion occurs
- The later cognitive-response approach is credited with providing insight into *why* people change attitudes in response to persuasive messages; it analyzes:

    what people attend to in a persuasive message

    how cognitive assessment influences attitudes

- The elaboration likelihood model is a cognitive-response theory contending that people engage in either high or low elaboration when attending to persuasive messages

    central-route processing: high elaboration of message content by focusing on information central to message

    peripheral-route processing: low elaboration of message content by focusing on information not central to message

SOURCE VARIABLES: WHO IS COMMUNICATING?

One factor that is a peripheral cue to the actual content of the persuasive communication is the deliverer of the message. Research indicates that the *source* of a communication is important in determining whether the message will be effective in producing attitude change (Jones et al., 2003). This is especially true when the recipient lacks the motivation to process the message arguments carefully (Petty et al., 1981). What makes one source a better persuader than another?

Low Credibility Is a Discounting Cue

More than 2,300 years ago, the Greek philosopher Aristotle specified one of the critical elements in a communicator's ability to persuade:

> We believe good men more fully and more readily than others; this is true generally whatever the question is, and absolutely true where exact certainty is impossible and opinions are divided . . . his character may almost be called the most effective means of persuasion he possesses. (Roberts, 1954, pp. 24–25)

Building on Aristotle's insights, contemporary researchers contend that those listening to the source of a persuasive message pay a good deal of attention to his or her *credibility* or believability (Cecil et al., 1996). The Yale group stated that credibility is mainly based on two factors: *expertise,* which is the amount of knowledge that a communicator is assumed to possess, and *trustworthiness,* which is the perceived intention of the communicator to deceive.

In this regard, think back to our chapter-opening story about alcohol consumption on college campuses. If you were a college administrator developing an ad campaign to change students' attitudes toward binge drinking, one of the biggest hurdles you would have to overcome is the credibility issue. Often, teenagers and young adults perceive persuasive messages from authority figures and governmental agencies regarding alcohol abuse as having low credibility (Johnston et al., 2003). As noted by social psychologist Lloyd Johnston, who tracks drug use trends among this age group, "I'm worried putting that tagline [a governmental affiliation] causes kids to dismiss the message they've just consumed because they're not sure they like who is giving it to them."

Propaganda, to be effective, must be believed. To be believed, it must be credible.

Hubert H. Humphrey, U.S. senator and vice president, 1911–1978

DISCOUNTING CUES

Not surprisingly, research has found that high-credibility sources are more effective in producing attitude change than are low-credibility sources, at least in the short run. A source's low credibility is a *discounting cue* that results in the audience rejecting the message. For example, in one study, Hovland and Walter Weiss (1951) asked American college students to read an article proposing that nuclear-powered submarines were both feasible and safe (at the time, no such submarines had yet been built). Some of those reading the article were told that the author was J. Robert Oppenheimer, the American physicist who supervised the construction of the atomic bomb. Others were told that the source was the Soviet newspaper *Pravda*. The researchers assumed that during the height of the cold war, the average American would perceive Oppenheimer as a highly credible source and would consider *Pravda* a low-credibility source. True to expectations, readers who believed the article was written by the highly credible Oppenheimer were more persuaded by its message immediately after reading it than those who believed they were reading a Soviet article.

THE SLEEPER EFFECT

If this was all there was to learn about source credibility, we might conclude that persuasion seems pretty straightforward and uncomplicated. Yet four weeks after the initial reading of the submarine article, Hovland and Weiss again measured their participants' attitudes toward nuclear-powered submarines and found a surprise. As you can see in figure 7.2, the highly credible Oppenheimer had lost some of his persuasive power, whereas *Pravda* had actually gained in persuasiveness. Similar studies by Hovland and Weiss revealed the same delayed effects; highly credible sources are more persuasive immediately after the message presentation than less credible sources, but over time the credibility gap weakens. The researchers called this enhanced, delayed effect that the low-credible source has on attitude change the **sleeper effect.**

What could explain the sleeper effect? Herbert Kelman and Hovland (1953) believed it occurs because people who receive a message from a low-credibility source eventually forget where they heard it and then are influenced by the message content alone. If true, this

We are not won by arguments that we can analyze but by tone and temper, by the manner which is the man himself.

Samuel Butler, English author, 1835–1902

Sleeper Effect

The delayed effectiveness of a persuasive message from a noncredible source.

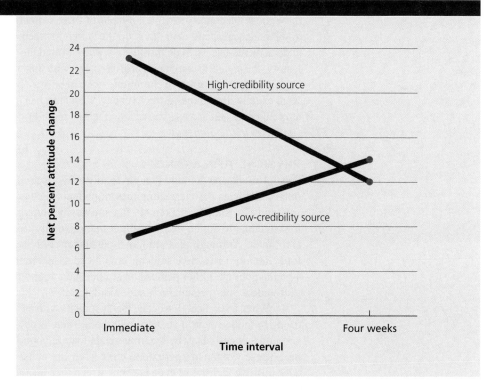

FIGURE 7.2

The Sleeper Effect

Immediately following the reception of a message, people are more likely to be persuaded by a highly credible source than one of low credibility. However, as Hovland and Weiss (1951) found, over time, the message becomes disassociated from its source, resulting in less agreement with the highly credible source and more agreement with the source having lower credibility. What is a possible explanation for this effect?

would also explain why the highly credible Oppenheimer lost some of his persuasive power over time—the credible source became disassociated from the message. To test this hypothesis, the researchers extended the Hovland and Weiss (1951) design by adding a condition in which participants were reminded of the source's identity before their attitudes were reassessed. If the sleeper effect occurred because people forgot that the persuasive message came from a low-credible source, then it could be eliminated by reestablishing this link. This is exactly what happened. Participants who were not reminded of the source showed the expected sleeper effect, but those who were reminded did not.

A recent meta-analysis of over seventy different sleeper effect studies found that the magnitude of this effect depends on the strength of the discounting cue (Kumkale & Albarracín, 2004). The more effective the discounting cue in suppressing the immediate impact of the persuasive message, the larger the sleeper effect. Not surprisingly, the meta-analysis also found that when the discounting cue is ineffective, there is no delayed increase in persuasion (that is, no sleeper effect). This meta-analysis and one other (Pratkanis et al., 1988) indicate that the sleeper effect most likely occurs when the following conditions are met:

1. The message must be convincing enough by itself to lead to persuasion.
2. People are sufficiently able and motivated to elaborate on the message arguments prior to receiving the discounting cue.
3. People are given information discounting the credibility of the source *following* the persuasive message, not before.
4. The impact of the discounting cue (the low-credibility information) decays in memory faster than the persuasive message.

Attractiveness Enhances Persuasiveness

During the 1920s, when feminists were demonstrating against women's inequality, Edward Bernays, the nephew of Sigmund Freud, was designing an ad campaign for the cigarette industry to persuade women to smoke cigarettes. He thought that cigarettes could serve as a "torch of freedom" symbol for women if he could somehow dramatically show attractive and "liberated" women using the product. Bernays arranged to have a group of attractive, "liberated," cigarette-smoking women marching in Manhattan's 1929 Easter Parade (Greaves, 1996). Women throughout the country saw photographs of these women in their local newspapers and in national magazines, and many took up the "torch of freedom" habit. Advertisers also collected endorsements from female movie stars who extolled the virtues of various brands. The rest is history: the cigarette company's profits soared with this newfound, "liberated-female" market.

Clearly, an attractive communicator can be very persuasive (Stanton et al., 1996). But what exactly determines attractiveness? Research has demonstrated that a communicator's attractiveness can be based on several factors, including *physical appearance, likability,* and *similarity to the audience.*

PHYSICAL APPEARANCE

Several studies have found that physically attractive persons are more effective in changing others' attitudes than less attractive individuals (Petty et al., 1997; Shavitt et al., 1994). In one study by Shelly Chaiken (1979), university undergraduates attempted to persuade fellow students to sign a petition to get the university to stop serving meat during breakfast and lunch. Although less attractive persuaders only secured signatures 32 percent of the time, the more attractive students convinced 41 percent of the students they approached to sign the petition. Other persuasion studies have found that good looks can sometimes even overcome a poor presentation style (Pallak, 1983).

When advertisers associate their products with attractive persons, do you think they are trying to induce central-route or peripheral-route processing in their target audience? Have you noticed how many beer commercials feature young, attractive women in skimpy clothing? These women are peripheral cues. They are consciously placed in commercials to induce positive feelings in male viewers, which then becomes associated with the beer through classical conditioning (see chapter 6, p. 179). This is attitude change without much thought—peripheral-route processing. Putting on your hypothetical college administrator hat again, if you were developing an ad campaign to change students' attitudes toward binge drinking, how could you use the powerful peripheral cue of attractiveness to enhance your message?

LIKABILITY

Besides physical appearance, being likable can also increase attractiveness. Indeed, merely saying nice things is often enough to get people to like you and thereby increase your ability to persuade (Drachman et al., 1978; Eagly & Chaiken, 1993). The power of being likable is not lost on those in the "image-making" business. Roger Ailes, a well-known public relations adviser to Republican presidents, believes likability is a persuader's most important quality:

> If you could master one element of personal communication that is more powerful than anything we've discussed, it is the quality of being *likable*. I call it the magic bullet, because if your audience likes you, they'll forgive just about everything else you do wrong. If they don't like you, you can hit every rule right on target and it doesn't matter. (Ailes, 1988, p. 81)

SIMILARITY

A third determinant of attractiveness is similarity. We are attracted to those who are similar to us. As a general rule, this attraction also results in us being influenced by similar others (Budesheim et al., 1996). For example, Theodore Dembroski and his colleagues (1978) found that when African American students heard an appeal from a dentist to engage in proper dental care, the message was more persuasive when it came from a dentist who was also African American rather than White.

Communicators can be similar to their audience in a number of ways (McCroskey et al., 1975; Petty & Wegener, 1998). One way is if they share attitudes and values ("Does she think like me?" "Are his morals like mine?"). Another way is if they have similar backgrounds ("Is he of my race or from my hometown?"). A third way is in terms of appearance ("Does he look like me?"). Of the different ways in which people could be similar to one another, perceived similarity in attitudes and values appears to be the most important in enhancing persuasion (Simons et al., 1970). This is why politicians try to present themselves as having attitudes and values in step with the majority: they understand that perceived similarity will lead to increased liking and greater persuasive power. This is also why effective campaigns to reduce binge drinking on college campuses use fellow students to deliver the persuasive messages: compared with nonstudents, student communicators are more likely to be perceived by the message recipients as sharing their attitudes, values, and interests (Johnston & White, 2003).

To please people is the greatest step toward persuading them.

Philip Dormer Stanhope, Earl of Chesterfield, 1694–1773

CRITICAL *thinking*

Commercial advertisers are acutely aware of the similarity effect and tailor their ads to enhance liking for their products. For example, television commercials are constructed in ways that reinforce the image of gender most familiar to and comfortable for their target audience at a particular time of the day. Over the next few days, observe the content of TV commercials in the morning, evening, or during weekend sports shows. Are there differences in the way women and men are portrayed?

SECTION SUMMARY

- A number of factors determine source persuasiveness:

    Highly *credible* sources are more persuasive, at least initially, than less credible sources

    Attractive sources are more persuasive than unattractive sources

MESSAGE VARIABLES: WHAT IS THE CONTENT?

Another question the Yale researchers were interested in answering was, what makes a message persuasive in its own right, independent of the source? Numerous studies have investigated the characteristics of a persuasive message, including such things as the effectiveness of using facts versus vivid images; fear and humor; the use of one-sided versus two-sided arguments; the order in which arguments are presented; and the number of times the message is repeated.

Vividness Can Bolster Evidence, But Sometimes It Undermines Persuasion

In trying to enhance persuasive arguments, we can cite facts, or we can infuse our message with vivid and colorful stories that will attract and hold our audience's attention (Green & Brock, 2000). Advertisers use both evidence-based appeals and vivid, graphic messages in trying to convince viewers to follow a certain course of action. For example, as part of your campaign to reduce binge drinking, you might create an evidence-based message targeting drunk driving by stating that "*Last year, over 1,400 college students were killed in alcohol-related automobile accidents.*" On the other hand, a vividness-based appeal (see photo on page 221) presents no data but instead offers a jarring and disturbing image making the negative consequences of drunk driving immediate and memorable.

Research strongly supports the notion that evidence-based appeals are effective in enhancing persuasive messages; yet while evidence enhances persuasion, not all evidence persuades. As already discussed, evidence is more immediately persuasive when attributed to a highly credible source rather than to one with low credibility (Reinard, 1988). Research also indicates that the persuasive power of evidence can be increased if it is combined with vivid imagery. For example, since 1978 utility companies have offered American consumers a free home audit to pinpoint how they can increase energy efficiency. Despite the valuable information given to them in these audits, only 15 percent of homeowners actually followed the recommendations of the auditor. Why were people not persuaded to take action when presented with all this evidence? To answer this question, Marti Gonzales and her colleagues (1988) interviewed homeowners and discovered that most of them had a hard time believing that such things as a small crack under a few doors could appreciably decrease energy efficiency. Based on this information, the researchers trained auditors to present their information in the following graphic and vivid terms:

> If you were to add up all the cracks around and under the doors of your home, you'd have the equivalent of a hole the size of a football in your living room wall. Think for a moment about all the heat that would escape from a hole that size. That's precisely why I'm recommending that you install weatherstripping. . . . And your attic totally lacks insulation. We call that a "naked attic." It's as if your home is facing winter not just without an overcoat, but without any clothing at all. (Gonzales et al., 1988, p. 1052)

Results indicated that auditors trained to use such vivid descriptions in presenting their evidence for greater energy efficiency dramatically increased their effectiveness in persuading consumers to have the recommended work done (61 percent compliance versus the previous 15 percent rate). Why does vividness increase persuasion? The most likely explanation is that vivid elements prime relevant information in memory, increasing the message recipient's ability to process the message (Sherman et al., 1990).

Although Gonzales's findings suggest that a vivid presentation can make solid evidence even more persuasive, further research indicates that under certain conditions, vividness can actually undermine the persuasiveness of a message. In one such study, Kurt Frey and Alice Eagly (1993) presented vivid or nonvivid persuasive messages to undergraduate volunteers. In one condition *(high attentional constraint),* students were instructed to pay close attention to this information, whereas in another condition *(low attentional constraint),* the information was presented as an incidental part of the laboratory situation with no instructions to pay attention to it. Although both types of messages were equally persuasive when students were instructed to pay close attention to them, nonvivid messages were more persuasive than the vivid ones when incidentally presented.

These results suggest that vividness may undermine persuasiveness when vivid elements interfere with the full comprehension of the persuasive message. Such interference is most likely when people's attention has not been constrained. That is, when not admonished to "pay attention" to a message, vivid elements in the message itself may cause people's attention to wander off on tangents so they miss the essential meaning of the message. Additional research indicates that this cognitive "wandering off" is most likely when the vivid elements are incongruent with the theme of the message itself (Smith & Shaffer, 2000). Vividness interfering with message elaboration is exactly what swindlers hope for when conning potential victims. When plying their trade, swindlers often use colorful language and provocative metaphors, because they have learned that such vivid speech interferes with a victim's ability to critically analyze what they are being told. Such diminished message elaboration decreases the likelihood that contradictions and inconsistencies will be discovered in the swindler's lies.

Fear Appeals Facilitate Persuasion if Certain Conditions Are Met

Would-be persuaders, whether they are making evidence-based appeals or using more graphically oriented arguments, often try to evoke fear in order to persuade. An antismoking ad tells you how your nicotine habit will shorten life expectancy. An insurance agent conjures up the frightening image of your family being thrown out of their home if you do not purchase sufficient life-insurance coverage. A presidential candidate suggests that if his opponent is elected, terrorists will run roughshod over the country. There is no doubt that fear appeals are used quite frequently in persuasion. But do they work?

Early research on the use of fear in persuasion suggested that it might be counterproductive. For example, Irving Janis and Seymour Feshbach (1953) found that people who watched a graphic and frightening lecture on the dangers of poor oral hygiene were less likely to follow the lecture recommendations than those who watched a less frightening lecture. Unfortunately, subsequent research generally was not able to replicate these findings and, instead, found that greater aroused fear led to more—not less—effective persuasion (Janis, 1967; Leventhal, 1970).

To explain the contradictory findings, Ronald Rogers and his colleagues proposed a **protection-motivation theory,** outlining the conditions under which fear facilitates attitude

There are two levers for moving man—interest and fear.

Napoleon Bonaparte, French general and emperor, 1769–1821

Protection-Motivation Theory

A theory proposing that fear induces both a self-protective response and an appraisal of whether the fear-arousing threat can be avoided.

change (Maddux & Rogers, 1983; Rogers & Prentice-Dunn, 1997). This theory hypothesizes that fear induces a motivation to protect the self, as well as influences a person's cognitive appraisal of the fear-arousing threat. Fear appeals can effectively persuade under the following four conditions: (1) the target of the message is convinced that the dangers mentioned are serious; (2) the target is convinced that the dangers are quite probable; (3) the target is convinced that the recommendations to avoid the dangers will be effective; and (4) the target believes that he or she can competently take the recommended action. The first two conditions in this persuasion process convince people that they should change their behavior, and the third and fourth conditions reassure them that they are personally capable of changing the necessary behavior in order to avoid the danger. If a person's self-beliefs indicate an ability to make the necessary behavioral changes, the fear-inducing message will likely be effective. Does this notion of being personally capable of changing one's own behavior sound familiar? It should, because it bears a striking similarity to the concept of *perceived behavioral control* in the theory of planned behavior discussed in chapter 6 (see p. 193).

Returning to the dental hygiene study by Janis and Feshbach in which fear did not induce change, more recent studies suggest that this effect may have been due to the participants either thinking less clearly or actually tuning out the message (Sengrupta & Johar, 2001). That is, at times a high fear appeal induces so much anxiety that the audience is unable to efficiently process later information in the appeal about how to avoid the danger. For example, Christopher Jepson and Chaiken (1990) measured participants' anxieties about cancer and then asked them to read and evaluate an article advocating regular checkups for cancer. Following this exercise, participants were asked to list all their thoughts about the article and as many of the arguments contained in the article. Those who were highly anxious about cancer listed fewer thoughts, remembered fewer arguments, and were ultimately less persuaded than those who were less anxious. This study and others suggest that if a fear-inducing message immobilizes its audience with anxiety, they may be unable to carefully process the message content concerning how to avoid the danger. Instead of promoting healthy change, the message may instead induce a feeling of helplessness. Although this is certainly an undesirable consequence of fear appeals, existing research indicates that if fear appeals are combined with information that one can do something about the danger, important behavioral changes can and do occur (Block & Keller, 1997; Mulilis et al., 2001).

Although protection-motivation theory provides important insights into how we respond to fear appeals, recent studies indicate that we are not as rational as the theory assumes. When feeling highly vulnerable to some threat, we often do not critically analyze the recommended actions to avoid the danger (Das & de Wit, 2003). Feeling vulnerable, we fall victim to the *confirmation bias,* which is the tendency to seek only information that verifies our beliefs (see chapter 5, pp. 155–156). Our desire to perceive the recommended actions as effective causes us to ignore information that might disconfirm our beliefs. This strong "desire to believe" that a highly threatening situation can be avoided places a great deal of power in the hands of those who are offering solutions (Landau et al., 2004).

Humor Increases Attention to a Message, But It May Interfere with Message Processing

Advertising executives believe that humor can persuade consumers to buy their products, which is why about 40 percent of all advertisements employ humor (Unger, 1996). Public relations consultants also believe that humor is an effective persuader, and they regularly recommend that their clients punch up their persuasive speeches with humorous anecdotes (Weinberger & Campbell, 1991). Even some recent student-designed ad campaigns to increase alcohol awareness on college campuses (see accompanying photo) have employed humor to change student drinking attitudes (Saltzman, 2002). Are they correct in their beliefs?

Research clearly shows that using humor in persuasive messages does increase people's *attention* to the message more than serious-sounding communication attempts (Duncan & Nelson, 1985). People are simply more likely to listen to someone who is trying to make them laugh, or at least smile, while trying to persuade them about a particular point

CRITICAL *thinking*

In addition to using humor, the anti-binge-drinking SMU ad also provides information on how much alcohol the typical SMU student consumes. Why might this information be effective in reducing binge drinking at SMU? When would reporting such normative information possibly promote—rather than reduce— binge drinking?

A FEW SMU STUDENTS
WERE DRUNK LAST WEEK.
The rest of us have the pictures to prove it.

A 2002 snapshot of SMU students shows that 84 percent of us don't miss classes because of drinking. This shows that we are part of a growing national trend. We enjoy partying with friends and do so responsibly. The survey shows that the vast majority of us drink once a week or less. We average five or fewer drinks in a night, haven't gotten into a fight because of drinking, don't drink and drive and have never been in trouble with authorities due to drinking either on or off campus. The next time you're out, remember that drinking responsibly is actually the most popular student activity.

Congratulations. And welcome to The Majority.

A student-sponsored anti-binge-drinking ad campaign at Southern Methodist University used humor as a method of persuading fellow students to drink responsibly. Is humor an effective persuasion technique? Research suggests that sometimes humor can actually interfere with a person's elaboration of persuasive message content. What is the key determining factor in whether humor facilitates or inhibits message processing? Do you think the SMU ad meets this standard?

of view. Persuaders who inject humor into their messages also tend to enhance their likability in the minds of the audience (Gruner, 1985). As we have already discussed, communicators can use this increased liking to persuade their audience to adopt their perspective on the issue under consideration, whether—in the case of alcohol consumption—it is to promote responsible drinking or simply to encourage the choice of one alcoholic beverage over another.

One of the problems with using humor, however, is that it may interfere with the listener's *comprehension* of the message, by directing attention away from the persuasive content (Cantor & Venus, 1983). That is, the jokes may be so funny that people only remember them and not the persuasive information. Thus, if a persuader merely wants to get people to notice the message, humor may be useful in this regard. However, as pointed out by the message-learning approach, attending to the message is only the first step in persuasion. With no message comprehension (step 2), any attitude change is likely to be extremely vulnerable to a counterpersuasive attack (Haugtvedt & Petty, 1992).

Because enabling listeners to comprehend the message is important in securing durable attitude change, some studies have more closely assessed the effects of humor on how people *process* persuasive messages. One such study, conducted by Steven Smith and his coworkers (1994), found that humor can either promote message processing or disrupt it. The key factor in determining whether processing or disruption occurs is the *relevance* of the humor to the evaluation of the message content. When humor is relevant to the content of the message, people appear to be more motivated to take a central route to persuasion and process the message arguments. However, when humor is irrelevant to the message content, people are likely to take a peripheral route and base their evaluation of the message merely on cues such as source credibility.

Given our previous discussion of fear and persuasion, it is interesting to note that humor may be effective in persuading certain individuals to take protective steps when facing potential health threats. In studies of persuasive appeals involving sunscreen use to avoid skin cancer and condom use to prevent AIDS, humorous messages appear to be more effective than nonhumorous messages for men and women high in psychological masculinity (Conway & Dubé, 2002). *Psychological masculinity* consists of an assertive, task-oriented approach to life, reflected in such personality characteristics as being independent, forceful, and dominant. Although men are on average higher than women in masculinity, these gender differences are shrinking (Twenge, 1997). Why might people high in psychological masculinity respond more favorably to humorous appeals related to health threats? As discussed in chapter 4 (p. 109–110), masculinity is associated with *manly emotion,* in which people exert control over their emotions, just as they try to exert control over other aspects of their lives. Persuasive messages that induce fear can hinder message elaboration if the perceived threat is high. For people who place a high value on controlling their emotions—that is, those high in masculinity—humor in the context of a fear-inducing message may be very appreciated because it helps them manage their fear, which then allows them to more effectively process the message.

In ending our analysis of humor, what can we conclude concerning whether it is helpful or hurtful to a persuasive message? Based on what we know so far, it seems to depend first on the *goal* of the persuasive message: humor will get you most people's attention, but it may interfere with them processing the important content of your persuasive message. However, it appears that you can circumvent this negative "humor effect" by employing humor that is *relevant* to your persuasive arguments. This relevant humor appears to motivate people to process the content of your message, which increases the likelihood that any ensuing attitude change will be less susceptible to decay.

Two-Sided Messages Inoculate Audiences Against Opposing Views Better Than One-Sided Messages

Besides humor, another factor in determining whether a message will be persuasive has to do with whether you present a one-sided or a two-sided message. A *one-sided* message is one in which you try to convince others to adopt your perspective by presenting only your arguments. In contrast, a *two-sided* message involves you acknowledging the opposing arguments in your pitch and attempting to refute them.

Hovland and his colleagues (1949), in a study conducted during World War II, attempted to determine whether one-sided or two-sided messages were more effective audience persuaders. Working in the Army's Information and Education Division immediately after the surrender of Nazi Germany, their objective was to convince American soldiers that the war was far from over and that the armed conflict against Japan would last at least two more years. Some soldiers heard a one-sided message that did not bring up opposing viewpoints, and other soldiers heard a two-sided message that also mentioned and then refuted the opposing viewpoints. As illustrated in figure 7.3, the effectiveness of the appeal depended on who was listening. A one-sided appeal was most effective with those who already believed that the war would be long, while a two-sided appeal worked better with those who initially believed that the war would be over soon.

Later research found that two-sided messages are more effective in persuading not only those who initially disagree, but also people who are either well informed on the topic or are going to be exposed to opposing viewpoints in the future (Crowley & Hoyer, 1994; Lumsdaine & Janis, 1953). In such circumstances, mentioning the opposition's arguments suggests that you are being an objective, fair-minded person, thereby increasing your trustworthiness and, thus, your effectiveness at persuasion (Bohner et al., 2003).

Besides increasing communicator trustworthiness, another important factor is operating in two-sided messages. For those who are soon going to hear the opposition state its case, raising and then refuting its arguments can *inoculate* these people against it, making it harder for them to be persuaded. William McGuire developed this inoculation approach to persuasion during the 1950s in partial response to cold war fears about Americans' susceptibility to communist propaganda from the Soviet Union. McGuire reasoned that people become vulnerable to propaganda when they are raised in a society that overprotects them from hearing things that

FIGURE 7.3

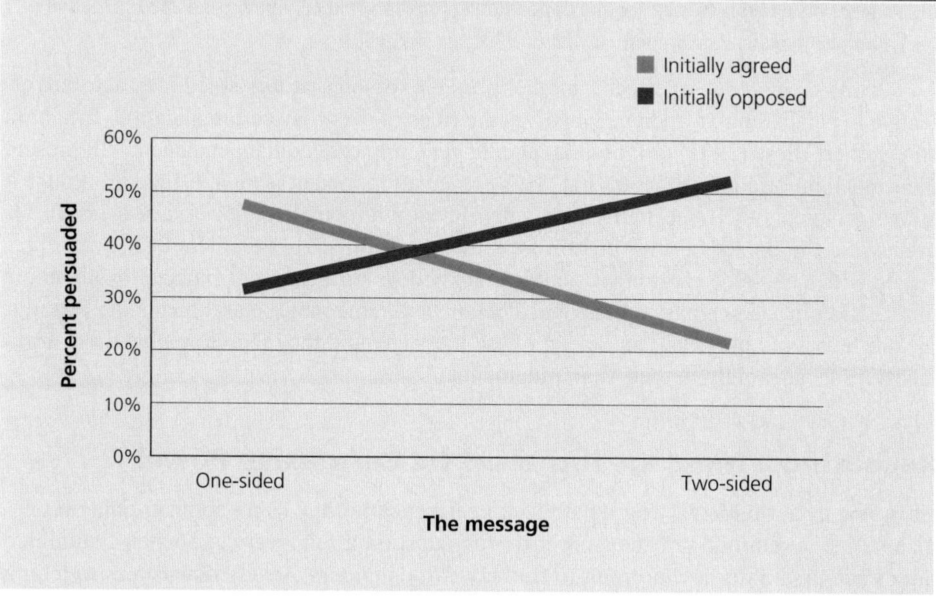

One-Sided Versus Two-Sided Appeals

Following Germany's defeat in World War II, American soldiers who initially agreed with a message that Japan was strong and that the war in the Pacific would last a long time were more persuaded by a one-sided appeal. In contrast, soldiers skeptical of this message were more persuaded by a two-sided appeal.

Source: Data from C. I. Hovland et al., *Experiments on Mass Communications*, Princeton University Press, 1949.

attack culturally shared beliefs. Using a biological analogy, he stated that people who are raised in such a "germ-free" environment would not have developed appropriate mechanisms to adequately defend themselves against attacking viruses (outside propaganda). However, just as administering a small dose of a dangerous virus will stimulate the body to develop defenses to fight off the disease, McGuire asserted that exposing people to a weakened dose of the attacking material would also stimulate the development of resistance-promoting counterarguments.

Research supports some of the basic elements of inoculation theory, and its principles have been effectively applied in many realms, including commercial advertising and political campaigning (McGuire, 1999; McGuire & Papageorgis, 1961). However, as the application of inoculation theory spread, McGuire had second thoughts about some of his basic theoretical assumptions. Two of his initial assumptions were that (1) outside beliefs were often dangerous and should be guarded against, and (2) the inoculation effect would only protect people from "dangerous" political perspectives, such as Soviet-style communism and other totalitarian belief systems; it could not be used to manipulate an audience. As you can see from the following commentary, McGuire came to recognize these early views as being naive:

I must confess that I felt like Mr. Clean when I started this immunization work because while everybody else was studying how to manipulate people, I was studying how to keep them from being manipulated. But now I appreciate more that the person has to be open to outside influence: if one had to learn everything from one's own experience, one probably wouldn't survive. . . . Immunizing somebody against change isn't always very healthy for the reason that people do have to be open to outside influence.

I am also uneasy because subsequent developments in advertising show that our immunization research can be used for questionable purposes. I remember a call I got from an advertising agency bigwig just after this research was publicized. He said, "Very interesting, Professor. I was really delighted to read about it." Somewhat righteously I replied, "Very nice of you to say that, Mr. Bigwig, but I'm really on the other side. You're trying to persuade people, and I'm trying to make them more resistant." "Oh, don't underrate yourself, Professor," he said. "What you're doing will be very helpful to us in reducing the effectiveness of our competitors." And so it has turned out. Before our immunization research, advertisements always ignored the opposition as if it didn't exist. But now mentioning the other brands and deflating their claims is becoming almost standard in the advertising of many product classes. Our immunization research has brought home to the ad agencies that with audiences likely to be exposed to strong ads for competing brands, it is more efficacious to mention the opposition claims in advance, but in weakened form that builds up resistance to them. (Evans, 1980, pp. 179–180)

Besides inoculation effects, another possible reason that two-sided messages are effective in persuading an audience involves the rules of everyday communication. Eric Igou and Herbert Bless (2003) propose that people generally expect that persuaders will present their most important arguments first. This presentation format is most efficient because it allows recipients the opportunity to rapidly develop a mental framework, or schema, for processing the presented information (see chapter 5, pp. 141–145). However, when presented with a two-sided argument, people quickly develop a different expectation about the information in the persuasive message. They now assume that the arguments the communicator favors are presented at the end of the message, and they therefore give these arguments a special weight in their final judgments.

Repeating a Message Increases Its Persuasive Power

Have you ever wondered why advertisers keep repeating the same commercials on television? I was reminded of the answer to this question a few years ago when I stumbled out of bed on a Saturday morning to find my two daughters already downstairs watching cartoons. Usually my wife and I limit their TV viewing, but this morning they literally caught us napping and had at least a sixty-minute dose of "Scooby-Doo," "Land of the Lost," and numerous commercials. Apparently the Trix rabbit had figured prominently in commercial airtime, for all my daughters wanted for breakfast was a bowl of Trix, "the fruity sweetened corn puff cereal with natural fruit flavors and eight essential vitamins and iron."

One reason television sponsors repeat commercials is because repetition tends to increase liking for the product due to the *mere exposure effect* discussed in chapter 6. But despite the effectiveness that repetitive messages can have on liking and, thus, persuasion, there are limits to its power. Repeated exposure seems to increase liking for stimuli that are initially perceived as neutral or positive, but it has the opposite effect on stimuli that are initially perceived as negative (Cacioppo & Petty, 1989). This undoubtedly explains why I hate "Snuggles," the little animated, stuffed bear in the fabric softener commercials of the same name. I was irritated by its squeaky, giggly voice when the commercials first appeared in the early 1980s, and my negative attitude has increased through repeated exposures over the years.

Repeated exposure to a product often leads to greater liking, except if one's initial reaction to the product is negative. Are there any products you dislike because the ads irritate you?

Another limitation of the mere exposure effect is that even when it is effective, it increases liking only up to a point. After too much exposure, liking will level off and, in some instances, even decline, an effect advertisers call *wear-out* (Smith & Dorfman, 1975). Wear-out effects tend to occur with ads that attract a great deal of attention when they first appear, such as humorous ads. One technique that advertisers use to overcome wear-out effects is to engage in *repetition with variation* (Pratkanis & Aronson, 1992). In this technique, they present the same information repeatedly, but the format of the ad is varied. For example, during the course of an hour of television viewing, you might see as many as four Energizer battery commercials featuring the pink Energizer-operated toy bunny, but each time the pointy-eared toy is shown in a different humorous context. Research indicates that such variation in repetition does generally succeed in reducing wear-out effects, and it may accomplish this by causing viewers to further elaborate—and thereby strengthen—their attitudes toward the product (Haugtvedt et al., 1994; Schumann et al., 1990).

SECTION SUMMARY

- Vividness can make solid evidence even more persuasive, but sometimes it undermines message elaboration
- Fear can persuade, yet it can also immobilize an audience with anxiety
- Humor increases message attention, but it can interfere with message comprehension
- Two-sided messages are effective in persuading those who

    initially disagree

    are well informed

    are going to be exposed to opposing viewpoints
- Message repetition increases persuasive power due to the mere exposure effect

CHANNEL VARIABLES: HOW IS THE MESSAGE TRANSMITTED?

Another important aspect of persuasion is the channel or medium of communication used to persuade an audience to adopt a particular attitude or course of action. In other words, how does the persuader deliver the message? Two aspects of the communication medium that have been investigated deal with the speed at which the message is delivered, and the style of speech that is used.

Rapid Speech Can Benefit Peripheral-Route Persuasion yet Often Hinders Central-Route Processing

Are fast-talking communicators any more successful at persuading an audience than those who speak more slowly? Research indicates that people who speak rapidly are generally more persuasive than those who speak more slowly because fast talkers convey the *impression* that they are more credible (Miller et al., 1976). Certain marketing studies also report this benefit of rapid speech—people seem to be more favorably disposed toward advertisements and the products advertised when the product spokesperson talks at a faster-than-normal rate of speech (LaBarbera & MacLachlan, 1979; Street & Brady, 1982). But is fast talking always beneficial to persuasion?

According to the elaboration likelihood model, fast talking will only be beneficial to the persuasive communicator when the audience's initial attitudinal position is *opposite* to that of the communicator (Petty & Wegener, 1998). This hypothesis is derived from the belief that rapid speech makes it difficult for a listener to adequately process and critically analyze the content of the message. Because the audience's counterarguing is "short-circuited" by the sheer speed at which the opposing viewpoints are presented, audience members are more likely to be persuaded by the message than if they had more time to scrutinize it. Put another way, the difficulty in processing rapid speech prompts the audience to abandon the central route, and instead, they take the peripheral route to persuasion. In contrast to the hypothesized benefits of rapid speech when the audience opposes the communicator, the elaboration likelihood model further predicts that fast talking will hurt the persuasive power of the message when it is presented to an audience that favors the communicator's point of view. Why? Because the arguments are presented so quickly, the audience cannot adequately process them and incorporate them into their existing belief system to further bolster their current attitudes on the issue.

Steven Smith and David Shaffer (1991) found support for this explanation in a study in which college students listened to persuasive messages arguing for or against raising the legal drinking age to 20. A survey conducted prior to the study revealed that the overwhelming majority of undergraduates on campus opposed such a law. Students heard the persuasive arguments either at a slow, normal, or rapid rate of speech. Consistent with the elaboration likelihood hypothesis, when students listened to arguments counter to their perspective, rapid speech suppressed the tendency to rebut the counterattitudinal message, and hence, listeners were more susceptible to persuasion. However, when students listened to arguments consistent with their own attitudes toward the drinking-age law, rapid speech inhibited favorable elaboration of the proattitudinal message, thus undermining its persuasive impact. These findings suggest that rapid speech may either promote or inhibit persuasion through its impact on message elaboration.

Powerful Speech Is Generally More Persuasive Than Powerless Speech

In addition to how fast a person talks, another speech-related factor influencing persuasion is the style in which a speech is delivered. For example, consider two people, Jessie and Tony, going to their boss to make persuasive arguments for a raise. First, let's see how Jessie states her case:

> "Uh . . . excuse me, sir? . . . Uh . . . could I have a minute of your time? . . . This may sound a little out of the ordinary, but, I've been with the company for one year now, you know, and . . . uhm, well, I was sort of wondering if we could talk about an increase in my salary? Uh . . . you know, since starting here, I've kind of been given a good deal of responsibilities that go beyond my job description, you know, and . . . uh . . . I've handled this additional work efficiently and professionally, you know, without complaining and without supervision, don't you think? I'm not an expert on how to run this company, you know, but I was wondering . . . uh . . . now that I have proven capable of handling this increased workload and responsibilities, you know, don't you think my salary should reflect this fact?"

Now, let's see how Tony presents these same arguments to his boss:

> "Excuse me, sir? Could I have a minute of your time? I've been with the company for one year now, and I would like to talk to you about an increase in my salary. Since starting here I've been given a good deal of responsibilities that go well beyond my job description, and I've handled this additional work efficiently and professionally without complaining and without supervision. Now that I have proven capable of handling this increased workload and responsibilities, I would like to have my salary reflect this fact."

The factual content of both messages is the same, yet they differ markedly in how the content is presented. Sociolinguists would say that Jessie's presentation is an example of *powerless speech,* while Tony's embodies *powerful speech* (Newcombe & Arnkoff, 1979). Powerless speech includes the following language forms:

CRITICAL *thinking*

When radio ads try to persuade you to buy tickets in state lotteries or to purchase their products in the hopes of later winning prizes, they are required by law to tell the listener the actual odds of winning. Have you noticed that when the spokespersons are trying to persuade you to spend your money they speak at a normal rate of speed, yet when they convey the odds of winning, their speech rate dramatically increases? Are they simply trying to save money by cutting down on the length of the commercial, or is there an equally important reason for this shift to fast-paced speech?

Hesitation Forms: "Uh" and "You know" indicate a lack of confidence or certainty.

Disclaimers: "This may sound out of the ordinary, but . . ." and "I'm not an expert, but . . ." ask the listener to be patient or refrain from criticism.

Qualifiers: "Sort of," "kind of," and "I guess" serve to tone down or blunt the force of an assertive statement.

Tag Questions: "I've handled this additional work efficiently and professionally, don't you think?" "That's the right thing to do, isn't it?" The added-on question turns an assertive statement into a plea for agreement.

Given the different delivery styles of Jessie and Tony, who do you think is more likely to persuade their boss to give them the raise? Not surprisingly, research finds that when people use a powerful speaking style, they are generally judged more competent and credible than when their style is powerless (Erickson et al., 1978; Newcombe & Arnkoff, 1979). This suggests that even when people have good and persuasive messages, they often fail to persuade if they weaken their message by the way they deliver it. Despite the fact that using powerful language adds an assertive "punch" to one's message, not everyone is taught to use this style of speech. Sociolinguist Robin Lakoff (1975) contends that because the status of women in society has been relatively powerless and marginal compared with men, they generally are neither socialized nor expected to express themselves as assertively and forcefully as men. True to this gender expectation, in conversation women are more likely than men to use qualifiers, ask tag questions, and use disclaimers (Crosby & Nyquist, 1977; Mulac & Lundell, 1986).

Although a powerful speaking style generally is more persuasive than a powerless one, under certain conditions, the communicator's sex may reverse this effect. For example, Linda Carli (1990) found that when women tried to persuade men to change their attitudes, using powerless speech was more effective than employing a more assertive style. On the other hand, when trying to persuade other women, breaking with convention and adopting a more powerful speaking style was more influential. The greater influence a powerless speaking style had on men occurred despite the fact that both male and female participants believed that women who spoke tentatively were less competent and knowledgeable than women who spoke assertively! As you can see in table 7.1, men perceived the woman who talked tentatively to be more trustworthy and likable, while women judged her to be less likable and trustworthy.

This study clearly suggests that there is a double standard in speaking style for women and men. The use of tentative speech appears to enhance a woman's ability to persuade a man at the same time that it reduces her ability to persuade another woman. Why might these differences exist? One possibility is that because women typically have lower social status than men, they must first demonstrate in conversations with them that they have no desire to compete for status—hence the use of powerless speech. When women conversationally acknowledge their lower status (for example, "I know I'm not an expert on this issue, but . . ." "Maybe we could . . ."), men may be more likely to consider their ideas and arguments (Meeker & Weitzel-O'Neill, 1977). Does this mean that women should adopt a powerless speaking style to improve their persuasive power with men? No. The use of such powerless language as a subtle persuasion technique will either compromise a woman's perceived competence or make it difficult for her to persuade an audience of both men and women. Instead, a second study by Carli and her coworkers (1995) suggests that an alternative method for female persuaders to use with a male audience is to combine assertive language with a *social nonverbal style* that communicates friendliness and affiliation (relaxed forward-leaning, smiling face, moderate eye contact). In this study, men were more inclined to like and be persuaded by a competent woman when she was also sociable than when she was merely competent. For a male audience, then, a sociable nonverbal style appears to take the perception of threat out of a competent woman's self-presentation, making her an effective agent of persuasion.

Public speaking is done in the public tongue, the national or tribal language; and the language of our tribe is the men's language. Of course women learn it. We're not dumb. If you can tell Margaret Thatcher from Ronald Reagan, or Indira Gandhi from General Somoza, by anything they say, tell me how. This is a man's world, so it talks a man's language.

Ursula LeGuin, U.S. author, 1983

Gender Differences in Speech Style and Persuasiveness

Carli (1990) found that there appears to be a double standard in persuasive speaking style for women and men, with tentative speech enhancing a woman's ability to persuade a man at the same time that it reduces her persuasiveness with a woman. In the table, higher scores reflect greater trustworthiness and likableness, and greater agreement with the persuasive message. What might explain these differences?

| | Sex of Listener | | | | | |
| | Agreement with Speaker | | Speaker Trustworthiness | | Speaker Likableness | |
Speaker	Male	Female	Male	Female	Male	Female
Male						
Tentative language	4.13	4.07	6.73	6.73	5.93	6.53
Assertive language	3.80	5.20	6.80	7.00	6.40	6.93
Female						
Tentative language	5.00	3.13	8.40	5.47	8.00	5.80
Assertive language	2.93	5.93	6.33	7.27	6.53	7.73

Source: Data from L. L. Carli, "Gender, Language, and Influence" in *Journal of Personality and Social Psychology,* 59:941-951, American Psychological Association, 1990.

SECTION SUMMARY

- Rapid speech can increase or decrease persuasiveness, depending on the audience's initial position and the message strength
- Speech style can boost or hinder persuasion:

    powerful speech generally increases persuasiveness

    powerless speech generally decreases persuasiveness

    female persuaders employing powerful speech may threaten male listeners if the persuaders do not also use a sociable nonverbal style

AUDIENCE VARIABLES: TO WHOM IS THE MESSAGE DELIVERED?

Now that we have discussed the source, the message, and the channel of persuasion, let's analyze certain characteristics of the target of persuasion that can also influence how the message is received. Some of these characteristics have to do with the mood, involvement, personality, self-concept, and age of the target.

Good Moods Generally Foster, but Sometimes Hinder, Persuasion

Early research on mood and persuasion indicated that people who are in a positive mood are more susceptible to persuasion than the average person. For example, Irving Janis and his colleagues (1965) had some people read persuasive messages while they ate a snack and drank soda, while others simply read the messages without the accompanying treats. Greater attitude change occurred among the "munchers" than among the "food-free" group. Similar effects were also found among people listening to pleasant music (Milliman, 1986).

Why do you think these effects might occur? Although some would contend that people in a good mood are easier to persuade simply because of classical conditioning principles (see chapter 6, pp. 179–181), the cognitive-response approach offers more complex explanations (Petty & Wegener, 1998). The *feelings-as-information* explanation suggest that whereas negative moods signal to people that something is wrong in their environment and that some action is necessary, positive moods have the opposite effect: they signal that everything is fine and no effortful thought is necessary (Isbell, 2004; Schwarz, 1990). As a result, people in a positive mood are more persuasible because they are less likely to engage in extensive processing of the presented arguments than those in a neutral or negative mood (Bohner et al., 1992; Ruder & Bless, 2003). This does not mean, as classical conditional principles would suggest, that people in a bad mood are more likely to react negatively to any arguments presented. On the contrary, they are simply less likely than those in a positive mood to be influenced by poor arguments.

While the feelings-as-information view contends that happy people rely on peripheral-route processing, an alternative cognitive-response explanation, the *hedonic-contingency* view, asserts that this is not always the case (Wegener & Petty, 1994). According to this perspective, happy people will engage in cognitive tasks that allow them to remain happy and will avoid those tasks that lower their mood. Research investigating this possible effect indicates that a happy mood can indeed lead to *greater* message elaboration than a neutral or sad mood when the persuasive message is either uplifting or not mood threatening (Wegener et al., 1995). Thus, it appears that happy people do not always process information less than neutral or sad people.

Although this research suggests that happy people can, under certain conditions, be less susceptible to persuasion because they engage in high message elaboration, there is another reason why happy moods can cause less persuasion. When happy people think that their positive mood might be biasing their evaluations toward accepting a persuasive message, they often consciously adjust their evaluations downward to compensate for this possible "good mood" effect (Ottati & Isbell, 1996). In such instances, happy people may actually overadjust and evaluate the message more negatively than they would if they were not happy (Isbell & Wyer, 1999).

Taken together, these studies suggest that although happy people are generally more susceptible to persuasion than neutral or sad people, certain conditions can erase or actually reverse this tendency (Bohner & Weinerth, 2001; Petty et al., 2001). First, when a persuasive message does not threaten happy people's moods, they are more likely to carefully scrutinize it and, thus, may be less persuasible than neutral or sad individuals. Second, when happy people are aware that their good moods may contaminate their thinking, they often adjust their evaluations of the message and become even harsher critics than others. Try to keep these points in mind the next time you attend a political campaign rally. The music preceding the speech, the euphoria permeating the audience, and any free food and drink dispensed by campaign workers are all designed to put you in an upbeat, festive mood. Will your joy in the moment cause you to be a "soft" or a "hard" sell? To a certain extent, the answer may depend on whether the candidate's speech is consistent with your upbeat mood and/or whether you self-reflect on the nature of your happiness prior to judging the candidate.

Degree of Message Elaboration Is Shaped Both by Issue and Impression Involvement

In some of the earliest work on how one's involvement in an issue can influence willingness to be persuaded, Muzafir Sherif and Hadley Cantril (1947) argued that attitudes that become closely associated with the self are highly resistant to change. Later studies by cognitively oriented researchers not only have supported this hypothesis, but also have identified at least two different types of involvement, each usually having a different effect on persuasion (Nienhuis et al., 2001; Petty & Cacioppo, 1990).

Issue involvement is a type of involvement in which the attitudinal issue under consideration has important consequences for the self. Involvement in an issue results in you being very attentive to the presented arguments and very active in critically analyzing their strengths and weaknesses (Petty & Cacioppo, 1979). A second type of involvement is *impression-relevant involvement* (also known as *response involvement*), in which the attitudinal issue does not have great personal relevance, but your attitudinal response will be scrutinized by others and receive either social approval or disapproval. In this form of involvement, you are more concerned about your self-presentation and the social acceptability of your attitudes than you are about the quality of the arguments surrounding the issue.

Michael Leippe and Roger Elkin (1987) conducted a study in which they sought to determine how these two different types of involvement might interact in a given situation. College students were first told that their university was seriously considering implementing comprehensive examinations. The researchers then manipulated issue involvement by either telling students that the policy, if adopted, would go into effect the following year and they would be participants in the process *(high issue involvement),* or that the policy would not be put into effect for some years (*low issue involvement*). Impression-relevant involvement was manipulated by telling some students they would discuss this issue with another student and a professor *(high impression-relevant involvement),* while others did not believe any public discussion would take place *(low impression-relevant involvement).* Which condition do you think yielded the most critical analysis? Actually, the only students who engaged in a critical analysis of the arguments were those who were both highly issue involved and weakly involved in terms of impression relevance. If students were strongly involved in terms of impression relevance, or weakly involved in terms of issue relevance, they largely ignored the strength of the arguments.

These findings suggest that if an issue has great personal relevance to an audience and they are not very concerned how others might judge their stance on the issue, they are likely to take a central route to persuasion. In such a scenario, the audience is most likely to be persuaded by strong, well-reasoned arguments. However, if issue relevance is low to an audience, or they are concerned how others might judge them, they are likely to take a peripheral route and be persuaded by a speaker who is popular and who can reassure them that this perspective is socially acceptable.

Individual Differences Affect Susceptibility to Persuasion

Three individual difference variables that appear to make people more or less susceptible to persuasion are one's *need for cognition,* level of *self-monitoring,* and *age.*

NEED FOR COGNITION

Involvement in an issue can be affected not only by the importance of the message to the self, but also by the tendency for people to desire cognitive challenges. The **need for cognition** is an individual preference for and tendency to engage in effortful cognitive activities. Cacioppo and Petty (1982) have designed a personality scale to measure individual differences in this need for cognition. Table 7.2 lists some of the items from this scale. People who are high in the need for cognition (high NFC) like to work on difficult cognitive tasks, analyze situations, and make subtle cognitive distinctions (Nair & Ramnaraya, 2000). Research has shown that high-NFC persons tend to take the central route to persuasion. In contrast, individuals with a low need for cognition (low NFC) are more likely to take mental shortcuts and follow a peripheral route (Cacioppo et al., 1996; Priester & Petty, 1995). As a result, the attitudes of low NFCs are easier to change than those of high NFCs (Shestowsky et al., 1998).

How does need for cognition influence attention to political campaigns and stability of political attitudes? During the 1984 presidential and vice-presidential debates, vot-

Need for Cognition

An individual preference for and tendency to engage in effortful cognitive activities.

TABLE 7.2

Need for Cognition Scale: Sample Items

Directions

These are sample items taken from the Need for Cognition Scale. If you agree with items 1, 3, 5, and 7 and disagree with items 2, 4, 6, and 8, you exhibit behaviors that are indicative of a person high in the need for cognition. If your responses to these items are exactly in the opposite direction, you may be low in the need for cognition. Based on your responses, which route to persuasion do you think you tend to take? [Items taken from Cacioppo & Petty, 1982]

1. I really enjoy a task that involves coming up with new solutions to problems.

2. Thinking is not my idea of fun.

3. The notion of thinking abstractly is appealing to me.

4. I like tasks that require little thought once I've learned them.

5. I usually end up deliberating about issues even when they do not affect me personally.

6. It's enough for me that something gets the job done; I don't care how or why it works.

7. I prefer my life to be filled with puzzles that I must solve.

8. I only think as hard as I have to.

ers high in the need for cognition were more likely to watch these events than were their low-NFC counterparts (Ahlering, 1987). Not only did they spend more time watching the debates, but the high-NFC voters also held more beliefs about the candidates than did those low in the need for cognition. The greater number of beliefs making up the overall attitudes held by the high-NFC voters toward the political candidates may well explain another finding that emerged from the 1984 election. Their attitudes toward the candidates eight weeks before the November election were significantly better predictors of their actual voting behavior than were the attitudes of the low NFCs (Cacioppo et al., 1986). This greater attitude-behavior persistence probably occurs because attitudes formed as a result of critically analyzing the relevant issues are more resistant to change than attitudes shaped by means of peripheral cues (Haugtvedt & Petty, 1992). In addition to the need for cognition, table 7.3 reviews some of the factors that influence central versus peripheral processing.

Man is but a reed, the weakest in nature, but he is a thinking reed.

Blaise Pascal, French scientist, 1625–1662

SELF-MONITORING

Another personality trait related to persuasion is *self-monitoring.* As discussed in chapters 4 and 5, people who are high in self-monitoring tend to use social cues to regulate their self-presentations, while low self-monitors are less concerned about the opinions of others and are more likely to behave according to their own personal preferences. Mark Snyder and Kenneth DeBono (1985) hypothesized that high and low self-monitors might differ in their susceptibility to two common persuasion techniques employed in advertising. One technique, the *soft sell,* emphasizes the visual image of the product or ad and is relatively unconcerned with the characteristics or ingredients of the product itself. The *hard sell,* on the other hand, is a technique that emphasizes the quality, value, and utility of the product and is less concerned with how the product is packaged. Snyder and DeBono believed that high self-monitors, who are sensitive to social cues indicating appropriate behavior in a particular setting, would be more persuaded by the soft-sell stress on images. On the other hand, they believed low self-monitors, who base their life

TABLE 7.3

Central Versus Peripheral Processing of Persuasive Messages

Route to Persuasion	Most Likely to Occur When	Effect on Attitudes
Central Route		
The person carefully scrutinizes all the available information in the persuasion environment in an attempt to determine the merits of the presented arguments.	People find the message personally relevant and involving. People are high in need for cognition. People are in a neutral or mildly negative mood. The communicator speaks at a normal rate of speed.	Attitudes tend to be strong, resistant to counterarguments, and predictive of behavior.
Peripheral Route		
Instead of actively thinking about the attitude object, the person relies on incidental cues and simple rules of thumb, such as the attractiveness of the communicator or the length of the message.	People find the message to be irrelevant and noninvolving. People are low in need for cognition. People are in a positive mood. The communicator speaks rapidly.	Attitudes tend to be weak, susceptible to counterarguments, and not predictive of behavior.

choices more on their internal attitudes, would be more influenced by hard-sell ads that focus on product information. As predicted, results indicated that high self-monitors not only favored image-oriented ads and were more willing to buy products (coffee, cigarettes, and whiskey) using such an approach, but they also were willing to pay more money for such products. In contrast, low self-monitoring individuals were more influenced by information-oriented ads that stressed product quality and utility (refer to figure 7.4).

This interesting set of findings has been supported in other studies as well (Celuch & Slama, 1995; Debono & Packer, 1991). It suggests that the image-conscious, high self-monitors will more likely be persuaded by the ad on the top of page 236 rather than the ad on the bottom. The reverse will be true for low self-monitoring persons. Yet, despite these differences in the persuasion techniques that high and low self-monitors are likely to respond to, both are susceptible to persuasion. As the functional approach to attitudes suggested in chapter 6, if you want to change someone's attitudes, you must first understand what the attitude does for the person—what *function* it serves.

AGE AND LIFE STAGE

I'm sure you have heard the old adage "You can't teach an old dog new tricks." In part, this saying reflects a common belief that while adolescents and young adults are highly susceptible to change, as people mature they become more fixed in their ways (Schuman & Scott, 1989). How true is this folk wisdom as it relates to persuasion?

According to the *impressionable years hypothesis,* people are most impressionable and susceptible to persuasion during the formative years of adolescence and young adulthood (Dawson & Prewitt, 1969). This period of heightened susceptibility is thought to be caused by young people grappling for the first time with a wide range of social and po-

To most people nothing is more troublesome than the effort of thinking.

James Bryce, British statesman, 1838–1922

FIGURE 7.4

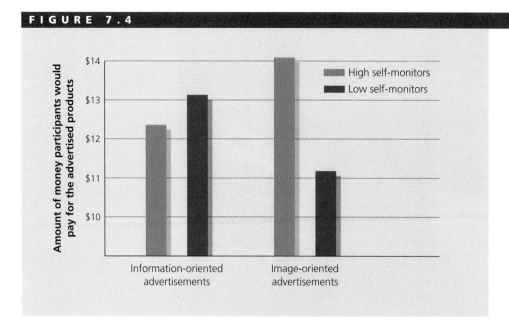

High and low self-monitors were asked how much they would pay for products presented in image-oriented or information-oriented ads. As predicted, high self-monitors were not only more willing than low self-monitors to purchase image-oriented products; they were willing to spend more money for such products. In contrast, low self-monitors were more influenced by the information-oriented ads that stressed product quality. Based on your knowledge of self-monitoring, how would you explain these findings?

litical issues upon which they begin to formulate opinions. Once these basic social and political orientations are acquired, they remain largely unchanged throughout the remaining adult years. Jon Krosnick and Duane Alwin (1989) found support for this hypothesis when they analyzed survey data collected from 2,500 Americans during national elections between 1956 and 1980. The attitudes of individual respondents toward several issues were measured at several points over a four-year period, and the results indicated that those 18 to 25 years old exhibited the most attitude change, followed by those 25 to 36 years old. No significant attitude change occurred among any of the older age groups (37 to 83 years old).

Although the impressionable years hypothesis seems plausible, a more recent series of studies suggests that it provides an incomplete picture of attitude change over the life cycle. Penny Visser and Krosnick (1998) pointed out that previous investigations—including Krosnick and Alwin's own study—mistakenly divided their samples into several discrete age groups and examined the average level of attitude change for each group. The problem with this technique of collapsing across a span of ages was that 65- to 80-year-olds often were grouped together. Because there are more 65-year-olds in the population than 80-year-olds, this grouping contained many more people at the younger end of the range than at the older end. Due to the relatively small number of truly old people in this "elderly" grouping, Visser and Krosnick suspected that averaging across these individuals masks changes that occur at the very end of the life cycle. To overcome this methodological problem, rather than arbitrarily breaking their samples into broad age subgroups, Visser and Krosnick used a more sophisticated statistical procedure (linear and nonlinear regression analysis) to allow them to use people's exact ages when assessing the relation between age and susceptibility to change. In six survey studies involving more than 8,500 participants, Visser and Krosnick analyzed age differences in people's attitudes toward such social and political issues as crime, race relations, defense spending, and international affairs. Consistent with the impressionable years hypothesis, young adults' attitudes were more susceptible to change than middle-age adults' attitudes. However, counter to the impressionable years hypothesis, after about age 60, attitude change became increasingly common with increasing age.

What accounts for these results? As discussed earlier (p. 214), strong attitudes are more resistant to change than weak attitudes. In chapter 6 you also learned that what makes

Image-oriented ad.

TAGHeuer
WHAT ARE YOU MADE OF ?

TIGER WOODS AND HIS LINK AUTOMATIC CHRONOGRAPH

SWISS AVANT-GARDE SINCE 1860

Information-oriented ad.

an attitude strong is acquiring more relevant information about it and becoming more personally involved so that the attitude is more important to you (p. 190). Visser and Krosnick found that attitude importance and perceived knowledge about attitude issues rose in early adulthood, peaked at about age 50, and then began to fall after about age 65. Thus, resistance to attitude change may increase between early and middle adulthood because we attach more importance to our social and political attitudes and think more frequently about them. This same resistance appears to decline later in life because the importance of these attitudes and our knowledge about the relevant issues surrounding them also declines. Their *life-stages hypothesis* contends that the greater susceptibility to attitude change in young adulthood and old age is partly due to the many role transitions that often occur in these two age groups. As their social roles change, young and elderly adults' perceptions of their social and political worlds also change, thereby undermining the strength of their attitudes. In addition, for the elderly, a decline in cognitive skills may render them less able to actively resist persuasion through counterarguing. These findings suggest that we may need to revise our "old dog" folk saying. It is not old dogs or young dogs who are most likely to resist learning new tricks. It is the middle-aged dogs who appear set in their ways.

CRITICAL *thinking*

If the life-stages hypothesis is correct that the attitudes of the young and the elderly are more susceptible to persuasion than the attitudes of middle-age adults, does this change any conclusions that we drew from the Bennington College study described in the Applications section of chapter 6?

AGE AND TIME PERSPECTIVE

Memory and persuasion research suggest that people are more likely to remember and be persuaded by messages that are more relevant to their current life goals and values (Blaney, 1986; Clary et al., 1994). Developmental research further suggests that life goals and values change as people age (Dittmann-Kohli & Westerhof, 1997; Staudinger et al., 1999). *Socioemotional selectivity theory* proposes that these changes partly result from a shift in *time perspective* as people age (Carstensen, 1998; Kennedy et al., 2001). According to this theory, many goals can be classified as either *knowledge related* or *emotionally meaningful*. Knowledge-related goals are concerned with acquiring new information and are oriented toward the future, whereas emotionally meaningful goals are concerned with feelings and emotional connection to others. When adults are young, time is perceived as open ended and knowledge-related goals tend to assume relatively high priority. As adults age, however, time is perceived as limited and knowledge-related goals become less relevant. Instead, emotionally meaningful goals become more important because they have more immediate payoffs (Carstensen et al., 1999; Fung et al., 2001).

How does this shift in time perspective affect persuasion? In a set of studies, Helene Fung and Laura Carstensen (2003) showed young and old adults advertisements for different products such as a camera, a desk lamp, and a line of watches. For each of the products, three versions of the advertisement were created. Each version was identical except for the slogan (see the photos on p. 238). The *emotionally meaningful ad* contained a slogan that appealed to emotions surrounding love and concern. The *knowledge-related ad* contained a slogan concerned with expanding horizons or achieving success in the future. The *control ad* had no slogan at all. Participants were randomly presented with different types of ads, but no participant saw more than one version of the same ad. After reviewing each ad for 30 seconds, participants evaluated each ad and later completed a recognition memory test for the brand names and slogans in the ads.

As expected, Fung and Carstensen found that the older participants not only preferred advertisements with emotionally meaningful appeal more than the younger participants, but they also remembered a higher proportion of information from such ads compared to the ads with knowledge-related appeal. These findings provide support for socioemotional selectivity theory's contention that as adults become elderly they place more emphasis on emotionally meaningful goals, as compared to knowledge-related goals. This increased emphasis on emotional meaning rather than acquiring new knowledge and skills appears to result from a shift in time perspective among the elderly: their future is limited so they focus on what will give them emotional meaning now.

It is important to note that additional research indicates that these age-related differences in goals are not fixed, but instead, appear changeable due to shifts in time perspective

Knowledge-related version

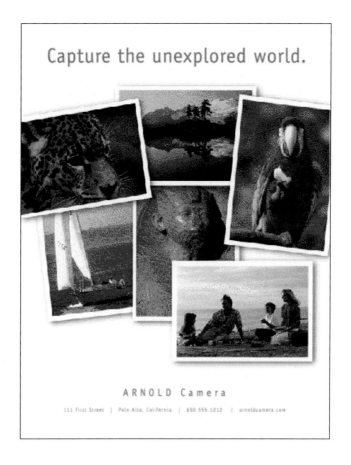

Emotionally meaningful version

(Fredrickson & Carstensen, 1990; Fung et al., 1999). In one additional condition in Fung and Carstensen's (2003) study, they manipulated participants' time perspective to determine whether this would influence their preferences for advertisements with emotionally meaningful appeal. Time perspective was experimentally manipulated by asking participants to imagine that they had just been told that a new medical advance would ensure that they would enjoy twenty more healthy years of life beyond their expected age of death. Elderly participants in this "expanded time perspective" condition no longer exhibited a preference for emotionally meaningful ads. This finding provides support for the hypothesis that time perspective—and not age itself—accounts for the observed age differences in ad preferences. As baby boomers age, marketing professionals may find these findings useful in shaping their ad campaigns for the expanding older population. If the current findings are valid, ads focusing on nostalgia and connecting emotionally to others should resonate with the elderly.

SECTION SUMMARY

- Audience factors that determine persuasion:

    Positive moods generally induce more persuasion than neutral or somber moods

    High self-involved audiences are more likely to take the central route to persuasion

    Low *need for cognition* persons or high *self-monitors* are more persuaded by peripheral cues

- Age effects (recent studies suggest a life-stages explanation):

    Middle-aged adults are most resistant to attitude change

    Young adults and the elderly are more easily persuaded

- Time perspective

    Older adults' more shortened time perspective causes them to be more influenced by ads emphasizing emotional meaning than young adults

THE ROLE OF THE SELF IN PERSUASION

When discussing persuasion, it is technically incorrect to state that persuaders change people's minds. Persuaders can present their persuasive arguments, couch it in powerful language, and associate it with pleasing stimuli, but they cannot actually change people's attitudes. Successful persuaders create the proper conditions under which individuals become *willing* to change their attitudes (Simons, 1971). This distinction may seem like hairsplitting, but it has raised important questions that have advanced our understanding of the persuasion process. At the heart of this discussion is the self.

By persuading others, we convince ourselves.

Junius, eighteenth-century English political pundit

Self-Generated Persuasion Is Very Effective

One of the first studies to explore the nature of self-generated persuasion was conducted by Kurt Lewin (1943, 1947) during World War II. The U.S. Department of Agriculture's Committee on Food Habits was attempting to increase the American public's consumption of meat products that, prior to the war, had generally been thrown away or used as pet food. These less desirable meats were kidneys, beef hearts, and intestines. The Agricultural Department asked Lewin to develop a way to persuade Americans that these undesirable foods were really not that bad. To accomplish this task, Lewin first enlisted a group of housewives as participants in the study and then divided them into two groups. The first group received a forty-five-minute lecture on the merits of intestinal meats. The speaker emphasized how eating these meats would provide more food for the troops overseas, which would greatly benefit the war effort. As recipes were distributed, the speaker described the many nutritional and economic advantages of intestinal meats and informed the women how she had successfully added them to her own family's diet.

In contrast to this first group, the second group of women received no lecture. Instead, after a brief introduction, the discussion leader asked the women, "Do you think that housewives like yourselves could be persuaded to participate in the intestinal meat program?" During the next forty-five minutes, the women brought up many of the same issues as in the lecture. The difference between the lecture and the discussion, however, was that the women in the discussion group were actively generating arguments for serving these relatively undesirable food products. What effect do you think this different information format had on their later culinary activities? While only 3 percent of the housewives in the lecture format group later served intestinal meats to their families, 32 percent of those who engaged in the self-persuasion discussion group served these food products.

As in most, if not all, of the persuasion techniques discussed thus far in the chapter, people who sell consumer products have learned how to employ the self-generated persuasion technique to boost sales. How might this work? Imagine that you are a door-to-door salesperson selling subscriptions to a local cable television network. Using the self-generated persuasion technique, you might knock on someone's door, introduce yourself and your product, and have the following conversation:

> You: Mr. Pantouflard, I'd like you to take a moment and imagine how cable TV will provide *you* with broader entertainment value. For example, how do you think cable TV will save you money and make your life easier?
>
> Mr. P.: Gee, let me think about that a bit. Hmm. Well, for one thing, if I had all those movies on HBO, I wouldn't have to waste time renting videos. I could just sit on my couch and tune in the flicks. That's appealing. Being a family man, I also wouldn't have to go to the movie theater and pay $30 for tickets and $20 for popcorn and refreshments. Heck, a night at the movies can cost more than an entire month's worth of cable TV and potato chips! Where do I sign up?!

Although this scene is a bit exaggerated, it is not too far off the mark from the actual technique a group of door-to-door cable TV salespersons employed in Tempe, Arizona. These salespersons were part of a study Larry Gregory and his colleagues conducted (1982), in which some salespersons used the self-generated persuasion strategy, while others simply told customers about the advantages of having cable. The results indicated that although less than 20 percent of the customers subscribed when they passively received the information, almost 50 percent subscribed when they themselves were asked to imagine using the service.

Taken together, the studies Lewin first conducted and those others later carried out suggest that getting people to actively generate arguments in favor of a certain course of action makes it more likely that their attitudes will change in the direction of these self-generated arguments. Why are these self-generated arguments more persuasive? One fundamental reason is that manipulations that encourage self-persuasion serve to increase how deeply people delve into their attitude structures and, therefore, how many self-relevant connections they make. Another reason is that when someone is actively trying to persuade you by presenting a set of arguments, you may respond negatively to this perceived manipulation of your thoughts (Rhodewalt & Davison, 1983). However, when you are encouraged to generate your own arguments, there is a much greater likelihood that you will adopt these ideas because they have been conceived by a trustworthy and credible source—yourself. Astute persuaders, therefore, allow their audience's positive attitudes concerning their own ideas to move them toward adopting the persuaders' point of view. This perspective is catching on among a growing number of alcohol and drug prevention programs in elementary and secondary schools. "It has to be highly interactive," says Zili Sloboda, senior research associate at the University of Akron Institute for Health and Social Policy. "Children have to be able to try it on in their own lives."

We Can Develop Attitude Certainty by Actively Trying to Counterargue

What happens when people successfully resist persuasion? The typical assumption has been that if persuasion is resisted, people's attitudes remain unchanged. Is this true?

Richard Petty and his colleagues (2002) question this widespread assumption and suggest instead that when people resist persuasion, they often become more confident in the attitude that was targeted. Successful resistance increases confidence in the attitude because people infer that their resistance was due to the validity of the attitude. The researchers further hypothesize that people will experience the greatest increase in attitude confidence after resisting messages they perceive as being very strong. In contrast, when people successfully defend their attitude against a weak attack, their confidence in the attitude should not increase because they cannot be certain that the attitude would have survived a strong challenge.

In a test of these hypotheses, Zakary Tormala and Petty (2002) conducted a study in which college students were presented with a proposal supposedly from the University's Board of Trustees to implement a new policy in two years requiring graduating seniors to pass a comprehensive exam in their major field of study (sound familiar?). As justification for the experiment, students were led to believe that the trustees wanted to assess students' reactions. In order to induce resistance to persuasion, participants in the experimental conditions—but not those in the control condition—next received the following instructions:

> The University's Board of Trustees would also like to gather all possible arguments that students can raise against the issue. After you read the proposal, we would like you to list your arguments *against* the exam policy.

Following these instructions, all participants were exposed to a persuasive message that contained two weak and two strong arguments on the issue. An example of a weak argument was that implementing the exams would allow the university to take part in a national trend. An example of a strong argument was that implementing the exams would increase the average starting salary of graduates. Participants in the *perceived strong arguments* condition were told that they were given only the strongest of all the arguments raised in favor of the exam policy, while those in the *perceived weak arguments* condition were informed that they were given only the weakest of all the arguments in favor of the policy.

After receiving the persuasive message, participants in the two experimental conditions—but not those in the control condition—were told to generate a list of as many counterarguments as they could. All participants then completed measures to assess their attitudes and attitude certainty toward the comprehensive exam proposal. Results found no group differences in attitude toward the exam proposal. However, as expected, the groups did differ in their later attitude confidence. When participants resisted what was described as a strong message, their attitude confidence increased compared with those who thought they received a weak message and from the no-message control group. Subsequent studies in this same series found that successful resistance to persuasion not only enhances people's confidence in their initial attitude, but it also renders the attitude more resistant to subsequent attacks and increases the likelihood that people will later behave in a manner consistent with the attitude (Tormala & Petty, 2002).

These studies demonstrate how counterarguing can produce successful and sustained resistance to persuasion. But what happens if the persuasive arguments are so strong that people cannot generate convincing counterarguments? Derek Rucker and Petty (2004) predicted that if people try to find fault in a persuasive message and fail, the new attitude resulting from this successful persuasion attempt will be held with more conviction and certainty. In testing this hypothesis, the researchers used the ever-popular scenario of telling students about a new proposal to require graduating seniors to pass a comprehensive exam. However, in this study, students in the two experimental conditions received very strong message arguments that were designed to be difficult to counterargue. An example of one of these hard-to-refute arguments was:

> Universities that implement senior comprehensive exams are given additional funding by a new government program that rewards performance-based education. For students, this

means that at least a 5% tuition decrease would accompany the passing of the exam proposal. In addition, to an immediate 5% tuition decrease, the government program provides funds to ensure that students' tuition will not be raised for a period of at least 5 years.

Before receiving the message arguments, participants in the experimental conditions were instructed to either focus on their thoughts while the message was presented *(thought condition)* or generate counterarguments to the message *(counterargument condition)*. Students in the control condition did not receive any persuasive message. All participants then completed measures to assess their attitudes and attitude certainty toward the comprehensive exam proposal.

The researchers found that students in the two experimental conditions—those who received the persuasive message—had more favorable attitudes toward the comprehensive exam proposal than students in the no-message control group. This suggests that the persuasive message was successful in securing attitude change. More important, these new attitudes were held with greater certainty in the *counterargument condition* than in the *thought condition.* In other words, when students were told to generate counterarguments toward a strong persuasive message, their failure to refute the message caused them to adopt a new attitude that was stronger than students who did not try to find fault with the message. Being impressed with how hard it was to counterargue, the active resisters became more confident in their new attitudes than did people who simply thought about the persuasive message without engaging in active resistance.

Considering these findings from the persuaders' point of view, when you are trying to persuade others and are convinced that you have very strong arguments that cannot be refuted, you might consider going against intuition and encourage your audience to try to find fault in your message. When audience members fail to find fault, they may say to themselves, "I changed my attitude even though I tried to fight the persuasive attempt. I now know that I have few negative thoughts about the message and my new attitude is a good one." In essence, this is another variation of self-generated persuasion.

Thus far, we have examined the conditions under which we may become impressed with our ability or our inability to counterargue a persuasive message. As demonstrated in these studies, being impressed with our resistance can lead to increased confidence in our initial attitude, but being impressed with our failure to resist can lead to increased confidence in our new attitude. But what if we are not so impressed with either our resistance or our lack of resistance?

In such instances, we should have less confidence in our attitudes. Consider first the case in which we are able to counterargue and resist persuasion, but we believe that our resistance was difficult or lacking in some way. Even though we do not change our attitude, we may now be less confident in the attitude, rendering it more susceptible to future persuasion attempts. In the case of failing to resist persuasion, if we believe that our changed attitude occurred because we did not try very hard to resist or that there were many distractions that prevented us from mounting a good defense, we may have less confidence in our new attitude. Figure 7.5 presents a summary of the key ideas developed by Petty and his colleagues (2004b) regarding the process of counterarguing and the conditions under which various outcomes are likely.

Employing Subtle Labels Can Nudge People into Attitude and Behavior Change

One final way the self can figure in persuasion is through the self-perception process: an effective persuader may nudge people into a desired course of action by convincing them that they are the *sort of people* who engage in this type of activity (Petty & Wegener, 1998). According to self-perception theory (see chapter 6, p. 182), people often come to know their attitudes and dispositions by inferring them from observations of their past behavior. When others begin to attribute certain dispositional qualities to us, self-perception theory contends that we look to our behavior for confirmation of the validity of this labeling. For example, suppose a friend tells you that you are a very insightful and "deep" person. Even though you may never have thought of yourself in this way, you may now recall incidents from your past when you exhibited particular wisdom, understanding, or the ability to ask penetrating questions (for example, you were the first child in your neighborhood to won-

FIGURE 7.5

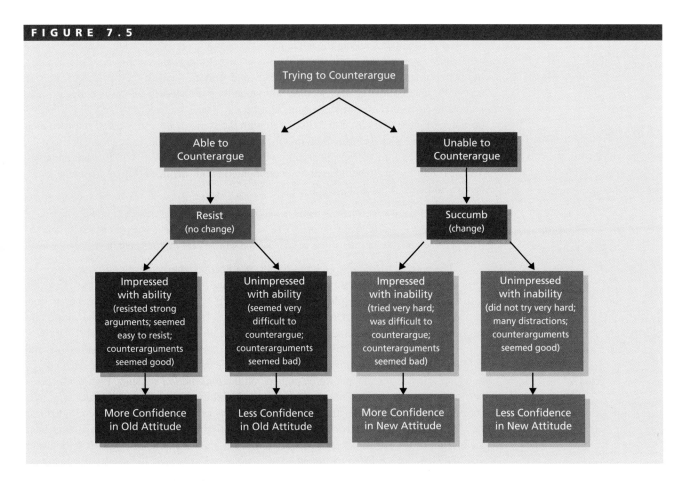

A Model of Attempted Resistance to Persuasion

Richard Petty and his colleagues (2004b) have outlined how attempts at counterarguing a persuasive message can either succeed or fail. Being impressed or unimpressed with one's ability to resist or not resist a persuasive message will either increase or decrease one's confidence in the new or old attitude.

Petty, R. E., Tormala, Z. L., & Rucker, D. D. (2004b). Resisting persuasion by counterarguing: An attitude strength perspective. In J. T. Jost, M. R. Banaji, & D. A. Prentice (Eds.). *Perspectivism in Social Psychology: The Yin and Yang of scientific progress* (pp. 37–51). Washington, DC: American Psychological Association.

der why Goofy, the Disney dog character, walked on his hind legs while Pluto, another Disney dog character, walked on all fours). This analysis of past behavior may lead you to conclude that your friend is correct—you are "deep."

Richard Miller and his coworkers (1975) conducted two interesting studies demonstrating the power of labels in changing an audience's behavior. Both studies took place in three fifth-grade classrooms in an inner-city Chicago public school. In the first study, the teachers in two of the three classrooms engaged in an eight-day ecology program, while the third classroom served as the control group. The teacher in the *attribution-persuasion* classroom first commended her students for being ecology minded and not throwing candy wrappers on the auditorium floor during that day's school assembly. She also told them that the janitor had said that their class was one of the cleanest in the building (this comment was a fabrication). During the week, whenever students picked up paper from the floor, the teacher would commend them for their ecology consciousness. During the middle of the school week, a large poster was pinned to the class bulletin board saying "We Are Anderson's Litter-Conscious Class." The next day, the principal visited their room, commented on how neat and orderly the students were, and then later sent a letter to the class stating:

> As I talked to your teacher, I could not help but notice how very clean and orderly your room appeared. A young lady near the teacher's desk was seen picking up around her desk. It is quite evident that each of you is very careful in your section.

On the eighth day, the janitor washed the classroom floor and left a note (actually written by the experimenters) telling the students it was easy to clean due to their neatness.

In the *information-persuasion* classroom, the students first went on a field trip during which their teacher talked about ecology and warned them of the dangers of littering and pollution. Following this lecture, the students pretended to be trash collectors and picked up litter as they came across it. During the week, the teacher talked about the importance of picking up litter and discussed with the students how they could improve their own classroom. She also told them that the school janitor had said he needed help from the students in keeping the floor clean, implying that such help would lead to adult approval. The next day the principal visited and commented about the need for tidy and neat classrooms, and later sent a letter stating:

> As I talked to your teacher, I could not help but notice that your room was in need of some cleaning. It is very important that we be neat and orderly in the upkeep of our school and classrooms. I hope each of you in your section will be very careful about litter.

The teacher also put up a large poster of a Peanuts character saying "Don't be a litterbug" with "Be neat" and "Don't litter" bordering it. Toward the end of the week, the teacher appointed several children to watch and see if people were neat outside the building as well as in the classroom. On the last day, a note was left on the board from the janitor (actually written by the experimenters) reminding the children to pick up papers off the floor.

Now in both classrooms, students learned that they should be ecology conscious and not litter. However, in the *attribution* classroom, students were repeatedly labeled as ecology minded, while no such labels were "pinned" on the *information* students. Figure 7.6 shows that students in the attribution classroom not only exhibited significantly greater nonlittering behavior two days after the eight-day treatment period, but their ecology-mindedness was found to still be intact two weeks following the first posttest. Indeed, three months later the teacher of the attribution class reported that her students were still significantly neater than they had been prior to treatment.

Using a similar labeling procedure with second-graders in the same school, the researchers significantly increased students' performance in mathematics. These studies, along with others, indicate that when people (especially those whose opinions we respect) make dispositional attributions about our behavior, we often will accept the given label and

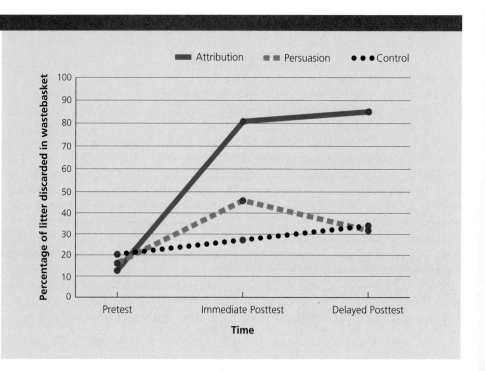

FIGURE 7.6

Attribution Versus Information Persuasion as a Means for Modifying Behavior

Miller and his colleagues taught fifth-graders in two separate classrooms not to litter and to clean up after others. How were they taught? Students in the attribution classroom were repeatedly told they were neat and tidy people, while those in the persuasion classroom were told they should be neat and tidy. The students who were labeled as neat and tidy not only littered less two days after the eight-day treatment period, but their ecology-mindedness was still intact two weeks later.

act in accordance with it in the future (Jenson & Moore, 1977; Kraut, 1973). That is, when we incorporate the labels that others assign to us into our own self-concepts, we will likely also begin acting in ways consistent with the labels.

This self-attribution process, which we previously discussed in chapter 5 as the *self-fulfilling prophecy* (pp. 156–159), usually does not occur instantaneously. Returning to the ecology study, during the first two days of the treatment, many of the students in the attribution condition did not agree with the ecology label. When the teacher told them that they were not the type of children who would litter, the students disagreed and stated that they would and did indeed litter. However, after repeatedly being called ecology minded by others, and given some time to observe their own behavior, these children began to adopt the ecology label quite strongly. They had accepted the dispositional attribution of being ecology-conscious children.

One of the advantages of using attributional statements in persuading people to change their attitudes and behavior is that in their guise as "truth statements," these labels may more easily slip past the defenses people ordinarily employ against more direct persuasive attempts. In other words, using attribution to persuade may be more successful because it is less easily recognized as persuasion, and thus, it is less likely to arouse resistance or counterarguing.

Having extolled the persuasive power of using labels to change people's attitudes and actions, I must add that there are limits to this attributional power. Labels are often rejected. As you will recall from chapter 3, self-concept change generally occurs only on those self-aspects about which people hold uncertain beliefs (Swann & Ely, 1984). When people hold very definite beliefs about themselves, they are very likely to reject any labels that contradict those beliefs. Thus, persuading through labeling is generally only going to have a chance for success when the audience has vaguely formulated conceptions of their personal attributes in the area under scrutiny. The lesson to be learned here is that you can use labels to persuade if the focus of change is not some attitude or behavior strongly associated with a central aspect of a person's self-concept.

SECTION SUMMARY

- Successful persuaders understand the role that the self plays in the persuasion process
- Actively self-generating arguments in favor of a position makes it more likely that people will persuade themselves
- Encouraging people to actively counterargue a message can strengthen or weaken either an existing attitude or a new attitude
- Subtly labeling persons may be sufficient to change their attitudes and behavior

FEATURED STUDY

SUBLIMINAL PRIMING AND PERSUASION

Strahan, E. J., Spencer, S. J., & Zanna, M. P. (2002). Subliminal priming and persuasion: Striking while the iron is hot. *Journal of Experimental Social Psychology, 38,* 556–568.

Psychologists have found substantial evidence that we can process a great deal of information below the level of our conscious awareness. When does this subliminal information affect our motivation to think and behave in certain ways? In the present study, the researchers hypothesized that although people perceive subliminal cues, those cues will not influence their motivation to take action unless they are already motivated to do so.

Method

Participants were eighty-one college students who received extra credit in their psychology courses for participating in what was described as a "marketing study" in which they would eat and drink and then evaluate a number of different products. To ensure that all participants would be initially at least somewhat thirsty when they arrived at the testing lab, they were instructed not to eat or drink anything for three hours prior to the experimental session. When they arrived, participants completed a mood scale that also measured their explicit level of thirst. Next they performed a "taste test" on two different types of cookies. Following this taste test, thirst was manipulated by telling half the participants "to cleanse their palate by drinking as much water as you want." The other participants received no water. After this manipulation, participants again completed the mood scale that included the explicit measure of thirst. Then, as part of a test administered by computer, the researchers subliminally exposed participants to neutral words (*pirate, won*) or thirst-related words (*thirst, dry*). Following this computer test, participants again completed the mood scale that contained the explicit rating of thirst. Finally, they performed a second taste test in which they judged two different types of Kool-Aid beverages. Participants were left alone in the room and told they could drink as much of the beverages as they desired. Following this taste test, participants were debriefed.

Results and Discussion

Participants who did not receive water after the first taste test reported feeling significantly thirstier than those who were given water, confirming that the manipulation of thirst was effective. The researchers hypothesized that the subliminal thirst priming procedure would affect how much participants drank when they were thirsty, but not when they were quenched. Consistent with this hypothesis, results indicated that the subliminal thirst primes had little impact on participants whose thirst had just been quenched, but they significantly increased consumption among those who were already thirsty (see figure 7.7). In other words, the subliminal thirst primes did not appear to generate a desire in people to begin drinking beverages, but they did appear to strengthen or sustain the desire for thirsty people to drink greater quantities of beverages.

These findings suggest that subliminal priming only affects people's behavior when they are already motivated to behave in a certain way. In other words, by themselves, subliminal messages should not be expected to automatically influence people's behavior. However, when they are already motivated, subliminal messages that are congruent with this motivational state may further energize people's behavior so that they behave more vigorously than they would without exposure to the subliminal messages. Additional laboratory studies have also supported this hypothesis (Jaskowski et al., 2003). Because of this possibility, there should be renewed debate about the potential use and abuse of subliminal procedures in persuasion.

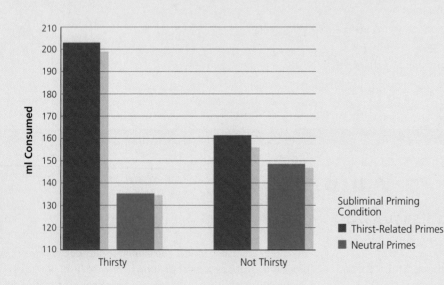

FIGURE 7.7

Amount of Liquid Consumed as a Function of Thirst and Subliminal Priming

Source: Strahan, E. J., Spencer, S. J., & Zanna, M. P. (2002). Subliminal priming and persuasion: Striking while the iron is hot. *Journal of Experimental Social Psychology, 38,* 556–568.

Subliminal Priming Condition
■ Thirst-Related Primes
■ Neutral Primes

APPLICATIONS

CAN YOU BE PERSUADED BY SUBLIMINAL MESSAGES?

*I*n the summer of 1957, advertising executive James Vicary claimed that he had induced customers at a New Jersey theater to dramatically increase their popcorn and coke purchases by secretly splicing the words *EAT POPCORN* and *DRINK COKE* into the Hollywood movie *Picnic* and flashing it before their eyes for a fraction of a second. These messages were *subliminal,* meaning that they were presented so fast or so faintly that they were just below the absolute threshold for conscious awareness. **Subliminal perception** is the processing of such information. Vicary's "study" created a sensation with the public, and, over the years people commonly cite it when they either talk or write about the powerful influence that subliminal messages can have on thought and action (Key, 1989). What they don't realize is that James Vicary fabricated the entire study in an attempt to attract customers to his failing marketing business (Weir, 1984).

Subliminal Perception

The processing of information that is just below the absolute threshold for conscious awareness.

A likely reason why Vicary's surprising claims were so uncritically accepted may be that they fit popular assumptions about the powers that new communication technologies can have over the attitudes and behavior of viewers (Wartella & Reeves, 1985). Indeed, almost 70 percent of people who have some knowledge of subliminal advertising believe that it can influence consumer buying habits (Zanot et al., 1983), and millions of people buy subliminal self-help tapes to help them lose weight, improve their memory, or increase their self-esteem (Pratkanis & Aronson, 1992). Yet is there any real scientific evidence that these efforts to subliminally persuade are effective?

Let us examine one representative study investigating subliminal persuasion and consumer purchasing. A few years after the popcorn/Coke results were reported, researchers conducted a field study of subliminal advertising effects with the help of an Indianapolis television station and a local grocery store chain (DeFleur & Petranoff, 1959). Over a period of several weeks, the television station ran a series of subliminal commercials for a food product. During the first week, the station ran a subliminal ad for the product, while during the second week this subliminal message was embedded in an ordinary advertisement for the product. Alone, the subliminal ad produced an unimpressive 1 percent increase in normal sales. However, when the subliminal message was coupled with the ordinary commercial, sales increased by a whopping 282 percent! Before you draw any hasty conclusions from this seemingly impressive sales figure, let's compare this increase with the sales figures for other products in the grocery store that had received consumer exposure through normal advertising during the same period of time. Ordinary advertisements without any subliminal messages increased sales, on average, by 2,509 percent! Although this study demonstrated the impor-

tance of control groups in experimental research, it did not provide any evidence whatsoever that subliminal messages have the slightest effect in persuading people to increase their product purchasing. Similar studies investigating subliminal advertising have also yielded nonsignificant effects (Trappey, 1996).

You can fool all the people all the time if the advertising is right and the budget is big enough.

Joseph E. Levine, U.S. film producer, 1984

Although there is no evidence that subliminal persuasion influences consumer behavior, what about those people who have used subliminal tapes and swear that their lives have been changed? Isn't this evidence that subliminal persuasion can be effective at least some of the time? This was the question that Anthony Pratkanis and his colleagues (1994) were interested in answering when they conducted a study of such self-help tapes. Participants were first pretested for their level of self-esteem and memory recall ability and then given an audiotape containing various pieces of classical music. The tape manufacturers

Although subliminal self-help tapes do not improve memory or increase self-esteem, they continue to do a brisk business. Their staying power in the marketplace is probably due to two factors: (1) a misperception by the public that subliminal persuasion can influence this type of attitude and behavior change, and (2) self-persuasion of consumers who likely experience postdecision dissonance after purchasing such pricey products

claimed that embedded within these self-help tapes were sub-liminal messages designed either to increase self-esteem (e.g., "I have high self-worth and high self-esteem") or to increase one's memory (e.g., "My ability to remember and recall is increasing daily."). However, the researchers purposely mislabeled half of the tapes, leading participants who received them to believe they had a memory tape when they really had a self-esteem tape, or vice versa. The remaining participants received the rest of the tapes, with correct labels. During the next five weeks, these volunteers listened daily to their tapes at home. After this exposure period, they were again given self-esteem and memory tests, and they were also asked whether they believed the tapes had been effective. Was there any evidence that participants experienced subliminal persuasion?

Pratkanis and his coworkers found no self-esteem or memory increases: the subliminal tapes were utterly ineffective. These null findings, however, stood in sharp contrast to the participants' beliefs about the tapes. Those who thought they had received the self-esteem tape tended to believe their self-esteem had increased, and those who thought they had been given the memory tape were more likely to believe that their memory had improved. This was true even if they had received a mislabeled tape! According to the researchers, these findings indicate that users of self-help audiotapes expect self-improvement through their use, and actually convince themselves that the improvement has taken place, when, in fact, it has not. Combined with the findings from other subliminal tape studies (Merikle & Skanes, 1992; Moore, 1995), this research suggests that whatever benefits people derive from such self-help products have little to do with the content of the subliminal messages. Instead, people's expectations and their desire to reduce cognitive dissonance ("I invested a lot of time and money in this tape, it must be good!") appear to be the sole means of influence operating here. When all is said and done, what very likely explains attitude and behavior change in those who use subliminal self-help products is good old-fashioned persuasion principles.

Before dismissing the possibility that subliminal persuasion can influence people's everyday attitudes and behavior, it must be kept in mind that subliminal perception does indeed exist. Numerous psychological studies indicate that

It is true that you may fool all the people some of the time; you can even fool some of the people all the time; but you can't fool all of the people all the time.

Abraham Lincoln, U.S. president, 1809–1865

perception without awareness can take place (Eimer & Schlaghecken, in press). More important, some of these studies, conducted under carefully controlled laboratory conditions, have been able to manipulate people's attitudes and behavior using subliminal stimuli. For example, in a series of experiments, Robert Bornstein and his colleagues (1987) found evidence for a *subliminal mere exposure effect*. Participants who were repeatedly exposed to subliminal stimuli (abstract geometric figures or people's faces) later expressed greater liking for those stimuli. Similarly, John Bargh and Tanya Chartrand (1999) found that participants who were subliminally exposed to achievement-oriented words (*strive, succeed, master*) while completing a "word search" puzzle were more likely to continue working on the puzzle task (57 percent) when signaled to stop than those in the control group (22 percent). These findings, along with others (Krosnick et al., 1992; Weisbuch et al., 2003), suggest that it still may be possible for a stimulus subliminally embedded in an advertisement to influence buyers' preferences.

The caveat to this possibility is that there are some important differences between the laboratory environment where these results were obtained and the real world where people would normally receive subliminal messages. In the carefully controlled settings where these subliminal effects have been found, participants paid a great deal of attention to the experimental stimuli. In watching the average media advertisement, people are considerably less attentive. Due to the viewer's wandering eye, it is much less likely that a subliminal stimulus embedded in an ad would be unconsciously processed. A second reason to doubt that these effects would occur outside the lab is that the duration of most of these subliminal effects appears to be very short, perhaps lasting only a few seconds. If the subliminal effects last only a short time, they are unlikely to influence product purchases. However, at least one recent set of studies has found evidence that people exposed to subliminal stimuli in the laboratory showed some effects seven days following exposure (Sohlberg & Birgegard, 2003). If this finding of longer duration effects can be replicated in future research, it is not beyond the realm of possibility that practitioners of persuasion could sometime in the future develop clever subliminal techniques that influence the thinking and behavior of the general public. The Featured Study in this chapter describes findings suggesting that advertisers may be able to subliminally persuade people who are already motivated to behave in a particular fashion. For example, people who are already hungry may be induced to eat more than usual after being exposed to subliminal eating messages. Future research will determine the actual potential use—and abuse—of subliminal procedures in persuasion.

THE BIG PICTURE

The first influential approach to understanding persuasion was the *message-learning approach,* which employed principles of learning theory to explain the distinctions between effective and ineffective persuasive communications. It is generally credited with providing important insights into *when* and *how* persuasion occurs, but it mistakenly viewed the message receiver as being relatively passive in the persuasion process. The more recent *cognitive-response* approach, which conceives of the message receiver as being an active agent in persuasion, employs cognitive theories. This approach has been most helpful in understanding *why* people change their attitudes when listening to persuasive messages. According to the elaboration likelihood model, recipients of persuasive messages either take the *central route* to persuasion by critically analyzing the message content or the *peripheral route* by attending to incidental cues surrounding the message. Which route is taken depends on many factors, including whether the issue is important to recipients, whether they have the time and/or the intellectual ability to analyze the message, and who or what happens to be around to distract or focus their attention. When combined with what is going on inside recipients' minds, message persuasiveness also depends on who is presenting the message, and how it is presented.

Persuasion is more than a textbook topic. The simple fact is that persuasive messages surround you, both those that you generate and those received from others. With the information learned in this chapter, do you now have a better understanding why some of these persuasion attempts are more effective than others? The repetition of radio and TV ads capitalizes on mere exposure effects. The celebrity product endorser or the physically attractive spokesperson is there as a peripheral cue to enhance your receptivity to the message. Fast-talking and wisecracking salespersons also use persuasion strategies that have ties to chapter material. First, they hope that their humor grabs your attention and increases your liking for them. Second, they count on their rapid speech serving as a peripheral cue of their expertise, while simultaneously rendering you less able to fully comprehend what they actually say. And what about your own persuasion attempts? Do you first try to induce a good mood in those you hope to persuade, banking on their happiness lowering their resistance to what you have to say?

Perhaps this is a mistake if your message is complex and in need of an audience ready to expend a great deal of cognitive effort. These examples illustrate the essential *message* of this chapter, which is that we are flexible social thinkers who rely on different cognitive strategies when evaluating information designed to change our attitudes and behavior.

WEB SITES
accessed through http://www.mhhe.com/franzoi4

Web sites for this chapter focus on persuasion, including an analysis of propaganda and recent research employing the elaboration likelihood model.

Propaganda Analysis Home Page

This Web page contains an analysis of common propaganda techniques, historical examples, and a bibliography of relevant publications.

John Cacioppo's Home Page

John Cacioppo, cocreator of the elaboration likelihood model, has a home page where you can learn more about his recent research and ideas.

CHAPTER 8

Prejudice and Discrimination

CHAPTER OUTLINE

PREVIEW *Over the years, prejudice research has examined both the social conditions that support and weaken intergroup intolerance, as well as the impact that such intolerance has on those who are its targets. How have social psychologists applied this knowledge to promote diversity acceptance and academic achievement in the schools?*

*Y*ou know who *they* are, don't you? *They* are different. *They* don't value what we value. *They* are disrespectful. *They're* pushy, greedy, dirty, ugly, unhealthy, stupid, and *they* aren't like us.

I like *them.* Some of my best friends are *them. They* like me because I'm not condescending, like other people. But do *they* always have to act like *they* do? Do *they* have to be so flamboyant? I just wish *they* would try to "fit in" more, be more normal, like us.

They have so much, and *they* took it from us. We value what is truly important, and *they* seem to value nothing. *They* are nothing like us. We need to watch out for *them. They* took advantage of us, and now it's payback time. *They* think *they're* so special, but *they* are not. We are the special ones. And we deserve what *they* have.

We feel sorry for *them.* It's not their fault that *they* are like that, but do we have to have *them* around us? *They* are so different. Can't we put *them* somewhere? *They* might hurt themselves, or someone else. *They're* strange and they make us uncomfortable. *They* would be better off by *themselves,* away from us.

We need to protect ourselves from *them. They* are trying to go where *they* don't belong. We have what *they* want. But we worked for what we have. *They're* lazy, and all *they* want to do is lay around while we work. *They* think we owe *them* something. *They* try to make us feel guilty, but *they're* the guilty ones. *They* are nothing like us.

Sure, there are a few good ones, but *they're* the exception that proves the rule. If you give *them* an inch, *they* take a mile. *They* aren't like us. You can't trust *them. They* act friendly, but you should hear what they say about us when *they're* alone. *They're* cunning, conceited, smug, condescending, and only looking out for *themselves.*

In the English language and in many other languages, the pronouns *us* and *them*—and their various linguistic cousins, such as *we, our, they,* and *their*—indicate the degree of social and psychological space between the writer or speaker and the social groups to which these pronouns refer (Nayar, 2002). As discussed in chapter 3 (p. 86), pronouns such as *we* and *us* represent an emotional identification with a group of people, an inclusion of them in our self-concept. In contrast, the pronouns *they* and *them* serve an exclusionary function, representing a psychologically distancing of ourselves from the target group. In this manner, the use of these pronouns repeatedly confirms and communicates our membership or nonmembership in relevant social groups (Helmbrecht, 2002; Pyykkö, 2002).

As illustrated by our chapter-opening monologues, social groups associated with the "distancing" *they* and *them* pronoun labels are valued much less than those with the "embracing" *we* and *us* labels. In this chapter, we examine the social psychology of intergroup intolerance, exploring its various forms, and the subtle and blatant ways such intolerance is expressed. We also analyze the many social, cognitive, and developmental causes of intergroup intolerance, and the consequences it has for those who are targeted. Finally, we explore research and theory concerning possible remedies.

WHAT DO WE MEAN BY PREJUDICE AND DISCRIMINATION?

Prejudice and *discrimination* are terms that very few people view positively, but they are a part of all human cultures. We generally go to great lengths to avoid having these terms used in describing us, and most of us realize that being the target of prejudice and

Who are the "they" people in your life? Who are the social groups that you view with automatic suspicion, condescension, and negativity? Are you aware of your own prejudices? Do you think it is possible to hold unconscious biases toward other groups?

discrimination is almost never a good thing. Yet what is prejudice? Can positive emotions lead to discriminatory treatment of a group that ultimately harms them? How is prejudice different from discrimination? Can you be prejudiced without knowing it? Can you be prejudiced without engaging in discrimination? Can you engage in discrimination without being prejudiced?

Prejudice Is an Attitude and Discrimination Is an Action

Prejudice and discrimination are closely tied yet distinct. On the most basic level, prejudice involves attitudes toward specific groups, while discrimination involves actions toward those groups (Brewer & Brown, 1998).

DEFINING PREJUDICE

The traditional definition of prejudice is that it is a *negative* attitude toward members of a specific group. This conventional view assumes that prejudice can be represented as a simple continuum of one emotion that varies in intensity from mild dislike to burning hatred. Recently, however, an increasing number of social scientists have criticized this definition. These critics believe that many forms of prejudice involve complex and contradictory emotions, combining positive attitudes toward group members on some dimensions with negative attitudes on other dimensions. They believe that it is misleading and overly simplistic to define prejudice solely in terms of varying degrees of dislike. As an example of their argument, consider the following hypothetical statement made by one person about women:

> I adore women. I love the way they look, the way they cook. I put women on a pedestal and worship them. But if a woman begins thinking she can "lord it over" a man, then she's a problem and is no good for anything.

Is this statement an expression of prejudice? Using the traditional definition as a guide, we would probably conclude that the first three sentences don't conform to the definition of prejudice, but the last sentence does. Yet critics of the traditional definition might argue that even underlying the first three sentences' seemingly positive evaluations is an underlying judgment that women are somehow undeserving of having a social status equal to men. Does it make sense to modify the traditional definition of prejudice to account for such thinking?

Prejudice

Attitudes toward members of specific groups that directly or indirectly suggest they deserve an inferior social status.

Although there is no clear consensus among prejudice researchers on how to define the concept, in this chapter **prejudice** is defined as attitudes toward members of specific groups that directly or indirectly suggest they deserve an inferior social status (Glick & Hilt, 2000). This definition has the advantage of being able to account for seemingly positive attitudes that prejudiced individuals often express toward other social groups that simultaneously justifies placing these groups into a lower social status. By allowing for the possibility of both positive and negative evaluations, this definition includes prejudices that are sometimes described as "ambivalent." This definition can also account for "upward-directed" prejudices, meaning prejudice expressed by members of lower-status groups toward groups that have higher status but are seen as undeserving of their higher rank. The prejudice expressed by some members of minority groups, some women's prejudice toward men, and some working-class resentment and envy of the upper social classes are all examples of this upward-directed prejudice.

DEFINING DISCRIMINATION

Discrimination

A negative action toward members of a specific social group.

In contrast to prejudice, there is relative consensus in social psychology when defining discrimination. For our purposes, we define **discrimination** as a negative and/or patronizing action toward members of specific groups (Brewer & Brown, 1998). Disliking, disrespecting, and/or resenting people because of their group membership are examples of prejudice. Physically attacking or failing to hire them for jobs because of their group membership are examples of discrimination (Hebl et al., 2002). As we learned in chapter 6, behavior does not always follow attitude. Similarly, discrimination is not an inevitable result of prejudice. For example, a storeowner who is prejudiced against Blacks might not act on this negative attitude because most of his customers are Black and he needs their business. In this case, the subjective norm (see chapter 6, p. 192) dictates against the storeowner acting on his prejudice.

It is also true that discrimination can occur without prejudice. Sometimes people who are not prejudiced engage in *institutional discrimination* by carrying out the discriminatory guidelines of institutions. For instance, certain real-estate agents show African American clients only houses located in Black or racially mixed neighborhoods even though they have no animosity toward African Americans (and may be Black themselves). They carry out this institutional practice, known as *redlining*, because they are following the guidelines of their superiors, who believe that integration will lower property values.

Prejudice Can Be Either Explicit or Implicit

A growing number of researchers believe that we can harbor prejudice even without being aware of it (Amodio et al., 2004a; Brendl et al., 2001; Levy & Banaji, 2002). Thus prejudice can be either explicit or implicit. **Explicit prejudice** involves consciously held prejudicial attitudes toward a group, while **implicit prejudice** involves unconsciously held prejudicial attitudes. This fairly recent perspective on prejudice mirrors similar developments in attitude research in general (see chapter 6, pp. 174–175). People with low explicit prejudice but high implicit prejudice toward a particular outgroup may not be aware of their negative bias. Therefore, while responding in negative ways toward outgroup members, these low explicit/high implicit prejudice individuals might honestly believe that they are nonprejudiced. In general, research suggests that implicit prejudice is more stable, enduring, and difficult to change than explicit prejudice (Dasgupta & Greenwald, 2001; Kim, 2003).

Despite the hidden nature of implicit prejudice, researchers can study its process using various techniques, including the Implicit Association Test (see chapter 6, p. 175) and brain-imaging technology (see chapter 3, p. 82). Researchers often employ both techniques in one study: using the Implicit Association Test to identify White individuals with high implicit racial prejudice and then using functional magnetic resonance imaging (fMRI) to scan their brains while they look at photos of familiar and unfamiliar black and white faces (O'Connor et al., 2000; Phelps et al., 2000). As depicted in figure 8.1, these studies find that the unfamiliar black faces are much more likely than the unfamiliar white faces to activate the *amygdala* in both the right and left cerebral hemispheres and the *anterior cingulate* in the frontal lobes. These brain structures are involved in emotional learning and play a crucial role in detecting threat and triggering fear (Phelps et al., 2000). No heightened amygdala and cingulate activity occurs when these high

Explicit Prejudice

Prejudicial attitudes that are consciously held, even if they are not publicly expressed.

Implicit Prejudice

Unconsciously held prejudicial attitudes.

FIGURE 8.1

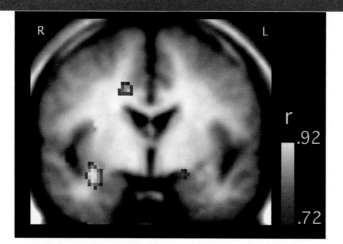

Measuring Implicit Prejudice Using Brain Scans

When White research participants with high scores on an implicit measure of racial prejudice (but low explicit prejudice scores) were shown photos of familiar and unfamiliar black and white faces, the unfamiliar black faces were much more likely than the unfamiliar white faces to activate the *amygdala* in both the right and left cerebral hemispheres of the brain, as well as the anterior cingulate in the frontal lobes (Phelps et al., 2000). These brain regions are associated with emotional responses and the brain's "alarm" system for threat, pain, and danger. What implications does the existence of implicit prejudice have for attempts at reducing intergroup hostility?

Source: Phelps, E. A., O'Connor, K. J., Cunningham, W. A., Funayama, E. S., Gatenby, J. C., & Gore, J. C., (2000). Performance on indirect measures of race evaluation predicts amygdala activation. *Journal of Cognitive Neuroscience, 12*, 729–738.

implicit/low explicit prejudiced participants view familiar black faces. These findings suggest that, despite not consciously reporting any negative racial attitudes toward African Americans, implicitly prejudiced Whites perhaps unknowingly feel some level of fear and negativity toward Black people. Similar findings have also been obtained from African American students when they viewed photos of white faces (Hart et al., 2000). As we will learn later in the chapter, the fact that implicit prejudice activates brain regions associated with fear and alarm without our awareness can result in biased perception and decision making.

There Are Three Basic Forms of Prejudice

Consistent with the updated conception of prejudice outlined in this chapter, Peter Glick and Susan Fiske (2001b) propose that there are three basic forms of prejudice that account for the different ways in which groups are perceived and treated. According to these theorists, the form of prejudice that is directed toward a particular group is determined by two social factors.

The first social factor is whether the target group is perceived as having a competitive or cooperative relationship with mainstream society. A group has a *competitive relationship* if they are perceived as intentionally grabbing resources for themselves at the expense of other groups. Examples of competitive groups would be rich and poor people, who are often perceived as unfairly taking or receiving societal resources. In contrast, a group has a *cooperative relationship* with mainstream society if they are perceived as undemanding (such as self-sufficient elderly people), contributing (such as homemakers raising children), or as needing help through no fault of their own (such as the disabled).

The second social factor is whether the target group is of relatively low or high social status within mainstream society. Examples of relatively *low-status* groups in the United States are poor people, women in general, homeless people, working-class people, gay men and lesbians, Blacks, Hispanics, Muslims, the disabled, housewives, and the elderly. Examples of relatively *high-status* groups are rich people, men in general, Whites in general, heterosexuals, middle-class Whites, highly educated people, Christians, Jews, Asians, and career women.

As depicted in table 8.1, if a group has relatively low social status and is perceived as having a competitive relationship with mainstream society, it is likely to become the target of *contemptuous prejudice,* characterized by exclusively negative attitudes of disrespect, resentment, and hostility. Contemptuous prejudice is most people's prototype for prejudice because it is characterized by uniformly negative attitudes; it most closely fits the traditional definition of prejudice (Hoffman et al., 2000). The blatant prejudices often expressed toward poor Whites, poor Blacks, homeless people, obese individuals, welfare recipients, lesbians and gay men, and illegal immigrants are examples of contemptuous prejudice. The contempt and disrespect that obese individuals often experience on a daily basis are also examples of this form of prejudice (Maranto & Stenoien, 2000).

In contrast to this easily recognized intergroup hostility, the other two forms of prejudice each represent a type of *ambivalent prejudice,* because they consist of both negative and positive attitudes. For instance, if a high-status group has a competitive relationship with mainstream society, it may become the target of *envious prejudice,* in which feelings of resentment and hostility are mixed with fear and envy, as well as with the positive emotions of respect and admiration. So-called model minorities—such as Jews and Asian Americans—are often targets of envious prejudice. Similarly, the mixed evaluations of feminists, Black professionals, and people in the upper classes of society are often rooted in envious prejudice. When a high-status outgroup is perceived as highly competent and threatening, the resulting envious prejudice can sometimes generate "hot" discrimination, in which the outgroup becomes a convenient target for high levels of frustration-fed aggression (Duckitt, 2001; Glick, in press).

Finally, a low-status group that has a cooperative or noncompetitive relationship with mainstream society may become the target of *paternalistic prejudice.* Paternalism is the care or control of subordinates in a manner suggesting a father's relationship with his children. The ambivalent attitudes expressed in this form of prejudice might involve patronizing affection and pity, mixed with condescension and disrespect. Sociologist Mary Jackman (1994) refers to paternalistic prejudice as the "velvet glove" approach to dominance, be-

TABLE 8.1

Three Forms of Prejudice Based on a Social Group's Relative Status and Its Relationship with Mainstream Society

Group's Relative Social Status	Group's Relationship with Mainstream Society	
	Cooperative	Competitive
High	***No Prejudice***	***Envious Prejudice***
Negative Emotions	None	Envy, fear, resentment hostility
Positive Emotions	Respect, admiration, affection	Grudging admiration of abilities
Behavior	Defer	Avoid, exclude, segregate, exterminate
Common Targets	Dominant groups perceived as generous, allies	Jews, Asian Americans, feminists, rich people, Black professionals
Low	***Paternalistic Prejudice***	***Contemptuous Prejudice***
Negative Emotions	Disrespect, condescension	Disrespect, resentment, hostility
Positive Emotions	Patronizing affection, pity, liking	None
Behavior	Personal intimacy, but role segregation	Avoid, exclude, segregate, exterminate
Common Targets	The elderly, the disabled, housewives, women in general, adolescents and young adults	Poor Whites, poor Blacks, homeless people, obese persons, welfare recipients lesbians and gay men, illegal immigrants

Adapted from: Glick, P. (in press). Sacrificial lambs dressed in wolves' clothing: Envious prejudice, ideology, and the scapegoating of Jews. In L. S. Newman & R. Erber (Eds.), *What social psychology can tell us about the holocaust.* Oxford: Oxford University Press.

cause dominant groups emphasize rewards rather than punishments in maintaining their control over subordinate groups. Although paternalism in intergroup relations often conjures up the nineteenth-century ideology of the "White man's burden," Jackman contends that it is still an identifiable and influential form of prejudice. The elderly, the disabled, housewives, women in general, and adolescents and young adults are often the targets of paternalistic prejudice (Chrisler, 2003; Viki et al., 2003).

Certain Groups Are More Acceptable Prejudice Targets Than Others

In all societies, some social groups are valued while other groups are stigmatized. A **stigma** is an attribute that discredits a person or a social group in the eyes of others. Stigmatized persons are not simply different from others, but society judges their difference to be discrediting. Individual members of society may vary in how they personally respond to a particular stigma, but everyone shares the knowledge that the characteristic in question, the "mark," is negatively valued and having it "spoils" the person's full humanity (Herek et al., in press; Link & Phelan, 2001). In a social cognitive sense, the stigma engulfs the person's entire identity. It becomes the central defining trait for that person (see chapter 4, p. 111), shaping the meaning of all other traits.

In his classic monograph, *Stigma: Notes on the Management of Spoiled Identity,* sociologist Erving Goffman (1963) distinguished the following three different categories of stigma:

1. *Tribal identities:* race, sex, ethnicity, religion, national origin
2. *Blemishes of individual character:* mental disorders, addictions, homosexuality, criminality

Stigma

An attribute that serves to discredit a person in the eyes of others.

3. *Abominations of the body:* physical deformities, physical disabilities, diseases, obesity

The concept of stigma is related to prejudice and discrimination because people who are stigmatized are almost always the targets of intolerance. Although many societal groups fall into one of the stigma categories, let us examine an example of "blemishes of individual character" (homosexuality/bisexuality) and "abominations of the body" (obesity). Later in the chapter we will examine intergroup intolerance associated with race-based and sex-based tribal identity stigmas.

HETEROSEXISM

During the first three-quarters of the twentieth century, the medical profession stigmatized lesbians and gay men as sexually deviant and mentally disturbed (Garnets et al., 2003; Minton, 2002). When rigorous scientific studies found no evidence of an association between homosexuality and psychopathology, the American Psychiatric Association finally changed its opinion in the mid-1970s and removed homosexuality as a diagnostic category for mental illness. Despite this clean bill of mental health from the scientific community, the Catholic Church has persisted in describing homosexual feelings as "ordered toward an intrinsic moral evil" and concludes that homosexuality "itself must be seen as an objective disorder" comparable to mental illness (Congregation for the Doctrine of the Faith, 1986, paragraph 3). Also, in the vast majority of states and municipalities, gay relationships have no legal status, and lesbians and gay men often lose the custody of their children when their homosexuality becomes known. This societal reaction is a classic example of stigma based on "blemishes of individual character," with homosexual and bisexual individuals being targets of contemptuous prejudice (refer back to p. 256).

Social scientists observing the continued contemptuous prejudice and discrimination directed at lesbians, gay men, and bisexuals have increasingly explained it in terms of a particular cultural ideology. **Heterosexism** is a system of cultural beliefs, values, and customs

Though your tissues gel, And you rot in hell, Don't feel gloomy, friend—It will never end. Happy Death, Faggot Fool.

From "Death Threat Christmas Cards" sent to gay students by a hate group at the University of Chicago

Heterosexism

A system of cultural beliefs, values, and customs that exalts heterosexuality and denies, denigrates, and stigmatizes any nonheterosexual form of behavior or identity.

Heterosexism is a system of cultural beliefs, values, and customs that exalts heterosexuality and stigmatizes homosexuality. In May 2004, when Massachusetts allowed lesbian and gay couples to legally marry, President Bush stated that he would push for a constitutional amendment banning same-sex marriages, and this issue fueled his re-election. Six months later, voters in 11 states approved constitutional bans on same-sex marriage and Republicans won key Senate and House races by characterizing Democrats as advocates for homosexuals. In the election, 22 percent of voters cited "moral values" as the most important issue of the campaign and 79 percent of those voters supported Bush and the Republican Party. Do you have an anti-gay bias? If so, do you view this as a justifiable type of prejudice?

that exalts heterosexuality and denies, denigrates, and stigmatizes any nonheterosexual form of behavior or identity (Fernald, 1995; Herek, 2004). Overt and blatant expressions of antigay attitudes, such as someone calling another person a "faggot" or a "dyke," are certainly examples of heterosexism. However, heterosexism can also operate on a more subtle level. Like the fish that doesn't realize it's wet, heterosexuals are so used to defining heterosexual behaviors as normal and natural that they cease to think of them as being a manifestation of sexuality. For instance, heterosexuals who don't look twice at a man and woman holding hands, hugging, or even kissing in public, often react very differently if the couple is of the same sex. Gay couples expressing affection in public are typically criticized for flaunting their sexuality. For further discussion of such subtle heterosexism, view the presentation on your Social Sense CD-ROM.

Although many cultures can be characterized as heterosexist, heterosexuals in those cultures who hold extremely negative attitudes toward gay men and lesbians differ in a number of ways from those with more accepting attitudes. In contrast to less-prejudiced individuals, heterosexuals who express antigay attitudes tend to

1. be male rather than female (Herek, 2000a, 2002).
2. hold traditional attitudes toward gender roles (Kite & Whitley, 1996).
3. be strongly religious and have membership in conservative religious organizations (Herek, 1987b, 2004; McFarland, 1989).
4. have friends who hold similarly negative attitudes (Franklin, 2000).
5. be racially prejudiced, sexist, and authoritarian (Basow & Johnson, 2000; Whitley, 1999).
6. have had less personal contact with gay men or lesbians (Herek & Capitanio, 1996; Sakalli-Ugurlu, 2002).

These findings indicate that those who have the most negative attitudes toward lesbians and gay men are those who conform most strongly to socially conservative—and even racist and sexist—value systems.

Why do heterosexual men have more negative attitudes than heterosexual women? Social scientists contend that this gender difference exists because many cultures emphasize the importance of heterosexuality in the male gender role (Herek, 2000b; Jellison et al., 2004). A defining characteristic of this *heterosexual masculinity* is to reject men who violate the heterosexual norm, namely gay males. This is also why heterosexual males express more negative attitudes toward gay men than toward lesbians. They perceive a male transgression of the heterosexual norm to be a more serious violation than that of a female transgression. As we will discuss in chapter 12 (p. 456), concern for not straying from the narrowly defined boundaries of heterosexual masculinity is also believed to be the main reason heterosexual male same-sex friendships are often lacking in emotional tenderness. This is especially true for males with strongly antigay attitudes (Devlin & Cowan, 1985).

The fact that people who hold strongly antigay attitudes also have friends who hold similar opinions is consistent with our previous discussion in chapter 6 (pp. 207–209) about the important role that reference groups play in the formation of attitudes. In the case of verbalizing antigay attitudes, Herek (1988) found that for men, but not for women, perceived social support in such attitude expression was very important. This gender difference suggests that expressing antigay attitudes helps some heterosexual males, especially those who are adolescents, to identify themselves as "real men" and be accepted into heterosexual friendship cliques.

WEIGHT PREJUDICE

Perhaps more so than facially unattractive individuals (see chapter 11, pp. 412–414), obese people in the United States are subjected to disdain and discrimination in their daily lives (Miller & Downey, 1999; Roehling, 1999). This greater prejudice is substantially due to the fact that most people view obesity as a condition that is controllable (Blaine et al., 2002). Thus, heavy individuals, unlike those who are facially unattractive, also are viewed as weak

Social Sense

View a presentation on heterosexism.

CRITICAL *thinking*

Try the following exercise. Listen to some of your favorite songs with lyrics involving romance. Do you tend to automatically imagine the person singing the song is expressing his or her love for a person of the other sex? If you do, does this tell us anything about your level of heterosexism? Now, actively imagine that the song is about same-sex love. How do you react to these lyrics and any visual images that come to mind? On the other hand, if you regularly imagine that the lyrics of popular songs involve same-sex love, is this an automatic process or does it usually take more cognitive effort on your part? How does this exercise illustrate your own personal experience of heterosexism?

willed, lazy, and self-indulgent (Weiner, 1995). In this sense, their stigma involves not only an "abomination of the body," but also a "blemish of individual character." Antifat prejudice is more pronounced in individualist cultures like the United States and Australia compared with collectivist cultures like Mexico and India, partly because individualists are more likely than collectivists to hold people accountable for personal outcomes (Crandall et al., 2001).

The prejudice and discrimination faced by obese people permeates both their personal and professional lives (Cossrow et al., 2001). They are less likely to be chosen as friends and romantic partners than normal weight persons, and they are treated in a less friendly manner by health care workers (Friedman & Brownell, 1995; Harris, 1990; Harvey & Hill, 2001; Hebl et al., 2003). The stigma of obesity is especially strong for women. One study even found that heavier college women were less likely than normal weight women to receive financial assistance from their own parents (Crandall, 1994). In the job market, obese individuals are discriminated against at every stage of employment, beginning with the hiring process and ending with the firing process (Roehling, 1999). Obesity is such a strong stigmatizing characteristic in our culture that it even affects how people evaluate individuals who are seen with obese persons. Michelle Hebl and Laura Mannix (2003) found that male job applicants were rated more negatively when seen with an overweight woman prior to their job interviews than when seen with a woman of normal weight. Goffman (1963) referred to this tendency for individuals who are associated with stigmatized people to face negative evaluations from others as **courtesy stigma.** This threat of negative evaluation causes many nonstigmatized people to avoid those who are stigmatized (Swim et al., 1999).

In the United States and Canada, antifat attitudes are stronger among men, Whites, and people with traditional gender roles compared with women, Blacks, and individuals with nontraditional gender roles (Glenn & Chow, 2002; Perez-Lopez et al., 2001). One explanation for these differences is that weight issues and the female thinness standard in North American culture is most closely associated with White, heterosexual beauty ideals that are closely aligned with traditional gender roles (see chapter 11, p. 419). A recent series of studies conducted by Bethany Teachman and her coworkers (2003) found that there is evidence of strong implicit antifat prejudice even among people with few explicit antifat attitudes. Further, this automatic and nonconscious negative reaction is very resistant to change. For example, even after informing research participants that obesity is mainly due to genetic factors, the researchers found no significant reduction in implicit prejudice to-

Courtesy Stigma

The tendency for individuals who are associated with stigmatized people to face negative evaluations from others.

The fat acceptance movement seeks to dispel myths and promote facts about fatness, and fights unfair discrimination on the basis of size or weight. Founders of the movement use the word *fat* because they believe that the word *overweight* begs the question "over what weight?" and *obese* suggests an unhealthy medical condition. Do you have an antifat bias? If so, do you view this as a justifiable type of prejudice?

ward obese individuals. When participants read stories of discrimination against obese persons to evoke empathy, diminished implicit bias was observed only among overweight participants. This last finding may be important, given that self-blame and internalizing negative social messages are common in obese individuals. Reminding obese persons about antifat discrimination may promote ingroup support and help them develop a positive social identity (Quinn & Crocker, 1998).

SECTION SUMMARY

- Prejudice involves attitudes toward members of specific groups that directly or indirectly suggest that they deserve an inferior social status
- Discrimination is a negative and/or patronizing action toward members of specific groups
- Explicit prejudices are consciously held, while implicit prejudices are unconsciously held
- The form of prejudice directed toward a group is determined by two social factors:

  Whether the target group is perceived as having a competitive or cooperative relationship with mainstream society

  Whether the target group is of low or high social status within mainstream society

- Contemptuous prejudice occurs when the target group has a competitive relationship with mainstream society and has low social status
- Envious prejudice occurs when the target group has a competitive relationship with mainstream society and has high social status
- Paternalistic prejudice occurs when the target group has a cooperative relationship with mainstream society and has low social status
- There are three different categories of stigma:

  Tribal identities

  Blemishes of individual character

  Abominations of the body

- Homosexuality is an example of a "blemish of individual character" stigma and it is related to the cultural ideology of heterosexism
- Obesity is an example of both a "blemish of individual character" stigma and an "abomination of the body" stigma, and it results in weight prejudice and discrimination

HOW DOES STEREOTYPING CAUSE PREJUDICE AND DISCRIMINATION?

Social psychologists are not only interested in establishing which people are likely to become targets of prejudice and discrimination, but they also seek to understand how basic psychological processes foster or inhibit such biases. As you may recall from chapter 5 (pp. 139–141), we naturally and automatically develop social categories based on people's shared characteristics. However, social categorization does not typically end with merely grouping people into categories. Once categorized, we begin to perceive people differently. Analyzing this tendency to perceive differences among human groups encompasses the next stage in our understanding of prejudiced thinking.

There is a tendency to perceive outgroup members as more similar to one another than members of one's own ingroup. This outgroup homogeneity effect can actually reverse and become an "ingroup homogeneity effect." When does this reversal occur?

Outgroup Homogeneity Effect

Perception of outgroup members as being more similar to one another than are members of one's ingroup.

CRITICAL *thinking*

Test your knowledge of racial and ethnic group stereotypes by writing down what you think are some of the positive and negative characteristics typically associated with the following social groups in North American culture: Anglo-Whites, Asians, Blacks, Jews, and Latinos. Once you have listed characteristics for each group, compare them with the research findings summarized in Appendix A. Does your knowledge of group stereotypes tell us anything about your degree of prejudice toward these racial and ethnic groups?

Outgroup Members Are Perceived as Being "All Alike"

How many times have you heard a woman say, "Well, you know men . . . They're all alike and they all want the same thing!" Likewise, how often have you heard men describing women in similar terms? This tendency to see members within a given outgroup as being more alike than members of one's ingroup is a consequence of social categorization. Research has shown that merely assigning people to different social groups can create this **outgroup homogeneity effect.** For example, Bernadette Park and Charles Judd found that on college campuses, sorority members, business majors, and engineering students all tend to perceive students in other campus social groups (those in other sororities or those with other majors) as more alike than those in their ingroup (Judd et al., 1991; Park & Rothbart, 1982).

What factors influence our tendency to see outgroups as uniform? Research indicates that this *illusion* of outgroup homogeneity is more likely to occur among competing than noncompeting groups (Judd & Park, 1988). It is also more likely when relatively few members in the outgroup are being judged (Mullen & Hu, 1989). Surprisingly, familiarity with the outgroup, such as the frequent and often intimate contact between men and women, does not appreciably change this tendency to see them as more alike than different (Lorenzi-Cioldi, 1993; Park et al., 1992).

Although we tend to perceive outgroups as being fairly uniform, our view of ingroup members is generally that they are relatively *distinct* and *complex.* For example, young adults tend to perceive others of their age as having more complex personalities than the elderly, whereas older adults hold exactly opposite beliefs (Brewer & Lui, 1984; Linville, 1982). Interestingly, the outgroup homogeneity effect actually reverses and becomes an "ingroup homogeneity effect" when members of *small groups* or *minority groups* compare their own group with the majority outgroup on attributes central to their social identity (Castano & Yzerbyt, 1998; Simon, 1992). This reversal is especially likely to occur when the ingroup members strongly identify with one another (Doosje et al., 1995; Simon et al., 1995). In such instances, by emphasizing their similarities with fellow ingroup members, minority group members affirm their social identity and perceive themselves as a unified, and therefore, similar group in comparison to the larger and seemingly more diverse comparison group.

Stereotypes Are Beliefs About Social Groups

Our tendency to perceive outgroup members as similar to one another sets the stage for developing beliefs about their personalities, abilities, and motives. These social beliefs, which are typically learned from others and maintained through regular social interaction, are

stereotypes (Lyons & Kashima, 2003; Schneider, 2004). Stereotypes are a type of *schema,* which is an organized structure of knowledge about a stimulus that is built up from experience and contains causal relations; it is a theory about how the social world operates (see chapter 5, pp. 141–145 for a review).

Like other types of schemas, stereotypes significantly influence how we process and interpret social information, even when we are not consciously aware that they have been activated from memory (Kawakami & Dovidio, 2001). In this sense, stereotypes are similar to prejudicial attitudes: they can nonconsciously influence our thoughts and actions. These *implicit stereotypes* can be automatically and nonconsciously activated by various stimuli. Once a stereotype is activated, we tend to see people within that social category as possessing the traits or characteristics associated with the stereotyped group (Hilton, 2000; Nosek et al., 2002a).

THE FUNCTIONS OF STEREOTYPED THINKING

In studying stereotyping, social psychologists have pondered what purpose it serves as a cognitive process. The quickness of stereotyped thinking is one of its most apparent qualities: being *fast,* it gives us a basis for immediate action in uncertain circumstances. In a very real sense, stereotypes are "shortcuts to thinking" that provide us with rich and distinctive information about individuals we do not personally know (Dijker & Koomen, 1996; Gilbert & Hixon, 1991). Not only do stereotypes provide us with a fast basis for social judgments, but stereotyping also appears to "free up" cognition for other tasks (Florack et al., 2001; Macrae et al., 1994). Thus, a second function of stereotyped thinking is that it is *efficient* and allows people to cognitively engage in other necessary activities. Daniel Gilbert (1989) suggests that this resource-preserving effect has an evolutionary basis. That is, expending cognitive resources as cheaply as possible enables perceivers to redirect their energy to more pressing concerns. This speed and efficiency of stereotype-based information apparently motivates people to rely on it over the more time-consuming method of getting to know a person as an individual (Pendry & Macrae, 1994).

One of the important reasons the activation of stereotypes often results in fast social judgments is that filtering social perceptions through a stereotype causes people to ignore information that is relevant but inconsistent with the stereotype (Bodenhausen, 1988; Dijksterhuis & Knippenberg, 1996). Thus, although stereotyping may be beneficial because it allows us to redirect our energies to other pressing cognitive activities, the cost appears to be that we may often make faulty social judgments about whomever we stereotype (Nelson et al., 1996).

STEREOTYPE CONTENT AND INTERGROUP RELATIONS

Although research has traditionally focused on the inaccuracy of stereotypes, a number of studies reveal that they often possess a "kernel of truth," and thus can lead to accurate social judgments (Ashton & Esses, 1999; Ryan, 2003). However, because stereotypes develop in a social environment in which groups are often regularly interacting with one another, each group's beliefs about the other are shaped and distorted by the interaction. The resulting stereotypes not only provide information about the group being stereotyped, they also reveal a good deal about the nature of the relationship between the groups (Rothbart, 2001).

The whole world is festering with unhappy souls: The French hate the Germans, the Germans hate the Poles; Italians hate Yugoslavs, South Africans hate the Dutch; And I don't like anybody very much!

Sheldon Harnick, American songwriter, b. 1924, from *The Merry Little Minuet*

Consistent with our previous discussion of the three basic forms of prejudice (envious, paternalistic, and contemptuous), the content of the stereotypes that one group has about another group are shaped by the target group's social status (low or high) and its perceived relationship with mainstream society (competitive or cooperative). Doctors, for example, are generally perceived as a high-status, cooperative group. As a result, most people view them with respect and even admiration, and doctors are often stereotyped as being intelligent, hardworking, and caring, although perhaps sometimes arrogant. In contrast, high-status, competitive groups are simultaneously envied and resented. Although these groups are stereotyped as being highly competent, they are also believed to have sinister motives. The stereotype of Jews being clever, good with money, but devious is an example of this envious-based stereotyping. Stereotypes surrounding low-status groups often have an air of

TABLE 8.2

Illusory Correlation

If Harriet tends to selectively remember only those deceptive business relationships with Jews and the honest ones with non-Jews, she is likely to develop an illusory correlation that Jews are more dishonest in their business dealings than non-Jews. This is so, even though the percentages of actual instances of business deception in the two groups is equal (5%). Can you think of any illusory correlations that people may have about a group in which you are a member?

Number of Business Relationships Harriet Has Been Exposed to in Her Life

	Deceptive Experiences	Honest Experiences
Jews	5	100
Non-Jews	25	500

condescension, but those associated with paternalistic prejudice include positive qualities. For example, sexist men might view women as being nurturing and "pure of heart" but inherently weak and incompetent, while sexist women might think of men as being likable and fun loving but hopelessly immature and irresponsible. In contrast to this mixture of positive and negative stereotype content, stereotypes of low-status, competitive groups are almost exclusively negative, such as the characteristics associated with homeless people, poor Whites, and obese individuals. Let us now examine how the cognitive foundation of prejudice-related stereotyping can be established and maintained.

Stereotypes Are Often Based on Illusory Correlations

When we stereotype people, we associate certain characteristics with them because of their group membership. As an example, Harriet might believe that Jews are more deceptive in their business dealings than non-Jews. When asked why she holds this belief, Harriet might recall a set of pertinent cases of either business deception or honesty from her own personal experiences or from the experience of others. As you can see in table 8.2, in recalling these instances, Harriet remembers those few cases that conform to her stereotype of Jews, but she forgets or explains away all those that clash with it. Based on this selective recall of past cases, Harriet concludes that there is an association between Jews and deception even though the correlation is no greater than it is for non-Jews. This example illustrates the power of an **illusory correlation,** which is the belief that two variables are associated with each other when no actual association exists.

> **Illusory Correlation**
>
> The belief that two variables are associated with each other when in fact there is little or no actual association.

At least two factors can produce an illusory correlation. The first is *associative meaning,* in which two variables are associated with each other because of the perceiver's preexisting beliefs. Because Harriet expects Jews to be more deceptive, she is not only more likely to notice possible instances of deception in her business dealings with Jews than in those with non-Jews, but she is also more likely to interpret ambiguous actions by Jews as reflecting sinister intentions. Numerous studies have found that people's preexisting attitudes and beliefs can predispose them to perceive associations that are truly illusory (Berndsen et al., 2002). Once the stereotype is activated, the person engages in biased processing of social information by attending to information consistent with the stereotype and ignoring that which contradicts it (Greenberg & Pyszczynski, 1985). Through this process of selective attention to information consistent with the stereotype, the stereotype proves resistant to change (Dovidio et al., 1986).

A second factor contributing to the development of illusory correlations is *shared distinctiveness,* in which two variables are associated because they share some unusual

FIGURE 8.2

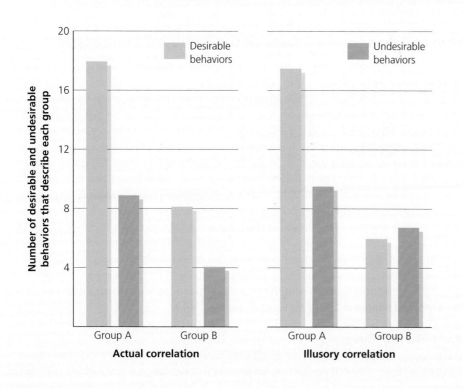

Actual correlation   **Illusory correlation**

Illusory Correlations and the Persistence of Stereotypes

In Hamilton and Gifford's (1976) study of illusory correlations, participants read sentences in which a person from Group A or Group B was associated with either a desirable or an undesirable behavior. As you can see in the actual correlation graph, both groups were described with the same proportion of desirable and undesirable behaviors, but only one-third of the provided information was about Group B members, making them the "minority group." The illusory correlation graph indicates that participants later overestimated the number of undesirable behaviors in the minority group (Group B), which suggests that people tend to perceive an illusory correlation between variables that stand out because they are unusual or deviant.

feature. According to this view, Harriet should develop an illusory correlation about Jews and dishonesty because both the minority group and the unfavorable trait are "infrequent" or "distinct" variables in the population. These two distinct variables are more likely to be associated in Harriet's memory simply because of their shared distinctiveness.

In an experiment demonstrating this effect, David Hamilton and Robert Gifford (1976) asked participants to read information about people from two different groups, "Group A" and "Group B." Twice as much information was provided about Group A than about Group B, making Group B the smaller or "minority group" in the study. In addition, twice as much of the information given about both groups involved desirable behaviors rather than undesirable actions. Desirable information included statements such as, "John, a member of Group A, visited a sick friend in the hospital." An example of an undesirable statement was, "Bob, a member of Group B, dropped litter in the subway station." Even though there was no correlation between group membership and the proportion of positive and negative information, participants perceived a correlation. As figure 8.2 shows, participants overestimated the frequency with which Group B, the "minority group," behaved undesirably. In this study, the members of the "minority group" (who were described only half as much as the "majority group") and the undesirable actions (which occurred only half as much as the desirable behaviors) were both distinctive aspects of participants' social perceptions. This shared distinctiveness resulted in their illusory correlation, a finding replicated in later studies (Mullen & Johnson, 1995).

Although selective attention to the infrequent behaviors of minority group members can create illusory correlations, what would happen if people's attention was diverted while they were observing the minority group's actions? Would this minimize the tendency to perceive illusory correlations? Research by Steven Stroessner and his colleagues (1992) found that when people are in either a positive or a negative mood, they are less likely to perceive an illusory correlation between minority group members and infrequent (that is, negative) actions. This research suggests that emotional arousal interferes with the cognitive processing necessary to encode into memory this infrequent or distinctive information about the minority group. Without this encoding, the illusory correlation effect is diminished.

Physical Appearance Cues Often Activate Stereotypes

Physical appearance cues play a critical role in either activating or defusing the stereotype process. Individuals whose physical characteristics closely match their culture's prototype for a particular social category are likely to be perceived as possessing the personal traits associated with that social category, even if they are not members of that category (McKelvie, 1993). Thus, for example, a man in North America with wide shoulders and a tapering V-shaped physique who also has a square jaw, small eyes, thin lips, and thick eyebrows is more likely to be thought of as being active, adventurous, forceful, independent, and coarse than a man with a pear-shaped body who has a round face, thick lips, high cheekbones, and long eyelashes. Similarly, when target persons who are known to be members of a particular social group do not come close to matching the *behavioral* prototype for that group, people are less likely to judge them based on that group's stereotype (Lord et al., 1991). Thus, if Antony is known to be homosexual, but is also known to be a "jock" who likes to hunt, fish, repair cars, and drink beer, he is less likely to be judged based on cultural gay stereotypes than a man who is simply known to be homosexual. This process of stereotype activation happens so quickly and automatically that we are often not aware it has happened (Bargh et al., 1996; Chen & Bargh, 1999).

RACE-BASED CUES

Due to socialization about what constitutes different racial categories, skin color and facial characteristics (such as shape of eyes, nose, and lips) are physical features that often automatically activate racial stereotypes among people of many different ethnicities in the United States, as well as in a number of countries around the world (Maddox, in press). When such race-based stereotype activation occurs, people generally associate more positive personality traits to those with lighter skin and Eurocentric facial features than those with darker skin and Afrocentric features (Blair et al., 2002; Livingston & Brewer, 2002; Maddox & Gray, 2002). Furthermore, the more Afrocentric the features of the target person in these studies, the more she or he is assumed to have the traits that are stereotypic of African Americans. Research suggests that when a person of any race makes a judgment on the basis of physical appearance, the target person's race-related features may influence social judgments in two ways (Blair et al., 2004; Judd et al., 2004). First, those features provide the basis for racial categorization, which then activates the relevant stereotypes. Second, those features may directly activate race-associated stereotypes even for a person who is not a member of the relevant race. Thus, a person with curly hair and/or a darker complexion who identifies himself as "White" and is also categorized by others as "White" may still be nonconsciously perceived by others as having characteristics stereotypically associated with Black males.

This tendency to negatively stereotype those with darker skin and Afrocentric facial features is even found among African Americans (Clark & Clark, 1939, 1947). For example, when African American teenagers were surveyed about their skin tone preferences (Anderson & Cromwell, 1977), they associated very light-brown skin with positive characteristics (the prettiest skin, the smartest girl, the children fathers like best) and black skin with more negative traits (the dumbest person, the person one would not like to marry, the color one would prefer not to be). Further, when African American children were read stories in which Black characters were portrayed in either stereotype-consistent or stereotype-inconsistent ways, they were more likely to remember stories when light-skinned Blacks were associated with positive traits and high-status occupations, or when dark-skinned Blacks were associated with negative traits and low-status occupations (Averhart & Bigler, 1997). These findings are consistent with the general observation that lighter-skinned Blacks attain higher status in society than darker-skinned Blacks (Hughes & Hertel, 1990). In fact, some social scientists contend that the social status gap between light- and dark-skinned Blacks in the United States is as large as the gap between Whites and Blacks (Hunter, 1998). Similar social status gaps are also found among lighter-skinned and darker-skinned Mexican Americans (Arce et al., 1987; Telles & Murguia, 1990).

RACE-BASED MISPERCEPTIONS OF WEAPONS

The negative effects of automatically stereotyping people with Afrocentric facial features can have real-world life-and-death consequences. For example, around midnight on February 4, 1999, four White New York City police officers were looking for a rape suspect in the Bronx when they saw 22-year-old Amadou Diallo, a West African immigrant, standing in his apartment building doorway. Stopping their car, they told Diallo to "freeze," but then they saw him reach into his pants' pocket. Fearing that this suspicious-looking man was reaching for a weapon, the officers drew their pistols and opened fire. Within five seconds they fired a total of forty-one shots at the unarmed Diallo, nineteen of which found their mark, killing him. The object that Diallo was reaching for was his wallet, which contained his ID. The officers were tried for murder but were acquitted of all charges on the grounds that although they made a mistake, their actions were justified (Fritsch, 2000).

Motivated by this high-profile case and the resulting charges of racism and racial profiling by law enforcement officers, Keith Payne (2001) conducted a series of studies to understand how the mere presence of a black face could cause people to misidentify harmless objects as weapons. In his research, Payne showed pictures of guns or tools to White participants and asked them to classify the objects as quickly as possible. Just prior to seeing an object, participants were primed by a brief presentation of either a white or a black face (see figure 8.3). Results indicated that when tools were immediately preceded by a black face, it was significantly more likely mistaken for a handgun compared with conditions in which this same tool was preceded with a white face. This stereotype difference emerged mainly when participants were required to react quickly, a condition that mimics the time pressure involved in real-world police confrontations like the Diallo shooting.

As you recall from our previous discussion of implicit prejudice (p. 255), when Whites with high implicit but low explicit race prejudice see an unfamiliar black face, brain regions that trigger fear and threat responses are activated. Combined with the present results, this research suggests that simply seeing a Black man may automatically and nonconsciously trigger a fear response in police officers. Further, under conditions that require quick and decisive action, this race-based reaction may result in police officers misperceiving harmless objects as weapons. This perceptual bias does not seem to simply reflect explicit prejudice toward African Americans. Instead, this effect appears to be caused by the racial stereotypes that exist in our culture (Judd et al., 2004).

Amadou Diallo, a native of West Africa, was shot 19 times by four New York City police officers who were looking for a rapist. When they saw Diallo and ordered him to "freeze," he reached in his pants pocket for his wallet and they mistakenly thought he had a gun. Was his killing caused by implicit racism?

FIGURE 8.3

Race and the Misperception of Weapons

After being primed by black or white faces, White participants were shown pictures of guns or tools and asked to classify the objects (Payne, 2001). When participants were required to react quickly, they were more likely to misidentify tools as guns after being primed with black faces rather than with white faces. How does this research provide insight into police shootings of unarmed suspects in real-world confrontations?

Source: Payne, B. K. (2001). Prejudice and perception: The role of automatic and controlled processes in misperceiving a weapon. *Journal of Personality and Social Psychology, 81,* 181–192.

Subsequent studies using computer-simulated "shooter/nonshooter" scenarios have verified these findings and have also found evidence suggesting that if a criminal suspect is Black versus White, people generally require less certainty that he is, in fact, holding a gun before they decide to shoot him (Greenwald et al., 2003; Payne et al., 2002). Importantly, this race-based bias was found among both African American and White participants (Correll et al., 2002). Thus, African American police officers may be as likely as White officers to misperceive that a Black man is holding a weapon and respond by shooting in self-defense. These studies also suggest that such race-based bias is very difficult to control because it is operating below a person's level of conscious awareness. However, results also indicate that when given ample time, people make few stereotypical misidentifications of weapons because their automatic, reflexive response is controlled and altered by more deliberate cognitive analysis. Of course, the problem here is that urging a police officer to react slowly during a confrontation with a potentially armed suspect can be extremely dangerous for the officer.

Though these studies suggest that bias in the decision to shoot may be widespread among police officers, it must be kept in mind that participants were not actual members of a police force. It is possible that police training may reduce this race-based shooter bias by teaching officers to focus on the presence of a weapon during confrontations rather than fixating on the target's race, but no such studies have yet been conducted.

Stereotype Subcategories Foster the Retention of Global Stereotypes

As noted earlier in the chapter (p. 262), many men and women describe members of the other sex as all having the same characteristics despite the fact that they have friends and lovers of the other sex who do not fit the stereotypical mold. Why don't these nonstereotypical acquaintances serve as a catalyst to alter people's stereotypes?

One explanation for why stereotypes survive such disconfirming evidence is that people create limited, specific *subtypes* or *subcategories* for individuals of the stereotyped group who do not match the global stereotype (Coats & Smith, 1999; Wyer et al., 2002). For example, Kay Deaux and her colleagues (1985) found that American college students distinguish at least five different subcategories of women: housewives, career women, athletes, feminists, and sex objects. When a man with a negative stereotype of women learns to respect a woman who does not fit this stereotype, he may retain his gender beliefs by concluding that this particular woman is not "like the rest of them." Instead of revising his global stereotype of women, the man creates a new subcategory in which to place this particular woman, thus leaving his global gender stereotype essentially unchanged.

For most stereotypes, very little overlap exists between the global stereotypes and the specific subcategories. For example, many White Americans' global stereotypes of African Americans tend to be primarily negative, while their stereotypes of African American businesspersons or athletes are primarily positive (Devine & Baker, 1991). In categorizing African Americans who are either businesspersons or athletes, many White Americans are more likely to identify them with their occupational role (either businessperson or athlete) rather than with their race (Black). This is perhaps why celebrities like Michael Jordan and Oprah Winfrey can be idolized by Whites who harbor negative racial stereotypes. For these people, the Michael Jordans and the Oprah Winfreys of the world are not like most others of their race. Because these Whites do not perceive them as representing the typical African American, such celebrities are unlikely to challenge the negative global stereotype these people hold. Thus, the creation of subcategories allows people to retain rigid and unflattering views of the social group in question.

People are most likely to create subcategories after encountering members of the stereotyped group who are *extremely different* from what they expect (Queller & Smith, 2002). In fact, if the members of the stereotyped group only moderately disconfirm people's expectations, no subcategories are likely to be created. Interestingly, when moderately disconfirming information does not lead to subcategorizing, this can have the effect of actually causing a small change in the overall stereotype. In other words, people from a negatively stereotyped group who only moderately disconfirm your stereotype are more effective in changing your beliefs than are people from that group who strongly disconfirm your stereotype. Thus, an African American woman who runs a modestly successful business is much more likely to change negative cultural stereotypes about African Americans being lazy than is the multimillionaire Oprah Winfrey.

In closing, when considering the resistance of stereotypes to change, keep in mind that they are a type of schema, and as such, they are designed to help us make fast social judgments with minimal cognitive effort. In dealing with new information in our social world, we are motivated to process and understand it using an existing schema, even in those instances when the information doesn't quite "fit" because assimilating it requires less cognitive effort than changing the schema (Piaget & Inhelder, 1969; Seta et al., 2003). Throughout life, one of the dilemmas in decision making and problem solving is whether to assimilate new information into existing schemas or to change those knowledge structures so that the new information can be better handled and understood. Our first inclination is to try to assimilate because it is cognitively easier to do so. However, if using an existing schema regularly results in poor decision making, we are motivated to expend cognitive effort and accommodate our schemas in an attempt to more successfully deal with the situation. It is this cognitive-efficiency motive that primarily creates the hurdle to stereotype change.

Stereotypical Thinking Is More Characteristic of the Powerful

Studies by Susan Fiske and Eric Dépret indicate that the tendency to think in stereotypical terms is partly related to a person's level of social power (Fiske, 1993; Fiske & Dépret, 1996). For example, in a business firm, secretaries know more about their bosses' personal habits and preferences than vice versa. Why is this so? Fiske and Dépret contend it is because powerful individuals in a social group exercise a good deal of control over the less powerful members. Due to this control, it is in the powerless person's best interests to pay close attention to those who have power (Dépret & Fiske, 1993). They pay particular attention to information about the powerful person that is inconsistent with the stereotype of

There are two ways of meeting difficulties. You alter the difficulties or you alter yourself to meet them.

Phyllis Bottome, English author, 1884–1963

CRITICAL *thinking*

One of the important functions of stereotyping is that it saves cognitive effort. Thus, when we are tired, we may be more likely to base our impressions of others on stereotypes. If this is true, during what times of the day are people likely to rely on stereotypes when judging others?

these individuals. This gives them knowledge about specific powerful persons that they cannot receive through simple reliance on stereotypes. Such knowledge is important, for it provides the powerless with some degree of power and control—power to better predict the powerful individuals' future actions, thus giving them a greater sense of control in their surroundings (Allen, 1996; Fiske & Dépret, 1996).

In contrast to the attentiveness of the powerless, research indicates that powerful people pay considerably less attention to those below them in the power hierarchy (Keltner & Robinson, 1997). When they do attend to those with little social power, the powerful are more likely to judge them based on social stereotypes. Fiske believes that people in power stereotype less powerful others for two primary reasons. First, due to their high-status position, more people are competing for their attention than is the case for the less powerful. Faced with time constraints brought on by these demands, the powerful are likely to rely on such cognitive shortcuts as stereotypes. This is *stereotyping by default.* Second, powerful people may want to maintain the status difference between themselves and the less powerful, and ignoring the individual qualities of the powerless is one way to keep them at a social distance and in "their proper place." This is *stereotyping by design* (Goodwin et al., 2000).

The tendencies of those with social power to ignore the individual qualities of their subordinates does not mean that the powerful always engage in stereotypical thinking when judging those below them in the status hierarchy. Research indicates that people, including the powerful, can be motivated to think of others in nonstereotypical ways by either appealing to their desire for accuracy and rewards (Keltner et al., 2003; Vescio et al., 2003), their concern for public accountability (Tetlock et al., 1989), their humanitarian or egalitarian values (Moskowitz et al., 1999), or their self-concepts as fair-minded and careful people (Fiske & Von Hendy, 1992). Again, these findings are consistent with the motivated-tactician model highlighted in chapter 5: as flexible social thinkers, we change our cognitive strategies based on what is currently motivating us.

Stigmatized Groups Respond to Negative Stereotypes with Opposition and Anxiety

As previously defined (p. 257), a stigma is an attribute that discredits a person or a social group in the eyes of others. Stigmatized people may internalize negative stereotypes and suffer serious damage to their self-esteem, but this is not an inevitable consequence (Kaiser & Major, in press; Major et al., 2003).

OPPOSITIONAL IDENTITIES

If you are a member of a stigmatized group, you may respond to negative stereotypes and discrimination by developing an *oppositional* identity, an identity based on opposition to the dominant culture (see chapter 3 for a discussion of the *ethnic identity search* stage). An oppositional identity defines your ingroup in ways that contrast with various outgroups (Ogbu, 1993). In this oppositional stance, you think, feel, and act the way you believe "authentic" members of your ingroup are supposed to act, and you judge other ingroup members by these same standards.

As a defensive strategy, oppositional identities can have both beneficial and hindering effects (Crocker & Major, 1989; Crocker & Quinn, 2000). On the positive side, they help stigmatized people cope with a hostile social environment by psychologically insulating them from loss of self-esteem. On the negative side, immersion in an identity that defines itself in terms of opposition to the dominant outgroup will likely constrict one's personal identity. For example, because academic tasks were long reserved for White Americans, Blacks who achieve academic excellence may be accused by other Blacks of "acting White" or being an "oreo" (being Black on the outside but White on the inside). For young African Americans who hold to an oppositional identity, committing themselves to academic excellence and learning to follow the academic standards of the school might be perceived as forsaking their ethnic identity (Smith & Moore, 2000). Unfortunately, by rejecting certain activities perceived as White, such as academic pursuits, many

Blacks have hindered themselves from fully taking advantage of civil rights advances (Bankston & Caldas, 1997).

Although rejecting pursuits that are important to mainstream economic success can create problems for a person, as described in chapter 3, a defensive oppositional identity is only one possible stage in developing ethnic identity. Many African Americans, for instance, do not identify at all with an oppositional identity, and others do so only marginally (Brookins et al., 1996; Fordham, 1985). For them, pursuing academic excellence does not create psychological conflict with their Black social identity. Instead, it is consistent with a central feature of the civil rights movement of the 1960s, namely, social advancement through educational achievement.

STEREOTYPE THREAT

In addition to the problem that oppositional identities pose to minority students' academic achievement, those enrolled in largely White schools and colleges often carry the extra burden of "representing their race" in academic pursuits. If you are one of only a few members of your race enrolled in a particular course, students not of your race may look on your performance as representing the "typical" student of your racial group. Accompanying this scrutiny is the added social stigma associated with your minority label, which often implies a suspicion of intellectual inferiority (Sigelman & Tuch, 1997).[1] Because these negative stereotypes are widely known throughout society, as the target of such stereotyping, you are susceptible to developing what Claude Steele (1997) identifies as **stereotype threat.** Stereotype threat is a disturbing awareness among members of a negatively stereotyped group that any of their actions or characteristics that fit the stereotype may confirm it as a self-characterization (Steele & Aronson, 1995; Steele et al., 2002). Physiological measures of people experiencing stereotype threat indicate that this uncomfortable psychological state creates an extra cognitive burden that reduces individuals' working memory capacity (Croizet et al., 2004; Schmader & Johns, 2003). In essence, people experiencing stereotype threat have a more difficult time concentrating on the task at hand and quickly remembering relevant information. This disruption in efficient thinking can occur even without the person consciously experiencing any anxiety (Blascovich et al., 2001b; Bosson et al., 2004).

The first evidence for the stereotype threat effect among African American college students came from a series of experiments conducted by Steele and Joshua Aronson (1995). In one of these studies, Black and White student volunteers were given a difficult English test. In the *stereotype threat condition,* the test was described as a measure of

Stereotype Threat

A disturbing awareness among members of a negatively stereotyped group that any of their actions or characteristics that fit the stereotype may confirm it as a self-characterization.

---

[1]Exceptions would be Asian students, who often are expected to perform better academically than others, including White students. Although this is a positive perception, it still burdens Asian students with the social pressure to positively represent their race in a way that White students rarely experience (Nakanishi & Nishida, 1995).

FIGURE 8.4

African-American Intellectual Test Performance and Stereotype Threat

Steele and Aronson (1995) administered a difficult English test to Black and White college students. When the test was described as a measure of intellectual ability (stereotype threat condition), Blacks performed worse than Whites. However, when it was not associated with ability (nonstereotype threat condition), no racial differences were found. How are these findings consistent with the stereotype threat hypothesis?

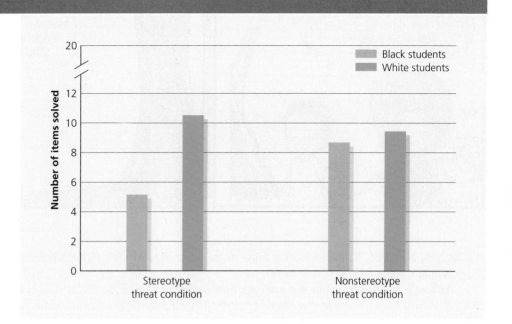

Social Sense

View a presentation of a stereotype threat experiment.

intellectual ability, while in the *nonstereotype threat condition,* it was described as a laboratory problem-solving task that did not measure intelligence. Because cultural stereotypes depict Blacks as intellectually inferior to Whites, the researchers presumed that describing the test as an intellectual measure would make this negative stereotype relevant to the Black students' performance. They also expected that making this stereotype relevant would induce concern in the Black students that they might confirm the stereotype ("If I do poorly, my performance will reflect badly on my race and on me"). Steele and Aronson hypothesized that the self-evaluation apprehension created by such thinking would interfere with the Black students' performance. In contrast, when the task was described as not measuring intelligence, researchers assumed that this would make the negative racial stereotype about ability *irrelevant* to the Black students' performance and, therefore, not arouse stereotype threat. As you can see in figure 8.4, consistent with the stereotype threat hypothesis, when the test was presented as a measure of ability, Blacks performed worse than Whites. However, when it was not associated with ability, no significant racial differences were found.

Stereotype threat has also been found among women in math classes. In one of the first studies documenting this effect, Steven Spencer and his colleagues (1999) gave male and female college students a difficult math test but divided it into two halves and presented it as two distinct tests. Half of the students were told that the first test was one on which men outperformed women, and that the second test was one on which there were no gender differences. The other students were told the opposite—test 1 was described as exhibiting no gender differences, but men outperformed women on test 2. As you can see in figure 8.5, consistent with the stereotype threat hypothesis, when told that the test yielded gender differences, women greatly underperformed in relation to men. However, when the test was described as not exhibiting any gender differences, women's underperformance disappeared. This dramatic change occurred even though the two tests were the same! View a dramatization of this study and comments by Claude Steele on your Social Sense CD-ROM.

Subsequent research has found that merely placing women in a room where men outnumber them is sometimes sufficient to induce stereotype threat and lower math performance (Inzlicht & Ben-Zeev, 2003). However, additional research suggests that women are less susceptible to stereotype threat in math performance when they have consistently had positive math experiences in school and also have parents and teachers who

FIGURE 8.5

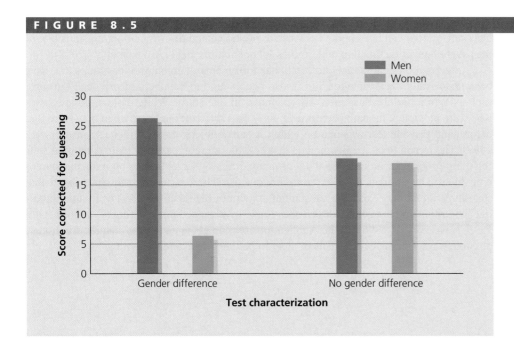

Stereotype Threat and Women's Math Performance

Spencer and his colleagues (1999) found that when a difficult math test was described as exhibiting gender differences (men outperforming women), women did indeed underperform. However, when the test was described as exhibiting no gender differences, women's underperformance disappeared. How do these results support the stereotype threat hypothesis?

encouraged and intentionally sheltered them from negative gender stereotypes (Oswald & Harvey, 2003). These high-achieving women not only have strong confidence in their math abilities, they also have little awareness of negative gender stereotypes in the area of math. Other studies find that women who become immersed and successful in academic math environments appear to insulate themselves from stereotype threat by *disidentifying* with feminine characteristics and behavior seen as incompatible with math success (such as being flirtatious or wearing a lot of makeup) but not with those feminine characteristics (such as being sensitive, nurturing, and having good fashion sense) perceived as unlikely to hinder such success (Pronin et al., 2004). Overall, this research suggests that one effective way to reduce the negative effects of stereotype threat among women regarding math performance is to discourage them from internalizing cultural gender beliefs related to *benevolent sexism,* a topic we discuss later in the chapter (pp. 289–290).

What happens when you are not as fortunate as these women and repeatedly experience stereotype threat? One likely consequence is that you will *disidentify* with whatever task is associated with the threatening scrutiny. For example, if the stereotype threat involves intellectual performance, you may change your self-concept so that academic achievement is no longer very important to your self-esteem. This sort of academic disidentification is much more common among African American students than among White American students, and it often begins in the lower elementary grades (Ambady et al., 2001; Osborne, 1995). Claude Steele describes this process of disidentification on your Social Sense CD-ROM.

In one experiment investigating disidentification, Brenda Major and her coworkers (1998) manipulated success and failure feedback on a supposed test of intelligence. White students reacted with higher self-esteem after success than after failure, but Black students' self-esteem was unaffected. These findings are consistent with the hypothesis that Black students tend to disengage their self-esteem from academic performance. A second experiment in this series found that, consistent with Steele's notion of stereotype threat, academic disidentification among African-American students is most likely to occur when negative racial stereotypes concerning Black intellectual inferiority are salient in an academic setting. Stereotype threat and academic disidentification also occur among American Indians, Hispanic Americans, lower-class Whites, and female students in male-dominated majors

Social Sense

View Claude Steele discussing disidentification

(Croizet & Claire, 1998; Inzlicht & Ben-Zeev, 2000). Although such disidentification protects self-esteem and is a coping response to prejudice and discrimination, it also is one of the psychological factors that undermines school achievement (Aronson et al., 2002).

Stereotype threat is most noticeable and problematic among social groups that have been historically disadvantaged, but it also occurs among members of privileged groups, such as White middle-class men. For example, in one study, White male undergraduates who were proficient in math performed poorly on a difficult math test when they were told beforehand that the test was one on which Asians outperformed Whites (Aronson et al., 1999). The lesson to be learned here is that negative stereotypes can create damaging self-fulfilling prophecies among members of many different social groups by inducing stereotype threat. The findings from all the studies discussed here raise the further possibility that stereotype threat may explain a substantial amount of the racial differences found in intelligence testing and the gender differences found in advanced math testing (Crawford et al., 1995; Neisser et al., 1996). In the Applications section at the end of the chapter, we discuss possible ways to reduce the effects of stereotype threat in academic settings.

SECTION SUMMARY

- The outgroup homogeneity effect is the tendency to perceive people in outgroups as more similar to one another than ingroup members
- Stereotypes are social beliefs typically learned from others and maintained through regular social interaction
- Two functions of stereotyped thinking:

    fast and efficient, but often faulty

- Stereotypes are often based on *illusory correlations,* meaning specific traits are believed to be characteristic of a social group when there are no actual associations
- Physical appearance cues are important in either activating or defusing the stereotype process
- Race-based cues automatically activate threat responses and negative stereotypes, which may contribute to shooter bias among law enforcement officers
- Unflattering global stereotypes are retained by stereotype subcategories
- Powerful people are more likely to stereotype the less powerful
- Stigmatized groups respond to negative stereotypes by

    developing oppositional identities

    experiencing stereotype threat

WHAT MOTIVES AND SOCIAL FACTORS SHAPE PREJUDICE AND DISCRIMINATION?

Beyond the role that negative stereotypes play in both the causes and effects of prejudice and discrimination, additional powerful motivational and social variables also exert a significant influence in the creation of intergroup intolerance (Gerstenfeld, 2002). In this section of the chapter we examine some of these causes, beginning with how group membership creates ingroup bias.

We Automatically Favor Ingroup Members Over Outgroup Members

We have already discussed how social categorization sets the stage for perceiving members of other groups as having similar characteristics and how such stereotyping can lead to intergroup intolerance. However, research by Henri Tajfel and his colleagues (1971) demonstrated that the simple act of categorizing people as ingroup or outgroup members affects how we evaluate and compare them, independent of stereotyping. To test their hypothesis that group membership is often sufficient to foster ingroup favoritism, these researchers created what they called *minimal groups,* which are groups selected from a larger collection of people using some trivial criterion such as eye color, a random number table, or the flip of a coin. The people comprising these newly created groups were strangers to one another and were never given the opportunity to get acquainted. In some studies, participants were individually taken into a room with the experimenter and asked how much money two other participants should be paid for a subsequent task. These two people were identified only by code numbers, indicating to the participant that one came from his or her own group and the other was a member of the other group. Although participants only knew the others' membership status, they proceeded to reward the ingroup person more than the outgroup person (Tajfel et al., 1971).

Subsequent research on minimal groups replicated these findings, indicating that people often habitually engage in **ingroup bias** when evaluating others. That is, if they observe two people performing the same task, one of whom is a member of their ingroup, their evaluations of the two people's performance will be biased in favor of the ingroup member. This ingroup favoritism may manifest itself by people selectively remembering ingroup persons' good behavior and outgroup members' bad behavior, or by selectively forgetting or trivializing ingroup members' bad behavior and outgroup members' good behavior (Sherman et al., 1998). Such selective information processing causes an overestimation of ingroup performance relative to outgroup performance. Because of this ingroup biasing, ingroup members are consistently rewarded more than outgroup members (Crisp et al., 2001; Reynolds et al., 2000).

Ingroup preference tends to be so automatically activated that simply using ingroup pronouns is often sufficient to arouse positive emotions, while using pronouns signifying outgroups can trigger negative emotions. Evidence for this effect comes from a series of studies conducted by Charles Perdue and his coworkers (1990), in which college students saw 108 seemingly randomly paired letter strings on a computer screen. Each pair of letter strings consisted of a nonsense syllable (*xeh, yof, laj*) presented with either an ingroup-designating pronoun (*we, us, ours*), an outgroup-designating pronoun (*they, them, theirs*), or, on the control trials, some other pronoun (*he, she, his, hers*). Students were told to quickly decide which letter string in each pair was a real word (*we-xeh, they-yof*). Unbeknownst to the students, one nonsense syllable was consistently paired with ingroup pronouns and another with outgroup pronouns. After the trials, students were asked to rate each of the nonsense syllables in terms of its degree of pleasantness-unpleasantness. As you can see from figure 8.6, students evaluated the nonsense words that had previously been paired with the ingroup pronouns as more pleasant than those paired with either outgroup pronouns or with the control pronouns. These results suggest that merely associating a previously neutral stimulus to words that designate either ingroup or outgroup affiliations is sufficient to create biased emotional responses. As you might guess, ingroup biasing is often subtle and not recognized as being unfair by either the target or the perpetrator.

One of the most popular explanations for *why* ingroup biasing occurs was offered by Tajfel and John Turner in their **social identity theory** (Tajfel & Turner, 1979; Turner, 1987). As you recall from chapter 3 (p. 83), besides our personal identity, another important aspect of our self-concept is our social identity, which derives from the groups to which we belong. Our social identity establishes *what* and *where* we are in social terms. Because our social identity forms a central aspect of our own self-definition, our self-esteem is partly determined by the social esteem of our ingroups. When our ingroups are successful, or even

Ingroup Bias

The tendency to give more favorable evaluations and greater rewards to ingroup members than to outgroup members.

Social Identity Theory

A theory suggesting that people seek to enhance their self-esteem by identifying with specific social groups and perceiving these groups as being better than other groups.

FIGURE 8.6

**Us and Them:
Ingroup Biasing**

How pervasive is ingroup biasing? Perdue and colleagues (1990) found that nonsense words that had previously been paired with ingroup pronouns (e.g., us) were evaluated as more "pleasant" than nonsense words that had been paired with either outgroup pronouns (e.g., them) or control pronouns (e.g., hers). This study suggests that the ingroup-outgroup distinction has such emotional meaning to people that it can even shape their evaluation of unfamiliar words.

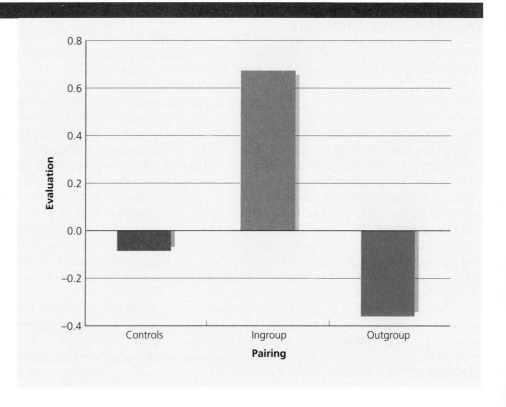

CRITICAL *thinking*

Based on the research you have just reviewed and the hypotheses derived from social identity theory, what is the relationship between "pride" and "prejudice"? How is this psychological process similar to the social reflection process (also known as "basking in reflected glory") observed in interpersonal relationships?

when members of our ingroups achieve some level of personal success, we can bask in their reflected glory. Consistent with several self-concept theories discussed in chapter 3, social identity theory asserts that we are motivated to achieve or maintain a high level of self-esteem. Therefore, when the social esteem of our ingroup is threatened, we attempt to maintain a positive social identity by engaging in ingroup biasing, perceiving our ingroup as being better than other groups.

Research generally supports social identity theory (Jackson et al., 1996; Weber, 1994). People who engage in ingroup biasing experience an increase in self-esteem compared with those who are not given the opportunity to express this bias (Rubin & Hewstone, 1998). Also as expected, members of lower-status groups—whose social esteem, by definition, is perpetually low—tend to engage in more ingroup biasing than members of higher-status groups (Ellemers et al., 1997). Finally, people who exhibit great pride in their ingroups and believe these groups are a central component of their own self-concept are more likely to engage in ingroup biasing than those who do not identify so strongly with their ingroups (Verkuyten et al., 1999).

In summary, research suggests that the way we are cognitively constructed predisposes us to be biased toward our ingroups. Social identity theory contends that the motive underlying this bias is a desire to indirectly enhance self-esteem by enhancing the social esteem of our ingroups. Yet what happens when we take this apparent inborn—and perhaps mild—tendency to perceive our ingroups as being better than other groups and mix it with "hot" intergroup competition, where one group's successes become the other group's failures? Hostility and violence are common results. Let us now examine how this escalation in intergroup conflict often occurs.

Intergroup Competition Can Lead to Prejudice

In 1996, "Beauty Island," a cosmetics store located in a predominantly Black Milwaukee neighborhood, was the target of boycotts, vandalism, and even attempted arson. The reason? Black community activists charged that the Korean-born owner's business was taking money out of the Black community. Amid a "Buy Black" message spray-painted on the side of the store and racial epithets hurled at the inhabitants, one protester stated, "This isn't just about Beauty Island, and it's not just about Milwaukee. It's about foreign merchants in the Black community." This example of racial prejudice and violence directed against a member of another social group is partly explained by *intergroup competition.* That is, when two groups compete for a limited number of scarce resources such as jobs, housing, consumer sales, or even food, one group's success becomes the other's failure and creates a breeding ground for prejudice (Duckitt & Mphuthing, 1998; Quillian, 1995).

REALISTIC GROUP CONFLICT THEORY

Examining the competitive roots for intergroup intolerance is exactly the perspective taken by **realistic group conflict theory** (Levine & Campbell, 1972). It argues that groups become prejudiced toward one another because they are in conflict over competition for scarce resources. The group conflict is considered "rational" or "realistic" because it is based on real competition. Contemptuous prejudice and envious prejudice are often fed by the intergroup competition examined by this theory. According to realistic group conflict theory, African Americans' hostility toward Asian Americans will increase if they believe that Asian shopkeepers in their neighborhoods are taking business opportunities away from them. Similarly, White Americans' prejudice toward African Americans will increase if Blacks are hired ahead of Whites due to affirmative-action programs. On the international scene, Americans' anti-Arab attitudes have substantially increased following the September 11th terrorist attacks (Oswald, in press).

Realistic group conflict theory contends that when groups are in conflict, two important changes occur in each group. The first change involves increased hostility toward the opposing outgroup, and the second change involves an intensification of ingroup loyalty. This pattern of behavior is referred to as **ethnocentrism** (Cunningham et al., 2004; Sumner, 1906). To better understand how ethnocentrism can develop due to conflict, let's examine one of the first experimental studies involving this psychological phenomenon.

THE ROBBERS CAVE EXPERIMENT

What happens if you randomly place people into one of two groups and manipulate circumstances to promote intergroup competition? This was the central question surrounding a classic field experiment designed by Muzafer Sherif and his colleagues (Sherif et al., 1961; Sherif & Sherif, 1956). They conducted the study in the summer of 1954 at a densely forested and hilly 200-acre camp that the researchers had created at Robbers Cave State Park, which is 150 miles southeast of Oklahoma City. Participants were twenty White, middle-class, well-adjusted 11- and 12-year-old boys who had never met one another before. In advance, the researchers divided the boys into two groups, with one group leaving by bus for the camp a day before the other. Upon arrival, each group was assigned a separate cabin out of sight of the other, and thus, neither knew of the other's existence. The camp counselors were actually researchers who unobtrusively observed and recorded day-to-day camp events as the study progressed.

The study had three phases. The first phase was devoted to *creating ingroups,* the second was devoted to *instilling intergroup competition,* and the third phase involved *encouraging intergroup cooperation.* During the first week of ingroup creation, each group separately engaged in cooperative activities such as hiking, hunting for hidden treasures, making meals, and pitching tents. As the week progressed, each group developed its own leader and unique social identity. One group named itself the "Rattlers," established a tough-guy group norm, and spent a good deal of time cursing and swearing. The other group called itself the "Eagles," and they instituted a group norm forbidding profanity. As the first week drew to a close, each group became aware of the other's existence. How do you think they responded? By making clear and undeniable ingroup-outgroup statements: "*They* better not be in *our* swimming hole!" "*Those* guys are using *our* baseball diamond again!"

During the second phase of the study, Sherif tested his main hypothesis that intergroup competition would cause prejudice. To do this, he created a weeklong tournament between the two groups, consisting of ten athletic events such as baseball, football, and tug-of-war. The winner of each event received points, and at the end of the week the group with

Realistic Group Conflict Theory

The theory that intergroup conflict develops from competition for limited resources.

Ethnocentrism

A pattern of increased hostility toward outgroups accompanied by increased loyalty to one's ingroup.

Sherif and his colleagues (1961) created intergroup hostility between two groups of boys (the "Eagles" and the "Rattlers") at a summer camp by having them compete against one another. In the top photo shown here, the Eagles grab and burn the Rattlers' group flag after losing a tug-of-war contest. Later (bottom photo), the Rattlers hang from a pole an Eagle's pair of jeans upon which they have painted, "The Last of the Eagles." Can you recall incidents from your own life where competition with another group resulted in the development of prejudicial attitudes and discriminatory behavior?

the most points received highly prized medals and impressive four-bladed pocketknives. True to Sherif's expectations, the intergroup conflict transformed these normal, well-adjusted boys into what a naive observer would have thought were "wicked, disturbed, and vicious" youngsters (Sherif, 1966, p. 58).

During this phase, the counselors heard a sharp increase in the number of unflattering names used to refer to outgroup members (for example, "pig" and "cheater"). The boys also rated their own group as being "brave," "tough," and "friendly," while those in the outgroup were "sneaky," "smart alecks," and "stinkers." This ingroup favoritism was also manifested in the boys' friendship preferences. Sherif, playing the role of camp handyman, asked the boys to tell him who their friends were at camp. The sharp division between the two groups was reflected in the fact that 93 percent of the friendship preferences were of the ingroup variety. If negative attitudes previously existed between ingroup members, they were now redirected against the outgroup. These findings indicate that one by-product of intergroup hostility is an increase in ingroup solidarity.

As the two groups competed in the various games, intergroup hostility quickly escalated from name-calling to acts of physical aggression. For example, at the end of the first tug-of-war contest, the losing Eagles demonstrated their outgroup attitudes by seizing and burning the Rattlers' group flag. Not to be outdone, the Rattlers raided the Eagles' cabin, overturning cots, ripping mosquito netting, and carrying off one of the Eagle's blue jeans as booty. The next day, armed with bats and sticks, the Eagles returned the favor. Then they retreated to their cabin, proceeded to stuff rocks in their socks, and waited for the next wave of Rattler reprisals.

Who ultimately won the valued prizes for which they were competing? The Eagles. Not surprisingly, the Rattlers thought they had been cheated. While the victors were taking a celebratory swim, the Rattlers stole their medals and knives. When the Eagles returned to find their prizes gone, the Rattlers admitted to the deed and told the incensed Eagles they could have them back . . . if they got down on their bellies and crawled for them! These are only a few of the incidents that occurred between the Eagles and the Rattlers. Intergroup hostility became so intense that members of the opposing groups held their noses whenever they passed by one another in camp.

This second phase of the study illustrates how easily hostility can develop between groups when they are brought into competition. The third phase of the experiment was designed to reverse the hostility, a task that proved to be much more difficult to accomplish. First, the researchers sought to determine whether simple noncompetitive contact between the groups would ease tensions. They tested this hypothesis during the first two days of phase three by bringing the groups together for some pleasant activity, such as a meal or a movie. The results were not encouraging. Both groups used each interaction as an opportunity to merely increase their mutual animosity for one another. During mealtimes, for example, food was more likely to be thrown at opposing group members than eaten.

This failure of simple contact to reduce hostility did not surprise Sherif and his colleagues. They hypothesized that to reduce intergroup conflict, they needed to introduce what they called a **superordinate goal,** which is a mutually shared goal that can be achieved only through intergroup cooperation. To test this hypothesis, the researchers arranged for a series of problem situations to develop over the course of the next six days. Each problem was urgent and involved both groups. The first problem was the "failure" of the camp's water supply. The groups initially responded to this emergency by trying to solve it on their own, without the other group's assistance. However, after converging on the source of the water problem, the camp water tank's plugged faucet, they cooperated in fixing it. A few days later, the camp truck "broke down" while the two groups were on an overnight camping excursion, and all the boys had to work together to pull it up a steep hill. Following this incident of cooperation, name-calling and negative outgroup stereotypes declined. Sherif, still in his guise as the camp handyman, again asked the boys who their friends were. Now, outgroup friendships had grown from a measly 7 percent average at the end of phase one to a rather robust 30 percent average, a significant increase in outgroup liking. In keeping with this newfound outgroup appreciation, at their final campfire the two groups decided to put on a joint entertainment program, consisting of skits and songs. When departing from camp the following day, the two groups insisted on traveling home on the same bus. On the way home, the Rattlers used money they had won in their previous competitions with the Eagles to buy milkshakes for everyone.

Taken as a whole, the Robbers Cave experiment is an excellent example of how ethnocentrism can develop when two groups compete for scarce resources. It also demonstrates that having a superordinate goal can lead to peaceful coexistence between previously antagonistic groups. Although this study used children as participants, similar results have also been obtained with adult samples (Jackson, 1993).

Despite the fact that the original theory assumed that prejudice develops due to real, tangible conflict between groups, more recent work demonstrates that the mere *perception* of conflict is often sufficient to fuel intolerance (Esses et al., 1998). For example, Michael Zárate and his colleagues (2004) found that when American research participants were led to believe that Mexican immigrants had similar skills and attributes as themselves, their sense of job security was threatened, which led to more negative attitudes toward immigrants. These findings suggest that when members of two groups share some important job-related skills, they may begin to view the other group as their rival, even where no actual rivalry exists. This is an important extension of realistic group conflict theory, and it also illustrates how attributing positive characteristics

Superordinate Goal

A mutually shared goal that can be achieved only through intergroup cooperation.

to a group—Americans who perceive Mexican immigrants as having useful skills—can trigger intergroup prejudice.

Prejudice Can Serve as a Justification for Oppression

What if two groups come in contact with one another, but one group is much more powerful than the other? In laboratory experiments, when groups are given different amounts of social power, members of high power groups discriminate more against outgroups than members of low power groups (Sachdev & Bourhis, 1987, 1991). **Social dominance theory** proposes that in all societies, groups can be organized in a hierarchy of power with at least one group being dominant over all others (Pratto, 1996; Sidanius & Pratto, 1999). Dominant groups enjoy a lopsided share of the society's assets, such as wealth, prestige, education, and health. In contrast, subordinate groups receive most of the society's liabilities, such as poverty, social stigma, illiteracy, poor health, and high levels of criminal punishment. History teaches us that the negative stereotypes and prejudicial attitudes that dominant groups develop about those they oppress serve to justify their continued oppression (Frederico & Sidanius, 2002; Sidanius et al., 2000). Contemptuous prejudice and paternalistic prejudice are the two forms of intolerance expressed by the oppressor group, while the prejudice that subordinate groups express toward those who oppress them is of the envious form.

A good deal of the prejudice in the history of the United States rests on social dominance. Europeans who founded this country did not arrive on uninhabited shores in the "New World." These settlers used their superior weapons to dominate and conquer the indigenous people of North America. At the same time that Europeans were colonizing North America, they were also capturing and buying Africans and transporting them to the colonies as slaves. They justified the inhuman exploitation that took place by stigmatizing both Native Americans and Africans as inferior races who needed civilizing.

Consistent with social dominance theory, research indicates that people develop less egalitarian beliefs toward outgroups as the social status of their own group increases in comparison to the target outgroups (Levin, 2004; Schmitt et al., 2003). A number of experimental studies have also demonstrated that developing prejudicial and stigmatizing attitudes toward the victims of one's own harmful actions is a common response (Georgesen & Harris, 2000; Rodriquez-Bailon et al., 2000). For example, Stephen Worchel and Virginia Mathie Andreoli (1978) found that when instructed to deliver electric shocks to a man when he responded incorrectly on a learning task, college students were more likely to dehumanize him than were students who were instructed to reward the man for correct answers. By dehumanizing and derogating their own victims, powerful exploiters can not only avoid thinking of themselves as villains, but they can also justify further exploitation (Quist & Resendez, 2002).

Old American textbooks illustrate the racist attitudes generated from such exploitation. For example, figure 8.7 is an excerpt from a popular high school geography book published in 1880 devoted to the "Races of Man" around the globe. The five listed races are classified in a descending order of capacity for civilization—the *Caucasian* races, the *Yellow* race, the *Negro* type, the *Malays,* and the *Indians.* Can you guess the race of the author of this civilized hierarchy? Particularly interesting about this section is how the White American author describes the two races that his social group had the most contact with, and whom they had historically treated so harshly. African tribes are described as living in a "savage or barbarous state," while the descendants of native Africans had "been Christianized and civilized" by Whites. What about the representatives of the native races of America, whose land had been taken by the same European descendants as the author of the text? According to the author, American Indians "have always shown but little capacity for civilization" (Swinton, 1880, p. 17). In these characterizations, we see how an oppressor group justifies its exploitation of less powerful groups by denigrating them.

Of course, not all members of dominant groups denigrate those below them in the status hierarchy. People differ in the degree to which they perceive their social world as a competitive jungle with "haves" and "have-nots" fighting to gain or maintain supremacy over the other. In-

Social Dominance Theory

A theory contending that societal groups can be organized in a power hierarchy in which the dominant groups enjoy a disproportionate share of the society's assets and the subordinate groups receive most of its liabilities.

The whites told only one side. Told it to please themselves. Told much that is not true. Only his own best deeds, only the worst deeds of the Indians, has the white man told.

Yellow Wolf of the Nez Perce Indians, 1940

Racism breeds racism in reverse.

Mary Brave Bird, Sioux (Lakota) Nation commentator, 1990

We first crush people to the earth, and then claim the right of trampling on them forever, because they are prostrate.

Lydia Maria Child, U.S. author and abolitionist, 1802–1880

FIGURE 8.7

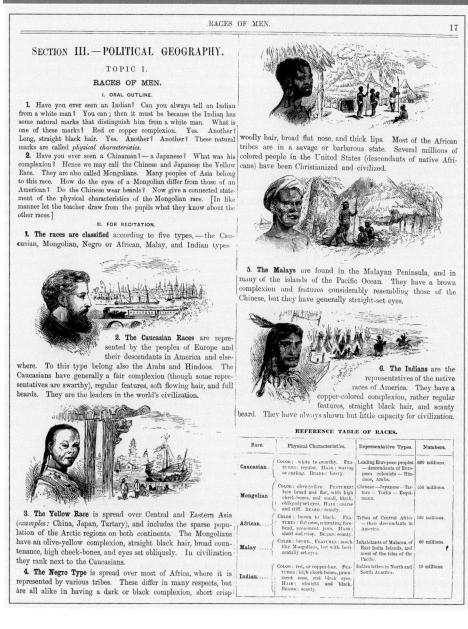

RACES OF MEN.   17

SECTION III.—POLITICAL GEOGRAPHY.

TOPIC I.

RACES OF MEN.

I. ORAL OUTLINE.

1. Have you ever seen an Indian? Can you always tell an Indian from a white man? You can; then it must be because the Indian has some natural marks that distinguish him from a white man. What is one of these marks? Red or copper complexion. Yes. Another? Long, straight black hair. Yes. Another? Another? These natural marks are called *physical characteristics.*

2. Have you ever seen a Chinaman?—a Japanese? What was his complexion? Hence we may call the Chinese and Japanese the Yellow Race. They are also called Mongolians. Many peoples of Asia belong to this race. How do the eyes of a Mongolian differ from those of an American? Do the Chinese wear beards? Now give a connected statement of the physical characteristics of the Mongolian race. [In like manner let the teacher draw from the pupils what they know about the other races.]

II. FOR RECITATION.

1. The races are classified according to five types,—the Caucasian, Mongolian, Negro or African, Malay, and Indian types.

2. The Caucasian Races are represented by the peoples of Europe and their descendants in America and elsewhere. To this type belong also the Arabs and Hindoos. The Caucasians have generally a fair complexion (though some representatives are swarthy), regular features, soft flowing hair, and full beards. They are the leaders in the world's civilization.

3. The Yellow Race is spread over Central and Eastern Asia (*examples*: China, Japan, Tartary), and includes the sparse population of the Arctic regions on both continents. The Mongolians have an olive-yellow complexion, straight black hair, broad countenance, high cheek-bones, and eyes set obliquely. In civilization they rank next to the Caucasians.

4. The Negro Type is spread over most of Africa, where it is represented by various tribes. These differ in many respects, but are all alike in having a dark or black complexion, short crisp

woolly hair, broad flat nose, and thick lips. Most of the African tribes are in a savage or barbarous state. Several millions of colored people in the United States (descendants of native Africans) have been Christianized and civilized.

5. The Malays are found in the Malayan Peninsula, and in many of the islands of the Pacific Ocean. They have a brown complexion and features considerably resembling those of the Chinese, but they have generally straight-set eyes.

6. The Indians are the representatives of the native races of America. They have a copper-colored complexion, rather regular features, straight black hair, and scanty beard. They have always shown but little capacity for civilization.

REFERENCE TABLE OF RACES.

Race.	Physical Characteristics.	Representative Types.	Numbers.
Caucasian	COLOR: white to swarthy. FEATURES: regular. HAIR: waving or curling. BEARD: heavy.	Leading European peoples — descendants of European colonists — Hindoos, Arabs.	600 millions.
Mongolian	COLOR: olive-yellow. FEATURES: face broad and flat, with high cheek-bones, and small, black, obliquely set eyes. HAIR: coarse and stiff. BEARD: scanty.	Chinese—Japanese—Tartars — Turks — Esquimaux.	550 millions.
African....	COLOR: brown to black. FEATURES: flat nose, retreating forehead, prominent jaws. HAIR: short and crisp. BEARD: scanty.	Tribes of Central Africa — their descendants in America.	180 millions.
Malay	COLOR: brown. FEATURES: much like Mongolian, but with horizontally set eyes.	Inhabitants of Malacca, of East India Islands, and most of the isles of the Pacific.	60 millions.
Indian.....	COLOR: red, or copper-hue. FEATURES: high cheek-bones, prominent nose, and black eyes. HAIR: straight and black. BEARD: scanty.	Indian tribes in North and South America.	10 millions.

An Example of Racist Attitudes in an Old American Textbook

The characterization of the various races in Swinton's text conveys the ingroup biases of the author. In comparing our own beliefs against the beliefs of this author of the nineteenth century, before we smugly assume a superior attitude of intergroup tolerance, we must ask ourselves how our current attitudes and beliefs toward different social groups will be judged by future generations. What sort of overlooked ingroup prejudices and biases permeate the text you are reading at this very moment? As the author of this social psychology book, I am sure my ingroup biases have occasionally made their way into my writing. Later, when discussing ways to monitor stereotypical thinking, we will examine how becoming aware of our current prejudices can steer us toward nonprejudiced thinking.

---

dividuals with a strong *social dominance orientation* desire and support the organization of societal groups in a status hierarchy, with designated "inferior" groups being dominated by designated "superior" groups (Sidanius & Pratto, 1999). Research suggests that this motivation to view the world in terms of a status hierarchy dominated by the powerful causes people to adopt belief systems and to seek out membership in groups that promote prejudice and social inequality (Dambrun et al., 2002; Guimond et al., 2003). On your Social Sense CD-ROM, view an interview with Jane Elliot where she discusses her "Blue Eyes-Brown Eyes" workshops that powerfully demonstrate the effect that social dominance has on the powerful and the powerless.

Authoritarianism Is Associated with Hostility Toward Outgroups

The idea that members of the same social group often respond differently to intergroup contact and conflict highlights the importance of considering personality and individual difference factors when studying prejudice and discrimination. One of the early inquiries into

Social Sense

Review the "Blue Eyes-Brown Eyes" Demonstration

prejudice-prone personalities was the work of Theodor Adorno and Else Frenkel-Brunswik, two social scientists who fled Nazi Germany during World War II. Motivated by their desire to explain the psychology underlying the mass genocide of millions of Jews and other "undesirables" by the Nazi regime, Adorno and Frenkel-Brunswik set out to discover how people with certain personality characteristics might be prone to intergroup hostility.

Along with their colleagues at the University of California at Berkeley, Adorno and Frenkel-Brunswik believed that the cause of extreme prejudice could be traced to personality conflicts developed during childhood (Adorno et al., 1950). Operating from a psychoanalytic perspective, and using survey, case study, and interview methods, they identified what they called the **authoritarian personality.** Based on their studies, the researchers concluded that authoritarians are submissive to authority figures and intolerant of those who are weak or different. The intergroup hostility they express toward lower status groups generally takes the form of contemptuous prejudice. Authoritarians also conform rigidly to cultural values and believe that morality is a matter of clear right and wrong choices. The instrument developed to measure authoritarian tendencies was called the *F-scale* (short for *Fascism*). People who expressed strong agreement with items such as the ones that follow were classified as having an authoritarian personality:

> Obedience and respect for authority are the most important virtues children should learn.

> People can be divided into two distinct classes: the weak and the strong.

> Homosexuals are hardly better than criminals and ought to be severely punished.

> What this country needs most, more than laws and political programs, is a few courageous, tireless, devoted leaders in whom the people can put their faith.

The Berkeley researchers believed that authoritarian personalities resulted from harsh childrearing practices that taught children to *repress* their hostility toward authority and, instead, to redirect or *displace* it onto less powerful targets who could not retaliate. Although this original theory is acknowledged as an important attempt to understand prejudice in terms of personality conflict and childrearing practices, questions about how people actually become authoritarians and criticisms of the Berkeley scientists' research methods resulted in this approach losing credibility by the late 1960s (Hiel et al., 2004).

In the 1980s, interest in the authoritarian personality was revived when Bob Altemeyer (1981, 1988) suggested that its origins have nothing to do with personality conflicts from childhood and instead are caused by people learning a prejudicial style of thinking during adolescence. Operating from a social learning perspective, Altemeyer contended that children who are socialized by authoritarian and strict disciplinarians develop similar tendencies because they model and reinforce this intolerant worldview. He further asserted that most of this social learning occurs during adolescence, with the principal modelers being parents and peers. Socialized to view their world as a dangerous and threatening place, and isolated from personal contact with nonconventional people or minorities, adolescents in authoritarian environments learn that it is acceptable to express hostility toward various outgroups.

A number of studies conducted over the past twenty years support Altemeyer's social learning view over the earlier psychoanalytic perspective (Duckitt & Fisher, 2003; Feldman & Stenner, 1997). What appears to motivate the prejudice of the authoritarian personality is not repressed parental conflict, but rather, a strong desire to identify with and conform to the existing social order, coupled with a learned sense of fearfulness and insecurity about the social world and a perception that other groups pose a threat to one's ingroup (Altemeyer, 2004; Jost et al., 2003). Individuals growing up in authoritarian households are most likely to adopt authoritarian attitudes and beliefs when they have strong needs for social order and conformity.

In many different societies, people with authoritarian personalities not only express greater antipathy toward threatening outgroups than the average person, but they are also more likely to act on their hostility (Lippa & Arad, 1999; Verkuyten & Hagendoorn, 1998). Authoritarians also tend to generalize their outgroup prejudices. For example, if they hate

Authoritarian Personality

A personality trait characterized by submissiveness to authority, rigid adherence to conventional values, and prejudice toward outgroups.

In the spring of 2004, the world became aware of widespread abuses of Iraqi detainees by U.S. occupying forces. This abuse was widely condemned throughout the world, as well as in the United States. Research indicates that authoritarians' distaste for outgroups causes them to be much more likely than nonauthoritarians to excuse such prisoner abuse during times of international conflict. How does research on the authoritarian personality relate to social dominance theory and the persecution of lower status groups?

Blacks, they are also likely to express hostility toward Jews, feminists, gay men and lesbians, the homeless, and people with AIDS (Pek & Leong, 2003; Whitley, 1999). Authoritarians' distaste for threatening outgroups is also reflected in greater support for their government's military actions against other countries during times of international tension. They not only support such actions, but they are also more likely to excuse atrocities committed by their own military forces during these interventions (Doty et al., 1997; Unger, 2002). On the home front, persons high in authoritarianism have a general bias against defendants in criminal proceedings—a definite outgroup (Narby et al., 1993). They pay more attention to the prosecuting attorney's arguments against the defendant than to the arguments presented by the defense attorney, and they are more influenced by incriminating evidence than the average person (Werner et al., 1982).

Besides identifying individual variations in authoritarianism, social scientists have also examined how it might vary on a societal level over time. An important catalyst for the manifestation of societal authoritarianism is *perceived social threat* (Burris & Rempel, 2004; Doty et al., 1991). That is, when societies undergo economic hardships and social upheaval, mildly authoritarian individuals may become motivated to join social, political, or religious organizations that express dogmatic and rigid social attitudes and preach intolerance of outgroups who are perceived as threats to the social order (Hunsberger, 1995; McCann, 1999). For example, in a series of archival studies of church membership patterns in the United States, Stuart McCann (1999) found that people were most attracted to intolerant religious teachings and authoritarian churches when the country was experiencing heightened social and economic threat. Similarly, longitudinal studies of South Koreans' social values between 1982 and 1996 found that as economic and military threats diminished, endorsement of authoritarian beliefs also diminished among the young and the educated portions of the population (Lee, 2003).

A DUAL-PROCESS MODEL OF PERSONALITY-INFLUENCED PREJUDICE

One of the more recent developments in the search for personality-influenced explanations of prejudice is John Duckitt's (2001, in press) contention that the individual difference characteristics of authoritarianism and social dominance orientation are more correctly identified as social attitudes and that they account for different types of outgroup prejudice. In explaining how these two social attitudes shape people's social-world beliefs and perceptions of outgroups, Duckitt developed a *dual-process model* in which he asserts that underlying authoritarianism and social dominance orientation are two different personality traits: social conformity and tough-mindedness.

As depicted in figure 8.8, in explaining the origins of the authoritarian personality, Duckitt asserts that individuals who are socialized by strict and punitive disciplinarians

CRITICAL *thinking*

The terrorist attacks in the United States in 2001 greatly increased Americans' perceived social threat. Based on authoritarianism research, what type of social consequences might we see in this country due to this heightened threat? Further, how might this same research explain the mind-set and behavior of the terrorists?

It's always a simple matter to drag the people along whether it's a democracy, a fascist dictator-ship, or a parliament, or a communist dictatorship. All you have to do is tell them they are being attacked, and denounce the pacifists for lack of patriotism, and exposing the country to great danger.

Herman Goring, Hitler's Commander of Nazi Storm Troopers, 1893–1946

FIGURE 8.8

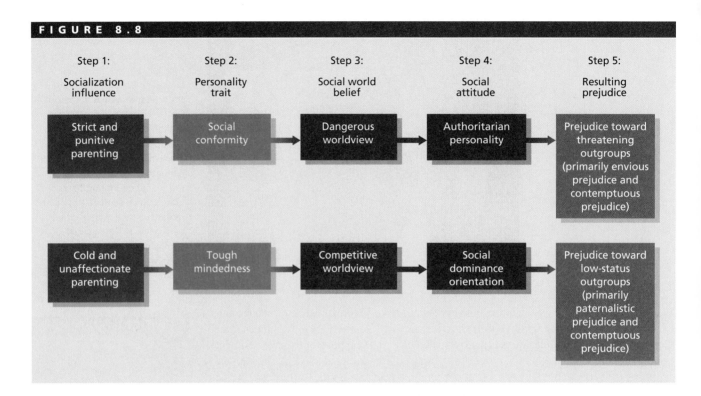

Step 1: Socialization influence	Step 2: Personality trait	Step 3: Social world belief	Step 4: Social attitude	Step 5: Resulting prejudice
Strict and punitive parenting	Social conformity	Dangerous worldview	Authoritarian personality	Prejudice toward threatening outgroups (primarily envious prejudice and contemptuous prejudice)
Cold and unaffectionate parenting	Tough mindedness	Competitive worldview	Social dominance orientation	Prejudice toward low-status outgroups (primarily paternalistic prejudice and contemptuous prejudice)

A Dual-Process Model of Personality-Influenced Prejudice

John Duckitt (in press) proposes that authoritarianism and social dominance orientation are shaped by different socialization and personality forces, resulting in different expressions of prejudice. Children raised by strict and punitive parents (step 1) develop a strong need for social conformity (step 2), and this sensitivity to authority and social conventions causes them to perceive their diverse social world as a threatening place (step 3). Their resulting authoritarian social attitudes (step 4) lead them to develop prejudice toward outgroups perceived as threatening their social order (step 5). In contrast, children raised in a cold and unaffectionate household (step 1) develop a tough-minded personality (step 2), which leads them to develop beliefs that their social world is ruthless and competitive (step 3). This worldview activates a desire for group power and social dominance (step 4), which causes them to develop prejudice toward low social status outgroups (step 5).

develop a strong need to conform to authority figures and social conventions. Because this desire for conformity is associated with the existing social order, these individuals develop a sensitivity to anything that might threaten this order. Thus, they tend to view the diversity in their social world as being dangerous and threatening. Motivated by social conformity and having threatening world-view beliefs, strong authoritarians develop prejudice toward outgroups they perceive as threatening their existing social order.

Regarding the development of a strong social dominance orientation, Duckitt proposes that people who are socialized in a cold and unaffectionate manner develop a tough-minded personality, in which they view the world as a ruthlessly competitive jungle where the strong win and the weak lose. In turn, this worldview activates a desire for group power, dominance, and superiority over others and a disdain for those who are weak or of low social status. The prejudices of people with a strong social dominance orientation are not triggered by perceptions that outgroups threaten social conventions and norms, but instead by perceptions that outgroups are weak or pose a threat to their own group's social status.

Recent studies provide preliminary support for this dual-process model of personality-based prejudices (Duckitt, in press; Duckitt et al., 2002; Esses et al., 2001). By emphasizing different socialization and personality forces in the shaping of different forms of prejudice, this dual-process model may provide a broader and more comprehensive understanding of the causes and dynamics of intergroup intolerance.

- People appear to be automatically biased toward ingroup members versus outgroup members
- Social identity theory asserts that prejudice and discrimination can result from people trying to increase or maintain self-esteem
- Realistic group conflict theory argues that groups become prejudiced toward one another because they are in conflict over competition for scarce resources
- Social dominance theory explains how dominant groups develop negative stereotypes and prejudicial attitudes toward those they oppress to justify their continued oppression
- Research on authoritarianism suggests that some forms of prejudice can be traced to personality and socialization factors

THE SOCIAL PSYCHOLOGY OF RACISM AND SEXISM

Now that we have examined some of the motivating forces underlying prejudice and discrimination, let us turn our attention to how two types of "tribal identity" stigmas—namely, race and sex—cause intergroup intolerance in contemporary society.

Modern-Day Racism Is More Ambivalent Than Openly Hostile

Prejudice and discrimination based on a person's racial background is called *racism*. Blatantly negative stereotypes based on beliefs in the racial superiority of one's own group, coupled with open opposition to racial equality, characterizes what is known as old-fashioned racism (McConahay, 1986). **Old-fashioned racism** involves contemptuous prejudice and often leads to movement *against* the despised group, including physical violence.

AVERSIVE RACISM

Although old-fashioned racism typified the perspective of many White Americans toward other racial groups throughout most of the history of this country, the vast majority of Whites today cannot be classified in this simple and straightforward fashion (Dovidio & Gaertner, 2000). Instead, researchers such as Samuel Gaertner and John Dovidio (1977, 2000) and Irwin Katz and R. Glen Hass (1988) assert that the fundamental nature of White Americans' current attitudes toward many racial groups, but especially toward African Americans, is complex and conflicted. They contend that on the one hand, the majority of Whites hold to egalitarian values that stress equal treatment of all people and a sympathy for social groups who have been mistreated in the past. Therefore, they sympathize with the victims of racial prejudice and tend to support public policies that promote racial equality. On the other hand, because of exposure to unflattering stereotypes and media images depicting African Americans as lazy, unmotivated, and violent, and due to simple ingroup-outgroup biases, these researchers believe that many Whites come to possess negative feelings and beliefs about Blacks that directly contradict their egalitarian values. The American individualist value of the Protestant work ethic, which emphasizes self-reliance and individual initiative in pursuing life goals, reinforces these negative social perceptions about Blacks. Given their own relative lack of personal experience with the negative impact of racial prejudice, many Whites tend to believe that anyone who works hard has a good chance of succeeding in life. Therefore, many of them conclude that at least part of the source of continued racial inequality is what they perceive as a low level of motivation and effort on the part of Blacks and other disadvantaged groups, such as American Indians and Latinos (Biernat et al., 1996).

Old-Fashioned Racism

Blatantly negative stereotypes based on beliefs in the racial superiority of one's own group, coupled with open opposition to racial equality.

According to this perspective on contemporary racism, the negative feelings engendered by Whites' perceptions of disadvantaged racial groups do not encompass anger or contempt, as in old-fashioned racism, but they do include uneasiness and even fear. As you recall, these are the precise emotions activated when Whites with high implicit and low explicit racial prejudice see an unfamiliar black face (refer back to pp. 255–256). Due to the fact that an egalitarian value system plays an important role in their self-concepts, this perspective assumes that many White Americans typically do not even acknowledge to themselves, much less to others, that they have these negative feelings. Because interacting with members of these other racial groups tends to make Whites aware of their negative—though not fully understood—racial feelings and beliefs, they avoid such interactions and, thus, avoid confronting their hidden prejudice (Nail et al., 2003). This is why the combination of both positive and negative beliefs and feelings about a particular racial group is called **aversive racism.** Interracial encounters make salient the attitudinal conflict, and this awareness threatens one's self-concept as a fair-minded person.

One study, conducted by Katz and Hass (1988), suggests that many White Americans may indeed have conflicting attitudes regarding African Americans. In this research, White college students first completed a questionnaire that either contained items measuring adherence to the individualist Protestant ethic of self-reliance, initiative, and hard work or contained egalitarian and humanitarian items stressing equal treatment of all people and empathy for those who are less fortunate (see table 8.3). When participants completed the questionnaire, the researchers administered a second questionnaire that measured their *explicit prejudice* toward Blacks. Because Katz and Hass believed that both sets of values were part of the participants' worldview, they predicted that their explicit prejudice would be influenced by whichever of these two values were made salient. Consistent with their hypothesis, when Whites were first primed by egalitarian statements, their subsequent prejudice scores went down. When they were primed by individualist work ethic statements, their prejudice scores went up. This is what one would expect if the participants held both value orientations. In any given situation, whichever one is made salient will exert the most influence over attitudes and behavior.

Aversive Racism

Attitudes toward members of a racial group that incorporate both egalitarian social values and negative emotions, causing one to avoid interaction with members of the group.

TABLE 8.3

Racial Ambivalence and Conflicting American Values

People with a strong Protestant ethic would agree with the sample items from the first scale, while those with a strong humanitarianism-egalitarianism value orientation would agree with the sample items from the scale bearing its name. If a White American believes in both of these value orientations, according to Katz and Hass (1988), what sort of attitudinal conflict might this create in their overall perceptions of African Americans or American Indians?

The Protestant Ethic (Sample Items from Katz & Hass, 1988)	Humanitarianism-Egalitarianism (Sample Items from Katz & Hass, 1988)
1. Most people who don't succeed in life are just plain lazy.	1. One should find ways to help others less fortunate than oneself.
2. Anyone who is willing to work hard has a good chance of succeeding.	2. There should be equality for everyone—because we are all human beings.
3. If people work hard enough they are likely to make a good life for themselves.	3. Everyone should have an equal chance and an equal say in most things.
4. Most people spend too much time in unprofitable amusements.	4. Acting to protect the rights and interests of other members of the community is a major obligation for all persons.

Research suggests that many White Americans have conflicting racial attitudes regarding other racial groups, but especially African Americans, American Indians, and Latinos. This research further suggests that many White Americans do not acknowledge even to themselves that they hold negative racial attitudes. Because interacting with members of these other racial groups tends to make Whites aware of their negative racial feelings and beliefs, they avoid such interactions and, thus, avoid confronting their hidden prejudice. What is the name for this modern form of racism? How do cultural beliefs and values shape this type of race-based prejudice?

Katz and Hass believe that another consequence of Whites having ambivalent attitudes toward minority groups is that it can cause them to act in a more extreme manner toward minority members than they would to other Whites (Katz et al., 1986). This tendency for responses to become more extreme when one holds ambivalent attitudes is called *response amplification,* and it can occur in either a favorable or an unfavorable direction, depending on the social context (Hass et al., 1991). Thus, Whites with ambivalent attitudes toward Blacks may act overfriendly and solicitous when being introduced to African Americans whom they perceive to be competent and ambitious. This is because such encounters discredit the negative components of their ambivalent attitudes. Likewise, they may react with great annoyance and anger when interacting with Blacks they judge to be incompetent and lazy, because the encounter discredits the positive component of their ambivalent attitudes. When either one of these components has been discredited in a given situation, the person's evaluative response is likely to be exaggerated in the opposing direction.

As you might guess, when aversive racists cannot easily avoid interacting with African Americans or with members of other minority groups for whom they hold similarly ambivalent attitudes, the resulting exchanges are often uncomfortable for both parties (Dovidio, 2001). During such interactions, aversive racists—who generally sincerely believe that they are not prejudiced—consciously focus on their egalitarian attitudes and actively monitor and regulate their self-presentations to convey warmth and friendliness. Simultaneously, they try to ignore their feelings of discomfort that are induced by their implicit prejudice. In contrast, based on past interactions with aversive racists, many minority group members have learned to not just attend to White individuals' consciously constructed self-presentations, but to also note their nonverbal behavior for evidence of implicit prejudice. Nonverbal behavior related to negative arousal and tension in face-to-face interactions includes such things as excessive blinking, gaze aversion, and forced smiles. When minority group members detect these behaviors, they feel more uncomfortable and less satisfied with the interaction than the aversive racists (Vorauer & Kumhyr, 2001). In other words, the research evidence suggests that because aversive racists pay most attention to their consciously held egalitarian attitudes and overtly friendly self-presentations, whereas their minority partners pay most attention to aversive racists' less consciously controlled—and less friendly—nonverbal behaviors, these two conversational partners often have different reactions to their interracial exchange (Devine et al., 1996; Dovidio et al., 2002b). While aversive racists often walk away feeling relieved that things "went well" and comforted by

He flattered himself on being a man without any prejudices; and this pretension itself is a very great prejudice.

Anatole France, French novelist and poet, 1844–1924

You learn about equality in history and civics, but you find out life is not really like that.

Arthur Ashe, professional tennis player, 1943–1993

the belief that they indeed are nonprejudiced, minorities often walk away feeling angry and certain that they have just encountered another prejudiced White person (Dovidio et al., 2002a).

WHAT ABOUT RACIAL PREJUDICE AMONG MINORITY GROUP MEMBERS?

Surveys asking African Americans about their experiences being targets of racial discrimination find that 60 percent or more report being targeted at some point in their lives, and more than half report having at least thirteen racial hassles in the past year (Kessler et al., 1999; Sellers & Shelton, 2003). Most racial hassles involve brief interactions with strangers in which respondents were ignored, overlooked, not given service, treated rudely, or perceived as a threat. Other minorities in the United States report comparable prejudice experiences (Stangor et al., 2003).

Because minorities are much more likely to be targets of racial discrimination than Whites, minority race bias is often overlooked or excused in the larger culture (Shelton, 2000). For example, at work, a Black person calling a White colleague *honky* would less likely be reprimanded or fired than a White person calling a Black colleague *nigger*. In such instances, the prejudice the Black employee expresses is often perceived to have a more justifiable reason underlying it than the prejudice the White employee expresses. Yet what do we know about the social psychological dynamics of minority group prejudice and race perception?

One important finding is that just as Whites' racial attitudes vary from positive to negative, so too do the racial attitudes of minorities. Despite being the target of prejudice from Whites, not all Blacks, Asians, Latinos, and American Indians are prejudiced against Whites (Shelton, 2000). Recent studies also suggest that although many Whites' attitudes toward Blacks stem from egalitarianism and the Protestant ethic, Blacks' racial attitudes originate primarily from perceptions of threat or conflict and their reaction to White racism (Montieth & Spicer, 2000). Thus, while many Whites' negative attitudes toward Blacks are related to their perceptions that Blacks are not living up to cherished values such as industriousness and perseverance, many Blacks' prejudicial attitudes toward Whites are related to their reactions to Whites' treatment of their race. It is likely that other minority groups' prejudicial attitudes toward Whites have similar origins.

A growing number of social psychologists believe that, just as Whites often have ambivalent attitudes toward various minority groups, minority groups have ambivalent attitudes toward Whites (Livingston, 2002). Minority group ambivalence may be caused by resenting the social power given to Whites in society, while simultaneously depending on this power to gain social status and financial rewards, or respecting Whites for certain positive traits associated with their group (Shelton, 2000). This represents a form of envious prejudice. Although Whites who hold ambivalent attitudes often avoid interracial exchanges, similarly conflicted minority members may not have the luxury of doing so, simply because of the sheer number of White people around them. However, the more frequent interracial encounters that minority group members engage in may pay them social dividends in the future. At least one study suggests that African Americans, regardless of whether or not they hold ambivalent attitudes toward Whites, develop more effective strategies for dealing with the psychological discomfort of interracial interactions than do White Americans (Hyers & Swim, 1998).

Another reason that minority groups' racial perceptions and attitudes might differ from that of Whites is that, because of their history of being the targets of oppression, people of color are much more likely to consider their race and ethnicity as an important aspect of their self-concepts. For example, when Charles Judd and his coworkers (1995) questioned Black and White Americans about their perceptions and attitudes toward each race, their findings suggested that differences in the ways in which these two groups are socialized to think about race increase the likelihood of misunderstandings and conflicts. Young Whites are generally socialized to avoid thinking about racial differences and stereotypes, because such thinking is considered the source of prejudice and discrimination. In contrast, young Blacks are typically socialized to emphasize their ethnic identity and to recognize the differences between themselves and Whites, because such thinking is considered to help them better deal with ongoing prejudice and discrimination.

As you have already learned in this chapter, both of these perspectives have psychological merit: stereotyping and recognizing group differences can lead to prejudice, and developing an ethnic identity can insulate one from many of the negative effects of prejudice. The former view emphasizes eliminating known causes of prejudice, while the latter perspective emphasizes protecting oneself from existing prejudice. To a certain extent, White Americans' racial views contend that an ideal society should be a "melting pot" or "colorblind," in which everyone is judged equally regardless of their race or ethnicity. In contrast, Black Americans tend to believe that eliminating their racial identity in a cultural melting pot would strip them of their most important defense against racism. Instead, their perspective on race contends that society is a "patchwork quilt" in which their group's unique strengths and qualities buffer them from ongoing racism. These two contrasting views on the wisdom of recognizing race in one's life and using it as a basis for making social judgments may partly explain why many Blacks and Whites hold different opinions about social issues such as affirmative action. Whereas Whites may believe that such programs create unhealthy racial divisions and emphasize group differences, Blacks may believe that these programs serve to correct the continuing unfair treatment of minorities in society. Here, once again, we see how differences in our definitions of social reality lead to sharply contrasting social judgments. Despite the merits in both viewpoints, some research indicates that the "patchwork quilt" perspective is more effective in reducing implicit racial bias than the color-blind perspective (Richeson & Nussbaum, 2004). Thus, extolling the virtues of multiculturalism may yield more positive outcomes for intergroup relations than color blindness (Blum, 2002; Bonilla-Silva, 2003).

The prejudice against color, of which we hear so much, is no stronger than that against sex. It is produced by the same cause, and manifested very much in the same way. The Negro's skin and the woman's sex are both prima facie evidence that they were intended to be in subjection to the white Saxon man.

Elizabeth Cady Stanton, U.S. feminist and abolitionist, 1815–1902

Sexism Has Both a Hostile and a Benevolent Component

Sexism is prejudice and discrimination based on a person's sex. Much as racism in Western societies is mostly discussed in terms of White hostility toward racial minority groups, sexism around the globe primarily focuses on the prejudice and discrimination that males direct at females. This is so because virtually all societies in the world are *patriarchal,* meaning that the social organization is such that males dominate females (Harris, 1991; Hoffman, 2001). Evolutionary theorists propose that the social dominance of men over women is probably due to the biology of human sexual reproduction, in which the competition between males for sexual access to females eventually resulted in men being more aggressive and having a stronger social dominance orientation than women. As outlined by social dominance theory (see p. 280), the patriarchal systems that resulted from males' greater dominance-seeking eventually led to the development of a sexist ideology to justify control over females (Krefting, 2003; Sidanius et al., 1995). The basic storyline of this ideology is that women are inferior and irrational creatures who need to be controlled by men. This patriarchal belief system underlying *old-fashioned sexism* justifies continued oppression and has many psychological similarities to old-fashioned racism.

Sexism

Any attitude, action, or institutional structure that subordinates a person because of her or his sex.

AMBIVALENT SEXISM

Unlike most dominant-subordinate relationships, in male-female relationships there is a great deal of intimacy: men are dependent on women as mothers, wives, and sexual/romantic partners. Historically, this intimacy has resulted in many sexist men idealizing women in traditional feminine roles: they cherish these women and want to protect them because these traditional relationships fulfill their dual desires for social dominance and intimacy. Peter Glick and Susan Fiske (1996) contend that this orientation toward women, which is based on both positive and negative attitudes (benevolence and hostility) rather than uniform dislike, constitutes **ambivalent sexism.** Recent studies indicate that the degree to which these views are held varies from culture to culture and is related to cultural differences in gender equality (Glick & Fiske, 2001a; Glick et al., 2004; Sakalli-Ugurlu & Glick, 2003). Although benevolent sexist beliefs lead people to express many positive attitudes about women, it shares common assumptions with hostile sexism; namely, that women belong in restricted domestic roles and are the "weaker" sex. Both beliefs serve to justify male social dominance. For example, in Turkey and Brazil, men and women who

We have mistresses for our enjoyment, concubines to serve our person, and wives for the bearing of legitimate offspring.

Demosthenes, Ancient Greek orator, 385–322 B.C.

Ambivalent Sexism

Sexism directed against women based on both positive and negative attitudes (hostility and benevolence), rather than uniform dislike.

Sexual Harassment

Unwelcome physical or verbal sexual overtures that create an intimidating, hostile, or offensive social environment.

endorse hostile and benevolent sexist beliefs toward women justify violence against wives when they challenge their husbands' authority or violate traditional gender roles (Glick et al., 2002). Spend a few minutes completing the Ambivalent Sexism Inventory in table 8.4.

Based on your understanding of cognitive dissonance theory (chapter 6, pp. 000–000), you might be wondering how ambivalent sexists avoid feeling conflicted about their positive and negative beliefs and attitudes toward women. Shouldn't people experience considerable dissonance if they simultaneously believe that women are inferior, ungrateful, sexual teasers who are also refined, morally superior goddesses? According to what we have already learned about the resiliency of negative stereotypes (refer back to pp. 268–269), ambivalent sexists could avoid cognitive dissonance by splitting women into "good" and "bad" stereotype subcategories that embody the positive and negative aspects of sexist ambivalence. Having subcategorized women in this polarized manner, the ambivalent sexist could justify treating the "bad" women with hostility, while treating the "good" women with benevolence.

In two separate studies, Glick and his colleagues (1997) found support for this hypothesis. When asked to spontaneously list the different "types" they use to classify women, men who scored high and low on the Ambivalent Sexism Inventory (ASI) generated many of the same subcategories, but ambivalent sexists evaluated their traditional and nontraditional female subcategories in a more polarized fashion than did the nonsexists. Among ambivalent sexists, career women evoked negative feelings (fear, envy, competitiveness, intimidation), and these negative evaluations were significantly correlated with the Hostile Sexism Scale of the ASI (Mean $r = .34$), but not with the ASI's Benevolent Sexism Scale (Mean $r = .12$). In contrast, homemakers elicited a variety of positive feelings (warmth, respect, trust, happiness), and these positive evaluations were significantly correlated with the Benevolent Sexism Scale (Mean $r = .21$), but not with the Hostile Sexism Scale (Mean $r = .02$). These findings suggest that, among ambivalent sexist men, specific female subcategories activate either hostility or benevolence, but not both. Apparently, reserving negative attitudes for nontraditional women and positive attitudes for those who are traditional allows sexist men to simultaneously hold contradictory views of women in general.

What about women who hold sexist attitudes toward other women? Do they also evaluate traditional and nontraditional female subcategories in a polarized benevolent-hostile manner? When female participants completed this same task, although sexist—as compared with nonsexist—women also evaluated career women less favorably and reported more positive feelings for homemakers, the Benevolent Sexism Scale did not significantly correlate with evaluations of either subcategory. These findings suggest that the sexism of women against other women is not of the polarized variety seen in sexist men, but instead, simply constitutes an expression of hostility toward women who have not adopted traditional feminine roles.

SEXUAL HARASSMENT

One manifestation of sexism of the hostile variety is **sexual harassment,** which is unwelcome physical or verbal sexual overtures that create an intimidating, hostile, or offensive social environment. Sexual harassment is a serious problem in virtually all countries in which women have entered the job market, with a large proportion of women being victimized at least once during their lifetime (Wasti et al., 2000). In the United States, sexual harassment charges against such high-profile public figures as Supreme Court Justice Clarence Thomas and Fox News Commentator Bill O'Reilly have highlighted a common problem in dealing with this issue. Put simply, sexual harassment is not an objective phenomenon: a behavior that is perceived as sexual harassment by one person may be casually shrugged off or viewed positively by others (Houston & Hwang, 1996; Kaiser & Miller, in press). This problem in identifying an incident as harassment is more common among men than among women (Frazier et al., 1995), especially when the incident involves gender-based insults (for example, "You and all other women are stupid") or unwanted sexual attention (for example, persistent flirting or sexual commentary). However, when the behavior in question consists of sexual coercion (for example, "Have sex with me or lose your job"), men are as likely as women to label it as sexual harassment (Burgess & Borgida, 1997).

TABLE 8.4

The Ambivalent Sexism Inventory

Instructions:

Below is a series of statements concerning men and women and their relationships in contemporary society. Please indicate the degree to which you agree or disagree with each statement using the following scale:

0 = Disagree strongly	3 = Agree slightly
1 = Disagree somewhat	4 = Agree somewhat
2 = Disagree slightly	5 = Agree strongly

_____ 1. No matter how accomplished he is, a man is not truly complete as a person unless he has the love of a woman.

_____ 2. Many women are actually seeking special favors, such as hiring policies that favor them over men, under the guise of asking for "equality."

_____ 3. In a disaster, women ought not necessarily be rescued before men.*

_____ 4. Most women interpret innocent remarks as being sexist.

_____ 5. Women are too easily offended.

_____ 6. People are often truly happy in life without being romantically involved with a member of the other sex.*

_____ 7. Feminists are not seeking for women to have more power than men.*

_____ 8. Many women have a quality of purity that few men possess.

_____ 9. Women should be cherished and protected by men.

_____ 10. Most women fail to appreciate fully all that men do for them.

_____ 11. Women seek to gain power by getting control over men.

_____ 12. Every man ought to have a woman whom he adores.

_____ 13. Men are complete without women.*

_____ 14. Women exaggerate problems they have at work.

_____ 15. Once a woman gets a man to commit to her, she usually tries to put him on a tight leash.

_____ 16. When women lose to men in a fair competition, they typically complain about being discriminated against.

_____ 17. A good woman should be set on a pedestal by her man.

_____ 18. There are actually very few women who get a kick out of teasing men by seeming sexually available and then refusing male advances.*

_____ 19. Women, compared with men, tend to have a superior moral sensibility.

_____ 20. Men should be willing to sacrifice their own well-being in order to provide financially for the women in their lives.

_____ 21. Feminists are making entirely reasonable demands of men.*

_____ 22. Women, as compared with men, tend to have a more refined sense of culture and good taste.

Scoring Instructions

Before summing either scale, first reverse the scores for the "" items:*

$$0 = 5, 1 = 4, 2 = 3, 3 = 2, 4 = 1, 5 = 0.$$

Hostile Sexism Scale Score: Add items 2,4,5,7,10,11,14,15,16,18,21

The average score for men is about 29, while the average score for women is about 20. Higher scores indicate greater degrees of hostile sexism.

Benevolent Sexism Scale Score: Add items 1,3,6,8,9,12,13,17,19,20,22

The average score for men is about 28, while the average score for women is about 24. Higher scores indicate greater degrees of benevolent sexism.

Total Ambivalent Sexism Inventory Score: Sum the Hostile Sexism Scale score and the Benevolent Sexism Scale score.

The average score for men is about 57, while the average score for women is about 44. Higher scores indicate greater degrees of ambivalent sexism.

Gender harassment is the least severe and most common form of sexual harassment, and it includes verbal and nonverbal behaviors that convey insulting, hostile, or degrading attitudes toward women. Based on our previous discussion, you will recognize gender harassment as an expression of hostile sexism. Men who are likely to engage in these types of harassing behaviors are those whose male identity has been threatened (Maas et al., 2003). Further, these men are most likely to direct their hostility toward women they perceive as feminists rather than women who conform to traditional gender roles, and they tend to engage in the harassing behavior when other men are present (Dall'Ara & Maas, 2000). Similar to one of the motives underlying heterosexual men's expressions of antigay attitudes (see p. 259), it appears that one of the motives fueling gender harassment is the need for men to reaffirm their heterosexual masculinity in front of other men.

In instances of *sexual coercion*, sexual harassment involves the misuse of power. Although women can be sexual harassers and men can be victims, women are overwhelmingly underrepresented in careers with the organizational power that would allow them to coerce others for sexual favors (Fitzgerald, 1993). Partly for this reason, sexual coercion is a social problem that women are much more likely to face than men. What type of man is most likely to engage in sexual coercion? Research indicates that men who associate sex with social dominance or power are most likely to sexually coerce a coworker (Pryor et al., 1995). Although they engage in sexual coercion, these men generally don't perceive their actions as inappropriate or a misuse of power (Fitzgerald, 1993). One reason for this lack of awareness is that, for these men, the connection between power and sex appears to be automatic and unconscious (Bargh et al., 1995). That is, the sexual harasser's tendency to automatically think in terms of sex in situations in which he has power blinds him to the inappropriate nature of his behavior.

One way in which power and sex may become associated in the harasser's own thought processes is through the type of behaviors exhibited in dominant-subservient role relationships. That is, subordinates typically treat power holders in a friendly, appreciative, and sometimes even worshipful manner (Jones, 1964). Instead of attributing the cause for these behaviors to their more powerful social role, harassers interpret such actions by female subordinates as indicating sexual attraction (Fiske, 1993). This tendency, coupled with the fact that men generally tend to misperceive a woman's friendliness as indicating sexual interest (see chapter 12, p. 457), creates a work environment where harassers often respond with unwelcomed sexual overtures (Stockdale, 1993).

Despite the negative impact sexual harassment has on their lives, most victims do not report these incidents, especially when the harassers are powerful men (Paludi & Barickman, 1991). Rather than seeking help from superiors within the organization, most women seek support from female friends and family members. In the United States, this is more true among Hispanic American women than their Anglo American counterparts (Cortina, 2004; Wasti & Cortina, 2002). The greater reluctance among Hispanic women to file a formal complaint may be due to "sexual silence" norms in Hispanic culture that discourage women from discussing sexual topics (Marin & Gomez, 1995). Finally, in addition to these restraints, victims of all ethnic and social backgrounds are often reluctant to report sexual harassment because all too often the charges are ignored or the offenders are given only token reprimands (Fitzgerald et al., 1995, 1997). One woman described her multiple experiences with sexual harassment on the job in the following way: "I lost or was forced out of my job each time, while my respective harassers are busily laying, tormenting, embarrassing, or firing people as we speak."

WHAT ABOUT SEXISM EXPRESSED BY WOMEN AGAINST MEN?

Similar to the greater acceptability of racial prejudice expressed by minority groups toward Whites, it is generally more acceptable in American society for women to express sexist attitudes toward men than vice versa. This is so, because in an egalitarian society, higher-status groups—such as men and Whites—are more likely to be considered fair game for criticism. In contrast, because low-status groups—such as women and minorities—have historically been the targets of discrimination by the higher-status groups, criticism of them is much more likely to call into question the critics' egalitarian credentials. What do social scientists know about the often overlooked expression of sexism by women against men?

One important finding is that just as men's sexism can be described as ambivalent, women also appear to simultaneously hold positive and negative attitudes about men (Glick & Fiske, 1999; Jackson et al., 2001). In childhood, girls exhibit signs of intergender hostility even before boys. Their antiboy attitudes may develop because of the frustration they often experience when interacting with boys, whose dominant play style of grabbing what they want and not taking turns clashes with girls' more polite style of asking for things and sharing play opportunities (Maccoby, 1990). Regardless of whether these conflicting play styles are due to biology, gender socialization, or some combination of the two, the greater power that boys exert in these cross-gender interactions creates resentment of that power among girls. Peter Glick and Lori Hilt (2000) suggest that this hostility represents an early-childhood version of many women's later resentment of patriarchy. Thus, just as patriarchal systems foster the expression of hostile sexism by men, they also create a similar intergender hostility in women.

During adolescence, as heterosexual teenagers grow increasingly interested in members of the other sex as romantic partners, the resulting emotional ties foster the development of benevolent attitudes (Glick & Fiske, 1996). The fact that male power in society can sometimes be used to protect and provide for women's welfare also contributes to the development of benevolent attitudes in both women and men. However, although both men and women develop benevolent attitudes toward the other sex, research suggests that women express much less benevolence than men (Glick & Fiske, 1999). Indeed, women's overall sexist attitudes toward men appear to be more hostile than benevolent, while men's overall sexist attitudes toward women are more clearly ambivalent, with levels of hostility and benevolence being fairly equal. The greater hostility expressed by women, as compared with men, may reflect the more negative experiences that women tend to have during intergender exchanges throughout their lives. This greater negativity is likely caused both by the frustration that women often experience due to men's more dominant interaction style, and by the fact that women are more likely than men to be the targets of sexual harassment and everyday sexism (Fitzgerald, 1993; Fitzgerald et al., 1997; Swim et al., 2001).

Like racism, sexism is a complex social problem. Although both men and women hold sexist attitudes and engage in sexist behavior, the ambivalent attitudes constituting male-initiated and female-initiated sexism are different. Current social psychological research suggests that these gender differences in expressing benevolence and hostility toward the other sex are best understood in terms of the respective historical roles that men and women have played as oppressors and oppressed. As a contemporary "actor" in this ongoing gender drama, you now have a better understanding of the social psychological dynamics surrounding sexism. With this knowledge, you are better equipped to redefine gender relations in your own life so that sexism is less problematic for you and for future generations.

SECTION SUMMARY

- Old-fashioned racism has declined and been largely replaced by *aversive racism*, which is a combination of both positive and negative beliefs and feelings about a racial group

- Blacks' and other minority groups' racial attitudes toward Whites originate primarily from perceptions of threat or conflict and their reaction to White racism

- Sexism is best conceptualized as involving *ambivalence*, based on both hostility and benevolence

- Sexual harassment can involve gender harassment, unwanted sexual attention, or sexual coercion

CAN WE REDUCE PREJUDICE AND DISCRIMINATION?

Having analyzed the psychological and social mechanisms underlying intergroup intolerance, let us now explore the prospects for reducing prejudice and discrimination. First, we examine whether changing people's thinking can reduce prejudice (an *individual-based approach*), and then we outline situational factors necessary to reduce intergroup intolerance (a *group-based approach*). Finally, the chapter ends with a brief look at two social psychological attempts to remedy some of the negative consequences of prejudice and discrimination in our educational system.

Social Scientists Differ on Whether Stereotyped Thinking Can Be Changed

Because prejudice and discrimination are often based on stereotypical thinking, some experts have suggested that positive changes can occur if people make a conscious effort to think more rationally and deductively. Others argue that such efforts are futile. Let's briefly explore both viewpoints, beginning with the more pessimistic perspective that stereotyped thinking cannot be changed.

ONE VIEW: STEREOTYPING IS INEVITABLE

A number of social scientists believe that stereotyped thinking is an adaptive mental strategy that has allowed us to survive as a species (Fox, 1992, Vaes et al., 2003). They contend that due to our biological makeup, we are locked in stereotyped thinking and there is no magic key to help us escape this particular cognitive domain. According to anthropologist Robert Fox, sensitivity training, consciousness raising, and even taking a social psychology course will not remove stereotyping from our daily thought processes.

> The whole point of this argument has been to show that we have no choice but to think in stereotypes. That is what a lot of basic thinking is. What is more, we are comfortable with such stereotyping, and our better selves only deplore the fact when some particular stereotype lacks social approval or conflicts with our current moralistic stereotyping. As long as it does not, we are happy to sink into it. Thus, in certain circles, "All big corporations are polluters" would not be challenged, whereas "all gay men are untrustworthy" would evoke

Are stereotyping and prejudice inevitable? Some social scientists believe that because stereotyping is often an automatic process, prejudiced thinking cannot be changed. Others contend that prejudice can be reduced by monitoring stereotypical thinking. What role do personal values play in successfully reducing prejudice? Can personal values actually fuel prejudice and discrimination?

horror. In other circles, of course, this would be reversed . . . as long as perceivable differences exist, we can only hope constantly to revise our stereotypes in a more favorable direction, not try to outlaw what is evidently not a disease of the mind but part of its basic constitution. We have to come to terms with the idea that prejudice is not a form of thinking but that thinking is a form of prejudice. (Fox, 1992, pp. 149, 151)

Although thinking in terms of stereotypes may be an automatic and inevitable process, and while it also is often socially beneficial, these advantages can, at times, be outweighed by the negative consequences of unmonitored stereotypical thinking. As we have already discussed, many stereotypes about various outgroups contain unflattering and demeaning characteristics. When they become activated, they can result in harmful biasing effects toward outgroup members who possess none of the objectionable qualities ascribed to their group. One of the disturbing possible implications of describing stereotyping as natural and inevitable is that it might appear to condone the prejudice and discrimination resulting from negative stereotypes. That is, some might conclude that we cannot—and we *should not*—do anything to change a type of thinking that helps us survive.

ANOTHER VIEW: STEREOTYPING CAN BE MONITORED

Not surprisingly, a number of social psychologists reject this conclusion. Michael Billig (1985), for example, argues that emphasizing categorization as the only useful and adaptive thought process in social cognition provides a one-sided account of human thinking. Although categorizing most certainly is useful, Billig contends that to *differentiate* between things within a given category is also useful. He asserts that it is too simplistic to think that it is always in a person's best interest to merely categorize.

Consistent with Billig's analysis, Patricia Devine and Margo Monteith (1999) believe that people can circumvent stereotypical thinking if they make a conscious effort to use more rational, inductive strategies. That is, even though individuals may have *knowledge* of a stereotype and may have relied on it in the past to make social judgments, their current *personal beliefs* may no longer be in agreement with the stereotype. Due to this change in circumstances, instead of making judgments based on the stereotype, they may now consciously decide to rely on their own personal beliefs (Monteith, 1993; Monteith et al., 1998).

For example, imagine that Clayton has grown up being taught that women are intellectually inferior to men. However, during the course of his life, Clayton has been exposed to people who do not fit this gender stereotype. Because of these experiences, as well as his desire to perceive himself as nonsexist, Clayton may begin to adopt a more egalitarian view of women. Although Clayton no longer accepts this stereotype, he has not eliminated it from his memory. Quite the contrary. During his relearning process, this stereotype remains a well-organized, frequently activated cognitive structure, and it is more accessible than his newly adopted personal beliefs. In fact, Clayton's unwanted stereotype will be most on his mind precisely when he is with women and feeling most anxious about saying the wrong thing (Lambert et al., 2003). In a very real sense, for a person like Clayton, censoring the negative stereotype and guarding against ingroup biasing takes conscious and deliberate attention—like trying to break a bad habit. As you may recall from chapter 6 (pp. 193–194), habits involve a good deal of automatic and unthinking responses, and because of this, they are often difficult to break. For people like Clayton, although the unwanted stereotype will likely be automatically activated as soon as he encounters a woman, the good news is that this stereotype is likely to become deactivated the longer the interaction continues (Kunda et al., 2002). This suggests that cognitively guarding against unwanted stereotypes is most important during the initial phases of an encounter with a person from the stereotyped group.

Figure 8.9 outlines how self-awareness and self-regulation (see chapter 3) may play a role in reducing prejudiced responses. Continuing with our example, whenever Clayton encounters a woman, the gender stereotype is involuntarily activated. If he does not consciously monitor his thoughts, he may automatically slip back into acting as though women were the intellectual inferiors of men (a *discrepant response*). Becoming aware of this discrepancy in his actions,

FIGURE 8.9

Reducing Prejudiced Responding Through Self-Regulation

According to Devine (1989) and Monteith (1993), when low prejudiced persons first begin to try to respond in a nonprejudiced manner toward previously denigrated outgroup members, stereotype activation often spontaneously triggers a discrepant (i.e., prejudiced) response, which subsequently triggers a series of discrepancy-associated consequences. This cognitive process is depicted by the arrows running vertically from top to bottom in the left side of the figure. Over time, through careful self-regulation of one's thoughts and attention to one's nonprejudiced standards, low prejudiced people break the "prejudice habit" and respond as depicted by the horizontal arrows at the top of the figure. If this model accurately describes how prejudiced behavior can be eliminated, what would be the first step you would need to take to reduce your own prejudiced responding?

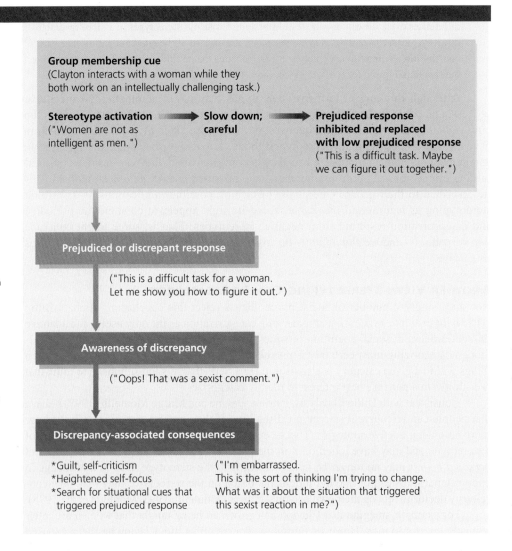

Group membership cue
(Clayton interacts with a woman while they both work on an intellectually challenging task.)

Stereotype activation → **Slow down;** → **Prejudiced response**
("Women are not as   **careful**   **inhibited and replaced**
intelligent as men.")   **with low prejudiced response**
                                                 ("This is a difficult task. Maybe
                                                 we can figure it out together.")

Prejudiced or discrepant response

("This is a difficult task for a woman.
Let me show you how to figure it out.")

Awareness of discrepancy

("Oops! That was a sexist comment.")

Discrepancy-associated consequences

*Guilt, self-criticism   ("I'm embarrassed.
*Heightened self-focus   This is the sort of thinking I'm trying to change.
*Search for situational cues that   What was it about the situation that triggered
 triggered prejudiced response   this sexist reaction in me?")

Clayton will experience *discrepancy-associated consequences.* These include feelings of guilt and self-criticism that will in turn motivate him to heighten his self-awareness and search for situational cues that may have spontaneously triggered this prejudiced response (Hing et al., 2002; Zuwerink et al., 1996). Through such attentiveness to prejudice-triggering cues, Clayton will slowly build up self-regulatory mechanisms that should produce more controlled and careful responses on future occasions (Kawakami et al., 2000; Monteith et al., 2002).

The importance of Devine and Monteith's perspective for reducing prejudice and discrimination is that it does not assume that prejudice is an inevitable consequence of the natural process of social categorization (Devine et al., 2002). People can avoid prejudiced responding (that is, discrimination) if low-prejudiced standards are central to their self-concept *and* they bring these standards to mind before acting. Thus, although automatic stereotype activation makes nonprejudiced responding difficult, research indicates that people can inhibit such intolerance through conscious and deliberate self-regulation (Blair et al., 2001; Gordijn et al., 2004; Rudman et al., 2001). However, the biggest stumbling block in unlearning prejudicial responding is that, as we discovered in chapter 3 (pp. 62–64), many people do not spontaneously engage in the self-awareness necessary to think about their own personal nonprejudiced standards (Monteith, 1996). If they do not think about these standards, there will be no guilt and internal conflict when they respond in a prejudicial manner. Yet if people do engage in self-awareness, they can learn to avoid using stereotypes in their social judgments (Kawakami et al., 2000).

A further implication of Devine and Monteith's perspective is that it draws some necessary boundaries around the pervasiveness of aversive racism among White Americans (refer back to pp. 285-288): not all Whites are desperately trying to hide their racial prejudices from themselves and others. Indeed, this perspective contends that many people, regardless of their race, sex, or sexual orientation, are motivated and consciously attempt to develop nonprejudicial thinking (Plant & Devine, 1998). Although it is not easy, and although it will undoubtedly induce instances of guilt and self-criticism, with conscious effort, prejudicial thinking can be reduced if you internalize egalitarian values and norms into your self-concept.

This perspective also holds out hope for reducing prejudice even among aversive racists. However, the cognitive hurdle here is that, unlike people who recognize that they sometimes engage in prejudiced thinking, aversive racists are convinced they are nonprejudiced, so they believe there is no need to monitor their thoughts for bias. How can their prejudiced thinking be reduced without them engaging in careful self-regulation? The answer is that someone else must point out to aversive racists the inconsistencies between their explicit and implicit attitudes, at least initially. Research by Leanne Son Hing and her coworkers (2002) indicates that when aversive racists are confronted with evidence exposing their hidden biases they tend to experience guilt and make conscious efforts to behave in a nonprejudiced manner. In essence, other people are playing the self-regulatory role for aversive racists, raising their consciousness and prompting them to reduce their prejudicial thinking and behavior.

The Contact Hypothesis Identifies Social Conditions That Can Reduce Intergroup Conflict

At the time of the original U.S. Supreme Court *Brown v. Board of Education* decision on school desegregation, Gordon Allport (1954) outlined how desegregation might reduce racial prejudice. Later, other social psychologists also contributed to what came to be known as the **contact hypothesis** (Amir, 1969; Hewstone, 1996). The contact hypothesis can be thought of as a blueprint for reducing hostility between groups that have had a history of conflict by manipulating situational variables. According to this perspective, intergroup contact will decrease hostility when specific situational conditions are met (refer to table 8.5).

EQUAL SOCIAL STATUS

The first necessary condition is that the groups interacting must be roughly *equal in social status*. When this condition is not met and traditional status imbalances are maintained, long-standing stereotypes that are largely based on status discrepancies are generally not revised (Gaertner & Dovidio, 2000). However, research indicates that when equal-status people from different racial and ethnic groups interact, such as soldiers in the U.S. Armed Services, racial stereotyping and prejudices decline (Pettigrew, 1969).

SUSTAINED CLOSE CONTACT

The second condition is that the two groups must have *sustained close contact*. Several public-housing studies conducted in the 1940s and 1950s demonstrated the importance of this condition in reducing prejudice. Reflecting on these social experiments in racial integration, Stuart Cook stated:

> One of the clearest findings of studies on the relation between intergroup contact and attitude change is that, while individuals rather quickly come to accept and even approve of association with members of another social group in situations of the type where they have experienced such association, this approval is not likely to be generalized to other situations unless the individuals have quite close personal relationships with members of the other group. (Cook, 1964, pp. 41–42)

Similarly, survey studies and field experiments in France, Great Britain, Germany, Finland, and the Netherlands confirm that intergroup friendships significantly reduce both subtle and blatant prejudice (Hewstone, 2003; Liebkind & McAlister, 1999; Pettigrew, 1997; van Dick et al., 2004). The sustained close contact necessary to reduce prejudice does not even have to be something that one directly experiences: simply knowing that some of your ingroup members

Contact Hypothesis

The theory that under certain conditions, direct contact between antagonistic groups will reduce prejudice.

Only equals can be friends.

Ethiopian proverb

You cannot judge another person until you have walked a mile in his moccasins.

American Indian proverb

TABLE 8.5

Reducing Prejudice Through Social Contact

Now that you have learned how to develop an individual program to reduce your own prejudice (refer back to figure 8.9), let's now set to work on reducing prejudice on a group level. According to the original contact hypothesis, intergroup prejudice can be reduced if the first four conditions listed below are met. Recently, Thomas Pettigrew has suggested a fifth necessary condition, friendship potential. Think about intergroup hostilities on your own college campus or in your local community. Perhaps this conflict involves men and women, gays and heterosexuals, or people from different racial groups. How could you develop a "Tolerance Campaign" utilizing these conditions?

Four Necessary Conditions in the Original Contact Hypothesis

1. *Equal Social Status:* Members of groups in conflict should interact in settings where everyone has roughly equal status.

2. *Sustained Close Contact:* Interaction between members of different groups should be one-on-one and should be maintained over an extended period of time.

3. *Intergroup Cooperation:* Members of different groups should engage in joint activities to achieve superordinate goals.

4. *Social Norms Favoring Equality:* There must be a clear social perception, largely fostered by group authority figures, that prejudice and discrimination are not condoned.

A Fifth Necessary Conditon in the Reformulated Contact Hypothesis

Friendship Potential: Developing friendships with outgroup members precipitates initial reductions in intergroup tensions and fosters emotional ties that are important in reducing prejudice over time.

And if a house be divided against itself, that house cannot stand.

The New Testament, Mark, 3:24–25

Let's go hand in hand, not one before another.

William Shakespeare, English dramatist and poet, 1564–1616

Social Sense

View a presentation on social contact and prejudice reduction.

have outgroup friends is often sufficient to reduce prejudice toward that outgroup (Wright et al., 1997). One likely reason school desegregation has not produced a significant reduction in racial prejudice is that students of different races generally avoid interacting with one another. That is, even though the school building is integrated, students segregate themselves on the bus and playground, and in the cafeteria and classroom. School officials often magnify the problem by separating students based on academic achievement, which results in advantaged White students and disadvantaged minority students having very little classroom contact (Epstein, 1985). One type of school activity that is fairly effective in reducing racial prejudice is team sports. When sports teams have a high percentage of minority athletes, there is a decrease in intergroup intolerance among the participants (Brown et al., 2003). View the presentation on your Social Sense CD-ROM for an example of how the close sustained contact in the masculine sport of football facilitated the acceptance of a teammate's homosexuality.

INTERGROUP COOPERATION

A third condition that can help reduce hostility is *intergroup cooperation.* As the Robbers Cave experiment demonstrated, animosity between the Rattlers and the Eagles subsided when they engaged in a joint activity to achieve mutually shared goals (*superordinate goals*). Similar results have been obtained in a variety of experimental and field settings, including school, work, and the armed forces (Desforges et al., 1997). One possible reason why cooperation reduces intergroup bias and hostility is that cooperating members of different social groups appear to cognitively *recategorize* one another into a new ingroup (Gaertner & Dovidio, 2000).

SOCIAL NORMS FAVORING EQUALITY

The fourth condition for successful conflict reduction is that there must be in place *social norms favoring equality* (Monteith et al., 1996). As demonstrated in chapter 6, social norms have a significant effect on determining people's behavioral intentions. Here is where au-

thority figures and group leaders play a pivotal role. If they publicly state support for equality, others are likely to follow their lead. If they oppose intergroup contact, prejudice reduction is unlikely (Crandall et al., 2002; Cook, 1984). This is one of the principal reasons why lesbians and gay men in the armed services continue to run the very real risk of physical and psychological abuse at the hands of fellow soldiers if their sexual orientation is revealed. Many of their superiors up the chain of command have consistently not favored acceptance or even tolerance for homosexual enlisted personnel (Herek, 2003). On the other hand, race, sex, and even sexual orientation tensions have been successfully defused in many work environments when supervisors make it clear that prejudicial statements and discriminatory actions will not be tolerated.

A FIFTH NECESSARY CONDITION?

Meta-analysis of numerous studies testing Allport's contact hypothesis indicate that intergroup contact, under the proper conditions, does indeed have a substantial effect in reducing prejudice toward outgroups (Pettigrew & Tropp, (2000). Based on the results of these studies, Thomas Pettigrew (1998) offered a reformulated version of the contact hypothesis, in which he added a fifth situational factor necessary for prejudice reduction, namely, *friendship potential.* Pettigrew argued that developing friendships with outgroup members is not only important in precipitating the initial reduction in intergroup tensions, but fostering these emotional ties becomes increasingly important in reducing prejudice over time. This reformulated model has received some empirical support (Carlson et al., 2003; Gaertner et al., 2000; Wagner et al., 2003). See the Featured Study for a description of one of these investigations.

BEYOND THE CONTACT HYPOTHESIS

One criticism of the contact hypothesis has been its overemphasis on changing the dominant group's prejudicial attitudes, while ignoring the attitudes of minority group members (Devine et al., 1996). To more effectively promote intergroup harmony, social scientists must also consider (1) the attitudes and beliefs of minority group members, and (2) the beliefs and anxieties of everyone involved in intergroup contact. For example, according to this perspective, during intergroup contact, minority group members may feel anxious because they fear being victimized and negatively evaluated (refer back to the *stereotype threat* discussion, pp. 271–274), while dominant group members may be anxious from fear of saying or doing something that might be interpreted as a sign of prejudice (Blascovich et al., 2001a; Shelton, 2003). The combined effect of this **intergroup anxiety** often creates difficulties in such social encounters, even in the absence of any real prejudicial attitudes (Hebl et al., 2000; Plant & Devine, 2003). Among low prejudiced individuals, those who have had very limited contact with the outgroup are the ones most likely to experience intergroup anxiety (Blair et al., 2003; Brown et al., 2001).

Most of the bigoted remarks I have heard and prejudice I have experienced came from people who were trying to be popular, not despised. They were following what they believed to be acceptable behavior in their group or sub-group, not deviating from it.

Clarence Page, U.S. author and social commentator, b. 1947

Progress is a nice word, but change is its motivator. And change has its enemies.

Robert Kennedy, U.S. senator, 1925–1968

Intergroup Anxiety

Anxiety due to anticipating negative consequences when interacting with an outgroup member.

> *If we accept and acquiesce in the face of discrimination, we accept the responsibility ourselves and allow those responsible to salve their conscience by believing that they have our acceptance and concurrence. . . . We should therefore, protest openly every-thing . . . that smacks of discrim-ination.*
>
> Mary McLeod Bethune, U.S. educator and civil rights activist, 1875–1955

When people experience this anxiety during intergroup exchanges, they often adopt a *protective self-presentation style,* in which they focus on trying not to make a bad impression, rather than trying to make a good one. Thus, they might talk less and generally act more cautiously than less anxious individuals. This strategy can backfire, however, because their outgroup partners may interpret their reticence as hostility. The good news is that if people place themselves in intergroup situations and have positive or even neutral contact with outgroup members, their intergroup anxiety will decrease (Britt et al., 1996; Hyers & Swim, 1998; Plant, 2004).

In the final analysis, no single strategy eliminates prejudice and discrimination from the vocabulary of intergroup relations (Aboud & Levy, 2000). Because of the manner in which we as a species process information from our social world, and because of the importance we place on our group affiliations, we will always need to be attentive to the way we judge others. Although there is nothing inherently wrong with social stereotyping, it can easily diminish our ability to see the shared humanity in those who fall outside the favored category of "we."

SECTION SUMMARY

- Social scientists differ in their opinion of whether people can stop stereotypical and prejudicial thinking
- Contact hypothesis identifies four conditions to reduce prejudice:

    Equal status interaction

    Intergroup cooperation

    Sustained close contact

    Social norms favoring equality

- A reformulated version of the contact hypothesis adds a fifth condition: friend-ship potential
- Intergroup anxiety hinders the development of greater understanding between conflicted social groups

FEATURED STUDY

INTERGROUP CONTACT, FRIENDSHIP, AND PREJUDICE REDUCTION

Eller, A., & Abrams, D. (2004). Come together: Longitudinal comparisons of Pettigrew's reformulated intergroup contact model and the common ingroup identity model in Anglo-French and Mexican-American contexts. *European Journal of Social Psychology, 34,* 229–256.

The present investigation involved two longitudinal field studies that primarily examined Pettigrew's (1998) reformulated model of the contact hypothesis. Both the original theory (Allport, 1954) and the reformulated model propose that intergroup contact will have positive effects on prejudice reduction when certain conditions are met. One of the goals of the present investigation was to determine how successful

Pettigrew's model would be in predicting prejudice reduction among people from groups with past histories of conflict. A second goal was to determine whether intergroup contact may have different prejudice-reducing effects in the short term than over the longer term.

Pettigrew's (1998) reformulation of Gordon Allport's contact hypothesis added a fifth situational factor necessary for prejudice reduction, namely, *friendship potential.* Pettigrew further argued that there are four processes that mediate prejudice reduction through contact: *learning about the outgroup, changing behavior, generating emotional ties,* and *ingroup reappraisal.* Finally, Pettigrew contended that intergroup contact will be most successful if the interacting members engage in different types of cognitive categorization of one another during different stages of contact. It is best during the early stages of contact if people *decategorize* outgroup members by interacting with them as individuals and not being concerned about their group membership. During the middle stage of intergroup contact, Pettigrew asserts that it is best if the interacting members engage in *salient categorization,* in which they recognize that they belong to different groups while learning to appreciate their interesting differences. Then, during the latter stages of intergroup contact, Pettigrew states that it is desirable if people engage in *recategorization,* in which they perceive themselves as sharing an overarching group membership with outgroup members. Recategorization is assumed to induce a maximum reduction in prejudice.

Method

The first study examined the effects of intergroup contact between British and French students at the University of Kent in England, the closest British university to France and a university with a rather high percentage of French citizens enrolled as students. In political and military terms, France constitutes Britain's oldest enemy. Despite recent alliances between these two countries, the attitudes of the British toward the French remain at best ambivalent. In Study 1, all ninety participants were both first-year students and English citizens who completed questionnaires at the beginning of the academic year and again six months later. The majority of the participants probably had minimal contact with citizens from France prior to arriving on campus. All students received course credit for their participation. The questionnaires completed by participants measured a host of attitudes, beliefs, and behaviors, including participants' level of identification as British citizens, their amount and quality of contact with French people at the university, their degree of intergroup anxiety when interacting with French people, their attitudes and beliefs about the French in general, and their degree of exposure to French culture.

The second study examined the effects of intergroup contact between Mexican and American employees of multinational corporations in Mexico. Similar to the Anglo-French context, Mexican American relations have been historically conflicted, with Mexicans' attitudes toward Americans being deeply ambivalent. In Study 2, 207 Mexicans working for multinational corporations mostly located in Mexico City completed questionnaires at their workplaces, with 87 of them completing the questionnaires again two years later. Participation was voluntary, with a $50 prize given to one participant in a later drawing. The questionnaires completed by the Mexican respondents were similar to those completed by the British students in Study 1. The translation of the questionnaire from English into Spanish was conducted by two native speakers of Spanish who were fluent in English, and it was back-translated by a bilingual person living in Mexico.

Results and Discussion

The general finding from these two longitudinal field studies was that contact in two different intergroup settings does have beneficial effects when it is characterized by friendship. In Study 1, British students who had more contact as friends with French students expressed less social distance toward the French, exhibited more learning about the French people, and engaged in more "pro-French" behavior than British students who had less of this friendship contact. Further, the longitudinal data indicated that contact with French students as friends significantly reduced British students' intergroup anxiety and led to significantly more positive attitudes toward the French people. Similarly, in Study 2, Mexicans who had more contact as friends with American coworkers expressed less social distance and greater emotional ties toward Americans, exhibited more learning about the American people, and engaged in more "pro-American" behavior than Mexicans who had less friendship contact. Further, over time, contact as friends with Americans significantly reduced Mexicans' social distance and led to significantly more positive attitudes toward Americans. Together, these results suggest that developing friendships with outgroup members is not only important in precipitating the initial reduction in intergroup tensions, but fostering these emotional ties becomes increasingly important in reducing prejudice over time. These findings are consistent with Pettigrew's reformulation of the contact hypothesis.

In addition, results also suggested that during the initial stages of intergroup contact, learning about the outgroup and behaving in a friendlier manner toward outgroup members were important in reducing prejudice. The researchers suggest that learning about the outgroup may have dispelled negative stereotypes, while acting friendlier toward outgroup members may have precipitated a shift toward more favorable attitudes that were consistent with this friendlier behavior. Regarding the form of categorization employed with respect to outgroup members at different phases of contact, decategorization was found to be the predominant categorization mode among the British students both early and later in their intergroup contact with French students, with recategorization being the second-most-common mode and salient categorization the least-common mode.

Among the Mexican participants, the dominant categorization mode at both time points was a combination of salient categorization and recategorization, in which the Mexican and American group identities were maintained within the context of an overarching inclusive group identity (the so-called dual identity). The researchers suggest that these differences in the categorization modes used by British and Mexican participants may be due to the fact that the British students' contact with their French counterparts was likely to be at its initial stages, while Mexican workers' contact with their American colleagues might have been at a more advanced stage. Alternatively, this difference might be due to the different status relationships represented in the two samples. English and French people have roughly equal levels of social status throughout the world, whereas Americans hold a higher-status position than Mexicans. Previous research has shown that lower-status group members favor a dual identity level of categorization. Although these findings are not entirely consistent with Pettigrew's model, the lack of consistency may be due to these societal factors or to limitations in the study's samples rather than problems with the theory.

One set of unexpected results from the longitudinal data in Study 2 was that Mexicans expressed heightened social distance and less positive general attitudes toward American the more they learned about American culture. The researchers suggest that this finding might reflect some kind of cultural resentment due to the saturation of American culture in Mexico: the more Mexicans learn about U.S. culture through films, newspapers, television, and the Internet, the less they like the objects of these portrayals.

Finally, this research represents one of the few longitudinal investigations of prejudice reduction and revealed that the causal direction of Pettigrew's model was largely supported. Future research needs to further analyze other factors that might strengthen or undermine beneficial intergroup contact.

APPLICATIONS

HOW CAN OUR SCHOOLS BOTH REDUCE INTERGROUP CONFLICT AND PROMOTE ACADEMIC ACHIEVEMENT?

*I*n 1971, Elliot Aronson was asked by the superintendent of the Austin, Texas, schools to devise a plan to reduce interracial tensions in the recently desegregated classrooms. After observing student interaction, Aronson realized that the social dynamics were strikingly similar to those described by Sherif in the Robbers Cave field experiment (refer back to pp. 277–279). Using that study and the contact hypothesis as guides, he and his colleagues developed a cooperative learning technique that came to be called the

Jigsaw Classroom

A cooperative group-learning technique designed to reduce prejudice and raise self-esteem.

jigsaw classroom (Aronson et al., 1978; Aronson & Thibodeau, 1992). The technique was so named because students had to cooperate in "piecing together" their daily lessons, much the way a jigsaw puzzle is assembled. Ten fifth-grade classrooms were introduced to this technique, and three additional classes served as control groups.

In the jigsaw classroom, students were placed in six-person, racially and academically mixed learning groups. The day's lesson was divided into six subtopics, and each student was responsible for learning one piece of this lesson and then teaching it to the other group members. With the lesson divided up in this manner, cooperation was essential for success. In contrast to traditional classroom learning, in which students compete against one another, the jigsaw classroom promoted superordinate goals. It also promoted racial harmony. Compared with students in the control classrooms in which traditional learning techniques were employed, students in the jigsaw groups showed a decrease in prejudice and an increase in liking for one another. Their liking for school also improved, as did their level of self-esteem. The cooperative learning also improved minority students' academic test scores, while White students' scores remained the same.

Since these studies were first conducted and reported meta-analysis of the results from similar cooperative classroom settings have found that the jigsaw method offers a promising way to improve race relations in desegregated schools by breaking down the "outgroup" barriers that drive a cognitive and emotional wedge between students (Miller & Davidson-Podgorny, 1987).

Another common social problem in academic settings is the failure of many minority students to perform up to their intellectual potential. For example, African American college students tend to underachieve academically, even when their college equivalency scores are equal to those of White students (Neisser et al., 1996). Based on our previous discussion of stereotype threat, this underachievement may be partly caused by two factors. First, the anxiety and/or extra cognitive burden associated with stereotype threat may directly impair Black students' academic achievement (Blascovich et al., 2001b). Second, following repeated instances of this anxiety-induced underperformance, many students may disidentify with academic achievement so that it is no longer important to their self-esteem.

To counteract these two negative effects of stereotype threat, social psychologists have been instrumental in developing a new—and still evolving—educational approach, known as *"wise" schooling*. An important component in wise schooling is to provide students with critical feedback concerning their academic progress in a manner that does not induce stereotype threat. Thus, instead of offering students stigmatizing remedial help, which often only reinforces doubts they may have about their intelligence and academic ability, wise schooling invites minority students to participate in a racially integrated and intellectually challenging learning program. Often working cooperatively, students receive the message that regardless of their current skill level, they have the ability to reach their academic potential. This message is

another important component in wise schooling: intelligence is not fixed and unchanging, but rather, through hard work it is expandable.

Beyond reducing stereotype threat, one impediment to improving the academic performance of members of historically stigmatized groups is convincing them that critical feedback regarding their academic efforts is not motivated by prejudice (Steele et al., 2002). African American students who enter college with high expectations of race-based rejection are more likely to perceive themselves as targets of discrimination on campus (Mendoza-Denton et al., 2002). How do such perceptions of race-based bias affect these students' academic motivation? In one study investigating this question, Black and White students at Stanford University were given the same critical feedback by a White evaluator about an essay they had written about their favorite teacher (Cohen et al., 1999). Compared with White students, Black students saw the feedback from the White critic as more biased. Seeing it that way, the Black students were less motivated to improve their essays for possible publication in a teaching journal than the White students. These Black students were talented writers, but their incorrect perception of racial prejudice caused them to not take the helpful feedback to heart.

If you consider the perspective of these students, how would you know whether criticism of your academic performance is based on prejudice or not? This is a question White students typically never have to ask. Is there any way over

this academic hurdle? Perhaps. In this same study, researchers found that there was one form of academic feedback that bridged this racial divide: telling students that the academic activity they were engaged in had *very high standards* and that after evaluating their performance the instructor believed that the student could meet those standards with *hard work*. Receiving this form of feedback, Black students perceived no bias and were highly motivated to improve their work. Apparently, this feedback conveyed to the Black students that they were not being judged by negative stereotypes about their group's intellectual abilities.

Research on wise schooling programs among low-income, minority, and female students indicate that, compared with control groups who receive conventional schooling, wise schooling fosters greater enjoyment of the academic process, greater identification with academic achievement and college-based careers, and higher grade point averages among stigmatized groups who are most likely to experience stereotype threat (Aronson et al., 2002; Good et al., 2003; Steele et al., in press). In a very real sense, like stereotype threat, wise schooling is another example of the self-fulfilling prophecy. Yet now, instead of teachers expecting little from their minority students and ultimately having their expectations confirmed when these students fail and drop out of school, teachers in wise schooling programs begin with high expectations and act on that conviction.

John Dovidio (2001) suggests that there have been three "waves" of scholarship in the study of prejudice. The first wave developed after World War II and conceived of prejudice as a form of personal psychopathology. The *authoritarian personality* is this wave's most identifiable theory. The second wave began in the 1950s and approached prejudice as more of a social problem, much like a social cancer that spread from person to person. A number of theories developed from this social perspective, including *realistic group conflict theory,* the *social contact hypothesis,* and *social identity theory.* This second wave, which peaked during the early 1990s, did not consider prejudice to be a manifestation of mental illness. Instead, it was conceptualized as an outgrowth of socialization, normal cognitive processes, and the natural desire to receive rewards and raise self-esteem. Now we are in the third wave of research on prejudice. Here, more attention is paid to understanding unconsciously held prejudicial attitudes, as well as how the targets of intergroup intolerance adapt to and cope with stigmatization. Examples of recent work in this third wave include *implicit prejudice, stereotype threat,* and *ambivalent sexism.* Together, these three research waves have deepened our understanding of how prejudice develops, spreads, and diminishes, as well as what consequences it has for both its targets and perpetrators.

We are far from being a nonprejudiced species. Our natural inclination to categorize people can set the stage for prejudice. It is also true that competition, ingroup loyalties, and social ideologies fan the flames of this tendency to see people as "them" rather than "us" (Lanning, 2002). However, as has been demonstrated throughout this text, our ability to reflect on our actions, our desire to act in ways consistent with our internalized personal beliefs, and our ability to reshape social reality means that prejudice can be reduced. If self-concept is truly a process of identification, what we need to do on an individual level is expand our ingroup identification to include humanity as a whole (Nier et al., 2001). In doing so, we will be able to see ourselves in those who were previously thought of as merely inferior "others." This is by no means an insignificant cognitive shift. As you will discover in chapter 12, when we include others in our self-concept, our resources become theirs to share, and their successes and failures become our own. Therefore, the first step in achieving a community with a low level of prejudice is to monitor our own thinking and action. The second step is to work collectively to change the perceptions of others. The question to ask yourself is whether you are ready to take that first step.

WEB SITES
accessed through http://www.mhhe.com/franzoi4

Web sites for this chapter focus on the nature of prejudice, including an analysis of ethnic stereotypes, sexual harassment, antigay prejudice, the history and psychology of hate crimes, and how to break prejudicial habits.

American Psychological Association

The American Psychological Association has Web pages that explore a number of issues related to prejudice and discrimination. For example, one Web page analyzes whether all of us have some degree of prejudice, as well as the possibility that we can break our prejudicial habits. Another Web page explores the history of hate crimes, including its prevalence, perpetrators, and emotional effects.

American Association of University Women

This Web site of the American Association of University Women has separate sites devoted to sexual harassment (Hostile Hallways: The AAUW Survey on Sexual Harassment in America's Schools) and gender discrimination in education ("Gender Gaps: Where Schools Still Fail Our Children").

Sexual Orientation: Science, Education, and Policy

This Web site features the work of Dr. Gregory Herek, a noted authority on antigay prejudice, and his Northern California Community Research Group. A number of the studies conducted by Herek and this group are cited in the present chapter.

UNDERSTANDING OUR PLACE WITHIN THE GROUP

$\mathcal{W}$e, as individuals, are creatures of the group (Miller & Prentice, 1994). Or, as sociologist George Herbert Mead (1934) pointed out so many years ago, it is the internalization of the group into the mind of the individual that gives us selfhood. Group dynamics are just that— vibrant and ever changing.

Chapter 9 examines how social power is used to influence our thoughts and behavior. How do personal, social, and cultural factors impact conformity? What happens to nonconformists or those who hold minority opinions in groups? How can we get others to comply to our requests? And how susceptible are we to the destructive commands of authority figures?

Chapter 10 looks more closely at the psychology of the group. How does a collection of people become a group? How does the group shape the behavior of individual members? Do groups make more cautious or more risky decisions than individuals? How do leaders emerge in a group, and are there different types of leaders? Finally, what happens when group interests and individual interests conflict?

CHAPTER **9**

Social Influence

CHAPTER OUTLINE

*A*merican Michael Newdow is not a popular person in most social circles. What makes this emergency-room doctor with a law degree so unpopular? Is it because he is a lifelong atheist living in a country where the vast majority of people believe in God and are members of some religious organization? His nonconformity to cultural religious practices certainly deviates from social norms, but most Americans generally tolerate and accept such dissent.

Newdow's unpopularity stems from the fact that he is determined to remove the phrase "under God" from the Pledge of Allegiance. Congress added this phrase to the pledge in 1954 during the height of the cold war to differentiate the United States from communist governments, which were mainly atheist. In defending his position, Newdow cited the clause in the U.S. Constitution that states "Congress shall make no law respecting an establishment of religion." Based on this clause, he filed a lawsuit against his daughter's school district, claiming that the addition of the words *under God* by Congress was unconstitutional. In June 2002, the 9th U.S. Circuit Court of Appeals agreed with him, ruling that the pledge in its present form should be outlawed in public schools. This court ruling created a firestorm of debate around the country and immediately transformed Newdow into a controversial public figure. Even his 9-year-old daughter and his daughter's mother do not support his efforts to change the Pledge. Undaunted, in March 2004, with only two years of legal experience, Newdow personally argued his case before the U.S. Supreme Court. He ultimately lost on a technicality when the Court ruled that Newdow had no legal right to file his claim because he does not have legal custody of his daughter.

Michael Newdow's dissent from the majority and his criticism of a popular cultural ritual opened him up to a great deal of public scorn. Do you think his dissent is trivial and a waste of time? Do you consider his argument of separating religion from government persuasive, or do you find it personally insulting? Why do you think he dissents from the majority? If Newdow lived in France, his minority belief about separating religion from politics would be a commonly held mainstream opinion. In 2004, the French National Assembly and Senate voted by an overwhelming majority to ban the conspicuous wearing of religious symbols—such as Muslim headscarves and Christian crucifixes—in public schools. The French legislation has come under fire from some Muslim, Christian, and human rights groups, including the U.S.-based Commission on International Religious Freedom, which argued that the law could violate international human rights standards. Some French students who oppose this new law contend they will continue to wear their religious symbols to school, even under the threat of fines or expulsion. Do you think their dissent is trivial? Do you perceive their defiance as insulting or praiseworthy? Why do you think they dissent from the majority?

For both Michael Newdow in the United States and the French students who refuse to remove their religious symbols, nonconformity invites social criticism and ridicule. Yet sometimes the risks of dissent are much higher. Consider the case of Farag Fouda, an Egyptian journalist who openly criticized Islamic extremism in the Middle East. Over a fourteen-year period from 1978 to 1992, Fouda defended religious toleration and was among the very first Arab intellectuals to warn against the dangers of the Taliban and Al Qaeda. In 1982, he published his first book championing the resumption of the Egyptian liberal movement that had been interrupted thirty years earlier when the military seized power and adopted a one-party system in his country.

Even though the largest liberal political party in Egypt initially welcomed Fouda and considered him part of a new generation of reformist intellectuals, things quickly changed in 1984 after the party chairman entered into a coalition with Muslim extremists. Fouda, a

Muslim himself, immediately denounced the coalition, arguing that these particular Muslims had clearly been hostile to democracy since 1928. When he failed to persuade the chairman to call off the coalition, Fouda resigned from the party. Over the next eight years, he wrote eight books warning his fellow Arabs about the dangers of religious fundamentalism, including Islamist extremist groups that were attacking art and artists and inciting their followers in universities to ban music concerts and destroy statues. Fouda always warned against mixing religion and politics. He stated, "The worst thing that has plagued our nation is the entrance of the religious scholars into politics, and what this led to in strange opinions and perverted thoughts." In 1992, a week after publicly criticizing Egyptian President Hosni Mubarak for restricting civil liberties, Fouda was assassinated by Muslim militants outside his Cairo office. He paid the ultimate personal price for dissent. Do you think his dissent was trivial and a waste of time? Do you consider his argument of separating religion from politics to have merit, or do you find it personally insulting? Why do you think he dissented from the majority?

WHAT IS SOCIAL INFLUENCE?

Social influence involves the exercise of social power by a person or group to change the attitudes or behavior of others in a particular direction (Cialdini & Goldstein, 2004). Our chapter-opening stories represent social influence involving the intersection of religion and politics, two important areas in many people's lives. In their actions, Newdow and Fouda were nonconformists trying to influence majority opinion concerning the separation of religious practices from governmental functions. In contrast, the dissenting French students were attempting to sway majority opinion in favor of allowing the expression of religious beliefs in a governmental setting.

Although all three cases involve people with minority opinions resisting or trying to change majority members' attitudes and behavior, social influence moves both up and down—and across—the social hierarchy of society. Those who can wield the power of societal institutions typically have much more influence than those outside the power structure (see social dominance theory in chapter 8, p. 280). In this chapter we examine the social psychology of influence in its various forms. Let's begin by identifying and defining the behavioral consequences of social influence.

Social Influence

The exercise of social power by a person or group to change the attitudes or behavior of others in a particular direction.

Sometimes when people dissent from the majority they are dealt with in the harshest of terms. Farag Fouda was an Egyptian journalist who openly criticized Islamic extremism in the Middle East and warned the world about the dangers of the Taliban and al Qaeda. A week after criticizing the Egyptian government for restricting civil liberties, Fouda was shot to death by Muslim extremists.

Three Behavioral Consequences of Social Influence Are Conformity, Compliance, and Obedience

Conformity

A yielding to perceived group pressure by copying the behavior and beliefs of others

Independence

Not being subject to control by others.

Compliance

Publicly acting in accord with a direct request.

Social psychologists typically identify three main behavioral consequences of social influence. The first consequence that we will examine is **conformity,** which is a yielding to perceived group pressure by copying the behavior and beliefs of others. To what degree do you conform to others' social influence? Consider the clothing you wear, the food you eat, the music you prefer, the religion you practice, and so on. How are these areas of your life influenced by the social standards of your friends, family, and larger culture? How about when you yawn after seeing someone else do so? Is this imitative response an example of conformity? What about when actively defying a particular group's influence? Are you then acting independently or are you simply conforming to another group's standards?

Sometimes it's difficult, if not impossible, to distinguish conformity from independence. Even though the former is a yielding to group standards and **independence** is being free of others' control, they often result in the same behavioral outcomes. We discuss this issue and many others in more detail later in the chapter.

The second behavioral consequence of social influence is **compliance,** which is publicly acting in accord with a direct request. In compliance, people responding to a direct request may privately agree or disagree with the action they are engaging in, or they may have no opinion about their behavior. Complying with a request upon which you have no personal attitude is not uncommon. Do you really think about what passing the salt to a dinner companion implies about your relationship with this person or your own values? Probably not. You simply comply out of habit. Now, consider for a moment a cultural ritual that you have probably engaged in on numerous occasions, namely, singing your country's national anthem. Being asked to stand and sing the national anthem during public ceremonies and before sporting events illustrates compliance. Prior to the terrorist attacks on September 11, 2001, many Americans stood and sang the "The Star-Spangled Banner" without considering the meaning of their actions. To them, it was a ritual they habitually complied with before all sporting events, and they did so in a mindless fashion (Langer, 1989). Following September 11th, however many Americans' previous mindless compliance to singing this song became decidedly mindful.

Have you ever granted a friend's request to copy your homework even though you believed it was the wrong thing to do? This *external compliance*—acting in accord with a direct request despite privately disagreeing with it—occurs because we are concerned how others might respond if we refuse them (Deutsch & Gerard, 1955; Tyler, 1997). On the other hand, we often comply with a request because we have a personal allegiance to the values and principles associated with it. Such *internal compliance* (or *internalization*) involves both acting and believing in accord with a request (Kelman, 1958). Agreeing to donate money to a social cause consistent with your own values is an instance of internal compliance. Expressing your patriotism by singing the national anthem or saying the Pledge of Allegiance (with or without the words *under God*) are also manifestations of the internalization process.

What happens when we do not respond by complying with others' requests? Well, they may simply shrug their shoulders and forget about it, or they may conclude that you're a jerk and resolve to return your noncompliance at an opportune future date. However, another possible response to noncompliance is to up the ante by trying to secure the third behavioral consequence of social influence; namely, obedience. **Obedience** is the performance of an action in response to a direct order, usually from a person of high status or authority. Because most of us are taught from childhood to respect and obey authority figures (parents, teachers, police officers), obedience to those of higher status is common and is often perceived as a sign of maturity. However, all things being equal, most people prefer being "asked" to do something (compliance) rather than being "ordered" (obedience). Obedient behavior is more likely than compliant behavior to imply a loss of personal freedom, which is a valued commodity by most people, especially in individualist cultures.

Obedience

The performance of an action in response to a direct order.

People with Social Power Are More Likely to Initiate Action

How powerful are you? I'm not referring to your physical strength, but your social strength. Do you exercise power or do you shrink from possessing it? There is a famous saying: "Power corrupts, and absolute power corrupts absolutely." Is there any truth to this assertion?

As previously defined, social influence is the exercise of social power to change people's attitudes or behavior in a particular direction. **Social power** refers to the force available to the influencer in motivating this change. This power can originate from having access to certain resources (for example, rewards, punishments, information) due to one's social position in society, or from being liked and admired by others (French & Raven, 1959; Raven, 2001). In most instances, those who are the targets of influence resent the use of social power when they perceive it as coercive and heavy-handed, but they often respond positively to "soft" power usage based on accepted social norms, expertise, and likability (Elias & Mace, 2004; Schwarzwald et al., 2004).

The findings from a number of empirical studies support the commonly held belief that possessing social power increases people's tendencies to take action, whereas powerlessness activates a general tendency to inhibit action (Anderson & Berdahl, 2002; Keltner et al., 2003). For example, when research participants are randomly assigned to experimental conditions with high or low social power, those given high power are more likely than those with low power to take action to achieve goals, even when their social power has nothing to do with the task at hand (Galinsky et al., 2003). This suggests that the possession of power in one context can lead to action in an unrelated context.

Why might people with social power be more likely to initiate action compared with those with low power? One reason is that having power makes people less dependent on others: they feel better equipped to act on their own without having to consider how others might impede or obstruct their actions. Because social power allows them to ignore or pay less attention to other people's viewpoints, powerful people tend to act more quickly, with less deliberation than those with low power (Greenspan et al., 2003). In essence, possessing power allows people to loosen the grip that social norms and standards typically exert on their behavior. With power, people can more easily and quickly exert their influence on the situation, including influencing those individuals in the situation. In fact, one avenue by which quick action is taken by the powerful is stereotyping: they judge the less powerful people around them based on stereotypes (Fiske, 1993). As discussed in chapter 8 (p. 269), although stereotyping often leads to errors in judgment, it does allow for quick decision making and action.

The fact that people with social power tend to be less concerned about the social consequences of their actions creates a paradox. The decisions made and the actions taken by those with high social power are much more likely to affect other people's lives than are the decisions and actions of those with little power. Thus, the people who have the biggest influence on others' lives are the very people who often seem to care less about the social consequences of their actions. Do you see a potential danger here for those with less power?

CRITICAL *thinking*

How might an individual's personality and behavior change as they gain or lose social power?

SECTION SUMMARY

- Social influence is the exercise of social power by a person or group to change the attitudes or behavior of others in a particular direction

- Conformity, compliance, and obedience represent the three main behavioral consequences of social influence

    Conformity: yielding to perceived group pressure

    Compliance: publicly acting in accord with a direct request

    Obedience: performance of an action in response to a direct order

- Social power increases people's tendencies to take action, perhaps because power gives them more freedom from social constraints

CLASSIC AND CONTEMPORARY CONFORMITY RESEARCH

To better understand social influence, let's begin by analyzing three classic conformity studies conducted more than forty years ago: Muzafir Sherif's work on norm development, Solomon Asch's work on group pressure, and Stanley Schachter's work on how people react to nonconformists. Analysis of each of these classic studies is followed by discussion of more recent studies that provide additional insight into the psychology of conformity.

Sherif's Norm Development Research Analyzed Conformity to an Ambiguous Reality

The first widely recognized conformity study was that of Turkish-born Muzafir Sherif, who in 1935 published his research on the development of social norms. Sherif's research was partly spurred by his disagreement with the prevailing individualist view of social psychology that a group was merely a collection of individuals and that no new group qualities arise when individuals form into a collective entity. Sherif countered that a group was more than the sum of its individuals' nongroup thinking, and he set out to test this hypothesis by studying how social norms develop in a group (Sherif, 1936).

In his study, Sherif enlisted college students into what was described as a visual perception experiment. Participants were individually placed in a small, totally darkened laboratory where, fifteen feet in front of them, a small dot of light appeared. They were told that after a short time the light would move, and their task would be to judge how far it moved. In all cases the light was left on for two seconds after the participants indicated the beginning of movement. Each participant made 100 light movement judgments. Although they did not realize it, the experimenter never actually moved the dot of light. What the participants perceived as light movement was really an optical illusion known as the autokinetic effect. The *autokinetic effect* refers to the fact that when someone stares at a stationary point of light in a darkened room where there is no frame of reference, it appears to move in various directions.

In this highly ambiguous situation, each participant's first few guesses were generally quite different from one another. However, after a few more trials, they settled on a consistent range of light movement. Thus, even though this was an optical illusion, participants assigned some order to the visual chaos, zeroing in on a stable estimate as if they were actually mastering this perceptual task. Yet because the light movement was illusory, there was not much consistency between those making their isolated judgments. One person would settle on a stable range of about two inches, while another would make an estimate of six inches. During the experiment's second phase, Sherif placed these same individuals together in groups of two and three and asked them to publicly announce their estimates after each trial. What ensued was not a free-for-all bickering of light movement experts. Instead, all participants tended to gradually change their estimates to be more similar to the others. Moving from their individual standards, they converged on an expected standard established by the group, known as a **social norm** (figure 9.1).

This demonstration of the process by which social norms develop is also an illustration of the more general process of social influence (Bar-Tal, 2000). Participants were in a fluid and ambiguous situation, and they looked to the group to help them define reality. They all conformed to an emerging social norm that was different from their individually developed standards. Interestingly, even though the data clearly indicated such social influence occurred, most of Sherif's participants denied that the others had influenced their own judgments. Sherif also found that the more uncertain participants were about the reality of the situation, the more they were influenced by others' opinions. For example, in a variation of the original experiment, Sherif had participants experience the autokinetic effect for the first time in a group setting rather than alone, and thus, they had not established their own individual norms. Under such circumstances, participants were even more influenced by others' view of reality, and convergence toward a common social norm occurred much faster than in the original group condition.

No written law has ever been more binding than unwritten custom supported by popular opinion.

Carrie Chapman Catt, U.S. women's suffrage and peace activist, 1859–1947

Social Norm

An expected standard of behavior and belief established and enforced by a group.

FIGURE 9.1

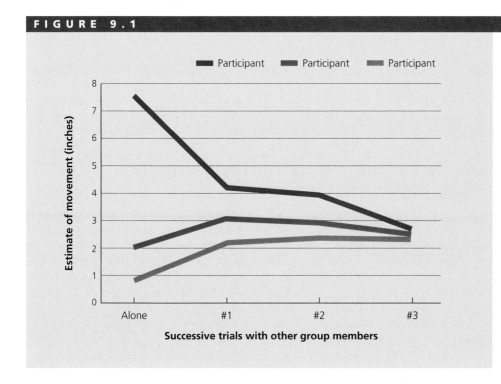

Successive trials with other group members

Norm Development

In Sherif's autokinetic experiments, when participants in three-person groups announced their individual judgments of light movement to one another, their initial divergent norms gradually converged over the course of the trials. In other words, in an ambiguous reality, the individuals established an expected standard (a social norm) of light movement. Can you think of instances in your own life where you and others established social norms to guide your own behavior and beliefs?

A third finding of Sherif's study was that when participants were uncertain about how to define reality, they were highly influenced by others who appeared confident. The basis for these findings came by placing a participant in the lab with a confederate who had been instructed to make all of his judgments within a predetermined range. As expected, the participant quickly adopted the confederate's range of judgments, and later used this social norm when placed in the autokinetic situation alone. In essence, faced with a confusing situation, people conformed to those who appeared confident in dealing with their surroundings, and they continued to be influenced by these opinions even in their absence.

The extent of the power that confident others can have over the less confident, and the durability of the social norms established in such a situation, was later explored by Robert Jacobs and Donald Campbell (1961). They exposed a single person to the autokinetic effect in the company of three confederates who made extreme judgments (light movement of sixteen inches). Even though these judgments were twelve inches larger than what people typically made, the participants strongly conformed, making judgments nearly as extreme as those of the confederates. Following the creation of the light movement norm in this "extreme" group, the researchers created successive generations of four-person groups to judge a series of thirty light movements, but in each generation they removed one of the extreme confederates and replaced him with a naive participant. By the fourth generation all confederates had been replaced, and the four-person group consisted of four actual participants. Although the extreme confederates were no longer in the group, their extreme group-derived norm continued to influence the judgment of successive generations of groups for quite some time. Jacobs and Campbell's study demonstrates experimentally a regularly occurring social phenomena—the views of past generations largely shape the thinking of current and future generations.

Taken together, these studies indicate that when faced with uncertainty about how to interpret or judge events, we are influenced by others, especially if they appear confident. Not only are we likely to conform to their view of reality, but we are likely to continue to use their perspective in rendering judgments even in their absence (Nye & Brower, 1996). This conformity forms the bedrock of the socialization process in all societies. First, we learn and practice common ways of conduct that are characteristic for our social group. Through rehearsal, we develop mental representations, or *schemas* (see

Never throw away hastily any old faith, tradition or convention . . . they are the result of the experience of many generations.

Sir Oliver Lodge, English physicist, 1851–1940

A stranger must conform to his host's customs.

Euripides, Greek dramatist, 5th century B.C.

To do exactly as your neighbors do is the only sensible rule.

Emily Post, U.S. hostess, 1873–1960

chapter 5, pp. 141–145), of how to behave according to these social norms. Our social environment—parents, friends, teachers, and popular culture—regularly communicate and enforce beliefs concerning which social norms should be used as guidelines for behavior in different situations. This socialization process helps us develop cognitive scripts for a wide variety of social situations. As discussed in chapter 5 (p. 142), these scripts—which contain perceptions of relevant social norms—guide our behavior and problem solving in the situation. Without this script learning, coordinated social interaction would be very difficult.

Specific Situations Can Automatically Activate Specific Social Norms

Over time and with experience and practice, social norms become associated with specific settings, so that the situation itself can activate mental representations of normative behaviors automatically. This idea that situations automatically activate social norms from memory is consistent with research discussed in chapters 5 and 8 showing that specific social groups often automatically activate stereotypes from memory (Dijksterhuis & Bargh, 2001). Both stereotype activation and norm activation illustrate how social stimuli can spontaneously trigger well-learned thoughts and responses.

In a series of experiments testing the ability of specific social environments to automatically activate situational norms, Dutch social psychologists Henk Aarts and Ap Dijksterhuis (2003) asked college students to perform two seemingly unconnected tasks on a computer. In the first "Picture Task," a photo either of the inside of an empty library or an empty platform at a railway station was shown on the computer screen for thirty seconds. Participants were told to examine the photo because they would answer questions about it later. Two-thirds of the students were also told that they would visit the depicted environment after the experiment. In one version of this experiment, upon completion of the first task, participants performed a "Word Recognition Task." They were told that when a word flashed on the computer screen, they were to decide as quickly as possible whether it was a meaningful word or a nonsense word. Four of the twelve meaningful words presented to participants represented normative behavior for a library setting (*silent, quiet, still, whisper*). The speed of their response was measured by how quickly they pressed "yes" or "no" keys indicating whether the word was meaningful or not. In a second version of this experiment, the word recognition task was replaced with a "Word Pronunciation Task," in which participants read aloud ten words that were presented on the computer screen. The intensity level of each spoken word was measured, although participants were not informed about this measurement until the end of their session.

What results were obtained in these two separate experiments? In the first experiment, Aarts and Dijksterhuis found that participants in the word recognition task were quicker at identifying library-related "quiet" words as meaningful if they had previously been exposed to the photo of the library rather than the train station photo. This finding suggests that the words related to the "silent" library norm were more readily accessible in memory, meaning that this situational social norm had been primed. As discussed in chapter 5 (p. 144), *priming* is the process by which recent exposure to certain stimuli or events increases the accessibility of certain memories, categories, or schemas. Priming is a good example of automatic thinking because it occurs spontaneously and nonconsciously. Similar results were found in the second experiment. These participants pronounced words in a quieter voice if they had previously been exposed to the library photo rather than the picture of the train station. Again, this finding suggests that the behavior of speaking softly occurred because the "silent" library norm had been primed. It should be added that in neither of these experiments did the participants make a conscious connection between looking at the photo of the library in the first task and responding to the word meanings or speaking the words in the second task. However, most important, in both studies these effects only occurred when participants thought they were later going to visit the library. Those partic-

Recent studies indicate that the anticipation of entering a specific situation often automatically—and nonconsciously—activates the relevant social norms for that situation, which then directly shapes people's behavior. Thus, while walking up to the library doors, the social norm of being quiet is activated, resulting in people's behavior becoming more subdued. This is an example of how social norms can directly shape behavior without any conscious thought.

ipants who had been shown the library photo but were not told that they would later visit the location showed neither of these effects.

Together, these findings suggest that the *anticipation* of entering a specific situation automatically heightens the accessibility of the relevant social norms for that situation from memory, which then can have a direct effect on subsequent behavior. In other words, when preparing to visit the library, the social norm of being quiet while in the library automatically becomes more accessible in your memory, which may result in your behavior becoming more subdued before you even open the library door. Do you see how these findings challenge a basic assumption of the theory of planned behavior, which is discussed in chapter 6 (pp. 191–194)? The theory of planned behavior contends that our perception of the social norms in a given situation *indirectly* influence our behavior by shaping our behavioral intentions. The present findings by Aarts and Dijksterhuis suggest that situational norms are able to guide social behavior *directly*. In essence, we have conformed to these situational norms so often that our norm-consistent behavior in the situation becomes a *habit* that occurs without conscious attention or monitoring.

Does this then mean that *all* situational norms guide social behavior directly? Of course not. Additional research by Aarts and Dijksterhuis (2003) suggest that only well-learned situational norms have the ability to directly guide social behavior. If situational norms are not well learned, they are not readily accessible in memory, and norm-consistent behavior is not spontaneously expressed. Further, even when situational norms are well learned, there are many instances in which we consciously consider how to match our behavior to these norms, and there are also many situations in which we consciously consider whether we should flout the relevant norms. However, norm-consistent automatic behavior is fairly common, and the cognitive resources we save by acting on automatic pilot allows us to consciously think about other matters, which can increase our overall social efficiency. After all, don't you enjoy an elegant meal better when you don't have to spend time thinking about which of the five utensils in front of you is the correct one to use when eating the next course? Or maybe you are like me and are still trying to master this particular situational norm.

Asch's Line Judgment Research Analyzed Conformity to a Unanimous Majority

In the spring of 1992, Los Angeles was rocked by its worst race riot in twenty-five years following a jury trial in which four White Los Angeles police officers were acquitted of using excessive force in the beating of Rodney King, a Black man.[1] The actual beating was captured on videotape, and most who viewed the tape believed that Mr. King was a victim of police brutality. One of the jurors, Virginia Loya, stated shortly after the trial that she initially favored a guilty verdict. Yet when the jury deliberated, the strength of her convictions waned as other jurors argued that King deserved the beating he received. In reflecting on her fellow jurors' thinking, Loya said, "The tape was the big evidence to me. They couldn't see. To me, they were people who were blind and couldn't get their glasses clean. If anything, I wish these people weren't so blind." Despite her belief that the other jurors were incorrectly assigning blame, Loya conformed to their judgment and changed her vote from guilty to not guilty on all counts but one. Why did she accept what she believed to be an incorrect judgment by the rest of the jurors? To understand her actions, we might be tempted to search for character flaws or an all-too-compliant personality structure. Yet in doing so, we would be overlooking the power of social influence and how group pressure can cause us to go against what our eyes tell us about social reality.

This account of an important jury trial bears a striking resemblance to the experience of participants in a classic study of conformity conducted by Solomon Asch (1951, 1952, 1956) fifty years ago. In a series of experiments, college students volunteered for what was described as a visual perception experiment. Upon arriving at the lab, they discovered that six other students would also be participating in the study. All six were confederates who were given prior instructions by Asch to behave a certain way. After the assembled students were seated around a table, Asch placed a card on an easel and pointed to a vertical line on the card that he said was the standard line. On this same card were three more vertical lines labeled "a," "b," and "c" (see figure 9.2). Asch explained that the students' task was to call out the letter corresponding to the line that was the same length as the standard line. Partic-

---

[1] The officers were later tried on charges that they violated Mr. King's civil rights. In this second trial, two of the officers were convicted and sentenced to prison.

In Asch's conformity experiments, individuals in seven-person groups publicly announced their judgments of which comparison line matched the standard line. Person 6, the only naive participant, appears perplexed and uneasy after the five people before him all chose the incorrect line. If you were in his place, would you have picked the correct line or conformed to the group's incorrect judgment?

FIGURE 9.2

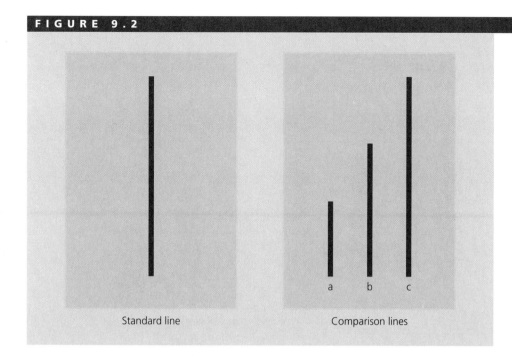

Standard line   Comparison lines

This is an example of the stimulus lines used in Asch's classic conformity experiments. Participants were asked to judge which of the three comparison lines were equal in length to the standard line.

ipants made a total of eighteen different line judgments and were seated so that five of the six confederates stated their judgments before the actual participant gave an opinion.

Undoubtedly, all participants in this study must have initially thought that their task would be simple, for it was obvious that "c" was the correct answer. For the first two trials, confederates picked the correct line, but thereafter, on a prearranged basis, they unanimously chose a clearly incorrect line in twelve of the remaining sixteen problems. What would the second-to-last student—the only "real" participant—do when faced with this dilemma? Would he conform to the judgment of others, or would he stick with what his eyes told him?

Although participants did differ in their degree of conformity, overall they conformed by naming the same incorrect line as the confederates on over one-third (37 percent) of the critical trials. Further, a large majority (76 percent) conformed to the incorrect judgments on at least one of the critical trials (see figure 9.3). In contrast, when other participants in a control condition made their judgments privately, less than 1 percent made errors (Asch, 1951). Similar to juror Virginia Loya, Asch's research participants demonstrated that many people can be induced to forgo what their own eyes tell them and, instead, conform to the incorrect judgment of others. These findings are consistent with later research indicating that people often find it easier to conform rather than challenge the unanimous opinions of others (Tanford & Penrod, 1984).

As discussed in previous chapters, many people prefer their attitudes, beliefs, and actions to fit into a consistent pattern. If this is true, how do people typically react to the reality of their own conforming behavior, especially when it seems to run counter to their private views? Research suggests that when faced with the choice of admitting that one has arbitrarily conformed to a group standard versus convincing oneself that the facts forced one's agreement with that standard, almost everyone attempts to reconstruct the facts (Buehler & Griffin, 1994). This sort of *postconformity change-of-meaning* allows conformers to justify their behavior and maintain cognitive consistency.

Although the Asch findings indicate the strength of social influence even when the group's judgment seems clearly misguided, they do not imply that we are merely slaves to others' judgments. As illustrated in figure 9.3, 24 percent of Asch's participants never followed the group on a single trial, and less than one-third conformed on more than half the trials. Likewise, in explaining why she dissented from the majority of the jurors on one count against one of the police officers after conforming to their not guilty judgment on all other counts, juror Loya stated, "They couldn't make me change my mind on guilty for [that officer]. I wasn't

Once conform, once do what other people do because they do it, and a lethargy steals over all the finer nerves and faculties of the soul. She becomes all outer show and inward emptiness; dull, callous, and indifferent.

Virginia Woolf, British novelist, 1882–1941

FIGURE 9.3

Degree of Conformity in Asch's Research

In judging line length, when faced with a group of people who picked incorrect lines, participants conformed to their false judgments on 33 percent of the trials. Although less than one-third conformed on more than half the judgmental trials, 76 percent conformed on at least one occasion. What type of social influence likely accounts for these effects?

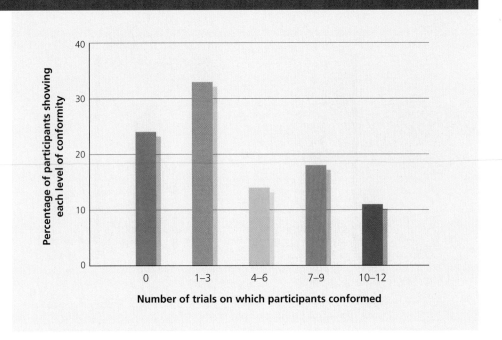

The fish dies because he opens his mouth.

Spanish proverb

Social Sense

View a simulation of the Asch experiment on your Social Sense CD-ROM.

Normative Social Influence

Conformity, compliance, or obedience based on a desire to gain rewards or avoid punishments (outcome dependence).

going to give in." As heartening as this act of independence may appear, the fact that people often are willing to go along with erroneous group judgments, or are willing to accept the judgments of others when they feel uncertain how to define their surrounding reality, suggests there are compelling social forces in need of further inquiry. Before reading further, check out a simulation of Asch's classic conformity experiment on your Social Sense CD-ROM.

Conformity Can Be Caused by Both Normative and Informational Influence

Let's explore a bit further the differing dilemmas that participants faced in the Sherif and Asch experiments. First, Sherif's participants found themselves in an ambiguous reality in which they undoubtedly felt less than confident about their own abilities to judge the movement of this fluctuating point of light. They could stumble along doing the best they could under the circumstances, or they could seek the guidance of others. Did the participants in the Asch experiments face a similar ambiguous reality? Hardly. In fact, in one form of the experiment, Asch (1952) tested sixteen naive participants and instructed a lone confederate to answer incorrectly, like the majority had in the original experiment. How did the naive participants respond when the confederate repeatedly picked the wrong lines? At first they were stunned, but soon they were laughing uproariously at each of his judgments! Clearly, there was no ambiguity here. The dilemma faced by Asch's original participants was deciding whether to maintain their own judgments and thereby stick out like a sore thumb, or go along with the group and thus avoid the uncomfortable stares and raised eyebrows of others. In the Asch study, by publicly adopting the opinions of others, participants demonstrated that "fitting in" was of greater concern to them than giving the correct answer. In the Sherif study, however, adopting the opinions of others was the avenue participants followed in their search for the correct answer.

In explaining the different social pressures in these two studies, Morton Deutsch and Henry Gerard (1955) suggested that group pressure derives from two sources: normative and informational influence. **Normative social influence** occurs when a person conforms, complies, or obeys to gain rewards or avoid punishments from another person or group (Kidwell et al., 2003). If Asch's participants changed their judgments because they were afraid others might laugh at them or evaluate them negatively, they were responding to normative pressure. However, if they modified their answers because they thought the unanimously responding confederates might have a more accurate view of the lines, then they were responding to informational pressure. **Informational social influence** occurs when the individual conforms, complies, or obeys to gain accurate information. We often look to groups for information, especially if we doubt our own judgment (Baron et al., 1996). Because it is unlikely that very many participants in the Asch studies actually believed that the group was correct in its line judgments, we are probably safe in concluding that their conformity was principally due to normative social influence rather than informational social influence. In the Sherif study, on the other hand, the conformity exhibited was more likely due to informational influence because light movement was extremely ambiguous.

These two different types of social influence reflect two different types of social dependence. Informational social influence reflects a form of social dependence called *information dependence,* which is dependence on others for information about the world that reduces uncertainty. Underlying normative social influence is the dependence on others for positive outcomes or rewards, which is called *outcome dependence* (also known as *normative dependence*). Therefore, the need to reduce uncertainty in a given situation leads to information dependence, while the need to gain acceptance or approval results in outcome dependence. Although in some cases these two mechanisms of influence operate separately, in many others they function simultaneously (Baron et al., 1996; Insko et al., 1985). This is likely what occurred as Virginia Loya deliberated with her fellow jurors in the Rodney King case. Faced with fellow jurors who pressured her to accept defense claims that the videotape did not tell the entire story (normative influence), the strength of her convictions weakened, and she may well have begun to more seriously consider their interpretation of events (informational influence).

Informational Social Influence

Conformity, compliance, or obedience based on a desire to gain information (information dependence).

Schachter's "Johnny Rocco" Study Investigated the Rejection of the Nonconformist

Thus far we have discussed the forces brought to bear on us so that we conform to the group's judgment. But what about those of us who do not knuckle under to this influence? How does a group typically respond to the nonconformist?

About the same time that Asch was conducting his group conformity research, Stanley Schachter (1951) provided an excellent experimental analysis of the consequences of not conforming to majority opinion. Schachter arranged for groups of eight to ten volunteers to form a "case study club" to discuss the case of a juvenile delinquent, Johnny Rocco, and then make a recommendation of what the authorities should do with Johnny. In making their recommendations, participants used a seven-point love-punishment rating scale ranging from a position 1 "loving" treatment of Johnny to a position 7 "punishment" treatment. Unknown to the participants, each group contained three confederates instructed to take a particular position in the discussion of Johnny. Expecting that the participants would select a position closer to the "loving" end of the scale, Schachter instructed his confederates to take differing positions. The "deviate" argued for position 7 throughout the discussion, acting unswayed by contrary opinions; the "slider" began at position 7 but slid toward the majority position of the group; the "mode" held the group's most agreed upon position throughout the discussion.

Have you ever felt like this in class? What sort of influence is operating here? Normative or informational? A clue: why are these students not raising their hands?

For Better Or For Worse © Lynn Johnston Productions. Dist. by Universal Press Syndicate. Reprinted with permission. All rights reserved.

How do you think the participants reacted to these three different positions during discussion, and how do you think they dealt with the deviate at the end, when their best efforts at persuasion failed to secure conformity? At first, participants communicated a great deal with the deviate and slider in an attempt to convince them to change their minds about Johnny. During this same time period, very little attention was paid to the right-thinking mode. Once participants concluded that the deviate was not going to alter his judgment, and once the slider adopted the group's position, communication toward them dropped sharply. If you think of this communication as an indicator of social pressure, these findings suggest that those who hold minority opinions become the focus of influence attempts until they either conform or convince the group that such attempts are fruitless. This direct persuasive communication is a form of normative influence.

At the end of group discussion, Schachter informed everyone that the group was simply too large for their next discussion and that he wanted them to decide who to retain in the group. Participants' responses provided the answer to how groups respond to nonconformists—the deviate was excluded from future discussions. A more recent meta-analysis of twenty-three Schachter-like "deviant" studies found that rejection by the group is most likely when there are only one or two nonconformists rather than a more substantial number (Tata et al., 1996). Additional research suggests that group members are least likely to tolerate dissension when it involves an important group value and the dissent is expressed in an intergroup context (Matheson et al. 2003). "Airing the group's dirty laundry" is perceived as a sign of disloyalty to the group and leads to very harsh judgments by the majority. Together, these studies provide compelling evidence that social rejection is the final, and perhaps most powerful, form of normative influence directed toward nonconformists (James & Olson, 2000). It is believed to be one of the primary causes of depression (Nolan et al., 2003).

In adolescence, many teenagers conform to their friends' alcohol and drug use to gain acceptance. For other teenagers with different group standards, acceptance entails forgoing these forms of harmful indulgences. In both instances, nonconformists are often banished from the group (Williams & Zadro, 2001). Ostracism is used as a social control mechanism at all age levels, and it is such a powerful tactic of social influence that it is even effective when used over the Internet (Williams et al., 2000; Zadro et al., 2004).

Brain-imaging studies indicate that the social pain we experience following rejection is neurologically similar to physical pain, with both originating in the brain's anterior cingulate cortex (Eisenberger et al., 2003). Why might social and physical pain have similar neural origins? Due to the fact that social bonds promote survival in most species of mammals, it is possible that during the course of human evolution our social attachment "alarm" system came under the control of the same brain area that already controlled the physical pain system. Because pain is the most primitive signal that "something is wrong," piggybacking the social attachment system onto the physical pain system would have kept young human children near their caregivers, thus increasing their chances of survival.

The greater neural activity in the anterior cingulate caused by social rejection may be associated with another consequence of being excluded by others: impairment in reasoning and logic. Recent studies suggest that when people believe they are going to be excluded by others, their reasoning and complex thinking skills suffer (Baumeister et al., 2002). Because the anterior cingulate plays a role in both the social attachment alarm system and in the process of self-regulation (see chapter 3, pp. 65–67), the threat of social exclusion may drain self-regulatory resources, causing a breakdown in the type of controlled thinking necessary for successful self-regulation.

There appear to be many cognitive and emotional costs incurred by those who are socially excluded. However, the negative effects of social exclusion are not solely directed at the person who is rejected by others. When people use their social power to ostracize someone, it typically comes at a psychological price. In a series of studies, Natalie Ciarocco and her coworkers (2001) found that ostracizing someone temporarily depletes the self's resources, making it more difficult to engage in self-regulation on other tasks. In other words, just as being shunned has a negative impact on our ability to think clearly, shunning someone takes substantial cognitive effort, and the stress is likely to make you less effective in

- Sherif's norm development research demonstrated that we:

    look to others when defining social reality

    are most influenced by people who appear confident

- Informational influence is social influence that derives its power from people's desire for accurate information

- Asch's line judgment experiments demonstrated that we

    often conform out of concern for "fitting in"

- Normative influence is social influence that derives its power from people's desire to gain rewards or avoid punishments

- Schachter's "Johnny Rocco" study demonstrated that cohesive groups react to nonconformers by

    first trying to persuade them

    rejecting nonconformists if persuasion is unsuccessful

other areas of your life. Thus, although ostracism is an effective way to "straighten out" nonconformers, those who use it are also likely to suffer from these strains of silence.

WHAT FACTORS INFLUENCE CONFORMITY?

Thus far, we have learned that people sometimes mindlessly conform due to the automatic activation of situational norms. We have also learned that people are likely to conform when they are uncertain about their own ability to make accurate judgments and others are confident, or when they are concerned about being negatively evaluated by others. What social and personal factors foster this uncertainty and concern?

Situational Factors Impact Conformity

In attempting to understand the conditions that facilitate conformity, social psychologists have paid particular attention to the social setting. The assumption is that these situational factors exert a social force on individuals that can cause uniform behavior.

GROUP SIZE

One situational factor contributing to conformity is the size of the influencing group. When Asch (1955) varied the number of unanimous confederates from one to fifteen, he found that conformity increased as group size increased, but only up to a certain size (figure 9.4). Conformity was near its peak level when the number of confederates was between three and four, and then actually tapered off so that there was no greater conformity with a group of fifteen confederates than with a group of three.

   Other research suggests that group size will only be a predictor of conformity levels in certain situations. Jennifer Campbell and Patricia Fairey (1989) found that group size is important when the social reality is clear (judgments are easy), but that the size of the group is relatively unimportant when the social reality is ambiguous (judgments are difficult). The explanation for this interaction effect has to do with what type of social influence is most potent in an ambiguous or clear reality. As previously discussed, when the reality is clear, whether you conform depends on the amount of normative influence the group can exert. Adding more people to the group (up to four or so) will increase normative influence, and thus, increase conformity. On the other hand, if the reality is ambiguous, informational

FIGURE 9.4

Group Size and Conformity

In Asch's (1955) conformity research, when the number of unanimous confederates was varied from one to fifteen, conformity approached its maximum level when the number of confederates was between three and four. Why do you think group size effects leveled off in this manner?

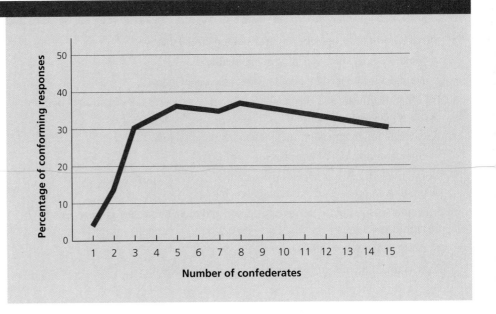

influence is more of a factor than normative influence. In this state of information dependence, one or two people may influence you just as well as three, four, or twenty-four.

GROUP COHESIVENESS AND TOPIC RELEVANCE

A group is termed cohesive when its members are highly attracted to one another. In general, cohesive groups engender more conformity than noncohesive groups (Christensen et al., 2004; Hogg, 1992). For example, in other conditions of Schachter's (1951) deviant study, he varied the cohesiveness of the group as well as the relevance of the contested discussion topic. When the group was highly cohesive and the topic was also highly relevant, the group exerted its greatest pressure on deviates and was most likely to reject nonconformists. These findings indicate that if groups with a strong sense of togetherness are discussing important topics, they will tend to be intolerant of those who hold differing opinions. The best examples of cohesive groups influencing members come from our own friendship networks. We are much more likely to accept their influence than that of others because of our respect for their opinions, our desire to please them, and our fear of rejection (Crandall, 1988).

SOCIAL SUPPORT

In Asch's study, what sort of effect do you think a single confederate picking the correct line would have on the conformity levels of the participants? Actually, Asch (1956) found that when one of the confederates picked the correct line, conformity dropped dramatically, to one-fourth the original levels. Research by Vernon Allen and John Levine (1969) indicates that a social supporter reduces conformity by diminishing the group's normative influence. In one of their studies, participants worked with four confederates on a visual perception task. Three of the confederates had previously been instructed to consistently agree on incorrect judgments. The fourth confederate either went along with the other confederates, agreed with the participant, or made a different incorrect judgment. Conformity was not only reduced when the fourth confederate agreed with the participant, but also when this confederate merely disagreed with all opinions, including the participants' opinions. In a second experiment (Allen & Levine, 1971), conformity was reduced even when the social supporter wore thick glasses and complained about not being able to see the visual displays!

These findings suggest that almost any dissent from the majority can diminish normative influence and thereby reduce conformity. Although breaking social consensus appears to be the crucial factor here, receiving social support early is more effective than receiving such support after normative pressures have already built up (Morris et al., 1977). Unfortunately, if this support is later removed, normative influence again is exerted. In one of Asch's studies, when the confederate who had previously agreed with the participant switched and began to conform to the majority opinion, the participants' own level of conformity returned to near the levels observed in the original experiments (Asch, 1955). Thus, to promote nonconformity in others, one should voice dissent, and do so early and consistently. Remember this bit of advice, for it will be important when we later discuss how minorities can exert influence in not only resisting majority opinion, but actually changing it.

Personal Factors Influence Conformity

The consensus is that situational forces are most important in determining whether we conform or not. Yet we are not machines who respond identically to these situational factors. Although specific personality traits related to conformity have been difficult to identify (McGuire, 1968), research does suggest that conforming to group pressure is related to our *values* and *self-concept.*

SELF-AWARENESS

As noted in chapter 3, whether behavior is more influenced by personal or social standards is at least partially determined by what aspect of the self is salient (private or public). When people are privately self-aware, they tend to act in line with their own personal standards, but social standards are more influential when people are publicly self-aware (Froming et al., 1982; Kallgren et al., 2000). Thus, being privately self-aware reduces conformity, while being publicly self-aware increases conformity.

SELF-PRESENTATION

The irony of yielding to social influence out of concern for how others might evaluate you is that in many cultures it is not desirable to be recognized as a conformist. Robert Cialdini and his coworkers (1974), for example, found that American college students generally perceived people as more intelligent if they do not yield to social influence—unless, of course, they were the ones trying to get others to conform! Further research found that often underlying the conformity and independence responses of people are calculated assessments of the impressions they are making on those present (Collins & Brief, 1995; Santee & Maslach, 1982). Conformity is most likely to occur when self-presenters are alone with those trying to influence them and when the conformity will be viewed as indicating intelligence or open-mindedness. On the other hand, open defiance of influence attempts is most likely under two conditions (Baumeister, 1982): (1) when others not involved in the influence attempt are present, and (2) when the attitude of those exerting the influence makes any subsequent yielding seem like weak-kneed surrender rather than intelligent decision making. Under such conditions, it would be difficult to conform and still maintain a public image of independence and autonomy.

THE DESIRE FOR PERSONAL CONTROL

Although self-presentation concerns may sometimes explain conformity and nonconformity, on other occasions we may resist social influence simply to feel that we personally control our own actions. Jack Brehm (Brehm, 1966; Brehm & Brehm, 1981) has proposed a **theory of psychological reactance,** which states that people believe they possess specific behavioral freedoms and that they will react against and resist attempts to limit this sense of freedom. For example, if parents demand that their daughter not date a certain boy, she might defy the parents as a way to restore a feeling of personal control over her own behavior. When reactance is aroused, the forbidden behavior (dating the disapproved boy) becomes more desirable. Similarly, if the daughter believes her parents are trying to coerce her into dating some other boy, reactance results in this boy becoming a much less desirable date than the forbidden male.

CRITICAL *thinking*

Imagine that you are conducting an Asch-type conformity experiment, yet you also want to test whether you can increase nonconformity by inducing public self-presentation concerns in your participants. What variable could you add to the standard Asch research design to test this possibility? That is, how could you alter the standard procedure to induce public self-presentation concerns? Would public self-presentation concerns lead to greater nonconformity when the line judgments were clear and easy or ambiguous and difficult? How might public self-awareness effects contaminate the findings?

I'm not gonna change the way I look or the way I feel to conform to anything. I've always been a freak. So I've been a freak all my life and I have to live with that, you know. I'm one of those people.

John Lennon, English rock musician, 1940–1980

Theory of Psychological Reactance

The theory that people believe they possess specific behavioral freedoms, and that they will react against and resist attempts to limit this sense of freedom.

Is the son's behavior an example of independence or anticonformity? How could his mother manipulate him to do what she desires by arousing his need to feel unique?

©*Zits Partnership. Reprinted with special permission of King Features Syndicate.*

Anticonformity

Opposition to social influence on all occasions, often caused by psychological reactance.

Jerry Burger (1987) found evidence indicating that individual differences in desire for personal control may partly explain susceptibility to social influence. In his study, he asked college students to rate the humor in a series of newspaper cartoons using a scale from 1 ("very unfunny") to 100 ("very funny"). In one condition, participants rated the cartoons alone, and in another condition, they rated them after hearing two other students' evaluations. These other students, being experimental confederates, had been instructed to rate the cartoons as being relatively funny (averaging 70 on the 100-point scale), even though Burger had specifically chosen cartoons that had previously been judged to be quite dull (average humor rating of only 25).

Prior to rating the cartoons, participants' desire for personal control (DPC) had been measured by a paper-and-pencil questionnaire. As you can see in table 9.1, DPC did not predict how students rated the cartoons when they were alone (both groups rated them as not very funny), but high DPC participants were less likely to agree with confederates' favorable ratings than were low DPCs. Although the high DPCs certainly were not immune to the confederates' influence, the results suggest that they appear to be better equipped to resist conformity than those who have a low desire for control.

Individuals may not conform to social pressures due to their desire for personal control, but this does not mean that they are necessarily acting independently. There are two different types of nonconformity responses. One is *independence,* which was previously defined as not being subject to others' control. The person who dates someone not because her parents approve or disapprove but because she genuinely likes her dating partner is demonstrating independence; psychological reactance does not play a factor in her behavioral choices. **Anticonformity,** on the other hand, is characterized by opposition to social influence on all occasions, and psychological reactance often explains these behavioral choices (Nail et al., 1996). The anticonformist would date people whom her parents disapproved and would not date those whom they approved. Thus, the actions of two people may be identical but may be motivated by very different desires. A person who has a strong desire for personal control could express this either through independence or anticonformity. Some people "take the road less traveled" not because they disagree with the group's direction, but by disagreeing they can satisfy their need for personal control.

GENDER AND CONFORMITY

Early social influence research found a slight tendency for women to conform more than men, but more recent studies find little, if any, gender differences (Eagly, 1987). Where small gender differences sometimes occur is in face-to-face encounters in which a person

TABLE 9.1

Desire for Control and Conformity: Are Unfunny Cartoons Judged Funny Due to Others' Favorable Ratings?

When students rated the humor of previously identified "unfunny" cartoons, high and low desire for personal control (DPC) individuals didn't significantly differ when rating the cartoons alone (higher scores mean funnier ratings), but high DPCs were significantly less likely to agree with confederates' favorable ratings (the Group condition) than were low DPCs. Based on these findings, which of these two groups are better equipped to resist conformity?

		Mean Humor Scores	
		Desire for Personal Control	
Condition		**Low**	**High**
	Alone	43.7	49.3
	Group	73.2	62.1

must openly disagree with others (Becker, 1986). Whatever small gender differences exist in susceptibility to influence appears to be due to the social roles that men and women have traditionally been socialized to assume in our culture, and to their concerns about self-presentation. That is, when people believe they are being observed, women tend to conform more and men tend to conform less than they do in more private settings (Eagly & Chravala, 1986). It is likely that in attempting to create a favorable impression when questions of conformity arise, people tend to fall back on well-learned patterns of behavior that are considered socially acceptable for their sex. If this analysis is correct, you would expect that as men and women adopt less traditional gender roles, such self-presentation concerns will diminish in importance, and whatever conformity differences there are will similarly diminish, if not disappear entirely.

Individualists and Collectivists Differ in Their Conformity Patterns

Does knowing a person's cultural background give you any insight into how he or she might respond to social influence? The guiding principle of individualism is that individual interests are more important than those of the group. In decided contrast, collectivism asserts that group interests should guide the thinking and behavior of individual members (Ho & Chiu, 1994). According to Harry Triandis and his colleagues, people from collectivist cultures are more concerned than individualists with gaining the approval of their group and feel shameful if they fail to get it (Hui & Triandis, 1986; Triandis, 1989). A person from an individualist culture, on the other hand, has a higher need or preference for autonomy from the group and a desire to feel unique. Because of these different orientations, people from collectivist cultures tend to be more conforming to their own group than individualists (Bond & Smith, 1996; Cialdini et al., 2001). This yielding to the group by collectivists is not considered to be a sign of weakness, as it is often perceived in our individualist culture, but rather it is believed to indicate self-control, flexibility, and maturity (White & LeVine, 1986).

Although these cultural differences suggest that conformity is generally more likely in a collectivist culture, this does not mean that collectivists submit to any and all group influence attempts. To understand social influence in such a culture, it is important to distinguish *ingroups* from *outgroups*. As described in chapter 3, an ingroup is a group to which you belong and which forms a part of your social identity, whereas an outgroup is any group

The man who never submitted to anything will soon submit to a burial mat.

Nigerian proverb

Social Sense

View an interview concerning culture and social influence.

with which you do not share membership. Research suggests that people from collectivist cultures perceive ingroup norms as universally valid and feel obligated to obey ingroup authorities. On the other hand, collectivists tend to distrust outgroup norms and, as a result, often are unwilling to yield to their influence (Triandis, 1972; Wosinska et al., 2001).

Most of the nonconformity that occurs in a collectivist culture is to the social norms of outgroups, not ingroups. This difference in the perceived validity of ingroup norms is one of the reasons that collectivist cultures tend to breed more conformity than individualist cultures. Therefore, a person from a collectivist culture such as traditional Greece might be very yielding to his family's and his village's influence attempts (his ingroup), yet be staunchly defiant of any pressure exerted by the distant national authorities (a perceived outgroup). When we consider those who belong to an individualist culture, although they too tend to trust ingroup norms more than outgroup norms, they are more likely than collectivists to question ingroup norms as well, especially when they run counter to their self-interests or when adherence to these social norms makes them feel average or ordinary (that is, nonunique). View an interview with social psychologist Shinovu Kitayama concerning culture and social influence on your Social Sense CD-ROM.

Under Certain Conditions, the Minority Can Influence the Majority

History is filled with stories of lone individuals or small, relatively powerless groups expressing unpopular views and enduring abuse from the majority until their views are eventually adopted. Our chapter-opening stories of Michael Newdow's attempt to remove the phrase "under God" from the Pledge of Allegiance and Farag Fouda's forceful criticism of Islamic extremism in the Middle East are examples of dissenters whose minority opinions may someday become widely accepted. The process by which dissenters produce change within a group is called **minority influence.**

Minority Influence

The process by which dissenters produce change within a group.

Commenting on what it takes to exert minority influence, nineteenth-century feminist Susan B. Anthony said, "Cautious, careful people always casting about to preserve their reputation and social standing, never can bring about a reform. Those who are really in earnest must be willing to be anything or nothing in the world's estimation." Social research bears out Ms. Anthony's pronouncement. Those who dissent from the majority, although generally perceived as competent, often are heartily disliked (Bassili & Provencal, 1988). Indeed, dissenters Fouda, Malcolm X, and Martin Luther King, Jr. were so heartily despised

Cross-cultural research suggests that people from a collectivist culture, such as the Chinese pictured here, tend to be more influenced by ingroup norms than people from individualist cultures.

by some people that they were murdered to eliminate their nonconforming voices. One consequence of the social isolation experienced by those in the minority is a hesitation in voicing their opinions. This tendency of those who hold a minority opinion to express that opinion less quickly than people who hold the majority opinion is called the **minority slowness effect.** People with a minority opinion are particularly slow in stating their views when they perceive the majority opinion to be widely held (Bassili, 2003). As articulated by Ms. Anthony, championing the minority viewpoint is not for the weak of heart.

When minority influence is expressed, how exactly does it operate? As previously discussed, movement to the majority position is often due to the common belief that there is truth in numbers (informational influence) and due to the concern for being accepted by those numbers (normative influence). Underlying this social influence is a generally positive judgment of and an attraction toward the majority by those being influenced (W. Wood et al., 1994). This favorable view of the majority often results in people adopting the majority opinion without much critical analysis. However, unlike the majority group, minority groups tend to be viewed negatively by others, and therefore, their viewpoints are subject to more critical analysis, and thus, need greater time to register with group members (Martin et al., 2003; Mugny & Perez, 1991). The good news for minority persuaders is that if their views are eventually adopted by the majority, these new attitudes and beliefs tend to be more resistant to change than those adopted from majority persuaders. Do you know why? As discussed in chapter 7, attitudes changed through critical analysis (*central-route processing*) are stronger and more resistant to change than attitudes changed through lazy thinking (*peripheral-route processing*).

French social psychologist Serge Moscovici (1980) contended that the most important factor in determining the effectiveness of minority group influence is the *style of behavior* used in presenting nonconforming views. For minorities to exert influence on majority members, they must consistently and confidently state their dissenting opinions (Moscovici & Mugny, 1983). In a demonstration of the importance of consistency in minority group influence, Moscovici and his colleagues (1969) asked groups of individuals to judge whether the color of projected blue slides was blue or green. Each group consisted of four participants and two confederates. In the *inconsistent minority condition* the confederates randomly varied calling the blue slide green and blue, while in the *consistent minority condition* they always claimed that it was green.

Figure 9.5 shows that when the confederates were inconsistent in labeling the blue slide green, their ability to influence the majority's opinion was negligible (1.25 percent).

Every society honors its live conformists and its dead troublemakers.

Mignon McLaughlin, U.S. author, 1963

Nelson Mandela was successful in changing the social and political landscape of South Africa despite his double minority status. One of his strengths was consistent and confident articulation of his ideas, coupled with a willingness to negotiate with white apartheid leaders.

FIGURE 9.5

Conformity to a Consistent and Inconsistent Minority

Moscovici, Lage, and Naffrechoux, (1969) found that the degree to which participants labeled a blue slide "green" was partly determined by whether they were tested alone (control condition), with a minority saying "green" inconsistently (inconsistent condition), or with a minority saying "green" consistently (consistent condition). Why is consistency so important for minority group influence?

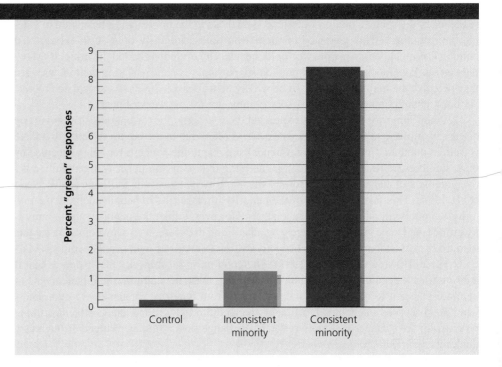

All men should have a drop of treason in their veins, if nations are not to go soft like so many sleepy pears.

Rebecca West, English novelist, 1892–1983

However, when the confederates were consistent, more than 8 percent of the time participants conformed to this minority point of view. In addition, after the color trials, those who were exposed to the consistent minority shifted the point on the blue-green color spectrum where they identified a color green instead of blue; now they called more stimuli "green" and fewer "blue." These findings not only suggest that a consistent minority can affect overt responses in the majority, but they also suggest that a unified minority can cause majority members to alter their private beliefs as well.

Although this research indicates that those sharing minority opinions must appear confident in consistently stating their views, other research indicates that minorities must walk a fine line in presenting their nonconforming opinions. They cannot appear dogmatic or rigid, for that will also reduce their influence (Nemeth et al., 1974). Therefore, for majority members to consider their perspective in the first place, the minority must come across as consistent and confident, but also flexible and open-minded. Nelson Mandela, a longtime opponent of the former apartheid government of South Africa, is an excellent example of a minority group leader (a minority in power but not in numbers) whose consistent, unwavering call for Black equality was combined with a nondogmatic approach to reform that won over many White South Africans. In 1994, he became the first president of a nonapartheid South Africa.

One other factor that also affects the ability of the minority to influence the majority is the *degree of difference* between the minority and the majority. *Single minorities* are individuals who differ from the majority only in terms of their beliefs, while *double minorities* are those who differ from the majority in terms of both beliefs and group membership (Martin, 1988). An example of a single minority is a heterosexual arguing for equal rights for gay people to the heterosexual majority. A gay person advocating such rights is a double minority. Research indicates that single minorities are more likely to exert influence over the majority than are double minorities (Alvaro & Crano, 1997). For example, in one study (Maass et al., 1982), conservative male participants engaged in a discussion of abortion with either a single (male confederate) or double (female confederate) minority. In these discussions, the minority consistently defended a liberal position rather than the conservative viewpoint of the male participants. Results indicated that the male participants perceived the double minorities (the liberal females) as having a stronger self-interest in the discussion, and they were less influenced by them than they were by the single minorities (the liberal males). By perceiving self-interest in the position of a double minority, it appears that people can more easily discount their arguments. Nelson Mandela recognized this tendency to discount double minorities in the struggle to put Black South Africans on an equal footing with their White counterparts. Some of the most effective influencers of White public opinion were fellow Whites who expressed antiapartheid beliefs.

Finally, minorities have the strongest influence when they take positions in the same direction as evolving cultural norms, but they are relatively ineffective when they argue against these emerging norms (Kiesler & Pallack, 1975). For example, during the early stages of the civil rights movement in the United States, Martin Luther King, Jr., and other civil rights activists espoused beliefs about equality and human justice that were in line with the emerging liberalism within the nation as a whole. Similarly, many political scientists predict that Farag Fouda's championing of social reform and democratic principles in Middle Eastern countries is consistent with slowly emerging norms in this region of the world. Although Fouda's political views are still largely rejected in most of these countries, if anti-American sentiment decreases in the coming years, prevailing norms may shift more in line with his position.

Overall, minorities are most successful in exerting influence on the majority when arguing for positions that are not too far from the prevailing majority position, and when they show a *consistent behavioral style* that the majority interprets as indicating *certainty* and *confidence*. On the other hand, minority influence will surely fail if the minority group *argues against evolving social norms* and exhibits a *rigid* style of negotiation with *inconsistently held beliefs*. In explaining why this is the case, Moscovici and Charlan Nemeth (1974) draw from the insights of Harold Kelley's attribution theory. As you remember from chapter 4, we tend to infer that the behavior of others is due to internal causes when (1) consensus is low (few others are behaving this way), (2) consistency is high (these people have behaved the same way over time), and (3) distinctiveness is low (they act this way in other situations). These conditions describe the behavior of strongly committed minorities. Not only are few others taking the belief position of the minority, but they consistently maintain this position over time and voice it in many varied situations. The logical conclusion that majority group members draw from all this information is that the voicing of such beliefs can only be due to deep and abiding personal convictions—convictions that perhaps should be seriously considered and scrutinized.

Even if minority groups follow a consistent avenue of persuasion, this does not mean that those holding majority beliefs will necessarily change. Remember, majority groups can impose sanctions and withdraw rewards from its members if they begin to espouse minority viewpoints, and this often is enough to maintain public compliance with majority opinions. Further, people's social identities generally consist of majority-held values and beliefs, and those aspects of the self-concept are resistant to change. However, although overt change toward minority positions may not readily take place, when majority members engage in critical analysis of these positions, it often stimulates *divergent thinking,* a cognitive process in which one considers a problem from varying perspectives (Gruenfel & Preston, 2000). What appears to initially motivate this enhanced scrutiny of the minority message is simply that it is different and unexpected (Baker & Petty, 1994). The benefit for the minority persuader is that this increased scrutiny often causes people to consider a wider variety of possible explanations or novel solutions to problems (Peterson & Nemeth, 1996).

Interestingly, when majority opinions eventually change due to the impact of the minority viewpoint, people often forget where they first heard their newly adopted views (refer to the *sleeper effect,* chapter 7, p. 217). In other words, the efforts of those who first propose minority positions often are not acknowledged when their influence attempts finally succeed. Such is the thankless job of the dissenter.

Conformity Is Sometimes Automatically Activated

Of the three behavioral consequences of social influence discussed in this chapter, conformity is the one that you are most likely to engage in with minimal thought. We have already discussed how simply thinking about entering a social setting can cause us to automatically

Based on what you learned in chapter 7 about gender differences in the effects of powerful speech on the ability to persuade, what is an alternative—or additional—interpretation of the findings from the Maass et al. (1982) experiment?

The power of a movement lies in the fact that it can indeed change the habits of people. This change is not the result of force but of dedication, of moral persuasion.

Steve Biko, South African political leader, 1946–1977

conform to the setting's social norms (see p. 316). Yet conformity can be automatically activated in ways having nothing to do with social norms (Dimberg et al., 2000; Epley & Gilovich, 1999). For example, I'm sure that you have had the experience of yawning after seeing someone else yawn or laughing when seeing others laugh. This *nonconscious mimicry* represents a type of conformity that we engage in within days of birth (Meltzoff & Moore, 1989). Make a happy, sad, or surprised face to a newborn and he or she will likely imitate the facial expression.

As discussed in chapter 4 (p. 107), evolutionary psychologists believe that this innate tendency to automatically imitate others' expressions is a survival reflex (Izard et al., 1995). For newborns, mimicking their mothers' gestures—especially facial gestures—helps establish an emotional bond between the two, making it more likely that the newborn will be nurtured and protected. In adulthood, mimicking others' expressions fosters positive feelings in those who are mimicked, even when they do not consciously notice the mimicry (van Baaren et al., 2004). Thus, nonconscious mimicry appears to create affiliation and rapport among people, and thereby fosters safety in groups.

SECTION SUMMARY

- Situational forces that influence conformity:

    the *size* of the influencing group

    the *cohesiveness* of the influencing group

    whether there is any *social support* for contrary positions
- Personal factors that influence conformity:

    private and public self-awareness

    self-presentational concerns

    desire for *personal control*

    gender differences are small and likely due to social roles
- *Collectivists* engage in more ingroup conforming than *individualists*
- *Minority group influence* is most likely when the minority group

    consistently and confidently states its dissenting views

    presents itself as flexible and open-minded
- Automatic imitation of others' gestures represents a type of unconscious conformity

COMPLIANCE

In trying to "get our way" with others, sometimes we forget the most direct route—simply asking them to do what we desire. However, because compliance involves a direct request, it generally induces more thinking and critical analysis by the target of social influence than conformity. As a compliance seeker, what strategies can you employ to increase the likelihood that others will grant your requests?

Three Factors That Foster Compliance Are Positive Moods, Reciprocity, and Giving Reasons

When people are roughly equal in social status, establishing the correct atmosphere or mood is especially important to increase compliance. Three factors that help create the proper atmosphere are to make people feel good, to do something for them, and to give them reasons for compliance. As you will discover, these factors also often reduce the likelihood that people will critically analyze the request.

POSITIVE MOOD

In the course of making requests, people soon discover that others are more likely to comply when they are in a good mood, especially if the requests are prosocial, such as helping others (Forgas, 1998). One reason for this is that people who are in good moods are simply more likely to be active and, thus, are more likely to engage in a range of behaviors, including granting requests (Batson et al., 1979). A second reason is that pleasant moods activate pleasant thoughts and memories, which likely makes people feel more favorable toward those making requests (Carlson et al., 1988). A third reason is that people in a happy mood are often less likely to critically analyze events, including requests, and thus, are more likely to grant them (Bless et al., 1996).

Because of this general awareness that good moods help create compliance, we often try to "butter someone up" before making a request. As discussed in chapter 4, this self-presentation strategy of *ingratiation* is designed to get others to view us favorably (Liden & Mitchell, 1988). Although people may be suspicious of ingratiators' motives after receiving their requests, the preceding flattery is still often effective in securing compliance (Kacmar et al., 1992).

Don't open a shop unless you know how to smile.

Jewish proverb

RECIPROCITY

How often have strangers offered you small gifts, such as flowers, pencils, or flags, and then asked you to donate money to their organization? If so, they were hoping that the token would lower your resistance to their request. The hope rested on a powerful social norm that people in all cultures follow, namely the **reciprocity norm.** Although this unwritten social norm helps to maintain fairness in social relationships by prescribing that favors or good deeds should be reciprocated, it can also be used to increase compliance (Uehara, 1995).

Research clearly demonstrates that giving someone a small gift or doing them a favor can easily lead to reciprocal compliance, especially if you seek compliance shortly after doing the good turn (Chartrand et al., 1999). For example, Dennis Regan (1971) had a college student work on a task with another student (a confederate) who acted in either a friendly or unfriendly manner. During a break, the confederate left and returned a few minutes later either with a soft drink for the student participant or with nothing. Shortly afterward, the confederate asked the student to buy twenty-five-cent raffle tickets. Those given the soft drink "gift" bought an average of two tickets, whereas those not given a soft drink bought only one. The effect of reciprocity was so strong that the students returned the favor even when the confederate had previously acted in an unlikable manner.

Reciprocity Norm

The expectation that one should return a favor or a good deed.

One does not give a gift without motive.

Mali proverb

A common technique to secure compliance from others is to first do them a favor or give them a gift. Due to the reciprocity norm, the recipients often then feel obligated to comply with a forthcoming request, such as a plea for monetary contributions. Who is likely to employ this technique in securing compliance?

Everyday experience tells us that reciprocity is commonly used as a strategy in making sales (Howard, 1995). Grocery stores provide free product samples. Insurance agents give away free pens or calendars. Car salespeople give potential customers new twenty-five-cent key rings—just right to hold the key to that new $25,000 automobile. In offering these "gifts," salespeople are often counting on the salience of the reciprocity norm overriding customers' careful consideration of the consequences of purchasing these products. Check out the interview with social psychologist Robert Cialdini on your Social Sense CD-ROM.

But it is not just professional salespeople who employ such tactics. Those who habitually use reciprocity to secure compliance are called *creditors,* because they try to keep others in their debt so they can cash in when necessary. People who are creditors tend to agree with statements such as "If someone does me a favor, it's a good idea to repay that person with a greater favor." Creditors know the power of indebtedness, and they work hard to make sure they are on the influential side of the reciprocity equation (Eisenberger et al., 1987). And they know all too well the wisdom of the proverb, "Beware of strangers bearing gifts."

GIVING REASONS

In granting someone's request, we often require a reason for complying. For instance, if you are in line at a grocery store with a small number of food items, and someone with only one item asks to go ahead because his sick grandmother is waiting for her cold medicine, you are likely to grant the request. The explanation given for his request strikes a responsive chord within you—it is "reasonable." Ellen Langer (1978) and her colleagues found evidence for the power of reason giving in gaining compliance when they had confederates try to cut in line ahead of others at a photocopying machine. In one condition the confederates gave no reason, merely asking, "May I use the photocopying machine to make five copies?" Sixty percent of those waiting complied with this "no reason" request. In another condition, when the confederates gave an explanation for their request ("May I use the photocopying machine to make five copies because I'm in a hurry?"), compliance increased to 94 percent, a significant difference. What Langer was interested in determining at this point was whether the actual content of the reason was important or whether any reason at all would suffice. To test this, she had her confederates try a third version of the request, where the reason given for cutting in line was really no explanation at all; it was merely a restatement of their desire to make copies ("May I use the photocopying machine to make five copies because I have to make copies?"). Surprisingly, this mere reiteration of a desire to make copies resulted in 94 percent compliance, identical to when an actual explanation was given ("I'm in a hurry").

Why does merely giving a reason—any reason—result in greater compliance? Giving reasons may be important because of our habitual desire to explain others' actions and our use of cognitive heuristics or "mental shortcuts" in arriving at these explanations (refer to chapter 5). We are especially likely to seek an explanation for behavior when it runs counter to the standard social norms (for example, cutting in front of someone in a line). We have also learned through experience that there are exceptions to these social norms, and when people ask to be granted an exception, it is expected that they will provide a reason why the exception should be granted. Because we believe that others are as concerned about acting appropriately as we are, we tend to assume that when someone gives us a reason for doing something, it must be worthy of an exception. As a result, we may often mindlessly grant a request accompanied by a reason because we assume the requester would not ask if the request was illegitimate. When my daughter Lillian was 2 years old, she had already learned the importance of giving reasons when seeking compliance from her parents. In asking to go outside she would say, "Can I go outside and play? Because I have to go outside and play." Based on Langer's findings, when it comes to securing compliance, Lillian had already developed sufficient social skills to do quite nicely in the adult world.

In summarizing this analysis of factors that affect compliance, additional insight is provided by the *elaboration likelihood model* of persuasion discussed in chapter 7 (pp. 213–216). As you recall, according to this model, persuasion can occur through either the thoughtful mode of central processing or the lazy mode of peripheral processing (Petty & Cacciopo,

A fair request should be followed by the deed in silence.

Dante Alighieri, Italian poet, 1265–1321

1986; Petty et al., 1995). Regarding compliance, the research discussed here suggests that positive moods, making the reciprocity norm salient, or providing reasons for why one should grant a request are all likely to foster compliance by inducing lazy peripheral processing of the requester's message. In other words, whenever any of these factors are present, the resulting compliance is less likely to be based on thoughtful consideration of the request.

Various Two-Step Compliance Strategies Are Effective for Different Reasons

Earlier, we discussed how "creditors" secure compliance by keeping tabs on others' debts to them. Professional creditors, such as insurance agents, car dealers, or door-to-door salespersons rely on more than just indebtedness to secure compliance to their sales requests. In making sales, they realize that it often takes more than a single plea to win over a potential customer. Social psychologists have studied how multiple requests, employed in different ways, can result in some very effective compliance techniques.

FOOT-IN-THE-DOOR

In chapter 6, we saw that many people feel pressure to remain consistent in their beliefs. Salespersons, recognizing this need for consistency, often employ a two-step compliance strategy known as the **foot-in-the-door technique.** In this strategy, the person secures compliance with a small request and then follows it up later with a larger, less desirable request. For example, imagine that a young woman knocks on your door and tells you she is gathering signatures on a petition supporting environmental protection. Would you be willing to sign? This question represents the first small request. Being proenvironment, you readily agree. After signing, the woman says she is also seeking money for her organization to better fight for the environment, and would you be willing to make a contribution? This is the second, larger request. Chances are, if you signed the petition you will also contribute some money. Joseph Schwarzwald and his coworkers (1983) found that, using a very similar scenario, they were able to produce a 75 percent increase in donations over a comparison request strategy involving no prior petition signing. Similar results have also been obtained in fund-raising efforts on the Internet (Gueguen & Jacob, 2001).

Meta-analyses of studies using the foot-in-the-door technique indicate that it is fairly reliable in securing compliance (Beaman et al., 1983; Cialdin & Trost, 1998). However, if people reject the small request, they are even less likely to comply with the larger request than those who were not approached with the small request (Snyder & Cunningham, 1975). Can you guess why? It appears that the foot-in-the-door effect causes a change in self-perception (Burger, 1999; Burger & Caldwell, 2003). In not granting the small first request, people may decide that they are not the type of person who grants those kinds of requests. Therefore, because of this new self-image, they are more likely to later reject the larger request. The same self-perception process operates for those who do grant the small request. They perceive themselves as cooperative, and therefore, later comply to the second, larger request in order to maintain their cooperative self-image. For this technique to work, the initial request must be large enough to cause people to think about the implications of their behavior, and they must believe they are freely complying (Gorassini & Olson, 1995).

DOOR-IN-THE-FACE

A second compliance technique that also uses multiple requests is in some sense the reverse of the foot-in-the door strategy. In the **door-in-the-face technique,** the person seeking compliance starts by asking for a very large favor—one the recipient is almost certain to reject. When the rejection occurs, the request is changed to a much less costly request. Securing this second request was the objective of the influencer from the start. The first rejection is the door in the face, and it is presumed that the second request stands a better chance of being accepted if it is preceded by this rejection (Cialdini & Trost, 1998). Phone solicitors for charities and other nonprofit organizations typically employ this technique by first asking people for a large donation and then reducing their request when the large request is refused. Likewise,

He that does not ask will never get a bargain.

French proverb

Foot-in-the-Door Technique

A two-step compliance technique in which the influencer secures compliance to a small request, and then later follows this with a larger, less desirable request.

CRITICAL *thinking*

How might the foot-in-the-door compliance strategy be combined with the effects of postdecision dissonance (see chapter 6, p. 200) to partly explain how some people initially become involved and then committed to religious or political cults?

Door-in-the-Face Technique

A two-step compliance technique in which, after having a large request refused, the influencer counteroffers with a much smaller request.

teenagers have been known to ask their parents whether they could go on an unsupervised weekend trip with their friends (a fabrication), and then respond to the inevitable refusal by asking whether they could at least join their friends at a local party (their actual goal).

A study by Robert Cialdini and his colleagues (1975) illustrates the effectiveness of this compliance strategy. College students were approached by teams of confederates who asked them to volunteer to spend two hours a week over the next year as "big brothers" or "big sisters" to juveniles in need of older role models. Not surprisingly, no one agreed to this request, which is exactly what Cialdini expected. But the confederates then followed this rejection with a second request: Would the students be willing to spend two hours just once taking the same kids to the zoo? Fifty percent agreed to this request. In a control condition, when this smaller request had been presented without being preceded by the large request, less than 17 percent of the students agreed to comply.

For the door-in-the-face effect to occur, three conditions must be met. First, the initial request must be very large so that when people refuse they make no negative inferences about themselves (for example, "I'm not a very generous person"). Second, the interval between the first and second requests must be relatively short so that the feeling of obligation is still salient. In contrast, a longer interval (weeks or even months) between the two requests can still be effective for the foot-in-the-door technique. Finally, the third condition is that the same person who made the first large request must make the subsequent smaller request. People perceive this second request as a concession by the requester that the first request was too large. Once this perceived concession occurs, due to the reciprocity norm, people feel pressure to reciprocate with a concession of their own—agree to the second request. Of the two sequential compliance techniques discussed thus far, the "face" approach has been shown to be more effective than the "foot" technique (Harari et al., 1980).

The door-in-the-face strategy is often used by both parties in negotiating contracts for such things as houses, cars, and salaries. Both parties begin with an economic position that is extremely favorable to themselves but very unfavorable to the other side. Following the initial proposal rejections, one or both of them might make concessions that are actually closer to what they really hope to obtain from the other. Often, those who make less reciprocal concessions and who are also less concerned with appearing unreasonable are the ones who secure the best deals (Pendleton & Batson, 1979).

THAT'S-NOT-ALL

That's-Not-All Technique

A two-step compliance technique in which the influencer makes a large request, then immediately offers a discount or bonus before the initial request is refused.

Closely related to the door-in-the-face technique is the **that's-not-all technique,** which involves the influencer making a large request, but then immediately offering a discount or bonus that makes the request more reasonable. Unlike the door-in-the-face technique, however, the person is not given the opportunity to reject the large request before it is reduced or "sweetened." The lowered price tags on store merchandise and the ads for "Buy One, Get One Free" deals are examples of this two-step compliance strategy.

Jerry Burger (1986) demonstrated the effectiveness of this tactic when he conducted a bake sale at Santa Clara University. On the table where the sale was taking place were a number of cupcakes with no indicated price. In one condition, when potential buyers asked how much one cupcake cost, they were given a high price. Then, before they could respond, they were also told that this price included a "bonus" bag of cookies. In a control condition, potential buyers were immediately shown the bag of cookies and told that they were included in the total price. Results indicated that 73 percent of those who experienced the that's-not-all tactic bought the sweets, versus only 40 percent of those who were offered everything up front.

In a second cupcake study, instead of the request being "sweetened" by a bonus, it was reduced in size. In the that's-not-all condition, people were told that the cupcakes cost $1.25 but that they would be sold to the buyer at $1.00, because the booth would be closing soon. In the control condition, people were merely told that the cupcakes cost $1.00. As shown in figure 9.6, the that's-not-all strategy was again more effective in selling cupcakes: 55 percent of those in this condition bought cupcakes, versus only 20 percent in the control condition.

FIGURE 9.6

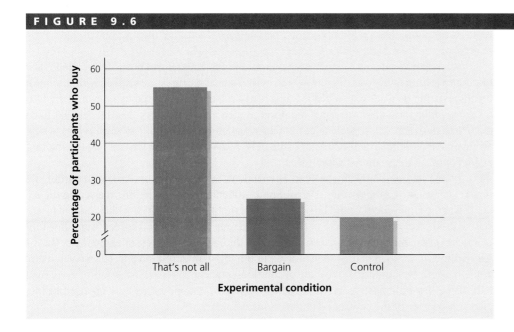

The effectiveness of the "that's-not-all" compliance technique was demonstrated in a campus bake sale. By far, the highest percentage of potential customers purchased cupcakes when the deal was "sweetened" by first stating one price and then lowering it before the customer could respond. When customers were told that the price had already been lowered (bargain) or when they were merely given the low price right away (control), purchases were much less likely.

Burger was also interested in determining whether the that's-not-all effect occurred only because the offered items were now a bargain, and so he created a third condition. In this *bargain* condition, the seller stated to the potential buyer that the cupcakes were now priced at $1.00, although formerly they were $1.25. The bargain condition only resulted in a 25 percent purchase rate (see figure 9.6). This finding suggests that the that's-not-all strategy is not just effective because it offers a bargain to the influence target, but there also appears to be a psychological potency created by the influencer personally sweetening the deal that lowers people's resistance to the request.

How exactly does the that's-not-all technique lower resistance? One possibility is that when the salesperson's request is reduced or sweetened, the customer may perceive this as a concession that the original request was unreasonable. Following the norm of reciprocity, the customer may now feel an increased obligation to reciprocate this act by agreeing to the better price (as in the door-in-the-face effect). Another possible way in which the that's-not-all technique may lower resistance is by altering the customer's "anchor point" against which the purchase decision is made (see chapter 5 discussion of the *anchoring and adjustment heuristic,* p. 148). That is, if customers are contemplating the purchase of a product for which they themselves don't have a fixed price in mind (such as cupcakes at a bake sale), the salesperson's costly first request sets the price standard, or anchor. When the second cheaper price immediately follows the costly price, it alters the anchor point and creates the impression that the product is a bargain.

Although the that's-not-all technique is effective, success appears to depend on targets responding rather mindlessly to the request (Pollock et al., 1998). For example, one recent study found that compliance occurs only when the initial request is within reason (Burger et al., 1999). If you first ask people to buy cupcakes for the extremely high price of $3.00 apiece, lowering your price to $1.00 is unlikely to induce compliance because the initial request appears ridiculous, and it places potential customers on guard. Now, instead of engaging in the type of "lazy" thinking discussed in chapter 5 (*heuristics*) and chapter 7 (*peripheral route processing*), the target is motivated to more critically analyze the offer. Under this greater scrutiny, compliance decreases.

LOW-BALLING

A few years ago I went shopping for a new car to replace my badly rusted "old reliable." After test driving one car, I made an offer that included my car as a trade-in for $700. The salesperson said we had a deal; he just had to get the manager's OK. After ten minutes, however, the salesperson returned looking forlorn, saying the manager would only take my trade-in for $300. Then with a big smile he declared, "And that means you can have *your* new car for only $400 more!"

What happened here? In the vernacular of the car dealer, I had been "low-balled." The **low-ball technique** is a strategy in which an influencer secures agreement with a request by understating its true cost. When the size of the request is increased by revealing the hidden costs, even though most people are disappointed and even angry that the deal has been made less desirable, they often stick to their initial commitment and proceed with the new arrangement (Gueguen et al., 2002). Fortunately, I was aware of the research on low-balling and recognized the scam for what it was.

In one low-balling study, psychology students were phoned and asked to participate in an experiment (Cialdini et al., 1978). Some students were told before answering the request that the experiment would begin at the undesirable time of 7 A.M. Other students were first asked if they would agree to participate, and only after they had agreed were they told that the experiment began at such an early hour (the low ball). As testament to the power of low-balling, more than half of the students in the low-ball condition agreed to participate, while fewer than one-third of the control condition students did so. Furthermore, more than half of the low-balled students actually kept their 7 A.M. appointment, as opposed to less than one-quarter of the control condition students.

Why does the low-ball procedure work? One important factor is the psychology of commitment. Once people make a decision, they tend to justify it to themselves by thinking of its positive aspects. As they become increasingly committed to their course of action, they grow more resistant to changing their minds. This is why car dealers will let you, the prospective buyer, sit in the showroom for a while before telling you that they require more money. During that time, they count on you fantasizing about "your new car" so that later you will pay the extra money to drive it off the lot. Yet, if you spend that time reviewing what you have learned here, you stand a better chance of leaving the showroom with a deal to your liking. In this case, knowledge truly is power—social influence power.

Low-Ball Technique

A two-step compliance strategy in which the influencer secures agreement with a request by understating its true cost.

Low-balling taken to new heights.

Dilbert © by Scott Adams. Reprinted by permission of United Features Syndicate, Inc.

- Factors that foster compliance:

    positive moods   reciprocity norm   providing reasons

- Compliance techniques that utilize multiple requests:

    foot-in-the-door   door-in-the-face   that's not all   low-balling

OBEDIENCE

As you can see from our overview of both conformity processes and compliance strategies, many social influence pressures are relatively hidden and subtly employed. In this respect, obedience differs from these other types of influence because it is overt and easily recognized as an exercise of power.

When an authority figure orders people to engage in a particular behavior, you might expect that their need for personal control would result in a good deal of disobedience. If the order was to engage in behavior that appeared to pose serious health risks to others, you might predict that wide-scale disobedience would occur. Would it? What would you do under such circumstances? To answer this question, let's explore the most discussed social psychological study ever conducted (Blass, 2000).

Milgram's Research Suggests That Obeying Destructive Commands Is More the Rule Than the Exception

Imagine that you have volunteered to participate in an experiment on learning. Upon arriving at the laboratory, you find that a 50-year-old man is also taking part in the study. The experimenter explains that the study will investigate the effects of punishment on the learning of word pairs. The punishment will be electrical shock. One of you will be the "teacher," and the other will be the "learner." A drawing of names determines that you will be the teacher. When the learner discovers that he will be receiving shocks, he tells the experimenter that he has a mild heart condition ("Nothing serious, but since electricity is being used I thought I should tell you"). The experimenter replies that while the shocks may be painful, they will not cause permanent tissue damage. The learner is then taken to an adjacent room where he is strapped into a chair and electrodes are attached to his arms. As this is being done, the experimenter explains that your task is to teach the learner a list of word pairs, to then test him on the list, and to administer punishment whenever he makes a mistake. In front of you is a shock generator, which has a row of thirty switches ranging from 15 to 450 volts. You are instructed to start at the lowest intensity level and to increase the shock by one switch (15 volts) for each subsequent learner error. To give you some idea of what the shock feels like, the experimenter gives you a 45-volt shock—and it hurts. You are a bit nervous now, but you do not say anything.

Once the study begins, the learner makes many mistakes, and you respond by flipping the shock switches. Starting at 75 volts, you hear through the intercom system the learner grunting and moaning in pain whenever you deliver the shocks. At 150 volts he demands to be released, shouting, "Experimenter! That's all! Get me out of here. My heart's starting to bother me now. I refuse to go on!" Now your nervousness becomes nail-biting anxiety. At 180 volts he shouts that he can no longer stand the pain. At 300 volts he says that he absolutely refuses to provide any more answers. Responding to this attempt by the learner to halt the study, the experimenter instructs you to treat the absence of a response as equivalent to an error and to deliver the appropriate level of shock. Even though the learner no

. . . far more, and far more hideous, crimes have been committed in the name of obedience than have ever been committed in the name of rebellion.

C. P. Snow, English novelist, 1905–1980

Obedience to the law is demanded as a right; not asked as a favor.

Theodore Roosevelt, U.S. president, 1858–1919

In schools all over the world, little boys learn that their country is the greatest in the world, and the highest honor that could befall them would be to defend it heroically someday. The fact that empathy has traditionally been conditioned out of boys facilitates their obedience to leaders who order them to kill strangers.

Myriam Miedzian, U.S. author, 1991

(Top) Stanley Milgram and the "shock generator," which he used in his obedience experiments. (Bottom) In this replication of the obedience experiment, the teacher (participant) had to force the learner's (confederate's) hand onto a shock plate. Less than one-third obeyed the experimenter under these conditions.

"Oh God, let's stop it."

A reluctant but obedient participant in the Milgram experiments, Milgram, 1963, p. 377

longer gives answers, he continues to scream in agony whenever your finger flips the shock generator switch. When you surpass the 330-volt switch, the learner not only does not give any answers, he falls silent, not to be heard from again. As you continue to increase the shock intensity, the labels under the switches now read, "Danger—Severe Shock" and you realize you are getting closer to the last switch, the 450-volt switch, which is simply labeled "XXX." You desperately want to stop, but when you hesitate, the experimenter first tells you, "Please continue," then "The experiment requires that you continue," then "It is absolutely essential that you go on," and finally, "You have no other choice, you must go on!"

What would you do? Would you disobey the experimenter's commands? When would you stop obeying? Is it possible that you would continue to deliver all the shocks, including the dangerous 450 volts, despite the learner's protests? How many of your friends do you think would obey the experimenter's orders if they were the teachers?

I'm guessing that your prediction is that you and your friends would disobey the experimenter's authority and refuse to continue the learning experiment well before the 450-

TABLE 9.2

Shock Levels at Which Milgram's Participants Disobeyed (n = 40) Compared to Predicted Disobedience by Psychiatrists

Voltage	Actual Number of Defectors	Percentage	Actual Cumulative % of Defectors	Predicted Cumulative % of Defectors
75	0	0.0	0.0	15
135	0	0.0	0.0	44
150	0	0.0	0.0	68
210	0	0.0	0.0	86
300	5	12.5	12.5	96
315	4	10.0	22.5	96
330	2	5.0	27.5	97
345	1	2.5	30.0	99
360–435	2	5.0	35.0	99
450[a]	0	0.0	35.0	99.9

[a]Although a team of psychiatrists predicted that only about one-tenth of 1 percent of the participants in the Milgram obedience research would fully obey the experimenter's commands and administer the highest shock level on the generator, in actuality, 65 percent of the participants fully obeyed the experimenter's commands. The first point at which participants began disobeying was when the learner refused or was unable to respond (the 300-volt level).

volt limit. If this is your prediction, you are in good company, for widespread disobedience is exactly what was predicted by college students, middle-class adults, and psychiatrists who were presented with this hypothetical scenario (Milgram, 1963). People in all three groups guessed that they would disobey by about 135 volts, and none thought they would go beyond 300 volts. The psychiatrists, when asked about other people's level of obedience, predicted that less than one-tenth of 1 percent of participants—one person out of one thousand—would obey the experimenter completely.

To determine the actual level of obedience, Milgram conducted this study at Yale University, using forty adult males who ranged in age from 20 to 50 years and who came from all walks of life. The drawing was rigged so that the participant always became the teacher. The learner was a confederate and received no actual shocks. Even his screams of protest and pain were prerecorded so that all participants heard exactly the same thing. To Milgram's astonishment, 65 percent of the participants (twenty-six out of forty) obeyed the experimenter completely, despite these convincing cries of agony from the learner. In fact, all participants who reached 450 volts obeyed the experimenter's command to continue with the procedure using the 450-volt switch until the experiment was halted a short time later. Table 9.2 provides a summary of when the disobedient participants refused to continue delivering shocks. As you can see, all obeyed up to 300 volts. View on your Social Sense CD-ROM an excerpt from one of Milgram's studies showing an actual participant ordered to deliver electrical shocks. Does he appear to be obeying willingly?

The simplest interpretation of these findings is that Milgram inadvertently recruited closet sadists who were more than willing to inflict pain on the hapless learner. However soothing this explanation would be to our collective psyches, it does not stand up to the available evidence (Darley, 1995). Milgram's participants were not suffering from any personality disorders that would cause them to enjoy their destructive obedience. In fact, their actions caused them a great deal of stress (Elms, 1995; Elms & Milgram, 1966). Participants were observed sweating, trembling, stuttering, biting their lips, and groaning as they struggled through the experimental procedure.

. . . Obedience, Bane of all genius, virtue, freedom, truth, makes slaves of men, and, of the human frame, a mechanized automaton.

Percy Bysshe Shelley, English poet, 1792–1822

Social Sense

View a presentation of Milgram's obedience study.

Some sense of their state of mind can be gleaned from remarks made by one of the fully obedient individuals who began the experiment calmly but became increasingly tense as the learner protested the shocks being delivered:

150 volts delivered: "You want me to keep going?"

165 volts delivered: "That guy is hollering in there. There's a lot of them here. He's liable to have heart condition. You want me to go?"

180 volts delivered: "He can't stand it! I'm not going to kill that man in there! You hear him hollering? He's hollering. He can't stand it. What if something happens to him? . . . I'm not going to get that man sick in there. He's hollering in there. You know what I mean? I mean I refuse to take the responsibility. He's getting hurt in there. He's in there hollering. Too many left here. Geez, if he gets them wrong. There's too many of them left. I mean who is going to take responsibility if anything happens to that gentleman?"

[The experimenter accepts responsibility]: "All right."

195 volts delivered: "You see he's hollering. Hear that. Gee, I don't know."

[The experimenter says, "The experiment requires that you go on"]: "I know it does, sir, but I mean—hugh—he don't know what he's in for. He's up to 195 volts."

210 volts delivered.

225 volts delivered.

240 volts delivered: "Aw no. You mean I've got to keep going up with the scale? No sir. I'm not going to kill that man! I'm not going to give him 450 volts!"

[The experimenter says, "The experiment requires that you go on."]: "I know it does, but that man is hollering there, sir. . . ."

Because the findings were so unexpected, Milgram carried out a number of variations of his experiment to better understand the conditions under which obedience and disobedience would be most likely. When college students and women served as participants, the same level of destructive obedience was found (Milgram, 1974). Different researchers also obtained similar results in several other countries, suggesting that these high levels of obedience were not solely an American phenomenon. Australia had a 68 percent obedience level (Kilham & Mann, 1974), Jordan was at 63 percent (Shanab & Yahya, 1977), and Germany was the highest at 85 percent (Mantell, 1971).

Some critics initially suggested that the high obedience was due to the prestige of Yale University and participants' presumed belief that no one at Yale would allow harm to come to anyone in the study (Baumrind, 1964; Orne, 1962). To test this possibility, Milgram (1965) moved the experimental site to a run-down office building in Bridgeport, Connecticut, with no noticeable affiliations with Yale. Although obedience decreased slightly, the difference was not significant—48 percent of the participants delivered the maximum shock level. Although switching locations from a prestigious to a nonprestigious institution did not have a significant effect on obedience, when the experimenter was replaced with an ordinary person (actually a confederate), obedience dropped to 20 percent. What these findings suggest is that the social role of "scientist" or "researcher" has sufficient prestige and authority to secure obedience, regardless of the social context (see Blass, 1996).

Although an authority figure is much more likely to be obeyed than a nonauthority, situational factors strengthen or weaken this influence. In a follow-up study, Milgram varied the proximity of the experimenter to the teacher. In one condition, the experimenter sat a few feet from the teacher as he delivered the electrical shocks to the learner. In a second condition, after giving initial instructions, the experimenter left the room and gave his orders by phone. In a third condition, the teacher received his instructions on a tape recorder and never actually met the experimenter. Findings from these three conditions indicated that obedience decreased as the distance to the experimenter increased. In fact, when the experimenter was absent, several participants administered shocks of a lower voltage than the experimenter called for.

The doctrine of blind obedience and unqualified submission to any human power, whether civil or ecclesiastical, is the doctrine of despotism.

Angelina Grimke, U.S. abolitionist and feminist, 1805–1879

In another series of experiments, the proximity of the learner to the teacher was varied (Milgram, 1974). In one condition, the learner and teacher were located in separate rooms without access to intercom systems, and thus, the teacher could not hear the learner's cries of protest and pain. The teacher's only knowledge of the victim's reaction was that he pounded on the adjoining wall at 300 volts and subsequently stopped responding to the word pairs. In another condition, the learner was seated in the same room only a few feet from the teacher. In a third condition, the learner sat right next to the teacher, resting his hand on a metal plate in order to receive the shock. At 350 volts, the learner refused to put his hand on the plate to receive the shock, and the experimenter then ordered the teacher to force the learner's hand onto the shock plate. In all of these studies, results indicated that the closer the teacher was to the learner, the lower the level of obedience.

In addition to testing for proximity and site effects, Milgram also investigated how group pressure might influence obedience. In one study, three teachers (two of them confederates) split up the duties previously assigned to one. The naive participant always was assigned the role of actually delivering the electrical shock, while the confederate-teachers read the word pairs and told the learner if his answers were correct. In one condition, the confederate-teachers simply followed the experimenter's commands and did not express any sympathy for the learner. In another condition, the confederates were openly rebellious—one refused to continue after 150 volts and the other quit at the 210-volt level. The first condition only slightly increased obedience (72 percent) above the original study's level, but the second condition resulted in complete obedience in only 10 percent of the participants.

The likely explanation for this sharp drop in obedience is that the open defiance of the confederates broke the social consensus of the situation and reduced the strength of the experimenter's social power. Did the participants in this study recognize the liberating effect that the rebellious confederate-teachers had on their own willingness to disobey the orders of the authority figure? No. Three-fourths of the participants who disobeyed believed that they would have stopped even without the other teachers' examples. Yet the previous studies strongly argue against this belief, suggesting that people seriously underestimate the impact that others have on their own behavior. Figure 9.7 summarizes the findings of some of these studies and identifies factors that foster and inhibit obedience.

Recently, François Rochot and his coworkers (2000) analyzed the audio recordings of one of Milgram's obedience studies to better understand how participants behaved over the course of the experiment. Results indicated that all participants were initially cooperative toward the experimenter, but this changed as the learner began complaining. What predicted obedience versus disobedience was the timing of participants' first firm opposition to the shocks they were told to administer to the learner. Those who firmly verbally opposed the experimenter by 150 volts all ended up defying his authority by disobeying. In contrast, only about half of the participants who began their verbal challenges after 150 volts ever disobeyed. Further, no disobedience ever occurred among those who never took a firm verbal stance against the experimenter. This reanalysis of one of Milgram's classic studies provides additional insights into the social psychological process of obedience and disobedience. It appears that a crucial factor in resisting the destructive commands of authority figures is an early and firm statement of opposition to what is transpiring.

Orders to Inflict Psychological Harm on Victims Are Also Likely to Be Obeyed

Milgram's experiments demonstrated the frightening willingness of people to inflict physical pain upon innocent victims due to the commands of authority figures. Two Dutch social psychologists, Wim Meeus and Quinten Raaijmakers (1986, 1995), conducted a series of experiments to determine whether people would be equally willing to obey the commands of authority figures in inflicting psychological pain on others.

In one study, when participants arrived at the lab, they met a man who told them he was there to take a test as part of a job interview. The applicant further stated that obtaining

Obedience is the mother of success, and the wife of security.

Aeschylus, Greek dramatist, 525–456 B.C.

group pressure

FIGURE 9.7

To determine what factors increase or decrease obedience beyond the baseline 65 percent level, Milgram varied the location of the experiment, the participant's proximity to the victim and the experimenter, and the presence of obedient or disobedient confederates. As you can see, all of these factors influenced obedience levels.

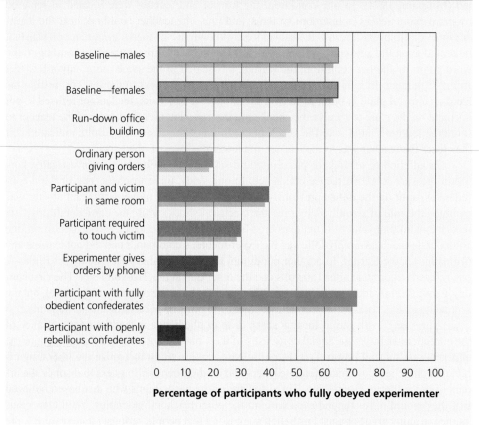

Percentage of participants who fully obeyed experimenter

the job depended on whether he passed the test. When the experimenter arrived, he took the participant aside and told him he was interested in people's ability to work under stress. To aid in this investigation, the participant was told to induce stress in the job applicant while he was taking the test. To induce stress, the participant was instructed to make a series of fifteen increasingly negative remarks about the applicant's performance and abilities as he read him the test items. Examples of some of the "stress remarks" were, "If you continue like this, you will fail the test," and "This job is much too difficult for you. You are more suited for lower functions." Actually, the applicant was a confederate who had been instructed to react to the stress remarks in a specified manner. First, he merely protested the distracting remarks. Next, he pleaded with the participant to stop making him nervous, and then he angrily refused to put up with such negative treatment. Finally, he fell into a state of despair. As the negative remarks escalated, the applicant's performance began to deteriorate and he eventually failed the test and lost the job. Whenever participants hesitated to deliver the next negative remark, the experimenter would order them to continue.

As in the Milgram studies, Meeus and Raaijmakers were interested in how many participants would follow the experimenter's orders through the entire set of stress remarks, despite the "fact" that their behavior was causing psychological harm to another. In a control condition in which the experimenter did not order hesitant participants to continue, everyone stopped before the fifteen stress remarks had been read. However, in the experimental condition in which orders were issued to reluctant participants, 92 percent of them—both males and females—obeyed fully.

In a follow-up to this study, Meeus and Raaijmakers (1987) attempted to determine whether obedience would be reduced if participants were forewarned about the nature of the task. With this in mind, they sent people a letter a day before they were to participate in the stress remark study and told them what they would be doing. This letter contained specific information that a job applicant might perform poorly on an exam due to their negative comments and thus lose a job he would normally obtain. Despite the opportunity to consider the implications of their actions away from the actual presence of the authority figure, the next day all participants fully obeyed the experimenters' commands.

In discussing the meaning of his obedience experiments, Milgram made the following remarks that would equally apply to Meeus and Raaijmakers's findings:

> The behavior revealed in the experiments reported here is normal human behavior but revealed under conditions that show with particular clarity the danger to human survival inherent in our make-up. And what is it we have seen? Not aggression, for there is no anger, vindictiveness, or hatred in those who shocked the victim. Men do become angry; they do act hatefully and explode in rage against others. But not here. Something far more dangerous is revealed: the capacity for man to abandon his humanity, indeed, the inevitability that he does so, as he merges his unique personality into larger institutional structures. This is a fatal flaw nature has designed into us, and which in the long run gives our species only a modest chance of survival. (1974, p. 188)

Observing Others Defy Authority Greatly Reduces Obedience

Milgram's commentary on his own obedience research paints a bleak picture of humankind's ability to resist destructive authoritarian pressure. Yet is the abandonment of our humanity as inevitable as he suggests? Perhaps the depth of Milgram's pessimism is partly due to the special circumstances created in his research design. In most of the obedience studies discussed thus far, a lone individual engages in destructive behavior after being placed in a situation in which he or she receives orders from an authority figure. What would happen if antisocial orders are delivered not to a lone individual but, rather, to an entire group of people? Would this collective be as malleable as the lone individual?

William Gamson and his colleagues (1982) explored this question when they recruited groups of people to participate in a purported discussion of community standards. Participants, scheduled in groups of nine, arrived at a local motel for the discussion and were greeted by the "coordinator." This coordinator told them that the proceedings would be videotaped for a large oil company that was being sued by a former manager of one of its local gas stations. This former employee was fired after the company learned he was living with a woman to whom he was not married. The company justified its actions by stating that its representatives must be beyond moral reproach. Despite this explanation by the coordinator, participants soon learned some additional information that cast a different light on the firing—the manager was fired after appearing on local TV, where he spoke out against higher gas prices.

Shortly after discussion began about whether the manager's lifestyle was morally offensive to those in the community, the coordinator interrupted and told three group members to argue on camera as if they were offended by the manager's lifestyle. A short time later, he again interrupted and told three more members to also act offended. Soon the coordinator had instructed all members to act offended on camera concerning the manager's lifestyle and to state that they would not do business at his gas station. Then he told them there was an affidavit to be signed and notarized that gave the oil company the right to introduce the videotapes as evidence in court, editing them as they saw fit.

As originally designed, some discussion groups were to include a confederate member who would either take a more or less active role in mobilizing rebellion against the oil company's actions. However, as the malicious intent of the videotaped discussion began to dawn on the actual group participants, they began to rebel on their own. One participant, when told to act offended before the videocamera, expressed his defiance by adopting a mocking, twangy accent and stating, "Next to ma waaf, ma car is my favritt

I hold it that a little rebellion now and then, is a good thing, and as necessary in the political world as storms in the physical. . . . It is a medicine for the sound health of government.

Thomas Jefferson, U.S. president, 1743–1826

Disobedience when it is not criminally but morally, religiously, or politically motivated is always a collective act and it is justified by the values of the collectivity and the mutual engagements of its members.

Social historian Michael Walzer, 1970

thing, an ah ain't sending neither of 'em tuh that gas stoishen." Some groups became so outraged at the company's attempts to use them to discredit the former employee that they threatened to forcibly confiscate the videotapes and expose the company to the local news media. Confronted by one outraged group after another, the researchers were forced to terminate the experiment due to fears that it was causing too much stress on the participants.

Why did this experiment result in such open disobedience when Milgram's research produced such widespread obedience? In both studies there were agents of authority, the experimenter and the coordinator. In both studies the original intention of participants was to obey the instructions of these authorities. In both studies the authorities overstepped the proper moral boundaries and began to demand unjust actions by the participants. The possibility that people generally became less prone to obedience over the twenty years separating these studies is not supported by an analysis of other obedience studies conducted during this time period (Blass, 1999). Instead the basic difference between these studies is that Milgram's participants were alone, whereas Gamson's were in groups. Because eight or nine of Gamson's group members were naive participants, the possibility of collective action always existed. Milgram's design, on the other hand, has never been tried with more than one naive participant in the teacher role, and so the possibility of collective action here has never been studied.

Although the Milgram design never tested more than one participant at a time, in one of his experiments he did use two confederates who posed as coteachers along with the actual participant. As discussed previously (see p. 343), when the participant observed others openly defying the destructive commands of the authority figure, he became much more willing to disobey as well. In a very real psychological sense, the rebellious confederates served as models for the participant's own disobedience. Similar findings were also obtained in Asch's conformity studies: social support allowed others to more easily express their own opinions.

(see p. 343)

> *One who breaks an unjust law that conscience tells him is unjust, and who willingly accepts the penalty of imprisonment in order to arouse the consciousness of the community over its injustice, is in reality expressing the highest respect for the law.*
>
> Martin Luther King, Jr., U.S. civil rights leader, 1929–1968

SECTION SUMMARY

- Obedience research indicates that

    almost two-thirds of Milgram's participants obeyed the destructive commands of an authority figure

    social support helps people follow their own beliefs when confronted by powerful others

TOWARD A UNIFIED UNDERSTANDING OF SOCIAL INFLUENCE

Although different factors are involved in the various forms of social influence discussed in this chapter, the task of social scientists is to discover common principles operating in the exercise of social power. In this section, we examine one theory that attempts to predict when influence attempts are most likely to succeed.

Social Impact Theory

The theory that the amount of social influence others have depends on their number, strength, and immediacy to those they are trying to influence.

Social Impact Theory States That Influence Is Determined by People's Number, Strength, and Immediacy

As developed by Bibb Latané (1981), **social impact theory** states that the amount of influence others have in a given situation (their social impact) is a function of three factors: their *number, strength,* and *immediacy.* This social impact operates like physical impact. For example, the

FIGURE 9.8

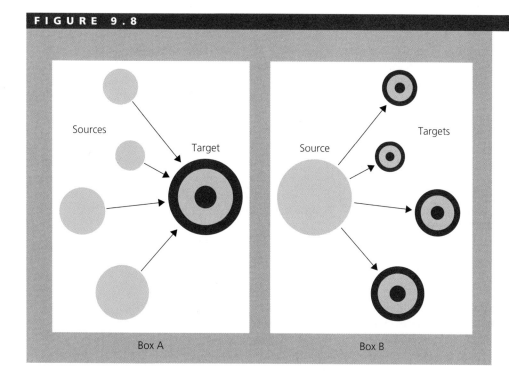

Box A   Box B

The Psychology of Social Impact: Source and Target Factors

According to social impact theory, the impact of other people on the target person depends on (a) the number of people present (number of source circles), the strength or importance of these people (size of the source circles), and their immediacy to the target person (nearness of the source circles to the target). Social impact increases as source factors increase. In addition, the total impact of other people on target persons depends on (b) the number of target persons (number of target circles), the strength of these targets (size of target circles), and their immediacy (nearness to one another). Social impact decreases as target factors increase.

amount of light falling on a surface depends not only on how many lights are turned on, but also on the strength or power of the bulbs and how close they are to the surface. Similarly, as illustrated in figure 9.8, Box A, a person will be more influenced by others when there are more of them, when they are stronger sources of influence, and when they are physically closer.

Although social impact theory predicts that people become more influential as their numbers increase, what about the "leveling off" effect found in the Asch (1956) conformity research? In that study, adding more confederates beyond three or four had little impact on conformity. Latané contends that this is due to another principle of social impact theory, which states that as the number of influencing persons increases, their individual impact decreases. Returning to the lightbulb analogy, when you turn on a second light in a room that previously had only one bulb illuminating it, the increased impact that the second light has on your sight is quite perceptible. Yet the impact of adding a fifteenth bulb to a room illuminated by fourteen lights is hardly seen at all. Latané claims that the same is true with individuals and their social impact on others: the second person has less impact than the first, and the nth person has less effect than the $(n-1)$th.

Latané states that the strength of would-be influencers depends on their status, expertise, and power. For example, in most circumstances, a police officer will have greater social impact than a mail carrier. Similarly, in the Milgram studies, the experimenter was more successful in securing obedience than an ordinary person. Finally, the immediacy of others is determined by their closeness to the individual in time or space. In other words, others will have greater social impact on you if they are actually present than if they are watching you on a monitor in another location or watching a videotape of your actions at a later date (Latané et al., 1995). In the obedience studies, people were more likely to obey the experimenter when he was physically present rather than when he gave orders over the phone.

Although social impact theory can explain the social influence exerted in the Asch and Milgram studies, how would it explain the *disobedience* in Gamson's oil company research? As you can see in figure 9.8, Box B, social impact theory also predicts that people are more likely to *resist* others' influence attempts when the social impact is dispersed among many strong and closely situated targets. In the oil company study, the social impact of the authority figure was divided among nine participants, not one, making disobedience easier. Similar disobedience occurred in the Milgram study when participants were in the presence of confederates who actively resisted the authority's orders. These findings indicate that when a group of

We must not confuse dissent with disloyalty.

Edward Murrow, news commentator, 1908–1965, during a "See It Now" broadcast on Wisconsin Senator Joseph R. McCarthy's campaign to fire and/or imprison all governmental employees who ever had any associations with socialist or communist political organizations (March 7, 1954)

individuals is confronted with the dictates of an immoral authority, there is always the possibility that the group will collectively redefine social reality and draw individual strength and conviction from the assembled others. With this group-originated conviction, they can more easily defy the social power of the authority. This same strength is simply not available to the lone individual, and therefore it is not surprising that obedience is more common here.

Having made the argument that groups can resist destructive obedience more effectively than the individual, I must also note that groups can often trigger destruction as well. You need only consider for a moment the death and suffering that has been caused by such group actions as lynchings, riots, and wars to recognize that groups are not a safeguard against destructive obedience. The power of groups can be used for either constructive or destructive purposes (see chapter 10). However, when prosocial values are made salient within a group setting, individual members can draw strength from those in their midst, enabling them to resist orders they consider immoral.

Over the years, social impact theory has been useful in predicting *when* other people will exert influence over someone's actions. More recently, Latané (2000) has expanded the theory to explain how ordinary communication between people can create a dynamic impact on their social thinking. In a series of studies, he and his coworkers have found that people who are physically closer and/or in regular direct contact with one another become more similar in their attitudes and beliefs than those separated by greater distances and infrequent contact (Huguet et al., 1998; Latané & L'Herrou, 1996). In essence, the social impact that these individuals regularly exert on one another appears to increase their similarity. Latané believes that this tendency for people to create like-minded *social clusters* when they regularly interact helps explain how regional differences may come to exist within a country, how minority viewpoints can survive within a larger culture, and why majority opinions in a culture tend to increase in size over time (Ramirez & Latané, 2001). In all of these instances, through the operation of what Latané calls *dynamic social impact*, people become organized into social clusters where they collectively reinforce one another's similarly held attitudes, values, and worldviews (Latané, 1997; Latané & Bourgeois, 1996).

College students' attitudes toward alcohol and their drinking tendencies are an example of how dynamic social impact can create like-minded social clusters. Campus surveys indicate that students who live in the same dormitory have more similar drinking patterns than students who live in different dorms (Bourgeois & Bowen, 2001). The social influence that dorm residents exert on one another in the course of their daily activities creates campus dormitories with distinct "personalities" regarding alcohol consumption. Residents in one building might identify themselves as the "party dorm," while students in another residence hall may have more restrictive attitudes and beliefs concerning excess drinking. Distinct social clusters can even develop on different floors of the same residence hall. One of the most noticeable effects of these distinct campus social clusters is that they tend to foster a misperception of campus drinking norms (Wechsler & Kuo, 2000). Further, because excess drinking is more likely to be noticed than moderate drinking, college students tend to overestimate how much alcohol their peers regularly consume, which by itself may encourage excess drinking (Lewis & Neighbors, in press). The good news is that, upon graduation, these same individuals develop new social clusters in their new work settings and new places of residence, which generally results in them adopting drinking norms more in line with full-time employment and adult role responsibilities (Bartholow et al., 2003b).

SECTION SUMMARY

- *Social impact theory* contends that the amount of influence people have is a function of three factors:

  their number   their strength   their immediacy

- Dynamic social impact can create social clusters of individuals who become more similar to each other as they interact

FEATURED STUDY

FALSELY ACCEPTING GUILT

Kassin, S. M., & Kiechel, K. L. (1996). The social psychology of false confessions: Compliance, internalization, and confabulation. *Psychological Science, 7,* 125–128.

Can people be induced to accept guilt for crimes they did not commit? In this experiment, researchers tested the following two hypotheses: (1) The presentation of false evidence can lead people who are in a heightened state of uncertainty to confess to an act they did not commit, and (2) these "false confessors" will internalize the confession and create details in memory consistent with this new guilt.

Method

Seventy-nine college students (forty males and thirty-nine females) participated, for extra course credit, in what they thought was a reaction time experiment. Participants were randomly assigned to one of four experimental conditions either involving high or low vulnerability, and either the presence or absence of a false incriminating witness. In each session, two people worked together on a computer "reaction" task. One of these people (a female confederate) read aloud a list of letters while the participant typed them on the computer keyboard. Before the session began, the participant was specifically warned not to press the "ALT" key because doing so would cause the program to crash and data to be lost. However, one minute after beginning work on the task, the computer ceased to function, and a highly agitated experimenter accused the participant of having pressed the forbidden key. In reality, the computer was rigged to stop functioning through no fault of the participant. When first accused, all participants denied responsibility for the computer damage. However, in the *false-witness* condition, the confederate disputed the participant's denial, testifying that she saw the participant press the forbidden key. In the *no-witness* condition, the confederate did not challenge the participant's denial, but simply stated that she did not see the key pressed. The participant's vulnerability was manipulated by varying the pace of the task. In the *high vulnerability* condition the confederate—following the beat of a metronome—read the letters at a frenzied pace of sixty-seven letters per minute, while in the *low vulnerability* condition the pace was set at a leisurely forty-three letters per minute.

The dependent measures involved three forms of social influence. To measure *external compliance,* the experimenter asked participants to sign a handwritten confession stating that they had hit the ALT key and caused the program to crash. To assess *internal compliance,* participants' private descriptions of what happened—told to a second confederate waiting outside the lab—were recorded and later coded for whether they unambiguously internalized guilt for what happened. To measure the *creation of memories,* the experimenter also asked participants to "recall" specific details of how they caused the computer program to crash. At the end of the session, participants were fully and carefully debriefed.

Results and Discussion

No gender differences were found on any of the dependent measures. Overall, 69 percent of the participants signed the confession, 28 percent exhibited internalization, and 9 percent created memories to support their false beliefs. As expected, participants in the high vulnerability condition were most susceptible to all three forms of social influence following the false accusation. In addition, regardless of the vulnerability condition, participants in the false witness conditions not only were more likely to sign a confession prepared by the experimenter, but they were also more likely to later admit their guilt to the second confederate. Finally, participants in the low vulnerability/no-witness condition were the least susceptible to these effects, while those in the high vulnerability/witness condition were the most susceptible. Although the false confessions coerced out of participants in this study are much less dramatic than many of the false confessions squeezed out of suspects in criminal cases, they do demonstrate that people can be induced to erroneously confess to crimes, and to believe in their own guilt, following the presentation of false evidence.

APPLICATIONS

COULD YOU BE PRESSURED TO FALSELY CONFESS TO A CRIME?

*I*n 1986 following a brutal murder of a woman in Clearwater, Florida, police invited Thomas Sawyer, a neighbor of the victim, to assist them in the investigation. They first flattered Sawyer by asking him to provide his own theory on how the murder occurred, and then used leading questions to shape his responses so that it fit the actual crime. When he was first accused of committing the crime, Sawyer vehemently denied the charge. To support their claim, the police lied to Sawyer about having "a lot of evidence" that implicated him in the murder. After hours of this sort of interrogation, Sawyer began to doubt his innocence, saying, "I honestly believe that I didn't do it. . . . I don't remember doing it. . . . You almost got me convinced I did, but. . . ." Finally, after sixteen hours of interrogation, Sawyer confessed to a crime he did not commit, stating, "I guess all the evidence is in, I guess I must have done it."

Sawyer's nightmare is an excellent example of how unusual influence can sometimes cause *internal compliance* (see p. 312). Internal compliance occurs when police interrogators' influence techniques are so effective that innocent suspects not only confess, but actually come to believe that they are indeed guilty (Zulawski & Wicklander, 2002). The influence operating here, namely informational, was observed in Sherif's autokinetic studies on group norm formation described earlier in this chapter. In contrast, false confessions can also occur through *external compliance* (see p. 312), where innocent suspects admit to crimes they know they did not commit in order to avoid further aversive interrogation. This form of normative influence was illustrated in Asch's conformity studies. Do you think you could fall prey to either one of these influence processes if you were a suspect in a crime you didn't commit?

Suspects generally make false confessions due to external compliance in exchange for penalty reductions. Here, their perceptions of the strength of the evidence against them—which police interrogators may highly exaggerate—significantly determines whether they will confess (Gudjonsson, 2003). Of course, many suspects will not falsely confess to a crime regardless of how strong the evidence appears. What distinguishes them from those who do? Not surprisingly, "resisters" are less susceptible to normative influence in general than are "confessors" (Gudjonsson, 1991).

By far, the most psychologically interesting confession is the one in which innocent defendants—anxious, confused, and desperately trying to make sense out of their current situation—actually come to believe that they committed the crime (Gudjonsson, 2001). This internalization of guilt is closely related to the creation of false memories, a topic extensively studied in cognitive psychology (Ost et al., 2001; Read, 1996). For obvious ethical reasons, psychologists cannot attempt to implant false memories of murder or sexual assault in research participants. However, Elizabeth Loftus and James Coan (1995) successfully implanted less traumatic

How do you think you would react to long hours of police interrogation, during which you were presented with damaging evidence linking you to a crime? Under such intense pressure from the authorities, are you certain that you would steadfastly maintain your innocence?

memories in five research participants ranging in age from 8 to 42. Following Loftus and Coan's instructions, trusted family members told these five individuals that, at age 5, they had been lost in a shopping mall for an extended time before being rescued by an elderly man. This information had the effect of convincing all participants that they indeed had been lost!

These and other studies demonstrate that false memories can be implanted into the minds of both children and adults (Ceci & Bruck, 1993; Kassin, 1997). In fact, research indicates that simply repeating imaginary events to people causes them to become more confident that they actually experienced these events (Zaragoza & Mitchell, 1996). Once constructed, these false memories may feel as real as—or even more real than—genuine memories (Brainerd et al., 1995). Susceptibility to such false memory construction is especially likely when people have been deprived of sleep, which is often the state of mind of crime suspects who are interrogated late at night (Blagrove, 1996).

How often do false confessions lead to miscarriages of justice? Based on a review of more than 400 cases in which innocent people were convicted of murder in the United States, Michael Radelet and his colleagues (1992) found that 14 percent (or 56 cases) were caused by false confessions. Similar percentages have been obtained in other countries (Sigurdsson & Gudjonsson, 1996). Although this figure is alarming, other research indicates that confessions in general are less important in securing a guilty verdict than is independent evidence. Few convictions are sustained on confession evidence alone, and it is estimated that a defendant's confession is pivotal in only 5 percent of cases (McConville, 1993).

Fortunately, few of you reading this text will ever be falsely accused of murder. However, all of you have been—and will continue to be—falsely accused of less serious transgressions. When facing your accusers, you will stand a better chance of successfully professing your innocence if you keep in mind the lessons of this chapter.

 THE BIG PICTURE

Earlier, when describing the situation confronting participants in Milgram's research, I asked whether you would have fully obeyed the experimenter's commands. This is a question I have asked myself over the years. Most people emphatically believe that they would resist the destructive commands and openly rebel. They further believe that those who would obey fully must be more aggressive, cold, and unappealing than the average person (Miller et al., 1973). How do we reconcile these beliefs with the actual experimental findings?

To answer this question, let me return to information presented in chapter 4. There is a widely held assumption—more common in individualist than in collectivist cultures—that people's actions are caused by internal dispositions rather than by external forces. This *fundamental attribution error* often results in a gross underestimation of the inherent power of the situation to shape behavior. The likely source for this belief in the power of the individual to act independent of situational forces resides in the desire of many people to believe that they have control over their own lives. This need to believe that the self is relatively uninfluenced by outside forces fosters a misrepresentation of how the social world actually operates.

Gunter Bierbrauer (1979) attempted to eliminate this misperception by having college students either observe a vivid reenactment of the Milgram experiment or play the role of obedient teachers themselves. Despite being exposed to the power that situational factors had in causing high levels of obedience, students still predicted that their friends would be only minimally obedient if they participated in Milgram's study. And even after being confronted by the social psychological facts, these students still essentially believed that only bad people do bad deeds, and good people only do good deeds. The danger in such a view of the social world is that it leaves us wide open to being manipulated by the very social forces we underestimate. Previous chapters have documented how the self and self-beliefs shape our interpretation and response to our social surroundings. In the matter of social influence, it is our *misinterpretation* of how the social world is constituted that helps to explain how we are so often easily manipulated. If our self-beliefs were not so firmly based on our power to remain uninfluenced by the wishes, desires, and dictates of others, we might be better able to recognize when we are in danger of falling prey to such social manipulation.

In closing this chapter on social influence, I'd like to introduce you to an excerpt from a humorous poem by Russell Edson (1976), in which a man awakens one morning to find strings coming through his window attached to his hands and feet.

> . . . I'm not a marionette, he says, his voice rising with the question, am I? Am I a marionette?
> One of the strings loosens and jerks as he scratches his head.
> . . . Hmmm, he says, I just wonder if I am a marionette?
> And then all the strings pull and jerk and he is jumping out of bed.

Now that he's up he'll just go to the window and see who's doing tricks with him when he's half asleep . . .

He follows the strings up into the sky with his eyes and sees a giant hand sticking through a cloud, holding a crossbar to which the strings are attached . . .

Hmmm, he says, that's funny, I never saw that crossbar before . . . I guess I am a marionette . . .

Based on your own newfound knowledge of the social influence process, you are undoubtedly more aware of the social strings to which you too are attached. The "anchor" for these social strings may well be based in an evolutionary past, predisposing you to be naturally receptive to others' influence. However, as Stanley Milgram's quote here in the margin reminds us, the difference between you and a marionette (and many other animal species) is that you can reflect on your own actions, and you can analyze the strings that bind you to your social world. Through such analysis, you can become less a puppet of other people's desires and more a coactor in a rich and interlocking web of social intercourse.

It may be that we are puppets—puppets controlled by the strings of society. But at least we are puppets with perception, with awareness. And perhaps our awareness is the first step to our liberation.

Stanley Milgram, social psychologist, 1933–1984

WEB SITES
accessed through http://www.mhhe.com/franzoi4

Web sites for this chapter focus on the social influence process, including the ordinary and extraordinary varieties.

Social Influence Web Site

This Web site is devoted to the psychological study of social influence, examining everyday and interpersonal influence, mindful versus mindless behavior, and the influence tactics used by cults.

AFF Cult Group Information

This Web site contains information about cults, mind control, and psychological manipulation. The recruitment and socialization practices of known cults are discussed, and former cult members tell their personal stories.

Social Psychology Network

Among other things, this large social psychology database offers links to other Web sites dealing with social influence, including those that discuss marketing and sales techniques, social influence countermeasures, and relevant research.

Stanley Milgram Web Site

The purpose of this Web site is to be a source of accurate information about the life and work of social psychologist Stanley Milgram.

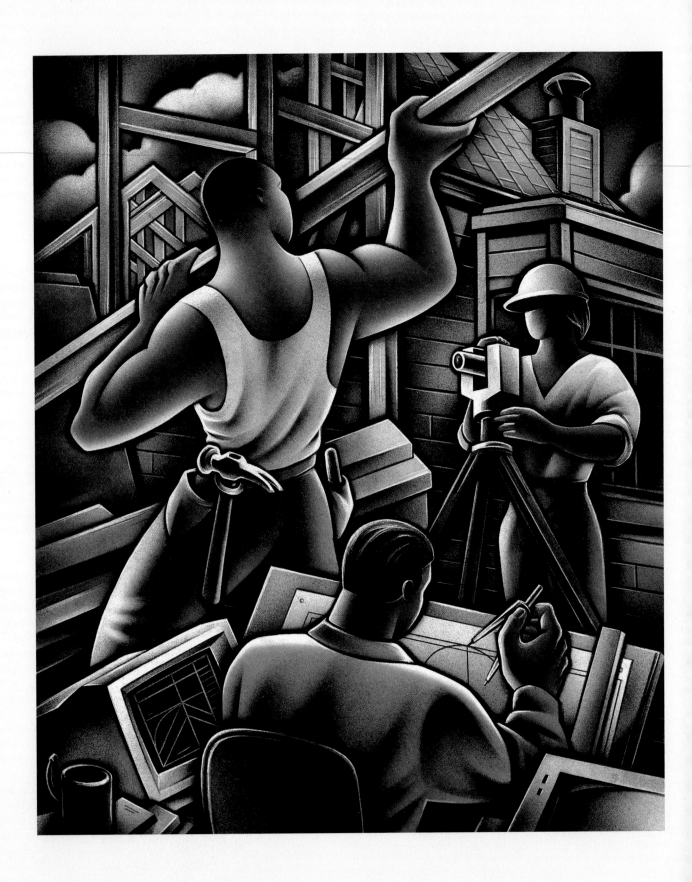

Group Behavior

CHAPTER OUTLINE

PREVIEW *The decision-making process of juries demonstrates the social psychology of small-group behavior, except for the fact that dissenters cannot be expelled. Yet how do jury size and rules concerning conviction influence the deliberation process?*

*I*n 1978, boyhood friends Jerry Greenfield and Ben Cohen opened a small home-made food shop in a converted gas station in Burlington, Vermont, with the help of a $4,000 bank loan. Their business plan, if you could call it that, was to sell high-quality food in a fun way, while using part of their profits to improve the quality of life of the community. Greenfield was given the title of president because they had put Cohen's name first when naming the business. Having little cash to pay for the building's extensive renovations, the two young businessmen promised their building contractor "free food for life" and named him as the third member on their board of directors. Greenfield and Cohen also offered lifetime free food to friends who helped with the renovations. Once open, they even extended their free food offer to a customer who regularly played ragtime and boogie-woogie tunes on the food shop's decrepit piano. Very quickly, this young business became a popular eating and entertainment spot, showing free summer movies on the outside wall of the store and having annual frog jumping, apple peeling, and stilt walking contests. The unofficial motto of the business became, "If it's not fun, why do it?" Attracted by this philosophy and the commitment to social responsibility, employees worked long hours for little pay to make the business a success.

Although only a handful of people and two unconventional leaders made up this business group in 1978, twenty years later it employed more than seven hundred people, had 150 franchises, and sold shares of its company on the stock market. True to their commitment to give back to the community, 7.5 percent of annual profits are donated to employee-managed philanthropic causes in this country and abroad. Have you guessed yet what kind of food Cohen and Greenfield serve to their customers? Do their first names, Ben and Jerry, jog your memory? Yes, their product is ice cream. Today, "Ben & Jerry's Homemade" has annual sales over $170 million and is widely regarded as a model for other socially responsible businesses.

How does a collection of individuals like those who initially formed around Ben Cohen and Jerry Greenfield come to perceive themselves as a group? What effect does group membership have on their subsequent thinking and behavior? How does leadership style influence group performance? The essential message of social psychology is that humans are social animals. Through the process of natural selection and evolutionary adaptation, we have inherited specialized skills from our ancestors that help us efficiently perform tasks that are essential for survival. Because our ancestors lived together in small groups, it makes evolutionary sense that many of these specialized skills relate to group behavior. In this chapter, we examine how specific social skills operate in a group context. But first, let's start with the most basic of questions: what is a group?

THE NATURE OF GROUPS

Group

Several interdependent people who have emotional ties and interact on a regular basis.

Although there is little agreement about how to precisely define a **group,** one common definition is that it consists of several interdependent people who have emotional ties, and who interact on a regular basis (Levine & Moreland, 1998; McGrath et al., 2000). By *interdependence,* I not only mean that members depend on one another to achieve group goals, but events that affect one member affect others as well. Therefore, members of Ben & Jerry's fledgling business not only relied on one another to create new marketing ideas and ice cream flavors, but they each were influenced by fellow members' personal joys and sorrows. Their lives were intertwined.

Groups Differ in Their Social Cohesiveness

Beyond this general definition, groups can be further distinguished by their *social cohesiveness,* or "groupiness" (Sherman & Johnson, 2003). As social cohesion increases, people think, feel, and act more like group members and less like isolated individuals (Fine & Holyfield, 1996). Members of highly cohesive groups have a greater desire to retain their membership than do those in low cohesive groups, and this cohesiveness allows the group to exert more influence on its members, which often leads to greater productivity (Gammage et al., 2001; Langfred, 1998). Such cohesiveness epitomized the atmosphere of Ben & Jerry's during its formative years: employees felt like it was "their" company and that together they could make a difference in the world. Two factors that affect group cohesion are *group size* and *member similarity and diversity*

GROUP SIZE

Although the size of the group in which animals live in a given habitat is partly determined by existing resources and other environmental limitations, comparative studies of various species indicate that the upper limit of group size is set by each species' cognitive abilities. Based on his analysis of humans and various nonhuman primate species (New and Old World monkeys and apes), Robin Dunbar (1993, 2002) concluded that the average size of a species' social group is directly related to what percentage of the species' brain is devoted to higher cognitive functions (the *neocortex ratio*). The group size identified by this relationship refers to the maximum number of individuals with whom an animal can maintain social relationships by personal contact. Subsequent research indicated that this relationship between group size and neocortex size involves the areas of the frontal lobes of the cerebral cortex, which are crucial for social cognition (Stuss et al., 2001). According to Dunbar (2000, 2003), animals cannot maintain the cohesion and integrity of groups larger than a size set by the information-processing capacity of their frontal lobes.

What is the upper limit of group size for which human brains are best adapted? As depicted in figure 10.1, Dunbar's calculations suggest that the relevant group size for modern humans is about 150 individuals, which approximates quite closely the observed sizes of clan-like groupings in contemporary and early human hunter-gatherer cultures. In contrast, the average group size among chimpanzees is about 50 individuals. Given that human brain size has remained unchanged over the past 250,000 years, we can assume that our current brain size is more a product of the evolutionary pressures of hunter-gatherer groups

Three stinking cobblers with their wits combined can equal the wisest philosopher.

Chinese folk saying

Groups often differ in terms of the degree to which their norms, roles, and status systems are articulated. For example, monthly Ben & Jerry corporate board meetings occasionally took place in Ben's swimming pool. Can you imagine a similar group structure at IBM or the U.S. Supreme Court?

© Ben & Jerry's Homemade Holdings, Inc. Used with permission of Ben & Jerry's Homemade Holdings, Inc. 1999.

FIGURE 10.1

Does Brain Size Limit the Size of Social Groups in Primates?

When Robin Dunbar (1993) plotted the average group size in different primate species against the percentage of the species' brain devoted to higher cognitive functions (the *neocortex ratio*), he found a positive linear relationship. In other words, as the neocortex size of monkeys' and apes' brains increased relative to other brain areas, the average size of a primate species social group also increased. The relevant group size for modern humans is about 150 individuals, which closely approximates the observed sizes of contemporary hunter-gatherer groups. If these findings are correct, do they have any implications for the type of social problems typically found in large metropolitan settings?

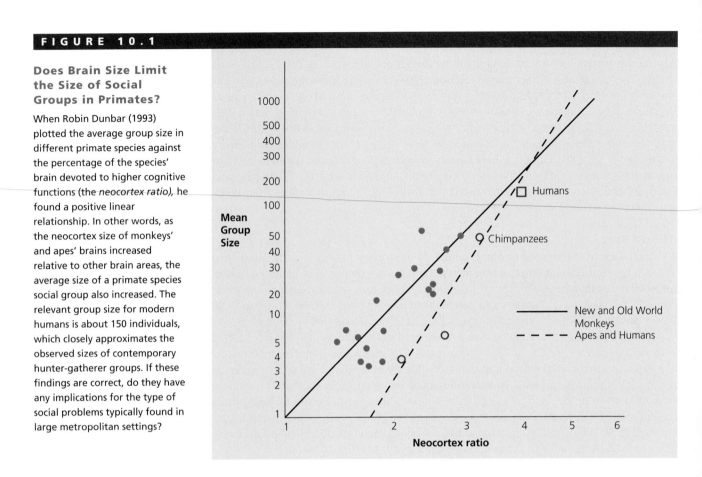

rather than the environmental demands people now face in technologically advanced cultures (Barrett et al., 2003). Dunbar contends that if this assumption is correct, then it is possible that our current brains are not well adapted to the very large social groupings sometimes found in modern societies.

Even in modern societies, most groups contain less than four persons (Mullen & Copper, 1994). As a group grows and as it reaches or exceeds the upper limit of our brain's capacity to process information on the individual members, there is a tendency for member participation to decline, power to become concentrated in the hands of a few, conflicts to increase, and cooperation to decrease (Hill & Dunbar, 2003; Wagner, 1995). Large groups make it harder for members to control what happens to them (Lawler, 1992), and as group size increases, members become more selfish and less group-focused because they perceive the impact of their own behavior on group success or failure being weaker and less identifiable (see *social loafing*, pp. 367–369).

MEMBER SIMILARITY AND DIVERSITY

Within groups, members tend to be more similar than different (Jackson et al., 1991). One reason for this similarity characteristic is that membership in most groups involves the performance of specific activities (for example, members of an aerobics class all exercise), and thus, people are drawn toward a specific group because they mutually share an interest in that group's activities. Another reason for within-group similarity is socialization. That is, in the process of socializing new members, attempts are made to mold them to the group's way of thinking and acting (see "There Are Five Phases to Group Membership," pp. 360–362). As discussed in chapter 7, similarity is often the "glue" of affiliation and liking. Thus, it is no surprise that when group members are dissimilar rather than similar, conflict and turnover are more likely (Ely & Thomas, 2001; Paletz et al., 2003).

Although member dissimilarity can be dangerous to groups, it can also provide benefits. As group tasks change and become more complex, and as the group's social environment changes, diversity among members gives the group more flexibility in adapting to these changes and may provide more accurate decision making (Watson et al., 1993; Yaniv, in press). For example, as North American culture has become more diverse and complex, many successful businesses have recognized the need to increase the diversity of their employees to better meet the challenges in the marketplace. Thus, although similarity tends to promote group cohesion, diversity can promote flexibility in group functioning.

What is the best strategy for capitalizing on the value of diversity? Recent studies suggest that groups become the most creative in solving problems when they celebrate and embrace the diversity of their members rather than minimizing these differences (Swann et al., 2003). This highlighting of diversity creates a social environment where members' distinct personal and social qualities are verified and validated by the group. Receiving such self-verification promotes satisfaction and commitment among members (Swann et al., 2000, 2002).

Group Structure Develops Quickly and Changes Slowly

One characteristic upon which groups differ is *structure,* the regular, stable patterns of behavior between members (Wilke, 1996). These group behavior patterns generally develop quickly and change slowly. Consider, for example, the loose management structure at Ben & Jerry's compared with the high structure at most major corporations. Monthly board meetings were occasionally held in Ben's swimming pool and the lines of authority within the company were only vaguely defined. When the company needed to hire a new corporate executive officer in 1995, they held a national "Yo! I Want to Be CEO!" contest with applicants instructed to send in 100-word applications.

In analyzing the structure of groups, social psychologists from different theoretical perspectives have identified a number of common elements (Poole et al., 2004). Three of the more important ones are social norms, social roles, and status systems.

SOCIAL NORMS

As defined in chapter 9, *social norms* are expected standards of behavior and belief established and enforced by a group. Some groups have norms for personal appearance (for example, shaved heads for Marine recruits), others have norms for opinions (for example, liberal views in environmental organizations), and most have norms for behavior (for example, profanity is forbidden in school classrooms). Sometimes, these norms are formally conveyed to group members in written guidelines, but most often, they are learned through everyday conversations or observing other members (Miller & Prentice, 1996). As demonstrated by Sherif's classic studies (see chapter 9), once norms are established, they tend to be stable over time, despite changes in group membership. Although social norms certainly increase conformity and reduce deviancy within groups, they also can enhance performance when structured in such a way as to reward effort, efficiency, and quality (Seashore, 1954).

SOCIAL ROLES

As defined in chapter 3, *social roles* are clusters of socially defined expectations that individuals in a given situation are expected to fulfill. In a group, roles often define the division of labor, and well-defined roles improve group dynamics and performance (Barley & Bechky, 1994). In some cases social roles *evolve* during group interaction, while in other cases people *import* a role into their new group that they enjoyed playing in previous groups (Rose, 1994). For instance, if you were known as a "good listener" in your high school friendship groups, you may import this role into your college friendships. Likewise, others may try to shape their "comedian" friendship role into the "class clown" role at school.

STATUS SYSTEMS

The third aspect of group structure is its *status system,* which reflects the distribution of power among members (Kaplan & Martin, 1999; Robinson & Balkwell, 1995). Status is a valued commodity in a group. Even in groups that do not have formal status systems, such

I am the people—the mob—the crowd—the mass. Do you know that all the great work of the world is done through me?

Carl Sandburg, U.S. poet and historian, 1878–1967.

By whom?

U.S. critic Dorothy Parker, when told she was outspoken, 1893–1967 as friendship cliques, members often differ in their prestige and authority. You can tell who has higher status in a group by paying attention to verbal and nonverbal behavior: higher-status members maintain greater eye contact, stand more erect; are more likely to criticize, command, or interrupt others; and not only speak more often but are also spoken to more often than those of lower status (Fournier et al., 2002; Leffler et al., 1982). Although status can be *achieved* by helping a group reach its goals, it is often *ascribed* rather than earned: people are given higher status simply because of who or what they are (Anderson et al., 2001; Ridgeway, 1991).

How exactly are these status differences created in the first place? According to **expectation states theory,** when group members first meet, they form expectations about each other's probable contributions to the achievement of group goals (Berger et al., 1985; Correll & Ridgeway, 2003). These expectations are not only based on members' *task-relevant characteristics,* such as social skills and past experience, but also on *diffuse status characteristics,* such as race, sex, age, and wealth (Balkwell & Berger, 1996; Wittenbaum, 1998). Those members whose characteristics produce higher expectations in fellow members are assigned higher status in the group. Thus, for example, White, middle-aged, wealthy men might be perceived as better potential leaders by other group members than young, poor, Hispanic women. Although these initial status assignments can be later modified based on actual performance, members who are unfairly given an initially low status will have trouble proving their worth to the group (Ridgeway, 1982). Because women have lower ascribed status than men in many groups, they report more dissatisfaction with their group status and must work harder to gain influence with other members (Foschi, 1996; Ridgeway, 2001).

As this brief overview suggests, there are many advantages to having high status in a group. Higher-status individuals have higher self-esteem, are better liked by other group members, and are more satisfied with their group relations than lower-status persons (Lovaglia & Houser, 1996). Further, when high-status individuals make decisions that lead to minor negative consequences for the group, they are more likely than lower-status members to be forgiven. However, when the bad decisions cause major negative group consequences, high-status persons are judged more harshly than those with low or medium status (Wiggins et al., 1965). This is one instance where high-status members can be treated very harshly by the group.

There Are Five Phases to Group Membership

An important, and often overlooked, characteristic of group membership is that it is a *temporal* process, meaning that change occurs over time, involving different *phases* (Arrow et al., 2004). Richard Moreland and John Levine's (1988, 2002) **temporal model of group membership** examines not only how people are changed through their membership in a group, but also how the group is changed by members' ideas and actions. Three psychological processes that propel people into and out of groups are the *ongoing evaluations* the individual and the group make of one another, the *feelings of commitment* that follow these evaluations, and the *role transitions* that result from these changes in commitment (Levine et al., 1998; Van Vugt & Hart, 2004). The two faces of evaluation that occur during the course of group membership involve (1) the degree to which the individual meets the needs of the group, and (2) the degree to which the group meets the needs of the individual.

According to Moreland and Levine, the temporal passage of the individual through the group generally occurs in an ordered set of five phases, with each phase associated with a different social role played by the individual. The movement from one membership phase to the next represents a role transition. In figure 10.2, the line of the bell-shaped curve represents the personal history of someone passing through all five phases of group membership. As people move up the line, their commitment to the group and the group's commitment to them strengthens. However, as they move down the line, this mutual commitment weakens.

In the *investigation phase,* the group seeks people who seem likely to be able to attain group goals, and prospective members look for groups that provide the opportu-

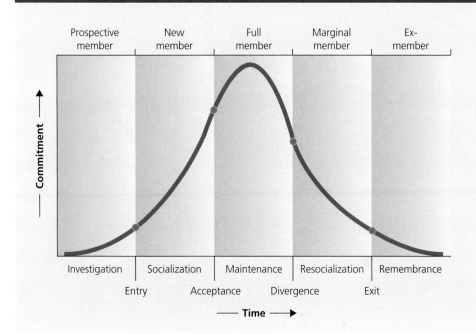

FIGURE 10.2

Prospective member | New member | Full member | Marginal member | Ex-member

Investigation | Socialization | Maintenance | Resocialization | Remembrance

Entry | Acceptance | Divergence | Exit

Commitment

⟶ **Time** ⟶

A Temporal Model of Group Membership

Based on Moreland and Levine's (1982) model of the phases of group membership, in what phase is commitment the greatest?

nity to satisfy personal needs. If both the individual's and the group's commitment levels are sufficiently strong, a prospective member enters the group. Although many groups have low entrance criteria and continually admit new members, other groups establish strict criteria and only periodically allow others to join. For these more formal groups, the entry of new members is almost always accompanied by some ceremony that acknowledges the newly established relationship between the group and the individual. Although many factors influence a group's tendency to be relatively open or closed to new members, groups that are unsuccessful or understaffed at key positions tend to be more accepting of new members than those that are successful or overstaffed (Cini et al., 1993).

In the *socialization phase,* the group tries to shape the new members' thinking and behavior so that they can and will make the maximum contribution to the group (Moreland & Levine, 2001; Ryan 2004). Groups accomplish this task through formal and informal indoctrination sessions and through "coaches" who model the appropriate thinking and behaviors (Shuval & Adler, 1980). While this socialization process is taking place the new members often try to change the group so that it will accommodate their needs (Swann et al., 2000). Newcomers can also bring fresh ideas into the group and increase innovation, but groups differ in their willingness to accept influence from new members (Levine et al., 2003). The socialization phase ends when the individual's and the group's commitment levels increase so that the individual becomes a full member of the group.

During the *maintenance phase,* the group attempts to define specialized roles for full members that maximize their contributions to the group's goals. In contrast, the full members often try to define their roles in the group to maximize personal needs. If the social influence that both parties exert results in a mutually satisfying agreement on the full member's role, commitment is increased on both sides. However, if role negotiation fails, both the member and the group will regard the relationship as less rewarding, and commitment to one another will decrease. The individual will now be viewed as a marginal member.

When full group members are relabeled as marginal, they enter the *resocialization phase,* in which both parties once again try to persuade the other to meet their expectations. If the group or the individual succeeds in convincing the other to accept their role expectations, or if a mutually agreeable compromise can be struck, the marginal member will once

I don't care to belong to any club that will have me as a member.

Groucho Marx, U.S. comedian, 1875–1977

For many student groups on college campuses (for example, political and religious groups, service organizations), new members are continuously accepted with little fanfare and few entrance criteria. In more formal groups, such as fraternities and sororities, prospective members are often admitted only during designated times, and only after being closely scrutinized and voted in by full members. A formal induction ceremony usually ushers these new members into the group.

again be regarded as a full member. As figure 10.2 shows, this essentially means that the person moves backward on the curve toward a higher commitment level. If, however, no agreement can be reached, the individual's and the group's commitment levels will fall even further, prompting the individual to exit the group. In the resulting *remembrance phase,* the group develops a consensus concerning the ex-member's contributions to the group's goals, and similarly, the ex-member reminisces about the benefits and costs of being a member of the group.

How does this model fit your experiences with various groups in your own life? Undoubtedly, many of you are currently associated with various groups and are in different phases of membership with many of them. A number of the social psychological processes that unfold in the different phases of group membership, such as majority and minority influence, have been discussed in chapter 9. Perhaps some of you have also noticed that the dynamics of group membership bears a striking similarity to the dynamics of romantic relationships, which we will discuss in chapter 12. The reason for this is simple: romantic relationships are often considered to be a type of group—the intimate dyad.

Although research generally indicates that people with high group commitment are much less likely to voluntarily leave a group than those with low commitment, there are instances when highly committed members decide to exit because they think their departure will benefit the group (Levine & Moreland, 2002; Zdaniuk & Levine, 2001). This type of scenario often occurs when highly committed members come to the conclusion that they are no longer adequately contributing to the group. Instead of "taking up space" that could be better filled by more productive individuals, these loyal members exit the group. Many employee retirements fall into this category.

The idea that members might place the welfare of the group ahead of their own is generally thought to be an exception to the rule in this model. In this sense, Moreland and Levine's depiction of the phases of group membership has an individualist bent to it. That is, there is an assumption that members conceive of their own personal goals as often diverging from group goals. In a collectivist culture, phases of group membership would be less affected by individual-group tensions (Abrams et al., 1998; Markus & Kitayama, 1994).

Groups Accomplish Instrumental Tasks and Satisfy Socioemotional Needs

Have you ever wondered why people join groups? Existing evidence suggests that they do so for several reasons, all of which can be traced to the accomplishment of *instrumental* tasks and the satisfaction of *socioemotional* or affiliation needs (Schachter, 1959). Put simply, people often join groups because they desire to achieve certain task-oriented goals that they cannot attain alone. For example, you will have a much better chance of extinguishing the fire in a burning building or of finding shelter for the homeless if you pursue these tasks within the supportive network of a group. In addition, becoming a group member provides the opportunity to satisfy such affiliative motives as the desire for approval, belonging, prestige, friendship, and even love. These mutual desires for task accomplishment and emotional fulfillment in a group setting are observed across many species and are an integral part of our evolutionary heritage

The work of Robert Bales, which began in the late 1940s, suggests that *accomplishing tasks* and *dealing with emotional and social relationships* are indeed the two principal functions of groups (Bales, 1970; Bales & Slater, 1955). Some groups are primarily task-oriented, while others are principally constituted to foster social relationships (Lickel et al., 2000; Sherman et al., 2002). Examples of *task-oriented* groups are work groups, such as a surgical team operating on a patient or factory workers assembling automobiles. Examples of *socioemotional* groups are friendship and family groups nurturing and emotionally supporting fellow members or neighbors organizing a summer block party.

Although some groups can be identified as more oriented toward one function than the other, almost all groups engage in at least some degree of both task and socioemotional activity. Indeed, Bales contends that this continual oscillation between task and socioemotional activities is what characterizes group process. As a group engages in task-oriented activities, members' feelings tend to be neglected, and this inattention creates group tension in the socioemotional area. However, when the group attempts to reduce these socioemotional tensions by paying more attention to members' feelings, task goals become temporarily sidetracked and this, in turn, creates task tension. According to Bales, groups constantly strive to strike a proper balance between their attention to task and socioemotional concerns so that they can keep group tension to a minimum. For example, imagine

When spiders unite, they can tie down a lion.

Ethiopian proverb

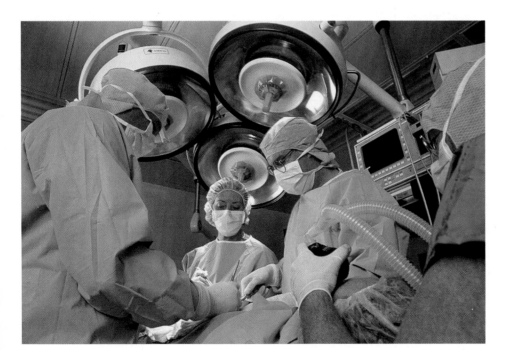

The two principal functions of groups are to accomplish tasks and to deal with emotional and social relationships. Would you guess that this group has more of a task orientation or a socioemotional orientation?

Two heads are better than one.

North American folk saying

that in pushing to complete a group project in one of your classes, you rub some of your classmates the wrong way. To try to restore group cohesion, you might bring a bag of doughnuts to class or do something else that will salve emotional hurts.

SECTION SUMMARY

- A group consists of several interdependent people who have emotional ties and interact on a regular basis
- Two factors that affect group cohesion:

    group size   member similarity and diversity
- Every group has a *structure,* consisting of

    social norms   social roles   status systems
- There are five phases to group membership, each with an associated social role:

    investigation phase—prospective member

    socialization phase—new member

    maintenance phase—full member

    resocialization phase—marginal member

    remembrance phase—ex-member
- Two main functions of groups:

    accomplish instrumental tasks

    satisfy socioemotional needs

GROUP INFLUENCE ON INDIVIDUAL BEHAVIOR

If one of the main functions of groups is to perform tasks, what factors influence the ability of people to successfully engage in task activities? In this section, we examine how the presence of others affects a person's work performance. The two types of situations investigated are (1) an individual performing an activity in the presence of an audience (*social facilitation*), and (2) an individual performing an activity as part of a larger group of performers (*social loafing*). We also examine how both being aroused and being hidden in the group can loosen one's behavioral inhibitions.

Social Facilitation Enhances Easy Tasks and Inhibits Difficult Tasks

As discussed in chapter 1, Norman Triplett (1897) conducted one of the first social psychological experiments investigating whether the presence of others enhanced or inhibited task performance. Subsequent experiments during the first quarter of the twentieth century found that the presence of others enhances the speed with which people perform relatively simple tasks but inhibits task efficiency in more complex activities (Allport, 1920; Travis, 1925). This *social facilitation* effect, as it came to be called, was also found in other animals, such as dogs, rats, birds, fish, and even ants and cockroaches (Chen, 1937; Gates & Allee, 1933). Although researchers extensively documented these divergent effects through the 1930s and 1940s, no one could explain *why* the presence of others would sometimes enhance and sometimes hinder individual performance. This explanatory conundrum ultimately led to a loss of interest in social facilitation as a research topic.

FIGURE 10.3

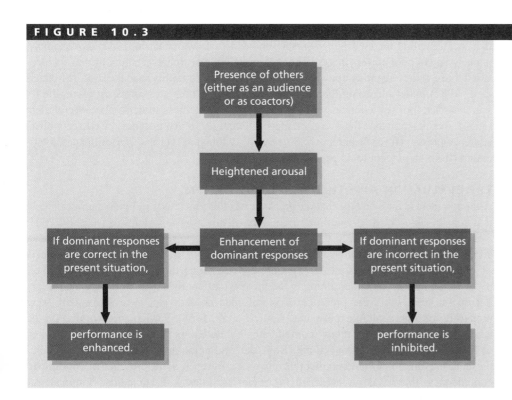

According to Zajonc (1965), the
presence of other people
increases arousal, which, in turn,
enhances the performance of
dominant responses. If the
dominant responses are correct,
performance will also be
enhanced. However, if the
dominant responses are incorrect,
performance will be inhibited.
Can you think of instances from
your own life in which the
presence of others had these two
contrasting effects on your
performance of different types of
tasks?

THE MERE-PRESENCE EXPLANATION

In the mid-1960s, Robert Zajonc (1965) renewed the field's interest in social facilitation by proposing a theory to reconcile the contradictory findings. His social facilitation theory involved three basic propositions or steps (see figure 10.3). First, he argued that all animals (including humans) are genetically predisposed to become physiologically aroused when around *conspecifics* (members of one's own species). This is so, he believed, because animals receive most of their rewards and punishments in life from conspecifics, and through the process of evolution have developed an innate arousal response due to their *mere presence.* Second, resurrecting an old behaviorist principle of learning (Hull, 1943), Zajonc stated that this physiological arousal enhances the performance of whatever response tendency is dominant (that is, well learned) in an animal. Third, and last, he contended that for well-learned tasks the correct responses are also the dominant responses, but for novel, unlearned tasks the dominant responses are the incorrect ones. What this means is that the presence of others will enhance correct execution of well-learned tasks, at the same time that it will interfere with or inhibit correct performance of novel, unlearned tasks.

Zajonc argued that when we perform a simple task like hand clapping, the mere presence of an audience increases our arousal, eliciting the dominant response, and we clap more vigorously than when we are alone and not aroused. Now, if instead, we calculated difficult math problems in front of others, our increased arousal would inhibit execution of this task because the correct answers are not dominant responses. They would only be dominant responses if we had them memorized. Taken together, these two different effects due to the presence of others—enhancement of correct performance on easy tasks and inhibition of correct performance on difficult tasks—are known as **social facilitation.** The reason the same term is used for both effects is that on both easy and difficult tasks, the performance of the dominant response is *facilitated* in others' presence. For easy tasks the correct response is dominant, and thus, the person's performance is enhanced. Yet for difficult tasks the correct response is not dominant, hence the decline in performance efficiency.

Numerous studies have been conducted to either specifically test Zajonc's theory or to more generally examine social facilitation. Two separate meta-analyses of more than

Social Facilitation

The enhancement of dominant
responses due to the presence of
others.

three hundred experiments involving more than twenty-five thousand participants indicates that social facilitation does indeed exist (Bond & Titus, 1983; Guerin, 1986). For example, in one study of pool players in a college student union, researchers first unobtrusively identified those who were either above or below average in their ability to make shots (Michaels et al., 1982). After recording their shooting accuracy without an audience present, the researchers had four confederates walk up and closely watch these students play several more rounds. Results indicated that the good players' accuracy in making shots increased with an audience present (from 71 percent to 80 percent), while poor players' performances deteriorated (from 36 percent to 25 percent).

THE EVALUATION-APPREHENSION EXPLANATION

Although there is little dispute that the presence of others increases individual arousal, there is a considerable debate concerning the nature of this arousal (Aiello & Douthitt, 2001; Strauss, 2002). Some contend that rather than being due to the mere presence of others, arousal is a result of *evaluation apprehension*—concern over being judged by others (Aiello & Svec, 1993; Cottrell, 1972). In one study supporting this explanation, participants worked on a task either alone, in the presence of confederates who were also working on the task, or in the presence of blindfolded confederates who supposedly were preparing for a perception experiment (Cottrell et al., 1968). Participants working on the task in the company of "seeing" confederates exhibited social facilitation effects when compared with those working alone. Both the evaluation-apprehension and the mere-presence explanations would predict this outcome. However, in the presence of blindfolded confederates, there was no evidence for social facilitation. Participants' dominant responses did not differ from those who were alone. Because the blindfolded confederates were physically present but could not evaluate the performance of participants, these findings support the evaluation-apprehension explanation at the same time they contradict the mere-presence explanation. Similar effects were found in other studies in which observers were present but not evaluating an individual's performance (Worringham & Messick, 1983). According to the evaluation-apprehension perspective, if people are present but not attending to another person's task performance, their presence is unlikely to produce social facilitation effects.

THE DISTRACTION-CONFLICT EXPLANATION

As appealing as the evaluation-apprehension explanation is, there are social facilitation effects it cannot explain. Recall that social facilitation has been observed in such animals as ants and cockroaches. Does this mean that insects "worry" about other insects evaluating them? Because this possibility is unlikely, other social scientists contend that heightened arousal is simply caused by a conflict between two tendencies (Baron, 1986). This *distraction-conflict theory* states that when an animal (human or other) is working on a task in the presence of other conspecifics, it experiences conflict regarding whether to attend to its companions or the task at hand. Distraction-conflict theorists contend that it is this conflict, and this conflict alone, that induces heightened arousal. Because conflict is a well-documented source of arousal, this perspective can explain both human and nonhuman social facilitation effects. In addition to social stimuli (that is, conspecifics) causing conflict, and thus arousal, the distraction-conflict theory hypothesizes that nonsocial objects that distract a performer can also induce conflict. True to this contention, loud noises and flashing lights have been found to produce the same enhancement/impairment effects produced by the presence of others (Pessin, 1933; Sanders & Baron, 1975; Wanshaffe, 2002). Therefore, the one advantage that the distraction-conflict theory has over the other two explanations is that it can explain task enhancement both in social and nonsocial settings (see figure 10.4).

Given the research discussed with the three theories of social facilitation, can we declare that one of them is clearly the best explanation of this phenomenon? Although the distraction-conflict theory can explain some instances of social facilitation that the other two theories cannot, no direct evidence indicates that conflict alone induces the heightened arousal we find in social situations. Thus, it is still possible that conflict and evaluation apprehension

FIGURE 10.4

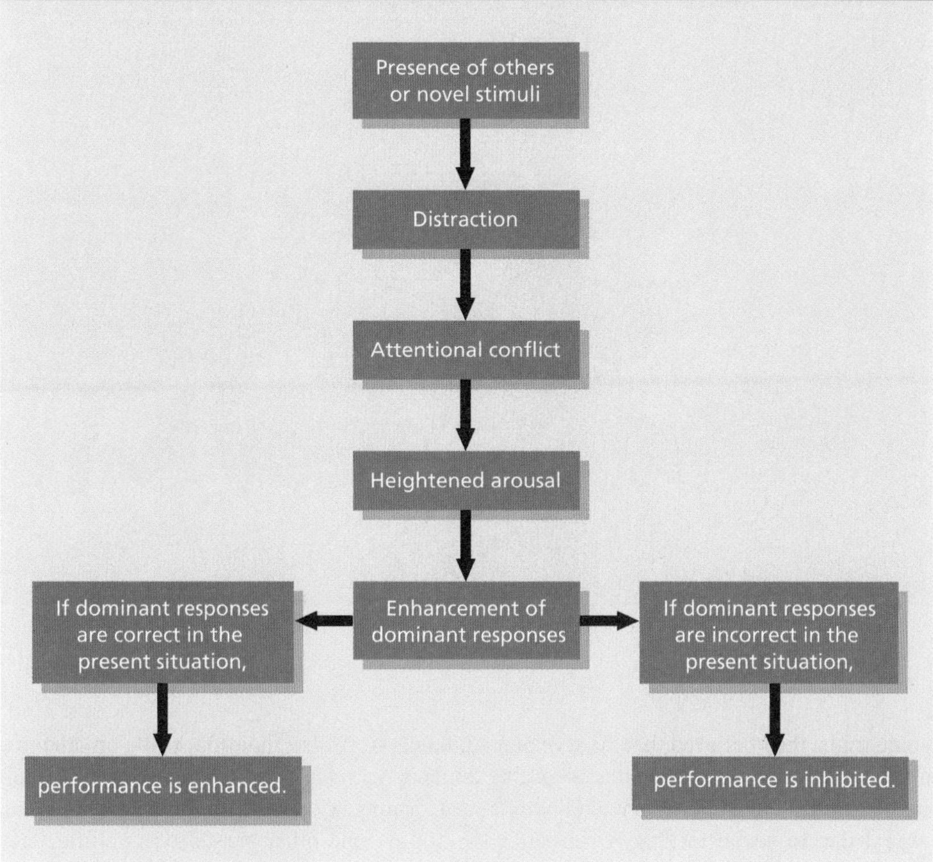

Distraction-Conflict Theory

According to the distraction-conflict theory, when one is working on a task, the presence of others or the presence of novel stimuli is distracting. This distraction produces a conflict between paying attention to the task and paying attention to these stimuli. This conflict causes arousal to increase, which leads to the social facilitation effects previously discussed.

simply enhance the arousal produced by mere presence. Currently, then, the most prudent conclusion to draw is that each theory adds to our understanding of social facilitation: others can affect our performance (1) by just being there, (2) as evaluators, and (3) by distracting us.

Social Loafing Occurs When Our Individual Output Becomes "Lost in the Crowd"

Social facilitation research identifies the conditions under which the presence of others can motivate individuals to enhance their performance. Usually this enhancement occurs when a person's efforts can be individually evaluated. Yet, what if the performers' efforts are *pooled* so that individually judging them is difficult or even impossible? Do you know what often happens? If you guessed that individuals work less hard under these conditions than when performing alone, you are correct. This group-induced reduction in individual output is known as **social loafing** (Karau & Williams, 1995).

Social Loafing

Group-induced reduction in individual output when performers' efforts are pooled and, thus, cannot be individually judged.

Early and Contemporary Research

French agricultural engineer Max Ringelman (1913) conducted the first empirical study suggesting such an effect in the 1880s. He found that people's efforts pulling on a rope or pushing a cart were less when they worked in a group than when they performed these tasks alone. More recently, social loafing has been documented in a host of behaviors. For example, Bibb Latané and his associates (1979) had six blindfolded college students sit in a semicircle and wear headphones that blasted sounds of people shouting into their ears. The students' task was to shout as loud as possible while listening to the headphone noise. On

Because of the diffusion of responsibility, people who perform a task as part of a group often exert themselves less than when they perform the task alone in front of others. How can the likelihood of social loafing be reduced?

Diffusion of Responsibility

The belief that the presence of other people in a situation makes one less personally responsible for the events that occur in that situation.

some trials, they believed that the five other students were also shouting, while on other trials they believed they were either shouting alone or with only one other person. In actuality, on all these trials only one student was performing. Consistent with what you would expect due to social loafing, when students thought one other person was yelling, they shouted 82 percent as intensely as when alone, and when they believed everyone was yelling, they shouted 75 percent as intensely.

Social loafing is not restricted to simple motor tasks like rope pulling or cheering; it also takes place when people perform cognitive tasks (Weldon & Gargano, 1988). In addition, cross-cultural research (Gabrenya et al., 1985) indicates that social loafing occurs in both individualist and collectivist societies, although the effect is not as strong in the latter (Karau & Williams, 1993).

What might explain social loafing? A likely explanation is that when people work in a group, they realize that their individual output will be "lost in the crowd." As a result, they feel less personally responsible for the outcome, and their performance effort declines (Comer, 1995). The cognitive process that group performers go through in feeling less personally responsible for task outcomes is known as the **diffusion of responsibility,** and in chapter 14 (pp. 549–551) we will examine how it causes a variation of social loafing, namely, bystanders to an emergency failing to aid victims.

REDUCING SOCIAL LOAFING

If social loafing is truly caused by a diffusion of responsibility, then it is also true that social loafing is not an inevitable consequence of people working together in groups. That is, if people's individual efforts can be judged while they work on a group task, they should not lose personal responsibility for their actions, and there should be no social loafing. This is exactly what was found in a variation of the cheering study (Williams et al., 1981). Here, as before, participants shouted alone or in groups. In some conditions, shouters were led to believe that their individual performance was being monitored; in other conditions they believed their output was never identifiable. Results indicated that if participants believed their individual shouting was being monitored, no performance drop off occurred in a group context. This study suggests that when group performers cannot conceal minimal effort from observers, social loafing is unlikely.

The fact that social loafing is greatly reduced when individual effort can be identified and evaluated suggests that evaluation apprehension can curtail minimal effort. But what if performers in a group are made aware of their own individual efforts or those of the group in comparison with a social standard without others being privy to this information? Would this private information still reduce social loafing on their part? Research indicates that it does (Harkins & Szymanski, 1989). This suggests that it is not necessary to convince individuals that others will identify their efforts. Simply providing them with a standard to evaluate their own performance, or even that of the entire group, is often sufficient to prevent social loafing. Thus, providing the potential for *evaluation*—even if it is only self-evaluation—seems to be the key to reduce the loss of individual output on a group task.

Although informing group members of the potential for evaluation may generally reduce loafing, how should known social loafers be handled? Short of physically rejecting lazy workers from the group, one common technique to increase their output is to socially shun them until they conform to the group productivity norm. Yet is such *social ostracism* effective? Kipling Williams and Kristin Sommer (1997) found that the effectiveness of this technique was different for female and male loafers. The women loafers reacted to social ostracism by socially acknowledging their feelings of rejection and openly questioning their own attractiveness and abilities. When given a chance to get back into the good graces of the group, the women worked hard to do so. In contrast, the men appeared to cope with ostracism by redirecting their interests toward nontask objects in their surroundings. Also, their concern for impression management caused the men to hide their emotions and to reinterpret the situation: they tended to perceive their separation from the group as being due to their own personal choice rather than something imposed on them. By engaging in these face-saving coping strategies, the men now had a lower need to seek the group's approval, and hence, they were more likely to continue loafing. Williams and Sommer speculate that these gender differences are due to most societies socializing women to be emotionally expressive and men to be nonexpressive. That is, women's learned response of attending to and expressing their emotions enhances the effectiveness of social ostracism as a control technique. For men, however, their learned response of directing their attention away from their emotions to other environmental stimuli dilutes the effectiveness of ostracism. These findings suggest that, although social ostracism may be an effective control strategy for social loafing in people who regularly attend to and publicly express their emotions, it may be ineffective for those who are psychologically invested in controlling any such public displays.

CAN ANONYMITY SOMETIMES IMPROVE GROUP PERFORMANCE?

So far, all the group activities resulting in social loafing that we have examined involved simple tasks. But if evaluation apprehension—either of the "social" or "self" variety—is the key to social loafing, then would working together at a complex, poorly learned task lower evaluation apprehension and, therefore, lead to better individual performance? Researchers addressed this question in a study in which people worked on a complex computer maze alongside a coworker (Jackson & Williams, 1985). In one condition, participants were led to believe that their scores would be combined with their coworker's so that no single performance could be identified. In another condition, they were told their individual scores would be identifiable. Results indicated that participants performed better on this complex task when they believed their individual efforts would *not* be evaluated than when they thought they would be. These interesting findings suggest that under conditions that usually produce social loafing (when one's individual efforts seemingly cannot be identified and evaluated) performance can actually be enhanced. Again, as before, the key to understanding this effect is that group performance allows task outcome responsibility to be diffused among fellow coactors. On simple tasks, this reduction in evaluation apprehension causes decreased output by individual actors. However, on poorly learned tasks, the reduction in evaluation apprehension—and presumably arousal—allows more careful concentration on the task at hand.

Imagine that you have been hired to design a training course to teach company employees how to efficiently use a complex computer program. How can you use the findings of social loafing research to design a training course that not only facilitates quick learning, but also encourages high productivity following learning?

Deindividuation Involves the Loss of Individual Identity

One Halloween night a few years ago, I heard a noise outside my house. Looking out the window, I saw a group of teenagers in masks and costumes carrying pumpkins—my pumpkins. I quickly went to the front porch and noticed that my lamppost light had been shattered by one of the pumpkins being thrown against it. Although I was barefoot and dressed in pajamas, I gave chase after these "hooligans." As I sprinted toward them, they took off running. They ran faster than I sprinted and I abruptly gave up the chase. As I ended my pursuit they stopped, too, and turned back to check me out. Standing there in the cold and the dark, it suddenly dawned on me that I was their "old geezer"—the feeble, angry man who chases pranksters on Halloween night. At that moment, memories of my own youthful Halloween escapades came back to haunt me. Just like me years ago, these "hooligans" were normally well-behaved adolescents who had been caught up in a one-night antisocial neighborhood romp. What caused them—and me, at that age—to act this way? Have you ever been in a similar situation and later wondered why you behaved so contrary to acceptable standards?

Group-Induced Lowering of Inhibitions

Social facilitation research demonstrates that groups can arouse us. Social loafing studies indicate that groups can also diffuse responsibility and lower evaluation apprehension. What happens when groups diffuse responsibility and lower evaluation apprehension at the same time that they arouse us? In such circumstances, our normal inhibitions may diminish, and we may engage in behaviors we normally avoid. This state of mind has come to be called **deindividuation.**

Deindividuation

The loss of individual identity and a loosening of normal inhibitions against engaging in behavior that is inconsistent with internal standards.

Deindividuation not only helps to explain the vandalism of many Halloween pranksters, but it also provides insight into other forms of collective antisocial behavior. Philip Zimbardo (1969) outlined the antecedents and consequences of a deindividuated state, noting that important contributing factors are *arousal, anonymity,* and *diffused responsibility.* Zimbardo argued that when people become deindividuated—by a combination of these factors—their inhibitions will be lowered and they will be much more likely to impulsively engage in such antisocial behavior as vandalism, aggression, and rioting. Steven Prentice-Dunn and Ronald Rogers (1980) believe that *accountability cues,* such as anonymity, tell people how far they can go without being held responsible for their actions. These cues loosen restraints against deviant behavior by altering a person's *cost-reward calculations.* For example, during a riot, people often think they won't be caught and punished for engaging in illegal activities, and this reassessment of the costs and rewards lowers their inhibitions. Although early investigators (Festinger et al., 1952) believed that deindividuation occurred only in groups, later research indicated that it could also be induced outside of a collective (Mullen, 1986).

One example of deindividuation causing antisocial consequences is when onlookers goad people who are threatening suicide. For example, while writing this chapter, I read a newspaper account of a distraught truck driver who committed suicide in his truck after passing motorists used citizens band radios to egg him on when they learned he was threatening to shoot himself. Similarly, in an analysis of newspaper accounts of people witnessing someone threatening suicide by jumping from a building or bridge, Leon Mann (1981) found that when a crowd of onlookers was large or masked by darkness (that is, deindividuated) they often jeered and encouraged the person to jump. Although large crowds and darkness facilitated the antisocial actions of onlookers during suicide attempts, when people were more easily identifiable—small crowds exposed by daylight—Mann found that they generally did not jeer the would-be jumper.

The perceived anonymity of the Internet causes some people to experience diffused responsibility while interacting in "chat rooms" or accessing pornographic material on various Web sites. Does this diffused responsibility loosen people's normal inhibitions? In one study investigating Internet-induced deindividuation, Christina Demetriou and Andrew Silke (2003) established a Web site to determine whether people who visited it to gain access to legal material would also try to access illegal and/or pornographic material at the site when they discovered it was available (no such material was actually available). Over a three-month period, a majority of the more than 800 visitors who entered the site to view the advertised legal materials also tried to access the illegal and/or pornographic material. Like actual groups, it appears that the "virtual" groups created on Internet sites have the capacity to induce deindividuation.

Because Halloween festivities tend to deindividuate celebrants, it is not surprising that researchers have used this annual event to investigate this process. In one such study, Ed Diener and his colleagues (1976) set up testing sites in twenty-seven homes throughout Seattle and waited for young trick-or-treaters to come calling. Some children arrived alone, and others came in groups. On some trials, the experimenter asked the children their names and where they lived, and on other trials they remained anonymous. Then, the experimenter showed the children a bowl of candy and told them to "take *one* of the candies." Then they were left alone with the candy bowl while hidden observers recorded how much candy the children actually took. The researchers discovered that, compared to those who were alone, children in a group were more than twice as likely to take extra candy. In addition, compared with children who identified themselves, those who remained anonymous were also more than twice as likely to take more than one piece of candy. As you can see in figure 10.5, the greatest candy stealing occurred when children were in a group and remained anonymous.

CAN DEINDIVIDUATION UNLEASH POSITIVE BEHAVIOR?

If deindividuation causes us to act more impulsively, could it also unleash prosocial behavior that we might normally inhibit? In an investigation of this question, Kenneth Gergen and his coworkers (1973) individually ushered eight college students—four women and four men—into a totally darkened room, where they were to spend the next hour. None of these students knew one another and all were told, "There are no rules as to what you should do together. At the end you will be escorted alone from the room and there will be no opportunity to meet the other individuals." A control group spent a similar hour in a lighted room. If you were in the "dark room" group, how do you think you would respond? Remember, no one knows your name and no one can even see you.

In this deindividuated state, "dark room" participants' affiliation desires were unleashed. They talked less than the control group, but they rated their conversations as more important. Ninety percent purposefully touched others, 50 percent hugged, and some even kissed. No one in the control group engaged in any of these activities. Few of the deindividuated participants disliked their experience—in fact, most enjoyed it immensely, and many asked if they could participate again without pay! This study and others indicate that

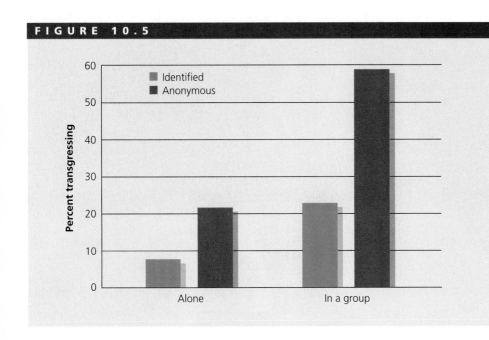

FIGURE 10.5

Effects of Deindividuation on Stealing Among Halloween Trick-or-Treaters

When trick-or-treating in a group or when anonymous, children were more likely to take extra Halloween candy. However, when both of these factors were present (group immersion and anonymity), candy stealing arose dramatically. What do these results tell us about the effects that deindividuation have on people's normal inhibitions?

deindividuation can encourage prosocial as well as antisocial behavior (Johnson & Downing, 1979; Spivey & Prentice-Dunn, 1990). Which type of behavior will occur depends on whether the situation encourages positive or negative actions.

DEINDIVIDUATION AND REDUCED SELF-AWARENESS

In explaining deindividuation, Diener (1980) argued that the crucial cognitive factor is a lack of self-awareness. Without such self-awareness, the deindividuated do not think of themselves as separate individuals and do not attend to their own inner values and behavioral standards (see chapter 3 for a discussion of self-awareness effects). To test this hypothesis, he and his coworkers conducted a second Halloween study in which, as before, experimenters waited for young trick-or-treaters to arrive to request candy (Beaman et al., 1979). After the children were asked to give their names, they were told to take only one candy each and were then left alone by the candy bowl. On some trials, a mirror was placed behind the bowl so that when the children reached for the candy they saw their own image in the mirror. On other trials, no mirror was present. As you may recall from chapter 3, a mirror induces self-awareness, a psychological state in which one is aware of oneself as an object of attention and is also more attentive to behavioral standards. In such a state, one is not deindividuated. Not surprisingly, in the *mirror present* condition, only 12 percent of the children took extra candy, yet when the mirror was absent, candy stealing increased to 34 percent. These results, and those of other investigations, suggest that *reduced self-awareness* is a component of deindividuation (Diener & Wallbom, 1976; Prentice-Dunn & Rogers, 1982): the deindividuated lose their sense of personal identity in a group by not engaging in self-awareness. Here, as in other aspects of social behavior discussed throughout the text, people abdicate their personal standards of conduct and fall prey to the influence of the immediate situation when they fail to take themselves as objects of attention.

CAN SOCIAL IDENTITY ACTIVATION EXPLAIN DEINDIVIDUATION?

Throughout the past forty some years of deindividuation research, the prevailing view has been that it is an expression of antinormative and disinhibited behavior caused by a loss of personal identity. More recently, however, Dutch social psychologists Tom Postmes and Russell Spears (1998) proposed that what we call antinormative and disinhibited behavior in such situations may actually be a behavioral expression of *conformity* to group norms specific to the situation. Arguing from a social identity perspective (see chapter 3), Postmes and Spears assert that deindividuating settings do not lead to a loss of personal identity and an

How could you use your knowledge of deindividuation when designing social environments to reduce crime?

These trick-or-treaters may exhibit deindividuation: they may be more likely to "sneak" extra candy in their costumes or their group make them feel anonymous and less self-aware. What is a simple way to "individuate" them?

acting on impulse, but instead, they facilitate a transition from a personal to a more social identity. The so-called antinormative behavior is really an expression of whatever group norm is salient in the situation. Whether they are taking extra candy and stealing pumpkins as Halloween pranksters or touching and hugging strangers in a pitch-black room, the deindividuated are simply conforming to the prevailing group norm of the moment.

Which of these two explanations is correct? Does deindividuation involve a loss of self-awareness and personal identity, or does it involve a shift from a personal identity to a social identity? Postmes and Spears's counterexplanation has received some empirical support (Kugihara, 2001; Spears et al., 2002), but a recent study suggests a possible resolution of this controversy. Brian Mullen and his coworkers (2003) recruited European American college students who had parents belonging to the same ethnic group (for example, Irish or Italian American) to answer a questionnaire concerning themselves and that aspect of their social identity related to ethnicity. There were three experimental conditions and one control condition in this study. Participants in the *mirror condition* completed the questionnaire while seated at a table in front of a small mirror. Participants in the *mask condition* were asked to wear a featureless, transparent mask while answering the questions, while those in the *family tree condition* were told to write the name of their ethnic group into the three boxes of a small family tree labeled "Father," "Mother," and "You," and to keep the family tree in front of them while completing the questionnaire. A control group simply completed the questionnaire with no manipulations of the testing setting. The questionnaire measured participants' current degree of self-awareness and their current degree of identification with their ethnic group. The researchers reasoned that if the conventional view of deindividuation is correct, participants in the mask condition would exhibit a decrease in both self-awareness and ethnic identity awareness (which is a form of social identity awareness). However, if the social identity explanation is correct, Mullen and his colleagues reasoned that the mask condition would cause an increase in ethnic identity awareness.

As expected, the mirror condition caused an increase in self-awareness and a decrease in ethnic identity awareness in participants, and the family tree condition caused a decrease in self-awareness and an increase in ethnic identity awareness. However, more importantly, the mask condition caused a decrease in both self-awareness and ethnic identity awareness, which is consistent with the conventional view of deindividuation, but inconsistent with the social identity explanation. As such, this study suggests that deindividuation involves different psychological processes than social identity awareness. This does not mean that certain crowd behavior is not sometimes caused by the activation of a common social identity among crowd members. However, it does suggest that deindividuation is a distinct psychological state, separate from social identification. The deindividuated mind-set of being "lost in the crowd" involves a psychological shifting of awareness away from the self; it does not appear to involve a shift from a personal identity to a social identity.

SECTION SUMMARY

- Social facilitation involves the enhancement of dominant responses due to the presence of others

- In social facilitation, others affect our performance:

    by their mere presence

    as evaluators

    by distracting us

- *Social loafing* occurs when the presence of coperformers reduces individual output because coperformers allow diffusion of task outcome responsibility

- *Deindividuation* occurs when people's normal inhibitions are diminished due to a loss of individual identity, triggered by anonymity and reduced self-awareness

DECISION MAKING IN GROUPS

Due to the fact that groups sometimes influence people to behave in ways that are antisocial, some social scientists have suggested that this is evidence that people in groups think and behave more irrationally than they would alone. Although this belief in the inferiority of group thinking and action may be partly a function of the individualist bias of these scientists (Markus & Kitayama, 1994), it is not a new view in the social sciences, nor is it unique to North American scholars. Over a century ago, French sociologists Gustave LeBon (1903) and Gabriel Tarde (1903) described people being magnetically drawn toward crowds, where they then develop a "collective mind." Although the research already discussed in this chapter indicates that people in groups can sometimes act in an inferior and impulsive manner (due to social loafing and deindividuation, respectively), you have learned in previous chapters that individuals acting alone can exhibit similar undesirable actions. Thus, group processes, like individual processes, are amply designed to foster both positive and negative outcomes (Kerr & Tindale, 2004). In this chapter section, we examine the decision-making process of groups and the conditions under which group decision making meets with success or failure.

Group Decision Making Occurs in Stages and Involves Various Decision Rules

In making decisions, groups typically move through four distinct stages (Forsyth, 1990). As depicted in figure 10.6, the *orientation stage* involves the group identifying the task it is trying to accomplish and the strategy it will use to solve it. As you will shortly discover, the

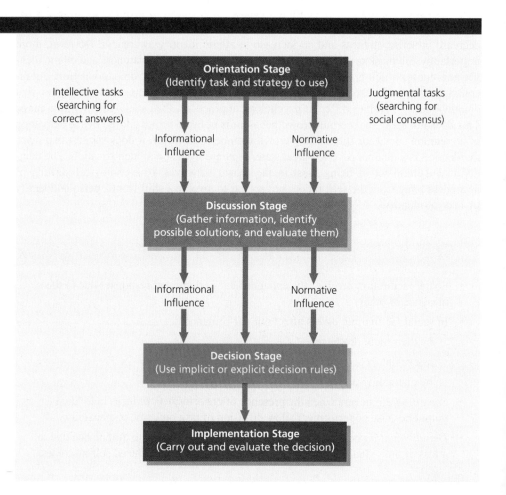

FIGURE 10.6

The Stages of Group Decision Making

Group decision making typically moves through four distinct stages: orientation, discussion, decision, and implementation. In what two stages are members' social influence attempts—either normative or informational—most apparent?

Intellective tasks (searching for correct answers)

Judgmental tasks (searching for social consensus)

Orientation Stage
(Identify task and strategy to use)

Informational Influence

Normative Influence

Discussion Stage
(Gather information, identify possible solutions, and evaluate them)

Informational Influence

Normative Influence

Decision Stage
(Use implicit or explicit decision rules)

Implementation Stage
(Carry out and evaluate the decision)

type of task presented to the group generally determines the strategy it chooses. In the *discussion stage,* the group gathers information, identifies possible solutions, and evaluates them. Members' influence attempts—either normative or informational—are most apparent in this second stage and in the following *decision stage.* In making decisions, the group relies on either implicit or explicit decision rules (see the section "Group Decision Rules"). Finally, in the *implementation stage,* the group first carries out the decision and then evaluates its effectiveness. Now that the stages have been outlined, let us examine the group dynamics in this process.

TWO TYPES OF DECISION-MAKING ISSUES

To a good degree, *how* a group makes a decision depends on what *kind* of decision it is making. Many of the issues on which groups make decisions can be located on a continuum (Laughlin, 1996). At one end of the continuum are *intellective* issues for which there are demonstrably correct solutions. Here, the group's task is to discover the "true" or "correct" answer. Scientists searching for a cure for AIDS or campers trying to determine how to put together a tent are both examples of groups struggling with an intellective task. In contrast, at the other end of the continuum are *judgmental* issues involving behavioral, ethical, or aesthetic judgments for which there are no demonstrably correct answers. Examples of judgmental tasks are members of an arts council deciding which artists are most worthy of receiving monetary awards, or corporate executives deciding how to market their products. In these types of cases, although the groups' decisions often involve weighing facts, the ultimate decision is principally based on the appeal to social norms and group consensus.

Research indicates that what type of issue a group believes it is working on will substantially determine the mode of influence members employ and how much information they try to gather in making their decision (Green, 1998). As you recall from chapter 9, there are two principal types of social influence: informational influence and normative influence. *Informational influence* occurs when a person accepts others' logical arguments and factual information in defining reality; *normative influence* involves accepting others' definition of reality based on the desire to win approval or avoid criticism. Informational influence is most likely to shape the discussion and decision stages when groups work on intellective tasks. The goal is to find and use any information that helps solve the problem. In reaching this goal, group members tend to engage in a thorough search for relevant information, and they are generally eager to share what they find with other members during the discussion stage. On the other hand, when working on judgmental tasks, normative influence is most likely to be used. Because there is no purely "correct" answer, the decision goal is to persuade other group members to accept your judgment. In reaching this goal, group members are less diligent in trying to uncover information, and some members may even withhold information during discussion if divulging it would weaken their arguments. Because of this different strategy, groups working on judgmental tasks tend to discuss only enough information to reach consensus (Wittenbaum & Stasser, 1996).

Although informational influence generally dictates decision making on intellective tasks, when groups have to make a quick decision, they often do not have the luxury of systematically searching for information during the discussion stage and instead must rely on more superficial or heuristic information processing (Karau & Kelly, 1992). In such instances, regardless of whether the task is judgmental or intellective, members tend to rely on normative influence when reaching a decision (Kelly et al., 1997).

MAJORITY INFLUENCE ON GROUP DECISIONS

Based on your previous reading of the social influence process in chapter 9, it should not be surprising that social psychologists have discovered that group decisions can be predicted with a good degree of accuracy from knowledge of members' initial preferences prior to a discussion of the issues (Davis, 1973). For example, interviews with members of 225 criminal juries found that in 97 percent of the cases the jury's final decision was the same as the one a majority of the jurors favored on the initial vote (Kalven & Zeisel, 1966). Similar results have also been obtained in *mock* (simulated) jury trials (Tanford

& Penrod, 1984). These findings suggest that if most of the group initially supports a particular position, discussion serves mainly to confirm or strengthen this popular view. The initial majority opinion wins over the entire group apparently due to the greater informational influence and normative influence that majority members have at their disposal. That is, group discussion is more likely to focus on majority-held opinions rather than opinions shared by the minority, and those sharing the majority opinion exert greater pressure to conform than do those who hold minority positions (Wittenbaum et al., 1999).

GROUP DECISION RULES

Although group discussion can affect individual judgments due to informational and normative influence, it's also true that the rules governing those decisions affect group decisions. That is, because group decision making requires some level of agreement or consensus among members, groups develop rules that determine when a sufficient level of consensus has been reached. A *group decision rule* is simply the required number of group members that must agree with a position for the group as a whole to adopt it. Common decision rules include the following:

> *Unanimity rule:* All group members must agree on the same position before a decision is finalized.
>
> *Majority-wins rule:* A group opts for whatever position is held by more than 50 percent of its members.
>
> *Plurality-wins rule:* When there is no clear majority, the group opts for the position that has the most support.

Decision rules may be explicit and formal, as is the case with the instructions given a jury to return a unanimous verdict, or they may be implicit and informal, such as a chairperson's intuitive assessment that the group sufficiently agrees on a previously disputed topic to consider it settled (Kaplan & Miller, 1983). Groups that use the unanimity rule are not only more thorough in discussing the issues than groups that employ the majority or plurality decision rules, but they also are more likely to use compromise in reaching a decision, which, not surprisingly, results in greater satisfaction with the final decision (Miller, 1989).

Group Discussion Enhances the Initial Attitudes of People Who Already Agree

Imagine that you are on Ben & Jerry's board of directors and tomorrow will be voting on whether to buy brownies for your Chocolate Fudge Brownie Bar ice cream sandwich from supplier A, which is a traditional business, or get them for the same price from supplier B, which is employing the homeless and doing wonderful things in its community. At first, the choice seems like a no-brainer, because giving business to supplier B fulfills your company's goal of social responsibility. Upon closer inspection, however, you discover that the traditional supplier has years of experience producing both high-volume and high-quality brownies, but the nontraditional supplier has never attempted to produce brownies in such huge quantities. In choosing supplier B, you run the risk that your own product could be compromised if the supplier cannot meet your high-volume, high-quality food requirements. In making a decision, what would be the *lowest* probabilities or odds of supplier B meeting your requirements you would consider acceptable? A five in ten chance? Seven in ten? Nine in ten? Would it surprise you to know that the level of risk you would settle on would likely be different if you made it on your own versus as part of the board?

ARE GROUP DECISIONS MORE OR LESS CAUTIOUS?

In the early 1960s, using hypothetical situations like the preceding one, James Stoner set out to test the commonly held belief that decision making by groups is more cautious than that made by individuals. To accomplish this task, Stoner (1961) asked management students to individually respond to twelve hypothetical dilemmas. When they completed these, he brought them together in groups with instructions to discuss each of the problems until they reached a unanimous decision as to what odds they would accept as a group. Unexpectedly, when Stoner compared the average odds of the groups with the average odds these people had endorsed as individuals, he found that the groups were actually *riskier* than the individuals on ten of the twelve items. During the next five years or so, subsequent research using similar hypothetical dilemmas found the same results across a wide variety of age and occupational groups and in dozens of different cultures—groups were riskier than individuals (Cartwright, 1971; Pruitt, 1971). This effect was initially known as the *risky shift*.

GROUP ENHANCEMENT OF INITIAL TENDENCIES

As researchers conducted more studies, they realized that not all decision dilemmas yielded a reliable risky shift. In fact, on some dilemmas, groups became reliably *more* cautious after discussion (Fraser et al., 1971; Knox & Safford, 1976). This was perplexing. How could group discussion produce both greater risk taking and greater conservativism? In time, researchers understood that what was occurring in these group discussions was not a consistent shift toward risk or caution but, rather, a tendency for discussion to *enhance* the initial attitudes of people who already agree (Moscovici & Zavalloni, 1969; Myers & Lamm, 1976). This group-produced enhancement or exaggeration of members' initial attitudes through discussion was called **group polarization,** and its basic nature is outlined in figure 10.7.

Group Polarization

Group-produced enhancement or exaggeration of members' initial attitudes through discussion.

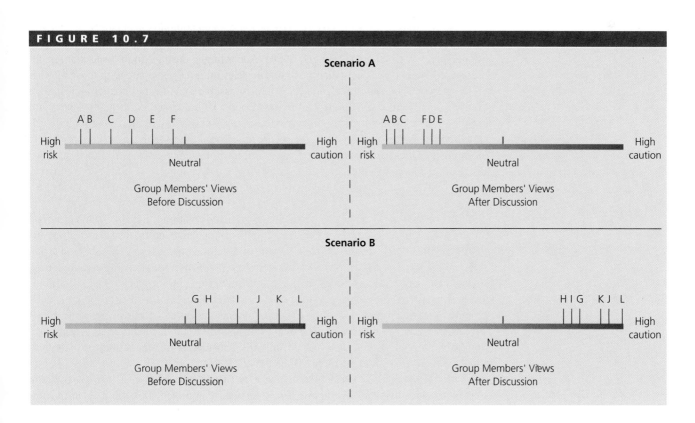

FIGURE 10.7

The Process of Group Polarization

In group polarization, discussion by group members enhances the initial attitudes or views of those who already agree, regardless of whether those views reflect caution or risk. Thus, in scenario A, prior to discussion, all members (A, B, C, D, E, and F) have varying degrees of support for engaging in a particular course of action, reflecting their willingness to take somewhat of a risk. Member "A" is most willing to take a risk and member "F" is least willing. Following discussion, the average opinion of the group members has shifted to being strongly in favor of the proposed group action (a shift to greater risk). Similarly, in scenario B, before discussing the issue, all members (G, H, I, J, K, and L) have varying degrees of opposition to the proposed course of action, with member "L" being most cautious and member "G" being least cautious. After discussion, the average opinion of the group members has shifted to being strongly opposed to the group action (a shift to greater caution).

Research indicates that group polarization is more likely to occur on important issues rather than trivial ones (Kerr, 1992). For example, based on high school students' responses to a racial attitudes questionnaire, David Myers and George Bishop (1970) classified them as high, medium, and low on prejudice. Groups of like-minded students then met to discuss racial issues. The researchers found that students who were initially low in prejudice were even *less* so after the group discussion. On the other hand, those who were moderately or highly prejudiced became even *more* prejudiced. Similar strengthening of initial attitudes is also found in many other group settings. In juries, for instance, group discussion tends to lead individual members to more extreme opinions about a defendant's guilt or innocence than they initially held (Myers & Kaplan, 1976). Surprisingly, even terrorist groups' actions may be shaped by group polarization effects. An analysis of terrorist organizations around the world found that these groups typically become more extreme only gradually over time (McCauley & Segal, 1987). Being relatively isolated from those who hold more moderate views, terrorists become more extreme as they interact with one another. The result is increased violence, something the individual members may never have initially endorsed.

WHAT PRODUCES GROUP POLARIZATION?

Several different explanations have been offered for the group polarization effect, but the two receiving the most attention and support are the *social comparison* and *persuasive arguments* perspectives. The social comparison view stresses the role of normative influence in the polarization process, while the persuasive arguments view focuses more exclusively on informational influence.

As you may recall from chapter 3 (p. 86), the social comparison perspective contends that we are motivated to self-evaluate, a process that we accomplish primarily by comparing ourselves with others (Festinger, 1954). Accordingly, during group discussion, members are concerned with how their positions on relevant issues compare with those of other group members (Goethals & Zanna, 1979). Most assume that they hold better views (more extreme in the valued direction) than others (Codol, 1975). However, through social comparison, individual members discover that they are not nearly as extreme in the socially valued direction as they initially thought. Because they want others to evaluate them positively (normative influence), discussants begin to shift toward even more extreme positions. Ultimately, this one-upmanship drives the group toward a decision that is either more conservative or more risky than individual members would otherwise have chosen (McGarty et al., 1992).

In contrast to this view, the persuasive arguments position states that group polarization involves *mutual persuasion.* According to this perspective, group discussion is not driven by the desire to be evaluated positively by oneself and others but by the desire to arrive at the correct or true solution. Here, the sheer strength of the arguments offered for certain decision choices is relevant (informational influence). Put simply, when people hear arguments from others, they learn new information. If even a slight majority of group members supports a particular position, most of the arguments presented will favor this view. Hearing more arguments in favor of their own position rather than against it, and hearing new supportive arguments that they had not initially considered, members gradually come to adopt even more extreme positions (Brauer et al., 1995).

Daniel Isenberg's (1986) meta-analysis of twenty-one different group polarization studies indicates that social comparison and persuasive argumentation often occur in combination to produce extreme group decisions. In an attempt to explain how these two forces could both produce group polarization, Martin Kaplan (1987) suggests that they may operate in different situations. That is, when the issue involves intellective tasks in which facts are weighed, group members will be primarily concerned with the information presented in people's arguments. In such a scenario, the persuasiveness of the arguments is what pushes their position toward extremity. However, when the issue involves judgmental tasks for which there are clearly no objectively right or wrong solutions, people are more likely to compare their views with those of others. Here, social comparison is more important in group polarization effects.

Based on the discussion of social influence processes in chapter 9, what type of individuals might be more susceptible to group polarization effects when working on judgmental tasks?

When a group becomes more concerned with maintaining group consensus than in critically analyzing their proposed course of action, they often engage in the defective decision making known as groupthink. Such a situation characterized the group dynamics of President George W. Bush and his cabinet during their decision to invade Iraq in 2003. To best prevent groupthink, what stage in group decision making should be principally targeted?

Groupthink Occurs When Consensus-Seeking Overrides Critical Analysis

On April 17, 1961, fourteen hundred American-armed Cuban exiles landed on the beaches of Cuba at the Bay of Pigs with the objective of overthrowing its communist government, led by Fidel Castro. The Central Intelligence Agency planned this counterrevolution, and President John Kennedy approved it after consulting with his advisers. Their belief was that the Cuban people would welcome the invading force and join them in overthrowing the communists. Nothing could have been further from the truth. Soon after landing on the beaches, loyal Castro forces captured the Cuban exiles. The Cuban citizenry rallied around their communist government, and the United States was humiliated on the world stage.

On March 19, 2003, President George W. Bush ordered the invasion of Iraq with the objective of overthrowing the dictatorial government of Saddam Hussein. The Central Intelligence Agency provided evidence indicating that Iraq had weapons of mass destruction and that Hussein's government was planning terrorist attacks with Osama bin Laden's al-Qaeda organization. Citing this evidence, President Bush approved a pre-emptive military strike. The Bush administration's belief was that they would achieve a quick and decisive victory, the Iraqi people would welcome the invading force, and America would become a beacon of hope for all people in the Middle East.

Like the Bay of Pigs invasion, nothing could have been further from the truth. Sixteen months following the invasion of Iraq, with American soldiers being killed daily, the U.S. Senate Select Committee on Intelligence issued a highly critical report on the decision making leading up to the war, charging that CIA analysts withheld information from Congress that did not support a military strike. Individual members of the committee also accused the Bush administration of being party to this distortion of information so that it could win public support for the war. In assessing the war's effects on the nation's security and prestige, Senate Committee member John Rockefeller stated, "Our credibility is diminished. Our standing in the world has never been lower. We have fostered a deep hatred of Americans in the Muslim world, and that will grow. As a direct consequence, our nation is more vulnerable today than ever before."

How could otherwise intelligent and competent people in two different presidential administrations make such poor decisions? In answering this question, Irving Janis (1982, 1996) contended that groups are sometimes susceptible to an extreme form of group polarization, which he called **groupthink.** This condition refers to a deterioration of mental efficiency, reality testing, and moral judgment in groups that have an excessive desire to reach consensus. According to Janis, groupthink emerges when maintaining a pleasant social atmosphere becomes more important than making the best decision.

Janis hypothesized that three major factors contribute to groupthink. The first factor is *high group cohesiveness.* Although a high level of cohesiveness among group members would seem to be a very positive group characteristic, it also is associated with increased conformity. That is, when people are strongly attracted to a group and want badly to be accepted by it, they are more likely to allow group members to influence their thinking and actions (t'Hart et al., 1993). Janis believed that when high cohesiveness is combined with the other two factors, namely a *threatening situational context* and *structural and procedural faults,* groups become more susceptible to groupthink. Regarding the situational context, Janis contended that groups faced with a threatening or stressful situation may value speed of decision making over accuracy. In addition, as we will discuss in chapter 11 (pp. 408–411), during times of stress people become more dependent on the reassuring support of others, which should increase the group's influence on individual members. According to Janis, structural and procedural faults that contribute to groupthink are a lack of systematic procedures for making and reviewing decisions, the isolation of the group from others, and a strong, directive leader who lets other members know what his or her inclinations are regarding the group's final decision choice.

SYMPTOMS OF GROUPTHINK

Janis believed three general ways (symptoms) tell whether a group is suffering from groupthink. These are as follows:

1. *An overestimation of one's ingroup.* Members develop an illusion of invulnerability and an unquestioned belief in the ingroup's own morality. During the Iraq War decision-making process, the Bush ingroup uncritically accepted the CIA's flawed information on Iraq's alleged weapons of mass destruction and their ties to al-Qaeda (after all, we had the best intelligence agency in the world, didn't we?) and operated on the false assumption that the U.S. military could simultaneously crush armed opposition and win the "hearts and minds" of the Iraqi people.

2. *Close-mindedness.* Members rationalize the correctness of their decisions and develop a stereotyped view of their opponents. "It was all about finding a way to do it. That was the tone of it," said Paul O'Neill, Bush's Treasury secretary. "The President saying, 'Go find me a way to do this.' " (Mackay, 2004) The CIA and Bush advisers, including Vice President Dick Cheney and Defense Secretary Donald Rumsfeld, were so convinced that Iraq had a program to develop weapons of mass destruction that they did not examine evidence that would have disconfirmed their beliefs and instead placed great weight on information provided by discredited Iraqi defectors. Later, Secretary of State Colin Powell told the Senate investigative panel that after the September 11th terrorist attacks, Deputy Defense Secretary Paul Wolfowitz "was always of the view that Iraq was a problem that had to be dealt with . . . And he saw this as one way of using this event." (Smith, 2004)

3. *Increased conformity pressure.* Members reject those who raise doubts about the group's assumptions and decisions, and they censor their own misgivings. With all this conformity pressure, members develop an illusion that everyone is in agreement, which serves to confirm the group's ill-chosen decisions. "Groupthink is more likely to arise when there is a strong premium on loyalty and when there is not a lot of intellectual range or diversity within a decision-

---

That is no use at all. What I want is men who will support me when I am in the wrong.

Lord Melbourne, British prime minister (1779–1848), reply to a politician's pledge: "I will support you as long as you are in the right."

---

making body," says political scientist Stephen Walt. "The Bush administration has been an unusually secretive group of like-minded people where a high premium is placed on loyalty." (Kemper, 2004)

RESEARCH ON GROUPTHINK

One reason why Janis's formulation of groupthink is so appealing is that it seeks to understand how the high stakes and high-pressure decision making of powerful groups within society can sometimes go terribly wrong. Besides the Iraq War and the invasion of Cuba, groupthink tendencies have been identified in such tragedies and political blunders as the decision to launch the space shuttle *Challenger* on its doomed mission in January of 1986 (Esser & Lindoerfer, 1989; Moorhead et al., 1991), and the decisions made by President Nixon and his advisers following the Watergate burglary (McCauley, 1989).

Perhaps the most comprehensive test of the Janis model was a study by Philip Tetlock and his colleagues (1992), in which they conducted a content analysis of the factual accounts of ten historic decisions that potentially involved groupthink. Consistent with Janis's model, results indicated that historic events involving disastrous decisions exhibited significantly more groupthink characteristics than those that led to successful decisions. Some of these groupthink characteristics were suspicion of outsiders, restriction of information exchange, and punishment of group dissenters. Also consistent with groupthink predictions, as groups became more concerned with maintaining group consensus, they began to exhibit more groupthink symptoms, which in turn resulted in more defective decision making. However, contrary to Janis's model, Tetlock and his colleagues did not find any evidence that group cohesiveness or situational threat were predictors of groupthink symptoms. However, later research found that cohesiveness does increase the risk of groupthink when it is accompanied by other risk factors, such as high stress or directive leaders who promote their own preferred solutions rather than encouraging alternative viewpoints (Ahlfinger & Esser, 2001; Hogg & Hains, 1998). These and other findings suggest that groupthink does exist, but it does not appear to function in the exact manner first proposed by Janis (Eaton, 2001; Granström & Stiwne, 1998; Paulus, 1998).

Due to the potential harm groupthink processes generate, what can groups do to prevent it? Based on the available evidence, the most important recommendation is to improve decision-making structures and procedures during the group's orientation stage (Schafer & Crichlow, 1996). Doing so will increase the likelihood that alternative perspectives will be fully weighed and considered during the discussion and decision stages. To facilitate this process, group leaders should encourage criticism and skepticism of all ideas, and once a decision has been reached, the group should return to the discussion stage so that members can express any lingering doubts. Approaching group decision making in this manner should facilitate the type of critical analysis that is the hallmark of success, both on the individual and the group levels (Kowert, 2002; Nemeth et al., 2001).

SECTION SUMMARY

- Most group decisions involve intellective or judgmental issues
    - intellective decisions are generally reached through informational influence
    - judgmental decisions typically rely on normative influence
- Group decisions also influenced by
    - formal and informal rules   members' initial positions
- Group polarization occurs when group discussion enhances the initial positions of members
- Groupthink is an extreme form of group polarization, which refers to a deterioration of mental efficiency, reality testing, and moral judgment resulting from an excess desire to reach consensus

LEADERSHIP

As previously mentioned, members of a group accept influence from others whom they believe have greater ability (Foddy & Smithson, 1996). In this chapter section, we examine these high-status individuals and the nature of their relationship with those who have lower status.

A Leader Is an Influence Agent

The person who exerts the most influence and provides direction and energy to the group is the **leader** (Pescosolido, 2001). This is the person who initiates action, gives orders, doles out rewards and punishments, settles disputes between fellow members, and pushes and pulls the group toward its goals. Many groups have only one leader; other groups have two or more individuals with equally high levels of influence. Generally, groups tend to have multiple leaders as their tasks become more diverse and complex (Fletcher & Käufer, 2003; Seers et al., 2003).

In their position of social influence, leaders are called on to perform two basic types of activities. *Task leadership* consists of accomplishing the goals of the group, and *socioemotional leadership* involves an attention to the emotional and interpersonal aspects of group interaction (Bales, 1970; Hare & Kent, 1994). The necessary qualities for effective task leadership are efficiency, directiveness, and knowledge about the relevant group task. Task leaders tend to have a directive style, giving orders and being rather impersonal in their dealings with group members. In contrast, friendliness, empathy, and an ability to mediate conflicts are important qualities for effective socioemotional leadership. A socioemotional leader's style is more democratic, with greater emphasis on delegating authority and inviting input from others (Fiedler, 1987).

In some groups, one person is the task leader and another person is the socioemotional leader (see the *contingency model,* pp. 360–362). At Ben & Jerry's, for example, Ben is more of a task leader than Jerry, who fits firmly in the mold of a socioemotional leader. Thus, early on they worked out an arrangement whereby affable Jerry did the hiring and, if things did not work out, Ben did the firing. In other groups, one leader performs both functions. In such instances, the leader must know when to be the taskmaster and when to be the supportive confidant—a difficult feat because the two leadership styles often conflict. Research indicates that individuals with a *flexible* leadership style know when to focus on task production and when to show concern for interpersonal relations. They also tend to receive the highest leadership ratings by other group members (Kirkpatrick & Locke, 1991).

One aspect of leadership that has not received adequate attention over the years is the role that *followers* play in legitimating the leader's influence. According to Edwin Hollander (1992), leaders and followers are involved in a *social exchange relationship.* The leader provides benefits to followers, such as direction, vision, a social identity, and the opportunity to attain goals, and followers reciprocate by becoming more responsive to that leader's influence (Haslam & Platow, 2001). Hollander (1961) describes this increased ability of the leader to influence group members as an accumulation of **idiosyncrasy credits.** These credits are earned over time by *competence* in helping the group achieve task goals and by conformity to group norms. Later on, these credits can be "cashed in" to prod group members into taking innovative actions that they would otherwise be reluctant to undertake. In a very real sense, early signs of competence and conformity by leaders earn the followers' confidence and trust, which later allows the leaders' nonconformity—that is, their innovation—to be tolerated by the group (Barbuto, 2000).

Transformational Leaders Take Heroic and Unconventional Actions

One of the earliest approaches to understanding leadership was to search for personality traits that caused some people and not others to become leaders. Unfortunately, few leader characteristics have been identified (Northouse, 2001). Leaders tend to be slightly more intelligent and taller than nonleaders, are more confident and adaptable, and, not surprisingly, have a higher desire for power (Chemers et al., 2000; Ottati & Deiger, 2002; Simonton, 1994). They also tend to be more charismatic, a quality that has prompted a number of researchers to analyze the psychological dynamics of *charismatic* or **transformational leaders.**

A transformational leader changes—or transforms—the outlook and behavior of followers, which allows them to move beyond their self-interests for the good of the group or society (Bass, 1997; Conger et al., 2000). The great leaders of the twentieth century, such as Mahatma Ghandhi and Jawaharlal Nehru in India, Franklin Roosevelt and Martin Luther King, Jr., in the United States, Nelson Mandela in South Africa, and even Adolf Hitler in Germany, all inspired tremendous changes in their respective societies by making supporters believe that anything was possible if they collectively worked toward a common good (as defined by the leader). The general view of transformational leaders is that they are "natural born" influence agents who inspire high devotion, motivation, and productivity in group members (Lowe et al., 1996). Because transformational leaders often use unconventional strategies that put them at risk, it is not uncommon for them to face severe physical hardships—and even death—in moving the group to its goals.

Survey, interview, and experimental studies suggest there are at least three core components to transformational leadership (Kirkpatrick & Locke, 1996; Rai & Sinha, 2000).

1. *Ability to communicate a vision.* A vision, which is a future ideal state embodying shared group values, is the main technique that transformational leaders use to inspire followers. In communicating a vision, leaders convey the expectation of high performance among followers and a confidence that they have the ability to reach the vision.

2. *Ability to implement a vision.* Transformational leaders use a variety of techniques to implement a vision, such as clarifying how task goals are to be accomplished, serving as a role model, providing individualized support, and recognizing accomplishments.

3. *Demonstrating a charismatic communication style.* Transformational leaders have a captivating communication style, in which they make direct eye contact, exhibit animated facial expressions, and use powerful speech and nonverbal tactics (refer to chapter 7, pp. 228–230).

Although the concept of transformational leadership has stimulated renewed interest in the trait approach to understanding leader influence, it explains only a small number of leaders. Further, even theorists studying these charismatic types admit that they are most likely to emerge during times of change, growth, and crisis (Barbuto, 1997; Bass, 1985). What about times of relative stability, and what about the majority of leaders who do not have these special qualities?

The Contingency Model Highlights Personal and Situational Factors in Leader Effectiveness

Instead of simply attending to special personality characteristics, an alternative approach to understanding leadership—which draws inspiration from Kurt Lewin's notion of *interactionism* (see chapter 1, p. 14)—is to view it as a combination of personal and situational factors. Such an approach is offered by Fred Fiedler's (1967, 1993) **contingency model of leadership.** This contingency model contends that people do not become effective leaders because they possess a particular set of personality traits but, rather, because their particular personality matches the circumstances of a particular group. In other words, the traits that make a leader effective are *contingent* on the circumstances the leader encounters. Fiedler's model has four basic components, the first dealing with leadership style and the remaining three encompassing the characteristics of the situation.

Transformatio

Leaders who change (transform) the outlook and behavior of followers so that they move beyond their self-interests for the good of the group or society.

The charismatic leader gains and maintains authority solely by proving his strength in life.

Max Weber, German sociologist, 1864–1920

An army of sheep led by a lion would defeat an army of lions led by a sheep.

Arab proverb

The art of leadership . . . consists in consolidating the attention of the people against a single adversary and taking care that nothing will split up that attention. . . . The leader of genius must have the ability to make different opponents appear as if they belonged to one category.

Adolf Hitler, ruler of Nazi Germany, 1889–1945

Contingency Model Leadership

The theory that leadership effectiveness depends both on whether leaders are task oriented or relationship oriented and on the degree to which they have situational control.

LEADERSHIP STYLE

Consistent with earlier research, Fiedler argued that there are two basic types of leaders. A *task-oriented leader* is one who gives highest priority to getting the work of the group accomplished and is much less concerned with the relations among group members. In contrast, a *relationship-oriented leader* assigns highest priority to group relations, with task accomplishment being of secondary concern. Vince Lombardi, who coached the Green Bay Packers football team in the 1960s, was a task-oriented leader. In describing his focus of concern as a leader, he stated, "Winning isn't everything, it's the *only* thing." Although Lombardi's leadership style was instrumental in the Packers winning five championships in nine years, it is doubtful that his style would be effective with a children's team, where coaches must attend to players' feelings and relations. Instead, this situation requires a relationship-oriented leader, one who would describe his or her coaching philosophy as fostering positive social relationships first ("Having fun is more important than winning or losing"). Fiedler believed that these contrasting leadership styles were a product of enduring personality traits, and thus, would be difficult or impossible to change.

To identify these two leadership styles, Fiedler developed the *Least Preferred Coworker Scale,* which asks leaders to evaluate the person in the group they like least. Fiedler found that leaders who evaluated their least preferred coworker (LPC) very negatively were primarily motivated to attain successful task performance and only secondarily motivated to seek good interpersonal relations among group members. These low LPC leaders fit the mold of the task-oriented leader. In contrast, Fiedler found that leaders who evaluated their LPCs positively were primarily motivated toward achieving satisfactory interpersonal relationships among the group members and only secondarily motivated to successfully complete group tasks. These high LPC leaders fit the mold of the relationship-oriented leader.

SITUATIONAL CONTROL

According to Fiedler, the favorability of the situation for task-oriented (low-LPC) and relationship-oriented (high-LPC) leaders will depend on the degree to which the situation allows them to exert influence over group members. This *situational control* depends on three factors:

1. *The leader's relations with the group.* The leader's personal relations with group members can range from very good to very poor and is similar to the previously discussed idiosyncrasy credits. Fiedler believes that leader/member relations is the most important factor determining the leader's influence on followers (Fiedler, 1967).

2. *Task structure.* How clearly defined are the goals and the tasks of the group? The amount of structure can vary a great deal, from clear to unclear.

3. *The leader's position power.* The power and authority inherent in the leadership position. Does the organization back the leader? Does the leader have the power to reward and punish followers? The leader's position power can vary from strong to weak.

Taking these three situational factors into consideration, a leader has high situational control when the leader/member relations are good, there is clear task structure, and the leader has strong position power. In contrast, poor leader/member relations, an unstructured task, and weak position power indicate low situational control.

There is no such thing as a perfect leader either in the past or present, in China or elsewhere. If there is one, he is only pretending, like a pig inserting scallions into its nose in an effort to look like an elephant.

Liu Shao-chíi, founding member of the Chinese Communist Party, 1898–1969

PREDICTING LEADER EFFECTIVENESS

How do leadership style and situational control interact to determine the effectiveness of a particular leader? As figure 10.8 shows, Fiedler hypothesizes that task-oriented (low-LPC) leaders are the most effective in situations in which they have either high or low situational control. In contrast, relationship-oriented (high-LPC) leaders should be associated with better group performance when they have only a moderate degree of control.

Why would this pattern of effectiveness be expected? Fiedler explains that under the difficult conditions of low situational control, groups need considerable guidance to be pro-

FIGURE 10.8

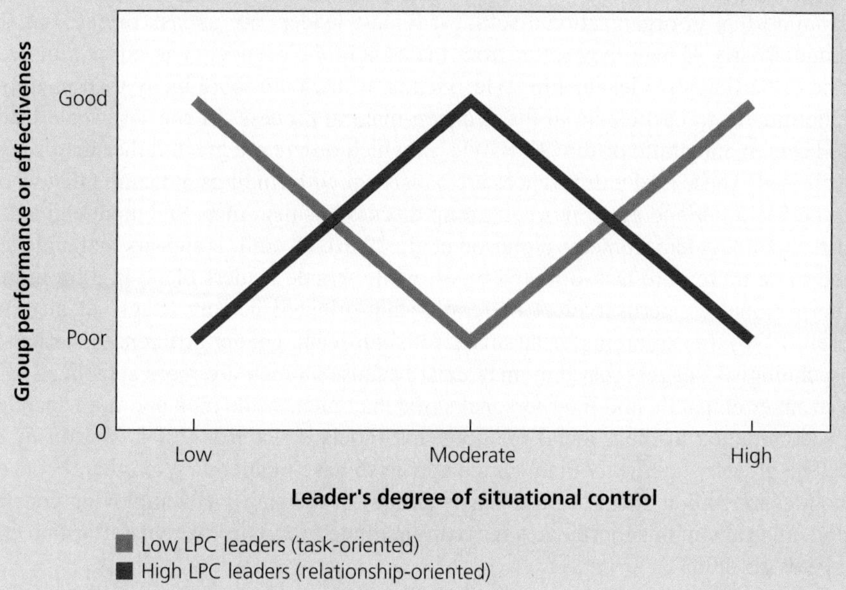

Predicting Group Effectiveness Based on Leadership Style and Situational Control

Based on your understanding of Fiedler's contingency theory of leadership and your reading of the figure, when are high LPC (relationship-oriented) leaders most effective in encouraging group productivity? How about low LPC (task-oriented) leaders?

ductive, and thus they will benefit from leaders who have this as their primary motivating goal. This challenging situation plays to the strengths of the task-oriented leader. In contrast, a relationship-oriented leader's more democratic style offers too little guidance in these low-control situations. When the situation in the group is very favorable, task-oriented leaders realize that their goal of task accomplishment is likely to be met and relationship-oriented leaders realize that they already enjoy good relations with their followers. With both leaders' primary motivating goals already achieved, they switch to achieving their respective secondary motives. For task-oriented leaders, their subsequent adoption of a more relaxed style increases group productivity, but the more directive style adopted by relationship-oriented leaders harms group performance because members perceive it as needless meddling. The only situation in which relationship-oriented leaders are more effective than task-oriented leaders is when they have only moderate situational control, such as when the task is unclear or the leader has little power. In such circumstances, a considerate, open-minded management approach should be best at rallying group support and fostering creative solutions to problems.

The contingency model has been tested in many natural and laboratory settings, and results generally support the model as outlined by Fiedler (Peters et al., 1985; Schriesheim et al., 1994). What we can learn from this research is that no one style of leadership is effective in all situations. Effective leadership requires a good fit between the leader's personal style and the demands of the situation. When the fit is not good, group productivity suffers (Ayman et al., 1995). And when a leader's style does not properly fit the situation, this mismatch also causes increased job stress and stress-related illnesses in the leader (Fiedler & Garcia, 1987; Graen & Hui, 2001)—a bad situation for all concerned. The limitation of this theory is that it assumes a leader can have only one style. Yet there is evidence that some leaders can adapt their style to meet the needs of the situation (Huczynski & Buchanan, 1996).

Gender and Culture Can Influence Leadership Style

Many authors who have extensive experience in organizations and who write nontechnical books for management audiences and the general public argue that male leaders and female leaders substantially differ in their style or approach to leadership (Loden, 1985). Is this true? Although the answer is not an emphatic no, research indicates that there are many more similarities than differences (Powell, 1990). In a meta-analysis of more than 150 studies of leadership in which men and women were compared, Alice Eagly and Blair Johnson (1990) found that in organizational settings, female leaders are as task oriented as their male counterparts. Where they differ from males is in their tendency to adopt a more democratic or participative leadership style. That is, women are more likely than men to invite subordinates to participate in the decision-making process. In contrast, male leaders tend to have an autocratic or directive style, in which orders are given rather than suggestions solicited. These leader differences are consistent with findings indicating that women tend to be friendlier and agree more in group discussions than men, and men tend to have higher rates of counterarguments (Johnson et al., 1996). Overall, it appears that male leaders tend to be more pure task-oriented types, while female leaders blend in a bit more of the interpersonal concerns typical of relationship-oriented leaders (Eagly et al., 1995; Helgesen, 1990). In explaining these small, yet significant, gender differences, various social psychologists suggest that they may exist because women are more socialized to develop stronger empathic and interpersonal skills than men, while men are more socialized to seek dominance in their social relationships (Foels & Pappas, 2004; Wilson & Liu, 2003). The greater superiority that women appear to have in attending to others' concerns and feelings may allow them to more easily adopt a leadership style employing considerable give-and-take with subordinates that can facilitate group productivity (Bartone et al., 2002; Peterson, 2003).

One impediment to women assuming leadership positions in mixed-sex groups is gender stereotypes. In many cultures around the world, the leader prototype is more closely associated with male stereotypes (Eagly & Karau, 2002). This masculinization of the leader role often leads to the perception that women are less qualified for elite leadership positions than men (Becker et al., 2002).

Moving from gender to cultural considerations, how might leadership style operate differently in individualist and collectivist cultures? A growing body of research suggests that the ideal leader may be different in these two cultures. Collectivists' concerns about group needs and interpersonal relations appear to foster a social climate in which nurturing, relationship-oriented leaders are highly desired by group members (Ayman & Chemers, 1983; Smith et al., 1990). In contrast, individualists are socialized to work alone, to concentrate on the task, and to emphasize achievement over socializing (Sanchez-Burks et al., 2000). This training appears to make individualists more responsive to task-oriented leaders.

One possible implication of these findings is that the previously discussed contingency model of leadership—which proposes that task-oriented leaders exhibit greater effectiveness in more varied situations than relationship-oriented leaders—may be better suited to explain leadership in individualist cultures than in those that are collectivist. Further, what about people living in multicultural societies like the United States and Canada who are also members of collectivist-oriented ethnic groups within these predominantly individualist societies? If you are a member of one of these ethnic groups, does your collectivist heritage cause you to respond to leaders somewhat differently than the typical individualist? It's possible. Jeffrey Sanchez-Burks and his coworkers (2000) found that Mexican Americans tend to be more responsive to relationship-oriented work groups than are Anglo Americans. These findings raise the possibility that even within an individualist society like the United States, how we respond to task-oriented versus relationship-oriented leaders may be partly determined by whether our ethnic heritage has individualist or collectivist roots.

SECTION SUMMARY

- A leader is the person who exerts the most influence and provides direction and energy to the group
- Transformational leaders are those who dramatically change the outlook and behavior of followers

Their attributes include the ability to

communicate and implement a vision

engage in charismatic communication

- In the contingency model of leadership, leader effectiveness is determined by the interaction of

the personal factor of *leadership style,* which involves task-oriented and relationship-oriented styles

three situational factors that provide the leader with situational control:

leader's relations with the group

task structure

leader's position power

- Although female leaders are as task oriented as male leaders, women tend to have a more democratic leadership style

- In collectivist cultures, relationship-oriented leaders may be more effective than they are in individualist cultures

GROUP INTERESTS VERSUS INDIVIDUAL INTERESTS

The idea that followers' responsiveness to certain types of leaders may partly depend on whether they are individualists or collectivists has relevance to the final topic in this chapter: individual interests versus group interests. Whenever individuals are involved in group activities, the possibility always exists that they will be faced with a situation in which their own immediate interests diverge from those of the group. How individuals resolve this conflict has been the subject of considerable attention by social psychologists over the years.

Scientists believe that the short-term profits realized by companies overlogging the South American rain forests will ultimately lead to long-term negative environmental consequences for millions of people. This situation is an example of a social dilemma. What are some strategies to promote more cooperative behavior?

Social Dilemmas Occur When Short-Term and Long-Term Interests Conflict

A **social dilemma** is any situation in which the most rewarding short-term choice for an individual will ultimately cause negative consequences for the group as a whole (Pruitt, 1998; Schroeder et al., 2003). A classic example of a social dilemma concerning how two or more people share a limited resource is the "tragedy of the commons" described by ecologist Garret Hardin (1968). Imagine a small town with a communal piece of land—the commons—available to all the townspeople's cattle. For many years the commons has been able to grow enough grass to support fifty cattle, one for each farmer. Now suppose that one farmer selfishly adds another cow to the commons to increase his milk production. Other farmers, noticing this addition, also add more cattle. Soon the farmers reap the results of their selfishness and competitiveness—the commons dies and all the cattle perish. By pursuing short-term individual gains, the farmers orchestrated a collective disaster. This type of social dilemma is known as a *resource dilemma.*

We read about numerous examples of resource dilemmas in the newspapers or confront them in our daily lives. The depletion of the South American rain forests brings timber companies short-term profits, but it poses a serious long-term threat to our environment. Even closer to home is the tendency for people to regularly use or benefit from certain public services, such as schools, libraries, parks, roads, public radio, and consumer groups, at the same time that they fail to contribute to their continued existence. If users do not contribute, the services will no longer be available. This willingness to use a public good, coupled with an unwillingness to contribute to it, has been called the *free-rider problem.*

In all social dilemmas, people are in a situation of *mixed motives* in which it is to their advantage both to cooperate and to act selfishly. Their short-term interests will be advanced if they act selfishly, but their long-term interests and those of the group will be advanced if they cooperate. Although you might expect that people would cooperate when such cooperation will enhance their long-term interests, this is often not the case. For example, in a study of resource dilemmas, Julian Edney (1979) had college students play a game in which ten metal nuts were placed into a bowl. They were told that the goal of the game was for each student to gather as many nuts as possible. They were further told that they could remove as many nuts from the bowl as they wished, and every ten seconds the number of nuts remaining in the bowl would be doubled. Despite the fact that the most rational choice for individual players was to leave the nuts in the bowl for a period of time so that they would multiply in numbers, this was not the typical strategy gameplayers adopted. Instead, when the game started, most players simply grabbed as many nuts as they could snatch from the grasp of others. Sixty-five percent of Edney's groups did not even make it past the first ten-second replacement period!

Have you noticed a psychological similarity between resource dilemmas and the phenomenon of social loafing examined earlier? In resource dilemmas, individuals deplete the group resource by taking from it more than their fair share, and in social loafing, individuals deplete group productivity (a group resource) by taking some of their own effort out of the collective effort. In both instances, being "lost in the crowd"—or deindividuated—allows members the protection necessary to behave selfishly (Williams et al., 1995). Although there are these similarities, research indicates that, unlike social loafing, fear and greed are two primary motives driving social dilemma decisions (Bruins et al., 1989). When people notice that others are taking a free ride or depleting collective resources, they abandon a socially responsible strategy and grab what they can (Kerr, 1983).

Social dilemmas are not limited to conflicts involving limited resources. Another type of dilemma, the *prisoner's dilemma,* derives its name from the research paradigm employed by social psychologists to study it. In its original format, the prisoner's dilemma involves a situation in which two men suspected of a crime are arrested by the police and placed into separate interrogation rooms (Luce & Raiffa, 1957). The district attorney is confident that the two together committed the crime but she does not have sufficient evidence to convict

FIGURE 10.9

Behavior of Prisoner A

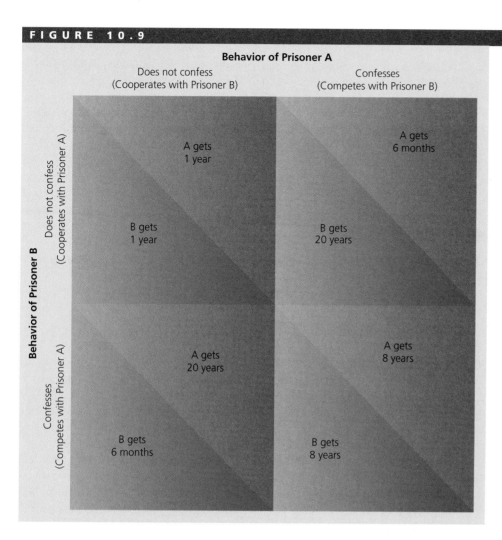

Does not confess
(Cooperates with Prisoner B)

Confesses
(Competes with Prisoner B)

Behavior of Prisoner B

Does not confess
(Cooperates with Prisoner A)

A gets
1 year

B gets
1 year

A gets
6 months

B gets
20 years

Confesses
(Competes with Prisoner A)

A gets
20 years

B gets
6 months

A gets
8 years

B gets
8 years

The Prisoner's Dilemma

In this form of social dilemma, two suspected criminals are interrogated separately and are given a choice: to confess or not to confess. If both cooperate with one another by staying silent, both get off with fairly light sentences (upper left). If both compete with one another by confessing, both receive moderate sentences (lower right). But if one confesses while the other stays silent, the confessor gets a very light sentence and the nonconfessor spends a long time in prison (lower left and upper right).

them. She approaches each suspect individually and tells him he has two alternatives: to confess to the crime the police are certain they both committed or not to confess. If they both do not confess, the district attorney states that she will charge them on some minor offense and each will get one year in prison. If both confess, they will be prosecuted, but the district attorney will recommend less than the most severe sentence; both will get eight years in prison. However, if one confesses and the other does not, then the one who confesses will receive a very lenient sentence of only six months for testifying against the other, but the one who holds out will get the maximum penalty of twenty years in prison. The essentials of the prisoner's dilemma are presented in figure 10.9, representing what will happen to each prisoner as a consequence of the four possible combinations of confessing and not confessing. Each prisoner knows that the other has the same options and knowledge as himself. Mutual nonconfession would produce a reasonably agreeable outcome for both; it would be their second choice of the four outcomes. However, the outcome most advantageous for one prisoner (getting six months) is necessarily the outcome that the other prisoner would least prefer (getting twenty years). Both prisoners would select mutual confession as their third choice among the outcomes. If you were in this situation, what would you do?

Numerous studies have used variations of the prisoner's dilemma to identify the factors that tip the balance toward cooperation or competition (Liberman et al., 2004). Frequently, the game is played over a series of trials so that players can alter their choices based on how their partner/competitor previously behaves. One variation entails two countries involved in an arms race, with each trial involving decision makers from each country choosing between competing (by building missiles) or cooperating (by building factories) with the other country. Initially in these multiple-trial games, competition typically occurs in the early trials, but then people begin to cooperate as they experience the negative consequences of competition and try to reduce them (Insko et al., 2001; Nowak & Sigmund, 1993). The findings from prisoner's dilemma studies and those involving resource dilemmas both suggest that many factors play a role in promoting cooperation versus competition in mixed-motives situations. Let us now turn our attention to those factors.

Cooperation Is Necessary to Resolve Social Dilemmas

The basic problem in resolving many social dilemmas is that it requires the cooperative efforts of numerous people. Yet all too often, people are unwilling to give up their short-term-gain strategies until the social dilemma becomes quite serious or they sustain many competitive losses (Yamagishi, 1988). Resolving social dilemmas is not easy under such conditions, but research reveals several ways to promote cooperation (Foddy et al., 1999)

SANCTIONING COOPERATIVE BEHAVIOR

Without a sanctioning system in place to regulate people's short-term interest strategies, cooperative group members are often taken advantage of by their more competitive neighbors (Koole et al., 2001). One way to increase the cooperation of selfish individuals is to force them to cooperate. Often this is accomplished by establishing an authority who will lead group members to set up guidelines of conduct that are consistent with the collective welfare of the group (Van Vugt & De Cremer, 1999). Interestingly, people who tend to be less cooperative and less trusting of others' behavior are more willing to contribute money to establish an authority that will punish others for noncooperative behavior (Yamagishi, 1986).

EDUCATION

A second way to solve a social dilemma is to educate group members. For example, in one study using a laboratory simulation of a water shortage, participants were told that they could draw water from a hypothetical lake, which would then renew itself by a small amount, much as rain replenishes a real lake (Allison & Messick, 1985). Those who understood the consequences of their actions behaved in a more socially responsible manner. Similarly, other studies have found that after receiving training in cooperation, even habitual competitors tend to become more cooperative and sustain this prosocial behavior over extended periods of time (Sheldon, 1999).

GROUP IDENTIFICATION

Solutions to social dilemmas also may be achieved by encouraging the adoption of a meaningful group identity (De Cremer & van Dijk, 2002; Van Vugt, 2001). For example, in resource dilemmas, people are more likely to cooperate if they think of the other users of limited resources as being a part of their ingroup rather than as mere competitors. In support of this hypothesis, research has found that when the salience of people's group identity is manipulated, they are more likely to exercise personal restraint in their use of an endangered resource (Brewer & Kramer, 1986). These findings suggest that if groups can develop a "sense of community" in their members, they may call on this group identification when it is crucial that individuals put collective needs ahead of immediate self-interest (Tyler & Blader, 2000).

PROMOTING A COOPERATIVE ORIENTATION

As we have already seen, not everyone automatically places cooperation ahead of competition when confronted with a social dilemma. This is because people differ in their *social value orientation,* which is a person's rules specifying how outcomes or resources should be divided between oneself and others (Van Lange, 1999). Those with a *cooperative orientation* seek to maximize joint gains, those with an *individualistic orientation* try to maximize their own well-being regardless of what happens to others, and those with a *competitive orientation* strive to outdo others by as much as possible. Cooperators see the long-term value of sustained mutual cooperation, and they focus on how the future can be better from the past (Parks et al., 2003). Not surprisingly, it is far easier to solve a social dilemma when you are dealing with cooperators rather than individualists or competitors (De Dreu & McCusker, 1997; Joireman et al., 2001). Recognizing this simple truth, and further realizing that a cooperative value system should be internalized early in life, educational programs have been established to teach children how to think and behave cooperatively rather than competitively in social interaction (Van Lange et al., 1997).

PROMOTING GROUP DISCUSSION

One final way to reduce the free-rider problem is simply to give people the opportunity to discuss the dilemma among themselves (Braver, 1995). Studies indicate that groups allowed to talk about the dilemma cooperate more than 95 percent of the time (van de Kragt et al., 1986). Why is discussion so effective? The most likely explanation appears to be that group discussion allows members to make explicit promises as to how they will behave, and these promises act as a binding social contract (Kiesler et al., 1996). If individual members hesitate to go along with this commitment to cooperate, group pressure is often sufficient to eventually secure compliance (Orbell et al., 1988).

Taking these strategies together, we can escape the destructive consequences of social dilemmas by (1) establishing guidelines and sanctions against self-serving behavior, (2) getting people to understand how their actions help or hurt everyone's long-term welfare, (3) encouraging people to develop a group identity, (4) fostering the internalization of social values that encourage cooperation rather than competition, and (5) promoting group discussion that leads to cooperation commitments.

Who see Me in all, And sees all in Me, For him I am not lost, And he is not lost for Me.

Bhagavad Gita ("The Lord's Song"), a sacred writing of Hinduism

It is our task in our time and in our generation to hand down undiminished to those who come after us, as was handed down to us by those who went before, the natural wealth and beauty which is ours.

John F. Kennedy, 35th U.S. president, 1917–1963

SECTION SUMMARY

- *Social dilemmas* occur when people's most rewarding short-term choices ultimately cause negative consequences for the group
- Factors that help resolve social dilemmas:

    sanctioning cooperative behavior

    education

    group identification

    promoting a cooperative orientation

    promoting group discussion

FEATURED STUDY

GROUP DECISION RULES IN CIVIL JURIES

Ohtsubo, Y., Miller, C. E., Hayashi, N., & Masuchi, A. (2004). Effects of group decision rules on decisions involving continuous alternatives: The unanimity rule and extreme decisions in mock civil juries. *Journal of Experimental Social Psychology, 40,* 320–331.

The civil jury system of the United States entrusts groups of twelve (or fewer) citizens with the task of resolving civil disputes between two or more conflicting parties. Many legal experts have expressed confidence in using juries to solve civil disputes, but others have reservations due in part to the high levels of damages that are sometimes awarded in certain cases. For example, in 1985 a jury of twelve Texas citizens assessed $11.1 billion in damages against Texaco for its improper interference in Pennzoil Company's bid to acquire Getty Oil Company. What social psychological processes might have contributed to such an extreme jury decision?

Research by Kaplan and Miller (1987) suggest that extreme damage awards may be influenced by the decision rule that is assigned to the jury to transform the preferences of the individual jurors into a final group decision. The two decision rules employed in the civil jury system in the United States are the unanimity rule, which stipulates that all jurors must agree on the same position before a decision is finalized, and the majority-wins rule, which stipulates that the jury will adopt whatever position is held by more than 50 percent of its members. Because the unanimity rule gives every jury member veto power over the group's decision, the researchers in the present research project hypothesized that jury decisions under that rule would be more influenced by extreme member opinions than jury decisions under the majority rule. They further hypothesized that when the initial distribution of jurors' preferences contains one or two opinions that recommend high punitive damages, the final jury decision will be larger under the unanimity rule than under the majority rule. Only the first of the two studies conducted by the researchers is described here.

Method

Participants were 282 college students (157 men and 125 women) enrolled in an introductory psychology class at a middle-size Japanese university. Participants were placed in six-person groups and randomly assigned to either a unanimity rule (twenty-four groups) or majority rule (twenty-three groups) condition. The defendant in the civil case they analyzed was a hospital whose allegedly negligent treatment left a newborn child with incurable disabilities. Pilot testing indicated that this case would likely produce an initial distribution of juror preferences containing at least one or two opinions that recommended high punitive damages. After reading the case, but before discussing it with fellow jurors, participants were asked to individually indicate their opinion about the appropriate level of punitive damages. Next each group was given twenty minutes to deliberate the case and make a group decision on the punitive damages. In the majority rule condition, participants were told that to reach a group decision, at least four members had to agree on the level of damages (if any) to be awarded. All groups were successful in reaching a decision within the time frame.

Results and Discussion

To test the first hypothesis, the correlation between the group decision and the initial preference of the most extreme group member (whose pre-discussion preference was highest) was computed separately for each decision rule condition. As hypothesized, although the correlation was significant in the unanimity rule condition ($r = .58$), it was not significant in the majority rule condition ($r = .01$). The difference between these correlations was significant, which indicates that group decisions took into account the preferences of the extreme members more under the unanimity rule than under majority rule. To test the second hypothesis, the damage awards decided by the unanimity rule were compared with those decided by groups under majority rule. Counter to expectations, the damage awards were not significantly different from one another, although they were in the expected direction.

These results suggest that when the initial preferences of one or two jury members recommend high punitive damages, jury decisions are influenced more by these extreme group members when juries operate under the unanimity rule than when they work under the majority rule. Because assigning the unanimity rule to civil juries appears to increase the likelihood of extreme decisions, some might consider the use of that rule undesirable compared with the use of the majority rules. However, this concern should be tempered because no significant differences in punitive damages were found in the present study. Further, a number of studies indicate that there are some real benefits in the greater consideration given minority opinions under the unanimity rule as compared with the majority rule (see Applications). Future research should further explore the upside and downside of these two decision rules in civil jury cases.

APPLICATIONS

HOW DO JURIES MAKE DECISIONS?

*I*n the Applications section of chapter 9, you learned how people can be coerced into confessing to a crime they did not commit. In this section, let's examine how juries weigh the evidence presented by both prosecution and defense attorneys. What goes on behind those closed doors once the jury has gone into seclusion to deliberate? Unfortunately for those interested in better understanding the social psychological dynamics of this process, federal and virtually all state laws forbid eavesdropping on jury deliberations. Ironically, the catalyst for these laws was the public outrage that ensued when a judge in the 1950s allowed University of Chicago researchers to tape-record the deliberations of five juries (Ferguson, 1955).

Due to the inaccessibility of real juries, social scientists have resorted to alternative means of gaining insight into the inner workings of this group (Wrightsman et al., 1987). Some of these are: (1) interviewing jurors once a verdict has been reached, (2) analyzing court records, and (3) simulating the jury deliberation process by staging simulated trials using mock juries. What do these studies tell us about the jury as a decision-making group?

The Deliberation Process

As in most groups, juries move through distinct stages in making their decisions (see p. 374). During the orientation stage, jurors pick a foreperson, set an agenda, and begin to get to know one another. Next, in the discussion stage, they tackle the task of reviewing the evidence. This review process and the following decision stage can generate considerable tension because

jurors often actively disagree with one another. As jurors move toward a decision in stage 3, the majority exerts pressure on dissenters to fall in line so that a unanimous verdict can be reached. Once consensus is within reach, the group tries to resolve the remaining differences and conflicts so that a verdict can be rendered. When no such consensus is reached, however, a jury does not have the option open to most other groups—rejecting nonconforming members. Instead, jurors who hold the majority opinion must continue to search for consensus with their minority counterparts. If after exhaustive and fruitless discussion, the jury proclaims itself hung and, if the judge agrees that further deliberation would be fruitless, a mistrial is declared.

As important as the deliberation process is to our legal system, in most cases the verdict is actually determined before the jurors even begin discussing the case. As previously discussed (see p. 375), Harry Kalven and Hans Zeisel (1966) found that in 97 percent of the court cases they reviewed, the jury's final decision was the same as the one a majority of the jurors favored on the initial vote before deliberation commenced. Similar results have been obtained in other studies (Sandys & Dillehay, 1995), suggesting that by the time the first vote is taken, the jury has generally already decided about the defendant's guilt. Does this then mean that group discussion of the facts does not significantly influence individual juror opinions? Maybe not. When jurors on fifty randomly selected felony cases were contacted by researchers and interviewed regarding their jury experience, they revealed that even when first-ballot votes were taken before formal discussion of the evidence, some informal discussion almost always took place

Better understanding the group dynamics of juries is of central concern not only to social scientists but also to those who must try to persuade the group to believe their interpretation of the evidence presented to them, namely, prosecutors and defense attorneys.

among individual jurors (Sandys & Dillehay, 1995). In such cases, it's possible that jurors were indeed influenced by the other jurors' opinions. In only 11 percent of these trials did the first ballot occur before any discussion or deliberation took place at all. These trials, then, represent individual juror first-ballot verdicts with the least amount of influence from other jurors. Did these individual first-ballot verdicts predict the jury's subsequent final verdicts? Interestingly, they did not, and thus, these findings suggest that the deliberation process may play a more significant role in shaping the verdicts of juries than was previously thought to be the case.

Although jurors holding minority viewpoints have little chance of dramatically shifting majority opinion, the research on minority influence described in chapter 9 suggests that jurors may be persuasive when their positions are not too far away from the prevailing majority position. Support for this hypothesis comes from a mock jury study that Nancy Pennington and Reid Hastie (1990) conducted, in which they found that a minority on a jury was often able to change the majority's minds on the degree of guilt of a defendant. This suggests that if ten out of twelve jurors believe a defendant is guilty of first-degree murder, though there is virtually no chance that the two dissenting jurors will be able to convince the majority that the defendant is innocent, they might be able to convince them to change their verdict to second-degree murder. Based on minority influence research, jurors holding minority positions would be most persuasive when they consistently and confidently state their dissenting views and, at the same time, come across as flexible and open-minded.

The Consequences of Small Juries

In the 1970 case of *Williams v. Florida,* the U.S. Supreme Court heard the appeal of a defendant who was convicted of armed robbery by a six-person jury instead of the traditional twelve-person jury. In their arguments, his lawyers contended that a six-person jury was biased against defendants because the possibility of juror dissent was greatly reduced with such a small group. The Supreme Court justices disagreed, ruling that in civil cases and state criminal cases not involving the death penalty, courts could use six-person juries instead of the traditional twelve. In making their rulings, the justices stated that there is no reason to believe that smaller juries will arrive at different decisions than the traditional jury. Is this true?

Although research indicates that jury size does not appear to affect rates of convictions or acquittals, a meta-analysis of studies involving fifteen thousand mock jurors who deliberated in over two thousand six-person or twelve-person juries found that smaller juries spend less time deliberating, recall less of the evidence, and are less likely to represent minority segments of the population (Saks & Marti, 1997). In addition, other studies have found that six-person juries are only half as likely to become hung than twelve-person juries (Kerr & MacCoun, 1985). Because trials resulting in hung juries often do so because of legitimate disagreements, it may be that smaller juries weaken a necessary safeguard in our legal system (Davis et al. 1997). One likely reason twelve-person juries are more likely to become deadlocked is that with more people in a group, there is a greater likelihood that more than one person will be dissenting from the majority. As Asch's (1956) conformity research suggests (see chapter 9, p. 319), when someone has a social supporter he or she is much more likely to resist majority pressure to conform.

The Consequences of Nonunanimous Verdicts

In 1972, the U.S. Supreme Court ruled in a split 5-4 decision that courts could accept verdicts based on less-than-unanimous majorities. The majority of the justices stated that a nonunanimous decision rule (for example, a guilty verdict by a 9 to 3 margin) would not adversely affect the jury, but four justices disagreed, arguing that it would reduce the intensity of deliberations and negatively affect the potential for minority influence. Was this Supreme Court decision consistent with the findings from scientific studies of juries? Based on your own understanding of group influence, do you think that people on a jury that needs only a 9-to-3 majority would engage in a different type of deliberation process than juries that require a unanimous decision?

Reid Hastie and his colleagues (1983) studied the deliberations of more than 800 people in sixty-nine different mock jury trials and found that juries with rules requiring less-than-unanimous verdicts behaved very differently than juries requiring unanimous verdicts. Their results indicated that majority-wins-rule juries (10-to-2 or 8-to-4 margins) are not only less likely to end up hung than unanimity-rule juries (12-to-0 margin), but they are also likely to render harsher verdicts—and do so in a relatively short period of time using a bullying persuasive style rather than relying on carefully reasoned arguments. Jurors who participate in these nonunanimous juries also emerge rating themselves as less informed, feeling less confident about their final decision, and perceiving their peers as more close-minded than jurors in the unanimous-rule groups (Nemeth, 1977). These findings clearly suggest that allowing nonunanimous verdicts is very likely to decrease the robustness of the arguments heard in deliberation. This, in turn, may well hinder the minority's ability to persuade the majority.

Today, only two states permit nonunanimous verdicts in criminal trials, but thirty-three states permit such verdicts in civil cases. Most civil cases today also employ six-member juries. Based on the research conducted since the Supreme Court loosened the restraints on jury size and unanimity, it appears that these changes result in faster and harsher trials by encouraging close-mindedness in jurors. The question we must ask ourselves is whether this is what we want to call "justice under the law."

THE BIG PICTURE

What I hope you understand by this time is that, although you are a unique individual in your own right, you are also a creature of the group (Miller & Prentice, 1994). In a psychological sense, you are not fully mature until you have internalized the group into your everyday thinking. As discussed in chapter 9, an important aspect of group living is the process of social influence. There is nothing inherently wrong with such influence—in fact, it is the social "stitching" that organizes the fabric of everyday life. Yet, in our individualist culture, the group has often been viewed with distrust and even condescension. It is true that you can sometimes act in an inferior and impulsive manner when in a group (due to *social loafing* and *deindividuation,* respectively), but you can also exhibit similar undesirable actions when acting alone. Thus, group processes, like individual processes, are amply designed to foster both positive and negative outcomes.

Whenever you become involved in a group, the possibility always exists that your own personal, self-focused interests will diverge from those of the collective. In such *social dilemmas,* your short-term interests will be advanced if you act selfishly, but your long-term interests and those of the group will be advanced if you cooperate. Resolving social dilemmas—and maintaining group membership itself—may be harder for individualists than collectivists. Based on your responses to the "Values Hierarchy Exercise" in chapter 1 (p. 19), do you think it would be difficult or easy for you to work to resolve social dilemmas when they arise in your own groups?

In summarizing the content of this chapter, contemporary social science confirms that the group fabric of human nature is strong. Yet, within the fabric of the group, you will find the creative weaving of the many interconnected selves. This unique blending of the self with others powers group dynamics. When you interact with group members, you are actively creating and recreating your social reality—yet you are often unaware of the situational forces that shape this reality. Despite the fact that you may think of yourself as being a relatively autonomous creature, your current understanding of group processes should tell you that much of this self-perceived independence is illusory. Regardless of your culture of origin, you are influenced by others, both singly and collectively. One of the most important goals of social psychology as a discipline is to increase knowledge of how the person—as a self—helps to weave the fabric of group life and how the paths of these individual life threads are influenced by one another. The better you understand the complex nature and influence of the group fabric, the better you will be able to weave your own unique, yet group-influenced, patterns.

WEB SITES
accessed through http://www.mhhe.com/franzoi4

Web sites for this chapter focus on why we form into groups, what needs and functions they serve, as well as the psychology of collective behavior and social institutions.

Why So Social an Animal?

This Web site by Donelson Forsyth presents a thorough analysis of why we form into groups, what needs they satisfy, and what functions they perform.

Center for Leadership Studies

This Web site for the Center for Leadership Studies contains the findings of recent studies on the social psychological dynamics of leaders as instruments of change within a group.

Self-Directed Work Teams

This Web site analyzes self-directed work teams, discussing research on group work and how to improve teamwork.

INTERACTING WITH OTHERS

*I*n this final book section (Part Four), we examine theory and research having to do with *how we interact with others.* Chapter 11 examines our desire to seek out others' company. Why do we seek affiliation? What characteristics of the situation and of others heighten our affiliation desires? Why are some of us more people-oriented than others, and why are some of us chronically worried about everyday social life?

Chapter 12 investigates how this interpersonal process can progress to friendship and romance. Do our early childhood experiences shape how we view intimacy? Do men and women differ in their friendship patterns and romantic desires? How can we understand the social psychology of love? What strengthens and weakens romantic relationships?

Chapter 13 explores the difficult issue of how social interaction can sometimes erupt into aggressive outbursts. To what degree are aggressive actions driven by our biology? Should we act out our aggressive desires to "purge" ourselves of their influence, or is this a strategy doomed to backfire on us? Are there certain regions of the country where aggressive outbursts are more likely? What influence do television and pornography have on our aggressive tendencies?

Finally, in Chapter 14 we scrutinize the helping process by trying to answer five basic questions: Why do we help others? When do we help others? Who among us is most likely to help? Who are we likely to help? And are there hidden costs for receiving help? In pursuing these questions, we will explore how inherited genetic tendencies, gender socialization, parental modeling, and political orientation can shape our helping tendencies. We will also examine the decisions we make in deciding to help—or not help—others in need.

Interpersonal Attraction

CHAPTER OUTLINE

*P*oet Lucy Grealy's (1994) book, *Autobiography of a Face,* relates the story of her childhood and young adulthood, a time of overwhelming physical pain caused by intensive chemotherapy and radiation treatments for facial bone cancer (Ewing's sarcoma) and numerous facial reconstructive surgeries. In treating the cancer, surgeons removed her jaw, leaving Lucy with a disfigured face that drew taunts from classmates. For example, on the first day of middle school she sat next to a table full of boys at lunch. They pointed and gawked, calling out loudly for all to hear, "What on earth is *that*?" "That is the ugliest girl I have *ever* seen!" For the first time, Lucy realized that she was not suitable girlfriend material. In the hallways she could look down and walk quickly to avoid seeing the stares and hearing the cruel remarks, but in the lunchroom she was a sitting duck. On an attractiveness scale ranging from 1 to 10 Lucy saw herself as lower than 1.

After weeks of enduring constant verbal abuse from these boys and with no one intervening on her behalf, Lucy went to her guidance counselor to complain. She was hoping he would reprimand the boys and perhaps even teach them some manners. Instead he offered to let Lucy spend her lunch period in the privacy of his office while he ate with the rest of the school staff. Lucy accepted because at least his office provided a sense of security. But it also made Lucy feel even more isolated, and she identified her face as the source of her unhappiness.

Very few people understand what it feels like to be the target of the type of verbal cruelty Lucy experienced. Yet many of us at some point in our lives have been shunned or rejected by others because one or more of our personal qualities does not measure up to others' standards of acceptability. **Interpersonal attraction** is the desire to approach another individual.

Besides physical appearance, what qualities influence your need to seek out others for interaction? What situational factors shape your desire to approach or avoid others? As a way to help you ponder these questions, try the following exercise. Think about your best friend. How did you first meet? On paper, list up to ten reasons why you were initially attracted to this person. These reasons could be profound or mundane. Now think about a casual friend. In addition to listing factors that initially attracted you, also identify reasons why you think this relationship hasn't come close to achieving the level of "best friend." Finally, think about someone you dislike. List the factors that shaped the course of this bad relationship. Now compare the three lists. How are they different? How are they similar? Can you develop any hypotheses about the nature of interpersonal attraction based on any patterns you observe?

As we study the "chemistry" of interpersonal attraction in this chapter, keep these lists handy and remember Lucy Grealy's story, for we will refer to them on more than one occasion. Following a discussion of two basic reasons why people affiliate, we examine how personal characteristics of the individual, situational factors, and characteristics of others influence the attraction process. Then we analyze how social interaction can be chronically problematic for some people and end by discussing ways to improve the interpersonal skills of the socially anxious and lonely. Then, in chapter 12, we will investigate how this interpersonal process can progress—and sometimes deteriorate—in close friendships and other intimate relationships.

Interpersonal Attraction

The desire to approach another individual.

Disfigured by facial bone cancer, poet Lucy Grealy learned early in life that most people judged her as having very low "relationship value." Why is physical appearance so important in interpersonal attraction?

AFFILIATION NEEDS

Have you ever wondered why your need to be around other people often changes due to your daily experiences? Have you ever questioned why your overall need to socialize is different from the expressed need of some of your friends and acquaintances? I'm guessing that the answer to both of these questions is yes. In this first section of chapter 11 you can explore how closely your personal musings on affiliation match the insights of social scientific theory and research.

Two Reasons for Affiliation Are Comparison and Exchange

Two factors that shape affiliation involve the desire to gain knowledge about ourselves and the world through *social comparison,* and the desire to secure psychological and material rewards through *social exchange.* These two reasons for seeking out others relate to our dependence on others for information (information dependence) and our dependence on others for positive outcomes (outcome dependence) that we first discussed in chapter 9. Can you guess which of these two factors is associated with the "cold" perspective of human nature, and which is associated with the "hot" perspective first introduced in chapter 1?

SOCIAL COMPARISON

According to Leon Festinger's (1954) **social comparison theory,** we human beings possess a strong need to have accurate views, both about our social world and about ourselves. As you may recall from our discussion of the social comparison process in chapter 3, one way to know ourselves and better understand our place in the social environment is to compare ourselves with others (Wedell & Parducci, 2000). The information that such social comparison provides is used to evaluate the self. According to Festinger, social comparison is most likely when we are in a state of *uncertainty* concerning a relevant self-aspect. He further hypothesized that we generally prefer to compare ourselves with *similar* others. Why? Because the more similar people are to us, the more likely we will be to use the information gained through social comparison in better understanding ourselves and our future actions.

> **Social Comparison Theory**
>
> The theory that proposes that we evaluate our thoughts and actions by comparing them with those of others.

To see how social comparison might be used, imagine trying to decide whether to take a particular course next semester. You know three people who were previously enrolled in the course: Juan, who is always the top student in every course; Vanessa, who usually receives similar grades as you; or Sarah, who is always on academic probation. Who would you seek out for information about the course? According to social comparison theory, you would go to Vanessa because of her academic similarity to you. Her opinions and observations, and her actual final grade, will be much more useful in predicting your own performance than information learned from Juan and Sarah.

We use social comparison not only to judge—and improve—ourselves, but as you will see in later chapter sections, we also use it to provide information about our emotions and perhaps even to choose our friends (Helgeson & Mickelson, 1995; Wood, 1996). Today, our understanding of social comparison processes is more complex than originally formulated by Festinger, but it still conforms to the general principles outlined here. This knowledge-based motive for affiliation reflects the "cold" perspective of human nature.

SOCIAL EXCHANGE

Although the desire to evaluate ourselves through social comparison is one reason for affiliation, a second theory explaining affiliation focuses more closely on the *interactions* between people. According to **social exchange theory,** people seek out and maintain those relationships in which rewards exceed costs, and they avoid or terminate relationships when costs are greater than rewards (Berscheid & Lopes, 1997). The assumption underlying this "hot" perspective on affiliation is that people are basically *hedonists*—they seek to maximize pleasure and minimize pain, and to do so at minimal cost. Operating from this assumption, the theory also states that people will be attracted to those who best reward them.

> **Social Exchange Theory**
>
> The theory that proposes that we seek out and maintain those relationships in which the rewards exceed the costs.

One of the earliest versions of social exchange theory was presented by sociologist George Homans (1958), who stated that all social relationships are like economic bargains in which each party places a value on the goods they exchange with one another. The "goods" exchanged could be either material (for example, money, flowers, food) or nonmaterial (for example, social influence, information, affection). For instance, teachers instruct students in various subjects (a nonmaterial good) in exchange for a certain amount of

CRITICAL *thinking*

Take out the three lists you created earlier for your best friend, casual friend, and disliked acquaintance. Examine your listed reasons for why each relationship developed in the way that it did. If you can, rank them in order of importance, with "1" being the "most important." Next, for each list, how many of your more important affiliation reasons (say, "1" through "5") can be identified as being primarily based on social comparison or social exchange needs? Finally, how are your three lists similar to or different from one another regarding social comparison and social exchange reasons?

money from their school districts (a material good). Similarly, a husband may do the grocery shopping, daily food preparation, and weekly yard work, and in exchange, his wife may do the laundry, dinner cleanup, and weekly vacuuming and dusting. Social exchange theory assumes that people keep track of the goods they exchange, and on some level they know whether their rewards are exceeding their costs.

John Thibaut and Harold Kelley (1959) stated that, when people are deciding whether to remain in a relationship, they will not consider the rewards and costs in isolation. Instead, the level of costs and rewards accruing in the current relationship will be compared with the possible rewards and costs available in alternative relationships. If no alternative relationships are available, or none appear appreciably more rewarding than the current one, the person will make no changes. This is one reason why some people remain in dissatisfying or even harmful relationships—they would rather receive some rewards than run the risk of receiving none at all (Rusbult & Martz, 1995). For much of Lucy Grealy's life she judged her overall value by how others responded to her face, which resulted in her putting up with less than stellar personal qualities in the men with whom she became romantically involved.

These two explanations for why we affiliate—the desire for social comparison and the desire for social exchange—do not exhaust the explanatory powers of current social psychological theories. Instead, they provide an anchoring point for the discussion that follows. With this in mind, let us now explore more specific aspects of interpersonal attraction.

Many Factors Influence Our Affiliation Desires

Survey studies of adolescents report that on average, they spend about 75 percent of their waking time with other people (Larson et al., 1982). When with others, teenagers tend to be happier, more alert, and more excited than when alone. Social interaction, however, is not just important to this age group. In an analysis of institutionalized infant orphans, higher death rates were found among infants whose physical needs had been met but who received very little social interaction and nurturance (Spitz, 1945). Additional research with nonhuman species and with human children raised in orphanages has found that being deprived of social and physical contact can adversely affect the ability of the brain and the hormonal system to cope with stress (Gunnar, 2000). Yet people also differ in their desire for affiliation. My father describes himself as a "real people person." He regularly organizes social activities, whether it's sporting events for neighborhood children or card clubs for fellow senior citizens. Are you like this, or do you instead prefer a more restricted range of social contact? Why do we differ in our general need for affiliation?

Although we are by nature social creatures, we often individually differ in our affiliation needs. How can differences in our nervous system or the culture we grow up in influence our tendency to seek social contact?

OUR EVOLUTIONARY HERITAGE

It appears that our *need to belong* is a powerful, fundamental, and extremely pervasive motivation (Baumeister & Leary, 1995; Gardner et al., 2000). When this need is unfulfilled due to social exclusion or rejection, we react in a variety of negative ways, including increased stress, anxiety, and self-defeating thinking and behavior, which are often followed by decreased physical health (Buckley et al., 2004; Twenge et al., 2003; Williams, 2001). Comparative studies of chimpanzees and monkeys suggest there is a biological basis for these affiliative desires (de Waal, 1989). As discussed in chapter 9 (p. 322), human brain-imaging studies indicate that the social pain we experience following rejection is neurologically similar to the affective distress associated with physical pain, with both originating in the brain's anterior cingulate cortex in the frontal lobes (Eisenberger et al., 2003). Evolutionary psychologists suggest that during the course of primate evolution the social attachment "alarm" system came under the control of the same brain area involved in pain detection because this promoted the goal of social connectedness. In other words, our tendency to seek out others, to make friends, and to form enduring close relationships seems to be an inherited trait that has helped us survive and reproduce (Bugental, 2000).

THE BRAIN AND CENTRAL NERVOUS SYSTEM ACTIVITY

Growing biological evidence indicates that individual differences in the need for affiliation involve differences in central nervous system arousability and brain activity related to the experience of positive and negative emotions. *Arousability* is the habitual degree to which stimulation produces arousal of the central nervous system (Stelmack & Geen, 1992). Research inspired by Hans Eysenck's (1990) work on introversion and extroversion suggests that introverts have inherited a nervous system that operates at a higher level of arousal than extroverts. For example, brain-imaging studies suggest that the anterior cingulate cortex—the brain's danger and pain alarm system—is more active among introverts than extroverts (Johnson et al., 1999). Because of this higher arousability, introverts avoid a great deal of social interaction and situational change in order to keep their arousal from reaching uncomfortable levels. Extroverts have the opposite problem. Because their nervous system normally operates at a relatively low level of arousal, they seek out situations that stimulate them (Bullock & Gilliland, 1993; Depue et al., 1994). For instance, while extroverted students prefer studying in relatively noisy settings where they can socialize with others, introverted students prefer studying in quiet, socially isolated settings (Campbell & Hawley, 1982). Socially active extroverts not only choose to perform tasks in noisy settings, they actually perform better in such settings (Geen, 1996).

Beyond arousability, extroverts appear to experience greater activation of dopamine pathways in the brain associated with reward and positive affect than introverts (Depue & Collins, 1999; Lucas et al., 2000). Further, when introverts and extroverts are shown positive images (for example, puppies, a happy couple, or sunsets), extroverts experience greater activation of brain areas that control emotion, such as the frontal cortex and the amygdala (Canli et al., 2001). This research suggests that introversion and extroversion are associated with distinct patterns of brain activity, and that the experience of positive affect may be a primary feature of extroversion. Overall, it appears that each of us is born with a nervous system that causes us to have varying degrees of tolerance for the stimulation resulting from social interaction, which may influence the emotions we experience in such settings. It is this biological difference that significantly shapes our affiliation desires.

CULTURE, GENDER, AND AFFILIATION

Beyond biological causes, affiliation needs also appear to be shaped by cultural variables. Geert Hofstede's (1980) study of twenty-two countries found a positive relationship ($r = .46$) between a culture's degree of individualism and its citizens' affiliation needs: the more individualist cultures had higher needs for affiliation. In explaining this finding, Hofstede stated that in individualist cultures, people are generally expected to individually develop their own relationships and to do so in many varied social settings. Because they develop social ties with people in various social groups, their relationships may be numerous, but they are not particularly intimate.

I'll do my thing and you do yours. If two people find each other—it's wonderful—If not, it can't be helped.

An oft-repeated individualist "prayer" written by Fritz Perls, German-born psychologist, 1893–1970

This affiliative, yet relatively nonintimate, approach to social relationships typifies our own culture. Individualist Americans have numerous relationships that are marked by friendliness and informality, but relatively few develop into deep and lasting friendships (Bellah et al., 1985; Stewart & Bennett, 1991). Whereas many Americans tend to restrict friendship to an area of common interest, collectivist Russians expect to form deep bonds with their friends and to have these intimate friendships extend over many years (Glenn, 1966). As Harry Triandis observed in his analysis of these possible cross-cultural affiliation differences:

> People in individualist cultures often have greater skills in entering and leaving new social groups. They make "friends" easily, but by "friends" they mean nonintimate acquaintances. People in collectivist cultures have fewer skills in making new "friends" but "friend" in their case implies a life-long intimate relationship with many obligations. So the quality of the friendships is different. This difference in quality may complicate our understanding of the construct of collectivism, since people in individualistic cultures are likely to *appear* more sociable, while intimacy is not a readily observable attribute. (Triandis et al., 1988, p. 325)

Although individualists' social relationships tend to be less intimate than those of collectivists, some individualists cultivate more intimacy than others. In North America, members of many ethnic and religious groups are taught to think of themselves as *interdependent* with close others and as defined by their social relationships (Oved, 1988). Girls are also more likely than boys to be raised to think, act, and define themselves in ways that emphasize their emotional connectedness to other individuals (Cross & Madson, 1997). This more socially connected *relational self* can be contrasted with the more solitary *independent self* typically taught to boys, which conceives of the person as independent and less interested in cultivating emotional relationships (Cross & Gore, 2002). As previously discussed in chapter 3 (pp. 73–74), this relationship-oriented interdependence has some psychological similarities to the group-oriented interdependence typical of collectivist cultures, but they are clearly distinct and different (Kanagawa et al., 2001; Kashima et al., 1995). The type of interdependence found in individualist cultures involves people emotionally relating to others as individuals, while the interdependence typical of collectivist cultures involves people's emotional and psychological ties to their group.

Table 11.1 contains the *Relational-Interdependent Self-Construal (RISC) Scale* Susan Cross and her colleagues (2000) developed to measure individual differences in people's tendency to define themselves in terms of their close relationships. People who score high on the RISC Scale are more committed to and involved in their social relationships and are more likely to consider the needs of others when making decisions than those who score low on the scale (Cross et al., 2000; Cross & Vick, 2001). Cross and her coworkers (2002) have also found that people who primarily define themselves in terms of close personal relationships (high RISCs) have a much richer network of cognitive associations in memory for relationship-oriented terms than people who are less likely to think of themselves in this manner. One consequence of this different way of defining the self is that high relational individuals have better memories for relational events than low relational persons. This might explain why women are more likely than men to remember birthdays, anniversaries, and who said what during an important personal encounter with a friend or loved one (Ross & Holmberg, 1993). Spend a few minutes completing and scoring the scale for yourself.

Based on this brief overview of possible influences on affiliation needs, we can tentatively conclude that the desire for affiliation is an important defining characteristic of our species, yet individuals differ in the expression of this need. For some, our optimal arousal level is fairly high, and we seek a great deal of social and nonsocial stimulation. For others, our optimal arousal level is relatively low, and we live our lives in a more socially introverted fashion. Within our pursuit of social relationships, we also differ in the degree of emotional connectedness we seek, and our culture substantially shapes this individual difference in seeking interdependence.

TABLE 11.1

Relational-Interdependent Self-Construal Scale

Instructions: Below is a series of statements concerning men and women and their relationships in contemporary society. Please indicate the extent to which you agree or disagree with each of these statements using the following scale:

Strongly disagree <u>1</u> 2 <u>3</u> <u>4</u> <u>5</u> <u>6</u> <u>7</u> Strongly agree

_____ 1. My close relationships are an important reflection of who I am.

_____ 2. When I feel very close to someone, it often feels to me like that person is an important part of who I am.

_____ 3. I usually feel a strong sense of pride when someone close to me has an important accomplishment.

_____ 4. I think one of the most important parts of who I am can be captured by looking at my close friends and understanding who they are.

_____ 5. When I think of myself, I often think of my close friends or family also.

_____ 6. If a person hurts someone close to me, I feel personally hurt as well.

_____ 7. In general, my close relationships are an important part of my self-image.

_____ 8. Overall, my close relationships have very little to do with how I feel about myself.*

_____ 9. My close relationships are unimportant to my sense of what kind of person I am.*

_____ 10. My sense of pride comes from knowing who I have as close friends.

_____ 11. When I establish a close friendship with someone, I usually develop a strong sense of identification with that person.

Directions for Scoring:

Two of the Relational-Interdependent Self-Construal (RISC) Scale items are reverse-scored; that is, for these items a lower rating actually indicates a higher level of relational-interdependence. Before summing the items for a total score, recode those with an asterisk ("*") so that 1 = 7, 2 = 6, 3 = 5, 5 = 3, 6 = 2, and 7 = 1.

When Cross, Bacon, and Morris developed the RISC in 2000, the mean score for 2,330 female college students was about 57, whereas the average score for 1,819 male college students was about 53, indicating significant differences between women and men. Higher scores indicate greater interest in developing close, committed social relationships.

SECTION SUMMARY

- Two basic reasons for interpersonal attraction are social comparison and social exchange:

  In social comparison, we seek out similar others for comparison purposes due to our need to have an accurate self and worldview

  In social exchange, we seek out others because of the social rewards exchanged in such interactions, and we maintain the relationships if the rewards exceed the costs

- Affiliation desires are influenced by

  evolutionary heritage

  biological arousability and other neural activity

  culture and gender

CHARACTERISTICS OF THE SITUATION AND ATTRACTION

Individual differences can foster social contact or withdrawal, but a number of situational factors also can trigger affiliation needs and interpersonal attraction. In the following sections, we consider three of the more important situational factors: proximity, familiarity, and anxiety.

Close Proximity Fosters Liking

One of the most powerful factors in determining whether you become friends with other people is their sheer *proximity* to you (Berscheid & Reis, 1998). Is this one of the reasons why you were initially attracted to your best friend? Chances are, most of your friends live in close proximity to you, or at least did so in the past.

Leon Festinger, Stanley Schachter, and Kurt Back (1950) conducted one of the earlier and better studies of how proximity influences social relationships when they investigated the development of friendships in married graduate student housing at the Massachusetts Institute of Technology. Following World War II, the university had randomly assigned these student families to available apartments in seventeen different buildings; therefore, virtually none of the residents knew one another prior to moving in. When residents were asked to name their three closest friends in the housing units, physical proximity was the single most important determinant of friendship choices. Not only did about two-thirds of the listed friends reside in the same building as those who nominated them, but about two-thirds lived on the same floor. Further, 41 percent of next-door neighbors were chosen compared with only 22 percent of those living two doors away and 10 percent of those at the end of the hall (see figure 11.1). Similar proximity effects have been found in urban housing projects for the elderly (Nahemow & Lawton, 1975), in freshmen college dormitories (Priest & Sawyer, 1967), in office work environments (Conrath, 1973), and even in classroom settings (Segal, 1974). In the latter study, police academy trainees who were assigned classroom seats based on the alphabetical order of their last names made friends with those who sat adjacent to them.

Finally, for you romantics, there even is evidence that proximity can affect intimate relationships. In an early sociological study, James Bossard (1932) plotted the residences of each applicant on 5,000 marriage licenses in Philadelphia and found a clear relation between proximity and love. Couples were more likely to get married the closer they lived to each other. This finding was replicated in later research as well (Ramsoy, 1966).

Based on the studies discussed in this section, you might think we have stumbled on a solution to the anger and violence in our world: move enemies next door to one another and soon they will be friends! Before you act on this newfound belief, let's consider one last study. Ebbe Ebbesen and his colleagues (1976) found that residents in a California condominium complex not only established most of their friendships with people who lived in the same housing units, but they also developed most of their enemies close by as well. Was proximity one of the contributing factors in the development of your own "bad relationship" listed earlier? Ebbesen explains this effect by stating that those who live closer to you are better able than those living farther away to spoil your happiness and peace of mind by having loud parties late at night, throwing trash on your lawn, and just generally getting on your nerves. Thus, although proximity typically leads to liking, the lamb lying down next to the lion is not likely to develop anything that could be called a friendship.

Familiarity Breeds Liking

Another important situational factor determining attraction is *familiarity,* the frequency of actual contact with individuals (Berscheid & Reis, 1998). As discussed in chapter 6, Robert Zajonc's (1968) *mere exposure hypothesis* proposes that repeated exposure to something or someone is sufficient, by itself, to increase attraction. This effect occurs in the absence of

FIGURE 11.1

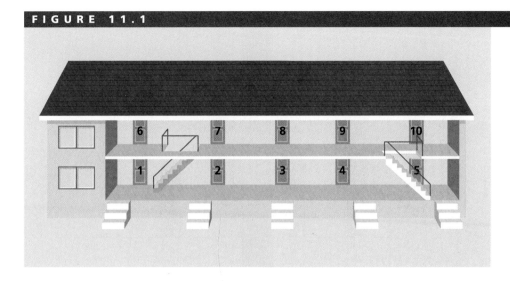

Proximity and Friendship Development

This schematic diagram of an apartment building in the Festinger et al. (1950) study shows the two floors containing five apartments each, connected by two staircases. Within each floor, people were more likely to be nominated as close friends if they lived in the middle apartments on their floors (apartments 3 and 8) rather than in the end apartments. Further, those who lived in the first-floor apartments near the staircases (apartments 1 and 5) tended to be nominated more than those living farther away from the stairs. The reason for this effect was that the residents living near the staircase had less "functional distance" from others in the building; people were more likely to bump into them as they came and went during the day. If you live—or have lived in an apartment complex—does this pattern of results mirror your own friendship patterns?

any information about the person or thing that is the object of attention, but it is strongest when somewhat positive feelings toward the person or thing already exist (Smith & Dorfman, 1975).

In one study examining mere exposure and liking for others, Susan Saegert and her colleagues (1973) asked undergraduate women to evaluate the taste of certain solutions, some that tasted good (various Kool-Aid flavors) and others that were rather unpleasant (vinegar, quinine, citric acid). The solutions were located in different rooms, which required participants to move from one tasting station to the next, sometimes being exposed to other tasters and other times tasting the solutions alone. The movement from room to room was carefully choreographed so that participants would be differentially exposed to one another. Finally, at the end of the testing, participants were asked to make one last set of evaluations—their degree of liking for each of the other participants. Consistent with the mere exposure effect, participants liked the people they had seen more often than those they had seen less frequently, regardless of the quality of the liquids they were tasting in the target person's presence.

The increased use of electronic mail and Internet chat rooms provides a new twist on the mere exposure effect because now people are regularly being exposed to others without ever physically meeting (Bargh & McKenna, 2004). The fact that familiarity can lead to liking in the absence of physical contact has been long recognized by advertising executives, whose raison d'être is to get people to like whatever it is they are selling. Finally, because we're discussing attraction to others, let's examine the electorate's exposure to political candidates during an election year. Joseph Grush and his colleagues (1978) analyzed the results from the 1972 congressional primaries and found that 83 percent of the primary winners could be predicted by the amount of media exposure they received! This candidate exposure effect has been replicated in numerous studies (Schaffner et al., 1981).

At present, it's not clear why familiarity leads to liking. One possibility is that it is part of our evolutionary heritage: we may have evolved to view unfamiliar objects or situations with caution, hesitation, and even fear (Bornstein, 1989). Such caution in the presence of the unfamiliar enhances our biological fitness because we are better prepared for danger. Only through repeated exposure to that which is unfamiliar does our caution and hesitation subside—the unfamiliar and potentially dangerous become familiar and safe, and thus, our positive feelings increase. Therefore, the mere exposure effect could have its roots in an evolutionarily adaptive tendency to be attracted toward those things that are familiar, because they are unlikely to pose a danger to our safety and health. According to this evolutionary perspective, then, familiarity doesn't breed contempt—it simply makes it more likely that we will breed!

FIGURE 11.2

Desire to Affiliate Among High and Low Anxious Individuals

Schachter (1959) found that research participants' desire to be with others depended on their level of anxiety and the similarity of their potential "waiting mates." His findings indicated that when anxious or fearful, people desire to affiliate with others who are also experiencing similar feelings. Based on these findings, how would you amend the old folk saying "Misery loves company" to better reflect how we react to anxious situations?

Source: Data from S. Schachter, *The Psychology of Affiliation,* Stanford University Press, 1959.

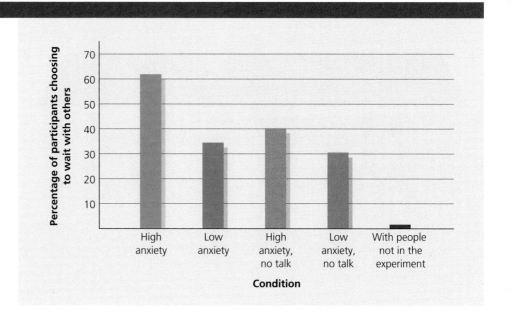

Our Affiliation Desires Increase with Anxiety

Although individuals differ in their habitual desire for affiliation, external events can also motivate people to seek out others. For example, do you recall what you did when you first learned about the terrorist attacks on New York City and Washington, DC, on September 11, 2001? If you are like most people, during that time of anxiety, grief, and uncertainty, you sought the companionship of others who were similarly affected by this tragedy. How can social psychological research and theory help us understand our need for others during such times of anxiety and crisis? Does misery love company?

SCHACHTER'S ANXIETY RESEARCH

In the late 1950s, Stanley Schachter attempted to answer this question by bringing female college students into the laboratory and creating a stressful event. In his initial study, Schachter (1959) introduced himself to the women as "Dr. Gregor Zilstein" of the Neurology and Psychiatry Department. He told them that they would receive a series of electrical shocks as part of an experiment on their physiological effects. In the "high-anxiety" condition, participants were told that the shocks would be quite painful but would cause no permanent damage. In the "low-anxiety" condition, they were led to believe that the shocks were virtually painless, no worse than a little tickle. In actuality, no shocks were ever delivered—the intent was merely to cause participants to believe that they soon would be receiving these shocks.

After hearing this information, the women were told there would be a ten-minute delay while the equipment was set up. They could spend this time waiting either in a room alone or in a room with another participant in the study. Their stated preference was the dependent variable. As soon as participants stated their preference, they were told the true purpose of the study. As figure 11.2 shows, 63 percent of those in the high-anxiety condition chose to wait with others, while only 33 percent of the women in the low-anxiety condition did so. Thus, it appears that high anxiety caused people to seek out others. Misery does indeed appear to love company.

Yet why did they desire affiliation? Perhaps others serve as a *social distraction* to anxious individuals, temporarily taking their minds off their anxiety. If this is the case, then anyone would be an acceptable "waiting mate" for these anxious individuals. To test this hypothesis, Schachter (1959) conducted a follow-up study identical to the first experiment except for one important variation: some of the high-anxiety participants were told they could either wait alone or with other students who weren't in the experiment but were in the building to see their advisers. If anxious people merely want to be around others, regardless of who they are, then these nonanxious students would be acceptable "waiting mates."

Results did not support this reasoning: high-anxiety participants overwhelmingly wanted to wait with others undergoing the same stress, and they were not interested in waiting with students who were not in the experiment (see figure 11.2). Schachter somewhat facetiously asserted that these findings added a new wrinkle to the old "Misery loves company" proverb—misery appears to only love *miserable* company. Put another way, when anxious or fearful, people desire to affiliate with others who are also experiencing similar feelings. But why?

As you might have guessed, Schachter (1959) conducted a third experiment to determine whether anxious participants were motivated to seek out similarly anxious others to share their thoughts about the impending event, or whether there was something more basic about this affiliation desire. If they sought out others to verbally discuss and compare information, then they shouldn't bother seeking out this company if it was made clear that such information exchange wasn't allowed. Schachter created such a scenario by having "Dr. Zilstein" inform certain high-anxiety participants that they could choose to wait with other participants, but they would not be allowed to discuss the upcoming experiment while in their presence. Even with these restrictions on information exchange, high-anxiety participants exhibited a greater desire to wait with others experiencing the same anxiety-producing event than did those in the low-anxiety condition (again, refer to figure 11.2). Thus, in addition to a specific desire to discuss their anxiety with others who were similarly anxious, these findings suggest that the *mere* presence of others also motivates the affiliative need. Of what possible benefit could their mere presence be to the anxious individuals?

Based on his previous work with Festinger, Schachter believed that *social comparison* was the motivating factor in these affiliation needs. Specifically, he believed that the high-anxiety participants wanted to wait with similarly threatened others not necessarily to talk to them, but rather, to compare the others' *emotional reactions* to the stressful event with their own. This social comparison process could occur even if they were not allowed to actually speak about their thoughts and feelings—observing similar others would suffice. As discussed in chapter 4, we tend to believe that we can gather a great deal of information about other people's state of mind by watching their nonverbal behavior. This was exactly what Schachter believed the anxious women in the "no-talking" condition were seeking when they chose to wait with other experimental participants. They could better evaluate their own emotional reactions to this experiment by comparing them with those of similarly distressed people.

Have you noticed that the information-seeking behavior exhibited by Schachter's research participants bears a striking similarity to those who participated in Sherif's autokinetic experiments, discussed in chapter 9 (p. 314)? In Sherif's experiments, when faced with uncertainty about how to interpret events ("How far did the dot of light move?"), people became dependent on others for information. Likewise, in Schachter's research, when people faced an uncertain future ("How worried should I be about the impending painful electrical shocks?"), they too looked toward those who might help them evaluate their circumstances. Although Sherif's research demonstrated that *information dependence* makes us more susceptible to others' influence, Schachter's work indicates that it also causes us to be drawn toward others in the first place to gather the necessary information to make social judgments. In this regard, Schachter's anxiety research marked the first major extension of social comparison theory. Subsequent research has largely supported Schachter's general conclusion that stress increases the desire to affiliate (Rofé, 1984; Taylor et al., 2003).

Common danger makes common friends.

Zara Neale Hurston, U.S. author, 1903–1960

LIMITATIONS AND WRINKLES IN THE ANXIETY-AFFILIATION EFFECT

One limitation to this stress-induced affiliation response has to do with people who are faced with an upcoming embarrassing event. When college students were told that they would soon be expected to suck on large nipples and baby pacifiers in the presence of an experimenter, most preferred to wait alone for the commencement of this embarrassing event (Sarnoff & Zimbardo, 1961). Further, if they did choose to affiliate, they preferred to do so with people who were not going to be in the same embarrassing experiment (Firestone et al., 1973). Under these circumstances, the type of social dependence most likely influencing participants' behavior was not information dependence but *outcome dependence*. Participants avoided social contact because they did not want anyone to know that they were about to engage in a series of infantile acts. For these individuals, affiliation was expected to increase, not decrease, the negative impact of the stressful situation. They only chose to affiliate when others had no knowledge of their impending embarrassment.

Besides this limitation to the anxiety-affiliation effect, there also is a "wrinkle" involved in this social comparison process. Although Schachter believed that anxious people affiliate with others who are similarly anxious in order to compare emotional states, this is not always so. Sometimes when anticipating a fearful event, people prefer not to be around those who are also fearful. Instead, they prefer someone who has already experienced the fearful event and who can tell them something about it. In such instances, people are seeking *cognitive clarity*—a desire to obtain information from others regarding the nature and dangerousness of the threat (Shaver & Klinnert, 1982). For example, a field study (Kulik & Mahler, 1989) found that the vast majority of hospital patients about to undergo coronary bypass surgery preferred to room with someone who had already undergone the procedure rather than with someone like them who had not yet had surgery (78 percent versus 22 percent). Subsequent research suggests that the cognitive clarity gained from having a postoperative heart patient as a roommate not only does the best job lowering anxiety but also results in faster recovery from surgery (Kulik et al., 1996). These findings and others like it suggest that our desire to affiliate when anxious is not only based on a need to compare our emotional state with others but also is fueled by our need to appraise the stressful situation itself—and such appraisal can provide us with both psychological and physical benefits (Kulik et al., 1994; Van der Zee et al., 1998).

AFFILIATION IN THE AFTERMATH OF A NATIONAL DISASTER

In Schachter's study, participants were introduced to a stressful scenario while alone and were then given the option to be with another person. In the real world, however, people are often actively interacting with others when stressful events occur. In such circumstances, the resulting stress and anxiety might cause a *change* rather than an increase in affiliation. Matthias Mehl and James Pennebaker (2003) observed this very pattern of affiliation in the aftermath of the September 11th terrorist attacks. The two social psychologists had just begun studying how adults cope with personal traumas when the terrorists struck, so they quickly shifted their study's focus onto how their participants interacted with others during this time of national crisis. Using small digital voice recorders that could be attached to clothing, participants' conversations were randomly recorded between 10:00 a.m. and 4:00 p.m. from September 10th to September 21st.

Did this real-world anxiety-inducing event cause an increase in people's affiliation desires? Apparently so, but not in the exact manner documented by Schachter. As depicted in figure 11.3, immediately after the terrorist attacks participants spent a good deal of time talking about the disaster, but discussions significantly decreased during the course of the week. For instance, during the forty-eight-hour period following the attacks, 28 percent of people's total conversations involved the event. By the fifth and sixth days this percentage had fallen below 20 percent, and by the ninth and tenth days only 3 percent of people's total conversations were about September 11th. During this time, people did not change their overall amount of interaction with others, but their interaction did shift from group and telephone conversations to in-person dyadic encounters. For instance, whereas less than 10 percent of total group conversations involved the attacks by days five and six, one-on-one in-person conversations about the event were still at 25 percent. Matthias and Pennebaker believe that the initial group interactions may have most efficiently satisfied people's information dependence, while the gradual shift to more one-on-one interactions best helped them psychologically cope with the event. These one-on-one conversations about the tragedy seemed to have a beneficial effect: people who best dealt with their stress were those who shifted from group discussions to one-on-one personal dialogues. Many Americans' cultural worldviews were challenged due to September 11th, and these one-on-one encounters may have provided the necessary intimacy and social support for people to reaffirm their shaken worldviews and reevaluate their beliefs and opinions (Davis & Macdonald, in press; Pyszczynski et al., 2003).

Overall, these results support Schachter's finding that stressful events heighten people's information dependence, and thereby, increase the likelihood of affiliation. However, the "wrinkle" provided by this study is that it demonstrates that when stressful

CRITICAL *thinking*

Immediately following the New York and Washington terrorist attacks, people around the country were highly anxious and uncertain about what was happening. How do you think information dependence and outcome dependence shaped their thoughts, feelings, and behavior during this time?

FIGURE 11.3

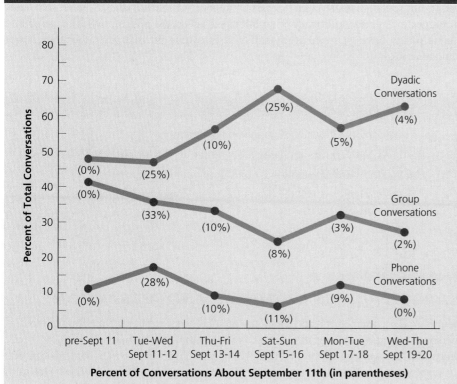

Percent of Total Conversations

80
70
60
50
40
30
20
10
0

Dyadic Conversations

(0%) (25%) (10%) (25%) (5%) (4%)

Group Conversations

(0%) (33%) (10%) (8%) (3%) (2%)

Phone Conversations

(0%) (28%) (10%) (11%) (9%) (0%)

pre-Sept 11   Tue-Wed   Thu-Fri   Sat-Sun   Mon-Tue   Wed-Thu
               Sept 11-12 Sept 13-14 Sept 15-16 Sept 17-18 Sept 19-20

Percent of Conversations About September 11th (in parentheses)

Social Interaction in the Aftermath of September 11, 2001

Following the terrorist attacks of September 11, 2001, people's amount of interaction with others did not significantly increase, but their interaction did shift from group and telephone conversations to in-person dyadic encounters. The percentage of dyadic, group, and phone conversations that involved the September 11th terrorist attacks during each two-day period are listed in parentheses. People who seemed to best cope with the stress caused by the disaster were those whose interactions shifted from group discussions to one-on-one personal dialogues. How do these findings provide further insight into the relationship between anxiety and affiliation?

Adapted from data in Mehl, M. R., & Pennebaker, J. W. (2003). The social dynamics of a cultural upheaval: Social interactions surrounding September 11, 2001. *Psychological Science, 14,* 579–585.

When anxious or fearful, we often seek out others who are also experiencing similar feelings. Such affiliation needs were dramatically demonstrated following the terrorist attacks on September 11, 2001. What sort of social dependence is likely operating in these cases? What sort of interaction appears to be the most beneficial—group or dyadic—in coping with the stress surrounding such tragedies?

events trigger anxiety in people, they are often already embedded in an existing social network, not socially isolated like the participants in Schachter's study. The present findings suggest that in the aftermath of a national disaster, the affiliation desires triggered by anxiety may be most successfully satisfied in dyadic interactions rather than large-group gatherings.

SECTION SUMMARY

- Situational factors influencing interpersonal attraction:

    Proximity: we form emotional bonds with those who are physically close to us

    Familiarity: we form emotional bonds through mere exposure

    Anxiety-inducing events: the desire for social comparison attracts us to similarly anxious others

CHARACTERISTICS OF OTHERS AND ATTRACTION

In fourth grade, a number of us began to rate members of the other sex in terms of their interpersonal appeal. I don't recall how this "rating game" began, but I do distinctly recall Colleen McCash walking up to me one morning and telling me that she liked Walter first, Chuckie second, John third, and me fourth. Wow! I was number four on Colleen McCash's boyfriend chart! I immediately moved her up two notches on my own chart, from fourth to second, just behind Jane Hauserman. I didn't listen very attentively that morning as our teacher talked about the colonization of America or the rotation of the earth on its axis. No, as the Europeans sailed and as the world turned, I rearranged again and again my girlfriend chart and wondered what Colleen would do when I told her she was now "number two" with me.

Today, looking back on my first systematic attempt to evaluate why others appealed to me, I realize that a number of factors figured into my assessments. First there was the girl's physical appearance—was she "cute"? Then, there was the matter of her personality—was she a "nice" person? Did we have similar interests? Finally, there was the consideration of her opinion of me—where did I fall on her "liking chart"? As you will see in the following sections, some of these qualities appear to be readily perceived and understood, while others are more subtle, requiring time by the perceiver to determine their presence or absence.

We Are Drawn Toward the Physically Attractive

As was mentioned in chapter 4, when we meet people, their physical appearance is generally the first thing we notice and remember (McArthur, 1982). What is the outcome of such attention to the physical self? As the life experiences of Lucy Grealy can attest, despite the frequently quoted folk sayings that "beauty is only skin deep" and "you can't judge a book by its cover," we tend to operate according to Aristotle's 2000-year-old pronouncement that "personal beauty is a greater recommendation than any letter of introduction." In other words, we have an *implicit personality theory* for physical attractiveness (see chapter 4, p. 112).

Physical Attractiveness Stereotype

The belief that physically attractive individuals possess socially desirable personality traits and lead happier lives than less attractive persons.

WHAT IS BEAUTIFUL IS GOOD

In one of the first studies of the **physical attractiveness stereotype,** Karen Dion, Ellen Berscheid, and Elaine [Walster] Hatfield (1972) asked college students to look at pictures of men and women who either were good-looking, average, or homely and to then evaluate their personalities. Results indicated that the students tended to assume that physically attractive persons possessed a host of socially desirable personality traits relative to those who were unattractive. This physical attractiveness effect has also been documented in Hollywood movies. Steven Smith and his coworkers (1999) asked people to watch the 100 most popular movies between 1940 and 1990 and to evaluate the movies' main characters. Consistent with the physical attractiveness stereotype, beautiful and handsome characters were significantly more likely to be portrayed as virtuous, romantically active, and successful than their less attractive counterparts. Over the past thirty-five years, many researchers have examined this stereotype, and two separate meta-analyses of these studies reveal that physically attractive people are perceived to be more sociable, successful, happy, dominant, sexually warm, mentally healthy, intelligent, and socially skilled than those who are unattractive (Eagly et al., 1991; Feingold 1992b). Spend a few minutes viewing the video clip regarding the physical attractiveness stereotype on your Social Sense CD-ROM.

Although these findings are based solely on samples from individualist cultures, the physical attractiveness stereotype also occurs in collectivist cultures, but its content is a bit different (Chen et al., 1997b). For example, Ladd Wheeler and Youngmee Kim (1997) found that, as in individualist cultures, physically attractive Koreans are perceived to be more sexually warm, mentally healthy, intelligent, and socially skilled than unattractive Koreans. However, consistent with the greater emphasis on harmonious relationships in collectivist cultures, physically attractive Koreans are also assumed to have higher integrity and to be more concerned for others than those who are physically unattractive. These findings suggest that although the physical attractiveness stereotype appears to be universal, its actual content is shaped by cultural values.

The positive glow generated by physical attractiveness is not reserved solely for adults. Attractive infants are perceived by adults as more likable, sociable, competent, and easy to care for than unattractive babies (Casey & Ritter, 1996; Karraker & Stern, 1990). In elementary school, cute children are more popular with their peers than unattractive children (Vaughn & Langlois, 1983), and there even is evidence that physical appearance may influence parents' and teachers' expectations (Martinek, 1981). For example, in one study by Dion (1972), female college students who were studying to become teachers read a negative evaluation of a child by her teacher after she had allegedly been caught throwing stones at a cat. Attached to each evaluation was a photo of either an attractive or unattractive child. When the child was attractive, the would-be teachers tended to excuse the negative behavior as being atypical, and they did not recommend punishment. However, the unattractive child was generally not given the benefit of the doubt—her negative behavior was more likely to be attributed to her personality. In a typical reaction to the attractive child's transgression, one of the college students remarked:

> She appears to be a perfectly charming little girl, well-mannered, basically unselfish. It seems that she can adapt well among children her age and make a good impression. . . . she plays well with everyone, but like anyone else, a bad day can occur. Her cruelty . . . need not be taken too seriously. (p. 211)

In contrast, the typical reaction to the unattractive child's negative behavior was captured in the following remark:

> . . . think the child would be quite bratty and would be a problem to teachers. . . . she would probably try to pick a fight with other children her own age. . . . she would be a brat at home. . . . all in all, she would be a real problem. (p. 211)

Can your degree of physical attractiveness have an impact on your earning potential and career success as an adult? Field and laboratory studies conducted in both individualist and collectivist cultures indicate that physical attractiveness does have a moderate impact on a variety of job-related outcomes, including hiring, salary, and promotion decisions (Chiu & Babcock, 2002; Collins & Ziebrowitz, 1995; Hosoda et al., 2003; Marlowe et al., 1996). In one representative study, Irene Frieze and her coworkers (1991) obtained information on the career success of more than 700 former MBA graduates of the 1973 to 1982 classes at the University of Pittsburgh. They also judged former students' facial attractiveness based on photos taken during their final year in school. Results indicated that there was about a $2,200 difference between the starting salaries of good-looking men and those with below average faces. For women, facial attractiveness did not influence their starting

Social Sense

View a clip discussing the physical attractiveness stereotype.

Beauty is power.

Arab proverb

salaries, but it did substantially impact their later salaries. Once hired, women who were above average in facial attractiveness typically earned $4,200 more per year than women who were below average in attractiveness. For attractive and unattractive men, this difference in earning power per year was $5,200. Further, although neither height nor weight affected a woman's starting salary, being 20 percent or more overweight reduced a man's starting salary by more than $2,000. Overall, the research literature informs us that physical appearance does indeed influence success on the job.

Is the Attractiveness Stereotype Accurate?

Based on our analysis thus far, it is clear that we tend to give beautiful people high marks on many socially desirable personality traits and, as a result, give them high social exchange value. But do the beautiful really have more desirable personalities? Overall, the answer is clearly no. Alan Feingold (1992b) conducted a meta-analysis of more than ninety studies that investigated whether physically attractive and physically unattractive people actually differed in their basic personality traits. His analysis indicated no significant relationships between physical attractiveness and such traits as intelligence, dominance, self-esteem, and mental health. Thus, even though we think good-looking people are more intelligent, dominant, happy, and mentally healthy than unattractive people, this is not really the case. Feingold did discover, however, that good-looking people do tend to be less socially anxious, more socially skilled, and less lonesome than those who are unattractive. One likely reason good-looking individuals are more at ease socially is that people generally seek out their company and respond favorably to them. As a result of this history of rewarding social encounters, the physically attractive have an increased sense of personal control when interacting with others (Diener et al., 1995).

Mark Snyder and his coworkers (1977) conducted an experimental demonstration of how such positive feedback can bolster social poise and confidence. They first gave college men information about a woman they soon would converse with on the telephone. Included in their information package was a photograph of the woman. Some of the men were given a photo of an attractive woman, while others saw an unattractive photo. Based on the research we have already discussed, Snyder and his colleagues assumed that the men would believe that the attractive woman would be more warm, likable, interesting, and outgoing than the unattractive woman. In reality, the women they talked to were not the women in either photo. As predicted, independent judges, who later listened to tape recordings of the phone conversations, rated the men who thought they were talking to an attractive woman as being more outgoing and sociable than those who believed they were conversing with an unattractive woman. Even more interesting was the response of the women on the other end of the line. Judges rated the women whose male partner thought they were attractive as being more warm, confident, animated, and attractive than the women whose partners thought they were unattractive. The same results were obtained in a related study when the roles were reversed and women were led to believe they were conversing with either an attractive or an unattractive man (Anderson & Bem, 1981). Together, these findings suggest that there is a *self-fulfilling prophecy* involved in the physical attractiveness stereotype. As discussed in chapter 5 (pp. 156–159), the self-fulfilling prophecy is the process by which someone's beliefs about another person can cause that person to behave in a manner that confirms those expectations. The apparent reason physically attractive people tend to be socially poised and confident is that those who interact with them convey the clear impression that they truly are very interesting and sociable individuals.

There Are Both Cultural Differences and Similarities in Attractiveness Standards

Our examination of the research evidence thus far suggests that we are drawn to physically attractive people like bees to honey. Yet, what makes a person physically attractive? Is there a universal standard that can be identified and measured?

Cross-cultural studies indicate that physical attractiveness—however defined—is more important for women than men (Ford & Beach, 1951; Townsend & Wasserman,

CRITICAL *thinking*

Consider again the findings from the Snyder et al. (1977) experiment and the Anderson and Bem (1981) study. When people thought that the individuals they were interacting with were physically attractive, they acted more outgoing and sociable toward them, which, in turn, resulted in those individuals acting more warm, confident, animated, and attractive. How do these findings relate to one of the basic messages of social psychology? Further, how can you generalize these findings beyond physical attractiveness effects to create a more pleasant and rewarding social world for yourself?

Research indicates that physical attractiveness standards vary cross-culturally. Yet, despite this variability, evolutionary theorists believe there still may be evidence of some universal attractiveness standards. Can you guess what these standards might be?

1997). Curiously, however, this relation between the importance of physical attractiveness and gender is reversed for homosexual partners. Physical attractiveness is an important quality for gay men, yet it is a less important feature for lesbians (Fawkner & McMurray, 2002; Harrison & Saeed, 1977). This suggests that men, regardless of their sexual orientation, place greater value on the physical appearance of a potential romantic partner than do either lesbians or heterosexual women.

Within a particular culture and during a particular time period, people are generally in agreement about what defines physical attractiveness (Langlois et al., 2000; Marcus & Miller, 2003). What is beautiful also often conforms to the current standards of the dominant social group. For example, consider the beauty standards of African Americans. Historically, fine facial features and light skin have been standards for physical attractiveness in North American culture, and African Americans mirrored these larger cultural preferences (Maddox & Gray, 2002). Light-skinned Blacks were not only more easily allowed into White society, they were also more accepted into affluent African American social clubs (Okazawa-Rey et al., 1986). Although White-defined attractiveness preferences have been challenged by various Black activists over the years, lighter skin tones are still perceived as more attractive by a majority of African Americans, especially in regard to Black women (Hill, 2002; Ross, 1997).

Historical records inform us that just as culture is not a static entity, neither is the concept of beauty. The Greeks revered the male body and, unlike our culture today, considered it more physically appealing than the female body (Fallon, 1990). During the Roman Empire, "thin was in," while being full-bodied was valued in the late Middle Ages (Garner et al., 1983). In the early to mid–nineteenth century, middle-class North American and European women strapped themselves into steel-framed corsets that, when tightened, would squeeze their waists to an eighteen-inch circumference to match the cultural ideal of the times—the delicate and frail Victorian woman. By the latter half of the century, the large influx of working-class immigrants to North America led to bustier, hippier, and heavy-legged women being the cultural ideal. This shift in attractiveness standards caused some young women to now worry about being too thin and frail. Acting on their concern, they ate more and often wore padding to make themselves look heavier. During the twentieth century, attractiveness standards for both women and men continued to change, providing little evidence for a universal beauty standard, at least for body build (Spitzer et al., 1999). A cross-cultural study by Jeanine Cogan and her colleagues (1996), for example, found that in contrast to American college students, college students in the West African country of Ghana more often rated larger body sizes as ideal for women.

About the time that many social scientists were reaching the conclusion that there were no universal attractiveness standards, evidence began to accumulate in cross-cultural studies that men worldwide are generally attracted to women who have a lower waist-to-hip ratio, meaning that the circumference of their waist is smaller than that of their hips (Furnham et al., 2003; Singh, 1993). The most desirable waist-to-hip ratio appears to be 0.7, so that a desirable woman with a waist of 25 inches would have a 35-inch hip size, or a desirable woman with a 35-inch waist would have 50-inch hips (Streeter & McBurney, 2003). Evolutionary psychologists contend that this 0.7 waist-to-hip ratio is universally perceived as attractive because it is a biologically accurate indicator that the woman is young, fertile, but currently not pregnant—and therefore sexually available (Crandall et al., 2001; Furnham et al., 2002). According to this argument, over the course of human evolution, those men who mated with women with a waist-to-hip ratio of about 0.70 were more likely to successfully conceive an offspring. Consistent with this reasoning, research findings indicate that deviations from the 0.70 ratio are associated with decreases in fertility (Van Hooff et al., 2000).

Although the 0.70 waist-to-hip ratio may be the generally preferred female body type, additional cross-cultural research indicates that this preference is sensitive to the reliability of a culture's food supply (Marlowe & Wetsman, 2001). For example, as depicted in figure 11.4, Judith Anderson and her colleagues' (1992) analysis of fifty-four societies found that heavy women were strongly favored in cultures where the availability of food was highly unpredictable (71 percent preference), but their popularity decreased in cultures with moderately or very reliable food supplies (40 percent preference). In contrast, slender women were not at all popular in cultures with unreliable food supplies, but their popularity increased to match heavy women when the culture's food supply was very reliable. The researchers believe that in environments that have periods of acute food shortages, male preference for heavy women is evolutionarily adaptive because fat represents stored calories. Put simply, heavy women carry a built-in food supply that helps them to not only survive food shortages, but also be fertile and produce offspring. Thus, in cultures where the food supply is

No woman can be too slim . . .

Wallis Simpson, the Duchess of Windsor, 1896–1986

FIGURE 11.4

Female Body Preferences Due to the Reliability of a Culture's Food Supply

Women with heavy bodies have relatively high waist-to-hip ratios, while women with slender bodies have relatively low waist-to-hip ratios. Cross-cultural research indicates that heavy women are considered more attractive in societies with highly unreliable food supplies. Evolutionary theorists believe this preference for heavy women over slender ones in environments with frequent food shortages has an evolutionary basis and has fostered our species survival. In environments with more reliable food supplies, why might men's preferences increase for women with lower waist-to-hip ratios?

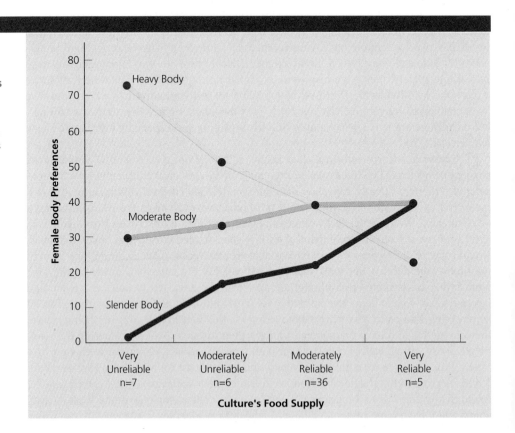

unreliable, the extra fat associated with a higher waist-to-hip ratio overrides the typical evolutionary advantage of choosing women with a lower ratio. For further information, check out the wrist-to-hip ratio discussion on the Social Sense CD-ROM.

Taking into consideration all the cross-cultural research we have reviewed here, it appears that—all things being equal—men prefer women with relatively low waist-to-hip ratios because this body type signifies youth, fertility, and current nonpregnancy. However, in environments where people face frequent food shortages, male preference shifts to a higher female waist-to-hip ratio because this body type signifies greater ability to both produce and nurse offspring when food is scarce.

Beyond body type, there is also evidence that there may be universal standards of *facial attractiveness*. For example, a number of studies indicate that we prefer faces in which the right and left sides are well matched, or *symmetrical* (Chen et al., 1997a; Mealey et al., 1999). Facial symmetry was one thing that Lucy Grealy's plastic surgeons tried unsuccessfully to restore in countless operations. Each time they used skin and bone grafts to restore a sense of symmetry to Lucy's face, the grafts would eventually be reabsorbed by her body.

What is so appealing about symmetry? Evolutionary psychologists contend that we prefer facial symmetry because symmetry generally indicates physical health and the lack of genetic defects, which are important attributes for a sexual partner to possess (Fink & Penton-Voak, 2002; Henderson & Anglin, 2003). In contrast, some perceptual psychologists propose that symmetrical faces are preferred because our perceptual system can process symmetrical stimuli with greater ease than asymmetrical stimuli (B. Jones et al., 2003). Currently, there is evidence supporting both explanations.

Besides symmetry influencing attractiveness, studies of people's perceptions of young men and women's individual faces and composite faces (computer-generated "averages" of all the individual faces), indicate that what people judge most attractive are faces that represent the "average" face in the population (Langlois et al., 1994). This tendency to define physical attractiveness according to the "average rule" has been found in many cultures (Jones & Hill, 1993; Pollard, 1995). Why might we perceive average faces as more attractive than more unusual faces? Drawing upon the insights of the *mere exposure effect*, Carol Langlois and her colleagues (1994) maintain that average faces are more attractive because they are more prototypically facelike and, thus, seem more familiar to us. Consistent with this hypothesis is research indicating that we are also more attracted to average dogs, fish, birds, and wristwatches (Halberstadt & Rhodes, 2003).

Evolutionary psychologists further contend that, besides symmetry and averageness, youthfulness and maturity figure into facial attractiveness judgments. Consistent with this hypothesis, a number of studies have found that possessing youthful or slightly *immature* facial features (large eyes, small nose, full lips, small chin, delicate jaw) enhances female attractiveness, while possessing *mature* facial characteristics related to social dominance (small eyes, broad forehead, thick eyebrows, thin lips, large jaw) increases the attractiveness of males (Cunningham, 1986; Johnston & Franklin, 1993; Keating, 1985). These preferences for mature facial features in males and slightly immature features in females suggest a dominant-submissive preference in heterosexual beauty standards. Although additional studies indicate that heterosexual women are also attracted to men with large eyes (an immature feature) and heterosexual men show a preference for women with high cheekbones (a mature feature), male preferences for youthfulness and female preferences for slightly more maturity appear to be the norm (Cunningham et al., 1990a).

What are the attributions people make of those with immature facial features? Based on their studies of infant faces, Leslie Zebrowitz and her colleagues contend that immature features serve as cues to inform people that the observed individual is dependent and helpless—like an infant (Andredetti et al., 2001; Zebrowitz, 1997). Accompanying these perceptions are attributions that adults with immature features are weaker, less dominant, and less intelligent than the average adult. In the workplace, these attributions result in baby-faced applicants being recommended for lower-status jobs than applicants with mature-looking faces (Zebrowitz et al., 1991).

Taken as a whole, these findings suggest a double bind that women face in their social lives. When they try to match physical attractiveness standards by using cosmetics to

Social Sense

View information on the waist-to-hip ratio.

Besides being young, a desirable sex partner—especially a woman—should also be fat.

Observations of the seminomadic Siriono Indians of Bolivia, 1946

One possible universal standard of beauty in women is youthfulness, while physical maturity may be somewhat more appealing in men. How might you explain this gender difference from an evolutionary perspective? How about from a cultural perspective?

enlarge the appearance of their eyes and lips and make their eyebrows thin, others may perceive them as more beautiful, but also as more weak and helpless. Understanding the effects these facial qualities can have on other people's evaluations, career-oriented women may think twice about trying to match current cultural beauty standards. Conforming to such standards may place them at a competitive disadvantage with their male colleagues.

From what is currently known about physical attractiveness standards, four general conclusions present themselves. First, there is a great deal of cultural variability in what people find beautiful or handsome, yet within cultures, consensus typically reigns. Second, female physical attractiveness is given more attention and scrutiny than male physical attractiveness by heterosexual men and women, but the opposite appears to be true for gay men and lesbians. Another way to state this is that regardless of their sexual orientation, males value physical attractiveness in their partners more than females. Third, symmetrical and average faces tend to be judged more attractive than asymmetrical and unusual faces, perhaps because the former qualities are associated with greater health and genetic strength. Finally, mature facial features seem to enhance male attractiveness more than female attractiveness. Therefore, maturity in men and youthfulness in women may be universal beauty standards. In a later section (pp. 426–428), we will discuss the possible reasons for these gender differences. Before doing so, let's explore the effect that these differing attractiveness standards have on women's and men's body perceptions.

WOMEN'S BODIES AS OBJECTS OF BEAUTY

Our culture, like many around the world, places a premium on physically attractive women. Starting at a very young age, from the Barbie dolls and toy makeup cases girls are encouraged to play with, to the close attention given to clothing fashion and other bodily adornments, females are taught that their body as an *object* is a significant factor in how others will judge their overall value. The pervasiveness of this attention is seen in the message conveyed in television commercials and magazine advertisements, where difficult-to-attain standards of female beauty are established, especially relating to weight (Posavac & Posavac, 1998). One consequence of this greater attention to the female form is that women of all age groups are more aware of and influenced by attractiveness standards than are men, and this heightened focus has a lasting negative impact on their body attitudes, or **body esteem** (Franzoi & Chang, 2000). Beginning in late childhood and early adolescence, girls not only experience more dissatisfaction with their bodies than boys, but they also experience a steady increase in this dissatisfaction over time (Feingold & Mazzella, 1998). By adulthood, negative affect is a pervasive quality of female body esteem, and women are more likely to habitually experience what researchers identify as *social physique anxiety*— anxiety about others observing or evaluating their bodies (Fredrickson et al., 1998; Sanderson et al., 2002). The women most likely caught in this "beauty trap" are those with a traditional feminine gender role (Franzoi, 1995; Martz et al., 1995).

Although women generally express greater dissatisfaction toward their bodies than do men, evidence shows that minority women and lesbians feel less pressure to conform to the unrealistic standard of thinness in the larger culture than White heterosexual women (Franzoi & Chang, 2002; Frisby, 2004; Lakkis et al., 1999). As a result, they are less concerned about dieting and weight loss. This healthier perspective appears to be partly due to a greater valuing of larger body sizes in minority and lesbian cultures, but it also may be a by-product of a more general tendency to reject White and heterosexual cultural standards, respectively (Share & Mintz, 2002; Webb et al., 2004). Yet, despite the fact that minority heterosexual women appear to have greater body satisfaction than White heterosexual women, this does not mean they are unconcerned about weight issues. In general, they are still more dissatisfied with their bodies—particularly their weight—than are heterosexual minority men (Harris, 1995; Mintz & Kashubeck, 1999). Similar ambivalent feelings are also experienced by young adult lesbians regarding the importance of weight and overall physical appearance (Beren et al., 1997). These findings suggest that although lesbians and minority women may adhere less to the dominant White heterosexual standard of female thinness, they are not immune to this beauty norm.

MEN'S BODIES AS INSTRUMENTS OF ACTION

In contrast to the way that most females are socialized, males are taught to view their bodies not as static objects of aesthetic beauty but more as dynamic instruments used to accomplish tasks in the world. Boys are typically trained for a world of action, where the ability of the body to adeptly move through physical space is more important than how it looks as a stationary object (Langlois & Downs, 1980). Thus, similar to the manner in which a young boy views a battle tank or a Matchbox car, he is also taught that power and function are more important criteria than visual appearance for evaluating his physical self. Because greater importance is placed on the body as a functioning unit in the daily experiences of males, they are more likely than women to judge their bodies as a unified whole and less as a collection of parts (Franzoi, 1995; Franzoi & Shields, 1984). Accompanying this more unified view of the body is a higher level of body esteem than typically found among women. One notable exception to this general finding is gay men. Like many heterosexual women, many gay men experience considerable pressure to conform to attractiveness standards that are difficult to attain (Silberstein et al., 1989). This heightened scrutiny of the body as a beauty object undoubtedly accounts for the lower levels of body esteem found in this population (Gettelman & Thompson, 1993; Lakkis et al., 1999).

Although men generally have more positive body esteem than women, their negative body attitudes are often linked to the large and muscular male body standard (Spitzer et al., 1999). This desire for muscles is not a new phenomenon, but heightened media and cultural attention to this masculine body ideal is playing a role in the increasing trend of male body dissatisfaction (Leit et al., 2001; Neumark-Sztainer et al., 1999). One example of this heightened cultural attention is that male action toys and male models in advertisements, which reflect the cultural ideal of the male body, have become substantially more muscular over the last thirty years (Pope et al., 1999, 2001). In an attempt to match this hypermuscular male standard, an increasing number of teenage boys and young men are taking anabolic steroids and untested dietary supplements, which can cause a variety of health problems (Labre, 2002). Before reading further, spend a few minutes completing and scoring the Body Esteem Scale in table 11.2.

Body Esteem

A person's attitudes toward his or her body.

The pursuit of beauty is much more dangerous nonsense than the pursuit of truth or goodness, because it affords a stronger temptation to the ego.

Northrop Frye, Canadian literary critic, 1912–1991

TABLE 11.2

What Are Your Attitudes Toward Your Body? The Body Esteem Scale

Instructions

Below are listed a number of body parts and functions. Please read each item and indicate how you feel about this part or function of your own body, using the following scale:

1 = Have strong negative feelings

2 = Have moderate negative feelings

3 = Have no feeling one way or the other

4 = Have moderate positive feelings

5 = Have strong positive feelings

_____ 1. body scent	_____ 13. chin	_____ 25. figure or physique
_____ 2. appetite	_____ 14. body build	_____ 26. sex drive
_____ 3. nose	_____ 15. physical coordination	_____ 27. feet
_____ 4. physical stamina	_____ 16. buttocks	_____ 28. sex organs
_____ 5. reflexes	_____ 17. agility	_____ 29. appearance of stomach
_____ 6. lips	_____ 18. width of shoulders	_____ 30. health
_____ 7. muscular strength	_____ 19. arms	_____ 31. sex activities
_____ 8. waist	_____ 20. chest or breasts	_____ 32. body hair
_____ 9. energy level	_____ 21. appearance of eyes	_____ 33. physical condition
_____ 10. thighs	_____ 22. cheeks/cheekbones	_____ 34. face
_____ 11. ears	_____ 23. hips	_____ 35. weight
_____ 12. biceps	_____ 24. legs	

Scoring Instructions and Standards

In 1984, Stephanie Shields and I developed the Body Esteem Scale (BES) which measures three different body esteem dimensions in men and women. For men, the dimensions are physical attractiveness, upper body strength, and physical condition, while for women they are sexual attractiveness, weight concern, and physical condition. To determine your score for each of the subscales for your sex, simply add up your responses for the items corresponding to each body esteem dimension. For example, for women, to determine self-judgments for the weight concern dimension of body esteem, add up the responses to the ten items comprising this subscale. For men, the items of "physical coordination" and "figure or physique" are on both the upper body strength and the physical condition dimensions. The subscale items— plus the means and standard deviations for 964 college men and women (Franzoi & Shields, 1984)—are listed below. How do you suppose your own body esteem has been influenced by your culture's physical attractiveness standards?

Women

Sexual attractiveness: *body scent, nose, lips, ears, chin, chest or breasts, appearance of eyes, cheeks/cheekbones, sex drive, sex organs, sex activities, body hair, face (Mean = 46.9, SD = 6.3)*

Weight concern: *appetite, waist, thighs, body build, buttocks, hips, legs, figure or physique, appearance of stomach, weight (Mean = 29.9, SD = 8.2)*

Physical condition: *physical stamina, reflexes, muscular strength, energy level, biceps, physical coordination, agility, health, physical condition (Mean = 33.3, SD = 5.7)*

Men

Physical attractiveness: *nose, lips, ears, chin, buttocks, appearance of eyes, cheeks/cheekbones, hips, feet, sex organs, face (Mean = 39.1, SD = 5.7)*

Upper body strength: *muscular strength, biceps, body build, physical coordination, width of shoulders, arms, chest or breasts, figure or physique, sex drive (Mean = 34.0, SD = 6.1)*

Physical condition: *appetite, physical stamina, reflexes, waist, energy level, thighs, physical coordination, agility, figure or physique, appearance of stomach, health, physical condition, weight (Mean = 50.2, SD = 7.7)*

Other People's Physical Appearance Influences Perceptions of Our Own Attractiveness

Sometimes factors other than one's actual appearance influence physical attractiveness judgments. In fact, sometimes it is the attractiveness of others that determines how we ourselves are judged. For example, people of average attractiveness tend to be judged more attractive when they are with a same-sex person who is very good-looking, but they are thought of as less attractive when with someone who is unattractive (Geiselman et al., 1984). This physical appearance *radiation effect* occurs when two people are observed simultaneously.

What happens when individuals are observed separately, one after the other? Interestingly, instead of sequential observations resulting in a radiation effect, they often lead to a *contrast effect*. People are generally judged more attractive after others have seen an unattractive same-sex person and less attractive when others have just seen someone who is very good-looking (Wedell et al., 1987). Consistent with earlier findings that men are more attentive to the physical attractiveness of potential and actual romantic partners, the contrast effect appears stronger in male than in female viewers (Kenrick et al., 1989).

Thus far we have only considered other people's judgments of our physical attractiveness. What about how we perceive our own physical appearance? In research Jonathan Brown and his colleagues (1992) conducted, female undergraduates evaluated their own physical attractiveness after being exposed to either an attractive or unattractive man or woman. Consistent with the contrast effect, participants' perceptions of their own beauty were greater after they were exposed to unattractive female targets than after they were exposed to attractive female targets (refer to figure 11.5). Male targets did not influence the women's self-perceptions. These findings have been replicated in a number of studies and indicate that social comparison does indeed influence self-perceptions of attractiveness (Evans, 2003; Grogan et al., 1996; Thornton & Maurice, 1997). Put simply, we feel prettier or more handsome after seeing same-sex persons who fall well below conventional beauty standards and less attractive after seeing "perfect 10s." Not surprisingly, this social comparison process has more of an effect on the self-evaluations of those of us who place a high importance on our physical appearance (Patrick et al., 2004).

One man: "How's your wife?"
Second man: "Compared to what?"

FIGURE 11.5

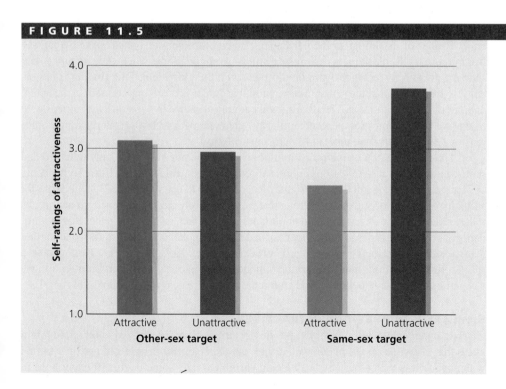

Self-Ratings of Attractiveness Following Exposure to Attractive and Unattractive Same-Sex and Other-Sex Individuals

When women evaluated their own physical attractiveness after being exposed to either an attractive or unattractive man or woman, their perceptions of their own beauty were greater after they were exposed to unattractive female targets than after they were exposed to attractive female targets. Male targets' attractiveness did not influence the women's self-perceptions. What do these findings tell us about how social comparison influences self-perceptions of attractiveness?

Birds of a Feather Really Do Flock Together

Imagine the following scene. It is the beginning of the fall semester in Ria's first year in college, and she has just checked into her dormitory room and will soon meet her new roommate. As she unpacks, Ria wonders what her roommate will be like. What is her race and ethnic background? What sort of music does she like? What are her politics? Does she like to party, or will she spend all her time studying? Abruptly, Ria's thoughts are interrupted by her new roommate entering. "Hi! I'm Kate," the tall, dark-haired woman exclaims as she smiles and extends her hand in greeting. "I guess we're roomies!"

This scene probably resonates with similar experiences you have had in your own life. In new surroundings, what sort of people do you typically seek out? Social psychological research generally indicates that we are attracted to those who are similar to us (Berscheid & Reis, 1998).

DEMOGRAPHIC SIMILARITY

Research on high school friendships found that students identified their best friends as those who were similar to them in sex, race, age, and year in school (Kandel, 1978). Theodore Newcomb (1961) further confirmed the magnetic-like power of similar demographics when he conducted a longitudinal study of friendship development in an all-male boardinghouse. The residents' liking for one another was significantly influenced by their sharing of similar demographic characteristics, and this effect extended beyond the initial getting-acquainted period. Similar results have also been obtained in studies of romantic relationships—we are attracted to those within our ingroups (Whitbeck & Hoyt, 1994).

ATTITUDINAL SIMILARITY

In Newcomb's boardinghouse study, similarity in age and family background not only influenced interpersonal attraction, but similarity in attitudes also provided mutual liking. Unlike physical and demographic characteristics, it generally takes time to learn another person's attitudes. In laboratory studies, Donn Byrne and his colleagues accelerated the getting-acquainted process by having participants complete attitude questionnaires and later "introducing" them to another person by having them read his or her responses to a similar questionnaire (Byrne & Nelson, 1965; Schoneman et al., 1977). As you might have already guessed, the researchers had actually filled out the questionnaire so that the answers were either similar or dissimilar to the participants' own attitudinal responses. As you can see from figure 11.6, participants expressed much stronger liking when they thought they shared a greater percentage of similar attitudes with the individual. This finding is important, for it suggests that the *proportion* of similar attitudes is more important than the actual *number* of similar attitudes. Thus, we should be more attracted to someone who agrees with us on four of six topics (66 percent similarity) than one with whom we share similar opinions on ten of twenty-five topics (40 percent similarity).

The attractive power of similar attitudes has been demonstrated not only in mixed and same-sex dyads but also in various cultures throughout the world (Byrne, 1997; Byrne et al., 1971). Indeed, as we learned in the "Johnny Rocco" study of chapter 9 (p. 321), our desire for attitudinal similarity is sufficiently strong that we will actively eject members from our groups if they refuse to share our attitudes on important issues. In fact, research indicates that the similarity of people's attitudes is more important in determining their attraction toward one another than the similarity of their personalities (Clore & Baldridge, 1968; Montoya & Horton, 2004). It is not surprising, then, that when trying to match up people into new friendship groups, we pay particular attention to their shared attitudinal characteristics (Chapdelaine et al., 1994).

SIMILARITY IN PHYSICAL ATTRACTIVENESS

Given that people generally favor the physically attractive, a visitor from outer space might guess that everyone on the planet would seek out the beautiful people and not be satisfied with anyone less than a perfect "10." Being earthlings with some degree of experience in these matters, we know this is not the case. In fact, researchers who have observed couples

To like and dislike the same things, that is indeed true friendship.

Gaius Crispus, Roman historian & politician, 86–34 B.C.

Live with wolves, howl like a wolf.

Russian proverb

CRITICAL *thinking*

To what degree has the similarity effect influenced your own personal relationships? Consider once again your "best friend" and "casual friend" lists. With whom do you share more similarities? Do these similarities fall into a particular category, such as shared values versus shared preferences?

FIGURE 11.6

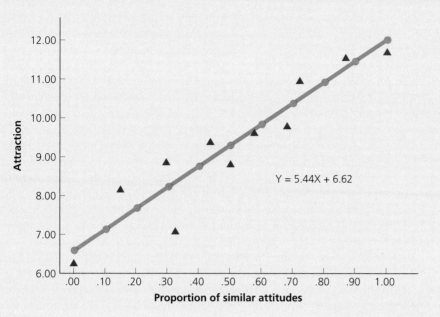

$$Y = 5.44X + 6.62$$

Similarity and Attraction

Donn Byrne and his colleagues found that the greater the proportion of similar attitudes held by people, the greater their attraction to one another. Does this type of relationship between attitude similarity and attraction help explain why you are attracted to or repelled by certain people in your own life?

in public settings have found that they are remarkably well matched in physical attractiveness (Feingold, 1988). One possible reason *why* we are attracted to potential romantic partners who are similar to us in physical attractiveness is that we estimate they have about the same social exchange value as us. Therefore, we are less likely to be rejected. In other words, we learn not to reach too far beyond our own attractiveness value when seeking romance.

This tendency to be attracted to others who are similar to us in particular characteristics, such as physical attractiveness, is known as the **matching hypothesis**, and it appears to be a socially shared belief (Stiles et al., 1996). We expect that people who have similar levels of physical attractiveness will be more satisfied as couples than those who are physically mismatched (Garcia & Khersonsky, 1997). True to form, physically similar couples are more intimate (kissing, holding hands) in public settings and report greater love for one another than the mismatched (Murstein, 1972). And studies in North America, Europe, and Asia indicate that matched couples are more likely to get married and stay married than those who are physically mismatched (Peterson & Miller, 1980; White, 1980b).

The attraction of those with similar looks is not exclusive to romantic relationships but is also found in same-sex friendships (Cash & Derlega, 1978). For example, research by Linda Carli and her colleagues (1991) found that similarly attractive roommates were more satisfied, felt their roommates were more satisfied, and were more likely to want the same roommates the next year than those roommates who were physically mismatched. For friendships between people who differ in their physical attractiveness, these easily discernible differences may cause a strain in the relationship. On the one hand, the more attractive partner may view his or her less attractive friend as a social handicap in certain settings (for example, pairing up with possible dates in a singles bar). On the other hand, despite the possible benefits of the radiation effect (see p. 421), the less attractive partner may become envious of all the attention the attractive friend receives.

WHY ARE SIMILAR OTHERS ATTRACTIVE?

Whether it is easily identifiable characteristics such as physical attractiveness and race, or factors that are harder to detect, such as one's attitudes and values, we seem to be drawn to those who are similar to us. Why is this so?

One reason is our desire for social comparison. As Schachter's anxiety experiments demonstrated, when we are uncertain about how to define social reality, we are drawn to

Matching Hypothesis

The proposition that people are attracted to others who are similar to them in particular characteristics.

"I'm gonna like this new kid," thought General Manager Glenn Habner.

Similarity provides the basis for mutual attraction.

Reprinted with special permission of King Features Syndicate.

those with whom we can best compare ourselves. Meeting others who share our views on important issues makes us feel better because it reassures us that essential aspects of our self-concept have social validity. According to this social comparison perspective, when others validate our own self-beliefs through agreement, we should develop positive attitudes toward them. In contrast, when others disagree with us, this questioning of our judgment may raise doubts in our own minds about our self-concept and worldview. The negative feelings created by such nonagreement should cause us to avoid these people in the future.

A second possible explanation is that our affinity for similar others is part of our evolutionary heritage. That is, our ancestors may have used similarity cues (physical and attitudinal) to detect those who were genetically similar to themselves. John Rushton (1989), for example, has found that friends tend to be more similar to one another on certain genetically determined characteristics than one would expect by chance. It's possible that humans have unconsciously been attracted to similar others because they share many of the same genes. If we become friends with these people and provide them with help when they are in need, as friends often do, we are increasing the probability that genes like our own will find their way to succeeding generations. It is this biological predisposition that may cause us to respond positively to those who appear to have "a bit of us in them."

Another reason why we may be attracted to similar others is that we like that which is familiar. As we have already discussed (p. 407), it may have been evolutionarily adaptive to perceive unfamiliar others with caution and distrust because of the dangers inherent in dealing with the unfamiliar (Bornstein, 1989). Due to this biological predisposition, we may perceive similar others as attractive because they *mimic* familiarity. That is, their similarity to us makes them seemingly familiar creatures! Thus, similarity may lead to liking because the similar appear familiar.

Although these evolutionary-based explanations are intriguing and merit further scientific inquiry, an explanation that has received greater attention and interest by social psychologists over the years is Fritz Heider's (1946, 1958) **balance theory,** which predates Leon Festinger's (1957) theory of cognitive dissonance. Like Festinger, Heider proposed that people desire cognitive consistency or "balance" in their thoughts, feelings, and social relationships (refer to chapter 6, p. 194). Because of this desire for consistency, balanced relationships should be rewarding, while imbalanced relationships—those in which a person holds inconsistent or discrepant thoughts—should be unpleasant. Between two people, balance is created when both parties value the same things.

Balance Theory

A theory that people desire cognitive consistency or balance in their thoughts, feelings, and social relationships.

Similarity leads to attraction. Balance theory proposes that this matching hypothesis is due to the need for cognitive consistency: we develop a liking relationship toward those things that are positively related to that which we value.

Consider again Ria and her new college roommate, Kate. As they get to know each other, imagine they discover that they both are feminists. According to balance theory, their mutual appreciation of the same social and political philosophy will facilitate the development of a mutual attraction toward each other (see figure 11.7a). This is so, Heider contended, because people develop a liking relationship toward those things that are positively related to that which they value.

To further illustrate balance theory, let's now imagine that Ria detests feminist thinking. According to the theory, this attitude dissimilarity may well push the two women toward an antagonistic relationship because Ria doesn't value something that Kate does (figure 11.7b). Although they now dislike one another, this relationship is also balanced.

What would make this relationship imbalanced? Imagine that the two roommates strike up a friendship before they discuss politics. Then one day, Kate pulls out her copy of *Ms.* magazine, and Ria tells her how much she hates feminism. Now their relationship is imbalanced (figure 11.5c), because Ria's dislike of that which Kate values is inconsistent with Ria and Kate's mutual liking. Recall that imbalanced relationships are unpleasant. This unpleasantness, Heider states, will motivate people to restore balance by making relationship

FIGURE 11.7

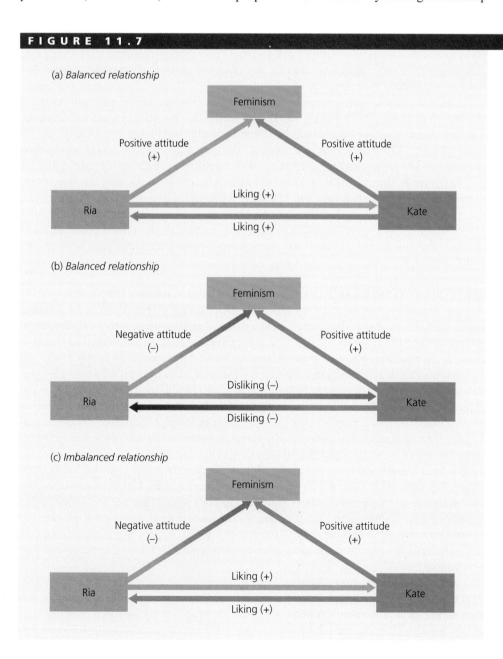

(a) *Balanced relationship*

(b) *Balanced relationship*

(c) *Imbalanced relationship*

Balanced and Imbalanced Relationships

According to Heider's balance theory, (a) two people who value the same thing (in this example, feminism) should develop a liking relationship with one another. However, (b) if one person values what the other detests, they should dislike one another. Both of these relationships are balanced because the people's feelings for one another are consistent with their attitudes toward the relevant topic (feminism). In addition, (c) if they mutually like one another but don't value the same thing, this should create a discomforting imbalance and a motivation to restore consistency and balance. How many different ways might Ria and Kate restore balance in their relationship?

thoughts consistent. In this case, balance could be restored if the two women change their attitudes toward each other, or if one of them could change her attitude toward feminism. A simple way to determine whether a relationship is balanced or imbalanced is to multiply the affective signs on the three sides of the triangle. If the product is positive, the relationship is balanced:

$$\text{a:} (+) \times (+) \times (+) = + \text{ and b:} (-) \times (+) \times (2) = +$$

If it is negative, the relationship is imbalanced:

$$\text{c:} (-) \times (+) \times (+) = -$$

Another way in which the strain of imbalance can be reduced is if *both* parties modify their attitudes so that they are more aligned with each other (Davis & Rusbult, 2001; Priester & Petty, 2001). In this instance, Kate and Ria could both become less strident in their own political beliefs, seeing some merit in the other's viewpoint.

We Are Also Attracted to "Complementary" Others

The tendency for similarity to lead to attraction is strong and pervasive. If you were asked to pick the most correct proverb describing the human condition, you would be well advised to choose "Birds of a feather flock together" over "Opposites attract." Having made this judgment, I must hasten to add that this does not mean that opposites cannot find affinity. According to both sociological and psychological theories of need *complementarity,* people choose relationships in which their basic needs can be mutually satisfied (Kerckhoff & Davis, 1962; Tracey, 1994). Sometimes this results in people with complementary characteristics (some would call them opposite traits) being attracted to one another (Tracey, 2004). For example, people who enjoy controlling social interactions (*dominants*) are more satisfied interacting with submissive people rather than dominant people (Dryer & Horowitz, 1997). Why? Because, in such situations, they are more likely to have their goal of control satisfied. The same is true of *submissives.* Their desire to have things decided for them is more likely to be satisfied when they interact with dominants, not submissives. This complementarity of personal traits is an example of a *compatible fit between differences.* Do you have any such complementary characteristics in your own best friendship?

MATE SELECTION BASED ON COMPLEMENTARY CHARACTERISTICS

Another example of complementary characteristics leading to attraction can be found in mate selection. As you learned earlier, in heterosexual relationships, men prefer a younger partner while women prefer older males. For example, David Buss (1989) found that in thirty-seven cultures around the world, men express a preference for women who are younger than themselves and women prefer men slightly older (except in Spain). This gender difference has been confirmed in both a large-scale national sample in the United States (Sprecher et al., 1994) and in a meta-analysis of forty different attractiveness studies including both North American and non-North American samples (Feingold, 1992a). In analyzing these findings (see figure 11.8), social scientists conclude that they reflect a *looks-for-status exchange* in mating relationships (Fletcher et al., 2004; Gutierres et al., 1999). Men are attracted to young women because female youth signifies beauty, and women are attracted to older men because male maturity signifies higher social status. The one exception to this general rule is that teenage boys report they are most attracted to women who are slightly older than they are, women in their fertile twenties (Kenrick et al., 1996). Overall these studies suggest that even though similarity generally leads to attraction, sexual sparks often fly if someone possesses a characteristic that you value but do not possess yourself.

If the looks-for-status exchange generally exists in heterosexual relationships, then a man who is physically unattractive should still be able to attract beautiful women if he has high social status. Likewise, a woman who does not have high social status should still be able to attract high-status men if she is physically attractive. One study confirming this par-

FIGURE 11.8

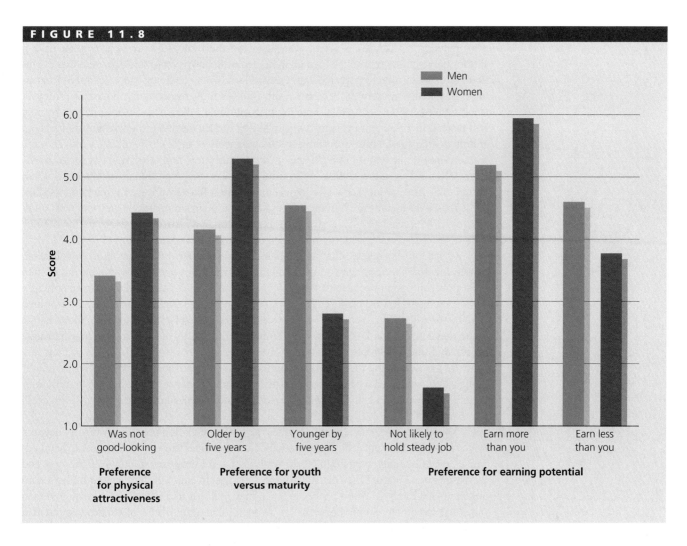

Gender Differences in Mate Selection Preferences

Sprecher, Sullivan, and Hatfield (1994) asked more than 1,300 English-speaking and Spanish-speaking Americans who were single and under the age of 35 to consider some possible assets and liabilities in a marriage partner and to indicate their willingness to marry someone possessing each of these characteristics. A score of "1" indicated "not at all," while a score of "7" indicated "very willing." All of the gender comparisons listed above are significant. What do these findings tell us about gender differences in heterosexual mate preferences?

Source: Data from S. Sprecher et al., "Mate Selection Preferences: Gender Differences Examined in a National Sample" in *Journal of Personality and Social Psychology,* *66:* 1074–1080, American Psychological Association, 1994.

ticular type of complementarity in romantic relationships asked college students to evaluate, as potential marriage partners, strangers who varied in physical attractiveness and social status (Townsend & Levy, 1990). Results indicated that high status compensated for a lack of male attractiveness. High-status men who were only moderately attractive were as appealing to women as highly attractive but only moderately successful men. No such status trade-off occurred in men's ratings of women; they preferred highly attractive but lower-status women. In other words, men can trade status for looks and women can trade looks for status, but reversing the trade—a woman trading status for looks or a man trading looks for status—is not nearly so common. Spend a few minutes viewing the video clip discussing attraction and mate selection on your Social Sense CD-ROM.

View excerpts from *Attraction and Mate Selection.*

Why do you think this looks-for-status complement exists worldwide? Do you think this effect is more influenced by biology or social conditions? The evolutionary perspective contends that what will be valued as desirable and attractive in men and women is that which increases their probability of producing offspring who will carry their genes to the next generation (Kenrick & Trost, 1987). Given the biological fact that women have a shorter time span to reproduce than do men, evolutionary psychologists assume that evolution predisposes men to perceive women who look *young* as being more desirable (that is, more physically attractive), because youth implies high reproductive potential (Alley & Cunningham, 1991). Using this same logic, evolutionary theorists also assume that women will instead favor male traits signifying an ability to provide and protect resources for them and their offspring. Thus, according to this perspective, instead of valuing youth in men, women should place more importance on status, ambition, and other signs of *social dominance* (Kenrick & Luce, 2000). As you might guess, the evolutionary perspective is not without its critics. Some see it as a logical explanation for why physical attractiveness standards exist that locates the human species within a larger comparative analysis with other species. Others see it as a social scientific explanation that justifies the perpetuation of male dominance and female subservience based on "the natural order of things."

A second perspective that attempts to explain gender differences in mate selection, namely, the *sociocultural* viewpoint, maintains that men seek beauty in a woman and women seek power in a man because of the widely different social statuses they have historically held in society (Howard et al., 1987). This social-exchange explanation argues that women have historically been excluded from power and are viewed by men as objects of exchange in the social marketplace. Men place a premium on the quality or the beauty of this exchange object, and that is why physical attractiveness is sought in a woman. Because of their historically low status and their restricted ability to socially advance based on their own individual skills, women have been forced to tie their social advancement with the status of their mate. Thus, women seek men who are socially dominant and can be "good providers" (Bernard, 1981).

Which of these perspectives provides the best explanation is currently a hotly debated topic (Rasmussen et al., 1998). If the sociocultural perspective is correct, recent social advances made by many women in North American and European countries (higher pay and increased social status) may cause shifts in the attractiveness preferences of both women and men (see Eagly & Wood, 1999). Women may look for more "beauty" in men, and men may look for more "economic status" in women. A handful of recent studies suggest that such changes may be taking place. In Spain, a content analysis of personal ads in newspapers found that although the overall preferences in what men and women seek in a mate are consistent with predictions from evolutionary theory, there is an age difference among women in their preferences that is consistent with the sociocultural perspective (Gil-Burmann et al., 2002). Unlike older women, those younger than the age of 40 seek mainly physical attractiveness in men, not socioeconomic status. These changes in mate preferences among the younger women may be at least partly caused by the newfound financial independence they are enjoying due to Spain's current economic prosperity. Similarly, Donald Strassberg and Stephen Holty (2003) examined male mate preferences by posting four "female seeking male" personal ads on two large Internet bulletin boards, but varied the ads slightly to highlight different characteristics in the imaginary women. Their analysis of over 500 e-mail responses found that the most popular ad was one in which the woman described herself as "financially independent . . . successful [and] ambitious." This ad generated over 50 percent more responses than the next most popular ad, which described a woman who was "lovely . . . very attractive and slim." If future studies provide additional evidence that mate preferences are indeed changing, this would not necessarily mean that evolutionary forces don't shape perceptions of attractiveness. It may simply mean that, in this instance, these inherited tendencies have been overridden by more powerful cultural forces.

We Like Those Who Like Us

The only way to have a friend is to be one.

Ralph Waldo Emerson, U.S. poet, 1803–1882

So far, we have discussed how attraction can be based on a number of personal and situational factors. Yet one very simple reason why people might make it on our "liking chart" is that we discover they like us. Research has shown that we like people who like us and say nice things about us (Berscheid & Reis, 1998, Wood & Kallgren, 1988). There is nothing surprising about reciprocal liking. Balance theory (Heider, 1958) asserts that we will develop a liking relationship toward anything that is positively related to something we value. Thus, if we learn that people like us, we should be more attracted to them because they value something we value—ourselves!

That we are attracted to those who like us raises the possibility that it is our perceptions of their liking for us, and not necessarily their true attitudes, that matter. In an interesting study, Rebecca Curtis and Kim Miller (1986) examined how people's interaction style changes once they believe that another likes or dislikes them. Upon arriving at the lab, participants were paired up, asked to spend five minutes getting to know one another, and then were separated. One half of this interaction pair was assigned to the target group and told that their partners (the perceivers) either liked or disliked them based on false information the experimenter provided. The experimenter stressed to the target person that she was interested in determining how the perceivers would act now that they had been given this false information about the targets. In actuality, the perceivers were never given any information at all. The experimenter's real goal was to manipulate the targets' perceptions, not the perceivers'. After this manipulation, the targets were asked to act as naturally as possible when they interacted again with the perceivers during a ten-minute discussion of current events.

Because this study is similar to the previously discussed phone experiments involving the physical attractiveness stereotype (Anderson & Bem, 1981; Snyder et al., 1977), it is not surprising that these false perceptions about the perceivers not only influenced the targets' behavior, they also influenced the perceivers' beliefs about their partner. Those targets who believed that the other person liked them disclosed more, had a more pleasant tone of voice and general attitude, and disagreed less with the perceiver than those who thought the perceiver disliked them. How did the perceivers evaluate their partners? They liked better those targets who had been led to believe that they were liked more than those who thought they were disliked. These findings suggest there is a *self-fulfilling prophecy* of liking, just as there is for the physical attractiveness stereotype. If we think others like us, we tend to act in ways that increase the likelihood that they will indeed like us. However, if we think they dislike us, our subsequent interaction style may fulfill the negative prophecy even if it is based on false information.

SECTION SUMMARY

- We are attracted to beautiful people
- Regarding the physical attractiveness stereotype, beautiful people are perceived to have better personalities and to lead healthier and happier lives; this stereotype is untrue, except that beautiful people are less socially anxious
- Cultures vary in their beauty standards, yet within cultures, consensus typically reigns
    - Men place a higher value on a physically attractive partner than do women
    - Women are judged more attractive if they have immature and dependent-looking facial features
    - Men are judged more attractive if they have mature facial characteristics related to social dominance
- Greater focus on the female body as a thin beauty object causes lower body esteem, especially among women with feminine gender roles
- Negative body esteem in men is often linked to the large and muscular male body standard
- We are attracted to those similar to us in their demographics, attitudes, and physical attractiveness
- We are attracted to those who have characteristics that complement our own
- We are attracted to those who like us

WHEN SOCIAL INTERACTION BECOMES PROBLEMATIC

Throughout this chapter we have examined factors that prompt us to seek out others. However, whenever we approach others, we risk rejection. Even if others do accept our social overtures, there is the further possibility that we may commit a social blunder that will cause them to form a negative impression of us. How do we respond to these social "land mines"?

Social Anxiety Can Keep Us Isolated from Others

Social anxiety is the unpleasant emotion we experience due to our concern with interpersonal evaluation (Leary & Kowalski, 1995). This anxiety is what causes us to occasionally (or frequently) avoid social interaction. We can experience social anxiety even when alone: simply anticipating social interaction is often sufficient to arouse it. For example, do you remember how you have sometimes felt just before a "big date" or an important job interview? The social jitters you experience are due to you anticipating an interaction in which you have a vested interest.

When socially anxious, we are less likely to initiate interactions, and when in an interaction, we talk less, sometimes stammer and stutter when we do speak, disclose less about ourselves, and occasionally even withdraw from the anxiety-producing situation altogether (Daly et al., 1997; McCroskey, 1997). This tendency to socially withdraw is not an effect characteristic of anxiety per se. As you have already discovered (see pp. 408–409), when we are anxious due to nonsocial factors, we often affiliate more, not less (Schachter, 1959). Therefore, avoiding affiliation generally occurs only when the source of the anxiety involves other people, either real or imagined.

Although almost everyone occasionally experiences social anxiety, some of us become victims of chronic social anxiety, or *social anxiousness*. Lucy Grealy was no stranger to social anxiousness. During adolescence, the main stabilizing influence in her life was her passionate love of horses and horse riding. Yet Lucy was petrified when the owner of the horse stables asked her to ride in shows:

> In practices I always wore a helmet with my hair hanging loose beneath it, but etiquette required that during shows my hair be tucked neatly up beneath the helmet, out of sight. I put this off until the very last minute, trying to act casual as I reached for the rubber band and hair net. This simple act of lifting my hair and exposing my face was among the hardest things I ever had to do, as hard as facing Dr. Woolf, harder than facing operations. I gladly would have undergone any amount of physical pain to keep my hair down. No one at the show grounds ever commented to me about it, and certainly no one there was going to make fun of me, but I was beyond that point. By then I was perfectly capable of doing it all to myself. (Grealy, 1994, p. 186)

The unfortunate consequence of social anxiousness is that it can trap a person into increasingly unpleasant social exchanges (DePaulo et al., 1990). Highly socially anxious people anxiously expect, readily perceive, and intensely react to rejection cues in their surroundings (Downey et al., 2004). For example, they are more attentive to faces with negative expressions than they are to those with positive or neutral expressions (Pishyar et al., 2004). This attentional bias in noticing negative social feedback results in highly anxious persons often acting in ways—avoiding eye contact, appearing nervous and jittery—that fulfill the self-prophecy (Pozo et al., 1991).

To understand the nature of social anxiety, keep in mind something stated early in the text about the self: as self-reflective creatures, we actively construct our social reality. Schachter's anxiety-affiliation research indicated that when unsure about our own emotional reactions, we often compare them with the reactions of similar others. Schachter (1964) took this insight and expanded on it in his **two-factor theory of emotions.** He proposed that if people are emotionally aroused but are not sure what they are feeling, they will

Social Anxiety

The unpleasant emotion people experience due to their concern with interpersonal evaluation.

I turn pale at the outset of a speech and quake in every limb and in all my soul.

Marcus Tullius Cicero, Roman philosopher and politician, 106–43 B.C.)

Two-Factor Theory of Emotions

A theory that emotional experience is based on two factors: physiological arousal and cognitive labeling of the cause of that arousal.

look for cues in their surroundings. If others are happy, they are likely to interpret their arousal as happiness. If others are anxious, they too are likely to feel anxious. Thus, according to Schachter, our emotions are based on two components: physiological arousal and cognitions about what that arousal means. Consistent with the two-factor theory of emotions, research indicates that the attributions we make concerning our physiological responses to a particular stimulus will often, but not always, determine our emotional reactions (Reisenzein, 1983).

To illustrate how this self-attributional process might influence social anxiety, James Olson (1988) asked Canadian college students to read a speech while wearing headphones. Some participants believed that the noise they were hearing over the headphones contained a subliminal sound that would make them feel tense and anxious. A second group was told that this subliminal sound would make them feel pleasantly relaxed and calm, and the control group was told the noise would do nothing. Just before reading the speech, a video camera was pointed at them to further induce arousal. Results indicated that those who believed they would feel tense and anxious due to the subliminal sound gave smoother, more fluent speeches than either the participants who expected to feel calm or those who were given no expectations.

Are these results surprising to you? Why would those who thought the noise would make them feel tense and anxious behave so calmly when speaking? The reason for this effect is **misattribution of arousal,** in which the explanation of the physiological symptoms of arousal is switched from the real source to some external source. In Olson's experiment, the presence of what was thought to be arousing subliminal noise provided a convincing, neutral label for symptoms actually caused by the speech task. Believing their anxiety was due to an external source having no association with the upcoming speech, these participants avoided the ever-increasing anxiety produced by fears of negative evaluation. Noticing their arousal, they told themselves: "This speech isn't making me anxious. My discomfort is caused by this noise." The other two groups could make no such attribution. Instead, after noticing their arousal, they likely thought: "Gosh, I'm really anxious! I don't know if I can get through this speech!"

Although misattribution of arousal can reduce social anxiety and thereby increase social functioning, there are limits to its effectiveness. The crucial factor is that the level of arousal must be relatively low so that its true cause is open to interpretation. When people are extremely aroused, they usually recognize its true source and, thus, are not likely to misattribute (Conger et al., 1976). Therefore, it is unlikely that prior to delivering a speech to a large audience, a person will incorrectly attribute her high anxiety to the distant sound of a droning lawnmower.

Loneliness Is the Consequence of Social Isolation

Although the anticipation of evaluation can make us anxious, how do you think you would react to being cut off from meaningful interaction with others? Because of our need for others, the loss of meaningful social exchange would likely be quite detrimental.

DEFINING AND MEASURING LONELINESS

Loneliness is defined as having a smaller or less satisfying network of social and intimate relationships than we desire (Green et al., 2001; Marangoni & Ickes, 1989). In understanding loneliness, keep in mind that this is a subjective experience, reflecting what we feel and think about our interpersonal life, and, as such, is not the same thing as solitude or being alone. We can spend long periods of time alone without feeling lonely, and we can also feel terribly lonely in a crowd. In fact, research has shown that lonely and nonlonely people do not differ in the *quantity* of their social interaction, but rather in the *quality* of such exchanges. Lonely people spend more time with strangers and acquaintances and less time with friends and family than those who are not lonely (Jones et al., 1985).

Similar to social anxiety, we can experience loneliness as both a short-lived *state* and a chronic, long-term *trait*. For example, when you first arrived on campus in your freshman

Misattribution of Arousal

A situation in which the explanation of the physiological symptoms of arousal is switched from the real source to another one.

Loneliness

Having a smaller or less satisfactory network of social and intimate relationships than one desires.

TABLE 11.3

Measuring Loneliness

Directions

Indicate how often each of the statements below is descriptive of you.

Circle one letter for each statement:

> O indicates "I often feel this way"
> S indicates "I sometimes feel this way"
> R indicates "I rarely feel this way"
> N indicates "I never feel this way"

1. How often do you feel unhappy doing so many things alone?	O	S	R	N
2. How often do you feel you have nobody to talk to?	O	S	R	N
3. How often do you feel you cannot tolerate being so alone?	O	S	R	N
4. How often do you feel as if nobody really understands you?	O	S	R	N
5. How often do you find yourself waiting for people to call or write?	O	S	R	N
6. How often do you feel completely alone?	O	S	R	N
7. How often do you feel you are unable to reach out and communicate with those around you?	O	S	R	N
8. How often do you feel starved for company?	O	S	R	N
9. How often do you feel it is difficult for you to make friends?	O	S	R	N
10. How often do you feel shut out and excluded by others?	O	S	R	N

Scoring

For each question, give yourself 1 point if you responded "never" (N), 2 points if you responded "rarely" (R), 3 points if you responded "sometimes" (S), and 4 points if you responded "often" (O). Your total loneliness score is computed by adding your score on each of the ten questions together.

Normative Data for This Loneliness Measure (Ten-Item Version) (Source unknown.)

Group	Average Score
College Students	20
Nurses	20
Public School Teachers	19
Elderly	16

Based on these normative data, a score above 30 in this version of the scale would indicate that the person is experiencing severe levels of loneliness.

Note: These are substitute items for the UCLA Loneliness Scale devised by Russell et al., 1978.

To whom can I speak today? I am heavy-laden with trouble through lack of an intimate friend.

The Man Who Was Tired of Life, 1990 B.C.

year, you may have experienced a temporary sense of loneliness until you became integrated into the college community. In contrast, some people suffer from chronic loneliness, regardless of the length of time they spend becoming acclimated to new social settings. Although loneliness is a subjective experience, social psychologists have developed objective measures to identify lonely people. One of the more commonly used measures is the UCLA Loneliness Scale (Russell et al., 1980), which asks people to indicate how often they experience such feelings. Spend a few minutes completing a variation of this scale in table 11.3, and then compare your score with the sample of other young adults.

Although almost everyone experiences loneliness, our recovery from it often depends on how we interpret and react to its perceived causes (Anderson et al., 1994). In an examina-

TABLE 11.4

Causal Attributions for Loneliness

Stability	Locus of Causality	
	Internal	**External**
Stable	"I'm too shy." "I don't know how to start new relationships."	"Other people don't try to make friends."
Unstable	"I'm lonely because I haven't tried hard enough to meet others. I can change that by letting others know I'm fun to be around."	"I'm lonely because I don't know anyone here. Things will get better as I meet others."

tion of the duration of loneliness experienced by first-year college students, Carolyn Cutrona (1982) found that it lasted longer among those who initially blamed themselves for their social isolation. That is, the chronically lonely made significantly more *internal, stable attributions* for their loneliness (for example, "I'm too shy" or "I don't know how to start a new relationship") than those who overcame their sense of isolation. Unfortunately, as can be seen in table 11.4, this sort of self-blaming can discourage people from seeking out others and can perpetuate their dissatisfaction with social relationships. On the other hand, Cutrona found that those who thought of loneliness as being caused by a combination of personal and external factors (for example, "I'm lonely because I don't know anyone here. Things will get better as I meet others") seemed to be more hopeful that they could make things change for the better. True to what would be expected from attribution theory (refer to chapter 4), these *external, unstable attributions* resulted in relatively short-lived loneliness for most of these students.

AGE, GENDER, CULTURE, AND LONELINESS

Who suffers the most from loneliness? Contrary to popular stereotypes, it is not the elderly. Numerous studies have identified the young—adolescents and young adults—as the loneliest age groups (Peplau et al., 1982). As people mature and move beyond the young adult years, their loneliness tends to decrease until relatively late in life, when factors such as poor health and the death of loved ones increase social isolation (Green et al., 2001). One reason why adolescents and young adults may be lonelier than older individuals is that young people face many more social transitions, such as falling in and out of love for the first time, leaving family and friends, and training and searching for a full-time job—all of which can cause loneliness (Oswald & Clark, 2003). Another reason for this decrease in loneliness with age is that as we mature, we often settle into long-term romantic relationships and marriages, where the accompanying emotional bonds contribute to overall mental health (Russell, 1982).

There are clear age differences in loneliness, but gender differences are not as clear-cut. Some studies have found a slight tendency for women to report greater loneliness than men, yet other studies fail to find any differences at all (Archibald et al., 1995; Brage et al., 1993). Despite any firm evidence for gender differences in the *degree* of loneliness, there does appear to be evidence that men and women feel lonely for different reasons. Men tend to feel lonely when deprived of group interaction; women are more likely to feel lonely when they lack one-to-one emotional sharing (Stokes & Levin, 1986). This different pattern of loneliness reflects a difference in the friendship patterns of women and men that we will discuss in chapter 12 (pp. 454–459).

I feel so lonesome I most wished I was dead.

Huck Finn in *The Adventures of Huckleberry Finn,* by Mark Twain

I see loneliness ooze damply from people's bodies, trail after them, trickling, widening, running deep, flowing on and on forever.

Kaneka Mitsuharu, 1977, Japanese poet

Regarding cultural differences in loneliness, a recent survey of people living in Canada, Turkey, and Argentina conducted by Ami Rokach and Hasan Bacanli (2001) found that the individualist Canadians not only experienced higher levels of loneliness than the collectivist Turks and Argentinians, they also had different perceptions of what caused their loneliness. Canadians were much more likely to explain their loneliness as being caused by personal inadequacies than the Argentinians and Turks. These cultural differences in loneliness are most likely due to the expectations that individualists and collectivists have about social relationships and the degree of help they receive in establishing social ties. While individualists are socialized to develop loosely knit relationships, and to do so by relying on their own social skills and initiative, collectivists are taught to develop tightly knit relationships within their existing group, and to do so with the assistance and supervision of ingroup members (Miller & Prentice, 1994; Tower et al., 1997). In a very real sense, the social world constructed by individualists is more likely to create loneliness in its members than the social world created by collectivists. Further, when loneliness is experienced, individualists are more likely than collectivists to explain it in terms of internal, stable factors ("I'm lonely because I'm personally inadequate"). As we have just learned, this type of self-blaming creates a mind-set that discourages lonely people from seeking out others. Overall, Rokach and Bacanli's findings suggest that the social world created in an individualist culture is not only more likely to cause loneliness, it is also more likely to perpetuate it.

SOCIAL SKILLS DEFICITS AND LONELINESS

Similar to the negative consequences of social anxiousness, chronically lonely people often think and behave in ways that reduce their likelihood of establishing new, rewarding relationships. Studies conducted with college students illustrate some of these self-defeating patterns of behavior. Typically, in these investigations, students who are strangers to one another are asked to briefly interact in either pairs or groups, after which they rate themselves and their partners on such interpersonal dimensions as friendliness, honesty, and openness. Compared with nonlonely individuals, lonely college students rate themselves negatively following such laboratory interactions. They perceive themselves as having been less friendly, less honest and open, and less warm (Christensen & Kashy, 1998; Jones et al., 1983). They also expect those who interact with them to perceive them in this negative manner. This expectation of failure in social interaction appears all the more hopeless to the chronically lonely because they believe that improving their social life is beyond their control (Duck et al., 1994).

If chronically lonely people were merely misperceiving their effect on others, you might expect that other people's positive feedback concerning their social competence would break down their misperceptions. The problem, however, is that the chronically lonely tend to lack social skills and, as a result, receive little positive reinforcement from others concerning their interaction style. Indeed, they are generally disliked or ignored by others, who see them as weak, unattractive, and insincere (Rotenberg et al., 1997).

What sort of social skills deficits do chronically lonely persons exhibit in their daily interactions? When conversing with another, the chronically lonely spend more time talking about themselves and take less interest in what their partner has to say than do nonlonely people (Jones et al., 1982). Consistent with the interaction style of those with low self-esteem, they also tend to perceive others in a negative light (Rotenberg & Kmill, 1992). When meeting such a person, new acquaintances often come away with negative impressions (Jones et al., 1983). Confronted with the negative social judgments accompanying this sort of inept social style, lonely individuals often immerse themselves in their occupations, withdraw into wish-fulfilling fantasies, or engage in self-destructive activities such as alcohol and drug abuse. Not surprisingly, lonely people often use the television, computer, and radio as substitutes for interpersonal relationships. Unfortunately, the content of a good deal of mass media programming focuses on failed relationships and sadness, which actually can deepen one's sense of social isolation (Davis & Kraus, 1989).

. . . Sitting down to one plate, that loneliest of all positions.

Caroline Gilman, U.S. author and educator, 1794–1888

SECTION SUMMARY

SECTION SUMMARY

- Social anxiety can cause people to avoid interaction, and chronic social anxiety can lead to increasingly unpleasant social exchanges

- Loneliness is an unpleasant subjective state in which a person has a smaller or less satisfying network of social and intimate relationships than desired

    Adolescents and young adults are the loneliest age groups

    As people mature, loneliness decreases until relatively late in life

    The chronically lonely often lack social skills

FEATURED STUDY

ALLEVIATION OF SPEECH ANXIETY

Savitsky, K., & Gilovich, T. (2003). The illusion of transparency and the alleviation of speech anxiety. *Journal of Experimental Social Psychology, 39,* 618–625.

The belief that one's thoughts, feelings, and emotions are more transparent to others than is actually the case is known as the *illusion of transparency.* This illusion derives from the difficulty people have in getting beyond their own subjective experience when trying to figure out how they appear to others. As a result, they exaggerate the degree to which their internal states "leak out" and overestimate the degree to which others can detect their private thoughts and feelings. The first goal in the present investigation was to collect unambiguous evidence of an illusion of transparency in the domain of public speaking. The second goal was to explore whether people's knowledge of the illusion of transparency can reduce their speech anxiety. In this two-study investigation, Study 1 found clear evidence of an illusion of transparency in the domain of public speaking. Participants asked to deliver speeches with little advanced preparation overestimated the extent to which their nervousness was apparent. The second study in this series, which is described here, investigated whether speech anxiety would be alleviated when speakers were told beforehand about the illusion of transparency.

Method

Participants were 117 undergraduate students with 77 serving as "speakers" and 40 serving as "observers." Upon individually reporting to the laboratory, speakers were informed that they would deliver a three-minute speech on race relations on campus. Speakers were then randomly assigned to one of three experimental conditions and were given five minutes to prepare. Those in the control condition were given no additional instructions, but the other speakers were told the following:

> I realize you might be anxious. It's perfectly natural to be anxious when confronted with a public speaking task. Many people become anxious not only because they're concerned about whether or not they'll do well, but also because they believe they will appear nervous to those who are watching. They're nervous about looking nervous.

For participants in the *informed condition* the experimenter continued by saying:

> I think it might help you to know that research has found that audiences can't pick up on your anxiety as well as you might expect. Psychologists have documented what is called an "illusion of transparency." [experimenter explains the illusion] . . . So, while you might be so nervous you're convinced that everyone can tell how nervous you are, in reality that's very rarely the case. What's inside of you typically manifests itself too subtly to be detected by others. With this in mind, you should just relax and try to do your best. Know that if you become nervous, you'll probably be the only one to know.

For speakers in the *reassured condition,* the experimenter provided verbal reassurances but did not inform them about the illusion:

> I think it might help you to know that you shouldn't worry much about what other people think. Psychologists have found that you don't need to be concerned about other people's impressions. This is hard to do because our own emotional experience of anxiety can be so strong, but past research has shown that we shouldn't be worried about this.

With this in mind, you should just relax and try to do your best. Know that if you become nervous, you probably shouldn't worry about it.

This condition was included to control for the possibility that any differences in the speeches of those in the informed and control conditions might be caused by the implicit suggestion that "one shouldn't worry" and not from speakers' appreciation of the illusion of transparency. After hearing these instructions, speakers delivered their speeches in front of a video camera and in the presence of an experimenter who was unaware of what experimental condition they were in. Speakers were also falsely informed that other members of the research team were observing them from behind a one-way mirror in the room. When finished, speakers rated the overall quality of their speech, along with their effectiveness as a speaker and the extent to which they were relaxed both before and during their speech. They also estimated how an observer who viewed their speech would rate its overall quality and their level of anxiety. Later, participants who were serving as "observers" viewed and evaluated eight to ten of these speeches, rating how relaxed the speakers appeared before giving their speech, how expressive they were, and how effective they were as a speaker. Each speech was evaluated by five observers.

Results and Discussion

Results indicated that speakers who were informed about the illusion of transparency and thereby were led to believe that their nervousness was not as apparent as they thought (but not speakers who were merely reassured not to worry) were able to escape the social anxiety typically caused by public speaking. The "informed" speakers delivered speeches that were rated more positively by observers than the speeches of those in the "reassured" and "control" conditions of the study. These findings lend support to the idea that "the truth can set you free" regarding the social psychology of speech giving. These results are also consistent with "cognitive modification" strategies that try to alter people's beliefs as a means of treating speech anxiety. Any time people are nervous over the prospect of appearing nervous, being informed about the illusion of transparency may be sufficient to help them alleviate their social anxiety.

APPLICATIONS

HOW CAN SOCIAL SKILLS TRAINING IMPROVE YOUR LIFE?

One of the most important obstacles that chronically lonely people must overcome is their lack of social skills (Solano & Koester, 1989). The same statement could also be made of those who experience high levels of social anxiousness, for they do not make good first impressions and often experience loneliness (Curran, 1977). This social deficiency is likely one of the more important causes of the low self-esteem of lonely and socially anxious individuals. It can also lead to a feeling of hopelessness and increased social withdrawal (Page, 1991). On the other hand, those who have well-developed social skills find it easy to talk to strangers, are perceived by others as friendly, are not easily angered, and possess high self-esteem.

What makes a person socially skilled? One of the most important factors determining social skill is the *amount of personal attention given to one's partner* in interaction (Kupke et al., 1979). People who are judged to be socially skilled direct more questions toward their conversational partners and make more positive personal statements about them. On the other hand, the unskilled are more self-focused and less responsive when conversing. Some social scientists suggest that this sort of "conversational narcissism," in which people habitually turn conversational topics to themselves without showing interest in their partners' topics, may be more prevalent in individualist cultures than in those with collectivist orientations (Vangelisti et al., 1990). These conversational narcissists have taken the individualist notion that personal needs are more important than group needs to the point where they ignore the interaction needs of others. The all-too-common price for such narcissism is social rejection.

A second factor related to social effectiveness is the *ability to recognize and conform to social norms*. People who have social skills problems often engage in situationally improper behavior. For example, they may make new acquaintances uncomfortable by disclosing very personal details about their lives. Although this sort of self-disclosure is important and valuable in intimate relationships, it is considered inappropriate when interacting with strangers and new acquaintances. Such norm violations generally discourage future encounters.

A third factor associated with social skill is *regulating one's mood prior to commencing social interaction*. Research indicates that people who are socially skilled monitor and impose constraints on their emotions prior to interacting with others (Lopes et al., 2004). Such mood regulation is especially necessary when interacting with strangers, due to the importance of first impressions. In general, when people anticipate interacting with a stranger, they try to regulate their mood in the direction of *neutrality,* regardless of whether their current mood is positive or negative (Erber et al., 1996). This self-imposed mood neutrality is sought because being perceived by new acquaintances as "cool" and "calm" is a socially desirable goal for most people, and a neutral mood is most consistent with attaining that goal. Further, during first encounters, arriving with a preexisting positive or negative mood might be interpreted by a new interaction partner as an attempt to impose one's own mood on her or him, which could lead to negative evaluations. The only times the socially skilled do not seek mood neutrality is when they know beforehand that the person they are about to meet shares their current mood, or when people are happy and they know that the person they are about to meet is depressed. In the latter instance, the failure to neutralize a happy mood might be a self-protective strategy employed by happy people. That is, they may not neutralize their positive emotions because they may believe that they will soon need their positive mood to buffer themselves against the contagious sadness of their interaction partner.

Given the fact that social skills promote greater relationship satisfaction, considerable research has been devoted

Social Skills Training

A behavioral training program designed to improve interpersonal skills through observation, modeling, role playing, and behavioral rehearsal.

to developing **social skills training** programs for both children and adults (Greca, 1993). These programs employ various learning techniques, including the observation and modeling of socially skilled trainers, role-playing various problematic social encounters, and observing one's own social interactions on videotape. The social skills taught in these training sessions cover such areas as initiating conversations, speaking fluently on the telephone, giving and receiving compliments, handling periods of silence, nonverbal methods of

communication, and actively listening to what others have to say in conversation (Kelly, 1997).

Training is usually conducted in groups. In a typical session, the instructor might show a videotape of a model starting a conversation inappropriately or failing to respond to someone's compliment. The group might then discuss ways in which the model could have acted more appropriately. Following this discussion, another videotape might be shown in which the model performs more effectively. Each person in the training group might then role-play a conversation while others observe and then provide feedback. This role playing might even be videotaped so that group members can see exactly how they had interacted. The session might end with a homework assignment for group members to start a conversation with a stranger during the following week.

A growing body of research indicates that those who participate in such training exercises show improvements in their social skills and an increased level of social satisfaction (Erwin, 1994; Margalit, 1995). In one such intervention study, Warren Jones and his colleagues (1982) taught lonely college men to increase their personal attention shown to female strangers during a series of dyadic interactions. They were first given information on the importance of paying attention to others in conversation, and then they interacted individually with four women in successive five-minute, taped conversations. Following these four dyadic interactions, the lonely men were next instructed how to ask questions of their conversational partners, how to refer to their partners while talking to them, and how to discuss topics of interest with their partners. Training consisted of modeling, practice interaction, and feedback. Compared with two control groups of lonely men who did not receive

Calvin and Hobbes   by Bill Watterson

People who possess the interpersonal skills necessary for daily living lead happier, more fulfilling lives than those who are lacking in these skills. Can you identify some of the more important factors determining social skills that Calvin has yet to master?

instruction in personal attention, the trained students subsequently reported feeling less lonely, less self-conscious, and less shy.

The particular skills emphasized in many training programs appear best suited to facilitate the *initiation* of social relationships. Although this is a necessary starting point, it is also important for people to learn skills for "deepening" relationships and overcoming interpersonal conflict. One study that attempted to train such skills was conducted by Robin Cappe and Lynn Alden (1986). They recruited twenty-six men and twenty-six women who were at least moderately socially impaired and exposed them to different types of training programs. Some recruits were instructed on four human relations skills necessary in developing and strengthening friendships: *active listening, empathic responding, communicating respect,* and *self-disclosure.* The instructors discussed and modeled each skill. Participants then practiced their own problematic social situations and incorporated these new skills into each situation. In addition to learning these social skills, participants also learned how to relax when feeling anxious. A second group of recruits was not given any social skills training, but merely learned how to relax in anxiety-producing situations. Finally, a third group received no training at all. Results indicated that the shy, socially avoidant individuals who received a combination of social skills training and relaxation instruction reported significantly greater improvements in their social functioning in the community than those who either received only relaxation training or no instruction at all. In addition, those who were given training in social skills were judged by independent observers to be more comfortable and skillful in social interactions than those in the other groups. A three-month follow-up assessment indicated that a greater proportion of those who had received the social skills training reported having made significant social changes in their lives. These events varied in social impact from minor ("I was able to join a club") to major ("I was able to date and am now engaged").

Taken together, these studies suggest that social skills training programs can, in a fairly short time, teach socially anxious and lonely people how to interact more effectively with others. The resulting interpersonal successes they experience can not only reduce their feeling of social isolation but also boost their sense of social competence and their overall level of self-esteem.

THE BIG PICTURE

In studying social psychology, have you noticed a recurring set of psychological principles that appear to shape people's thoughts and actions? These two psychological cousins are the general desire to be liked and accepted by others and the general desire to have an accurate view of things. They correspond to the "hot" and "cold" perspectives on the nature of human behavior first mentioned in chapter 1. You can see these two principles operating in your self-enhancement and self-verification motives, in your social judgments, and in your ability to exert and be susceptible to social influence. These principles also shape your attraction to others. According to *social exchange theory,* you seek out and maintain those relationships that make you feel good about yourself and bring you more rewards than costs. According to *social comparison theory,* you seek out similar others for accurate comparison so that you can judge and improve yourself.

What you have learned about the psychology of relationships should prove useful in the coming years. As you seek the company of others, remember that a self-fulfilling prophecy is associated with the "desire to be liked" principle. If you approach new social settings thinking that others will like you, you will probably act in ways that fulfill this prophecy. However, if you expect rejection, your subsequent interaction style may fulfill the negative prophecy, even if it is based on false information.

Also keep in mind that although almost everyone experiences loneliness, your recovery often depends on how you interpret and react to its perceived causes. People who make *internal, stable attributions* for their loneliness ("I just don't know how to make new friends") tend to be chronically lonely, while those who make *external, unstable attributions* ("I'm lonely because I don't know anyone here") are generally only temporarily lonely. The advice to be gleaned from this research is that you should be careful *what* you think you are, for you will likely behave consistent with those self-beliefs. Here again is an example of how the self is an active participant in creating its social reality.

WEB SITES

accessed through http://www.mhhe.com/franzoi4

Web sites for this chapter focus on research and theory on interpersonal relationships, as well as an analysis of shyness, social anxiety, and loneliness.

International Society for the Study of Personal Relationships

This Web site for the International Society for the Study of Personal Relationships lists information about interpersonal relationship publications and conferences, as well as links to other relevant sites.

Shyness Institute

This Web page is a gathering of network resources for people seeking information and services for shyness and social anxiety.

American Psychological Association

The American Psychological Association Web site contains a Web page that discusses research indicating that the Internet increases social isolation among users.

Intimate Relationships

CHAPTER OUTLINE

PREVIEW *Jealousy can cause irreparable harm to romantic relationships. What are some of the short-term and long-term strategies that you can use to constructively resolve jealousy?*

*I*n Robert Munsch's (1986) children's book, *Love You Forever,* he tells a movingly off-beat story about a mother-son relationship. It begins with the mother holding her new baby and slowly rocking him back and forth while singing the following verse:

> I'll love you forever,
> I'll like you for always,
> As long as I'm living
> my baby you'll be.

As the child grows, he gets into all sorts of messes and squabbles and does a nice job aging the mother. Despite these hassles of childrearing, each night as he slept, the mother would look into his room, crawl across the floor, and look up over the side of the bed. If he was truly asleep, she carefully picked him up, slowly rocked him back and forth, and sang her song to him.

When he grew up and moved across town, sometimes the mother would strap a ladder to her car late at night, drive to her son's house, climb into his room and crawl to the foot of his bed. If he was truly asleep, she carefully picked up this full-grown man and slowly rocked him back and forth, singing her song as she gazed into his peaceful face.

Well, one day when the mother was old and feeble, she phoned her son and told him to come over quickly because she was very sick. When he arrived, the mother tried to sing her song but could not finish. Instead then, the grown-up son carefully picked up his mother, held her in his arms, and began to slowly rock her back and forth. As he rocked her, he sang the following verse:

> I'll love you forever,
> I'll like you for always,
> As long as I'm living
> my Mommy you'll be.

Robert Munsch's book, *Love You Forever,* is a funny but moving depiction of the positive emotional bonds that parents have with their children. What sort of attachment style (see pp. 447–448) do you think the son in this story developed?

Later, when he returned to his own home, he went to his newborn daughter's room where she peacefully slept. Reaching down, he gently picked her up in his arms, held her close, and slowly began to rock her back and forth. As he rocked her, he sang:

I'll love you forever,
I'll like you for always,
As long as I'm living
my baby you'll be.

The deeply tender and nurturing feelings expressed in Robert Munsch's story mirror the story that psychologists tell about intimate relationships: children learn about intimacy and love during the first few years of life, and this forms the basis for how they will interact with others in later years. In chapter 11, you learned that people differ in their affiliation needs, and that women are more likely than men to seek an emotional connectedness to other individuals (see p. 404). Now, you will continue this analysis by examining the intimacy experienced in parent-child interactions, friendships, and romantic relationships, each of which offers its own unique contributions to people's health and welfare (Felmlee & Sprecher, 2000). This is a journey you have traveled before. Yet now, instead of trying to understand friendship and love simply by immersing yourself in the experience, you will survey the social psychological literature to better understand how scientists explain the communion of selves. Your social psychological journey begins with a discussion of what is encompassed in the term *intimacy*.

WHAT IS INTIMACY?

Imagine that you overhear another person make a disparaging remark about someone you love. How would you feel, and how might you respond? Now imagine that the one you care about has succeeded on an important task. Or done very poorly. How would this influence your mood? If you are like most people, you would *share* with that person the emotional highs and lows accompanying these events. **Intimacy** refers to sharing that which is inmost with others (McAdams, 1988). The word itself is derived from the Latin *intimus*, which means "inner" or "inmost."

Intimacy Involves Including Another in Your Self-Concept

As you recall from chapter 3, William James conceived of the "self as object" (or self-concept) as being a process of identification, expanding and contracting to include that which one values. Arthur Aron and Elaine Aron (1986, 1997) employ James's notion of *self-expansion* in their analysis of intimacy. They contend that in intimate relationships, we seek to psychologically expand ourselves by acting as if some or all aspects of our partner are part of our own selves (Aron et al., 2001). The degree to which our partner is included in our self-concept is an indicator of our level of relationship intimacy. Figure 12.1 provides a schematic illustration of different levels of intimacy through this self-expansion process.

This removal of psychological boundaries between people so that one experiences another as part of him- or herself is often identified as the most important distinguishing feature of intimacy (Cross & Gore, 2002). Yet if intimacy is really an inclusionary experience, can researchers detect it by studying the structure and the process of the self? A number of social psychologists respond with an affirmative yes to this question. They contend that in memory this inclusion of the other in the self is represented by a direct link between the self and the close other, so that activating either memories of the self or the close other will automatically activate memories of both persons and their associated traits (Mashek et al., 2003). The implication of this theory is that people will think about and respond to intimate others very similarly to the way they think about and respond to themselves. Let us examine various research areas where evidence for this inclusionary process has been found.

Each friend represents a world in us, a world possibly not born until they arrive, and it is only by this meeting that a new world is born.

Anaïs Nin, U.S. novelist, 1903–1977

Intimacy

Sharing that which is inmost with others.

A friend is, as it were, a second self.

Marcus Tullius Cicero, Roman statesman, 106–43 B.C.

FIGURE 12.1

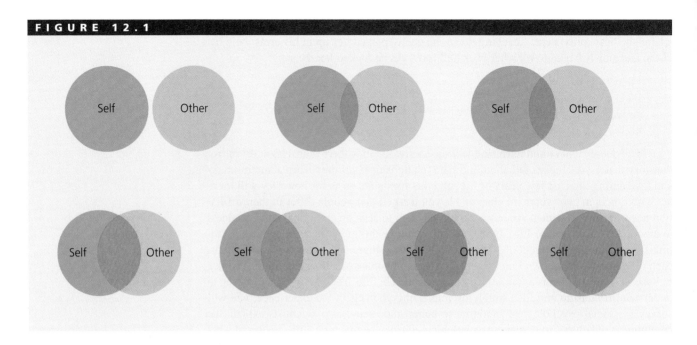

Inclusion of Other in the Self

This is a schematic illustration of seven different degrees of self-other relatedness, from no inclusion of the other in the self to an immersion of the other in one's self. Which of the pictures best describes different intimate relationships in your own life?

We are molded and remolded by those who have loved us; and, though the love may pass, we are nevertheless their work, for good or ill.

Francois Mauriac, French novelist, 1885–1970

SELF-SCHEMAS

One way in which intimate relationships reflect the inclusion of the other in the self-concept is in what constitutes self-concept ingredients, or *self-schemas.* As discussed in chapter 3, traits that we identify as being important in our self-concepts are recognized as being self-descriptive more quickly than traits that are not relevant to our self-concepts (Markus, 1977). Research comparing the self-schemas of strangers, friends, and married couples has found that as the intimacy bond deepens between two people, they begin to incorporate some of the other's self-schemas into their own self-concepts. As a result of this cognitive blurring of the self-other distinction, people involved in intimate relationships need less time to recognize self-descriptive traits if the traits are also shared with their partner (Aron et al., 1991; E. Smith et al., 1999). For example, imagine that Ann and Stephanie are involved in an intimate relationship. Ann has self-schemas consisting of such traits as independent, tidy, and industrious. Stephanie sees herself as independent, industrious, and athletic. The speed at which they can individually process and recall self-descriptive traits will be faster for traits they share (independent, industrious) rather than those upon which they differ. Even though Ann has a self-schema for "tidy" and Stephanie has a self-schema for "athletic," because the intimate other does not share this trait, it takes them longer to identify it as being self-descriptive.

THE ATTRIBUTION PROCESS

As discussed in chapter 4, when we make attributions about events, the perspective we have of our own versus others' behavior results in the *actor-observer effect*—we attribute our own behavior to external causes but that of others to internal factors (McCall et al., 2000). This self-other discrepancy has been found to be much less pronounced when the "other" is more intimate with the self (Nisbett et al., 1973). In other words, when explaining the actions of someone for whom we care a great deal, the attributions we infer are more similar to those we would have for our own actions versus those of the average person on the street (Gardner et al., 2002; Lavin, 1987).

TABLE 12.1

Exchange Versus Communal Relationships

Exchange Relationships (Governed by concern for equity)	Communal Relationships (Governed by responsiveness to the other's needs)
1. Person motivated by a desire to have a "fair" relationship	1. Person motivated by a desire to please the other person
2. Person desires to be immediately repaid for favors	2. Person dislikes being immediately repaid for favors
3. Person feels exploited when favors are not returned	3. Person does not feel exploited when favors are not returned
4. Person keeps track of who is contributing what to the relationship	4. Person does not keep track of who is contributing what to the relationship
5. Helping one's partner doesn't elevate one's mood	5. Helping one's partner elevates one's mood

RESOURCE ALLOCATION

Resource allocation is another way we include others within our self-concept. People in an intimate relationship make less of a distinction between self and other when allocating resources than do those who are less intimate (Aron et al., 1991). This is so because if another is included in your self-concept, your resources are also her or his resources. Imagine two couples going out to dinner together, one pair deeply in love, the other on their first date. During the course of the meal, the two lovers eat from each other's plate, reaching for morsels of food without asking permission. If, in a similar manner, one person from the nonintimate pair reached for the other's food, it would likely be interpreted as very bad manners—an encroachment on the other's personal resources.

COMMUNAL VERSUS EXCHANGE RELATIONSHIPS

The different disbursement of resources to an intimate other naturally leads to another quality indicative of the "self-inclusion of other" perspective. In most of our everyday relationships, we operate on the principle of *exchange* by carefully tallying our costs and balancing those against our rewards to determine whether we should maintain the relationship. However, a number of studies demonstrate that when we are involved in intimate relationships, we often do not think about our rewards and costs as if we were balancing our bank accounts (Mills & Clark, 1994). Instead, these *communal relationships* are organized according to the principle that people are to be given what they need, with little concern for what we will receive in return (Medvene et al., 2000). Thus, in intimate relationships, we treat our loved ones' needs as if they were our own. Because these intimate others are important elements in our own self-concept, our needs and their needs are intertwined and often indistinguishable. Table 12.1 summarizes the differences between these two different types of relationships.

If I have no love, I am nothing. . . . Love is patient; love is kind and envies no one. Love is never boastful, nor conceited, nor rude; never selfish, not quick to take offence. Love keeps no score of wrongs; does not gloat over other men's sins, but delights in the truth. . . . Love will never come to an end.

I Corinthians 13

TRANSACTIVE MEMORY

One final way that the self-inclusion of the other is manifested is in the use of *transactive memory*. Daniel Wegner and his colleagues (1991) found that people in intimate relationships have a shared memory system for encoding, storing, and retrieving information that is greater than either of their individual memories. In this transactive memory, each partner enjoys the benefits of the pair's memory by taking responsibility for remembering just those items that fall clearly to her or him (Andersson & Rönnberg, 1997; Hollingshead, 2001). For a romantic couple living together, this may involve one person remembering the proper place for all the workroom tools, while the other remembers where the special dinnerware and napkins are stored. If each person learns in a general way what the other knows in detail, the two can share the detailed memories enjoyed by both. Through updating one another on what is in each other's knowledge area, the partners further embellish their transactive memory (Engestrom et al., 1990).

In summary, these studies illustrate the utility of viewing close relationships as including the other in the self-concept. Partners who are high in intimacy are concerned about the other's welfare and happiness, often even more than their own (Cross et al., 2000). The rewards shared by intimates go far beyond "warm fuzzies." Cross-cultural studies find that having successful intimate relationships is among our most important life goals and aspirations, and it is the only factor that consistently predicts happiness in every country studied (Diener et al., 1999; Reis & Gable, 2003). Let us now examine the foundation for these intimacy beliefs.

SECTION SUMMARY

- *Intimacy* is an inclusion of others in one's self-concept, and manifests itself in

  self-schemas

  attribution processes

  resource allocation

  communal relationships

  transactive memory

PARENT-CHILD ATTACHMENT AND LATER ADULT RELATIONSHIPS

The strong emotional bond that develops between infants and their caregivers is known as **attachment,** and it is considered the cornerstone for all other relationships in a child's life (Cummings & Cummings, 2002). This bond is not unique to humans but is found in most species of birds and mammals (Graves & Hennesy, 2000; Mason, 1997). Before reading further, watch a Brief Social Sense CD-ROM video concerning the evolutionary significance of attachment.

Attachment Is an Inborn Adaptive Response

Biological processes and genetic tendencies spark the emotional bond of attachment. Human infants have an inborn attachment response that is observable within minutes of birth, beginning with attempts to suckle their mother's breasts (the *rooting instinct*) and the ability to grasp and hold fast when startled (the *Moro reflex).* Within days, newborns recognize and prefer the face, voice, and smell of their mother to those of unfamiliar people, and they spontaneously imitate their caretakers' facial expressions (Gopnik et al., 1999). New mothers are similarly predisposed to bond with their infants. During labor and later when breast-feeding their children, mothers produce the *oxytocin* hormone, which has a positive influence on parenting behavior. Both human and animal studies indicate that individuals with higher levels of oxytocin more strongly desire companionship and take better care of their young than those with lower levels (Maestripieri, 2001).

British psychiatrist John Bowlby (1969) was one of the first social scientists to systematically study the attachment process. Based on his analysis of human infants and the young of other species, Bowlby proposed that attachment is part of many species' genetic

Attachment

The strong emotional bond an infant forms with its primary caregiver.

Social Sense

View a presentation on the survival value of the attachment process heritage, with its evolutionary function being the protection of immature, highly vulnerable animals. Infants who cling or remain close to their parents are better protected from predators and thus stand a better chance of surviving to adulthood than those who wander away from parental care.

In his evolutionary analysis of attachment, Bowlby proposed a standard pattern of three responses produced by infants of many species when they become separated from their primary caregivers: protest, despair, and detachment. *Protest* is the first strategy employed following parental separation, and it is characterized by infants creating a ruckus. Infants who wail and scream are likely to draw their parents near, thus increasing the likelihood that they will be protected and fed. However, if this protest strategy does not succeed, Bowlby reasoned that the next best survival strategy is for infants to remain quiet (*despair*), thus reducing the likelihood of attracting the attention of predators. Finally, if left unattended for long periods, infants will develop emotional *detachment* and begin to behave independently.

Children Develop Different Attachment Styles

One of Bowlby's associates, Mary Ainsworth (1989), took his basic ideas about attachment and studied how human infants develop different *attachment styles.* Ainsworth reasoned that although our biological heritage may propel us toward caregivers, the basic principles of reinforcement theory suggest that the caregiver's response will influence the strength of this desire to establish such proximity. Subsequent research on parent-child attachment indicated that as infants interact with their parents they develop either optimistic or pessimistic beliefs about human relationships (Meins, 1999; Moss et al., 2004). Children with parents who are nurturing and sensitively responsive to their needs develop a *secure attachment* style characterized by a belief that they are worthy of others' love and that people can be trusted. In marked contrast, children with parents who are inattentive to their needs develop an *insecure attachment* style characterized by a belief that they are unworthy love objects and that others cannot be relied upon (Huth-Bocks et al., 2004).

From a social cognitive perspective, one way to understand attachment styles is that they consist of people's cognitive representations of what constitutes love and intimacy. In

The affection of mothers for their offspring is at least partly based on the hormones present during the birth process and later during nursing. Whether children develop a secure versus an insecure attachment style is significantly determined by the parenting style of the primary caregiver. Parents who are sensitively responsive to their children's needs foster secure attachment, while parents who are inattentive to their infants' needs foster insecure attachment.

essence, children with different attachment styles have different *prototypes* for intimate relationships (Fehr, 1993). As you recall from chapter 5 (p. 141), a prototype is the most representative member of a category. If an adult or another child behaves in a warm and affectionate manner toward them, securely attached children quickly recognize this as an overture for intimacy, but insecurely attached children will be less likely to do so because the behavior does not match their "intimate relationship" prototype. This difficulty in associating nurturing intimacy with the cognitive category of "intimate relationships" signals trouble for the social world of the insecurely attached.

Generally speaking, throughout childhood insecurely attached children exhibit less social competence and lower levels of self-esteem and self-concept complexity than children with secure attachment (Schulman et al., 1994). Insecurely attached children often exhibit contradictory social behavior, sometimes initiating social contact, but then unexpectedly spurning others' social advances. This vacillating pattern of approach-avoidance invites social rejection from peers, which then serves to confirm the child's original sense of insecurity and distrust.

Although attachment is a universal feature among humans, the nature of the attachment styles that children eventually develop also is shaped by culture (Harwood et al., 1995; Rothbaum et al., 2000). For example, both U.S. and German children are far more likely than Japanese children to develop a type of insecure attachment style characterized by avoiding intimacy with the mother (Cole, 1992). These cultural differences are probably due to different views on how to raise children in individualist and collectivist cultures. Parents in the United States and Germany try to foster independence at an earlier age, and thus, they discourage their children from staying near them and are more likely to give them toys or food when they cry rather than picking them up. In contrast, Japanese parents do not promote independence, and thus, they rarely leave their children alone and quickly pick them up when they cry.

Childhood Attachment Styles Influence Adult Romantic Relationships

Up until the mid-1980s, all research on attachment styles focused on children and adolescents' social relationships. Then, in 1987, social psychologists Cindy Hazan and Philip Shaver developed self-report measures of secure and insecure attachment styles derived from the work of Ainsworth and other developmental psychologists. Hazan and Shaver were interested in determining whether these attachment styles might affect adult romantic relationships. Inserting their attachment measures into a "love quiz" printed in a local newspaper, they asked respondents questions about their current romantic relationships. The results of this pioneering study found that the percentage of adults who endorsed each attachment style were similar to the figures obtained in studies of infant-parent attachment (Campos et al., 1983). Hazan and Shaver also found that securely attached adults reported more positive relationships with their parents than did adults with insecure attachment styles.

After the publication of this research, many social psychologists began exploring how attachment styles influenced the nature and quality of adult social relationships and found that they were consistent with the findings for children (Conger et al., 2000; Green & Campbell, 2000; Scharf et al., 2004). One of the additional discoveries from the infant and adult studies was that attachment styles are best thought of as being determined by two basic attitudes: (1) the extent to which one's self-esteem is positive or negative, and (2) the extent to which one perceives others as trustworthy (a positive attitude) or untrustworthy (a negative attitude). In turn, these two basic attitudes cause different reactions whenever intimacy becomes an issue: low self-esteem triggers anxiety and low interpersonal trust triggers avoidance (Mikulincer & Shaver, 2003). As depicted in figure 12.2, this new conception of attachment—which is still consistent with Ainsworth's original research—yields four kinds of attachment style (Brennan et al., 1998; Fraley & Spieker, in press).

Individuals with a **secure attachment style** have positive self-esteem and believe that people are basically loving and trustworthy, and therefore, they experience low anxiety and low avoidance in their social relationships. Securely attached adults easily become close to others, expect intimate relationships to endure, and handle relationship conflict constructively (Feeney & Kirkpatrick, 1996; Morrison et al., 1997). In college, securely attached

What is love? Ask him who lives, what is life. Ask him who adores, what is God . . . [Love] is that powerful attraction towards all that we conceive, or fear, or hope beyond ourselves, when we find within our own thoughts the chasm of an insufficient void, and seek to awaken in all things that are, a community with what we experience within ourselves.

Percy Bysshe Shelley, English poet, 1792–1824

Secure Attachment Style

An expectation about social relationships characterized by trust, a lack of concern with being abandoned, and a feeling of being valued and well liked.

FIGURE 12.2

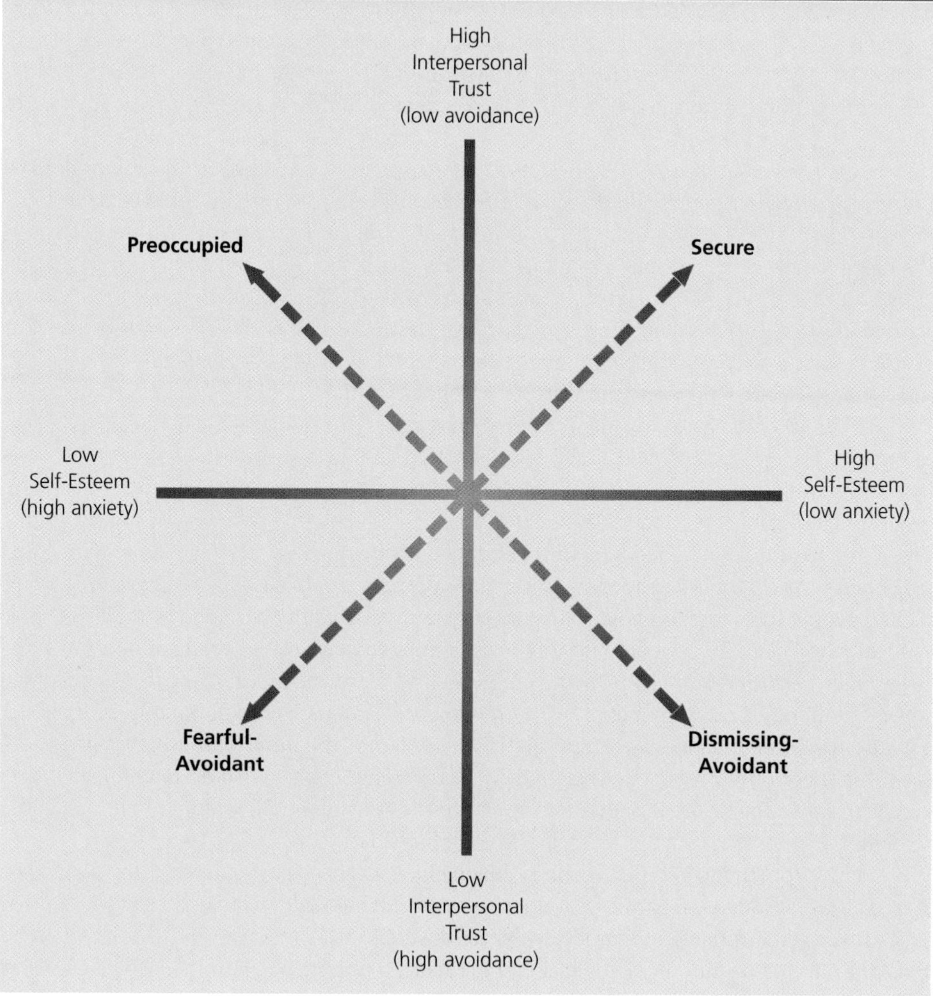

High
Interpersonal
Trust
(low avoidance)

Preoccupied

Secure

Low
Self-Esteem
(high anxiety)

High
Self-Esteem
(low anxiety)

Fearful-
Avoidant

Dismissing-
Avoidant

Low
Interpersonal
Trust
(high avoidance)

Four Attachment Styles Based on Perceptions of Self-Worth and Others' Trustworthiness

Derived from Bowlby's cross-species analysis of attachment and Ainsworth's research on child-parent attachment styles, the current perspective on attachment style is that it is shaped by two basic attitudes: (1) the degree to which one's self-esteem is positive or negative, and (2) the degree to which one perceives others as trustworthy or untrustworthy. High self-esteem persons experience low anxiety whereas persons with low self-esteem experience high anxiety whenever intimacy becomes an issue. Further, persons with high interpersonal trust respond with little or no avoidance during intimate encounters, but those with low interpersonal trust respond with avoidance. Together, these two dimensions of self-esteem and interpersonal trust identify four adult attachment styles: *secure, preoccupied, dismissing-avoidant, and fearful-avoidant.* Which attachment style is associated with the most successful intimate relationships?

first-year students adjust better to university life and have higher achievement aspirations than students with other attachment styles (Elliot & Reis, 2003; Mattanah et al., 2004).

Although persons with a **preoccupied attachment style** have positive expectations that people will be loving and trustworthy, they have a negative view of themselves as not being worthy of others' love. Thus, they are low on avoidance but high on anxiety. They desperately seek out intimate relationships, but they tend to be obsessed and preoccupied with their friends and romantic partners, and they fear that their friendship and love will not be reciprocated. Preoccupied individuals' often judge their self-worth in terms of their physical attractiveness, and their orientation toward sexual activity is strongly shaped by their insecurity and strong intimacy needs (Davis; Park et al., 2004). They tend to have sex as a way to feel valued by their partners or as a means to induce their partners to love them more (Schachner & Shaver, 2004).

In contrast to the belief by secure and preoccupied people that others are basically loving and trustworthy, people with a **dismissing-avoidant attachment style** have little faith in other people, and thus, they avoid them. They are uncomfortable becoming intimate, find it hard to trust others, have difficulty even recognizing expressions of warmth and empathy from others, and often withdraw from relationships when conflicts arise (Mikulincer, 1998; Mikulincer & Arad, 1999). Due to their positive self-esteem and lack of self-insight, dismissing-avoidant individuals typically experience little interpersonal

Preoccupied Attachment Style

An expectation about social relationships characterized by trust, but combined with a feeling of being unworthy of others' love and a fear of abandonment.

Dismissing-Avoidant Attachment Style

An expectation about social relationships characterized by low trust and avoidance of intimacy, combined with high self-esteem and compulsive self-reliance.

Fearful-Avoidant Attachment Style

An expectation about social relationships characterized by low trust and avoidance of intimacy, combined with a feeling of being unworthy of others' love and a fear of rejection.

CRITICAL *thinking*

The self-sufficient cowboy who keeps to himself and doesn't engage in idle chitchat is one of the great icons of the American West. Hollywood actors John Wayne, Gary Cooper, and Clint Eastwood personified this extreme form of individualism in many of their film roles. Today, Hollywood uses this same rugged, individualist personality in creating the lead male role in action adventure films (Bruce Willis, Sylvester Stallone, John Travolta). What attachment style would you say these film characters most often represent? Is this an attachment style we should be placing in our male cultural role models?

anxiety (Gjerde et al., 2004). In fact, they are generally confident—even arrogant—but because they do not trust others they exhibit a compulsive self-reliance. Unlike preoccupied individuals who are motivated to engage in sexual activity to reduce insecurity and foster intense intimacy, dismissives are likely to have sex simply because they enjoy it or because they can then brag about it and increase their status with their social group (Schachner & Shaver, 2004).

Finally, similar to dismissives, persons with a **fearful-avoidant attachment style** do not trust others, but unlike dismissives, they also have a low opinion of themselves and therefore experience a great deal of anxiety in interpersonal settings. Fearful-avoidant individuals expect to be rejected by others, and they have a heightened attentiveness and reaction to angry and sad facial expressions (Niedenthal et al., 2003). Like preoccupied individuals, fearful-avoidants base their self-worth on their physical level of attractiveness (Parker et al., 2004). As you might guess, this attachment style is associated with negative interpersonal experiences and the abuse of alcohol to reduce anxiety in social settings (McNally et al., 2003). Fearful-avoidants often have a history of psychological, physical, or sexual abuse (Bartholomew, 1990; Bartholomew et al., 2001).

Research that has examined the childhood experiences of adults who differ in attachment styles finds that the securely attached report positive family relationships when young, while the insecurely attached rate their childhood family environments as emotionally cold and openly conflicted (Klohnen & Bera, 1998). These findings suggest that securely attached people have learned how to foster intimacy while adults with one of the three insecure attachment styles have unwittingly learned how to destroy it. The dismissing-avoidant lover tends to starve intimacy by being emotionally distant and aloof, while the preoccupied lover smothers intimacy by being overly possessive, jealous, and emotionally demanding. Finally, fearful-avoidant lovers perhaps have the worst dilemma because they want approval, but not only do they not feel worthy of receiving it, they also do not believe others can be trusted. So they avoid intimacy in relationships, thinking it is safer to fantasize about a relationship instead of actually trying to establish one.

Is it surprising to you that securely attached lovers are the most desired partners by the vast majority of adults, regardless of their own attachment style (Chappell & Davis, 1998)? Does it further surprise you that the two least desirable attachment styles in romantic relationships are the dismissing-avoidants and the fearful-avoidants (Pietromonaco & Carnelly, 1994)? What is it about securely attached people that makes them so desirable? Given the warmth and openness that securely attached people bring to romantic relationships, it is not surprising that securely attached adults are attracted to each other and are the happiest couples (Kirkpatrick & Davis, 1994; Senchak & Leonard, 1992). For other securely attached people, a secure partner confirms their expectations of love: they each share the same intimate relationship prototype. When securely attached people are romantically involved with insecure partners there is prototype mismatch, but secure types can buffer the negative effects that their partners bring to the relationship, providing the emotional stability necessary to disconfirm negative expectations (Feeney, 2003). If the secure partner consistently encourages openness, trust, and acceptance, the insecure partner may gradually change her or his beliefs about intimacy and/or her or his own feelings of self-worth. This involves the adoption of a new prototype of the category "intimate relationship" that conforms to the secure attachment style.

The idea that attachment styles can change is a relatively new one (Davila & Sargent, 2003). Recent studies suggest that although childhood attachment style does predict adulthood attachment style with reasonable accuracy, changes can occur (Waters et al., 2000; Weinfield et al., 2000). Yet the change may not always be for the better. Just as parental divorce or physical abuse can cause a child to slip from a secure to an insecure style, a romantic couple containing at least one insecure partner or a relationship fraught with conflict can destroy a person's secure attachment style. In one study investigating married couples expecting their first child, women became more insecure in their attachment style when they received less support and more anger from their husbands (Simpson et al., 2003). It appears that people are most likely to undergo attachment style changes when they grapple with stressful, life-altering events that expose them to experiences that challenge their existing attachment beliefs. These stressful events could be either positive or negative in nature. Upon evaluation and reflection, if they change one or both of the basic attitudes underlying their current attachment style, their orientation toward intimate relationships will either become more optimistic or pessimistic. This ability to significantly revise core attitudes and beliefs is another example of the dynamic nature of the self.

SECTION SUMMARY

- Attachment evolved to keep the young close to adults where they are better protected from predators
- Parent-child attachment patterns influence later childhood peer relations and intimate adult relationships
- Attachment style is shaped by two basic attitudes: (1) the degree to which one's self-esteem is positive or negative, and (2) the degree to which one perceives others as trustworthy or untrustworthy
- Four adult attachment styles:

    Secure attachment style: high self-esteem and high trustworthiness

    Preoccupied attachment style: low self-esteem and high trustworthiness

    Dismissing-avoidant attachment style: high self-esteem and low trustworthiness

    Fearful-avoidant attachment style: low self-esteem and low trustworthiness
- People with a secure attachment style have more successful intimate relationships later in life than those who are insecurely attached

FRIENDSHIP

As children mature, they not only form emotional ties to family members, but they also form friendships with their peers. Although intimacy is expressed in both social arenas, friendship appears to have a very different function from that of family relationships (Elbedour et al., 1997; Side, 2004). While relationships with relatives are based on largely nonvoluntary forces, relationships based on friendship are primarily voluntary and mutually satisfying. The distinction between friends and family is summed up in the old saying, "you can pick your friends, but not your family."

Self-Disclosure Shapes Friendship Development and Maintenance

Social scientists and the ordinary person generally make distinctions between two different levels of friendship (Blieszner & Adams, 1992). *Superficial friendships* are formed and maintained because they are rewarding and are based on the principle of exchange. *Developed friendships,* in contrast, are based not only on rewards but also on friends' mutual concern for each other's welfare (Lydon et al., 1997). One of the prime avenues for creating developed friendships is through **self-disclosure,** which is the revealing of personal information about oneself to other people (Vittengl & Holt, 2000). Individuals who do not avail themselves of this type of intimate communication tend to have dysfunctional relationships and experience greater loneliness than those who reveal their private self-aspects to friends and lovers (Stokes, 1987).

SOCIAL PENETRATION THEORY

Irving Altman and Dalmas Taylor (1973) sought to explain the self-disclosure process in their **social penetration theory.** According to Altman and Taylor, the development of a relationship is associated with communication moving gradually from a discussion of

Self-Disclosure

The revealing of personal information about oneself to other people.

Social Penetration Theory

A theory that describes the development of close relationships in terms of increasing self-disclosure.

FIGURE 12.3

The Theory of Social Penetration

According to Altman and Taylor's (1973) theory of social penetration, the amount of information people disclose early in a relationship is rather narrow and shallow, yet as the relationship progresses, self-disclosure becomes broader (covering a wider range of topics) and deeper (revealing more personal information).

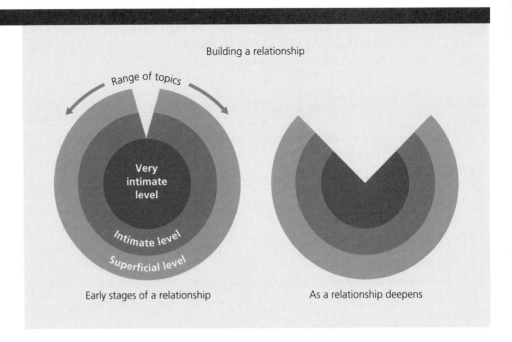

Fondness is a poor substitute for friendship.

Anna Green Winslow, Canadian poet, 1759–1780

superficial topics to more intimate exchanges. During the first initial interactions, people are likely to discuss such impersonal topics as the weather, sports events, or popular culture. If this superficial discussion is rewarding, they may broaden and deepen the social exchange by covering a wider range of topics and choosing to divulge more personal and sensitive information. As you can see in figure 12.3, when discussion topics move from the very narrow and shallow range to a broader and deeper scope, the intimacy level also increases (Laurenceau et al., 1998). In a very real sense, the process of relationship development involves the proper "pacing" of self-disclosure so that one avoids negative reactions if personal revelations are too large or too small.

During first meetings, new acquaintances usually follow the norm of *self-disclosure reciprocity*—they match each other's level of self-disclosure, revealing more when the other person does so, and decreasing personal revelations if the other person becomes reticent (Omarzu, 2000). In most first encounters, self-disclosure reciprocity is useful in building a mutually satisfying level of information exchange that benefits relationship development. However, if one person ignores this gradual self-disclosure process and instead reveals a great deal of personal information, there is a good chance the recipient will feel threatened with this premature rush to intimacy and will evaluate the discloser negatively (Kaplan et al., 1974). Once the relationship progresses beyond the superficial stage and intimacy barriers have been lowered, this tit-for-tat exchange of personal information is not as important and occurs much less frequently (Altman, 1973). In fact, in an intimate relationship, instead of reciprocating with self-disclosure, a partner may simply offer support and understanding (Archer, 1979).

What happens to self-disclosure in troubled friendships? In their theory, Altman and Taylor also discuss the dynamics of what they called *depenetration,* which is the disengagement from an intimate relationship. When intimate relationships are in trouble, some people emotionally withdraw by engaging in less breadth and depth in their personal revelations (Baxter, 1987). Other people reduce the number of topics they discuss but increase the depth of their self-disclosure (Tolstedt & Stokes, 1984). The deeply personal feelings and beliefs that are disclosed are usually negative and are designed to accuse and hurt the other person. Thus, just as self-disclosure can build a relationship and provide it with a solid emotional foundation, it can also serve to weaken and tear it down.

Although social penetration theory's description of a gradual and orderly pattern of increasing self-disclosure fits most developing friendships and romantic relationships (Collins & Miller, 1994), not all intimate relationships progress in this fashion. In some, the type of intimate self-disclosure normally seen in long-term relationships develops almost immediately. For example, in studies of friends, roommates, and dating partners, John Berg found that some relationships just "click" right from the start rather than gradually becoming close over time (Berg, 1984; Berg & Clark, 1986). Berg explained that this early exchange of highly personal information occurs because the respective partners make quick judgments that the other person fits their prototype of the ideal friend or romantic partner. In situations in which people immediately become best friends or lovers, self-disclosure does not serve to deepen the relationship in the same way that it does in the more common and gradually developing relationships described by social penetration theory. Instead, when the partners recognize that this is an intimate relationship, the highly personal self-disclosure begins to flow.

He who has nothing has no friends.

Greek proverb

CULTURAL DIFFERENCES IN SELF-DISCLOSURE

Research indicates that there are cultural differences in self-disclosure tendencies (Adams & Anderson, in press). North Americans tend to disclose more about themselves in a wider variety of social settings than people from collectivist cultures such as China, Japan, and the West African nation of Ghana (Chen, 1995; Sanders et al., 1991). These differences in self-disclosure practices do not mean that Americans have more intimate relationships than people from China or Japan (refer to chapter 11, pp. 403–405), but they may be rooted in their respective individualist and collectivist orientations. For example, in chapter 3 (p. 72), we discussed research indicating that many individualist Americans have a need to feel unique or distinct from others (Pratt, 1991; Triandis, 1989). Perhaps the willingness to reveal private self-aspects through self-disclosure provides individualists with the opportunity to identify and share their uniqueness.

These self-disclosure differences may also be partly due to preferred communication channels within the respective cultures. In many Western societies, social expressiveness tends to be a sign of social competence and is valued as an avenue to intimacy, yet in Eastern cultures such as Japan, China, and Korea, oral communication skills are not as highly valued. In fact, being socially *nonexpressive* is often interpreted as an indication of emotional strength and trustworthiness (Russell & Yik, 1996). Although great value is not placed on social expressiveness in these collectivist cultures, it is considered virtuous to be able to quickly and accurately interpret and respond to others' vaguely expressed feelings and desires before they have to be clearly articulated (Barnlund, 1989). In this kind of cultural context, self-disclosing one's desires or fears may be considered inappropriate, because others are expected to "read" them through indirect means.

When same-sex friends get together, their main reason for doing so is to talk. The conversation of female friends, however, tends to be more intimate than that of male friends. What might explain these gender differences?

Gender Differences Exist in Heterosexual Friendships

Although both men and women value friendship throughout their lives, research suggests certain gender differences in heterosexual friendship patterns from childhood through adulthood (Fehr, 2003; Winstead, 1986).

INTIMACY

One notable gender difference involves the level of emotional expressiveness within same-sex friendships. Put simply, women's friendships tend to be more intimate and involve more emotional sharing than men's friendships (Oswald et al., 2004; Way et al., 2001). This specific gender difference is part of a larger pattern of gender-based behavior found in same-sex friendships. That is, when men and women interact with same-sex friends, they are more likely to conform to gender stereotypes than when interacting with other-sex friends: men are more dominant and women are more agreeable (Suh et al., 2004).

Initially, research conducted in the 1970s and 1980s suggested that in contrast to the friendships of women, men's friendships are more likely to revolve around shared activities (Sherrod, 1989). Paul Wright (1982) characterized this seemingly different orientation toward friendship as *face-to-face* versus *side-by-side:* women spend a good deal of time together talking about personal and intimate matters, and men spend the majority of their time together working or playing, with considerably less personal self-disclosure. Even though these contrasting descriptions of men's and women's friendships have an appealing simplicity, later studies found that they were just that—too simplistic. Research by Steve Duck and Wright (1993) found that both women *and* men meet most often just to talk. They also discovered that although women are indeed more emotionally expressive than men in their friendships, they are just as likely as men to engage in shared activities. Therefore, it is misleading to describe men's friendships as being exclusively side-by-side encounters and women's friendships as being exclusively face-to-face interactions.

One important point to keep in mind is that even though women tend to have more intimate friendships than men, this does not mean that *all* men's friendships are less emotionally expressive than the average women's friendships. In all such comparisons, we are discussing *group averages.* The general consensus among social scientists is that although some aspects of these intimacy differences between men and women may be weakly rooted in biology, they are primarily caused by gender socialization. Indeed, Dorie Williams (1985) has found that both men and women who possess personality traits associated with psychological femininity report being more intimate in their same-sex friendships than men and women who exhibit few feminine traits. Perhaps because women's same-sex friendships are generally more intimate, they also regard them more favorably than do men (Wright & Scanlon, 1991). This greater intimacy in female friendships is expressed in a number of ways.

SELF-DISCLOSURE

In a meta-analysis of 205 studies, Kathryn Dindia and Mike Allen (1992) found that women generally self-disclose more than men, especially in intimate relationships. Their analysis indicates that women self-disclose more than men to their same-sex friends and other-sex romantic partners, but men and women do not differ in their disclosure to male friends. They also found that these gender differences, although not as great as once thought, have shown no evidence of reduction during the past thirty years. More recent studies confirm these findings: women emphasize self-disclosure and emotional support more than men in their friendships (Fehr, 2003; Oswald et al., 2004).

What is it about gender socialization that leads to less intimate self-disclosure among men? Research suggests that males in North American culture appear to be governed by a more rigid set of gender rules than females, especially regarding emotional expression (Bank & Hansford, 2000; Timmers et al., 1998). As a result, a man is likely to have a harder time acting vulnerable and dependent. This restriction on male emotional expressiveness was demonstrated in a study in which male and female participants read a story about a man

TABLE 12.2

Do You Self-Disclose Differently to Your Male and Female Friends?

Instructions:

Think of a close male friend and a close female friend. Indicate for the topics listed below the degree to which you have disclosed to each person using the following scale:

Discussed not at all   0   1   2   3   4   *Discussed fully and completely*

Male Friend		**Female Friend**
_____	1. My personal habits.	_____
_____	2. Things I have done that I feel guilty about.	_____
_____	3. Things I wouldn't do in public.	_____
_____	4. My deepest feelings.	_____
_____	5. What I like and dislike about myself.	_____
_____	6. What is important to me in life.	_____
_____	7. What makes me the person I am.	_____
_____	8. My worst fears.	_____
_____	9. Things I have done that I am proud of.	_____
_____	10. My close relationships with other people.	_____
_____ Total score		Total score _____

You can determine your overall self-disclosure score for each of your friends by adding up the scores in the column. The higher the score, the greater the self-disclosure to the person. Is there an appreciable difference between these two scores? If there is a difference, does it correspond to what has been found in more systematic investigations of self-disclosure in intimate relationships?

or a woman who appeared to be extremely upset while flying in a plane (Derlega & Chaikin, 1976). The reason this individual was so upset was that his or her mother had just suffered a nervous breakdown. Noticing this agitation, the person sitting next to the individual inquired as to whether he or she was anxious about flying. In one condition, participants read that the individual concealed the problem by replying, "Yes, I guess I am. I haven't flown that much before." In another condition, the character in the story revealed the actual problem. After reading the story, participants were asked to estimate the character's degree of psychological adjustment. Results indicated that if the character was depicted as a man, he was considered to be more unstable if he disclosed his mother's real problem than if he concealed it. For a female character, the results were exactly opposite: not disclosing was judged more indicative of maladjustment. Male and female participants did not differ in their assessments. Both men and women considered the emotionally expressive male and the inexpressive female to be maladjusted. These results, and similar findings from other studies, suggest that one important reason men disclose less than women is that for them to reveal tender and vulnerable feelings—to let down their emotional guard—is to run the risk of inviting negative evaluations from both men and women (Chelune, 1976; Felmlee, 1999).

Before reading further, take a few minutes and complete the self-disclosure questionnaire in table 12.2. If possible, ask some of your male and female friends to complete it as well, so that you can informally test for some of the gender differences we have discussed concerning friendship self-disclosure.

PHYSICAL TOUCHING

Beyond verbal communication, men and women also differ in the degree to which they engage in physical contact with a same-sex friend (Felmlee, 1999). In North American culture, both heterosexual men and women view hugging and other forms of physical intimacy among men as less appropriate than among male-female and female-female pairings (Derlega et al., 2001). Generally, men are only encouraged to hug one another when they are involved in sporting events where expressions of physical intimacy are consistent with the masculine gender role (Mormon & Floyd, 1998). This injunction against male physical intimacy is not the norm in many European, Latin, African, and Middle Eastern cultures (Axtell, 1993; DiBaise & Gunnoe, 2004).

In one study investigating this physical touching taboo in the United States, Val Derlega and his colleagues (1989) asked friends and heterosexual dating partners to act out an imaginary scene where one person was greeting the other at the airport after returning from a trip. The greetings were photographed and later evaluated by judges for the intimacy of physical contact, ranging from no touch at all to combinations of hugging and kissing. As figure 12.4 shows, dating partners exhibited the highest levels of physical intimacy: all of them engaged in a combination of hugging and kissing. When friendship touching was analyzed, male friends employed significantly less touching than did either female friends or mixed-sex friends. Further investigation of participants' perceptions of physical touch indicated that men were more likely than women to interpret touching as an indication of sexual desire.

THE AVOIDANCE OF INTIMACY IN MALE FRIENDSHIPS

Why are male friendships less intimate than female friendships, and why is there this social injunction against men being emotionally expressive? A number of social scientists contend that avoidance of emotional expressiveness is due to males being socialized to conform to *heterosexual masculinity,* which entails valuing masculine traits related to power and control, while devaluing feminine traits related to the expression of tenderness and vulnerability (Brendan, 2002). As previously noted, men are most likely to conform to gender stereotypes and the norms surrounding heterosexual masculinity when in the company of other men. One important aspect of heterosexual masculinity involves the denigration of male homosexuality because it is perceived to be the antithesis of masculinity (Herek, 2000b). For a man to express warmth, nurturance, or caring toward another man is often interpreted as an indication of homosexuality (Derlega et al., 2001). Thus, being masculine requires men to avoid acting in ways that might indicate homosexuality, including ex-

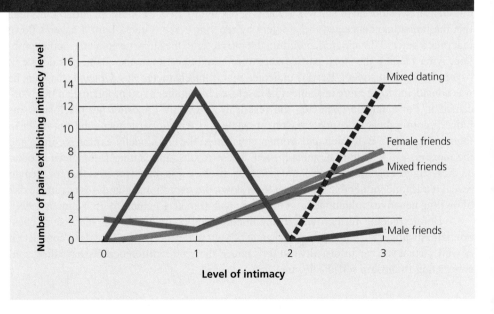

FIGURE 12.4

Gender Differences in Touching During Social Interaction

How do men and women differ with respect to touching when greeting a friend or dating partner? In North American cultures, physical intimacy is highest among dating partners, second highest among female friends and mixed-sex friends, and lowest among male friends. Have you observed and/or experienced such gender differences in your own life?

pressing warmth, tenderness, and affection in friendships with other men (Theodore & Basow, 2000).

The contemporary conception of masculinity as not encompassing tenderness and affection in male friendships is a fairly recent historical development in North American culture (Williams, 1992). According to historians, until the late nineteenth century, a man could express tender affection for an intimate male friend without fearing the disapproval of others (Rotundo, 1989). This all changed around the 1880s, when *homosexuality* and *heterosexuality* came to be defined as clearly distinct and nonoverlapping social roles. Masculinity was redefined to exclude "manly love" (Nardi, 1992a). As we move through the twenty-first century, the changes in gender roles may eventually lead men to feel less constrained in their expression of tenderness and affection toward other men. Until that time, however, male heterosexual friendships in the United States and Canada will generally lack the emotional intensity and gratification of the average female friendship.

Cross-Sex Heterosexual Friendships Gravitate to an "Intimacy Mean"

From our review of past research, we can conclude that women's friendships are typically more intimate and openly expressive than those of men. Yet what happens when men and women are friends? Roughly 40 percent of young men and 30 percent of young women have one or more cross-sex friends. In these friendships, there is a gravitation to the "intimacy mean." Men tend to be more emotionally open and self-disclosing than they are with their male friends, while women disclose less and are not as intimate as they are with their women friends (Monsour, 1997). Generally, heterosexual men believe their female friends provide more emotional support and security than their male friends, but not as much as women with whom they have romantic relationships. Women, on the other hand, do not perceive their cross-sex friendships as being that intimate, and they are likely to turn to female friends for highly personalized interaction (Wright & Scanlon, 1991).

Although cross-sex friendships are quite common, as in all friendships, similarity attracts. Heidi Reeder (2003) found that young adults who have a nontraditional gender-role orientation (masculine women and feminine men) have a higher proportion of cross-sex friendships than those with a traditional orientation (feminine women and masculine men). In other words, consistent with the matching hypothesis (chapter 11, p. 423), men and women are more likely to form friendships with the other sex when they have interests and personality traits that are traditionally associated with the other sex.

The biggest problem or challenge in cross-sex friendships is sexual tension (Werking, 1997). One-fourth of cross-sex friendship failures are due to problems caused by romantic and/or sexual desires, with men being more likely than women to experience such desires (Bleske-Rechek & Buss, 2001; Schneider & Kenny, 2000). This gender difference may occur because men not only tend to view sex as the primary means of achieving intimacy with women, but they also tend to misinterpret certain signs of affection (for example, physical touching) as indicating sexual desire (Haselton & Buss, 2000).

Although most cross-sex friendships do not have these problems, survey research by Walid Afifi and Sandra Faulkner (2000) suggest that half of all college students have engaged in sexual activity with an other-sex friend on at least one occasion, and one-third have engaged in sexual activity on multiple occasions. When sex occurs, it does not necessarily change the friendship into a romantic relationship, nor does it necessarily end the friendship. If the two parties freely discuss the sexual contact and can agree on what it means to their relationship, the experience is likely to build trust and confidence in the friend's intentions and feelings.

Additional research indicates that sexual contact is much more common among cross-sex friendships that are relatively new than among those that are of longer duration (Reeder, 2000). One possible explanation for this finding is that it reflects the natural decline in sexual passion that occurs over time in most sexually based relationships (see pp. 463–467 for a discussion of passionate love). A second possible reason why sexual contact is less common in longer-term friendships is that partners recognize that for them to preserve the

Friendship is love without wings.

George Gordon (Lord Byron), English poet, 1788–1824

Many people have cross-sex friendships. In such relationships, men are often more emotionally open and self-disclosing than they are with their male friends. In contrast, women tend to be less intimate than they are with their women friends. Why might these differences exist? What tends to be the biggest problem in cross-sex friendships?

friendship, sexual urges must decrease, or at least be safely regulated. Related to this explanation is a third explanation contending that the lower levels of sexual contact in longer-term friendships mainly reflect the fact that cross-sex friends who don't redirect their sexual attraction eventually define themselves as romantic partners and, thus, are no longer included in studies of friendship. As we await the insights from future research, we can say that cross-sex friendship is an important source of intimacy for both men and women, it may be more highly valued by men than women, and issues of sexuality often have to be managed and negotiated to sustain these relationships over time (Messman et al., 2000).

Gender Differences Disappear in Same-Sex Homosexual Friendships

Sexual orientation appears to play an important role in shaping the same-sex friendship patterns of men and women. Survey studies by Peter Nardi and Drury Sherrod (1994) find that, in contrast to heterosexuals, the same-sex friendships of gay men are as intimate as those of lesbians. This different same-sex friendship pattern among homosexuals and heterosexuals is partly due to heterosexual men avoiding intimacy in same-sex friendships out of fear of being labeled homosexual. Although many gay men are justifiably wary of expressing affection toward one another in heterosexual surroundings because of fear of assault, no such anxiety exists in the gay community. Another reason greater intimacy occurs in gay male friendships is that for both gay men and lesbians, gay friends are frequently viewed as family (Nardi, 1992c). This is so because their biological families often reject them or do not fully accept them as family members (Oswald, 2000). Faced with these intimacy roadblocks, many gay people turn to friendships for their emotional well-being. As a gay man explained:

> Friends become part of my extended family. A lot of us are estranged from our families because we're gay and our parents don't understand or don't want to understand. . . . I can't talk to them about my relationships. I don't go to them; I've finally learned my lesson: family is out. Now I've got a close circle of friends that I can sit and talk to about anything, I learned to do without the family. (Kurdek & Schmitt, 1987, p. 65)

Another difference between homosexual and heterosexual same-sex friendships is that sexual intimacy is much more likely in homosexual friendships. Just as sexual desires often become salient in heterosexual cross-sex friendships, they are a common issue in homosexual same-sex friendships. In both cases, the sexual orientation of the two people can conceivably lead to sexual activity and, thus, pose problems or challenges to the friendship. Nardi and Sherrod's (1994) survey research suggests that about two-thirds of gay men and about one-half of lesbians have had sexual contact with their same-sex "close" or "best" friend, which is comparable to the sexual contact level found in heterosexual cross-sex friendships. As in these heterosexual friendships, sex among homosexual same-sex friends is much more likely early in the relationship than later (Nardi, 1992b, 1992c), undoubtedly due to the same previously discussed psychological and/or physiological forces. Although more research is needed to better understand the social psychological dynamics underlying homosexual same-sex friendship, clearly it provides gay men and lesbians with a vital source of intimacy—and often a surrogate "family"—in a social environment that is often hostile toward their lifestyle.

SECTION SUMMARY

- Social penetration theory describes the development of relationships in terms of movement from superficial to more intimate levels of self-disclosure
- People from individualist cultures may self-disclose more than those from collectivist societies
- Women self-disclose more than men
- Same-sex heterosexual female friendships are more emotionally intimate than same-sex heterosexual male friendships
- The biggest problem in cross-sex friendships is sexual tension
- Same-sex friendships of gay men are as intimate as those of lesbians

ROMANTIC RELATIONSHIPS

About the time that my friends and I entered the fifth grade, we began to view girls as potential romantic partners. Being boys and having a history of doing things as a "pack," we often approached prepubescent romance as a group activity. Gathered in the basement of one of our houses, we would first discuss which girl in our class we would call on the phone, and then, which of us would be the group's offering to her. It was a simple game. Look up the phone number, make the call, ask the question, and then congratulate or tease the member of the group who had been either rejected or embraced (at this age, only in a social sense) by the girl on the other end of the line.

I believe myself that romantic love is the source of the most intense delight that life has to offer.

Bertrand Russell, British philosopher, 1872–1970

> "Hello, is this Marsha?"
> (Pause)
> "Never mind who this is. Listen, do you want to go with John Despins?"
> (Another pause, the length of which was positively correlated with impending rejection.)
> "What?! No?!!" (Then in a hurried attempt to save face for John, the caller turned the rejection on its head.) "Yeah, well he doesn't want to go with you either!"

To a certain degree, the collective esteem of the entire group rose slightly with each individual "phone embrace" and dipped a bit with each rejection. After all, it was an indication of our popularity as a group with the fifth-grade girls. If the girl said yes to our friend, perhaps one of her friends—maybe even the highly coveted Colleen McCash—would "go with" one of his lucky friends.

The psychological drama and tension generated in these early attempts at discovering where one stood in the minds of those who were confusingly and romantically coveted were played out in increasing degrees of sophistication in the coming years. Each time, psychological costs and rewards were riding on every attempt to secure the embrace of another. In the remaining sections of this chapter we turn our attention to the psychological nature of romantic love, and to the factors that foster and inhibit it.

Culture Shapes How We Think About Romantic Love

Although romantic love can be found in all recorded time periods, it has undergone numerous social transformations (Hatfield & Rapson, 2002). The ancient Greeks considered romantic love a form of madness that would "wound" you, and thus, the Greek god of love (Eros) was armed with a bow and a quiver of arrows. Romantic love was experienced almost exclusively outside of marriage and was more likely to be homosexual in nature rather than heterosexual (Bullough, 1976). During the Roman era, homosexual love—considered a "Greek vice"—gave way to heterosexual love. Yet the free-born Roman male's self-conception as a world conqueror led him to view romantic love as a game played outside of marriage. Keeping with this view of love as a game, the Romans were one of the first Western societies to institutionalize divorce (Gathorne-Hardy, 1981). Later, as Christianity became more entrenched as an institution within Roman society, sex came to be viewed as a corrupting influence, tolerated only in marriage. Romantic love was not highly valued. During the Middle Ages (A.D. 1000–1300), European aristocrats practiced courtly love. Romance was no longer a game, even though it still occurred outside of marriage. Courtly love was considered majestic and spiritual and, in theory, was never consummated (Murstein, 1974). It struck at first sight, conquered all, accepted no substitutes, and was a consuming passion of both agony and ecstasy.

Cross-cultural research indicates that associating romantic love with marriage typically occurs when people are free to choose their own partners (Rosenblatt & Cozby, 1972), although for centuries before and after courtly love, marriage was arranged by parents and based almost exclusively on political and property considerations. Beginning in the seventeenth and eighteenth centuries, as these more traditional considerations declined in importance, romantic love began to make some limited headway into marital arrangements (Stone, 1977). This new association of love and marriage first appeared in England but spread faster in the New World of North America, where social class considerations were not so rigidly defined. Although love was now considered possible—and perhaps even desirable—within marriage, early-twentieth-century marriage educators in America still counseled against basing marital choice on this "romantic impulse" (Burgess, 1926). The irrational nature of romantic love was believed to dangerously undermine what should be a very serious, prudent, and rational decision. However, as marriages became more egalitarian and more focused on mutual satisfaction, romance became even more attractive. With this increased desire for romance within marriage came a greater willingness to end marriages that had lost their romantic spark (Scanzoni, 1979).

Today, our Western conception of romantic love is an amalgam of past formulations. It is generally no longer considered a form of madness, but it is something many of us believe we "fall into" and cannot control. Love leads to happiness, but we can also be hurt in love. Love is possible both within and outside of marriage, and as we explore more fully in the next section, it can be either heterosexual or homosexual in nature.

HETEROSEXIST VIEWS OF ROMANTIC LOVE

Despite the fact that between 2 to 5 percent of the world's adult population is primarily or exclusively attracted to their own sex, until fairly recently virtually all research on romantic relationships focused on heterosexual dating and marriage (Gonsiorek & Weinrich, 1991). The lack of research on homosexual romantic relationships, coupled with heterosexist beliefs that denigrated homosexuality, allowed cultural stereotypes to shape social perceptions by creating myths about the gay lifestyle (Herek, 1991).

One of the main myths is that people who are gay drift from one sexual liaison to another and are unsuccessful in developing enduring, committed romantic relationships

FIGURE 12.5

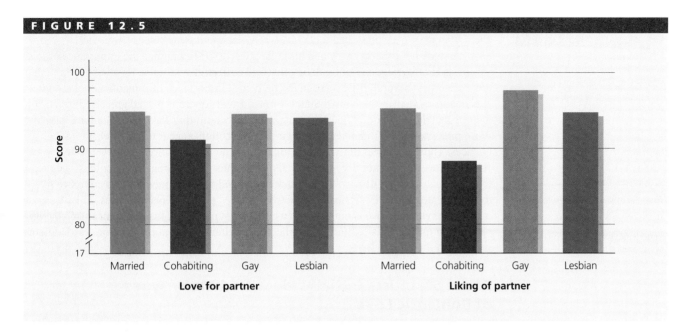

Expressed Love and Liking in Homosexual and Heterosexual Romantic Relationships

In a study of married, heterosexual cohabiting, gay, and lesbian monogamous couples, Kurdek and Schmitt (1986) obtained a liking and a loving score from each partner, which could range from a low of 17 to a high of 117. Higher scores indicated greater liking/loving. Results indicated that there were no differences in expressed love for one's partner between any of the different types of romantic relationships. In addition, the married, gay, and lesbian relationships expressed equally high amounts of liking of their partners. In contrast, heterosexual cohabiting couples had lower liking scores than the other couples. This study and others of its kind have dispelled the myth that gay couples are less capable of developing satisfying romantic relationships than are heterosexual couples.

(De Cecco, 1988). Yet actual surveys indicate that between 40 and 60 percent of gay men and between 45 and 80 percent of lesbians are currently in a steady relationship (Peplau et al., 1997). Gay and lesbian couples do break up more frequently than married couples, but this is also true of heterosexual couples who also don't have the formal institution of marriage to stabilize their relationships (Adams & Jones, 1997; Kurdek, 1998).

As you can see in figure 12.5, lesbians, gay men, and heterosexuals involved in monogamous romantic relationships all tend to score high on scales that evaluate liking and love for one's partner, and all tend to be equally well adjusted and satisfied (Eldridge & Gilbert, 1990; Kurdek & Schmitt, 1986). Based on our previous discussion of heterosexual men being less emotionally expressive, it isn't surprising to find that homosexual romantic love—especially lesbian love—tends to be *more* emotionally intimate than heterosexual love (Kurdek, 1997, 2003; Schreurs & Buunk, 1994). These findings indicate that, counter to cultural stereotypes, many lesbians and gay men establish lifelong partnerships, and the psychological dynamics in these relationships are more similar to than different from married heterosexual partnerships. Regardless of whether we are heterosexual or homosexual, our romantic relationships follow a similar psychological course and are influenced by many of the same personal, situational, and cultural factors.

INDIVIDUALIST VERSUS COLLECTIVIST VIEWS

In general, people from Western cultures view love as a positive experience. However, in a cross-cultural study of love, Philip Shaver and his coworkers (1991) found that not all contemporary cultures share this perspective. In fact, people of China have a more pessimistic outlook on romantic love than most Western cultures (Rothbaum & Tsang, 1998). Consistent with ancient traditions, most contemporary Chinese associate romance with sorrow, pain, and unfulfilled affection. What do they think of the Western view of love? They regard

Many years ago I chased a woman for almost two years, only to discover that her tastes were exactly like mine: we both were crazy about girls.

Groucho Marx, American comedian, 1895–1977

There is only one happiness in life, to love and be loved.

George Sand (pen name of Amandine Dupin), French novelist, 1804–1876

it as unrealistically optimistic. In a very real sense, how we experience love speaks volumes about who we are as individuals and what we are as a culture (Dion & Dion, 1991).

A study by Robert Levine and his colleagues (1995) examined the importance of love as a basis for marriage in both individualist and collectivist cultures. Results indicated that there are cross-cultural differences in the perceived importance of romantic love. Individualist countries such as the United States, England, and Australia placed great importance on love in marriage, while collectivist countries such as India, Pakistan, Thailand, and the Philippines rated it as much less important. These beliefs appear to have behavioral consequences. Those countries placing great importance on love had higher marriage rates, lower fertility rates, and higher divorce rates. Other studies indicate that while collectivists tend to select mates who will best "fit in" to the extended family, individualists are more likely to select mates who are physically attractive or have "exciting" personalities. This does not mean, however, that love is not a part of a collectivist marriage. Instead, it means that, compared with individualist cultures, in collectivist cultures it is more common for people to marry, and then fall in love.

Social Scientists Initially Identified Many Types of Romantic Love

Acknowledging that there is more than one way to experience love, in the 1970s social scientists began developing multidimensional theories that identified various forms or styles of love. For example, Canadian sociologist John Lee's (1977) *typology of love styles* identified three primary styles of love—*eros* (passionate love), *ludus* (game-playing love), and *storge* (friendship love). Lee contended that these primary love styles could be combined to form three secondary love styles: *pragma* (pragmatic love), which contains storge and ludus elements; *mania* (possessive love), which is a compound of eros and ludus; and *agape* (altruistic love), which combines elements of eros and storge. According to Lee, the six different love styles are equally valid ways of loving, and it is the relationship that is styled, not the lover. Thus, one could have a romantic relationship that is intense and passionate (eros), and then develop one that starts as a friendship and slowly leads to a lasting commitment (storge). Clyde and Susan Hendrick (1986, 2003) developed questionnaires to assess Lee's different love styles. Table 12.3 lists sample items for each style.

Similar to Lee, in the 1980s Robert Sternberg (1986, 1997) proposed a *triangular theory of love* in which seven different types of love consisted of different degrees of passion, intimacy, and commitment. Although Sternberg's and Lee's multidimensional theories were helpful in providing a framework to examine romantic love, later empirical attempts to pin down a specific set of love categories were not entirely successful (Fletcher et al., 2000; Masuda, 2003). However, the two types of love that have been consistently found in all studies and that appear to be the most fundamental are *passionate love* and *companionate love* (Hendrick & Hendrick, 2003). Let us examine what social psychologists have learned about these two forms of romantic love.

For Better or For Worse® by Lynn Johnston

TABLE 12.3

Measuring Six Basic Styles of Love

Listed below are sample items from Hendrick and Hendrick's love scale, which was designed to measure the six styles of love identified by Lee (1977). Read through the various items and think about your current or past relationships. Which style or styles characterize each of these relationships? According to Lee, people could experience many different styles of love during their lives.

Eros

1. My lover and I were attracted to each other immediately after we first met.
2. Our lovemaking is very intense and satisfying.
3. My lover fits my ideal standards of physical beauty/handsomeness.

Ludus

1. I try to keep my lover a little uncertain about my commitment to him/her.
2. I have sometimes had to keep two of my lovers from finding out about each other.
3. I enjoy playing the "game of love" with a number of different partners.

Storge

1. It is hard to say exactly when my lover and I fell in love. (Our friendship merged gradually into love over time.)
2. Love is really a deep friendship, not a mysterious, mystical emotion.
3. My most satisfying love relationships have developed from good friendships.

Pragma

1. I consider what a person is going to become in life before I commit myself to him/her.
2. I try to plan my life carefully before choosing a lover.
3. A main consideration in choosing a lover is how he/she reflects on my family.

Mania

1. Sometimes I get so excited about being in love that I can't sleep.
2. When I am in love, I have trouble concentrating on anything else.
3. If my lover ignores me for a while, I sometimes do stupid things to get his/her attention back.

Agape

1. I would rather suffer myself than let my lover suffer.
2. I cannot be happy unless I place my lover's happiness before my own.
3. I would endure all things for the sake of my lover.

Passionate Love Can Be Triggered by Excitation Transfer

Joyce and Louis have been dating for three weeks and are passionately in love. The last thing Joyce thinks about before falling asleep and the first thing she thinks about upon awakening is her Louis. Across town, Louis is trying to stay awake while he feigns interest in his coworker's latest design project. The previous night, he tossed and turned for hours in bed, being both exhilarated by his love for Joyce and riddled with anxiety that she might not feel the same toward him. Now, in less than five hours, twenty-six minutes, and thirty-two seconds he will see her again.

Does this sound familiar? Do Louis and Joyce's feelings bring a pleasant, perhaps even pained, smile of recognition to your face? If so, you are a member of that not-so-elite group who since time immemorial experienced something deliciously joyful and painful: passionate love. According to Elaine Hatfield (1988), **passionate love** is "a state of intense

When love is not madness, it is not love.

Spanish proverb

Passionate Love

A state of intense longing for union with another.

FIGURE 12.6

Love Activated in the Brain

When neuroscientists study the brain activity of people experiencing passionate love as they gaze at photos of their loved ones they find increased activity in the caudate nucleus. This primitive part of the brain processes dopamine and plays a key role in the "reward and pleasure system."

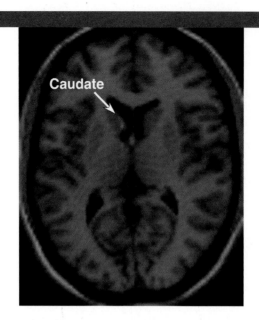

Caudate

When you are beside me my heart sings; a branch it is, dancing, dancing before the Wind Spirit in the moon of strawberries. When you frown upon me, beloved, my heart grows dark. . . . the shadows of clouds darken, then with your smile comes the sun.

Anonymous Ojibway poem

longing for union with another" (p. 193). It is a type of love that we feel with our bodies— a warm-tingling, body rush, stomach-in-a-knot kind of love. Indeed, neuroscientists have found evidence that passionate love produces changes in brain chemistry, which causes focused attention, concentrated motivation to attain a reward, and a sense of giddiness that is primarily fueled by one of nature's most powerful stimulants, dopamine (Barber, 2002; Kurup & Kurup, 2003).

Brain scans of romantically involved individuals who report high levels of passionate love for their partner find that many brain areas become active when they view photos of their beloved (Bartels & Zeki, 2000; Fisher, 2004). Compared with the brain activity produced when they view photos of friends, love-struck individuals experience increased activity in the *caudate nucleus*, a large, C-shaped region that sits near the center of the brain (see figure 12.6). This very primitive brain area not only directs bodily movement, it also plays a key role in the brain's "reward and pleasure system." In addition to activation of the caudate nucleus, passionate lovers also experience increased activity in other regions of the reward system, including areas of the septum and a brain region that is activated when people eat chocolate. Additional studies indicate that when we believe that our passionate love may be reciprocated, regions of the prefrontal cortex responsible for higher-order thinking join in the pursuit, planning tactics, exercising proper restraint, and monitoring our progress toward the goal of romantic bliss (Fisher, 1998, 2004).

Passionate love is experienced most intensely during the early stages of a romantic relationship. According to Ellen Berscheid and Hatfield (1974), passionate love is produced, or at least enhanced, during these first romantic encounters due to a rather interesting transference of arousal from one stimulus to another. As a way to introduce you to this phenomenon, let me tell you how I met my wife.

In the winter of 1982 I had recently arrived in Bloomington, Indiana, to begin a three-year postdoctoral fellowship at Indiana University. One evening I attended a modern dance concert. When I purchased my ticket, the ticketer ripped it in two and gave me half, instructing me to remember the number on my ticket stub because it would later be used as part of the performance. Indeed. The dance company's performance pieces were extremely avant-garde, and just before beginning the last one, they brought a hat on stage filled with all the ticket stubs. If your ticket stub number was called, you were supposed to walk on stage and become part of the performance. Upon hearing this, I instinctively sunk lower in my seat. Ever since my sister had tried to teach me to dance the "twist" and the "pony" in the early 1960s—while laughing uncontrollably—I have always felt self-conscious on the dance floor (an excellent example of classical conditioning). As luck would have it, my number was called by one of the performers, a tall attractive woman, with long blonde hair. Maybe this wouldn't be so bad after all, I thought as I walked onstage. But what did she want me to do? You guessed it, learn a complicated dance step in front of the entire audience. My heart began to beat rapidly and my face became flushed, but I concentrated as best I could as she led me through the steps. Halfway through the routine, in the middle of a big leg swing, my brand-new reversible belt buckle popped completely off my belt and shot across the dance floor! The dancer laughed, the audience roared. I was mortified. Somehow I finished the dance routine and sat down. Later, whenever I would see this dancer around town, my heart would race and my face would become flushed as I relived "the incident." She never took notice of me during these near encounters, but now I certainly had her number. What were my feelings toward her? Attraction coupled with anxiety. Eight months later, I finally introduced myself when our paths crossed again, and we began dating. A year and a half later we were married.

In explaining the initial encounter with my future wife, social psychological research suggests that my acute embarrassment may have actually sparked a romantic attraction toward her. Drawing on Schachter's (1964) two-factor theory of emotion described in chapter 11 (p. 430), Berscheid and Hatfield (1974) contend that passionate love is likely to occur when three conditions are met. The first condition is that you must learn what love is and come to expect that you will eventually fall in love. Second, you must meet someone who fits your preconceived beliefs of an appropriate lover. And third, while in this person's presence, you must experience a state of physiological arousal. How does this arousal become passionate love? Recall that Schachter's theory of emotion asserts that people use external cues to label their arousal states. When arousal occurs in the presence of an appropriate love object, you may well interpret this arousal as romantic and sexual attraction. Dolf Zillmann (1984) has called this psychological process—in which arousal caused by one stimulus is

Capilano Canyon Suspension Bridge, Vancouver, British Columbia. Dutton and Aron (1974) tested the romantic attribution of arousal hypothesis on this bridge, 230 feet above the Capilano River. Their research is discussed on p. 466.

Excitation Transfer

A psychological process in which arousal caused by one stimulus is transferred and added to arousal elicited by a second stimulus.

We don't believe in rheumatism and true love until after the first attack.

Marie von Ebner-Eschenbach

transferred and *added* to arousal elicited by a second stimulus—**excitation transfer.** In such instances, our increased romantic interest can be traced to the transfer of arousal from one source to the object of our newfound affections.

Donald Dutton and Arthur Aron (1974) tested this romantic attribution of arousal hypothesis on two bridges at a popular tourist site in North Vancouver, British Columbia. One of the bridges, the Capilano Canyon Suspension Bridge, is 5 feet wide, 450 feet long, and constructed of wooden boards attached to wire cables that span the Capilano River at a height of 230 feet. This bridge is not for those with a fear of heights—it wobbles as you walk on it and it sways in the wind. Nearby, there is another bridge that does not set your heart aflutter. It is solidly built out of heavy wood and stands only ten feet above a small, peaceful stream.

In their experiment, whenever an unaccompanied male began to walk across either bridge, he was approached by a male or female research assistant and asked to write an imaginative story in response to a picture while standing on the bridge. The assistant also told the man that if he wanted to receive information about the study's results he could give her (or him) a phone call. Dutton and Aron found that the men who were approached by a woman on the suspension bridge told stories with the highest sexual imagery of all the experimental groups. As you can see in figure 12.7, these men were also more likely than any of the other groups to call the assistant. Apparently, they had attributed their arousal, which was undoubtedly principally caused by the swaying bridge, to the female assistant.

Although this is one interpretation of the results, can you think of another possibility? Perhaps the men who chose to walk across the dangerous-looking suspension bridge were more adventurous, both sexually and physically, than the men who chose the safer bridge. If this were the case, then it was their more adventurous personalities that caused both the bridge choice and the phoning of the female assistant. Dutton and Aron ruled out this possibility by repeating the experiment, but this time using only the suspension bridge. Half of the men were asked to write their stories as they stood on the bridge, while the others were approached after they had completed their walk and had calmed down. As expected, increased sexual imagery and phone calls were only associated with the condition in which men were approached as they crossed the bridge. Excitation transfer, not adventurous personalities, explained the men's actions.

FIGURE 12.7

Sexual Attraction Under Conditions of High Anxiety

A male or female research assistant asked men to write an imaginative story in response to a picture while either standing on a solid 10-foot-high bridge or a wobbly 230-foot-high bridge. Men who were approached by the female assistant on the wobbly bridge were much more likely to later call her, supposedly to learn more about the study's findings. These men's imaginative stories also contained the highest sexual imagery of all the groups. How do these findings support the misattribution of arousal hypothesis?

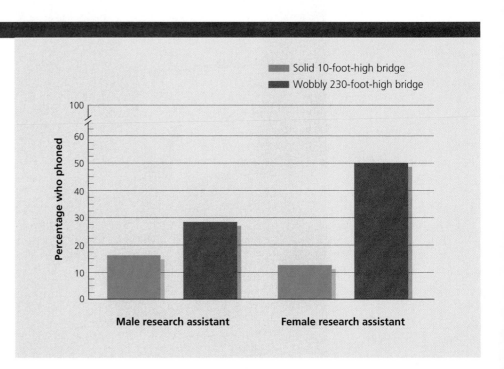

The two-factor theory of emotion emphasizes the role our thoughts and beliefs play in accounting for our states of arousal. Yet other social psychologists suggest that a different mechanism may explain why fear and anxiety intensifies romantic feelings (Kenrick & Cialdini, 1977; Riordan & Tedeschi, 1983). Referring to the anxiety-affiliation studies discussed in chapter 11, Douglas Kenrick and Robert Cialdini (1977) proposed that in some circumstances the presence of others tends to calm anxious people. They argued that the reason the men on the suspension bridge were attracted to the female assistant was not because they thought she aroused them, but because she in fact calmed them down. The men associated her with a reduction of anxiety, and that led to greater liking for her. Therefore, it is not transferred arousal that increases romantic feelings, but it is the emotional "comfort" people provide that increases their attractiveness.

This explanation of romantic attraction, although providing an alternative interpretation of the Dutton and Aron findings, soon ran into trouble based on the findings of another series of arousal studies. In one experiment, male participants' arousal was manipulated by having them run in place for either two minutes or fifteen seconds (White et al., 1981). As soon as the men completed this exercise, they watched a videotape of a woman they expected to meet sometime later. In one condition, the woman was made to look and sound attractive, while in another condition she appeared unattractive. After watching the videotape, the men rated the woman's attractiveness.

One thing to keep in mind about this experiment is that the men who participated did not experience any anxiety or fear, and thus Kenrick and Cialdini's arousal reduction explanation would predict no differences due to this exercise-induced arousal. Yet this arousal did heighten the men's emotional responses toward the target woman. Men who had exercised for two minutes evaluated the physically attractive woman as more attractive and the physically unattractive woman as less attractive than those who had exercised for only fifteen seconds. These findings suggest that arousal from a nonsexual stimulus can intensify a person's initial emotional reaction to a potential romantic partner, be it either positive or negative.

In a meta-analysis of thirty-three experiments, Craig Foster and his coworkers (1998) confirmed that excitation transfer does influence attractiveness. They also found that this effect is strongest when the source of arousal is ambiguous, but it can occur even when people know the person to whom they are attending does not primarily cause their arousal. In other words, simply being aroused—regardless of its source—facilitates whatever is the most natural response in that situation. If the target person is good-looking and reasonably meets our criteria for a romantic partner, we automatically become more attracted, and the attraction is stronger if the source of arousal is ambiguous. However, if the person is not good-looking or in some other way is an unsuitable romantic partner, we become less attracted.

Finally, one recent study found that amorous excitation transfer toward a stranger is less likely to occur when we are with our romantic partner. In this study, researchers approached people at amusement parks as they were either waiting to begin or as they had just finished a roller-coaster ride (Meston & Frohlich, 2003). Participants were shown a photo of a person of the other sex who was of average attractiveness and asked to evaluate the individual on attractiveness and dating desirability. They were also asked to rate the attractiveness of the person sitting next to them on the roller coaster. Consistent with the excitation transfer hypothesis, women and men who were not riding with a romantic partner rated the photo of the other-sex stranger higher in attractiveness and dating desirability immediately after finishing the ride as compared to just prior to taking the ride. For those who were riding with a romantic partner, there were no significant rating differences between persons entering and exiting the ride. These results not only confirm previous findings, but they also raise the possibility that the relatively automatic arousal-attraction effect becomes "deactivated"—or perhaps we are less conscious of its effect—when we are with a current romantic partner.

For now, the lesson to be learned from all these studies is that when our ticket is pulled out of the hat of romance, it may not matter whether our romantic feelings are initially triggered by excitation transfer or "the real thing," but we'd better hope that our potential romantic partner's initial reaction toward us is one of attraction rather than repulsion, for excitation transfer may heighten either to equal degrees.

Will he always love me? I cannot read his heart. This morning my thoughts are as disordered as my black hair.

Harikawa, Japanese poet, 1135–1165

I am your clay. You are my clay. In life we share a single quilt. In death we will share our coffin.

Kuan Tao-sheng, Chinese poet and painter, 1262–1319

As a romantic relationship grows, the emotional highs and lows of passionate love subside. What then predicts relationship satisfaction and longevity is the couple's degree of companionate love.

Companionate Love Is More Stable and Enduring Than Passionate Love

Let's consider again the romantic relationship of Joyce and Louis. Yes, they did become more certain about each other's love. Yet as time has passed, the hot flames of passion have cooled to warm embers. Having grown up watching movie stars convulse with passion whenever they embrace on the silver screen, Joyce and Louis are disillusioned to discover that the intensity of their feelings no longer matches Hollywood's depiction of love. They feel very close, like best buddies, but the passion ebbs and flows. They wonder to themselves, "Is this what love becomes?" Social psychologists investigating the course of romantic relationships might reply, "Yes, in most cases, this is what becomes of romantic love . . . if you're lucky." Why is this so?

One reason the emotional roller-coaster ride of early love slows over time to a more smooth and steady experience is the fact that passion generally burns itself out. Passionate love is considered to be a relatively short-lived type of love, more typical of the early stages of a romantic relationship when one's partner's love is less certain (Brehm, 1988). Indeed, passionate love thrives on the thrill and uncertainty of winning over another's affections. As we settle into a romantic relationship, the emotional freshness and uncertainty of passionate love is replaced by a more certain and dependable type of love—if love survives at all.

In defining this less impassioned, more enduring **companionate love,** Hatfield (1988) states that it is "the affection we feel for those with whom our lives are deeply entwined" (p. 205). Companionate love exists between close friends as well as between lovers. It develops out of a sense of certainty in each other's love and respect, and a feeling of genuine mutual understanding (Sprecher, 1999).

Another difference between passionate love and companionate love is the beliefs that one has about one's partner. In the early stages of romantic relationships, when passions run high, lovers tend to see their partners through rose-colored glasses (Brehm, 1988). Their partners are "perfect," the "ideal man or woman," their "dream come true." As passion fades and couples develop companionate love based on mutual understanding, this idealization of one's beloved often gives way to a more realistic view. Yet, as we will discuss more fully later in the chapter (p. 473), although companionate love is a more reality-based love, successful and happy romantic partners are those who tend to see each other's imperfections in the best possible light.

Evolutionary psychologists propose that sex-driven passionate love and commitment-driven companionate love evolved to meet different human needs (Diamond, 2003; Fisher, 1998, 2004). According to this theory, sexual desire is governed by the *sexual mating system,* in which the goal is to sexually reproduce and thereby pass one's genes on to the next generation. In contrast, companionate love is governed by the *attachment system,* in which the goal is to establish and maintain a strong emotional bond between two people. As discussed earlier, attachment is a part of our evolutionary heritage that developed to foster childrearing and maximize the newborn's survival. Likewise, the attachment bond that develops between two parents in companionate love also ensures the survival of offspring. Parents who love each other are more likely to stay together to raise their children, and there is strength in numbers. According to this evolutionary perspective, then, the sexual desire typical of passionate love fuels the sexual mating system, ensuring that a new generation is born into this world. In turn, the sharing and commitment typical of companionate love fuels the attachment system, ensuring that enough members of the new generation will survive childhood.

Women and Men May Differ in Their Experience of Love

Although I have described the sexual desire associated with passionate love as preceding the strong emotional bonding associated with companionate love, there is evidence that women and men differ in the degree to which their experience of romantic love adheres to this pattern (Rose & Zand, 2000). Would it surprise you to learn that women appear more likely than

Companionate Love

The affection we feel for those with whom our lives are deeply entwined.

To be in love is merely to be in a state of perpetual anesthesia—to mistake an ordinary young woman for a goddess.

H. L. Mencken, U.S. social critic, 1880–1956

men to feel sexually attracted toward others only after feeling romantically attracted to them? Or to pose this question somewhat differently, would it surprise you to learn that, in regard to love, men may be more driven by their passions and women may be more driven by their affections?

When college students were asked what they thought caused sexual desire, both sexes strongly agreed that the causes were often different for women and men (Peplau & Garnets, 2000; Regan et al., 2000). The most widely endorsed causes of female sexual desire were interpersonal experiences related to companionate love, whereas the most widely endorsed causes of male desire were biological processes and a physical "need" for sex. Thus, it appears that women tend to emphasize emotional intimacy as more of a necessity for sexuality than men. The same gender difference exists among homosexual adults. Like heterosexual women, lesbians are less likely than gay and heterosexual men to desire or engage in casual sex (Peplau et al., in press).

In thinking about these gender differences within the contexts of the sexual mating system and the attachment system, men appear more focused than women on the sexual mating aspect of this process that we identify as passionate love, whereas women are more focused than men on the attachment aspect that we identify as companionate love. For women more than men, the goal of sex is intimacy, and the best context for pleasurable sex is a committed relationship. For men, this is less true (Peplau, 2003). Of course, this does not mean that women are not interested in casual sex and men do not seek committed romantic relationships. It simply means that gender differences in motivational tendencies regarding sex and intimacy appear to exist. However, these are only tendencies, and many women and men do not fit these general patterns.

But wait a second. Over the years, a number of studies suggest that in some ways heterosexual men have a more romantic view of love than heterosexual women (Hobart, 1958; Spaulding, 1970; Sprecher & Toro-Morn, 2002). That is, men are more likely to believe in love at first sight, in love as the basis for marriage and for overcoming obstacles, and to believe that their romantic partners and their relationships will be perfect (Hendrick et al., 1984). True to these beliefs, other studies indicate that men tend to fall in love faster and fall out of love more slowly than women (Dion & Dion, 1985). They also are less likely than women to break up a premarital romance (Fletcher, 2002; Hill et al., 1979). This does not mean that women are unromantic. Women are typically at least as emotionally involved as their partners once they fall in love. In fact, they are more likely than men to report feeling intense romantic sensations such as euphoria and giddiness for their partner, and to have more vivid memories of past romantic relationships (Dion & Dion, 1973; Harvey et al., 1986). In assessing these findings, it appears that men are more eager to fall in love than women, but once a man and a woman take the plunge, the woman's emotional expressiveness is at least equal to that of her partner's. If this indeed is the way men and women typically approach romance, the next question comes begging. Why is it that men appear very willing to fall in love, while women initially take a more cautious approach? Further, how do these differences relate to the already discussed gender differences in the experience of passionate and companionate love?

In keeping with our previous analysis, evolutionary theorists contend that the different approaches to love that men and women exhibit are principally due to the different investment the two sexes have in the results of sexual bonding, namely, the children that are born (Buss, 1995; Kenrick & Simpson, 1997). To maximize the probability that his genes will live on in future generations, it is to a man's advantage to establish sexual intimacy as quickly as possible in a relationship and to have frequent sexual encounters with many different women. Sparking passionate love is the means to this end. If a man can establish sexual intimacy early in a relationship, he could theoretically court one woman after another and therefore be a big winner in reproductive fitness. For a woman, a more discriminating approach is needed in choosing a mate because she has a limited number of eggs that can be fertilized during her time of reproduction. This biological limitation means the best strategy for women is to forestall passionate feelings, and instead, carefully judge their potential partners' strengths and weaknesses so they can identify men with the best genes. Thus, according to evolutionary

Rank creates its rules: A woman is asked about her husband, a man is asked about his rank.

From the Palace of Nefertari, 1554–1070 B.C.

Marriage, to women as to men, must be a luxury, not a necessity; an incident of life, not all of it. And the only possible way to accomplish this great change is to accord to women equal power in the making, shaping and controlling of the circumstances of life.

Susan B. Anthony, U.S. women's rights pioneer, 1820–1906

theorists, it is adaptive for men to emphasize passion and fall in love quickly, while the female evolutionary injunction is to move slowly in matters of love and emphasize commitment.

Although the evolutionary approach provides a plausible explanation for why men fall in love quickly while women are more cautious, how might it explain the fact that men are more reluctant than women to end a romantic relationship? From an evolutionary perspective, it might seem to make more sense for men to fall in and out of love quickly, because such a strategy of numerous, short romantic relationships will maximize their chances of passing their genes on to future generations. One possible explanation offered by evolutionary theorists about why men fall out of love more slowly than women is that they have less to lose in a romantic relationship. Because they don't have to worry about a ticking biological clock and the risks of pregnancy, they can waste more time than women in a relationship that is going nowhere.

In contrast to this evolutionary explanation's focus on genetic predispositions, the sociocultural perspective highlights cultural practices and the social distribution of power. According to sociocultural theorists, in most cultures around the world men and women are traditionally born with different social statuses, with men's *ascribed* status being considerably higher than that of women (Howard et al., 1987). Due to this cultural practice, young men tend to have greater expectations about their social and economic security than young women. Men may therefore feel they can afford to let their emotions and passions rule their mate selection: their status will be determined by them alone, and not their partner's status. On the other hand, being aware of the sexual inequality in their culture, women might be more likely to believe that their future status will be determined more by their mates' status than their own. Women may therefore believe they cannot afford the luxury of only following their emotions and may adopt a more pragmatic approach to love. This sociocultural explanation is consistent with the data presented in chapter 11 indicating that men place more importance on physical attractiveness in choosing a partner, while women emphasize social status.

Similarly, the sociocultural perspective further suggests that heterosexual men may fall in love quickly and out of love slowly because they are starved for intimacy due to their inability to express love and tenderness to their male friends. As discussed earlier, because males are socialized to value heterosexual masculinity, their same-sex friendships tend to lack intimacy. Therefore, often the only outlet they have to express warmth, tenderness, and deep affection is in a romantic relationship with a woman. This greater dependence on romantic relationships for emotional support is true for both married and unmarried hetero-sexual men (Tschann, 1988). Thus, it may be that heterosexual men tend to fall in love more quickly and be less willing to end a romantic relationship because they place all their emo-tional "eggs" in this romantic basket. In contrast, women are more likely to spread their emotional eggs around, placing a number of them in their same-sex friendships.

Although I have been contrasting the evolutionary and cultural viewpoints, a grow-ing number of social scientists believe that these two perspectives may often complement—rather than compete with—each other (Schaller, 1997). Cultural explanations of why women and men differ in their approach to and experience of love emphasize the different social roles and positions of power that the two sexes traditionally hold in society. In other words, they focus on how existing social conditions differentially influence the thinking and decision making of women and men regarding love. Yet what are the origins of these gen-der roles and cultural status systems? Evolutionary explanations focus on how these differ-ences might have initially arisen due to evolutionary selection pressures. Perhaps the ultimate "best" explanation for gender differences in love may describe how selection pres-sures that operated in our prehuman ancestors shaped certain patterns of social behavior, leaving modern women and men with certain *capacities* to possibly react differently to love. Yet the degree to which women and men actually manifest these inherited capacities may well be decided by current social and environmental forces (Malach, 2001). In other words, culture and social learning may either enhance or override these inherited capacities.

SECTION SUMMARY

- Cultural and historical views of romance vary
- Two types of romantic love consistently found in all studies are passionate love and companionate love
- Passionate love is a relatively short-lived type of romantic love, more typical of the early stages of romance, when one's partner's love is less certain
- Companionate love is a slower developing and more enduring type of romantic love that develops out of a sense of certainty in each other's love and respect
- Sex-driven passionate love and commitment-driven companionate love may have evolved to meet different human needs
- Cultural and/or evolutionary forces may explain why women and men often differ in their experience of love

WILL LOVE ENDURE?

More than one million divorces occur each year in the United States, and more than half of all marriages end in divorce (U.S. Bureau of the Census, 1998). Outside of marriage, the mortality rate of romantic relationships is even higher. Although the odds that love will en-dure are not good, we all know people who have built loving and satisfying relationships lasting many years. In this section we examine some of the factors that contribute to satis-faction and conflict in romance.

Partners Are Satisfied When the Ratio Between Their Rewards and Costs Are Similar

As stated in chapter 11, social exchange theory is based on the assumption that all relation-ships are like economic bargains in which each party tries to maximize their rewards while minimizing their costs. Although intimate relationships tend to be based on attention to other people's needs rather than one's own, it would be naive to believe that once people fall in love they cease to consider their relationship rewards and costs. Indeed, one important factor determining whether a romantic relationship will endure is the perception the partners have about what they give to and receive from each other. How are these rewards and costs tabulated?

One theory that provides a sensible explanation for how rewards and costs are analyzed in an intimate relationship is a special type of exchange model known as **equity theory** (Adams, 1965). This theory contends that people in a romantic relationship don't try to maximize their rewards and minimize their costs but, instead, are most satisfied when the *ratio* between the rewards and costs is similar for both partners. If one partner receives more rewards from the relationship but also makes greater contributions to it, the relationship is still equitable.

For the sake of illustration, consider again our imaginary couple, Joyce and Louis, who are now married and have a young baby. Joyce has put her career on hold to stay home, and despite the drudgery of household duties, she derives great pleasure in witnessing her child's development. Regarding Louis's perceptions, his career is advancing nicely, but it keeps him from his family for extended periods. Yet overall, he too is still pleased with their marriage. Employing some arbitrary numbers to describe these costs and rewards, let's say that Joyce's rewards equal 40, and Louis's benefits amount to 25. Even though Joyce receives more relationship rewards than Louis, the relationship is equitable because her costs are higher: 32 to Louis's 20. As you can see, the basic equation suggests a balanced or equitable relationship:

$$\frac{40}{32} \quad = \quad \frac{25}{20} \quad = \quad \frac{5}{4}$$

Joyce's ratio Louis' ratio Relationship ratio

If these two ratios were not equal, equity theory would predict that both partners would become distressed and would try to restore balance. How would this distress be manifested? The partner who is *overbenefited* should feel guilty about the inequity, while the one who is *underbenefited* should experience anger and depression. Research indicates that inequity does indeed produce these negative emotions in both dating and married couples (Gleason et al., 2003; Hatfield et al., 1982; Schafer & Keith, 1980). However, although people who are overbenefited tend to feel guilty, they generally are very satisfied and contented with the relationship. This is not the case for the underbenefited. Their anger and depression cause a great deal of dissatisfaction with the relationship (Sprecher, 1992). Given the stress that this inequity produces, it is not surprising that inequitable relationships are less likely to endure (Walster et al., 1978).

Self-Esteem Can Both Facilitate and Undermine Romantic Love

Beyond the weighing of relationship costs and rewards, how is our capacity for success in romance affected by our feelings of self-worth? A commonly held belief is that self-love is a necessary precondition for loving others. For example, Nathaniel Branden, a writer of popular self-esteem books, specifically states that "If you do not love yourself, you will be unable to love others" (Branden, 1994, pp. 7–8). Is this true?

Based on our discussion of attachment styles, this claim appears misleading. There is little evidence that people with high self-esteem are more capable of loving others than those with low self-esteem (Campbell & Baumeister, 2001). Indeed, some studies find that people with low self-esteem have more intense experiences of love than those with high self-esteem, although this love is often fed by insecurity, such as that found among people with a preoccupied attachment style (Dion & Dion, 1975; Hendrick & Hendrick, 1986).

Self-esteem may not be related to the capacity to love, but it is related to loving in a way that maintains intimacy. Those with low self-esteem often doubt the strength of their partners' love and tend to constantly seek reassurance from loved ones (Joiner et al., 1992; Murray et al., 2001). This emotional neediness can prove burdensome to a romantic partner and thus may cause problems in the relationship. Therefore, low self-esteem may at times be harmful to relationship health. However, research also suggests that some forms of high self-esteem can harm romantic relationships (Schuetz, 1998). For instance, indi-

Equity Theory

The theory that people are most satisfied in a relationship when the ratio between rewards and costs is similar for both partners.

viduals with unstable high self-esteem (see chapter 3, p. 81) tend to respond to relationship problems with jealousy and even violence, especially when their self-esteem is threatened (Baumeister et al., 1996). On the other hand, people identified as *narcissists*—meaning those with grandiose self-concepts, feelings of superiority, and a strong need for power and acclaim—view love as a game and are fickle, selfish, and insensitive lovers (Campbell et al., 2002). Together, these studies suggest that there is no simple relationship between self-esteem and the durability of romantic relationships. Relationship intimacy can be threatened both by the type of low self-esteem that requires constant emotional reassurance, and by certain types of high self-esteem that induce either hostility when challenged or selfish gamesmanship. Returning to the previously discussed attachment studies (pp. 447–451), the type of self-esteem that is best suited to foster intimacy is that possessed by people with secure attachment styles: self-love that is stable and sufficiently strong to handle relationship conflict in a constructive manner (Morrison et al., 1997).

Perceiving Partners in the Best Possible Light Leads to Satisfying Relationships

My parents have been married for more than fifty-five years. For me, they epitomize the happily married couple, and I use their photo on page 467 to illustrate companionate love. Over the years, one thing that I have noticed about my parents' love is how it seems to be partly based on *positive illusions.* Example: Although I believe my mother is a truly wonderful person, the way my father describes her would lead you to conclude that she is simultaneously being considered for both sainthood and "Ms. Universe." With apologies to my mother, the questions this example begs are the following: Are my father's embellishments of my mother's virtues a healthy ingredient in their relationship? Does it promote a happier marriage?

For many years, most psychologists asserted that lasting satisfaction in romantic relationships depends on people understanding their partners' real strengths and weaknesses (Brickman, 1987; Swann et al., 1994). Although it is hard to argue against the benefits of an occasional good dose of reality, a number of studies suggest that we have a need to perceive our romantic relationships as being better than others' (Gagné & Lydon, 2001; Sanderson & Evans, 2001). Yet how can we satisfy this need if we insist on scrutinizing our partner's flaws? The answer to this question may be that, if we want happiness in love, we should allow our desire to feel good about our romantic relationships to dominate our desire to critically analyze relationship imperfections (Rusbult et al., 2000; Sedikides et al., 1998). Just as there is a *self-serving bias* that leads people with high self-esteem to see themselves in the best possible light (see chapter 4, pp. 126–127), people in happy romantic relationships tend to attribute their partners' positive behaviors to dispositional causes ("their wonderful personality") and their negative behaviors to situational factors ("a bad day"). This *partner-enhancing bias* not only makes lovers feel better and increases relationship trust (Miller & Rempel, 2004), research suggests that it can also create a self-fulfilling prophecy (Drigotas et al., 1999).

In a series of studies, Sandra Murray and her colleagues discovered that an important component of a satisfying, stable romantic relationship is the ability to mix positive illusion with sober reality when perceiving one's partner. That is, those who can see virtues in their partners that their partners cannot even see in themselves tend to be happier with the relationship than those who perhaps have a more realistic view (Murray & Holmes, 1999). For instance, in one longitudinal study, dating couples who idealized each other more during the initial stages of their romance reported greater increases in satisfaction and decreases in conflicts and doubts over the course of a year than couples who saw each other in a more realistic light (Murray et al., 1996b). In addition, during the year, the targets of these positive illusions actually incorporated these idealized images into their own self-concepts. Similar findings were also obtained with married couples (Murray & Holmes, 1997). These studies suggest that partners who idealize each other often create a self-fulfilling prophecy. By taking a "leap of faith" and seeing imperfect relationships in

Things become better when you expect the best instead of the worst.

Norman Vincent Peale, 1899–1993, minister and author)

Earlier in the chapter you learned that passionate love is associated with perceiving one's partner through rose-colored glasses. This idealization, however, often gives way to a more realistic view with the development of companionate love. Yet, if companionate love is more enduring than passionate love, how can the present findings—that perceiving one's partner in somewhat ideal terms leads to greater romantic happiness than perceiving her/him realistically—be explained?

somewhat idealized ways, people not only satisfy their need to feel that their relationships are better than most other relationships, but they create the conditions necessary for their positive illusions to be realized.

Partners Who Can "Read" Each Other's Thoughts and Feelings are Happier

Research with both dating and married couples indicate that people are happiest in their romantic relationships when they believe they have found their kindred spirit, someone who understands them and shares their experiences (Murray et al., 2002). Although we have just learned that positive illusions might facilitate the belief that one has found the "perfect match," couldn't there also be benefits to accurately reading your partner's thoughts and feelings? In other words, can accuracy in reading your partner coexist with positive illusions about your partner?

Let's first examine the likely relationship between your accuracy in judging a person and the level of intimacy you have with her or him. From a social cognitive perspective, the accuracy of person perception should increase as intimacy increases. Why? When trying to understand the thoughts and actions of a stranger you only have access to her or his immediate behavior, which you then filter through your implicit personality theories and general all-purpose stereotypes to arrive at a judgment (see chapter 4, pp. 112–113). Stereotype–driven judgments are not known for their accuracy. In contrast, when judging a romantic partner, you can compare his or her current behavior to a treasure trove of knowledge of the person's past actions, which is part of a highly detailed theory of him or her as a specific person interacting in a variety of social relationships. These intimate person judgments should be relatively accurate. Are they? Further, does their degree of accuracy predict relationship satisfaction?

New Zealand social psychologists Geoff Thomas and Garth Fletcher (1997) have investigated the ability of relationship partners to read each other's thoughts and feelings, an interpersonal skill they call *mind reading* (also known as *empathic accuracy*). In one of their typical studies, either married or dating couples are videotaped while they discuss two serious problems in their relationship. Couples are instructed to try to resolve the problems during this ten-minute discussion. After completing this task, couples are separated and partners independently review a videotape of the discussion, stopping the tape whenever they recall experiencing a thought or emotion, and writing it down. Next, the researchers give each partner the time points the other partner had noted and ask each person to review the tape a second time, but now give their best guess as to what their partner was thinking and feeling at the indicated time points. Raters later assess the similarity between the pairs of statements from the two partners to determine each one's accuracy in reading the other's thoughts and feelings. For comparison purposes, friends of the couple and strangers also review these tapes and guess what each person was thinking and feeling at the selected time points.

The central findings from these studies (Thomas et al., 1997) are that couples average close to a 50 percent accuracy rate in assessing what their partners were thinking and feeling, which is significantly more accurate than friends of the dating partners (41 percent accuracy) or strangers (39 percent). A more recent study by Thomas and Fletcher (2003) using the same methodology not only replicated these findings, but also found evidence that women exhibit superior mind-reading accuracy than men, and that superior mind reading is related to higher relationship satisfaction and closeness. Additional research suggests that superior mind readers have higher verbal skills and engage in more complex and effortful thinking when making attributions of others' behavior than inferior mind readers (Davis & Kraus, 1997; Fletcher, 2002; Fletcher et al., 1986). In other words, people who regularly critically analyze social interaction and who are also adept at verbal interaction are more accurate in reading their partner's thoughts and feelings, which appears to benefit the relationship.

Is superior mind reading always a good thing for romantic relationships? Maybe not. A series of studies by Jeffry Simpson and William Ickes find that partners in highly committed romantic relationships are sometimes motivated to inaccurately read their partners' minds, such as when they avoid acknowledging that their lover is having carnal thoughts and feelings about another person (Ickes & Simpson, 2001; Simpson et al., 2003). In such instances, engaging in positive illusions may protect relationship satisfaction. Overall, it appears that accurate mind reading in romance increases intimacy and satisfaction with the relationship when the partners' thoughts and feelings are not threatening to the relationship (Ickes, 2003). However, when these thoughts and feelings pose a danger, positive illusions protect relationship happiness.

Social Support Predicts Relationship Satisfaction

In the majority of Western cultures, most people involved in long-term romantic relationships consider their partners to be their best friends and the persons they would most likely turn to for support in times of need (Pasch et al., 1997). Receiving such support has important benefits, including a decrease in stress and an increase in physical health and happiness, while simultaneously increasing satisfaction and commitment to the relationship (Coyne et al., 2001; Dehle et al., 2001; Feeney, 2004). Of course, when couples are angry at each other, they are less likely to seek or provide support, and this nonsupport can be very damaging to the relationship (Abbey et al., 1985). Withholding support causes the most damage to those relationships that are already troubled; satisfied couples are much more likely than dissatisfied couples to excuse nonsupport from their partners (Frazier et al., 2003).

Due to the fact that girls in North American culture are raised to think, act, and define themselves in ways that emphasize their emotional connectedness to others more than boys (see chapter 11, p. 404), perhaps it is not surprising that at least one study found that recently married women desire significantly greater support from their spouses than do recently married men (Xu & Burleson, 2001). Of course, this does not mean that newlywed husbands do not desire or benefit from spousal support. In fact, a recent study suggests that husbands and wives in new marriages may depend equally on satisfying spousal support when dealing with the stress of marital conflict (Heffner et al., 2004). Further, a longitudinal study of married couples found that lower levels of depression were associated with both women and men receiving a good deal of *emotional support* (tenderness and understanding) and *information support* (advice and guidance) from their partners during the previous six months (Cutrona & Suhr, 1994).

Unfortunately for women involved in heterosexual romantic relationships, their skill in providing social support appears to be greater than that of their male partners (Vinokur & Vinokur-Kaplan, 1990; Wheeler et al., 1983). As already noted, whereas female socialization fosters the development of these *relationship-enhancing* behaviors, male socialization is more likely to promote the development of *individual-enhancing* behaviors, such as independence and control. This gender difference may explain why women are better mind readers than men in romantic relationships and also why marriage is more beneficial to men than to women: men marry people who, on average, have a good deal of training and experience in providing care and nurturance to others, while women marry people who, on average, have spent a lot of time learning how to be independent of others!

How does this gender difference influence social support among lesbian and gay couples? A five-year longitudinal study by Lawrence Kurdek (1998) suggests that although the "double dose" of relationship-enhancing skills that lesbians bring to romantic relationships results in somewhat higher levels of intimacy than that found among heterosexual couples, it doesn't lead to higher levels of relationship satisfaction. For gay couples, while their "double dose" of individual-enhancing skills may explain why they tend to have a higher need for autonomy than heterosexual couples, it doesn't lead to lower levels of relationship satisfaction.

Because males are the dominant sex in virtually all societies, their gender socialization more closely mirrors the dominant values of the culture than female socialization. As our society becomes more egalitarian on gender issues, it's possible that these gender differences may diminish as we socialize boys and girls in more similar ways. The question is, in which direction will the shift take place? Will it move toward more relationship-enhancing behaviors or toward more individual-enhancing behaviors? The answer to this question will be partly determined by the values you bring to future romantic relationships, and the extent to which you shape the gender and relationship beliefs of coming generations.

We Are Meaner to Those We Love Than We Are to Strangers

Despite the many emotional joys we derive from long-term intimate relationships, this closeness can also be the source of frequent frustrations and annoyances. A common reaction to these "aggravations of the heart" is to emotionally lash out at those we profess to love (Miller, 1997). For example, studies of married people interacting with either their spouses or strangers during casual conversation and while working on a problem-solving task found that they were much more polite, agreeable, and attentive to the strangers than to their spouses (Birchler et al., 1975). They not only interrupted their spouses, but they also often openly criticized and belittled them. The communication problems that result from this social insensitivity can gradually weaken lovers' emotional bonds (Kurdek, 1991, 1994).

How do those who transgress against their partners perceive their actions? In an investigation of hurtful behavior in romantic relationships, Jessica Cameron and her coworkers (2002) asked heterosexual college student couples to describe a past transgression in which one of them had been the victim and the other had been the perpetrator in a negative relationship event. Realizing that almost everybody involved in a romantic relationship at some point causes harm to their partner, the researchers randomly assigned participants to either the "perpetrator" or "victim" role. Perpetrators were told to suggest possible negative episodes from their relationship in which they had upset their partner, while victims were instructed to assist their partner in settling upon the most appropriate transgression. Cameron and her colleagues found that during the subsequent retelling of the chosen negative event, the partner who was the perpetrator had a very different perception of the event and its aftermath than the partner who was the victim. In contrast to victims' descriptions of the transgression, perpetrators were more likely to minimize their own blameworthiness, justify their actions, ignore the negative consequences to their partners, and perceive greater improvement in themselves and in the relationship since the transgression (see figure 12.8).

These findings suggest that when people behave badly in an intimate relationship, they are motivated to dissociate themselves from their undesirable actions. One way to accomplish this goal is for perpetrators to convince themselves that their actions were not really that bad, and further, their "bad" behavior was in many ways an ultimately "good thing" for them and the relationship. In interpreting these results, keep in mind that participants were randomly assigned to the perpetrator and victim roles. If the assignment had gone the other way, then the persons chosen for the victim role would have been the perpetrators. Presumably, they also would then have changed their assessments of both the event and how it had affected their relationship. In other words, this tendency to engage in such self-serving remembrances of harmful relationship behavior is something that all of us are potentially capable of doing.

When a relationship becomes troubled, harmful transgressions increase in frequency. People who feel emotionally snubbed respond by behaving badly toward their partner (Murray et al., 2003). In fact, couples headed for a breakup tend to be unable or unwilling to terminate the expression of negative emotions (Halford et al., 1990). For example, in a four-year longitudinal study of married couples, John Gottman and Robert Levenson (1992) discovered that those relationships that end in divorce tend to involve people who nag and whine a great deal and don't listen very well to their partner's concerns. When troubled couples interact, they often fall into what Gottman (1979) calls a *negative reciprocity cycle,* where positive behaviors tend to be ignored and negative behaviors are reciprocated. Although troubled couples may realize the damage they are inflicting on their relationship with each glare, harsh word, and slammed door, they nevertheless persist in these destructive actions. Happy couples, on the other hand, argue in a more constructive fashion (Blais et al., 1990). When they complain to each other, they also recognize the validity of the other person's feelings and viewpoint (Koren et al., 1980). This tendency to take their partner's point of view when arguing (a psychological state known as *perspective-taking*) is important in maintaining relationship health (Arriaga & Rusbult, 1998).

FIGURE 12.8

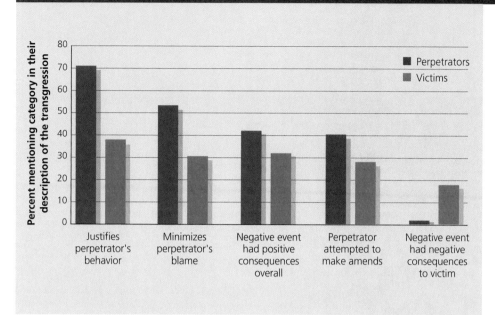

Perpetrators' and Victims' Perceptions of a Negative Relationship Event

When romantic couples were randomly assigned to describe a past transgression in which one of them had been the victim and the other had been the perpetrator in a negative relationship event, Jessica Cameron and her coworkers (2002) found that perpetrators and victims had decidedly different perceptions of the event and its aftermath. Compared with their partner victim, perpetrators minimized their blame, justified their actions, and downplayed the event's negative consequences. Perpetrators also were more likely than victims to state that they had attempted to make amends for the negative event and that the event ultimately had positive consequences for the relationship. Because participants were randomly assigned to the perpetrator and victim roles, what do the findings suggest about our capacity to delude ourselves when we act badly in romantic relationships?

People Use Different Strategies to Cope with a Troubled Relationship

How do people typically react when a romantic relationship becomes dissatisfying? Caryl Rusbult and her coworkers have identified four strategies people use in coping with a troubled relationship (Rusbult et al., 1986a, 1987, 2001). Their level of commitment to the relationship influences the strategies they choose, or find themselves using. The more satisfied and the more invested partners are, the more committed they will be to work on solutions to maintain and improve the relationship (Arriaga & Agnew, 2001; Bui et al., 1996). Figure 12.9 illustrates the primary qualities of these four strategies.

In dealing with conflict, Rusbult contends that some people may take a passively constructive approach by exhibiting *loyalty.* They simply wait, hoping that things will improve on their own. Individuals who adopt this strategy are often afraid to "rock the boat," so they say nothing and pray that their loyalty will keep the relationship afloat. Others, especially men, adopt the passively destructive strategy of *neglect.* They "clam up" and ignore their partners or spend less time with them. When together, neglectful persons often treat their partners poorly by constantly criticizing them for things unrelated to the real problem. Those who don't know how to deal with their negative emotions, or aren't motivated to improve the relationship but also aren't ready to end it, tend to employ this strategy. When people do conclude that the relationship is not worth saving, they *exit,* which is an active, yet destructive, strategy. A much more constructive and active strategy is *voice.* People discuss their problems, seek compromises, consult therapists, and attempt to salvage a relationship they still highly value.

Rusbult and her colleagues (1986b) have found that one determinant of the strategies that people choose to employ in dealing with their dissatisfaction is their level of psychological masculinity and femininity. In survey studies involving lesbian, gay male, and heterosexual women and men, individuals with many feminine personality traits were much more likely to react constructively to relationship problems. They either actively searched for an acceptable resolution, or, if a solution did not seem possible, they remained quietly loyal to the relationship. In contrast, those who had many masculine traits and few feminine

Love doesn't just sit there, like a stone, it has to be made, like bread; re-made all the time, made new.

Ursula K. LeGuin, U.S. science fiction writer, b. 1929

FIGURE 12.9

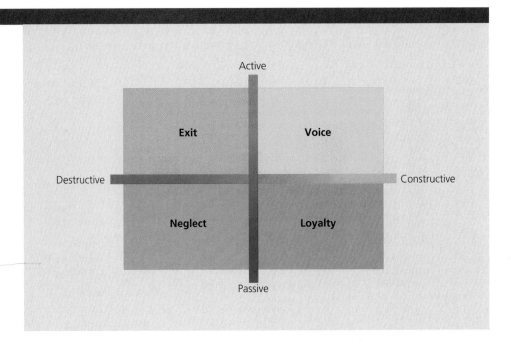

A Typology of Basic Coping Strategies

In dealing with relationship conflict people employ different strategies, which differ in terms of the dimensions of active-passive and constructive-destructive. In dealing with dissatisfactions in romantic relationships in your own life, which of these four basic strategies have you used?

traits tended to respond destructively when trouble developed in their relationships. They either passively neglected the problems and allowed things to deteriorate further, or they actively threatened to exit. These patterns were true for both men and women, regardless of sexual orientation. More generally, other studies indicate that high levels of femininity in one or both partners are associated with higher levels of relationship satisfaction and commitment (Lamke et al., 1994; Stets & Burke, 1996). In addition, longitudinal studies of married couples indicate that masculinity's negative impact on relationship satisfaction is due to the influence of the undesirable masculine personality traits in men (but not in women) related to arrogance and aggressiveness, and not due to the more desirable masculine traits related to independence and assertiveness (Bradbury et al., 1995).

Overall, these findings suggest that through the acquisition of feminine personality traits, people learn to react to relationship problems in a constructive manner (Ickes, 1985). On the other hand, acquiring undesirable masculine traits is downright destructive to relationship survival. Why might this be the case? As already mentioned, feminine traits are characterized by a communal orientation of warmth, intimacy, and a concern with interpersonal relations. On the other hand, masculine traits are characterized by a more individualistic orientation of power, dominance, and a concern with achieving instrumental (that is, work) goals. People with many feminine personality characteristics are more interested in resolving conflict through emotional sharing and compromise, whereas those with mostly masculine characteristics, especially those that are undesirable, prefer reaching decisions on their own and imposing their will on others. When described in this manner, it isn't surprising that these two gender orientations often achieve different results when conflicts arise in romance.

Romantic Breakups Often Cause Emotional Distress

When romantic relationships fail, it is relatively rare that the breakup is mutually desired. In both heterosexual dating relationships and marriages, women tend to initiate the breakup (Hagestad & Smyer, 1982; Rubin et al., 1981). One possible reason for this gender difference is that women appear to be more attentive to and sensitive about relationship problems (Ptacek & Dodge, 1995).

In both heterosexual and homosexual relationships, the partner who initiates the breakup tends to suffer less distress, but this effect is much more apparent for men than

When a romantic relationship ends, social support received from friends and family can help people cope with their emotional pain.

women in heterosexual romance (Frazier & Cook, 1993; Helgeson, 1994). Men also tend to suffer more than women when they are romantically rejected. A possible explanation for this effect involves the traditional gender roles taught to men and women. First, because power and control are central aspects of the traditional male gender role (Garfinkel, 1985), men may experience greater self-esteem threat and emotional distress when their partner takes relationship control away from them by ending the romance. Second, because heterosexual men tend to place all their emotional eggs in their romantic baskets, they may suffer more emotional pain when the bottom falls out of the relationship and those eggs are smashed (Barbee et al., 1990).

A similar effect is found regarding the ideologies of individualism and collectivism. In a study of romantic breakups in both the United States and Puerto Rico, Harry Triandis and his colleagues (1988) found that people with a more individualist orientation were the loneliest following a breakup. As discussed in chapter 11 (p. 404), individualists' greater loneliness is most likely due to their less extensive social support network. When romantic relationships fall apart, individualists have fewer people to soothe their emotional pain than collectivists.

In coping with the loss of love, men and women are equally likely to spend considerable time talking to themselves about the relationship ("I'm lucky to have dumped that jerk!" "I've learned a valuable lesson"), distracting themselves by engaging in physical activities or doing things to improve their looks and sex appeal. However, women are more likely than men to cry, talk things over with their friends, read self-help books, and consult a therapist to better understand their feelings (Orimoto et al., 1993). These results suggest that women, more than men, tend to spend time following a breakup attending to their emotional needs in ways that may promote increased understanding so future relationships can be more satisfying.

People who deal best with the loss of romantic love are those who have a supportive social network; that is, friends and family from whom they can receive emotional sustenance and encouragement (Holahan et al., 1997; Milardo & Allan, 1997). In such times of stress, this support network provides the recent victims of love with a "buffer" from the full force of their loss (Thoits, 1982). The support that a social network offers could be either emotional or financial assistance, and its purpose is to help people overcome their loss and reestablish a sense of normalcy in their daily activities.

Despite the turmoil that love often brings to our lives, most of us yearn for romance even after experiencing romantic failure. Some call this persistence a form of addiction, but others describe the desire for romantic intimacy as an expression of one of the most basic human needs, the desire to share and immerse oneself as completely as possible in the life and love of another who has become an integral part of one's self-concept.

- A number of factors determine whether love will endure or fade:

  Romantic relationships are happiest when the ratio between the rewards and costs is similar for both partners

  The positive self-esteem typical of securely attached individuals fosters romantic satisfaction

  Couples who idealize each other tend to have happier relationships than those who have more realistic views

  Accurate mind reading increases relationship satisfaction when partners' thoughts and feelings are not threatening

  Receiving social support from one's partner increases satisfaction and commitment to the relationship

  Troubled couples often are unable or unwilling to terminate the expression of negative emotions toward each other

- In dealing with relationship dissatisfaction, we typically employ four distinct strategies: loyalty, neglect, voice, and exit

- Losers in love cope best when they have a supportive social network

FEATURED STUDY

MATE POACHING ACROSS CULTURES

Schmitt, D. P. (2004). Patterns and universals of mate poaching across 53 nations: The effects of sex, culture, and personality on romantically attracting another person's partner. *Journal of Personality and Social Psychology, 86,* 560–584.

Mate poaching is the process of trying to attract someone who is already in a romantic relationship. In practice, mate poaching often takes the form of a short-term sexual liaison. In some cases, mate poachers desire a more enduring relationship with the desired person. As you might guess, this process is filled with many special challenges and potential obstacles and dangers. The present study examined the psychology of mate poaching from a cross-cultural perspective. The objective was to determine the frequency of mate poaching across cultures, the type of person most likely to engage in this process, and the importance of culture in shaping the features of mate poaching. The first hypothesis was that more men than women attempt and succumb to short-term mate poaching across all world regions, and more women than men receive and are successful at short-term mate poaching. The second hypothesis in this study was that world regions with more demanding environments have lower rates of short-term mate poaching. The reasoning here

is that in demanding environments there is a greater need for joint parental care of children to ensure their health and safety, and thus, fidelity is highly valued and more enforced than in cultures with less demanding environments. The third hypothesis was that world regions with more men than women have higher rates of mate poaching by men, whereas regions with more women than men have higher rates of mate poaching by women. Finally, the last hypothesis was that gender differences in short-term mate poaching are larger in regions with traditional gender-role ideologies and smaller in regions with liberal gender-role ideologies. The reasoning here is that male and female poaching habits are most different in those cultures that enforce strong gender-based beliefs about proper behavior.

Method

As part of the International Sexuality Description Project, 16,954 participants from fifty-three nations were administered an anonymous survey about experiences with romantic attraction. Several national samples failed to reach the designated sample size of 100 men and 100 women, so the fifty-three nations were collapsed into ten basic world regions for data analysis. The ten world regions included North America, South America, Western Europe, Eastern Europe, Southern Europe, the Middle East, Oceania, South/Southeast Asia, and East Asia. Participants in most samples were recruited as volunteers, some received course credit for participation, and others received a small monetary reward for participation. Return rates for college student samples were around 95 percent, while return rates for community samples were around 50 percent.

Results and Discussion

Consistent with hypothesis 1, either for the purpose of having a short-term sexual relationship or for the purpose of forming a new long-term mating alliance, the occurrence of attempting at least one mate poach is significantly higher for men (60 percent) than women (40 percent) across all regions. Further, for all world regions, gender differences in short-term mate-poaching attempts were small to moderate in magnitude, confirming the hypothesis that men expend more mating effort on short-term mateships than women. Results also indicated that among those who have attempted to poach, the success rate is substantial, often over 80 percent. Nearly 70 percent of participants report that someone has tried to poach them, and around 50 percent of those who have been tempted by a would-be poacher have yielded to the attempt. Men were significantly more likely to succumb to short-term poaching than women. These findings suggest that mate poaching is a culturally universal human experience and that it coevolved as part of the human condition. Mate poaching also undoubtedly triggers strong feelings of jealousy and even aggression from those who are poached.

A consistent pattern of poaching personality characteristics emerged across most world regions. Those who attempt to poach another's partner are especially extraverted, disagreeable, unconscientious, and lustful. Similarly, common targets of mate poaching have high levels of extraversion, openness, attractiveness, and lustfulness. Regarding environmental factors, regions with fewer resources tend to have lower rates of short-term poaching than regions with more resources. These results suggest that in resource-poor environments humans pursue more long-term, monogamous mating strategies, whereas in resource-rich settings they are more likely to pursue short-term mating strategies, including poaching.

Regarding the last two hypotheses, results indicated that as the ratio of women to men increases, women are more likely to engage in both short-term and long-term mate poaching. No similar effects were found for men. In explaining why an excess of women, but not men, led to more poaching by both sexes, the researcher speculated that when women are abundant and men are a scarce resource, men may be able to command more promiscuity on the part of women, and the entire mating system may shift toward promiscuity. Finally, as predicted, as women's access to resources increases across regions due to liberal gender roles, their rates of short-term poaching increase and gender differences in short-term poaching decrease.

Overall, the results of the present study suggest that the influence of culture on human mate poaching is profound. Although proportionately more men than women seek short-term mate poaches across all world regions, this effect is tempered by several cultural factors, including changes in the resources in the environment, greater gender equality, and changes in the ratio of men to women in the culture.

APPLICATIONS

WHAT CAUSES JEALOUSY AND HOW CAN YOU COPE WITH IT?

esides the many other problems that can besiege an intimate relationship, jealousy can also contribute to relationship failure. **Jealousy** is the negative emotional reaction experienced when a relationship that is important to a person's self-concept is threatened by a real or imagined rival (Harris, 2004; Parrott & Smith, 1993). In most cases, the threat is another person, but people can also feel jealous about their partner's time involvement with work, hobbies, and family obligations (Buunk & Bringle, 1987). Some people mistakenly believe that jealousy indicates the depths of a partner's love and, thus, is a healthy sign in romantic relationships. In actuality, research demonstrates that it indicates the degree of a lover's dependence and, thus, is a sign of relationship insecurity (Marelich et al., 2003; Salovey & Rodin, 1991). It also triggers a host of negative feelings and behaviors and tends to lower self-esteem (Buunk & Dijkstra, 2001; Mathes et al., 1985).

Despite the negative and unpleasant effects brought on by jealousy, some people consciously try to manipulate situations

Jealousy

The negative emotional reaction experienced when a relationship that is important to a person's self-concept is threatened by a real or imagined rival.

> O! Beware my lord, of jealousy;
> It is the green-eyed monster which doth mock.

William Shakespeare, English dramatist 1564–1616, from *Othello.*

to make their partners jealous. For example, a survey of college students found that one-third of young women and one-fifth of young men flirt with others or talk about former lovers in an attempt to gain their current lover's attention and to strengthen the relationship (White, 1980a). Those who tried to induce jealousy stated they were more involved in the relationship than were their partners. In most cases, however, the actual consequences of these tactics were that they hurt, not helped, the relationship.

Are There Gender Differences in Romantic Jealousy?

Although jealousy can develop in friendships and family relationships, romantic jealousy appears to be the strongest and most destructive form (Felson, 1997; Puente & Cohen, 2003). Both women and men experience the "green-eyed monster," but several evolutionary psychologists propose that the two sexes are aroused by different triggering events (Buss et al., 2000; Symons, 1979; Daly & Wilson, 1996). According to these theorists, due to natural selection pressures, men are genetically predisposed to become upset over a mate's *sexual* infidelity, while women are predisposed to become upset over a mate's *emotional* infidelity. For a man, his mate's sexual philandering increases the risk that the children he supports are not his own. This is a serious male problem from a fitness point of view because it sharply reduces a man's ability to pass his genes on to the next generation. In contrast, a woman cannot be tricked into bringing up an offspring not her own. Therefore, from a fitness perspective, she should be less concerned over the simple act of sexual infidelity in her mate. What should concern her about these sexual dalliances is the loss of her mate's emotional involvement in the relationship because that could result in him withdrawing his resources for her and her offspring. This is why women should be particularly upset over a mate's emotional infidelity. Using the terminology of our Featured Study, men should be more upset than women by the consequences of short-term poaching of their mates, while women should be more upset than men by the consequences of long-term mate poaching.

Is there empirical support for this theory that jealousy has different evolutionary-based triggers in women and men? Yes and no. Studies that typically support this theory have used a forced-choice hypothetical scenario in which research participants are asked to imagine a romantic relationship where their partner is either having sex with someone else or is falling in love with someone else. Participants were then asked to choose which of the two types of infidelity would be more upsetting to them. In the United States, this scenario typically produces a significant gender effect: between 40 and 60 percent of the men report they would be more upset by sexual infidelity, whereas around 75 percent of the women report that emotional infidelity would be worse. Similar gender differences have also been found in some European and Asian countries, but in China, Korea, Germany, New

Zealand, and Holland the percentage of men choosing sexual infidelity as worse drops to as little as 25 to 30 percent (Brase et al., in press; Buss et al., 2000; Buunk et al., 1996; Geary et al., 1995; Mullen & Martin, 1994). Taking these studies together, it appears that the evolutionary-based theory of gender differences in jealousy has mixed support (Sabini & Green, 2004).

In reviewing these findings, some social cognitive theorists have argued that the gender differences that have been found may not reflect inherited sex-based tendencies. Instead, they may simply indicate that women and men draw different conclusions about what infidelity means about their partner's love for them (Harris, 2003a, 2003b). According to this view, men tend to think sexual infidelity is more distressing because they believe that if a woman is having sex with another man she is probably also in love with him. In other words, sexual infidelity implies emotional infidelity. In contrast, because women tend to believe that men can have sex without being in love, a man's sexual infidelity does not necessarily imply emotional infidelity. So, for women, emotional infidelity is much worse than sexual infidelity. This theory of gender differences in jealousy has found support in two American studies and one Dutch study (DeSteno & Salovey, 1996; Dijkstra et al., 2001; Harris & Christenfeld, 1996). However, when Christine Harris (2002, 2003b) studied young adults and older adults who reported having actual experience with a mate's infidelity, no gender differences in jealous responses were found: both women and men reported focusing slightly more on emotional aspects of their partner's infidelity.

So where are we in our understanding of jealousy in women and men? Regardless of whether gender differences in jealousy are primarily caused by evolutionary-based natural selection pressures or relatively complex cognitive analysis, substantial gender differences probably do not exist (DeSteno et al., 2002). Further, instead of natural selection pressures shaping different inborn responses in men and women, it is at least equally likely that natural selection shaped fairly general jealousy mechanisms that evolved outside the mating context as a response to competition between siblings in a family (Harris, 2004). In nonhuman species, sibling rivalry is not uncommon. For example, among black eagles, the older sibling in the nest routinely kills the younger one. In humans, infants as young as six months express the type of emotional displeasure typically associated with jealousy when their mothers interact with a lifesize doll or a similar-aged peer in their presence (Hart et al., 1998). Although more research is needed, it is possible that romantic jealousy has its genetic roots in sibling rivalry and not in the sex-linked human mating system.

Coping with Jealousy

Regardless of the ultimate origins of jealousy in humans, what types of coping strategies, both of the constructive and destructive variety, could you employ in contending with this destructive emotion? Jeff Bryson (1977) suggests that all

TABLE 12.4

Different Ways of Coping with Jealousy

		Relationship Maintaining Behaviors	
		Yes	**No**
Self-Esteem Maintaining Behaviors	**Yes**	Negotiating a mutually acceptable solution	Verbal/physical attacks against the partner or rival
	No	Clinging to the relationship	Self-destructive behaviors

jealousy-coping strategies boil down to two major goal-oriented behaviors:

1. Attempts to maintain the relationship
2. Attempts to maintain one's own self-esteem

As can be seen in table 12.4, if jealous individuals desire to maintain both the relationship and their self-esteem, they will try to negotiate a mutually satisfying solution with their partners. This constructive and active strategy corresponds to Rusbult's notion of relationship *voice.* However, if jealous individuals desire to maintain their romantic relationships regardless of the loss of self-esteem, they may swallow their pride and put up with the jealousy-inducing behavior. This passive approach corresponds to Rusbult's notion of relationship *loyalty.* In contrast to these relationship-maintaining strategies, those who are more concerned with self-esteem maintenance often use verbal and physical attacks against their partner or rival. Likewise, jealous people who are not principally attempting to either maintain the relationship or bolster their self-esteem often employ self-destructive behavior.

In commenting on these different coping strategies, Sharon Brehm (1992) brings up a good point: the jealous should think about both the short-term and long-term consequences of their coping responses *before* acting. For example, verbally or physically attacking your partner may temporarily intimidate him or her into staying in the relationship while it also shores up your own sagging self-

esteem, but in the long run, it will push your partner away and lower your self-worth. Similarly, begging and pleading with your partner to end another romance may succeed in the short run, but it will threaten your self-esteem as it reduces your partner's attraction to you.

A survey of young adults conducted by Peter Salovey and Judith Rodin (1988) found that the strategy of *self-reliance* was the most effective in reducing jealousy. This strategy involved jealous individuals *containing emotional outbursts, maintaining daily routines,* and *reevaluating the importance of the relationship.* Another strategy that reduced depression and anger among the jealous was *self-bolstering,* which involved thinking positively about oneself and doing nice things for oneself. Similarly, Elaine Hatfield and Richard Rapson (1993) found that encouraging people to make new friends, or to get a job, or to go back to school helped them to think better of themselves, which in turn reduced their jealousy.

The general recommendations coming from all this jealousy work is that the best antidotes to the "green-eyed monster" are to (1) avoid emotional outbursts that are destructive to you and others, and (2) develop a feeling of self-confidence about your ability to act and survive independent of the relationship. In the final analysis, even though intimacy involves an inclusion of the other in our self-concept, our own health and the health of the relationship depends on our ability to develop a sense of self independent of our partners

THE BIG PICTURE

So what have you learned about intimacy? Do you recognize a connection between the type of attachment style that you developed with your parents and your expectations about friendships and romantic relationships? What about the different types of romantic love? In contrast to the common Hollywood depiction of passion being the cornerstone of romance, research clearly indicates that companionship is what best supports an enduring romantic relationship. Of course, passion is important, but its primary function is not to preserve your romantic relationship as much as it is to spark the initial attraction. As the relationship progresses and is sustained by your mutual companionship, passion will likely diminish, but it will probably also sporadically reignite, reminding each of you about your sensual chemistry. Hopefully, this knowledge will inoculate you against habitually entering and leaving relationships in search of the fantasy lover whose passion never fades.

Although "true love" usually does not match the idealized Hollywood version, an important component of a satisfying, stable romantic relationship is the ability to mix positive illusion with sober reality when perceiving your partner. As with your own self-perceptions, overlooking faults and exaggerating virtues in your partner will not only satisfy the need to feel that your relationship is better than most others, but it can actually create the conditions necessary for your positive illusions to become realized. Here again is an example of how you can shape your social reality and create self-fulfilling prophecies.

Although you have the power to substantially shape the course of your intimate relationships, you can run into problems if you believe that they are invulnerable to outside influences. Despite the folk-saying that "no third party can break up a happy relationship," research suggests that friends' and family members' approval or disapproval of your romantic relationships will significantly determine whether they survive or fail (Sprecher & Felmlee, 1992). In addition, although you might believe that "love conquers all," numerous studies indicate that outside influences such as money problems and job stress not only promote hostility in romantic relationships, but they also make partners less emotionally supportive of each other, all of which contribute to breakups (Lynch et al., 1997).

As you have learned from the attachment studies reviewed in this chapter, the important people in the early years of your life significantly shaped what you expect from intimate relationships and how you behave with those you love. In the coming years, your success in developing and nurturing your intimate relationships will not only determine the quality of your own life, it will also largely shape the next generation's views of intimacy issues.

WEB SITES
accessed through http://www.mhhe.com/franzoi4

Web sites for this chapter focus on research and theory on adult attachment dynamics and the psychology of personal relationships.

Adult Attachment Lab

This Web page for the Adult Attachment Lab, which is directed by Dr. Phillip Shaver at the University of California at Davis, advances understanding of adult attachment dynamics. Here you will find an overview of self-report measures of adult attachment security, as well as recent studies conducted from the lab.

International Society for the Study of Personal Relationships

The International Society for the Study of Personal Relationships has a Web site that endeavors to stimulate and support scholarship and research on personal relationships.

Social Cognition and Personal Relationships

At this Web site you can learn about the formation, evolution, maintenance, and dissolution of intimate relationships.

CHAPTER 13

Aggression

CHAPTER OUTLINE

*M*itchell Johnson, age 13, was angry after being "dumped" by his girlfriend. He was mad at everybody, and he told some of his classmates at Westside Middle School in Jonesboro, Arkansas, that he was going to shoot all the girls who had ever broken up with him. "Tomorrow you all find out if you live or die," he bragged. Eleven-year-old Andrew Golden, also of Jonesboro, was already known in his neighborhood as a bully who regularly threatened other children. He also was well tutored by his father, an official of a local gun club, in shooting rifles, shotguns, and pistols. On the afternoon of March 24, 1998, these two boys executed a plan that relied on Andrew's deadly expertise to fulfill Mitchell's promise of revenge. Shortly after lunch, dressed in camouflage clothing and armed with their families' handguns and semiautomatic rifles, Mitchell and Andrew lured the student body of the middle school onto the playground with a false fire alarm and then opened fire from a nearby woods. Their weapons were aimed at girls, the target of Mitchell's anger. Within fifteen seconds, four students and one teacher had been fatally shot, and eleven others had been wounded, including Mitchell's former girlfriend. All the victims were female.

The following year, two students at Columbine High School in Littleton, Colorado—Eric Harris and Dylan Klebold—sought revenge from fellow students for perceived slights and mistreatment by athletes. Armed with guns and explosives, they murdered thirteen people and wounded twenty-one others before turning their guns on themselves. Nationwide, an average of more than twenty-four students are killed each year in school-related shootings. Each time school shootings occur, the media interviews experts to help people understand why such deadly acts of violence occur in our culture. What could cause people, much less children, to behave so violently? Biology? Family environment? Culture? These are some of the questions we address in this chapter. Hopefully, by its end, we will have a better understanding of the social psychological dynamics of various forms of aggression.

WHAT IS AGGRESSION?

Before we try to understand aggression similar to the Westside Middle School shootings, we first need to define the concept. What is aggression, and how can we distinguish between different types? Also, what is the nature of gender and self-esteem differences in aggressive responding?

Social Psychologists Define Aggression as "Intentional Harm"

Aggression

Any form of behavior that is intended to harm or injure some person, oneself, or an object.

Although there is no universally agreed upon definition of **aggression,** one of the more common ones social psychologists use is that it is any form of behavior that is intended to harm or injure some person, oneself, or an object (Björkqvist & Niemelä, 1992). Using this definition, we can clearly conclude that Mitchell Johnson and Andrew Golden committed an aggressive act against students and teachers at the middle school. In firing their weapons, they *intended* to harm the people on the playground.

To test whether you can identify other aggressive actions based on this definition, read the following vignette and try to identify five acts of aggression.

A thief fires a gun at a man he is trying to rob, but the bullet misses the mark and the man is uninjured. Panicked, the man accidentally knocks down a young girl as he flees the scene, and she badly cuts her knee on the pavement. Later, the girl screams in pain as a doctor puts five stitches in her knee to stop the bleeding. Upon finishing, the doctor asks the girl how badly it hurts. Still crying and now very angry, she grabs his moustache and yanks with all her might and sneers, "That's how much it hurts!" The next day, the thief is arrested and his cellmate verbally berates him for being such an inept burglar. Depressed and angry, the thief smashes his fist into the concrete cell wall, fracturing three fingers. While in the infirmary being treated for his injury, the thief angrily kicks and dents a waste container. In response, the attending medical assistant angrily shouts at the thief that if he does not calm down immediately he will face solitary confinement.

Can you correctly identify the five aggressive acts in this injury-filled story? What about the thief shooting but missing his intended victim? No harm, no aggression? Even though the bullet missed its mark, this is still an aggressive action because it was the intention of the thief to harm the man. In the second action, although the robbery victim's behavior caused injury to the girl, this is not an example of aggression because the man had no intention of hurting the child or anyone else. Neither is the behavior of the doctor treating the girl's wound an aggressive action. Although his actions caused pain and he performed those actions intentionally, the goal was to help the girl recover from her previous injury. Although the man and the doctor did not perform any aggressive actions, the little girl did. In pulling the doctor's moustache, she intentionally tried to seek retribution for the hurt she believed he caused. What about the thief's cellmate? The psychological harm intended in such verbal abuse qualifies this as an aggressive action. The fourth instance of aggression involved the prisoner's self-inflicted injury: intentional actions that cause harm to oneself are considered aggressive, even if they are impulsive. Finally, aggression can be directed against inanimate objects, as was the case when the thief kicked the waste container. The medical assistant's angry response to this outburst is not an example of aggression, but rather, illustrates assertiveness. *Assertiveness* is the ability to express yourself and your rights without violating the rights of others. People sometimes mistakenly label assertiveness as aggression. However, unlike aggression, assertiveness is designed not to hurt others.

> *The wish to hurt, the momentary intoxication with pain, is the loophole through which the pervert climbs into the minds of ordinary men.*
>
> Jacob Bronowski, British biologist

> *You cannot shake hands with a clenched fist.*
>
> Indira Gandhi, India's first woman prime minister, 1917–1984

A Distinction Has Traditionally Been Made Between "Instrumental" and "Hostile" Aggression

There is a long history in social psychology—and in general psychology as well—distinguishing between two "types" of aggression, namely, instrumental and hostile (Geen, 1990). The aggression the thief used in his robbery attempt is an example of instrumental aggression. **Instrumental aggression** is the intentional use of harmful behavior to achieve some other goal. In the robbery attempt, the thief used aggression as an instrument to achieve his real goal, which was obtaining the victim's money. The aggression that occurs in a military context is also often instrumental in nature. Here, the principal goal may be either to defend one's own territory or to confiscate the enemy's land. As a general rule, aggressive acts carried out with the objective of gaining material, psychological, or social benefits all fit our instrumental definition. In addition, aggression carried out to avoid punishment would also be classified as instrumental aggression. Research indicates that observers perceive acts of instrumental aggression differently depending on their perceptions of the aggressor's motives. People who are perceived to engage in instrumental aggression fed by a desire to obtain rewards are evaluated more negatively and are thought to be less moral than those who appear to be motivated by a desire to avoid punishment (Reeder et al., 2002).

In contrast to this type of aggression, the Westside Middle School and the Columbine shootings and most of the other aggressive instances in the imaginary vignette were examples of hostile aggression. **Hostile aggression** is triggered by anger, and the goal of the intentionally harmful behavior is simply to cause injury or death to the victim. Mitchell Johnson's goal and the goal of Eric Harris and Dylan Klebold was to kill those who had angered them. Similarly, the girl attacking the doctor, the thief smashing his hand against the wall, and the thief then destroying a medicine cabinet were all instances in which the aggressor's principal goal was to cause injury to another person or thing.

Instrumental Aggression

The intentional use of harmful behavior so that one can achieve some other goal.

Hostile Aggression

The intentional use of harmful behavior, triggered by anger, in which the goal is simply to cause injury or death to the victim.

Is this primarily an example of instrumental or hostile aggression?

Reprinted with special permission of King Features Syndicate, Inc.

Carl's wife offers him proof that, yes, she was planning to serve "that stupid stringy Italian stuff" again.

Anger is a short madness.

Quintus Horatius Flaccus, Roman poet, 65–8 B.C.

In thinking about instrumental and hostile aggression, it is important to keep in mind how they differ. Instrumental aggression is motivated by the anticipation of rewards or the avoidance of punishment. In that sense, it can be thought of as being relatively deliberate and rational. On the other hand, hostile aggression is not really motivated by the anticipation of rewards or the avoidance of punishments, even though these may indeed be ultimate consequences of the aggressive act. Instead, this type of aggression is often impulsive and irrational. There is a goal, but it is simply the desire to cause harm to the victim (Wann et al., 2003).

Research suggests that highly aggressive individuals can be distinguished by the degree to which they engage in instrumental and hostile aggression (Berkowitz, 1994b). *Instrumental aggressors* tend to use "proactive" force in a cool and collected manner to attain their objectives (Atkins et al., 2001). Many robbers and schoolyard bullies fall into this category. In contrast, *hostile aggressors* tend to use "reactive" force in a highly emotional and impulsive manner. Their crimes often entail excessive use of violence due to their tempers getting out of hand. Hostile aggressors are especially likely to perceive danger in their world and to respond to ambiguous stimuli with aggression (Bushman, 1996).

Although the distinction between instrumental and hostile aggression has been useful in helping researchers grasp the complex problem of human violence, a growing number of social psychologists are criticizing it as being too simplistic (Bushman & Anderson, 2001; Weinshenker & Siegel, 2002). The simple fact is that many aggressive actions cannot be neatly placed into only one of the categories. For example, a child may angrily hit another child who has taken her favorite toy, and then she may retrieve the toy while the victim cries. The motives underlying this aggression are both the infliction of pain (hostile aggression) and the recovery of the favored toy (instrumental aggression). In such instances, no clear distinctions can be made between hostile and instrumental aggression. In other instances, aggression might start out instrumentally, yet then turn hostile. For example, a soldier's cool and methodical firing of a weapon at a hidden enemy may turn into impulsive rage when one of his comrades is killed. Because of this problem of multiple motives, in the coming years social psychologists will likely revise this classic distinction to better represent the often complex motivational nature of aggression.

Gender and Personality Moderate the Expression of Aggression

Research has found considerable evidence that individual differences in aggression are relatively stable, meaning that some people are more prone to aggressive outbursts than others (Farrington, 1994). Attempts to better understand these individual differences have resulted in studies examining gender and personality as variables likely to moderate the expression of aggression.

GENDER

A widespread belief in our culture is that men are more aggressive than women. Does social psychological research support this cultural belief? The answer is yes and no. Meta-analytic studies indicate that males and females do differ in one important kind of aggression: physical aggression. That is, males are more likely than females to engage in aggression that produces pain or physical injury (Eagly & Steffen, 1986a). This gender difference in willingness to cause physical injury is more pronounced (1) among children than adults, and (2) for unprovoked aggression than for provoked aggression (Bettencourt & Miller, 1996; Pellegrini & Bartini, 2001). In contrast, men and women are very similar to one another in their verbal aggression and in expressing feelings of anger (Tavris, 1989).

Although gender differences are considerably smaller than what gender stereotypes suggest, women and men do appear to have different social representations of their physical aggression. In a series of studies, British social psychologist Anne Campbell and her colleagues found that women viewed their aggression as being stress-induced and precipitated by a loss of self-control that erupts into an antisocial act (Campbell et al., 1996, 1997b). They uniformly perceived their aggression as a negative experience. Men, in contrast, perceived their aggression as a means of exerting control over others and reclaiming power and self-esteem. Unlike women, men often believed that resorting to physical violence was a positive experience. The researchers contend that these gender differences in the experience of physical aggression may mean that the more spontaneous and unplanned behaviors typical of hostile aggression are more descriptive of the antisocial actions of women, while the more planned and calculated actions of instrumental aggression are more descriptive of male aggression.

One form of aggression that researchers largely ignored for many years is *indirect aggression,* a form of social manipulation in which the aggressor attempts to harm another person without a face-to-face encounter. Gossiping, spreading bad or false stories about someone, telling others not to associate with a person, and revealing someone's secrets are all examples of indirect aggression. The field studies by Finnish social psychologists Kaj Björkqvist and Kirsti Lagerspetz (see figure 13.1) found that among adolescents in Finland, girls were more likely than boys to use indirect aggression (Björkqvist et al., 1992; Lagerspetz et al., 1988). Their research further indicated that while male physical aggression decreased significantly during adolescence, teenage girls continued to exhibit higher levels of indirect aggression at all age levels. Subsequent studies in other countries found similar preferences for indirect aggression among girls and women (Campbell, 1999; Fujihara et al., 1999; Theron et al., 2000). Together, they suggest we need to reexamine the "peaceful female" stereotype.

One important question emerging from these studies is: Why might females be more likely to choose indirect rather than direct aggressive means? Björkqvist and Lagerspetz suggest four possible reasons. One explanation is that girls are discouraged more than boys from engaging in direct acts of aggression. Because of this different gender socialization pattern, females may use more indirect aggression simply because it is more socially acceptable (Campbell, 1999). Another possibility involves the social structure of same-sex peer groups during childhood and adolescence. Girls typically form small, intimate play

FIGURE 13.1

Gender Comparisons in Aggressive Strategies

In a study of the aggressive styles used by adolescents in Finland, Björkqvist and his colleagues (1992) found that verbal aggression (for example, yelling, insulting, name-calling) is the most used by both boys and girls. Boys display more physical aggression (hitting, kicking, shoving), whereas girls utilize more indirect forms of aggression (gossiping, writing nasty notes about another, telling bad or false stories).

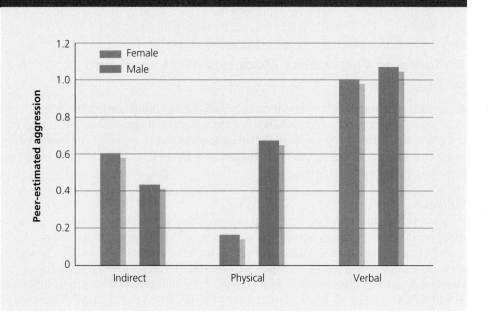

groups, while boys' groups tend to be bigger and less defined (Maccoby, 1990). Björkqvist and Lagerspetz suggest that indirect aggression may be more effective in the intimate social settings girls usually inhabit because such surroundings create greater opportunities to discover and pass on personal information about others. A third possibility has to do with the relative physical strengths of the two sexes. Women, typically being smaller than men, may have learned that indirect forms of aggression are more effective and less costly than direct personal attack. Finally, because research indicates that indirect retaliation to aggression is more common in older than in younger children, Lagerspetz and Björkqvist (1994) suggest that the greater use of indirect means by females during adolescence may reflect their earlier social maturation.

In our examination of gender differences in aggression, we must also consider the impact that culture has on females' willingness to act in an aggressive manner. Although a good deal of cross-cultural research indicates that women are less physically aggressive than men and less likely to commit homicide (Daly & Wilson, 1988), a number of societies encourage and teach women to be physically aggressive. For example, in her study of aggression among the islanders of Margarita, Venezuela, anthropologist H. B. Kimberley Cook (1992) discovered that aggression was an integral aspect of being a woman in Margarita. As one elderly woman told her:

> Women in Margarita are "guapa" (physically strong). When we fight, we punch and tear each other's hair. A long time ago, I had a fight with a woman. I chased her all around the ranchería. When I caught her, I grabbed her by the hair and pushed her face into the mud. She was screaming, but I wouldn't let go. I was stronger and I laughed. She didn't talk to me for years afterwards, but later we became friends again. (Cook, 1992, p. 156)

Unlike many women in North America, Margariteño women do not relate their aggression to a loss of self-control. Instead, their antisocial actions are an exercise of control, usually employed against other women in disputes over authority or jealousy concerning a man. When combined with the findings from other cross-cultural aggression studies (Burbank, 1987), Cook's observations illustrate that although women are less lethal and generally less physically aggressive than men, they are by no means the "gentle sex." As a species, we all share the capacity to cause harm to one another.

Although males appear to be more physically aggressive than females, research suggests that females engage in more indirect aggression, such as spreading bad or false stories about others, or revealing someone's secrets. Why might these gender differences exist?

PERSONALITY

A major program of research conducted by Italian social psychologist Gian Vittorio Caprara and his associates (1994, 1996) indicates that three personality traits consistently related to aggression are irritability (the tendency to explode at the slightest provocation), rumination (the tendency to retain feelings of anger following provocation), and emotional susceptibility (the tendency to experience feelings of discomfort and inadequacy). Additional research indicates that adolescents who score low on the personality trait of *agreeableness*—with low scores associated with irritability, ruthlessness, and rudeness—tend to have high levels of both direct and indirect aggression (Gleason et al., 2004). Together, these findings suggest that highly aggressive people have a hard time controlling their emotions: they not only have quick tempers, but they also "stew in their own angry juices" following a confrontation.

The fact that aggressive-prone individuals tend to experience feelings of inadequacy is relevant to research discussed in chapter 3 (p. 81) suggesting that aggression is one way some people seek to maintain or restore their self-esteem. For many years, it was thought that only low self-esteem individuals were susceptible to these types of aggressive outbursts, but there actually is little evidence to support this claim. For example, depressed people are less aggressive than nondepressed people, and individuals who are shy and self-deprecating are underrepresented among populations of violent criminals (Baumeister & Boden, 1998). A comprehensive review of the research literature suggests that aggression is more commonly a result of threats to highly favorable views of the self and is most likely to occur when a person's high self-esteem is fragile and unstable (Baumeister et al., 1996; Kernis, in press). Apparently, in these instances, aggression is a defensive reaction to avoid having to make any downward revision of self-esteem (Kirkpatrick et al., 2002; Tangney et al., 1992).

One puzzling aspect of habitual, hot-tempered aggression is that it occurs despite the aggressor often experiencing long-term negative consequences, such as losing friends or being arrested and jailed. Why don't these aggressive-prone individuals learn from their mistakes? A series of studies suggest that a possible reason for these aggressive individuals often not taking long-term consequences into account is that they tend to be habitually impulsive (Joireman et al., 2003). Instead of thinking of future consequences, many aggressive-prone individuals focus on the immediate consequences of their aggressive behavior, which they perceive as beneficial (for example, winning an argument or preserving their self-esteem).

Delegitimizing Outgroups Promotes and Justifies Aggression

Our analysis in this chapter primarily focuses on interpersonal acts of aggression, but violence also occurs on the group level. Indeed, it has been estimated that approximately 36 million people have died in wars fought over the past 100 years and at least 119 million more have been killed by government genocide, massacres, and other mass killings (Bond, 2004; Rosenberg & Mercy, 1991). In comparing interpersonal versus intergroup acts of aggression, research indicates that group-initiated aggression is often more intense and harmful (Meier & Hinsz, 2004). What are some of the psychological factors that make collective aggression more likely and also more deadly?

As discussed in chapter 8, *realistic group conflict theory* contends that when groups are in conflict, two important changes occur in each group. The first change involves increased hostility toward the opposing outgroup, while the second change involves an intensification of ingroup loyalty (Staub, 2004). This pattern of behavior is referred to as ethnocentrism (see p. 277). Both of these changes took place in the United States following the terrorist attacks of September 11, 2001: hatred of Islamic terrorist Osama bin Laden and his followers grew, as did patriotism. Similar changes had already taken place among the terrorists and their supporters long before the attack (Cooper, 2001; Crenshaw, 2000). In fact, the terrorists' hostility was carried to such an extreme that they cognitively placed the United States—the target outgroup—into an extremely negative social category that excluded us from acceptable norms and values (Bar-Tal, 1990; Struch & Schwartz, 1989). This process of **delegitimization** effectively removes the target outgroup from the perceived world of humanity, and thus, ingroup members do not feel inhibited about aggressing against them (Bandura et al., 1996; Mandel, 2002). *They* are not like us. *They* are trying to destroy our way of life. *They* deserve our aggression.

Delegitimization often follows incidents of harm to one's ingroup by members of an outgroup (Freyd, 2002; Gerstenfeld, 2002). For example, shortly after the United States' invasion of Iraq, most Americans viewed Iraqi citizens with sympathy and compassion, considering them victims of Saddam Hussein's repressive regime. However, one year later, many Americans' attitudes toward Iraqi citizens had become hostile due to daily reports of U.S. soldiers being killed by Iraqis who opposed the foreign occupation. Likewise, many Iraqi citizens were initially grateful for the removal of their dictator by American troops. Yet, when these same troops were perceived as causing the deaths of many innocent Iraqis, Iraqis' attitudes toward American soldiers became increasingly hostile. Throughout both countries, political leaders, social commentators, and ordinary citizens increasingly defined the opposing country or faction within the country as an "evil" group that must be hunted down and destroyed. For further information on delegitimization, view the presentation on your Social Sense CD-ROM.

Collective aggression not only has negative consequences for those who are delegitimized, it also hurts the aggressor group. In a cross-national study of 110 countries, Dane Archer and Rosemary Gartner (1984) found a strong tendency for violent crime to increase after major wars, in both defeated and victorious nations. This increase in aggression was found among civilians as well as war veterans, which suggests that there is a generalized behavioral shift across society concerning how to resolve disputes. Carol and Melvin Ember (1994) confirmed this finding in a subsequent study of 186 societies. The likely reason for this effect is that war legitimizes violence as an acceptable remedy for conflict. The social norms of cultures that go to war indirectly endorse aggression as "the correct way to behave." Based on these findings, Ember and Ember (1994) offer the following recommendation:

> If we want to reduce the likelihood of interpersonal violence in our society, we may mostly
> need to reduce the likelihood of war, which would minimize the need to socialize for
> aggression and possibly reduce the likelihood of all violence. (p. 643)

Delegitimization

The process of cognitively placing an outgroup into an extremely negative social category that excludes them from acceptable norms and values, thereby eliminating inhibitions against harming them.

Social Sense

View a presentation on *Delegitimization and Genocide..*

- Aggression involves any form of behavior that is intended to harm or injure some person, oneself, or an object
- Instrumental aggression is the use of harmful behavior to achieve some other goal
- In hostile aggression, harming another is the goal of the attack
- Men are more physically aggressive, but women engage in more indirect aggression
- Personality traits found in aggressive-prone persons:

    irritability   rumination   emotional susceptibility

- Extreme outgroup hostility leads to delegitimization, which eliminates aggressive inhibitions against outgroup members

THE BIOLOGY OF AGGRESSION

Besides deaths resulting from collective aggression, each year in the United States, nearly 20,000 people are killed in violent assaults. Worldwide, more than 563,000 homicides occur each year, representing a global rate of roughly 10.7 for every 100,000 individuals (Mercy & Hammond, 1999). Even when people do not directly participate in aggressive acts themselves, many enjoy watching others do so in action adventure films or sporting events (Mustonen, 1997). Aggression even manifests itself in the play guns and toy soldiers we produce and purchase for our children's enjoyment. And judging from their faces as they play with these toys, enjoyment is what it often brings them. Based on these observations, is it reasonable to conclude that the human race has an inborn tendency for aggression?

Evolution Shaped Our Aggressive Behavior Patterns

A number of social scientists concur with the judgment that we are an innately aggressive species. In fact, for more than 100 years, many biologically oriented scientists have argued that aggression in humans—as well as aggression in other species—can be understood as an adaptive response to the environment. Evolutionary psychologists believe that males of many species, including our own, are more aggressive and have a stronger social dominance orientation than females (see chapter 8, pp. 280–281), because aggression and dominance-seeking have been the primary ways males have gained sexual access to females (Buss & Duntley, 2003). That is, by physically intimidating—and sometimes even killing—less aggressive males, the more aggressive males became socially dominant and thus were more likely to sexually reproduce. Unlike males, females' reproductive success did not depend on their level of aggression. Over many generations, this difference in the importance of aggression and dominance-seeking in male and female reproductive success led to genetically based differences in male and female aggression.

One important point to keep in mind about evolutionary theory is that it assumes that aggression increases the likelihood that an individual will survive and successfully reproduce. However, unlike earlier instinct theories that emphasized individual survival (Lorenz, 1966), modern evolutionary theories stress genetic survival (Buss & Shackelford, 1997). From this perspective, genetic survival necessitates that aggression should be selective because relatives share many more of the same genes than strangers. In other words, relatives should not be attacked, for this reduces the likelihood that one's gene pool will be passed on

The impulse to mar and to destroy is as ancient and almost nearly as universal as the impulse to create. The one is an easier way than the other of demonstrating power.

Joseph Wood Krutch, 1893–1970, U.S. author and critic

FIGURE 13.2

**Murder Rates
Around the Globe**

A United Nations study reported that not only does the murder rate vary widely from country to country, but also that the murder rates within many countries change substantially from year to year. Do these data suggest that evolutionary based explanations of aggression are false? How might you explain the data by considering both evolutionary and cultural factors in your analysis?

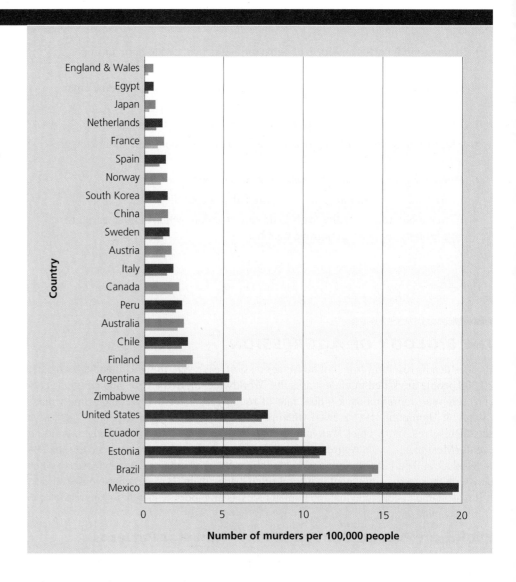

to future generations. In general, research supports this hypothesis: aggression is much more likely to be directed against nonrelatives, and when relatives are attacked, they tend to be "relatives by marriage." For example, stepchildren, who by definition do not have genetic ties to one of their parents, are much more likely to be abused and killed than are other children (Daly & Wilson, 1991). A similar pattern is found in other animal species (Lore & Schultz, 1993).

One problem with solely relying on an evolutionary-based explanation for aggression in humans is that—as figure 13.2 illustrates—levels of aggression vary so widely across cultures. A related problem is that wide differences in aggression occur within cultures over time. For example, 300 years ago, Sweden had one of the highest documented rates of interpersonal violence in the Western world, and today it has one of the lowest (Lagerspetz, 1985). Genetic changes in human groups over such a short (in terms of evolution) time period are simply not possible. Instead, social and cultural factors are the more likely causes. Of course, this does not mean that evolutionary factors do not influence human aggression. It simply means that evolutionary forces, by themselves, cannot adequately explain human aggression.

Biological Factors Influence Aggressive Behavior

Beyond focusing on how aggressive tendencies may have been shaped over hundreds of thousands of generations, scientists also study whether individual aggressive tendencies are inherited and whether hormonal fluctuations influence later aggressive responses.

War nourishes war.

Johann Schiller, German writer and philosopher, 1759–1805

BEHAVIOR GENETICS

Research on identical and fraternal twins in the field of behavior genetics suggests that our individual aggressiveness may be partly due to inheritance (Miles & Carey, 1997). That is, twins who share exactly the same genetic material (identical twins) tend to have more similar aggressive tendencies than twins who share only 50 percent of the same genes (fraternal twins). The problem with this research, however, is that parents tend to treat identical twins more similarly than fraternal twins, and thus, it is difficult for twin studies to clearly distinguish between biological and environmental determinants of aggression (McCord, 1994). In addition, animal studies suggest that environmental factors, such as stress and nutrition, can actually cause certain genes to become activated or deactivated, resulting in even identical twins not having the same active genetic makeup (McClearn, 1993). For the time being, then, although heritability undoubtedly influences human aggression, its degree of influence is still unknown (Plomin et al., 1990).

HORMONAL ACTIVITY

Several studies suggest that chemical messengers in the bloodstream, known as hormones, influence human aggression (Adelson, 2004; Herbert & Martinez, 2001). For example, one study found that people who had been institutionalized for attempted suicide (self-directed aggression) or extreme aggressiveness had lower than average levels of serotonin, a hormone that is associated with the ability to control aggressive impulses (Marazzitti et al., 1993).

Other studies have found higher than normal levels of the male hormone testosterone in highly aggressive individuals of both sexes (Carlson, 2004; Dabbs et al., 1987). These findings suggest that high testosterone levels may either directly cause aggression or indirectly cause it by encouraging social dominance and competitiveness (Mazur & Booth, 1998). However, other evidence suggests an opposite causal path: testosterone levels are sometimes affected by the outcome of competition. For example, in one study of male tennis players, winners' testosterone levels increased after the match while losers' hormonal levels decreased (Mazur & Lamb, 1980). Similar hormonal changes occur among nonhuman primates following competition in which they either gain or lose status in their social groups. Among humans, the positive and negative emotions accompanying success and failure appear to be what cause the changes in testosterone level (McCaul et al., 1992).

These studies suggest that there is no simple causal relationship between hormone levels and aggression in humans or other animals. Heightened testosterone levels may make aggression more likely, but aggression—or even nonaggressive competition—may cause changes in testosterone levels. The message that can be taken from this research and the other studies reviewed in this section is that biological variables—evolutionary history, genetic inheritance, and level of hormone activity—contribute to the general aggressiveness of the person (Geen, 1998). Unlike early instinct theories, contemporary biologists and evolutionary theorists do not argue that aggressive behavior is determined by some inborn fixed tendency. Instead, they propose that these biological background variables influence how we respond to situational provocations. Although a growing number of social psychologists are acknowledging the impact that biological factors can have on our capacity for aggression, the vast majority still believe that the form that the aggression takes, as well as its intensity, is influenced most by the many psychological, social, and cultural forces that we will discuss in the remaining chapter sections (Hinde, 1990; Robarchek, 1989).

SECTION SUMMARY

- Evolutionary theorists contend that aggressive tendencies are selective and based on the principle of genetic survival
- Biological research suggests that individual differences in aggressiveness are partly due to inheritance and hormonal changes

AGGRESSION AS A REACTION TO NEGATIVE AFFECT

Japanese are world-famous for their politeness. One notable exception to this courteous behavior is a 200-year-old event that takes place just before midnight on New Year's Eve in Ashikaga, a city fifty miles north of Tokyo. In what outsiders might consider to be a very strange festival, people walk in a procession up a dark mountain road to the Saishoji Temple, screaming curses at those who have frustrated them during the previous twelve months. "You idiot!" "Give me a raise!" "My teacher is stupid!" Although these words of blame, hostility, and anger would almost never be directed at the real sources of the Japanese's frustration, participants believe the screaming is beneficial. Is such behavior really beneficial to people? Does it reduce aggressive tendencies?

The Frustration-Aggression Hypothesis Asserts That Aggression Is Always the Product of Frustration

If you had asked a group of social psychologists these questions in 1939, they most likely would have replied that releasing pent-up frustrations in this manner was a very good idea. At that time, John Dollard, Neal Miller, Leonard Doob, O. H. Mowrer, and Robert Sears had just published their now classic monograph, *Frustration and Aggression,* which outlined what came to be the most popular theory of aggression in the social sciences, namely the **frustration-aggression hypothesis.** They defined frustration as any external condition that prevents you from obtaining the pleasures you had expected to enjoy. In other words, if you are prevented from doing something that you want to do, you become frustrated. The original theory had three main propositions. The first proposition was that frustration always elicits the drive to attack others. The second proposition was that every act of aggression could be traced to some previous frustration (this essentially meant that all aggression is of the hostile variety). The third proposition was that engaging in aggression causes **catharsis,** which is the reduction in the aggressive drive following an aggressive act.

Research supports the general proposition that frustration can cause aggression. For example, archival studies have found a negative correlation between economic conditions and lynchings of African Americans in the pre-1930s South (Hepworth & West, 1988; Hovland & Sears, 1940; Tolnay & Beck, 1995). When Southern states experienced economic depression due to a drop in cotton prices, White southerners appeared to vent their frustration by lynching Blacks. In other words, African Americans became the scapegoats of White displaced aggression. Other studies have found a correlation between the loss of jobs in communities and an increase in child abuse and other violent behavior (Catalano et al., 1993; Steinberg et al., 1981).

Although this research has established a link between frustration and aggression, additional studies indicate that this link is subject to a rapid rate of decay (Green et al., 1998). If frustration is not acted upon quickly (often less than an hour), people are unlikely to aggress (Buvinic & Berkowitz, 1976). Frustration is most likely to produce an inclination to aggress when the person believes the hindrance was unfair and deliberate (Batson et al., 2000; Pedersen et al., 2000). Thus, if someone catches your heel and sends you tumbling to the ground, you are less likely to hold it against him if you believe it was an accident rather than deliberate. Another basis for criticizing the theory was its contention that frustration was the root cause of all aggression. Subsequent research has clearly shown that frustration is simply one among many causes of aggression.

Finally, the claim that aggressive tendencies are reduced following the expression of aggression has been subjected to a great deal of scientific scrutiny. Although this notion of catharsis reflects a common belief that people can purge themselves of powerful emotions by "letting off steam" or "getting it off their chests," little empirical evidence supports this proposition. For example, in one representative study, Shahbaz Mallick and Boyd McCandless (1966) had third-grade girls and boys work on a block-construction task in pairs. What the young participants did not realize, however, was that the child working with them was

---

Frustration-Aggression Hypothesis

The theory that frustration causes aggression.

Catharsis

The reduction in the aggressive drive following an aggressive act.

I have enjoyed all the pleasures that revenge can give.

Marie Madeleine de La Fayette, French countess and novelist, 1634–1692

FIGURE 13.3

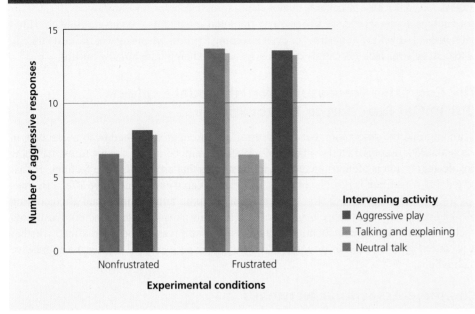

Does Children's Aggressive Play Have a Cathartic Effect?

In contradiction to the catharsis hypothesis, Mallick and McCandless (1966) found that children who had been frustrated by a "clumsy" child confederate showed no reduction in their aggressive responses after engaging in imaginary aggression. What did reduce aggression in the frustrated children was being told that the confederate's clumsiness had been caused by fatigue and strain (talking and explaining condition). What do these findings suggest about recommendations that aggression can be decreased by having people engage in make believe violence?

a confederate who had been instructed to either allow participants to complete the block-construction task or to act very clumsy and impede completion. Immediately following this frustrating or nonfrustrating experience, participants performed an intervening activity for about eight minutes. This activity either involved shooting a toy gun at a target or talking with the experimenter. Half of the children who talked with the experimenter were told during the course of the conversation that their partner had been tired and upset, while the rest merely engaged in neutral talk with the experimenter. At the end of this intervening activity, the young confederate was brought into another room, supposedly to work on another block-construction task. Each of the naive participants then was given an opportunity to hinder the confederate's progress by pushing a "hurt" button that would disrupt the confederate's work. Aggression was measured by the number of times the child pushed the button. As figure 13.3 shows, frustration generally increased aggression, except when participants were told that fatigue and emotional strain caused the confederate's clumsiness. This finding replicates previously discussed research indicating that aggression is much more likely following intentional rather than unintentional frustration. More important for our discussion of catharsis, however, is the fact that children's aggressive play did not result in any reduction in the number of attacks on the frustrator. Put simply, there is no evidence in these findings for catharsis. Engaging in make-believe violence does not purge aggressive drives.

Direct acts of aggression also do not cause catharsis. In fact, a number of experiments indicate that people who are given the opportunity to aggress directly against someone who has frustrated them often become more aggressive, not less so (Buss, 1966; Geen, 1968). Sociologist Murray Straus's research indicates that this sort of escalation of aggression is a common pattern in domestic violence. Family conflicts often begin with verbal quarreling, which then escalates to screaming and yelling, and finally to physical aggression (Straus & Gelles, 1990). In contrast, households that engage in little or no verbal aggression rarely ever experience physical violence (less than half of 1 percent). Despite the lack of research support for catharsis, the popular media and many mental health professionals continue to advocate its use. For example, a common belief among many marriage counselors is that "couples who fight [verbally] together, stay together"—as long as they do not engage in vindictive verbal attacks. As Straus points out, however, the research literature indicates that once verbal aggression begins, it is difficult to keep it within manageable bounds. In such

No more tears now. I will think about revenge.

Mary, Queen of Scots, 1542–1587

instances, advocating the venting of anger through aggressive means may be worse than useless—it may cause a general increase in aggressive behavior (Bushman, 2002). This does not mean you should keep your frustrations and anger bottled up inside yourself. However, instead of yelling at others—or even punching a pillow when angry—the best strategy is to convey your feelings calmly and clearly, without being intentionally hurtful.

The Cognitive-Neoassociationist Model Explains Our Initial Reaction to Provocation

Realizing that the association between frustration and aggression had been overstated, in the late 1960s Leonard Berkowitz (1969, 1989) developed a new theory to explain how hostile aggression is often triggered by circumstances that arouse negative feelings. He asserted that frustration is just one of many factors that can stimulate negative affect. Besides frustration, other aversive factors such as pain, extreme temperatures, and encountering disliked people can also cause negative affect. It is this negative affect, and not frustration itself, that stimulates the inclination to aggress. The stronger the negative affect, whether it is caused by frustration or by some other aversive experience, the greater the aggressive inclination.

COGNITIVE-ASSOCIATIVE NETWORKS

Berkowitz named his theory the **cognitive-neoassociationist model** because he believes that when we experience negative affect due to some unpleasant condition, this affect is encoded into memory and becomes cognitively associated with specific types of negative thoughts, emotions, physiological responses, and reflexive behaviors (see figure 13.4). Although these cognitive-associative networks are initially weak, the more they are activated, the stronger they become (Ratcliff & McKoon, 1994). When these associations are sufficiently strong, activating any one of them will likely activate the others, a process known as *priming* (see chapter 5, p. 144). Thus, when we recall a past occasion in which we were extremely angry, this memory may prime hostile thoughts, angry feelings, and even anger/aggression-related reflexive actions, such as clenched fists and gritted teeth. One important implication of this theory is that even when our surroundings do not elicit negative affect, simply thinking about aggression can set us on the path to its activation (Miller et al., 2003).

INITIAL "FIGHT" OR "FLIGHT" TENDENCIES

In addition to describing how cognitive-associative networks are formed, the cognitive-neoassociationist model further proposes that an aversive event initially activates, not one, but two different networks at the same time. One network is related to the impulsive aggression-related tendencies already described (the fight response), while the other is related to impulsive escape-related tendencies (the flight response). Whether we react to negative affect with "fight" or "flight" depends on our (1) genetic predispositions, (2) prior conditioning and learning, and (3) attention to aspects of the situation that facilitate or inhibit aggression (Berkowitz, 1993). Because our present objective is to understand how aversive events lead to aggression, we will concentrate on the fight-response side of this model (the left side of figure 13.4).

"UNTHINKING" AGGRESSIVE RESPONSES

One thing to keep in mind is that the cognitive processes discussed thus far are simply impulsive reactions to negative affect, and thus, they represent only the potential first stage in aggression. The negative thoughts, emotions, and reflexive actions evoked in the cognitive-associative networks at this stage are primitive, or rudimentary, and have yet to be shaped and developed by higher-order cognitive processes. If this more-sophisticated thinking does not come into play, we may simply lash out with anger or aggression. According to Berkowitz (1994a), this type of "unthinking" or impulsive aggression is most likely to occur when we are engaged in highly routine activities and thus are not consciously monitoring our thoughts, feelings, or actions.

Cognitive-Neoassociationist Model

A theory of impulsive aggression that aversive events produce negative affect, which stimulates the inclination to aggress.

No man can think clearly when his fists are clenched.

George Jean Nathan, American critic and writer, 1882–1958

FIGURE 13.4

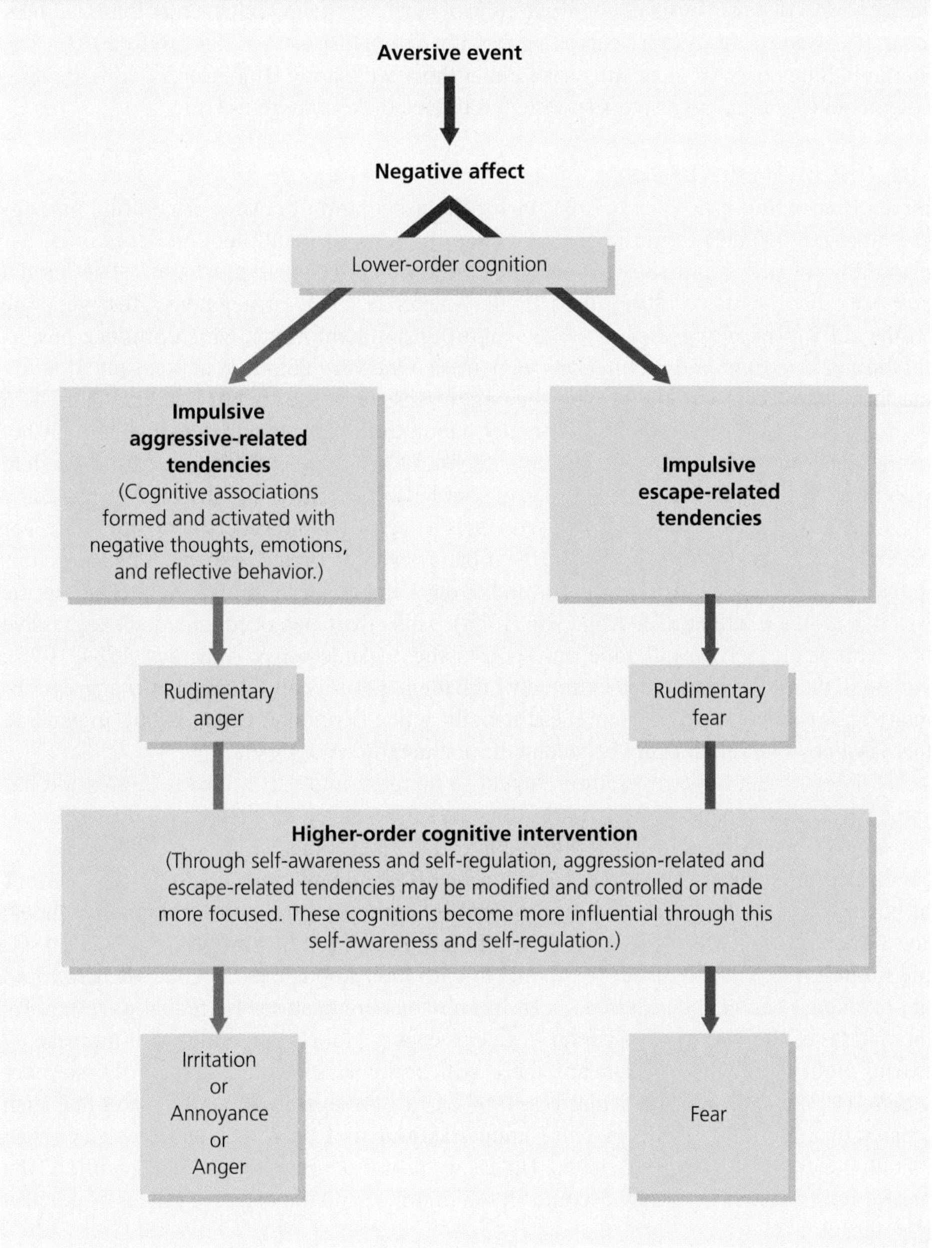

Aversive event

↓

Negative affect

Lower-order cognition

Impulsive aggressive-related tendencies
(Cognitive associations formed and activated with negative thoughts, emotions, and reflective behavior.)

Impulsive escape-related tendencies

Rudimentary anger

Rudimentary fear

Higher-order cognitive intervention
(Through self-awareness and self-regulation, aggression-related and escape-related tendencies may be modified and controlled or made more focused. These cognitions become more influential through this self-awareness and self-regulation.)

Irritation
or
Annoyance
or
Anger

Fear

Cognitive-Neoassociationist Model of Hostile Aggression

Leonard Berkowitz's theory of impulsive aggression states that aversive events produce negative affect. This negative affect, in turn, stimulates the inclination to aggress. How can this aggressive inclination be "short-circuited"?

HIGHER-ORDER COGNITIVE INTERVENTION

Although aggression is likely if we reflexively respond to negative affect, a very different outcome often occurs if higher-order cognitive processes are activated. This represents stage two in the aggressive response. The cognitive-neoassociationist model contends that if these aggression-related tendencies are subjected to higher-level thinking, they are often modified and controlled. What causes the aggression-related tendencies in stage one to come under the control of the more complex cognitive processes of stage two? Research suggests that these cognitive control mechanisms are activated when we become self-aware and attend to what we are thinking, feeling, and doing (Mischel et al., 1996). Thus, when frustrated, we may try to make sense of our negative feelings before acting. If we conclude that no one is to blame for the aversive event, our anger will likely subside. Similarly, we

When anger rises, think of the consequences.

Confucius, Chinese philosopher, 551–479 B.C.

may assign blame to a particular person but still conclude that retaliation is an inappropriate response. Because of these cognitive control mechanisms in higher-order thinking, negative affect does not always lead to aggression (Kuppens et al., 2004). Of course, after thinking things over we may still strike out at those we blame. Higher-order thinking does not guarantee a nonaggressive response, but it does make it more likely.

THE "HEAT HYPOTHESIS"

Beyond providing a better explanation for the association between frustration and aggression, the primary importance of the cognitive-neoassociationist model is in its explanation of our impulsive and affect-driven reactions to aggression. The model proposes that events resulting in particularly intense levels of negative affect generate strong activation of aggression-related cognitions and emotions, which produce powerful feelings of anger and inclinations to aggress. One very common unpleasant situation that has often been associated with such aggressive responses is hot weather. Consistent with the cognitive-neoassociationist model, laboratory experiments demonstrate that hot temperatures increase hostile thoughts and feelings (Anderson et al., 1995). Also consistent with the model is the finding of an upward spiral effect, in which the discomfort caused by high temperatures is related to increased levels of aggression (Anderson et al., 1997). For example, archival studies suggest that the urban riots that erupted in many American cities in the 1960s were most likely to occur on hot days and then to diminish in intensity as the weather cooled (Carlsmith & Anderson, 1979). This effect also occurs for such aggressive behaviors as murder, assault, rape, and spousal abuse (Anderson & Anderson, 1984, 1996). Although there is evidence that extremely high temperatures can actually lower aggression-related crimes due to people being less socially active (Rotton & Cohn, 2000), in general, there is a positive relationship between hot weather and hot tempers.

The fact that hot temperatures appear to increase impulsive, hostile aggression has some interesting practical implications. First, it suggests that the frequency of hostile outbursts could be reduced in temperature-controlled environments. For example, using air-conditioning in prisons might reduce the problems of inmate violence. Similar reductions of hostile aggression might also be achieved by controlling the temperatures in schools and work environments. Of course, air-conditioning will not create harmony in these settings, but it may make it easier for people to curb their impulse to lash out when annoyed or provoked. Second, the heat hypothesis has obvious implications for global warming. By the middle of the twenty-first century, we can expect global temperatures to increase by two to eight degrees, which means there will be many more hot days in the summer months (U.S. House of Representatives, 1994). Craig Anderson (2001) estimates that such temperature increases could increase annual serious and deadly assaults by more than 24,000 incidents in the United States. Unless we discover some way to "air-condition" the planet, future generations may become all too familiar with the negative effects of the heat hypothesis.

AGGRESSIVE CUES AS "TRIGGERS" OF AGGRESSION

One question many people were asking following the Westside Middle School shootings was whether the presence of guns in the two boys' homes actually triggered their aggression. Leonard Berkowitz would certainly consider this a distinct possibility. In addition to anger eliciting aggression, Berkowitz believes that the presence of aggression-associated cues in the environment can act as triggers for hostile outbursts by making aggressive thoughts more accessible. An aggression-associated cue is anything that is associated with either violence or unpleasantness. The most obvious aggressive cues are weapons, such as guns, knives, and clubs, while less obvious cues are negative attitudes and unpleasant physical characteristics. Numerous studies indicate that the presence of aggression-associated cues does indeed trigger aggression (Anderson et al., 1998; Lindsay & Anderson, 2000).

Aggression-associated cues can also heighten aggression. In a meta-analysis of twenty-three studies, Michael Carlson and his coworkers (1990) found strong support for the hypothesis that aggression-associated cues enhance aggressiveness among people who

Anger blows out the lamp of the mind.

Robert Ingersoll, American politician, 1833–1899

Man only becomes dangerous when he is equipped with weapons.

Sir Edmund Leach, British social anthropologist, b. 1910

TABLE 13.1

Facts Concerning Firearm Violence in the U.S.: Aggression-Eliciting Cues?

1. Over 35 percent of U.S. households contain at least one firearm, and in half of those households the guns are loaded and/or easily accessible to children.

2. Guns kept in the home for self-protection are 43 times more likely to kill someone you know than to kill in self-defense.

3. The death rate of American children from guns is 12 times higher than in 25 other industrialized countries combined.

4. By the teen years, most homicides and suicides occur with firearms.

5. The risk of homicide in the home is three times greater and the risk of suicide in the home is five times greater for those households with guns.

6. Almost half of all deaths among African-American male teenagers involve firearms.

7. Handguns are increasingly being marketed as tools of self-defense for women. However, crime statistics indicate that for every one instance that a woman uses a handgun to kill a stranger in self-defense, 239 women are murdered with handguns. Often, the handguns used in these murders came from the woman's own household.

are already angry. This finding may go a long way in explaining the fact that a handgun kept in the home for self-protection is forty-three times more likely to kill a friend or family member than to be used in killing intruders (refer to table 13.1). When domestic disputes erupt, the presence of firearms may enhance the aggressiveness of the angry parties, resulting in tragic consequences. As Berkowitz explains this effect, "Guns not only permit violence, they can stimulate it as well. The finger pulls the trigger, but the trigger may also be pulling the finger" (Berkowitz, 1968, p. 22).

An important caveat to Berkowitz's statement is that the weapons effect depends on the meaning people attach to guns and other weapons. For many people, guns are associated in memory to concepts related to aggression and hostility because they are viewed as instruments designed and used to hurt and kill people. Yet what about people who view guns less as objects of aggression against other people and more as objects they use only for sport? If these people associate guns with having fun outdoors on weekends when they hunt for wild game, are they unlikely to have aggressive thoughts when in the presence of hunting guns? A series of studies conducted by Bruce Bartholow and his colleagues (2005) indicate that this appears to be the case. They found that although both hunting rifles and assault weapons served as cues to aggression for people with no prior hunting experience, only assault weapons served as an aggressive cue for hunters. Instead of priming negative thoughts and emotions, guns associated with animal hunting tended to activate nonaggressive responses among hunters. These findings suggest that an object serves as a cue to aggression only if it is closely linked with aggression-related concepts in memory.

What are the possible implications of these findings for social debates concerning gun ownership? One implication is that guns used for hunting are less likely to prime the sort of negative emotions and thoughts that lead to crimes of passion than guns used for protection. Consistent with this reasoning, a survey of over 6,000 middle school students found that owning a pistol or handgun in order to gain respect or to frighten others was associated with extremely high levels of antisocial behavior, such as bullying, physical aggression, and delinquency (Cunningham et al., 2000). In contrast, students who owned hunting rifles and shotguns engaged in only slightly greater antisocial behavior than students who did not own guns of any kind. Returning to Berkowitz's previous statement of the "trigger pulling the

The Weapons Effect

Because many people perceive guns as harmful and dangerous, they associate these objects in memory with aggression and hostility. Research indicates that aggression-associated cues can trigger aggressive outbursts in people. However, Bruce Bartholow and his colleagues (2005) found that although both hunting rifles and assault weapons serve as cues to aggression for people with no prior hunting experience, only assault weapons serve as an aggressive cue for hunters. Why might this be the case?

finger," it appears that handguns and assault weapons are likely to "itch" more fingers than hunting rifles.

Alcohol Consumption Increases the Likelihood of Aggression

. . . O thou invisible spirit wine, if thou hast no name to be known by,

let us call thee devil! . . .

O God, that men should put an enemy

in their mouths to steal away their brains!

That we should, with joy, pleasure, revel

and applause, transform into beasts!

William Shakespeare, *Othello* (II, iii)

Although weapons may trigger aggressive outbursts in those who are already angry, it has long been assumed that the consumption of alcohol causes people to become more easily angered and hostile. Both correlational and experimental research support this assumption. Numerous studies conducted in various countries have found a strong correlation between alcohol intoxication and a host of different types of aggression, including domestic abuse, assault, rape, and homicide (Bachman & Peralta, 2002; Busch & Rosenberg, 2004; Leonard & Quigley, 1999). Experimental studies have also found that when people drink beverages containing enough alcohol to make them legally intoxicated, they tend to behave more aggressively or respond more strongly to provocation than do persons who consume nonalcoholic drinks (Giancola & Zeichner, 1997; MacDonald et al., 2000).

Why does the consumption of alcohol increase aggression? Few researchers contend that alcohol provides a direct biochemical stimulus to aggression. Instead, the general view is that alcohol weakens people's restraints against aggression by adversely affecting more controlled, effortful thinking while simultaneously leaving more automatic, impulsive responses relatively unaffected (Bartholow et al., 2003a; Ito et al., 1996). Some researchers believe that this weakening of restraints, or *disinhibition,* is partly caused by an interruption of one's ability to process and respond to the meaning of complex and subtle situational cues (Hull & Bond, 1986; Johnson et al., 2000). In other words, when provoked, people who are drunk are much less attentive than those who are sober to such inhibiting cues as the provocateur's intent and the possible negative consequences of violence. For example, in a shock-competition experiment, Kenneth Leonard (1989) found that alcohol did not influence participants' reactions to their competitors' explicit aggressive or nonaggressive signals, but it did interfere with their understanding of subtle aggressive signals. That is, following an aggressive exchange, intoxicated participants were more likely than those who

What are some ways researchers believe alcohol increases aggressive outbursts?

were sober to misinterpret their competitors' subtly announced intentions of nonaggression as being aggression-as-usual.

Inattention to personal and social standards of nonviolence can also cause disinhibition. As discussed in chapter 3 (p. 61), we are more attentive to personal and social standards of behavior when self-aware. However, alcohol consumption reduces self-awareness (Hull, 1981; Hull et al., 1986), and this can lead to impulsive, nonnormative actions, such as aggression. Thus, intoxicated people not only have problems attending to external cues that might defuse their inclinations to aggress, but they also have problems attending to internalized behavioral standards that might also inhibit aggression.

A third way this disinhibition effect may occur is through people's expectations of how alcohol will affect behavior. Perhaps you have heard people excuse a drunken individual's verbal aggression by saying, "It's the liquor talking." Such statements imply that it is not the drunken person misbehaving, but rather, it is the alcohol that is to blame. If people learn that normally inappropriate behavior is often excused when performed under the influence of alcohol, they may engage in those behaviors when drinking (Cameron & Stritzke, 2003; Gelles, 1993). From this perspective, alcohol's effect on aggression is due to a *learned disinhibition.* In support of this viewpoint, research indicates that people sometimes become more aggressive not just when they have consumed alcohol, but also when they think they have consumed it (Lang et al., 1975). There is also evidence that some men who ordinarily disapprove of hitting a woman believe that being in an intoxicated state gives them a socially acceptable excuse to abuse their spouses (Straus & Gelles, 1990).

Undoubtedly, both the chemically induced disinhibiting effects of alcohol and its learned disinhibiting effects offer us possible explanations of why alcohol consumption causes aggression. Alcohol not only reduces self-awareness and disrupts our ability to adequately process situational cues that would normally inhibit our aggressive behavior, but it also provides us with a ready excuse for responding in such an antisocial manner.

Excitation Transfer Can Intensify Hostility-Based Aggression

You may recall that in chapter 12 (pp. 463–468) we discussed how passionate love is kindled sometimes by transferring emotional arousal from one source to the love object. Dolf Zillmann (1994) called this psychological process—in which arousal caused by one stimulus is transferred and added to arousal elicited by a second stimulus—excitation transfer. According to Zillmann, excitation transfer is not restricted to romantic attraction; it can also explain aggressive outbursts.

CRITICAL *thinking*

How might alcohol impair judgment and, thus, lead to the kind of aggressive outbursts found in domestic violence cases?

Drunkeness . . . is the highway to hell. . . .

Elizabeth Joceline, English author, 1566–1622

For example, in one study, male participants were either provoked or treated in a neutral manner by an experimental confederate (Zillmann et al., 1972). Then, half of them engaged in strenuous physical exercise while the rest did not. Following a brief delay, participants were then given the opportunity to shock the confederate they had interacted with earlier (of course, no actual shocks were actually delivered). As expected, angered men who had exercised chose stronger shock levels than did those who had not been angered or who had not exercised. In other words, the elevation of excitation due to physical exertion energized aggression only in those who had been angered. No longer thinking about the arousing effects of the exercise, it was fairly easy for these previously angered men to transfer this arousal to the now-salient disliked confederate. In the unangered men, however, the increased excitation had no consequence because they had not experienced any feelings, either positive or negative, toward the confederate.

Besides physical exercise, increased aggression through excitation transfer can also occur due to such arousing stimuli as loud noise, vigorous music, violent movies, and even sexual scenes (Anderson, 1997; Zillmann, 1983). Thus, no matter what produces heightened excitation, the arousal can energize whatever aggressive urges we may be having at the moment. Excitation transfer may partly explain why violence sometimes erupts among sports fans of rival teams during games. Aroused by the excitement of the contest, ordinarily civilized fans may become violent when angered by an incident on or off the field of play. Excitation transfer is an even more likely explanation for why warriors throughout the ages have engaged in such energizing practices as dancing, chanting, and drum beating before going into battle. Undoubtedly, they discovered that such activities intensified their anger and aggressive inclinations.

CRITICAL *thinking*

In addition to excitation transfer, how else might violence erupt among rival sports fans? Consider factors already discussed in this chapter, as well as those discussed in the prejudice and discrimination chapter.

SECTION SUMMARY

- The frustration-aggression hypothesis proposes that
    blocking a person's goal-directed behavior produces frustration
    frustration increases the aggressive drive
- The cognitive-neoassociationist model asserts that
    frustration is just one of many factors that can stimulate negative affect
    negative affect stimulates the inclination to aggress
    aggressive tendencies are often modified by higher-level thinking
- Hostile aggression can also be sparked by
    heat   alcohol intoxication   excitation transfer

LEARNING AGGRESSIVE BEHAVIOR

Now that we have examined how negative affect can sometimes trigger aggressive outbursts, let us explore how our social environment can shape aggressive behavior. In families where adults use violence, children grow up being much more likely to use it themselves (Guille, 2004; Tjaden & Thoennes, 2000). In communities where aggression is considered a sign of manhood, aggressive behaviors are eagerly and consciously transmitted from generation to generation, especially among males (Rosenberg & Mercy, 1991). Yet how does this learning take place?

Social Learning Theory Emphasizes the Acquisition and Maintenance of Aggressive Behavior

Albert Bandura, one of the leading proponents of **social learning theory,** contends that people learn when to aggress, how to aggress, and against whom to aggress (Bandura, 1979; Bandura & Walters, 1963). This social learning of appropriate behavior, shaped by operant

Social Learning Theory

A theory that social behavior is primarily learned by observing and imitating the actions of others, and secondarily by being directly rewarded and punished for our own actions.

conditioning principles (see chapter 6, p. 181), occurs through both direct and indirect means.

THE REWARDS OF AGGRESSION

Any behavior that is rewarded, or reinforced, is more likely to occur in the future. Therefore, if people act aggressively and receive rewards, they are more likely to act aggressively at some later date. The rewards could be material, such as candy or money, or they could be social, such as praise or increased status and self-esteem (Branscombe & Wann, 1994). When behavior, like aggression, is repeatedly not rewarded, or is even punished, this will generally lead to a reduction in the frequency of the behavior. Psychologists call this weakening and eventual termination of behavior *extinction*. Extinction of aggressive actions is exactly what parents are aiming at when they give children "time-outs" following harmful outbursts.

Although withdrawing rewards can lead to the extinction of aggressive behavior, an inconsistent pattern of reward withdrawal can do more harm than good. This is because like any behavior that people learn and utilize, aggression does not have to be rewarded each time it occurs. In fact, an important principle of learning is that both people and other animals show greater resistance to the extinction of a behavior when it has been rewarded only intermittently rather than continuously. In one study demonstrating this principle, young children were rewarded for hitting a doll (Cowan & Walters, 1963). Half were rewarded every time they acted aggressively, but the others were rewarded only periodically. In both instances, the rewards increased the children's aggressive behavior. However, when the experimenters stopped the rewards, the children who had been only periodically reinforced continued to hit the doll longer than those whose aggressiveness had been continuously reinforced. Because in real life people are not always reinforced for their aggressive activities, this study suggests that such periodic reinforcement is ideally suited to the prevention of extinction, not the weakening of aggressive behavior.

OBSERVATIONAL LEARNING

Although learning does occur through direct reinforcement, we most often learn by watching and imitating others without being directly rewarded for doing so. This observational learning is also known as social modeling, because the learner imitates the model. Children are most likely to pay attention to and model the behavior of those with whom they have a nurturing relationship and who also have social control over them (Bandura & Huston, 1961; Pettit, 2004). Parents are prime candidates as role models, but behavior can also be observed and modeled from television, books, and other mass media sources (Basow, 1986).

In perhaps the most well-known series of observational learning experiments, Bandura and his colleagues (1961) set out to determine whether children would imitate the behavior of an aggressive adult model. In these studies, a child was first brought into a room to work on an art project. In another part of the room, an adult was playing quietly with Tinker Toys. Near these toys was a mallet and a Bobo doll, which is a big, inflatable clownlike toy that is weighted at the bottom so that when it is pushed or punched down it will quickly bounce back to an upright position. In the experimental condition, after playing with the Tinker Toys for a minute, the adult stood up, walked over to the Bobo doll, and began to attack it. She punched the doll, kicked it, hit it with the mallet, and even sat on it. As she pummeled the clown doll, she yelled out, "Sock him in the nose! . . . Kick him! . . . Knock him down!" In the control condition, the adult simply played quietly and nonaggressively with her toys for ten minutes. After witnessing either the aggressive or nonaggressive adult model, the child was led into another room filled with many wonderful toys. However, before the child could play with these treasures, the experimenter aroused frustration by saying that these were her best toys and she must "save them for the other children." The child was then led to a third room, containing both aggressive and nonaggressive toys, including a Bobo doll.

What did children typically do in this third room? If they had witnessed the nonaggressive adult model, they played calmly. However, if they had been exposed to the aggressive adult, they were likely to beat up the Bobo doll, often shouting the same things at the clown during their attack as the previous adult model. Similar results were

Bandura's Bobo doll studies clearly indicate that children can learn aggressive behavior through modeling the aggressive actions of an adult.

Social Sense

View excerpts from the Bobo Doll study.

obtained when the child had no direct exposure to the adult but merely saw a film of the adult attacking the doll. Other experimental variations demonstrated that children were more likely to imitate same-sex models (boys imitating men and girls imitating women) than those of the other sex. View actual footage of the Bobo Doll study on your Social Sense CD-ROM. Taken as a whole, these studies indicate that observing adult aggression can not only lower children's aggressive inhibitions; it can also teach them how to aggress.

As with direct aggression, the observational learning experiments demonstrated that children are likely to imitate others' aggressive acts if social models are rewarded for their behavior. For example, Mary Rosekrans and Willard Hartup (1967) had preschool children watch an adult model aggress against a Bobo doll. These aggressive actions were either praised ("Good for you! I guess you really fixed him that time") or scolded ("Now look what you've done, you've ruined it") by another adult. After watching this interaction, the children were allowed to play with the same toys. Another group of children who had not been exposed to the aggressive model also played with the toys. Results indicated that the children who had watched the aggressive model being rewarded were significantly more aggressive in their play behavior than the children in the other two groups (refer to figure 13.5). This study and others reveal that children do not unthinkingly imitate a model's actions. Rather, they copy the actions of others who have been rewarded, not punished.

Although these findings might leave you with the impression that aggressive models who are punished have little negative impact on children's later behavior, this is not necessarily the case. The research demonstrates that children are less likely to imitate the actions of punished aggressors. Does this mean these children fail to learn the aggressive behavior, or does it mean they simply inhibit the expression of these behaviors? In a study similar to Rosekrans and Hartup's experiment, Bandura (1965) offered all the children in the study a reward if they could imitate the aggressive behavior of the model that they had previously observed. Every single one of the participants could mimic the model's aggressive actions, even those who had seen the punished model. Thus, observing someone being punished for

FIGURE 13.5

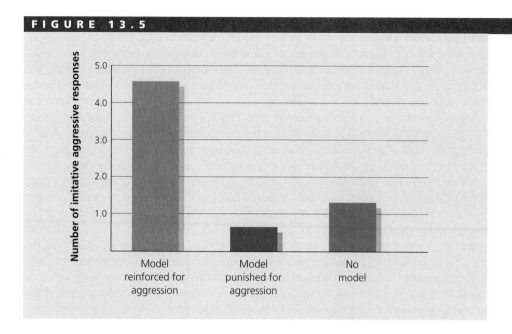

Modeling Aggression as a Function of Reinforcement and Punishment

Children were much more likely to imitate the aggressive behavior of an adult model if the adult had been rewarded rather than punished. Can you imagine how these social learning principles might exert their influence among children playing on a grade-school playground?

aggression does not prevent the learning of aggression—it simply inhibits its expression in certain circumstances. When children believe aggressive expression will lead to rewards, their inhibitions generally evaporate.

THE FORMATION OF AGGRESSIVE SCRIPTS

Borrowing a concept from cognitive psychology, Rowell Huesmann (1986b, 1988) proposed that aggression—like other social behavior—is controlled by scripts. As first outlined in chapter 5, *a script* is a preconception about how a series of events is likely to occur, which is developed and stored in memory and used as a guide for behavior and problem solving. Based on many social learning experiments (for example, Bandura's Bobo doll studies), Huesmann contends that children develop **aggressive scripts** by observing other people's aggressive actions. For instance, if children learn from their parents or friends that the proper way to respond to insults or other social slights is to physically or verbally assault their protagonists, when they are later actually insulted by someone, an aggressive script will be recalled from memory. This script not only provides the child with a prediction about what is likely to happen in this situation, but it also prescribes the proper way to act. Huesmann believes that the more exposure children have to aggressive role models, the greater the number of detailed aggressive scripts they will encode into memory. Those with strongly developed aggressive scripts are likely to choose an aggressive solution to social conflict because it will seem to them to be the best and most natural way to respond to such circumstances.

Aggressive Scripts

Guides for behavior and problem solving that are developed and stored in memory and are characterized by aggression.

Media and Video Violence Fosters Aggressive Behavior

Facts: According to the National Television Violence Study, more than 60 percent of all TV shows contain some violence. One-fourth of all violent interactions involve handguns. In almost three-fourths of the violent acts depicted, perpetrators go unpunished. When violence occurs on children's programs, two-thirds of the time it is depicted as funny, and rarely (5 percent of the time) are children shown any long-term negative consequences for victims. Only 13 percent of reality programs that depict violence present any alternatives to violence or show how it can be avoided. (Federman, 1998)

Although aggressive scripts most commonly form by observing people with whom we regularly interact, research suggests that these scripts also can develop by viewing media violence (Anderson et al., 2003a, 2003b). Experimental studies indicate that immediately after watching violent television shows or movies, children act more aggressively in their play behavior and are more likely to choose aggressive solutions to social problems than those not exposed to such violence (Bushman & Huesmann, 2001). Further, three separate meta-analyses of laboratory and field experiments conducted over the past half-century demonstrate that exposure to media violence enhances children's and adolescents' aggression in interactions with strangers, classmates, and friends (Hearold, 1986; Paik & Comstock, 1994; Wood et al., 1991).

Longitudinal studies have also found a link between media violence and aggression. In perhaps the best of these studies—previously discussed in chapter 2—Leonard Eron and Huesmann collected data on 856 people in the state of New York when they were about 8 years old, then again when they were 19, and finally when they were about 30 years of age (Eron & Huesmann, 1984; Huesmann, 1986a). Their results: Early exposure to TV violence was related to later aggression, but only among the males. Boys who preferred to watch violent television shows when they were 8 years of age were significantly more aggressive ten years later, even after controlling for their initial level of aggressiveness. In addition, as figure 13.6 illustrates, the 8-year-old boys who had the strongest preference for violent shows were much more likely to have been convicted of a serious crime by the time they reached the age of 30. These findings suggest that the frequent viewing of televised violence contributes to later aggressive behavior beyond what you would expect due to stable aggressive traits.

Similar findings have been obtained in Europe, except that the European studies found no gender differences in the negative effects of TV violence (Huesmann & Eron, 1986a). What appears to influence children's later aggressiveness is their *identification* with aggressive TV characters. Children who watch a lot of TV violence when they are young and identify with aggressive TV characters are most likely to become highly aggressive in late childhood, adolescence, and even young adulthood (Anderson & Bushman, 2002). Based on these lab, field, and longitudinal studies, solid evidence indicates that repeated exposure to violence on television can encourage children to develop aggressive scripts that make later antisocial conduct more likely (Huesmann & Miller, 1994; Johnson et al., 2002).

What about the violence often depicted in music videos and in music lyrics? Music executives and some pop psychologists often assert that watching violent music videos and listening to violent music lyrics provide teenagers and young adults the opportunity to harm-

There is absolutely no evidence, none, that playing a violent video game leads to aggressive behavior.

Doug Lowenstein, president of the Interactive Digital Software Association, May 12, 2000

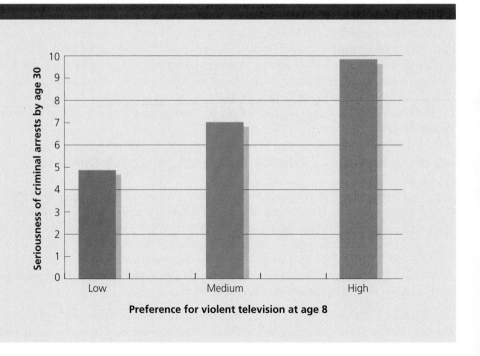

FIGURE 13.6

Childhood Preference for Violent Television and Later Aggressive Behavior

Boys who show a high preference for violent television shows at age 8 have been found to exhibit greater aggressive behavior later in life, as indicated by the number of criminal convictions by age 30. Does this mean that TV violence caused their later aggression?

Preference for violent television at age 8

lessly "vent" their aggressive emotions and thoughts. Although our previous analysis of the catharsis hypothesis seriously questions this assertion (see p. 498), is there any scientific evidence that this sort of media violence directly causes increased physical aggression?

Unfortunately, no experimental studies have yet examined how exposure to such music affects youths' physically aggressive behavior. However, several studies have examined how music videos affect adolescents' aggressive thinking and attitudes. In one such study involving young African American men, exposure to violent rap music videos increased endorsement of violent behavior in response to a hypothetical conflict situation (Johnson et al., 1995). Similarly, college students shown rock music videos containing violence subsequently reported a greater acceptance of antisocial behavior compared with students in a control group (Hansen & Hansen, 1990). Regarding the effects of music lyrics, a recent series of five experiments found consistent evidence that songs with violent lyrics increase aggression-related thoughts and feelings of hostility in listeners (Anderson et al., 2003b). Overall, the implication of these findings is that watching and/or listening to violent music causes people to not only be more accepting of antisocial behavior, but it also creates an emotional state of mind that is more likely to provoke aggressive responses. In other words, watching and listening to angry, violent music does not provide the kind of cathartic release that some people might lead you to believe.

In addition to the negative effects of watching or listening to violent media, research also indicates that playing violent video games has similar detrimental effects (Gentile et al., 2004; Krahé & Moller, 2004). Despite the denials from the video-game industry, at least two separate meta-analyses of existing video-game studies involving over 3,000 participants found that exposure to high video-game violence is associated with heightened aggression in the real world among young adults and children (Anderson, 2004; Anderson & Bushman, 2001). There were no gender differences in these effects. The active nature of playing video games, which often involves intense emotional engagement on the part of participants, is particularly troubling to many social scientists because it is likely to lead to strong identification with the aggressive characters that participants are directing in the games (Uhlmann & Swanson, 2004).

Beyond the learning of aggressive scripts and the priming of aggressive thoughts and emotions, another possible negative effect of exposure to media and video violence is emotional blunting or *desensitization,* which means simply becoming indifferent to aggressive outbursts. For example, in a series of experiments conducted by Ronald Drabman and Margaret Thomas, children who had just watched a violent movie were less concerned when they observed other youngsters fighting and were slower to stop the fight than a control group of children who had not seen the movie. This desensitization to violence was also observed in college students who watched a lot of violent TV programs. When their physiological responses were monitored, the heavy consumers exhibited the weakest levels of arousal when observing both fictional and realistic aggression (Drabman & Thomas, 1975; Thomas et al., 1977). These findings suggest that people who watch a lot of media-generated violence become habituated to violence in other aspects of their lives (Carnagey et al., 2004). Because they are less anxious and bothered by aggressive behavior, they may be more inclined to use the aggressive scripts they have learned as a means to solve social confrontations.

Another way in which media and video violence may increase aggression is through cognitive priming. According to Berkowitz (1984), the aggression-associated cues in television programs and films can cognitively prime a host of aggressive ideas and violent emotions, which in turn may trigger aggressive actions. Brad Bushman and Russell Geen (1990) found support for the priming hypothesis in experiments investigating the effects of media violence on viewers' thoughts and emotional responses. In these studies, college students wrote down the thoughts they had while watching excerpts from such violent movies as *48 Hours* and *The French Connection.* A control group watched a nonviolent scene from the TV series *Dallas.* Results indicated that viewers who watched the most aggressive episodes had the most aggressive thoughts, experienced the strongest increase in anger-related feelings, and had the greatest physiological arousal. The same effects have been found when people play violent video games (Anderson & Bushman, 2001; Anderson & Dill, 2000).

Of course, this does not mean that all or even most children and young adults who regularly view or listen to media violence or play violent video games will begin terrorizing their schools and neighborhoods. However, while exposure to such staged violence is not the primary cause of aggression among the young, it may be the one factor that is easiest to control and reduce (Hamilton, 1998; Wilson et al., 1998).

The "Culture of Honor" Encourages Male Violence

Cross-cultural research suggests that societies in which the economy is based on the herding of animals have more male violence than farming societies. For example, among the Native American cultures of North America, the herding Navajos were famous for their warring tendencies, while the farming Zunis tended to be nonviolent (Farb, 1978). Within given societies, researchers have also observed this contrast in aggression. In East African cultures, for instance, herders are easily provoked to violence, while farmers go out of their way to get along with their neighbors (Edgerton, 1971). Social psychologists Richard Nisbett and Dov Cohen (1996) believe that the greater violence exhibited by herding people is due to their **culture of honor,** which is a belief system that prepares men to protect their reputation by resorting to violence. In cultures that place a high value on honor, males learn from childhood that it is important to project a willingness to fight to the death against insults and to vigorously protect their property—specifically, their animals—from theft. Nisbett and Cohen hypothesize that this culture of honor is more necessary in herding than in farming societies because herders' assets (animals) are more vulnerable to theft—and thus, more in need of aggressive protection—than are the assets of farmers (land).

How does this culture of honor theory relate to contemporary violence in the United States? First, in an archival analysis of crime statistics in this country, Nisbett and Cohen found that the southern and western states, which were settled by people whose economy was originally based on herding, have higher levels of current violence related to honor than the northern states, which were originally settled by farmers (Cohen, 1996; Cohen & Nisbett, 1994). Honor-related violence involves arguments, brawls, and lovers' triangles where a person's public prestige and honor have been challenged. Second, the cultures of the South and West are also more likely to approve of violence as indicated by viewership of violent TV programs, subscriptions to violent magazines, hunting license applications, and national guard enrollments (Baron & Straus, 1989; Lee, 1995). Third, in a series of experimental studies, Cohen and Nisbett also found that, when insulted, young White men from the South not only became more stressed and angry than young White men from the North, but they also were more prepared to respond to insults with aggression (Cohen et al., 1996).

What these multimethod studies suggest is that southern and western White men tend to be more physically aggressive than northern White men in certain situations because they have been socialized to live by a code of honor that calls for quick and violent responses to threats to their property or personal integrity. Although the vast majority of these men no longer depend on herding for their livelihood, they still live by the culture of honor of their ancestors, and this code of conduct continues to be legitimated by cultural institutions (Cohen, 1998; Cohen & Vandello, 1998). Ironically, "honor" cultures tend to have very strong norms of politeness and hospitality. This emphasis on elaborate politeness may have developed as a way to reduce the likelihood that honor-bound men would be insulted during daily interactions. However, the anger suppression resulting from such politeness norms has the unfortunate effect of making it difficult to accurately perceive other people's anger until it has reached the boiling point, triggering aggression on their part.

Interestingly, similar regional differences in violence are not found among young African American males: Black southern men are not more violent than Black northern men. Thus, this hypothesized culture of honor in the south and west is unique to White males. Having stated this, however, both psychologists and sociologists note that the higher incidence of violence among inner-city African American males than among African American males in rural or suburban areas may be partly related to a similar honor code (Anderson, 1994; Cohen et al., 1998). Thus, just as a culture of honor may exist among southern and western White men, in the inner-city street culture there may also be a culture of honor that makes violent outbursts more likely. That is, in the inner city, where it is extremely difficult to pull oneself out of poverty by legal means, and where police provide little protection from crime and physical attack, young Black males may strive to gain and maintain respect by responding violently to any perceived insults.

Culture of Honor

A belief system in which males are socialized to protect their reputation by resorting to violence.

- In social learning theory, aggression occurs because it has been rewarded in the past
- Observational learning can foster the development of aggressive scripts
- Exposure to media violence promotes antisocial conduct
- The culture of honor is a belief system that prepares men to protect their reputation by resorting to violence

SEXUAL AGGRESSION

Would it surprise you to know that in the past quarter century forcible rape has increased by 21 percent, making it the largest increase among all major crimes (Magid et al., 2004; Von et al., 1991)? Or what about the fact that more than 100,000 women in the United States report being raped each year—about one every six minutes (Federal Bureau of Investigation, 2001)? Does this fact surprise you? These statistics are grim reminders concerning the dangers women face in American society. Yet rape is certainly not confined to the U.S. borders. It is a worldwide phenomenon, most common in societies characterized by male violence and a social ideology of male dominance (Jewkes & Abrahams, 2002; Muir & Macleod, 2003; Sanday, 1981).

Although less common, men are also the victims of sexual assault. In this section we analyze three possible determinants of sexual aggression, namely pornography, sexual scripts, and jealousy.

Pornography Promotes a Belief in the "Rape Myth" and May Increase Male Violence Against Women

Erotica is typically defined as sexually suggestive or arousing material that is nonviolent and respectful of all persons portrayed. In contrast, **pornography** is the combination of sexual material with abuse or degradation in a manner that appears to endorse, condone, or encourage such behavior (Brown, 2003; Russell, 1993). Pornography is objectionable not for its sexual content, but rather, its abusive and degrading portrayal of another person, usually a female. Experimental studies demonstrate that exposure to erotic material generally elicits a pleasant emotional response and increased sexual arousal in both men and women, which usually results in them being less aggressive (Davis & Bauserman, 1993; Donnerstein et al., 1987). A different pattern appears to hold for people's response to pornography, as you will soon discover.

Pornography

The combination of sexual material with abuse or degradation in a manner that appears to endorse, condone, or encourage such behavior.

THE RAPE MYTH

In a content analysis of 428 pornographic paperback books, sociologist Donald Smith (1976) found that physical abuse was a common theme in sexual encounters between men and women. Twenty percent of all sex episodes depicted in these books involved rape. The story line focused on the victim's initial fear and terror at being attacked, followed by an awakening of her sexual desire as it proceeded. In more than 97 percent of these rape depictions, the victims experienced an orgasm during the sexual assault. Similar story themes are found in sexually oriented home videos (Cowan & Campbell, 1994).

This false belief that deep down, women enjoy forcible sex and find it sexually exciting is known as the **rape myth.** People who believe in the rape myth are less likely to empathize with rape victims and are more likely to blame victims for causing the assault (Frese et al., 2004; Jimenez & Abreu, 2003). A number of studies indicate that heterosexual men are much more likely than heterosexual women to believe in the rape myth (Burt, 1980; Payne et al., 1999). Although the definition of the rape myth is framed to include only

Rape Myth

The false belief that, deep down, women enjoy forcible sex and find it sexually exciting.

women as targets, recent studies suggest that a similar myth exists for gay men: that is, some people falsely believe that gay men have an unconscious desire to be raped. As with the traditional rape myth, heterosexual men are most likely to endorse rape myths regarding gay men; gay men are least likely to endorse such beliefs (Davies & McCartney, 2003). Together, these findings suggest that the people who are most likely to strongly endorse false beliefs about sexual assault are males who have hostile attitudes toward the victim group (either women or gay men).

Not surprisingly, convicted rapists generally hold strong beliefs regarding the rape myth (Scully, 1985), but more disturbingly, there is evidence that exposure to pornography also increases ordinary men's rape myth beliefs. In one such study, Neil Malamuth and James Check (1981) arranged for Canadian college students to attend commercial movies at campus theaters. Half of the students saw two nonviolent romantic movies, *A Man and a Woman* and *Hooper*. The other students saw two sexually aggressive films, *Swept Away* and *The Getaway,* in which women characters in both films become sexually aroused by a sexual assault and romantically attracted to their assailant. Several days later, these same students were asked to complete a class questionnaire about their attitudes toward rape and other forms of aggression against women (refer to table 13.2 and table 13.3). None of the students realized that the questionnaire and the movies were connected in any way.

Results indicated that exposure to the two films portraying sexual aggression increased male viewers' acceptance of interpersonal aggression against women and tended to increase their acceptance of rape myths (see figure 13.7). In contrast, females' acceptance of interpersonal aggression against women and of rape myths decreased after watching these sexually aggressive films. These data indicate that exposure to films that seem to condone sexual violence against women can cause men to become more accepting of such violence. Another disturbing fact about these findings is that they were not obtained by exposing men to pornographic material typically found in adult X-rated movies, but rather were obtained from exposure to commercially successful R-rated films that contained pornographic elements in their story lines. Subsequent studies have replicated these results (Oddone-Paolucci et al., 2000).

DOES PORNOGRAPHY PROVOKE MALE AGGRESSION AGAINST WOMEN?

Thus far, we have learned that exposure to sexually violent films can cause men to become more accepting of false beliefs about rape and to have greater tolerance for violence against women. However, does this translate into men actually becoming more aggressive toward women? In an attempt to answer this question, social psychologists have conducted two separate lines of research: (1) lab experiments in which exposure to violent pornography is manipulated to see how it affects laboratory aggression, and (2) survey research on whether the prevalence of pornography in a particular geographic region is related to sexual assault.

Regarding lab experiments, a series of studies conducted by Edward Donnerstein and his colleagues suggest that although male-to-male aggression is no greater after exposure to violent pornography, male-to-female aggression is significantly increased (Donnerstein & Malamuth, 1997). In one representative study, Donnerstein and Leonard Berkowitz (1981) demonstrated that how rape is depicted in films is crucial in determining male viewers' later aggression. First, male participants were either angered or not by either a male or a female confederate and then were either shown a neutral, erotic, or one of two violent pornographic films. In both the sexually violent films, two men raped a woman, but each film had a different ending. In one ending shown to some participants, the victim is smiling and not resisting as she experiences sexual gratification at being raped (rape myth ending). In the other ending, the victim is in obvious pain and emotional turmoil, and conveys disgust and humiliation at being raped (realistic negative ending).

As can be seen in figure 13.8, males who had been angered by the female confederate and who had watched a sexually violent film administered more intense shocks to the female confederate, regardless of the film victim's own emotional reaction to being raped. However, when they were not angry, males who had been exposed to the rape film delivered intense shocks to the female confederate only when the film depicted the woman as enjoying the experience. These results are consistent with other investigations of aggression

Everyone knows that murder is wrong, but a strange myth has grown up, and been seized on by filmmakers, that rape is really not so bad, that it may even be a form of liberation for the victim, who may be acting out what she secretly desires—and perhaps needs—with no harm done.

Lord Harlech, British Film Board

TABLE 13.2

Rape Myths Acceptance Scale

Directions

There are nineteen items on this scale. For items 1 to 11, use the following seven-point scale to indicate your degree of agreement or disagreement:

Strongly disagree   1   2   3   4   5   6   7   *Strongly agree*

_____ 1. A woman who goes to the home or apartment of a man on their first date implies that she is willing to have sex.

_____ 2. Any female can get raped.

_____ 3. One reason that women falsely report a rape is that they frequently have a need to call attention to themselves.

_____ 4. Any healthy woman can successfully resist a rapist if she really wants to.

_____ 5. When women go around braless or wearing short skirts and tight tops, they are just asking for trouble.

_____ 6. In the majority of rapes, the victim is promiscuous or has a bad reputation.

_____ 7. If a girl engages in necking or petting and she lets things get out of hand, it is her own fault if her partner forces sex on her.

_____ 8. Women who get raped while hitchhiking get what they deserve.

_____ 9. A woman who is stuck-up and thinks she is too good to talk to guys on the street deserves to be taught a lesson.

_____ 10. Many women have an unconscious wish to be raped, and may then unconsciously set up a situation in which they are likely to be attacked.

_____ 11. If a woman gets drunk at a party and has intercourse with a man she's just met there, she should be considered "fair game" to other males at the party who want to have sex with her too, whether she wants to or not.

Note: For items 12 and 13, use the following scale to answer the questions:

1 = About 0%   *2 = About 25%*   *3 = About 50%*   *4 = About 75%*   *5 = About 100%*

_____ 12. What percentage of women who report a rape would you say are lying because they are angry and want to get back at the man they accuse?

_____ 13. What percentage of reported rapes would you guess were merely invented by women who discovered they were pregnant and wanted to protect their own reputation?

Note: For items 14 to 19, read the statement below and use the following scale to indicate your response:

1 = Always   *2 = Frequently*   *3 = Sometimes*   *4 = Rarely*   *5 = Never*

A person comes to you and claims s/he was raped. How likely would you be to believe their statement if the person were

_____ 14. your best friend?

_____ 15. an Indian woman?

_____ 16. a neighborhood woman?

_____ 17. a young boy?

_____ 18. a Black woman?

_____ 19. a White woman?

Note: Once you have indicated your response to each item, reverse the scoring for item 2 (1 = 7, 2 = 6, 3 = 5, 5 = 3, 6 = 2, 7 = 1). Then add up your total score. The higher your total score, the greater your belief in the rape myths. The mean total score in Burt's (1980) original sample of 598 American adults (average age of 42 years) was 86.6, with a standard deviation of 11.9. How does your total score compare with Burt's original sample? Are you more or less likely to believe in the rape myths than these American adults? Have your friends complete this scale as well. How do your beliefs about the rape myths compare with their beliefs?

Total score: _____

TABLE 13.3

Acceptance of Interpersonal Violence Scale

Directions

Use the following seven-point scale to indicate your degree of agreement or disagreement to the six items on this scale:

Strongly disagree   1   2   3   4   5   6   7   Strongly agree

_____ 1. People today should not use "an eye for an eye and a tooth for a tooth" as a rule for living.

_____ 2. Being roughed up is sexually stimulating to many women.

_____ 3. Many times a woman will pretend she doesn't want to have intercourse because she doesn't want to seem loose, but she's really hoping the man will force her.

_____ 4. A man is never justified in hitting his wife.

_____ 5. Sometimes the only way a man can get a cold woman turned on is to use force.

_____ 6. A wife should move out of the house if her husband hits her.

Note: Once you have indicated your response to each item, reverse the scoring for items 1, 4, and 6 (1 = 7, 2 = 6, 3 = 5, 5 = 3, 6 = 2, 7 = 1). Then add up your total score. The higher your total score, the greater your acceptance of interpersonal violence. The mean total score for Burt's (1980) sample of 598 American adults was 29.8 and a standard deviation of 5.9. How does your score compare to this sample? What about your friends? How do your beliefs about interpersonal violence compare with theirs?

Total score: _____

FIGURE 13.7

The Effects of Mass Media Exposure on Acceptance of Violence Against Women

Malamuth and Check (1981) found that men who had watched sexually violent commercial films were more accepting of interpersonal violence against women and were more accepting of the rape myth than men who were not exposed to such violent entertainment. What effect did such exposure have on women viewers?

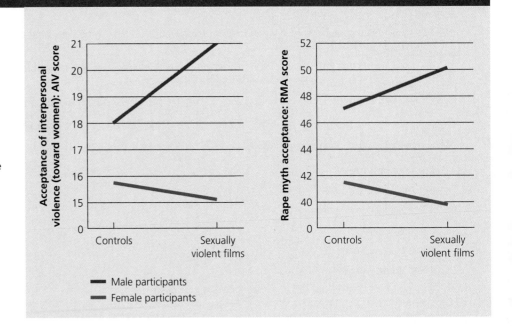

of a nonsexual nature, in which for nonangered individuals, victim pain cues tend to reduce aggression by inducing empathy. However, for highly angered individuals, a victim's pain can actually provoke increased aggression (Geen, 1978). Why this is the case is a matter of speculation. One possible explanation is that anger raises the threshold for empathy toward the victim's plight (Hartmann, 1969). Another explanation is Berkowitz's notion of aggression-associated cues (p. 502). For males who have been angered, watching a woman

FIGURE 13.8

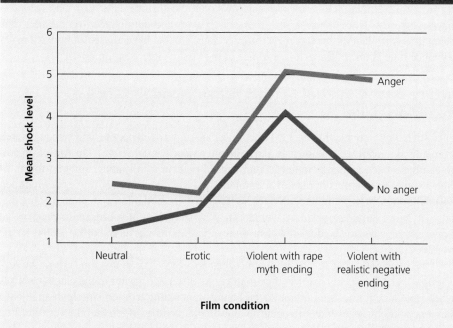

Mean shock level

6
5
4
3
2
1

Neutral   Erotic   Violent with rape myth ending   Violent with realistic negative ending

Film condition

Anger

No anger

How Does the Film Victim's Reaction to Rape Affect Male Viewers' Subsequent Level of Aggression Toward Women?

Men who had been angered by a female confederate and who had then watched a sexually violent film administered more intense shocks to the female confederate, regardless of the film victim's own emotional reaction to being raped. How were these men's reactions different from males who were not angered by the female confederate, but who also were exposed to one of the two rape films?

become the victim of sexual aggression may not only cause arousal, it may also associate women with aggression. Later, in a situation in which aggression is a behavioral option, the presence of a woman might be a sufficient aggression-eliciting cue for the already aroused male.

Although Donnerstein's overall findings and those of other experiments (Hui, 1986) suggest that men who watch violent pornography are more likely to engage in aggressive behaviors toward women, survey studies of actual sex crimes do not generally support this conclusion. For example, Danish social psychologist Berl Kutchinsky (1971, 1985) reasoned that if pornography increases male sexual aggression against women, then sexual crimes should rise when pornography laws are relaxed. In an early test of this hypothesis, he gathered crime statistics for the time periods prior to and following the legalization of hard-core pornography in Denmark in the late 1960s. What he found was exactly opposite of what would be expected based on the experimental literature: the increased availability of pornography coincided with a decrease in sex offenses against children, while the number of reported rapes remained unchanged. Kutchinsky (1991) later extended his research by looking at rates of rape and nonsexual assault from 1964 to 1984 in Denmark, Sweden, Germany, and the United States. In all four countries, new laws made pornography much more available during the late 1960s and early 1970s. Did this increased availability of pornography coincide with an increase in sexual assault? Crime statistics indicate that rape rates only increased in the United States, but this change coincided with a similar increase in nonsexual violent crimes. Kutchinsky argued that this simultaneous increase in rapes and assaults is consistent with the belief that rape is primarily an act of violence rather than of sexual arousal. These results seem to suggest that the increased availability of pornography does not seem to directly contribute to increased sexual offenses (Bauserman, 1996).

So where are we in our understanding of the effects of pornography on men's sexual beliefs and aggressive actions toward women? There appears to be generally good support for the hypothesis that exposure to violent pornography increases men's acceptance of the rape myth. However, the contradictory findings in the experimental and survey literature regarding a possible pornography-aggression link suggest that additional research is necessary before we can reach any firm conclusions. In the meantime, research by Murray Straus and his colleagues has led them to suggest that rape rates are shaped by two sets of social forces (Baron & Straus, 1987, 1989). The first is *social disorganization,* which is brought about as a society experiences increases in poverty, urbanization, and divorce—the very social ills that the United States has increasingly experienced since the 1960s. The second is *hypermasculinity,* which is the desire to exercise power and dominance over women. The rape myth is a product of this hypermasculinity. The role that hypermasculinity plays in acquaintance rape is one of the primary topics of the next chapter section.

Culture-Based Sexual Scripts Make Acquaintance Rape More Likely

Forced sexual intercourse that occurs either on a date or between people who are acquainted or romantically involved is known as **acquaintance rape** (or *date rape*). On American college campuses, acquaintance rapes account for 85 percent of all rapes, and one-fourth of college women are victims of rape or attempted rape (Koss et al., 1987; Yancey & Hummer, 2003). Although surveys indicate that the vast majority of both men and women agree that sexual advances should stop when a woman says no, nearly half of young adults believe that when a woman says no she does not always mean it (Adams-Curtis & Forbes, 2004; Krahé et al., 2000).

One explanation for this belief that no does not always mean no comes from the sexual scripts that adolescents learn as they mature. As discussed earlier in the chapter, scripts provide guidance for people in their social behavior, enabling them to anticipate the goals, behaviors, and outcomes likely to occur in a particular setting. Much like the way children can learn aggressive scripts by watching violent television programs, adolescents and adults can also learn societal *sexual scripts* that make sexual aggression more likely in a dating relationship.

THE RESISTANT FEMALE ROLE

The common belief that no does not always mean no is based on the traditional sexual script in which the woman's role is to act resistant to sex and the man's role is to persist in his sexual advances despite the woman's protests (Alksnis et al., 1996). Charlene Muehlenhard and Lisa Hollabaugh (1988) found that some women do indeed appear to sometimes go along with this traditional sexual script in their relationships with men. In a questionnaire administered to more than 600 undergraduate women, the researchers asked them to recall whether they had ever been in the following situation with a man:

> You were with a guy who wanted to engage in sexual intercourse and you wanted to also, but for some reason you indicated that you didn't want to, although you had every intention to and were willing to engage in sexual intercourse. In other words, you indicated "no" and you meant "yes."

Thirty-nine percent of the respondents reported that they had indeed been in such a situation at least once with a man—saying no to sexual intercourse when they really meant yes. More recent studies suggest that the true instances of token resistance to sex by women are closer to 10 percent rather than the 39 percent figure reported by Muehlenhard and Hollabaugh, and they are most likely to occur in later-stage dating relationships (Shotland & Hunter, 1995).

Even if this lower estimate is accurate, why might one in ten women put up this sort of token resistance to sex? One possible explanation has to do with our culture's double standard for sexual activity between men and women. Put simply, frequent sexual activity outside of marriage has always been more socially acceptable for men than for women. Although it is socially acceptable for women to appear "sexy," they run the risk of being negatively labeled "promiscuous" or "loose" if they appear to be too sexually eager. Faced with this double standard, some women may see engaging in token resistance as a rational behavior to deflect this sort of negative social attribution.

The danger in employing this sexual script, however, is that it not only discourages honest communication between men and women, but it also perpetuates restrictive gender roles and encourages men to ignore women's refusals. Having encountered a

Acquaintance Rape

Forced sexual intercourse that occurs either on a date or between people who are acquainted or romantically involved. Also known as date rape.

woman who employed token resistance to sex might reinforce a man's belief in the rape myth—that is, he may believe that all a woman needs is a little encouragement or even force to overcome her inhibitions. This belief, in turn, may precipitate later acquaintance rapes. Thus, the small minority of women who use token resistance not only put themselves in danger, but they also endanger the majority of women who mean no when they say no.

THE PREDATOR MALE ROLE

Even though evidence shows that some women send mixed signals regarding their own sexual desires, this in no way justifies forced sex. It cannot be stressed enough that acquaintance rape occurs when a man refuses to stop his sexual aggression. Surveys on college campuses indicate that roughly 12 to 15 percent of male respondents admit having used force or violence to try to obtain sex against another's will (Sigelman et al., 1984). In an even more alarming series of survey findings, when asked to rate their likelihood of raping a woman if they could be absolutely assured that they would not be arrested or punished, between 35 and 51 percent of college male respondents state that there is at least "some possibility" of them doing so (Malamuth, 1981).

Although sexual gratification is clearly a motive in rape, studies of convicted rapists have found that they view rape as an aggressive conquest that validates their sense of hypermasculinity (Groth, 1979). Based on this work, social scientists have identified the desire to exercise power and dominance over women as key factors in sexual aggression (Malamuth & Thornhill, 1994). Similarly, in studies using college samples, men who either had a history of sexual aggression or were more accepting of violence against and dominance over women were also more likely to be sexually aroused by depictions of rape and to be insensitive to others' feelings (Dean & Malamuth, 1997; Porter & Critelli, 1994). Together, this research suggests that enjoyment of sexual dominance is a more important motive in sexual assault than sexual gratification (Chiroro et al., 2004).

Researchers have identified characteristics of both the victimizer and the victim that closely correspond to the sexual scripts already discussed (Osman, 2003; Willan & Pollard, 2003). A victim often does not clearly communicate the limits of acceptable behavior to someone who persists after initial sexual advances have been discouraged. Instead of employing the highly effective tactic of declaring to her attacker, "This is rape and I'm calling the cops," a victim of acquaintance rape tends to be nonassertive or in the habit of giving mixed messages. The victim of acquaintance rape often has problems with forcefully conveying a clear message of no, and the victimizer often misperceives the actions of the victim, interpreting passivity as permission. He tends to be more sexually active than other men and treats women as if they were his property. An acquaintance rapist also generally has a history of antisocial behavior and displays a lot of anger and hostility toward women (Abrams et al., 2003; Allison & Wrightsman, 1993). Because he believes that women often need a little force to enjoy sex, the victimizer does not believe that acquaintance rape is rape, even after he has committed this crime. View the presentation on your Social Sense CD-ROM for an example of how male sexual scripts can contribute to sexual assault.

Social Sense

View a presentation on male sexual scripts and rape.

Sexual Jealousy Often Leads to Intimate Violence

Sexual aggression does not entail only sexual assault and rape. As discussed in chapter 12, jealousy between lovers or former lovers can often lead to aggression. More American and Canadian women are injured by men with whom they have a romantic relationship than are injured in automobile accidents, armed robberies, and stranger rape combined (Grandin & Lupri, 1997; Zlotnick et al., 1998). The prime reason given for such aggression by the victims and the victimizers is sexual jealousy (Daly & Wilson, 1996). In the United States, more than half of all women murdered are the victims of partner homicide, while in Canada the figure is about 40 percent (Browne & Williams, 1989; Sev'er et al., 2004). Similarly, a

Brute force, the law of violence, rules to a great extent in the poor man's domicile; and woman is little more than his drudge.

Sarah Moore Grimkè, U.S. abolitionist and feminist, 1792–1873

Learning and practicing sexual scripts in which men act as "predators" and women play the "resistant" role promotes sexual aggression and acquaintance rape. Couples who are sexually attracted to one another should put aside these traditional, limiting gender roles and engage in open, honest communication. In such exchanges, a refusal of sexual intimacy should be accepted as such.

woman who kills her male lover generally does so to protect herself from his jealousy-induced physical assaults (see table 13.4).

The fact that heterosexual men have a greater tendency to respond violently when they discover or suspect their romantic partner of infidelity may be because society has historically sanctioned this sort of response in men but not in women. Indeed, wife beating occurs in more societies around the globe than any other type of domestic violence, and it is reinforced within male peer networks (Brownridge & Halli, 2002; Capaldi et al., 2001; McQuestion, 2003).

Although virtually all research investigating jealousy and violence has focused on heterosexual relationships, some studies have also documented the occurrence of violence in relationships of gay men and lesbians (Levy & Lobel, 1991; Waterman et al., 1989). Like their heterosexual counterparts, gay men and lesbians who batter seek to achieve, maintain, and demonstrate power over their partners to meet their own needs and desires. Surprisingly, however, lesbians appear to be at least as likely as gay men to victimize their partners (Walkner-Haugrud et al., 1997). Given the previously reported findings that women tend to be less physically aggressive than men (p. 491), why would lesbian relationships not have lower abuse levels? Several researchers suggest that it might be due to the tendency for lesbian couples to socially isolate themselves more from society than gay couples (Lockhart et al., 1994; Renzetti, 1993). This kind of isolation tends to lead to overdependence on one's partner and, borrowing from research on heterosexual couples, increases the likelihood of relationship violence (Pagelow, 1984). These findings suggest that, regardless of sexual orientation, when couples become overly dependent on one another, jealousy-based abuse becomes more likely.

TABLE 13.4

Domestic Abuse Among Couples in the United States and Canada

Some Facts

Women are the victims of abuse eleven times more often than men.

One out of ten men carries out at least one violent act toward his wife or live-in girlfriend each year.

Two million women are beaten every year, one every sixteen seconds.

Approximately fourteen hundred women are killed by their husbands each year.

The U.S. Surgeon General has ranked abuse by husbands and partners as the leading cause of injuries to women aged 15 to 44.

Statistically, one woman in four will be physically assaulted by a partner or ex-partner during her lifetime.

Risk Factors

Previous domestic abuse is the highest risk factor for future violence. Couples with any two of the factors listed below are twice as likely to experience violence as those with none. For those with seven or more of these factors, the abuse rate is 40 times higher.

- Male unemployed
- Male uses illegal drugs at least once each year
- Partners have different religious backgrounds
- Male saw father hit mother
- Couple isolates themselves within the relationship
- Male has blue-collar occupation, if employed
- Male did not graduate from high school
- Male is between 18 and 30 years of age
- Male or female uses severe violence toward children in home
- Total family income is below the poverty line

Getting Help

The national information and referral centers listed below handle domestic-violence calls from male and female victims as well as abusers, whether gay or straight.

In the United States:

National Domestic Violence Hotline, Phone #: 1-800-799-SAFE
National Center for Victims of Crime, Phone #: 1-800-FYI-CALL

In Canada:

CAVEAT (Canadians Against Violence Everywhere Advocating for its Termination),
Phone #: 1-800-622-8328
Or contact local mental health organizations.

In a study of relationship violence among college students, James Makepeace (1989) found evidence suggesting two distinct types of courtship violence, one more typical of early-stage relationships and the other more characteristic of later stages. *Predatory violence* appears to be most common in the early stages of romantic relationships, especially first dates. Here, the primary motivation of the aggressor is to sexually exploit his partner. Physical aggression is used to gain sex, and thus, this violence describes the previously discussed acquaintance rape. These relationships usually break up. Those romantic relationships that advance to the more intimate stages of steady dating, and later, engagement and living together, increasingly focus the couple's attention on how to socialize as a couple and how to define the status of the relationship itself. Here, the violence that occurs tends to be relational; that is, primarily motivated by jealousy and rejection. What is disturbing about *relational violence* is that the victims often fail to leave their relationships, and they tend not to notify authorities or seek professional help.

A likely reason why the victims of relational violence fail to terminate these destructive relationships has to do with their heavy psychological and emotional involvement with their partners. Evidence for this explanation comes from Makepeace's finding that the victims of relational violence who were engaged or living with their victimizer were much less likely to end the relationship than those who were only steadily dating. Makepeace believes that in the advanced stages of courtship, the costs of walking away from a relationship, however abusive, are substantially higher compared with earlier stages. Victimizers, realizing that their abused partners are now less likely to leave, become less restrained in acting on their aggressive tendencies. Unfortunately, an escalation of physical and psychological abuse often results.

SECTION SUMMARY

- Exposure to violent pornography increases men's acceptance of rape myths
- Experimental studies suggest that violent pornography increases men's aggression toward women, but survey research does not generally support this conclusion
- Sexual aggression may also be fostered through cultural sexual scripts:
  women expected to act resistant to sex
  men expected to persist in their sexual advances regardless of women's protests
- Relational aggression caused by sexual jealousy is more likely in the advanced stages of romance

---

REDUCING AGGRESSION

As you see from our review, many different causes underlie human aggression. The resulting psychological and physical injury has naturally led social psychologists to try to determine how aggressive responses can be minimized. In this final section, we examine some relatively effective strategies.

Punishment Can Both Decrease and Increase Aggression

Punishment is the most common treatment societies have employed to control aggression. Following such timeworn prescriptions as "an eye for an eye and a tooth for a tooth," legal systems throughout the world often use aggression to punish violent criminals, sometimes resorting to the ultimate punishment—death. Exercising this extreme form of punishment will certainly "relieve" convicted criminals of their aggressive tendencies, but short of killing aggressors, is punishment a truly effective technique?

Three conditions are necessary for punishment to have a chance of being effective (Bower & Hilgard, 1981). First, the punishment must be *prompt,* administered quickly after the aggressive action. Second, it must be *relatively strong* so that its aversive qualities are duly noted by the aggressor. And third, it must be *consistently applied* so that the aggressor knows that punishment will likely follow future aggressive actions. But even if these conditions are met, reduced aggression is not guaranteed. If potential aggressors are extremely angry, threats of punishment preceding an attack are unlikely to inhibit aggression (Baron, 1973). Here, the strength of the anger supersedes any concerns about the negative consequences of aggression. Likewise, the cognitive-neoassociationist model would suggest that punishment following aggression may actually provoke counteraggression in the aggressor-turned-victim, because such punishment might provoke even more intense anger.

In further considering the effectiveness of using punishment to reduce aggression, one should be even more wary of using aggression in doling out punishment. Based on the research inspired by social learning theory, it is entirely possible that employing violent punishment as a treatment for aggression may simply teach and encourage observers to copy these violent actions. That is, the aggressive punisher may serve as an aggressive model. This is exactly the process underlying the continuing cycle of family violence—observing adult aggression appears to encourage rather than discourage aggression in children (Hanson et al., 1997).

Taking these factors into account, even though punishment may reduce aggressive behavior under certain circumstances, it does not teach the aggressor new prosocial forms of behavior. The aggressive behaviors are not being replaced by more productive kinds of actions, but are most likely only being temporarily suppressed. For this reason, punishment by itself is unlikely to result in long-term changes in behavior.

Inducing Incompatible Responses Can Inhibit Aggression

Have you ever been in a situation in which you were about to hit or verbally lash out at someone, when suddenly someone breaks the tension and dissipates your anger by making you laugh? As a youngster, my father often used this strategy whenever I became angry with all the "injustices" that he and my mother imposed upon me. As I stood there red-faced and fuming, he might make a funny gesture or suggest that my face looked as though it was about to explode like a firecracker. Suddenly my anger was transformed into giggles, and my parents were no longer the enemy who needed to be vanquished.

Using a well-established principle in psychology that states that all organisms are incapable of engaging in two incompatible responses, or of experiencing two incompatible emotions at the same time, Robert Baron (1983) has argued that inducing responses or emotions incompatible with anger or overt aggression may effectively deter such actions. In one field experiment that encapsulates the basic findings of many other studies investigating this *incompatible response strategy,* Baron (1976) instructed a research confederate driving a car near campus to frustrate other male motorists. The confederate accomplished this task by stopping at a traffic light and then hesitating for fifteen seconds before driving on when the light turned from red to green. Because motorists honk their horns frequently to express irritation (Turner et al., 1975), two observers sitting in a parked car nearby recorded whether the frustrated drivers honked their horns. This was the dependent measure of aggression.

Three different stimuli were introduced when the light was still red in order to determine whether incompatible responses would reduce the motorists' tendencies to aggress (honk). In one experimental condition, the induced incompatible response was empathy—a female confederate wearing a bandage on her leg hobbled across the street on crutches. In the second condition, humor was induced by this same confederate crossing the street wearing an outlandish clown mask. Finally, in the third experimental condition, mild sexual arousal was induced—the female confederate wore a very brief and revealing outfit while crossing the street. In addition to these experimental conditions, Baron also included two control conditions. In one (distraction), the confederate crossed the street dressed in conservative clothing, while in the other (control), she was absent entirely from the scene. As you can see in table 13.5, consistent with the incompatible response hypothesis, inducing empathy, humor, and mild sexual arousal resulted in less horn honking and a greater delay in horn honking than in either of the control conditions. These findings suggest that inducing incompatible responses in potential aggressors can inhibit overt aggressive behavior.

Violence and injury enclose in their net all that do such things, and generally return upon him who began.

Lucretius Carus, Ancient Roman philosopher-poet, 99–55 B.C.

RITICAL *thinking*

"Road rage" has unfortunately become an all-too-familiar term we read and hear about to describe violent outbursts by people driving cars. How could you use social psychological knowledge to reduce the likelihood of "road rage" on city streets and highways?

TABLE 13.5

Aggression-Inhibiting Influence of Incompatible Responses

Inducing empathy, humor, and mild sexual arousal in frustrated drivers resulted in less horn honking and a greater delay in horn honking than in the control and distraction conditions. How do these findings support the incompatible response hypothesis?

Dependent Measure	Experimental Conditions				
	Control	Distraction	Empathy	Humor	Mild Sexual Arousal
Percentage of drivers honking	90	89	57	50	47
Latency of honking (seconds)	7.19	7.99	10.73	11.94	12.16

Teaching Nonaggressive Responses to Provocation Can Effectively Control Aggression

Beyond the rather simple strategies of punishment and induction of incompatible emotions, social psychologists have also relied on the considerable cognitive abilities of human beings in constructing more elaborate techniques for controlling aggression (Dunn, 2001).

SOCIAL MODELING: TEACHING BY EXAMPLE

Just as destructive models can teach people how to act aggressively, social learning theorists contend that nonaggressive models can urge observers to exercise restraint in the face of provocation. In an experiment supporting this claim, research participants who watched a nonaggressive model exhibit restraint in administering shocks to a "victim" in a learning experiment were subsequently less aggressive than those who observed an aggressive model (Baron & Kepner, 1970).

Besides reducing aggression by modeling nonaggressive behavior, aggression can also be controlled by having an authority figure condemn the behavior of aggressive individuals. For example, research demonstrates that if a child watches violence on television in the presence of an adult who condemns the violence, the child is less likely to later imitate this aggression (Hicks, 1968; Horton & Santogrossi, 1978). This bit of knowledge was not lost on my wife and me in raising our children. On numerous occasions while watching television with our daughters, the screen would suddenly erupt with violent images so quickly that we did not have time to change the channel. Each time this happened we condemned the violence. These efforts had an impact. When Lillian was 4 years old, we were watching a Looney Toons cartoon and Elmer Fudd suddenly pulled out a shotgun and blew the head off of Daffy Duck. Without missing a beat Lillian turned to us and said, "Boy, that wasn't very nice was it? People shouldn't be so mean."

INTERNALIZING ANTIAGGRESSION BELIEFS

As we have discussed throughout the text, when people internalize certain beliefs and attitudes into their self-concept, they are more likely to act in ways consistent with those beliefs and attitudes. Recognizing the important role that the self plays in behavior change, social scientists have devised a cognitive strategy to facilitate the internalization of antiviolent beliefs by simply having people think of reasons why aggression is a bad idea. For example, in one study, when children were prompted to generate reasons why it was bad to imitate TV violence, this intervention was effective in later reducing the impact that TV violence had on their attitudes and behavior regarding aggression (Huesmann et al., 1983). Generating these antiviolent beliefs apparently caused the children to incorporate them into their self-concepts and overall worldview. The subsequent reduction in aggression through this "belief ownership" was still measurable two years after the initial intervention.

APOLOGIES AS AGGRESSION CONTROLLERS

The fact that people can reason and develop explanations for their actions and those of others also explains why apologies can effectively reduce anger and aggression. An experiment by Ken-ichi Ohbuchi and his coworkers (1989) demonstrated this aggression-reducing effect of apologies. In the experiment, Japanese college students were embarrassed by their poor performance while working on a complex experimental task. The reason they did so poorly was that the experimenter's assistant committed a series of errors in presenting the experimental materials to them. When the experimenter learned of each participant's poor performance, he roundly criticized the assistant, who then either apologized for causing the participants to fail, or said nothing. After this, participants were asked to rate the assistant on several dimensions and were told that these ratings would be used as a basis for the assistant's grade. A public apology in the experimenter's presence significantly reduced the participants' hostility in these ratings. This study is important because it suggests that merely offering an apology can defuse another's hostile aggression.

There is a gender difference in willingness to apologize, with women being more willing than men to take responsibility for a perceived social transgression (Gonzales et al., 1990). In fact, women tend to become more apologetic when severely reproached for a social transgression, while men respond more defensively to severe reproaches (Hodgins & Liebeskind, 2003). Underlying this greater unwillingness of men to offer apologies is a fear of "losing face" or social status in such confrontations (Hodgins et al., 1996). These gender differences may partly explain why men are more likely than women to be involved in physical altercations.

SOCIAL SKILLS TRAINING

The art of apologizing is just one skill in a larger repertoire of interpersonal skills learned through the process of socialization. As children mature, their impulsive aggressive reactions to anger and conflict are often replaced by more socially acceptable responses, such as negotiation, compromise, and cooperative problem solving. However, children with low intelligence are less likely to learn these prosocial skills and, therefore, are more likely to retain a combative interpersonal style that invites aggression and further interferes with their intellectual development (Huesmann et al., 1987). For these antisocial children, and for adults who have trouble managing their own aggression, deliberately and consciously teaching them alternative nonaggressive strategies can be extremely beneficial.

Social skills training can take many forms, including the role playing of nonaggressive behaviors, modeling the prosocial actions of others, or generating nonaggressive alternative solutions to conflict. In one twelve-session intervention program employing some of these cognitive strategies, Nancy Guerra and Ronald Slaby (1990) found that male and female juvenile delinquents not only showed increased skills in solving social problems, but they also exhibited a significant decrease in their aggressive beliefs and actions. This study, and others like it (McCarthy-Tucker et al., 1999), indicate that aggressive behavior can be changed by teaching people to replace maladaptive thoughts and behaviors with ones that foster social harmony and conflict resolution.

REDUCING EXPOSURE TO VIOLENCE

An essential ingredient in reducing aggressive responses is to diminish people's exposure to violence. Recent studies indicate that aggressive behavior in children is significantly reduced when they spend less time watching violent television shows and playing violent video games (Rosenkoetter et al., 2004). One such study examined third- and fourth-grade students at two comparable schools over a six-month period (Robinson et al., 2001). In one of the schools, TV and video-game exposure was reduced by one-third by encouraging students and parents to engage in alternative forms of home entertainment, while in the other school no effort was made to reduce exposure. The researchers found that children at the intervention school were subsequently less aggressive on the playground than students at the control school, especially those students who were initially rated as most aggressive by their classmates.

- Punishment can both increase and decrease aggression
- Inducing incompatible responses can inhibit aggression
- Nonaggressive responding can occur through:

  social modeling

  internalizing antiaggression beliefs

  offering apologies

  social skills training

  reducing exposure to violence

FEATURED STUDY

SEXUALLY AGGRESSIVE MEN'S COGNITIVE ASSOCIATIONS ABOUT WOMEN, SEX, HOSTILITY, AND POWER

Leibold, J. M., & McConnell, A. R. (2004). Women, sex, hostility, power, and suspicion: Sexually aggressive men's cognitive associations. *Journal of Experimental Social Psychology, 40,* 256–263.

Social interactions between men and women about mutual sexual interest are often ambiguous. This ambiguity has spurred investigations of sexually aggressive men's perceptions of sexual information, including the types of situational cues they use and the associations they have in memory between concepts such as power and sex. The researchers hypothesized that sex is an important core concept for how sexually aggressive men represent women in memory. In the present study they predicted that men who are more sexually aggressive will have stronger associations between women and sex, women and hostility, women and power, and women and suspicion than less sexually aggressive men.

Method

After 213 male college students completed a questionnaire measuring their frequency and degree of sexually aggressive behaviors, 39 respondents who scored at the extreme ends were recruited by phone for the laboratory portion of the study. Of these participants, 20 men reported no sexually aggressive behaviors in past romantic relationships and 19 men reported engaging in some degree of sexually aggressive behaviors.

For the laboratory portion of the study, ten female and ten male images (head and shoulder color photos) were used for decision task primes. The female images had been

pretested and were rated as feminine, nonmasculine, typical, and attractive, while the male images had been previously rated as masculine, nonfeminine, typical, and attractive. Twelve target words represented the four concepts of interest: *sex* (sex, naked, and erotic), *hostile* (hostile, rage, and angry), *power* (power, influence, and dominate), and *suspicious* (suspicious, doubt, and sneaky). These words had been pretested as strongly associated to the relevant concept but as unrelated to the other three concepts. In addition, a set of eight neutral target words (for example, window, song) and twenty nonwords (for example, werlof, niwood) were included so that an equal number of words and nonwords were target.

When participants arrived at the lab, they were individually seated at a computer and were told that they would simultaneously perform two tasks: attending to images for a subsequent memory task and making judgments about words. The instructions regarding a later memory task of visual images were provided so that participants would pay attention to the images on the computer screen, which served as priming stimuli. After each visual prime was presented for 313 milliseconds on the computer screen, a target word appeared in its place and participants decided as quickly as possible whether the string of letters was a meaningful word or a nonsense word. The computer measured how quickly participants made a response for each decision task. Of particular importance was the quickness of responding to the tasks involving the female image primes compared to those with the male image primes for all target words. After completing the decision tasks, participants were instructed to write down as many of the target words as they could recall in five minutes. Participants were then debriefed.

Results and Discussion

For each participant, two mean image response latencies were calculated for each target word, one for trials preceded by a female image prime and one for trials preceded by a male image prime. Results indicated that men who previously reported that they had engaged in more sexually aggressive behaviors toward women had stronger associations in memory between women and sex, stronger associations in memory between women and hostility, and better recall for sex-related concepts than men who had not reported engaging in any sexually aggressive behaviors. Further, men who showed stronger women-sex and women-hostility associations showed better recall for sex-related concepts.

These findings of stronger cognitive associations between women and sex and between women and hostility for more sexually aggressive men are consistent with the *Confluence Model* of sexual aggression (Malamuth, 2003; Malamuth et al., 1995). This model hypothesizes that two pathways additively lead to sexually aggressive behaviors: first, hostile masculinity encourages men to affirm their masculinity through sexual aggression, and second, a desire for sex that is noncommittal, unrestricted, and promiscuous encourages men to also engage in sexual aggression. The present findings provide insights into the social cognitive processes underlying these two pathways to sexual aggression.

APPLICATIONS

HOW CAN ACQUAINTANCE RAPE BE PREVENTED?

Given that sexual assault is all too commonly found within dating relationships, an increasing number of rape prevention programs are being developed to not only train women how to protect themselves, but also change the attitudes, beliefs, and behaviors of potential rapists, namely, ordinary men. Listed here are some of the common elements in these acquaintance rape prevention programs (Foubert, 2000; Schewe, 2002):

Targeting the rape myth: Discrediting the rape myth is one of the most widely used—and effective— techniques in rape education programs (Hinck & Thomas, 1999; Johansson-Love & Geer, 2003). Generally, participants first read or view fictional depictions of women becoming sexually aroused while being raped, followed by the presentation of the scientific and medical facts of rape trauma. One problem with most rape prevention programs is that they only target rape myths for female victims, despite the fact that 10 percent of rape victims are men.

Sexual communication training: As previously discussed, men are more likely than women to misinterpret friendliness from another person as sexual interest. Educating people about how such sexual misunderstandings come about has been shown to have a positive influence on beliefs and attitudes about rape and violence (Foshee et al., 1998).

Discussing negative sexual scripts: Many programs accompany sexual communication training with discussions of the contrasting sexual scripts learned by most women and men that contribute to acquaintance rape (Pacifici et al., 2001).

Inducing empathy: Empathy is a feeling of compassion and tenderness for people who experience pain, loss, or other unfortunate circumstances in their lives. Because people who experience empathy are less likely to believe that victims caused their own plight, rape prevention programs that deliberately structure their presentation to induce empathy for sexual assault victims are more effective than programs that do not focus on empathy arousal (O'Donohue et al., 2003).

Role playing: After learning about the rape myth, negative sexual scripts, and sexual miscommunication, participants often engage in role-playing exercises. These role-playing activities involve practicing caring ways to refuse and respond to sexual advances, as well as responsibly handling sexual rejection (Pacifici et al., 2001).

Nonconfrontational approaches: When discussing rape myths, male misperceptions, and male "predators," trainers must be careful not to cast male participants into the "enemy" camp. Inducing defensiveness and alienation in male participants is one of the surest ways to guarantee that desirable changes will not take place (Dallager & Rosen, 1993). Instead, effective trainers adopt a nonconfrontational approach. When discussing cultural ideologies that promote rape, they emphasize the point that men are also victims of these ideologies because they are taught to behave according to a very restrictive hypermasculine role.

These are some of the basic elements in many acquaintance rape prevention programs. Yet, an effective program has more than just these elements—*time duration* of the training is also important. Rape education researchers contend that training programs that meet only once or twice are insufficient in effectively challenging rape-supportive ideology

Effective acquaintance rape prevention programs are designed to accomplish numerous goals, including debunking the rape myth, increasing sexual communication, learning about negative sexual scripts, and inducing empathy for sexual assault victims. When presenting these programs to mixed-sex groups, should trainers use confrontational tactics with male participants?

(Schaeffer & Nelson, 1993). Instead, they strongly recommend that classes meet weekly over several months. Such a format is ideally suited for a college course.

Kimberly Lonsway and her colleagues (1998) evaluated one such semester-long college program (Campus Acquaintance Rape Education, or CARE) that incorporates the course elements just listed. Their findings indicate that it is effective in changing beliefs and behaviors regarding sexual communication and sexual assault. For example, students who participated in the CARE program were subsequently less accepting of cultural rape myths and adversarial sexual beliefs than students who took a human sexuality course. The

CARE students also became more willing and able to directly express themselves and assert their needs in ways that facilitated increased sexual communication in a dating relationship. In a two-year follow-up survey, Lonsway and her colleagues found that the CARE participants remained less accepting of cultural rape myths than students who were enrolled in the human sexuality course, but there were no group differences in endorsement of adversarial sexual beliefs. Although more research is needed in how to best design and implement rape prevention training programs, this study suggests that the changes that take place in such venues can have a lasting, positive impact.

THE BIG PICTURE

Nonviolence is the answer to the crucial political and moral questions of our time; the need for man to overcome oppression and violence without resorting to oppression and violence. Man must evolve for all human conflict a method which rejects revenge, aggression and retaliation. The foundation of such a method is love.
    Rev. Martin Luther King, Jr., 1964

If we could point to one single strategy to effectively control aggression in a wide range of settings, it would simply be the adoption of the nonviolent philosophy practiced by civil rights leader Martin Luther King. Indeed, research suggests that forgiving others' aggressive acts against us can actually enhance our own health by lowering stress and increasing a sense of personal control (Witvliet et al., 2001). Unfortunately, because the widespread adoption of a nonviolent philosophy will not take place anytime soon, we are left with a number of imperfect intervention strategies, each of which has a reasonable chance of reducing aggression when certain conditions are met.

The cognitive-neoassociationist model tells us that impulsive aggression is most likely to occur when we are engaged in highly routine activities and thus are not consciously monitoring our thoughts, feelings, or actions. However, if these aggression-related tendencies are subjected to higher-level thinking, we can often modify and control them. What causes these aggression-related tendencies to come under the control of more complex cognitive processes? Self-awareness, one of our great human gifts. Use this gift to control your own aggression. When you become angry, try to make sense of your negative feelings before reacting. Analyze the implications of your actions and consider alternative nonaggressive responses. By bringing into play these cognitive control mechanisms, the link between negative affect and aggression can be short-circuited.

In summary, although our present ability to control aggression may seem meager at best, keep in mind that our analysis of aggression reveals that this is a highly complex phenomenon. It not only springs from a number of psychological sources (for example, anger, fear of punishment, desire for rewards), but it also appears to be shaped by a variety of environmental factors. For me, in some respects, the various forms of aggression in society today seem like a modern-day Hydra. In Greek mythology, the Hydra was a terribly dangerous nine-headed serpent that was exceedingly difficult to kill. Whenever one head was chopped off, two grew back. Fortunately for the ancient Greeks, the Hydra was finally destroyed by their superhero, Hercules. There are no superheroes in contemporary social psychology, nor in the larger society. Yet if we ever hope to slay our Hydra, it will entail a Herculean task by all elements of society.

WEB SITES
accessed through http://www.mhhe.com/franzoi4

Web sites for this chapter focus on research and theory on family violence, acquaintance rape, violence on television, and recommendations on how to control anger before it leads to aggression.

Minnesota Center Against Violence and Abuse

This is the Web site for the Minnesota Center Against Violence and Abuse listing links to education and training resources, papers and reports on aggression, and resource materials for teaching about family violence.

American Psychological Association

The American Psychological Association Web site has a number of relevant Web pages, including one that examines research on the psychological effects of television violence and another on how to control anger before it leads to aggression.

"Friends" Raping Friends: Could It Happen to You?

This is a Web site devoted to the facts about acquaintance rape, including its causes and consequences, and how to avoid situations that might lead to acquaintance rape.

Center for the Study and Prevention of Violence

This is the Web site for the Center for the Study and Prevention of Violence, which has fact sheets on violence, research summaries, and a list of papers you can request.

National Consortium on Violence Research

This is the Web site for the National Consortium on Violence Research, which is a research and training center specializing in violence research. The mission of the consortium is to advance basic scientific knowledge about the causes or factors contributing to interpersonal violence.

International Society for Research on Aggression

This Web site is devoted to the scientific study of aggression and violence around the world.

CHAPTER 14

Prosocial Behavior: Helping Others

CHAPTER OUTLINE

O n the morning of September 11, 2001, television viewers watched as thousands of people died inside the twin towers of New York's World Trade Center and the Pentagon Building in Washington, DC, following terrorist attacks by followers of Osama Bin Laden. As this tragedy unfolded, Michael Benfante and John Cerqueira were racing for the exits on the sixty-eighth floor of the Trade Center's south tower. Then they noticed a woman sitting helplessly behind a set of glass doors. She was a stranger to them. Diagnosed with juvenile rheumatoid arthritis at age 3, Tina Hansen had been confined to a wheelchair most of her life. And now she was trapped inside a burning building. Benfante and Cerqueira had to make a quick decision. If they continued running down the stairs, they might get out alive. What were their chances if they stopped to help this woman? Putting aside their own safety, the two men strapped Hansen into a lightweight chair and carried her out of the building, reaching the street just minutes before their tower began to collapse.

New York City Fire Chief Peter Ganci, Jr., arrived at the World Trade Center just after the collapse of the first tower. Immediately, Ganci took charge and led people to safety. Then, amid the choking dust and blinding smoke, he continued ushering terrified survivors and injured fellow firefighters away from the second collapsing tower. A witness saw Ganci still trying to rescue people as gigantic panes of glass and steel girders rained down on him. "Even at the very end he was helping someone," said fire chaplain John Delendick.

At the same time, in Washington, DC, Lieutenant Colonel Patty Horoho, an army health-policy officer, ran from her damaged section of the Pentagon to set up a triage center for survivors. Reverting to her earlier training as a certified nurse, Horoho treated more than seventy-five injured people over the next four hours. "I felt like my life and career had been a preparation for this moment," said Horoho. "I truly believe that is why I could take charge."

The willingness to help is not reserved solely for life-threatening situations, nor is it unique to Americans. Throughout the world, people provide aid and comfort to those in need. In this chapter, we address and try to answer five basic questions. First, why do we help? Second, when do we help? Third, who is most likely to help? Fourth, whom do we help? And fifth, are there hidden costs for those who receive help?

WHAT IS PROSOCIAL BEHAVIOR?

Before tackling these five helping questions, let's begin by defining our topic and briefly discussing the notion that there may be two basic forms of helpful actions.

Prosocial Action Is Voluntary and Benefits Others

Prosocial Behavior

Voluntary behavior that is carried out to benefit another person.

Prosocial behavior is voluntary behavior that is carried out to benefit another person (Batson & Powell, 2003). This definition excludes beneficial actions that are not performed voluntarily or are not performed with the intention of helping another. Thus, if Tina Hansen had forced Michael Benfante and John Cerqueira at gunpoint to carry her out of the building, their actions would not be considered prosocial because they really would have had no *choice* in rendering assistance. Likewise, if a terrified person fleeing from the burning towers accidentally pushed someone out of the path of falling debris, this action also would not be prosocial because the pushing was unintentional and was not meant to benefit another. On the other hand, the actions of Benfante, Cerqueira, and Ganci in New York and those of Horoho in Washington perfectly fit our definition because they were freely chosen and the intention was to benefit another.

All of us have had personal experiences of helping and being helped by others. Sometimes our prosocial actions involve little cost, while at other times our helping can entail considerable time, money, and even personal danger. Have you ever wondered how your own degree of helpfulness compares with that of others' prosocial tendencies? If you have, spend a few minutes responding to the Helping-Orientation Questionnaire items (Romer et al., 1986) in table 14.1.

Beyond the basic definition, philosophers and a number of social scientists have traditionally described two forms of helpful behavior that are based on very different motives. For example, nineteenth-century philosopher Auguste Comte (1875) contended that **egoistic helping**—in which the person wants something in return—is based on *egoism*, because the ultimate goal of the helper is to increase his or her own welfare. In contrast, Comte stated that **altruistic helping,** in which the person expects nothing in return, is based on *altruism,* because the ultimate goal is to increase another's welfare (Batson et al., 2002a).

As we discuss later in the chapter, social scientists disagree on whether any useful distinctions can be made between egoistic and altruistic helping, and some argue that all helping is ultimately egoistic in nature. Based on your responses to the questionnaire, what best describes your reactions to others in need of help? Are you generally helpful? If you are, do you think any of your helpfulness could be described as ultimately motivated by altruism rather than mere egoism?

Gender Influences Helping

Beyond egoism and altruism, do you think your willingness to help is influenced by whether you are a woman or a man? Alice Eagly and Maureen Crowley's (1986) meta-analytic review of 172 helping behavior studies indicates that men and women differ in their willingness to engage in certain prosocial actions: men generally help more than women, and they are more likely than women to help strangers. These gender differences are greatest when there is an audience, when there is potential danger involved in helping, and when the person in need is

Egoistic Helping

A form of helping in which the ultimate goal of the helper is to increase his or her own welfare.

Altruistic Helping

A form of helping in which the ultimate goal of the helper is to increase another's welfare without expecting anything in return.

Immediately following the September 11th terrorist attacks, many people on the scene of the tragedies ignored risks to their own lives and helped others. Why might men be more likely than women to take life-threatening risks in such situations? Are there other situations in which women tend to be more helpful than men?

TABLE 14.1

Helping-Orientation Questionnaire

Directions

While reading these descriptions of hypothetical situations, imagine yourself in each of them and pick the action that best describes what you would do:

1. You have come across a lost wallet with a large sum of money in it, as well as identification of the owner. You
    A. return the wallet without letting the owner know who you are.
    B. return the wallet in hopes of receiving a reward.
    C. keep the wallet and the money.
    D. leave the wallet where you found it.

2. A person in one of your classes is having trouble at home and with schoolwork. You
    A. help the person as much as you can.
    B. tell the person not to bother you.
    C. leave the person alone to work out his or her own problems.
    D. agree to tutor the person for a reasonable fee.

3. When it comes to cooperation when you would rather not, you usually
    A. cooperate if it is helpful to others.
    B. cooperate if it is helpful to yourself.
    C. refuse to get involved.
    D. avoid situations where you might be asked to cooperate.

4. A neighbor calls you and asks for a ride to a store that is six blocks away. You
    A. refuse, thinking you will never need a favor from him (or her).
    B. explain that you are too busy at the moment.
    C. immediately give the ride and wait while the neighbor shops.
    D. consent if the neighbor is a good friend.

5. You are approached by someone asking for a contribution to a well-known charity. You
    A. give if there is something received in return.
    B. refuse to contribute.
    C. give whatever amount you can.
    D. pretend you are in a hurry.

6. You are in a waiting room with another person. If you heard a scream in the adjoining room and the other person failed to respond, you would
    A. help the screaming person whether the other person helps or not.
    B. help the screaming person only if the other person does too.
    C. wait to see if the screaming continues.
    D. leave the room.

7. When asked to volunteer for a task in which you will receive no pay, you
    A. avoid or put off answering.
    B. explain that you don't agree with the objectives to be accomplished and therefore couldn't volunteer.
    C. compromise and help if you will receive some recognition.
    D. volunteer without question.

Scoring

The information below shows which answers on the Helping-Orientation Questionnaire indicate altruistic helping, egoistic helping, and unhelpful behavior. It also shows the percentage of people who gave each answer in a recent survey. Do your responses indicate that your helping orientation is predominantly altruistic, egoistic, or unhelpful?

Item	Altruistic Helping	Egoistic Helping	Unhelpful Behavior
1.	A (38%)	B (47%)	C,D (15%)
2.	A (86%)	D (4%)	B,C (10%)
3.	A (61%)	B (20%)	C,D (19%)
4.	C (33%)	D (56%)	A,B (11%)
5.	C (70%)	A (4%)	B,D (26%)
6.	A (50%)	B (10%)	C,D (40%)
7.	D (35%)	C (27%)	A,B (39%)

female. Although these differences appear real, they apply most to nonroutine prosocial acts such as offering help to strangers in distress. When other forms of prosocial behavior—such as helping a friend or caring for children—are studied, women generally prove to be more helpful than men. For example, women are more likely than men to provide social and emotional support to others (Shumaker & Hill, 1991), and they also are more willing to serve as caretakers for children and the elderly (Trudeau & Devlin, 1996). In addition, among children, there are few gender differences in helping, and the few differences that have been found indicate that girls tend to be a bit more helpful than boys (Eisenberg et al., 1996).

Based on these findings, we can make two tentative conclusions. First, women and men appear to be helpful in different ways. Second, these differences become stronger from childhood to adulthood and are most apparent when gender roles are salient. Consistent with the culturally valued male role of heroic rescuer, men are more likely than women to place themselves in danger when rendering assistance. In contrast, women are more likely than men to provide longer-term help involving empathy and caretaking, qualities consistent with the feminine gender role.

CRITICAL *thinking*

What sort of cultural role models might influence the "helping habits" of boys and girls? How might greater gender-role flexibility influence male and female helping tendencies?

SECTION SUMMARY

- *Prosocial behavior* is voluntary behavior carried out to benefit another, and comes in two forms:

   egoistic helping: the helper's ultimate goal is to increase her or his own welfare

   altruistic helping: the helper's ultimate goal is to increase another's welfare with no self-benefit expected

- Women and men appear to be helpful in different ways

   men are more likely to help in dangerous situations

   women are more likely to provide long-term help

   these gender differences increase from childhood to adulthood and when gender roles are salient

WHY DO WE HELP?

As already noted, some social scientists believe that people sometimes help solely to benefit another, while at other times they help in order to achieve some personal gain. In addition, it has also been suggested that because of inborn characteristics, people may be predisposed to prosocial behavior.

Helping Is Consistent with Evolutionary Theory

As discussed in previous chapters, one principle of evolutionary theory is that any social behaviors that enhance reproductive success (the conception, birth, and survival of offspring) will continue to be passed on from one generation to the next. However, to reproduce, an animal must first survive. Often, an animal's survival depends on how well it can compete with other members of its own species for limited resources. This evolutionary fact would seem to dictate that animals should be selfish, looking out first and foremost for themselves. Yet what of the seemingly selfless act of helping?

Ethologists and evolutionary psychologists have documented countless instances in which animals have put their own lives at risk to protect other members of their own species from danger (Fouts, 1997; Wilson, 1996). For example, a chimpanzee foraging for food with its troop will often emit a warning call to alert the others about a nearby predator. By calling out, this chimp is the one most likely to be caught by the predator. As this example illustrates, helping others can be downright deadly. When you are dead, your reproductive days are over. Thus, from an evolutionary perspective, how could helping be advantageous to reproduction?

KIN SELECTION

Kin Selection

A theory that people will exhibit preferences for helping blood relatives because this will increase the odds that their genes will be transmitted to subsequent generations.

As previously outlined in the chapter 13 discussion of aggression, evolutionary theorists contend that it is not individual survival that is important, but rather, it is *gene* survival that promotes reproductive fitness (Archer, 1991). Because your blood relatives share many of your same genes, by promoting their survival you can also preserve your genes even if you don't survive the helpful act. This principle of **kin selection** states that you will exhibit preferences for helping blood relatives because this will increase the odds that your genes will be transmitted to subsequent generations (Zahavi, 2003).

Although the principle of kin selection explains why we are more likely to help those who are related to us by blood, it does not explain the countless incidents of people helping total strangers. Stranger helping is found not only among humans but among other species as well. For example, female chimpanzees, lions, dolphins, and bluebirds have been observed taking care of nonrelated newborns deserted by their mothers (Conner & Norriss, 1982; Goodall, 1986). Given this fact, how can evolutionary theorists explain prosocial behavior that extends beyond one's family?

RECIPROCAL HELPING

Reciprocal Helping (also known as reciprocal altruism)

An evolutionary principle stating that people expect that anyone helping another will have that favor returned at some future time.

Robert Trivers (1971) has described a way in which helping strangers could have arisen through natural selection. This principle, which he called *reciprocal altruism,* involves mutual helping, usually separated in time. However, because "altruism" refers to motives and Trivers was merely referring to behavior, we will use the more accurate term **reciprocal helping** when referring to this mutual helping. According to this principle, people are likely to help strangers if it is understood that the recipient is expected to return the favor at some time in the future. In such a world of reciprocal helping, the cost of aiding another is more than offset by the later returned help (Kurzban, 2003). For reciprocal helping to evolve, the benefit to the recipient must be high and the cost to the helper must be relatively low. In addition, the likelihood of their positions being reversed in the future must also be high, and there must be a way to identify "cheaters"—those who do not reciprocate (Brown & Moore, 2000).

A good example of reciprocal helping is *social grooming.* In many species, one individual cleans the other's fur or feathers, and later, the "groomee" returns the favor (Matheson & Bernstein, 2000). Grooming is a low-cost activity (only time lost) that returns high benefits to the recipient (removing disease-carrying parasites). Trivers (1983) believes that reciprocal helping is most likely to evolve in a species when certain conditions exist. Three of these conditions are (1) *social group living,* so that individuals have ample opportunity to give and receive help, (2) *mutual dependence,* in which species survival depends on cooperation, and (3) the *lack of rigid dominance hierarchies,* so that reciprocal helping will enhance each animal's power.

Considerable research supports both kin selection and reciprocal helping among humans and other animals. For example, when threatened by predators, squirrels are much more likely to warn genetically related squirrels and squirrels with which they live than unrelated squirrels or those from other areas (Sherman, 1985). Similarly, across a wide variety of human cultures, relatives receive more help than nonrelatives, especially if the help involves considerable costs, such as being a kidney donor (Borgida et al., 1992). Reciprocal helping is also common in humans, and, consistent with evolutionary-based mechanisms to prevent cheating, when people are unable to reciprocate, they tend to experience guilt and shame (Fehr & Gaechter, 2002; Wonderly, 1996).

Taken together, this research suggests that there may be mechanisms for the genetic transmission of helpful inclinations from generation to generation. Yet unlike many species where altruistic behavior is closely tied to genetic heritage, human genes influence behavior in a more indirect manner (Kruger, 2003). As I have stated throughout this text, although ancient evolutionary forces may have left us with *capacities* (such as the capacity to behave altruistically), current social and environmental forces encourage or discourage the actual development and use of those capacities.

Social Norms Define the Rules of Helping Others

Although prosocial behavior may have a genetic basis, it makes sense that social mechanisms would develop to enforce these evolutionarily adaptive helping strategies (Nesse, 2000; Simon, 1990). Chapter 9 discussed how general rules of conduct, known as *social norms,* prescribe how people should generally behave. These shared expectations are backed up by the proverbial carrot and stick: the threat of group punishment if the norms are not obeyed and the promise of rewards for conforming. Prosocial norms are expectations to behave selflessly in bestowing benefits on others. Three social norms that serve as guidelines for prosocial behavior deal with *reciprocity, responsibility,* and *justice.*

The first of these prosocial norms, the *norm of reciprocity,* is based on maintaining fairness in social relationships. As discussed in chapters 9 and 12, this norm prescribes that people should be paid back for whatever they give us. Regarding prosocial behavior, this means helping those who help us (Brown & Moore, 2000; Gouldner, 1960). As mentioned in the previous section, this norm also explains the discomfort that people typically experience when they receive help but cannot give something back in return.

In comparison to the reciprocity norm, the other two prosocial norms dictate that people should help due to a greater awareness of what is right. For instance, the **norm of social responsibility** states that we should help when others are in need and dependent on us (Bierhoff, 2002). Acting on this norm, adults feel responsible for the health and safety of children, teachers have a sense of duty and obligation to their students, and police and firefighters believe they must help even at the risk of their own lives. This social responsibility norm requires help-givers to render assistance regardless of the recipient's worthiness and without an expectation of being rewarded (Nunner-Winkler, 1984). Unfortunately for the needy of the world, even though most people endorse the social responsibility norm, they often do not act in accordance with it. One reason for this nonadherence is that people also often believe in social justice (Darley, 2001). In contrast to the dependent-driven social responsibility norm, the **norm of social justice** stipulates that people should help only when they believe that others *deserve* assistance (Batson, 2002b). How does one become a "deserving" person? Melvin Lerner (1980, 1997) contends that at least in North American society, people become entitled to the deserving label by either possessing socially desirable personality characteristics or by engaging in socially desirable behaviors. Thus, according to the social justice norm, if "good" people encounter unfortunate circumstances, they deserve our help and we have a duty to render assistance.

POLITICAL DIFFERENCES

During the past two U.S. presidential campaigns, George W. Bush's political advisers attempted to dispel public perceptions that the Republican Party was relatively unsympathetic to the needy by portraying their candidate as a "compassionate conservative." Is there any truth in associating compassion with liberal versus conservative political ideologies?

As previously discussed in chapter 8 (pp. 285–287), American democracy was founded on the sometimes conflicting value orientations of *individualism* (or self-reliance) and *egalitarianism* (equal treatment of groups and sympathy for the disadvantaged). Because conservatives emphasize individualism and liberals emphasize egalitarianism in their respective political ideologies, they often develop different positions regarding the obligations society should have toward the disadvantaged (Dionne, 1991). In explaining poverty, for example, conservatives tend to make dispositional attributions, blaming poverty on self-indulgence, laziness, or low intelligence. In contrast, liberals tend to make situational attributions, perceiving the poor as victims of social injustice. As a result of these different social beliefs and attributions, liberals generally favor, whereas conservatives oppose, increased spending on social programs for the disadvantaged (Biernat et al., 1996; Kluegel & Smith, 1986).

If you don't look out for others, who will look out for you?

Whoopi Goldberg, comedian, actress and social activist for the homeless, b. 1949

Norm of Social Responsibility

Social norm stating that we should help when others are in need and dependent on us.

Norm of Social Justice

A social norm stating that we should help only when we believe that others deserve our assistance.

Help the weak ones that cry for help, help the prosecuted and the victim . . . they are the comrades that fight and fall.

Nicola Sacco, Italian-born anarchist, 1891–1927

If a free society cannot help the many who are poor, it cannot save the few who are rich.

John F. Kennedy, 35th U.S. President, 1917–1963

Research also suggests that conservatives are less willing to help victims of natural disasters than liberals. In a national sample of over 1,000 adults following floods in the Mississippi and Ohio River valleys, Linda Skitka (1999) found that people with a conservative political orientation consistently held flood victims more responsible for their plight and for resolving it than did those with a liberal orientation. Invoking the social justice norm, conservatives were even reluctant to provide public support for immediate humanitarian aid (clean water, food, shelter) to those who had not taken actions to protect themselves against flood risks. Although liberals were significantly more compassionate in their willingness to provide immediate help, like conservatives, they were unenthusiastic about using federal disaster assistance to financially bail out victims.

Overall, these studies suggest that, when faced with those who need help in situations not immediately life-threatening, liberals are more likely to adhere to the norm of social responsibility, while conservatives adhere more closely to the norm of social justice. In other words, "compassionate conservativism" is a more discriminating approach to helping others than that practiced by liberals, who have been accused by conservatives as having "bleeding hearts" when it comes to assisting those who are disadvantaged.

CULTURAL DIFFERENCES

Research conducted in both individualist and collectivist cultures indicates that the norm of reciprocity may be universal (Gergen et al., 1975). Regarding the norm of social responsibility, a number of cross-cultural studies have found that adult members of collectivist cultures are not only more likely to help others of their ingroup than are members of individualist cultures, but they also express greater enjoyment in meeting these social obligations than do individualists (Bontempo et al., 1990). Similar cross-cultural differences have also been obtained when studying children's prosocial actions. For example, children from the collectivist cultures of Kenya, Mexico, and the Philippines were found to be much more helpful than children from the United States (Whiting & Edwards, 1988). A likely reason for this difference is that collectivists are much more likely than individualists to stress ingroup cooperation and individual sacrifice. In such a context, people may feel greater moral obligation to help than if they grew up in a less group-oriented environment.

Joan Miller and her colleagues (1990) found support for this perspective in a study of the moral reasoning of Hindus in India and of Americans. Participants read a series of hypothetical situations in which the main character in the story failed to help someone experiencing a life-threatening, a moderately serious, or a minor need. The needy person either was the main character's child, best friend, or a stranger. As table 14.2 shows, Hindu respondents tended to perceive helping as the main character's social responsibility in all conditions, even when the need was minor. This means they believed that in all situations, giving help should be dictated by social norms and not by the personal norms of the potential helper. In comparison, American respondents believed that the norm of social responsibility should only be dictated in life-threatening cases or when parents were faced with moderately serious needs of their children. In all other instances, Americans believed that the main character's decision to help should be based on his or her own personal norms of help giving and should not be subject to social regulation.

How do these cross-cultural findings fit in with the previously discussed results regarding Americans' liberal-conservative distinctions in helping orientation? Overall, it appears that collectivist Indian culture holds to a broader and more stringent view of social responsibility than does the individualist American culture (Miller, 1994). For life-threatening needs of both strangers and loved ones and for moderately serious needs of one's family members, both Indians and Americans are likely to subscribe to the social responsibility norm. However, for needs of friends and strangers that are not life threatening, Americans are generally less likely than Indians to subscribe to the social responsibility norm. This cultural difference appears to be especially apparent for Americans with a conservative political ideology rather than those with a liberal ideology.

What about Americans with an ethnic heritage rooted in collectivism? Are they more helpful than Americans with more of an individualist heritage? Ronnie Janoff-Bul-

CRITICAL *thinking*

Following the terrorist attacks of September 11, 2001, liberal and conservative politicians did not differ in endorsing massive economic assistance to New York City. Does this unified response contradict Skitka's research findings?

An individual has not started living until he can rise above the narrow confines of his individualist concerns to the broader concerns of all humanity.

Martin Luther King, Jr., African American civil rights leader, 1929–1968

TABLE 14.2

Percentage of Hindus and Americans Saying People Have an Obligation to Help Others

When asked to state their opinion on people's social responsibility to help, collectivist Hindus believed that helping was one's responsibility as a parent, friend, and stranger, even when the need was minor. In contrast, Americans believed the social responsibility norm only extended to life-threatening situations or when parents had children with moderately serious needs.

	Hindus			Americans		
	Parent	Friend	Stranger	Parent	Friend	Stranger
Extreme need	99	99	100	100	98	96
Moderate need	98	100	99	95	78	55
Minor need	96	97	88	61	59	41

man and Hallie Leggatt (2002) tested this hypothesis by having Latino-American and Anglo-American college students complete a questionnaire assessing the extent to which they felt obligated to help and wanted to help across a variety of social situations. Results mirrored the cross-cultural findings for people with collectivist versus individualist orientations. Although respondents from both ethnic groups reported a strong sense of obligation to help close friends and family members in need, the more collectivist Latinos expressed a greater desire to engage in these expected behaviors than the more individualist Anglos. In addition, Latino students also felt a stronger sense of social obligation and desire to help more distant family members and friends than did Anglo students. The two ethnic groups did not differ in their motivation to help strangers. Thus, similar to cross-cultural studies, these findings suggest that individualist and collectivist orientations in the United States have predictable effects on helping motivation, with collectivist-oriented Americans perceiving help giving as both more obligatory ("I must help") and more personally desirable ("I want to help") than Americans with a more individualist orientation.

In closing, it should be noted that the individualist-collectivist cultural differences discussed here appear to apply only to ingroup helping. When those needing help are clearly members of an outgroup, research suggests that collectivists may at times be less helpful than individualists (L'Armand & Pepitone, 1975; Lonner & Adamopoulos, 1997). In this case, "compassionate collectivism" does not extend to those who are seen as "them" rather than "us."

Learning to Be a Helper Involves Both Observation and Direct Reinforcement

The research we have discussed thus far informs us that culture and political beliefs influence our adherence to helping norms. However, although many people subscribe to the same helping norms, they differ in their tendencies to act consistently with these norms. The internalization of prosocial values begins in the preschool years, and parents and other adults play a significant role in this developmental process (Grusec et al., 2002). Just as chapter 13 outlined how aggression can be learned through modeling and direct reinforcement, we now examine how prosocial behavior is similarly learned.

OBSERVATIONAL LEARNING IN CHILDREN

According to social learning theorists, observational learning or modeling can influence the development of helping in at least two ways (Rosenkoetter, 1999; Rushton, 1980). First, it can initially teach children how to engage in helpful actions. Second, it can show children what is likely to happen when they actually engage in helpful (or selfish) behavior. In

Does research suggest that people from a collectivist culture like India are more or less likely to give assistance to a stranger than people from the individualist-oriented United States? Does the severity of the need appear to matter in willingness to help in these two cultures?

If I can stop one Heart from breaking
I shall not live in vain
If I can ease one Life the Aching
Or cool one Pain
Or help one fainting Robin
Unto his Nest again
I shall not live in Vain.

Emily Dickinson, American poet, 1830–1886

this learning process, what models *say* and what they *do* both shape the observers' prosocial behaviors.

For example, in one study, sixth-grade girls played a game to win chips that could be traded for candy and toys (Midlarsky et al., 1973). Prior to actually playing, each of the girls watched a woman play the game. In the *charitable* condition, the adult put some of the chips she won into a jar labeled "money for poor children" and then urged the girl to think about the poor children who would "love to receive the prizes these chips can buy." In the *selfish* condition, the adult model also urged the child to donate chips to the poor children, but she did so after putting all her chips into a jar labeled "my money." Results indicated a clear effect of prosocial modeling. Girls who had observed the charitable model donated more chips to the poor than those who had seen the selfish model.

Although this study demonstrates that what one does has more effect on children than what one says, subsequent studies have shown that *preaching* can have a delayed effect in influencing prosocial behavior. In one of these studies, J. Philippe Rushton (1975) had children observe a same-sex adult model being either generous or selfish with her or his winning tokens from a game. Regardless of their actual behavior, some of the models told the watching child that one should be generous ("We should share our tokens . . ."), while others preached that one should be selfish ("We should not share our tokens . . ."). As in the previous study, the models' behavior had clear effects on the children's immediate helping, but what the models said had little immediate impact (see figure 14.1). However, two months later, in a retest of their willingness to help, something interesting happened. Although the children who had observed the charitable models were still more helpful than those who had watched the selfish models, children exposed to the models who preached generosity now donated more of their winnings to charity than those children who heard models preach selfishness. By far the most generous were those children previously exposed to models who had acted consistently with their prosocial preachings. In addition, the models preaching generosity but behaving selfishly produced the most giving in the selfish model condition.

This study, along with others (Moore & Eisenberg, 1984), suggests that although children are more likely to be influenced by adults' deeds rather than their words, over the course

FIGURE 14.1

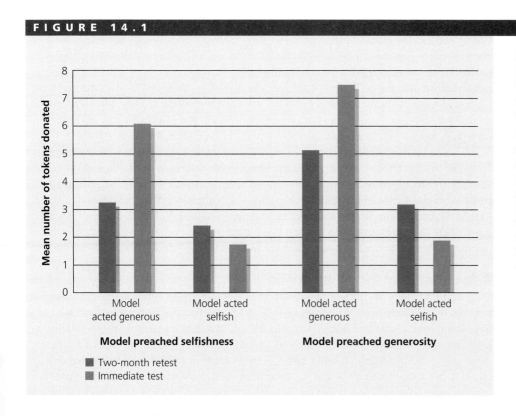

Model preached selfishness   Model preached generosity

- ■ Two-month retest
- ■ Immediate test

Immediate and Long-Term Effects of Modeling and Preaching on Children's Generosity

Children observed an adult model acting either generously or selfishly and also listened to them preach either generosity or selfishness. How did the model's behavior and preaching influence the children's immediate willingness to donate tokens? What about their willingness to donate two months later?

of time, preaching generosity can have some positive effect on children's prosocial tendencies, even if it comes from people who do not practice what they preach. The finding that selfish people can, over time, promote prosocial behavior by preaching generosity is interesting, but why might this be the case? Wouldn't listeners simply discount a hypocrite's words?

In the short run, a hypocrite's preachings do appear to be discounted. However, in chapter 7 we learned that although people with low credibility (like a hypocrite) are not very persuasive immediately after they present their message, over time listeners forget where they heard it and then are influenced by the message content alone. This delayed effectiveness of a persuasive message from a noncredible source is known as the *sleeper effect* (see p. 217). In Rushton's study, although the children initially seemed to dismiss the selfish models' preachings of generosity, over time they were somewhat persuaded by the message content because they forgot where it originated.

PROSOCIAL MODELING IN ADULTS

Modeling prosocial behavior is not confined to children. In one study conducted in a natural setting, motorists who simply saw someone helping a woman change a flat tire were more likely to later stop and assist a second woman who was in a similar predicament (Bryan & Test, 1967). In another experiment (Rushton & Campbell, 1977), female college students interacted with a friendly woman as part of a study on social interaction (this was not the true purpose, and the woman was a confederate of the researchers). When the fabricated study was completed, the two women left the lab together and passed a table staffed by people asking for blood donations. When participants were asked first, only 25 percent agreed, and none actually followed through on their pledge six weeks later. However, when the confederate was asked first and signed up to donate blood, 67 percent of the participants also agreed to give blood, and 33 percent actually fulfilled their commitment.

THE LASTING CONSEQUENCES OF MODELING

A number of studies have revealed the critical importance that prosocial parental modeling plays in the lives of extraordinary helpers. For example, a study of civil rights activists in the late 1950s and 1960s found that previous parental modeling of prosocial behavior distinguished those who made many personal sacrifices from those who participated in only one or two freedom rides or marches. The fully committed activists had parents who had been excellent prosocial models when the activists were children, while the parents of the partially committed tended to be inconsistent models, often preaching prosocial action but not actually practicing it (Rosenhan, 1970). These findings mesh nicely with the previously discussed experiment by Rushton (1975). Combined with other studies, they indicate that adults' modeling of altruism can have a powerful effect on the altruistic tendencies of children that can last well into adulthood (Fogelman, 1996; Oliner & Oliner, 1988).

Based on this knowledge, social scientists believe they can make a clear recommendation to parents on how to raise children who will help those in need. Put simply, parents who try to instill prosocial values only by preaching and not by modeling altruism will likely raise children who are only weakly altruistic. Parents who not only preach altruism, but also let their prosocial actions serve as guidelines for their children's behavior, are much more likely to foster altruism in the next generation. In a very real sense, to be effective altruistic teachers, one must not only "talk the talk," but also "walk the walk."

REWARDING PROSOCIAL BEHAVIOR

Although observing the prosocial actions of others can shape children's and adults' own helping, the *consequences* of their actions will often determine whether they continue to engage in prosocial behavior. Social rewards, such as praise, are generally more effective reinforcers than material rewards, such as money (Grusec, 1991). In one such "praise" experiment conducted by Rushton and Goody Teachman (1978), children were first induced to behave generously by having generosity modeled to them as in the previously described game-token studies. When the children donated some of their winnings to an orphan named Bobby, the model either praised the child for his or her imitative generosity (*reward condition*) by saying "Good for you, that's really nice of you," or scolded the child (*punishment condition*) by saying "That's kind of silly for you to give to Bobby. Now you will have fewer tokens for yourself." There was also a no-reinforcement condition in which the adult said nothing. As you can see in figure 14.2, children who were praised gave more to Bobby on later trials than did children who were scolded. The effects of being either rewarded or punished for prosocial behavior were so strong that they still influenced how much the chil-

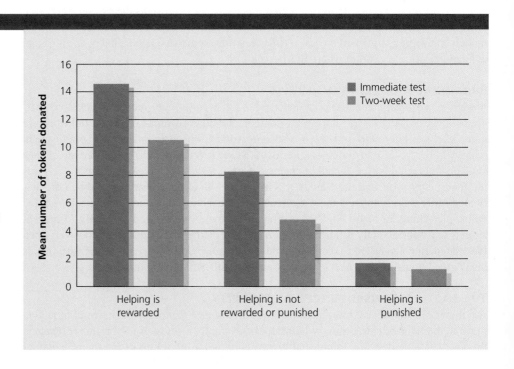

FIGURE 14.2

The Effects of Positive Reinforcement and Punishment on Model-Induced Generosity in Children

Do rewards and punishment affect children's willingness to help others? Rushton and Teachman (1978) either praised, criticized, or said nothing to children who donated tokens to an orphan named Bobby. How did these different consequences influence the children's subsequent willingness to donate tokens?

dren gave to Bobby two weeks later. This study demonstrates that verbal praise or scolding by an adult model can either strengthen or weaken children's level of generosity.

Reinforcement also influences adult helping. For example, imagine yourself walking along the main street in your hometown and being approached by a woman who asks how to get to a local department store. After giving her directions you continue along your way. Shortly, you pass by another woman who accidentally drops a small bag and continues walking, unaware that she has lost this possession. Would you return the bag to her? Do you think your decision to help the second woman would be influenced by how the first woman responded to your attempt to help her?

This was the question that researchers asked in a naturalistic study conducted on the streets of Dayton, Ohio, using just this scenario (Moss & Page, 1972). In the *reward* condition, the woman asking for directions rewarded her helper by saying, "Thank you very much, I really appreciate this." In contrast, in the *punishment* condition the woman responded to help by saying, "I can't understand what you're saying, never mind, I'll ask someone else." Researchers found that when people were rewarded by the first woman, 90 percent of them helped the second woman. However, when punished by the first woman, only 40 percent helped in the later situation. As in the study with children, this adult study suggests that people's future decisions to help are often influenced by the degree to which current helpful efforts are met by praise or rebuke.

SECTION SUMMARY

- In kin selection, we exhibit preferences for helping blood relatives because this increases the odds that our genes will be transmitted to subsequent generations
- In reciprocal helping, aiding strangers can be adaptive because any helpful act or favor is expected to be returned
- Relevant social norms that promote helping:

    reciprocity norm: help those who help you

    social responsibility norm: help those in need or those dependent on you

    social justice norm: help those who deserve assistance

- Liberals adhere more to the social responsibility norm, while conservatives adhere more to the social justice norm
- Collectivist cultures hold to a broader and more stringent view of social responsibility than individualist cultures
- Prosocial behavior that is rewarded will become stronger
- Parents who model prosocial behavior raise children who become helpful adults

WHEN DO WE HELP?

In chapter 2, you learned how social psychological research is sometimes motivated by the researcher's desire to explain some real-life incident that has received wide news coverage. One of the most memorable examples of a real-life event spurring social psychological research was the Kitty Genovese case, which occurred on March 13, 1964, in the New York City borough of Queens. At 3:20 A.M. Kitty Genovese was returning home from her job as a bar manager when a man attacked her with a knife near her apartment building. She screamed, "Oh, my God! He stabbed me. Please help me!" As her cry rang out in the night, at least thirty-eight of her neighbors went to their windows to see what was going on. Within moments, Kitty Genovese's assailant stabbed her again, and then got into his car and drove away.

Despite the fact that Ms. Genovese was on the ground and in obvious need of help, not one of her neighbors came to her aid. No one called the police or an ambulance, but one

While neighbors listened to her cries for help, Kitty Genovese was repeatedly stabbed outside her apartment building on the night of March 31, 1964. Despite this obvious emergency, no one came to her aid and no one even called the police until she had already died from her wounds. This incident prompted social psychologists John Darley and Bibb Latané to study the conditions that inhibit bystanders from helping in emergencies.

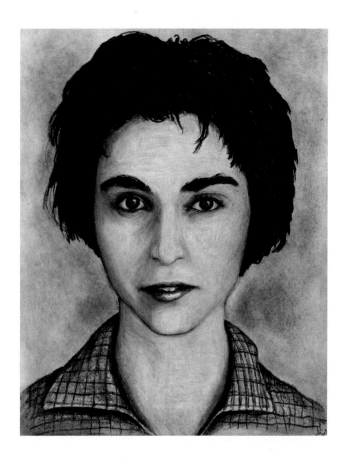

Social Sense

View a social psychological analysis of the Kitty Genovese murder.

couple did pull up chairs to their window and turn out the lights to see more clearly. Fifteen minutes passed. As Ms. Genovese was crawling toward the back of her apartment building in search of safety, the assailant returned again. Now a watching neighbor reached for the phone to call police, but his wife told him, "Don't; thirty people have probably called by now." Yet no one had alerted the police. Within seconds, the killer, finding Ms. Genovese slumped against the stairs, struck again, this time stabbing her eight times and sexually assaulting her. Twenty minutes after she died, someone finally phoned the police, who arrived on the scene within two minutes. View a social psychological analysis of the Kitty Genovese murder on your Social Sense CD-ROM.

Bystander Intervention Involves a Series of Decisions

The apathy of Kitty Genovese's neighbors was the topic of news stories, commentaries, religious sermons, and dinner conversation for some time. The question everyone was asking was "Why were these bystanders so callous to her suffering?" Two people who discussed the murder at length were social psychologists John Darley and Bibb Latané. Years later, Darley recalled the content of their discussion:

> Latané and I, shocked as anybody else, met over dinner a few days after this terrible incident had occurred and began to analyze this process in social psychological terms. . . . First, social psychologists ask not how are people different or why are the people who failed to respond monsters, but how are all people the same and how might anybody in that situation be influenced not to respond. Second, we asked: What influences reach the person from the group? We argued for a several-step model in which a person first had to define the situation. Emergencies don't come wearing signs saying "I am an emergency." In defining an event as an emergency, one looks at other people to see their reactions to the situation and interpret

the meaning that lies behind their actions. Third, when multiple people are present, the responsibility to intervene does not focus clearly on any one person. . . . You feel a diffusion of responsibility in that situation and you're less likely to take responsibility. We argued that these two processes, definition and diffusion, working together, might well account for a good deal of what happened. (Evans, 1980, pp. 216–217)

According to the **bystander intervention model,** which eventually emerged as a result of this dinner discussion, being helpful during an emergency involves not just one decision, but a series of five decisions. As you can see from figure 14.3 (p. 546), at each point in this five-step process, one decision results in no help being given, while the other decision takes the bystander one step closer to intervention.

The first thing that you, as a potential helper, must do is *notice that something unusual is happening.* Unfortunately, in many social settings, countless sights and sounds flood our senses. Because it is impossible to attend to all this stimuli, and because we may be preoccupied with something else, a cry for help could conceivably go completely unnoticed. This *stimulus overload effect* is more likely to occur in densely populated urban environments than in rural settings (Milgram, 1970). Indeed, it is one of the likely reasons why there is a negative correlation between population density and helping (Levine, 2003). That is, throughout the world, people who live in more crowded cities are less likely to help strangers in need of assistance than those who live in less densely populated urban centers (Levine et al., 1994; Yousif & Korte, 1995). Another reason it is sometimes difficult to notice things out of the ordinary is that what is unusual in one setting may be a normal occurrence in another. For example, in some neighborhoods, a person lying unconscious on the sidewalk may be extremely unusual and cause passersby to take notice. Yet, in other neighborhoods, this same person may be one of many streetpeople who live and sleep outdoors much of the year—an all too common sight that passersby generally would take little, if any, notice of.

As a bystander to an emergency, if you do indeed notice that something unusual is happening, you move to the second step in the decision-making process: *deciding whether something is wrong and help is needed.* Returning to the previous example, if you pass by an unconscious man on the sidewalk you may ask yourself, "Did he suffer a heart attack or is he merely sleeping?" This is an extremely important decision, because if you decide he is merely sleeping you will continue on your way. But what if you are mistaken? One evening a few years ago, students in a fraternity house at the University of Wisconsin saw a man and a woman having sex near their residence. They quickly realized this was highly unusual behavior (the first decision step), but they did not define the situation as an emergency (the second decision step). Instead of intervening in what they perceived to be consensual sex, the onlookers yelled encouragement to the couple below. Only later did they learn that they were actually watching a rape. Incorrectly defining the situation led to their nonintervention.

When you define the situation as an emergency, the bystander intervention model states that the third decision you must make is *determining the extent to which you have responsibility to help.* According to Latané and Darley, one factor that may play a role in your decision to help or not is whether an appropriate authority figure is nearby. For instance, imagine sitting in your car at a busy intersection and noticing that in the car ahead of you, two people are arguing heatedly. Suddenly, one of these quarrelers begins hitting the other with a club. This is definitely unusual and it is clearly an emergency. The pertinent question now is, do you have responsibility to come to the victim's aid? Further, imagine that to your immediate right is a police car with two officers sitting inside. If you decide that it is their responsibility to render assistance, you will likely assume the role of an unresponsive bystander.

Let's continue this hypothetical emergency situation, but now imagine that there is no police car in sight. Faced with the reality of a clear emergency, you still may not help if you convince yourself that all the other motorists watching this incident could help just as well as you. The presence of these other potential helpers, like the presence of authority figures, may cause you to feel less personally responsible for intervening.

If you assume responsibility for helping, a fourth decision you must make is *the appropriate form of assistance to render.* But in the heat of the moment, what if you are not sure what

Bystander Intervention Model

A theory that whether bystanders intervene in an emergency is a function of a five-step decision-making process.

FIGURE 14.3

The Model of Bystander Intervention: A Five-Step Decision Process

As outlined by Latané and Darley (1970), the decision to help someone involves a five-step process. At any step, a bystander's decision could lead to either further analysis of the situation or to nonintervention.

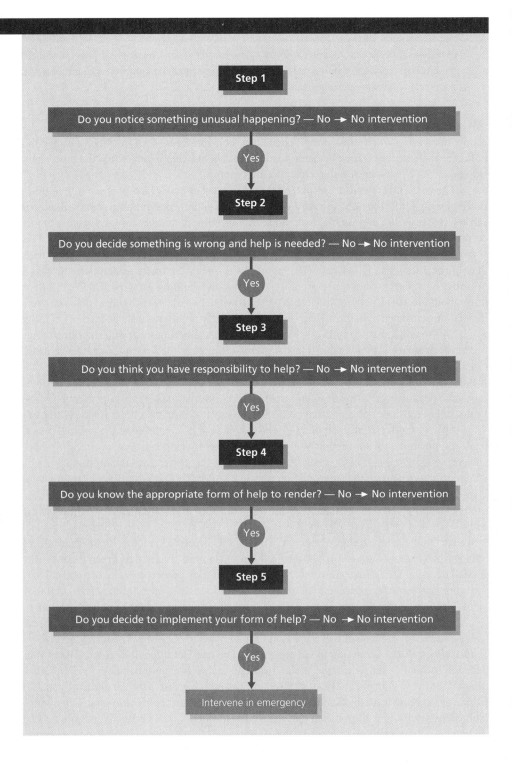

Step 1

Do you notice something unusual happening? — No → No intervention

Yes

Step 2

Do you decide something is wrong and help is needed? — No → No intervention

Yes

Step 3

Do you think you have responsibility to help? — No → No intervention

Yes

Step 4

Do you know the appropriate form of help to render? — No → No intervention

Yes

Step 5

Do you decide to implement your form of help? — No → No intervention

Yes

Intervene in emergency

to do? You may become paralyzed with uncertainty about exactly how to render assistance. Unable to decide, you may not offer any help at all. Children are particularly likely not to have the appropriate skills or confidence to make a decision at this stage in the helping process.

Finally, if you notice something unusual, interpret it as an emergency, assume responsibility, and decide how best to help, you still must decide whether to *implement your course of prosocial action.* If you have decided to run to the car where the person is being beaten and intervene, you must now act on this intention. However, due to fear of injury or concern about testifying at a future trial, you may decide not to implement your previous decision and remain a passive bystander.

As you can see from the outline of this model, Latané and Darley believe that the decision to intervene in a possible emergency involves a rather complex set of decisions. As a bystander, if you make an incorrect choice at any point in this process, you will not intervene. Two social psychological processes that often operate in emergency situations are the *audience inhibition effect* and the *diffusion of responsibility*. The inhibition effect can short-circuit helping at step 2 in the bystander intervention model, and diffusion of responsibility occurs in step 3.

Outcome and Information Dependence Produce the Audience Inhibition Effect

Many emergency situations are not clearly defined as such, but rather, have some degree of ambiguity. You may realize that something unusual is happening (step 1 in the model), but you are not sure that it's an emergency (step 2). This is exactly what happened after the hijacked planes hit the twin towers. Many people inside both buildings were unsure whether their lives were in danger, and this hesitation prevented some of them from escaping in time.

In one study designed to investigate bystander uncertainty, Latané and Darley (1968) recruited male college students for a study on problems of urban life. When a research participant arrived at the laboratory, he was ushered into a room, given a questionnaire, and then was left alone to complete it. Soon, what looked like white smoke (but wasn't) began to enter the room through a small wall vent. Within six minutes, the smoke was so thick it was difficult to see. The dependent variable was whether or not the participant would leave the room to report the problem before the six minutes had elapsed. What do you think happened?

When working alone, most participants usually hesitated a moment upon first seeing the smoke, but then walked over to the vent to investigate. In 75 percent of the trials, the participant finally left the room to report the emergency. In a second experimental condition, groups of three naive participants were seated in the room when smoke began to pour from the vent. In all trials, participants looked to one another to help them decide if there was an emergency, but in only 38 percent of these three-person groups did even a single person report the incident before the six-minute mark. Although 55 percent of the participants in the *alone* condition reported the smoke within the first two minutes, only 12 percent of the three-person groups did so. Finally, in a third condition, two confederates, acting like research participants, joined the one real participant in the room. As it began to fill with smoke, the confederates acted unconcerned. If the real participant asked them any questions, they replied "I dunno" and continued working on the questionnaire. In the presence of these unconcerned confederates, only 10 percent of the participants reported the smoke. The other 90 percent coughed, rubbed their eyes, and opened the window, but they did not leave the room. These findings, summarized in figure 14.4 (p. 548), indicate that when others are present, people not only are less likely to define a potentially dangerous situation as an emergency, but they also respond more slowly to the possible emergency. This **audience inhibition effect** is particularly likely when other people are acting calmly.

In another investigation of the inhibition effect, Latané and Judith Rodin (1969) set up a situation in which some other person, besides the research participant, was in possible danger. First, a female researcher set participants to work on a questionnaire and then left through a collapsible curtained doorway to work in an adjoining office. From their room, participants could hear her shuffling papers and opening and closing drawers. After four minutes, the researcher turned on a tape recorder that broadcast the sound of her climbing on a chair to reach a stack of papers on a bookcase. Participants then heard the researcher's scream, quickly followed by a loud crash. "Oh, my God, my foot. . . . I . . . I . . . can't move . . . it," she moaned. "Oh . . . my ankle. . . . I . . . can't get this . . . thing . . . off me." After about two minutes of moaning, the woman could be heard dragging herself out of her office.

Audience Inhibition Effect

People are inhibited from helping for fear that other bystanders will evaluate them negatively if they intervene and the situation is not an emergency.

FIGURE 14.4

The Audience Inhibition Effect

When a room began filling with white smoke, people were much less likely to report the incident—and did so more slowly—when they were with others rather than alone. What two types of social dependence are interacting here to create the audience inhibition effect?

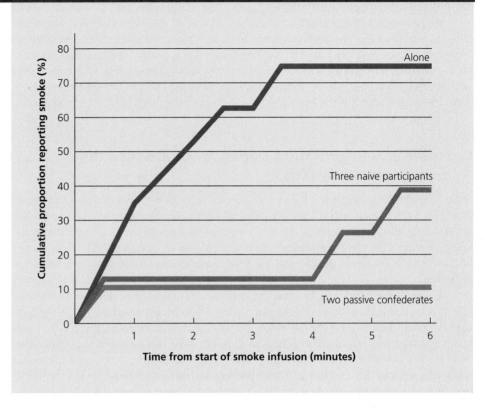

Social Sense

View an interview with social psychologist John Darley.

Seventy percent of the participants who were alone in the room tried to help by pulling open the curtain or running out the other door to find help. Consistent with the audience inhibition effect, when two strangers were sitting in the room, only 40 percent of the time did either of them help. When the two people sitting in the room were friends, at least one of them helped in 70 percent of the trials. Even though this is the same percentage of helping as in the *alone* condition, it still indicates an inhibition effect because two people were present. If these two friends did not inhibit each other's response, then helping should have occurred in 91 percent of the trials ($70\%_{\text{friend 1}} + (70\% \times \text{remaining } 30\%_{\text{friend 2}}) = 91\%$).[1] Finally, in the last condition, a naive participant sat in the room with a confederate who acted unconcerned and nonchalant about the ruckus behind the curtain. Again, consistent with the inhibition effect, in this setting the participant tried to help only 7 percent of the time. View social psychologist John Darley's comments on this research and watch a recreation of this study on your Social Sense CD-ROM.

To better understand why the inhibition effect occurs, let's return to two concepts previously discussed in chapter 9, namely *information dependence* and *outcome dependence.* As discussed in that chapter, when we are not clear about how to define a particular situation, we are likely to become dependent on others for a definition of social reality. Thus, when a group of people witnesses a possible emergency, each person bases his or her interpretation of the event partly or exclusively on the reaction of others (information dependence). The problem with this information seeking in an emergency is that in our culture

---

[1] Why would less inhibition occur in a friend's presence than in a stranger's presence? Shortly, I will discuss the likely reason for the inhibition effect. For now, suffice it to say that as opposed to being with strangers, with friends we are generally less likely to be concerned about embarrassing ourselves by overreacting to a situation.

we have learned that it is not socially acceptable to "lose your cool." If we become agitated and excitable during a crisis, we run the risk of being negatively evaluated by others (outcome dependence). Due to this concern, we will often pretend to be calm while witnessing an emergency. Acting cool and calm, they then observe others' behavior as a clue as how to define what they all are witnessing. However, because everyone else is also assuming this calm exterior, what we observe is a group of calm bystanders who, by their nonplussed demeanor, are defining the situation as a nonemergency.

In ambiguous emergency situations, then, the fear of being negatively evaluated (outcome dependence), combined with the tendency to look to others for further information (information dependence), results in the audience inhibition effect. In both the "smoke" study and the "woman in distress" study, the presence of others and their behavior significantly inhibited helping. Postexperimental debriefings indicated that some of those who did not intervene claimed they were either unsure of what had occurred or did not think the situation was very serious. Russell Clark and Larry Word (1972), in a replication of the Latané and Rodin study, made the situation even less ambiguous by allowing participants in the adjoining room to not only hear the crash of the person (this time a man) falling and his subsequent moaning, but now they could also feel the floor shake with the force of the crash. With this reduction in ambiguity, every single participant helped, regardless of the number of bystanders. However, when the situation was made more ambiguous (the victim did not cry out in pain), helping occurred only 30 percent of the time. In addition, as with the previous studies, participants in groups were less likely to help than those who were alone. This study clearly indicates that the audience inhibition effect is driven by our fear of being negatively evaluated. Indeed, those of us who are especially sensitive to embarrassment are the most likely to experience inhibition in emergencies (Tice & Baumeister, 1985). Thus, in an ambiguous emergency situation, we seem to be thinking, "What if I cause a big fuss by intervening and there is no emergency? I'll look like a fool and be mortified." However, if that fear of committing a social faux pas is reduced due to clear emergency signals, our inhibitions are greatly reduced and we are more likely to help.

Diffusion of Responsibility Increases with the Number of Bystanders

Fear of embarrassment is one reason we do not intervene in some emergencies, but what about those situations in which someone clearly needs help but no one raises a finger to come to the victim's aid? Surely some other social psychological factor is operating. For example, the neighbors of Kitty Genovese, sitting in their own separate apartments, heard her cries for help and correctly understood what was happening. However, they knew—or assumed—that others were also watching this drama unfold below them. Darley and Latané believed that this realization that others could also help diffused the neighbors' own feelings of individual responsibility (step 3 in the model). They called this response to others' presence the *diffusion of responsibility*—the belief that the presence of other people in a situation makes one less personally responsible for events that occur in that situation (see chapter 10, p. 368).

In an attempt to simulate the social psychological factors present in the Genovese case, Darley and Latané (1968) designed an experiment in which they placed people in separate areas from which they then heard a victim cry for help. In this study, New York University students thought they were participating in a discussion about the kinds of personal problems undergraduates typically face in a large urban environment. They were also told that to avoid embarrassment, they each would be placed in separate booths and would talk to one another using an intercom system. To further ensure they wouldn't be inhibited, the experimenter said he would not eavesdrop on their conversation. The way the intercom system worked was that only one person could speak at a time, and the others had to merely listen.

The study included three different conditions. Some participants were told the discussion would be with just one other student, while others were told they were either part of a three-person or a six-person group. In reality, all the other discussion participants were merely tape recordings. Discussion began with the first speaker stating that he was an epileptic who was prone to seizures when studying hard or when taking exams. When everyone else had spoken, the first speaker began to talk again, but now he was speaking in a loud and increasingly incoherent voice:

> I-er-um-I think I-I need-er-if-if could-er-er-somebody er-er-er-er-er-er-er give me a little-er-give me a little help here because-er-I-er-I'm-er-er-h-h-having a-a-a real problem-er-right now and I-er-if somebody could help me out it would-it would-er-er s-s-sure be-sure be good . . . because-er-there-er-er-a cause I-er-I-uh-I've got a-a one of the-er-seizure-er-things coming on and-and-and I could really-er-use some help so if somebody would-er-give me a little h-help-uh-er-er-er-er-er c-could somebody-er-er-help-er-uh-uh-uh (choking sounds). . . . I'm gonna die-er-er-I'm . . . gonna die-er-help-er-er-seizure-er-[chokes, then quiet]. (Darley & Latané, 1968, p. 379)

How did participants respond to this concocted, yet convincing, emergency? It depended on the number of bystanders they thought were also aware of the epileptic's seizure. When participants thought they were the only ones listening to the emergency unfold, 85 percent of them left their booths to help before the victim's pleas for help were choked off. When they thought they were one of five bystanders, only 31 percent reacted in a similar prosocial manner. When participants thought there was one other bystander aware of the emergency, helping was intermediate, with 62 percent helping. Not only was helping less likely as the number of bystanders increased, but the *speed* of rendering assistance was significantly slower as well. As you can see from figure 14.5, when participants thought there were four other bystanders, it took them three times longer to take any action (if they helped at all) than it did in the alone condition.

Where are they who claim kindred with the unfortunate?

Caroline Lamb, English novelist, 1785–1828

FIGURE 14.5

The Diffusion of Responsibility Effect

When participants heard over an intercom system someone having a seizure, how did the number of perceived bystanders influence their speed and willingness to help the victim?

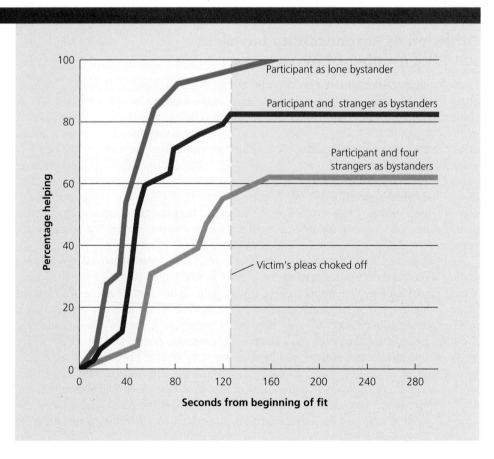

More than fifty subsequent laboratory and naturalistic studies have confirmed this diffusion of responsibility effect (Latané & Nida, 1981). On average, when participants believed they were the only bystander to an emergency, 75 percent of them helped, compared with only 53 percent who were in the presence of others. Diffusion of responsibility also occurs when people need help on the Internet (Barron & Yechiam, 2002). For example, in one study, more than 4,800 people were monitored in 400 different Internet chat groups over a month's time to determine the amount of time it took a bystander to render assistance to someone who asked for help (Markey, 2000). Results indicated that it took longer for people to receive help as the number of people present in a computer-mediated chat group increased. However, this diffusion of responsibility was virtually eliminated and help was received more quickly when help was asked for by specifying a bystander's name.

Despite the clear evidence that the presence of others influences people's decision to help, in postexperimental interviews participants in all of Latané and Darley's experiments tended to deny that others' assumed presence had any effect on their actions (or inactions). As discussed in chapter 9, underestimating the effect that others have on your behavior makes it more likely that you will fall prey to their influence. After all, how can you guard against not falling into the nonhelpful mode when you don't recognize how the simple presence of others can change your feelings of personal responsibility?

CRITICAL *thinking*

Do you think you would find these same bystander effects among people whose jobs regularly deal with helping others? How might you test whether the situational context or the salience of their "helping" social roles would influence their tendency to intervene?

Bystander Intervention Is Also Shaped by Emotional Arousal and Cost-Reward Assessments

Latané and Darley's bystander intervention model is best at explaining why people in a group of bystanders often don't interpret an event as an emergency, as well as why they often don't help even when it's clearly defined. Although this model provides a number of important pieces to the bystander puzzle, its focus is on the social problem of *nonintervention.* Yet why *do* we often decide to actually intervene in an emergency?

Jane Piliavin and her colleagues (1981) attempted to answer this question by developing a theory of bystander intervention that extends and complements Latané and Darley's model. These researchers added to the decision-making equation a consideration of bystanders' emotional arousal during an emergency and their assessment of the costs of helping and not helping. Essentially, their work focuses on the second half of Latané and Darley's model, namely, deciding on personal responsibility (step 3), deciding what to do (step 4), and implementing action (step 5).

How might information dependence and outcome dependence inhibit bystanders from defining a situation as an emergency? If they do define the situation as an emergency, how might the presence of others inhibit intervention?

FIGURE 14.6

The Influence of Costs and Rewards on Direct Helping

According to Piliavin and Piliavin (1972), the type of response a moderately aroused observer will have to someone's need for help will be influenced by his or her assessment of the combination of personal costs for direct help and costs for no help to the victim. According to this model, when are bystanders most and least likely to help?

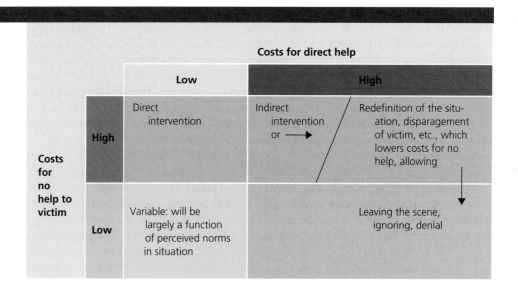

		Costs for direct help		
		Low	High	
Costs for no help to victim	**High**	Direct intervention	Indirect intervention or →	Redefinition of the situation, disparagement of victim, etc., which lowers costs for no help, allowing
	Low	Variable: will be largely a function of perceived norms in situation	Leaving the scene, ignoring, denial	

Arousal:Cost-Reward Model

A theory that helping or not helping is a function of emotional arousal and analysis of the costs and rewards of helping.

According to their **arousal:cost-reward model** of helping, witnessing an emergency is emotionally arousing and is generally experienced as an uncomfortable tension that we, as bystanders, seek to decrease (Gaertner & Dovidio, 1977). This tension can be reduced in several different ways. We could intervene and thereby decrease our arousal, but we could also reduce arousal by either ignoring danger signs or benignly interpreting them as nothing to worry about. In addition to these avenues of action, we could reduce arousal by simply fleeing the scene. Which behavior we choose will be a function of our analysis of the costs and rewards for helping and for not helping. What are the costs to the bystander for helping? This could involve a host of expenditures, including loss of time, energy, resources, health (even life), as well as the risk of social disapproval and embarrassment if the help is not needed or is ineffective. Counterbalancing the costs of helping are the costs of not helping. These might include serious harm to the ignored victim and subsequent public scorn of the nonhelpful bystander. Realizing that one did not render assistance could also lead bystanders to engage in self-blame and experience loss of self-esteem.

According to Piliavin and her colleagues (refer to figure 14.6), if the costs of helping are low and the costs of not helping are high, bystanders will likely intervene. In contrast, if these costs are reversed (high helping costs and low not-helping costs), bystanders are unlikely to render assistance. If both types of costs are low, intervention will depend on the perceived social norms in the situation. The most difficult situation for bystanders is one in which the costs for helping and for not helping are both high. Here, the arousal:cost-reward model suggests two likely courses of action. One is for bystanders to intervene indirectly by calling the police, an ambulance, or some other professional helping source. Another course of action is for bystanders to redefine the situation in a way that results in them not helping. Here, they could decide there really is no emergency after all, or that someone else will help, or that the victim deserves to suffer.

None of the heroes who risked or sacrificed their lives during the terrorist attacks behaved according to this model. Faced with a situation of high costs to themselves for helping and high costs to victims for not helping, these people put their own safety concerns aside. Thus, this theory's consideration of these two cost factors cannot explain the behavior of heroes, but it does explain the behavior of more ordinary bystanders in emergency situations. For instance, imagine that you are walking down the street when you hear a child screaming in pain. Directing your gaze toward the screams, you see a lone young girl who has slammed a car door on one of her hands. In this situation, you will likely directly intervene because: (1) the costs of not helping are high—the girl may seriously injure her hand if it is not removed from the door's grip soon, and you will experience terrible guilt if you don't help; and (2) the costs of helping are low—opening the car door will require little effort or loss of time, and helping will not put you in any danger.

Now, imagine that the child is not screaming in pain because her hand is caught in a door, but rather because an adult is beating her with a stick. Now, what will you do? Here, both the costs of not helping and helping are high—the girl may be seriously hurt and you will experience guilt if you don't stop the beating, but the adult could seriously injure you if you intervene. Faced with these high costs, you may help indirectly by calling the police or by yelling from a safe distance for the adult to stop. Sadly, you might also convince yourself that the child must deserve the beating she is getting and continue on your way.

Now, imagine that the child is screaming in pain because an adult is spanking her bottom with moderate force. In this situation, both the costs of not helping and helping are probably low. Not intervening will probably not cause serious physical injury to the child, and intervening may only result in the adult telling you to mind your own business. If your perception of cultural norms is that spanking children is an unacceptable response to misbehavior, you may try to stop the punishment. Otherwise, you are unlikely to intervene.

Finally, imagine the same scene as in the previous paragraph, but now let's add that you are rushing to an important job interview. If you try to stop the spanking you run the very real risk of arriving late. Here, your costs for helping are high and the costs for not helping are low. Weighing these factors, you are likely to continue on your way, perhaps muttering about the misguided actions of the adult but justifying your nonintervention to yourself ("If I didn't have this appointment, I'd give that adult a piece of my mind!").

A number of studies support the arousal:cost-reward model's hypothesis that people often weigh the costs of helping and not helping prior to rendering assistance (Dovidio et al., 1991; Fritzsche et al., 2000). For example, Lance Shotland and Margaret Straw (1976) staged a realistic fight between a man and a woman on an elevator. In one condition, 65 percent of the time bystanders intervened when the woman shouted, "Get away from me! I don't know you!" However, in another condition bystanders helped only 19 percent of the time when the woman shouted, "Get away from me! I don't know why I ever married you!" These differences in helping were apparently due to perceived costs. People who watched videotapes of the fights perceived the woman as being in greater danger when with the stranger than when with the husband. They also believed that the combatants would be more likely to turn on them if they tried to intervene in the "domestic" fight rather than the "stranger" fight. Thus, the "stranger" condition was perceived to involve higher costs for not helping and lower costs for helping than the "husband" condition.

Another study investigating the costs for helping and the costs for not helping was conducted on the Philadelphia subway system when a male confederate carrying a cane collapsed (Piliavin & Piliavin, 1972). In one condition, the victim had a thin trickle of fake blood slip from his mouth as he fell, while in a second condition he did not. The researchers assumed that the presence of blood would increase the costs of intervening, because contact with blood for most people is repulsive. It was further assumed that bystanders would interpret the presence of blood to mean that the victim was in more danger than if no blood was visible. Thus, the "blood" condition was hypothesized to cause conflicting thoughts that would impede intervention ("The man needs help, but yikes! Look at that blood!"). True to these predictions, the unbloodied victim was directly helped more often (95 percent of the time) and more quickly than the bloody victim (helped 65 percent of the time). In one trial of the study, two teenagers witnessed the man collapse and rose to help but then saw the blood. "Oh, he's bleeding!" gasped one of them. Both promptly sat down.

Positive and Negative Moods Can Either Increase or Decrease Helping

Beyond the influence that fellow bystanders and perceived costs can have on prosocial behavior, research also demonstrates that people's willingness to help is affected by the mood they happen to be in when assistance is needed.

GOOD MOODS AND GENEROSITY

Imagine this scene. Ralph bounds out of his psychology class feeling on top of the world because he has achieved one of the highest scores on his midterm exam. As he happily walks back to his apartment, he notices a woman carrying a tall stack of papers. Suddenly, the stack slips from her grasp and begins flying in all directions across campus. Without hesitation, Ralph springs into action and helps retrieve the errant papers.

Would Ralph have been so willing to help if he was in a less positive mood? Perhaps not. Research consistently indicates that good moods lead to more prosocial behavior. For example, in one study, Alice Isen (1970) administered a series of tests to college students and teachers, later telling them they had either performed very well or very poorly. Still others were told nothing at all about their performance. In addition to these three experimental conditions, a control group was not administered any tests at all. The participants who had "succeeded" at the tests were later more likely to help a woman struggling with an armful of books than any of the other participants. This *good mood effect* following success has been replicated in other studies (Klein, 2003), and additional research indicates that people are more likely to help others on sunny days than on cloudy ones (Cunningham, 1979), after finding money or being offered a tasty treat (Isen & Levin, 1972), and even after listening to uplifting music or a comedian deliver a funny routine (North et al., 2004; Wilson, 1981).

Why do positive moods lead to greater helping? Several possibilities have been offered. One is that when we are in a positive mood, we are more likely to perceive other people as "nice," "honest," and "decent," and thus deserving of our help (Isen, 1987). Another possibility is that we help others to enhance or prolong our good mood (Wegener & Petty, 1994). A third reason might be that, when happy, we are less likely to be absorbed in our own thoughts ("stewing in our own juices"), and thus, we are more attentive to others' needs (McMillen et al., 1977). A fourth possibility is that good moods increase the likelihood that we think about the rewarding nature of social activities in general. With the rewarding properties of helping being salient, our helping becomes more likely (Cunningham et al., 1990b). This enhanced attentiveness to the rewarding properties of helping may explain why good moods increase helpfulness only when the helpful task is expected to be pleasant. If helping is expected to entail unpleasant and aversive experiences, happy people are no more helpful than others (Isen & Simmonds, 1978; Rosenhan et al., 1981).

BAD MOODS AND SEEKING RELIEF

What about negative moods and helping? Rewind your thoughts to Ralph and his psychology midterm. As the "string-puller" of all fictional characters in this text, I will now change Ralph's exam grade from "A" to "F." Now, instead of bounding out of class, he trudges. Given his present somber mood, will he still dart around campus retrieving wayward sheets of paper? Surprisingly, he might. Isen and her coworkers (1973) found that people who believed they had failed at an experimental task were more likely to help another person than those who did not experience failure. Although this response certainly seems to contradict the good mood effect just described, one possible link between the two is the rewarding properties of helping. Because helping others often makes us feel good about ourselves, when feeling bad we may help as a way of *escaping* our mood—just as we help when we are in a good mood to maintain that mood.

Feeling guilty can also increase helping. Michael Cunningham and his colleagues (1980) conducted a field study in which individuals were approached on the street by a young man who asked them to use his camera to take his picture for a class project. The problem for the would-be helpers was that the camera had been rigged to malfunction. When the helpers realized the camera was not working, the young man examined it closely and asked the helpers if they touched any of the dials. He then informed them that it would have to be repaired. The researchers assumed that such an encounter would induce a certain degree of guilt in these individuals. As they continued on their way, these now guilty people passed a young woman who suddenly dropped a file folder containing some papers. How do you think they responded to this needy situation? Eighty percent of those who were led to believe that they had broken the young man's camera helped the female stranger pick up her papers. Only

40 percent of the passersby who had no broken-camera experience paused to help. Another field study found that Roman Catholics were more likely to donate money to a charity just prior to making their confession of sins to a priest—when their guilt level should have been high—rather than immediately after being absolved of those sins (Harris et al., 1975).

Although these studies demonstrate that negative moods can lead to prosocial behavior, other studies suggest that when we experience extremely negative moods, such as grief or depression, we may be so focused on our own emotional state that we simply don't notice others' needs and concerns (Carlson & Miller, 1987). Still other studies suggest that even when experiencing less severe negative moods, we are less likely to help than those who are in good moods (Isen, 1984). Robert Cialdini and Douglas Kenrick (1976) attempted to explain why this is the case by proposing that when we are in a bad mood, our decision to help is often based on a simple self-serving question: Will helping make us feel better? This **negative state relief model** asserts that when we are in a bad mood, if the perceived benefits for helping are high and the costs are low, the expected *reward value* for helping will be high, and thus, we will likely help to lift our own spirits. However, if the perceived benefits and costs are reversed so that the reward value is low, we are unlikely to help. Essentially, this model predicts that bad moods are more likely to lead to helping than neutral moods when helping is easy and highly rewarding.

Despite the fact that the negative state relief model has generated considerable scientific debate over whether it accurately depicts foul mood effects, even its proponents have pointed out the limits of its application (Cialdini & Fultz, 1990). First, research indicates that increased helping due to bad moods is much more common among adults than children (Kenrick et al., 1979). One probable explanation for this age difference is that children are less likely to have learned the self-rewarding properties of helping—that it can pull one out of a bad mood. A second limitation is that the model specifies that only mildly negative feelings such as sadness, guilt, and temporary depression will increase helping. More intense negative emotions, such as hostile anger and resentment, result in decreased helping. Finally, because the helping exhibited by adults in a bad mood is of a self-serving nature, if sad or guilty people get their spirits raised from some other source (such as being complimented or hearing a funny joke), they will no longer have a need to help others (Cunningham et al., 1980). Figure 14.7 summarizes the effects that both bad moods and good moods have on helping.

Negative State Relief Model

A theory suggesting that for those in a bad mood, helping others may be a way to lift their own spirits if the perceived benefits for helping are high and the costs are low.

How might inducing guilt prompt people to help others? What might be the motivation of the helper in such a situation?

FIGURE 14.7

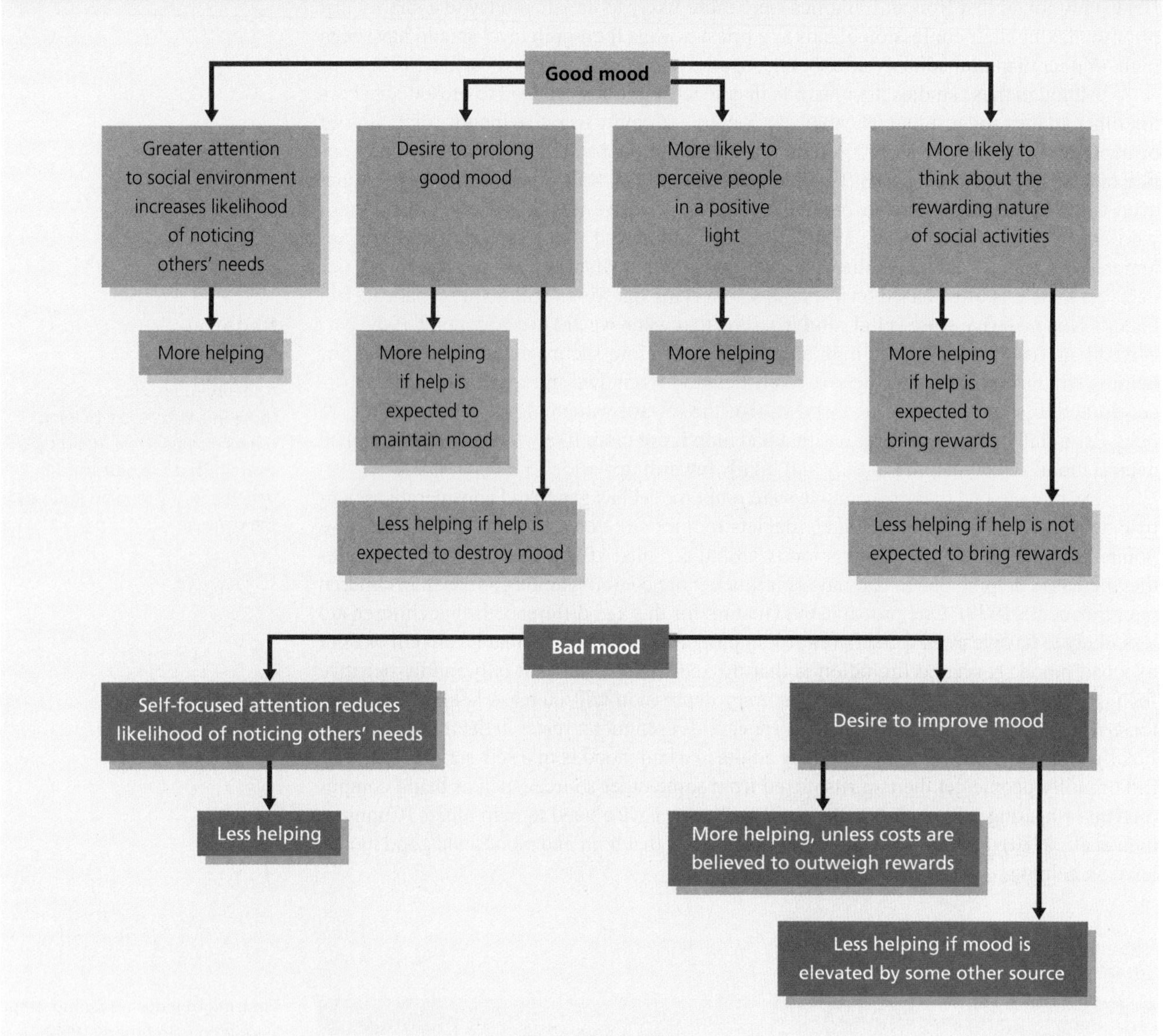

Good mood

| Greater attention to social environment increases likelihood of noticing others' needs | Desire to prolong good mood | More likely to perceive people in a positive light | More likely to think about the rewarding nature of social activities |

More helping

More helping if help is expected to maintain mood

Less helping if help is expected to destroy mood

More helping

More helping if help is expected to bring rewards

Less helping if help is not expected to bring rewards

Bad mood

Self-focused attention reduces likelihood of noticing others' needs

Desire to improve mood

Less helping

More helping, unless costs are believed to outweigh rewards

Less helping if mood is elevated by some other source

The Varied Effects of Mood on Helping

Depending on the circumstances, positive and negative moods can either increase or decrease helping.

SECTION SUMMARY

- The model of bystander intervention focuses on the influence that bystanders have on prosocial behavior:

  audience inhibition effect: bystanders inhibit people from defining dangerous situations as emergencies

  diffusion of responsibility: bystanders make people feel less personally responsible for helping

- The arousal: cost-reward model focuses attention on the perceived costs of prosocial behavior

- Greater helping often follows good moods, but we may sometimes try to eliminate negative moods by helping others

DOES TRUE ALTRUISM REALLY EXIST?

The three previously discussed explanations of the conditions under which people are most likely to help others (arousal:cost-reward model, good mood effect, and negative state relief model), all assume there is an *egoistic* motive underlying prosocial behavior. All three explanations contend that helpful bystanders are ultimately trying to improve their own well-being by helping. Is egoism all there is underlying prosocial action?

The Empathy-Altruism Hypothesis Contends That Empathy Produces Altruistic Motivation

Although not denying that helping is often motivated by a desire to fulfill egoistic needs, Daniel Batson (1991) and others (Hoffman, 1981; Krebs, 1975) have argued that sometimes our prosocial actions are truly *altruistic* (motivated solely by the desire to increase the welfare of another). In Batson's **empathy-altruism hypothesis,** he proposes that we typically experience two kinds of emotional reactions upon witnessing someone else suffer. One reaction, **personal distress,** is an unpleasant state of arousal in which we become preoccupied with our own anxiety upon viewing the victim's plight. Another reaction, **empathy,** is a feeling of compassion and tenderness for the victim (Duan 2000). Batson contends that these two contrasting emotional reactions to a victim's plight—one focused on our own well-being (personal distress) and the other focused on the victim's (empathy), result in very different motivations.

Regarding the negative arousal state of personal distress, the greater our personal distress as a bystander, the more we will be motivated to have it reduced. Batson believes that Piliavin's arousal:cost-reward model does a good job of explaining how we respond to personal distress. Because reduction of this unpleasant arousal state is the primary motivation underlying personal distress, we will likely flee the stress-producing situation if at all possible. However, if we cannot easily escape, we will likely lend assistance in order to reduce our own unpleasant arousal. Described in this manner, one can clearly see that helping caused by personal distress is egoistic in nature.

Like personal distress, empathy for someone who is suffering will likely be an unpleasant emotion. However, unlike personal distress, empathy will not be satisfied by flight. Instead, Batson's empathy-altruism hypothesis contends that when we experience empathy, the stronger the feelings of compassion for the victim, the greater our motivation to help. Thus, when we feel great empathy, we are motivated more by our desire to improve the victim's welfare than attend to our own.

Support for the empathy-altruism hypothesis has been found in a number of studies in which bystanders' empathy or personal distress has been manipulated. In one of these studies, Batson and his coworkers (1981) had pairs of female college students participate in a task seemingly investigating how people work under aversive conditions. One participant was the "worker" who received electric shocks at random intervals during two trial periods; the other student observed the worker on a closed-circuit television as she performed the task. In actuality, the worker was a confederate. When the first aversive work trial began, the worker's facial expressions and body movements indicated that she found the shocks to be extremely uncomfortable. At the end of this trial, the worker explained that she had been traumatized by electric shocks in an accident as a child, and now, even mild shocks were often very painful. Responding to this "dilemma," the researcher asked the observer—who was naturally disturbed by this story—whether she would be willing to help the woman by trading places with her on the last trial. Batson and his colleagues predicted two factors would determine how participants responded to this dilemma: (1) whether or not they felt personal distress or empathy, and (2) whether or not they could flee this aversive situation.

Regarding the first factor, the experimenters assumed that everyone would experience arousal when witnessing the victim's plight, and that they would naturally attribute this arousal both to sympathy for the victim (empathy), and to personal discomfort (personal distress). To more clearly direct participants' interpretation of their arousal, the experimenters

Empathy-Altruism Hypothesis

A theory that experiencing empathy for someone in need produces an altruistic motive for helping.

Personal Distress

An unpleasant state of arousal in which people are preoccupied with their own emotions of anxiety, fear, or helplessness upon viewing a victim's plight.

Empathy

A feeling of compassion and tenderness upon viewing a victim's plight.

gave them a fictional drug, "Millentana" (a cornstarch placebo), as part of another study just prior to observing their partner being shocked. All participants were told that Millentana had a side effect. In the *empathy* condition, Batson and his coworkers wanted the participants to misattribute any feelings of personal distress to the drug and not to the victim's plight. To achieve this result, they said that the drug "produces a clear feeling of uneasiness and discomfort, a feeling similar to that you might experience while reading a particularly distressing novel." Due to this misattribution of personal distress to Millentana, the researchers assumed that participants in the empathy condition would perceive their emotional response to the victim to be primarily empathy. In contrast, those in the *personal distress condition* were told that the drug "produces a clear feeling of warmth and sensitivity, a feeling similar to that you might experience while reading a particularly touching novel." Following a similar logic, the experimenters assumed that these people would misattribute feelings of empathy to Millentana and perceive their emotional response to the victim to be primarily personal distress. Participants' subsequent self-reports indicated that the experimenters were successful in manipulating the women's emotional responses in the desired directions.

Regarding the second factor, ease of escape was manipulated by the instructions participants had previously received concerning their role as observer. In the *easy-escape* condition, they were told they would observe only the first trial, while in the *difficult-escape* condition, participants were told they would observe both trials.

How do you think these different emotional reactions affected willingness to help the victim? As can be seen in table 14.3, regardless of whether escape was difficult or easy, empathic observers tended to help by deciding to trade places with the confederate. On the other hand, the personally distressed observers chose to flee when fleeing was easy; they helped only if that was the only way to relieve their own discomfort. These findings are perfectly consistent with the empathy-altruism hypothesis.

In a replication of this experiment, instead of manipulating empathy and personal-distress arousal by giving people a placebo drug, Batson and his coworkers (1983) asked participants to describe their emotions after watching the confederate suffer. Based on these responses, participants were categorized as being either personally distressed or empathic. As in the previous experiment, the empathic observers chose to help regardless of how easy or difficult it was to escape. Likewise, those who experienced personal distress tended to flee if they could, and only helped if fleeing was not an option. Overall, the pattern that emerged in five separate studies is that, regardless of ease or difficulty of escape, empathic individuals provided help about 75 percent of the time. Likewise, those who experienced personal distress and could not escape easily tended to help at approximately the same level, about 79 percent. In contrast, when escape was easy for the personally distressed, their level of helping dropped dramatically, to only about 30 percent.

CRITICAL *thinking*

How could you design a donation pitch to members of a local community center to help starving people in a foreign country, knowing that some message receivers will react with empathy, while others will react with personal distress?

TABLE 14.3

Percentage of Participants Willing to Help Due to Their Emotional Response to the Victim and Their Ability to Escape

Participants who experienced empathy when observing the victim's suffering were more likely to help regardless of whether it was easy or difficult to escape the situation. In contrast, those who experienced personal distress generally helped only when escape was difficult. How do these findings support the empathy-altruism hypothesis?

| | Predominant Emotional Response | |
Escape Condition	Personal Distress	Empathy
Easy	33	83
Difficult	75	58

Based on these and other findings that are consistent with the empathy-altruism hypothesis (Batson et al., 2002b; Sibicky et al., 1995), can we conclude that people who help due to empathy are motivated by true altruism? Certainly, Batson and many other social scientists think there is compelling scientific evidence for this view (see Batson, 2002a, for a review). Further, true altruism seems to best explain the actions of the helpers in our chapter-opening story. Although some researchers still contend that the case for genuine altruism is still to be proven (Cialdini et al., 1997), the consensus is that this sort of selfless helping does exist and is a part of human nature.

There Are Individual Differences in Empathic Responding

In addition to exploring the role that *situational* empathy and personal distress play in prosocial behavior, researchers have also examined whether we differ in our habitual tendencies to experience these contrasting emotions. In other words, can these different emotional experiences be thought of as personality *traits?* Mark Davis (1980) has developed a personality measure that assesses individual differences in empathy (what he calls *empathic concern*) and personal distress. People who score high on empathic concern are those who habitually feel warmth and compassion for unfortunate others, while those who score high on personal distress tend to become anxious and uneasy when seeing others in need of help.

Studies of fraternal and identical twins indicate that individual differences in empathy and personal distress may be partly due to genetic factors (Davis et al., 1994; Zahn-Wexler et al., 1992). That is, high empathy and high personal distress people appear to have an inherited sensitivity to emotional experiences that causes them to react more strongly to the observed experiences of others. Before reading further, spend a few minutes answering the items in table 14.4. Based on your responses, are you high or low on empathic concern and personal distress?

Research indicates that individuals high in empathic concern not only are more willing to put themselves in situations in which the experience of sympathy for another is likely, but they also are generally more willing to help people in trouble than are those low in empathic concern (Unger & Thumuluri, 1997). For example, in an analysis of people's responses to the annual Jerry Lewis muscular dystrophy telethon, Davis (1983) found that people with high empathic concern were more likely to watch the telethon and to contribute their time, effort, and money as a result. In contrast, people high in personal distress showed no such tendency. We can conclude from this research that people who typically feel compassion for unfortunate others tend to be drawn toward situations in which their feelings of sympathy will be aroused. When exposed to other's misfortunes, they don't remain passive bystanders, but rather, they tend to take action to try to relieve the suffering. In this regard, the experience of caring for others represents a central self-concept value for those high in empathic concern (Emmons & Diener, 1986).

In addition to these trait-based differences in empathic responding, Batson and his coworkers (1996) found evidence that a past experience with a need may facilitate, or even create, empathy for other people experiencing that need. However, this possible effect was found for women only, not men. The researchers suggest that this gender difference might reflect a difference in how men and women are typically socialized to respond to esteem-threatening experiences. That is, girls in North American culture are socialized to value *emotional relatedness* to others, possibly causing them to deal with suffering by moving toward others and seeking social support, which also increases their likelihood of helping. In contrast, boys are socialized to devalue emotional expression, and instead, value *independence* and *self-defense*. This may cause them to deal with suffering by pulling away from others, and thus, decreasing their help giving.

The possibility that men are more likely than women to avoid feeling empathy due to their upbringing raises the further issue that sometimes we might all be wary of feeling empathy out of concern for the costs of helping. This *empathy-avoidance hypothesis* assumes that we have an implicit knowledge of the empathy-helping relationship, and this knowledge sometimes causes us to actively avoid feeling empathy when we believe the cost of helping will be high. Research indicates that empathy avoidance may well explain some instances of nonintervention. For example, in a series of experiments, when people believed

TABLE 14.4

Measuring Empathic Concern and Personal Distress

Instructions

To discover your level of empathic concern and personal distress, read each item below and then, using the following response scale, indicate how well each statement describes you.

0 = Extremely uncharacteristic (not at all like me)
1 = Uncharacteristic (somewhat unlike me)
2 = Neither characteristic nor uncharacteristic
3 = Characteristic (somewhat like me)
4 = Extremely characteristic (very much like me)

Empathic Concern Scale

_____ 1. When I see someone being taken advantage of, I feel kind of protective toward them.

_____ 2. When I see someone being treated unfairly, I sometimes don't feel very much pity for them.*

_____ 3. I often have tender, concerned feelings for people less fortunate than me.

_____ 4. I would describe myself as a pretty soft-hearted person.

_____ 5. Sometimes I don't feel very sorry for other people when they are having problems.*

_____ 6. Other people's misfortunes do not usually disturb me a great deal.*

_____ 7. I am often quite touched by things that I see happen.

Personal Distress Scale

_____ 1. When I see someone who badly needs help in an emergency, I go to pieces.

_____ 2. I sometimes feel helpless when I am in the middle of a very emotional situation.

_____ 3. In emergency situations, I feel apprehensive and ill-at-ease.

_____ 4. I am usually pretty effective in dealing with emergencies.*

_____ 5. Being in a tense emotional situation scares me.

_____ 6. When I see someone hurt, I tend to remain calm.*

_____ 7. I tend to lose control during emergencies.

Scoring Your Responses

Several of the items on these two scales are reverse-scored; that is, for these items a lower rating actually indicates a higher level of empathic concern or personal distress. Before summing the items, recode those with an asterisk (*) so that 0 = 4, 1 = 3, 3 = 1, 4 = 0.

Gender Differences in Empathic Concern and Personal Distress

Davis (1980) has found the following gender differences in levels of empathic concern and personal distress.

Empathic concern	Personal distress
Male mean = 19.04	Male mean = 9.46
Female mean = 21.67	Female mean = 12.28

Are your scores above or below the mean for your sex?

that helping a homeless man would entail considerable time and effort, they actively avoided situations in which their empathy for this man would be aroused (Shaw et al., 1994). These findings suggest that even normally soft-hearted people can steel themselves to the suffering of others if they avoid an empathic connection. Consider this the next time you pass a homeless person on the street. Are you actively avoiding an empathic response because the perceived costs of helping are too great?

S E C T I O N S U M M A R Y

- The empathy-altruism hypothesis contends that:

    bystanders who experience empathy will help to provide comfort for victims

    bystanders who experience personal distress will only help victims to reduce their own negative arousal state

- Because empathy motivates helping, people sometimes actively avoid experiencing empathy when the cost of helping is high

WHOM DO WE HELP?

Thus far we have examined the *why, when,* and *who* of helping. Now it is time to ask the question, *whom* do we help? Are some people more likely to receive help than others?

We Tend to Help Similar Others

Perceiving a needy person as similar to us tends to increase our willingness to lend assistance. For example, gay men were more willing than heterosexuals to volunteer at an AIDS service organization, and their willingness to help was strongest when their social identity as "gay men" was most salient (Simon et al., 2000). Similarly, in another study, when a person in need of help was identified as heterosexual, heterosexual bystanders were more likely to render assistance than when the needy person was identified as gay or lesbian (Ellis & Fox, 2001). In other words, we appear to be most willing to help ingroup members who need assistance.

As discussed in chapter 5, we often rely on physical cues in guessing people's ingroup-outgroup status. One salient physical cue often used in categorizing needy people into ingroups and outgroups is the clothes they wear. In one study conducted on college campuses in the early 1970s, researchers had confederates ask fellow students for a dime to make a phone call. The confederates asked for this help when either dressed conservatively or in a countercultural ("hippie") fashion. Fewer than half the students gave the dime to those dressed differently from themselves. Two-thirds did so for those dressed similarly (Emswiller et al., 1971). It is likely that the would-be helpers made assumptions about the social and political beliefs of the person-in-need based on what they wore. Clothing was a symbol for these hidden qualities.

Similarity of beliefs does indeed influence help giving. During the 1972 presidential campaign, Stuart Karabenick and his colleagues (1973) convinced Nixon and McGovern workers to "accidentally" drop campaign leaflets as people walked by on their way to vote. If passersby supported the candidate of the needy campaign worker, they were much more likely to help pick up the spilled leaflets than if they supported the other candidate.

One characteristic that exhibits an inconsistent, yet intriguing, pattern of similarity bias is *race.* In a review of helping studies investigating race as a predictor of aid giving, Faye Crosby and her colleagues (1980) found a same-race helping bias in less than half the studies. The remaining studies either showed no discrimination or a different-race helping bias. Does this inconsistent and even contradictory pattern of findings mean that no relation exists for race? Not necessarily. The studies that found greater different-race helping than same-race helping generally involved face-to-face interactions. As discussed in chapter 8, in most social quarters it's no longer acceptable to publicly engage in racial discrimination. It's possible that people today are generally biased toward their own race but hide this bias to avoid social disapproval. In fact, at times, they may even bend over backward to prove that they are not prejudiced. If this explanation is true, then people should be less likely to help someone from another race if they can attribute their unhelpful response to factors other than race.

This is exactly what has been found in a number of studies. For example, Samuel Gaertner and John Dovidio (1977) found that White female college students were less likely to help a needy Black woman than a needy White woman if they could diffuse responsibility among other bystanders. When they were the only bystander to the female victim's plight, and thus unable to diffuse responsibility, there was no difference in their help giving. Studies like this one, then, suggest that race similarity does increase helping. Or, looking at this similarity effect as a *dissimilarity* effect, when people are provided with an excuse not to help, racial discrimination in helping is more likely.

Although similarity may generally lead to greater helping, even a casual observer of the cultural scene can tell you that this is not the case when we consider whom male helpers prefer to assist. In a review of twenty-five studies that compared help received by male and female victims, Alice Eagly and Maureen Crowley (1986) found there was an overall tendency for men to provide more frequent help to women, not men. Women helpers, in contrast, did not show any gender bias. Although male helpers are acting out of line with the similarity effect, they are behaving perfectly in accord with the male gender role, which nurtures helping that is heroic and chivalrous—and is generally directed toward the benefit of female victims. In many cases, the help that men offer to women is clearly egoistic in nature; they more frequently help attractive than unattractive women (West & Brown, 1975).

We Help Deserving Others, but We Also Blame Victims

As discussed earlier in the chapter (p. 537), whether people receive help in times of need will partly depend on others' inferences about the causes of their troubles. Following the principles of attribution theory discussed in chapter 4, we are more likely to help someone if we attribute the cause of their problems to external or uncontrollable factors rather than internal ones. For example, college students state that they would be more willing to lend an acquaintance money or give them their lecture notes if the need arose due to an uncontrollable cause, such as illness, rather than an internal, controllable cause, such as laziness (Weiner, 1980). Similarly, as previously mentioned, liberals' greater willingness than conservatives to help the poor and other disadvantaged people is substantially shaped by what they believe caused these unfortunate events in the first place (Dionne, 1991; Skitka, 1999). Put simply, if we believe people could not have prevented their predicament, we are more likely to help.

The reason we are more likely to help deserving others is due to the *norm of social justice* discussed earlier in the chapter. However, the problem in making inferences about the cause of a victim's troubles, and thereby deciding if she or he deserves our help, is that most of us believe in a just world. As discussed in chapter 5 (p. 159), the *just-world belief* is a belief that the world is a fair and equitable place, with people getting what they deserve (Hafer, 2000a, 200b; Lerner, 1997). One unfortunate consequence of this belief is that we tend to make defensive attributions when explaining the plight of victims. That is, we blame people for their misfortunes, and by doing so, we reassure ourselves that the world is just and that we aren't likely to fall victim to similar circumstances.

Although many people believe in a just world, individual differences exist in the extent to which this belief is held (refer back to table 5.2 p. 159). Because those with a strong just-world belief are more likely to be unsympathetic to victims, it's not surprising to find that they generally are also less likely to help those in need. Does this mean that people who are strong believers in a just world are always unhelpful bystanders? No. When a victim's suffering can be easily and promptly corrected, strong believers in a just world are much more likely to help than when the problems are of a widespread and enduring nature (Bierhoff et al., 1991). The likely reason for this effect is that helping someone who needs just a little bit of assistance to get back on track confirms the just-world believer's perception that the truly deserving will not be unfairly punished. Thus, firm believers in a just world are much more likely to be onetime contributors to little Billy's heart operation fund than they are to be continuing contributors to a fund in search of a cure for AIDS or a program to promote affordable housing for the poor.

SECTION SUMMARY

- We are most likely to help similar others
- We also are most likely to help deserving others
- One unfortunate consequence of believing in a just world is that we tend to blame people for their misfortunes

ARE THERE HIDDEN COSTS FOR HELP RECIPIENTS?

Throughout the chapter we have examined some of the factors that inhibit bystanders to provide assistance to others, but what if help is given? How do recipients typically respond? And what might prevent a person in need from asking for help?

Being Unable to Reciprocate Help Can Create Stress

Throughout the world, people recognize that receiving help is a mixed blessing. Those who receive help often respond with feelings of relief and gratitude, but they also often feel embarrassed, indebted, and even inferior (Nadler, 1991). The contradictory feelings that often flow from prosocial actions help to explain why victims are sometimes less than gracious recipients of a helping hand. The potential that help giving has for producing resentment and hostility is aptly recognized in an Indian proverb that states, "Why do you hate me? I never even helped you" (Nadler & Fisher, 1986, p. 82).

> *. . . It is natural to avoid those to whom we have been too much obliged.*
>
> Héloise, French abbess, 1098–1164

In attempting to explain why receiving help may at times evoke unpleasant emotions, social psychologists have turned their attention to the fact that in exchange relationships (refer to chapter 12, p. 445), people are especially attentive to *reciprocity*—a mutual exchange of resources. *Equity theory* (chapter 12, p. 472) contends that people seek to maintain equity in their social relationships by keeping the exchange ratio of resources balanced, and they feel distressed when inequity exists (Hatfield et al., 1978). When people receive help, they commonly experience a feeling of inequity, because by definition, they realize they have a more favorable ratio of rewards to contributions than does the helper. Under such circumstances, recipients of help are motivated to restore actual equity by trying to return the favor (Greenberg & Frisch, 1972). But what happens if they cannot reciprocate?

Research indicates that recipients not only find nonreciprocal helping distressful, but they also are less likely to ask for assistance in the first place if they don't think they can repay the person in some way (Riley & Eckenrode, 1986). If they aren't in a position to refuse the help, they also might sometimes deal with their inability to restore equity by resenting the helper (Gross & Latané, 1974). In essence, help-givers may be resented if they don't allow recipients to restore equity in some way and thereby allow those who have been helped to live up to the reciprocity norm.

Receiving Help Can Threaten Self-Esteem

The notion that receiving help may produce inequity and feelings of distress in a relationship suggests that it may also pose a threat to the recipient's self-esteem. For instance, in our individualist culture we place a high premium on self-reliance, and this value often is a key defining feature of our self-concept. Receiving help from someone puts us into a dependent role that is contrary to this individualistic value. According to Jeffrey Fisher and Arie Nadler's **threat-to-self-esteem model,** if receiving help contains such negative self-messages, we are likely to feel threatened and respond negatively (Nadler & Fisher, 1986). More specifically, this model states that when receiving help, we can perceive it as either *self-supporting* or *self-threatening.* Aid will be supportive to the extent that it (1) conveys caring for the recipient and (2) provides real benefits (Dakof & Taylor, 1990). It will be threatening to the extent that it (1) implies an inferiority-superiority relationship between recipient and helper and (2) conflicts with important cultural values of self-reliance and independence (Dunkel-Schetter et al., 1992).

Beyond the qualities of the help itself, qualities of the helper and the recipient's own level of self-esteem will also determine whether aid is seen as supportive or threatening. Being helped by a friend, sibling, or a *similar* person is more likely to prompt social comparison, which in turn may call into question the recipient's level of competence (Searcy & Eisenberg, 1992). This is especially true when the helpful task involves something important to the recipient's self-concept. For example, if you are an aspiring psychologist who does not understand the subtleties of a particularly complex theory, asking a fellow student probably would be more threatening to your self-esteem than to ask your psychology professor. Why? The threat-to-self-esteem model would hypothesize that asking a fellow student for help would be more likely to reflect negatively on your own level of competence in this area than seeking help from the professor, a person who is clearly dissimilar to you in psychological training and knowledge (Nadler et al., 1983).

In one experiment testing this hypothesis, Nadler (1987) asked Israeli high school students to solve a series of anagrams when working alongside a same-sex partner. While describing the anagrams task the researchers told half of the students that their performance would provide accurate information on their intelligence and creativity. The rest were told that the task had no association with any important intellectual qualities. All the students were also told that during the task, they could ask their partner for help if they wished. Just before they began the anagrams, they were shown an attitude questionnaire their partner had supposedly completed a few minutes earlier. Half of these questionnaires were constructed to be similar to the participants' own attitude questionnaire responses, while the others were dissimilar in content. The question of interest was under what conditions the students would be most likely to avoid help seeking.

Consistent with the threat-to-self-esteem model, students were less likely to seek help from their partners when they believed they were similar to them, especially when the task was defined as requiring skills important to self-esteem, namely, intelligence and creativity. This reluctance to ask for help from similar others was greatest among adolescents high in self-esteem, who supposedly had the most self-regard to lose on these important personal qualities. One positive consequence of this self-esteem threat is that people who feel threatened in this manner become motivated to develop the necessary skills so that in the future, they will not have to seek help.

Given our previous discussion of gender differences in providing aid (with men tending to assume the role of the chivalrous helper of women), it is not surprising to find that

---

Threat-to-Self-Esteem Model

A theory stating that if receiving help contains negative self-messages, recipients are likely to feel threatened and respond negatively.

A charitable deed must be done as a duty which man owes to man, so that it conveys no idea of the superiority of the giver or the inferiority of the receiver.

The Koran 2:262, Sacred Scripture of Islam

The gods help them that help themselves.

Aesop, Greek folk hero & teller of fables, sixth century B.C.

When we need help on a task, we prefer that it comes from someone similar to us, such as a friend. The dilemma we sometimes face, however, is that if this task requires skills important to our self-esteem, we may feel threatened and, as a result, come to resent the help and the helper. Whom do you think is most likely to react in this manner, those high in self-esteem or those low in self-esteem?

men are more reluctant than women to ask for help (Barbee et al., 1993; Corney, 1990). After all, how often do you see Bruce Willis or Sylvester Stallone-type characters asking for help in the movies? Such help seeking is more frowned upon for men than women and therefore poses a more serious threat to their self-esteem (Smith & DeWine, 1991). Evidence also shows that when heterosexual individuals seek help from someone of the other sex, men are more likely to prefer that it come from an unattractive woman, and women are more likely to prefer help from an attractive man (Nadler et al., 1982). This different pattern of help seeking can be explained as a function of traditional gender roles and self-esteem threat. For a traditional (masculine) heterosexual man, acting dependent toward an attractive woman would be perceived as imperiling his "macho" image in her eyes, but for a traditional (feminine) heterosexual woman, acting dependent toward an attractive man would be thought of as increasing, not decreasing, her appeal. In summary, then, our assessments of what effect such help seeking will have on our self-esteem will largely determine whether and from whom we will seek help.

SECTION SUMMARY

- The threat-to-self-esteem model hypothesizes that if receiving help poses a threat to self-esteem, the recipient may respond negatively, disparaging the help and the helper

- Help recipients may resent help-givers if they are not given the opportunity to return the favor in some way

FEATURED STUDY

CAN IMAGINING THE PRESENCE OF OTHERS INDUCE THE BYSTANDER EFFECT?

Garcia, S. M., Weaver, K., Moskowitz, G. B., & Darley, J. M. (2002). Crowded minds: The implicit bystander effect. *Journal of Personality and Social Psychology, 83,* 843–853.

Bystander intervention studies have consistently demonstrated that the presence of others inhibits helping behavior. However, this research also shows that if individuals know that others cannot possibly help, then bystander apathy will not occur; individuals will behave as if alone. Yet is the presence of actual people necessary to induce the bystander effect? Is it possible that simply imagining others may induce a similar mental state of diffused responsibility, regardless of whether those others are available to respond?

Research on *priming* suggests that merely activating knowledge structures from memory can influence people's social perceptions and behavior. In the present study, researchers sought to determine whether merely activating the construct of *group* in the mind of participants could result in the bystander apathy effect. The hypothesis was that merely *priming* the presence of others at Time 1 can affect helping behavior on a completely unrelated task at Time 2, even when the primed others cannot possibly contribute to the helping task. If one of the concepts associated with *group* is diminished responsibility, then less helping should occur. Study 3 in a five-study investigation is described here.

Method

One hundred and twenty-nine college students from three different universities participated in the study. Students were approached while they sat alone at campus student centers. Participants completed a two-page questionnaire, which included a *group prime* on page one. The *group condition* read as follows: "Imagine you won a dinner for yourself and 10 of your friends at your favorite restaurant." The *one-person control condition* was similar but focused on only one friend:

"Imagine you won a dinner for yourself and a friend at your favorite restaurant." Next, all participants answered the filler question: "What time of day would you most likely make your reservation?" The choices were 5 P.M., 6 P.M., 7 P.M., 8 P.M., 9 P.M., or 10 P.M.. In the *neutral control condition,* participants only read the filler question, which was slightly modified to "What time of day would you make a dinner reservation?"

Helping behavior was operationalized as volunteering to help out with an experiment. Thus, on page 2 of the questionnaire all participants read the following: "In addition to this survey, we are conducting a brief experiment in another room. How much time are you willing to spend on this other experiment?" At this point, participants checked off one of the following minute intervals: 0 minutes, 2 minutes, 5 minutes, 10 minutes, 15 minutes, 20 minutes, 25 minutes, and 30 minutes. After the questionnaires were collected, participants were debriefed about the true nature of the study.

Results and Discussion

Consistent with the experimenters' prediction, participants who imagined a group of ten people at Time 1 offered less helping assistance at Time 2 than did participants in either of the two control conditions. Even though the participants in the group condition imagined their friends, these imagined friends were not in the immediate vicinity to offer helping behavior assistance. Hence, these results suggest that others need not be physically present for diffusion of responsibility to be created. In other words, merely imagining a group can lead to lessened levels of responsibility for helping in a given situation. The priming of group representations appears to simultaneously prime notions of lack of responsibility that disrupt helping behavior. Future research should explore under what conditions this *implicit bystander effect* is likely to be induced.

APPLICATIONS

CAN SOCIAL PSYCHOLOGICAL KNOWLEDGE ENHANCE PROSOCIAL BEHAVIOR?

Shortly after 6 P.M. on September 5, 1993, a nude man was seen running through Cornell University's campus. Suddenly, he stopped at the College Avenue Bridge and began climbing over the railing so that he could jump into the deep gorge below. Yet before he could commit suicide, some students grabbed and held him to the ground until police arrived. Although hundreds of people saw him run past and head toward the bridge, only a handful chose to intervene. These Good Samaritans later admitted that they might not have helped if not for the quick thinking of Cornell undergraduate Gretchen Goldfarb. "Something just clicked," Goldfarb said, in explaining how she realized that this was an emergency and not simply a prank. What was it that "clicked" in her mind? Social psychological knowledge. A few days earlier, she had learned in her psychology class about Darley and Latané's bystander intervention research, which demonstrated that people often do not help in emergencies unless someone first takes action. Armed with this knowledge, she admonished fellow bystanders to grab the man. In that moment, her application of social psychological knowledge played a pivotal role in saving a life.

Learning About the Barriers to Helping

Few of you will ever have your prosocial character tested like those who risked their lives saving people at the Pentagon and the World Trade Center. It is much more likely, however, that you will find yourself in an emergency situation like the one Gretchen Goldfarb experienced. Perhaps the most disturbing set of findings discussed in this chapter is the tendency of bystanders to fail to act when someone needs help. Because emergencies are often not clearly defined as such, and because of the potential for embarrassment if one intervenes and there is no actual emergency, the presence of others inhibits prosocial responding. However, as Goldfarb's story demonstrates, social psychological knowledge truly can release you from such inhibition.

In an empirical demonstration of the empowering effects of such knowledge, Arthur Beaman and his coworkers (1978) randomly assigned students to listen to either a lecture on Latané and Darley's bystander intervention research or to a topic irrelevant to helping. Two weeks later, while participating in a seemingly unrelated study, these same students walked past a person lying on the ground. A confederate who accompanied the student acted unconcerned at this possible emergency. How did the students react? Only 25 percent of those not previously exposed to the bystander intervention lecture stopped to offer assistance. This low prosocial response rate is consistent with Latané and Darleys own findings. Undoubtedly, these students took their cue from their unconcerned companion and defined the situation as a nonemergency. In contrast, students who had previously learned about the paralyzing effects of fellow bystanders on the intervention process acted very differently. Forty-three percent stopped to help the person. These findings suggest that simply knowing about the social barriers to helping can free one from their antisocial effects.

Jane Piliavin, codeveloper of the arousal: cost-reward model, believes that in addition to this knowledge-created awareness of the social dynamics of emergency situations, we must also understand that in our individualistic society we have been socialized to leave people alone and to mind our own business. Such training can effectively inhibit intervention:

> In our society, we are trained from an early age to see the problems of other people as "none of our business," to close our feelings off from others' experiences. We have only recently "discovered" child abuse, spouse abuse, incest, and other family "traditions" because of the sanctity of the home and respect for others' privacy. This tendency saves all of us a great deal of emotional distress, but it contributes to the bureaucratization of helping in our society and, we believe, to the increasing alienation and self-absorption of which we all are currently being accused. We may need more training as busybodies; respect for privacy prevents empathic arousal, and directs one's attention to the costs of intervention, specifically the cost of being thought "intrusive." (Piliavin et al., 1981, p. 254)

Piliavin and her colleagues state that in classes in which they have discussed the social psychological research and theories of helping, students repeatedly report an increased attentiveness and responsiveness to emergencies. In a very real and important sense, then, making people aware of the social dynamics of emergencies and the inhibiting effects of socialization may be an important key to unlocking people's prosocial tendencies.

In this chapter, we addressed five basic questions about helping: Why do we help? When do we help? Who is most likely to help? Whom do we help? And, are there hidden costs for those who receive help? Now, let's turn the tables a bit: What if *you* are the one who needs help? How can you use your social psychological knowledge to increase the likelihood that others will assist you?

The *bystander intervention model* provides valuable insights in this regard, for it tells you that deciding to intervene in a possible emergency involves a rather complex set of decisions. If bystanders make an incorrect decision at any point in this process, they will not help you. Faced with these facts, as the victim, you must attack and neutralize the psychological factors that cause nonintervention. Essentially, you need to capitalize on the self's ability to construct social reality. You can do so by actively and forcefully altering people's social perceptions so that they adopt helping social roles.

The first psychological hurdle is the *audience inhibition effect,* in which the fear of being negatively evaluated, combined with the tendency to look to others for further information, leads bystanders to identify emergencies as nonemergencies. As the victim, you can eliminate this inhibition by clearly letting everyone know that this is an emergency and you need help.

After clearing this hurdle, you must next attack the *diffusion of responsibility,* which is bystanders' tendency to believe they are less personally responsible for helping when others are present. Here, you should implore specific people to help you, because it's hard to deny assistance when singled out of the crowd.

Finally, because some people may want to help but are unsure what to do, you can overcome this last hurdle by specifically giving them instructions ("You! Call an ambulance!" "You! Gather my belongings and bring them to me!"). Using your most authoritative voice will further increase obedience. And obedience is exactly what you are seeking here. In all likelihood, you probably won't need to direct everyone who is assisting you. Once you get the ball rolling, others are likely to spring into action on their own. However, the more quickly you consciously transform the social dynamics to facilitate helping, the better off you will be. Gretchen Goldfarb can attest to this social fact. View some final advice of receiving help in an emergency from social psychologist John Darley on your Social Sense CD-ROM.

Social Sense

View an interview with social psychologist John Darley on receiving help in an emergency.

WEB SITES
accessed through http://www.mhhe.com/franzoi4

Web sites for this chapter focus on research and theory on helping, including how to raise children to be more altruistic and personal life stories of people who help others.

American Psychological Association

The American Psychological Association has a Web page that offers suggestions on how to raise children to be more altruistic, and supports the suggestion with relevant theories.

Giraffe Project Heroes Program

This Web site highlights the personal life stories of people who stick their necks out for the common good.

The Altruistic Personality and Prosocial Behavior Institute

This Web site is devoted to the institute founded in 1982 by Dr. Samuel Oliner and Dr. Pearl Oliner, who recognized the need for more research into the areas of altruism and prosocial behavior.

A NOTE FROM THE AUTHOR

Appendix A contains possible answers to the critical thinking sidebars in chapters 1 to 14. In reading and comparing them with your own responses, analyze each answer's strengths and weaknesses. If you would like to help me improve my responses for the next edition, please drop me a line with your suggestions (or questions) using my e-mail address (Stephen.Franzoi@marquette.edu). For those critical thinking sidebar questions that asked you to provide personal recollections from your own experiences, I have understandably not provided a possible answer.

CHAPTER 1: INTRODUCING SOCIAL PSYCHOLOGY

Question: Why do you think that some social psychologists have named Adolf Hitler as the one person who had the greatest impact on the development of social psychology?

Possible Answer: Adolf Hitler had a profound, albeit indirect, impact on the development of social psychology. As the leader of Nazi Germany during World War II, his persecution of Jews and intellectuals resulted in the mass exodus of many of Europe's leading scholars from Germany and other Nazi-occupied countries to the United States. Upon arriving in this country, these scholars exerted an immediate and lasting influence on their respective fields of study, including social psychology, which was still in its infancy as a science. Yet these refugees from Hitler's persecution not only shaped the direction and content of theory and research in social psychology. They also became mentors for many of the young American social psychologists who were able to attend college and graduate school under the G.I. Bill after serving as soldiers overseas fighting Hitler's armies. In addition, because of World War II, social psychology in the United States was able to demonstrate to the government that its theories and findings could be put to practical use in solving problems that aided the war effort against Hitler's Germany (and Japan). These wartime successes led to increased government funding of social psychological research when the war was over, which proved vital to the field's development. For these reasons, Hitler can be given indirect credit for shaping the field of social psychology.

CHAPTER 2: RESEARCH METHODS IN SOCIAL PSYCHOLOGY

Question: Prior to conducting research, what precautions do you think social psychologists should take to ensure that the people who participate in their research will not be harmed? Should they be allowed to study people without their consent?

Possible Answer: Just as you can never guarantee that someone won't be hurt taking a walk around the block, you cannot guarantee that participants in a social scientific study will never be harmed. However, what you can do is examine all aspects of your study so that all reasonable precautions are taken to minimize participant risk. Whenever the choice is between securing the welfare of the study or the welfare of the participant, you must always place the participant's welfare first. This means that some studies will simply not be conducted.

In most cases, social scientists should only study people with their "informed consent," meaning that they are provided with enough information about the research to be able to make a conscious choice to participate or not. In some cases, however, it may be necessary to study people without their informed consent. For instance, when researchers study helping behavior, they may stage a fake emergency in a public setting—for example, a person collapsing on the street—and then observe the responses of bystanders. In such a natural setting, you cannot ask people for permission to include them in the study beforehand.

Question: Imagine that you are the leader of a team of researchers studying social psychological topics at a university. Under your tutelage, students are learning about the research process while working on your team. Besides instructing them on the proper scientific methods, statistical procedures, and ethical standards to adopt when conducting research, what advice would you give them concerning how they should approach scientific problems in their work?

Possible Answer: In 1973, social psychologist William McGuire wrote an important article on how social psychologists should approach scientific problems. This article, "The Yin and Yang of Progress in Social Psychology," suggested that researchers adopt an Eastern philosophical approach to problem solving that defies conventional notions of logic by simultaneously entertaining contradictory and opposing explanations of reality. This approach to "doing" social psychology McGuire called *perspectivism,* and it requires that scientists engage in oppositional thinking when developing theories and hypotheses. When a scientist develops a hypothesis from a theory, she must also consider how other theories might also account for this hypothesis, and she must also develop an opposing hypothesis that is also derived from multiple theories. This approach to thinking about scientific problems frees the scientist's mind from being bound by the logic of only one explanation of events. Social psychologist

Mahzarin Banaji (2004), a former graduate student of McGuire's, asserts that the student members of a research team with this perspectivist philosophy would feel safe and even elated when research findings run counter to their hypotheses. Instead of feeling that they somehow "failed" the leader of their research team, these students would view these findings as providing them with an opportunity to entertain alternative explanations that are closer to providing an accurate accounting of the social behavior under study. To learn more about perspectivism, check out the book, *Perspectivism in Social Psychology,* edited by John T. Jost, Mahzarin R. Banaji, and Deborah A. Prentice published in 2004 by the American Psychological Association.

Question: What are some similarities and some differences between "random assignment" and "random selection"?

Possible Answer: One similarity is that both of these research procedures are meant to serve as a safeguard against researchers unconsciously allowing their opinions and preferences to influence subject participation. Further, as their names imply, both random selection and random assignment involve the reliance upon a chance selection procedure. The difference is that while random selection has to do with giving everyone in the population being studied an equal chance of being included in the study, random assignment involves giving everyone who is already in the study an equal chance of being exposed to every level of the study's treatment conditions. Random assignment is associated with experimental designs in which there are different treatment conditions, whereas random selection is more often associated with survey research (although it is sometimes used in experiments).

Question: If you were a member of your college's institutional review board and a research proposal similar to the Milgram obedience study was submitted for approval, what questions would you ask to determine its risk/benefit ratio? Based on your assessment, would you approve the study?

Possible Answer: Using the risk/benefit ratio, you would weigh the potential risks to the participants against the study's potential benefits to society, with greater weight given to the participants' welfare. While assessing a Milgram-type study proposal, you might ask whether there was any other way the researchers could conduct the study to minimize participant stress. In essence, because of the deception being used, full informed consent could not be obtained. As such, you might ask the researchers whether they were going to let the participants know up front that they could not reveal all the details of the purpose and procedures to be used in the study. You might also ask the researchers how they would respond to a participant who asked them to stop the study. Would they stop the study after the first request? Because of the deception and the destructive obedience that is being studied, you would probably also ask the researchers to specifically detail their debriefing procedures, because these would need to be as sensitive and detailed as possible. You might also require follow-up interviews with participants to determine whether there

were any delayed stress responses and further require that free counseling opportunities with a mental health professional be made available to participants if they wanted to discuss their research experience.

Would you approve a Milgram-type study? You might decide to do so only if it was seeking to shed light on an aspect of obedience that had not already been investigated. Given the fact that there already have been a number of Milgram obedience replications, you might find it difficult to justify approving another replication of the original study given the possible harm to participants. However, in considering your own answer to this question, keep in mind the following thought: the decision not to grant a request to conduct research on a particular topic also has ethical implications. If you do not allow certain research to be conducted because the behavior in question is socially undesirable or destructive when it naturally occurs in the "real world," the social sciences are likely to have crucial gaps in their knowledge base, and these gaps may prevent scientists from developing useful intervention strategies to lessen people's future suffering. What will be potentially lost by not allowing this study to go forward? These are just a few of the tough questions that you would grapple with as a member of an institutional review board.

CHAPTER 3: THE SELF

Question: According to the strength model of self-regulation, when would a parent or a spouse be most likely to engage in domestic violence due to losing control of their emotions?

Possible Answer: According to this theory, each act of self-regulation depletes the limited energy available for this purpose. Thus, immediately after exercising self-regulation in one activity, people will find it harder to regulate their behavior in an unrelated activity. From this perspective, domestic violence is most likely to occur when self-regulatory resources have been recently depleted. Thus, when abusers have just finished controlling or regulating their behavior—for example, working hard to prepare a meal when they would rather be relaxing, or holding their temper in check when talking to their employer on the phone—they are more susceptible to not being able to control their aggressive tendencies toward family members.

Question: How would you design a study, using Markus's "me"/"not me" response format, to document the disappearance of a specific self-schema—say "sexiness"—from people's self-concept along the lines of James's notion of emotional identification? Would this be a longitudinal study or would you instead test people of different age groups?

Possible Answer: You could first identify young adult participants who were either schematic or aschematic for this particular self-attribute and then periodically test their response latencies for sexiness-related words that were embedded within a long list of nonrelated words. You might also test their recall of past incidents in which they acted in a sexy manner. Of course, this memory probing would also have to be embedded within many other memory probes in order not to raise participants' suspicions about all these "sexiness" questions. This retesting could be done over the course of many years, and you might hypothesize that the latencies would become longer and the recall of incidents more infrequent as they age. Given the amount of time, money, and energy necessary to conduct such a longitudinal study, you might decide to go forward with this project only if it was part of a much larger study of these individuals involving other research hypotheses so that you would get more of a "return" on your research investment.

A far simpler study could be conducted using what is called a cross-sectional design, in which you simultaneously test participants from different age groups. You might simply hypothesize that young adult participants would be more self-schematic for "sexiness" than older adults. The problem with this cross-sectional design is that you probably would have a harder time interpreting your results compared with the previously described longitudinal format. For instance, if you did find evidence to support your hypothesis, it might be difficult to determine whether this effect was due to age differences or generational differences. Is it that people's emotional identification with "sexiness" lessens with age, or is it perhaps that the elderly grew up in a time where "sexiness" was associated with sinfulness, and thus, they were much less likely to emotionally identify with it than young adults today? Teasing apart these two possibilities is much harder in a cross-sectional study.

Question: If you were to tell someone to "just be yourself," what would that mean to them depending on whether they were from an individualist or a collectivist culture?

Possible Answer: When Chie Kanagawa and her colleagues (2001) asked that question of U.S. and Japanese college students, they received decidedly different responses. For the Americans, the statement implied a self comprised of personal attributes that were not influenced by the situation they happened to be in at the time. Further, these attributes reflected the Americans' unique qualities, and these qualities were mostly positive. In contrast, for the Japanese, the statement implied a self that was defined by the relationships inherent in the situation. Here, "being yourself" meant constructing a self-presentation that was fairly self-critical and would help one fit into the situation. This research suggests that, for individualists, "being yourself" assumes a relatively fixed and stable self-concept made up of generally positive personal attributes. For collectivists, "being yourself" assumes a self that changes according to the situation to better fit in with the group.

Question: Based on Trzesniewski and her coworkers' (2003) research on the stability of self-esteem across the life-span, during what stage in life (besides early childhood) would you likely be most successful in changing self-esteem?

Possible Answer: Middle childhood and early adolescence are times when self-esteem stability is relatively low. Because of the fluctuations that occur in self-esteem during this period of life, it may offer an important window of opportunity for programs designed to increase self-esteem levels. Indeed, research suggests that programs designed to increase the self-esteem of children and adolescents are often successful and have beneficial effects for a wide variety of social behaviors (DuBois, in press; Haney & Durlak, 1998).

Question: If low self-esteem people are likely to reject your attempts to increase their feelings of self-worth, what strategy might you use to feed their self-enhancement needs without triggering their need for self-verification?

Possible Answer: Self-verification needs are most likely to override self-enhancement needs when low self-esteem people are presented with positive feedback that, if accepted, would require a major change in their self-concepts. Research suggests that low self-esteem persons can engage in direct forms of self-enhancement when the positive feedback is not related to a highly important aspect of their self-concepts (Seta et al., 1999). Thus, you could offer low self-esteem people subtle praise and other positive feedback that will make them feel good and hopefully boost their feelings of self-worth, without being so strong as to make them uncomfortable.

Question: People with low implicit self-esteem don't like themselves but are not typically consciously aware of this negative self-regard. If you were a therapist, how might you use classical conditioning techniques to unconsciously increase a person's low implicit self-esteem?

Possible Answer: Classical conditioning is a type of learning first identified by Russian physiologist Ivan Pavlov, in which a neutral stimulus acquires the capacity to elicit a response after being repeatedly paired with another stimulus that naturally elicits that response. In this nonconscious learning, the two stimuli are repeatedly paired until the presence of one evokes the expectation of the other. In a recent study, Jodene Baccus and her coworkers (2004) used classical conditioning techniques to increase implicit self-esteem. How did they accomplish this task? Sitting at a computer, research participants were told that a word would appear randomly in some area of the computer screen and their task was to use the computer mouse to click on the word as quickly as possible. They were also told that doing so would cause an image to be displayed briefly (for 400 milliseconds) in that same area. Whenever a word appeared on the screen that the participants had previously noted was self-descriptive, it was paired with an image of a smiling face. The participants completed 240 trials, with 80 of those trials involving self-relevant words. Results indicated that those participants who were repeatedly exposed to pairings of self-relevant words with smiling faces showed enhanced implicit self-esteem compared with participants in a control condition. Although more research is needed to further understand this learning process, the finding in this study suggests that feelings of low self-esteem are not set in stone in childhood, but might be raised at a later time using basic learning principles.

Question: If your ethnic heritage is relevant to who you think you are, what stage are you at in Phinney's model? Is this model an accurate portrayal of your own ethnic identity development?

This answer will be unique to your personal experiences.

Question: Our self-esteem will often be threatened when we compare ourselves with those superior to us on some task. However, a review of the literature indicates that upward comparison can sometimes lead to higher self-esteem (Collins, 1996). How do you think this particular self-enhancement effect might occur?

Possible Answer: Upward social comparison is generally regarded as a threat to self-esteem, but people often compare themselves with others who have better abilities and attributes than their own. Such upward comparison provides useful information, and it doesn't always lead to more negative self-evaluations. Rebecca Collins' (1996) meta-analysis of studies testing upward comparison effects found that people sometimes make upward comparisons in hopes of enhancing their self-esteem by discovering ways to improve themselves and by identifying attributes they share with their "betters."

CHAPTER 4: SELF-PRESENTATION AND PERSON PERCEPTION

Question: Do you think that people raised in collectivist cultures might sometimes have different self-presentation concerns than persons raised in individualist cultures?

Possible Answer: As discussed in chapter 3 (pp. 72–74), people in collectivist cultures tend to have a more interdependent view of themselves than those in individualist cultures. As a result, collectivists may often be more concerned than individualists about presenting the appropriate public self to their group. In Asian collectivist cultures, "saving face" or avoiding public embarrassment is more important than in individualist cultures. For example, in Japan, there are "convenience agencies" (*benriya*) that supply customers with rented "friends" who become additional guests at their weddings, mourners at family funerals, or romantic partners at important parties. Such extreme measures to manage others' impressions also occur in individualist cultures, but they may be more common in a social environment in which interdependent selves are more salient.

Question: Of the different self-presentation strategies that you employed today, under what circumstances and with whom were they used? Which ones achieved the desired effect? Was there one strategy that you frequently employed? If you didn't use any, why was this the case?

This answer will be unique to your personal experiences.

Question: How might an evolutionary theorist explain the gender differences in decoding nonverbal communication? That is, from an evolutionary perspective, why would it be more beneficial for females than males to have good nonverbal skills?

Possible Answer: According to the evolutionary perspective, human beings, along with all other species on the planet, have evolved in ways that maximize the chances of their genes being passed on to their offspring so that these gene traits survive from generation to generation. Because only women could bear and breast-feed infants, evolutionary theorists contend that they evolved to take on the more nurturing and empathic role of domestic caretaker. To be a good nurturer of infants who cannot yet convey their desires through spoken language, being very attentive to nonverbal signals of sickness or distress would be very beneficial. Thus, women who were nonverbally skilled would be most likely to have offspring who survived through this vulnerable age period. Over thousands of generations, a sex difference may have emerged based on this natural selection pressure on women.

Question: Health experts have grown increasingly alarmed about AIDS among young adults because most of this population are not practicing safe sex by using condoms (Langer et al., 2001). How might young adults' implicit personality theories about safe-sex partners be shaping their decisions not to use condoms?

Possible Answer: A survey conducted by Diane Kimble and her colleagues (1992) found that young adults tend to have a well-developed and generally accepted set of ideas regarding who are safe sexual partners. Who are these sexually "safe" individuals? People who one knows and likes are perceived not to be a risk. As one respondent summed up this view, "When you get to know the person . . . as soon as you begin trusting the person . . . you don't really have to use a condom" (p. 926). Risky people, on the other hand, are those one does not know well, who are older, and are overanxious for sex. Kimble and her coworkers interpreted the young adults' tendencies not to practice safe sex with partners they knew and liked as being due to their reluctance to link the risk of disease with loving or caring relationships. Unfortunately, the criteria these people use to judge AIDS risk is totally unrelated to a person's HIV status. Individuals who operate from such a belief system run the very real risk of exposure to AIDS and possibly death.

Question: Why might someone argue that correspondent inference theory would not have been developed in a collectivist culture? Put another way, what individualist assumption is at the core of this theory?

Possible Answer: A correspondent inference is an inference that the action of an actor corresponds to, or is indicative of, a stable personal characteristic. In developing correspondent inference theory, Jones and Davis assumed that people have a preference for explaining people's behavior in terms of their personalities, and that external attributions are merely default options, made only when internal causes cannot be found. This assumption makes perfect sense in an individualist culture, in which people are socialized to think of themselves and others as personally controlling their own actions, and that their rights and desires are at least as important as those of the group. Yet in a collectivist culture, where people are socialized to think first about the rights and desires of the group, it's likely that much greater attention would be paid to external causes of behavior than in an individualist culture. Because of these differences in cultural orientation, it's likely that correspondent inference theory would not have been developed in a collectivist culture.

Question: Based on your understanding of correspondent inference theory, why do you think the fundamental attribution error is also known as the *correspondence bias?*

Possible Answer: A correspondent inference is an inference that the actor's action corresponds to, or is indicative of, a stable personal characteristic. According to correspondent inference theory, people are motivated to make correspondent inferences because doing so increases their confidence that they can predict other actors' behavior in the future. The fundamental attribution error is the tendency to overestimate the impact of dispositional causes and underestimate the impact of situational causes when explaining actors' behavior. In other words, it reflects an overzealous desire to make a correspondent inference. Thus it could be called a *correspondence bias.*

CHAPTER 5: THINKING ABOUT OUR SOCIAL WORLD

Question: How is the spontaneous self-concept discussed in chapter 3 related to schemas and priming effects?

Possible Answer: As defined in chapter 3, a spontaneous self-concept is that aspect of the self-concept that becomes salient and activated in a particular setting. In essence, a spontaneous self-concept is a self-schema or a set of self-schemas that have been situationally activated. Priming is the process by which recent exposure to certain stimuli or events increases the accessibility of certain schemas. Thus, for example, if you notice a parent comforting a crying child just as you walk into a store, your self-schema of empathy might be

activated. Upon entering the store, this spontaneous empathic self-concept may cause you to take notice of the donation box for "Needy Children" at the service desk, prompting you to donate money to the cause.

Question: If the representativeness heuristic is stereotyping operating in reverse, does that mean that stereotyping is also a heuristic?

Possible Answer: Yes, stereotyping is definitely a heuristic. Like other heuristics, stereotyping provides a "shortcut in thinking" by supplying us with rich and distinctive information—but not necessarily accurate information—about individuals we do not personally know. Stereotypes provide us with a fast basis for social judgments, and they also "free up" cognition for other tasks. Stereotyping will be discussed more fully in chapter 8.

Question: In the days and weeks following the suicide attacks at the Pentagon and World Trade Center by Arab terrorists, FBI officer around the country were flooded with calls from citizens reporting possible leads and suspects. Virtually every person who was perceived as being suspicious was of Arab descent. What cognitive heuristic was being used in making these social judgments? Why do you think people were relying on this heuristic?

Possible Answer: People were relying on the representativeness heuristic, which involves the tendency to judge the category membership of things based on how closely they match the typical or average member of that category, Anyone who had physical characteristics, clothing, or a surname perceived to be associated with people from Middle Eastern cultures were much more likely judged as a possible terrorist,. Further, Americans were primed to place people into the "terrorist" category because of the wide news coverage of the September 11th attacks. In this atmosphere of terrorist-saturated news coverage and discussion, Americans perceived future terrorist attacks to be quite likely, and many people believed they were possible targets. This tendency to judge the frequency or probability of an event in terms of how easy it is to think of examples of that event is known as the availability heuristic. The availability heuristic contributed to people relying on the representativeness heuristic.

Question: Why might a neuroscientist argue that the hindsight bias is triggered by some of the same neurological activity that creates the storyline of dreams?

Possible Answer: Social psychologists explain the hindsight bias as an attempt to make sense out of a surprising outcome; in essence, inserting missing causal connections so that our story of the event makes sense given the outcome. The part of our brains that does this cognitive work is the left hemisphere of the central cortex, what neuroscientist Mike Gazzaniga (2000) describes as the brain's "interpreter." The left hemisphere always strives to assign some rational meaning to behavior, even when there is none.

According to the *activation-synthesis theory* of dreaming, a dream is the left hemisphere's attempt to interpret the random neural activity initiated in the midbrain during sleep (Hobson & McCarley, 1977; Hobson et al., 1998). Thus, the neurological activity that triggers the hindsight bias may involve some of the same neural activity that triggers dreams, with the right hemisphere helping construct most of the dream's visual features.

Question: Can you think of personal life situations in which the false consensus effect contributed to either misunderstandings and conflicts between you and other people or smoother interactions?

Possible Answer: The tendency to believe that your own attitudes, opinions, and beliefs are more common than they really are is known as the false consensus effect. Some possible social misunderstandings due to the false consensus effect might involve angry responses from others due to you acting on your assumptions that most people you meet share your political or social attitudes and beliefs. However, due to your false consensus assumptions, you might act more warm and personable toward others, which results in them responding in kind. If the truth about the false consensus is not discovered, your false assumptions would promote smooth interactions.

Question: Do you think that a judge's beliefs about the guilt or innocence of a defendant in a criminal trial could create a self-fulfilling prophecy among the jury, even if the judge does not voice her opinions?

Possible Answer: Actually, several studies have investigated this very question. What they have found is that although judges may not directly convey to the jury their beliefs about the defendant's guilt or innocence, their nonverbal behavior and instructions to the jury prior to them beginning deliberations can influence jurors' decisions (Halverson et al., 1997). For example, scowling or smiling in the general direction of a defendant by a judge can signal to jurors some important information about the judge's beliefs, and this information can steer the evaluative direction of subsequent deliberations. It has been estimated that the effect of such subtle influence is sufficient to potentially increase the rate of guilty findings by 14 percent for a jury instructed by a judge who believes a defendant to be guilty (Rosenthal, 2003).

CHAPTER 6: ATTITUDES

Question: Which values on the Values Hierarchy questionnaire were more important for you? Can you identify ways in which these values have influenced your attitudes and behavior?

This answer will be unique to your personal experiences.

Question: How do implicit and explicit attitudes relate to the self-perception process?

Possible Answer: Bem's self-perception theory proposes that we often do not know our attitudes, but simply infer them from our behavior. However, implicit attitude research demonstrates how implicit attitudes can unknowingly shape behavior. One possibility is that self-perception theory actually explains how implicit attitudes sometimes become explicit attitudes. Of course, this explanation is a reinterpretation of Bem's original theory of self-perception. In step 1, an implicit attitude prompts a person to behave a certain way, and then in step 2, self-reflection prompts the person to form an explicit attitude that is consistent with the already-existing implicit attitude.

In my example of teaching, prior to reflecting on my past actions and developing an explicit positive attitude toward teaching this course, my behavior in the course was guided by my implicit positive attitude. Thus, self-reflection did not create a new attitude where none existed before, but instead, reflecting on my past behavior helped me consciously recognize that I already had an unconscious positive attitude. If this explanation is correct, self-reflection can be thought of as facilitating the formation of explicit attitudes due to the behavioral effects of pre-existing implicit attitudes. For additional reading on topics related to this one, check out Timothy Wilson's (2002) book, *Strangers to Ourselves: Discovering the Adaptive Unconscious.*

Question: Is there any wisdom in parents admonishing their children to straighten their posture and to avoid slouching? How might the manner in which parents try to correct slouching destroy these possible benefits?

Possible Answer: Yes there is, because studies suggest that upright postures cannot only cause you to feel happier, but they can also cause you to have a more favorable attitude toward things in general. Yet these are subtle effects and could be easily destroyed by parents forcing their children to engage in this behavior. In such instances, the feeling of children that their parents are trying to control their behavior may well be sufficient to create the exact opposite mood! Thus, to capitalize on these positive posture effects, parents should steer clear of orders and threats.

Question: In terms of Daniel Katz' four functions of attitudes, which functions do you think clothing attitudes serve for most people?

Possible Answer: Our attitudes toward clothing are undoubtedly shaped by satisfying such biological needs as maintaining our body temperature at a comfortable and safe level (not too hot and not too cold, but "just right"). Clothes that also allow us to move comfortably are generally favored over those that restrict our movements. We tend to prefer clothes that do not cause physical pain. All of these factors point to the *adjustment function:* We will develop positive attitudes toward clothing that brings us rewards or helps us avoid punishment. We also tend to like clothing that expresses important aspects of our self-concept, especially our values and social identities. For example, a study of Japanese and Korean women found that their preferences in clothing were associated with factors including traditions, culture, public morals, and racial consciousness (Shoyama et al., 2003). The fact that people are more likely to wear clothing associated with their sports team following a victory rather than after a defeat is further evidence for the *value-expressive* nature of clothing.

Question: What are some possible confounding variables in the LaPiere study?

Possible Answer: One problem with the LaPiere study was that the behavioral measures of actually serving the Chinese couple when they showed up at managers' doorsteps created a conflict between the managers' positive attitudes toward making money versus their negative attitudes toward serving Chinese. In contrast, the previously obtained self-report measures concerning whether the managers would serve Chinese presented no such conflict for them because it was simply a hypothetical situation. Another possible problem was that LaPiere did not know whether the person who responded to the mailed questionnaire was the same person who decided whether to serve LaPiere's Chinese companions when they arrived at the manager's place of business.

CHAPTER 7: PERSUASION

Question: Advertisers design their ads to capitalize on the similarity effect. Did you observe differences in the way women and men are portrayed in TV ads that correspond to this effect?

Possible Answer: Even with the more balanced portrayal of the two sexes in TV commercials today, they are still constructed in ways that reinforce the image of gender most familiar to and comfortable for their target audience at a particular time of the day. R. Stephen Craig (1992) found that daytime ads, which are typically aimed at the female homemaker, focus on images of the traditional American household, with the wife taking care of the domestic family needs and the husband holding a position of authority at home and at the office. In contrast, weekend commercials targeted at the male sports viewer frequently exclude women and children altogether. These ads—dominated by alcohol and automotive products—stress traditional stereotypes of masculinity, such as the importance of being strong, daring, rugged, independent, and competitive. When women do appear in weekend commercials, they are generally portrayed in either subservient roles to men (for example, secretary or flight attendant) or as sexual objects. The traditional gender stereotyping in daytime and weekend commercials stands in sharp contrast to those shown during the evening and geared toward dual-career couples and single working women. Here, women are more likely to be portrayed in positions of authority and in settings away from home than they are in daytime ads. Men, in contrast, are more likely to be portrayed as a parent or spouse, and more in settings at home than they are on weekend TV. Thus, Craig's analysis suggests that how men and women are portrayed in North American TV ads today depends on who is watching. Evening commercials represent a more sophisticated and balanced portrayal of gender roles, but daytime and weekend ads reflect more traditional orientations.

Question: In addition to using humor, the anti-binge drinking SMU ad also provides information on how much alcohol the typical SMU student consumes. Why might this information be effective in reducing binge drinking at SMU? When would reporting such normative information possibly promote—rather than reduce—binge drinking?

Possible Answer: Providing information to fellow students on how much alcohol the typical SMU student consumes may be effective in reducing binge drinking *if* the campus drinking average is fairly low. *Social norms* campaigns that inform students that most students don't drink excessively can effectively reduce binge drinking. However these same social norms campaigns may actually promote binge drinking on campuses where student drinking is very high. Thus, this persuasive approach should be used cautiously, because it can backfire.

Question: Why is it that when radio lottery advertisers are trying to persuade you to spend your money, they speak at a normal rate of speed, yet when they convey the odds of winning, their speech rate dramatically increases? Are they simply trying to save money by cutting down on the length of the commercial, or is there an equally important reason for this shift to fast-paced speech?

Possible Answer: Although research indicates that fast talkers are generally more persuasive than slow talkers due to listeners' impressions that they are more credible, this is not why fast talking is used when announcing the odds of winning. Instead, a message that is presented very quickly is difficult to process and critically analyze, and this is exactly what the advertisers are counting on. They don't want listeners to elaborate on the message that their chances of winning the lottery are about equal to the likelihood that they will be struck by lightning while sitting in their living rooms!

Question: If the hypothesis is correct that the greater attitude change among the young isn't due to an age difference in openness to change, but rather is due to young adults encountering more negative experiences than their elders, does this change any conclusions that we drew from the Bennington College study?

Possible Answer: The Bennington College study demonstrated the important role that reference groups can play in attitude formation and attitude endurance. Although Duane Alwin and his colleagues (1991) asserted that their Bennington College findings were consistent with the "impressionable years" hypothesis, these findings are also consistent with the more recent "negative experiences" hypothesis. Whether inducements to change attitudes are from greater impressionability among young adults or from greater negative experiences they encounter does not change the basic conclusions regarding the importance of reference groups in attitude formation and endurance.

CHAPTER 8: PREJUDICE AND DISCRIMINATION

Question: Do you automatically imagine that popular songs are about other-sex love? If you do, does this tell us anything about your level of heterosexism? How do you react to these lyrics when you imagine that they are about same-sex love? If you regularly imagine that popular songs involve same-sex love, does this usually take more cognitive effort on your part?

Possible Answer: Whether or not you automatically imagine the lyrics of romantic songs are about heterosexual love tells us little, if anything, about your level of heterosexism. Instead, regardless of your sexual orientation, such imagining simply illustrates how our culture is dominated by heterosexual assumptions about romantic relationships. Yet, it's likely that how you react to imagining homosexual romance in these same lyrics does provide some indication of your level of heterosexism. Given the fact that heterosexual romantic love is our cultural norm, if you regularly imagine that popular songs involve same-sex love, this probably takes more cognitive effort, or at least it may have in the past.

Question: What do you think are the stereotypes associated with Anglo-Whites, Asians, Blacks, Jews, and Latinos in North American culture? Does your knowledge of these stereotypes tell us anything about your degree of prejudice toward these racial and ethnic groups?

Possible Answer: Common stereotypes of these groups are listed on page 576. Sometimes, people will deny knowledge of negative stereotypes of other groups out of fear that admitting to such knowledge is a sign of their own personal prejudice toward these groups. However, by itself, knowledge of these stereotypes tells us nothing about a person's degree of prejudice toward these racial and ethnic groups. Indeed, due to its personal relevance, you may have more extensive knowledge about the negative stereotypes associated with your own group than any other groups.

Question: One of the important functions of stereotyping is that it saves cognitive effort. Thus, when we are tired, we may be more likely to base our impressions of others on stereotypes. If this is true, during what times of the day are people likely to rely on stereotypes when judging others?

Possible Answer: Have you ever heard of "morning" and "night" people? Morning people wake up early, with a good deal of energy and alertness, but are ready to retire before 10:00 P.M. Night persons, on the other hand, stay up much later in the evening, and have a hard time getting up early in the morning (Thoman, 1999). About 25 percent of us are "night persons," 25 percent are "morning persons," and the remaining 50 percent fall somewhere between these two extremes. This different sleep pattern appears to be related to differences in circadian body temperatures. Not surprisingly, in one study, college students who were identified as morning persons obtained better grades in early-morning classes than in evening classes. The exact opposite effect was found for students classified as night persons (Guthrie et al., 1995).

Question: Can you think of a negative stereotype about Whites relative to Blacks that might cause White individuals to experience stereotype threat in a particular area of pursuit, thereby motivating them to disidentify with this activity?

Possible Answer: A common negative stereotype about Whites is that they do not have the physical skills to compete against Blacks in most sports. This was the primary theme in the basketball movie *White Men Can't Jump.* When competing against Black basketball players, White players may become aware of this negative stereotype, experience stereotype threat, and underperform.

In an experimental demonstration of this effect, Jeff Stone and his colleagues (1999) described a golf task to White and Black college students as either diagnostic of "natural athletic ability" or "sports intelligence." White students performed worse than a control group when the task was thought to be associated with natural ability, while Black students performed worse than a control group when the task was framed as measuring intelligence. In a second experiment involving only White students, the researchers found that when the golf task was described as measuring natural athletic ability, those who performed worst were students who had previously stated that their self-esteem was significantly associated with success in athletic endeavors.

One likely consequence of regularly experiencing stereotype threat in athletic competition is that Whites may disidentify with sports achievement and choose to identify with other endeavors, such as academic achievement. In other words, they change their self-concept so that sports achievement is no longer very important to their self-esteem. Of course, this disidentification process does not have the negative impact on Whites' future career prospects as does Blacks' disidentification with academic achievement. Why? Because athletic performance, unlike academic performance, is seldom associated with career success in adulthood.

Question: How would social identity theory explain the relationship between "pride" and "prejudice"?

Possible Answer: There is a positive correlation between pride and prejudice. To indirectly increase or protect our own self-esteem, we try to bask in the reflected glory of our own group's esteem. To increase this group esteem, we may disparage and discriminate against other groups whose successes might reflect negatively on our own group's accomplishments. This intergroup process is psychologically identical to what we do in our interpersonal relationships when our friends are competing against other people for material and social rewards. In judging the competition, we tend to highlight our friends' good points and their competitors' bad points, while downplaying or forgetting our friends' bad points and their competitors' good points. In both cases, the result is that we actively construct a negative bias against other groups and individuals whose successes might indirectly threaten our own self-esteem.

Question: The terrorist attacks in the United States in 2001 greatly increased Americans' perceived social threat. Based on authoritarianism research, what type of social consequences might we see in this country due to this heightened threat? Further, how might this same research explain the mind-set and behavior of the terrorists?

Possible Answer: Authoritarianism research suggests that people with mild authoritarian tendencies may become more dogmatic and rigid in their social attitudes following such attacks. Thus, what we might expect from these people is a call for civil rights laws to be temporarily (or permanently) set aside to allow the government to identify and punish possible terrorists. President Bush implemented such a policy two months after the attacks when he announced that suspected foreign terrorists would be prosecuted in secret military tribunals rather than in civilian courts.

Authoritarian personalities will also generalize their outgroup prejudices toward groups within American culture that they perceive as "not real Americans." Due to their submission to established, legitimate authority figures, authoritarians are likely to severely criticize anyone who does not support the government's military or civil actions. When there is armed conflict with foreign countries, people with authoritarian tendencies are more likely to excuse atrocities committed by the United States.

Regarding the mind-set and actions of the terrorists, from news accounts it appears that they have a very rigid and dogmatic worldview. The popularity of this authoritarian mind-set in the Middle East may be substantially driven by the severe economic and physical hardships that the Arab people have endured for so many years. The prevalence of this authoritarian thinking does not bode well for any kind of negotiated settlement.

CHAPTER 9: SOCIAL INFLUENCE

Question: How might an individual's personality and behavior change as they gain or lose social power?

Possible Answer: If social power increases people's tendencies to take action, then as people gain power they should exhibit a decreased sensitivity to threats (Croizet & Claire, 1998). Their increased power should cause them to develop a more decisive behavioral style, marked by increased confi-

dence. Their personalities may become more extraverted and they may engage in a wider range of behaviors. They may now approach social situations looking more toward acquiring rewards rather than avoiding losses. What about those who lose power? If powerlessness activates a general tendency to inhibit action, then as people lose power they should show an increased sensitivity to threats. Their behavioral style should become indecisive, marked by decreased confidence. Likewise, their personalities may become more introverted, they may engage in a narrower range of behaviors, and they may approach situations looking to avoid losses rather than acquiring rewards.

Question: What variable could you introduce to the standard Asch research design to test the possibility that inducing public self-presentation concerns in your participants would increase nonconformity?

Possible Answer: Because nonconformity may increase when others not involved in the influence attempt are present, you could have an experimental condition in which nonparticipants observe the line judgment tasks. If public self-presentation concerns significantly influence conformity, then this condition should result in greater nonconformity than in the standard Asch condition. This effect should occur when the line judgments are clear and easy, but probably won't occur when judgments are ambiguous and difficult. Instead, because the presence of an audience also induces public self-awareness—which leads to greater conformity to social standards—it's possible that ambiguous and difficult judgmental tasks will lead to greater conformity than in the standard Asch condition.

Question: What is an alternative—or additional— interpretation of the findings from the Maass et al. (1982) experiment that relate to the chapter 7 discussion of gender differences in the effects of powerful speech on persuasion?

Possible Answer: Linda Carli's (1990) research found that women who use a powerful speaking style when trying to persuade men to change their attitudes may be less successful than male persuaders due to the male audience being "put off" by the assertive female persuader. It's possible that the "double minority" results in the Maass et al. Experiment are partly due to this gender bias effect. That is, the conservative male participants in this experiment are the sort of men who would most likely be defensive when listening to an assertive woman's persuasive message.

Question: How might the foot-in-the-door compliance strategy be combined with the effects of postdecision dissonance to partly explain how some people initially become involved and then committed to religious or political cults?

Possible Answer: In the foot-in-the-door strategy, a person who complies with a small request is more likely to later comply to a larger, less desirable request from the same person. Converts to cults are initially drawn to them by agreeing to read the cult's literature or agreeing to attend one meeting. The compliance with these small requests are used by cult members to secure even greater degrees of compliance later on. Of course, cult members also tend to act very warm and accepting toward possible recruits, thus making it more likely that they will want to seek greater ties to this group.

When the recruits do commit themselves to the cult, postdecision dissonance may exert its influence. Now, the attractive aspects of not joining and the unattractive aspects of joining are inconsistent with the decision to join the cult. Because this is viewed by new recruits as an important life decision, they will likely experience quite a bit of postdecision dissonance. According to cognitive dissonance theory, the new members will try to reduce the dissonance by only focusing on the positive aspects of the cult, while simultaneously focusing on only the negative aspects of their previous life. Other cult members, both new and old, will eagerly reinforce this sort of thinking—often because they too need to justify their own decision to join—and the new members' allegiance to the cult is immensely strengthened.

CHAPTER 10: GROUP BEHAVIOR

Question: In chapter 8 you learned how ingroup biases can lead to prejudice and discrimination. How might the knowledge of how ingroup biases can lead to prejudice and discrimination help you better understand the process by which the *diffuse status characteristics* of group members significantly determines their power in the group?

Possible Answer: When observing an ingroup member and an outgroup member performing the same task, performance evaluations will tend to be biased in favor of the ingroup member. This ingroup bias may manifest itself by people selectively remembering ingroup members' good behavior and outgroup members' bad behavior, or by selectively forgetting or trivializing ingroup members' bad behavior and outgroup members' good behavior. In a group, the ingroup biasing that will usually have the biggest consequences for how much power and status members individually attain is the biasing exhibited by those members who hold "gatekeeping" roles. Gatekeepers are usually high-status members who give other members access to similar high-status positions. Gatekeepers will tend to single out those members in the group whom they perceive to be "one of them." Often this means they will prefer members who are similar to them on such diffuse status characteristics as race, sex, age, and wealth.

Question: Imagine that you have been hired to design a training course to teach company employees how to efficiently use a complex computer program. How can you use the findings of social loafing research to design a training course that not only facilitates quick learning, but also encourages high productivity following learning?

Possible Answer: Research indicates that people can learn complex tasks more quickly when they believe their individual efforts are not being evaluated, such as when they are performing as part of a larger group. This is the type of situation that also often leads to social loafing on well-learned tasks. In both situations, group performance allows task outcome responsibility to be diffused among fellow coperformers. To facilitate employees learning a complex computer program, you could design the training so that their individual efforts are not evaluated. This could be accomplished by training employees in a group setting. Group coperformance should reduce their evaluation apprehension—and presumably their arousal—and allow them to more carefully concentrate on the task at hand.

Once the employees have mastered the computer program, you could then either monitor their individual performance to reduce social loafing, or—if you didn't want to be so Orwellian—you could simply allow them to monitor their own performance by providing them with individual performance feedback. Both strategies have been found to be effective in reducing social loafing.

Question: How could you use your knowledge of deindividuation when designing social environments to reduce crime?

Possible Answer: If it is true that anonymity serves as an accountability cue causing people to believe that they will not be held accountable for their actions, then environments should be designed to reduce feelings of anonymity. Large mirrors, bright lighting, and even the presence of surveillance cameras (even if they are nonfunctional) will make it much less likely that people will feel anonymous. Large mirrors and surveillance cameras will also induce public self-awareness, making it more likely that people will be attentive to social standards.

Question: Based on social influence research, what type of individuals might be more susceptible to group polarization effects when working on judgmental tasks?

Possible Answer: When the task is judgmental, people who are more concerned with how others will evaluate them will be more influenced by others' opinions. If they sense that the "socially acceptable" judgment is in a particular direction, they are likely to leapfrog over others to arrive at the most group-praiseworthy position. It's also possible that people with a high need for individuation—a desire to feel unique—may try to grab the most extreme position in the socially acceptable direction to "stand on top of the crowd."

CHAPTER 11: INTERPERSONAL ATTRACTION

Question: How many of your more important affiliation reasons for your lists can be identified as being primarily based on social comparison or social exchange needs? How are your three lists similar to or different from one another regarding social comparison and social exchange reasons?

This answer will be unique to your personal experiences.

Question: Immediately following the New York and Washington terrorist attacks, people around the country were highly anxious and uncertain about what was happening. How do you think information dependence and outcome dependence shaped their thoughts, feelings, and behavior during this time?

Possible Answer: Information dependence caused confused and anxious people to seek out one another so that they could gain an understanding of what was taking place. With this information, they could properly define and then respond to the unfolding events. Such information was most critical to individuals in the buildings attacked by the terrorists, because their lives depended on them correctly defining the situation as an emergency. Outcome dependence involves being dependent on others for rewards. While watching the horrendous events on television in the company of others, people may have monitored the expression of certain emotions (public displays of crying or prejudicial comments about Arab Americans) out of concern over how others might react. I know one person who watched news reports at work all day with coworkers despite not wanting to do so. Her explanation about why she did not walk away was that she was concerned that her colleagues would think of her as heartless if she left.

Question: How do the findings from the Snyder et al. (1977) experiment and the Anderson and Bem (1981) study relate to one of the basic messages of social psychology? Further, how can you generalize these findings beyond physical attractiveness effects to create a more pleasant and rewarding social world for yourself?

Possible Answer: One of the basic messages of social psychology is that we actively create and re-create our social reality. The better you understand the psychological dynamics of this social constructive process, the better equipped you will be to shape your reality in the manner you desire. In a larger sense, the findings from these two studies point out that if you treat other people as if they are attractive and a joy to be around, they not only will appreciate and seek out your company, but—if they weren't before—they are now more likely to become people who really are attractive and a joy to be around! This topic also relates to the "We like those who like us" discussion later in the chapter (p. 428).

Question: How has the similarity effect influenced your own personal relationships?

This answer will be unique to your personal experiences.

CHAPTER 12: INTIMATE RELATIONSHIPS

Question: What attachment style would you say the self-sufficient cowboy/action film characters most often represent? Is this an attachment style we should be placing in our male cultural role models?

Possible Answer: Securely attached adults easily become close to others, expect intimate relationships to endure, perceive others as generally trustworthy, and handle relationship conflict constructively. This type of an adult would be a very positive role model as a Hollywood movie figure. Unfortunately, this is definitely not how male cowboy/action film characters are typically portrayed. Thus, you already know that these characters are not the best role models for children and adults regarding intimate relationships. Yet it gets even worse. These male film characters represent the absolute worst attachment style for intimacy, namely, an avoidant one. Avoidant adults are uncomfortable with intimacy, have a hard time trusting others, and often express hostility during relationship conflicts. I guess that last difficulty would explain all the dead bodies that they leave in their wake. These cowboy/action characters sometimes tug at the audience's heartstrings by disclosing that "true love" is very hard to find and hold onto. Usually, there is a woman in their past who emotionally scarred them by either dying or rejecting them. Adults who watch these movies with children would be well advised to point out to the children afterward why Mr. Cowboy/Action Figure has such a hard time finding true love, and why imitation is not recommended.

Question: Is there an inherent conflict between individualist values and the interdependence necessary to maintain romantic love?

Possible Answer: Because individualists are raised to be autonomous and independent, perhaps they would have greater difficulty than collectivists maintaining an intimate relationship that is defined by partners depending on each other. The curious irony is that although individualists are more likely to marry due to romantic love, the way they've been socialized may make it less likely that their marriages will survive and their love will be nurtured. This is especially true for individualist males, who are most likely to be the ones socialized to be independent and relatively emotionally distant from others. However, because women are more likely socialized to be interdependent in their relations with other people, they may be best equipped to foster relationship success.

Question: If companionate love is more enduring than passionate love, how can you explain the findings that perceiving one's partner in somewhat ideal terms leads to greater romantic happiness than perceiving her/him realistically?

Possible Answer: The giddy, roller-coaster emotional ride associated with passionate love doesn't usually endure in a romantic relationship, but, rather, gives way to a more emotionally balanced form of romantic love, namely, companionate love. Passionate love can still exert its influence, but companionate love is the most influential. Yet, even with these romantic facts generally recognized, one manifestation of the importance of passion in an intimate relationship is revealed in the findings we are presently discussing. Put simply, those romantic relationships that have this "partner idealization" tendency appear to be the extra special romantic relationships, the ones that are perhaps closest to the enduring and happy relationships depicted in Hollywood movies (not necessarily including all the heavy breathing). They also would fall into the category that Sternberg (p. 462) calls "consummate love" and that Lee (p. 462) calls "agape" (altruistic love).

CHAPTER 13: AGGRESSION

Question: How might alcohol impair judgment and, thus, lead to the aggressive outbursts found in domestic violence cases?

Possible Answer: When people are intoxicated with alcohol, they are less likely to engage in self-awareness. Because self-awareness is necessary for self-regulation, and because self-regulation is part of the higher-level thinking necessary to control aggressive impulses, intoxication will make aggressive outbursts more likely.

Question: In addition to excitation transfer, how else might violence erupt among rival sports fans?

Possible Answer: One obvious factor is the negative affect sports fans experience following a bad turn of events for their team or an outright defeat. The aggressive tendencies sparked by this negative affect are less likely to be modified by higher-level thinking due to the fans' high arousal level. In addition, sporting events often take place outdoors in hot weather or indoors in hot, cramped facilities. Both arenas could heighten aggression due to the heat effect. Finally, avid sports fans strongly identify with their teams, and this social identity can lead to strong prejudices against the fans of rival teams, which can erupt into discriminatory violence.

Question: How could you use social psychological knowledge to reduce the likelihood of "road rage" on city streets and highways?

Possible Answer: You could employ Robert Baron's incompatible response strategy, in which you induce some emotional response in drivers that is likely to be incompatible with anger-induced aggression. Brooklyn, New York, employed this strategy by posting signs along the highway containing "knock-knock" jokes. You could also encourage radio stations with "happy" programming formats to advertise their dial numbers on billboards that drivers could see. Another way to use billboards would be to use the insights of social learning theory: remind adults that they are role models for children and how they behave while driving will be observed and learned by younger passengers and drivers. This strategy might engage higher-order cognitive processes in angry drivers—as proposed by Berkowitz's cognitive-neoassociationist model—so that their anger doesn't precipitate aggression.

CHAPTER 14: PROSOCIAL BEHAVIOR: HELPING OTHERS

Question: What sort of cultural role models might influence the "helping habits" of boys and girls? How might greater gender role flexibility influence male and female helping tendencies?

Possible Answer: Social modeling studies suggest that children are most likely to imitate the behavior of people with whom they strongly identify, and for most children, this means same-sex adults. Thus, to foster good helping habits in children, existing cultural role models for boys and girls could be enlisted to convey this message to children in public service announcements.

In Hollywood movies, most leading-male actors play the traditional masculine role of helping people in dangerous situations, while being rather unwilling or ineffective in providing more mundane, long-term help, such as caring for children and the elderly. The underlying message in many of these movies is that this kind of assistance is unmanly and less important. Yet, in everyday living, this form of help is needed far more frequently than dangerous helping.

In contrast, most leading-female actors play characters with less gender stereotyped roles. As such, they are often depicted as being willing to intervene in both dangerous situations and in those requiring nurturance and long-term care to needy others. This greater flexibility in helping responses reflects the greater gender flexibility available to women in contemporary culture. For instance, girls are generally allowed to engage in more nontraditional gender behavior than boys. As a result, you might expect that girls will learn to help in a wider variety of situations than boys.

Question: Following the terrorist attacks of September 11, 2001, liberal and conservative politicians did not differ in endorsing massive economic assistance to New York City. Does this unified response contradict Skitka's research findings?

Possible Answer: First, it is always difficult to predict how individuals or groups will respond to specific events, even when guided by research findings that suggest that certain behaviors are more likely when certain conditions are met. Having restated this cautionary note about scientific research, the terrorist attacks differ significantly from the type of disasters Skitka studied. While Skitka's research examined how liberals and conservatives responded to the victims of natural disasters, the terrorist attacks were by no means "natural." The widespread belief by both liberal and conservative politicians was that the terrorist victims were innocent of any blame in the disaster, they could not have anticipated its occurrence, and they were now dependent upon others for assistance. Here, both the social responsibility and the social justice norms were strongly salient. In such a scenario, social psychological research would predict that political differences are unlikely. Thus, the response to this event does not appear to contradict Skitka's research findings.

Question: Do you think you would find these same bystander effects among people whose jobs regularly deal with helping others? How might you test whether the situational context or the salience of their "helping" social roles would influence their tendency to intervene?

Possible Answer: You probably would not find the same degree of bystander effects among nurses, doctors, and police officers because their experience and skill at handling emergencies would make it less likely that they would (1) worry about overreacting in possible emergency situations and (2) assume that other bystanders have as much responsibility to help as them. It's likely that their tendency to diffuse responsibility would be further reduced if their "helping" social roles were currently salient to them, because they would be even more aware of the social norms regarding helping for their occupations. It's also likely that doctors' and nurses' willingness to help will be greater in those situations in which their occupations best prepare them, namely, emergencies involving medical attention. However, because police officers are trained to intervene in both physically dangerous and medical emergencies, it's likely that there would be few differences in their willingness to respond. You might test these hypotheses in an experiment by having doctors, nurses, and police officers participate in a typical bystander intervention study, but (1) vary the degree to which their occupations are socially salient, and (2) vary the type of emergency (medical or physical endangerment) that they witness.

Question: How could you design a donation pitch to members of a local community center to help starving people in a foreign country, knowing that some message receivers will react with empathy, while others will react with personal distress?

Possible Answer: First, you want to convey an emotionally arousing message concerning how desperately these people need the audience's help. For those individuals who experience empathy, you can simply ask for their donations. However, for those who experience personal distress, you have to deal with the fact that they will try to escape the situation to reduce their distress. Thus, you need to make it difficult for them to escape the distress without donating money. You might set up your talk so that it precedes a dinner or event that everyone in attendance generally enjoys. Then, inform the audience that the enjoyable event will commence as soon as the donations reach a specified amount. This scenario is admittedly heavy-handed, but it should induce those who are experiencing personal distress to help in order to facilitate their own escape from this unpleasantly arousing situation.

APPENDIX B

THE PROFESSION OF SOCIAL PSYCHOLOGY

At this point, some of you might be wondering how people become social psychologists and where they typically find employment today. Actually, there is no simple answer to either question, but let's briefly explore the typical path to a career in social psychology.

BECOMING A SOCIAL PSYCHOLOGIST

The vast majority of today's social psychologists majored in psychology as undergraduates. In their senior year many of them then applied to graduate programs in social psychology or social/personality psychology (sometimes these two areas of study are merged). Although master's degree programs do exist, almost all psychologists who identify themselves as social psychologists have a Ph.D. Earning a doctorate in social psychology generally takes at least four years of graduate training and entails extensive coursework in theory, statistics, and research methodology.

In graduate school, budding social psychologists often begin specializing in a particular area of the discipline, such as attitude change, social influence, or self-esteem. They then create a *research program* in which hypotheses are systematically tested and theories developed or extended. The graduate student's dissertation generally represents the clearest articulation of this research program. Often the dissertation builds on the research program of the more experienced social psychologists who trained the graduate student. Once social psychologists earn a Ph.D., they either seek employment in their profession or go on for further training. This *postdoctoral training,* if pursued, is often made possible by government-sponsored research grants offered at various universities. In these postdoctoral programs, social psychologists continue to develop their research programs and gain greater expertise in their field of specialization.

WHO EMPLOYS THE SOCIAL PSYCHOLOGIST?

Although becoming an expert in one's chosen field has its own intrinsic rewards, most people would lose sight of these inner perks if there was no accompanying job. Let's spend some time on the all-important second question of employment possibilities for the social psychologist. The answer to this question depends, to a great extent, on whether the work of the social psychologist is mainly geared toward theory testing and knowledge advancement or whether it entails mostly applying such knowledge to real-life situations. Most of the social psychologists with Ph.D.s—roughly 75 percent—are employed by colleges or universities. There, social psychologists spend the majority of their time conducting basic re-search, teaching undergraduates about their discipline's insights, and training future social psychologists in their graduate programs. It is in these academic pursuits that the knowledge base of the field is principally developed.

Once enough has been learned about a specific topic that is relevant to current problems in society, academic social psychologists may attempt to apply this knowledge to promote human welfare. This wedding of basic and applied scientific interests and activities was first championed by Kurt Lewin in the 1940s (see chapter 1, p. 9). What he called *action research* combines basic theoretical research and social action in a coordinated program. Although in recent years academic social psychologists have shown an increased interest in such action research, in general, it does not dominate the daily schedule of the average academician.

Those social psychologists who devote most of their energies to applying their knowledge of social behavior to real-life situations are much more likely to be employed outside academic settings. Instead of trying to primarily develop theories of social behavior as academic social psychologists often do, nonacademic applied social psychologists typically utilize already formulated theories to effect changes in the social world. Listed below are brief descriptions of seven of the more prominent applied areas where academic action researchers and nonacademic applied social psychologists are working and having an impact.

Crime and the legal system: Up until about thirty years ago, the only psychologists regularly consulted by the courts were clinical psychologists. However, since the mid-1970s an increasing number of social psychologists have studied and applied their knowledge to many different aspects of the legal system. Some of their primary areas of contribution have been in better understanding police interrogation, jury selection and decision making, eyewitness testimony, legal bargaining and negotiation, and the fairness of bail-setting and sentencing procedures (see Applications, chapters 9 and 10).

Health and health care: Most of the diseases that lead to deaths in our society are largely caused by human behaviors. As the discipline that analyzes the dynamic interplay between the person and the situation, social psychology is uniquely qualified to assist people in changing their unhealthy lifestyles. Currently, social psychological work on health behavior emphasizes three different approaches: (1) applying existing theories to health problems (for example, the *theory of planned behavior,* see pp. 191-194), (2) developing new theories specifically to solve health problems (for example, *protection-motivation theory,* see p. 221) and (3) identifying specific social and personality factors that affect health (for example, *optimistic and pessimistic explanatory style,* see pp. 161-164).

Counseling and mental health: Social psychology shares a great deal of common ground with both counseling and clinical psychology. In recent years, a growing number of social psychologists have begun working with both clinical and counseling psychologists—or have actually received training in clinical or counseling psychology—in an attempt to better understand the social psychology of mental health. As with general health care already described, social psychological work on mental health emphasizes applying existing theories to health problems (see Applications in chapter 3), developing new theories specifically to solve health problems (see Applications in chapter 11), and identifying specific social and personality factors that affect mental health (see Applications in chapter 12).

Organizational behavior: More than 90 percent of the people living in the United States will work for an organization during their lifetime. From personnel selection and training to leadership and labor-management relations, social psychology has greatly contributed to the understanding and improvement of organizational functioning. Some of the topics studied by applied social psychologists in organizational settings involve group structure and leadership (see pp. 383-385), the phases of membership (see pp. 360-362), participative management, and job satisfaction.

Education and learning: Dating back to the famous 1954 Supreme Court school desegregation case, *Brown v. Board of Education,* in which many eminent social psychologists provided expert testimony (Clark & Clark, 1947; Stephan, 1980), the discipline has played an important role in understanding the social variables that can facilitate and impede learning. Some of the important areas of contribution have been in understanding classroom self-fulfilling prophecies (see pp. 156-159), the benefits of cooperative learning, and how to educate students with differing abilities.

Environmental effects: Largely an offshoot of social psychology, *environmental psychology* studies the interactions and relations between people and their environments. Traditionally, most of the work in this area has emphasized how the physical environment influences people's thoughts, feelings, and behavior (see *temperature and aggression,* p. 502). However, more recent work has examined how human actions can affect the environment (refer to *social dilemmas,* pp. 388-391).

Politics and public policy: Social psychologists have worked to gain insight into the political process by studying such topics as political reference groups (see Applications, chapter 6), negative campaigning, and international negotiating. In relation to directly influencing public policy, some social psychologists adopt an *advocacy role*—speaking and working for particular social reforms—by using their expertise to mobilize legislators, courts, or disadvantaged groups to enact social changes. Some areas where social psychologists have attempted—with varying degrees of success—to influence public policy has been in pornography (see pp. 513-519), gun control (see p. 503), school desegregation (see p. 302), and hate-crime legislation.

NEW CONNECTIONS

Regardless of whether social psychologists work in an applied setting or a university environment, their ultimate goal is to use the scientific discipline's body of knowledge to improve the quality of people's lives. Two very interesting new connections that are developing in the twenty-first century are with the fields of social neuroscience and computer science:

Social neuroscience: As outlined throughout this textbook, social psychology is developing increasing integrative efforts with biology. A growing body of research and theory in social psychology is exploring how neural activity in the brain is associated with a number of social psychological processes, including self-awareness, self-regulation, attitude formation and change, and prejudice. Similarly, recent studies are also revealing insights into the psychobiology underlying the influences of positive affect on motivated cognition (Ashby et al., 1999; Miller & Keller, 2000). This increased collaboration between social psychology and neuroscience is largely due to the development of more accurate measures of physiological changes. Although the numbers of social psychologists who pursue such research is still relatively small, the knowledge they acquire concerning the biology of social behavior will undoubtedly play a role in reshaping existing theories.

Computer science: The Internet and other electronic communication media are altering the way we interact and influence one another. Social psychological theory and research in such areas as group dynamics and interpersonal attraction will provide much needed insights into knowledge networking in the computer sciences. For example, how might access to the Internet both promote and reduce feelings of loneliness? Similarly, how can videoconferencing be made more effective? What social formats are good for such meetings? To what degree will these "virtual groups" operate according to the same social psychological principles as normal groups? Social psychologists are in a unique position to explore these questions.

As you can see, social psychology continues to expand its areas of inquiry, developing more sophisticated methods and theories that hopefully will provide greater insights into the social process. For those of you who might be interested in obtaining more information about graduate programs and career opportunities in social psychology, contact the Society for Personality and Social Psychology (SPSP) and the American Psychological Association (APA) through their web sites.

 WEB SITES

Society for Personality and Social Psychology (SPSP)

The Society for Personality and Social Psychology (SPSP) offers a Web site for those who might be interested in obtaining more information about graduate programs and career opportunities in social psychology. Membership in SPSP is open to students as well as professionals—anyone interested in social psychology and personality is welcome to join.

American Psychological Association (APA)

The American Psychological Association offers a Web page containing suggestions on career planning in psychology, including what are the typical salaries in psychology and what nonacademic careers are available to people.

GLOSSARY

A

Acquaintance Rape
Forced sexual intercourse that occurs either on a date or between people who are acquainted or romantically involved. Also known as date rape.

Actor-Observer Effect
The tendency for people to attribute their own behavior to external causes but that of others to internal factors.

Aggression
Any form of behavior that is intended to harm or injure some person, oneself, or an object.

Aggressive Scripts
Guides for behavior and problem solving that are developed and stored in memory and are characterized by aggression.

Altruistic Helping
A form of helping in which the ultimate goal of the helper is to increase another's welfare without expecting anything in return.

Ambivalent Sexism
Sexism directed against women based on both positive and negative attitudes (*hostility* and *benevolence*), rather than uniform dislike.

Anchoring and Adjustment Heuristic
A tendency to be biased toward the starting value or anchor in making quantitative judgments.

Anticonformity
Opposition to social influence on all occasions, often caused by psychological reactance.

Applied Research
Research designed to increase the understanding of and solutions to real-world problems by using current social psychological knowledge.

Archival Research
A descriptive scientific method in which already-existing records are examined.

Arousal: Cost-Reward Model
A theory that helping or not helping is a function of emotional arousal and analysis of the costs and rewards of helping.

Attachment
The strong emotional bond between an infant and a caregiver.

Attitude
A positive or negative evaluation of an object.

Attribution
The process by which people use information to make inferences about the causes of behavior or events.

Audience Inhibition Effect
People are inhibited from helping for fear that other bystanders will evaluate them negatively if they intervene and the situation is not an emergency.

Authoritarian Personality
A personality trait characterized by submissiveness to authority, rigid adherence to conventional values, and prejudice toward outgroups.

Availability Heuristic
The tendency to judge the frequency or probability of an event in terms of how easy it is to think of examples of that event.

Aversive Racism
Attitudes toward members of a racial group that incorporate both egalitarian social values and negative emotions, causing one to avoid interaction with members of the group.

B

Balance Theory
A theory that people desire cognitive consistency or balance in their thoughts, feelings, and social relationships.

Basic Research
Research designed to increase knowledge about social behavior.

Belief
An estimate of the probability that something is true.

Body Esteem
A person's attitudes toward his or her body.

Bystander Intervention Model
A theory that whether bystanders intervene in an emergency is a function of a five-step decision-making process.

C

Category
A mental grouping of objects, ideas, or events that share common properties. Also known as concept.

Catharsis
The reduction in the aggressive drive following an aggressive act.

Central Route to Persuasion
Persuasion that occurs when people think carefully about a communication and are influenced by the strength of its arguments.

Central Traits
Traits that exert a disproportionate influence on people's overall impressions, causing them to assume the presence of other traits.

Cerebral Cortex
The wrinkled-looking outer layer of the brain that coordinates and integrates all other brain areas into a fully functioning unit. This is the brain's "thinking" center, and is much larger in humans than in other animals.

Characterization-Correction Model
A dual-process model that contends we initially automatically characterize people's behavior as being caused by dispositional factors and then later correct attribution to better account for situational factors.

Classical Conditioning
Learning through association, when a neutral stimulus (conditioned stimulus) is paired with a stimulus (unconditioned stimulus) that naturally produces an emotional response.

Cognitive Consistency
The tendency to seek consistency in one's cognitions.

Cognitive Dissonance
A feeling of discomfort caused by performing an action that is inconsistent with one's attitudes.

Cognitive-Neoassociationist Model
A theory of impulsive aggression that aversive events produce negative affect, which stimulates the inclination to aggress.

Collectivism
A philosophy of life stressing the priority of group needs over individual needs, a preference for tightly knit social relationships, and a willingness to submit to the influence of one's group.

Companionate Love
The affection we feel for those with whom our lives are deeply entwined.

Compliance
Publicly acting in accord with a direct request.

Confederate
An accomplice of an experimenter whom research participants assume is a fellow participant or bystander.

Confirmation Bias
The tendency to seek information that supports our beliefs while ignoring disconfirming information.

Conformity
A yielding to perceived group pressure.

Contact Hypothesis
The theory that under certain conditions, direct contact between antagonistic groups will reduce prejudice.

Contingency Model of Leadership
The theory that leadership effectiveness depends both on whether leaders are task oriented or relationship oriented, and on the degree to which they have situational control.

Control Theory of Self-Regulation
A theory contending that, through self-awareness, people compare their behavior to a standard, and if there is a discrepancy, they work to reduce it.

Correlation Coefficient
A statistical measure of the direction and strength of the linear relationship between two variables, which can range from −1.00 to +1.00.

Correlational Research
Research designed to examine the nature of the relationship between two or more naturally occurring variables.

Correspondent Inference
An inference that the action of an actor corresponds to, or is indicative of, a stable personal characteristic.

Counterfactual Thinking
The tendency to evaluate events by imagining alternative versions or outcomes to what actually happened.

Courtesy Stigma
The tendency for individuals who are associated with stigmatized people to face negative evaluations from others.

Covariation Principle
A principle of attribution theory stating that for something to be the cause of a particular behavior, it must be present when the behavior occurs and absent when it does not occur.

Cultural Frame Switching
The process by which biculturalists switch between different culturally appropriate behaviors depending on the context.

Culture
The total lifestyle of a people from a particular social grouping, including all the ideas, symbols, preferences, and material objects that they share.

Culture of Honor
A belief system in which males are socialized to protect their reputation by resorting to violence.

D

Debriefing
A procedure at the conclusion of a research session in which participants are given full information about the nature and hypotheses of the study.

Deception
A research technique that provides false information to persons participating in a study.

Deindividuation
The loss of a sense of individual identity and a loosening of normal inhibitions against engaging in behavior that is inconsistent with internal standards.

Delegitimization
The process of cognitively placing an outgroup into an extremely negative social category that excludes them from acceptable norms and values, thereby eliminating inhibitions against harming them.

Dependent Variable
The experimental variable that is measured because it is believed to depend on the manipulated changes in the independent variable.

Diffusion of Responsibility
The belief that the presence of other people in a situation makes one less personally responsible for the events that occur in that situation.

Discounting Principle
A principle of attribution theory stating that whenever there are several possible causal explanations for a particular event, people tend to be much less likely to attribute the effect to any particular cause.

Discrimination
A negative action toward members of a specific social group.

Dismissing-Avoidant Attachment Style
An expectation about social relationships characterized by low trust and avoidance of intimacy, combined with high self-esteem and compulsive self-reliance.

Door-in-the-Face Technique
A two-step compliance technique in which, after having a large request refused, the influencer counteroffers with a much smaller request.

Dual Attitudes
The simultaneous possession of contradictory implicit and explicit attitudes toward the same object.

Dual-Process Models of Social Cognition
Theories of social cognition which propose that people employ two broad cognitive strategies to understand and respond to social stimuli, one involving effortless thinking and the other involving effortful thinking.

E

Egoistic Helping
A form of helping in which the ultimate goal of the helper is to increase his or her own welfare.

Elaboration Likelihood Model
A theory that persuasive messages can cause attitude change in two ways, each differing in the amount of cognitive effort or elaboration it requires.

Embarrassment
An unpleasant emotion experienced when we believe that others have good reason to think a flaw has been revealed in us.

Empathy
A feeling of compassion and tenderness upon viewing a victim's plight.

Empathy-Altruism Hypothesis
A theory proposing that experiencing empathy for someone in need produces an altruistic motive for helping.

Equity Theory
The theory that people are most satisfied in a relationship when the ratio between rewards and costs is similar for both partners.

Ethnic Identity
An individual's sense of personal identification with a particular ethnic group.

Ethnocentrism
A pattern of increased hostility toward outgroups accompanied by increased loyalty to one's ingroup.

Evolution
The genetic change due to natural selection.

Evolutionary Psychology
An approach to psychology based on the principle of natural selection.

Excitation Transfer
A psychological process in which arousal caused by one stimulus is transferred and added to arousal elicited by a second stimulus.

Expectation States Theory
A theory that states that the development of group status is based on members' expectations of others' probable contributions to the achievement of group goals. These expectations are shaped not only by members' *task-relevant characteristics* but also by *diffuse-state characteristics,* such as race, sex, age, and wealth.

Experimental Methods
Research designed to test cause-effect relationships between variables.

Explicit Attitude
A consciously held attitude.

Explicit Cognition
Deliberate judgments or decisions of which we are consciously aware.

Explicit Prejudice
Prejudicial attitudes that are consciously held, even if they are not publicly expressed.

Explicit Self-Esteem
A person's conscious and deliberate evaluation of his or her self-concept.

External Attribution
An attribution that locates the cause of an event to factors external to the person, such as luck, or other people, or the situation.

External Validity
The extent to which a study's findings can be generalized to people beyond those in the study itself.

F

False Consensus Effect
The tendency to overestimate how common one's own attitudes, opinions, and beliefs are in the general population.

False Uniqueness Effect
The tendency to underestimate how common one's own desirable traits and abilities are in the general population.

Fearful-Avoidant Attchment Style
An expectation about social relationships characterized by low trust and avoidance of intimacy, combined with a feeling of being unworthy of others' love and a fear of rejection.

Foot-in-the-Door Technique
A two-step compliance technique in which the influencer secures compliance to a small request, and then later follows this with a larger, less desirable request.

Frontal Lobe
The region of the cerebral cortex situated just behind the forehead that is involved in the coordination of movement and higher mental processes, such as planning, social skills, and abstract thinking. This is the area of the brain that is the originator of self processes.

Frustration-Aggression Hypothesis
The theory that frustration causes aggression.

Functional Approach
Attitude theories that emphasize that people develop and change their attitudes based on the degree to which they satisfy different psychological needs. To change an attitude, one must understand the underlying function that attitude serves.

Fundamental Attribution Error
The tendency to overestimate the impact of dispositional causes and underestimate the impact of situational causes on other people's behavior.

G

Gender Identity
The knowledge that one is a male or a female and the internalization of this fact into one's self-concept.

Gender Schema
A cognitive structure for processing information based on its perceived male or female qualities.

Genes
The biochemical units of inheritance for all living organisms.

Group
Two or more people who interact with and influence one another over a period of time, and who depend on one another and share common goals and a collective identity.

Group Polarization
Group-produced enhancement or exaggeration of members' initial attitudes through discussion.

Groupthink
A deterioration of mental efficiency, reality testing, and moral judgment in a group that results from an excessive desire to reach consensus.

H

Heterosexism
A system of cultural beliefs, values, and customs that exalts heterosexuality and denies, denigrates, and stigmatizes any nonheterosexual form of behavior or identity.

Heuristics
Timesaving mental shortcuts that reduce complex judgments to simple rules of thumb.

Hindsight Bias
The tendency, once an event has occurred, to overestimate our ability to have foreseen the outcome.

Hostile Aggression
The intentional use of harmful behavior in which the goal is simply to cause injury or death to the victim.

Hypotheses
Specific propositions or expectations about the nature of things derived from a theory.

I

Ideology
A set of beliefs and values held by the members of a social group, which explains its culture both to itself and to other groups.

Idiosyncrasy Credits
Interpersonal influence that a leader earns by helping the group achieve task goals and by conforming to group norms.

Illusory Correlation
The belief that two variables are associated with each other when in fact there is little or no actual association.

Implicit Association Test (IAT)
A technique for measuring implicit attitudes and beliefs based on the idea that people will give faster responses to presented concepts that are more strongly associated in memory.

Implicit Attitude
An attitude that is activated automatically from memory, often without the person's awareness that she or he possesses it.

Implicit Cognition
Judgments or decisions that are under the control of automatically activated evaluations occurring without our awareness.

Implicit Personality Theory
Assumptions or naive belief systems people make about which personality traits and behaviors go together.

Implicit Prejudice
Unconsciously held prejudicial attitudes.

Implicit Self-Esteem
A person's unconscious and unintentional evaluation of his or her self-concept.

Impression Formation
The process by which one integrates various sources of information about another into an overall judgment.

Independence
Not being subject to control by others.

Independent Self
A way of conceiving the self in terms of unique, personal attributes and as a being that is separate and autonomous from the group.

Independent Variable
The experimental variable that the researcher manipulates.

Individualism
A philosophy of life stressing the priority of individual needs over group needs, a preference for loosely knit social relationships, and a desire to be relatively autonomous of others' influence.

Informational Social Influence
Conformity, compliance, or obedience based on a desire to gain information (information dependence).

Informed Consent
A procedure by which people freely choose to participate in a study only after

they are told about the activities they will perform.

Ingroup
A group to which we belong and that forms a part of our social identity.

Ingroup Bias
The tendency to give more favorable evaluations and greater rewards to ingroup members than to outgroup members.

Institutional Review Boards (IRBs)
A panel of scientists and nonscientists who ensure the protection and welfare of research participants by formally reviewing researchers' methodologies and procedures prior to data collection.

Instrumental Aggression
The intentional use of harmful behavior so that one can achieve some other goal.

Interaction Effect
An experimental result that occurs when two independent variables in combination have different effects on the dependent variable than when alone.

Interactionism
An important perspective in social psychology that emphasizes the combined effects of both the person and the situation on human behavior.

Interdependent Self
A way of conceiving the self in terms of social roles and as a being that is embedded in and dependent on the group.

Intergroup Anxiety
Anxiety due to anticipating negative consequences when interacting with an outgroup member.

Internal Attribution
An attribution that locates the cause of an event to factors internal to the person, such as personality traits, moods, attitudes, abilities, or effort.

Internal Validity
The extent to which cause-and-effect conclusions can validly be made in a study.

Interpersonal Attraction
The desire to approach another individual.

Intimacy
Sharing that which is inmost with others.

J

Jealousy
The negative emotional reaction experienced when a relationship that is important to a person's self-concept is threatened by a real or imagined rival.

Jigsaw Classroom
A cooperative group-learning technique designed to reduce prejudice and raise self-esteem.

Just-World Belief
A belief that the world is a fair and equitable place, with people getting what they deserve in life.

K

Kin Selection
A theory that people will exhibit preferences for helping blood relatives because this will increase the odds that their genes will be transmitted to subsequent generations.

L

Leader
The person who exerts the most influence on group behavior and beliefs.

Learned Helplessness
The passive resignation produced by repeated exposure to negative events that are perceived to be unavoidable.

Loneliness
Having a smaller or less satisfactory network of social and intimate relationships than one desires.

Low-Ball Technique
A two-step compliance strategy in which the influencer secures agreement with a request by understanding its true cost.

M

Matching Hypothesis
The proposition that people are attracted to others who are similar to them in particular characteristics, such as attitudes and physical attractiveness.

Mere Exposure Effect
The tendency to develop more positive feelings toward objects and individuals the more we are exposed to them.

Meta-Analysis
A statistical technique for combining information from many studies to objectively determine whether specific variables have important effects across these studies.

Minority Influence
The process by which dissenters produce change within a group.

Minority Slowness Effect
The tendency of those who hold a minority opinion to express that opinion less quickly than people who hold the majority opinion.

Misattribution of Arousal
A situation in which the explanation of the physiological symptoms of arousal is

switched from the real source to another one.

Motivated-Tactician Model
An approach to social cognition that conceives of people as being flexible social thinkers who choose among multiple cognitive strategies based on their current goals, motives, and needs.

N

Natural Selection
The process by which organisms with inherited traits best suited to the environment reproduce more successfully than less well-adapted organisms over a number of years. Natural selection leads to evolutionary changes.

Naturalistic Observation
A form of observational method that investigates behavior in its natural environment.

Need for Cognition
An individual preference for and tendency to engage in effortful cognitive activities.

Negative State Relief Model
A theory suggesting that for those in a bad mood, helping others may be a way to lift their own spirits if the perceived benefits for helping are high and the costs are low.

Negativity Effect
The tendency for negative traits to be weighted more heavily than positive traits in impression formation.

Nonconscious Mimicry
The tendency to adopt the behaviors, postures, or mannerisms of interaction partners without conscious awareness or intention.

Nonverbal Behavior
Communicating feelings and intentions without words.

Norm of Social Justice
A social norm stating that we should help only when we believe that others deserve our assistance.

Norm of Social Responsibility
A social norm stating that we should help when others are in need and dependent on us.

Normative Social Influence
Conformity, compliance, or obedience based on a desire to gain rewards or avoid punishments (outcome dependence).

O

Obedience
The performance of an action in response to a direct order.

Observational Research
A scientific method involving systematic qualitative and/or quantitative descriptions of behavior.

Observer Bias
Occurs when preconceived ideas held by the researcher affect the nature of the observations made.

Old-Fashioned Racism
Blatantly negative stereotypes based on White racial superiority, coupled with open opposition to racial equality.

Operant Conditioning
A type of learning in which behavior is strengthened if followed by reinforcement and weakened if followed by punishment.

Operational Definition
A scientist's precise description of how a variable has been quantified so that it can be measured.

Optimistic Explanatory Style
A habitual tendency to attribute negative events to external, unstable, and specific causes, and positive events to internal, stable, and global causes.

Outgroup
Any group with which we do not share membership.

Outgroup Homogeneity Effect
Perception of outgroup members as being more similar to one another than are members of one's ingroup.

P

Participant Observation
A descriptive scientific method where a group is studied from within by a researcher who records behavior as it occurs in its usual natural environment.

Passionate Love
A state of intense longing for union with another.

Peripheral Route to Persuasion
Persuasion that occurs when people do not think carefully about a communication and instead are influenced by cues that are irrelevant to the content or quality of the communication.

Person Perception
The process by which we come to know about other people's temporary states and enduring dispositions (also called *social perception*).

Personal Distress
An unpleasant state of arousal in which people are preoccupied with their own emotions of anxiety, fear, or helplessness upon viewing a victim's plight.

Persuasion
The process of consciously attempting to change attitudes through the transmission of some message.

Pessimistic Explanatory Style
A habitual tendency to attribute negative events to internal, stable, and global causes, and positive events to external, unstable, and specific causes.

Physical Attractiveness Stereotype
The belief that physically attractive individuals possess socially desirable personality traits and lead happier lives than less attractive persons.

Population
All the members of an identifiable group from which a sample is drawn.

Pornography
The combination of sexual material with abuse or degradation in a manner that appears to endorse, condone, or encourage such behavior.

Positivity Bias
The tendency for people to evaluate individual human beings more positively than groups or impersonal objects.

Prejudice
Attitudes toward members of specific groups that directly or indirectly suggest they deserve an inferior social status.

Preoccupied Attachment Style
An expectation about social relationships characterized by trust but combined with a feeling of being unworthy of others' love and a fear of abandonment.

Primacy Effect
The tendency for the first information received to carry more weight than later information on one's overall impression.

Priming
The process by which recent exposure to certain stimuli or events increases the accessibility of certain memories, categories, or schemas.

Prosocial Behavior
Voluntary behavior that is carried out to benefit another person.

Protection-Motivation Theory
A theory proposing that fear induces both a self-protective response and an appraisal of whether the fear-arousing threat can be avoided.

Prototype
The most representative member of a category.

R

Random Assignment
Placement of research participants into experimental conditions in a manner that guarantees that all have an equal chance of being exposed to each level of the independent variable.

Random Selection
A procedure for selecting a sample of people to study in which everyone in the population has an equal chance of being chosen.

Rape Myth
The false belief that, deep down, women enjoy forcible sex and find it sexually exciting.

Realistic Group Conflict Theory
The theory that intergroup conflict develops from competition for limited resources.

Recency Effect
The tendency for the last information received to carry greater weight than earlier information.

Reciprocal Helping
(Also known as reciprocal altruism.) An evolutionary principle stating that people expect that anyone helping another will have that favor returned at some future time.

Reciprocity Norm
The expectation that one should return a favor or a good deed.

Reference Group
A group to which people orient themselves, using its standards to judge themselves and the world.

Replication
Repeating a study using different participants in an attempt to duplicate previous findings.

Representativeness Heuristic
The tendency to judge the category membership of things based on how closely they match the "typical" or "average" member of that category.

S

Sample
A group of people who are selected to participate in a research study.

Schema
A schema is an organized structure of knowledge about a stimulus that is built up from experience and that contains causal relations; it is a theory about how the social world operates.

Scientific Method
A set of procedures used to gather, analyze, and interpret information in a way that reduces error and leads to dependable generalizations.

Script
A schema that describes how a series of events is likely to occur in a well-known situation, and which is used as a guide for behavior and problem solving.

Secure Attachment Style
An expectation about social relationships characterized by trust, a lack of concern with being abandoned, and a feeling of being valued and well liked.

Self
A symbol-using individual who can reflect on his/her own behavior.

Self-Affirmation Theory
A theory predicting that people will often cope with specific threats to their self-esteem by reminding themselves of other unrelated but cherished aspects of their self-concept.

Self-Awareness
A psychological state in which one takes oneself as an object of attention.

Self-Concept
The sum total of a person's thoughts and feelings that defines the self as an object.

Self-Consciousness
The habitual tendency to engage in self-awareness.

Self-Disclosure
The revealing of personal information about oneself to other people.

Self-Discrepancies
Discrepancies between our self-concept and how we would ideally like to be (*ideal self*) or believe others think we should be (*ought self*).

Self-Enhancement
The process of seeking out and interpreting situations so as to attain a positive view of oneself.

Self-Esteem
A person's evaluation of his or her self-concept.

Self-Evaluation Maintenance Model
A theory predicting under what conditions people are likely to react to the success of others with either pride or jealousy.

Self-Fulfilling Prophecy
The process by which someone's expectations about a person or group leads to the fulfillment of those expectations.

Self-Handicapping
Actions that people take to sabotage their performance and enhance their opportunity to excuse anticipated failure.

Self-Monitoring
The tendency to use cues from other people's self-presentations in controlling one's own self-presentations.

Self-Perception Theory
The theory that we often infer our internal states, such as our attitudes, by observing our behavior.

Self-Regulation
The ways in which people control and direct their own actions.

Self-Schema
A cognitive structure that represents how you think about yourself in a particular domain and how you organize your experiences in that domain.

Self-Serving Bias
The tendency to assign an internal locus of causality for our positive outcomes and an external locus for our negative outcomes.

Self-Verification
The process of seeking out and interpreting situations so as to confirm one's self-concept.

Sexism
Any attitude, action, or institutional structure that subordinates a person because of her or his sex.

Sexual Harassment
Unwelcome physical or verbal sexual overtures that create an intimidating, hostile, or offensive social environment.

Sleeper Effect
The delayed effectiveness of a persuasive message from a noncredible source.

Social Anxiety
The unpleasant emotion people experience due to their concern with interpersonal evaluation.

Social Categorization
The process of forming categories of people based on their common attributes.

Social Cognition
The way in which we interpret, analyze, remember, and use information about the social world.

Social Comparison Theory
The theory that proposes that we evaluate our thoughts and actions by comparing them to those of others.

Social Desirability Bias
A type of response bias in surveys in which people respond to a question by trying to portray themselves in a favorable light rather than responding in an accurate and truthful manner.

Social Dilemma
Any situation in which the most rewarding short-term choice for an individual will ultimately cause negative consequences for the group as a whole.

Social Dominance Theory
A theory contending that societal groups can be organized in a power hierarchy in which the dominant groups enjoy a disproportionate share of the society's assets and the subordinate groups receive most of its liabilities.

Social Exchange Theory
The theory that proposes that we seek out and maintain those relationships in which the rewards exceed the costs.

Social Facilitation
The enhancement of dominant responses due to the presence of others.

Social Identities
Aspects of a person's self-concept based on his or her group memberships.

Social Identity Theory
A theory suggesting that people seek to enhance their self-esteem by identifying with specific social groups and perceiving these groups as being better than other groups

Social Impact Theory
The theory that the amount of social influence others have depends on their number, strength, and immediacy to those they are trying to influence.

Social Influence
The exercise of social power by a person or group to change the attitudes or behavior of others in a particular direction.

Social Learning Theory
A theory that social behavior is primarily learned by observing and imitating the actions of others, and secondarily by being directly rewarded and punished for our own actions.

Social Loafing
Group-induced reduction in individual output when performers' efforts are pooled, and thus, cannot be individually judged.

Social Neuroscience
The study of the relationship between neural processes of the brain and social processes.

Social Norm
An expected standard of behavior and belief established and enforced by a group.

Social Penetration Theory
A theory that describes the development of close relationships in terms of increasing self-disclosure.

Social Power
The force available to the influencer to motivate attitude or behavior change.

Social Psychology
The scientific discipline that attempts to understand and explain how the thought, feeling, and behavior of individuals are influenced by the actual, imagined, or implied presence of others.

Social Role
A cluster of socially defined expectations that individuals in a given situation are expected to fulfill.

Social Role Theory
The theory that virtually all of the documented behavioral differences between males and females can be accounted for in terms of cultural stereotypes about gender and the resulting social roles that are taught to the young.

Social Skills Training
A behavioral training program designed to improve interpersonal skills through observation, modeling, role playing, and behavioral rehearsal.

Stereotype
Beliefs about people that put them into categories and don't allow for individual variation.

Stereotype Threat
A disturbing awareness among members of a negatively stereotyped group that any of their actions or characteristics that fit the stereotype may confirm it as a self-characterization.

Stigma
An attribute that serves to discredit a person in the eyes of others.

Strategic Self-Presentation
Conscious and deliberate efforts to shape other people's impressions in order to gain power, influence, sympathy, or approval.

Subliminal Conditioning
Classical conditioning that occurs in the absence of conscious awareness of the stimuli involved.

Subliminal Perception
The processing of information that is below one's threshold of conscious awareness.

Superordinate Goal
A mutually shared goal that can be achieved only through intergroup cooperation.

Surveys
Structured sets of questions or statements given to a group of people to measure their attitudes, beliefs, values, or behavioral tendencies.

Symbolic Interaction Theory
A contemporary sociological theory, inspired by Mead's insights and based on the premise that the self and social reality emerge due to the meaningful communication among people.

T

Temporal Model of Group Membership
A theory of group membership describing the changes that occur over time in members and in the group due to their mutual influence and interdependence.

That's-Not-All Technique
A two-step compliance technique in which the influencer makes a large request, then immediately offers a discount or bonus before the initial request is refused.

Theory
An organized system of ideas that seeks to explain how two or more events are related.

Theory of Planned Behavior
The theory that people's conscious decisions to engage in specific actions are determined by their attitudes toward the behavior in question, the relevant subjective norms, and their perceived behavioral control.

Theory of Psychological Reactance
The theory that people believe they possess specific behavioral freedoms, and that they will react against and resist attempts to limit this sense of freedom.

Thought Suppression
The attempt to prevent certain thoughts from entering consciousness.

Threat-to-Self-Esteem Model
A theory stating that if receiving help contains negative self-messages, recipients are likely to feel threatened and respond negatively.

Transformational Leader
A leader who changes (transforms) the outlook and behavior of followers (also referred to as a charismatic leader).

Two-Factor Theory of Emotions
A theory that emotional experience is based on two factors: physiological arousal and cognitive labeling of the cause of that arousal.

V

Values
Enduring beliefs about important life goals that transcend specific situations.

Variables
In scientific research, things that can be measured and that can vary.

REFERENCES

Aaker, J. L., Benet-Martinez, V., & Garolera, J. (2001). Consumption symbols as carriers of culture: A study of Japanese and Spanish brand personality constructs. *Journal of Personality and Social Psychology, 81,* 492–508.

Aarts, H., & Dijksterhuis, A. (2000). Habits as knowledge structures: Automaticity in goal-directed behavior. *Journal of Personality and Social Psychology, 78,* 53–63.

Aarts, H., & Dijksterhuis, A. (2003). The silence of the library: Environment, situational norm, and social behavior. *Journal of Personality and Social Psychology, 84,* 18–28.

Abbey, A., Abramis, D. J., & Caplan, R. D. (1985). Effects of different sources of social support and social conflict on emotional well-being. *Basic and Applied Social Psychology, 6,* 111–129.

Abelson, R. P. (1972). Are attitudes necessary? In B. T. King & E. McGinnies (Eds.), *Attitudes, conflicts, and social change.* New York: Academic Press.

Abelson, R. P. (1982). Three modes of attitude-behavior consistency. In M. P. Zanna, E. T. Higgins, & C. P. Herman (Eds.), *Consistency in social behavior: The Ontario symposium* (Vol. 2, pp. 131–147). Hillsdale, NJ: Erlbaum.

Aboud, F. E., & Levy, S. R. (2000). Interventions to reduce prejudice and discrimination in children and adolescents. In S. Oskamp (Ed.), *Reducing prejudice and discrimination* (pp. 269–293). Mahwah, NJ: Erlbaum.

Abrams, D., & Hogg, M. A. (2004). Metatheory: Lessons from social identity research. *Personality and Social Psychology Review, 8,* 98–106.

Abrams, D., Ando, K., & Hinkle, S. (1998). Psychological attachment to the group: Cross-cultural differences in organizational identification and subjective norms as predictors of workers' turnover intentions. *Personality and Social Psychology Bulletin, 24,* 1027–1039.

Abrams, D., Viki, G. T., Masser, B., & Böhner, G. (2003). Perceptions of benevolent and hostile sexism in victim blame and rape proclivity. *Journal of Personality and Social Psychology, 84,* 111–125.

Abramson, L. Y., Seligman, M. E. P., & Teasdale, J. (1978). Learned helplessness in humans: Critique and reformulation. *Journal of Abnormal Psychology, 87,* 358–372.

Adamopoulos, J. (1999). The emergence of cultural patterns of interpersonal behavior. In J. Adamopoulos & Y. Kashima (Eds.), *Social psychology and cultural context* (pp. 63–76). Thousand Oaks, CA: Sage.

Adams-Curtis, L. E., & Forbes, G. B. (2004). College women's experiences of sexual coercion: A review of cultural, perpetrator, victim, and situational variables. *Trauma, Violence, and Abuse, 5,* 91–122.

Adams, G., & Anderson, S. L. (in press). The cultural grounding of closeness and intimacy. In D. Mashek & A. Aron (Eds.), *Handbook of closeness and intimacy.* Mahwah, NJ: Erlbaum.

Adams, J. M., & Jones, W. H. (1997). The conceptualization of marital commitment: An integrative analysis. *Journal of Personality and Social Psychology, 73,* 1177–1196.

Adams, J. S. (1965). Inequity in social exchange. In L. Berkowitz (Ed.), *Advances in experimental social psychology* (Vol. 2, pp. 267–299). New York: Academic Press.

Adelson, R. (2004). Hormones, stress and aggression: A vicious cycle. *Monitor on Psychology, 35,* 18–19.

Adorno, T. W., Frenkel-Brunswik, E., Levinson, D., & Sanford, R. (1950). *The authoritarian personality.* New York: Harper.

Afifi, W. A., & Faulkner, S. L. (2000). On being "just friends": The frequency and impact of sexual activity in cross-sex friendships. *Journal of Social and Personal Relationships, 17,* 205–222.

Ahlering, R. F. (1987). Need for cognition, attitudes, and the 1984 presidential election. *Journal of Research in Personality, 21,* 100–102.

Ahlfinger, N. R., & Esser, J. K. (2001). Testing the groupthink model: Effects of promotional leadership and conformity predisposition. *Social Behavior and Personality, 29,* 31–41.

Aielllo, J. R., & Douthitt, E. A. (2001). Social facilitation from Triplett to electronic performance monitoring. *Group Dynamics, 5,* 163–180.

Aiello, J. R., & Svec, C. M. (1993). Computer monitoring of work performance: Extending the social facilitation framework to electronic presence. *Journal of Applied Social Psychology, 23,* 537–548.

Ailes, R. (1988). *You are the message.* New York: Doubleday.

Ainsworth, M. D. S. (1989). Attachments beyond infancy. *American Psychologist, 44,* 709–716.

Ajzen, I. (1985). From intentions to actions: A theory of planned behavior. In J. Kuhl & J. Beckmann (Eds.), *Action control: From cognition to behavior* (pp. 11–39). New York: Springer-Verlag.

Ajzen, I. (1988). *Attitudes, personality, and behavior.* Chicago: Dorsey.

Ajzen, I. (1991). The theory of planned behavior. *Organizational Behavior and Human Decision Processes, 50,* 179–204.

Ajzen, I. (1996). The social psychology of decision making. In E. T. Higgins & R. M. Sorrentino (Eds.), *Handbook of motivation and cognition: Foundations of social behavior* (Vol. 2, pp. 297–325). New York: Guilford.

Ajzen, I. (2001). Nature and operation of attitudes. *Annual Review of Psychology, 52,* 27–58.

Ajzen, I., & Holmes, W. H. (1976). Uniqueness of behavioral effects in causal attribution. *Journal of Personality, 44,* 98–108.

Ajzen, I., Brown, T. C., & Carvajal, F. (2004). Explaining the discrepancy between intentions and actions: The case of hypothetical bias in contingent valuation. *Personality and Social Psychology Bulletin, 30,* 1108–1121.

Albarracín, D. (2002). Cognition in persuasion: An analysis of information processing in response to persuasive communications. In M. P. Zana (Ed.), *Advances in experimental social psychology* (Vol. 34, pp. 61–130). New York: Academic Press.

Albarracín, D., Johnson, B. T., Fishbein, M., & Muellerleile, P. A. (2001). Theories of reasoned action and planned behavior as models of condom use: A meta-analysis. *Psychological Bulletin, 127,* 142–161.

Alicke, M. D., LoSchiavo, F. M., Zerbst, J., & Zhang, S. (1997). The person who outperforms me is a genius: Maintaining perceived competence in upward social comparison. *Journal of Personality and Social Psychology, 73,* 781–789.

Alicke, M. D., Yurak, T. J., & Vredenburg, D. S. (1996). Using personal attitudes to judge others: The roles of outcomes and consensus. *Journal of Research in Personality, 30,* 103–119.

Alksnis, C., Desmarais, S., & Wood, E. (1996). Gender differences in scripts for types of dates. *Sex Roles, 34,* 321–336.

Allen, B. P. (1996). African Americans' and European Americans' mutual attributions: Adjective generation technique (AGT) stereotyping. *Journal of Applied Social Psychology, 26,* 884–912.

Allen, V. L., & Levine, J. M. (1969). Consensus and conformity. *Journal of Experimental Social Psychology, 5,* 389–399.

Allen, V. L., & Levine, J. M. (1971). Social support and conformity: The role of independent assessment of reality. *Journal of Experimental Social Psychology, 7,* 48–58.

Alley, T. R., & Cunningham, M. R. (1991). Averaged faces are attractive, but very attractive faces are not average. *Psychological Science, 2,* 123–125.

Allison, J. A., & Wrightsman, L. S. (1993). *Rape: The misunderstood crime.* Newbury Park: Sage.

Allison, S. T., & Messick, D. M. (1985). Effects of experience on performance in a replenishable resource trap. *Journal of Personality and Social Psychology, 49,* 943–948.

Allman, J. M. (1998). *Evolving brains.* New York: W. H. Freeman.

Allman, J. M., & Hasenstaub A. (1999). Brains, maturation times, and parenting. *Neurobiology of Aging, 20,* 447–454.

Allport, F. H. (1920). The influence of the group upon association and thought. *Journal of Experimental Psychology, 3,* 159–182.

Allport, F. H. (1924). *Social psychology.* Boston: Houghton Mifflin.

Allport, G. W. (1935). Attitudes. In C. Murchison (Ed.), *The handbook of social psychology* (pp. 798–844). Worcester, MA: Clark University Press.

Allport, G. W. (1954). *The nature of prejudice.* Cambridge, MA: Addison-Wesley.

Allport, G. W. (1985). The historical background of social psychology. In G. Lindzey & E. Aronson (Eds.), *Handbook of social psychology* (Vol. I, 3rd ed., pp. 1–46). New York: Random House.

Alluisi, E. A., & Warm, J. S. (1990). Things that go together: A review of stimulus-response compatibility and related effects. In R. W. Proctor & T. G. Reeve (Eds.), *Stimulus-response compatibility: An integrated perspective* (pp. 3–30). Amsterdam: North Holland.

Altemeyer, B. (1981). *Right-wing authoritarianism.* Winnipeg: University of Manitoba Press.

Altemeyer, B. (1988). *Enemies of freedom: Understanding right-wing authoritarianism.* San Francisco: Jossey-Bass.

Altemeyer, B. (2004). Highly dominating, highly authoritarian personalities. *Journal of Social Psychology, 144,* 421–447.

Altheide, D. L. (2000). Identity and the definition of the situation in a mass-mediated context. *Symbolic Interaction, 23,* 1–27.

Altman, I. (1973). Reciprocity of interpersonal exchange. *Journal of Theory of Social Behavior, 3,* 249–261.

Altman, I., & Taylor, D. A. (1973). *Social penetration theory: The development of interpersonal relationships.* New York: Holt, Rinehart.

Álvarez, R. (2001). The social problem as an enterprise: Values as a defining factor. *Social Problems, 48,* 3–10.

Alvaro, E. M., & Crano, W. D. (1997). Indirect minority influence: Evidence for leniency in source evaluation and counterargumentation. *Journal of Personality and Social Psychology, 72,* 949–964.

Alwin, D. F., Cohen, R. L., & Newcomb, T. M. (1991). *Political attitudes over the life span: The Bennington women after fifty years.* Madison: University of Wisconsin Press.

Alwin, D. F., Cohen, R. L., & Newcomb, T. M. (1991). *Political attitudes over the lifespan: The Bennington women after fifty years.* Madison, WI: University of Wisconsin Press.

Ambady, N., Shih, M., Kim, A., & Pittinsky, T. L. (2001). Stereotype susceptibility in children: Effects of identity activation on quantitative performance. *Psychological Science, 12,* 385–390.

American Psychological Association. (1982). *Ethical principles in the conduct of research with human participants.* Washington, DC: Author.

Ames, D. R. (2004). Inside the mind reader's tool kit: Projection and stereotyping in mental state inference. *Journal of Personality and Social Psychology, 87,* 340–353.

Amir, Y. (1969). Contact hypothesis in ethnic relations. *Psychological Bulletin, 71,* 319–342.

Amodio, D. M., Harmon-Jones, E., Devine, P. G., Curtin, J. J., Hartley, S. L., & Covert, A. E. (2004a). Neural signals for the detection of unintentional race bias. *Psychological Science, 15,* 88–93.

Amodio, D. M., Shah, J. Y., Sigelman, J., Brazy, P. C., & Harmon-Jone, E. (2004b). Implicit regulatory focus associated with asymmetrical frontal cortical activity. *Journal of Experimental Social Psychology, 40,* 225–232.

Amsterdam, B. (1972). Mirror self-image reactions before age two. *Developmental Psychobiology, 5,* 297–305.

Andersen, S. M., & Glassman, N. S. (1996). Responding to significant others when they are not there: Effects on interpersonal inference, motivation, and affect. In R. M. Sorrentino & E. T. Higgins (Eds.), *Handbook of motivation and cognition* (pp. 262–321). New York: Guilford.

Anderson, C. A. (1997). Effects of violent movies and trait hostility on hostile feelings and aggressive thoughts. *Aggressive Behavior, 23,* 161–178.

Anderson, C. A. (2001). Heat and violence. *Current Directions in Psychological Science, 10,* 33–38.

Anderson, C. A. (2004). An update on the effects of playing violent video games. *Journal of Adolescence, 27,* 113–122.

Anderson, C. A., & Anderson, D. C. (1984). Ambient temperature and violent crime: Tests of the linear and curvilinear hypotheses. *Journal of Personality and Social Psychology, 46,* 91–97.

Anderson, C. A., & Anderson, K. B. (1996). Violent crime rate studies in philosophical context: A destructive testing approach to heat and Southern culture of violence effects. *Journal of Personality and Social Psychology, 70,* 740–756.

Anderson, C. A., & Bushman, B. J. (1997). External validity of "trivial" experiments: The case of laboratory aggression. *Review of General Psychology, 1,* 19–41.

Anderson, C. A., & Bushman, B. J. (2001). Effects of violent video games on aggressive behavior, aggressive cognition, aggressive affect, physiological arousal, and prosocial behavior: A meta-analytic review of the scientific literature. *Psychological Science, 12,* 353–359.

Anderson, C. A., & Bushman, B. J. (2002). Media violence and the American public revisited. *American Psychologist, 57,* 448–450.

Anderson, C. A., & Dill, K. E. (2000). Video games and aggressive thoughts, feelings, and behavior in the laboratory and in life. *Journal of Personality and Social Psychology, 78,* 772–790.

Anderson, C. A., Benjamin, A. J., & Bartholow, B. D. (1998). Does the gun pull the trigger? Automatic priming effects of weapon pictures and weapon names. *Psychological Science, 9,* 308–314.

Anderson, C. A., Berkowitz, L., Donnerstein, E., Huesmann, L. R., Johnson, J. D., Linz, D., Malamuth, N. M., & Wartella, E. (2003a). The influence of media on violence on youth. *Psychological Science in the Public Interest, 4,* 81–110.

Anderson, C. A., Bushman, B. J., & Groom, R. W. (1997). Hot years and serious and deadly assault: Empirical tests of the heat hypothesis. *Journal of Personality and Social Psychology, 73,* 1213–1223.

Anderson, C. A., Carnagey, N. L., & Eubanks, J. (2003b). Exposure to violent media: The effects of songs with violent lyrics on aggressive thoughts and feelings. *Journal of Personality and Social Psychology, 84,* 960–971.

Anderson, C. A., Deuser, W. E., & DeNeve, K. M. (1995). Hot temperatures, hostile affect, hostile cognition, and arousal: Tests of a general model of affective aggression. *Personality and Social Psychology Bulletin, 21,* 434–448.

Anderson, C. A., Miller, R. S., Riger, A. L., Dill, J. C., & Sedikides, C. (1994). Behavioral and characterological attributional styles as predictors of depression and loneliness: Review, refinement, and test. *Journal of Personality and Social Psychology, 66,* 549–558.

Anderson, C., & Berdahl, J. L. (2002). The experience of power: Examining the effects of power on approach and inhibition tendencies. *Journal of Personality and Social Psychology, 83,* 1362–1377.

Anderson, C., & Cromwell, R. L. (1977). "Black is beautiful." And the color preferences of Afro-American youth. *Journal of Negro Education, 46,* 76–88.

Anderson, C., John, O. P., Keltner, D., & Kring, A. M. (2001). Who attains social status? Effects of personality and physical attractiveness in social groups. *Journal of Personality and Social Psychology, 81,* 116–132.

Anderson, D. E., DePaulo, B. M., & Anfield, M. E. (2002). The development of deception detection skill: A longitudinal study of same-sex friends. *Personality and Social Psychology Bulletin, 28,* 536–545.

Anderson, D. E., DePaulo, B. M., Anfield, M. E., Tickle, J. J., & Green, E. (1999). Beliefs about cues to deception: Mindless stereotypes or untapped wisdom? *Journal of Nonverbal Behavior, 23,* 67–88.

Anderson, E. (1994). The code of the streets. *Atlantic Monthly, 5,* 81–94.

Anderson, J. L., Crawford, C. B., Nadeau, J., & Lindberg, T. (1992). Was the Duchess of Windsor right? A cross-cultural review of the socioecology of ideals of female body shape. *Ethology and Sociobiology, 13,* 197–227.

Anderson, N. H. (1968). A simple model for information integration. In R. B. Abelson, E. Aronson, W. J. McGuire, M. J. Rosenberg, & P. H. Tannenbaum (Eds.), *Theories of cognitive consistency: A sourcebook* (pp. 731–743). Chicago: Rand McNally.

Anderson, N. H. (1981). *Foundations of information integration theory.* New York: Academic Press.

Anderson, S. M., & Bem, S. L. (1981). Sex typing and androgyny in dyadic interaction: Individual differences in responsiveness to physical attractiveness. *Journal of Personality and Social Psychology, 41,* 74–86.

Andersson, J., & Rönnberg, J. (1997). Cued memory collaboration: Effects of friendship and type of retrieval cue. *European Journal of Cognitive Psychology, 9,* 273–287.

Andreoletti, C., Zebrowitz, L. A., & Lachman, M. E. (2001). Physical appearance and control beliefs in young, middle-aged, and older adults. *Personality and Social Psychology Bulletin, 27,* 969–981.

Ansolabehere, S., & Iyengar, S. (1995). *Going negative: How attack ads shrink and polarize the electorate.* New York: Free Press.

Arce, C. H., Murguia, E., & Frisbie, W. P. (1987). Phenotype and life chances among Chicanos. *Hispanic Journal of Behavioral Sciences, 9,* 19–32.

Archer, D., & Gartner, R. (1984). *Violence and crime in cross-national perspective.* New Haven, CT: Yale University Press.

Archer, J. (1991). Human sociobiology: Basic concepts and limitations. *Journal of Social Issues, 47,* 11–26.

Archer, R. L. (1979). Role of personality and the social situation. In G. J. Chelune (Ed.), *Self-disclosure* (pp. 28–58). San Francisco: Jossey-Bass.

Archibald, F. S., Bartholomew, K., & Marx, R. (1995). Loneliness in early adolescence: A test of the cognitive discrepancy model of loneliness. *Personality and Social Psychology Bulletin, 21,* 296–301.

Armitage, C. J., & Conner, M. (1999). The theory of planned behaviour: Assessment of predictive validity and "perceived control." *British Journal of Social Psychology, 38*, 35–54.

Armitage, C. J., & Conner, M. (2000). Attitudinal ambivalence: A test of three key hypotheses. *Personality and Social Psychology Bulletin, 26*, 1421–1432.

Armony, J. L., & LeDoux, J. E. (2000). How danger is encoded: Toward a systems, cellular, and computational understanding of cognitive-emotional interactions in fear. In M. S. Gazzaniga (Ed.), *The new cognitive neurosciences* (2nd ed., pp. 1067–1080). Cambridge, MA: MIT Press.

Aron, A., & Aron, E. N. (1986). *Love as the expansion of self: Understanding attraction and satisfaction.* New York: Hemisphere.

Aron, A., & Aron, E. N. (1997). Self-expansion motivation and including other in the self. In S. Duck (Ed.), *Handbook of personal relationships: Theory, research and interventions* (2nd ed., pp. 251–270). Chichester, England: Wiley.

Aron, A., Aron, E. N., & Norman, C. (2001). Self-expansion model of motivation and cognition in close relationships and beyond. In G. J. O. Fletcher & M. S. Clark (Eds.), *Blackwell handbook of social psychology: Interpersonal processes.* Malden, MA: Blackwell.

Aron, A., Aron, E. N., Tudor, M., & Nelson, G. (1991). Close relationships as including other in the self. *Journal of Personality and Social Psychology, 60*, 241–253.

Aronoff, J., Woike, B. A., & Hyman, L. M. (1992). Which are the stimuli in facial displays of anger and happiness? Configurational bases of emotion recognition. *Journal of Personality and Social Psychology, 62*, 1050–1066.

Aronson, E. (1969). The theory of cognitive dissonance: A current perspective. In L. Berkowitz (Ed.), *Advances in experimental social psychology* (Vol. 4, pp. 1–34). New York: Academic Press.

Aronson, E., & Carlsmith, J. M. (1963). Effect of the severity of threat on the devaluation of a forbidden behavior. *Journal of Abnormal and Social Psychology, 66*, 584–588.

Aronson, E., & Mills, J. (1959). The effect of severity of initiation on liking for a group. *Journal of Abnormal and Social Psychology, 59*, 177–181.

Aronson, E., & Thibodeau, R. (1992). The jigsaw classroom: A cooperative strategy for reducing prejudice. In J. Lynch, C. Modgil, & S. Modgil (Eds.), *Cultural diversity in the schools.* London: Falmer Press.

Aronson, E., Stephan, C., Sikes, J., Blaney, N., & Snapp, M. (1978). *The jigsaw classroom.* Beverly Hills, CA: Sage.

Aronson, J., Blanton, H., & Cooper, J. (1995). From dissonance to disidentification: Selectivity in the self-affirmation process. *Journal of Personality and Social Psychology, 68*, 986–996.

Aronson, J., Fried, C. B., & Good, C. (2002). Reducing the effects of stereotype threat on African American college students by shaping theories of intelligence. *Journal of Experimental Social Psychology, 38*, 113–125.

Aronson, J., Lustina, M. J., Good, C., Keough, K., Steele, C. M., & Brown, J. (1999). When White men can't do math: Necessary and sufficient factors in stereotype threat. *Journal of Experimental Social Psychology, 35*, 29–46.

Arriaga, X. B., & Agnew, C. R. (2001). Being committed: Affective, cognitive, and conative components of relationship commitment. *Personality and Social Psychology Bulletin, 27*, 1190–1203.

Arriaga, X. B., & Rusbult, C. E. (1998). Standing in my partner's shoes: Partner perspective taking and reactions to accommodative dilemmas. *Personality and Social Psychology Bulletin, 24*, 927–948.

Arrow, H., Poole, M. S., Henry, K. B., Wheelan, S., & Moreland, R. (2004). Time, change, and development: The temporal perspective on groups. *Small Group Research, 35*, 73–105.

Asch, S. E. (1946). Forming impressions of personality. *Journal of Abnormal and Social Psychology, 41*, 258–290.

Asch, S. E. (1951). Effects of group pressure upon the modification and distortion of judgments. In H. Guetzkow (Ed.), *Groups, leadership, and men.* Pittsburgh, PA: Carnegie Press.

Asch, S. E. (1952). *Social psychology.* Englewood Cliffs, NJ: Prentice-Hall.

Asch, S. E. (1955, November). Opinions and social pressure. *Scientific American, 31–35.*

Asch, S. E. (1956). Studies of independence and conformity: A minority of one against a unanimous majority. *Psychological Monographs, 70* (Whole No. 416).

Asch, S. E., & Zukier, H. (1984). Thinking about persons. *Journal of Personality and Social Psychology, 46*, 1230–1240.

Ash, M. G. (1992). Cultural contexts and scientific change in psychology: Kurt Lewin in Iowa. *American Psychologist, 47*, 198–207.

Ashby, F. G., Isen, A. M., & Turken, A. U. (1999). A neuropsychological theory of positive affect and its influence on cognition. *Psychological Review, 106*, 529–550.

Ashton, M. C., & Esses, V. M. (1999). Stereotype accuracy: Estimating the academic performance of ethnic groups. *Personality and Social Psychology Bulletin, 25*, 225–236.

Atkins, M. S., Osborne, M. L., Bennett, D. S., Hess, L. E., & Halperin, J. M. (2001). Children's competitive peer aggression during reward and punishment. *Aggressive Behavior, 27*, 1–13.

Averhart, C. J., & Bigler, R. S. (1997). Shades of meaning: Skin tone, racial attitudes, and constructive memory in African American children. *Journal of Experimental Child Psychology, 67*, 363–388.

Axsom, D. (1989). Cognitive dissonance and behavior change in psychotherapy. *Journal of Experimental Social Psychology, 21*, 149–160.

Axtell, R. E. (1993). *Gestures: The do's and taboos of body language around the world* (3rd ed.). New York: Wiley.

Ayman, R., & Chemers, M. M. (1983). The relationship of supervisory behavior ratings to work group effectiveness and subordinate satisfaction among Iranian managers. *Journal of Applied Psychology, 68*, 338–341.

Ayman, R., Chemers, M. M., & Fiedler, F. (1995). The contingency model of leadership effectiveness: Its level of analysis. Special Issue: Leadership: The multiple-level approaches (Part I). *Leadership Quarterly, 6*, 147–167.

Ayyash-Abdo, H. (2001). Individualism and collectivism: The case of Lebanon. *Social Behavior and Personality, 29*, 503–518.

Babad, E., Kaplowitz, H., & Darley, J. (1999). A "classic" revisited: Students' immediate and delayed evaluations of a warm/cold instructor. *Social Psychology of Education, 3*, 81–102.

Baccus, J. R., Baldwin, M. W., & Packer, D. J. (2004). Increasing implicit self-esteem through classical conditioning. *Psychological Science, 15*, 498–502.

Bachman, R., & Peralta, R. (2002). The relationship between drinking and violence in an adolescent population: Does gender matter? *Deviant Behavior, 23*, 1–19.

Bachnik, J. M. (1992). The two "faces" of self and society in Japan. *Ethos, 20*, 3–32.

Backman, C. W. (1983). Toward an interdisciplinary social psychology. In L. Berkowitz (Ed.), *Advances in experimental social psychology* (Vol. 14, pp. 219–261). New York: Academic Press.

Bagozzi, R. P. (1981). Attitudes, intentions, and behavior: A test of some key hypotheses. *Journal of Personality and Social Psychology, 41*, 607–627.

Baker, S. M., & Petty, R. E. (1994). Majority and minority influence: Source-position imbalance as a determinant of message scrutiny. *Journal of Personality and Social Psychology, 67*, 5–19.

Bales, R. F. (1970). *Personality and interpersonal behavior.* Fort Worth, TX: Holt, Rinehart.

Bales, R. F., & Slater, P. E. (1955). Role differentiation. In T. Parsons & R. F. Bales (Eds.), *Family, socialization, and interaction processes* (pp. 259–306). Glencoe, IL: Free Press.

Balkwell, J. W., & Berger, J. (1996). Gender, status, and behavior in task situations. *Social Psychology Quarterly, 59*, 273–283.

Ball-Rokeach, S. J., Rokeach, M., & Grube, J. W. (1984). *The great American values test: Influencing behavior and belief through television.* New York: Free Press.

Banaji, M. R. (2004). The opposite of a great truth is also true: Homage to koan #7. In J. T. Jost, M. R. Banaji, & D. A. Prentice (Eds.). *Perspectivism in social psychology: The yin and yang of scientific progress* (pp. 127–140). Washington, DC: American Psychological Association.

Banaji, M. R. (in press). Social psychology of stereotypes. In N. J. Smelser & P. B. Bates (Eds.), *International encyclopedia of the social and behavioral sciences.* New York: Elsevier/North Holland.

Banaji, M. R., Bazerman, M. H., & Chugh, D. (2003, December). How (un)ethical are you? *Harvard Business Review, 5526*, 1–11.

Bandura, A. (1965). Influences of models' reinforcement contingencies on the acquisition of initiative responses. *Journal of Personality and Social Psychology, 1*, 589–593.

Bandura, A. (1979). The social learning perspective: Mechanism of aggression. In H. Toch (Ed.), *Psychology of crime and criminal justice.* New York: Holt, Rinehart.

Bandura, A. (1986). *Social foundations of thought and action: A social-cognitive theory.* Englewood Cliffs, NJ: Prentice-Hall.

Bandura, A., & Huston, A. C. (1961). Identification as a process of incidental learning. *Journal of Abnormal and Social Psychology, 63*, 575–582.

Bandura, A., & Walters, R. H. (1963). *Social learning and personality development.* New York: Holt, Rinehart.

Bandura, A., Barbaranelli, C., Caprara, G. V., & Pastorelli, C. (1996). Mechanisms of moral disengagement in the exercise of moral agency. *Journal of Personality and Social Psychology, 71,* 364–374.

Bandura, A., Ross, D., & Ross, S. A. (1961). Transmission of aggression through imitation of aggressive models. *Journal of Abnormal and Social Psychology, 63,* 575–582.

Bank, B. J., & Hansford, S. L. (2000). Gender and friendship: Why are men's best same-sex friendships less intimate and supportive? *Personal Relationships, 7,* 1–23.

Bankston, C. L. III, & Caldas, S. J. (1997). The American school dilemma: Race and scholastic performance. *The Sociological Quarterly, 38,* 423–429.

Bar-Tal, D. (1990). Causes and consequences of delegitimization: Models of conflict and ethnocentrism. *Journal of Social Issues, 46,* 65–81.

Bar-Tal, D. (2000). *Shared beliefs in a society: Social psychological analysis.* Thousand Oaks, CA: Sage.

Barbee, A. P., Cunningham, M. R., Winstead, B. A., Derlega, V. J., Gulley, M. R., Yankeelov, P. A., & Druen, P. B. (1993). Effects of gender role expectations on the social support process. *Journal of Social Issues, 49,* 175–190.

Barbee, A. P., Gulley, M. R., & Cunningham, M. R. (1990). Support seeking in personal relationships. *Journal of Social and Personal Relationships, 7,* 531–540.

Barber, N. (2002). *The science of romance: Secrets of the sexual brain.* Amherst, NY: Prometheus Books.

Barbuto, J. E., Jr. (1997). Taking the charisma out of transformational leadership. *Journal of Social Behavior and Personality, 12,* 689–697.

Barbuto, J. E., Jr. (2000). Influence triggers: A framework for understanding follower compliance. *Leadership Quarterly, 11,* 365–387.

Bardi, A., & Schwartz, S. H. (2003). Values and behavior: Strength and structure of relations. *Personality and Social Psychology Bulletin, 29,* 1207–1220.

Bargh, J. A., & Chartrand, T. L. (1999). The unbearable automaticity of being. *American Psychologist, 54,* 462–479.

Bargh, J. A., & McKenna, K. Y. A. (2004). The Internet and social life. *Annual Review of Psychology, 55,* 573–590.

Bargh, J. A., & Pietromonaco, P. (1982). Automatic information processing and social perception: The influence of trait information presented outside of conscious awareness on impression formation. *Journal of Personality and Social Psychology, 43,* 437–449.

Bargh, J. A., Chen, M., & Burrows, L. (1996). Automaticity of social behavior: Direct effects of trait construct and stereotype activation on action. *Journal of Personality and Social Psychology, 71,* 230–244.

Bargh, J. A., Raymond, P., Pryor, J. B., & Strack, F. (1995). Attractiveness of the underling: An automatic power-sex association and its consequences for sexual harassment and aggression. *Journal of Personality and Social Psychology, 68,* 768–781.

Barley, S. R., & Bechky, B. A. (1994). In the backrooms of science: The work of technicians in science labs. *Work and Occupations, 21,* 85–126.

Barnlund, D. C. (1989). *Communicative styles of Japanese and Americans.* Belmont, CA: Wadsworth.

Baron, L., & Straus, M. A. (1987). Four theories of rape: A macrosociological analysis. *Social Problems, 34,* 467–489.

Baron, L., & Straus, M. A. (1989). *Four theories of rape in American society: A state-level analysis.* New Haven, CT: Yale University Press.

Baron, R. A. (1973). Threatened retaliation from the victim as an inhibitor of physical aggression. *Journal of Research in Personality, 7,* 103–115.

Baron, R. A. (1976). The reduction of human aggression: A field study of the influence of incompatible reactions. *Journal of Applied Social Psychology, 6,* 260–274.

Baron, R. A. (1983). The control of human aggression: A strategy based on incompatible responses. In R. G. Geen & E. I. Donnerstein (Eds.), *Aggression: Theoretical and empirical reviews* (Vol. 2, pp. 173–190). New York: Academic Press.

Baron, R. A. (1986). Self-presentation in job interviews: When there can be "too much of a good thing." *Journal of Applied Social Psychology, 16,* 16–28.

Baron, R. A., & Kepner, C. R. (1970). Model's behavior and attraction toward the model as determinants of adult aggressive behavior. *Journal of Personality and Social Psychology, 14,* 335–344.

Baron, R. S. (1986). Distraction-conflict theory: Progress and problems. In L. Berkowitz (Ed.), *Advances in experimental social psychology* (Vol. 19, pp. 1–40). New York: Academic Press.

Baron, R. S., Vandello, J. A., & Brunsman, B. (1996). The forgotten variable in conformity research: Impact of task importance on social influence. *Journal of Personality and Social Psychology, 71,* 915–927.

Barrett, L., Dunbar, R., & Lycett, J. (2002). *Human evolutionary psychology.* Princeton, NJ: Princeton University Press.

Barrett, L., Henzi, P., & Dunbar, R. (2003). Primate cognition: From 'what now?' to 'what if?' *Trends in Cognitive Sciences 7,* 494–497.

Barron, G., & Yechiam, E. (2002). Private e-mail requests and the diffusion of responsibility. *Computers in Human Behavior, 18,* 507–520.

Barsalou, L. W. (1991). Deriving categories to achieve goals. In M. I. Posner, (Ed.), *The psychology of learning and motivation* (Vol. 27, pp. 1–64). New York: Academic Press.

Bartels, A., & Zeki, S. (2000). The neural basis of romantic love. *Neuroreport, 11,* 3829–2834.

Bartholomew, K. (1990). Avoidance of intimacy: An attachment perspective. *Journal of Social and Personal Relationships, 7,* 147–178.

Bartholomew, K., Kwong, M. J., & Hart, S. D. (2001). Attachment. In W. J. Livesley (Ed.). *Handbook of personality disorders: Theory, research, and treatment* (pp. 196–230). New York: Guilford.

Bartholow, B. D., Anderson, C. A., & Carnagey, N. L. (2005). Interactive effects of life experience and situational cues on aggression: The weapons priming effect in hunters and nonhunters. *Journal of Experimental Social Psycholog, 41,* 48–60.

Bartholow, B. D., Pearson, M. A., Gratton, G., & Fabiani, M. (2003a). Effects of alcohol on person perception: A social cognitive neuroscience approach. *Journal of Personality and Social Psychology, 85,* 627–638.

Bartholow, B. D., Sher, K. J., & Krull, J. L. (2003b). Changes in heavy drinking over the third decade of life as a function of collegiate fraternity and sorority involvement: A prospective, multilevel analysis. *Health Psychology, 22,* 616–626.

Bartlett, F. C. (1932). *Remembering: A study in experimental and social psychology.* London: Cambridge University Press.

Bartone, P. T., Snook, S. A., & Tremble, T. R., Jr. (2002). Cognitive and personality predictors of leader performance in West Point cadets. *Military Psychology, 14,* 321–338.

Bartz, J. A., & Lydon, J. E. (2004). Close relationships and the working self-concept: Implicit and explicit effects of priming attachment on agency and communion. *Personality and Social Psychology Bulletin, 30,* 1389–1401.

Basow, S. A. (1986). *Gender stereotypes: Traditions and alternatives* (2nd ed.). Monterey, CA: Brooks/Cole.

Basow, S. A., & Johnson, K. (2000). Predictors of homophobia in female college students. *Sex Roles, 42,* 391–404.

Bass, B. M. (1985). *Leadership and performance beyond expectations.* New York: Free Press.

Bass, B. M. (1997). Does the transactional/ transformational leadership paradigm transcend organizational and national boundaries? *American Psychologist, 52,* 130–139.

Bassett, J. F., Cate, K. L., & Dabbs, J. M., Jr. (2002). Individual differences in selfpresentation style: Driving an automobile and meeting a stranger. *Self & Identity, 1,* 281–288.

Bassili, J. N. (2003). The minority slowness effect: Subtle inhibitions in the expression of views not shared by others. *Journal of Personality and Social Psychology, 84,* 261–276.

Bassili, J. N., & Provencal, A. (1988). Perceiving minorities: A factor-analytic approach. *Personality and Social Psychology Bulletin, 14,* 5–15.

Batson, C. D. (1991). *The altruism question: Toward a social psychological answer.* Hillsdale, NJ: Erlbaum.

Batson, C. D. (2002a). Addressing the altruism question experimentally. In S. G. Post, & L. G. Underwood (Eds.), *Altruism and altruistic love: Science, philosophy, & religion in dialogue* (pp. 89–105). London: Oxford University Press.

Batson, C. D. (2002b). Justice motivation and moral moitivation. In M. Ross, D. T. Miller, & T. Dale (Eds.), *The justice motive in everyday life* (pp. 91–106). New York: Cambridge University Press.

Batson, C. D., & Powell, A.A. (2003). Altruism and prosocial behavior. In T. Millon, & M. J. Lerner (Eds.), *Handbook of psychology: Personality and social psychology, Vol. 5* (pp. 463–484). New York: Wiley.

Batson, C. D., Ajmad, N., Lishner, D. A., & Tsang, J. (2002a). Empathy and altruism. In C. R. Snyder, & S. J. Lopez. (Eds.). *Handbook of positive psychology* (pp. 485–498). London: Oxford University Press.

Batson, C. D., Bowers, M. J., Leonard, E. A., & Smith, E. C. (2000). Does personal morality exacerbate or restrain retaliation after being harmed? *Personality and Social Psychology Bulletin, 26,* 35–45.

Batson, C. D., Chang, J., Orr, R., & Rowland, J. (2002b). Empathy, attitudes and action: Can feeling for a member of a stigmatized group motivate one to help the group? *Personality and Social Psychology Bulletin, 28,* 1656–1666.

Batson, C. D., Coke, J. S., Chard, F., Smith, D., & Taliaferro, A. (1979). Generality of the "glow of goodwill": Effects of mood on helping and information acquisition. *Social Psychology Quarterly, 42,* 176–179.

Batson, C. D., Duncan, B. D., Ackerman, P., Buckley, T., & Birch, K. (1981). Is empathic emotion a source of altruistic motivation? *Journal of Personality and Social Psychology, 40,* 290–302.

Batson, C. D., O'Quinn, K., Fultz, J., Vanderplas, N., & Isen, A. M. (1983). Influence of self-reported distress and empathy on egoistic versus altruistic motivation to help. *Journal of Personality and Social Psychology, 45,* 706–718.

Batson, C. D., Sager, K., Garst, E., Kang, M., Rubchinsky, K., & Dawson, K. (1997). Is empathy-induced helping due to self-other merging? *Journal of Personality and Social Psychology, 73,* 495–509.

Batson, C. D., Sympson, S. C., Hindman, J. L., Decruz, P., Todd, R. M., Weeks, J. L., Jennings, G., & Burris, C. T. (1996). "I've been there, too": Effect on empathy of prior experience with a need. *Personality and Social Psychology Bulletin, 22,* 474–482.

Battaglia, D. M., Richard, F. D., Datteri, D. L., & Lord, C. G. (1998). Breaking up is (relatively) easy to do: A script for the dissolution of close relationships. *Journal of Social and Personal Relationships, 15,* 829–845.

Baumeister, R. F. (1982). A self-presentational view of social phenomena. *Psychological Bulletin, 91,* 3–26.

Baumeister, R. F. (1991). *Escaping the self: Alcoholism, spirituality, masochism, and other flights from the burden of selfhood.* New York: Basic Books.

Baumeister, R. F. (1993). Understanding the inner nature of low self-esteem: Uncertain, fragile, protective, and conflicted. In R. F. Baumeister (Ed.), *Self-esteem: The puzzle of low self-regard* (pp. 201–218). New York: Plenum.

Baumeister, R. F. (1998). The self. In D. T. Gilbert, S. T. Fiske, & G. Lindzey (Eds.), *The handbook of social psychology* (4th ed., Vol. 1, pp. 680–740). New York: McGraw-Hill.

Baumeister, R. F., & Boden, J. M. (1998). Aggression and the self: High self-esteem, low self-control, and ego threat. In R. Geen & E. Donnerstein (Eds.), *Human aggression: Theories, research, and implications for social policy* (pp. 111–138). San Diego, CA: Academic Press.

Baumeister, R. F., & Heatherton, T. F. (1996). Self-regulation failure: An overview. *Psychological Inquiry, 7,* 1–15.

Baumeister, R. F., & Ilko, S. A. (1995). Shallow gratitude: Public and private acknowledgment of external help in accounts of success. *Basic and Applied Social Psychology, 16,* 191–209.

Baumeister, R. F., & Jones, E. E. (1978). When self-presentation is constrained by the target's knowledge: Consistency and compensation. *Journal of Personality and Social Psychology, 36,* 608–618.

Baumeister, R. F., & Leary, M. R. (1995). The need to belong: Desire for interpersonal attachments as a fundamental human motivation. *Psychological Bulletin, 117,* 497–529.

Baumeister, R. F., & Twenge, J. M. (2003). The social self. In T. Millon & M. J. Lerner. (Eds.), *Handbook of psychology: Personality and social psychology* (Vol. 5, pp. 327–352). New York: Wiley.

Baumeister, R. F., & Vohs, K. D. (2002). Self-regulation and the executive function of the self. In M. R. Leary & J. P. Tangney (Eds.), *Handbook of self and identity* (pp. 197–217). New York: Guilford Press.

Baumeister, R. F., & Vohs, K. D. (Eds.) (2004). *Handbook of self-regulation: Research, theory, and applications.* New York: Guilford.

Baumeister, R. F., Bratslavsky, Muraven, M., & Tice, D. M. (1998). Ego depletion: Is the active self a limited resource? *Journal of Personality and Social Psychology, 74,* 1252–1265.

Baumeister, R. F., Heatherton, T. F., & Tice, D. M. (1994). *Losing control: How and why people fail at self-regulation.* San Diego: Academic Press.

Baumeister, R. F., Smart, L., & Boden, J. M. (1996). Relation of threatened egotism to violence and aggression: The dark side of high self-esteem. *Psychological Review, 103,* 5–33.

Baumeister, R. F., Tice, D. M., & Hutton, D. G. (1989). Self-presentational motivations and personality differences in self-esteem. *Journal of Personality, 57,* 547–579.

Baumeister, R. F., Twenge, J. M., & Nuss, C. K. (2002). Effects of social exclusion on cognitive processes: Anticipated aloneness reduces intelligent thought. *Journal of Personality and Social Psychology, 83,* 817–827.

Baumrind, D. (1964). Some thoughts on ethics of research: After reading Milgram's "Behavioral Study of Obedience." *American Psychologist, 19,* 421–423.

Baumrind, D. (1996). The discipline controversy revisited. *Family Relations, 45,* 405–414.

Bauserman, R. (1996). Sexual aggression and pornography: A review of correlational research. *Basic and Applied Social Psychology, 18,* 405–427.

Baxter, L. A. (1987). Self-disclosure and relationship disengagement. In V. Derlega & J. H. Berg (Eds.), *Self-disclosure: Theory, research, and therapy* (pp. 155–174). New York: Plenum.

Beach, S. R. H., & Tesser, A. (2000). Self-evaluation maintenance and evolution: Some speculative notes. In J. Suls & L. Wheeler (Eds.), *Handbook of social comparison: Theory and research,* (pp. 123–140). New York: Kluwer Academic/Plenum.

Beaman, A. L., Barnes, P. J., Klentz, B., & McQuirk, B. (1978). Increasing helping rates through information dissemination: Teaching pays. *Personality and Social Psychology Bulletin, 9,* 181–196.

Beaman, A. L., Cole, M., Preston, M., Klentz, B., & Steblay, N. M. (1983). Fifteen years of the foot-in-the-door research: A meta-analysis. *Personality and Social Psychology Bulletin, 9,* 181–186.

Beaman, A. L., Klentz, B., Diener, E., & Svanum, S. (1979). Self-awareness and transgression in children: Two field studies. *Journal of Personality and Social Psychology, 37,* 1835–1846.

Becker, B. J. (1986). Influence again: Another look at studies of gender differences in social influence. In J. S. Hyde & M. C. Linn (Eds.), *The psychology of gender: Advances through meta-analysis.* Baltimore: Johns Hopkins University Press.

Becker, J., Ayman, R., & Korabik, K. (2002). Discrepancies in self/subordinates' perceptions of leadership behavior: Leader's gender, organizational context and leader's self-monitoring. *Group and Organization Management, 27,* 226–244.

Bell, K. L., & DePaulo, B. M. (1996). Liking and lying. *Basic and Applied Social Psychology, 18,* 243–266.

Bell, S. T., Kuriloff, P. J., & Lottes, I. (1994). Understanding attributions of blame in stranger-rape and date-rape situations: An examination of gender, race, identification, and students' social perception of rape victims. *Journal of Applied Social Psychology, 24,* 1719–1734.

Bellah, R., Madsen, R., Sullivan, W., Swindler, A., & Tipton, S. (1985). *Habits of the heart: Individualism and commitment in American life.* Berkeley: University of California Press.

Bem, D. J. (1965). An experimental analysis of self-persuasion. *Journal of Experimental Social Psychology, 1,* 199–218.

Bem, D. J. (1967). Self-perception: An alternative interpretation of cognitive dissonance phenomena. *Psychological Review, 74,* 183–200.

Bem, D. J. (1972). Self-perception theory. In L. Berkowitz (Ed.), *Advances in experimental social psychology* (Vol. 6). New York: Academic Press.

Bem, S. L. (1981). Gender schema theory: A cognitive account of sex typing. *Psychological Review, 88,* 354–364.

Bem, S. L. (1993). *The lenses of gender: Transforming the debate on sexual inequality.* New Haven: Yale University Press.

Benet-Martínez, V., & Karakitapoglu-Aygun, Z. (2003). The interplay of cultural values and personality in predicting life-satisfaction: Comparing Asian- and European-Americans. *Journal of Cross-Cultural Psychology, 34 ,* 38–61.

Benet-Martínez, V., Leu, J., Lee, F., & Morris, M. (2002). Negotiating biculturalism: Cultural frame-switching in biculturals with "oppositional" vs. "compatible" cultural identities. *Journal of Cross-Cultural Psychology, 33 ,* 492–516.

Bentler, P. M., & Speckart, G. (1981). Attitudes "cause" behaviors: A structural equation analysis. *Journal of Personality and Social Psychology, 40,* 226–238.

Beren, S. E., Hayden, H. A., Wilfley, D. E., & Striegel-Moore, R. H. (1997). Body dissatisfaction among lesbian college students. *Psychology of Women Quarterly, 21,* 431–445.

Berg, J. H. (1984). The development of friendships between roommates. *Journal of Personality and Social Psychology, 46,* 346–356.

Berg, J. H., & Clark, M. S. (1986). Differences in social exchange between intimate and other relationships: Gradually evolving or quickly apparent? In V. J. Derlega & B. A. Winstead (Eds.), *Friendship and social interaction* (pp. 101–128). New York: Springer-Verlag.

Berger, J., Wagner, D. G., & Zelditch, M. (1985). Expectation states theory: Review and assessment. In J. Berger & M. Zelditch (Eds.), *Status, rewards, and influence* (pp. 1–72). San Francisco: Jossey-Bass.

Berglas, S., & Jones, E. E. (1978). Drug choice as a self-handicapping strategy in response to noncontingent success. *Journal of Personality and Social Psychology, 36,* 405–417.

Berkowitz, L. (1968, September). Impulse, aggression and the gun. *Psychology Today,* pp. 18–22.

Berkowitz, L. (1969). The frustration-aggression hypothesis revisited. In L. Berkowitz (Ed.), *Roots of aggression* (pp. 1–28). New York: Atherton.

Berkowitz, L. (1984). Some effects of thoughts on anti- and prosocial influences of media events: A cognitive-neoassociation analysis. *Psychological Bulletin, 95,* 410–427.

Berkowitz, L. (1989). Frustration-aggression hypothesis: Examination and reformulation. *Psychological Bulletin, 106,* 59–73.

Berkowitz, L. (1993). *Aggression: Its causes, consequences, and control.* New York: McGraw-Hill.

Berkowitz, L. (1994a). Is something missing? Some observations prompted by the cognitive-neoassociationist view of anger and emotional aggression. In L. R. Huesmann (Ed.), *Aggressive behavior: Current perspectives* (pp. 35–57). New York: Plenum.

Berkowitz, L. (1994b). On the escalation of aggression. In M. Potegal & J. F. Knutson (Eds.), *The dynamics of aggression: Biological and social processes in dyads and groups* (pp. 33–41). Hillsdale, NJ: Erlbaum.

Bernard, J. (1981). The good-provider role: Its rise and fall. *American Psychologist, 36,* 1–12.

Bernard, M. M., Maio, G. R., & Olson, J. M. (2003). The vulnerability of values to attack: Inoculation of values and value-relevant attitudes. *Personality and Social Psychology Bulletin, 29,* 63–75.

Bernichon, T., Cook, K. E., & Brown, J. D. (2003). Seeking self-evaluative feedback: The interactive role of global self-esteem and specific self-views. *Journal of Personality and Social Psychology, 84,* 194–204.

Berscheid, E., & Hatfield (Walster), E. (1974). A little bit about love. In T. Huston (Ed.), *Foundations of interpersonal attraction* (pp. 355–381). New York: Academic Press.

Berscheid, E., & Hatfield, E. (1969). *Interpersonal attraction.* Reading, MA: Addison-Wesley.

Berscheid, E., & Lopes, J. (1997). A temporal model of relationship satisfaction and stability. In R. J. Sternberg & M. Hojjat (Eds.), *Satisfaction in close relationships* (pp. 129–159). New York: Guilford.

Berscheid, E., & Reis, H. T. (1998). Attraction and close relationships. In D. Gilbert, S. Fiske, & G. Lindzey (Eds.), *The handbook of social psychology* (4th ed., Vol. 2, pp. 193–281). New York: McGraw-Hill.

Betsch, T., Plessner, H., Schwieren, C. (2001). I like it but I don't know why: A value-account approach to implicit attitude formation. *Personality and Social Psychology Bulletin, 27,* 242–253.

Bettencourt, B. A., & Miller, N. (1996). Gender differences in aggression as a function of provocation: A meta-analysis. *Psychological Bulletin, 119,* 422–447.

Bhargava, R. (1992). *Individualism in social science: Forms and limits of a methodology.* Oxford: Clarendon Press.

Bierbauer, G. (1979). Why did he do it? Attribution of obedience and the phenomenon of disposi-tional bias. *European Journal of Social Psychology, 9,* 67–84.

Bierhoff, H. W. (2002). Just world, social responsibility, and helping behavior. In M. Ross & D. T. Miller (Eds.). *The justice motive in everyday life* (pp. 189–203). New York: Cambridge University Press.

Bierhoff, H. W., Klein, R., & Kramp, P. (1991). Evidence for the altruistic personality from data on accident research. *Journal of Personality, 59,* 263–280.

Biernat, M., Vescio, T. K., & Theno, S. A. (1996). Violating American values: A "value congruence" approach to understanding outgroup attitudes. *Journal of Experimental Social Psychology, 32,* 387–410.

Billig, M. (1985). Prejudice, categorization and particularization: From a perceptual to a rhetorical approach. *European Journal of Social Psychology, 15,* 79–104.

Birchler, G. R., Weiss, R. L., & Vincent, J. P. (1975). Multimethod analysis of social reinforcement exchange between maritally distressed and nondistressed spouse and stranger dyads. *Journal of Personality and Social Psychology, 31,* 349–360.

Birnbaum, M. H. (2004). Methodological and ethical issues in conducting social psychology research via the Internet. In C. Sansone, C. C. Morf, & A. T. Panter (Eds.), *Handbook of methods in social psychology* (pp. 359–382). Thousand Oaks, CA: Sage.

Björkqvist, K., & Niemelä, P. (1992). New trends in the study of female aggression. In K. Björkqvist & P. Niemelä (Eds.), *Of mice and women: Aspects of female aggression* (pp. 3–16). San Diego, CA: Harcourt Brace Jovanovich.

Björkqvist, K., Lagerspetz, K. M. J., & Kaukiainen, A. (1992). Do girls manipulate and boys fight? Developmental trends regarding direct and indirect aggression. *Aggressive Behavior, 18.*

Blagrove, M. (1996). Effects of length of sleep deprivation on interrogative suggestibility. *Journal of Experimental Psychology: Applied, 2,* 48–59.

Blaine, B., & Crocker, J. (1993). Self-esteem and self-serving biases in reactions to positive and negative events: An integrative review. In R. Baumeister (Ed.), *Self-esteem: The puzzle of low self-regard* (pp. 55–85). New York: Plenum.

Blaine, B. E., DiBlasi, D. M., & Connor, J. M. (2002). The effect of weight loss on perceptions of weight controllability: Implications for prejudice against overweight people. *Journal of Applied Biobehavioral Research, 7,* 44–56.

Blair, I. V., Judd, C. M., & Chapleau, K. M. (2004). The influence of Afrocentric facial features in criminal sentencing. *Psychological Science, 15,* 674–679.

Blair, I. V., Judd, C. M., Sadler, M. S., & Jenkins, C. (2002). The role of Afrocentric features in person perception: Judging by features and categories. *Journal of Personality and Social Psychology, 83,* 5–25.

Blair, I. V., Ma, J. E., & Lenton, A. P. (2001). Imagining stereotypes away: The moderation of implicit stereotypes through mental imagery. *Journal of Personality and Social Psychology, 81,* 828–841.

Blair, I. V., Park, B., & Bachelor, J. (2003). Understanding intergroup anxiety: Are some people more anxious than others? *Group Processes and Intergroup Relations, 6,* 151–169.

Blais, M. R., Sabourin, S., Boucher, C., & Vallerand, R. J. (1990). Toward a motivational model of couple happiness. *Journal of Personality and Social Psychology, 59,* 1021–1031.

Blakely, G. L., Andrews, M. C., & Fuller, J. (2003). Are chameleons good citizens? A longitudinal study of the relationship between self-monitoring and organizational citizenship behavior. *Journal of Business & Psychology, 18,* 131–144.

Blaney, P. H. (1986). Affect and memory: A review. *Psychological Bulletin, 99,* 229–246.

Blank, H., Fischer, V., & Erdfelder, E. (2003). Hindsight bias in political elections. *Memory, 11,* 491–504.

Blascovich, J. (2002). Social influence within immersive virtual environments. In R. Schroeder (Ed.), *The social life of avatars* (pp. 127–145). New York: Springer-Verlag.

Blascovich, J. (2003). The virtual social animal. Sage Presidential Address to the 4th Annual Meeting of the Society of Personality and Social Psychology. February 6, Los Angeles, CA.

Blascovich, J., Mendes, W. B., Hunter, S. B., Lickel, B., & Kowai-Bell, N. (2001a). Perceiver threat in social interactions with stigmatized others. *Journal of Personality and Social Psychology, 80,* 253–267.

Blascovich, J., Spencer, S. J., Quinn, D., & Steele, C. (2001b). African Americans and high blood pressure: The role of stereotype threat. *Psychological Science, 12,* 225–229.

Blass, T. (1984). Social psychology and personality: Toward a convergence. *Journal of Personality and Social Psychology, 47,* 1013–1027.

Blass, T. (1996). Attribution of responsibility and trust in the Milgram obedience experiment. *Journal of Applied Social Psychology, 26,* 1529–1535.

Blass, T. (1999). The Milgram paradigm after 35 years: Some things we now know about obedience to authority. *Journal of Applied Social Psychology, 29,* 955–978.

Blass, T. (Ed.). (2000). *Obedience to authority: Current perspectives on the Milgram paradigm.* Mahwah, NJ: Erlbaum.

Bleske-Rechek, A. L., & Buss, D. M. (2001). Opposite-sex friendship: Sex differences and similarities in initiation selection and dissolution. *Personality and Social Psychology Bulletin, 27,* 1310–1323.

Bless, H., Clore, G. L., Schwarz, N., Golisano, V., Rabe, C., and Wölk, M. (1996). Mood and the use of scripts: Does a happy mood really lead to mindlessness? *Journal of Personality and Social Psychology, 71,* 665–679.

Blieszner, R., & Adams, R. G. (1992). *Adult friendship.* Newbury Park, NJ: Sage.

Block, L. G., & Keller, P. A. (1997). Effects of self-efficacy and vividness on the persuasiveness of health communication. *Journal of Consumer Psychology, 6,* 31–54.

Blum, L. (2002). *"I'm not a racist, but . . ."* The moral quandary of race. Ithaca, NY: Cornell University Press.

Bodenhausen, G. V. (1988). Stereotypic biases in social decision making: Testing process models of stereotype use. *Journal of Personality and Social Psychology, 55,* 726–737.

Bodenhausen, G. V. (1990). Stereotypes as judgmental heuristics: Evidence of circadian variations in discrimination. *Psychological Science, 1,* 319–322.

Bohner, G., & Weinerth, T. (2001). Negative affect can increase or decrease message scrutiny: The affect interpretation hypotheses. *Personality and Social Psychology Bulletin, 27,* 1417–1428.

Bohner, G., Crow, K., Erb, H., & Schwarz, N. (1992). Affect and persuasion: Mood effects on the processing of message content and context cues and on subsequent behaviour. *European Journal of Social Psychology, 22,* 511–530.

Bohner, G., Einwiller, S., Erb, H.- P., & Siebler, F. (2003). When small means comfortable: Relations between product attributes in two-sided advertising. *Journal of Consumer Psychology, 29.*

Boldero, J., & Francis, J. (2000). The relation between self-discrepancies and emotion: The moderating roles of self-guide importance, location relevance, and social self-domain centrality. *Journal of Personality and Social Psychology, 78,* 38–52.

Bolino, M. C., & Turnley, W. H. (2003). More than one way to make an impression: Exploring profiles of impression management. *Journal of Management, 29,* 141–160.

Bonanno, G. A., Keltner, D., Noll, J. G., Putnam, F. W., Trickett, P. K., LeJeune, J., & Anderson, C. (2002). When the face reveals what words do not: Facial expressions of emotion, smiling, and the willingness to disclose childhood sexual abuse. *Journal of Personality and Social Psychology, 83,* 94–110.

Bond, C. F., Jr., & Titus, L. J. (1983). Social facilitation: A meta-analysis of 241 studies. *Psychological Bulletin, 94,* 265–292.

Bond, C. F., Jr., Thomas, B. J., & Paulson, R. M. (2004). Maintaining lies: The multiple-audience problem. *Journal of Experimental Social Psychology, 40,* 29–40.

Bond, M. H. (2004). Culture and aggression—From context to coercion. *Personality and Social Psychology Review, 8,* 62–78.

Bond, R., & Smith, P. B. (1996). Culture and conformity: A meta-analysis of studies using Asch's (1952b, 1956) line judgment task. *Psychological Bulletin, 119,* 111–137.

Bonilla-Silva, E. (2003). *Racism without racists: Color-blind racism and the persistence of racial inequality in the United States.* Lanham, MD: Roman & Littlefield.

Bontempo, R., Lobel, S., & Triandis, H. (1990). Compliance and value internalization in Brazil and the U.S. *Journal of Cross-Cultural Psychology, 21,* 201–213.

Borgida, E., Conner, C., & Manteufel, L. (1992). Understanding living kidney donation: A behavioral decision-making perspective. In S. Spacapan & S. Oskamp (Eds.), *Helping and being helped* (pp. 183–212). Newbury Park, CA: Sage.

Bornstein, G., Kugler, T., & Ziegelmeyer, A. (2004). Individual and group decisions in the centipede game: Are groups more "rational" players? *Journal of Experimental Social Psychology, 40,* 599–605.

Bornstein, R. F. (1989). Exposure and affect: Overview and meta-analysis of research, 1968–1987. *Psychological Bulletin, 106,* 265–289.

Bornstein, R. F., Leone, D. R., & Galley, D. J. (1987). The generalizability of subliminal mere exposure effects: Influence of stimuli perceived without awareness on social behavior. *Journal of Personality and Social Psychology, 53,* 1070–1079.

Bossard, J. (1932). Residential propinquity as a factor in marriage selection. *American Journal of Sociology, 38,* 219–224.

Bosson, J. K., Brown, R. P., Zeigler-Hill, V., & Swann, W. B., Jr. (2003). Self-enhancement among people with high explicit self-esteem: The moderating role of implicit self-esteem. *Self & Identity, 2,* 169–187.

Bosson, J. K., Haymovitz, E. L., & Pinel, E. C. (2004). When saying and doing diverge: The effects of stereotype threat on self-reported versus non-verbal anxiety. *Journal of Experimental Social Psychology, 40,* 247–255.

Bourgeois, M. J., & Bowen, A. (2001). Self-organization of alcohol-related attitudes and beliefs in a campus housing complex: An initial investigation. *Health Psychology, 20,* 434–437.

Boven, L. V., White, K., Kamida, A., & Gilovich, T. (2003). Intuitions about situational correction in self and others. *Journal of Personality and Social Psychology, 85,* 249–258.

Bower, G. H., & Hilgard, E. R. (1981). *Theories of learning* (5th ed.). Englewood Cliffs, NJ: Prentice Hall.

Bowlby, J. (1969). *Attachment and loss.* Vol. I. *Attachment.* New York: Wiley.

Boysen, S. T., & Himes, G. T. (1999). Current issues and emerging theories in animal cognition. *Annual Review of Psychology, 50,* 683–705.

Brackett, M. A., Lopes, P. N., Ivcevic, Z., Mayer, J. D., & Salovey, P. (2004). Integrating emotion and cognition: The role of emotional intelligence. In D. Dai & R. J. Sternberg (Eds.), *Motivation, emotion, and cognition: Integrating perspectives on intellectual functioning* (pp. 175–194). Mahwah, NJ: Lawrence Erlbaum.

Bradbury, T. N., Campbell, S. M., & Fincham, F. D. (1995). Longitudinal and behavioral analysis of masculinity and femininity in marriage. *Journal of Personality and Social Psychology, 68,* 328–341.

Brage, D., Meredith, W., & Woodward, J. (1993). Correlates of loneliness among midwestern adolescents. *Adolescence, 28,* 685–693.

Brainerd, C. J., Reyna, V. F., & Brandse, E. (1995). Are children's false memories more persistent than their true memories? *Psychological Science, 6,* 359–364.

Branden, N. (1994). *The six pillars of self-esteem.* New York: Bantam Books.

Brandstätter, V., Lengfelder, A., & Gollwitzer, P. M. (2001). Implementation intentions and efficient action initiation. *Journal of Personality and Social Psychology 81,* 946–960.

Branscombe, N. R., & Wann, D. L. (1994). Collective self-esteem consequences of outgroup derogation when a valued social identity is on trial. *European Journal of Social Psychology, 24,* 641–651.

Branscombe, N. R., Schmidtt, M. T., & Harvey, R. D. (1999). Perceiving pervasive discrimination among African-Americans: Implications for group identification and well-being. *Journal of Personality and Social Psychology, 77,* 135–149.

Brase, G. L., Caprar, D., & Voracek, M. (in press). Sex differences in responses to relationship threats in England and Romania. *Journal of Social and Personal Relationships.*

Brauer, M., Judd, C. M., & Gliner, M. D. (1995). The effects of repeated expressions on attitude polarization during group discussions. *Journal of Personality and Social Psychology, 68,* 1014–1029.

Braver, S. L. (1995). Social contracts and the provision of public goods. In D. A. Schroeder (Ed.), *Social dilemmas: Perspectives on individuals and groups* (pp. 69–86). Westport, CT: Praeger.

Breckler, S. J. (1984). Empirical validation of affect, behavior, and cognition as distinct components of attitude. *Journal of Personality and Social Psychology, 52,* 384–389.

Brehm, J. W. (1966). *A theory of psychological reactance.* New York: Academic Press.

Brehm, S. S. (1988). Passionate love. In R. J. Sternberg & M. L. Barnes (Eds.), *The psychology of love* (pp. 232–263). New Haven, CT: Yale University Press.

Brehm, S. S. (1992). *Intimate relationships.* New York: McGraw-Hill.

Brehm, S. S., & Brehm, J. W. (1981). *Psychological reactance: A theory of freedom and control.* New York: Academic Press.

Brendan, G. (2002). "I've always tolerated it but . . .": Heterosexual masculinity and the discursive reproduction of homophobia. In A. Coyle & C. Kitzinger, Celia (Eds.), *Lesbian and gay psychology: New perspectives* (pp. 219–238). Malden, MA: Blackwell.

Brendl, C. M., Markman, A. B., & Messner, C. (2001). How do indirect measures of evaluation work? Evaluating the inference of prejudice in the Implicit Association Test. *Journal of Personality and Social Psychology, 81,* 760–773.

Brennan, K. A., Clark, C. L., & Shaver, P. R. (1998). Self-report measurement of adult attachment: An integrative overview. In J. A. Simpson & W. S. Rholes (Eds.), *Attachment theory and close relationships* (pp. 46–76). New York: Guilford.

Brewer, M. B. (2004). Taking the social origins of human nature seriously: Toward a more imperialist social psychology. *Personality and Social Psychology Review, 8,* 107–113.

Brewer, M. B., & Brown, R. J. (1998). Intergroup relations. In D. T. Gilbert, S. T. Fiske, & G. Lindzey (Eds.), *The handbook of social psychology* (4th ed.). New York: McGraw-Hill.

Brewer, M. B., & Kramer, R. K. (1986). Choice behavior in social dilemmas: Effects of social identity, group size, and decision framing. *Journal of Personality and Social Psychology, 50,* 543–549.

Brewer, M. B., & Lui, L. (1984). Categorization of the elderly by the elderly: Effects of perceiver's category membership. *Personality and Social Psychology Bulletin, 10,* 585–595.

Brickman, P. (1987). *Commitment, conflict, and caring.* Englewood Cliffs, NJ: Prentice-Hall.

Briñol, P., & Petty, R. E. (2003). Overt head movements and persuasion: A self-validation analysis. *Journal of Personality and Social Psychology, 84,* 1123–1139.

Bristow, D. N., & Sebastian, R. J. (2001). Holy cow! Wait til next year! A closer look at the brand loyalty of Chicago Cubs baseball fans. *Journal of Consumer Marketing, 18,* 256–275.

Britt, T. W., Boniecki, K. A., Vescio, T. K., Biernat, M., & Brown, L. M. (1996). Intergroup anxiety: A person 3 situation approach.

Personality and Social Psychology Bulletin, 22, 1177–1188.

Brody, L. R., & Hall, J. A. (1993). Gender and emotion. In M. Lewis & J. M. Haviland (Eds.), *Handbook of emotions* (pp. 447–460). New York: Guilford.

Brookins, C. C., Anyabwile, T. M., & Nacoste, R. (1996). Exploring the links between racial identity attitudes and psychological feelings of closeness in African-American college students. *Journal of Applied Social Psychology, 26,* 243–264.

Brown, D. (2003). Pornography and erotica. In J. Bryant & D. Roskos-Ewoldsen (Eds.), *Communication and emotion: Essays in honor of Dolf Zillmann. LEA's communication series* (pp. 221–253). Mahwah, NJ: Lawrence Erlbaum.

Brown, J. D. (1993). Motivational conflict and the self: The double-bind of low self-esteem. In R. F. Baumeister (Ed.), *Self-esteem: The puzzle of low self-regard* (pp. 117–130). New York: Plenum.

Brown, J. D., & Dutton, K. A. (1995). The thrill of victory, the complexity of defeat: Self-esteem and people's emotional reactions to success and failure. *Journal of Personality and Social Psychology, 68,* 712–722.

Brown, J. D., & Marshall, M. A. (2001). Self-esteem and emotion: Some thoughts about feelings. *Personality and Social Psychology Bulletin, 27,* 575–584.

Brown, J. D., Novick, N. J., Lord, K. A., & Richards, J. M. (1992). When Gulliver travels: Social context, psychological closeness, and self-appraisals. *Journal of Personality and Social Psychology, 62,* 717–727.

Brown, K. T., Brown, T. N., Jackson, J. S., Sellers, R. M., & Manuel, W. J. (2003). Teammates on and off the field? White student athletes. *Journal of Applied Social Psychology, 33,* 1379–1403.

Brown, R., Maras, P., Masser, B., Vivian, J., & Hewstone, M. (2001). Life on the ocean wave: Testing some intergroup hypotheses in a naturalistic setting. *Group Processes and Intergroup Relations, 4,* 81–97.

Brown, W. M., & Moore, C. (2000). Is prospective altruist-detection an evolved solution to the adaptive problem of subtle cheating in cooperative ventures? Supportive evidence using the Wason selection task. *Evolution and Human Behavior, 21,* 25–37.

Browne, A., & Williams, K. R. (1989). Exploring the effect of resource availability and the likelihood of female-perpetrated homicides. *Law and Society Review, 23,* 75–94.

Brownridge, D. A., & Halli, S. S. (2002). Double jeopardy?: Violence against immigrant women in Canada. *Violence & Victims, 17,* 455–471.

Brownstein, A. L., Read, S. J., & Simon, D. (2004). Bias at the racetrack: Effects of individual expertise and task importance on predecision reevaluation of alternatives. *Personality and Social Psychology Bulletin, 30,* 891–904.

Bruins, J. J., Liebrand, W. P., & Wilke, H. A. (1989). About the saliency of fear and greed in social dilemmas. *European Journal of Social Psychology, 19,* 155–162.

Bruner, J. S., & Taguiri, R. (1954). Person perception. In G. Lindzey (Ed.), *Handbook of social psychology* (Vol. 2, pp. 634–654). Reading, MA: Addison-Wesley.

Bruner, J. S., Goodnow, J. J., & Austin, G. A. (1956). *A study of thinking.* New York: Wiley.

Brus, M. (May 21, 1998). My friend Steve Glass, the conartist. *The Daily Pennsylvanian.* http://www.dailypennsylvanian.com

Bryan, J. H., & Test, N. A. (1967). Models and helping: Naturalistic studies in aiding behavior. *Journal of Personality and Social Psychology, 6,* 400–407.

Bryant, F. B., & Guilbault, R. L. (2002). "I knew it all along" eventually: The development of hindsight in reaction to the Clinton impeachment verdict. *Basic & Applied Social Psychology, 24,* 27–41.

Bryson, J. B. (1977). Situational determinants of the expression of jealousy. In H. Sigall (Chair), *Sexual jealousy.* Symposium presented at the annual meeting of the American Psychological Association, San Francisco.

Buck, R. (1977). Nonverbal communication of affect in preschool children: Relationships with personality and skin conductance. *Journal of Personality and Social Psychology, 35,* 225–236.

Buckley, K. E., Winkel, R. E., & Leary, M. R. (2004). Reactions to acceptance and rejection: Effects of level and sequence of relational evaluation. *Journal of Experimental Social Psychology, 40,* 14–28.

Budesheim, T. L., Houston, D. A., & DePaola, S. J. (1996). Persuasiveness of in-group and out-group political messages: The case of negative political campaigning. *Journal of Personality and Social Psychology, 70,* 523–534.

Buehler, R., & Griffin, D. (1994). Change of meaning effects in conformity and dissent: Observing construal processes over time. *Journal of Personality and Psychology, 67,* 984–996.

Bugental, D. (2000). Acquisition of the algorithms of social life: A domain-based approach. *Psychological Bulletin, 126,* 187–219.

Bui, K.-V. T., Peplau, L. A., & Hill, C. T. (1996). Testing the Rusbult model of relationship commitment and stability in a 15-year study of heterosexual couples. *Personality and Social Psychology Bulletin, 22,* 1244–1257.

Bullock, W. A., & Gilliland, K. (1993). Eysenck's arousal theory of introversion-extroversion: A converging measures investigation. *Journal of Personality and Social Psychology, 64,* 113–123.

Bullough, V. L. (1976). *Sexual variance in society and history.* Chicago: University of Chicago Press.

Burbank, V. K. (1987). Female aggression in cross-cultural perspective. *Behavior Science Research, 21,* 70–100.

Burger, J. M. (1981). Motivational biases in the attribution of responsibility for an accident: A meta-analysis of the defensive-attribution hypothesis. *Psychological Bulletin, 90,* 496–512.

Burger, J. M. (1986). Increasing compliance by improving the deal: The that's-not-all technique. *Journal of Personality and Social Psychology, 51,* 277–283.

Burger, J. M. (1987). Desire for control and conformity to a perceived norm. *Journal of Personality and Social Psychology, 53,* 355–360.

Burger, J. M. (1999). The foot-in-the-door compliance procedure: A multiple-process analysis and review. *Personality and Social Psychology Bulletin, 3,* 303–325.

Burger, J. M., & Caldwell, D. F. (2003). The effects of monetary incentives and labeling on the foot-in-the-door effect: Evidence for a self-perception process. *Basic and Applied Social Psychology, 25,* 235–241.

Burger, J. M., Reed, M., DeCesare, K., Rauner, S., & Rozolis, J. (1999). The effects of initial request size on compliance: More about the that's-not-all technique. *Basic and Applied Social Psychology, 21,* 243–249.

Burgess, D., & Borgida, E. (1997). Sexual harassment: An experimental test of sex-role spillover theory. *Personality and Social Psychology Bulletin, 23,* 63–75.

Burgess, E. W. (1926). The romantic impulse and family disorganization. *Survey, 57,* 290–294.

Burris, C. T., & Rempel, J. K. (2004). "It's the end of the world as we know it": Threat and the spatial-symbolic self. *Journal of Personality and Social Psychology, 86,* 19–42.

Burt, M. (1980). Cultural myths and supports for rape. *Journal of Personality and Social Psychology, 38,* 217–230.

Busch, A. L., & Rosenberg, M. S. (2004). Comparing women and men arrested for domestic violence: A preliminary report. *Journal of Family Violence, 19,* 49–57.

Bushman, B. J. (1996). Individual differences in the extent and development of aggressive cognitive-associative networks. *Personality and Social Psychology Bulletin, 22,* 811–819.

Bushman, B. J. (2002). Does venting anger feed or extinguish the flame? Catharsis, rumination, distraction, anger, and aggressive responding. *Personality and Social Psychology Bulletin, 28,* 724–731.

Bushman, B. J., & Anderson, C. A. (2001). Is it time to pull the plug on the hostile versus instrumental aggression dichotomy? *Psychological Review, 108,* 273–279.

Bushman, B. J., & Baumeister, R. F. (1998). Threatened egotism: Narcissism, self-esteem, and direct and displaced aggression: Does self-love or self-hate lead to violence? *Journal of Personality and Social Psychology, 75,* 219–229.

Bushman, B. J., & Geen, R. G. (1990). Role of cognitive-emotional mediators and individual differences in the effects of media violence on aggression. *Journal of Personality and Social Psychology, 58,* 156–163.

Bushman, B. J., & Huesmann, L. R. (2001). Effects of televised violence on aggression. In D. Singer & J. Singer (Eds.), *Handbook of children and the media* (pp. 223–254). Thousand Oaks, CA: Sage.

Buss, A. H. (1966). Instrumentality of aggression, feedback, and frustration as determinants of physical aggression. *Journal of Personality and Social Psychology, 3,* 153–162.

Buss, A. H. (1980). *Self-consciousness and social anxiety.* San Francisco: W. H. Freeman.

Buss, D. M. (1989). Sex differences in human mate preferences: Evolutionary hypotheses tested in 37 cultures. *Behavioral and Brain Sciences, 12,* 1–49.

Buss, D. M. (1995). Evolutionary psychology: A new paradigm for psychological science. *Psychological Inquiry, 6,* 1–30.

Buss, D. M., & Duntley, J. D. (2003). Homicide: An evolutionary psychological percpective and implications for public policy. In R. W. Bloom & N. Dess (Eds.), *Evolutionary psychology and violence: A primer for policymakers and public policy advocates* (pp. 115–128). Westport, CT: Praeger.

Buss, D. M., & Kenrick, D. T. (1998). Evolutionary social psychology. In D. T. Gilbert, S. T. Fiske, & G. Lindzey (Eds.), *The handbook of social psychology* (Vol. II, pp. 982–1026). Boston, MA: McGraw-Hill.

Buss, D. M., & Shackelford, T. K. (1997). Human aggression in evolutionary psychological perspective. *Clinical Psychology Review, 17,* 605–619.

Buss, D. M., & Shackelford, T. K., Choe, J., Buunk, B. P., & Dijkstra, P. (2000). Distress about mating rivals. *Personal Relationships, 7,* 235–243.

Bussey, K., & Bandura, A. (1999). Social cognitive theory of gender development and differentiation. *Psychological Review, 106,* 676–713.

Butterworth, G. (1992). Origins of self-perception in infancy. *Psychological Inquiry, 3,* 103–111.

Buunk, B. J., & Bringle, R. G. (1987). Jealousy in love relationships. In D. Perlman & S. Duck (Eds.), *Intimate relationships: Development, dynamics, and deterioration* (pp. 123–147). Newbury Park, CA: Sage.

Buunk, B. J., & van der Laan, V. (2002). Do women need female role models? Subjective social status and the effects of same-sex and opposite-sex comparisons. *Revue Internationale de Psychologie Sociale, 15,* 129–155.

Buunk, B. P., & Dijkstra, P. (2001). Evidence from a homosexual sample for a sex-specific rival-oriented mechanism: Jealousy as a function of a rival's physical attractiveness and dominance. *Personal Relationships, 8,* 391–406.

Buunk, B., Angleitner, A., Oubaid, V., & Buss, D. M. (1996). Sex differences in jealousy in evolutionary and cultural perspective: Tests from the Netherlands, Germany, and the United States. *Psychological Science, 7,* 359–363.

Buvinic, M. L., & Berkowitz, L. (1976). Delayed effects of practiced versus unpracticed responses after observation of movie violence. *Journal of Experimental Social Psychology, 12,* 283–293.

Byrne, D. (1997). An overview (and underview) of research and theory within the attraction paradigm. *Journal of Social and Personal Relationships, 14,* 417–431.

Byrne, D., & Nelson, D. (1965). Attraction as a linear function of proportion of positive reinforcements. *Journal of Personality and Social Psychology, 1,* 659–663.

Byrne, D., Gouaux, C., Griffitt, W., Lamberth, J., Murakawa, N., Prasad, M. B., & Ramirez, M., III. (1971). The ubiquitous relationship: Attitude similarity and attraction. A cross-cultural study. *Human Relations, 24,* 201–207.

Cacioppo, J. T. (2004). Common sense, intuition, and theory in personality and social psychology. *Personality and Social Psychology Review, 8,* 114–122.

Cacioppo, J. T., & Berntson, G. C. (2001). The affect system and racial prejudice. In J. A. Bargh & D. K. Apsley (Eds.), *Unraveling the complexities of social life: A festschrift in honor of Robert B. Zajonc* (pp. 95–110). Washington, DC: American Psychological Association.

Cacioppo, J. T., & Petty, R. E. (1982). The need for cognition. *Journal of Personality and Social Psychology, 42,* 116–131.

Cacioppo, J. T., & Petty, R. E. (1989). Effects of message repetition on argument processing, recall, and persuasion. *Basic and Applied Social Psychology, 10,* 3–12.

Cacioppo, J. T., Berntson, G. G., Lorig, T. S., Norris, C. J., Rickett, E., & Nusbaum, H. (2003). Just because you're imaging the brain doesn't mean you can stop using your head: A primer and set of first principles. *Journal of Personality and Social Psychology, 85,* 650–661.

Cacioppo, J. T., Hawkley, L. C., & Bernston, G. G. (2003). The anatomy of loneliness. *Current Directions in Psychological Science, 12,* 71–74.

Cacioppo, J. T., Lorig, T. S., Nusbaum, H. C., & Bernston, G. G. (2004). Social neuroscience: Bridging social and biological systems. In C. Sansone, C. C. Morf, & A. T. Panter (Eds.), *Handbook of methods in social psychology* (pp. 383–404). Thousand Oaks, CA: Sage.

Cacioppo, J. T., Marshall-Goodell, B. S., Tassinary, L. G., & Petty, R. E. (1992). Rudimentary determinants of attitudes: Classical conditioning is more effective when prior knowledge about the attitude stimulus is low than high. *Journal of Experimental Social Psychology, 28,* 207–233.

Cacioppo, J. T., Petty, R. E., Feinstein, J. A., & Jarvis, W. B. G. (1996). Dispositional differences in cognitive motivation: The life and times of individuals varying in need for cognition. *Psychological Bulletin, 119,* 197–253.

Cacioppo, J. T., Petty, R. E., Kao, C. F., & Rodriguez, R. (1986). Central and peripheral routes to persuasion: An individual differences perspective. *Journal of Personality and Social Psychology, 51,* 1032–1043.

Cacioppo, J. T., Priester, J. R., & Berntson, G. G. (1993). Rudimentary determinants of attitudes II: Arm flexion and extension have differential effects on attitudes. *Journal of Personality and Social Psychology, 65,* 5–17.

Calvin, W. H. (1996). *How brains think.* New York: Basic Books.

Cameron, C. A., & Stritzke, W. G. K. (2003). Alcohol and acquaintance rape in Australia: Testing the presupposition model of attributions about responsibility and blame. *Journal of Applied Social Psychology, 33,* 983–1008.

Cameron, J. E. (in press). A three-factor model of social identity. *Self & Identity.*

Cameron, J. J., Ross, M., & Holmes, J. G. (2002). Loving the one you hurt: Positive effects of recounting a transgression against an intimate partner. *Journal of Experimental Social Psychology, 38,* 307–314.

Campbell, A. (1999). Staying alive: Evolution, culture, and women's intrasexual aggression. *Behavioral and Brain Sciences, 22,* 203–252.

Campbell, A., Muncer, S., Guy, A., & Banim, M. (1996). Social representations of aggression: Crossing the sex barrier. *European Journal of Social Psychology, 26,* 135–147.

Campbell, A., Muncer, S., & Odber, J. (1997a). Aggression and testosterone: Testing a bio-social model. *Aggressive Behavior, 23,* 229–238.

Campbell, A., Sapochnik, M., & Muncer, S. (1997b). Sex differences in aggression: Does social representation mediate form of aggression? *British Journal of Social Psychology, 36,* 161–171.

Campbell, J. B., & Hawley, C. W. (1982). Study habits and Eysenck's theory of extraversion-introversion. *Journal of Research in Personality, 16,* 139–146.

Campbell, J. D., & Fairey, P. J. (1989). Informational and normative routes to conformity: The effect of faction size as a function of norm extremity and attention to the stimulus. *Journal of Personality and Social Psychology, 57,* 457–468.

Campbell, R. S., & Pennebaker, J. W. (in press). The secret life of pronouns: Flexibility in writing style and physical health. *Psychological Science.*

Campbell, W. K., & Baumeister, R. F. (2001). Is loving the self necessary for loving another? An examination of identity and intimacy? In M. Clark & G. Fletcher (Eds.), *The Blackwell handbook of social psychology: Vol. 2. Interpersonal processes* (pp. 437–456). London: Blackwell.

Campbell, W. K., & Sedikides, C. (1999). Self-threat magnifies the self-serving bias: A meta-analytic integration. *Review of General Psychology, 3,* 23–43.

Campbell, W. K., Foster, C. A., & Finkel, E. J. (2002). Does self-love lead to love for others? A story of narcissistic game playing. *Journal of Personality and Social Psychology, 83,* 340–354.

Campos, J. J., Barrett, K., Lamb, M. E., Goldsmith, H. H., & Sternberg, C. (1983). Socioemotional development. In M. M. Haith & J. J. Campos (Eds.), *Handbook of child psychology (4th ed.): Vol. 2. Infancy and developmental psychobiology* (pp. 783–915). New York: Wiley.

Canli, T., Zhao, Z., Desmond, J. E., Kang, E., Gross, J., & Gabrieli, J. D. E. (2001). An fMRI study of personality influences on brain reactivity to emotional stimuli. *Behavioral neuroscience, 115,* 33–42.

Cantor, J. R., & Venus, P. (1983). The effect of humor on recall of a radio advertisement. *Journal of Broadcasting, 24,* 13–22.

Capaldi, D., Dishion, T. J., Sttolmiiler, M., & Yoerger, K. (2001). Aggression toward female partners by at-risk young men: The contribution of male adolescent friendships. *Developmental Psychology, 37,* 61–73.

Caporael, L. R. (2001). Parts and whole: The evolutionary importance of groups. In C. Sedikides & M. B. Brewer (Eds.), *Individual self, relational self, collective self* (pp. 241–258). Philadelphia: Psychology Press.

Cappe, R. F., & Alden, L. E. (1986). A comparison of treatment strategies for clients functionally impaired by extreme shyness and social avoidance. *Journal of Consulting and Clinical Psychology, 54,* 796–801.

Caprara, G. V., Barbaranelli, C., & Zimbardo, P. G. (1996). Understanding the complexity of human aggression: Affective, cognitive, and social dimensions of individual differences in propensity toward aggression. *European Journal of Personality, 10,* 133–155.

Caprara, G. V., Perugini, M., & Barbaranelli, C. (1994). Studies of individual differences in aggression. In M. Potegal & J. F. Knutson (Eds.), *The dynamics of aggression: Biological and social processes in dyads and groups* (pp. 123–153). Hillsdale, NJ: Erlbaum.

Carli, L. L. (1990). Gender, language, and influence. *Journal of Personality and Social Psychology, 59,* 941–951.

Carli, L. L. (1999). Cognitive reconstruction, hindsight, and reactions to victims and perpetrators. *Personality and Social Psychology Bulletin, 25,* 966–979.

Carli, L. L., Ganley, R., & Pierce-Otay, A. (1991). Similarity and satisfaction in roommate relationships. *Personality and Social Psychology Bulletin, 17,* 419–426.

Carli, L. L., LaFleur, S. J., & Loeber, C. C. (1995). Nonverbal behavior, gender, and influence. *Journal of Personality and Social Psychology, 68,* 1030–1041.

Carlsmith, J. M., & Anderson, C. A. (1979). Ambient temperature and the occurrence of collective violence: A new analysis. *Journal of Personality and Social Psychology, 37,* 337–344.

Carlson, C. I., Wilson, K. D., & Hargrave, J. L. (2003). The effect of school racial composition on Hispanic intergroup relations. *Journal of Social and Personal Relationships, 20,* 203–220.

Carlson, M., & Miller, N. (1987). Explanation of the relation between negative mood and helping. *Psychological Bulletin, 102,* 91–108.

Carlson, M., Charlin, V., & Miller, N. (1988). Positive mood and helping behavior: A test of six hypotheses. *Journal of Personality and Social Psychology, 55,* 211–299.

Carlson, M., Marcus-Newhall, A., & Miller, N. (1990). The effects of situational aggressive cues: A quantitative review. *Journal of Personality and Social Psychology, 58,* 622–633.

Carlson, N. R. (2004). *Physiology of behavior.* Boston: Allyn & Bacon.

Carnagey, N. L., Bushman, B. J., & Anderson, C. A. (2004). *Video game violence desensitizes players to real world violence.* Manuscript submitted for publication.

Carretie, L., Hinojosa, J. A., & Mercado, F. (2003). Cerebral patterns of attentional habituation to emotional visual stimuli. *Psychophysiology, 40,* 381–388.

Carstensen, L. L. (1998). A life-span approach to social motivation. In J. Heckhausen & C. Dweck (Eds.), *Motivation and self-regulation across the life span* (pp. 341–364). New York: Cambridge University Press.

Carstensen, L. L., Isaacowitz, D., & Charles, S. T. (1999). Taking time seriously: A theory of socioemotional selectivity. *American Psychologist, 54,* 165–181.

Carter, P. L. (2003). "Black" cultural capital, status positioning, and schooling conflicts for low-income African American youth. *Social Problems, 50,* 136–155.

Cartwright, D. (1971). Risk taking by individuals and groups: An assessment of research employing choice dilemmas. *Journal of Personality and Social Psychology, 20,* 245–261.

Caruso, E., Epley, N., & Bazerman, M. (2004). *Leader of the packed: The costs and benefits of perspective taking in group endeavors.* Unpublished manuscript.

Carver, C. S., & Scheier, M. F. (1981). *Attention and self-regulation: A control-theory approach to human behavior.* New York: Springer-Verlag.

Carver, C. S., & Scheier, M. F. (1998). *On the self-regulation of behavior.* Cambridge, UK: Cambridge University Press.

Casey, R. J., & Ritter, J. M. (1996). How infant appearance informs: Child care providers' responses to babies varying in appearance of age and attractiveness. *Journal of Applied Developmental Psychology, 17,* 495–518.

Cash, T. F., & Derlega, V. J. (1978). The matching hypothesis: Physical attractiveness among same-sexed friends. *Personality and Social Psychology Bulletin, 4,* 240–243.

Casselden, P. A., & Hampson, S. E. (1990). Forming impressions from incongruent traits. *Journal of Personality and Social Psychology, 59,* 253–262.

Cast, A. D., Stets, J. E., & Burke, P. J. (1999). Does the self conform to the views of others? *Social Psychology Quarterly, 62,* 68–82.

Castano, E., & Yzerbyt, V. Y. (1998). The highs and lows of group homogeneity. *Behavioural Processes, 42,* 219–238.

Castro, V. S. (2003). *Acculturation and psychological adaptation.* Westport, CT: Greenwood Press.

Catalano, R., Dooley, D., Novaco, R. W., Wilson, G., & Hough, R. (1993). Using ECA survey data to examine the effect of job layoffs on violent behavior. *Hospital and Community Psychiatry, 44,* 874–879.

Caughey, J. L. (1984). *Imaginary social worlds: A cultural approach.* Lincoln: University of Nebraska Press.

Ceci, S. J., & Bruck, M. (1993). Suggestibility of the child witness: A historical review and synthesis. *Psychological Bulletin, 113,* 403–439.

Cecil, H., Evans, R. I., & Stanley, M. A. (1996). Perceived believability among adolescents of health warning labels on cigarette packs. *Journal of Applied Social Psychology, 26,* 502–519.

Celuch, K., & Slama, M. (1995). "Getting along" and "getting ahead" as motives for self-presentation: Their impact on advertising effectiveness. *Journal of Applied Social Psychology, 25,* 1700–1713.

Chaiken, S. (1979). Communicator physical attractiveness and persuasion. *Journal of Personality and Social Psychology, 37,* 1387–1397.

Chaiken, S. (1980). Heuristic versus systematic information processing and the use of source versus message cues in persuasion. *Journal of Personality and Social Psychology, 39,* 752–766.

Chaiken, S. (1987). The heuristic model of persuasion. In M. P. Zanna, J. M. Olson, & C. P. Herman (Eds.), *Social influence: The Ontario symposium* (Vol. 5, pp. 3–39). Hillsdale, NJ: Erlbaum.

Chaiken, S., & Baldwin, M. W. (1981). Affective-cognitive consistency and the effect of salient behavioral information on the self-perception of attitudes. *Journal of Personality and Social Psychology, 41,* 1–12.

Chaiken, S., & Trope, Y. (1999). (Eds.). *Dual-process theories in social psychology.* New York: Guilford.

Chaiken, S., Pomerantz, E. M., & Giner-Sorolla, R. (1995). Structural consistency and attitude strength. In R. E. Petty & J. A. Krosnick (Eds.), *Attitude strength: Antecedents and consequences* (pp. 387–412). Mahwah, NJ: Erlbaum.

Chang, L., Hau, K. T., & Guo, A. M. (2001). The effect of self-consciousness on the expression of gender views. *Journal of Applied Social Psychology, 31,* 340–351.

Chapdelaine, A., Kenny, D. A., & LaFontana, K. M. (1994). Matchmaker, matchmaker, can you make me a match? Predicting liking between two unacquainted persons. *Journal of Personality and Social Psychology, 67,* 83–91.

Chaplin, W. F., Phillips, J. B., Brown, J. D., Clanton, N. R., & Stein, J. L. (2000). Handshaking, gender, personality, and first impressions.

Journal of Personality and Social Psychology, 79, 110–117.

Chapman, G. B., & Johnson, E. J. (1999). Anchoring, activation and the construction of value. *Organizational Behavior and Human Decision Processes, 79,* 120–138.

Chapman, G. B., & Johnson, E. J. (2002). Incorporating the irrelevant: Anchors in judgments of belief and value. In T. Gilovich, D. Griffin, & D. Kahneman (Eds.), *Heuristic and biases: The psychology of intuitive judgment* (pp. 617–624). New York: Cambridge University Press.

Chappell, K. D., & Davis, K. E., (1998). Attachment partner choice and partner perception: An experimental test of the attachment-security hypothesis. *Personal Relationships, 5,* 327–342.

Chartrand, T. L., & Bargh, J. A. (1999). The chameleon effect: The perception-behavior link and social interaction. *Journal of Personality and Social Psychology, 76,* 893–910.

Chartrand, T. L., Cheng, C. M., & Jefferis, V. E. (2002). You're just a chameleon: The automatic nature and social significance of mimicry. In M. Jarymowicz & R. K. Ohme (Eds.), *Natura automatyzmow (Nature of automaticity)* (pp. 19–24). Warszawa: IPPAN & SWPS.

Chartrand, T. L., Maddux, W. W., & Lakin, J. L. (in press). Beyond the perception-behavior link: The ubiquitous utility and motivational moderators of nonconscious mimicry. In R. Hassin, J. Uleman, & J. A. Bargh (Eds.), *Unintended thought 2: The new unconscious.* New York: Oxford University Press.

Chartrand, T., Pinckert, S., & Burger, J. M. (1999). When manipulation backfires: The effects of time delay and requester on the foot-in-the-door technique. *Journal of Applied Social Psychology, 29,* 211–221.

Check out a description of the elaboration likelihood model by Richard Petty Social Sense CD-ROM.

Chelune, G. J. (1976). Reactions to male and female disclosure at two levels. *Journal of Personality and Social Psychology, 34,* 1000–1003.

Chemers, M. M., Watson, C. B., & May, S. T. (2000). Dispositional affect and leadership effectiveness: A comparison of self-esteem, optimism, and efficacy. *Personality and Social Psychology Bulletin, 26,* 267–277.

Chen, A. C., German, C., & Zaidel, D. W. (1997a). Brain asymmetry and facial attractiveness: Facial beauty is not simply in the eye of the beholder. *Neuropsychologia, 35,* 471–476.

Chen, F. F., & Kenrick, D. T. (2002). Repulsion or attraction? Group membership and assumed attitude similarity. *Journal of Personality and Social Pscyhology, 83,* 111–125.

Chen, G. (1995). Differences in self-disclosure patterns among Americans versus Chinese. *Journal of Cross-Cultural Psychology, 26,* 84–91.

Chen, H., Yates, B. T., & McGinnies, E. (1988). Effects of involvement on observers' estimates of consensus, distinctiveness, and consistency. *Personality and Social Psychology Bulletin, 14,* 468–478.

Chen, M., & Bargh, J. A. (1999). Consequences of automatic evaluation: Immediate behavioral predispositions to approach or avoid the stimulus. *Personality and Social Psychology Bulletin, 25,* 215–224.

Chen, N. Y., Shaffer, D. R., & Wu, C. (1997b). On physical attractiveness stereotyping in Taiwan: A revised sociocultural perspective. *Journal of Social Psychology, 137,* 117–124.

Chen, S. (2001). The role of theories in mental representations and their use in social perception: A theory-based approach to significant-other representations and transference. In G. B. Moskowitz (Ed), *Cognitive social psychology: The Princeton symposium on the legacy and future of social cognition* (pp. 125–142). Mahwah, NJ: Erlbaum.

Chen, S. C. (1937). Social modification of the activity of ants in nest-building. *Physiological Zoology, 10,* 420–436.

Chen, S., Shecter, D., & Chaiken, S. (1996). Getting at the truth or getting along: Accuracy-versus impression-motivated heuristic and systematic processing. *Journal of Personality and Social Psychology, 71,* 262–275.

Chiroro, P., Bohner, G., Viki, G. T., & Jarvis, C. I. (2004). Rape myth acceptance and rape proclivity: Expected dominance versus expected arousal as mediators in acquaintance-rape situations. *Journal of Interpersonal Violence, 19.*

Chiu, C., Hong, Y., & Dweck, C. S. (1997). Lay dispositionism and implicit theories of personality. *Journal of Personality and Social Psychology, 73,* 19–30.

Chiu, C., Morris, M. W., Hong, Y., & Menon, T. (2000). Motivated cultural cognition: The impact of implicit cultural theories on disposition attribution varies as a function of need for closure. *Journal of Personality and Social Psychology,78,* 247–259.

Chiu, R. K., & Babcock, R. D. (2002). The relative importance of facial attractiveness and gender in Hong Kong selection decisions. *The International Journal of Human Resources Management, 13,* 141–155.

Choi, I., & Nisbett, R. E. (1998). Situational salience and cultural differences in the correspondence bias and in the actor-observer bias. *Personality and Social Psychology Bulletin, 24,* 949–960.

Choi, I., & Nisbett, R. E. (2000). Cultural psychology of surprise: Holistic theories and recognition of contradiction. *Journal of Personality and Social Psychology, 79,* 890–905.

Choi, I., Nisbett, R. E., & Norenzayan, A. (1999). Causal attribution across cultures: Variation and universality. *Psychological Bulletin, 125,* 47–63.

Chrisler, J. C. (2003). Ageism: The equal opportunity oppression. *Psychology of Women Quarterly, 27,* 187–188.

Christensen, L. (1988). Deception in psychological research: When is its use justified? *Personality and Social Psychology Bulletin, 14,* 664–675.

Christensen, P. N., & Kashy, D. A. (1998). Perceptions of and by lonely people in initial social interaction. *Personality and Social Psychology Bulletin, 24,* 322–329.

Christensen, P. N., Rothgerber, H., Wood, W., & Matz, D. C. (2004). Social norms and identity relevance: A motivational approach to normative behavior. *Personality and Social Psychology Bulletin, 30,* 1295–1309.

Church, A. T., Ortiz, F. A., Katigbak, M. S., Avdeyeva, T. V., Emerson, A. M., Flores, J., & Reyes, J. I. (2003). Measuring individual and cultural differences in implicit trait theories. *Journal of Personality and Social Psychology, 85,* 332–347.

Cialdini, R. B., & Fultz, J. (1990). Interpreting the negative mood-helping literature via "mega" analysis: A contrary view. *Psychological Bulletin, 107,* 210–214.

Cialdini, R. B., & Goldstein, N. J. (2004). Social influence: Compliance and conformity. *Annual Review of Psychology, 55,* 591–621.

Cialdini, R. B., & Kenrick, D. T. (1976). Altruism as hedonism: A social development perspective on the relationship of negative mood state and helping. *Journal of Personality and Social Psychology, 34,* 907–914.

Cialdini, R. B., & Trost, M. R. (1998). Social influence: Social norms, conformity, and compliance. In D. T. Gilbert, S. T. Fiske, & G. Lindzey (Eds.), *The handbook of social psychology* (4th ed., Vol. 2, pp. 151–192). New York: McGraw-Hill.

Cialdini, R. B., Borden, R. J., Thorne, A., Walker, M. R., Freeman, S., & Sloan, L. R. (1976). Basking in reflected glory: Three (football) field studies. *Journal of Personality and Social Psychology, 34,* 366–375.

Cialdini, R. B., Braver, S. L., & Lewis, S. K. (1974). Attributional bias and the easily persuaded other. *Journal of Personality and Social Psychology, 30,* 631–637.

Cialdini, R. B., Brown, S. L., Lewis, B. P., Luce, C., & Neuberg, S. L. (1997). Reinterpreting the empathy-altruism relationship: When one into one equals oneness. *Journal of Personality and Social Psychology, 67,* 481–494.

Cialdini, R. B., Cacioppo, J. T., Bassett, R., & Miller, J. A. (1978). Low-ball procedure for producing compliance: Commitment then cost. *Journal of Personality and Social Psychology, 36,* 463–476.

Cialdini, R. B., Trost, M., & Newsom, J. (1995). Preference for consistency: The development of a valid measure and the discovery of surprising behavioral implications. *Journal of Personality and Social Psychology, 69,* 318–328.

Cialdini, R. B., Vincent, J. E., Lewis, S. K., Catalan, J., Wheeler, D., & Darby, B. L. (1975). Reciprocal concessions procedure for inducing compliance: The door-in-the-face technique. *Journal of Personality and Social Psychology, 31,* 206–215.

Cialdini, R. B., Wosinska, W., Barrett, D. W., Butner, J., & Gornik-Durose, M. (2001). The differential impact of two social influence principles on individual and collectivists in Poland and the United States. In W. Wosinska, R. B. Cialdini, D. W. Barrett, & J. Reykowski (Eds), *The practice of social influence in multiple cultures* (pp. 33–50). Mahwah, NJ: Erlbaum.

Ciarocco, N. J., Sommer, K. L., & Baumeister, R. F. (2001). Ostracism and ego depletion: The strains of silence. *Personality and Social Psychology Bulletin, 27,* 1156–1163.

Cini, M. A., Moreland, R. L., & Levine, J. M. (1993). Group staffing levels and responses to prospective and new group members. *Journal of Personality and Social Psychology, 65,* 723–734.

Clark, K. B., & Clark, M. (1947). Racial identification and preferences in Negro children. In T. M. Newcomb & T. L. Hartley (Eds.), *Readings in social psychology* (pp. 167–178). New York: Holt.

Clark, K. B., & Clark, M. P. (1939). The development of self and the emergence of racial identifications in Negro preschool children. *Journal of Social Psychology, 10,* 591–599.

Clark, R. D., III, & Word, L. E. (1972). Why don't bystanders help? Because of ambiguity? *Journal of Personality and Social Psychology, 24,* 392–400.

Clary, E. G., Snyder, M., Ridge, R. D., Miene, P. K., & Haugen, J. A. (1994). Matching messages to motives in persuasion: A functional approach to promoting volunteerism. *Journal of Applied Social Psychology, 24,* 1129–1149.

Clore, G. L., & Baldridge, B. (1968). Interpersonal attraction: The role of agreement and topic interest. *Journal of Personality and Social Psychology, 9,* 340–346.

Coats, S., & Smith, E. R. (1999). Perceptions of gender subtypes: Sensitivity to recent exemplar activation and in-group/out-group differences. *Personality and Social Psychology Bulletin, 25,* 515–526.

Codol, J. P. (1975). On the so-called "superior conformity of the self" behavior: Twenty experimental investigations. *European Journal of Social Psychology, 5,* 457–501.

Cogan, J. C., Bhalla, S. K., Sefa-Dedeh, A., & Rothblum, E. D. (1996). A comparison study of United States and African students on perceptions of obesity and thinness. *Journal of Cross-Cultural Psychology, 27,* 98–113.

Cohen, D. (1996). Law, social policy, and violence: The impact of regional cultures. *Journal of Personality and Social Psychology, 70,* 961–978.

Cohen, D. (1998). Culture, social organization, and patterns of violence. *Journal of Personality and Social Psychology, 75,* 408–419.

Cohen, D., & Nisbett, R. E. (1994). Self-protection and the culture of honor: Explaining southern violence. *Personality and Social Psychology Bulletin, 20,* 551–567.

Cohen, D., & Vandello, J. A. (1998). Meanings of violence. *Journal of Legal Studies, 27,* 501–518.

Cohen, D., Nisbett, R. E., Bowdle, B., & Schwarz, N. (1996). Insult, aggression, and the southern culture of honor: An "experimental ethnography." *Journal of Personality and Social Psychology, 70,* 945–960.

Cohen, D., Vandello, J. A., & Rantilla, A. K. (1998). The sacred and the social: Cultures of honor and violence. In P. Gilbert & B. Andrews (Eds.), *Shame: Interpersonal behavior, psychopathology, and culture* (pp. 261–282). Oxford: Oxford University Press.

Cohen, G. L., Steele, C. M., & Ross, L. D. (1999). The mentor's dilemma: Providing critical feedback across the racial divide. *Personality and Social Psychology Bulletin, 25,* 1302–1318.

Cohen, R. L., & Alwin, D. F. (1993). Bennington women of the 1930s: Political attitudes over the life course. In K. D. Hulberet, & D. T. Schuster (Eds.), *Women's lives through time: Educated American women of the twentieth century* (pp. 117–139). San Francisco, CA: Jossey-Bass.

Coker, D. R. (1984). The relationships among gender concepts and cognitive maturity. *Sex Roles, 10,* 19–31.

Cole, M. (1992). Culture in development. In M. H. Bornstein & M. E. Lamb (Eds.), *Developmental psychology: An advanced textbook* (3rd ed.). Hillsdale, NJ: Erlbaum.

Collins, B. E., & Brief, D. E. (1995). Using person-perception vignette methodologies to uncover the symbolic meanings of teacher behaviors in the Milgram paradigm. *Journal of Social Issues, 51,* 89–106.

Collins, M. A., & Ziebrowitz, L. A. (1995). The contributions of appearance to occupational outcomes in civilian and military settings. *Journal of Applied Social Psychology, 25,* 129–163.

Collins, N. L., & Miller, L. C. (1994). Self-disclosure and liking: A meta-analytic review. *Psychological Bulletin, 116,* 457–475.

Collins, R. L. (1996). For better or worse: The impact of upward social comparison on self-evaluations. *Psychological Bulletin, 119,* 51–69.

Colombo, J. (1995). Cost, utility, and judgments of institutional review boards. *Psychological Science, 6,* 318–319.

Comer, D. R. (1995). A model of social loafing in real work groups. *Human Relations, 48,* 647–667.

Compton, R. J., Williamson, S., Murphy, S. G., & Heller, W. (2002). Hemispheric differences in affective response: Effects of mere exposure. *Social Cognition, 20,* 1–16.

Comte, I. A. (1875). *Systems of positive polity* (Vol. 1). London: Longmans, Green. (First published 1851.)

Conger, J. A., Kanungo, R. N., & Menon, S. T. (2000). Charismatic leadership and follower effects. *Journal of Organizational Behavior, 21,* 747–767.

Conger, J. D., Conger, A. J., & Brehm, S. S. (1976). Fear level as a moderator of false feedback effects in snake phobics. *Journal of Consulting and Clinical Psychology, 44,* 135–141.

Conger, R. D., Cui, M., Bryant, C. M., & Elder, G. H., Jr. (2000). Competence in early adult romantic relationships: A developmental perspective on family influences. *Journal of Personality and Social Psychology, 79,* 224–237.

Congregation for the Doctrine of the Faith. (1986). *Letter to the bishops of the Catholic church on the pastoral care of homosexual persons.* Vatican City: Author.

Conner, R. C., & Norriss, K. S. (1982). Are dolphins reciprocal altruists? *American Naturalist, 119,* 358–374.

Conrath, D. W. (1973). Communication patterns, organizational structure, and man: Some relationships. *Human Factors, 15,* 459–470.

Conway, L. G., & Schaller, M. (2002). On the verifiability of evolutionary psychological theories: An analysis of the psychology of scientific persuasion. *Personality and Social Psychology Review, 6,* 152–160.

Conway, M., & Dubé, L. (2002). Humor in persuasion on threatening topics: Effectiveness is a function of audience sex role orientation. *Personality & Social Psychology Bulletin, 28,* 863–873.

Cook, G. I., Marsh, R. L., & Hicks, J. L. (2003). Halo and devil effects demonstrate valenced-based influences on source-monitoring decisions. *Consciousness and Cognition, 12,* 257–278.

Cook, H. B. K. (1992). Matrilocality and female aggression in Margarite ño society. In K. Björkqvist & P. Niemelä (Eds.), *Of mice and women: Aspects of female aggression* (pp. 149–162). San Diego, CA: Harcourt Brace Jovanovich.

Cook, S. W. (1964). Desegregation: A psychological analysis. In W. W. Charters, Jr., & N. L. Gage (Eds.), *Readings in the social psychology of education.* Boston: Allyn & Bacon.

Cook, S. W. (1984). Cooperative interaction in multiethnic contexts. In N. Miller & M. Brewer (Eds.), *Groups in contact: The psychology of desegregation.* New York: Academic Press.

Cook, T. D., & Shadish, W. R. (1994). Social experiments: Some developments over the past fifteen years. *Annual Review of Psychology, 45,* 545–580.

Cooley, C. H. (1902). *Human nature and the social order.* New York: Scribner's Press.

Cooper, H. H. A. (2001). Terrorism: The problem of definition revisited. *American Behavioral Scientist, 44,* 881–893.

Corby, N. H., Jamner, M. S., & Wolitski, R. J. (1996). Using the theory of planned behavior to predict intention to use condoms among male and female injecting drug users. *Journal of Applied Social Psychology, 26,* 52–75.

Corney, R. (1990). Sex differences in general practice attendance and help seeking for minor illness. *Journal of Psychosomatic Research, 34,* 525–534.

Correll, J., Park, B., Judd, C. M., & Wittenbrink, B. (2002). The police officer's dilemma: Using ethnicity to disambiguate potentially threatening individuals. *Journal of Personality and Social Psychology, 83,* 1314–1329.

Correll, S. J., & Ridgeway, C. L. (2003). Expectation states theory. In J. Delamater (Ed.). *Handbook of social psychology and social research* (pp. 29–51). New York: Kluwer Academic/Plenum.

Cortina, L. M. (2004). Hispanic perspectives on sexual harassment and social support. *Personality and Social Psychology Bulletin, 30,* 570–584.

Cossrow, N. H. F., Jeffery, R. W., & McGuire, M. T. (2001). Understanding weight stigmatization: A focus group study. *Journal of Nutrition Education, 33,* 208–214.

Cottrell, N. B. (1972). Social facilitation. In C. G. McClintock (Ed.), *Experimental social psychology* (pp. 185–236). New York: Holt.

Cottrell, N. B., Wack, D. L., Sekerak, G. J., & Rittle, R. H. (1968). Social facilitation of dominant responses by the presence of an audience and the mere presence of others. *Journal of Personality and Social Psychology, 9,* 245–250.

Cowan, G., & Campbell, R. R. (1994). Racism and sexism in interracial pornography: A content analysis. *Psychology of Women Quarterly, 18,* 323–338.

Cowan, P. A., & Walters, R. H. (1963). Studies of reinforcement of aggression: I. Effects of scheduling. *Child Development, 34,* 543–551.

Coyne, J. C., Rohrbaugh, M. J., Shoham, V., Sonnega, J. S., Nicklas, J. M., & Cranford, J. A. (2001). Prognostic importance of marital quality for survival of congestive heart failure. *American Journal of Cardiology, 88,* 526–529.

Craig, R. S. (1992). The effect of television day part on gender portrayals in television commercials: A content analysis. *Sex Roles, 26,* 197–211.

Crandall, C. S. (1988). Social contagion of binge eating. *Journal of Personality and Social Psychology, 55,* 588–598.

Crandall, C. S. (1994). Do parents discriminate against their overweight daughters? *Personality and Social Psychology Bulletin, 21,* 724–735.

Crandall, C. S., D'Anello, S., Sakalli, N., Lazarus, E., Wieczorkowska, G., & Feather, N. T. (2001). An attribution-value model of prejudice: Anti-fat attitudes in six nations. *Personality and Social Psychology Bulletin, 27,* 30–37.

Crandall, C. S., Eshleman, A. E., & O'Brien, L. (2002). Social norms and the expression and suppression of prejudice: The struggle for internalization. *Journal of Personality and Social Psychology, 82,* 359–378.

Crano, W. D. (1995). Attitude strength and vested interest. In R. E. Petty & J. A. Krosnick (Eds.), *Attitude strength: Antecedents and consequences* (pp. 131–157). Mahwah, NJ: Erlbaum.

Crawford, M., Chaffin, R., & Fitton, L. (1995). Cognition in social context. Special Issue: Psychological and psychobiological perspectives on sex differences in cognition: I. Theory and research. *Learning and Individual Differences, 7,* 341–362.

Crenshaw, M. (2000). The psychology of terrorism: An agenda for the 21st century. *Political Psychology, 21,* 405–420.

Crisp, R. J., Hewstone, M., & Rubin, M. (2001). Does multiple categorization reduce intergroup bias? *Personality and Social Psychology Bulletin, 27,* 76–89.

Crites, S. L., Cacioppo, J. T., Gardner, W. L., & Berntson, G. G. (1995). Bioelectrical echoes from evaluative categorization: II. A late positive brain potential that varies as a function of attitude registration rather than attitude report. *Journal of Personality and Social Psychology, 68,* 997–1013.

Crocker, J., & Luhtanen, R. K. (2003). Level of self-esteem and contingencies of self-worth: Unique effects on academic, social, and financial problems in college students. *Personality and Social Psychology Bulletin, 29,* 701–712.

Crocker, J., & Major, B. (1989). Social stigma and self-esteem: The self-protective properties of stigma. *Psychological Review, 96,* 608–630.

Crocker, J., & Quinn, D. M. (2000). Social stigma and the self: Meanings, situations, and self-esteem. In T. F. Heatherton, R. E. Kleck, M. R. Hebl, & J. G. Hull (Eds.), *The social psychology of stigma* (pp. 153–183). New York: Guilford.

Crocker, J., Karpinski, A., Quinn, D. M., & Chase, S. K. (2003). When grades determine self-worth: Consequences of contingent self-worth for male and female engineering and psychology majors. *Journal of Personality and Social Psychology, 85,* 507–516.

Crocker, J., Luhtanen, R., Blaine, B., & Broadnax, S. (1994). Collective self-esteem and psychological well-being among White, Black, and Asian college students. *Personality and Social Psychology Bulletin, 20,* 503–513.

Crocker, J., Major, B., & Steele, C. (1998). Social stigma. In D. T. Gilbert, S. T. Fiske, & G. Lindzey (Eds.), *The handbook of social psychology* (4th ed.). New York: McGraw-Hill.

Croizet, J-C., & Claire, T. (1998). Extending the concept of stereotype threat to social class: The intellectual underperformance of students from low socioeconomic backgrounds. *Personality and Social Psychology Bulletin, 24,* 588–594.

Croizet, J-C., Després, G., Gauzins, M-E., Huguet, P., Leyens, J-P., & Méot, A. (2004). Stereotype threat undermines intellectual performance by triggering a disruptive mental load. *Personality and Social Psychology Bulletin, 30,* 721–731.

Crosby, F., & Nyquist, L. (1977). The female register: An empirical study of Lakoff's hypothesis. *Language in Society, 6,* 313–322.

Crosby, F., Bromley, S., & Saxe, L. (1980). Recent unobtrusive studies of black and white discrimination and prejudice: A literature review. *Psychological Bulletin, 87,* 546–563.

Cross, S. E. , & Morris, M. L. (2003). Getting to know you: The relational self-construal, relational cognition, and well-being. *Personality and Social Psychology Bulletin, 29,* 512–523.

Cross, S. E., & Gore, J. (2002). Cultural models of the self. In M. Leary & J. Tangney (Eds.), *Handbook of self and identity (*pp. 536–564). New York: Guilford.

Cross, S. E., & Gore, J. S. (in press).The relational self-construal and the construction of closeness. In A. Aron & D. Mashek (Eds.), *The handbook of closeness and intimacy.* Hillsdale, NJ: Lawrence Earlbaum Associates, Inc.

Cross, S. E., & Madson, L. (1997). Models of the self: Self-construals and gender. *Psychological Bulletin, 122,* 5–37.

Cross, S. E., & Vick, N. (2001). The interdependent self-construal and social support: The case of persistence in engineering. *Personality and Social Psychology Bulletin, 27,* 820–832.

Cross, S. E., Bacon, P. L., & Morris, M. L. (2000). The relational-interdependent self-construal and relationships. *Journal of Personality and Social Psychology, 78,* 791–808.

Cross, S. E., Morris, M. L., & Gore, J. S. (2002). Thinking about oneself and others: The relational-interdependent self-construal and social cognition. *Journal of Personality and Social Psychology, 82,* 399–418.

Cross, W. E. (1991). *Shades of black: Diversity in African-American identity.* Philadelphia: Temple University Press.

Crowley, A. E., & Hoyer, W. D. (1994). An integrative framework for understanding two-sided persuasion. *Journal of Consumer Research, 20,* 561–574.

Culos-Reed, S. N., Brawley, L. R., Martin, K. A., & Leary, M. R. (2002). Self-presentation concerns and health behaviors among cosmetic surgery patients. *Journal of Applied Social Psychology, 32,* 560–569.

Cummings, E. M., & Cummings, J. S. (2002). Parenting and attachment. In M. H. Bornstein (Ed.), *Handbook of parenting: Vol. 3. Being and becoming a parent* (2nd ed., pp. 35–58). Mahwah, NJ: Erlbaum.

Cunningham, M. R. (1979). Weather, mood, and helping behavior: Quasi-experiments with the sunshine samaritan. *Journal of Personality and Social Psychology, 37,* 1947–1956.

Cunningham, M. R. (1986). Measuring the physical in physical attractiveness: Quasi-experiments on the sociobiology of female facial beauty. *Journal of Personality and Social Psychology, 50,* 925–935.

Cunningham, M. R., Barbee, A. P., & Pike, C. L. (1990a). What do women want: Facialmetric assessment of multiple motives in the perception of male physical attractiveness. *Journal of Personality and Social Psychology, 59,* 61–72.

Cunningham, M. R., Shaffer, D. R., Barbee, A. P., Wolff, P. L., & Kelley, D. J. (1990b). Separate processes in the relation of elation and depression to helping: Social versus personal concerns. *Journal of Experimental Social Psychology, 26,* 13–33.

Cunningham, M. R., Steinberg, J., & Grev, R. (1980). Wanting to and having to help: Separate motivation for positive mood and guilt-induced helping. *Journal of Personality and Social Psychology, 38,* 181–192.

Cunningham, P. B., Henggeler, S. W., Limber, S. P., Melton, G. B., & Nation, M. A. (2000). Patterns and correlates of gun ownership among nonmetropolitan and rural middle school students. *Journal of Clinical Child Psychology, 29,* 432–442.

Cunningham, W. A., Johnson, M. K., Gatenby, J. C., Gore, J. C., & Banaji, M. R. (2003). Neural components of social evaluation. *Journal of Personality and Social Psychology, 85,* 639–649.

Cunningham, W. A., Nelzek, J. B., & Banaji, M. R. (2004). Implicit and explicit ethnocentrism: Revisiting the ideologies of prejudice. *Personality and Social Psychology Bulletin, 30,* 1332–1346.

Cunningham, W. A., Preacher, K. J., & Bonaji, M. R. (2001). Implicit attitude measures: Consistency, stability, and convergent validity. *Psychological Science, 12,* 163–170.

Curran, J. P. (1977). Skills training as an approach to the treatment of heterosexual-social anxiety: A review. *Psychological Bulletin, 84,* 140–157.

Curtis, R. C., & Miller, K. (1986). Believing another likes or dislikes you: Behaviors making the beliefs come true. *Journal of Personality and Social Psychology, 51,* 284–290.

Cutrona, C. (1982). Transition to college: Loneliness and the process of social adjustment. In L. A. Peplau & D. Perlman (Eds.), *Loneliness: A sourcebook of current theory, research and therapy* (pp. 291–309). New York: Wiley.

Cutrona, C. E., & Suhr, J. A. (1994). Social support communication in the context of marriage: An analysis of couples' supportive interactions. In B. B. Burleson, T. L. Albrecht, & I. G. Sarason (Eds.), *Communication of social support: Messages, relationships, and community* (pp. 113–135). Thousand Oaks, CA: Sage.

Dabbs, J. M., Frady, R. F., Carr, T. S., & Besch, N. F. (1987). Saliva testosterone and criminal violence in young adult prison inmates. *Psychosomatic Medicine, 49,* 174–182.

Dakof, G. A., & Taylor, S. E. (1990). Victims' perceptions of social support: What is helpful from whom? *Journal of Personality and Social Psychology, 58,* 80–89.

Dall'Ara, E., & Maas, A. (2000). Studying sexual harassment in the laboratory: Are egalitarian women at higher risk? *Sex Roles, 41,* 681–704.

Dallager, C., & Rosen, L. A. (1993). Effects of a human sexuality course on attitudes toward rape and violence. *Journal of Sex Education & Therapy, 19,* 193–199.

Daly, J. A., Caughlin, J. P., & Stafford, L. (1997). Correlates and consequences of social-communicative anxiety. In J. A. Daly, J. C. McCroskey, J. Ayres, T. Hopf, & D. M. Ayres (Eds.), *Avoiding communication: Shyness, reticence, and communication apprehension* (2nd ed., pp. 21–71). Creskill, NJ: Hampton Press.

Daly, M., & Wilson, M. (1988). *Homicide.* New York: Aldine De Gruyer.

Daly, M., & Wilson, M. (1991). A reply to Gelles: Stepchildren are disproportionately abused, and diverse forms of violence can share causal factors. *Human Nature, 2,* 419–426.

Daly, M., & Wilson, M. I. (1996). Violence against stepchildren. *Current Directions in Psychological Science, 5,* 77–81.

Daly, M., & Wilson, M. I. (1996). Violence against stepchildren. *Current Directions in Psychological Science, 5,* 77–81.

Damasio, A.R., Anderson, S.W. (2003). The frontal lobes. In K. M. Heilman and E. Valenstein (Eds.), *Clinical neuropsychology,* (4th Ed). New York: Oxford University Press.

Dambrun, M., Guimond, S., & Duarte, S. (2002). The impact of hierarchy-enhancing vs. attenuating academic major on stereotyping: The mediating role of perceived social norm. *Current Research in Social Psychology, 7,* 114–136.

Dana, E. R., Lalwani, N., & Duval, S. (1997). Objective self-awareness and focus of attention following awareness of self-standard discrepancies: Changing self or changing standards of correctness. *Journal of Social and Clinical Psychology, 16,* 359–380.

Dardenne, B., & Leyens, J.-P. (1995). Confirmation bias as a social skill. *Personality and Social Psychology Bulletin, 21,* 1229–1239.

Darley, J. M. (1995). Constructive and destructive obedience: A taxonomy of principal-agent relationships. *Journal of Social Issues, 51,* 125–154.

Darley, J. M. (2001). Citizens' sense of justice and the legal system. *Current Directions in Psychological Science, 10,* 10–13.

Darley, J. M., & Latanè, B. (1968). Bystander intervention in emergencies: Diffusion of responsibility. *Journal of Personality and Social Psychology, 8,* 377–383.

Darwin, C. (1859). *On the origin of species by natural selection.* New York: New York University Press, 1988.

Darwin, C. (1871). *The descent of man.* London: John Murray.

Darwin, C. (1872). *Expression of emotion in man and animals.* London: Murray.

Das, E. H. H. J., & de Wit, J. B. F. (2003). Fear appeals motivate acceptance of action recommendations: Evidence for a positive bias in the processing of persuasive messages. *Personality and Social Psychology Bulletin, 29,* 650–664.

Dasgupta, N., & Greenwald, A. G. (2001). On the malleability of automatic attitudes: Combating automatic prejudice with images of admired and disliked individuals. *Journal of Personality and Social Psychology, 81,* 800–814.

Davies, M. F. (1994). Private self-consciousness and the perceived accuracy of true and false personality feedback. *Personality and Individual Differences, 17,* 697–701.

Davies, M., & McCartney, S. (2003). Effects of gender and sexuality on judgements of victim blame and rape myth acceptance in a depicted male rape. *Journal of Community and Applied Social Psychology, 13,* 391–398.

Davila, J., & Sargent, E. (2003). The meaning of life (events) predicts changes in attachment security. *Personality and Social Psychology Bulletin, 29,* 1383–1395.

Davis, C. G., & Macdonald, S. L. (in press). Threat appraisals, distress, and the development of positive life changes following 9/11 in a Canadian sample. *Cognitive Behavioural Therapy.*

Davis, C. G., Lehman, D. R., Silver, R. C., Wortman, C. B., & Ellard, J. H. (1996). Self-blame following a traumatic life event: The role of perceived avoidability. *Personality and Social Psychology Bulletin, 22,* 557–567.

Davis, C. G., Lehman, D. R., Wortman, C. B., Silver, R. C., & Thompson, S. C. (1995). The undoing of traumatic life events. *Personality and Social Psychology Bulletin, 21,* 109–124.

Davis, C. M., & Bauserman, R. (1993). Exposure to sexually explicit materials: An attitude change perspective. In J. Bancroft (Ed.), *Annual Review of Sex Research* (Vol. 4, pp. 121–209). Mt. Vernon, IA: Society for the Scientific Study of Sex.

Davis, D., Shaver, P. R., & Vernon, M. L. (2004). Attachment style and subjective motivations for sex. *Personality and Social Psychology Bulletin, 30,* 1076–1090.

Davis, J. H. (1973). Group decision and social interaction: A theory of social decision schemes. *Psychological Review, 80,* 97–125.

Davis, J. H., Au, T., Hulbert, L., Chen, X., & Zarnoth, P. (1997). Effects of group size and procedural influence on consensual judgments of quantity: The example of damage awards and mock civil juries. *Journal of Personality and Social Psychology, 73,* 703–718.

Davis, J. L., & Rusbult, C. E. (2001). Attitude alignment in close relationships. *Journal of Personality and Social Psychology, 81,* 65–84.

Davis, M. H. (1980). A multidimensional approach to individual differences in empathy. *Psychological Documents, 10,* 85.

Davis, M. H. (1983). Empathic concern and the muscular dystrophy telethon: Empathy as a multidimensional construct. *Personality and Social Psychology Bulletin, 9,* 223–229.

Davis, M. H., & Franzoi, S. L. (1986). Adolescent loneliness, self-disclosure, and private self-consciousness: A longitudinal investigation. *Journal of Personality and Social Psychology, 51,* 595–608.

Davis, M. H., & Kraus, L. A. (1989). Social contact, loneliness, and mass media use: A test of two hypotheses. *Journal of Applied Social Psychology, 19,* 1100–1124.

Davis, M. H., & Kraus, L. A. (1997). Personality and empathic accuracy. In W. Ickes (Ed.), *Empathic accuracy* (pp. 144–168). New York: Guilford Press.

Davis, M. H., Luce, C., & Kraus, S. J. (1994). The heritability of characteristics associated with dispositional empathy. *Journal of Personality, 62,* 369–391.

Davis, T. L. (1995). Gender differences in masking negative emotions: Ability or motivation? *Developmental Psychology, 31,* 660–667.

Dawson, E., Gilovich, T., & Regan, D. T. (2002). Motivated reasoning and performance on the Wason Selection Task. *Personality & Social Psychology Bulletin, 28,* 1379–1387.

Dawson, R. E., & Prewitt, K. (1969). *Political socialization.* Boston: Little, Brown.

De Cecco, J. P. (1988). *Gay relationships.* Binghampton, NY: Haworth.

De Cremer, D., & van Dijk, E. (2002). Reactions to group success and failure as a function of identification level: A test of the goal-transformation hypothesis in social dilemmas. *Journal of Experimental Social Psychology, 38,* 435–442.

De Dreu, C. K. W., & McCusker, C. (1997). Loss frames and cooperation in two-person social dilemmas: A transformational analysis. *Journal of Personality and Social Psychology, 72,* 1093–1106.

de Waal, F. (1989). *Peacemaking among primates.* Cambridge, MA: Harvard University Press.

de Waal, F. (2002). *The ape and the sushi master: Cultural reflections of a primatologist.* New York: Basic Books.

Dean, K. E., & Malamuth, N. M. (1997). Characteristics of men who aggress sexually and of men who imagine aggressing: Risk and moderating variables. *Journal of Personality and Social Psychology, 72,* 449–455.

Deaux, K. (1996). Social identification. In E. T. Higgins & A. W. Kruglanski (Eds.), *Social psychology: Handbook of basic principles* (pp. 777–798). New York: Guilford.

Deaux, K., Winton, W., Crowley, M., & Lewis, L. L. (1985). Levels of categorization and content of gender stereotypes. *Social Cognition, 3,* 145–167.

Debono, K., & Packer, M. (1991). The effects of advertising appeal on perceptions of product quality. *Personality and Social Psychology Bulletin, 17,* 194–200.

DeFleur, M. L., & Petranoff, R. M. (1959). A televised test of subliminal persuasion. *Public Opinion Quarterly, 23,* 168–180.

Dehle, C., Larsen, D., Landers, J. E. (2001). Social support in marriage. *Special Issue: American Journal of Family Therapy, 29,* 307–324.

Delgado-Gaitan, C. (1994). Socializing young children in Mexican-American families: An intergenerational perspective. In P. M. Greenfield & R. R. Cocking (Eds.), *Cross-cultural roots of minority child development* (pp. 55–86). Hillsdale, NJ: Erlbaum.

Dembroski, T. M., Lasater, T. M., & Ramirez, A. (1978). Communicator similarity, fear arousing communications, and compliance with health care recommendations. *Journal of Applied Social Psychology, 8,* 254–269.

Demetriou, C., & Silke, A. (2003). A criminological Internet "sting": Experimental evidence of illegal and deviant visits to a website trap. *British Journal of Criminology, 43,* 213–222.

DeNeve, K. M., & Cooper, H. (1998). The happy personality: A meta-analysis of 137 personality traits and subjective well-being. *Psychological Bulletin, 124,* 197–229.

DePaulo, B. M. (1992). Nonverbal behavior and self-presentation. *Psychological Bulletin, 111,* 230–243.

DePaulo, B. M., & Bell, K. L. (1994). Truth and investment: Lies are told to those who care. *Journal of Personality and Social Psychology, 71,* 703–716.

DePaulo, B. M., & Bell, K. L. (1996). Truth and investment: Lies are told to those who care. *Journal of Personality and Social Psychology, 71,* 703–716.

DePaulo, B. M., & Friedman, H. S. (1998). Nonverbal communication. In D. T. Gilbert, S. T. Fiskle, & G. K. Lindsey (Eds.), *The handbook of social psychology* (4th ed., Vol. 2, pp. 3–40). New York: McGraw-Hill.

DePaulo, B. M., & Pfeifer, R. L. (1986). On-the-job experience and skill at detecting deception. *Journal of Applied Social Psychology, 16,* 249–267.

DePaulo, B. M., Charlton, K., Cooper, H. M., Lindsay, J. J., & Muhlenbruck, L. (1997). The accuracy-confidence correlation in the detection of deception. *Personality and Social Psychology Review, 1,* 346–357.

DePaulo, B. M., Epstein, J. A., & LeMay, C. S. (1990). Responses of the socially anxious to

the prospect of interpersonal evaluation. *Journal of Personality, 58,* 623–640.

DePaulo, B. M., Kashy, D. A., Kirkendol, S. E., Wyer, M. M., & Epstein, J. A. (1996). Lying in everyday life. *Journal of Personality and Social Psychology, 70,* 979–995.

DePaulo, B. M., Lindsay, J. J., Malone, B. E., Muhlenbruck, L., Charlton, K., & Cooper, H. (2003). Cues to deception. *Psychological Bulletin, 129,* 74–112.

Dèpret, E. F., & Fiske, S. T. (1993). Social cognition and power: Some cognitive consequences of social structure as a source of control deprivation. In G. Weary, F. Gleicher, & K. Marsh (Eds.), *Control motivation and social cognition* (pp. 176–202). New York: Springer-Verlag.

Depue, R. A., & Collins, P. F. (1999). Neurobiology of the structure of personality: Dopamine, facilitation of incentive motivation, and extraversion. *Behavioral and Brain Sciences, 22,* 491–569.

Depue, R. A., Luciana, M., Arbisi, P., Collins, P., & Leon, A. (1994). Dopamine and the structure of personality: Relation to agonist-induced dopamine activity to positive emotionality. *Journal of Personality and Social Psychology, 67,* 485–498.

Derlega, V. J., Catanzaro, D., & Lewis, R. J. (2001). Perceptions about tactile intimacy in same-sex and opposite-sex pairs based on research participants' sexual orientation. *Psychology of Men and Masculinity, 2,* 124–132.

Derlega, V. J., Lewis, R. J., Harrison, S., Winstead, B. A., & Costanza, R. (1989). Gender differences in the initiation and attribution of tactile intimacy. *Journal of Nonverbal Behavior, 13,* 83–96.

Derlega, V., & Chaikin, A. L. (1976). Norms affecting self-disclosure in men and women. *Journal of Consulting and Clinical Psychology, 44,* 376–380.

Desforges, D. M., Lord, C. G., Pugh, M. A., Sia, T. L., Scarberry, N. C., & Ratcliff, C. D. (1997). Role of group representativeness in the generalization part of the contact hypothesis. *Journal of Applied Social Psychology, 19,* 183–204.

DeSteno, D. A., & Salovey, P. (1996). Evolutionary origins of sex difference in jealousy? Questioning the fitness of the model. *Psychological Science, 7,* 367–372.

DeSteno, D., Bartlett, M. Y., Braverman, J., & Salovey, P. (2002). Sex differences in jealousy: Evolutionary mechanism or artifact of measurement? *Journal of Personality and Social Psychology, 83,* 1103–1116.

Deutsch, M., & Gerard, H. B. (1955). A study of normative and informational social influence upon individual judgment. *Journal of Abnormal and Social Psychology, 51,* 629–636.

Devine, P. G. (1989). Stereotypes and prejudice: Their automatic and controlled components. *Journal of Personality and Social Psychology, 56,* 5–18.

Devine, P. G., & Baker, S. M. (1991). Measurement of racial stereotype subtyping. *Personality and Social Psychology Bulletin, 17,* 44–50.

Devine, P. G., & Monteith, M. J. (1999). Automaticity and control in stereotyping. In S. Chaiken & Y. Trope (Eds.), *Dual process theories in social psychology* (pp. 339–360). New York: Guilford.

Devine, P. G., Evett, S. R., & Vasquez-Suson, K. A. (1996). Exploring the interpersonal dynamics of intergroup contact. In R. M. Sorrentino & E. T. Higgins (Eds.), *Handbook of motivation and cognition: The interpersonal context* (Vol. 3, pp. 423–464). New York: Guilford.

Devine, P. G., Plant, E. A., Amodio, D. M., Harmon-Jones, E., & Vance, S. L. (2002). The regulation of explicit and implicit race bias: The role of motivations to respond without prejudice. *Journal of Personality and Social Psychology, 83,* 835–848.

Devlin, P. K., & Cowan, G. A. (1985). Homophobia, perceived fathering, and male intimate relationships. *Journal of Personality Assessment, 49,* 467–473.

DeVos, G. (1985). Dimensions of the self in Japanese culture. In A. Marsella, G. DeVos, & F. L. K. Hsu (Eds.), *Culture and self* (pp. 149–184). London: Tavistock.

Diamond, L. M. (2003). What does sexual orientation orient? A biobehavioral model distinguishing romantic love and sexual desire. *Psychological Review, 110,* 173–192.

Diaz, T. (1999). *Making a killing: The business of guns in America.* Free Press.

DiBaise, R., & Gunnoe, J. (2004). Gender and culture differences in touching behavior. *Journal of Social Psychology, 144,* 49–62.

Diekmann, K., Tenbrunsel, A. E., & Galinsky, A. D. (2003). From self-prediction to self-defeat: Behavioral forecasting, self-fulfilling prophecies, and the effect of competititve expectations. *Journal of Personality and Social Psychology, 85,* 672–683.

Diener, E. (1980). Deindividuation: The absence of self-awareness and self-regulation in group members. In P. B. Paulus (Ed.), *Psychology of group influence* (pp. 209–242). Hillsdale, NJ: Erlbaum.

Diener, E., & Wallbom, M. (1976). Effects of self-awareness on antinormative behavior. *Journal of Research in Personality, 10,* 107–111.

Diener, E., Fraser, S. C., Beaman, A. L., & Kelem, R. T. (1976). Effects of deindividuation variables on stealing among Halloween trick-or-treaters. *Journal of Personality and Social Psychology, 33,* 178–183.

Diener, E., Suh, E. M., Lucas, R. E., & Smith, H. L. (1999). Subjective well-being: Three decades of progress. *Psychological Bulletin, 125,* 276–302.

Diener, E., Wolsie, B., & Fujita, F. (1995). Physical attractiveness and subjective well-being. *Journal of Personality and Social Psychology, 69,* 120–129.

Dijker, A. J., & Koomen, W. (1996). Stereotyping and attitudinal effects under time pressure. *European Journal of Social Psychology, 26,* 61–74.

Dijksterhuis, A., & Bargh, J. A. (2001). The perception-behavior expressway: the automatic effects of social perception on social behavior. In M. P. Zanna (Ed.), *Advances in experimental social psychology* (Vol. 33, pp. 1–40). San Diego, CA: Academic Press.

Dijksterhuis, A., & Knippenberg, A. V. (1996). The knife that cuts both ways: Facilitated and inhibited access to traits as a result of stereotype activation. *Journal of Experimental Social Psychology, 32,* 271–288.

Dijkstra, P., Groothof, H. A. K., Poel, G. A., Laverman, T. T. G., Schrier, M., & Buunk, B. P. (2001). Sex differences in the events that elicit jealousy among homosexuals. *Personal Relationships, 8,* 41–54.

Dimberg, U., Thunberg, M., & Elmehed, K. (2000). Unconscious facial reactions to emotional facial expressions. *Psychological Science, 11,* 86–89.

Dindia, K., & Allen, M. (1992). Sex differences in self-disclosure: A meta-analysis. *Psychological Bulletin, 112,* 106–124.

Dion, K. K. (1972). Physical attractiveness and evaluations of children's transgressions. *Journal of Personality and Social Psychology, 24,* 285–290.

Dion, K. K., & Dion, K. C. (1975). Self-esteem and romantic love. *Journal of Personality, 43,* 39–57.

Dion, K. K., & Dion, K. L. (1985). Personality, gender, and the phenomenology of romantic love. In P. R. Shaver (Ed.), *Self, situations and behavior: Review of personality and social psychology* (Vol. 6, pp. 209–239). Beverly Hills, CA: Sage.

Dion, K. K., & Dion, K. L. (1991). Psychological individualism and romantic love. *Journal of Social Behavior and Personality, 6,* 17–33.

Dion, K. K., Berscheid, E., & [Walster] Hatfield, E. (1972). What is beautiful is good. *Journal of Personality and Social Psychology, 24,* 285–290.

Dion, K. L., & Dion, K. K. (1973). Correlates of romantic love. *Journal of Consulting and Clinical Psychology, 41,* 51–56.

Dionne, E. J., Jr. (1991). *Why Americans hate politics.* New York: Simon & Schuster.

Dittmann-Kohli, F., & Westerhof, G. J. (1997). The SELE-Sentence completion Questionnaire: A new instrument for the assessment of personal meanings in aging research. *Anuario de Psicologia, 73,* 7–18.

Ditto, P. H., Scepansky, J. A., Munro, G. D., Apanovich, A. M., & Lockhart, L. K. (1998). Motivated sensitivity to preference-inconsistent information. *Journal of Personality and Social Psychology, 75,* 53–69.

Dodgson, P. G., & Wood, J. V. (1998). Self-esteem and the cognitive accessibility of strengths and weaknesses after failure. *Journal of Personality and Social Psychology, 75,* 178–197.

Dodwell, P. (2002). *Brave new mind: A thoughtful inquiry into the nature and meaning of mental life.* New York: Oxford University Press.

Donahue, M. J. (1985). Intrinsic and extrinsic religiousness: Review and meta-analysis. *Journal of Personality and Social Psychology, 48,* 400–419.

Donnerstein, E., & Berkowitz, L. (1981). Victim reactions in aggressive erotic films as a factor in violence against women. *Journal of Personality and Social Psychology, 41,* 710–724.

Donnerstein, E., & Malamuth, N. (1997). Pornography: Its consequences on the observer. In L. B. Schlesinger, & E. Revitch (Eds.), *Sexual dynamics of anti-social behavior* (2nd ed., pp. 30–49). Springfield, IL: Thomas.

Donnerstein, E., Linz, D., & Penrod, S. (1987). *The question of pornography.* New York: Free Press.

Doosje, B., Ellemers, N., & Spears, R. (1995). Perceived intragroup variability as a function of group status and identification. *Journal of Experimental Social Psychology, 31,* 410–436.

Dordick, G. A. (1997). *Something left to lose: Personal relations and survival among New York's homeless.* Philadelphia: Temple University Press.

Dorfman, J., Shames, V. A., & Kihlstrom, J. F. (1996). Intuition, incubation, and insight: Implicit cognition in problem solving. In G. Underwood (Ed.), *Implicit cognition* (pp. 257–296). Oxford: Oxford University Press.

Doty, R. M., Peterson, B. E., & Winter, D. G. (1991). Threat and authoritarianism in the United States, 1978–1987. *Journal of Personality and Social Psychology, 61,* 629–640.

Doty, R. M., Winter, D. G., Peterson, B. E., & Kemmelmeier, M. (1997). Authoritarianism and American students' attitudes about the Gulf War, 1990–1996. *Personality and Social Psychology Bulletin, 23,* 1133–1143.

Dovidio, J. F. (2001). On the nature of contemporary prejudice: The third wave. *Journal of Social Issues, 57,* 829–849.

Dovidio, J. F., & Gaertner, S. L. (2000). Aversive racism and selection decisions: 1989 and 1999. *Psychological Science, 11,* 315–319.

Dovidio, J. F., Evans, N., & Tyler, R. B. (1986). Racial stereotypes: The contents of their cognitive representations. *Journal of Experimental Social Psychology, 22,* 22–37.

Dovidio, J. F., Gaertner, S. L., Kawakami, K., & Hodson, G. (2002a). Why can't we just get along? Interpersonal biases and interracial distrust. *Cultural Diversity and Ethnic Minority Psychology, 8,* 88–102.

Dovidio, J. F., Kawakami, K., & Beach, K. R. (2001). Implicit and explicit attitudes: Examination of the relationship between measures of intergroup bias. In R. Brown & S. L. Gaertner (Eds.), *Blackwell handbook of social psychology: Vol. 4. Intergroup relations* pp. 175–197). Oxford, UK: Blackwell.

Dovidio, J. F., Kawakami, K., & Gaertner, S. L. (2002b). Implicit and explicit prejudice and interracial interaction. *Journal of Personality and Social Psychology, 82,* 62–68.

Dovidio, J. F., Piliavin, J. A., & Clark, R. D., III (1991). The arousal:cost reward model and the process of intervention: A review of the evidence. In M. S. Clark (Ed.), *Review of personality and social psychology: Vol. 12. Prosocial behavior* (pp. 86–118). Newbury Park, CA: Sage.

Downey, G., Mougios, V., Ayduk, O., London, B. E., & Shoda, Y. (2004). Rejection sensitivity and the defensive motivational system, *Psychological Science, 15,* 668–673.

Drabman, R. S., & Thomas, M. H. (1975). Does TV violence breed indifference? *Journal of Communications, 25*(4), 86–89.

Drachman, D., DeCarufel, A., & Insko, C. A. (1978). The extra credit effect in interpersonal attraction. *Journal of Experimental Social Psychology, 14,* 458–467.

Drigotas, S. M., Rusbult, C. E., Wieselquist, J., & Whitton, S. W. (1999). Close partner as sculptor of the ideal self: Behavioral affirmation and the Michelangelo phenomenon. *Journal of Personality and Social Psychology, 77,* 293–323.

Dryer, D. C., & Horowitz, L. M. (1997). When do opposites attract? Interpersonal complementarity versus similarity. *Journal of Personality and Social Psychology, 72,* 592–603.

Duan, C. (2000). Being empathic. The role of motivation to empathize and the nature of target emotions. *Motivation & Emotion, 24,* 29–50.

DuBois, D. L. (in press). Promoting the self-esteem of children. In T. P. Gullotta & M. Bloom (Eds.) & L. Bond (Section Ed.), *Encyclopedia of primary prevention and health promotion: Childhood.* New York: Kluwer Academic/Plenum.

Duck, S., & Wright, P. H. (1993). Reexamining gender differences in same-gender friendships: A close look at two kinds of data. *Sex Roles, 28,* 709–727.

Duck, S., Pond, K., & Leatham, G. (1994). Loneliness and the evaluation of relational events. *Journal of Social and Personal* Relationships, *11,* 253–276.

Duckitt, J. (2001). A dual-process cognitive-motivational theory of ideology and prejudice. In M. P. Zanna (Ed.). *Advances in experimental social psychology,* Vol. 33 (pp. 41–113). San Diego, CA: Academic Press.

Duckitt, J. (2001). A dual-process cognitive-motivational theory of ideology and prejudice. In M. P. Zanna (Ed.). Advances in experimental social psychology (Vol. 33, pp. 41–113). San Diego, CA: Academic Press.

Duckitt, J. (in press). Personality and prejudice. In J. F. Dovidio, P. Glick, & L. Rudman (Ed.), *Reflecting on the nature of prejudice.* Malden, MA: Blackwell Press.

Duckitt, J., & Fisher, K. (2003). The impact of social threat on worldview and ideological attitudes. *Political Psychology, 24,* 199–222.

Duckitt, J., & Mphuthing, T. (1998). Group identification and intergroup attitudes: A longitudinal analysis in South Africa. *Journal of Personality and Social Psychology, 74,* 80–85.

Duckitt, J., Wagner, C., Du Plessis, I., & Birum, I. (2002). The psychological bases of ideology and prejudice. Testing a dual process model. *Journal of Personality and Social Psychology, 83,* 75–93.

Duclos, S. E., Laird, J. D., Schneider, E., Sexter, M., Stern, L., & Van Lighten, O. (1989). Emotion-specific effects of facial expressions and postures on emotional experience. *Journal of Personality and Social Psychology, 57,* 100–108.

Dunbar, R. (2002). Brains on two legs: Group size and the evolution of intelligence. In F. B. M. de Waal (Ed.). Tree of origin: *What primate behavior can tell us about human social evolution* (pp. 173–191). Cambridge, MA: Harvard University Press.

Dunbar, R. (2003). Solution of the social brain. *Science, 302,* 1160–1161.

Dunbar, R. I. M. (1993). Coevolution of neocortical size, group size and language in humans. *Behavioral and Brain Sciences, 16,* 681–735.

Dunbar, R. I. M. (2000). Causal reasoning, mental rehearsal and the evolution of primate cognition. In C. Heyes & L. Huber (Eds.), *Evolution of cognition* (pp. 205–221). Cambridge, MA: MIT Press.

Duncan, C. P., & Nelson, J. E. (1985). Effects of humor in a radio advertising experiment. *Journal of Advertising, 14,* 33–40.

Dunkel-Schetter, C., Blasband, D. E., Feinstein, L. G., & Herbert, T. B. (1992). Elements of supportive interactions: When are attempts to help effective? In S. Spacapan & S. Oskamp (Eds.), *Helping and being helped: Naturalistic studies* (pp. 83–114). Newbury Park, CA: Sage.

Dunn, J. (2001). The development of children's conflict and prosocial behaviour: Lessons from research on social understanding and gender. In J. Hill & B. Maughan (Eds.), *Conduct disorders in childhood and adolescence: Cambridge child and adolescent psychiatry* (pp. 49–66). New York: Cambridge University Press.

Dunning, D. (1999). A newer look: Motivated social cognition and the schematic representation of social concepts. *Psychological Inquiry, 10,* 1–11.

Dunning, D. (2004). But what would a balanced approach look like? *Behavioral and Brain Sciences, 27.*

Dunning, D., Leuenberger, A., & Sherman, D. A. (1995). A new look at motivated inference: Are self-serving theories of success a product of motivational forces? *Journal of Personality and Social Psychology, 69,* 58–68.

Dutton, D. G., & Aron, A. P. (1974). Some evidence for heightened sexual attraction under conditions of high anxiety. *Journal of Personality and Social Psychology, 30,* 510–517.

Duval, S., & Wicklund, R. A. (1972). *A theory of objective self-awareness.* New York: Academic Press.

Eagly, A. H. (1987). *Sex differences in social behavior: A social-role interpretation.* Hillsdale, NJ: Erlbaum.

Eagly, A. H. (1992). Uneven progress: Social psychology and the study of attitudes. *Journal of Personality and Social Psychology, 63,* 693–710.

Eagly, A. H. (1996). Differences between women and men: Their magnitude, practical importance, and political meaning. *American Psychologist, 50,* 158–159.

Eagly, A. H., & Chaiken, S. (1993). *The psychology of attitudes.* Fort Worth, TX: Harcourt Brace Jovanovich.

Eagly, A. H., & Chravala, C. (1986). Sex differences in conformity: Status and gender-role interpretations. *Psychology of Women Quarterly, 10,* 203–220.

Eagly, A. H., & Crowley, M. (1986). Gender and helping behavior: A meta-analytic review of the social psychological literature. *Psychological Bulletin, 100,* 283–308.

Eagly, A. H., & Johnson, B. T. (1990). Gender and leadership style: A meta-analysis. *Psychological Bulletin, 108,* 233–256.

Eagly, A. H., & Steffen, V. J. (1986a). Gender and aggressive behavior: A meta-analytic review of the social psychological literature. *Psychological Bulletin, 100,* 309–330.

Eagly, A. H., & Wood, W. (1999). The origins of sex differences in human behavior. *American Psychologist, 54,* 408–423.

Eagly, A. H., Ashmore, R. D., Makhijani, M. G., & Longo, L. C. (1991). What is beautiful is good, but . . .: A meta-analytic review of research on the physical attractiveness stereotype. *Psychological Bulletin, 110,* 107–128.

Eagly, A. H., Karau, S. J. (2002). Role congruity theory of prejudice toward female leaders. *Psychological Review, 109,* 573–598.

Eagly, A. H., Karau, S. J., & Makhijani, M. G. (1995). Gender and the effectiveness of leaders: A meta-analysis. *Psychological Bulletin, 117,* 125–145.

Eaton, J. (2001). Management communication: The threat of groupthink. *Corporate Communications, 6,* 183–192.

Ebbesen, E. B., Kjos, G. L., & Konecni, V. J. (1976). Spatial ecology: Its effects on the choice of friends and enemies. *Journal of Experimental Social Psychology, 12,* 505–518.

Echabe, A. E. & Garate, J. F. V. (1994). Private self-consciousness as moderator of the importance of attitude and subjective norm: The prediction of voting. *European Journal of Social Psychology, 24,* 285–293.

Echabe, A. E., Rovira, D. P., & Garate, J. F. V. (1988). Testing Ajzen and Fishbein's attitudes model: The prediction of voting. *European Journal of Social Psychology, 18,* 181–189.

Edgerton, R. (1971). *The individual in cultural adaptation.* Berkeley: University of California Press.

Edney, J. J. (1979). The nuts game: A concise commons dilemma analog. *Environmental Psychology and Nonverbal Behavior, 3,* 252–254.

Edson, R. (1976). *The intuitive journey and other works.* New York: Harper & Row.

Edwards, K., & Smith, E. E. (1996). A disconfirmation bias in the evaluation of arguments. *Journal of Personality and Social Psychology, 71,* 5–24.

Eimer, M., & Schlaghecken, F. (in press). Links between conscious awareness and response inhibition: Evidence from masked priming. *Psychonomic Bulletin and Review.*

Eisenberg, N., Martin, C. L., & Fabes, R. A. (1996). Gender development and gender effects. In D. C. Berliner & R. C. Calfee (Eds.), *Handbook of educational psychology* (pp. 358–396). New York: Prentice-Hall.

Eisenberger, N. I., Lieberman, M. D., & Williams, K. D. (2003). Does rejection hurt? An fMRI study of social exclusion. *Science, 302,* 290–292.

Eisenberger, R., Cotterell, N., & Marvel, J. (1987). Reciprocation ideology. *Journal of Personality and Social Psychology, 53,* 743–750.

Ekman, P. (1994). Strong evidence for universals in facial expressions: A reply to Russell's mistaken critique. *Psychological Bulletin, 115,* 268–287.

Ekman, P., & Friesen, W. V. (1974). Detecting deception from the body or face. *Journal of Personality and Social Psychology, 29,* 288–298.

Ekman, P., & O'Sullivan, M. (1991). Who can catch a liar? *American Psychologist, 46,* 913–920.

Ekman, P., Friesen, W. V., & O'Sullivan, M. (1988). Smiles when lying. *Journal of Personality and Social Psychology, 54,* 414–420.

Ekman, P., Friesen, W. V., O'Sullivan, M., Chan, A., Diacoyanni-Tarlatzis, I., Heider, K., Krause, R., LeCompte, W. A., Pitcairn, T., Ricci-Bitti, P. E., Scherer, K., Tomita, M., & Tzavaras, A. (1987). Universals and cultural differences in the judgments of facial expressions of emotion. *Journal of Personality and Social Psychology, 53,* 712–717.

Elbedour, S., Shulman, S., & Kedem, P. (1997). Adolescent intimacy: A cross-cultural study. *Journal of Cross-Cultural Psychology, 28,* 5–22.

Eldridge, N. S., & Gilbert, L. A. (1990). Correlates of relationship satisfaction in lesbian couples. *Psychology of Women Quarterly, 14,* 43–62.

Elias, S. M., & Mace, B. L. (2004). Social power in the classroom: Student attributions for compliance. *Journal of Applied Social Psychology, 34.*

Ellemers, N., Rijswijk, W. V., Roefs, M., & Simons, C. (1997). Bias in intergroup perceptions: Balancing group identity with social reality. *Personality and Social Psychology Bulletin, 23,* 186–198.

Eller, A., & Abrams, D. (2004). Come together: Longitudinal comparisons of Pettigrew's reformulated intergroup contact model and the common ingroup identity model in Anglo-French and Mexican-American contexts. *European Journal of Social Psychology, 34.*

Elliot, A. J., & Reis, H. T. (2003). Attachment and exploration in adulthood. *Journal of Personality and Social Psychology, 85,* 317–331.

Elliott, G. C. (2001). The self as social product and social force: Morris Rosenberg and the elaboration of a deceptively simple effect. In T. J. Owens, S. Stryker, & N. Goodman (Eds.), *Extending self-esteem theory and research: Sociological and psychological currents* (pp. 10–28). Cambridge: Cambridge University Press.

Ellis, A. P. J., West, B. J., Ryan, A. M., & DeShon, R. P. (2002). The use of impression management tactics in structured interviews: A function of question type? *Journal of Applied Psychology, 87,* 1200–1208.

Ellis, J., & Fox, P. (2001). The effect of self-identified sexual orientation on helping behavior in a British sample: Are lesbians and gay men treated differently? *Journal of Applied Social Psychology, 31,* 1238–1247.

Ellsworth, P. C., & Mauro, R. (1998). Psychology and law. In D. T. Gilbert, S. T. Fiske, & G. Lindzey (Eds.), *The handbook of social psychology* (4th ed., Vol. 2, pp. 684–732). New York: McGraw-Hill.

Elms, A. C. (1975). The crisis of confidence in social psychology. *American Psychologist, 30,* 967–976.

Elms, A. C. (1994). Keeping deception honest: Justifying conditions for social scientific research strategems. In E. Erwin, S. Gendin, & L. Kleiman (Eds.), *Ethical issues in scientific research: An anthology* (pp. 121–140). New York: Garland.

Elms, A. C. (1995). Obedience in retrospect. *Journal of Social Issues, 51,* 21–31.

Elms, A. C., & Milgram, S. (1966). Personality characteristics associated with obedience and defiance toward authoritative command. *Journal of Experimental Research in Personality, 1,* 282–289.

Ely, R. J., & Thomas, D. A. (2001). Cultural diversity at work: The effects of diversity perspectives on work group processes and outcomes. *Administrative Science Quarterly, 46,* 229–273.

Ember, C. R., & Ember, M. (1994). War, socialization, and interpersonal violence: A cross-cultural study. *Journal of Conflict Resolution, 38,* 620–646.

Emmons, R. A., & Diener, E. (1986). A goal-affect analysis of everyday situational choices. *Journal of Research in Personality, 20,* 309–326.

Emswiller, T., Deaux, K., & Willits, J. E. (1971). Similarity, sex, and requests for small favors. *Journal of Applied Social Psychology, 1,* 284–291.

End, C. M., Kretschmar, J. M., & Dietz-Uhler, B. (2004). College students' perceptions of sports fandom as a social status determinant. *International Sports Journal, 8,* 114–123.

Engestrom, Y., Brown, K., Engestrom, R., & Koistinen, K. (1990). Organizational forgetting: An activity-theoretical perspective. In D. Middleton & D. Edwards (Eds.), *Collective remembering* (pp. 137–168). Newbury Park, CA: Sage.

Epley, N., & Gilovich, T. (1999). Just going along: Nonconscious priming and conformity to social pressure. *Journal of Experimental Social Psychology, 35,* 578–589.

Epley, N., & Gilovich, T. (2001). Putting adjustment back in the anchoring and adjustment heuristic: Differential processing of self-generated and experimenter-provided anchors. *Psychological Science, 12,* 391–396.

Epley, N., & Huff, C. (1998). Suspicion, affective response, and educational benefit as a result of deception in psychology research. *Personality and Social Psychology Bulletin, 24,* 759–768.

Epley, N., Van Boven, L., & Caruso, E. M. (2004). Balance where it really counts. *Behavioral and Brain Sciences, 27.*

Epstein, J. L. (1985). After the bus arrives: Resegregation in desegregated schools. *Journal of Social Issues, 41,* 23–43.

Epstein, S. (1973). The self-concept revisited, or a theory of a theory. *American Psychologist, 28,* 404–416.

Epstein, S., & Morling, B. (1995). Is the self motivated to do more than enhance and verify itself? In M. H. Kernis (Ed.), *Efficacy, agency, and self-esteem* (pp. 9–30). New York: Plenum.

Erber, R., Wegner, D. M., & Therriault, N. (1996). On being cool and collected: Mood regulation in anticipation of social interaction. *Journal of Personality and Social Psychology, 70,* 757–766.

Erickson, B., Lind, E. A., Johnson, B. C., & O'Barr, W. M. (1978). Speech style and impression formation in a court setting: The effects of "powerful" and "powerless" speech. *Journal of Experimental Social Psychology, 14,* 266–279.

Eron, L. D. (1963). Relationship of TV viewing habits and aggressive behavior in children. *Journal of Abnormal and Social Psychology, 67,* 193–196.

Eron, L. D., & Huesmann, L. R. (1984). The control of aggressive behavior by changes in attitudes, values, and the conditions of learning. In R. J. Blanchard & D. C. Blanchard (Eds.), *Advances in the study of aggression* (Vol. 1, pp. 139–171). New York: Academic Press.

Eron, L. D., Huesmann, L. R., Lefkowitz, M. M., & Walder, L. O. (1972). Does television violence cause aggression? *American Psychologist, 27,* 253–263.

Erwin, P. G. (1994). Effectiveness of social skills training with children: A meta-analytic study. *Counseling Psychology Quarterly, 7,* 305–310.

Esser, J. K., & Lindoerfer, J. S. (1989). Groupthink and the space shuttle Challenger accident: Toward a quantitative case analysis. *Journal of Behavioral Decision Making, 2,* 167–177.

Esses, V. M., Dovidio, J. F., Jackson, L. M., & Armstrong, T. L. (2001). The immigration dilemma: The role of perceived group competition, ethnic prejudice, and national identity. *Journal of Social Issues, 57,* 389–412.

Esses, V. M., Jackson, L. M., & Armstrong, T. L. (1998). Intergroup competition and attitudes toward immigrants and immigration: An instrumental model of group conflict. *Journal of Social Issues, 54,* 699–724.

Evans, P. C. (2003). "If only I were thin like her, maybe I could be happy like her": The self implications of associating a thin female ideal with life success. *Psychology of Women Quarterly, 27,* 209–214.

Evans, R. I. (1980). *The making of social psychology: Discussions with creative contributors.* New York: Gardner Press.

Eysenck, H. J. (1990). Biological dimensions of personality. In L. A. Pervin (Ed.), *Handbook of personality theory and research* (pp. 244–276). New York: Guilford.

Fagot, B. I. (1985). Changes in thinking about early sex role development. *Developmental Review, 5,* 83–98.

Fallon, A. (1990). Culture in the mirror: Sociocultural determinants of body image. In T. F. Cash & T. Pruzinsky (Eds.), *Body images: Development, deviance, and change* (pp. 80–109). New York: Guilford.

Farb, P. (1978). *Man's rise to civilization: The cultural ascent of the Indians of North America.* New York: Penguin.

Farnham, S. D., Greenwald, A. G., & Banaji, M. R. (1999). Implicit self-esteem. In D. Abrams & M. A. Hogg (Eds.), *Social identity and social cognition* (pp. 230–248). Oxford: Blackwell.

Farr, R. M. (1996). *The roots of modern social psychology.* Cambridge, MA: Blackwell.

Farrington, D. P. (1994). Childhood, adolescent, and adult features of violent males. In L. R. Huesmann (Ed.), *Aggressive behavior: Current perspectives* (pp. 215–240). New York: Plenum.

Fawkner, H. J., & McMurray, N. (2002). Body image in men: Self-reported thoughts, feelings, and behaviors in response to media images. *International Journal of Men's Health, 1,* 137–162.

Fazio, R. H. (1990). Multiple processes by which attitudes guide behavior: The MODE model as an integrative framework. In M. P. Zanna (Ed.), *Advances in experimental social psychology* (Vol. 23, pp. 75–109). New York: Academic Press.

Fazio, R. H. (1995). Attitudes as object-evaluation associations: Determinants, consequences, and correlates of attitude accessibility. In R. E. Petty & J. A. Krosnick (Eds.), *Attitude strength: Antecedents and consequences* (pp. 247–282). Mahwah, NJ: Erlbaum.

Fazio, R. H. (2001). On the automatic activation of associated evaluations. An overview. *Cognition and emotion, 14,* 1–27.

Fazio, R. H., & Williams, C. J. (1986). Attitude accessibility as a moderator of the attitude-perception and attitude-behavior relations. *Journal of Personality and Social Psychology, 51,* 505–514.

Fazio, R. H., Zanna, M. P., & Cooper, J. (1977). Dissonance and self-perception: An integrative view of each theory's proper domain of application. *Journal of Experimental Social Psychology, 13,* 464–479.

Federal Bureau of Investigation (Oct. 22, 2001). *Crime in the United States.* http://www.fbi.gov/pressrel/pressrel01/cius2000.htm

Federico, C. M. (2004) Predicting attitude extremity: The interactive effects of schema development and the need to evaluate and their mediation by evaluative integration. *Personality and Psychology Bulletin, 30,* 1281–1294.

Federman, J. (1998). (Ed). *National Television Violence Study, Vol. 3.* (1998). Thousand Oaks, CA: Sage.

Feeney, B. C., & Kirkpatrick, L. A. (1996). Effects of adult attachment and presence of romantic partners on physiological responses to stress. *Journal of Personality and Social Psychology, 70,* 255–270.

Feeney, J. A. (2003). The systemic nature of couple relationships: An attachment perspective. In P. Erdman & T. Caffery (Eds.). *Attachment and family systems: Conceptual, empirical, and therapeutic relatedness.* (pp. 139–163). New York: Brunner/Mazel.

Fehr, B. (2003). Intimacy expectations in same-sex friendships: A prototype interaction-pattern model. *Journal of Personality and Social Psychology, 86,* 265–284.

Fehr, E. (1993). How do I love thee. . .? Let me consult my prototype. In S. Duck (Ed.). *Understanding personal relationships: Individuals in relationships* (Vol. 1, pp. 87–120). Newbury Park, CA: Sage.

Fehr, E., & Gaechter, S. (2002). Altruistic punishment in humans. *Nature, 415,* 137–140.

Feingold, A. (1988). Matching for attractiveness in romantic partners and same-sex friends: A meta-analysis and theoretical critique. *Psychological Bulletin, 104,* 226–235.

Feingold, A. (1992a). Gender differences in mate selection preferences: A test of the parental investment model. *Psychological Bulletin, 112,* 125–139.

Feingold, A. (1992a). Gender differences in mate selection preferences: A test of the parental investment model. *Psychological Bulletin, 112,* 125–139.

Feingold, A. (1992b). Good-looking people are not what we think. *Psychological Bulletin, 111,* 304–341.

Feingold, A., & Mazzella, R. (1998). Gender differences in body image are increasing. *Psychological Science, 9,* 190–195.

Fejfar, M. C., & Hoyle, R. H. (2000). Effect of private self-awareness on negative affect and self-referent attribution: A qualitative review. *Personality and Social Psychology Review, 4,* 132–142.

Feldman, S., & Stenner, K. (1997). Perceived threat and authoritarianism. *Political Psychology, 18,* 741–770.

Felmlee D. H., & Sprecher, S. (2000). Close relationships and social psychology: Intersections and future paths. *Social Psychology Quarterly, 63,* 365–376.

Felmlee, D. H. (1999). Social norms in same- and cross-gender friendships. *Social Psychology Quarterly, 62,* 53–67.

Felson, R. B. (1997). Anger, aggression, and violence in love triangles. *Violence and victims, 12,* 345–362.

Fenigstein, A., & Vanable, P. A. (1992). Paranoia and self-consciousness. *Journal of Personality and Social Psychology, 62,* 129–138.

Fenigstein, A., Scheier, M. F., & Buss, A. H. (1975). Public and private self-consciousness: Assessment and theory. *Journal of Consulting and Clinical Psychology, 43,* 522–527.

Ferguson, G. (1955). Legal research on trial. *Judicature, 39,* 78–82.

Ferguson, M. J., & Bargh, J. A. (2004). Liking is for doing: The effects of goal pursuit on automatic evaluation. *Journal of Personality and Social Psychology, 87,* 557–572.

Fernald, J. L. (1995). Interpersonal heterosexism. In B. Lott, & D. Maluso (Eds.), *The social psychology of interpersonal discrimination* (pp. 80–117). New York: Guilford.

Ferrari, J. R., & Tice, D. M. (2000). Procrastination as a self-handicap for men and women: A task-avoidance strategy in a laboratory setting. *Journal of Research in Personality, 34,* 73–83.

Festinger, L. (1954). A theory of social comparison processes. *Human Relations, 7,* 117–140.

Festinger, L. (1957). *A theory of cognitive dissonance.* Stanford, CA: Stanford University Press.

Festinger, L., & Carlsmith, J. M. (1959). Cognitive consequences of forced compliance. *Journal of Abnormal and Social Psychology, 47,* 382–389.

Festinger, L., Pepitone, A., & Newcomb, T. (1952). Some consequences of deindividuation in a group. *Journal of Abnormal and Social Psychology, 47,* 382–389.

Festinger, L., Reicken, H. W., & Schachter, S. (1956). *When prophecy fails.* Minneapolis: University of Minnesota Press.

Festinger, L., Schachter, S., & Back, K. (1950). *Social pressures in informal groups: A study of a housing community.* New York: Harper.

Fiedler, F. E. (1967). *A theory of leadership effectiveness.* New York: McGraw-Hill.

Fiedler, F. E. (1987, September). When to lead, when to stand back. *Psychology Today,* pp. 26–27.

Fiedler, F. E. (1993). The leadership situation and the black box in contingency theories. In M. M. Chemers & R. Ayman (Eds.), *Leadership theory and research: Perspectives and directions* (pp. 1–28). San Diego, CA: Academic Press.

Fiedler, F. E., & Garcia, J. E. (1987). *New approaches to effective leadership.* New York: Wiley.

Fiedler, K. (2004). Tools, toys, truisms, and theories: Some thoughts on the creative cycle of theory formation. *Personality and Social Psychology Review, 8,* 123–131.

Fiedler, K., Walther, E., & Nickel, S. (1999). Covariation-based attribution: On the ability to assess multiple covariates of an effect. *Personality and Social Psychology Bulletin, 25,* 607–622.

Figueredo, A. J., Landau, M. J., & Sefcek, J. A. (2004). Apes and angels: Adaptionism versus panglossianism. *Behavioral and Brain Sciences, 27.*

Fine, G. A., & Elsbach, K. D. (2000). Ethnography and experiment in social psychological theory building: Tactics for integrating qualitative field data with quantitative lab data. *Journal of Experimental Social Psychology, 36,* 51–76.

Fine, G. A., & Holyfield, L. (1996). Secrecy, trust, and dangerous leisure: Generating group cohesion in voluntary organizations. *Social Psychology Quarterly, 59,* 22–38.

Fink, B., & Penton-Voak, I. (2002). Evolutionary psychology of facial attractiveness. *Current Directions in Psychological Science, 11,* 154–158.

Firestone, I. J., Kaplan, K. J., & Russell, J. C. (1973). Anxiety, fear, and affiliation with similar state versus dissimilar state others: Misery sometimes loves miserable company. *Journal of Personality and Social Psychology, 26,* 409–414.

Fishbein, M. (1980). A theory of reasoned action: Some applications and implications. In H. E.

Howe, Jr. & M. M. Page (Eds.), *Nebraska symposium on motivation, 1979* (Vol. 27, pp. 65–116). Lincoln: University of Nebraska Press.

Fishbein, M., & Ajzen, I. (1975). *Beliefs, attitude, intention, and behavior: An introduction to theory and research.* Reading, MA: Addison-Wesley.

Fishbein, M., & Coombs, F. S. (1974). Basis for decision: An attitudinal analysis of voting behavior. *Journal of Applied Social Psychology, 4,* 95–124.

Fisher, H. E. (1998). Lust, attraction, and attachment in mammalian reproduction. *Human Nature, 9,* 23–52.

Fisher, H. E. (2004). *Why we love: The nature and chemistry of romantic love.* New York: Henry Holt.

Fiske, A. P., & Haslam, N. (1996). Social cognition is thinking about relationships. *Current Directions in Psychological Science, 5,* 143–148.

Fiske, A. P., Kitayama, S., Markus, H. R., & Nisbett, R. E. (1998). The cultural matrix of social psychology. In D. T. Gilbert, S. T. Fiske, & G. Lindzey (Eds.), *The handbook of social psychology* (Vol. II, pp. 915–981). Boston, MA: McGraw-Hill.

Fiske, S. T. (1993). Controlling other people: The impact of power on stereotyping. *American Psychologist, 48,* 621–628.

Fiske, S. T. (2004). Developing a program of research. In C. Sansone, C. C. Morf, & A. T. Panter (Eds.), *Handbook of methods in social psychology* (pp. 71–90). Thousand Oaks, CA: Sage.

Fiske, S. T., & Cox, M. G. (1979). Person concepts: The effect of target familiarity and descriptive purpose on the process of describing others. *Journal of Personality, 47,* 136–161.

Fiske, S. T., & Dèpret, E. (1996). Control, interdependence and power: Understanding social cognition in its social context. In W. Stroebe & M. Hewstone (Eds.), *European review of social psychology* (Vol. 7, pp. 31–61). New York: Wiley.

Fiske, S. T., & Neuberg, S. L. (1990). A continuum model of impression formation, from category-based to individuating processes: Influence of information and motivation on attention and interpretation. In M. P. Zanna (Ed.), *Advances in experimental social psychology* (Vol. 23). New York: Academic Press.

Fiske, S. T., & Von Hendy, H. M. (1992). Personality feedback and situational norms can control stereotyping processes. *Journal of Personality and Social Pscycology, 62,* 577–596.

Fitzgerald, L. F. (1993). Sexual harassment: Violence against women in the workplace. *American Psychologist, 48,* 1070–1076.

Fitzgerald, L. F., Drasgow, F., Hulin, C. L., Gelfand, M. J., & Magley, V. J. (1997). Antecedents and consequences of sexual harassment in organizations: A test of an integrated model. *Journal of Applied Psychology, 82,* 578–589.

Fitzgerald, L. F., Swan, S., & Fischer, K. (1995). Why didn't she just report him? The psychological and legal implications of women's responses to sexual harassment. *Journal of Social Issues, 51,* 117–138.

Fletcher, G. (2002). *The new science of intimate relationships.* Malden, MA: Blackwell.

Fletcher, G. J. O., Danilovics, P., Fernandez, G., Peterson, D., & Reeder, G. D. (1986). Attributional complexity: An individual differences measure. *Journal of Personality and Social Psychology, 51,* 875–884.

Fletcher, G. J. O., Simpson, J. A., & Thomas, G. (2000). The measurement of perceived relationship quality components: A confirmatory factor analytic approach. *Personality and Social Psychology Bulletin, 26,* 340–354.

Fletcher, G. J. O., Tither, J. M., O'Loughlin, C., Friesen, M., & Overall, N. (2004). Warm and homely or cold and beautiful? Sex differences in trading off traits in mate selection. *Personality and Social Psychology Bulletin, 30,* 659–672.

Fletcher, J. K., & Käufer, K. (2003). Shared leadership. In C. L. Pearce & J. A. Conger (Eds.), *Shared leadership. Reframing the hows and whys of leadership.* (pp. 21–47). Thousand Oaks, CA: Sage.

Florack, A., Scarabis, M., & Bless, H. (2001). When do associations matter? The use of automatic associations toward ethnic groups in person judgments. *Journal of Experimental Social Psychology, 37,* 518–524.

Foddy, M., & Smithson, M. (1996). Relative ability, paths of relevance, and influence in task-oriented groups. *Social Psychology Quarterly, 59,* 140–153.

Foddy, M., Smithson, M., Schneider, S., & Hogg, M. (Eds.). (1999). *Resolving social dilemmas: Dynamic, structural, and intergroup aspects.* Philadelphia: Psychology Press.

Foels, R., & Pappas, C. J. (2004). Learning and unlearning the myths we are taught: Gender and social dominance orientation. *Sex Roles, 50,* 743–757.

Fogelman, E. (1996). Victims, perpetrators, bystanders, and rescuers in the face of genocide and its aftermath. In C. B. Strozier & M. Flynn (Eds.), *Genocide, war, and human survival* (pp. 87–97). Lanham, MD: Rowman & Littlefield.

Follette, W. C., Davis, D., & Kemmelmeier, M. (2003). Ideals and realities in the development and practice of informed consent. In W. O'Donohue & K. Ferguson (Eds.), *Handbook of professional ethics for psychologists: Issues, questions, and controversies* (pp. 195–226). Thousand Oaks, CA: Sage.

Ford, C. S., & Beach, F. A. (1951). *Patterns of sexual behavior.* New York: Harper & Row.

Fordham, S. (1985). *Black student school success as related to fictive kinship: Final report.* The National Institute of Education, Washington, D.C.

Forgas, J. P. (1998). Asking nicely? The effects of mood on responding to more or less polite requests. *Personality and Social Psychology Bulletin, 24,* 173–185.

Forrest, J. A., & Feldman, R. S. (2000). Detecting deception and judge's involvement: Lower task involvement leads to better lie detection. *Personality and Social Psychology Bulletin, 26,* 118–125.

Förster, J., & Strack, F. (1996). Influence of overt head movements on memory for valenced words: A case of conceptual-motor compatibility. *Journal of Personality and Social Psychology, 71,* 421–430.

Forsyth, D. R. (1990). *Group dynamics* (2nd ed.). Pacific Grove, CA: Brooks/Cole.

Foschi, M. (1996). Double standards in the evaluation of men and women. *Social Psychology Quarterly, 48,* 237–254.

Foshee, V. A., Bauman, K. F., Arriaga, X. B., Koch, G. G., & Linder, G. F. (1998). An evaluation of safe dates, an adolescent dating violence prevention program. *American Journal of Public Health, 88,* 45–50.

Foster, C. A., Witcher, B. S., Campbell, W. K., & Green, J. D. (1998). Arousal and attraction: Evidence for automatic and controlled processes. *Journal of Personality and Social Psychology, 74,* 86–101.

Foubert, J. D. (2000). The longitudinal effects of a rape-prevention program on fraternity men's attitudes, behavioral intent, and behavior. *Journal of American College Health, 48,* 158–163.

Fournier, M. A., Moskowitz, D. S., & Zuroff, D. C. (2002). Social rank strategies in hierarchical relationships. *Journal of Personality and Social Psychology, 83,* 425–433.

Fouts, R. (1997). *Next of kin: What chimpanzees have taught me about who we are.* New York: William Morrow.

Fox, D. R. (1985). Psychology, ideology, utopia, and the commons. *American Psychologist, 40,* 48–58.

Fox, R. (1992). Prejudice and the unfinished mind: A new look at an old failing. *Psychological Inquiry, 3,* 137–152.

Fraley, R. C., & Spieker, S. J. (in press). Are infant attachment patterns continuously or categorically distributed? A taxometric analysis of strange situation behavior. *Developmental Psychology.*

Frank, M. G., & Gilovich, T. (1989). Effect of memory perspective on retrospective causal attributions. *Journal of Personality and Social Psychology, 57,* 399–403.

Franklin, K. (2000). Antigay behaviors among young adults: Prevalence, patterns and motivators in a noncriminal population. *Journal of Interpersonal Violence, 15,* 339–362.

Franzoi, S. L. (1995). The body-as-object versus the body-as-process: Gender differences and gender considerations. *Sex Roles, 33,* 417–437.

Franzoi, S. L., & Chang, Z. (2000). The sociocultural dynamics of the physical self: How does gender shape body esteem? In J. A. Holstein & G. Miller (Eds.), *Perspectives on social problems* (pp. 179–201). Stamford, CT: JAI Press.

Franzoi, S. L., & Chang, Z. (2002). The body esteem of Hmong and Caucasian young adults. *Psychology of Women Quarterly, 26,* 89–91.

Franzoi, S. L., & Davis, M. H. (2005). Self-awareness and self-consciousness. In V. Derlega, B. Winstead, & W. Jones (Eds.), *Personality: Contemporary theory and research* (pp. 281–308) (3rd ed.). Belmont, CA: Thomson Wadsworth.

Franzoi, S. L., & Shields, S. A. (1984). The body esteem scale: Multidimensional structure and sex differences in a college population. *Journal of Personality Assessment, 48,* 173–178.

Fraser, C., Gouge, C., & Billig, M. (1971). Risky shifts, cautious shifts, and group polarization. *European Journal of Social Psychology, 1,* 7–30.

Frazier, P. A., & Cook, S. W. (1993). Correlates of distress following heterosexual relationship dissolution. *Journal of Social and Personal Relationships, 10,* 55–67.

Frazier, P. A., Cochran, C. C., & Olson, A. M. (1995). Social science research on lay defini-

tions of sexual harassment. *Journal of Social Issues, 51,* 21–37.

Frazier, P. A., Tix, A. P., & Barnett, C. L. (2003). The relational context of social support: Relational satisfaction moderates the relation between enacted support and distress. *Personality and Social Psychology Bulletin, 29,* 1133–1146.

Frederico, C. M., & Sidanius, J. (2002). Racism, ideology, and affirmative action revisited: the antecedents and consequences of "principled objections" to affirmative action. *Journal of Personality and Social Psychology, 82,* 488–502.

Fredricks, A. J., & Dossett, D. L. (1983). Attitude-behavior relations: A comparison of the Fishbein-Ajzen and the Bentler-Speckart models. *Journal of Personality and Social Psychology, 45,* 501–512.

Fredrickson, B. L., & Carstensen, L. L. (1990). Choosing social partners: How age and anticipated endings make people more selective. *Psychology and Aging, 5,* 335–347.

Fredrickson, B. L., Roberts, T., Noll, S. M., Quinn, D. M., & Twenge, J. M. (1998). That swimsuit becomes you: Sex differences in self-objectification, restrained eating, and math performance. *Journal of Personality and Social Psychology, 75,* 269–284.

Freedman, J. L. (1965). Long-term behavioral effects of cognitive dissonance. *Journal of Experimental Social Psychology, 1,* 145–155.

Freedman, J. L. (1984). Effect of television violence on aggressiveness. *Psychological Bulletin, 96,* 227–246.

French, J. R. P., & Raven, B. H. (1959). The bases of social power. In D. Cartwright (Ed.), *Studies in social power.* Ann Arbor: University of Michigan Press.

Frenkl, O. J., & Doob, A. N. (1976). Post-decision dissonance at the polling booth. *Canadian Journal of Behavioral Science, 8,* 347–350.

Frese, B., Moya, M. L., & Megias, J. L. (2004). Social perception of rape: How rape myth acceptance modulates the influence of situational factors. *Journal of Interpersonal Violence, 19,* 143–161.

Frey, D., & Schulz-Hardt, S. (2001). Confirmation bias in group information seeking and its implications for decision making in administration, business and politics. In F. Butera, & G. Mugny (Eds.), *Social influence in social reality: Promoting individual and social change* (pp. 53–73). Ashland, OH: Hogrefe & Huber.

Frey, K. P., & Eagly, A. H. (1993). Vividness can undermine the persuasiveness of messages. *Journal of Personality and Social Psychology, 65,* 32–44.

Freyd, J. J. (2002). In the wake of terrorist attack, hatred may mask fear. *Analyses of Social Issues and Public Policy, 2,* 5–8.

Friedman, H. S., & Miller-Herringer, T. (1991). Nonverbal display of emotion in public and private: Self-monitoring, personality, and expressive cues. *Journal of Personality and Social Psychology, 61,* 766–775.

Friedman, M. A., & Brownell, K. D. (1995). Psychological correlates of obesity: Moving to the next generation of research. *Psychological Bulletin, 117,* 3–20.

Frieze, I. H., Olson, J. E., & Russell, J. (1991). Attractiveness and income for men and women in management. *Journal of Applied Social Psychology, 21,* 1039–1057.

Frings, C., & Wentura, D. (2003). Who is watching big brother? TV consumption predicted by masked affective priming. *European Journal of Social Psychology, 33,* 779–791.

Frisby, C. M. (2004). Does race matter? Effects of idealized images on African American women's perceptions of body esteem. *Journal of Black Studies, 34,* 323–347.

Fritsch, J. (2000, February 26). The Diallo verdict: The overview; 4 officers in Diallo shooting are acquitted of all charges. *The New York Times,* p. A1.

Fritzsche, B. A., Finkelstein, M. A., & Penner, L. A. (2000). To help or not to help: Capturing individuals' decision policies. *Social Behavior and Personality, 28,* 561–578.

Froming, W. J., Corley, E. B., & Rinker, L. (1990). The influence of public self-consciousness and the audience's characteristics on withdrawal from embarrassing situations. *Journal of Personality, 58,* 603–622.

Froming, W. J., Nasby, W., & McManus, J. (1998). Prosocial self-schemas, self-awareness, and children's prosocial behavior. *Journal of Personality and Social Psychology, 75,* 766–777.

Froming, W. J., Walker, G. R., & Lopyan, K. J. (1982). Public and private self-awareness: When personal attitudes conflict with societal expectations. *Journal of Experimental Social Psychology, 18,* 476–487.

Fujihara, T., Kohyama, T., Andreu, J. M., & Ramirez, J. M. (1999). Justification of interpersonal aggression in Japanese, American and Spanish students. *Aggressive Behavior, 25,* 185–195.

Funder, D. C. (1999). *Personality judgment: A realistic approach to person perception.* New York: Academic Press.

Fung, H. H., & Carstensen, L. L. (2003). Sending memorable messages to the old: Age differences in preferences and memory for advertising. *Journal of Personality and Social Psychology, 85,* 163–178.

Fung, H. H., Carstensen, L. L., & Lang, F. R. (2001). Age-related patterns in social networks among European-Americans and African-Americans: Implications for socioemotional selectivity across the life span. *International Journal of Aging and Human Development, 52,* 185–206.

Fung, H. H., Carstensen, L. L., & Lutz, M. A. (1999). Influence of time on social preferences: Implications for life-span development. *Psychology and Aging, 14,* 595–604.

Furnham, A., McClelland, A., & Omer, L. (2003). A cross-cultural comparison of ratings of perceived fecundity and sexual attractiveness as a function of body weight and waist-to-hip ratio. *Psychology Health and Medicine, 8,* 219–230.

Furnham, A., Moutafi, J., & Baguma, P. (2002). A cross-cultural study on the role of weight and waist-to-hip ratio on female attractiveness. *Personality and Individual Differences, 32,* 729–745.

Gabrenya, W. K., Jr., Wang, Y. E., & Latané, B. (1985). Social loafing on an optimizing task: Cross-cultural differences among Chinese and Americans. *Journal of Cross-Cultural Psychology, 16,* 223–242.

Gabrieli, J. D. E. (1999). The architecture of human memory. In J. K. Foster & M. Jelicic (Eds.). *Memory: Systems, process, or function.* (pp. 205–231). Oxford, England: Oxford University Press.

Gaertner, S. L., & Dovidio, J. F. (1977). The subtlety of white racism, arousal, and helping behavior. *Journal of Personality and Social Psychology, 35,* 691–707.

Gaertner, S. L., & Dovidio, J. F. (2000). *Reducing intergroup bias: The common ingroup identity model.* Philadelphia, PA: Psychology Press.

Gaertner, S. L., Dovidio, J. F., Banker, B. S., Houlette, M., Johnson, K. M., & McGlynn, E. A. (2000). Reducing intergroup conflict: From superordinate goals to decategorization, recategorization, and mutual differentiation. *Group Dynamics: Theory, Research, and Practice, 4,* 98–114.

Gagnè, F. M., & Lydon, J. E. (2001). Mindset and relationship illusions: The moderating effects of domain specificity and relationship commitment. *Personality and Social Psychology Bulletin, 27,* 1144–1155.

Gaines, S. O., Jr. (1995). Relationships between members of cultural minorities. In J. T. Wood & S. Duck (Eds.), *Understudied relationships: Off the beaten track* (pp. 51–88). Thousand Oaks, CA: Sage.

Galinsky, A. D., & Moskowitz, G. B. (2000). Counterfactuals as behavioral primes: Priming the simulation heuristic and consideration of alternatives. *Journal of Experimental Social Psychology, 36,* 384–409.

Galinsky, A. D., Gruenfeld, D. H., & Magee, J. C. (2003). From power to action. *Journal of Personality and Social Psychology, 85,* 453–466.

Gallese, V., & Goldman, A. (1998). Mirror neurons and the stimulation theory of mind-reading. *Trends in Cognitive Sciences, 2,* 493–501.

Gallup, G. G., Jr. (1977). Self-recognition in primates: A comparative approach to the bidirectional properties of consciousness. *American Psychologist, 32,* 329–338.

Gammage, K. L., Carron, A. V., & Estabrooks, P. A. (2001). Team cohesion and individual productivity: The influence of the norm of reciprocity and the identifiability of individual effort. *Small Group Research, 32,* 3–18.

Gamson, W. A., Fireman, B., & Rytina, S. (1982). *Encounters with unjust authority.* Homewood, IL: Dorsey Press.

Gangestad, S. W., & Simpson, J. A. (2000). The evolution of human mating: Trade-offs and strategic pluralism. *Behavioral and Brain Sciences, 23,* 573–644.

Gangestad, S. W., & Snyder, M. (2000). Self-monitoring: Appraisal and reappraisal. *Psychological Bulletin, 126,* 530–555.

Garcia, S. D., & Khersonsky, D. (1997). "They are a lovely couple": Further examination of perceptions of couple attractiveness. *Journal of Social Behavior and Personality, 12,* 367–380.

Garcia, S. M., Weaver, K., Moskowitz, G. B., & Darley, J. M. (2002). Crowded minds: The implicit bystander effect. *Journal of Personality and Social Psychology, 83,* 843–853.

Gardner, W. L., Gabriel, S. & Hochschild, L. (2002). When you and I are "we," you are not threatening: The role of self-expansion in social comparison. *Journal of Personality and Social Psychology, 82,* 239–251.

Gardner, W. L., Gabriel, S., & Lee, A. Y. (1999). "I" value freedom, but "we" value relationships: Self-construal priming mirrors cultural differences in judgment. *Psychological Science, 15,* 321–326.

Gardner, W. L., Pickett, C. L., & Brewer, M. B. (2000). Social exclusion and selective memory: How the need to belong influences memory for social events. *Personality and Social Psychology Bulletin, 26,* 486–496.

Garfinkel, P. (1985). *In a man's world.* New York: New American Library.

Garner, D. M., Garfinkel, P. E., & Olmsted, M. P. (1983). An overview of sociocultural factors in the development of anorexia nervosa. In L. D. Darby, P. E. Garfinkel, D. M. Garner, & D. V. Coscina (Eds.), *Anorexia nervosa: Recent developments in research.* New York: Alan R. Liss.

Garnets, L. D., Herek, G. M., & Levy, B. (2003). Violence and victimization of lesbians and gay men. Mental health consequences. In L. D. Garnets & D. Kimmel (Eds.). *Psychological perspectives on lesbian, gay, and bisexual experience* (2nd ed.). (pp. 188–206). New York: Columbia University Press.

Gates, M. F., & Allee, W. C. (1933). Conditioned behavior of isolated and grouped cockroaches on a simple maze. *Journal of Comparative Psychology, 15,* 331–358.

Gathorne-Hardy, J. (1981). *Marriage, love, sex and divorce.* New York: Summit Books.

Gawronski, B. (2003). On difficult questions and evident answers: Dispositional inference from role-constrained behavior. *Personality and Social Psychology Bulletin, 29,* 1459–1475.

Gawronski, B., & Strack, F. (2004). On the prepositional nature of cognitive consistency: Dissonance changes explicit, but not implicit attitudes. *Journal of Experimental Social Psychology, 40.*

Gazzaniga, M. S. (Ed.). (2000). *The new cognitive neuroscience* (2nd ed.). Cambridge, MA: The MIT Press.

Geary, D. C., Rumsey, M., Bow-Thomas, C. C., & Hoard, M. K. (1995). Sexual jealousy as a facultative trait: Evidence from the pattern of sex differences in adults from China and the United States. *Ethology and Sociobiology, 16,* 355–383.

Gecas, V. (2001). The self as a social force. In T. J. Owens, S. Stryker, & N. Goodman (Eds.), *Extending self-esteem theory and research: Sociological and psychological currents* (pp. 85–100). Cambridge: Cambridge University Press.

Geen, R. G. (1968). Effects of frustration, attack, and prior training on aggressiveness upon aggressive behavior. *Journal of Personality and Social Psychology, 9,* 316–321.

Geen, R. G. (1978). Some effects of observing violence upon the behavior of the observer. In B. Maher (Ed.), *Progress in experimental personality research* (Vol. 8). New York: Academic Press.

Geen, R. G. (1990). *Human aggression.* Stony Stratford: Open University Press.

Geen, R. G. (1996). Preferred stimulation levels in introverts and extraverts: Effects on arousal and performance. *Journal of Personality and Social Psychology, 46,* 1303–1312.

Geen, R. G. (1998). Aggression and antisocial behavior. In D. T. Gilbert, S. T. Fiske, & G. Lindzey (Eds.), *The handbook of social psychology* (4th ed.). New York: McGraw-Hill.

Geiselman, R. E., Haight, N. A., & Kimata, L. G. (1984). Context effects in the perceived physical attractiveness of faces. *Journal of Experimental Social Psychology, 20,* 409–424.

Gelfand, M. J., Fitzgerald, L. F., & Dragsow, F. (1995). The structure of sexual harassment: A confirmatory analysis across cultures and setting. *Journal of Vocational Behavior, 47,* 164–177.

Gelles, R. J. (1993). Alcohol and other drugs are associated with violence: They are not its cause. In R. J. Gelles & D. R. Loseke (Eds.), *Current controversies on family violence* (pp. 182–196). Newbury Park, CA: Sage.

Gentile, D. A., Lynch, P. J., Linder, J. R., & Walsh, D. A. (2004). The effects of violent video game habits on adolescent hostility: Aggressive behaviors and school performance. *Journal of Adolescence, 27,* 5–22.

Georgesen, J. C., & Harris, M. J. (2000). The balance of power: Interpersonal consequences of differential power and expectancies. *Personality and Social Psychology Bulletin, 26,* 1239–1257.

Georgopoulos, A. P., Whang, K., Georgopoulos, M.-A., Tagaris, G. A., Amirikan, B., Richter, W., Kim, S.-G., & Ugurbil, K. (2001). Functional magnetic resonance imaging of visual object construction and shape discrimination: Relations among task, hemispheric liberalization, and gender. *Journal of Cognitive Neuroscience, 13,* 72–89.

Gerard, H. B., & Mathewson, G. C. (1966). The effects of severity of initiation on liking for a group: A replication. *Journal of Experimental Social Psychology, 2,* 278–287.

Gergen, K. J., Ellsworth, P., Maslach, C., & Seipel, M. (1975). Obligation, donor resources, and reactions to aid in 3 cultures. *Journal of Personality and Social Psychology, 43,* 462–474.

Gergen, K. J., Gergen, M. M., & Barton, W. H. (1973). Deviance in the dark. *Psychology Today, 7,* 129–130.

Gerlach, A. L., Wilhelm, F. H., & Roth, W. T. (2003). Embarrassment and social phobia: The role of parasympathetic activation. *Journal of Anxiety Disorders, 17,* 197–210.

Gerstenfeld, P. B. (2002). A time to hate: Situational antecedents of intergroup bias. *Analyses of Social Issues and Public Policy, 2,* 61–67.

Gervey, B. M., Chiu, C., Hong, Y., & Dweck, C. S. (1999). Differential use of person information in decisions about guilt versus innocence: The role of implicit theories. *Personality and Social Psychology Bulletin, 25,* 17–27.

Gettleman, T. E., & Thompson, J. K. (1993). Actual differences and stereotypical perceptions in body image and eating disturbance: A comparison of male and female heterosexual and homosexual samples. *Sex Roles, 29,* 545–562.

Giancola, P. R., & Zeichner, A. (1997). The biphasic effects of alcohol on human physical aggression. *Journal of Abnormal Psychology, 106,* 598–607.

Gibbons, F. X., & McCoy, S. B. (1991). Self-esteem, similarity, and reactions to active versus passive downward comparison. *Journal of Personality and Social Psychology, 60,* 414–424.

Gibbons, F. X., Carver, C. S., Scheier, M. F., & Hormuth, S. E. (1979). Self-focused attention and the placebo effect: Fooling some of the people some of the time. *Journal of Experimental Social Psychology, 15,* 263–274.

Gibbons, F. X., Lane, D. J., Gerrard, M., Reis-Bergan, M., Lautrup, C. L., Pexa, N. A., & Blanton, H. (2002). Comparison-level preferences after performance: Is downward comparison theory still useful? *Journal of Personality and Social Psychology, 83,* 865–880.

Gibson, B., & Sachau, D. (2000). Sandbagging as a self-presentational strategy: Claiming to be less than you are. *Personality and Social Psychology Bulletin, 26,* 56–70.

Giddens, A. (1981). *Profiles and critiques of social theory.* London: Macmillan.

Gil-Burmann, C., Pelaez, F., & Sanchez, S. (2002). Mate choice differences according to sex and age: An analysis of personal advertisements in Spanish newspapers. *Human nature, 13,* 493–508.

Gilbert, D. T. (1989). Thinking lightly about others: Automatic components of the social inference process. In J. Uleman & J. Bargh (Eds.), *Unwanted thought: Limits of awareness, intention, and control* (pp. 189–211). New York: Guilford.

Gilbert, D. T. (1998). Ordinary personalogy. In D. T. Gilbert, S. T. Fiske, & G. Lindzey (Eds.), *The handbook of social psychology* (4th ed., Vol. 2, pp. 89–150). New York: McGraw-Hill.

Gilbert, D. T., & Hixon, J. G. (1991). The trouble of thinking: Activation and application of stereotypic beliefs. *Journal of Personality and Social Psychology, 60,* 509–517.

Gilbert, D. T., Pelham, B. W., & Krull, D. S. (1988). On cognitive busyness: When person perceivers meet persons perceived. *Journal of Personality and Social Psychology, 54,* 733–740.

Gill, M. J., & Swann, W. B., Jr. (2004). On what it means to know someone: A matter of pragmatics. *Journal of Personality and Social Psychology, 86,* 405–418.

Gilovich, T., & Griffin, D. (2002). Introduction—heuristics and biases: Then and now. In T. Gilovich, D. Griffin, & D. Kahneman (Eds.), *Heuristic and biases: The psychology of intuitive judgment* (pp. 1–18). New York: Cambridge University Press.

Gilovich, T., & Savitsky, K. (2002). Like goes with like: The role of representativeness in erroneous and pseudo-scientific beliefs. In T. Gilovich, D. Griffin, & D. Kahneman (Eds.), *Heuristic and biases: The psychology of intuitive judgment* (pp. 617–624). New York: Cambridge University Press.

Gilovich, T., Medvec, V. H., & Chen, S. (1995). Commission, omission, and dissonance reduction: Coping with regret in the "Monty Hall" problem. *Personality and Social Psychology Bulletin, 21,* 182–190.

Gjerde, P. F., Onishi, M., & Carlson, K. S. (2004). Personality characteristics associated with romantic attachment: A comparison of interview and self-report methodologies. *Personality and Social Psychology Bulletin, 30,* 1402–1415.

Gleason, K. A., Jensen-Campbell, L. A., & Richardson, D. S. (2004). Agreeableness as a predictor of aggression in adolescence. *Aggressive Behavior, 30,* 43–61.

Gleason, M. E. J., Iida, M., Bolger, N., & Shrout, P. E. (2003). Daily supportive equity in close relationships. *Personality and Social Psychology Bulletin, 29,* 1036–1045.

Glenn, C. V., & Chow, P. (2002). Measurement of attitudes toward obese people among a Canadian sample of men and women. *Psychological Reports, 91,* 627–640.

Glenn, E. S. (1966). *Mind, culture and politics.* Cited in Stewart, E. C., & Bennett, M. J. (1991). *American cultural patterns: A cross-cultural perspective* (p. 102). Yarmouth, ME: Intercultural Press.

Glick, P., & 15 coauthors. (2004). Bad but bold: Ambivalent attitudes toward men predict gender inequality in 16 nations. *Journal of Personality and Social Psychology, 86,* 713–728.

Glick, P., & Fiske, S. T. (1996). The ambivalent sexism inventory: Differentiating hostile and benevolent sexism. *Journal of Personality and Social Psychology, 70,* 491–512.

Glick, P., & Fiske, S. T. (1999). The ambivalence toward men inventory: Differentiating hostile and benevolent beliefs about men. *Psychology of Women Quarterly, 23,* 519–536.

Glick, P., & Fiske, S. T. (2001a). Ambivalent sexism. In M. P. Zanna (Ed.), *Advances in experimental social psychology* (pp. 115–188). San Francisco: Academic Press.

Glick, P., & Fiske, S. T. (2001b). Ambivalent stereotypes as legitimizing ideologies: Differentiating paternalistic and resentful prejudice. In J. T. Jost & B. Major (Eds.), *The psychology of legitimacy: Emerging perspectives on ideology, justice, and intergroup relations.* New York: Cambridge University Press.

Glick, P., & Hilt, L. (2000). From combative children to ambivalent adults: The development of gender prejudice. In T. Eckes & M. Trautner (Eds.), *Developmental social psychology of gender.* Hillsdale, NJ: Erlbaum.

Glick, P., Diebold, J., Bailey-Werner, B., & Zhu, L. (1997). The two faces of Adam: Ambivalent sexism and polarized attitudes toward women. *Personality and Social Psychology Bulletin, 23,* 1323–1334.

Glick, P., Sakalli-Ugurlu, N., Ferreira, M. C., & de Souza, M. A. (2002). Ambivalent sexism and attitudes toward wife abuse in Turkey and Brazil. *Psychology of Women Quarterly, 26,* 292–297.

Godfrey, D. K., Jones, E. E., & Lord, C. G. (1986). Self-promotion is not ingratiating. *Journal of Personality and Social Psychology, 50,* 106–115.

Goethals, G. R., & Zanna, M. P. (1979). The role of social comparison in choice shifts. *Journal of Personality and Social Psychology, 37,* 1469–1476.

Goethals, G. R., Messick, D. M., & Allison, S. T. (1991). The uniqueness bias: Studies of constructive social comparison. In J. Suls & T. A. Wills (Eds.), *Social comparison: Contemporary theory and research.* Hillsdale, NJ: Erlbaum.

Goffman, E. (1959). *The presentation of self in everyday life.* Garden City, NY: Doubleday.

Goffman, E. (1963). *Stigma: Notes on the management of spoiled identity.* Englewood Cliffs, NJ: Prentice-Hall.

Goldberg, C. (2003, May 18). Privacy an issue in brain imaging: Machines can track unconscious preferences, fear. *Boston Globe.*

Goldberg, E. (2001). *The executive brain: Frontal lobes and the civilized mind.* New York: Oxford University Press.

Gollwitzer, P. M., & Schaal, B. (1998). Metacognition in action: The importance of implementation intentions. *Personality and Social Psychology Review, 2,* 124–136.

Gonnerman, M. E., Jr., Parker, C. P., Lavine, H., & Huff, J. (2000). The relationship between self-discrepancies and affective states: The moderating roles of self-monitoring and standpoints on the self. *Personality and Social Psychology Bulletin, 26,* 810–819.

Gonsiorek, J. C., & Weinrich, J. D. (1991). The definition and scope of sexual orientation. In J. C. Gonsiorek & J. D. Weinrich (Eds.), *Homosexuality: Research implications for public policy* (pp. 1–12). Newbury Park, CA: Sage.

Gonzales, M. H., Aronson, E., & Costanzo, M. (1988). Increasing the effectiveness of energy auditors: A field experiment. *Journal of Applied Social Psychology, 18,* 1049–1066.

Gonzales, M. H., Pederson, J. H., Manning, D. J., & Wetter, D. W. (1990). Pardon my gaffe: Effects of sex, status, and consequence severity on accounts. *Journal of Personality and Social Psychology, 58,* 610–621.

Good, C., Aronson, J., & Inzlicht, M. (2003). Improving adolescents' standardized test performance: An intervention to reduce the effects of stereotype threat. *Applied Developmental Psychology, 24,* 645–662.

Goodall, J. (1986). *The chimpanzees of Gombe.* Cambridge, MA: Harvard University Press.

Goodwin, S. A., Gubin, A., Fiske, S. T., & Yzerbyt, V. Y. (2000). Power can bias impression processes: Stereotyping subordinates by default and by design. *Group Processes & Intergroup Relations, 3,* 227–256.

Gopnik, A., Meltzoff, A. N., & Kuhl, P. K. (1999). *The scientist in the crib: Minds, brains, and how children learn.* New York: William Morrow.

Gorassini, D. R., & Olson, J. M. (1995). Does self-perception change explain the foot-in-the-door effect? *Journal of Personality and Social Psychology, 69,* 91–105.

Gordijn, E. H., Hindriks, I., Koomen, W., Dijksterhuis, A., & Knippenberg, A. V. (2004). Consequences of stereotype suppression and internal suppression motivation: a self-regulation approach. *Personality and Social Psychology Bulletin, 30,* 212–224.

Gordon, R. A. (1996). Impact of ingratiation on judgments and evaluations: A meta-analytic investigation. *Journal of Personality and Social Psychology, 71,* 54–70.

Göregenli, M. (1997). Individualist-collectivist tendencies in a Turkish sample. *Journal of Cross-Cultural Psychology, 28,* 787–794.

Gosling, S. D. (2004). Another route to broadening the scope of social psychology: Ecologically valid research. *Behavioral and Brain Sciences, 27.*

Gottman, J. M. (1979). *Marital interaction.* New York: Academic Press.

Gottman, J. M., & Levenson, R. W. (1992). Marital processes predictive of later dissolution: Behavior, physiology, and health. *Journal of Personality and Social Psychology, 63,* 221–233.

Gouldner, A. W. (1960). The norm of reciprocity: A preliminary statement. *American Sociological Review, 25,* 161–178.

Graen, G. B., & Hui, C. (2001). Approaches to leadership: Toward a complete contingency model of face-to-face leadership. In M. Erez & U. Kleinbeck (Eds), *Work motivation in the context of a globalizing economy* (pp. 211–225). Mahwah, NJ: Erlbaum.

Graham, S. R. (1992). What does a man want? *American Psychologist, 47,* 837–841.

Grandin, E., & Lupri, E. (1997). Intimate violence in Canada and the United States: A cross-national comparison. *Journal of Family Violence, 12,* 417–443.

Granström, K., & Stiwne, D. (1998). A bipolar model of groupthink: An expansion of Janis's concept. *Small Group Research, 29,* 32–56.

Graves, F. C., & Hennessy, M. B. (2000). Comparison of the effects of the mother and an unfamiliar adult female on cortisol and behavioral responses of pre- and postweaning guinea pigs. *Developmental Psychobiology, 36,* 91–100.

Grealy, L. (1994). *Autobiography of a face.* Boston: Houghton Mifflin.

Greaves, L. (1996). *Smoke screen: Women's smoking and social control.* Halifax, Canada: Fernwood.

Greca, A. M. la. (1993). Social skills training with children: Where do we go from here? *Journal of Clinical Child Psychology, 22,* 288–298.

Green, C. W. (1998). Normative influence on the acceptance of information technology: Measurement and effects. *Small Group Research, 29,* 85–123.

Green, D. P., Glaser, J., & Rich, A. (1998). From lynching to gay bashing: The elusive connection between economic conditions and hate crime. *Journal of Personality and Social Psychology, 75,* 82–92.

Green, J. D., & Campbell, W. K. (2000). Attachment and exploration in adults: Chronic and contextual accessibility. *Personality and Social Psychology Bulletin, 26,* 452–461.

Green, J. D., & Sedikides, C. (1999). Affect and self-focused attention revisited: The role of affect orientation. *Personality and Social Psychology Bulletin, 25,* 104–119.

Green, L. R., Richardson, D. S., Lago, T., & Schatten-Jones, E. C. (2001). Network correlates of social and emotional loneliness in young and older adults. *Personality and Social Psychology Bulletin, 27,* 281–288.

Green, M. C., & Brock, T. C. (2000). Transportation in the persuasiveness of public narratives. *Journal of Personality and Social Psychology, 79,* 701–721.

Greenberg, J., & Pyszczynski, T. (1985). The effect of an overheard slur on evaluations of the target: How to spread a social disease. *Journal of Experimental Social Psychology, 21,* 61–72.

Greenberg, M. S., & Frisch, D. M. (1972). Effects of intentionality on willingness to reciprocate a favor. *Journal of Experimental Social Psychology, 8,* 99–111.

Greenfield, P. M. (1994). Independence and interdependence as developmental scripts: Implications for theory, research, and practice. In P. M. Greenfield & R. R. Cocking (Eds.), *Cross-cultural roots of minority child development* (pp. 1–37). Hillsdale, NJ: Erlbaum.

Greenland, K., & Brown, R. (1999). Categorization and intergroup anxiety in contact between British and Japanese nationals. *European Journal of Social Psychology, 29,* 503–521.

Greenspan, D. H., Keltner, D. J., & Anderson, C. (2003). The effects of power on those who possess it: How social structure can affect social cognition. In G. A. Bodenhausen & A. J. Lambert (Eds.), *Foundations of social cognition: A festschrift in honor of Robert S.*

Wyer, Jr. (pp. 237–261). Washington, DC: American Psychological Association.

Greenwald, A. G. (1980). The totalitarian ego: Fabrication and revision of personal history. *American Psychologist, 35,* 603–618.

Greenwald, A. G., & Pratkanis, A. R. (1984). The self. In R. S. Weyer & T. K. Srull (Eds.), *The handbook of social cognition* (Vol. 3). Hillsdale, NJ: Erlbaum.

Greenwald, A. G., McGhee, D. E., & Schwartz, J. L. K. (1998). Measuring individual differences in implicit cognition: The implicit association test. *Journal of Personality and Social Psychology, 74,* 1464–1480.

Greenwald, A. G., Nosek, B. A., & Banaji, M. R. (2003). Understanding and using the implicit association test: I. An improved scoring algorithm. *Journal of Personality and Social Psychology, 85,* 197–216.

Greenwald, A. G., Oakes, M. A., & Hoffman, H. G. (2003). Targets of discrimination: Effects of race on responses to weapons holders. *Journal of Experimental Social Psychology, 39,* 399–405.

Gregory, G. D., Munch, J. M., & Peterson, M. (2002). Attitude functions in consumer research: Comparing value-attitude relations in individualist and collectivist cultures. *Journal of Business Research, 55,* 933–942.

Gregory, W. L., Cialdini, R. B., & Carpenter, K. M. (1982). Self-relevant scenarios as mediators of likelihood estimates and compliance: Does imagining make it so? *Journal of Personality and Social Psychology, 43,* 89–99.

Grogan, S., Williams, Z., & Conner, M. (1996). The effects of viewing same-gender photographic models on body esteem. *Psychology of Women Quarterly, 20,* 569–575.

Gross, A. E., & Latanè, J. G. (1974). Receiving help, reciprocation, and interpersonal attraction. *Journal of Applied Social Psychology, 4,* 210–223.

Gross, S. R., & Miller, N. (1997). The "golden section" and bias in perceptions of social consensus. *Personality and Social Psychology Review, 1,* 241–271.

Groth, A. N. (1979). *Men who rape: The psychology of the offender.* New York: Plenum.

Gruenfeld, D. H., & Preston, J. (2000). Upending the status quo: Cognitive complexity in U.S. Supreme Court justices who overturn legal precedent. *Personality and Social Psychology Bulletin, 26,* 1013–1022.

Gruner, C. R. (1985). Advice to the beginning speaker on using humor: What the research tells us. *Communication Education, 34,* 142–147.

Grusec, J. E. (1991). The socialization of empathy. In M. S. Clark (Ed.), *Review of personality and social psychology: Vol. Prosocial behavior* (pp. 9–33). Newbury Park, CA: Sage.

Grusec, J. E., Davidov, M., & Lundell, L. (2002). In P. K. Smith, & C. H. Hart (Eds.). *Blackwell handbook of childhood social development. Blackwell handbooks of developmental psychology* (pp. 457–474). Malden, MA: Blackwell.

Grush, J. E., McKeough, K. L., & Ahlering, R. F. (1978). Extrapolating laboratory exposure to actual political elections. *Journal of Personality and Social Psychology, 36,* 257–270.

Gudjonsson, G. H. (1991). Suggestibility and compliance among alleged false confessors and resisters in criminal trials. *Medicine, Science, and the Law, 31,* 147–151.

Gudjonsson, G. H. (2001). False confession. *Psychologist, 14,* 588–591.

Gudjonsson, G. H. (2003). *The psychology of interrogations and confessions: A handbook.* New York: Wiley.

Gueguen, N., & Jacob, C. (2001). Fund-raising on the Web: The effect of an electronic foot-in-the-door on donation. *Cyberpsychology and Behavior, 4,* 705–709.

Gueguen, N., Pascual, A., & Dagot, L. (2002). Low-ball and compliance to a request: An application in a field setting. *Psychological Reports, 91,* 81–84.

Guerin, B. (1986). Mere presence effects in humans: A review. *Journal of Personality and Social Psychology, 22,* 38–77.

Guerra, N. G., & Slaby, R. G. (1990). Cognitive mediators of aggression in adolescent offenders: 2. Intervention. *Developmental Psychology, 26,* 269–277.

Guille, L. (2004). Men who batter and their children: An integrated review. *Aggression and Violent Behavior, 9,* 129–163.

Guimond, S., Dambrun, M., Michinov, M., & Duarte, S. (2003). Does social dominance generate prejudice? Integrating individual and contextual determinants of intergroup cognitions. *Journal of Personality and Social Psychology, 84,* 697–721.

Gunnar, M. R. (2000). Early adversity and the development of stress reactivity and regulation. In C. Nelson (Ed.), *The effects of adversity on neurobehavioral development: Minnesota Symposia on Child Psychology, Vol. 31* (pp. 163–200).

Guthrie, J. P., Ash, R. A., & Bendapudi, V. (1995). Additional validity evidence for a measure of morningness. *Journal of Applied Psychology, 80,* 186–190.

Gutierres, S. E., Kenrick, D. T., & Partch, J. J. (1999). Beauty, dominance, and the mating game: Contrast effects in self-assessment reflect gender differences in mate selection. *Personality and Social Psychology Bulletin, 25,* 1126–1134.

Hadaway, C. K., Marler, P. L., & Chaves, (1993). What the polls don't show: A closer look at U.S. church attendance. *American Sociological Review, 58,* 741–752.

Hafer, C. L. (2000a). Do innocent victims threaten the belief in a just world? Evidence from a modified stroop task. *Journal of Personality and Social Psychology, 79,* 165–173.

Hafer, C. L. (2000b). Investment in long-term goals and commitment to just means drive the need to believe in a just world. *Personality and Social Psychology Bulletin, 26,* 1059–1073.

Hagestad, G. O., & Smyer, M. A. (1982). Dissolving long-term relationships: Patterns of divorcing in middle age. In S. Duck (Ed.), *Personal relationships, 4: Dissolving relationships* (pp. 155–188). New York: Academic Press.

Halberstadt, J., & Rhodes, G. (2003). It's not just average faces that are attractive: Computer-manipulated averageness makes birds, fish, and automobiles attractive. *Psychonomic Bulletin and Review, 10,* 149–156.

Halford, W. K., Hahlweg, K., & Dunne, M. (1990). The cross-cultural consistency of marital communication associated with marital distress. *Journal of Marriage and the Family, 52,* 487–500.

Hall, J. A. (1978). Gender effects in decoding nonverbal cues. *Psychological Bulletin, 85,* 845–875.

Hall, J. A. (1984). *Nonverbal sex differences: Communication accuracy and expressive style.* Baltimore: Johns Hopkins University Press.

Hall, S., & Brannick, M. T. (2002). Comparison of two random-effects methods of meta-analysis. *Journal of Applied Psychology, 87,* 377–389.

Halverson, A. M., Hallahan, M., Hart, A. J., & Rosenthal, R. (1997). Reducing the biasing effects of judges' nonverbal behavior with simplified jury instruction. *Journal of Applied Psychology, 82,* 590–598.

Ham, J., & Vonk, R. (2003). Smart and easy: Co-occurring activation of spontaneous trait inferences and spontaneous situational inferences. *Journal of Experimental Social Psychology, 39,* 434–447.

Hamann, S. B., Ely, T. D., Hoffman, J. M., & Kilts, C. D. (2002). Ecstasy and agony: Activation of the human amygdala in positive and negative emotion. *Psychological Science, 13,* 135–141.

Hamilton, D. L., & Gifford, R. K. (1976). Illusory correlation in interpersonal judgments. *Journal of Experimental Social Psychology, 12,* 392–407.

Hamilton, D. L., & Sherman, S. J. (1996). Perceiving persons and groups. *Psychological Review, 103,* 336–355.

Hamilton, J. T. (1998). *Channeling violence: The economic market for violent television programming.* Princeton, NJ: Princeton University Press.

Hammond, K. R. (2004). The wrong standard: Science, not politics, needed. *Behavioral and Brain Sciences, 27.*

Hampson, S. E. (1988). The dynamics of categorization and impression formation. In T. K. Srull & R. S. Wyer, Jr. (Eds.), *Advances in social cognition: Vol. 1. A dual process model of impression formation* (pp. 77–82). Hillsdale, NJ: Erlbaum.

Haney, P., & Durlak, J. A. (1998). Changing self-esteem in children and adolescents: A meta-analytic review. *Journal of Clinical Child Psychology, 27,* 423–433.

Hansen, C. H., & Hansen, R. D. (1988). Finding the face in the crowd: An anger superiority effect. *Journal of Personality and Social Psychology, 54,* 917–924.

Hansen, C. H., & Hansen, R. D. (1990). Rock music videos and antisocial behavior. *Basic and Applied Social Psychology, 11,* 357–369.

Hanson, R. K., Cadsky, O., Harris, A., & Lalonde, C. (1997). Correlates of battering among 997 men: Family, history, adjustment, and attitudinal differences. *Violence and Victims, 12,* 191–208.

Harari, H., Mohr, D., & Hosey, K. (1980). Faculty helpfulness to students: A comparison of compliance techniques. *Personality and Social Psychology Bulletin, 6,* 373–377.

Harbus, A. (2002). The medieval concept of the self in Anglo-Saxon England. *Self & Identity, 1,* 77–97.

Hardin, C. D. (2004). (Self-)conceptions as social actions. In J. T. Jost, M. R. Banaji, & D. A. Prentice (Eds.), *Perspectivism in social psychology: The yin and yang of scientific progress* (pp. 161–172). Washington, DC: American Psychological Association.

Hardin, G. (1968). The tragedy of the commons. *Science, 162,* 1243–1248.

Hare, A. P., & Kent, M. V. (1994). Leadership. In A. P. Hare, H. H. Blumberg, M. F. Davies, & M. V. Kent (Eds.), *Small group research: A handbook* (pp. 155–166). Norwood, NJ: Ablex.

Haritatos, J., & Benet-Martínez, V. (2002). Bicultural identities: The interface of cultural, personality, and socio-cognitive processes. *Journal of Research in Personality, 6,* 598–606.

Harkins, S. G., & Symanski, K. (1989). Social loafing and group evaluation. *Journal of Personality and Social Psychology, 56,* 934–941.

Harmon-Jones, E. (2000). Cognitive dissonance and experienced negative affect: Evidence that dissonance increases experienced negative affect even in the absence of aversive consequences. *Personality and Social Psychology Bulletin, 26,* 1490–1501.

Harmon-Jones, E., & Devine, P. G. (2003). Introduction to the special section on social neuroscience. *Journal of Personality and Social Psychology, 85,* 589–593.

Harmon-Jones, E., & Mills, J. (Eds.). (1999). *Cognitive dissonance: Progress on a pivotal theory in social psychology.* Washington, DC: American Psychological Association.

Harré, R. (1984). *Personal being: A theory for individual psychology.* Cambridge, MA: Harvard University Press.

Harrè, R. (1999). Discourse and the embodied person. In D. J. Nightingale & J. Cromby (Eds.), *Social constructionist psychology: A critical analysis of theory and practice* (pp. 97–112). Buckingham: Open University Press.

Harris, C. R. (2002). Sexual and romantic jealousy in heterosexual and homosexual adults. *Psychological Science, 13,* 7–12.

Harris, C. R. (2003a). A review of sex differences in sexual jealousy, including self-report data, psychophysiological responses, interpersonal violence, and morbid jealousy. *Personality and Social Psychology Review, 7,* 102–128.

Harris, C. R. (2003b). Factors associated with jealousy over real and imagined infidelity: An examination of the social-cognitive and evolutionary psychology perspectives. *Psychology of Women Quarterly, 27,* 319–329.

Harris, C. R. (2004). The evolution of jealousy. *American Scientist, 92,* 62–71.

Harris, C. R., & Christenfeld, N. (1996). Gender, jealousy, and reason. *Psychological Science, 7,* 364–366.

Harris, M. (1991). *Cultural anthropology* (3rd ed.). New York: HarperCollins.

Harris, M. (1999). *Theories of culture in postmodern times.* Walnut Creek, CA: Alta Mira Press

Harris, M. B. (1990). Is love seen as different for the obese? *Journal of Applied Social Psychology, 20,* 1209–1224.

Harris, M. B., Benson, S. M., & Hall, C. L. (1975). The effects of confession on altruism. *Journal of Social Psychology, 96,* 187–192.

Harris, M. J., Milich, R., Corbitt, E. M., Hoover, D. W., & Brady, M. (1992). Self-fulfilling effects of stigmatizing information on children's social interactions. *Journal of Personality and Social Psychology, 63,* 41–50.

Harris, S. M. (1995). Family, self, and sociocultural contributions to body-image attitudes of African-American women. *Psychology of Women Quarterly, 19,* 129–145.

Harrison, A., & Saeed, L. (1977). Let's make a deal: An analysis of revelations and stipulations in lonely hearts advertisements. *Journal of Personality and Social Psychology, 35,* 257–264.

Hart, A. J., Whalen, P. J., Shin, L. M., McInerney, S. C., Fischer, H., & Rauch, S. L. (2000). Differential response in the human amygdala to racial outgroup vs. ingroup face stimuli. *Neuroreport, 11,* 2351–2355.

Hart, S., Field, T., del Valle, C., & Letourneau, M. (1998). Infants protest their mothers' attending to an infant-size doll. *Social Development, 7,* 54–61.

Hartley, T. R., Ginsburg, G. P., Heffner, K. (1999). Self-presentation and cardiovascular reactivity. *International Journal of Psychophysiology, 32,* 75–88.

Hartley, W. S. (1970). *Manual for the twenty statements problem.* Kansas City, MO: Department of Research, Greater Kansas City Mental Health Foundation.

Hartmann, D. P. (1969). Influence of symbolically modeled instrumental aggression and pain cues on aggressive behavior. *Journal of Personality and Social Psychology, 11,* 280–288.

Harvey, E. L., & Hill, A. J. (2001). Health professionals' views of overweight people and smokers. *International Journal of Obesity, 25,* 1253–1261.

Harvey, J. H., Flanary, R., & Morgan, M. (1986). Vivid memories of vivid loves gone by. *Journal of Social and Personal Relationships, 3,* 359–373.

Harwood, R. L., Miller, J. G., & Irizarry, N. L. (1995). *Culture and attachment: Perceptions of the child in context.* New York: Guilford Press.

Haselton, M. G., & Buss, D. M. (2000). Error management theory: A new perspective on biases in cross-sex mind reading. *Journal of Personality and Social Psychology, 78,* 81–91.

Haslam, S. A., & Platow, M. J. (2001). The link between leadership and followership: How affirming social identity translates vision into action. *Personality and Social Psychology Bulletin, 27,* 1469–1479.

Hass, R. G., Katz, I., Rizzo, N., Bailey, J., & Eisenstadt, D. (1991). Cross-racial appraisal as related to attitude ambivalence and cognitive complexity. *Personality and Social Psychology Bulletin, 17,* 83–92.

Hastie, R., Penrod, S., & Pennington, N. (1983). *Inside the jury.* Cambridge, MA: Harvard University Press.

Hastorf, A., & Cantril, H. (1954). They saw a game: A case study. *Journal of Abnormal and Social Psychology, 49,* 129–134.

Hatfield, E. (1988). Passionate and companionate love. In R. J. Sternberg & M. L. Barnes (Eds.), *The psychology of love* (pp. 191–217). New Haven, CT: Yale University Press.

Hatfield, E., & Rapson, R. L. (1993). *Love, sex, and intimacy: Their psychology, biology, and history.* New York: HarperCollins.

Hatfield, E., & Rapson, R. L. (2002). Passionate love and sexual desire: Cultural and historical perspectives. In A. L. Vangelisti & H. T. Reis (Eds.), *Stability and change in relationships. Advances in personal relationships* (pp. 306–324). New York: Cambridge University Press.

Hatfield, E., Aronson, E., Abrahams, D., & Rottman, L. (1966). The importance of physical attractiveness in dating behavior. *Journal of Personality and Social Psychology, 4,* 508–516.

Hatfield, E., Greenberger, E., Traupmann, J., & Lambert, P. (1982). Equity and sexual satisfaction in recently married couples. *Journal of Sex Research, 18,* 18–32.

Hatfield, E., Walster, G. W., & Piliavin, J. (1978). Equity theory and helping relationships. In L. Wispé (Ed.), *Altruism, sympathy and helping* (pp. 115–139). New York: Academic Press.

Hau, K. T., & Salili, F. (1991). Structure and semantic differential placement of specific causes: Academic causal attributions by Chinese students in Hong Kong. *International Journal of Psychology, 26,* 175–193.

Haugtvedt, C. P., & Petty, R. E. (1992). Personality and persuasion: Need for cognition moderates the persistence and resistance of attitude changes. *Journal of Personality and Social Psychology, 63,* 308–319.

Haugtvedt, C. P., Schumann, D. W., Schneier, W. L., & Warren, W. L. (1994). Advertising repetition and variation strategies: Implications for understanding attitude strength. *Journal of Consumer Research, 21,* 176–189.

Hawkins, S. A., & Hastie, R. (1990). Hindsight: Biased judgments of past events after the outcomes are known. *Psychological Bulletin, 107,* 311–327.

Hayes, G. J. (2003). Institutional review boards: Balancing conflicting values in research. In W. O'Donohue & K. Ferguson (Eds.), *Handbook of professional ethics for psychologists: Issues, questions, and controversies* (pp. 101–112). Thousand Oaks, CA: Sage.

Hazan, C., & Shaver, P. (1987). Romantic love conceptualized as an attachment process. *Journal of Personality and Social Psychology, 52,* 511–524.

Hearold, S. (1986). A synthesis of 1043 effects of television on social behavior. In G. Comstock (Ed.), *Public communication and behavior* (Vol. 1, pp. 66–133). New York: Academic Press.

Heath, L., Acklin, M., & Wiley, K. (1991). Cognitive heuristics and AIDS risk assessment among physicians. *Journal of Applied Social Psychology, 21,* 1859–1867.

Heatherton, T. F., & Baumeister, R. F. (1991). Binge eating as escape from self-awareness. *Psychological Bulletin, 110,* 86–108.

Heatherton, T. F., Macrae, C. N., & Kelley, W. M. (2004). What the social brain sciences can tell us about the self. *Current Directions in Psychological Science, 13,* 190–193.

Hebl, M. R., & Mannix, L. M. (2003). The weight of obesity in evaluating others: A mere proximity effect. *Personality & Social Psychology Bulletin, 29,* 28–38.

Hebl, M. R., Foster, J. B., Mannix, L. M., & Dovidio, J. F. (2002). Formal and interpersonal discrimination: A field study of bias toward homosexual applicants. *Personality and Social Psychology Bulletin, 28,* 815–825.

Hebl, M. R., Tickle, J., & Heatherton, T. F. (2000). Awkward moments in interactions between nonstigmatized and stigmatized individuals. In T. F. Heatherton, R. E. Kleck, M. R. Hebl, & J. G. Hull (Eds.), *The social psychology of stigma* (pp. 273–306). New York: Guilford.

Hebl, M. R., Xu, J., & Mason, M. F. (2003). Weighing the care: Patients' perceptions of physician care as a function of gender and weight. *International Journal of Obesity, 27,* 269–275.

Hecht, M. A., & LaFrance, M. (1998). License or obligation to smile: The effect of power and sex on amount and type of smiling. *Personality and Social Psychology Bulletin, 24,* 1332–1342.

Heffner, K. L., Ginsburg, G. P., & Hartley, T. R. (2002). Appraisals and impression management opportunities: Person and situation influences on cardiovascular reactivity. *International Journal of Psychophysiology, 44,* 165–175.

Heffner, K. L., Kiecolt-Glaser, J. K., Loving, T. J., Glaser, R., & Malarkey, W. B. (2004). Spousal support satisfaction as a modifier of physiological responses to marital conflict in younger and older couples. *Journal of Behavioral Medicine, 11.*

Heider, F. (1946). Attitudes and cognitive organization. *Journal of Psychology, 21,* 107–112.

Heider, F. (1958). *The psychology of interpersonal relations.* New York: Wiley.

Heimpel, S. A., Wood, J. V., Marshall, M. A., & Brown, J. D. (2002). Do people with low self-esteem want to feel better? Self-esteem differences in motivation to repair negative moods. *Journal of Personality and Social Psychology, 82,* 128–147.

Heine, S. J., & Lehman, D. R. (1997). Culture, dissonance, and self-affirmation. *Personality and Social Psychology Bulletin, 23,* 389–400.

Heine, S. J., & Lehman, D. R. (1999). Culture, self-discrepancies, and self-satisfaction. *Personality and Social Psychology Bulletin, 25,* 915–925.

Helgesen, S. (1990). *The female advantage: Women's ways of leadership.* New York: Doubleday.

Helgeson, V. S. (1994). Long-distance romantic relationships: Sex differences in adjustment and breakup. *Personality and Social Psychology Bulletin, 20,* 254–265.

Helgeson, V. S., & Mickelson, K. D. (1995). Motives for social comparison. *Personality and Social Psychology Bulletin, 21,* 1200–1209.

Helmbrecht, J. (2002). Grammar and function of we. In A. Duszak (Ed.), *Us and others: Social identities across languages, discourses and cultures* (pp. 31–49). Amsterdam: John Benjamins.

Henderson-King, D., & Stewart, A. J. (1999). Educational experiences and shifts in group consciousness: Studying women. *Personality and Social Psychology Bulletin, 25,* 390–399.

Henderson, J. A., & Anglin, J. M. (2003). Facial attractiveness predicts longevity. *Evolution and Human Behavior, 24,* 351–356.

Hendrick, C., & Hendrick, S. (1986). A theory and method of love. *Journal of Personality and Social Psychology, 50,* 392–402.

Hendrick, C., & Hendrick, S. S. (2003). Romantic love: Measuring cupid's arrow. In S. J. Lopez & C. R. Snyder (Eds.). *Positive psychological assessment: A handbook of models and measures* (pp. 235–249). Washington, DC: American Psychological Association.

Hendrick, C., Hendrick, S., Foote, F. H., & Slapion-Foote, M. J. (1984). Do men and women love differently? *Journal of Social and Personal Relationships, 1,* 177–195.

Hepworth, J. T., & West, S. G. (1988). Lynchings and the economy: A time-series reanalysis of

Hovland and Sears (1940). *Journal of Personality and Social Psychology, 55,* 239–247.

Herbert, J., & Martinez, M. (2001). Neural mechanisms underlying aggressive behaviour. In J. Hill & B. Maughan (Eds.), *Conduct disorders in childhood and adolescence: Cambridge child and adolescent psychiatry* (pp. 67–102). New York: Cambridge University Press.

Herek, G. M. (1987). Religious orientation and prejudice: A comparison of racial and sexual attitudes. *Personality and Social Psychology Bulletin, 13,* 34–44.

Herek, G. M. (1988). Heterosexuals' attitudes toward lesbians and gay men: Correlates and gender differences. *Journal of Sex Research, 25,* 451–477.

Herek, G. M. (1991). Myths about sexual orientation: A lawyer's guide to social science research. *Law and Sexuality: A Review of Lesbian and Gay Legal Issues, 1,* 133–172.

Herek, G. M. (2000a). Sexual prejudice and gender: Do heterosexuals' attitudes toward lesbians and gay men differ? *Journal of Social Issues, 56,* 251–266.

Herek, G. M. (2000b). The psychology of sexual prejudice. *Current Directions in Psychological Science, 9,* 19–22.

Herek, G. M. (2002). Gender gaps in public opinion about lesbians and gay men. *Public Opinion Quarterly, 66,* 40–46.

Herek, G. M. (2003). Why tell if you're not asked? Self-disclosure, intergroup contact, and heterosexuals' attitude toward lesbians and gay men. In L. D. Garnets & D. C. Kimmel (Eds.). *Psychological perspectives on lesbian, gay, and bisexual experiences* (2nd ed.). (pp. 188–200). New York: Columbia University Press.

Herek, G. M. (2004). Beyond "homophobia": Thinking about sexual prejudice and stigma in the twenty-first century. *Sexuality Research and Social Policy, 1,* 6–24.

Herek, G. M., & Capitanio, J. P. (1996). "Some of my best friends": Intergroup contact, concealable stigma, and heterosexuals attitudes toward gay men and lesbians. *Personality and Social Psychology Bulletin, 22,* 412–424.

Herek, G. M., & Capitanio, J. P. (1998). Symbolic prejudice or fear of infection? A functional analysis of AIDS-related stigma among heterosexual adults. *Basic and Applied Social Psychology, 20,* 230–241.

Herek, G. M., Widaman, K. F., & Capitanio, J. P. (in press). When sex equals AIDS: Symbolic stigma and inaccurate beliefs about sexual transmissioin of AIDS among U.S. adults. *Social Problems.*

Hermans, D., De Houwer, J., & Eelen, P. (2001). A time course analysis of the affective priming effect. *Cognition and Emotion, 15,* 143–165.

Hewstone, M. (1996). Contact and categorization: Social psychological interventions to change intergroup relations. In C. N. Macrae, C. Stangor, & M. Hewstone (Eds.), *Stereotypes and stereotyping* (pp. 323–368). New York: Guilford.

Hewstone, M. (2003). Intergroup contact: Panacea for prejudice? *Psychologist, 16,* 352–355.

Hewstone, M., & Brown, R. J. (1986). Contact is not enough: An intergroup perspective on the "contact hypothesis." In M. Hewstone & R. Brown (Eds.), *Contact and conflict in intergroup encounters* (pp. 1–44). Oxford: Basil Blackwell.

Heyman, J., & Ariely, D. (2004). Effort for payment: A tale of two markets. *Psychological Science, 15,* 787–793.

Hicks, D. (1968). Short- and long-term retention of affectively-varied modeled behavior. *Psychonomic Science, 11,* 369–370.

Hiel, A. V., Pandelaere, M., & Duriez, B. (2004). The impact of need for closure on conservative beliefs and racism: Differential mediation by authoritarian submission and authoritarian dominance. *Personality and Social Psychology Bulletin, 30,* 824–837.

Higgins, E. T. (1987). Self-discrepancy: A theory relating self and affect. *Psychological Review, 94,* 319–340.

Higgins, E. T. (1996). The "self digest": Self-knowledge serving self-regulatory functions. *Journal of Personality and Social Psychology, 71,* 1062–1083.

Higgins, E. T. (2000). Social cognition: Learning about what matters in the social world. *European Journal of Social Psychology, 30,* 3–39.

Higgins, E. T. (2004). Making a theory useful: Lessons handed down. *Personality and Social Psychology Review, 8,* 138–145.

Higgins, E. T., Bond, R. N., Klein, R., & Strauman, T. (1986). Self-discrepancies and emotional vulnerability: How magnitude, accessibility, and type of discrepancy influence affect. *Journal of Personality and Social Psychology, 51,* 5–15.

Higgins, E. T., Rholes, W. S., & Jones, C. R. (1977). Category accessibility and impression formation. *Journal of Experimental Social Psychology, 13,* 141–154.

Higgins, R. L., & Harris, R. N. (1988). Strategic "alcohol" use: Drinking to self-handicap. *Journal of Social and Clinical Psychology, 6,* 191–202.

Hill, C. T., Rubin, Z., & Peplau, L. A. (1979). Breakups before marriage: The end of 103 affairs. In G. Levinger & O. C. Moles (Eds.), *Divorce and separation* (pp. 64–82). New York: Basic Books.

Hill, M. E. (2002). Skin color and the perception of attractiveness among African Americans. Does gender make a difference? *Social Psychological Quarterly, 65,* 77–91.

Hill, R. A., & Dunbar, R. (2003). Social network size in humans. *Human Nature, 14,* 53–72.

Hilton, P. R. (2000). *Stereotypes, cognition, and culture.* East Sussex: Psychology Press.

Hinck, S. S., & Thomas, R. W. (1999). Rape myth acceptance in college students: How far have we come? *Sex Roles, 40,* 815–832.

Hinde, R. A. (1990). The interdependence of the behavioural sciences. *Philosophical Transactions of the Royal Society of London, B 329,* 217–227.

Hing, L. S. S., Li, W., & Zanna, M. P. (2002). Inducing hypocrisy to reduce prejudicial responses among aversive racists. *Journal of Experimental Social Psychology, 38,* 71–78.

Hirt, E. R. (1990). Do I see only what I expect? Evidence for an expectancy-guided retrieval model. *Journal of Personality and Social Psychology, 58,* 937–951.

Hirt, E. R., Deppe, R. K., & Gordon, L. J. (1991). Self-reported versus behavioral self-handicapping: Empirical evidence for a theoretical distinction. *Journal of Personality and Social Psychology, 61,* 981–991.

Hirt, E. R., McCrea, S. M., & Boris, H. I. (2003). "I know you self-handicapped last exam": Gender differences in reactions to self-handicapping. *Journal of Personality and Social Psychology, 84,* 177–193.

Hirt, E. R., McCrea, S. M., & Kimble, C. E. (2000). Public self-focus and sex differences in behavioral self-handicapping: Does increasing self-threat still make it "just a man's game"? *Personality and Social Psychology Bulletin, 26,* 1131–1141.

Hirt, E. R., Zillmann, D., Erickson, G. A., & Kennedy, C. (1992). Costs and benefits of allegiance: Changes in fans' self-ascribed competencies after team victory versus defeat. *Journal of Personality and Social Psychology, 63,* 724–738.

Ho, D. Y.-F., & Chiu, C.-Y. (1994). Component ideas of individualism, collectivism, and social organization: An application in the study of Chinese culture. In U. Kim, H. C. Triandis, C. Kâğitçibşi, S. C. Choi, & G. Yoon (Eds.), *Individualism and collectivism: Theory, method, and applications* (pp. 137–156). Thousand Oaks, CA: Sage.

Hobart, C. W. (1958). The incidence of romanticism during courtship. *Social Forces, 36,* 364–367.

Hobson, J. A., & McCarley, R. W. (1977). The brain as a dream state generator: An activation-synthesis hypothesis of the dream process. *The American Journal of Psychiatry, 134,* 1335–1348.

Hobson, J. A., Stickgold, R., & Pace-Schott, E. F. (1998). The neuropsychology of REM sleep dreaming. *NeuroReport, 9*(3), R1–R14.

Hodges, S. D., Klaaren, K. J., & Wheatley, T. (2000). Talking about safe sex: The role of expectations and experience. *Journal of Applied Social Psychology, 2,* 330–349.

Hodgins, H. S., & Liebeskind, E. (2003). Apology versus defense: Antecedents and consequences. *Journal of Experimental Social Psychology, 39,* 297–316.

Hodgins, H. S., Liebeskind, E., & Schwartz, W. (1996). Getting out of hot water: Facework in social predicaments. *Journal of Personality and Social Psychology, 71,* 300–314.

Hoelzl, E., Kirchler, E., & Rodler, C. (2002). Hindsight bias in economic expectations: I knew all along what I want to hear. *Journal of Applied Psychology, 87,* 437–443.

Hoffman, J. (2001). *Gender and sovereignty: Feminism, the state and international relations.* New York: Palgrave.

Hoffman, L. E. (1992). American psychologists and wartime research on Germany, 1941–1945. *American Psychologist, 47,* 264–273.

Hoffman, L. G., Hevesi, A. G., Lynch, P. E., Gomes, P. J., Chodorow, N. J., Roughton, R. E., Frank, B., & Vaughn, S. (2000). Homophobia: Analysis of a "permissible" prejudice: A public forum of the American Psychoanalytic Association and the American Psychoanalytic Foundation. *Journal of Gay & Lesbian Psychotherapy, 4,* 5–53.

Hoffman, M. L. (1981). Is altruism part of human nature? *Journal of Personality and Social Psychology, 40,* 121–137.

Hofstede, C. (1980). *Culture's consequences: International differences in work related values.* Beverly Hills, CA: Sage.

Hogg, M. A. (1992). *The social psychology of group cohesiveness: From attraction to social identity.* London: Harvester-Wheatsheaf.

Hogg, M. A., & Abrams, D. (1988). *Social identifications: A social psychology of intergroup relations and group processes.* London: Routledge.

Hogg, M. A., & Hains, S. C. (1998). Friendship and group identification: A new look at the role of cohesiveness in groupthink. *European Journal of Social Psychology, 28,* 323–341.

Holahan, C. J., Moos, R. H., & Bonn, L. (1997). Social support, coping, and psychological adjustment: A resource model. In G. R. Pierce, B. Lakey, I. G. Sarason, & B. R. Sarason (Eds.), *Sourcebook of social support and personality* (pp. 169–186). New York: Plenum.

Holden, R. R., Wood, L. L., & Tomashewski, L. (2001). Do response time limitations counteract the effect of faking on personality inventory validity? *Journal of Personality and Social Psychology, 81,* 160–169.

Holland, R. W., Meertens, R. M., & Van Vugt, M. (2002). Dissonance on the road: Self-esteem as a moderator of internal and external self-justification strategies. *Personality and Social Psychology Bulletin, 28,* 1713–1724.

Holland, R. W., Verplanken, B., & van Knippenberg, A. (2003). From repetition to conviction: Attitude accessibility as a determinant of attitude certainty. *Journal of Experimental Social Psychology, 39,* 594–601.

Hollander, E. P. (1961). Some effects of perceived status on responses to innovative behavior. *Journal of Abnormal and Social Psychology, 63,* 247–250.

Hollander, E. P. (1992). The essential interdependence of leadership and followership. *Current Directions in Psychological Science, 1,* 71–75.

Hollingshead, A. B. (2001). Cognitive interdependence and convergent expectations in transactive memory. *Journal of Personality and Social Psychology, 81,* 1080–1089.

Hollon, S. D., Shelton, R. C., & Loosen, P. T. (1991). Cognitive therapy and pharmacotherapy for depression. *Journal of Consulting and Clinical Psychology, 58,* 88–99.

Holstein, J. A., & Miller, G. (Eds.). (2000). *Perspectives on social problems, Vol. 12.* Stamford, CT: JAI Press.

Holtgraves, T. (2004). Social desirability and self-reports: Testing models of socially desirable responding. *Personality and Social Psychology Bulletin, 30,* 161–172.

Homans, G. C. (1958). Social behavior as exchange. *American Journal of Sociology, 63,* 597–606.

Honeycutt, J. M. (2003). *Imagined interactions: Daydreaming about communication.* Cresskill, NJ: Hampton Press.

Hong, L. K., & Duff, R. W. (2002). Modulated participant-observation: Managing the dilemma of distance in field research. *Field Methods, 14,* 190–196.

Hong, Y. Y., Benet-Martínez, Chiu, C. Y., & Morris, M. W. (2003). Boundaries of cultural influence: Construct activation as a mechanism for cultural differences in social perception. *Journal of Cross-cultural Psychology, 34,* 453–464.

Hong, Y. Y., Ip, G., Chiu, C. Y., Morris, M., & Menon, T. (2001). Cultural identity and dynamic construction of the self: Collective duties and individual rights in Chinese and American cultures. *Social Cognition, 19,* 251–268.

Hong, Y. Y., Morris, M. W., Chiu, C.Y., & Benet-Martínez, V. (2000). Multicultural minds: A dynamic constructivist approach to culture and cognition. *American Psychologist, 55,* 709–720.

Horton, R. W., & Santogrossi, D. A. (1978). The effect of adult commentary on reducing the influence of televised violence. *Personality and Social Psychology Bulletin, 4,* 337–340.

Hosoda, M., Stone-Romero, E. F., & Coats, G. (2003). The effects of physical attractiveness on job-related outcomes: A meta-analysis of experimental studies. *Personnel Psychology, 56,* 431–462.

Houston, S., & Hwang, N. (1996). Correlates of the objective and subjective experiences of sexual harassment in high school. *Sex Roles, 34,* 189–204.

Hovland, C. I., & Sears, R. R. (1940). Minor studies in aggression: VI. Correlation of lynchings with economic indices. *Journal of Personality, 9,* 301–310.

Hovland, C. I., & Weiss, W. (1951). The influence of source credibility on communication effectiveness. *Public Opinion Quarterly, 15,* 635–650.

Hovland, C. I., Janis, I. L., & Kelley, H. H. (1953). *Communication and persuasion.* New Haven, CT: Yale University Press.

Hovland, C. I., Lumsdaine, A. A., & Sheffield, F. D. (1949). *Experiments on mass communication.* Princeton, NJ: Princeton University Press.

Howard, D. J. (1995). "Chaining" the use of influence strategies for producing compliance behavior. *Journal of Social Behavior and Personality, 10,* 169–185.

Howard, J. A., Blumstein, P., & Schwartz, P. (1987). Social evolutionary theories? Some observations on preferences in human mate selection. *Journal of Personality and Social Psychology, 53,* 194–200.

Hoyt, W. T. (2000). Rater bias in psychological research: When is it a problem and what can we do about it? *Psychological Methods, 5,* 64–86.

Huczynski, A., & Buchanan, D. (1996). Can leaders change their styles? In J. Billsberry (Ed.), *The effective manager: Perspectives and illustrations* (pp. 42–46). Thousand Oaks, CA: Sage.

Huesmann, L. R. (1986a). The effects of film and television violence among children. In S. J. Katz & P. Vesin (Eds.), *Children and the media* (pp. 101–128). Paris: Centre International de l'Enfance.

Huesmann, L. R. (1986b). Psychological processes promoting the relation between exposure to media violence and aggressive behavior by the viewer. *Journal of Social Issues, 42,* 125–140.

Huesmann, L. R. (1988). An information processing model for the development of aggression. *Aggressive Behavior, 14,* 125–139.

Huesmann, L. R., & Eron, L. D. (Eds.). (1986). *Television and the aggressive child: A cross-national comparison.* Hillsdale, NJ: Erlbaum.

Huesmann, L. R., & Miller, L. S. (1994). Long-term effects of repeated exposure to media violence in childhood. In L. R. Huesmann (Ed.), *Aggressive behavior: Current perspectives* (pp. 153–186). New York: Plenum.

Huesmann, L. R., Eron, L. D., & Yarmel, P. W. (1987). Intellectual functioning and aggression. *Journal of Personality and Social Psychology, 52,* 232–240.

Huesmann, L. R., Eron, L. D., Klein, R., Brice, P., & Fischer, P. (1983). Mitigating the imitation of aggressive behaviors by changing children's attitudes about media violence. *Journal of Personality and Social Psychology, 44,* 899–910.

Hugenberg, K., & Bodenhausen, G. V. (2004). Category membership moderates the inhibition of social identitites. *Journal of Experimental Social Psychology, 40,* 233–238.

Hughes, M., & Hertel, B. R. (1990). The significance of color remains: A study of life chances, mate and ethnic consciousness among black Americans. *Social Forces, 68,* 1105–1120.

Huguet, P., Latanè, B., & Bourgeois, M. (1998). The emergence of a social representation of human rights via interpersonal communication: Empirical evidence for the convergence of two theories. *European Journal of Social Psychology, 28,* 831–846.

Hui, C. H. (1986). Fifteen years of pornography research: Does exposure to pornography have any effects? *Bulletin of the Hong Kong Psychological Society, 14,* 41–62.

Hui, C. H., & Triandis, H. C. (1986). Individualism-collectivism, a study of cross-cultural researchers. *Journal of Cross-Cultural Psychology, 17,* 225–248.

Hull, C. L. (1943). *Principles of behavior: An introduction to behavior theory.* New York: Appleton-Century-Crofts.

Hull, J. G. (1981). A self-awareness model of the causes and effects of alcohol consumption. *Journal of Abnormal Psychology, 90,* 586–600.

Hull, J. G. (2002). Modeling the structure of self-knowledge and the dynamics of self-regulation. In A. Tesser, D. Stapel, & J. Woods (Eds.), *Self and motivation: Emerging psychological perspectives* (pp. 173–203). Washington, DC: American Psychological Association.

Hull, J. G., & Bond, C. F., Jr. (1986). Social and behavioral consequences of alcohol consumption and expectancy: A meta-analysis. *Psychological Bulletin, 99,* 347–360.

Hull, J. G., & Young, R. D. (1983). Self-consciousness, self-esteem, and success-failure as determinants of alcohol consumption in male social drinkers. *Journal of Personality and Social Psychology, 44,* 1097–1109.

Hull, J. G., Reilly, N. P., & Ennis, L. C. (1990). Self-consciousness, role discrepancy, and depressive affect. In R. Schwarzer & R. Wicklund (Eds.), *Anxiety and self-focused attention* (pp. 27–40). London: Harwood Academic.

Hull, J. G., Young, R. D., & Jouriles, E. (1986). Applications of the self-awareness model of alcohol consumption: Predicting patterns of use and abuse. *Journal of Personality and Social Psychology, 51,* 790–796.

Hunsberger, B. (1995). Religion and prejudice: The role of religious fundamentalism, quest, and right-wing authoritarianism. *Journal of Social Issues, 51,* 113–129.

Hunter, M. (1998). Colorstruck: Skin color stratification in the lives of African American women. *Sociological Inquiry, 68,* 517–535.

Huskinson, T. L. H., & Haddock, G. (2004). Individual differences in attitude structure: Variance in the chronic reliance on affective and cognitive information. *Journal of Experimental Social Psychology, 40,* 82–90.

Huth-Bocks, A. C., Levendosky, A. A., Bogat, G. A., & von Eye, A. (2004). The impact of maternal characteristics and contextual variables on infant-mother attyachment. *Child Development, 75,* 480–496.

Hutnik, N. (1991). *Ethnic minority identity: A social psychological perspective.* New York: Oxford University Press.

Hyatt, C. W., & Hopkins, W. D. (1994). Self-awareness in bonobos and chimpanzees: A comparative perspective. In S. T. Parker, R. W. Mitchell, & M. L. Boccia (Eds.), *Self-awareness in animals and humans: Developmental perspectives* (pp. 248–253). Cambridge, UK: Cambridge University Press.

Hyers, L., & Swim, J. (1998). A comparison of the experiences of dominant and minority group members during an intergroup encounter. *Group Process and Intergroup Relations, 1,* 143–163.

Iacoboni, M., Lieberman, M. D., Knowlton, B. J., Molnar-Szakacs, I., Moritz, M., Throop, C. J., & Fiske, A. P. (2004). Watching social interactions produces dorsomedial prefrontal and medial parietal BOLD fMRI signal increases compared to a resting baseline. *NeuroImage.*

Iacoboni, M., Woods, R., Brass, M., Bekkering, H., Mazziotta, J. C., & Rizzolatti, G. (1999). Cortical mechanisms of human imitation. *Science, 286,* 2526–2528.

Ichheiser, G. (1934). Über zurechnungstäuschungen. [About misattributions]. *Monatsschrift für Kriminalpsycholgie und Strafrechtsreform, 25,* 129–142.

Ichheiser, G. (1943). Misinterpretations of personality in everyday life and the psychologist's frame of reference. *Character and Personality, 12,* 145–160.

Ickes, W. (1985). Sex-role influences in dyadic interaction: A theoretical model. In C. Mayo & N. Henley (Eds.), *Compatible and incompatible relationships* (pp. 187–208). New York: Springer-Verlag.

Ickes, W. (2003). *Everyday mind reading: Understanding what other people think and feel.* Amherst, NY: Prometheus Books.

Ickes, W., & Simpson, J. A. (2001). Motivatinal aspects of empathic accuracy. In G. J. O. Fletcher & M. Clark (eds.), *The Blackwell handbook of social psychology: Interpersonal processes* (pp. 229–249). Oxford, England: Blackwell.

Igou, E. R., & Bless, H. (2003). Inferring the importance of arguments: Order effects and conversational rules. *Journal of Experimental Social Psychology, 39,* 91–99.

Illes, J., & Raffin, T. A. (2002). Neuroethics: An emerging new discipline in the study of brain and cognition. *Brain and Cognition, 50,* 341–344.

Inglehart, R., & Baker, W. (2000). Modernization, cultural change and the persistence of traditional values. *American Sociological Review, 65,* 19–51.

Inglehart, R., & Oyserman, D. (in press). Individualism, autonomy and self-espression: The human development syndrome. In H. Vinken, J. Soeters, & P. Ester (Eds.), *Comparing cultures: Dimensions of culture in a comparative perspective.* Leiden, The Netherlands: Brill.

Ingram, R. E. (1990). Self-focused attention in clinical disorders: Reviews and a conceptual model. *Psychological Bulletin, 107,* 156–176.

Inman, M. L., McDonald, N., & Ruch, A. (in press). Boasting and firsthand and secondhand impressions: A new explanation for the positive teller-listener extremity effect. *Basic and Applied Social Psychology.*

Inman, M. L., Reichl, A. J., & Baron, R. S. (1993). Do we tell less than we know or hear less than we are told? Exploring the teller-listener extremity effect. *Journal of Experimental Social Psychology, 29,* 528–550.

Insko, C. A., Schopler, H. J., Gaertner, G., Wildschutt, T., Kozar, R., Pinter, B., Finkel, E. J., Brazil, D. M., Cecil, C. L., & Montoya, M. R. (2001). Interindividual-intergroup discontinuity reduction through the anticipation of future sinterraction. *Journal of Personality and Social Psychology, 80,* 95–111.

Insko, C. A., Smith, R. H., Alicke, M. D., Wade, J., & Taylor, S. (1985). Conformity and group size: The concern with being right and the concern with being liked. *Personality and Social Psychology Bulletin, 11,* 41–50.

Inzlicht, M., & Ben-Zeev, T. (2000). A threatening intellectual environment: Why females are susceptible to experiencing problem-solving deficits in the presence of males. *Psychological Science, 11,* 365–371.

Inzlicht, M., & Ben-Zeev, T. (2003). Do high-achieving female students underperform in private? The implicatioins of threatening environments on intellectual processing. *Journal of Educational Psychology, 95,* 796–805.

Isbell, L. M. (2004). Not all happy people are lazy or stupid: Evidence of systematic processing in happy moods. *Journal of Experimental Social Psychology, 40,* 341–349.

Isbell, L. M., & Wyer, R. S. (1999). Correcting for mood-induced bias in the evaluation of political candidates: The roles of intrinsic and extrinsic motivation. *Personality and Social Psychology Bulletin, 25,* 237–249.

Isen, A. M. (1970). Success, failure, attention, and reactions to others: The warm glow of success. *Journal of Personality and Social Psychology, 15,* 294–301.

Isen, A. M. (1984). Toward understanding the role of affect in cognition. In S. R. Wyer & T. K. Srull (Eds.), *Handbook of social cognition* (Vol. 3, pp. 179–236). New York: Academic Press.

Isen, A. M. (1987). Positive affect, cognitive processes, and social behavior. In L. Berkowitz (Ed.), *Advances in experimental social psychology* (Vol. 20, pp. 203–253). New York: Academic Press.

Isen, A. M., & Levin, P. A. (1972). Effect of feeling good on helping: Cookies and kindness. *Journal of Personality and Social Psychology, 21,* 384–388.

Isen, A. M., & Simmonds, S. F. (1978). The effect of feeling good on a helping task that is incompatible with good mood. *Social Psychology Quarterly, 41,* 346–349.

Isen, A. M., Horn, N., & Rosenhan, D. L. (1973). Effects of success and failure on children's generosity. *Journal of Personality and Social Psychology, 27,* 239–247.

Isenberg, D. (1986). Group polarization: A critical review and meta-analysis. *Journal of Personality and Social Psychology, 50,* 1141–1151.

Ishii-Kuntz, M. (1989). Collectivism or individualism? Changing patterns of Japanese attitudes. *Social Science Review, 73,* 174–179.

Ito, T. A., & Urland, G. R. (2003). Race and gender on the brain: Electrocortical measures of attention to the race and gender of multiply categorizable individuals. *Journal of Personality and Social Psychology, 85,* 616–626.

Ito, T. A., Miller, N., & Pollock, V. E. (1996). Alcohol and aggression: A meta-analysis on the moderating effects of inhibitory cues, triggering effects, and self-focused attention. *Psychological Bulletin, 120,* 60–82.

Iwao, S. (1989). Social psychology's models of social behavior: Is it not time for West to meet East? Unpublished manuscript. Keio University, Institute for Communications Research, Tokyo, Japan.

Izard, C. E. (1994). Innate and universal facial expressions: Evidence from developmental and cross-cultural research. *Psychological Bulletin, 115,* 288–299.

Izard, C. E., Fantauzzo, C. A., Castle, J. M., Haynes, O. M., Rayias, M. F., & Putnam, P. H. (1995). The ontogeny and significance of infants' facial expressions in the first 9 months of life. *Developmental Psychology, 31,* 997–1013.

Jaśkowski, P., Skalska, B., & Verleger, R. (2003). How the self controls its "automatic pilot" when processing subliminal information. *Journal of Cognitive Neuroscience, 15,* 911–920.

Jackman, M. R. (1994). *The velvet glove: Paternalism and con??? in gender class and race relations.* Berkeley: University of California Press.

Jackson, J. W. (1993). Realistic group conflict theory: A review and evaluation of the theoretical and empirical literature. *Psychological Record, 43,* 395–413.

Jackson, J., & Williams, K. D. (1985). Social loafing on difficult tasks: Working collectively can improve performance. *Journal of Personality and Social Psychology, 49,* 937–942.

Jackson, L. A., Sullivan, L. A., Harnish, R., & Hodge, C. N. (1996). Achieving positive social identity: Social mobility, social creativity, and permeability of group boundaries. *Journal of Personality and Social Psychology, 70,* 241–254.

Jackson, L. M., Esses, V. M., & Burris, C. T. (2001). Contemporary sexism and discrimination: The importance of respect for men and women. *Personality and Social Psychology Bulletin, 27,* 48–61.

Jackson, S. E., Brett, J. F., Sessa, V. I., Cooper, D. M., Julin, J. A., & Peyronnin, K. (1991). Some differences make a difference: Individual dissimilarity and group heterogeneity as correlates of recruitment, promotions, and turnover. *Journal of Applied Psychology, 76,* 675–689.

Jacobs, R. C., & Campbell, D. T. (1961). The perpetuation of an arbitrary tradition through several generations of a laboratory microculture. *Journal of Abnormal and Social Psychology, 62,* 649–658.

James, L. M., & Olson, J. M. (2000). Jeer pressure: The behavioral effects of observing ridicule of others. *Personality and Social Psychology Bulletin, 26,* 474–485.

Jamieson, D. W., Lydon, J. E., & Zanna, M. P. (1987). Attitude and activity preference similarity: Differential bases of interpersonal attraction for low and high self-monitors. *Journal of Personality and Social Psychology, 53,* 1052–1060.

Janis, I. L. (1967). Effects of fear arousal on attitude change: Recent developments in theory and experimental research. In L. Berkowitz (Ed.), *Advances in experimental social psychology* (Vol. 3, pp. 166–224). New York: Academic Press.

Janis, I. L. (1982). *Groupthink* (2nd ed.). Boston: Houghton Mifflin.

Janis, I. L. (1996). Groupthink. In J. Billsberry (Ed.). *The effective manager: Perspectives and illustrations* (pp. 166–178). Thousand Oaks, CA: Open University Press.

Janis, I. L., & Feshbach, S. (1953). Effects of fear-arousing communications. *Journal of Abnormal and Social Psychology, 48,* 78–92.

Janis, I. L., Kaye, D., & Kirschner, P. (1965). Facilitating effects of "eating while reading" on responsiveness to persuasive communications. *Journal of Personality and Social Psychology, 1,* 17–27.

Janoff-Bulman, R., & Leggatt, H. K. (2002). Culture and social obligation: When "shoulds" are perceived as "wants." *Journal of Research in Personality, 36,* 260–270.

Jarvis, W. B. G., & Petty, R. E. (1996). The need to evaluate. *Journal of Personality and Social Psychology, 70,* 172–194.

Jefferis, V. E., van Baaren, R., & Chartrand, T. L. (2003). *The functional purpose of mimicry for creating interpersonal closeness.* Manuscript under review, The Ohio State University.

Jeffrey, L. R., Miller, D., & Linn, M. (2001). Middle school bullying as a context for the development of passive observers to the victimization of others. In R. A. Geffner & M. Loring (Eds.). *Bullying behavior: Current issues, research, and interventions (*pp. 143–156). Binghamton, NY: Haworth Maltreatment and Trauma Press/The Haworth Press.

Jellison, W. A., McConnell, A. R., & Gabriel, S. (2004). Implicit and explicit measures of sexual orientation attitudes: Ingroup preferences and related behaviors and beliefs among gay and straight men. *Personality and Social Psychology Bulletin.*

Jenson, R. E., & Moore, S. G. (1977). The effect of attribute statements on cooperativeness and competitiveness in school-age boys. *Child Development, 48,* 305–307.

Jepson, C., & Chaiken, S. (1990). Chronic issue-specific fear inhibits systematic processing of persuasive communications. *Journal of Social Behavior and Personality, 5,* 61–84.

Jewkes, R., & Abrahams, N. (2002). The epidemiology of rape and sexual coercion in South Africa: An overview. *Social Science and Medicine, 55,* 1231–1244.

Jimenez, J. A., & Abreu, J. M. (2003). Race and sex effects on attitudinal perceptions of acquaintance rape. *Journal of Counseling Psychology, 50,* 252–256.

Joe, J. R. (1994). Revaluing Native-American concepts of development and education. In P. M. Greenfield & R. R. Cocking (Eds.), *Cross-cultural roots of minority child development* (pp. 107–113). Hillsdale, NJ: Erlbaum.

Johansson-Love, J., & Geer, J. H. (2003). Investigation of attitude change in a rape prevention program. *Journal of Interpersonal Violence, 18,* 84–99.

John, O. P., Cheek, J. M., & Klohnen, E. C. (1996). On the nature of self-monitoring: Construct explication with Q-sort ratings. *Journal of Personality and Social Psychology, 71,* 763–776.

Johnson, C., Clay-Warner, J., & Funk, S. J. (1996). Effects of authority structures and gender on interaction in same-sex task groups. *Social Psychology Quarterly, 59,* 221–236.

Johnson, D. L., Wiebe, J. S., Gold, S. M., Andreasen, N. C., Hichwa, R. D., Watkins, G. L., et al. (1999). Cerebral blood flow and personality: A positron emission tomography study. *American Journal of Psychiatry, 156,* 252–257.

Johnson, J. D., Jackson, L. A., & Gatto, L. (1995). Violent attitudes and deferred academic aspirations: Deleterious effects of exposure to rap music. *Basic and Applied Social Psychology, 16,* 27–41.

Johnson, J. D., Noel, N. E., & Sutter-Hernandez, J. (2000). Alcohol and male acceptance of sexual aggression: The role of perceptual ambiguity. *Journal of Applied Social Psychology, 30,* 1186–1200.

Johnson, J. G., Cohen, P., Smailes, E. M., Kasen, S., & Brook, J. S. (2002). Television violence and aggressive behavior during adolescence and adulthood. *Science, 295, 2468–2471.*

Johnson, R. D., & Downing, R. L. (1979). Deindividuation and valence of cues: Effects of prosocial and antisocial behavior. *Journal of Personality and Social Psychology, 37,* 1532–1538.

Johnston, J. H., Driskell, J. E., & Salas, E. (1997). Vigilant and hypervigilant decision making. *Journal of Applied Psychology, 82,* 614–622.

Johnston, K. L., & White, K. M. (2003). Binge-drinking: A test of the role of group norms in the theory of planned behaviour. *Psychology and Health, 18,* 63–77.

Johnston, L. D., O'Malley, P. M., & Bachman, J. G. (2003). *Monitoring the Future national survey results on drug use, 1975–2002. Volume II: College students and adults ages 19–40* (NIH Publication No. 03–5376). Bethesda, MD: National Institute on Drug Abuse.

Johnston, V. S., & Franklin, M. (1993). Is beauty in the eye of the beholder? *Ethology and Sociobiology, 14,* 183–199.

Joiner, T. E., Alfano, M. S., & Metalsky, G. I. (1992). When depression breeds contempt: Reassurance seeking, self-esteem and rejection of depressed college students and their roommates. *Journal of Abnormal Psychology, 12,* 112–134.

Joireman, J. A., Lasane, T. P., Bennett, J., Richards, D., & Solaimani, S. (2001). Integrating social value orientation and the consideration of future consequences within the extended form activation model of proenvironmental behavior. *British Journal of Social Psychology, 40,* 133–145.

Joireman, J., Anderson, J., & Strathman, H. (2003). The aggression paradox: Understanding links among aggression, sensation seeking, and the consideration of future consequences. *Journal of Personality and Social Psychology, 84,* 1287–302.

Jonas, E., Schulz-Hardt, S., Frey, D., & Thelan, N. (2001). Confirmation bias in sequential information search after preliminary decisions: An expansion of dissonance theoretical research on selective exposure to information. *Journal of Personality and Social Psychology, 80,* 557–571.

Jones, B. C., Little, A. C., & Perrett, D. I. (2003). Why are symmetrical faces attractive? In S. P. Shohov (Ed.), *Advances in psychology research* (Vol. 19, pp. 145–166). Hauppauge, NY: Nova Science.

Jones, D., & Hill, K. (1993). Criteria of facial attractiveness in five populations. *Human Nature, 4,* 271–296.

Jones, E. E. (1964). *Ingratiation.* New York: Appleton-Century-Crofts.

Jones, E. E. (1990). *Interpersonal perception.* New York: W. H. Freeman.

Jones, E. E. (1998). Major developments in five decades of social psychology. In D. T. Gilbert, S. T. Fiske, & G. Lindzey (Eds.), *The handbook of social psychology* (4th ed., Vol. 1, pp. 3–57). New York: McGraw-Hill.

Jones, E. E., & Davis, K. E. (1965). A theory of correspondent inferences: From acts to dispositions. In L. Berkowitz (Ed.), *Advances in experimental social psychology* (Vol. 2, pp. 219–266). New York: Academic Press.

Jones, E. E., & Harris, V. A. (1967). The attribution of attitudes. *Journal of Experimental Social Psychology, 3,* 1–24.

Jones, E. E., & Nisbett, R. E. (1972). The actor and the observer: Divergent perceptions of the causes of behavior. In E. E. Jones, D. E. Kanouse, H. H. Kelley, R. E. Nisbett, S. Valins, & B. Weiner (Eds.), *Attribution: Perceiving the causes of behavior* (pp. 79–94). Morristown, NJ: General Learning Press.

Jones, E. E., & Pittman, T. S. (1982). Toward a general theory of strategic self-presentation. In J. Suls (Ed.), *Psychological perspectives on the self.* Hillsdale, NJ: Erlbaum.

Jones, E. E., & Wortman, C. (1973). *Ingratiation: An attributional approach.* Morristown, NJ: General Learning Press.

Jones, E. E., Davis, K. E., & Gergen, K. J. (1961). Role playing variations and their informational value for person perception. *Journal of Abnormal and Social Psychology, 63,* 302–310.

Jones, E. E., Rock, L., Shaver, K. G., Goethals, G. R., & Ward, L. M. (1968). Pattern of performance and ability attribution: An unexpected primacy effect. *Journal of Personality and Social Psychology, 10,* 317–340.

Jones, L. W., Sinclair, R. C., & Courneya, K. A. (2003). The effects of source credibility and message framing on exercise intentions, behaviors and attitudes: An integration of the elaboration likelihood model and prospect theory. *Journal of Applied Social Psychology, 33,* 179–196.

Jones, W. H., Carpenter, B. N., & Quintana, D. (1985). Personality and interpersonal predictors of loneliness in two cultures. *Journal of Personality and Social Psychology, 48,* 1503–1511.

Jones, W. H., Hobbs, S. A., & Hockenbury, D. (1982). Loneliness and social skills deficits. *Journal of Personality and Social Psychology, 42,* 682–689.

Jones, W. H., Sansone, C., & Helm, B. (1983). Loneliness and interpersonal judgments. *Personality and Social Psychology Bulletin, 9,* 437–441.

Jordan, C. H., Spencer, S. J., & Zanna, M. P. (2003). "I love me . . . I love me not": Implicit self-esteem, explicit self-esteem, and defensiveness. In S. J. Spencer, S. Fein, M. P. Zanna, & J. M. Olson (Eds.), *Motivated social perception: The Ontario symposium* (Vol. 9, pp. 117–145). Mahwah, NJ: Erlbaum.

Josephs, R. A., Bosson, J. K., & Jacobs, C. G. (2003). Self-esteem maintenance processes: Why low self-esteem may be resistant to change. *Personality and Social Psychology Bulletin, 29,* 920–933.

Josephs, R. A., Larrick, R. P., Steele, C. M., & Nisbett, R. E. (1992). Protecting the self from the negative consequences of risky decisions.

Journal of Personality and Social Psychology, 62, 26–37.

Jost, J. T., Banaji, M. R., & Prentice, D. A. (Eds.). (2004). *Perspectivism in social psychology: The yin and yang of scientific progress.* Washington, DC: American Psychological Association.

Jost, J., Glaser, J., Kruglanski, A., & Sulloway, F. (2003). Political conservatism as motivated social cognition. *Psychological Bulletin, 129,* 339–375.

Judd, C. M., & Park, B. (1988). Out-group homogeneity: Judgments of variability at the individual and group levels. *Journal of Personality and Social Psychology, 54,* 778–788.

Judd, C. M., Blair, I. V., & Chapleau, K. M. (2004). Automatic stereotypes vs. automatic prejudice: Sorting out the possibilities in the Payne (2001) weapon paradigm. *Journal of Experimental Social Psychology, 40,* 75–81.

Judd, C. M., Park, B., Ryan, C., Brauer, M., & Kraus, S. (1995). Stereotypes and ethnocentrism: Diverging interethnic perceptions of African American and White American youth. *Journal of Personality and Social Psychology, 69,* 460–481.

Judd, C. M., Ryan, C. S., & Park, B. (1991). Accuracy in the judgment of in-group and out-group variability. *Journal of Personality and Social Psychology, 61,* 366–379.

Judd, M., & Brauer, M. (1995). Repetition and evaluative extremity. In R. E. Petty & J. A. Krosnick (Eds.), *Attitude strength: Antecedents and consequences* (pp. 43–71). Mahwah, NJ: Erlbaum.

Judge, T. A., & Bono, J. E. (2001). Relationship of core self-evaluations traits—self-esteem, generalized self-efficacy, locus of control, and emotional stability—with job satisfaction and job performance: A meta-analysis. *Journal of Applied Psychology, 86,* 80–92.

Jussim, L. (1989). Teacher expectations: Self-fulfilling prophecies, perpetual biases, and accuracy. *Journal of Personality and Social Psychology, 57,* 469–480.

Jussim, L., Yen, H., & Aiello, J. R. (1995). Self-consistency, self-enhancement, and accuracy in reactions to feedback. *Journal of Experimental Social Psychology, 31,* 322–356.

Kacmar, K. M., Delery, J. E., & Ferris, G. R. (1992). Differential effectiveness of applicant impression management tactics on employment interview decisions. *Journal of Applied Social Psychology, 22,* 1250–1272.

Kåğitçibşi, C. (1994). A critical appraisal of individualism and collectivism: Toward a new formulation. In U. Kim, H. C. Triandis, C. Kåğitçibşi, S. Choi, & G. Yoon (Eds.), *Individualism and collectivism: Theory, method, and applications* (pp. 52–65). Thousand Oaks, CA: Sage.

Kahneman, D. (1995). Varieties of counterfactual thinking. In N. J. Roese & J. M. Olson (Eds.), *What might have been: The social psychology of counterfactual thinking* (pp. 375–396). Hillsdale, NJ: Erlbaum.

Kahneman, D., & Frederick, S. (2002). Representativeness revisited: Attribute substitution in intuitive judgment. In T. Gilovich, D. Griffin, & D. Kahneman (Eds.), *Heuristic and biases: The psychology of intuitive judgment* (pp. 49–81). New York: Cambridge University Press.

Kahneman, D., & Tversky, A. (1973). On the psychology of prediction. *Psychological Review, 80,* 237–251.

Kahneman, D., & Tversky, A. (1982). The simulation heuristic. In D. Kahneman, P. Slovic, & A. Tversky (Eds.), *Judgment under uncertainty: Heuristics and biases.* New York: Cambridge University Press.

Kaiser, C. R., & Major, B. (in press). Judgments of deserving and the emotional consequences of stigmatization. In C. W. Leach & L. Tiedens (Eds.), *The social life of emotions.*

Kaiser, C. R., & Miller, C. T. (in press). A stress and coping perspective on confronting sexism. *Psychology of Women Quarterly.*

Kaiser, C. R., Vick, S. B., & Major, B. (2004). A prospective investigation of the relationship between just-world beliefs and the desire for revenge after September 11, 2001. *Psychological Science, 15,* 503–506.

Kallgren, C. A., & Wood, W. (1986). Access to attitude-relevant information in memory as a determinant of attitude-behavior consistency. *Journal of Experimental Social Psychology, 22,* 328–338.

Kallgren, C. A., Reno, R. R., & Cialdini, R. B. (2000). A focus theory of normative conduct: When norms do and do not affect behavior. *Personality and Social Psychology Bulletin, 26,* 1002–1012.

Kalven, H., Jr., & Zeisel, H. (1966). *The American jury.* Boston: Little, Brown.

Kanagawa, C., Cross, S. E., & Markus, H. R. (2001). "Who am I?" The cultural psychology of the conceptual self. *Personality and Social Psychology Bulletin, 27,* 90–103.

Kanazawa, S. (1992). Outcome or expectancy? Antecedent of spontaneous causal attribution. *Personality and Social Psychology Bulletin, 18,* 659–668.

Kandel, D. B. (1978). Similarity in real-life adolescent friendship pairs. *Journal of Personality and Social Psychology, 36,* 306–312.

Kaplan, K. J., Firestone, I. J., Degnore, R., & Morre, M. (1974). Gradients of attraction as a function of disclosure probe intimacy and setting formality: On distinguishing attitude oscillation from attitude change—Study one. *Journal of Personality and Social Psychology, 30,* 638–646.

Kaplan, M. F. (1987). The influencing process in group decision making. In C. Hendrick (Ed.), *Review of personality and social psychology: Group processes* (Vol. 8, pp. 189–212). Beverly Hills, CA: Sage.

Kaplan, M. F., & Martin, A. M. (1999). Effects of differential status of group members on process and outcome of deliberation. *Group Processes and Intergroup Relations, 2,* 347–364.

Kaplan, M. F., & Miller, C. E. (1983). Group discussion and judgment. In P. B. Paulus (Ed.), *Basic group processes* (pp. 65–94). New York: Springer-Verlag.

Karabenick, S. A., Lerner, R. M., & Beecher, M. D. (1973). Relation of political affiliation to helping behavior on election day, November 7, 1972. *Journal of Social Psychology, 91,* 223–227.

Karasawa, K. (1995). An attributional analysis of reactions to negative emotions. *Personality and Social Psychology Bulletin, 21,* 456–467.

Karasawa, M. (2003). Projecting group liking and ethnocentrism on ingroup members: False consensus effect of attitude strength. *Asian Journal of Social Psychology, 6,* 103–116.

Karau, S. J., & Kelly, J. R. (1992). The effects of time scarcity and time abundance on group performance quality and interaction process. *Journal of Experimental Social Psychology, 28,* 542–571.

Karau, S. J., & Williams, K. D. (1993). Social loafing: A meta-analytic review and theoretical integration. *Journal of Personality and Social Psychology, 65,* 681–706.

Karau, S. J., & Williams, K. D. (1995). Social loafing, research findings, implications, and future directions. *Current Directions in Psychological Science, 4,* 134–140.

Karpinski, A. (2004). Measuring self-esteem using the implicit association test: The role of the other. *Personality and Social Psychology Bulletin, 30,* 22–34.

Karraker, K. H., & Stern, M. (1990). Infant physical attractiveness and facial expression: Effects on adult perceptions. *Basic and Applied Social Psychology, 11,* 371–385.

Kashima, Y. (1987). Conceptions of person: Implications in individualism/collectivism research. In C. Kåğitçibşi, (Ed.), *Growth and progress in cross-cultural psychology* (pp. 104–112). Lisse, The Netherlands: Swets & Zeitlinger.

Kashima, Y., & Foddy, M. (2002). Time and self: The historical construction of the self. In Y. Kashima, M. Foddy, & M. Platow (Eds.), *Self and identity: Personal, social and symbolic* (pp. 181–206). Mahwah, NJ: Erlbaum.

Kashima, Y., & Kerekes, A. R. Z. (1994). A distributed memory model of averaging phenomena in person impression formation. *Journal of Experimental Social Psychology, 30,* 407–455.

Kashima, Y., Kokubo, T., Kashima E. S., Boxall, D., Yamaguchi, S., & Macrae, K. (2004). Culture and self: Are there within-culture differences in self between metropolitan areas and regional cities? *Personality and Social Psychology Bulletin, 30,* 816–823.

Kashima, Y., Siegel, M., Tanaka, K., & Kashima, E. S. (1992). Do people believe behaviours are consistent with attitudes? Towards a cultural psychology of attribution processes. *British Journal of Social Psychology, 31,* 111–124.

Kashima, Y., Yamaguchi, S., Kim, U., Choi, S-C., Gelfand, M. J., & Yuki, M. (1995). Culture, gender, and self: A perspective from individualism-collectivism research. *Journal of Personality and Social Psychology, 69,* 925–937.

Kashy, D. A., & DePaulo, B. M. (1996). Who lies? *Journal of Personality and Social Psychology, 70,* 1037–1051.

Kassin, S. M. (1997). The psychology of confession evidence. *American Psychologist, 52,* 221–233.

Kassin, S. M., & Kiechel, K. L. (1996). The social psychology of false confessions: Compliance, internalization, and confabulation. *Psychological Science, 7,* 125–128.

Katkin, E. S., Wiens, S., & Ohman, A. (2001). Nonconscious fear conditioning, visceral perception, and the development of gut feeling. *Psychological Science, 12,* 366–370.

Katz, D. (1960). The functional approach to the study of attitudes. *Public Opinion Quarterly, 24,* 163–204.

Katz, I., & Hass, R. G. (1988). Racial ambivalence and American value conflict: Correlational and prime studies of dual cognitive structures. *Journal of Personality and Social Psychology, 55,* 893–905.

Katz, I., Wackenhut, J., & Hass, R. G. (1986). Racial ambivalence, value duality, and behavior. In J. F. Dovidio & S. L. Gaertner (Eds.), *Prejudice, discrimination, and racism* (pp. 35–60). New York: Academic Press.

Katz, P. (1986). Gender identity: Development and consequences. In R. Ashmore & F. Del Boca (Eds.), *The social psychology of female-male relations* (pp. 21–67). Orlando, FL: Academic Press.

Kawakami, K., & Dovidio, J. F. (2001). The reliability of implicit stereotyping. *Personality and Social Psychology Bulletin, 27,* 212–225.

Kawakami, K., Dovidio, J. F., Moll, J., Hermsen, S., & Russin, A. (2000). Just say no (to stereotyping): Effects of training in the negation of stereotypic associations on stereotype activation. *Journal of Personality and Social Psychology, 78,* 871–888.

Keating, C. F. (1985). Gender and the physiognomy of dominance and attractiveness. *Social Psychology Quarterly, 48,* 61–70.

Keating, C. F., Mazur, A., Segall, M. H., Cysneiros, P. G., DiVale, W. T., Kilbride, J. E., Komin, S., Leahy, P., Thurman, B., & Wirsing, R. (1981). Culture and the perception of social dominance from facial expression. *Journal of Personality and Social Psychology, 40,* 601–614.

Kelley, H. H. (1950). The warm-cold variable in first impressions of persons. *Journal of Personality, 18,* 431–439.

Kelley, H. H. (1967). Attribution theory in social psychology. In D. L. Vine (Ed.), *Nebraska symposium on motivation.* Lincoln: University of Nebraska Press.

Kelley, H. H. (1972). Causal schemata and the attribution process. In E. Jones, D. Kanouse, H. Kelley, R. Nisbett, S. Valms, & B. Weiner (Eds.), *Attribution: Perceiving the causes of behavior.* Morristown, NJ: General Learning Press.

Kelly, J. R., Jackson, J. W., & Hutson-Comeaux, S. L. (1997). The effects of time pressure and task differences on influence modes and accuracy in decision-making groups. *Personality and Social Psychology, 23,* 10–22.

Kelly, L. (1997). Skills training as a treatment for communication problems. In J. A. Daly, J. C. McCroskey, J. Ayres, T. Hopf, & D. M. Ayres (Eds.), *Avoiding communication: Shyness, reticence, and communication apprehension* (2nd ed., pp. 331–365). Creskill, NJ: Hampton Press.

Kelman, H. C. (1958). Compliance, identification and internalization: Three processes of attitude change. *Journal of Conflict Resolution, 2,* 51–60.

Kelman, H. C. (1998). The place of ethnic identity in the development of personal identity: A challenge for the Jewish family. *Studies in Contemporary Jewry: An Annual* (pp. 3–26). New York: Oxford University Press.

Kelman, H. C., & Hovland, C. I. (1953). "Reinstatement" of the communicator in delayed measurement of opinion change. *Journal of Abnormal and Social Psychology, 48,* 327–335.

Keltner, D., & Anderson, C. (2000). Saving face for Darwin: The functions and uses of embarrassment. *Current Directions in Psychological Science, 9,* 187–192.

Keltner, D., & Robinson, R. J. (1997). Defending the status quo: Power and bias in social conflict.

Personality and Social Psychology Bulletin, 23, 1066–1077.

Keltner, D., Gruenfeld, D. H., & Anderson, C. (2003). Power, approach, and inhibition. *Psychological Review, 110,* 265–284.

Kemmelmeier, M. (2001). Private self-consciousness as a moderator of the relationship between value orientations and attitudes. *Journal of Social Psychology, 141,* 61–74.

Kemmelmeier, M., Davis, D., & Follette, W. C. (2003). Seven "sins" of misdirection? Ethical controversies surrounding the use of deception in research. In W. O'Donohue & K. Ferguson (Eds.), *Handbook of professional ethics for psychologists: Issues, questions, and controversies* (pp. 227–256). Thousand Oaks, CA: Sage.

Kemper, V. (2004, July 10). "Groupthink" led to decision to attack Iraq. *Los Angeles Times.*

Kennedy, Q., Fung, H. H., & Carstensen, L. L. (2001). Aging, time estimation and emotion. In S. H. McFadden & R. C. Atchley (Eds.), *Aging and the meaning of time* (pp. 51–74). New York: Springer.

Kenny, D. A. (2004). PERSON: A general model of interpersonal perception. *Personality and Social Psychology Review, 8,* 265–280.

Kenrick, D. T., & Cialdini, R. B. (1977). Romantic attraction: Misattribution versus reinforcement explanations. *Journal of Personality and Social Psychology, 35,* 381–391.

Kenrick, D. T., & Luce, C. L. (2000). An evolutionary life-history model of gender differences and similarities. In T. Eckes & H. M. Trautner (Eds.), *The developmental social psychology of gender* (pp. 35–63). Mahwah, NJ: Erlbaum.

Kenrick, D. T., & Maner, J. K. (2004). One path to balance and order in social psychology: An evolutionary perspective. *Behavioral and Brain Sciences, 27.*

Kenrick, D. T., & Simpson, J. A. (1997). Why social psychology and evolutionary psychology need one another. In J. A. Simpson & D. T. Kenrick (Eds.). *Evolutionary Social Psychology.* Mahwah, NJ: Erlbaum, 1–20.

Kenrick, D. T., & Trost, M. R. (1987). A biosocial theory of heterosexual relationships. In K. Kelly (Ed.), *Families, males, and sexuality.* Albany: State University of New York Press.

Kenrick, D. T., Baumann, D. J., & Cialdini, R. B. (1979). A step in the socialization of altruism as hedonism: Effects of negative mood on children's generosity under public and private conditions. *Journal of Personality and Social Psychology, 37,* 747–755.

Kenrick, D. T., Gabrielidis, C., Keefe, R. C., & Cornelius, J. S. (1996). Adolescents' age preferences for dating partners: Support for an evolutionary model of life-history strategies. *Child Development, 67,* 1499–1511.

Kenrick, D. T., Gutierres, S. E., & Goldberg, L. L. (1989). Influence of popular erotica on judgments of strangers and mates. *Journal of Experimental Social Psychology, 25,* 159–167.

Kerckhoff, A. C., & Davis, K. E. (1962). Value consensus and need complementarity in mate selection. *American Sociological Review, 27,* 295–303.

Kernis, M. H. (in press). Toward a conceptualization of optimal self-esteem. *Psychological Inquiry.*

Kernis, M. H., Paradise, A. W. (2002). Distinguishing between secure and fragile forms of high self-esteem. In E. L. Deci & R. M. Ryan

(Eds.), *Handbook of self-determinatioin research* (pp. 339–360). Rochester, NY: University of Rochester Press.

Kernis, M. H., Paradise, A. W., Whitaker, D. J., Wheatman, S. R., & Goldman, B. N. (2000). Master of one's psychological domain? Not likely if one's self-esteem is unstable. *Personality and Social Psychology Bulletin, 26,* 1297–1305.

Kerr, N. L. (1983). Motivation losses in small groups: A social dilemma. *Journal of Personality and Social Psychology, 45,* 819–828.

Kerr, N. L. (1992). Issue importance and group decision making. In S. Worchel, W. Wood, & J. A. Simpson (Eds.), *Group process and productivity* (pp. 68–88). Newbury Park, CA: Sage.

Kerr, N. L., & MacCoun, R. J. (1985). The effects of jury size and polling method on the process and product of jury deliberation. *Journal of Personality and Social Psychology, 48,* 349–363.

Kerr, N. L., & Tindale, R. S. (2004). Group performance and decision making. *Annual Review of Psychology, 55,* 623–655.

Kessler, R. C., Mickelson, K. D., & Williams, D. R. (1999). The prevalence, distribution, and mental health correlates of perceived discrimination in the United States. *Journal of Health and Social Behavior, 40,* 208–230.

Key, W. B. (1989). *The age of manipulation.* New York: Holt.

Kidwell, B., Brinberg, D., & Turrisi, R. (2003). Determinants of money management behavior. *Journal of Applied Social Psychology, 33,* 1244–1260.

Kierstead, M. D. (1981, April 6). The Shetland pony. *The New Yorker,* pp. 40–48.

Kiesler, C. A., & Pallak, M. S. (1975). Minority influence: The effect of majority reactionaries and defectors, and minority and majority compromisers, upon majority opinion and attraction. *European Journal of Social Psychology, 5,* 237–256.

Kiesler, S., Sproull, L., & Waters, K. (1996). A prisoner's dilemma experiment on cooperation with people and human-like computers. *Journal of Personality and Social Psychology, 70,* 47–65.

Kihlstrom, J. F. (2004). Is there a "people are stupid" school in social psychology. *Behavioral and Brain Sciences, 27.*

Kilham, W., & Mann, L. (1974). Level of destructive obedience as a function of transmitter and executant roles in the Milgram obedience paradigm. *Journal of Personality and Social Psychology, 29,* 696–702.

Kim, D-Y. (2003). After the South and North Korea summit: Malleability of explicit and implicit national attitudes of South Koreans. *Peace and Conflict: Journal of Peace Psychology, 9,* 159–170.

Kim, U. (1994). Individualism and collectivism: Conceptual clarification and elaboration. In U. Kim, H. C. Triandis, C. Kǎğıtçibşi, S. Choi, & G. Yoon (Eds.), *Individualism and collectivism: Theory, method, and applications* (pp. 19–40). Thousand Oaks, CA: Sage.

Kim, U., & Choi, S.-H. (1994). Individualism, collectivism, and child development: A Korean perspective. In P. M. Greenfield & R. R. Cocking (Eds.), *Cross-cultural roots of minority child development* (pp. 227–257). Hillsdale, NJ: Erlbaum.

Kimble, D. L., Covell, N. H., Weiss, L. H., Newton, K. J., & Fisher, J. D. (1992). College students use implicit personality theory instead of safer sex. *Journal of Applied Social Psychology, 22,* 921–933.

Kimble, G. A. (1989). Psychology from the standpoint of a generalist. *American Psychologist, 44,* 491–499.

Kimmel, A. J. (2004). Ethical issues in social psychology research. In C. Sansone, C. C. Morf, & A. T. Panter (Eds.), *Handbook of methods in social psychology* (pp. 45–70). Thousand Oaks, CA: Sage.

Kinder, D. R. (1998). Attitude and action in the realm of politics. In D. T. Gilbert, S. T. Fiske, & G. Lindzey (Eds.), *The handbook of social psychology* (4th ed., Vol. 2, pp. 778–867). New York: McGraw-Hill.

Kirkpatrick, L. A., & Davis, K. E. (1994). Attachment style, gender, and relationship stability: A longitudinal analysis. *Journal of Personality and Social Psychology, 66,* 502–512.

Kirkpatrick, L. A., Waugh, C. E., Valencia, A., & Webster, G. D. (2002). The functional domain specificity of self-esteem and the differential prediction of aggression. *Journal of Personality and Social Psychology, 82,* 756–767.

Kirkpatrick, S. A., & Locke, E. A. (1991). Leadership: Do traits matter? *Academy of Management Executives, 5(2),* 48–60.

Kirkpatrick, S. A., & Locke, E. A. (1996). Direct and indirect effects of three core charismatic leadership components on performance and attitudes. *Journal of Applied Psychology, 81,* 36–51.

Kite, M. E., & Whitley, B. E., Jr. (1996). Sex differences in attitudes toward homosexual persons, behaviors, and civil rights: A meta-analysis. *Personality and Social Psychology Bulletin, 22,* 336–353.

Kjaer, K. W., Nowak, M., & Lou, H. C. (2002). Reflective self-awareness and conscious states: PET evidence for a common midline parietofrontal core. *NeuroImage, 17,* 1080–1086.

Klahr, D., & Simon, H. A. (1999). Studies of scientific discovery: Complementary approaches and convergent findings. *Psychological Bulletin, 125,* 524–543.

Klauer, C. K., Ehrenberg, K., & Wegener, I. (2003). Crossed categorization and stereotyping: Structural analyses, effect patterns, and dissociative effects of context relevance. *Journal of Experimental Social Psychology, 39,* 332–354.

Klein, G. (1996). The effect of acute stressors on decision making. In J. Driskell & E. Salas (Eds.), *Stress and human performance* (pp. 49–88). Mahwah, NJ: Erlbaum.

Klein, W. M. P. (2003). Effects of objective feedback and "single other" or "average other" social comparison feedback on performance judgments and helping behavior. *Personality and Social Psychology Bulletin, 29,* 418–429.

Klein, W. M., & Weinstein, N. D. (1997). Social comparison and unrealistic optimism about personal risk. In B. P. Buunk & F. X. Gibbons (Eds.), *Health, coping and well-being* (pp. 25–61). London, UK: Erlbaum.

Kling, K. C., Hyde, J. S., Showers, C. J., & Buswell, B. N. (1999). Gender differences in self-esteem: A meta-analysis. *Psychological Bulletin, 125,* 470–500.

Klinger, L. J., Hamilton, J. A., & Cantrell, P. J. (2001). Children's perceptions of aggressive and gender-specific content in toy commercials. *Social Behavior and Personality, 29,* 11–20.

Klohnen, E. C., & Bera, S. (1998). Behavioral and experiential patterns of avoidantly and securely attached women across adulthood: A 31–year longitudinal perspective. *Journal of Personality and Social Psychology, 74,* 211–223.

Kluegel, J. R., & Smith, E. R. (1986). *Beliefs about inequality.* New York: Aldine.

Knapp, M. L., Stafford, L., & Daly, J. A. (1986). Regrettable messages: Things people wish they hadn't said. *Journal of Communication, 36,* 40–58.

Knight, R. T., & Grabowecky, M. (1995). Escape from linear time: Prefrontal cortex and conscious experience. In M. S. Gazzaniga (Ed.), *The cognitive neurosciences* (pp. 1357–1371). Cambridge, MA: MIT Press.

Knox, R. E., & Inkster, J. A. (1968). Postdecision dissonance at posttime. *Journal of Personality and Social Psychology, 8,* 319–323.

Knox, R. E., & Safford, R. K. (1976). Group caution at the race track. *Journal of Experimental Social Psychology, 12,* 317–324.

Koch, S. (1981). Psychology and its human clientele: Beneficiaries or victims? In R. A. Kasschau & F. S. Kessel (Eds.), *Psychology and society: In search of symbiosis* (pp. 24–47). New York: Holt, Rinehart.

Koestner, R., Bernieri, F., & Zuckerman, M. (1992). Self-regulation and consistency between attitudes, traits, and behaviors. *Personality and Social Psychology Bulletin, 18,* 52–59.

Koffka, K. (1935). *Principles of gestalt psychology.* London: Routledge.

Köhler, W. (1929). *Gestalt psychology.* New York: Liveright.

Komatsu, L. K. (1992). Recent reviews of conceptual structure. *Psychological Bulletin, 112,* 500–526.

Koole, S. L., Jager, W., van den Berg, A. E., Vlek, C. A. J., & Hofstee, W. K. B. (2001). On the social nature of personality: Effects of extraversion, agreeableness, and feedback about collective resource use on cooperation in a resource dilemma. *Personality and Social Psychology Bulletin, 27,* 289–301.

Koren, P., Carlton, K., & Shaw, D. (1980). Marital conflict: Relations among behaviors, outcomes, and distress. *Journal of Consulting and Clinical Psychology, 48,* 460–468.

Koss, M. P., Gidycz, C. A., & Wisniewski, N. (1987). The scope of rape: Incidence and prevalence of sexual aggression and victimization in a national sample of higher education students. *Journal of Consulting and Clinical Psychology, 55,* 162–170.

Kowert, P. A. (2002). *Groupthink or deadlock: When do leaders learn from their advisors?* Albany, NY: State University of New York Press.

Krahe, B., & Moller, I. (2004). Playing violent electronic games, hostile attributional style, and aggression-related norms in German adolescents. *Journal of Adolescence, 27,* 53–69.

Krahé, B., Scheinberger-Olwig, R., & Koplin, S. (2000). Ambiguous communication of sexual intentions as a risk marker of sexual aggression. *Sex roles, 1,* 313–337.

Kraut, R. E. (1973). Effects of social labeling on giving to charity. *Journal of Experimental Social Psychology, 9,* 551–562.

Kraut, R., Olson, J., Banaji, M., Bruckman, A., Cohen, J., & Couper, M. (in press). Psychological research online: Opportunities and challenges. *American Psychologist.*

Krebs, D. L. (1975). Empathy and altruism. *Journal of Personality and Social Psychology, 32,* 1134–1146.

Krefting, L. A. (2003). Intertwined discourses of merit and gender: Evidence from academic employment in the USA. *Gender, Work and Organization, 10,* 260–278.

Kristiansen, C. M., & Hotte, A. M. (1996). Morality and the self: Implications for the when and how of value-attitude behavior relations. In C. Seligman, J. Olson, & M. P. Zanna (Eds.), *The psychology of values: The Ontario symposium* (Vol. 8). Mahwah, NJ: Erlbaum.

Kristiansen, C. M., & Zanna, M. P. (1994). The rhetorical use of values to justify social and intergroup attitudes. *Journal of Social Issues, 50,* 47–65.

Krosnick, J. A. (1999). Survey research. *Annual Review of Psychology, 50,* 537–567.

Krosnick, J. A., & Alwin, D. F. (1989). Aging and susceptibility to attitude change. *Journal of Personality and Social Psychology, 59,* 1140–1152.

Krosnick, J. A., Betz, A. L., Jussim, L. J., & Lynn, A. R. (1992). Subliminal conditioning of attitudes. *Personality and Social Psychology Bulletin, 18,* 152–162.

Krueger, J. (1998). Enhancement bias in descriptions of self and others. *Personality and Social Psychology Bulletin, 24,* 505–516.

Krueger, J. (2001). Null hypothesis significance testing: On the survival of a flawed method. *American Psychologist, 56,* 16–26.

Krueger, J. I., & Funder, D. C. (2004). Towards a balanced social psychology: Causes, consequences and cures for the problem-seeking approach to social behavior and cognition. *Behavioral and Brain Sciences, 27.*

Krueger, J. I., Ham, J. J., & Linford, K. M. (1996). Perceptions of behavioral consistency: Are people aware of the actor-observer effect? *Psychological Science, 7,* 259–264.

Krueger, J. I., Hasman, J. F., Acevedo, M., & Villano, P. (2003). Perceptions of trait typicality in gender stereotypes: Explaining the role of attribution and categorization processes. *Personality and Social Psychology Bulletin, 29,* 108–116.

Kruger, D. J. (2003). Evolution and altruism: Combining psychological mediators with naturally selected tendencies. *Evolution and Human Behavior, 24,* 118–125.

Kruger, J., & Dunning, D. (1999). Unskilled and unaware of it: How difficulties in recognizing one's own incompetence lead to inflated self-assessments. *Journal of Personality and Social Psychology, 77,* 1121–1134.

Kruglanski, A. W. (1996). Motivated social cognition: Principles of the interface. In E. T. Higgins & A. W. Kruglanski (Eds.), *Social psychology: Handbook of basic principles* (pp. 493–520). New York: Guilford Press.

Kruglanski, A. W. (2001). That "vision thing": The state of theory in social and personality psychology at the edge of the new millennium. *Journal of Personality and Social Psychology, 80,* 871–875.

Kruglanski, A. W., & Freund, T. (1983). The freezing and unfreezing of lay inferences: Effects on impressional primacy, ethnic stereotyping, and numerical anchoring. *Journal of Experimental Social Psychology, 19,* 448–468.

Kruglanski, A. W., & Webster, D. M. (1996). Motivated closing of the mind: "Seizing" and "freezing." *Psychological Review, 103,* 263–283.

Krull, D. S. (2001). On partitioning the fundamental attribution error: Dispositionalism and the correspondence bias. In G. B. Moskowitz (Ed.), *Cognitive social psychology: The Princeton symposium on the legacy and future of social cognition* (pp. 211–227). Mahwah, NJ: Erlbaum.

Krull, D. S., & Dill, J. C. (1996). On thinking first and responding fast: Flexibility in social inference processes. *Personality and Social Psychology Bulletin, 22,* 949–959.

Krull, D. S., & Erickson, D. J. (1995). Inferential hopscotch: How people draw social inferences from behavior. *Current Directions in Psychological Science, 13,* 35–38.

Krull, D. S., Loy, M. H.-M., Lin, J., Wang, C.-F., Chen, S., & Zhao, X. (1999). The fundamental attribution error: Correspondence bias in individualist and collectivist cultures. *Personality and Social Psychology Bulletin, 25,* 1208–1219.

Kugihara, N. (2001). Effects of aggressive behaviour and group size on collective escape in an emergency: A test between a social identity model and deindividuation theory. *British Journal of Social Psychology, 40,* 575–598.

Kühnen, U., & Oyserman, D. (2002). Thinking about the self influences thinking in general: Cognitive consequences of salient self-concept. *Journal of Experimental Social Psychology, 38,* 492–499.

Kühnen, U., Hannover, B., & Schubert, B. (2001). The semantic-procedural interface model of the self: The role of self-knowledge for context-dependent versus context-independent modes of thinking. *Journal of Personality and Social Psychology, 80,* 397–409.

Kulig, J. W. (2000). Effects of forced exposure to a hypothetical population on false consensus. *Personality and Social Psychology Bulletin, 26,* 629–636.

Kulik, J. A., & Mahler, H. I. M. (1989). Stress and affiliation in a hospital setting: Preoperative roommate preferences. *Personality and Social Psychology Bulletin, 15,* 183–193.

Kulik, J. A., Mahler, H. I. M., & Earnest, A. (1994). Social comparison and affiliation under threat: Going beyond the affiliate-choice paradigm. *Journal of Personality and Social Psychology, 66,* 301–309.

Kulik, J. A., Mahler, H. I. M., & Moore, P. J. (1996). Social comparison and affiliation under threat: Effects on recovery from major surgery. *Journal of Personality and Social Psychology, 71,* 967–979.

Kulynych, J. (2002). Legal and ethical issues in neuroimaging research: Human subjects protection, medical privacy and the public communication of research results. *Brain and Cognition, 50,* 345–357.

Kumkale, G. T., & Albarracín, D. (2004). The sleeper effect in persuasion: A meta-analytic review. *Psychological Bulletin, 130,* 143–172.

Kunda, Z. (1999). *Social cognition: Making sense of people.* Cambridge, MA: MIT Press.

Kunda, Z. (Ed.). (2000). *Social cognition: Making sense of people.* Cambridge, MA: The MIT Press.

Kunda, Z., Davies, P. G., Adams, B. D., & Spencer, S. J. (2002). The dynamic time course of

stereotype activation: Activation, dissipation, and resurrection. *Journal of Personality and Social Psychology, 82,* 283–299.

Kupke, T., Hobbs, S. A., & Cheney, T. H. (1979). Selection of heterosocial skills: I. Criterion-related validity. *Behavior Therapy, 10,* 327–335.

Kuppens, P., Van Mechelen, I., & Meulders, M. (2004). Every cloud has a silver lining: Interpersonal and individual differences determinants of anger-related behaviors. *Personality and Social Psychology Bulletin, 30,* 1550–1564.

Kurdek, L. A. (1991). The dissolution of gay and lesbian couples. *Journal of Social and Personal Relationships, 8,* 265–278.

Kurdek, L. A. (1994). Areas of conflict for gay, lesbian, and heterosexual couples: What couples argue about influences relationship satisfaction. *Journal of Marriage and the Family, 56,* 923–934.

Kurdek, L. A. (1997). Adjustment to relationship dissolution in gay, lesbian, and heterosexual partners. *Personal Relationships, 4,* 145–161.

Kurdek, L. A. (1998). Relationship outcomes and their predictors: Longitudinal evidence from heterosexual married, gay cohabiting, and lesbian cohabiting couples. *Journal of Marriage and the Family, 60,* 553–568.

Kurdek, L. A. (2003). Differences between gay and lesbian cohabiting couples. *Journal of Social and Personal Relationships, 20,* 411–436.

Kurdek, L. A., & Schmitt, J. P. (1986). Relationship quality of partners in heterosexual married, heterosexual cohabiting, and gay and lesbian relationships. *Journal of Personality and Social Psychology, 51,* 711–720.

Kurdek, L. A., & Schmitt, J. P. (1987). Perceived emotional support from families and friends in members of homosexual, married, and heterosexual cohabiting couples. *Journal of Homosexuality, 14,* 57–68.

Kurup, R. K., & Kurup, P. A. (2003). Hypothalamic digoxin, hemispheric dominance, and neurobiology of love and affection. *International Journal of Neuroscience, 113,* 721–729.

Kurzban, R. (2003). Biological foundations of reciprocity. In E. Ostrom, J. Walker (Eds.), *Trust and reciprocity: Interdisciplinary lessons from experimental research. A volume in the Russell Sage Foundation series on trust* (pp. 105–127). New York: Sage.

Kuschel, R. (1998). The necessity for code of ethics in research. *Psychiatry Today: Journal of the Yugoslav Psychiatric Association, 30,* 247–274.

Kutchinsky, B. (1971). Towards an explanation of the decrease in registered sex crimes in Copenhagen. *Technical report of the Commission on Obscenity and Pornography* (Vol. 7, pp. 263–310). Washington, DC: U.S. Government Printing Office.

Kutchinsky, B. (1985). Pornography and its effects in Denmark and the United States: A rejoinder and beyond. *Comparative Social Research, 8,* 301–330.

Kutchinsky, B. (1991). Pornography and rape: Theory and practice? *International Journal of Law and Psychiatry, 14,* 47–64.

L'Armand, K., & Pepitone, A. (1975). Helping to reward another person: A cross-cultural analysis. *Journal of Personality and Social Psychology, 31,* 189–198.

LaBarbera, P., & MacLachlan, J. (1979). Time compressed speech in radio advertising. *Journal of Marketing, 43,* 30–36.

Labre, M. P. (2002). Adolescent boys and the muscular male body ideal. *Journal of Adolescent Health, 30,* 233–242.

LaFrance, M., & Broadbent, M. (1976). Group rapport: Posture sharing as a nonverbal indicator. *Group and Organization Studies, 1,* 328–333.

Lagerspetz, K. (1985). Are wars caused by aggression? In F. L. Denmark (Ed.), *Social/ecological psychology and the psychology of women.* New York: Elsevier (North-Holland).

Lagerspetz, K. M. J., & Björkqvist, K. (1994). Indirect aggression in boys and girls. In L. R. Huesmann (Ed.), *Aggressive behavior: Current perspectives* (pp. 131–150). New York: Plenum.

Lagerspetz, K. M. J., Björkqvist, K., & Peltonen, T. (1988). Is indirect aggression typical of females? Gender differences in aggressiveness in 11- to 12-year-old children. *Aggressive Behavior, 14,* 403–414.

Lakin, J. L., & Chartrand, T. L. (2003). Using nonconscious behavioral mimicry to create affiliation and rapport. *Psychological Science, 14,* 334–339.

Lakkis, J., Ricciardelli, L. A., & Williams, R. J. (1999). Role of sexual orientation and gender-related traits in disordered eating. *Sex Roles, 31,* 1–16.

Lakoff, R. T. (1975). *Language and woman's place.* New York: Harper & Row.

Lambert, A. J., Payne, B. K., Jacoby, L. L., Shaffer, L. M., Chasteen, A. L., & Khan, S. R. (2003). Stereotypes as dominant responses: On the "social facilitation" of prejudice in anticipated public contexts. *Journal of Personality and Social Psychology, 84,* 277–295.

Lamke, L. K., Sollie, D. L., Durbin, R. G., & Fitzpatrick, J. A. (1994). Masculinity, femininity and relationship satisfaction: The mediating role of interpersonal competence. *Journal of Social and Personal Relationships, 11,* 535–554.

Lan, P.-C. (2003). Negotiating social boundaries and private zones: The micropolitics of employing migrant domestic workers. *Social Problems, 50,* 525–549.

Landau, M. J., Solomon, S., Greenberg, J., Cohen, F., Pyszczyhski, T., Arndt, J., Miller, C. H., Ogilvie, D. M., & Cook, A. (2004). Deliver us from evil: The effects of mortality salience and reminders of 9/11 on support for President George W. Bush. *Personality and Social Psychology Bulletin 3???,* 1136–1150.

Lang, A. R., Goeckner, D. J., Adesso, V. J., & Marlatt, G. A. (1975). Effects of alcohol on aggression in male social drinkers. *Journal of Abnormal Psychology, 84,* 508–518.

Langer, E. J. (1978). Rethinking the role of thought in social interaction. In J. H. Harvey, W. Ickes, & R. F. Kidd (Eds.), *New directions in attribution research* (Vol. 2, pp. 35–58). Hillsdale, NJ: Erlbaum.

Langer, E. J. (1989). Minding matters: The consequences of mindlessness-mindfulness. In L. Berkowitz (Ed.), *Advances in experimental social psychology* (Vol. 22, 137–173). San Diego: Academic Press.

Langer, L. M., Warheit, G. J., & McDonald, L. P. (2001). Correlates and predictors of risky sexual practices among a multi-racial/ethnic sample of university students. *Social Behavior and Personality, 29,* 133–144.

Langfred, C. W. (1998). Is group cohesiveness a double-edged sword? An investigation of the effects of cohesiveness on performance. *Small Group Research, 29,* 124–143.

Langlois, J. H., Kalakanis, L., Rubenstein, A. J., Larson, A., Hallam, M., & Smoot, M. (2000). Maxims or myths of beauty? A meta-analytic and theoretical review. *Psychological Bulletin, 126,* 390–423.

Langlois, J. H., Roggman, L. A., & Musselman, L. (1994). What is average and what is not average about attractive faces? *Psychological Science, 5,* 214–220.

Langolis, J. H., & Downs, A. C. (1980). Mothers, fathers, and peers as socialization agents of sex-typed behaviors in young children. *Child Development, 51,* 1237–1247.

Lanning, K. (2002). Reflections on September 11: Lessons from four psychological perspectives. *Analysis of Social Issues and Public Policy, 2,* 27–34.

Lanzetta, J. T., & Orr, S. P. (1986). Excitatory strength of expressive faces: Effects of happy and fear expressions and context on the extinction of a conditioned fear response. *Journal of Personality and Social Psychology, 50,* 190–194.

LaPiere, R. T. (1932). Attitudes vs. actions. *Social Forces, 13,* 230–237.

L'Armand, K., & Pepitrone, A. (1975). Helping to reward another person: A cross-cultural analysis, *Journal of Personality and Social Psychology, 31,* 189–198.

Larsen, R. J. (2000). Toward a science of mood regulation. *Psychological Inquiry, 11,* 129–141.

Larson, R., Csikszentmihalyi, M., & Graef, R. (1982). Time alone in daily experience: Loneliness or renewal? In L. A. Peplau & D. Perlman (Eds.), *Loneliness: A sourcebook of current theory, research and therapy* (pp. 40–53). New York: Wiley-Interscience.

LatanÇ, B. (2000). Pressures to uniformity and the evolution of cultural norms: Modeling dynamic social impact. In D. R. Ilgen & C. L. Hulin (Eds.), *Computational modeling of behavior in organizations: The third scientific discipline* (pp. 189–220). Washington, DC: American Psychological Association.

Latanè, B. (1981). The psychology of social impact. *American Psychologist, 36,* 343–356.

Latanè, B. (1997). Dynamic social impact: The social consequences of human interaction. In C. McGarty & S. A. Haslam (Eds.), *The message of social psychology: Perspectives on mind in society* (pp. 200–220). Cambridge, MA: Blackwell.

Latanè, B., & Bourgeois, M. J. (1996). Experimental evidence for dynamic social impact: The emergence of subcultures in electronic groups. *Journal of Communication, 46,* 35–47.

Latanè, B., & Darley, J. M. (1968). Group inhibition of bystander intervention in emergencies. *Journal of Personality and Social Psychology, 10,* 215–221.

Latanè, B., & Darley, J. M. (1970). *The unresponsive bystander: Why doesn't he help?* Englewood Cliffs, NJ: Prentice-Hall.

Latanè, B., & L'Herrou, T. (1996). Spatial clustering in the conformity game: Dynamic social impact in electronic groups. *Journal of Personality and Social Psychology, 70,* 1218–1230.

Latanè, B., & Nida, S. (1981). Ten years of research on group size and helping. *Psychological Bulletin, 89,* 308–324.

Latanè, B., & Rodin, J. (1969). A lady in distress: Inhibiting effects of friends and strangers on bystander intervention. *Journal of Experimental Social Psychology, 5,* 189–202.

Latanè, B., Liu, J. H., Nowak, A., Bonevento, M., & Zheng, L. (1995). Distance matters: Physical space and social impact. *Personality and Social Psychology Bulletin, 21,* 795–805.

Latanè, B., Williams, K., & Harkins, S. (1979). Many hands make light the work: The causes and consequences of social loafing. *Journal of Personality and Social Psychology, 37,* 822–832.

Laughlin, P. R. (1996). Group decision making and collective induction. In E. Witte & J. Davis (Eds.), *Understanding group behavior: Vol. 1. Small group processes and interpersonal relations* (pp. 61–80). Hillsdale, NJ: Erlbaum.

Laurenceau, J. P., Barrett, L. F., & Pietromonaco, P. R. (1998). Intimacy as an interpersonal process: The importance of self-disclosure, partner disclosure, and perceived partner responsiveness in interpersonal exchanges. *Journal of Personality and Social Psychology, 74,* 1238–1251.

Lavin, T. J. (1987). Divergence and convergence in the causal attributions of married couples. *Journal of Marriage and the Family, 49,* 71–80.

Lavrakas, P. J. (1993). *Telephone survey methods: Sampling, selection, and supervision* (2nd ed.), Newbury Park, CA: Sage.

Lawler, E. J. (1992). Affective attachments to nested groups: A choice-process theory. *American Sociological Review, 57,* 327–339.

Lazarus, R. S. (1984). On the primacy of cognition. *American Psychologist, 39,* 124–129.

Leary, M. R. (1996). *Self-presentation: Impression management and interpersonal behavior.* Boulder, CO: Westview Press.

Leary, M. R., & Kowalski, R. M. (1995). *Social anxiety.* New York: Guilford.

Leary, M. R., Nezlek, J. B., Downs, D., Radford-Davenport, J., Martin, J., & McMullen, A. (1994). Self-presentation in everyday interactions: Effects of target familiarity and gender composition. *Journal of Personality and Social Psychology, 67,* 664–673.

Leary, M. R., Tambor, E. S., Terdal, S. K., & Downs, D. L. (1995). Self-esteem as an interpersonal motive: The sociometer hypothesis. *Journal of Personality and Social Psychology, 68,* 518–530.

LeBon, G. (1903). *Psychologie des foules [The psychology of the crowd].* Paris: Alcan.

Leck, K., & Simpson, J. (1999). Feigning romantic interest: The role of self-monitoring. *Journal of Research in Personality, 33,* 69–91.

LeDoux, J. (1998). *The emotional brain.* New York: Simon & Schuster.

Lee, A-R. (2003). Stability and change in Korean values. *Social Indicators Research, 62–63,* 93–117.

Lee, A. Y. (2001). The mere exposure effect: An uncertainty reduction explanation revisited. *Personality & Social Psychology Bulletin, 27,* 1255–1266.

Lee, J. A. (1977). A typology of styles of loving. *Personality and Social Psychology Bulletin, 3,* 173–182.

Lee, R. S. (1995). Regional subcultures as revealed by magazine circulation patterns. *Cross-Cultural Research, 29,* 91–120.

Lee, T. M. C., Liu, H.-L., Tan, L.-H., Chan, C. C. H., Mahankali, S., Feng, C.-M., Hou, J., Fox, P. T., & Gao, J.-H. (2002). Lie detection by functional magnetic resonance imaging. *Human Brain Mapping, 15,* 157–164.

Leffler, A., Gillespie, D. L., & Conaty, J. C. (1982). The effects of status differentiation on nonverbal behavior. *Social Psychology Quarterly, 45,* 153–161.

Leibold, J. M., & McConnell, A. R. (2004). Women, sex, hostility, power, and suspicion: Sexually aggressive men's cognitive associations. *Journal of Experimental Social Psychology, 40,* 256–263.

Leippe, M. R., & Eisenstadt, D. (1994). The generalization of dissonance reduction: Decreasing prejudice through induced compliance. *Journal of Personality and Social Psychology, 67,* 395–413.

Leippe, M. R., & Elkin, R. A. (1987). When motives clash: Issue involvement and response involvement as determinants of persuasion. *Journal of Personality and Social Psychology, 52,* 269–278.

Leit, R. A., Pope, H. G., & Gray, J. J. (2001). Cultural expectations of muscularity in men: The evolution of *Playgirl* centerfolds. *International Journal of Eating Disorders, 29,* 90–93.

Leonard, K. (1989). The impact of explicit aggressive and implicit nonaggressive cues on aggression in intoxicated and sober males. *Personality and Social Psychology Bulletin, 15,* 390–400.

Leonard, K. E., & Quigley, B. M. (1999). Drinking and marital aggression in newlyweds: An event-based analysis of drinking and the occurrence of husband marital aggression. *Journal of Studies on Alcohol, 60.*

Lerner, M. J. (1980). *The belief in a just world: A fundamental delusion.* New York: Plenum.

Lerner, M. J. (1997). What does the belief in a just world protect us from: The dread of death or the fear of undeserved suffering? *Psychological Inquiry, 8,* 29–32.

Leung, K., & Chan, D. K.-S. (1999). Conflict management across cultures. In J. Adamopoulos & Y. Kashima (Eds.), *Social psychology and cultural context* (pp. 177–188). Thousand Oaks, CA: Sage.

Leventhal, H. (1970). Findings and theory in the study of fear communications. In L. Berkowitz (Ed.), *Advances in experimental social psychology* (Vol. 5, pp. 119–186). New York: Academic Press.

Levin, S. (2004). Perceived group status differences and the effects of gender, ethnicity, and religion on social dominance orientation. *Political Psychology, 25,* 31–48.

Levine, J. M., & Moreland, R. L. (1998). Small groups. In D. Gilbert, S. T. Fiske, & G. Lindzey (Eds.), *Handbook of social psychology* (4th ed.). New York: McGraw-Hill.

Levine, J. M., & Moreland, R. L. (2002). Group reactions to loyalty and disloyalty. In S. R. Thye & E. J. Lawler (Eds.), *Group cohesion, trust and solidarity: Advances in group processes* (Vol. 19, pp. 203–228). New York: Elsevier Science/JAI Press.

Levine, J. M., Choi, H.-S., & Moreland, R. L. (2003). Newcomer innovation in work teams. In P. B. Paulus (Ed.), *Group creativity: Innovation through collaboration* (pp. 202–224). London: Oxford University Press.

Levine, J. M., Moreland, R. L., & Ryan, C. S. (1998). Group socialization and intergroup relations. In C. Sedikides, J. Schopler, & C. A. Insko (Eds.), *Intergroup cognition and intergroup behavior* (pp. 283–308). Mahwah, NJ: Erlbaum.

Levine, R. A., & Campbell, D. T. (1972). *Ethnocentrism.* New York: Wiley.

Levine, R. V. (2003). The kindness of strangers. *American Scientist, 91,* 226–233.

Levine, R. V., Martinez, T. S., Brase, G., & Sorenson, K. (1994). Helping in 36 U.S. cities. *Journal of Personality and Social Psychology, 67,* 69–82.

Levine, R., Sata, S., Hashimoto, T., & Verma, J. (1995). Love and marriage in eleven cultures. *Journal of Cross-Cultural Psychology, 26,* 554–571.

Levy B. R., & Banaji, M. R. (2002). Implicit ageism. In T. D. Nelson (Ed.), *Ageism: Stereotyping and prejudice against older persons* (pp. 49–75). Cambridge, MA: MIT Press.

Levy, B., & Lobel, K. (1991). Lesbian teens in abusive relationships. In B. Levy (Ed.), *Dating violence: Young women in danger* (pp. 203–208). Seattle, WA: Seal Press.

Lewin, K. (1936). *Principles of topological psychology.* New York: McGraw-Hill.

Lewin, K. (1943). Forces behind food habits and methods of change. *Bulletin of the National Research Council, 8,* 35–65.

Lewin, K. (1947). Group decision and social change. In T. M. Newcomb & E. L. Hartley (Eds.), *Readings in social psychology* (pp. 330–344). New York: Holt.

Lewin, K. (1951). Problems of research in social psychology. In D. Cartwright (Ed.), *Field theory in social science* (pp. 155–169). New York: Harper & Row.

Lewin, K., Lippitt, R., & White, R. K. (1939). Patterns of aggressive behavior in experimentally created "social climates." *Journal of Social Psychology, 10,* 271–299.

Lewis, M. A., & Neighbors, C. (in press). Gender-specific misperceptions of college student drinking norms. *Psychology of Addictive Behaviors.*

Lewis, M., & Brooks, J. (1978). Self-knowledge in emotional development. In M. Lewis & L. Rosenblum (Eds.), *The development of affect* (pp. 205–226). New York: Plenum.

Leyens, J.-P. (1990). Intuitive personality testing: A social approach. In J. Extra, A. van Knippenberg, J. van der Pligt, & M. Poppe (Eds.), *Fundamentele sociale psychologie* [Basic social psychology] (Vol. 4, pp. 3–20). Tilburg, The Netherlands: Tilburg University Press.

Leyens, J.-P. (Ed.). (1991). Prolegomena for the concept of implicit theories of personality. *European Bulletin of Cognitive Psychology, 11,* 131–136.

Leyens, J.-P., & Dardenne, B. (1994). La perception et connaissance d'autrui [People perception]. In M. Richelle, J. Requin, & M. Robert (Eds.), *Traité de psychologie expérimentale* [Handbook of experimental psychology] (Vol. 2, pp. 81–132). Paris: Presses Universitaires de France.

Leyens, J.-P., Camino, L., Parke, R. D., & Berkowitz, L. (1975). Effects of movie violence on aggression in a field setting as a function of group dynamics and cohesiveness. *Journal of Personality and Social Psychology, 32,* 346–360.

Liberman, A., & Chaiken, S. (1996). The direct effect of personal relevance on attitudes. *Personality and Social Psychology Bulletin, 22,* 269–279.

Liberman, V., Samuels, S. M., & Ross, L. (2004). The name of the game: Predictive power of reputations versus structural labels in determining prisoner's dilemma game moves. *Personality and Social Psychology Bulletin, 30,* 1175–1185.

Lickel, B., Hamilton, D. L., Lewis, A., Sherman, S. J., Wieczorkowska, G., & Uhles, A. N. (2000). Varieties of groups and the perception of group entitativity. *Journal of Personality and Social Psychology, 78,* 223–246.

Liden, R. C., & Mitchell, T. R. (1988). Ingratiatory behaviors in organizational settings. *Academy of Management Review, 13,* 572–587.

Lieberman, M. D. (2003). Reflective and reflexive judgment processes: A social cognitive neuroscience approach. In J. P. Forgas, K. Williams, & W. V. Hippel (Eds.), *Social judgments: Implicit and explicit processes* (pp. 44–67). New York: Cambridge University Press.

Lieberman, M. D., & Pfeifer, J. H. (in press). The self and social perception: Three kinds of questions in social cognitive neuroscience. In A. Easton, & N. Emery (Eds.), *Cognitive neuroscience of emotional and social behavior.* Philadelphia: Psychology Press.

Lieberman, M. D., Gaunt, R., Gilbert, D. T., & Trope, Y. (in press). Reflection and reflexion: A social cognitive neuroscience approach to attributional inference. *Advances in Experimental Social Psychology.*

Liebkind, K., & McAlister, A. L. (1999). Extended contact through peer modeling to promote tolerance in Finland. *European Journal of Social Psychology, 29,* 765–780.

Likert, R. (1932). A technique for the measurement of attitudes. *Archives of Psychology, 140,* 5–53.

Linder, D. E., Cooper, J., & Jones, E. E. (1967). Decision freedom as a determinant of the role of incentive magnitude in attitude change. *Journal of Personality and Social Psychology, 6,* 245–254.

Lindsay, J. J., & Anderson, C. A. (2000). From antecedent conditions to violent actions: A general affective aggression model. *Personality and Social Psychology Bulletin, 26,* 533–547.

Link, B. G., & Phelan, J. C. (2001). Conceptualizing stigma. *Annual Review of Sociology, 27,* 363–385.

Linville, P. W. (1982). The complexity-extremity effect and age-based stereotyping. *Journal of Personality and Social Psychology, 42,* 193–211.

Lipkus, I. M. (1991). The construction and preliminary validation of a Global Belief in a Just World Scale and the exploratory analysis of the Multidimensional Belief in a Just World Scale. *Personality and Individual Differences, 12,* 1171–1178.

Lipkus, I. M., & Bissonnette, V. L. (1996). Relationships among belief in a just world, willingness to accommodate, and marital well-being. *Personality and Social Psychology Bulletin, 22,* 1043–1056.

Lipkus, I. M., Dalbert, C., & Siegler, I. C. (1996). The importance of distinguishing the belief in a just world for self versus for others: Implications for psychological well-being. *Personality and Social Psychology Bulletin, 22,* 666–677.

Lippa, R., & Arad, S. (1999). Gender, personality, and prejudice: The display of authoritarianism and social dominance in interviews with college men and women. *Journal of Research in Personality, 33,* 463–493.

Livingston, R. W. (2002). The role of perceived negativity in the moderation of African Americans' implicit and explicit racial attitudes. *Journal of Experimental Social Psychology, 38,* 405–413.

Livingston, R. W., & Brewer, M. B. (2002). What are we really priming? Cue-based versus category-based processing of facial stimuli. *Journal of Personality and Social Psychology, 82,* 5–18.

Lockhart, L. L., White, B. A., Causby, V., & Isaac, A. (1994). Letting out the secret: Violence in lesbian relationships. *Journal of Interpersonal Violence, 9,* 469–492.

Lockwood, P. (2002). Could it happen to you? Predicting the impact of downward comparisons on the self. *Journal of Personality and Social Psychology, 82,* 343–358.

Loden, M. (1985). *Feminine leadership or how to succeed in business without being one of the boys.* New York: Times Books.

Lofland, J., & Lofland, L. (1995). *Analyzing social settings: A guide to qualitative observation and analysis* (3rd ed.). Belmont, CA: Wadsworth.

Loftus, E. F., & Coan, D. (1995). The construction of childhood memories. In D. Peters (Ed.), *The child witness in context: Cognitive, social and legal perspectives.* New York: Kluwer.

Lonner, W. J., & Adamopoulos, J. (1997). Culture as antecedent to behavior. In Dr. J. Berry, & Y. H. Poortinga (Eds.), *Handbook of cross-cultural psychology: Vol. 1. Theory and method* (2nd ed., pp. 43–83). Needham Heights, MA: Allyn & Bacon.

Lonsway, K. A., Klaw, E. L., Berg, D. R., Waldo, C. R., Kothari, C., Mazurek, C. J., & Hegeman, K. E. (1998). Beyond "no means no": Outcomes of an intensive program to train peer facilitators for campus acquaintance rape education. *Journal of Interpersonal Violence, 13,* 73–92.

Lopes, P. N., Brackett, M. A., Nezlek, J. B., Schütz, A., Sellin, I., & Salovey, P. (2004). Emotional intelligence and social interaction. *Personality and Social Psychology Bulletin, 30,* 1018–1034.

Lord, C. G., Desforges, D. M., Ramsey, S. L., Trezza, G. R., & Lepper, M. R. (1991). Typicality effects in attitude-behavior consistency: Effects of category discrimination and category knowledge. *Journal of Experimental Social Psychology, 27,* 550–575.

Lore, R., & Schultz, L. A. (1993). Control of human aggression: A comparative perspective. *American Psychologist, 48,* 16–25.

Lorenz, K. (1966). *On aggression.* New York: Harcourt, Brace & World.

Lorenzi-Cioldi, F. (1993). They all look alike, but so do we . . . sometimes: Perceptions of in-group and out-group homogeneity as a function of sex and context. *British Journal of Social Psychology, 32,* 111–124.

Lottes, I. L., & Kuriloff, P. J. (1994). The impact of college experience on political and social attitudes. *Sex Roles, 31,* 31–54.

Lovaglia, J. J., & Houser, J. A. (1996). Emotional reactions and status in groups. *American Sociological Review, 61,* 867–883.

Lowe, K. B., Kroeck, K. G., & Sivasubramaniam, N. (1996). Effectiveness correlates of transformational and transactional leadership: A meta-analytic review. *Leadership Quarterly, 7,* 385–391.

Lucas, R. E., Diener, E., Grob, A., Suh, E., & Shao, L. (2000). Cross-cultural evidence for the fundamental features of extraversion. *Journal of Personality and Social Psychology, 79,* 452–468.

Luce, R. D., & Raiffa, H. (1957). *Games and decisions.* New York: Wiley.

Luginbuhl, J., & Palmer, R. (1991). Impression management aspects of self-handicapping: Positive and negative effects. *Personality and Social Psychology Bulletin, 17,* 655–662.

Lumsdaine, A., & Janis, I. (1953). Resistance to counterpropaganda produced by a one-sided versus a two-sided propaganda presentation. *Public Opinion Quarterly, 17,* 311–318.

Lupfer, M. B., Weeks, M., & Dupuis, S. (2000). How pervasive is the negativity bias in judgments based on character appraisal? *Personality and Social Psychology Bulletin, 26,* 1353–1366.

Lydon, J. E., Jamieson, D. W., & Holmes, J. G. (1997). The meaning of social interactions in the transition from acquaintanceship to friendship. *Journal of Personality and Social Psychology, 73,* 536–548.

Lynch, J. W., Kaplan, G. A., & Shema, S. J. (1997). Cumulative impact of sustained economic hardship on physical, cognitive, psychological, and social functioning. *New England Journal of Medicine, 337,* 1889–1895.

Lynch, M. (1994). Developmental psychology. In D. Matsumoto (Ed.), *People: Psychology from a cultural perspective* (pp. 65–81). Pacific Grove, CA: Brooks/Cole.

Lyons, A., & Kashima, Y. (2003). How are stereotypes maintained through communication? The influence of stereotype sharedness. *Journal of Personality and Social Psychology, 85,* 989–1005.

Lyubomirsky, S., Caldwell, N. D., & Nolen-Hoeksema, S. (1998). Effects of ruminative and distracting responses to depressed mood on retrieval of autobiographical memories. *Journal of Personality and Social Psychology, 75,* 166–177.

Ma, V., & Schoeneman, T. J. (1997). Individualism versus collectivism: A comparison of Kenyan and American self-concepts. *Basic and Applied Social Psychology, 19,* 261–273.

Maas, A., Cadinu, M., Guarnieri, G., & Grasselli, A. (2003). Sexual harassment under social identity threat: The computer harassment paradigm. *Journal of Personality and Social Psychology, 85,* 853–870.

Maass, A., Clark, R. D., III, & Haberkorn, G. (1982). The effects of differential ascribed category membership and norms on minority influence. *European Journal of Social Psychology, 12,* 89–104.

Maccoby, E. E. (1990). Gender and relationships: A developmental account. *American Psychologist, 45,* 513–520.

MacDonald, G., & Nail, P. R. (in press). Attitude change and the public-private attitude distinction. *British Journal of Social Psychology.*

MacDonald, G., Zanna, M. P., & Holmes, J. G. (2000). An experimental test of the role of alcohol in relationship conflict. *Journal of Experimental Social Psychology, 36,* 182–193.

Mackay, N. (2004, January 11). Former Bush aide: U.S. plotted Iraq invasion long before 9/11. *Sunday Herald.*

Macrae, C. N., Hewstone, M., & Griffiths, R. J. (1993). Processing load and memory for stereotype-based information. *European Journal of Social Psychology, 23,* 77–87.

Macrae, C. N., Milne, A. B., & Bodenhausen, G. V. (1994). Stereotypes as energy-saving devices: A peek inside the cognitive toolbox. *Journal of Personality and Social Psychology, 66,* 37–47.

Maddox, K. B. (in press). Perspectives on racial phenotypicality bias. *Personality and Social Psychology Bulletin.*

Maddox, K. B., & Gray, S. A. (2002). Cognitive representations of Black Americans: Reexploring the role of skin tone. *Personality and Social Psychology Bulletin, 28,* 250–259.

Maddux, J. E., & DuCharme, K. A. (1997). Behavioral intentions in theories of health behavior. In D. S. Gochman (Ed.), *Handbook of health behavior research I: Personal and social determinants* (pp. 133–151). New York: Plenum.

Maddux, J. E., & Rogers, R. W. (1983). Protection motivation and self-efficacy: A revised theory of fear appeals and attitude change. *Journal of Experimental Social Psychology, 19,* 469–479.

Maestripieri, D. (2001). Biological bases of maternal attachment. *Current Directions in Psychological Science, 10,* 79–82.

Magid, D. J., Houry, D., Koepsell, T. D., Ziller, A., Soules, M. R., & Jenny, C. (2004). The epidemiology of female rape victims who seek immediate medical care: Temporal trends in the incidence of sexual assault and acquaintance rape. *Journal of Interpersonal Violence, 19,* 3–12.

Maio, G. R., & Olson, J. M. (2000). Emergent themes and potential approaches to attitude function: The function-structure model of attitudes. In G. R. Maio & J. M. Olson (Eds.), *Why we evaluate: Functions of attitudes* (pp. 417–442). Mahwah, NJ: Erlbaum.

Major, B., Kaiser, C. R., & McCoy, S. K. (2003). It's not my fault: When and why attributions to prejudice protect well-being. *Personality and Social Psychology Bulletin, 29,* 772–781.

Major, B., Spencer, S., Schmader, T., Wolfe, C., & Crocker, J. (1998). Coping with negative stereotypes about intellectual performance: The role of psychological disengagement. *Personality and Social Psychology Bulletin, 24,* 34–50.

Makepeace, J. (1989). Dating, living together, and courtship violence. In M. A. Pirog-Good & J. E. Stets (Eds.), *Violence in dating relationships: Emerging social issues* (pp. 94–107). New York: Praeger.

Malach, P. A. (2001). The role of gender and culture in romantic attraction. *European Psychologist, 6,* 96–102.

Malamuth, N. M. (1981). Rape fantasies as a function of exposure to violent sexual stimuli. *Archives of Sexual Behavior, 10,* 33–47.

Malamuth, N. M. (2003). Criminal and noncriminal sexual aggressors: Integrating psychopathy in a hierarchial–mediational conference model *Annual New York Academy of Science, 989,* 33–58.

Malamuth, N. M., & Check, J. V. P. (1981). The effects of mass media exposure on acceptance of violence against women: A field experiment. *Journal of Research in Personality, 15,* 436–446.

Malamuth, N. M., & Thornhill, N. W. (1994). Hostile masculinity, sexual aggression, and gender-

based domineeringness in conversations. *Aggressive Behavior, 20,* 185–193.

Malamuth, N. M., Linz, D., Heavey, C. L. Barnes, G. & Acker M, (1995). Using the confluence model of sexual aggression to predict men's conflict with women: A 10- year follow-up study. *Journal of Personality and Social Psychology, 69,* 353–369.

Mallick, S. K., & McCandless, B. R. (1966). A study of catharsis of aggression. *Journal of Personality and Social Psychology, 4,* 591–596.

Mandel, D. R. (2002). Evil and the instigation of collective violence. *Analyses of Social Issues and Public Policy, 2,* 101–108.

Mandel, D. R. (2003). Counterfactuals, emotions, and context. *Cognition and Emotion, 17,* 139–159.

Mandel, D. R., & Lehman, D. R. (1996). Counterfactual thinking and ascriptions of cause and preventability. *Journal of Personality and Social Psychology, 71,* 450–463.

Mann, L. (1981). The baiting crowd in episodes of threatened suicide. *Journal of Personality and Social Psychology, 41,* 703–709.

Mantell, D. M. (1971). The potential for violence in Germany. *Journal of Social Issues, 27,* 101–112.

Marangoni, C., & Ickes, W. (1989). Loneliness: A theoretical review with implications for measurement. *Journal of Social and Personal Relationships, 6,* 93–128.

Maranto, C. L., & Stenoien, A. F. (2000). Weight discrimination: A multidisciplinary analysis. *Employee Responsibilities and Rights Journal, 12,* 9–24.

Marazziti, D., Rotondo, A., Presta, S., Pancioloi-Guadagnucci, M. L., Palego, L., & Conti, L. (1993). Role of serotonin in human aggressive behavior. *Aggressive Behavior, 19,* 347–353.

Marcus, D. K., & Miller, R. S. (2003). Sex differences in judgments of physical attractiveness: A social relations analysis. *Personality and Social Psychology Bulletin, 29,* 325–335.

Marcus, D. K., Wilson, J. R., & Miller, R. S. (1996). Are perceptions of emotion in the eye of the beholder? A social relations analysis of judgments of embarrassment. *Personality and Social Psychology Bulletin, 22,* 1220–1228.

Marelich, W. D., Gaines, S. O. Jr., & Branzet M. R. (2003). Commitment, insecurity and arousability: Testing a transactional model of jealousy. *Representative Research in Social Psychology, 27,* 23–31.

Margalit, M. (1995). Effects of social skills training for students with an intellectual disability. *International Journal of Disability, Development and Education, 42,* 75–85.

Marin, B. V., & Gomez, C. A. (1995). Latino culture and sex: Implications for HIV prevention. In M. C. Zeq & J. Garcia (Eds.), *Psychological interventions and research with Latino populations.* Needham Heights, MA: Allyn & Bacon.

Mark, M. M., & Mellor, S. (1991). Effect of self-relevance of an event on hindsight bias: The foreseeability of a layoff. *Journal of Applied Psychology, 76,* 569–577.

Mark, M. M., Boburka, R. R., Eyssell, K. M., Cohen, L. L., & Mellor, S. (2003). "I couldn't have seen it coming": The impact of negative self-relevant outcomes on retrospections about foreseeability. *Memory, 11,* 443–454.

Markey, P. M. (2000). Bystander intervention in computer-mediated communication. *Computers in Human Behavior, 16,* 183–188.

Markman, A. B. (1999). *Knowledge representation.* Mahwah, NJ: Erlbaum.

Markus, H. R. (1977). Self-schemata and processing information about the self. *Journal of Personality and Social Psychology, 35,* 63–78.

Markus, H. R., & Kitayama, S. (1991). Culture and the self: Implications for cognition, emotion, and motivation. *Psychological Review, 98,* 224–253.

Markus, H. R., & Kitayama, S. (1994). A collective fear of the collective: Implications for selves and theories of selves. *Personality and Social Psychology Bulletin, 20,* 568–579.

Markus, H. R., Kitayama, S., & Heiman, R. J. (1996). Culture and "basic" psychological principles. In E. T. Higgins & A. W. Kruglanski (Eds.), *Social psychology: Handbook of basic principles* (pp. 857–913). New York: Guilford.

Markus, H. R., Smith, J., & Moreland, R. L. (1985). Role of the self-concept in the perception of others. *Journal of Personality and Social Psychology, 49,* 1494–1512.

Marlowe, C. M., Schneider, S. L., & Nelson, C. E. (1996). Gender and attractiveness biases in hiring decisions: Are more experienced managers less biased? *Journal of Applied Psychology, 81,* 11–21.

Marlowe, F., & Wetsman, A. (2001). Preferred waist-to-hip ratio and ecology. *Personality and Individual Differences, 30,* 481–489.

Marrow, A. J. (1969). *The practical theorist: The life and work of Kurt Lewin.* New York: Basic Books.

Marrow, A. J. (1969). *The practical theorist: The life and work of Kurt Lewin.* New York: Basic Books.

Marsh, H. W., Craven, R. G., & Debus, R. (1991). Self-concepts of young children 5 to 8 years of age: Measurement and multidimensional structure. *Journal of Educational Psychology, 83,* 377–392.

Marsh, K. L., Julka, D. L. (2000). A motivational approach to experimental tests of attitude functions theory. In G. R. Maio & J. M. Olson (Eds.), *Why we evaluate: Functions of attitudes* (pp. 271–294). Mahwah, NJ: Erlbaum.

Martin, R. (1988). Ingroup and outgroup minorities: Differential impact upon public and private responses. *European Journal of Social Psychology, 18,* 39–52.

Martin, R., Hewstone, M., & Martin, P. Y. (2003). Resistance to persuasive messages as a function of majority and minority source status. *Journal of Experimental Social Psychology, 39,* 585–593.

Martinek, T. J. (1981). Physical attractiveness: Effects on teacher expectations and dyadic interactions in elementary school children. *Journal of Sport Psychology, 3,* 196–205.

Martz, D. M., Handley, K. B., & Eisler, R. M. (1995). The relationship between feminine gender role stress, body image, and eating disorders. *Psychology of Women Quarterly, 19,* 493–508.

Maruyama, G. (2004). Program evaluation, action research, and social psychology: A powerful blend for addressing applied problems. In C. Sansone, C. C. Morf, & A. T. Panter (Eds.), *Handbook of methods in social psychology* (pp. 429–442). Thousand Oaks, CA: Sage.

Marwell, G., Aiken, M. T., & Demerath, N. J., III. (1987). The persistence of political attitudes among 1960s civil rights activists. *Public Opinion Quarterly, 51,* 383–399.

Mashek, D. J., Aron, A., & Boncimino, M. (2003). Confusion of self with close others. *Personality and Social Psychology Bulletin, 29,* 382–392.

Maslow, A. H. (1970). *Motivation and personality.* New York: Harper & Row.

Mason, W. A. (1997). Discovering behavior. *American Psychologist, 52,* 713–720.

Mast, M. S., & Hall, J. A. (in press). When is dominance related to similing? Assigned dominance, dominance preference, trait dominance, and gender as moderators. *Sex Roles.*

Masuda, M. (2003). Meta-analyses of love scales: Do various love scales measure the same psychological constructs? *Japanese Psychological Research, 45,* 25–37.

Mathes, E. W., Adams, H. E., & Davies, R. M. (1985). Jealousy: Loss of relationship rewards, loss of self-esteem, depression, anxiety, and anger. *Journal of Personality and Social Psychology, 48,* 1552–1561.

Matheson, K., Cole, B., & Majka, K. (2003). Dissidence from within: Examining the effects of intergroup context on group members' reactions to attitudinal opposition. *Journal of Experimental Social Psychology, 39,* 161–169.

Matheson, M. D., & Bernstein, I. S. (2000). Grooming, social bonding, and agonistic aiding in rhesus monkeys. *American Journal of Primatology, 51,* 177–186.

Maticka-Tyndale, E., & Herold, E. S. (1999). Condom use on spring-break vacation: The influence of intentions, prior use, and context. *Journal of Applied Social Psychology, 29,* 1010–1027.

Matlin, M., & Stang, D. (1978). *The pollyanna principle: Selectivity in language, memory, and thought.* Cambridge, MA: Schenkman.

Matsumoto, D. (1992). American-Japanese cultural differences in the recognition of universal facial expressions. *Journal of Cross-Cultural Psychology, 23,* 72–84.

Mattanah, J. F., Hancock, G. R., & Brand, B. L. (2004). Parental attachment, separation-individuation, and college student adjustment: A structural equation analysis of mediational effects. *Journal of Counseling Psychology, 51,* 213–225.

Mazur, A., & Booth, A. (1998). Testosterone and dominance in men. *Behavioral and Brain Sciences, 21,* 353–397.

Mazur, A., & Lamb, T. A. (1980). Testosterone, status, and mood in human males. *Hormones and Behavior, 14,* 236–246.

McAdam, G. (1989). The biographical consequences of activism. *American Sociological Review, 54,* 744–760.

McAdams, D. P. (1988). Personal needs and personal relationships. In S. Duck (Ed.), *Handbook of personal relationships: Theory, research, and interventions* (pp. 7–22). New York: Wiley.

McArthur (Zebrowitz), L. Z. (1982). Judging a book by its cover: A cognitive analysis of the relationship between physical appearance and stereotyping. In A. H. Hastorf & A. M. Isen (Eds.), *Cognitive social psychology* (pp. 149–211). New York: Elsevier/North Holland.

McAuliffe, S. P., & Knowlton, B. J. (2001). Hemispheric differences in object identification. *Brain and Cognition, 45,* 119–128.

McCall, M., & Nattrass, K. (2001). Carding for the purchase of alcohol: I'm tougher than other clerks are! *Journal of Applied Social Psychology, 31,* 2184–2194

McCall, M., Reno, R. R., Jalbert, N., & West, S. G. (2000). Communal orientation and attributions between the self and other. *Basic and Applied Social Psychology, 22,* 301–308.

McCann, S. J. H. (1999). Threatening times and fluctuations in American church memberships. *Personality and Social Psychology Bulletin, 25,* 325–336.

McCarthy-Tucker, S., Gold, A., & Garcia, E., III. (1999). Effects of anger management training on aggressive behavior in adolescent boys. *Journal of Offender Rehabilitation, 29,* 129–141.

McCaul, K. D., Gladue, B. A., & Joppa, M. (1992). Winning, losing, mood, and testosterone. *Hormones and Behavior, 26,* 486–504.

McCauley, C. (1989). The nature of social influence in groupthink: Compliance and internalization. *Journal of Personality and Social Psychology, 57,* 250–260.

McCauley, C. R., & Segal, M. E. (1987). Social psychology of terrorist groups. In C. Hendrick (Ed.), *Group processes and intergroup relations: Review of personality and social psychology* (Vol. 9, pp. 231–256). Newbury Park, CA: Sage.

McClearn, G. E. (1993). Behavioral genetics: The last century and the next. In R. Plomin & G. E. McClearn (Eds.), *Nature, nurture, and psychology.* Washington, DC: American Psychological Association.

McConahay, J. B. (1986). Modern racism, ambivalence, and the modern racism scale. In S. L. Gaertner & J. Dovidio (Eds.), *Prejudice, discrimination, and racism: Theory and research.* New York: Academic Press.

McConville, M. (1993). *Corroboration and confession: The impact of a ride requiring that no conviction can be sustained on the basis of confession evidence alone.* London: HMSO. (Royal Commission on Criminal Justice Research Study No. 13).

McCord, J. (1994). Aggression in two generations. In L. R. Huesmann (Ed.), *Aggressive behavior: Current perspectives* (pp. 241–251). New York: Plenum.

McCoy, S. K., & Major, B. (in press). Group identification moderates emotional responses to perceived prejudice. Personality and Social Psychology Bulletin.

McCroskey, J. C. (1997). Willingness to communicate, communication apprehension, and self-perceived communication competence: Conceptualizations and perspectives. In J. A. Daly, J. C. McCroskey, J. Ayres, T. Hopf, & D. M. Ayres (Eds.), *Avoiding communication: Shyness, reticence, and communication apprehension* (2nd ed., pp. 75–108). Creskill, NJ: Hampton Press.

McCroskey, J. C., Richmond, V. P., & Daly, J. A. (1975). The development of a measure of perceived homophily in interpersonal communication. *Human Communication Research, 1,* 325–332.

McCullough, M. E., Bellah, C. G., Kilpatrick, S. D., & Johnson, J. L. (2001). Vengefulness: Relationships with forgiveness, rumination, well-being, and the Big Five. *Personality and Social Psychology Bulletin, 27,* 601–610.

McDougall, W. (1908). *An introduction to social psychology*. London: Methuen.

McFarland, S. G. (1989). Religious orientation and the targets of discrimination. *Journal for the Scientific Study of Religion, 28,* 324–336.

McGarty, C. (1999). *Categorization in social psychology*. London: Sage.

McGarty, C., & Haslam, S. A. (1997). Introduction and a short history of social psychology. In C. McGarty & S. A. Haslam (Eds.), *The message of social psychology: Perspectives on mind in society* (pp. 1–19). Cambridge, MA: Blackwell.

McGarty, C., Turner, J. C., Hogg, M. A., David, B., & Wetherell, M. S. (1992). Group polarization as conformity to the prototypical group member. *British Journal of Social Psychology, 31,* 1–19.

McGarty, C., Yzerbyt, V. Y., & Spears, R. (Eds.). (2002). *Stereotypes as explanations: The formation of meaningful beliefs about social groups*. New York: Cambridge University Press.

McGowan, S. (2002). Mental representations in stressful situations: The calming and distressing effects of significant others. *Journal of Experimental Social Psychology, 38,* 152–161.

McGrath, J. E., Arrow, H., & Berdahl, J. L. (2000). The study of groups: Past, present, and future. *Personality and Social Psychology Review, 4,* 95–105.

McGuire, W. J. (1968). Personality and susceptibility to social influence. In E. F. Borgatta & W. W. Lambert (Eds.), *Handbook of personality theory and research*. Chicago: Rand McNally.

McGuire, W. J. (1973). The yin and yang of progress in social psychology: Seven koan. *Journal of Personality and Social Psychology, 26,* 446–456.

McGuire, W. J. (1999). *Constructing social psychology: Creative and critical processes*. Cambridge: Cambridge University Press.

McGuire, W. J. (2004). A perspectivist approach to theory construction. *Personality and Social Psychology Review, 8,* 173–182.

McGuire, W. J., & Papageorgis, D. (1961). The relative efficacy of various types of prior belief-defense in producing immunity against persuasion. *Journal of Abnormal and Social Psychology, 62,* 327–337.

McGuire, W. J., McGuire, C. V., Child, P., & Fujioka, T. (1978). Salience of ethnicity in the spontaneous self-concept as a function of one's ethnic distinctiveness in the social environment. *Journal of Personality and Social Psychology, 36,* 511–520.

McKelvie, S. J. (1993). Stereotyping in perception of attractiveness, age, and gender in schematic faces. *Social Behavior and Personality, 21,* 121–128.

McKenna, F. P., & Albery, I. P. (2001). Does unrealistic optimism change following a negative experience? *Journal of Applied Social Psychology,. 31,* 1146–1157.

McKenna, F. P., Stanier, R. A., & Lewis, C. (1991). Factors underlying illusory self-assessments of driving skill in males and females. *Accident Analysis and Prevention, 23,* 45–52.

McMillen, D. L., Sander, D. V., & Solomon, G. S. (1977). Self-esteem, attentiveness, and helping behavior. *Personality and Social Psychology Bulletin, 3,* 257–261.

McMullen, M. N., & Markman, K. D. (2000). Downward counterfactuals and motivation: The wake-up call and the Pangloss effect. *Personality and Social Psychology Bulletin, 26,* 575–584.

McNally, A. M., Palfai, T. P., Levine, R. V., & Moore, B. M. (2003). Attachment dimensions and drinking-related problems among young adults: the mediational role of coping motives. *Addictive Behaviors, 28,* 1115–1127.

McQuestion, M. J. (2003). Endogenous social effects on intimate partner violence in Colombia. *Social Science Research, 32,* 335–345.

Mead, G. H. (1934). *Mind, self, and society*. Chicago: University of Chicago Press.

Mealey, L., Bridgstock, R., & Townsend, G. C. (1999). Symmetry and perceived facial attractiveness: A monozygotic co-twin comparison. *Journal of Personality and Social Psychology, 76,* 151–158.

Medvene, L. J., Teal, C. R., & Slavich, S. (2000). Including the other in self: Implications for judgments of equity and satisfaction in close relationships. *Journal of Social and Clinical Psychology, 19,* 396–419.

Meeker, B. F., & Weitzel-O'Neill, P. A. (1977). Sex roles and interpersonal behavior in task-oriented groups. *American Sociological Review, 42,* 91–105.

Meeus, W. H. J., & Raaijmakers, Q. A. W. (1986). Administrative obedience: Carrying out orders to use psychological administrative violence. *European Journal of Social Psychology, 16,* 311–324.

Meeus, W. H. J., & Raaijmakers, Q. A. W. (1987). Administrative obedience as a social phenomenon. In W. Doise & S. Moscovici (Eds.), *Current issues in European social psychology,* (Vol. 2, pp. 183–230). Cambridge, England: Cambridge University Press.

Meeus, W. H. J., & Raaijmakers, Q. A. W. (1995). Obedience in modern society: The Utrecht studies. *Journal of Social Issues, 51,* 155–175.

Mehl, M. R., & Pennebaker, J. W. (2003). The social dynamics of a cultural upheaval: Social interactions surrounding September 11, 2001. *Psychological Science, 14,* 579–585.

Mehlman, R. C., & Snyder, C. R. (1985). Excuse theory: A test of the self-protective role of attributions. *Journal of Personality and Social Psychology, 49,* 994–1001.

Meier, B. P., & Hinsz, V. B. (2004). A comparison of human aggression committed by groups and individuals: An interindividual-intergroup discontinuity. *Journal of Experimental Social Psychology, 40,* 551–559.

Meins, E. (1999). Sensitivity, security, and internal working models: Bridging the transmission gap. *Attachment and Human Development, 1,* 325–342.

Mellars, P. A. (1996). *The Neanderthal legacy*. Princeton, NJ: Princeton University Press.

Mellers, B., Hertwig, R., & Kahneman, D. (2001). Do frequency representations eliminate conjunction effects? An exercise in adversarial collaboration. *Psychological Science, 12,* 269–275.

Meltzoff, A. N., & Moore, M. K. (1989). Imitation in newborn infants: Exploring the range of gestures imitated and the underlying mechanisms. *Developmental Psychology, 25,* 954–962.

Mendoza-Denton, R., Downey, G., Purdie, V. J., Davis, A., & Pietrzak, J. (2002). Sensitivity to status-based rejection: Implications for African American students' college experience. *Journal of Personality and Social Psychology, 83,* 896–918.

Mercy, J. A., & Hammond, W. R. (1999). Combining action and analysis to prevent homicide. In M. D. Smith & M. A. Zahn (Eds.), *Homicide: A sourcebook of social research* (pp. 297–310). Thousand Oaks, CA: Sage.

Merikle, P. M., & Skanes, H. E. (1992). Subliminal self-help audiotapes: A search for placebo effects. *Journal of Applied Psychology, 77,* 772–776.

Merton, R. (1948). The self-fulfilling prophecy. *Antioch Review, 8,* 193–210.

Mesquita, B., & Frijda, N. (1992). Cultural variations in emotions: A review. *Psychological Bulletin, 112,* 179–204.

Messman, S. J., Canary, D. J., & Hause, K. S. (2000). Motives to remain platonic, equity, and the use of maintenance strategies in opposite-sex friendships. *Journal of Social and Personal Relationships, 17,* 67–94.

Meston, C. M., & Frohlich, P. F. (2003). Love at first fright: Partner salience moderates roller-coaster-induced excitation transfer. *Archives of Sexual Behavior, 32,* 537–544.

Meyer, J. P., & Koebl, S. L. M. (1982). Dimensionality of students' causal attributions for test performance. *Personality and Social Psychology Bulletin, 8,* 31–36.

Michaels, J. W., Blommel, J. M., Brocato, R. M., Linkous, R. A., & Rowe, J. S. (1982). Social facilitation and inhibition in a natural setting. *Replications in Social Psychology, 2,* 21–24.

Midlarsky, E., Bryan, J. H., & Brickman, P. (1973). Aversive approval: Interactive effects of modeling and reinforcement on altruistic behavior. *Child Development, 44,* 321–328.

Mikulincer, M. (1998). Adult attachment style and individual differences in functional versus dysfunctional experiences of anger. *Journal of Personality and Social Psychology, 74,* 513–524.

Mikulincer, M., & Arad, D. (1999). Attachment, working models, and cognitive openness in close relationships: A test of chronic and temporary accessibility effects. *Journal of Personality and Social Psychology, 77,* 710–725.

Mikulincer, M., & Shaver, P. R. (2003). The attachment behavioral system in adulthood: Activation, psychodynamics, and interpersonal processes. *Advances in Experimental Social Psychology, 35,* 53–152.

Milardo, R. M., & Allan, G., (1997). Social networks and marital relationships. In S. Duck (Ed.), *Handbook of personal relationships: Theory, research and interventions* (2nd ed., pp. 506–522). Chichester, England: Wiley.

Miles, D. R., & Carey, G (1997). Genetic and environmental architecture of human aggression. *Journal of Personality and Social Psychology, 72,* 207–217.

Milgram, S. (1963). Behavioral study of obedience. *Journal of Abnormal and Social Psychology, 67,* 371–378.

Milgram, S. (1965). Some conditions of obedience and disobedience to authority. *Human Relations, 18,* 57–76.

Milgram, S. (1970). The experience of living in cities. *Science, 167,* 1461–1468.

Milgram, S. (1974). *Obedience to authority: An experimental view*. New York: Harper & Row.

Milgram, S. (1992). *The individual in a social world: Essays and experiments.* Reading, MA: Addison-Wesley.

Millar, M. G., & Millar, K. U. (1996). The effects of direct and indirect experience on affective and cognitive responses and the attitude-behavior relation. *Journal of Experimental Social Psychology, 32,* 561–579.

Miller, A. G., Gillen, B., Schenker, C., & Radlove, S. (1973). Perception of obedience to authority. *Proceedings of the 81st Annual Convention of the American Psychological Association, 8,* 127–128.

Miller, C. E. (1989). The social psychological effects of group decision rules. In P. B. Paulus (Ed.), *Psychology of group influence* (2nd ed., pp. 327–355). Hillsdale, NJ: Erlbaum.

Miller, C. T., & Downey, K. T. (1999). A meta-analysis of heavyweight and self-esteem. *Personality and Social Psychology Review, 3,* 68–84.

Miller, C. T., & Felicio, D. M. (1990). Person-positivity bias: Are individuals liked better than groups? *Journal of Experimental Social Psychology, 26,* 408–420.

Miller, D. T., & Prentice, D. A. (1994). The self and the collective. *Personality and Social Psychology Bulletin, 20,* 451–453.

Miller, D. T., & Prentice, D. A. (1996). The construction of norms and standards. In E. T. Higgins & A. W. Kruglanski (Eds.), *Social psychology: Handbook of basic principles* (pp. 799–829). New York: Guilford.

Miller, D. T., & Turnbull, W. (1990). The counterfactual fallacy: Confusing what might have been with what ought to have been. *Social Justice Research, 4,* 1–19.

Miller, J. G. (1984). Culture and the development of everyday social explanation. *Journal of Personality and Social Psychology, 46,* 961–978.

Miller, J. G. (1988). Bridging the content-structure dichotomy: Culture and the self. In M. H. Bond (Ed.), *The cross-cultural challenge to social psychology* (pp. 266–281). Beverly Hills, CA: Sage.

Miller, J. G. (1994). Cultural diversity in the morality of caring: Individually oriented versus duty-based interpersonal moral codes. *Cross-Cultural Research, 28,* 3–39.

Miller, J. G., Bersoff, D. M., & Harwood, R. L. (1990). Perceptions of social responsibilities in India and in the United States: Moral imperatives or personal decisions? *Journal of Personality and Social Psychology, 58,* 33–47.

Miller, L. C., Cooke, L. L., Tsang, J., & Morgan, F. (1992). Should I brag? Nature and impact of positive and boastful disclosures for women and men. *Human Communication Research, 18,* 364–399.

Miller, M. L., & Thayer, J. F. (1989). On the existence of discrete classes in personality: Is self-monitoring the current joint to carve? *Journal of Personality and Social Psychology, 57,* 143–155.

Miller, N., & Davidson-Podgorney, G. (1987). Theoretical models of intergroup relations and the use of cooperative teams as an intervention for desegregated settings. In C. Hendrick (Ed.), *Group processes and intergroup relations: Review of personality and social psychology* (Vol. 9, pp. 41–67). Beverly Hills, CA: Sage.

Miller, N., Maruyama, G., Beaber, R. J., & Valone, K. (1976). Speed of speech and persuasion. *Journal of Personality and Social Psychology, 34,* 615–624.

Miller, N., Pedersen, Earleywine, M., & Pollock, V. E. (2003). A theoretical model of triggered displaced aggression. *Personality and Social Psychology Review, 7,* 75–97.

Miller, P. J. E., & Rempel, J. K. (2004). Trust and partner-enhancing attributions in close relationships. *Personality and Social Psychology Bulletin, 30,* 695–705.

Miller, R. L., Brickman P., & Bolen, D. (1975). Attribution versus persuasion as a means of modifying behavior. *Journal of Personality and Social Psychology, 31,* 430–441.

Miller, R. S. (1987). Empathic embarrassment: Situational and personal determinants of reactions to the embarrassment of another. *Journal of Personality and Social Psychology, 53,* 1061–1069.

Miller, R. S. (1995). Embarrassment and social behavior. In J. P. Tangney & K. W. Fischer (Eds.), *Self-conscious emotions: The psychology of shame, guilt, embarrassment, and pride* (pp. 322–339). New York: Guilford.

Miller, R. S. (1997). We always hurt the ones we love: Aversive interactions in close relationships. In R. M. Kowalski (Ed.), *Aversive interpersonal behaviors* (pp. 11–29). New York: Plenum.

Miller, R. S., & Schlenker, B. R. (1985). Egotism in group members: Public and private attributions of responsibility for group performance. *Social Psychology Quarterly, 48,* 85–89.

Miller, S. A. (1995). Parents' attributions for their children's behavior. *Child Development, 66,* 1557–1584.

Milliman, R. E. (1986). The influence of background music on the behavior of restaurant patrons. *Journal of Consumer Research, 13,* 286–289.

Mills, J., & Clark, M. S. (1994). Communal and exchange relationships: Controversies and research. In R. Erber & R. Gilmour (Eds.), *Theoretical frameworks for personal relationships* (pp. 29–42). Hillsdale, NJ: Erlbaum.

Minton, H. L. (2002). *Departing from deviance: A history of homosexual rights and emancipatory science in America.* Chicago: University of Chicago Press.

Mintz, L. B., & Kashubeck, S. (1999). Body image and disordered eating among Asian American and Caucasian college students: An examination of race and gender differences. *Psychology of Women Quarterly, 23,* 781–796.

Mischel, W., Cantor, N., & Feldman, S. (1996). Principles of self-regulation: The nature of willpower and self-control. In E. T. Higgins & A. W. Kruglanski (Eds.), *Social psychology: Handbook of basic principles* (pp. 329–360). New York: Guilford Press.

Mita, T. H., Dermer, M., & Knight, J. (1977). Reversed facial images and the mere-exposure hypothesis. *Journal of Personality and Social Psychology, 35,* 597–601.

Mitchell, R. W., & Anderson, J. R. (1993). Discrimination learning of scratching, but failure to obtain imitation and self-recognition in a long-tailed macaque. *Primates, 34,* 301–309.

Miyamoto, Y., & Kitayama, S. (2002). Cultural variation in correspondence bias: The critical role of attitude diagnosticity of socially constrained behavior. *Journal of Personality and Social Psychology, 83,* 1239–1248.

Money, J., & Ehrhardt, A. A. (1972). *Man and woman, boy and girl.* Baltimore: Johns Hopkins University Press.

Monsour, M. (1997). Communication and cross-sex friendship across the lifecycle: A review of the literature. *Communication Yearbook, 20,* 375–414.

Monteith, M. J. (1993). Self-regulation of prejudiced responses: Implications for progress in prejudice-reduction efforts. *Journal of Personality and Social Psychology, 65,* 469–485.

Monteith, M. J. (1996). Affective reactions to prejudice-related discrepant responses: The impact of standard salience. *Personality and Social Psychology Bulletin, 22,* 48–59.

Monteith, M. J., & Spicer, C. V. (2000). Contents and correlates of Whites' and Blacks' racial attitudes. *Journal of Experimental Social Psychology, 36,* 125–154.

Monteith, M. J., Ashburn-Nardo, L., Voils, C. I., & Czopp, A. M. (2002). Putting the brakes on prejudice: On the development and operation of cues for control. *Journal of Personality and Social Psychology, 83,* 1029–1050.

Monteith, M. J., Deneen, N. E., & Tooman, G. D. (1996). The effect of social norm activation on the expression of opinions concerning gay men and blacks. *Basic and Applied Social Psychology, 18,* 267–288.

Monteith, M. J., Sherman, J. W., & Devine, P. G. (1998). Suppression as a stereotype control strategy. *Personality and Social Psychology Review, 2,* 63–82.

Montepare, J. M., & Zebrowitz-McArthur, L. (1988). Impressions of people created by age-related qualities of their gaits. *Journal of Personality and Social Psychology, 55,* 547–556.

Montoya, R. M., & Horton, R. S. (2004). On the importance of cognitive evaluation as a determinant of interpersonal attraction. *Journal of Personality and Social Psychology, 86,* 696–712.

Moore, B. S., & Eisenberg, N. (1984). The development of altruism. *Annals of Child Development, 1,* 107–174.

Moore, T. E. (1995). Subliminal self-help auditory tapes: An empirical test of perceptual consequences. *Canadian Journal of Behavioural Science, 27,* 9–20.

Moorhead, G., Ference, R., & Neck, C. P. (1991). Group decision fiascoes continue: Space shuttle Challenger and a revised groupthink framework. *Human Relations, 44,* 539–550.

Moreland, R. L., & Levine, J. M. (1988). Group dynamics over time: Development and socialization in small groups. In J. E. McGrath (Ed.), *The social psychology of time* (pp. 151–181). Newbury Park, CA: Sage.

Moreland, R. L., & Levine, J. M. (2001). Socialization in organizations and work groups. In M. E. Turner (Ed.)., *Groups at work: Theory and research: Applied social research* (pp. 69–112). Mahwah, NJ: Erlbaum.

Moreland, R. L., & Levine, J. M. (2002). Socialization and trust in work groups. *Group Processes and Intergroup Relations, 5,* 185–201.

Morf, C. C., & Rhodewalt, R. (1993). Narcissism and self-evaluation maintenance: Explorations in object relations. *Personality and Social Psychology Bulletin, 19,* 668–676.

Morling, B., & Epstein, S. (1997). Compromises produced by the dialectic between self-verification and self-enhancement. *Journal of Personality and Social Psychology, 73,* 1268–1283.

Mormon, M. T., & Floyd, K. (1998). "I love you, man": Overt expressions of affection in male-male interaction. *Sex Roles, 38,* 871–881.

Morrill, C., & Fine, G. A. (1997). Ethnographic contributions to organizational sociology. *Sociological Methods and Research, 25,* 424–451.

Morris, M. W., & Larrick, R. P. (1995). When one cause casts doubt on another: A normative analysis of discounting in causal attribution. *Psychological Review, 102,* 331–355.

Morris, W. N., Miller, R. S., & Spangenberg, S. (1977). The effects of dissenter position and task difficulty on conformity and response to conflict. *Journal of Personality, 45,* 251–266.

Morrison, T. L., Urquiza, A. J., & Goodlin-Jones, B. L. (1997). Attachment, perceptions of interaction, and relationship adjustment. *Journal of Social and Personal Relationships, 14,* 627–642.

Moscovici, S. (1980). Toward a theory of conversion behavior. In L. Berkowitz (Ed.), *Advances in experimental social psychology* (Vol. 13, pp. 2209–2239). New York: Academic Press.

Moscovici, S., & Mugny, G. (1983). Minority influence. In P. B. Paulus (Ed.), *Basic group processes* (pp. 41–64). New York: Springer-Verlag.

Moscovici, S., & Nemeth, C. (1974). Social influence II: Minority influence. In C. Nemeth (Ed.), *Social psychology: Classic and contemporary integrations* (pp. 217–249). Chicago: Rand McNally.

Moscovici, S., & Zavalloni, M. (1969). The group as a polarizer of attitudes. *Journal of Personality and Social Psychology, 12,* 125–135.

Moscovici, S., Lage, E., & Naffrechoux, M. (1969). Influences of a consistent minority on the responses of a majority in a color perception task. *Sociometry, 32,* 365–380.

Moskalenko, S., & Heine, S. J. (2003). Watching your troubles away: Television viewing as a stimulus for subjective self-awareness. *Personality and Social Psychology Bulletin, 29,* 76–85.

Moskowitz, G. B., Gollwitzer, P. M., Wasel, W., & Schaal, B. (1999). Preconscious control of stereotype activation through chronic egalitarian goals. *Journal of Personality and Social Psychology, 77,* 167–184.

Moss, E., Bureau, J.-F, Cyr, C., Mongeau, C., & St. Laurent, D. (2004). Correlates of attachment at age 3: Construct validity of the preschool attachment classification system. *Developmental Psychology, 40,* 323–334.

Moss, M. K., & Page, R. A. (1972). Reinforcement and helping behavior. *Journal of Applied Social Psychology, 2,* 360–371.

Muehlenhard, C. L., & Hollabaugh, L. C. (1988). Do women sometimes say no when they mean yes? The prevalence and correlates of women's token resistance to sex. *Journal of Personality and Social Psychology, 54,* 872–879.

Mugny, G., & Perez, J. A. (1991). *The social psychology of minority influence.* Cambridge, England: Cambridge University Press.

Muir, G., & Macleod, M. D. (2003). The demographic and spatial patterns of recorded rape in a large UK metropolitan area. *Psychology, Crime & Law, 9,* 345–355.

Mulac, A., & Lundell, T. L. (1986). Linguistic contributors to the gender-linked language effect. *Journal of Language and Social Psychology, 5,* 81–101.

Mulilis, J. P., Duval, T. S., & Rombach, D. (2001). Personal responsibility for tornado preparedness: Commitment or choice? *Journal of Applied Social Psychology, 31,* 1659–1688.

Mullen, B. (1986). Atrocity as a function of lynch mob composition: A self-attention perspective. *Personality and Social Psychology Bulletin, 12,* 187–197.

Mullen, B., & Copper, C. (1994). The relation between group cohesiveness and performance: An integration. *Psychological Bulletin, 115,* 210–227.

Mullen, B., & Hu, L. (1989). Perceptions of ingroup and outgroup variability: A meta-analytic integration. *Basic and Applied Social Psychology, 10,* 233–252.

Mullen, B., & Johnson, C. (1995). Cognitive representation in ethnophaulisms and illusory correlation in stereotyping. *Personality and Social Psychology Bulletin, 21,* 420–433.

Mullen, B., & Riordan, C. A. (1988). Self-serving attributions for performance in naturalistic settings: A meta-analytic review. *Journal of Applied Social Psychology, 18,* 3–22.

Mullen, B., & Suls, J. (1982). Know thyself: Stressful life changes and the ameliorative effect of private self-consciousness. *Journal of Experimental Social Psychology, 18,* 43–55.

Mullen, B., Migdal, M. J., & Rozell, D. (2003). Self-awareness, deindividuation, and social identity: Unraveling theoretical paradoxes by filling empirical lacunae. *Personality and Social Psychology Bulletin, 29,* 1071–1081.

Mullen, P. E., & Martin, J. (1994). Jealousy: A community study. *British Journal of Psychiatry, 164,* 35–43.

Muller, S. L., Williamson, D. A., & Martin, C. K. (2002). False consensus effect for attitudes related to body shape in normal weight women concerned with body shape. *Eating and Weight Disorders, 7,* 124–130.

Munsch, R. (1986). *Love you forever.* Ontario, Canada: Firefly Books, Limited.

Muraven, M., & Slessareva, E. (2003). Mechanisms of self-control failure: Motivation and limited resources. *Personality and Social Psychology Bulletin, 29,* 894–906.

Muraven, M., Tice, D. M., & Baumeister, R. F. (1998). Self-control as limited resource: Regulatory depletion patterns. *Journal of Personality and Social Psychology, 74,* 774–789.

Murphy, P. L., & Miller, C. T. (1997). Postdecisional dissonance and the commodified self-concept: A cross-cultural examination. *Personality and Social Psychology Bulletin, 23,* 50–62.

Murphy, S. T. (2001). Feeling without thinking: Affective primacy and the nonconscious processing of emotion. In J. A. Bargh & D. K. Apsley (Eds.), *Unraveling the complexitities of social life: A festschrift in honor of Robert B. Zajonc* (pp. 39–53). Washington, DC: American Psychological Association.

Murray, S. L., & Holmes, J. G. (1997). A leap of faith? Positive illusions in romantic relationships. *Personality and Social Psychology Bulletin, 23,* 586–604.

Murray, S. L., & Holmes, J. G. (1999). The (mental) ties that bind: Cognitive structures that predict relationship resilience. *Journal of Personality and Social Psychology, 77,* 1228–1244.

Murray, S. L., Bellavia, G., Rose, P., & Griffin, D. W., (2003). Once hurt, twice hurtful: How perceived regard regulates daily marital interactions. *Journal of Personality and Social Psychology, 84,* 126–147.

Murray, S. L., Holmes, J. G., & Griffin, D. W. (1996b). The benefits of positive illusions: Idealization and the construction of satisfaction in close relationships. *Journal of Personality and Social Psychology, 70,* 79–98.

Murray, S. L., Holmes, J. G., Bellavia, G., Griffin, D. W., & Dolderman, D. (2002). Kindred spirits? The benefits of egocentrism in close relationships. *Journal of Personality and Social Psychology, 82,* 563–581.

Murray, S. L., Holmes, J. G., Griffin, D. W., Bellavia, G., & Rose, P. (2001). The mismeasure of love: How self-doubt contaminates relationship beliefs. *Personality and Social Psychology Bulletin, 27,* 423–436.

Murstein, B. I. (1972). Physical attractiveness and marital choice. *Journal of Personality and Social Psychology, 22,* 8–12.

Murstein, B. I. (1974). *Love, sex, and marriage through the ages.* New York: Springer.

Musch, J., & Reips, U.-D. (2000). A brief history of Web experimenting. In M. H. Birnbaum (Ed.), *Psychological experiments on the Internet* (pp. 61–87). San Diego, CA: Academic Press.

Musolf, G. R. (2003). *Structure and agency in everyday life: An introduction to social psychology.* Lanham, MD: Rowman & Littlefield.

Mussweiler, T., & Bodenhausen, G. V. (2002). I know you are, but what am I? Self-evaluative consequence of judging in-group and out-group members. *Journal of Personality and Social Psychology, 82,* 19–32.

Mussweiler, T., & Rüter, K. (2003). What friends are for! The use of routine standards in social comparison. *Journal of Personality and Social Psychology, 85,* 467–481.

Mussweiler, T., & Strack, F. (2000). The use of category and exemplar knowledge in the solution of anchoring tasks. *Journal of Personality and Social Psychology, 78,* 1038–1052.

Mustonen, A. (1997). Nature of screen violence and its relation to program popularity. *Aggressive Behavior, 23,* 281–292.

Myers, D. G., & Bishop, G. D. (1970). Discussion effects on racial attitudes. *Science, 169,* 778–789.

Myers, D. G., & Kaplan, G. D. (1976). Group-induced polarization in simulated juries. *Personality and Social Psychology Bulletin, 2,* 63–66.

Myers, D. G., & Lamm, H. (1976). The group polarization phenomenon. *Psychological Bulletin, 83,* 602–627.

Nadler, A. (1987). Determinants of help seeking behaviour: The effects of helper's similarity, task centrality and recipient's self-esteem. *European Journal of Social Psychology, 17,* 57–67.

Nadler, A. (1991). Help-seeking behavior: Psychological costs and instrumental benefits. In M. S. Clark (Ed.), *Prosocial behavior: Review of personality and social psychology* (Vol. 12, pp. 290–311). Newbury Park, CA: Sage.

Nadler, A., & Fisher, J. D. (1986). The role of threat to self-esteem and perceived control in recipient reactions to help: Theory development and empirical validation. In L. Berkowitz (Ed.), *Advances in experimental social psychology* (Vol. 19, pp. 81–122). New York: Academic Press.

Nadler, A., Fisher, J. D., & Ben-Itzhak, S. (1983). With a little help from my friend: Effects of single or multiple act aid as a function of donor and task characteristics. *Journal of Personality and Social Psychology, 44,* 310–321.

Nadler, A., Shapiro, R., & Ben-Itzhak, S. (1982). Good looks may help: Effects of helper's physical attractiveness and sex of helper on males' and females' help-seeking behavior. *Journal of Personality and Social Psychology, 42,* 90–99.

Nahemow, L., & Lawton, M. P. (1975). Similarity and propinquity in friendship formation. *Journal of Personality and Social Psychology, 32,* 205–213.

Nail, P. R., Harton, H. c., & Decker, B. P. (2003). Political orientation and modern versus aversive racism: Tests of Dovidio and Gaertner's integrated model. *Journal of Personality and Social Psychology, 84,* 754–770.

Nail, P. R., VanLeeuwen, M. D., & Powell, A. B. (1996). The effectance versus the self-presentational view of reactance: Are importance ratings influenced by anticipated surveillance? *Journal of Social Behavior and Personality, 11,* 573–584.

Nair, K. U., & Ramnarayan, S. (2000). Individual differences in need for cognition and complex problem solving. *Journal of Research in Personality, 34,* 305–328.

Nakanishi, D.-T., & Nishida, T. Y. (Eds.). (1995). *The Asian American educational experience.* New York: Routledge.

Narby, D. J., Cutler, B. L., & Moran, G. (1993). A meta-analysis of the association between authoritarianism and jurors' perceptions of defendant culpability. *Journal of Applied Psychology, 78,* 34–42.

Nardi, P. M. (1992a). Seamless souls: An introduction to men's friendships. In P. M. Nardi (Ed.), *Men's friendships* (pp. 1–14). Newbury Park, CA: Sage.

Nardi, P. M. (1992b). Sex, friendship, and gender roles among gay men. In P. M. Nardi (Ed.), *Men's friendships* (pp. 173–185). Newbury Park, CA: Sage.

Nardi, P. M. (1992c). That's what friends are for: Friends as family in the gay and lesbian community. In K. Plummer (Ed.), *Modern homosexualities* (pp. 108–120). New York: Routledge.

Nardi, P. M., & Sherrod, D. (1994). Friendship in the lives of gay men and lesbians. *Journal of Social and Personal Relationships, 11,* 185–199.

National Institute on Alcohol Abuse and Alcoholism. (2002). *Task Force of the National Advisory Council on Alcohol Abuse and Alcoholism A Call to Action: Changing the Culture of Drinking at U.S. Colleges.* (2002). Washington, DC: National Institutes of Health.

Nayar, B. (2002). Ideological binarism in the identities of native and non-native English speakers. In A. Duszak (Ed.), *Us and others: Social identities across languages, discourses and cultures* (pp. 463–480).

Neighbors, C., Larimer, M. E., Geisner, I. M., & Knee, C. R. (in press). Feeling controlled and drinking motives among college students: Contingent self-esteem as a mediator. *Self & Identity.*

Neisser, U., Boodoo, G., Bouchard, T. J., Jr., Boykin, A. W., Brody, N., Ceci, S. J., Halpern, D. F., Loehlin, J. C., Perloff, R., Sternberg, R. J., & Urbina, S. (1996). Intelligence: Knowns and unknowns. *American Psychologist, 51,* 77–101.

Nelson, K. (1986). *Event knowledge: Structure and function in development.* New York: Erlbaum.

Nelson, T. E., Acker, M., & Manis, M. (1996). Irrepressible stereotypes. *Journal of Experimental Social Psychology, 32,* 13–28.

Nemeth, C. (1977). Interactions between jurors as a function of majority vs. unanimity decision rules. *Journal of Applied Social Psychology, 7,* 38–56.

Nemeth, C. J., Connell, J. B., Rogers, J. D., & Brown, K. S. (2001). Improving decision making by means of dissent. *Journal of Applied Social Psychology, 31,* 48–58.

Nemeth, C. J., Swedlund, M., & Kanki, B. (1974). Patterning of the minority's responses and their influence on the majority. *European Journal of Social Psychology, 4,* 53–64.

Nesse, R. M. (2000). How selfish genes shape moral passions. *Journal of Consciousness Studies, 7,* 227–231.

Neuberg, S. L., Judice, T. N., & West, S. G. (1997). What the Need for Closure Scale measures and what it does not: Toward differentiating among related epistemic motives. *Journal of Personal and Social Psychology, 72,* 1396–1412.

Neumann, R., Hülsenbeck, K., & Seibt, B. (2004). Attitudes towards people with AIDS and avoidance behavior: Automatic and reflective bases of behavior. *Journal of Experimental Social Psychology, 40,* 543–550.

Neumark-Sztainer, D., Story, M., Falkner, N. H., Beuhring, T., & Resnick, M. D. (1999). Sociodemographic and personal characteristics of adolescents engaged in weight loss and weight/muscle gain behaviors: Who is doing what? *Preventative Medicine, 28,* 40–50.

Newby-Clark, I. R., McGregor, I., & Zanna, M. P. (2002). Thinking and caring about cognitive inconsistency: When and for whom does attitudinal ambivalence feel uncomfortable? *Journal of Personality and Social Psychology, 82,* 157–166.

Newcomb, M. D., Rabow, J., & Hernandez, A. C. R. (1992). A cross-national study of nuclear attitudes, normative support, and activist behavior: Additive and interactive effects. *Journal of Applied Social Psychology, 22,* 780–800.

Newcomb, T. M. (1943). *Personality and social change: Attitude formation in a student community.* New York: Dryden.

Newcomb, T. M. (1951). Social psychological theory: Integrating individual and social approaches. In J. Rohrer & M. Sherif (Eds.), *Social psychology at the crossroads.* New York: Harper.

Newcomb, T. M. (1958). Attitude development as a function of reference groups. In E. E. Maccoby, T. M. Newcomb, & E. L. Hartley (Eds.), *Readings in social psychology* (3rd ed., pp. 265–275). New York: Holt, Rinehart.

Newcomb, T. M. (1961). *The acquaintance process.* New York: Holt, Rinehart.

Newcomb, T. M., Koenig, K. E., Flacks, R., & Warwick, D. P. (1967). *Persistence and change: Bennington College and its students after twenty-five years.* New York: Wiley.

Newcombe, N., & Arnkoff, D. B. (1979). Effect of speech style and sex of speaker on person perception. *Journal of Personality and Social Psychology, 37,* 1293–1303.

Newman, L. S. (2001). A cornerstone for the science of interpersonal behavior? Person perception and person memory, past, present, and future. In G. B. Moskowitz (Ed.) *Cognitive social psychology: The Princeton symposium on the legacy and future of social cognition* (pp. 191–207). Mahwah, NJ: Erlbaum.

Newman, M. L., Berry, D. S., & Richards, J. M. (2003). Lying words: Predicting deception from linguistic styles. *Personality and Social Psychology Bulletin, 29,* 665–675.

Nezlek, J. B., & Leary, M. R. (2002). Individual differences in self-presentational motives in daily social interaction. *Personality and Social Psychology Bulletin, 28,* 211–223.

Nezlek, J. B., & Plesko, R. M. (2003). Affect- and self-based models of relationships between daily events and daily well-being. *Personality and Social Psychology Bulletin, 29,* 584–596.

Nickerson, R. S. (2000). Null hypothesis significance testing: A review of an old continuing controversy. *Psychological Methods, 5,* 241–301.

Niedenthal, P. M., Brauer, M., Robin, L., & Innes-Ker, è. H. (2003). Adult attachment and the perception of facial expression of emotion. *Journal of Personality and Social Psychology, 82,* 419–433.

Nienhuis, A. E., Manstead, A. S. R., & Spears, R. (2001). Multiple motives and persuasive communication: Creative elaboration as a result of impression motivation and accuracy motivation. *Personality and Social Psychology Bulletin, 27,* 118–132.

Nier, J. A., Gaertner, S. L., Dovidio, J. F., Banker, B. S., & Ward, C. M. (2001). Changing interracial evaluations and behavior: The effects of a common ingroup identity. *Group Processes and Intergroup Relations, 4,* 299–316.

Nimchinsky, E. A., Gilissen, E., Allman, J. M., Perl, D. P., Erwin, J. M., & Hof, P. R. (1999). A neuronal morphologic type unique to humans and great apes. *Proceedings of the National Academy of Sciences, 96,* 5268–5273.

Nisbett, R. E., & Cohen, D. (1996). *Culture of honor: The psychology of violence in the south.* Boulder, CO: Westview Press.

Nisbett, R. E., Caputo, C., Legant, P., & Marecek, J. (1973). Behavior as seen by the actor and as seen by the observer. *Journal of Personality and Social Psychology, 27,* 154–164.

Nix, G., Watson, C., Pyszcznski, T., & Greenberg, J. (1995). Reducing depressive affect through external focus of attention. *Journal of Social and Clinical Psychology, 14,* 36–52.

Nolan, S. A., Flynn, C., & Garber, J. (2003). Prospective relations between rejection and depression in young adolescents. *Journal of Personality and Social Psychology, 85,* 745–755.

Nolen-Hoeksma, S., Girgus, J. S., & Seligman, M. E. P. (1992). Predictors and consequences of childhood depressive symptoms: Five year longitudinal study. *Journal of Abnormal Psychology, 101,* 405–422.

Norenzayan, A., & Nisbett, R. E. (2000). Culture and causal cognition. *Current Directions in Psychological Science, 9,* 132–135.

Norenzayan, A., Choi, I., & Nisbett, R. E. (2002). Cultural similarities and differences in social inference: Evidence from behavioral predictions and lay theories of behavior. *Personality and Social Psychology Bulletin, 28,* 109–120.

North, A. C., Tarrant, M., & Hargreaves, D. J. (2004). The effects of music on helping behavior: A field study. *Environment & Behavior, 36,* 266–275.

Northouse, P. G. (2001). *Leadership: Theory and practice* (2nd ed.). Thousand Oaks, CA: Sage.

Norton, M. I., Monin, B., Cooper, J., & Hogg, M. A. (2003). Vicarious dissonance: Attitude change from the inconsistency of others. *Journal of Personality and Social Psychology, 85,* 47–62.

Nosek, B. A., Banaji, M., & Greenwald, A. G. (2002a). Harvesting implicit group attitudes and beliefs from a demonstration web site. *Group Dynamics, 6,* 101–115.

Nosek, B. A., Banaji, M., & Greenwald, A. G. (2002b). Math = male, me = female, therefore math ≠ me. *Journal of Personality and Social Psychology, 83,* 44–59.

Nowak, A. (2004). Dynamical minimalism: Why less is more in psychology. *Personality and Social Psychology Review, 8,* 183–192.

Nowak, M., & Sigmund, K. (1993). A strategy of win-stay, lose-shift that outperforms tit-for-tat in the Prisoner's Dilemma game. *Nature, 364,* 56–58.

Nunner-Winkler, G. (1984). Two moralities? A critical discussion of an ethic of care and responsibility versus an ethic of rights and justice. In W. M. Kurtines & J. L. Gewiirtz (Eds.), *Morality, moral behavior and moral development* (pp. 348–361). New York: Wiley.

Nyberg, L., Forkstam, C., Petersson, K. M., Cabeza, R., & Ingvar, M. (2002). Brain imaging of human memory systems: Between-systems similarities and within-system differences. *Cognitive Brain Research, 13,* 281–292.

Nye, J. L., & Brower, A. M. (Eds.). (1996). *What's social about social cognition? Research on socially shared cognition in small groups.* Thousand Oaks, CA: Sage.

O'Connor, K. J., Cunningham, W. A., Funayama, E. S., Gatenby, J. C., Gore, J. C., & Banaji, M. R. (2000). Performance on indirect measures of race evaluation predicts amygdala activation. *Journal of Cognitive Neuroscience, 12,* 729–738.

O'Donnell, C. R. (1995). Firearm deaths among children and youth. *American Psychologist, 50,* 771–776.

O'Donohue, W., Yeater, E. A., & Fanetti, M. (2003). Rape prevention with college males: The roles of rape myth acceptance, victim empathy, and outcome expectancies. *Journal of Interpersonal Violence, 18,* 513–531.

O'Farrell, T., & Murphy, C. M. (1995). Marital violence before and after alcoholism treatment. *Journal of Consulting and Clinical Psychology 63,* 256–262.

O'Mahen, H. A., Beach, S. R. H., & Tesser, A. (2000). Relationship ecology and negative communication in romantic relationships: A self-evaluative maintenance perspective. *Personality and Social Psychology Bulletin, 26,* 1343–1352.

Ochsner, K. N., & Lieberman, M. D. (2001). The emergence of social cognitive neuroscience. *American Psychologist, 56,* 717–734.

Oda, Ryo. (2001). Lemur vocal communication and the origin of human language. In T. Matsuzawa (Ed), *Primate origins of human cognition and behavior* (pp. 115–134). New York, NY: Springer-Verlag.

Oddone-Paolucci, E., Genuis, M., & Violato, C. (2000). A meta-analysis of the published research on the effects of pornography. In C. Violato & E. Oddone-Paolucci (Eds.), *The changing family and child development* (pp. 48–59). Aldershot, England: Ashgate.

Ogbu, J. U. (1993). Differences in cultural frame of reference. *International Journal of Behavioral Development, 16,* 483–506.

Ohbuchi, K., Kamdea, M., & Agarie, N. (1989). Apology as aggression control: Its role in mediating appraisal of and response to harm. *Journal of Personality and Social Psychology, 56,* 219–227.

Öhman, A., Lundqvist, D., & Esteves, F. (2001). The face in the crowd revisited: A threat advantage with schematic stimuli. *Journal of Personality and Social Psychology, 80,* 381–396.

Ohtsubo, Y., Miller, C. E., Hayashi, N., & Masuchi, A. (2004). Effects of group decision rules on decisions involving continuous alternatives: The unanimity rule and extreme decisions in mock civil juries. *Journal of Experimental Social Psychology, 40,* 320–331.

Oishi, S., Diener, E. F., Lucas, R. E., & Suh, E. M. (1999). Cross-cultural variations in predictors of life satisfaction: Perspectives from needs and values. *Personality and Social Psychology Bulletin, 25,* 980–990.

Okazawa-Rey, M., Robinson, T., & Ward, J. V. (1986). Black women and the politics of skin color and hair. *Women's Studies Quarterly, 14,* 13–14.

Oliner, S. P., & Oliner, P. M. (1988). *The altruistic personality: Rescuers of Jews in Nazi Europe.* London: Free Press.

Olson, J. M. (1988). Misattribution, preparatory information, and speech anxiety. *Journal of Personality and Social Psychology, 54,* 758–767.

Olson, J. M., & Roese, N. J. (1995). The perceived funniness of humorous stimuli. *Personality and Social Psychology Bulletin, 21,* 908–913.

Olson, K. R., Lambert, A. J., & Zacks, J. M. (2004). Graded structure and the speed of category verification: On the moderating effects of anticipatory control for social vs. non-social categories. *Journal of Experimental Social Psychology, 40,* 239–246.

Omarzu, J. (2000). A disclosure decision model: Determining how and when individuals will self-disclose. *Personality and Social Psychology Review, 4,* 174–185.

Orbell, J. M., van de Kragt, A. J. C., & Dawes, R. M. (1988). Explaining discussion-induced cooperation. *Journal of Personality and Social Psychology, 54,* 811–819.

Orimoto, L., Hatfield, E., Yamakawa, R., & Denney, C. (1993). Gender differences in emotional reactions and coping strategies following a break-up. Reported in E. Hatfield & R. Rapson (1996), *Love, sex, and intimacy: Their psychology, biology, and history* (p. 231). Needham Heights, MA: Allyn & Bacon.

Ormel, J., & Schaufeli, W. B. (1991). Stability and change in psychological distress and their relationship with self-esteem and locus of control: A dynamic equilibrium model. *Journal of Personality and Social Psychology, 60,* 288–299.

Orne, M. T. (1962). On the social psychology of the psychological experiment: With particular reference to demand characteristics and their implications. *American Psychologist, 17,* 776–783.

Orpen, C. (1996). The effects of ingratiation and self promotion tactics on employee career success. *Social Behavior and Personality, 24,* 213–214.

Ortmann, A., & Hertwig, R. (1997). Is deception acceptable? *American Psychologist, 52,* 746–747.

Osborne, J. W. (1995). Academics, self-esteem, and race: A look at the underlying assumptions of the disidentification hypothesis. *Personality and Social Psychology Bulletin, 21,* 449–455.

Osborne, R. E. (2002). "I may be homeless, but I'm not helpless": The costs and benefits of identifying with homelessness. *Self and Identity, 1,* 43–52.

Osman, S. L. (2003). Predicting men's rape perceptions based on the belief that "no" really means "yes". *Journal of Applied Social Psychology, 33,* 683–692.

Ost, J., Costall, A., & Bull, R. (2001). False confessions and false memories: A model for understanding retractors' experiences. *Journal of Forensic Psychiatry, 12,* 549–579.

Oswald, D. L. (in press). Predicting anti-Arab reactions: The role of threats, social categories, and personal ideologies. *Basic and Applied Social Psychology.*

Oswald, D. L., & Clark, E. M. (2003). Best friends forever?: High school best friendships and the transition to college. *Personal Relationships, 10,* 187–196.

Oswald, D. L., & Harvey, R. D. (2003). A Q-methodological study of women's subjective perspectives on mathematics. *Sex Roles, 49,* 133–142.

Oswald, D. L., Clark, E. M., & Kelly, C. M. (2004). Friendship maintenance behaviors: An analysis of individual and dyad behaviors. *Journal of Social and Clinical Psychology, 23,* 413–441.

Oswald, R. F. (2000). A member of the wedding? Heterosexism and family ritual. *Journal of Social and Personal Relationships, 17,* 349–368.

Ottati, V. C., & Deiger, M. (2002). Visual cues and the candidate evaluation process. In V. C. Ottati & R. S. Tindale, J. Edwards, F. B. Bryant, L. Heath, D. C. O'Connell, Y. Suarez-Balcazar, & E. J. Posavac (Eds.). *The social psychology of politics. Social psychological applications to social issues* (pp. 75–87). New York: Kluwer Academic/Plenum.

Ottati, V. C., & Isbell, L. M. (1996). Effects of mood during exposure to target information and subsequently reported judgments: An on-line model of misattribution and correction. *Journal of Personality and Social Psychology, 71,* 39–53.

Oved, Y. (1988). *Two hundred years of American communes.* New Brunswick, NJ: Transaction Press.

Oyserman, D. (1993). The lens of personhood: Viewing the self and others in a multicultural society. *Journal of Personality and Social Psychology, 65,* 993–1009.

Oyserman, D., & Packer, M. J. (1996). Social cognition and self-concept: A socially contextualized model of identity. In J. L. Nye & A. M. Brower (Eds.), *What's social about social cognition: Research on socially shared cognition in small groups* (pp. 175–201). Thousand Oaks, CA: Sage.

Oyserman, D., Bybee, D., Terry, K., & Hart-Johnson, T. (in press). Possible selves as roadmaps. *Journal of Research in Personality.*

Oyserman, D., Coon, H. M., & Kemmelmeier, M. (2002). Rethinking individualism and collectivism: Evaluation of theoretical assumptions and meta-analysis. *Psychological Bulletin, 128,* 3–72.

Oyserman, D., Sakamoto, I., & Lauffer, A. (1998). Cultural accommodation: Hybridity and the framing of social obligation. *Journal of Personality and Social Psychology, 74,* 1606–1618.

Pacifici, C., Stoolmitler, M., & Miller, C. (2001). Evaluating a prevention program for teenagers on sexual coercion: A differential effectiveness approach. *Journal of Consulting and Clinical Psychology, 69,* 552–559.

Page, R. M. (1991). Loneliness as a risk factor in adolescent hopelessness. *Journal of Research in Personality, 25,* 189–195.

Pagelow, M. (1984). *Family violence.* New York: Praeger.

Paik, H., & Comstock, G. (1994). The effects of television violence on anti-social behavior: A meta-analysis. *Communication Research, 21,* 516–546.

Paletz, S. B. F., Peng, K., Erez, M., & Maslach, C. (2003). Ethnic composition and its differential impact on group processes in diverse teams. *Small Group Research, 20,* 1–31.

Pallak, S. R. (1983). Salience of a communicator's physical attractiveness and persuasion: A heuristic versus systematic processing interpretation. *Social Cognition, 2,* 158–170.

Paludi, M., & Barickman, R. B. (1991). *Academic and workplace sexual harassment.* Albany: State University of New York Press.

Park, B. (1986). A method for studying the development of impressions of real people. *Journal of Personality and Social Psychology, 51,* 907–917.

Park, B., & Rothbart, M. (1982). Perception of outgroup homogeneity and levels of social categorization: Memory for the subordinate attributes of ingroup and outgroup members. *Journal of Personality and Social Psychology, 42,* 1051–1068.

Park, B., Ryan, C. S., & Judd, C. M. (1992). Role of meaningful subgroups in explaining differences in perceived variability for in-groups and out-groups. *Journal of Personality and Social Psychology, 63,* 553–567.

Park, L. E., Crocker, J., & Mickelson, K. D. (2004). Attachment styles and contingencies of self-worth. *Personality and Social Psychology Bulletin, 30,* 1243–1254.

Park, Y., Killen, M., Crystal, D. S., & Watanabe, K. (2003). Korean, Japanese, and U.S. students' judgments about peer exclusion: Evidence for diversity. *International Journal of Behavioral Development, 27,* 555–565.

Parke, R. D., & Buriel, R. (1998). Socialization in the family: Ethnic and ecological perspectives. In W. Damon & N. Eisenberg (Eds.), *Handbook of child psychology: Vol. 3. Social, emotional, and personality development* (5th ed., pp. 463–552). New York: Wiley.

Parker, S. T., Langer, J., & McKinney, M. L. (Eds.). (2000). *Biology, brains, and behavior: The evolution of human development.* School of American Research Advanced Seminar Series.

Parks, C. D., Sanna, L. J., & Posey, D. C. (2003). Retrospection in social dilemmas: How thinking about the past affects future cooperation. *Journal of Personality and Social Psychology, 84,* 988–996.

Parnell, R. J., & Buchanan-Smith, H. M. (2001). Animal behaviour: An unusual social display by gorillas. *Nature, 412,* 294.

Parrott, W. G., & Smith, R. H. (1993). Distinguishing the experiences of envy and jealousy. *Journal of Personality and Social Psychology, 64,* 906–920.

Pasch, L. A., Bradbury, T. N., & Sullivan, K. T. (1997). Social support in marriage: An analysis of intraindividual and interpersonal components. In G. R. Pierce, B. Lakey, I. G. Sarason, & B. R. Sarason (Eds.), *Sourcebook of social support and personality* (pp. 229–256). New York: Plenum.

Patrick, H., Neighbors, C., & Knee, C. R. (2004). Appearance-related social comparisons: The role of contingent self-esteem and self-perceptions of attractiveness. *Personality and Social Psychology Bulletin, 30,* 501–514.

Patterson, F. G. P., & Cohen, R. H. (1994). Self-recognition and self-awareness in lowland gorillas. In S. T. Parker, R. W. Mitchell, & M. L. Boccia (Eds.), *Self-awareness in animals and humans: Developmental perspectives* (pp. 273–290). Cambridge, UK: Cambridge University Press.

Paulhus, D. L., & Levitt, K. (1987). Desirable responding triggered by affect: Automatic egotism? *Journal of Personality and Social Psychology, 52,* 245–259.

Paulus, P. B. (1998). Developing consensus about groupthink after all these years. *Organizational Behavior and Human Decision Processes, 73,* 1–13.

Payne, B. K. (2001). Prejudice and perception: The role of automatic and controlled processes in misperceiving a weapon. *Journal of Personality and Social Psychology, 81,* 181–192.

Payne, B. K., Lambert, A. J., & Jacoby, L. L. (2002). Best laid plans: Effects of goals on accessibility bias and cognitive control in race-based misperceptions of weapons. *Journal of Experimental Social Psychology, 38,* 384–396.

Payne, D. L., Lonsway, K. A., & Fitzgerald, L. F. (1999). Rape myth acceptance: Exploration of its structure and its measurement using the Illinois Rape Myth Acceptance Scale. *Journal of Research in Personality, 33,* 27–68.

Pedersen, W. C., Gonzales, C., & Miller, N. (2000). The moderating effect of trivial triggering provocation on displaced aggression. *Journal of Personality and Social Psychology, 78,* 913–927.

Peeters, G. (2003). Positive-negative asymmetry in the human information search and decision-making: Five basic and applied studies on voting behavior. In S. P. Shohov (Ed.), *Advances in psychology research,* (Vol. 19, pp. 61–92). Hauppauge, NY: Nova Science Publishers.

Pek, J. C. X., & Leong, F. T. L. (2003). Sex-related self-concepts, cognitive styles and cultural values of traditionality-modernity as predictors of general and domain-specific sexism. *Asian Journal of Social Psychology, 6,* 31–49.

Pelham, B. W., & Wachsmuth, J. O. (1995). The waxing and waning of the social self: Assimilation and contrast in social comparison. *Journal of Personality and Social Psychology, 69,* 825–838.

Pellegrini, A. D., & Bartini, M. (2001). Dominance in early adolescent boys: Affiliative and aggressive dimensions and possible functions. *Merrill-Palmer Quarterly, 47,* 142–163.

Pendleton, M. G., & Batson, C. D. (1979). Self-presentation and the door-in-the-face technique for inducing compliance. *Personality and Social Psychology Bulletin, 5,* 77–81.

Pendry, L. F., & Macrae, C. N. (1994). Stereotypes and mental life: The case of the motivation but thwarted tactician. *Journal of Experimental Social Psychology, 30,* 303–325.

Peng, K., & Nisbett, R. E. (1999). Culture, dialectics, and reasoning about contradiction. *American Psychologist, 54,* 741–754.

Pennington, N., & Hastie, R. (1988). Explanation-based decision making: Effects of memory structure on judgment. *Journal of Experimental Psychology: Learning, Memory, and Cognition, 14,* 521–533.

Pennington, N., & Hastie, R. (1990). Practical implications of psychological research on juror and jury decision making. *Personality and Social Psychology Bulletin, 16,* 90–105.

Pennington, N., & Hastie, R. (1992). Explaining the evidence: Tests of the story model for juror decision making. *Journal of Personality and Social Psychology, 62,* 189–206.

Peplau, L. A. (2003). Human sexuality: How do men and women differ? *Current Directions in Psychological Science, 12,* 37–40.

Peplau, L. A., & Garnets, L. D. (2000). A new paradigm for understanding women's sexuality and sexual orientation. *Journal of Social Issues, 56,* 329–350.

Peplau, L. A., Bikson, T. K., Rook, K. S., & Goodchilds, J. D. (1982). Being old and living alone. In L. A. Peplau & D. Perlman (Eds.), *Loneliness: A sourcebook of current theory, research and therapy* (pp. 327–347). New York: Wiley.

Peplau, L. A., Cochran, S. D., & Mays, V. M. (1997). A national survey of the intimate relationships of African American lesbians and gay men: A look at commitment, satisfaction, sexual behavior and HIV disease. In B. Greene & G. Herek (Eds.), *Psychological perspectives on lesbian and gay issues: Ethnic and cultural diversity among lesbians and gay men.* Newbury Park, CA: Sage.

Peplau, L. A., Fingerhut, A., & Beals, K. (in press). Sexuality in the relationships of lesbians and gay men. In J. Harvey, A. Wenzel, & S. Sprecher (Eds.), *Handbook of sexuality in close relationships.* Mahwah, NJ: Erlbaum.

Perdue, C. W., Dovidio, J. F., Gurtman, M. B., & Tyler, R. B. (1990). Us and them: Social categorization and the process of intergroup bias. *Journal of Personality and Social Psychology, 59,* 475–486.

Perez-Lopez, M. S., Lewis, R. J., & Cash, T. F. (2001). The relationship of antifat attitudes to other prejudicial and gender-related attitudes. *Journal of Applied Social Psychology, 31,* 683–697.

Pescosolido, A. T. (2001). Informal leaders and the development of group efficacy. *Small Group Research, 32,* 74–93.

Pessin, J. (1933). The comparative effects of social and mechanical stimulation on memorizing. *American Journal of Psychology, 45,* 263–270.

Peters, L. H., Hartke, D. D., & Pohlmann, J. T. (1985). Fiedler's contingency theory of leadership: An application of the meta-analytic procedures of Schmidt and Hunter. *Psychological Bulletin, 97,* 274–285.

Peterson, B. E. (2003). Authoritarianism and methodological innovation. *Analyses of Social Issues and Public Policy, 3,* 185–187.

Peterson, C. S., & Steen, T. A. (2002). Optimistic explanatory style. In C. R. Snyder & S. J. Lopez (Eds.), *Handbook of positive psychology* (pp. 244–256). London: Oxford University Press.

Peterson, C., & Seligman, M. E. P. (1987). Explanatory style and illness. *Journal of Personality, 55,* 237–265.

Peterson, C., Maier, S. F., & Seligman, M. E. P. (1993). *Learned helplessness: A theory for the age of personal control.* New York: Oxford University Press.

Peterson, C., Seligman, M. E. P., & Vaillant, G. E. (1988). Pessimistic explanatory style is a risk factor for physical illness: A thirty-five-year longitudinal study. *Journal of Personality and Social Psychology, 55,* 23–27.

Peterson, C., Seligman, M. E. P., Yurko, K. H., Martin, L. R., & Friedman, H. S. (1998). Catastrophizing and untimely death. *Psychological Science, 9,* 127–130.

Peterson, J. L., & Miller, C. (1980). Physical attractiveness and marriage adjustment in older American couples. *Journal of Psychology, 105,* 247–252.

Peterson, R. S., & Nemeth, C. J. (1996). Focus versus flexibility: Majority and minority influence can both improve performance. *Personality and Social Psychology Bulletin, 22,* 14–23.

Petrie, K. J., Booth, R. J., & Pennebaker, J. W. (1998). The immunological effects of thought suppression. *Journal of Personality and Social Psychology, 75,* 1264–1272.

Pettigrew, T. F. (1969). Racially separate or together? *Journal of Social Issues, 25,* 43–69.

Pettigrew, T. F. (1997). Generalized intergroup contact effects on prejudice. *Personality and Social Psychology Bulletin, 23,* 173–185.

Pettigrew, T. F. (1998). Intergroup contact theory. *Annual Review of Psychology, 49,* 65–85.

Pettigrew, T. F., & Tropp, L. R. (2000). Does intergroup contact reduce prejudice? Recent meta-analytic findings. In S. Oskamp (Ed). *Reducing prejudice and discrimination. The Claremont Symposium on Applied Social Psychology* (pp. 93–114). Mahwah, NJ: Erlbaum.

Pettit, G. S. (2004). Violent children in developmental perspective. Risk and protective factors and the mechanisms through which they (may) operate. *Current Directions in Psychological Science, ???,* 194–197.

Petty, R. E. (1997). The evolution of theory and research in social psychology: From single to multiple effect and process models of persuasion. In C. McGarty & S. A. Haslam (Eds.), *The message of social psychology: Perspectives on mind in society* (pp. 268–290). Oxford, England: Blackwell.

Petty, R. E. (2004). Multi-process models in social psychology provide a more balanced view of social thought and action. *Behavioral and Brain Sciences, 27.*

Petty, R. E., & Cacioppo, J. T. (1979). Issue involvement can increase or decrease persuasion by enhancing message-relevant cognitive responses. *Journal of Personality and Social Psychology, 37,* 1915–1926.

Petty, R. E., & Cacioppo, J. T. (1984). Source factors and the elaboration likelihood model of persuasion. *Advances in Consumer Research, 11,* 668–672.

Petty, R. E., & Cacioppo, J. T. (1986). *Communication and persuasion: Central and peripheral routes to attitude change.* New York: Springer-Verlag.

Petty, R. E., & Cacioppo, J. T. (1990). Involvement and persuasion: Tradition versus integration. *Psychological Bulletin, 107,* 367–374.

Petty, R. E., & Wegener, D. T. (1998). Attitude change: Multiple roles for persuasion variables. In D. Gilbert, S. Fiske, & G. Lindzey (Eds.), *The handbook of social psychology* (4th ed., pp. 323–390). New York: McGraw-Hill.

Petty, R. E., Briñol, P., & Tormala, Z. L. (2002). Thought confidence as a determinant for persuasion: The self-validation hypothesis. *Journal of Personality and Social Psychology, 82,* 722–741.

Petty, R. E., DeStono, D., & Rucker, D. D. (2001). The role of affect in attitude change. In J. P. Forgas (Ed.), *Handbook of affect and social cognition* (pp. 212–233). Mahwah, NJ: Erlbaum.

Petty, R. E., Haugtvedt, C. P., & Smith, S. M. (1995). Elaboration as a determinant of attitude strength: Creating attitudes that are persistent, resistant, and predictive of behavior. In R. E. Petty & J. A. Krosnick (Eds.), *Attitude strength: Antecedents and consequences.* Hillsdale, NJ: Erlbaum.

Petty, R. E., Ostrom, T. M., & Brock, T. C. (1981). Historical foundations of the cognitive response approach to attitudes and persuasion. In R. E. Petty, T. M. Ostrom, & T. C. Brock (Eds.), *Cognitive responses in persuasion* (pp. 5–29). Hillsdale, NJ: Erlbaum.

Petty, R. E., Rucker, D., Bizer, G., & Cacioppo, J.T. (2004a). The elaboration likelihood model of persuasion. In J. S. Seiter & G. H. Gass (Eds.), *Perspectives on persuasion, social influence and compliance gaining* (pp. 65–89). Boston: Allyn & Bacon.

Petty, R. E., Tormala, Z. L., & Rucker, D. D. (2004b). Resisting persuasion by counterarguing: An attitude strength perspective. In J. T. Jost, M. R. Banaji, & D. A. Prentice (Eds.), *Perspectivism in social psychology: The yin and yang of scientific progress* (pp. 37–51). Washington, DC: American Psychological Association.

Petty, R. E., Wegener, D. T., & Fabrigar, L. R. (1997). Attitudes and attitude change. *Annual Review of Psychology, 48,* 609–647.

Pezzo, M. V. (2003). Surprise, defense, or making sense: What removes hindsight bias? *Memory, 11,* 421–441.

Phelps, E. A., O'Connor, K. J., Cunningham, W. A., Funayama, E. S., Gatenby, J. C., & Gore, J. C., (2000). Performance on indirect measures of race evaluation predicts amygdala activation. *Journal of Cognitive Neuroscience, 12,* 729–738.

Phinney, J. S. (1991). Ethnic identity and self-esteem: A review and integration. *Hispanic Journal of Behavioral Sciences, 13,* 193–208.

Phinney, J. S. (1993). A three-stage model of ethnic identity development. In M. Bernal & G. Knight (Eds.), *Ethnic identity: Formation and transmission among Hispanics and other minorities* (pp. 61–79). Albany: State University of New York Press.

Phinney, J. S., & Kohatsu, E. (1997). Ethnic and racial identity and mental health. In J. Schulenberg, J. Maggs, & K. Hurrelmann (Eds.), *Health risks and developmental transitions during adolescence,* pp. 420–443. New York: Cambridge University Press.

Phinney, J. S., Cantu, C. L., & Kurtz, D. A. (1997). Ethnic and American identity and self-esteem. *Journal of Youth and Adolescence, 26,* 165–185.

Piaget, J., & Inhelder, B. (1969). *The psychology of the child.* New York: Basic Books.

Pietromonaco, P. R., & Carnelley, K. B. (1994). Gender and working models of attachment: Consequences for perception of self and romantic relationships. *Personal Relationships, 1,* 3–26.

Piliavin, J. A., & Piliavin, I. M. (1972). The effect of blood on reactions to a victim. *Journal of Personality and Social Psychology, 23,* 253–261.

Piliavin, J. A., Dovidio, J. F., Gaertner, S. L., & Clark, R. D., III. (1981). *Emergency intervention.* New York: Academic Press.

Pilkington, C. J., & Smith, K. A. (2000). Self-evaluation maintenance in a larger social context. *British Journal of Social Psychology, 39,* 213–227.

Pion, G. M., Mednick, M. T., Astin, H. S., Hall, C. C. I., Kenkel, M. B., Keita, G. P., Kohut, J. L., & Kelleher, J. C. (1996). The shifting gender composition of psychology: Trends and implications for the discipline. *American Psychologist, 51,* 509–528.

Pishyar, R., Harris, L. M., & Menzies, R. G. (2004). Attentional bias for words and faces in social anxiety. *Anxiety, Stress, and Coping, 17,* 23–36.

Plant, E. A. (2004). Responses to interracial interaction over time. *Personality and Social Psychology Bulletin, 30,* 1458–1471.

Plant, E. A., & Devine, P. G. (1998). Internal and external motivation to respond without prejudice. *Journal of Personality and Social Psychology, 75,* 811–832.

Plant, E. A., & Devine, P. G. (2003). The antecedents and implications of interracial anxiety. *Personality and Social Psychology Bulletin, 29,* 790–801.

Pleban, R., & Tesser, A. (1981). The effects of relevance and quality of another's performance on interpersonal closeness. *Social Psychology Quarterly, 44,* 278–285.

Plomin, R., Nitz, K., & Rowe, D. C. (1990). Behavior genetics and aggressive behavior in childhood. In M. Lewis & S. Miller (Eds.), *Handbook of developmental psychopathology* (pp. 119–133). New York: Plenum.

Plous, S. (1989). Thinking the unthinkable: The effects of anchoring on likelihood estimates of nuclear war. *Journal of Applied Social Psychology, 19,* 67–91.

Pohl, R. F., Bender, M., & Lachman, G. (2002). Hindsight bias around the world. *Experimental Psychology, 49,* 270–282.

Poldrack, R. A., & Wagner, A. D. (2004). What can neuroimaging tell us about the mind? Insights from prefrontal cortex. *Current Directions in Psychological Science, 13,* 177–181.

Pollard, J. S. (1995). Attractiveness of composite faces: A comparative study. *International Journal of Comparative Psychology, 8*(2), 77–83.

Pollock, C. L., Smith, S. D., Knowles, E. S., & Bruce, H. J. (1998). Mindfulness limits compliance with the that's-not-all technique. *Personality and Social Psychology, 24,* 1153–1157.

Pomerantz, E. M., Ruble, D. N., & Bolger, N. (2004). Supplementing the snapshots with video footage: Taking a developmental approach to understanding social psychological phenomena. In C. Sansone, C. C. Morf, & A. T. Panter (Eds.), *Handbook of methods in social psychology* (pp. 405–425). Thousand Oaks, CA: Sage.

Pontari, B. A., & Schlenker, B. R. (2000). The influence of cognitive load on self-presentation: Can cognitive busyness help as well as harm social performance? *Journal of Personality and Social Psychology, 78,* 1092–1108.

Poole, M. S., Hollingshead, A. B., McGrath, J. E., & Moreland, R. L. (2004). Interdisciplinary perspectives on small groups. *Small Group Research, 35,* 3–16.

Pope, H. G., Jr., Olivardan, R., Borowiecki, J., & Cohane, G. H. (2001). The growing commercial value of the male body: A longitudinal survey of advertising in women's magazines. *Psychotherapy and Psychosomatics, 70,* 189–192.

Pope, H. G., Olivardia, R., Gruber, A., & Borowiecki, J. (1999). Evolving ideals of male body image as seen through action toys. *International Journal of Eating Disorders, 26,* 65–72.

Porter, J. F., & Critelli, J. W. (1994). Self-talk and sexual arousal in sexual aggression. *Journal of Social and Clinical Psychology, 13,* 223–239.

Porter, S., & Yuille, J. C. (1996). The language of deceit: An investigation of the verbal clues to deception in the interrogation context. *Law and Human Behavior, 20,* 443–458.

Posavac, H. D., & Posavac, S. S. (1998). Exposure to media images of female attractiveness and concern with body weight among young women. *Sex Roles, 38,* 187–201.

Postmes, T., & Spears, R. (1998). Deindividuation and antinormative behavior: A meta-analysis. *Psychological Bulletin, 123,* 238–259.

Powell, G. N. (1990). One more time: Do female and male managers differ? *Academy of Management Executive, 4,* 68–75.

Powers, T. A., & Zuroff, D. C. (1988). Interpersonal consequences of overt self-criticism: Comparison with neutral and self-enhancing presentations of self. *Journal of Personality and Social Psychology, 54,* 1054–1062.

Pozo, C., Carver, C. S., Wellens, A. R., & Scheier, M. F. (1991). Social anxiety and social perception: Construing others' reactions to the self. *Personality and Social Psychology Bulletin, 17,* 355–362.

Pratkanis, A. R., & Aronson, E. (1992). *Age of propaganda: The everyday use and abuse of persuasion.* New York: W. H. Freeman.

Pratkanis, A. R., Eskenazi, J., & Greenwald, A. G. (1994). What you expect is what you believe (But not necessarily what you get): A test of the effectiveness of subliminal self-help audiotapes. *Basic and Applied Social Psychology, 15,* 251–276.

Pratkanis, A. R., Greenwald, A. G., Leippe, M. R., & Baumgardner, M. H. (1988). In search of reliable persuasion effects: III. The sleeper effect is dead. Long live the sleeper effect. *Journal of Personality and Social Psychology, 54,* 203–218.

Pratt, D. D. (1991). Conceptions of self within China and the United States: Contrasting foundations for adult education. *International Journal of Intercultural Relations, 15,* 285–310.

Pratto, F. (1996). Sexual politics: The gender gap in the bedroom, the cupboard, and the cabinet. In D. Buss & N. Malamuth (Eds.), *Sex, power, and conflict: Evolutionary and feminist perspectives* (pp. 179–230). New York: Oxford University Press.

Prentice, D. A. (1987). Psychological correspondence of possessions, attitudes, and values. *Journal of Personality and Social Psychology, 53,* 993–1003.

Prentice, D. A. (2004). Values and evaluations. In J. T. Jost, M. R. Banaji, & D. A. Prentice (Eds.). *Perspectivism in Social Psychology: The yin and yang of scientific progress* (pp. 69–81). Washington, DC: American Psychological Association.

Prentice, D. A., Trail, T. E., & Cantor, N. (2001). *Making choices and living with the consequences: Values, activities, and well-being among college students.* Unpublished manuscript, Princeton University.

Prentice-Dunn, S., & Rogers, R. W. (1982). Effects of public and private self-awareness on deindividuation and aggression. *Journal of Personality and Social Psychology, 43,* 503–513.

Prentice-Dunn, S., & Rogers. R. W. (1980). Effects of deindividuating situational cues and aggressive models on subjective deindividuation and aggression. *Journal of Personality and Social Psychology, 39,* 104–113.

Priest, R. F., & Sawyer, J. (1967). Proximity and peership: Bases of balance in interpersonal attraction. *American Journal of Sociology, 72,* 633–649.

Priester, J. R., & Petty, R. E. (1995). Source attributions and persuasion: Perceived honesty as a determinant of message scrutiny. *Personality and Social Psychology Bulletin, 21,* 637–654.

Priester, J. R., & Petty, R. E. (2001). Extending the bases of subjective attitudinal ambivalence: Interpersonal and intrapersonal antecedents of evaluative tension. *Journal of Personality and Social Psychology, 80,* 19–34.

Priester, J. R., Cacioppo, J. T., & Petty, R. E. (1996). The influence of motor processes on attitudes toward novel versus familiar semantic stimuli. *Personality and Social Psychology Bulletin, 22,* 442–447.

Pronin, E., Steele, C. M., & Ross, L. (2004). Identity bifurcation in response to stereotype threat: Women and mathematics. *Journal of Experimental Social Psychology, 40,* 152–168.

Pruitt, D. G. (1971). Choice shifts in group discussion: An introductory review. *Journal of Personality and Social Psychology, 20,* 339–360.

Pruitt, D. G. (1998). Social conflict. In D. Gilbert, S. T. Fiske, & G. Lindzey (Eds.), *Handbook of social psychology* (4th ed.). New York: McGraw-Hill.

Pryor, J. B., Giedd, J. L., & Williams, K. B. (1995). A social and psychological model for predicting sexual harassment. *Journal of Social Issues, 51,* 69–84.

Pryor, J. B., Reeder, G. D., Yeadon, C., & Hesson-McInnis, M. (2004). A dual-process model of reactions to perceived stigma. *Personality and Social Psychology, 87,* 436–452.

Ptacek, J. T., & Dodge, K. L. (1995). Coping strategies and relationship satisfaction in couples. *Personality and Social Psychology Bulletin, 21,* 76–84.

Puente, S., & Cohen, D. (2003). Jealousy and the meaning (or nonmeaning) of violence. *Personality and Social Psychology Bulletin, 29,* 449–460.

Pye, L. W. (1996). The state and the individual: An overview interpretation. In B. Hook (Ed.), *The individual and the state in China* (pp. 16–42). Oxford: Clarendon Press.

Pyszczynski, T. A., Solomon, S., & Greenberg, J. (2003). *In the wake of 9/11: The psychology of terror.* Washington, DC: American Psychological Association.

Pyszczynski, T., & Greenberg, J. (1992). *Hanging on and letting go: Understanding the onset, maintenance, and remission of depression.* New York: Springer-Verlag.

Pyykkö, R. (2002). Who is "us" in Russian political discourse? In A. Duszak (Ed.), *Us and others: Social identities across languages, discourses and cultures* (pp. 233–264). Amsterdam: John Benjamins.

Queller, S., & Smith, E. R. (2002). Subtyping versus bookkeeping in stereotype learning and change: Connectionist simulations and empirical findings. *Journal of Personality and Social Psychology, 82,* 300–313.

Querido, J. G., Warner, T. D., & Eyberg, S. M. (2002). Parenting styles and child behavior in African American families of preschool children. *Journal of Clinical Child Psychology, 31,* 272–277.

Quillian, L. (1995). Prejudice as a response to perceived group threat: Population composition and anti-immigrant and racial prejudice in Europe. *American Sociological Review, 60,* 586–611.

Quinn, D. M., & Crocker, J. (1998). When ideology hurts: Effects of belief in the Protestant ethic and feeling overweight on the psychological well-being of women. *Journal of Personality and Social Psychology, 77,* 402–414.

Quiñones-Vidal, E., López-Garcia, J. J., Peñaranda-Ortega, M., & Tortosa-Gil, F. (2004). The nature of social and personality psychology as reflected in JPSP, 1965–2000. *Journal of Personality and Social Psychology, 86,* 435–452.

Quist, R. M., & Resendez, M. G. (2002). Social dominance threat: Examining social dominance theory's explanation of prejudice as legitimizing myths. *Basic and Applied Social Psychology, 24,* 287–293.

Radelet, M. L., Bedau, H. A., & Putnam, C. E. (1992). *In spite of innocence: Erroneous convictions in capital cases.* Boston: Northeastern University Press.

Rai, S., & Sinha, A. K. (2000). Transformational leadership, organizational commitment, and facilitating climate. *Psychological Studies, 45,* 33–42.

Räikkönen, K., Matthews, K. A., Flory, J. D., Owens, J. F., & Gump, B. B. (1999). Effects of optimism, pessimism, and trait anxiety on ambulatory blood pressure and mood during everyday life. *Journal of Personality and Social Psychology, 76,* 104–113.

Ramirez, J. M., & Latané, B. (2001). Dynamic social impact theory predicts regional variation in, and the development of social representations of, aggression. In J. M. Ramirez & D. S. Richardson (Eds.), *Cross-cultural approaches to research on aggression and reconciliation* (pp. 9–21). Huntington, NY: Nova Science.

Ramsoy, N. R. (1966). Assortive mating and the structure of cities. *American Journal of Sociology, 31,* 773–786.

Rao, N., McHale, J. P., & Pearson, E. (2003). Links between socialization goals and child-rearing practices in Chinese and Indian mothers. *Infant and Child Development, 12,* 475–492.

Rasmussen, J. L., Rajecki, D. W., Ebert, A. A., Lagler, K., Brewer, C., & Cochran, E. (1998). Age preferences in personal advertisements: Two life history strategies or one matching tactic? *Journal of Social and Personal Relationships, 15,* 77–89.

Ratcliff, R., & McKoon, G. (1994). Retrieving information from memory: Spreading-activation theories versus compound-cue theories. *Psychological Review, 101,* 177–184.

Raven, B. H. (2001). Power/interaction and interpersonal influence: Experimental investigations and case studies. In A. Lee-Chai & J. Bargh (Eds.), *The use and abuse of power: Multiple perspectives on the causes of corruption* (pp. 217–240). Philadelphia, PA: Psychology Press.

Read, J. D. (1996). From a passing thought to a false memory in 2 minutes: Confusing real and illusory events. *Psychonomic Science and Review, 3,* 105–111.

Redding, R. E. (2001). Sociopolitical diversity in psychology. *American Psychologist, 56,* 205–215.

Reeder, G. D., Kumar, S., Hesson-McInnis, M. S., & Trafimow, D. (2002). Inferences about the morality of an aggressor: The role of perceived motive. *Journal of Personality and Social Psychology, 83,* 789–803.

Reeder, H. M. (2000). "I like you . . . as a friend": The role of attraction in cross-sex friendship. *Journal of Social and Personal Relationships, 17,* 329–348.

Reeder, H. M. (2003). The effect of gender role orientation on same- and cross-sex friendship formation. *Sex Roles, 49,* 143–152.

Reeve, J. (1992). *Understanding motivation and emotion.* Fort Worth, TX: Harcourt Brace.

Regan, D. T. (1971). Effects of a favor and liking on compliance. *Journal of Experimental Social Psychology, 7,* 627–639.

Regan, D. T., & Gilovich, T. (2004). Social psychological research isn't negative, and its message fosters compassion. *Behavioral and Brain Sciences, 27.*

Regan, D. T., & Kilduff, M. (1988). Optimism about elections: Dissonance reduction at the ballot box. *Political Psychology, 9,* 101–107.

Regan, P. C., Levin, L., Sprecher, S., Christopher, F. S., & Cate, R. (2000). Partner preferences: What characteristics do men and women desire in their short-term sexual and long-term romantic partners? *Journal of Psychology & Human Sexuality, 12,* 1–21.

Reich, A. A. (2004). What you expect is not always what you get: The roles of extremity, optimism, and pessimism in the behavioral confirmation process. *Journal of Experimental Social Psychology, 40,* 199–215.

Reinard, J. C. (1988). The empirical study of the persuasive effects of evidence: The status after fifty years of research. *Human Communications Research, 15,* 3–59.

Reinecke, J., Schmidt, P., & Ajzen, I. (1996). Application of the theory of planned behavior to adolescents' condom use: A panel study. *Journal of Applied Social Psychology, 26,* 749–772.

Reis, H. T., & Gable, S. L. (2003). Toward a positive psychology of relationships. In C. L. M. Keyes & J. Haidt (Eds.), *Flourishing: Positive psychology and the life well-lived* (pp. 129–159).

Reisenzein, R. (1983). The Schachter theory of emotion: Two decades later. *Psychological Bulletin, 94,* 239–264.

Reisman, J. M. (1984). Friendliness and its correlates. *Journal of Social and Clinical Psychology, 2,* 143–155.

Renner, K.-H., Laux, L., Schütz, A., & Tedeschi, J. T. (in press). The relationship between self-presentation styles and coping with social stress. *Anxiety, Stress, and Coping.*

Renzetti, C. (1993). Violence in lesbian relationships. In M. Hensen & M. Hareway (Eds.), *Battering and family therapy: A feminist perspective* (pp. 188–199). Newbury Park, CA: Sage.

Reynolds, K. J., Turner, J. C., & Haslam, S. A. (2000). When are we better than them and they worse than us? A closer look at social discrimination in positive and negative domains. *Journal of Personality and Social Psychology, 78,* 64–80.

Rhodewalt, F., & Davison, J., Jr. (1983). Reactance and the coronary-prone behavior pattern: The role of self-attribution in response to reduced behavioral freedom. *Journal of Personality and Social Psychology, 44,* 220–228.

Richeson, J. A., & Nussbaum, R. J. (2004). The impact of multiculturalism versus color-blindness on racial bias. *Journal of Experimental Social Psychology, 40,* 417–423.

Ridgeway, C. L. (1982). Status in groups: The importance of motivation. *American Sociological Review, 47,* 76–88.

Ridgeway, C. L. (1991). The social construction of status value: Gender and other nominal characteristics. *Social Forces, 70,* 367–386.

Ridgeway, C. L. (2001). Gender, status, and leadership. *Journal of Social Issues, 57,* 637–655.

Ridley, M., & Dawkins, R. (1981). The natural selection of altruism. In J. P. Rushton & R. M. Sorrentino (Eds.), *Altruism and helping behavior: Social personality, and developmental perspectives.* Hillsdale, NJ: Erlbaum.

Riggs, J. M., & Gumbrecht, L. B. (in press). Correspondence bias and American sentiment in the wake of September 11, 2001. *Journal of Applied Social Psychology.*

Riley, D., & Eckenrode, J. (1986). Social ties: Subgroup differences in costs and benefits. *Journal of Personality and Social Psychology, 51,* 770–778.

Ringelmann, M. (1913). Research on animate sources of power: The work of man. *Annales de l'Institut National Agronomique, 2e serietome XII,* 1–40.

Riordan, C. A., & Tedeschi, J. T. (1983). Attraction in aversive environments: Some evidence for classical conditioning and negative reinforcement. *Journal of Personality and Social Psychology, 44,* 683–692.

Rizzolatti, G., Craighero, L., & Fadiga, L.(2002). The mirror system in humans. In M. I. Stamenov & V. Gallese (Eds.), *Mirror neurons and the evolution of brain and language: Advances in consciousness research* (pp. 37–59). University di Parma: Bulgarian Academy of Sciences.

Robarchek, C. (1989). Primitive warfare and the ratomorphic image of mankind. *American Anthropologist, 91,* 903–920.

Roberts, B. W., & Helson, R. (1997). Changes in culture, changes in personality: The influence of individualism in a longitudinal study of women. *Journal of Personality and Social Psychology, 72,* 641–651.

Roberts, R. E., Phinney, J. S., Masse, L. C., Chen, Y., Roberts, C. R., & Romero, A. (1999). The structure of ethnic identity of young adolescents from diverse ethno cultural groups. *Journal of Early Adolescence, 19,* 301–322.

Roberts, W. R. (1954). *Aristotle.* New York: Modern Library.

Robins, R. W., & Beer, J. S. (2001). Positive illusions about the self: Short-term benefits and long-term costs. *Journal of Personality and Social Psychology, 80,* 340–352.

Robins, R. W., Gosling, S. D., & Craik, K. H. (1999). An empirical analysis of trends in psychology. *American Psychologist, 54.*

Robins, R. W., Spranca, M. D., & Mendelsohn, G. A. (1996). The actor-observer effect revisited: Effects of individual differences and repeated social interactions on actor and observer attributions. *Journal of Personality and Social Psychology, 71,* 375–389.

Robinson, D. T., & Balkwell, J. W. (1995). Density, transitivity, and diffuse status in task-oriented groups. *Social Psychology Quarterly, 58,* 241–254.

Robinson, T. N., Wilde, M. L., Navracruz, L. C., Haydel, K. F., & Varady, A. (2001). Effects of reducing children's television and video game use on aggressive behavior: A randomized controlled trial. *Archives of Pediatrics and Adolescent Medicine, 155,* 17–23.

Roccas, S., & Brewer, M. B. (2002). Social identity complexity. *Personality and Social Psychology Review, 6,* 88–106.

Rochot, F., Maggioni, O., & Modigliani, A. (2000). The dynamics of obeying and opposing authority: A mathematical model. In T. Blass, (Ed.), *Obedience to authority: Current perspectives on the Milgram paradigm* (pp. 161–192). Mahwah, NJ: Erlbaum.

Rodriguez-Bailon, R., Moya, M., & Yzerbyt, V. (2000). Why do superiors attend to negative stereotypic information about their subordinates? Effects of power legitimacy on social perception. *European Journal of Social Psychology, 30,* 651–671.

Roehling, M. (1999). Weight-based discrimination in employment: Psychological and legal aspects. *Personnel Psychology, 52,* 969–1016.

Roese, N. J. (1997). Counterfactual thinking. *Psychological Bulletin, 121,* 133–148.

Roese, N. J., Hur, T., & Pennington, G. L. (1999). Counterfactual thinking and regulatory focus: Implications for action versus inaction and sufficiency versus necessity. *Journal of Personality and Social Psychology, 77,* 1109–1120.

Rofé, Y. (1984). Stress and illness: A utility theory. *Psychological Review, 91,* 235–250.

Rogers, C. R. (1947). Some observations on the organization of personality. *American Psychologist, 2,* 358–368.

Rogers, R. W., & Prentice-Dunn, S. (1997). Protection motivation theory. In D. S. Gochman (Ed.), *Handbook of health behavior research I: Personal and social determinants* (Vol. 1, pp. 113–132). New York: Plenum.

Rogoff, B., Paradise, R., Arauz, R. M., Correa-Chavez, M., & Angelillo, C. (2003). Firsthand learning through intent participation. *Annual Review of Psychology, 54,* 175–203.

Rohan, M. J. (2000). A rose by any name? The values construct. *Personality and Social Psychology Review, 4,* 255–277.

Rokach, A., & Bacanli, H. (2001). Perceived causes of loneliness: A cross-cultural comparison. *Social Behavior and Personality, 29,* 169–182.

Rokeach, M. (1973). *The nature of human values.* New York: Free Press.

Romer, D., Gruder, C. L., & Lizzadro, T. (1986). A person-situation approach to altruistic behavior. *Journal of Personality and Social Psychology, 51,* 1001–1012.

Rosch, E. H. (1978). Principles of categorization. In E. Rosch & B. L. Lloyd (Eds.), *Cognition and categorization.* Hillsdale, NJ: Erlbaum.

Rosch, E., & Mervis, C. B. (1975). Family resemblances: Studies in the internal structure of categories. *Cognitive Psychology, 7,* 573–605.

Rose, J. (1994). Communication challenges and role functions of performing groups. *Small Group Research, 25,* 411–432.

Rose, S., & Zand, D. (2000). Lesbian dating and courtship from young adulthood to midlife. *Journal of Gay and Lesbian Social Services, 11,* 77–104.

Rosekrans, M., & Hartup, W. (1967). Imitative influences of consistent and inconsistent response consequences to a model on aggressive behavior in children. *Journal of Personality and Social Psychology, 7,* 429–434.

Rosenberg, M. L., & Mercy, J. A. (1991). Assaultive violence. In M. L. Rosenberg & M. A. Fenley (Eds.), *Violence in America: A public health approach* (pp. 14–50). New York: Oxford University Press.

Rosenblatt, P. C., & Cozby, P. C. (1972). Courtship patterns associated with freedom of choice of spouse. *Journal of Marriage and the Family, 34,* 689–695.

Rosenhan, D. L. (1970). The natural socialization of altruistic autonomy. In J. Macaulay & L. Berkowitz (Eds.), *Altruism and helping behavior.* New York: Academic Press.

Rosenhan, D. L., Salovey, P., & Hargis, K. (1981). The joys of helping: Focus of attention mediates the impact of positive affect on altruism. *Journal of Personality and Social Psychology, 40,* 899–905.

Rosenkoetter, L. I. (1999). The television situation comedy and children's prosocial behavior. *Journal of Applied Social Psychology, 29,* 979–993.

Rosenkoetter, L. I., Rosenkoetter, S. E., Ozretich, R. A., & Acock, A. C. (2004). Mitigating the harmful effects of violent television. *Journal of Applied Developmental Psychology, 25,* 25–47.

Rosenthal, R. (1991). Teacher expectancy effects: A brief update 25 years after the Pygmalion experiment. *Journal of Research in Education, 1,* 3–12.

Rosenthal, R. (2002). Covert communication in classrooms, clinics, courtrooms, and cubicles. *American Psychologist, 57,* 839–849.

Rosenthal, R. (2003). Covert communication in laboratories, classrooms, and the truly real world. *Current Directions in Psychological Science, 12,* 151–154.

Rosenthal, R., & Jacobson, L. (1968). *Pygmalion in the classroom: Teacher expectation and pupils' intellectual development.* New York: Holt.

Ross, E. A. (1908). *Social psychology: An outline and sourcebook.* New York: Macmillan.

Ross, L. (1977). The intuitive psychologist and his shortcomings: Distortions in the attribution process. In L. Berkowitz (Ed.), *Advances in experimental social psychology* (Vol. 10, pp. 174–221). New York: Academic Press.

Ross, L. E. (1997). Mate selection preferences among African-American college students. *Journal of Black Studies, 27,* 554–569.

Ross, L., Amabile, T. M., & Steinmetz, J. L. (1977a). Social roles, social control, and biases in social perception processes. *Journal of Personality and Social Psychology, 35,* 485–494.

Ross, L., Greene, D., & House, P. (1977b). The "false consensus effect": An egocentric bias in social perception and attribution processes. *Journal of Experimental Social Psychology, 13,* 279–301.

Ross, M. A., & Holmberg, D. (1993). Are wives' memories for events in relationships more vivid than their husbands' memories? *Journal of Social and Personal Relationships, 9,* 585–604.

Ross, M., & Miller, D. T. (Eds.). (2002). *The justice motive in everyday life.* New York: Cambridge University Press.

Rossano, M. J. (2003). *Evolutionary psychology: The science of human behavior and evolution.* Hoboken, NJ: John Wiley.

Rotenberg, K. J., & Kmill, J. (1992). Perception of lonely and nonlonely persons as a function of individual differences in loneliness. *Journal of Social and Personal Relationships, 9,* 325–330.

Rotenberg, K. J., Bartley, J. L., & Toivonen, D. M. (1997). Children's stigmatization of chronic loneliness in peers. *Journal of Social Behavior and Personality, 12,* 577–584.

Rothbart, M. (2001). Category Dynamics and the Modification of Outgroup Stereotypes. In S. Gaertner and R. Brown (Eds.), *Blackwell Handbook in Social Psychology, Volume 4 (Intergroup Processes),* (pp. 45–64). Oxford, UK: Blackwell Publishers.

Rothbaum, F., & Tsang, B. Y-P. (1998). Lovesongs in the United States and China: On the nature of romantic love. *Journal of Cross-Cultural Psychology, 29,* 306–319.

Rothbaum, F., Weisz, J., Pott, M., Miyake, K., & Morelli, G. (2000). Attachment and culture: Security in the United States and Japan. *American Psychologist, 55,* 1093–1104.

Rothstein, H. R., McDaniel, M. A., & Borenstein, M. (2002). Meta-analysis: A review of quantitative cumulation methods. In F. Drasgow & N. Schmitt (Eds.), *Measuring and analyzing behavior in organizations: Advances in measurement and data analysis. The Jossey-Bass business & management series.* San Francisco: Jossey-Bass.

Rotton, J., & Cohn, E. G. (2000). Violence is a curvilinear function of temperature in Dallas: A replication. *Journal of Personality and Social Psychology, 78,* 1074–1081.

Rotundo, A. (1989). Romantic friendships: Male intimacy and middle-class youth in the northern United States, 1800–1900. *Journal of Social History, 23,* 1–25.

Rowatt, W. C., Cunningham, M. R., & Druen, P. B. (1998). Deception to get a date. *Personality and Social Psychology Bulletin, 24,* 1228–1242.

Rowe, D. C., Chassin, L., Presson, C., & Sherman, S. J. (1996). Parental smoking and the "epidemic" spread of cigarette smoking. *Journal of Applied Social Psychology, 26,* 437–454.

Rowe, D. J. (2003, November 14). "Fabulist" Stephen Glass calls biopic of his life my own personal horror film. *Suburban Chicago Newspapers.* http://www.suburbanchicagonews.com/entertainment/e14glass.htm

Rozell, E. J., & Gundersen, D. E. (2003). The Effects of Leadership Impression Management on Group Perceptions of Cohesion, Consensus, and Communication, *Small Group Research, 34,* 197–222.

Rozin, P. (2001). Social psychology and science: Some lessons from Solomon Asch. *Personality and Social Psychology Review, 5,* 2–14.

Rozin, P., & Royzman, E. B. (2001). Negativity bias, negativity dominance, and contagion. *Personality and Social Psychology Review, 5,* 296–320.

Rubin, M., & Hewstone, M. (1998). Social identity theory's self-esteem hypothesis: A review and some suggestions for clarification. *Personality and Social Psychology Review, 2,* 40–62.

Rubin, Z., Peplau, L. A., & Hill, C. T. (1981). Loving and leaving: Sex differences in romantic attachments. *Sex Roles, 7,* 821–835.

Rucker, D. D., & Petty, R. E. (2004). When resistance is futile: Consequences of failed counterarguing for attitude certainty. *Journal of Personality and Social Psychology, 86,* 219–235.

Ruder, M., & Bless, H. (2003). Mood and the reliance on the ease of retrieval heuristic. *Journal of Personality and Social Psychology, 85,* 20–32.

Rudman, L. A., Ashmore, R. D., & Gary, M. L. (2001). "Unlearning" automatic biases: The malleability of implicit prejudice and stereotypes. *Journal of Personality and Social Psychology, 81,* 856–868.

Rudmin, F. (1999). Ichheiser, Gustav. In J.A. Garraty (Ed.), *American national biography* (nr. 11), New York: Oxford University Press.

Rusbult, C. E., & Martz, J. M. (1995). Remaining in an abusive relationship: An investment model analysis of nonvoluntary dependence. *Personality and Social Psychology Bulletin, 21,* 558–571.

Rusbult, C. E., Johnson, D. J., & Morrow, G. D. (1986a). Impact of couple patterns of problem solving on distress and nondistress in dating relationships. *Journal of Personality and Social Psychology, 50,* 744–753.

Rusbult, C. E., Morrow, G. D., & Johnson, D. J. (1987). Self-esteem and problem-solving behaviour in close relationships. *British Journal of Social Psychology, 26,* 293–303.

Rusbult, C. E., Olsen, N., Davis, J. L., & Hannon, P. A. (2001). Commitment and relationship maintenance mechanisms. In J. Harvey & A. Wenzel (Eds.), *Close romantic relationships: Maintenance and enhancement* (pp. 87–113). Manwah, NJ: Erlbaum.

Rusbult, C. E., Van Lange, P. A. M., Wildschut, T., Yovetich, N. A., & Verette, J. (2000). Perceived superiority in close relationships: Why it exists and persists. *Journal of Personality and Social Psychology, 79,* 521–545.

Rusbult, C. E., Zembrodt, I., & Iwaniszek, J. (1986b). The impact of gender and sex-role orientation on responses to dissatisfaction in close relationships. *Sex Roles, 15,* 1–20.

Ruscher, J. B., Fiske, S. T., & Schnake, S. B. (2000). The motivated tactician's juggling act: Compatible vs. incompatible impression goals. *British Journal of Social Psychology, 39,* 241–256.

Rushton, J. P. (1975). Generosity in children: Immediate and long term effects of modeling, preaching, and moral judgment. *Journal of Personality and Social Psychology, 31,* 459–466.

Rushton, J. P. (1980). *Altruism, socialization, and society.* Englewood Cliffs, NJ: Prentice-Hall.

Rushton, J. P. (1989). Genetic similarity in male friendships. *Ethology and Sociobiology, 10,* 361–373.

Rushton, J. P., & Campbell, A. C. (1977). Modeling, vicarious reinforcement and extraversion on blood donating in adults: Immediate and long term effects. *European Journal of Social Psychology, 7,* 297–306.

Rushton, J. P., & Teachman, G. (1978). The effects of positive reinforcement, attributions, and punishment on model-induced altruism in children. *Personality and Social Psychology Bulletin, 4,* 322–325.

Russell, D. (1982). Types of loneliness. In L. A. Peplau & D. Perlman (Eds.), *Loneliness: A sourcebook of current theory, research and therapy* (pp. 81–104). New York: Wiley.

Russell, D. E. H. (1993). *Making violence sexy: Feminist views on pornography.* New York: Teachers College Press.

Russell, D., Peplau, L. A., & Cutrona, C. E. (1980). The revised UCLA Loneliness Scale: Concurrent and discriminant validity evidence. *Journal of Personality and Social Psychology, 39,* 472–480.

Russell, J. A., & Yik, S. M. (1996). Emotion among the Chinese. In M. H. Bond (Ed.), *The handbook of Chinese psychology.* Hong Kong, China: Oxford University Press.

Ryan, C. S. (2003). Stereotype accuracy. *European Review of Social Psychology, 13,* 75–109.

Ryan, C. S. (in press). Stereotype accuracy. In W. Stroebe & M. Hewstone (Eds.), *European review of social psychology* (Vol. 13). Chichester, UK: John Wiley.

Ryan, C. S., Robinson, D. R., & Hausmann, R. M. (2004). Group socialization, uncertainty reduction and the development of new members' perceptions of group variability. In V. Yzerbyt, C. M. Judd, & O'Corneille (Eds.), *The psychology of group perception: Contributions to the study of homogeneity, entitativity, and essentialism.* Psychology Press.

Ryckman, R. M., Robbins, M. A., Thornton, B., Kaczor, L. M., Gayton, S. L., & Anderson, C. V. (1991). Public self-consciousness and physique stereotyping. *Personality and Social Psychology Bulletin, 17,* 400–405.

Saarni, C. (1999). *The development of emotional competence.* New York: Guilford.

Sabini, J., & Green, M. C. (2004). Emotional responses to sexual and emotional infidelity. Constants and differences across genders samples, and methods. *Personality and Social Psychology Bulletin, 30,* 1375–1388.

Sabini, J., Garvey, B., & Hall, A. L. (2001). Shame and embarrassment revisited. *Personality and Social Psychology Bulletin, 27,* 104–117.

Sachdev, I., & Bourhis, R. Y. (1987). Status differentials and intergroup behaviour. *European Journal of Social Psychology, 17,* 277–293.

Sachdev, I., & Bourhis, R. Y. (1991). Power and status differentials in minority and majority group relations. *European Journal of Social Psychology, 21,* 1–24.

Saegert, S. C., Swapp, W., & Zajonc, R. B. (1973). Exposure, context, and interpersonal attraction. *Journal of Personality and Social Psychology, 25,* 234–242.

Sakalli-Ugurlu, N. (2002). The relationship between sexism and attitudes toward homosexuality in a sample of Turkish college students. *Journal of Homosexuality, 42,* 53–64.

Sakalli-Ugurlu, N., & Glick, P. (2003). Ambivalent sexism and attitudes toward women who engage in premarital sex in Turkey. *Journal of Sex Research, 40,* 296–302.

Saks, M. J., & Marti, M. W. (1997). A meta-analysis of the effects of jury size. *Law and Human Behavior, 21,* 451–468.

Salovey, P., & Rodin, J. (1988). Coping with envy and jealousy. *Journal of Social and Clinical Psychology, 7,* 15–33.

Salovey, P., & Rodin, J. (1991). Provoking jealousy and envy: Domain relevance and self-esteem threat. *Journal of Social and Clinical Psychology, 10,* 395–413.

Salovey, P., Rothman, A. J., & Rodin, J. (1998). Health behavior. In D. T. Gilbert, S. T. Fiske, & G. Lindzey (Eds.), *The handbook of social psychology* (4th ed., Vol. 2, pp. 633–683). New York: McGraw-Hill.

Saltzman, S. (2002, November 27). Ad majors raise alcohol awareness. *SMU Daily Campus.* www.smudailycampus.com/vnews/display.v/ART/2002/11/27/3de442356f80b

Sampson, E. E. (1988). The debate on individualism: Indigenous psychologies of the individual and their role in personal and societal functioning. *American Psychologist, 43,* 15–22.

Sanchez-Burks, J., Nisbett, R. E., & Ybarra, O. (2000). Cultural styles, relational schemas, and prejudice against outgroups. *Journal of Personality and Social Psychology, 79,* 174–189.

Sanday, P. (1981). The socio-cultural context of rape: A cross-cultural study. *Journal of Social Issues, 37,* 5–27.

Sanders Thompson, V. L. (1991). Perceptions of race and race relations which affect African-American identification. *Journal of Applied Social Psychology, 21,* 1502–1516.

Sanders, G. S., & Baron, R. S. (1975). The motivating effects of distraction on task performance. *Journal of Personality and Social Psychology, 32,* 956–963.

Sanders, J. A., Wiseman, R. L., & Matz, S. I. (1991). Uncertainty reduction in acquaintance relationships in Ghana and the United States. In S. Ting-Toomey & F. Korsenny (Eds.), *Cross-cultural interpersonal communication* (pp. 79–98). Newbury Park, CA: Sage.

Sanderson, C. A., & Evans, S. M. (2001). Seeing one's partner through intimacy-colored glasses: An examination of the processes underlying the intimacy goals-relationship satisfaction link. *Personality and Social Psychology Bulletin, 27,* 463–473.

Sanderson, C. A., Darley, J. M., & Messinger, C. S. (2002). "I'm not as thin as you think I am": The development and consequences of feeling discrepant from the thinness norm. *Personality and Social Psychology Bulletin, 28,* 172–183.

Sandys, M., & Dillehay, R. C. (1995). First-ballot votes, predeliberation dispositions, and final verdicts in jury trials. *Law and Human Behavior, 19,* 175–195.

Sanna, L. J., & Mark, M. M. (1995). Self-handicapping, expected evaluation, and performance: Accentuating the positive and attenuating the negative. *Organizational Behavior and Human Decision Processes, 64,* 84–102.

Sanna, L. J., & Turley, K. J. (1996). Antecedents to spontaneous counterfactual thinking: Effects of expectancy violation and outcome valence. *Personality and Social Psychology Bulletin, 22,* 906–919.

Sanna, L. J., Chang, E. C., & Meier, S. (2001). Counterfactual thinking and self-motives. *Personality and Social Psychology Bulletin, 27,* 1023–1034.

Sansone, C., Morf, C. C., & Panter, A. T. (2004). The research process: Of big pictures, little details, and the social psychological road in between. In C. Sansone, C. C. Morf, & A. T. Panter (Eds.),

Handbook of methods in social psychology (pp. 3–16). Thousand Oaks, CA: Sage.

Santee, R. T., & Maslach, C. (1982). To agree or not to agree: Personal dissent amid social pressure to conform. *Journal of Personality and Social Psychology, 42,* 690–700.

Sargent, M. J., & Bradfield, A. L. (2004). Race and information processing in criminal trials: Does the defendant's race affect how the facts are evaluated? *Personality and Social Psychology Bulletin, 30,* 985–994.

Sarnoff, I., & Zimbardo, P. G. (1961). Anxiety, fear, and social affiliation. *Journal of Abnormal and Social Psychology, 62,* 356–363.

Savin, H. B. (1973). Professors and psychological researchers: Conflicting values in conflicting roles. *Cognition, 2,* 147–149.

Savitsky, K., & Gilovich, T. (2003). The illusion of transparency and the alleviation of speech anxiety. *Journal of Experimental Social Psychology, 39,* 618–625.

Savitsky, K., Epley, N., & Gilovich, T. (2001). Do others judge us as harshly as we think? Overestimating the impact of our failures, shortcomings, and mishaps. *Journal of Personality and Social Psychology, 81,* 44–56.

Scanzoni, J. (1979). Social exchange and behavioral interdependence. In R. L. Burgess & T. L. Huston (Eds.), *Social exchange in developing relationships.* New York: Academic Press.

Schachner, D. A., & Shaver, P. R. (2004). Attachment dimensions and sexual motives. *Personal Relationships, 11,* 179–195.

Schachter, S. (1951). Deviation, rejection and communication. *Journal of Abnormal and Social Psychology, 46,* 190–207.

Schachter, S. (1959). *The psychology of affiliation.* Stanford, CA: Stanford University Press.

Schachter, S. (1964). The interaction of cognitive and physiological determinants of emotional state. In L. Berkowitz (Ed.), *Advances in experimental social psychology* (Vol. 1, pp. 49–80). New York: Academic Press.

Schacter, D. L., & Badgaiyan, R. D. (2001). Neuroimaging of priming: New perspectives on implicit and explicit memory. *Current Directions in Psychological Science, 10,* 1–4.

Schacter, D. L., & Buckner, R. L. (1998). On the relations among priming, conscious recollection, and intentional retrieval: Evidence from neuroimaging research. *Neurobiology of Learning and Memory, 70,* 284–303.

Schaeffer, A. M., & Nelson, E. S. (1993). Rape-supportive attitudes: Effects of on-campus residence and education. *Journal of College Student Development, 34,* 175–179.

Schafer, M., & Crichlow, S. (1996). Antecedents of groupthink: A quantitative study. *Journal of Conflict Resolution, 40,* 415–435.

Schafer, R. B., & Keith, P. M. (1980). Equity and depression among married couples. *Social Psychology Quarterly, 43,* 430–435.

Schaffner, P. E., Wandersman, A., & Stang, D. (1981). Candidate name exposure and voting: Two field studies. *Basic and Applied Social Psychology, 2,* 195–203.

Schaller, M. (1997). Beyond "competing," beyond "compatible." *American Psychologist, 52,* 1379–1380.

Scharf, M., Mayseless, O., & Kivenson-Baron, I. (2004). Adolescents' attachment representations and developmental tasks in emerging adulthood. *Developmental Psychology, 40,* 430–444.

Schaufeli, W. B. (1988). Perceiving the causes of unemployment: An evaluation of the causal dimensions scale in a real-life situation. *Journal of Personality and Social Psychology, 54,* 347–356.

Scheier, M. F. (1980). Effects of public and private self-consciousness on the public expression of personal beliefs. *Journal of Personality and Social Psychology, 39,* 514–521.

Scheier, M. F., & Carver, C. S. (1977). Self-focused attention and the experience of emotion: Attraction, repulsion, elation, and depression. *Journal of Personality and Social Psychology, 35,* 625–636.

Scheier, M. F., & Carver, C. S. (1980). Private and public self-attention, resistance to change, and dissonance reduction. *Journal of Personality and Social Psychology, 39,* 390–405.

Scher, S. J., & Rauscher, F. (Eds.). (2003). *Evolutionary psychology: Alternative approaches.* New York's Kluwer Press.

Schewe, P. A. (2002). Guidelines for developing rape prevention and risk reduction intervention: Lessons from evaluation research. In P. Schewe (Ed.), *Preventing violence in relationships: Developmentally appropriate interventions across the life span* (pp. 107–136). Washington, DC: American Psychological Association.

Schimmack, U., Oishi, S., Furr, R. M., & Funder, D. C. (2004). Personality and life satisfaction: A facet-level analysis. *Personality and Social Psychology Bulletin, 30,* 1062–1075.

Schlenker, B. R. (1980). *Impression management: The self-concept, social identity, and interpersonal relations.* Monterey, CA: Brooks/Cole.

Schlenker, B. R. (2003). Self-presentation. In M. R. Leary & J. P. Tangney (Eds.), *Handbook of self and identity* (pp. 492–518). New York: Guilford Press.

Schlenker, B. R., & Britt, T. W. (2001). Strategically controlling information to help friends: Effects of empathy and friendship strength on beneficial impression management. *Journal of Experimental Social Psychology, 37,* 357–372.

Schlenker, B. R., & Wowra, S. A. (2003). Carryover effects of feeling socially transparent or impenetrable on strategic self-presentation. *Journal of Personality and Social Psychology, 85,* 871–880.

Schliemann, A. D., Carraher, D. W., & Ceci, S. (1997). Everyday cognition. In J. W. Berry, P. R. Dasen, & T. S. Saraswathi (Eds.), *Handbook of cross-cultural psychology: Vol. 2. Basic processes and human development* (pp. 177–216). Boston: Allyn & Bacon.

Schmader, T., & Johns, M. (2003). Converging evidence that stereotype threat reduces working memory capacity. *Journal of Personality and Social Psychology, 85,* 440–452.

Schmader, T., & Major, B. (1999). The impact of ingroup vs outgroup performance on personal values. *Journal of Experimental Social Psychology, 35,* 47–67.

Schmeichel, B. J., Vohs, K. D., & Baumeister, R. F. (2003). Intellectual performance and ego depletion: Role of the self in logical reasoning and other information processing. *Journal of Personality and Social Psychology, 85,* 33–46.

Schmidt, G., & Weiner, B. (1988). An attributional-affect-action theory of behavior: Replications of judgments of helping. *Personality and Social Psychology Bulletin, 14,* 610–621.

Schmitt, D. P. (2004). Patterns and universals of mate poaching across 53 nations: The effects of sex, culture, and personality on romantically attracting another person's partner. *Journal of Personality and Social Psychology, 86,* 560–584.

Schmitt, M. T., Branscombe, N. R., & Kapen, D. M. (2003). Attitudes toward group-based inequality: Social dominance or social identity? *British Journal of Social Psychology, 42,* 161–186.

Schnall, S., & Laird, J. D. (2003). Keep smiling: Enduring effects of facial expressions and postures on emotional experience and memory. *Cognition and Emotion, 17,* 787–797.

Schnall, S., Abrahamson, A., & Laird, J. D. (2002). Premenstrual syndrome and misattribution: A self-perception, individual differences perspective. *Basic and Applied Social Psychology, 24,* 215–228.

Schneider, C. S., & Kenny, D. A. (2000). Cross-sex friends who were once romantic partners: Are they platonic friends now? *Journal of Social and Personal Relationships, 17,* 451–466.

Schneider, D. J. (2004). *The psychology of stereotyping.* New York: Guilford Press.

Schoneman, P. H., Byrne, D., & Bell, P. A. (1977). Statistical aspects of a model for interpersonal attraction. *Bulletin of the Psychonomic Society, 9,* 243–246.

Schreurs, K. M. G., & Buunk, B. P. (1994). Intimacy, autonomy, and relationship satisfaction in Dutch lesbian couples and heterosexual couples. *Journal of Psychology and Human Sexuality, 7,* 41–57.

Schriesheim, C. A., Tepper, B. J., & Tetrault, L. A. (1994). Least preferred coworker score, situational control, and leadership effectiveness: A meta-analysis of contingency model performance predictions. *Journal of Applied Psychology, 79,* 561–573.

Schroeder, D. A., Steel, J. E., Woodell, A. J., & Bembenek, A. F. (2003). Justice within social dilemmas. *Personality and Social Psychology Review, 7,* 374–387.

Schubert, T. W., & Häfner, M. (2003). Contrast from social stereotypes in automatic behavior. *Journal of Experimental Social Psychology, 39,* 577–584.

Schuetz, A. (1998). Self-esteem and interpersonal strategies. In J. P. Forgas, K. D. Williams, & L. Wheeler (Eds.), *The social mind: Cognitive and motivational aspects of interpersonal behavior.* New York: Cambridge University Press.

Schulman, S., Elicker, J., & Sroufe, A. (1994). Stages of friendship growth in preadolescents as related to attachment history. *Journal of Social and Personal Relationships, 11,* 341–361.

Schuman, H. (1995). Attitudes, beliefs, and behavior. In K. S. Cook, G. A. Fine, & J. S. House (Eds.), *Sociological perspectives on social psychology* (pp. 68–89). Boston: Allyn & Bacon.

Schuman, H. (2002). Sense and nonsense about surveys. *Contexts, 1,* 40–47.

Schuman, H., & Scott, J. (1987). Problems in the use of survey questions to measure public opinion. *Science, 236,* 957–959.

Schuman, H., & Scott, J. (1989). Generations and collective memories. *American Sociological Review, 54,* 359–381.

Schumann, D. W., Petty, R. E., & Clemons, D. S. (1990). Predicting the effectiveness of different strategies of advertising variation: A test of the repetition-variation hypotheses. *Journal of Consumer Research, 17,* 192–202.

Schuster, B., Forsterling, F., & Weiner, B. (1989). Perceiving the causes of success and failure: A cross-cultural examination of attributional concepts. *Journal of Cross-Cultural Psychology, 20,* 191–213.

Schwartz, S. H. (1994). Are there universal aspects in the content and structure of values? *Journal of Social Issues, 50,* 19–45.

Schwartz, S. H. (1997). Values and culture. In D. Munro, S. Carr, & J. Schumaker (Eds.), *Motivation and culture* (pp. 69–84). New York: Routledge.

Schwartz, S. H. (2003). Mapping and interpreting cultural differences around the world. In H. Vinken, J. Soeters, & P. Ester (Eds.), *Comparing cultures: Dimensions of culture in a comparative perspective.* Leiden, The Netherlands: Brill.

Schwartz, S. H., & Bardi, A. (2001). Value hierarchies across cultures: Taking a similarities perspective. *Journal of Cross-Cultural Psychology, 32,* 268–290.

Schwartz, S. H., & Boehnke, K. (2002). *Evaluating the structure of human values with confirmatory factor analysis.* Manuscript submitted for publication.

Schwartz, S. H., & Sagiv, L. (1995). Identifying culture specifics in the content and structure of values. *Journal of Cross-Cultural Psychology, 26,* 92–116.

Schwarz, N. (1990). Feelings as information: Informational and motivational functions of affective states. In E. T. Higgins & R. M. Sorrentino (Eds.), *Handbook of motivation and cognition: Foundations of social behavior* (Vol. 2, pp. 527–561). New York: Guilford.

Schwarz, N. (1998). Warmer and more social: Recent developments in cognitive social psychology. *Annual Review of Sociology, 24,* 239–264.

Schwarz, N. (2003). Self-reports in consumer research: The challenge of comparing cohorts and cultures. *Journal of Consumer Research, 29,* 588–594.

Schwarz, N., & Vaughn, L. A. (2002). The availability heuristic revisited: Ease of recall and content of recall as distinct sources of information. In T. Gilovich, D. Griffin, & D. Kahneman (Eds.), *Heuristics and biases: The psychology of intuitive judgment* (pp. 103–119). New York: Cambridge University Press.

Schwarz, N., Bless, H., Strack, F., Klumpp, G., Rittenauer-Schatka, & Simons, A. (1991b). Ease of retrieval as information: Another look at the availability heuristic. *Journal of Personality and Social Psychology, 61,* 195–202.

Schwarz, S., & Stahlberg, D. (2003). Strength of hindsight bias as a consequence of meta-cognitions. *Memory, 11,* 395–410.

Schwarzwald, J., Bizman, A., & Raz, M. (1983). The foot-in-the-door paradigm: Effects of second request size on donation probability and donor generosity. *Personality and Social Psychology Bulletin, 9,* 443–450.

Schwarzwald, J., Koslowsky, M., & Ochana-Levin, T. (2004). Usage of and compliance with power tactics in routine versus nonroutine work settings. *Journal of Business and Psychology, 18,* 385–395.

Scully, D. (1985). *The role of violent pornography in justifying rape.* Paper prepared for the Attorney General's Commission on Pornography Hearings, Houston, TX.

Searcy, E., & Eisenberg, N. (1992). Defensiveness in response to aid from a sibling. *Journal of Personality and Social Psychology, 62,* 422–433.

Searle, J. R. (1995). Ontology is the question. In P. Baumgartner & S. Payr (Eds.). *Speaking minds: Interviews with twenty eminent cognitive scientists* (p. 202–213). Princeton, NJ: Princeton University Press.

Sears, D. O. (1983). The person-positivity bias. *Journal of Personality and Social Psychology, 44,* 233–250.

Sears, D. O., & Funk, C. L. (1991). The role of self-interest in social and political attitudes. In M. Zanna (Ed.), *Advances in experimental social psychology* (pp. 2–91). San Diego: Academic Press.

Sears, D. O., & Henry, P. J. (2003). The origins of symbolic racism. *Journal of Personality and Social Psychology, 85,* 259–275.

Seashore, S. E. (1954). *Group cohesiveness in the industrial work group.* Ann Arbor, MI: Institute for Social Research.

Sedikides, C., & Skowronski, J. J. (1997). The symbolic self in evolutionary context. *Personality and Social Psychology Review, 1,* 80–102.

Sedikides, C., & Strube, M. J. (1997). Self-evaluation: To thine own self be good, to thine own self be sure, to thine own self be true, and to thine own self be better. In M. P. Zanna (Ed.), *Advances in experimental social psychology* (Vol. 29, pp. 209–269). San Diego: Academic Press.

Sedikides, C., Campbell, W. K., Reeder, G. D., & Elliot, A. J. (1998). The self-serving bias in relational context. *Journal of Personality and Social Psychology, 74,* 378–386.

Seeman, M. (1997). The elusive situation in social psychology. *Social Psychology Quarterly, 60,* 4–13.

Seers, A., Keller, T., & Wilkerson, J. M. (2003). Can team members share leadership? In C. L. Pearce & J. A. Conger (Eds.), *Shared leadership: Reframing the hows and whys of leadership* (pp. 77–102). Thousand Oaks, CA: Sage.

Segal, M. W. (1974). Alphabet and attraction: An unobtrusive measure of the effect of propinquity in a field setting. *Journal of Personality and Social Psychology, 30,* 654–657.

Segerstrom, S. C., Taylor, S. E., Kemeny, M. E., & Fahey, J. L. (1998). Optimism is associated with mood, coping, and immune change in response to stress. *Journal of Personality and Social Psychology, 74,* 1646–1655.

Segura, S., & McCloy, R. (2003). Counterfactual thinking in everyday life situations: Temporal order effects and social norms. *Psicologica, 24,* 1–15.

Seligman, M. E. P. (1991). *Learned optimism.* New York: Alfred A. Knopf.

Seligman, M. E. P., & Maier, S. F. (1967). Failure to escape traumatic shock. *Journal of Experimental Psychology, 74,* 1–9.

Sellers, R. M., & Shelton, J. N. (2003). The role of racial identity in perceived racial discrimination. *Journal of Personality and Social Psychology, 84,* 1079–1092.

Senchak, M., & Leonard, K. E. (1992). Attachment styles and marital adjustment among newlywed couples. *Journal of Social and Personal Relationships, 9,* 51–64.

Sengrupta, J., & Johar, G. V. (2001). Contingent effects of anxiety on message elaboration and persuasion. *Personality and Social Psychology Bulletin, 27,* 139–150.

Senior, C., Ward, J., & David, A. S. (2002). Representational momentum and the brain: An investigation into the functional necessity of V5/MT. *Visual Cognition, 9,* 81–92.

Seta, J. J., Donaldson, S., & Seta, C. E. (1999). Self-relevance as a moderator of self-enhancement and self-verification. *Journal of Research in Personality, 33,* 442–462.

Seta, J. J., Seta, C. E., & McElroy, T. (2003). Attributional biases in the service of stereotype-maintenance: A schema-maintenance through compensation analysis. *Personality and Social Psychology Bulletin, 29,* 151–163.

Sevér, A., Dawson, M., & Johnson, H. (2004). Lethal and nonlethal violence against women by intimate partners: Trends and prospects in the United States, the United Kingdom, and Canada. *Violence Against Women, 10,* 563–576.

Shanab, M. E., & Yahya, K. A. (1977). A behavioral study of obedience in children. *Journal of Personality and Social Psychology, 35,* 530–536.

Share, T. L., & Mintz, L. B. (2002). Differences between lesbians and heterosexual women in disordered eating and related attitudes. *Journal of Homosexuality, 42,* 89–106.

Shaver, P. R., Wu, S., & Schwartz, J. C. (1991). Cross-cultural similarities and differences in emotion and its representation: A prototype approach. In M. S. Clark (Ed.), *Review of personality and social psychology* (Vol. 13, pp. 175–212). Beverly Hills, CA: Sage.

Shaver, P., & Klinnert, M. (1982). Schachter's theories of affiliation and emotion: Implications of developmental research. In L. Wheeler (Ed.), *Review of personality and social psychology* (Vol. 3). Beverly Hills, CA: Sage.

Shavitt, S., Swan, S., Lowery, T. M., & Wänke, M. (1994). The interaction of endorser attractiveness and involvement in persuasion depends on the goal that guides message processing. *Journal of Consumer Psychology, 3,* 137–162.

Shaw, J. (2003). Automatic for the people: How representations of significant others implicitly affect goal pursuit. *Journal of Personality and Social Psychology, 84,* 661–681.

Shaw, L. L., Batson, C. D., & Todd, R. M. (1994). Empathy avoidance: Forestalling feeling for another in order to escape the motivational consequences. *Journal of Personality and Social Psychology, 67,* 879–887.

Sheeran, P. (2002). Intention-behavior relations: A conceptual and empirical review. In M. Hewstone & W. Stroebe (Eds.), *European review of social psychology* (Vol. 12, pp. 1–36). Chichester, England: Wiley.

Sheeran, P., Orbell, S., & Trafimow, D. (1999). Does the temporal stability of behavioral intentions moderate intention-behavior and past behavior-future behavior relations? *Personality and Social Psychology Bulletin, 25,* 721–730.

Sheldon, K. M. (1999). Learning the lessons of tit-for-tat: Even competitors can get the message. *Journal of Personality and Social Psychology, 77,* 1245–1253.

Shelton, J. N. (2000). A reconceptualization of how we study issues of racial prejudice. *Personality and Social Psychology Review, 4,* 374–390.

Shelton, J. N. (2003). Interpersonal concerns in social encounters between majority and minority group members. *Group Processes and Intergroup Relations, 6,* 171–185.

Shepperd, J. A., & Socherman, R. E. (1997). On the manipulative behavior of low Machiavellians: Feigning incompetence to "sandbag" an opponent. *Journal of Personality and Social Psychology, 72,* 1448–1459.

Shepperd, J. A., Ouellette, J. A., & Fernandez, J. K. (1996). Abandoning unrealistic optimism: Performance estimates and the temporal proximity of self-relevant feedback. *Journal of Personality and Social Psychology, 70,* 844–855.

Sherif, M. (1935). A study of some social factors in perception. *Archives of Psychology, 27* (187), 1–60.

Sherif, M. (1936). *The psychology of social norms.* New York: Harper.

Sherif, M. (1966). *In common predicament: Social psychology of intergroup conflict and cooperation.* Boston: Houghton Mifflin.

Sherif, M., & Cantril, H. (1947). *The psychology of ego-involvements: Social attitudes and identifications.* New York: Wiley.

Sherif, M., & Sherif, C. W. (1956). *An outline of social psychology.* New York: Harper & Brothers.

Sherif, M., Harvey, O. J., White, B. J., Hood, W. R., & Sherif, C. (1961). *Intergroup conflict and cooperation: The Robbers' Cave experiment.* Norman, OK: Oklahoma Book Exchange.

Sherman, J. W., & Klein, S. B. (1994). Development and representation of personality impressions. *Journal of Personality and Social Psychology, 67,* 972–983.

Sherman, J. W., Klein, S. B., Laskey, A., & Wyer, N. A. (1998). Intergroup bias in group judgment processes: The role of behavioral memories. *Journal of Experimental Social Psychology, 34,* 51–65.

Sherman, P. W. (1985). Alarm calls of Belding's ground squirrels to aerial predators: Nepotism or self-preservation? *Behavioral Ecology and Sociobiology, 17,* 313–323.

Sherman, R. C., Buddie, A. M., Dragan, K. L., End, C. M., & Finney, L. J. (1999). Twenty years of *PSPB:* Trends in content, design, and analysis. *Personality and Social Psychology Bulletin, 25,* 177–187.

Sherman, S. J., & Johnson, A. L. (2003). Perceiving groups: How, what, and why? In G. A. Bodenhausen & A. J. Lambert (Eds.), *Foundations of social cognition: A festschrift in honor of Robert S. Wyer, Jr.* (pp. 155–180). Washington, DC: American Psychological Association.

Sherman, S. J., Castelli, L., & Hamilton, D. L. (2002). The spontaneous use of a group typology as an organizing principle in memory. *Journal of Personality and Social Psychology, 82,* 328–342.

Sherman, S. J., Mackie, D. M., & Driscoll, D. M. (1990). Priming and the differential use of dimensions in evaluation. *Personality and Social Psychology Bulletin, 16,* 405–418.

Sherrod, D. (1989). The influence of gender on same-sex friendships. In C. Hendrick (Ed.), *Review of personality and social psychology: Vol. 10. Close relationships* (pp. 164–186). Newbury Park, CA: Sage.

Shestowsky, D., Wegener, D. T., & Fabrigar, L. R. (1998). Need for cognition and interpersonal influence: Individual differences in impact on dyadic decisions. *Journal of Personality and Social Psychology, 74,* 1317–1328.

Shields, S. A. (2002). *Speaking from the heart: Gender and the social meaning of emotion.* Cambridge: Cambridge University Press.

Shinha, J. B. P. (2003). Trends toward indigenization of psychology in India. In K.-S. Yang, K.-K. Hwang, P. B. Pedersen, & I. Daibo (Eds.), *Progress in Asian social psychology: Conceptual and empirical contributions* (pp. 11–27). Westport, CT: Praeger.

Shoda, Y., Mischel, W., & Peake, P. K. (1990). Predicting adolescent cognitive and self-regulatory competencies from preschool delay of gratification: Identifying diagnostic conditions. *Developmental Psychology, 26,* 978–986.

Shotland, R. L., & Hunter, B. A. (1995). Women's "token resistant" and compliant sexual behaviors are related to uncertain sexual intentions and rape. *Personality and Social Psychology Bulletin, 21,* 226–236.

Shotland, R. L., & Straw, M. K. (1976). Bystander response to an assault: When a man attacks a woman. *Journal of Personality and Social Psychology, 34,* 990–999.

Shoyama, S., Tochihara, Y., & Kim, J. (2003). Japanese and Korean ideas about clothing colors for elderly people: Intercountry and intergenerational differences. *Color Research and Application, 28,* 139–150.

Shrauger, J. S. (1975). Responses to evaluation as a function of initial self-perceptions. *Psychological Bulletin, 82,* 581–596.

Shumaker, S. A., & Hill, D. R. (1991). Gender differences in social support and physical health. *Health Psychology, 10,* 102–111.

Shuval, J. T., & Adler, I. (1980). The role of models in professional socialization. *Social Science and Medicine, 14,* 5–14.

Sibicky, M. E., Schroeder, D. A., & Dovidio, J. F. (1995). Empathy and helping: Considering the consequences of intervention. *Basic and Applied Social Psychology, 16,* 435–453.

Sidanius, J., & Pratto, F. (1999). *Social dominance: An intergroup theory of social hierarchy and oppression.* New York: Cambridge University Press.

Sidanius, J., Levin, S., Liu, J., & Pratto, F. (2000). Social dominance orientation, anti-egalitarianism and the political psychology of gender: An extension and cross-cultural replication. *European Journal of Social Psychology, 30,* 41–67.

Sidanius, J., Pratto, F., & Brief, D. (1995). Group dominance and the political psychology of gender: A cross-cultural comparison. *Political Psychology, 16,* 381–396.

Side, K. (2004). Broken promises. *Psychology of Women Quarterly, 28,* 100–101.

Sigelman, C. K., Berry, C. J., & Wiles, K. A. (1984). Violence in college students' dating relationships. *Journal of Applied Social Psychology, 5,* 530–548.

Sigelman, L., & Tuch, S. A. (1997). Metastereotypes: Blacks' perceptions of Whites' stereotypes of Blacks. *Public Opinion Quarterly, 61,* 87–101.

Sigurdsson, J. F., & Gudjonsson, G. H. (1996). Psychological characteristics of "false confessors": A study among Icelandic prison inmates and juvenile offenders. *Personality and Individual Differences, 20,* 321–329.

Silberstein, L. R., Mishkind, M. E., Striegel-Moore, R. H., Timko, C., & Rodin, J. (1989). Men and their bodies: A comparison of homosexual and heterosexual men. *Psychosomatic Medicine, 51,* 337–346.

Silvia & O'Brien (2004). *Journal of Social and Clinical Psychology, 23,* 475–489.

Silvia, P. J., & Duval, T. S. (2001a). Objective self-awareness theory: Recent progress and enduring problems. *Personality and Social Psychology Review, 5,* 230–241.

Silvia, P. J., & Duval, T. S. (2001b). Predicting the interpersonal targets of self-serving attributions. *Journal of Experimental Social Psychology, 37,* 333–340.

Silvia, P. J., & O'Brien, M. E. (in press). Self-awareness and constructive functioning: Revisiting "The human experience." *Journal of Social and Clinical Psychology.*

Simon, B. (1992). Intragroup differentiation in terms of ingroup and outgroup attributes. *European Journal of Social Psychology, 22,* 407–413.

Simon, B., Pantaleo, G., & Mummendey, A. (1995). Unique individual or interchangeable group member? The accentuation of intragroup differences versus similarities as an indicator of the individual self versus the collective self. *Journal of Personality and Social Psychology, 69,* 106–119.

Simon, B., Stürmer, S., & Steffens, K. (2000). Helping individuals or group members? The role of individual and collective identification in AIDS volunteerism. *Personality and Social Psychology Bulletin, 26,* 497–506.

Simon, H. (1990). A mechanism for social selection and successful altruism. *Science, 250,* 1665–1668.

Simons, H. W. (1971). Persuasion and attitude change. In L. L. Barker & R. J. Kibler (Eds.), *Speech communication behavior: Perspectives and principles* (pp. 227–248). Englewood Cliffs, NJ: Prentice-Hall.

Simons, H. W., Berkowitz, N. N., & Moyer, R. J. (1970). Similarity, credibility, and attitude change: A review and a theory. *Psychological Bulletin, 73,* 1–16.

Simonton, D. K. (1994). *Greatness: Who makes history and why?* New York: Guilford.

Simonton, D. K. (1998). Historiometric methods in social psychology. *European Review of Social Psychology, 9,* 267–293.

Simonton, D. K. (2001, July 22). Comment on Kruglanski's "state of theory" article to Society of Personality and Social Psychology Internet Listserve members.

Simpson, J. A., Rholes, W. S., Campbell, L., & Wilson, C. L. (2003). Changes in attachment orientations across the transition to parenthood. *Journal of Experimental Social Psychology, 39,* 317–331.

Singelis, T. M., Triandis, H. C., Bhawuk, D. S., & Gelfand, M. (1995). Horizontal and vertical dimensions of individualism and collectivism: A theoretical and measurement refinement. *Cross-Cultural Research, 29,* 240–275.

Singh, D. (1993). Adaptive significance of female physical attractiveness: Role of waist-to-hip ratio. *Journal of Personality and Social Psychology, 65,* 293–307.

Singh, R., & Teoh, J. B. P. (2000). Impression formation from intellectual and social traits: Evidence for behavioral adaptation and cognitive processing. *British Journal of Social Psychology, 39,* 537–554.

Sivacek, J., & Crano, W. D. (1982). Vested interest as a moderator of attitude-behavior consistency. *Journal of Personality and Social Psychology, 43,* 210–221.

Skinner, B. F. (1938). *The behavior of organisms.* New York: Appleton-Century-Crofts.

Skitka, L. J. (1999). Ideological and attributional boundaries on public compassion: Reactions to individuals and communities affected by a natural disaster. *Personality and Social Psychology Bulletin, 25,* 793–808.

Sloman, S. A. (2002). Two systems of reasoning. In T. Gilovich, D. Griffin, & D. Kahneman (Eds.) *Heuristics and biases: The psychology of intuitive judgment* (pp. 379–396). Cambridge, England: Cambridge University Press.

Smith, A. E., Jussim, L., & Eccles, J. (1999). Do self-fulfilling prophecies accumulate, dissipate, or remain stable over time? *Journal of Personality and Social Psychology, 77,* 548–565.

Smith, A., & Berard, S. P. (1982). Why are human subjects less concerned about ethically problematic research than human subjects committees? *Journal of Applied Social Psychology, 12,* 209–221.

Smith, D. (1976, August). *Sexual aggression in American pornography: The stereotype of rape.* Paper presented at the American Sociological Association meetings, New York City.

Smith, E. R., & Henry, S. (1996). An ingroup becomes part of the self: Response time evidence. *Personality and Social Psychology Bulletin, 22,* 635–642.

Smith, E. R., Coats, S., & Walling, D. (1999). Overlapping mental representations of self, ingroup, and partner: Further response time evidence for a connectionist model. *Personality and Social Psychology Bulletin, 25,* 873–882.

Smith, E. R., Fazio, R. H., & Cejka, M. A. (1996). Accessible attitudes influence categorization of multiply categorizable objects. *Journal of Personality and Social Psychology, 71,* 888–898.

Smith, G. F., & Dorfman, D. D. (1975). The effect of stimulus uncertainty on the relationship between frequency of exposure and liking. *Journal of Personality and Social Psychology, 31,* 150–155.

Smith, G. L., & DeWine, S. (1991). Perceptions of subordinates and requests for support: Are males and females perceived differently when seeking help? *Organizational Studies, 16,* 408–427.

Smith, G. T., Hohlstein, L. A., & Atlas, J. G. (1989, August). *Race differences in eating disordered behavior and eating-related experiences.* Paper presented at the 97th annual convention of the American Psychological Association, New Orleans, LA.

Smith, J. M., & Szathmáry, E. (1995). *The major transitions in evolution.* Oxford, England: W. H. Freeman.

Smith, M. B. (2002). Self and identity in historical/sociocultural context: "Perspectives on selfhood" revisited. Y. Kashima, M. Foddy, & M. Platow (Eds.), *Self and identity: Personal, social and symbolic* (pp. 229–243). Mahwah, NJ: Erlbaum.

Smith, M. B., Bruner, J. S., & White, R. W. (1956). *Opinions and personality.* New York: Wiley.

Smith, N. K., Cacioppo, J. T., Larsen, J. T., & Chartrand, T. L. (2003). May I have your attention please: Electrocortical responses to positive and negative stimuli. *Neuropsychologia, 41,* 171–183.

Smith, P. B., Peterson, M. F., Bond, M., & Misumi, J. (1990). Leadership style and leader behaviour in individualistic and collectivist cultures. In S. Iwawaki, Y. Kashima, & K. Leung (Eds.), *Innovations in cross-cultural psychology* (pp. 76–85). Amsterdam: Swets & Zeitlinger.

Smith, R. J. (2004, July 23). Operational relationship with Al Qaeda discounted. *Washington Post.* (p. A01).

Smith, S. M., & Shaffer, D. R. (1991). Celerity and cajolery: Rapid speech may promote or inhibit persuasion through its impact on message elaboration. *Personality and Social Psychology Bulletin, 17,* 663–669.

Smith, S. M., & Shaffer, D. R. (2000). Vividness can undermine or enhance message processing: The moderating role of vividness congruency. *Personality and Social Psychology Bulletin, 26,* 769–779.

Smith, S. M., Haugtvedt, C. P., & Petty, R. E. (1994). Humor can either enhance or disrupt message processing: The moderating role of humor relevance. Unpublished manuscript.

Smith, S. M., McIntosh, W. D., & Bazzani, D. G. (1999). Are the beautiful good in Hollywood? An investigation of the beauty-and-goodness stereotype on film. *Basic and Applied Social Psychology, 21,* 69–80.

Smith, S. S., & Moore, M. R. (2000). Intraracial diversity and relations among African Americans: Closeness among Black students at a dominantly White University. *American Journal of Sociology, 106,* 1–39.

Snodgrass, J. G., & Thompson, R. L. (1997). *The self across psychology: Self-recognition, self-awareness, and the self-concept.* New York: New York Academy of Sciences.

Snyder, M. (1974). The self-monitoring of expressive behavior. *Journal of Personality and Social Psychology, 30,* 526–537.

Snyder, M. (1987). *Public appearances/private realities: The psychology of self-monitoring.* New York: Freeman.

Snyder, M., & Cunningham, M. R. (1975). To comply or not to comply: Testing the self-perception explanation of the foot-in-the-door phenomenon. *Journal of Personality and Social Psychology, 31,* 64–67.

Snyder, M., & DeBono, K. G. (1985). Appeals to image and claims about quality: Understanding the psychology of advertising. *Journal of Personality and Social Psychology, 49,* 586–597.

Snyder, M., & Gangestad, S. (1982). Choosing social situations: Two investigations of self-monitoring processes. *Journal of Personality and Social Psychology, 43,* 123–135.

Snyder, M., & Simpson, J. A. (1984). Self-monitoring and dating relationships. *Journal of Personality and Social Psychology, 47,* 1281–1291.

Snyder, M., & Swann, W. B. (1978). Hypothesis-testing processes in social interaction. *Journal of Personality and Social Psychology, 36,* 1202–1212.

Snyder, M., Tanke, E. D., & Berscheid, E. (1977). Social perception and interpersonal behavior: On the self-fulfilling nature of social stereotypes. *Journal of Personality and Social Psychology, 35,* 656–666.

Sohlberg, S., & Birgegard, A. (2003). Persistent complex subliminal activation effects: First experimental observations. *Journal of Personality and Social Psychology, 85,* 302–316.

Solano, C. H., & Koester, N. H. (1989). Loneliness and communication problems: Subjective anxiety or objective skills? *Personality and Social Psychology Bulletin, 15,* 126–133.

Son Hing, L. S., Li, W., & Zanna, M. P. (2002). Inducing hypocrisy to reduce prejudicial responses among aversive racists. *Journal of Experimental Social Psychology, 38,* 71–78.

Sorrentino, R. M. (2003). Motivated perception and the warm look: Current perspectives and future directions. In S. J. Spencer, S. Fein, M. P. Zanna, & J. M. Olson (Eds.), *Motivated social perception: The Ontario symposium,* Vol. 9, pp. 299–316. Mahwah, NJ: Erlbaum.

Sorrentino, R. M., & Higgins, E. T. (1986). Motivation and cognition: Warming to synergism. In R. M. Sorrentino & E. T. Higgins (Eds.), *The handbook of motivation and cognition: Foundations of social behavior* (pp. 3–19). New York: Guilford.

Spaulding, C. (1970). The romantic love complex in American culture. *Sociology and Social Research, 55,* 82–100.

Spears, R., Lea, M., Corneliussen, R. A., Postmes, T., & ter Haar, W. (2002). Computer-mediated communication as a channel for social resistance: The strategic side of SIDE. *Small Group Research, 33,* 555–574.

Spencer-Rodgers, J., Peng, K., Wang, L., & Hou, Y. (2004). Dialectical self-esteem and East-West differences in psychological well-being. *Personality and Social Psychological Bulletin, 30,* 1416–1432.

Spencer, S. J., Steele, C. M., & Quinn, D. M. (1999). Stereotype threat and women's math performance. *Journal of Experimental Social Psychology, 35,* 4–28.

Spitz, R. A. (1945). Hospitalism: An inquiry into the genesis of psychiatric conditions in early childhood. In A. Freud (Ed.), *The psychoanalytic study of the child* (Vol. 1, pp. 53–74). New York: International Universities Press.

Spitzer, B. L., Henderson, K. A., & Zivian, M. T. (1999). Gender differences in population versus media body sizes: A comparison over four decades. *Sex Roles, 40,* 545–565.

Spivey, C. B., & Prentice-Dunn, S. (1990). Assessing the directionality of deindividuated behavior: Effects of deindividuation, modeling, and private self-consciousness on aggressive and prosocial responses. *Basic and Applied Social Psychology, 11,* 387–403.

Sprecher, S. (1992). How men and women expect to feel and behave in response to inequity in close relationships. *Social Psychology Quarterly, 55,* 57–69.

Sprecher, S. (1999). "I love you more today than yesterday": Romantic partners' perceptions of changes in love and related affect over time. *Journal of Personality and Social Psychology, 76,* 46–53.

Sprecher, S., & Felmlee, D. (1992). The influence of parents and friends on the quality and stability of romantic relationships: A three wave longitudinal investigation. *Journal of Marriage and the Family, 54,* 888–900.

Sprecher, S., & Toro-Morn, M. (2002). A study of men and women from different sides of earth to determine if men are from Mars and women are from Venus in their beliefs about love and romantic relationships. *Sex Roles, 46,* 131–147.

Sprecher, S., Metts, S., Burleson, B., Hatfield, E., & Thompson, A. (1995). Domains of expressive interaction in intimate relationships: Associations with satisfaction and commitment. *Family Relations, 44,* 1–8.

Sprecher, S., Sullivan, Q., & Hatfield, E. (1994). Mate selection preferences: Gender differences examined in a national sample. *Journal of Personality and Social Psychology, 66,* 1074–1080.

Staats, A. W., & Staats, C. K. (1958). Attitudes established by classical conditioning. *Journal of Abnormal and Social Psychology, 57,* 37–40.

Staats, A. W., Staats, C. K., & Crawford, H. L. (1962). First-order conditioning of meaning and the parallel conditioning of a GSR. *Journal of General Psychology, 67,* 159–167.

Stagner, R. (1986). Reminiscences about the founding of SPSSI. *Journal of Social Issues, 42,* 35–42.

Stamps, A. E., III. (2002). Meta-analysis. In R. B. Bechtel & A. Churchman (Eds.), *Handbook of environmental psychology* (pp. 222–232). New York: Wiley.

Stangor, C., & McMillan, D. (1992). Memory for expectancy-congruent and expectancy-incongruent information: A review of the social and social developmental literatures. *Psychological Bulletin, 111,* 42–61.

Stangor, C., Lynch, L., Duan, C., & Glass, B. (1992). Categorization of individuals on the basis of multiple social features. *Journal of Personality and Social Psychology, 62,* 207–218.

Stangor, C., Swim, J. K., Sechrist, G. B., DeCoster, J., & Van Allen, K. L. (2003). Ask, answer, and announce: Three stages in perceiving and responding to discrimination. *European Review of Social Psychology, 14.*

Stanovich, K. E. (2004). Balance in psychological research: The dual process perspective. *Behavioral and Brain Sciences, 27.*

Stanovich, K. E., & West, R. F. (2002). Individual differences in reasoning: Implications for the rationality debate? In T. Gilovich, D. Griffin, & D. Kahneman (Eds.). *Heuristics and biases: The psychology of intuitive judgment.* (pp. 421–440). Cambridge, England: Cambridge University Press.

Stanton, W. R., Currie, G. D., Oei, T. P. S., & Silva, P. A. (1996). A developmental approach to influences on adolescents' smoking and quitting. *Journal of Applied and Developmental Psychology, 17,* 307–319.

Stapel, D. A., Koomen, W., & Spears, R. (1999). Framed and misfortuned: Identity salience and the whiff of scandal. *European Journal of Social Psychology, 29,* 397–402.

Staub, E. (2004). Understanding and responding to group violence: Genocide, mass killing, and terrorism. In F. M. Moghaddam & A. J. Marsella. (Eds.), *Understanding terrorism: Psychosocial roots, consequences, and interventions* (pp. 151–168). Washington, DC: American Psychological Association.

Staudinger, U. M., Freund, A. M., Linden, M., & Maas, I. (1999). Self, personality, and life regulation: Facets of psychological resilience in old age. In P. B. Baltes & K. U. Mayer (eds), *The Berline Aging Study: Aging from 70 to 100* (pp. 302–328). New York: Cambridge University Press.

Steele, C. M. (1988). The psychology of self-affirmation: Sustaining the integrity of the self. In L. Berkowitz (Ed.), *Advances in experimental social psychology* (Vol. 21, pp. 261–302). New York: Academic Press.

Steele, C. M. (1997). A threat in the air: How stereotypes shape intellectual identity and performance. *American Psychologist, 52,* 613–629.

Steele, C. M., & Aronson, J. (1995). Stereotype threat and the intellectual test performance of African-Americans. *Journal of Personality and Social Psychology, 68,* 797–811.

Steele, C. M., & Josephs, R. A. (1990). Alcohol myopia: Its prized and dangerous effects. *American Psychologist, 45,* 921–933.

Steele, C. M., & Liu, T. J. (1981). Making the dissonant act unreflective of self: Dissonance avoidance and the expectancy of a value-affirming response. *Personality and Social Psychology Bulletin, 7,* 393–397.

Steele, C. M., Spencer, S. J., & Aronson, J. (2002). Contending with group image: The psychology of stereotype and social identity threat. In M. P. Zanna (Ed.), *Advances in experimental social psychology* (Vol. 34, pp. 379–440). San Diego: Academic Press.

Steele, C. M., Spencer, S. J., & Lynch, M. (1993). Self-image resilience and dissonance: The role of affirmational resources. *Journal of Personality and Social Psychology, 64,* 885–896.

Steele, C. M., Spencer, S. J., Hummel, M., Carter, K., Harber, K., Schoem, D., & Nisbett, R. (in press). African-American college achievement: A "wise" intervention. *Harvard Educational Review.*

Steinberg, L. D., Catalano, R., & Dooley, D. (1981). Economic antecedents of child abuse and neglect. *Child Development, 52,* 975–985.

Steinberg, L., & Morris, A. S. (2001). Adolescent development. *Annual Review of Psychology, 52,* 83–110.

Steinberg, L., Dornbusch, S. M., & Brown, B. B. (1992). Ethnic differences in adolescent achievement: An ecological perspective. *American Psychologist, 47,* 723–729.

Stelmack, R. M., & Geen, R. G. (1992). The psychophysiology of extraversion. In A. Gale & M. W. Eysenck (Eds.), *Handbook of individual differences: Biological perspectives* (pp. 227–254). New York: Wiley.

Stephan, W. G. (1980). A brief historical overview of school desegregation. In W. G. Stephan & J. R. Feagin (Eds.), *School desegregation: Past, present, and future* (pp. 3–24). New York: Plenum.

Stephan, W., Stephan, C., & de Vargas, M. (1996). Emotional expression in Costa Rica and the United States. *Journal of Cross-Cultural Psychology, 27,* 147–160.

Stepper, S., & Strack, F. (1993). Proprioceptive determinants of emotional and nonemotional feelings. *Journal of Personality and Social Psychology, 64,* 211–220.

Sternberg, R. J. (1986). A triangular theory of love. *Psychological Review, 93,* 119–135.

Sternberg, R. J. (1997). Construct validation of a triangular love scale. *European Journal of Social Psychology, 27,* 313–335.

Stets, J. E., & Burke, P. J. (1996). Gender, control, and interaction. *Social Psychology Quarterly, 59,* 193–220.

Stevens, C. K., & Kristof, A. L. (1995). Making the right impression: A field study of applicant impression management during job interviews. *Journal of Applied Psychology, 80,* 587–606.

Stewart, E. C., & Bennett, M. J. (1991). *American cultural patterns: A cross-cultural perspective.* Yarmouth, ME: Intercultural Press.

Stiles, W. B., Walz, N. C., Schroeder, M. A. B., Williams, L. L., & Ickes, W. (1996). Attractiveness and disclosure in initial encounters of mixed-sex diads. *Journal of Social and Personal Relationships, 13,* 303–312.

Stockdale, M. S. (1993). The role of sexual misperceptions of women's friendliness in an emerging theory of sexual harassment. *Journal of Vocational Behavior, 42,* 84–101.

Stokes, J. P. (1987). The relation of loneliness and self-disclosure. In V. J. Derlega & J. H. Berg (Eds.), *Self-disclosure: Theory, research, and therapy* (pp. 175–202). New York: Plenum.

Stokes, J., & Levin, I. (1986). Gender differences in predicting loneliness from social network characteristics. *Journal of Personality and Social Psychology, 51,* 1069–1074.

Stone, J. (2003). Self-consistency for low self-esteem in dissonance processes: The role of self-standards. *Personality and Social Psychology Bulletin, 29,* 846–858.

Stone, J., Lynch, C. I., Sjomeling, M., & Darley, J. M. (1999). Stereotype threat effects on Black and White athletic performance. *Journal of Personality and Social Psychology, 77,* 1213–1227.

Stone, J., Wiegand, A. W., Cooper, J., & Aronson, E. (1997). When exemplification fails: Hypocrisy and the motive for self-integrity. *Journal of Personality and Social Psychology, 72,* 54–65.

Stone, L. (1977). *The family, sex and marriage in England: 1500–1800.* New York: Harper & Row.

Stoner, J. A. F. (1961). *A comparison of individual and group decisions involving risk.* Unpublished master's thesis, MIT, Cambridge, MA.

Storms, M. D. (1973). Videotape and the attribution process: Reversing actors' and observers' points of view. *Journal of Personality and Social Psychology, 27,* 165–175.

Strack, F., & Deutsch, R. (2004). Reflective and impulsive determinants of social behavior. *Personality and Social Psychology Review, 8,* 220–247.

Strack, F., & Deutsch, R. (in press). Reflective and impulsive determinants of social behavior. *Personality and Social Psychology Review.*

Strack, F., Martin, L. L., & Stepper, S. (1988). Inhibiting and facilitating conditions of facial expressions: A nonobtrusive test of the facial feedback hypothesis. *Journal of Personality and Social Psychology, 54,* 768–777.

Strahan, E. J., Spencer, S. J., & Zanna, M. P. (2002). Subliminal priming and persuasion: Striking while the iron is hot, *Journal of Experimental Social Psychology, 38,* 556–568.

Strassberg, D. S., & Holty, S. (2003). An experimental study of women's Internet personal ads. *Archives of Sexual Behavior, 32,* 253–260.

Stratham, A., & Rhoades, K. (2001). Gender and self-esteem: Narrative and efficacy in the negotiation of structural factors. In T. J. Owens, S. Stryker, & N. Goodman (Eds.), *Extending self-esteem theory and research: Sociological and psychological currents* (pp. 255–284). Cambridge: Cambridge University Press.

Straus, M. A., & Gelles, R. J. (1990). *Physical violence in American families: Risk factors and adaptations to violence in 8,145 families.* New Brunswick, NJ: Transaction.

Straus, M. A., Gelles, R. J., & Steinmetz, S. K. (1980). *Behind closed doors: Violence in the American family.* Garden City, NY: Doubleday/Anchor.

Strauss, B. (2002). Social facilitation in motor tasks: A review of research and theory. *Psychology of Sport and Exercise, 3,* 237–256.

Street, R. L., Jr., & Brady, R. M. (1982). Speech rate acceptance ranges as a function of evaluative domain, listener speech rate, and communication context. *Communication Monographs, 49,* 290–308.

Streeter, S. A., & McBurney, D. H. (2003). Waist-to-hip ratio and attractiveness: New evidence and a critique of a "critical test." *Evolution and Human Behavior, 24,* 88–98.

Striegel-Moore, R. H., Silberstein, L. R., & Rodin, J. (1993). The social self in bulimia nervosa: Public self-consciousness, social anxiety, and perceived fraudulence. *Journal of Abnormal Psychology, 102,* 297–303.

Stroessner, S. J., Hamilton, D. L., & Mackie, D. M. (1992). Affect and stereotyping: The effect of induced mood on distinctiveness-based illusory correlations. *Journal of Personality and Social Psychology, 62,* 564–576.

Struch, N., & Schwartz, S. H. (1989). Intergroup aggression: Its predictor and distinctness from in-group bias. *Journal of Personality and Social Psychology, 56,* 364–373.

Stryker, S. (1997). "In the beginning there is society": Lessons from a sociological social psychology. In C. McGarty & S. A. Haslam (Eds.), *The message of social psychology: Perspectives on mind in society* (pp. 315–327). Cambridge, MA: Blackwell.

Stuphorn, I. S., Brown, J. W., & Schall, J. D. (2003). Performance monitoring by the anterior cingulated cortex during saccade countermanding. *Science, 302,* 120–122.

Stuss, D. T., Gallup, G. G., & Alexander, M. P. (2001). The frontal lobes are necessary for "theory of mind." *Brain, 124,* 279–286.

Suh, E. J., Moskowitz, D. S., Fournier, M. A., & Zuroff, D. C. (2004). Gender relationships: Influences on agentic and communal behaviors. *Personal Relationships, 11,* 41–59.

Suls, J., & Fletcher, B. (1985). Self-attention, life stress, and illness: A prospective study. *Psychosomatic Medicine, 47,* 469–481.

Sumner, W. (1906). *Folkways.* New York: Ginn.

Sussman, N. M. (2000). The dynamic nature of cultural identity throughout cultural transitions: Why home is not so sweet. *Personality and Social Psychology Review, 4,* 355–373.

Swann, W. B., Jr. (1984). Quest for accuracy in person perception: A matter of pragmatics. *Psychological Review, 91,* 457–477.

Swann, W. B., Jr. (1990). To be adored or to be known? The interplay of self-enhancement and self-verification. In E. T. Higgins & R. M. Sorrentino (Eds.), *Handbook of motivation and cognition: Foundations of social behavior* (Vol. 2, pp. 408–448). New York: Guilford.

Swann, W. B., Jr. (1997). The trouble with change: Self-verification and allegiance to the self. *Psychological Science, 8,* 177–183.

Swann, W. B., Jr., & Ely, R. J. (1984). A battle of wills: Self-verification versus behavioral confirmation. *Journal of Personality and Social Psychology, 46,* 1287–1302.

Swann, W. B., Jr., Bosson, J. K., & Pelham, B. W. (2002). Different partners, different selves: The verification of circumscribed identities. *Personality and Social Psychology Bulletin, 28*, 1215–1228.

Swann, W. B., Jr., De La Ronde, C., & Hixon, J. G. (1994). Authenticity and positive strivings in marriage and courtship. *Journal of Personality and Social Psychology, 66*, 857–869.

Swann, W. B., Jr., Griffin, J. J., Predmore, S., & Gaines, B. (1987). The cognitive-affective crossfire: When self-consistency confronts self-enhancement. *Journal of Personality and Social Psychology, 52*, 881–889.

Swann, W. B., Jr., Kwan, V. S. Y., Polzer, J. T., & Milton, L. P. (2003). Fostering group identification and creativity in diverse groups: The role of individuation and self-verification. *Personality and Social Psychology Bulletin, 29*, 1396–1406.

Swann, W. B., Jr., Milton, L. P., & Polzer, J. T. (2000). Should we create a niche or fall in line? Identity negotiation and small group effectiveness. *Journal of Personality and Social Psychology, 79*, 238–250.

Swann, W. B., Jr., Rentfrow, P. J., & Guinn, J. S. (2002). Self-verification: The search for coherence. In C. R. Snyder & S. J. Lopez (Eds.), *Handbook of positive psychology* (pp. 366–381). New York: Oxford University Press.

Sweeney, P. D., Anderson, K., & Bailey, S. (1986). Attributional style in depression: A meta-analytic review. *Journal of Personality and Social Psychology, 50*, 974–991.

Swim, J. K., Ferguson, M. J., & Hyers, L. L. (1999). Avoiding stigma by distancing. *Basic and Applied Social Psychology, 21*, 61–68.

Swim, J. K., Hyers, L. L., Cohen, L. L., & Ferguson, M. J. (2001). *Everyday sexism: Evidence for its incidence, nature, and psychological impact from three daily diary studies.* Manuscript submitted for publication.

Swinton, W. (1880). *A complete course in geography: Physical, industrial, and political.* New York: Ivison, Blakeman, Taylor, & Co.

Symons, D. (1979). *The evolution of human sexuality.* New York: Oxford University Press.

t'Hart, P., Rosenthal, U., & Kouzmin, A. (1993). Crisis decision making: The centralization thesis revisited. *Administration and Society, 25*, 12–45.

Tajfel, H. (1982). *Social identity and intergroup relations.* Cambridge, England: Cambridge University Press.

Tajfel, H., & Turner, J. (1979). An integrative theory of intergroup conflict. In W. G. Austin & S. Worchel (Eds.), *The social psychology of intergroup relations.* Monterey, CA: Brooks/Cole.

Tajfel, H., Billig, M. G., Bundy, R. P., & Flament, C. (1971). Social categorization and intergroup behavior. *European Journal of Social Psychology, 1*, 149–178.

Tam, S.-f., Man, W.-k., & Ng, J. Y.-y. (2003). Eastern and western perspectives in social psychological research on rehabilitation. In K.-S. Yang, K.-K. Hwang, P. B. Pedersen, & I. Daibo (Eds.), *Progress in Asian social psychology: Conceptual and empirical contributions* (pp. 291–316). Westport, CT: Praeger.

Tanford, S., & Penrod, S. (1984). Social influence model: A formal integration of research on majority and minority influence. *Psychological Bulletin, 95*, 189–225.

Tangney, J. P., Wagner, P., Fletcher, C., & Gramzow, R. (1992). Shamed into anger? The relation of shame and guilt to anger and self-reported aggression. *Journal of Personality and Social Psychology, 62*, 669–675.

Tarde, G. (1903). *The laws of imitation.* (Elsie Clews Parson, Trans.). New York: Henry Holt. (Original work published in 1890).

Tata, J., Anthony, T., Lin, H., Newman, B., Tang, S., Millson, M., & Sivakumar, K. (1996). Proportionate group size and rejection of the deviate: A meta-analytic integration. *Journal of Social Behavior and Personality, 11*, 739–752.

Tavris, C. (1989). *Anger: The misunderstood emotion.* New York: Touchstone Books.

Taylor, J., & Riess, M. (1989). "Self-serving" attributions to valenced causal factors: A field experiment. *Personality and Social Psychology Bulletin, 15*, 337–348.

Taylor, S. E. (1998). The social being in social psychology. In D. T. Gilbert, S. T. Fiske, & G. Lindzey (Eds.), *The handbook of social psychology* (4th ed., pp. 58–95). New York: McGraw-Hill.

Taylor, S. E. (2004). Preparing for social psychology's future. *Journal of Experimental Social Psychology, 40*, 139–141.

Taylor, S. E., & Brown, J. D. (1988). Illusion and well-being. A social psychological perspective on mental health. *Psychological Bulletin, 103*, 193–210.

Taylor, S. E., & Fiske, S. T. (1975). Point of view and perceptions of causality. *Journal of Personality and Social Psychology, 32*, 439–445.

Taylor, S. E., Klein, L. C., Gruenewald, T. L., Gurung, R. A. R., & Fernandes-Taylor, S. (2003). In J. Suls & K. A. Wallston (Eds.), *Social psychological foundations of health and illness. Blackwell series in health psychology and behavioral medicine* (pp. 314–331). Malden, MA: Blackwell.

Taylor, S. E., Lerner, J. S., Herman, D. K., Sage, R. M., & McDowell, N. K. (2003). Portrait of the self-enhancer: Well adjusted and well liked or maladjusted and friendless? *Journal of Personality and Social Psychology, 84*, 165–176.

Teachman, B. A., Gapinski, K. D., Brownell, K. D., Rawlins, M., & Jeyaram, S. (2003). Demonstrations of implicit anti-fat bias: The impact of providing causal information and evoking empathy. *Health Psychology, 22*, 68–78.

Telles, E. E., & Marguia, E. (1990). Phenotype discrimination and income differences among Mexican Americans. *Social Science Quarterly, 71*, 682–696.

Tesser, A. (1988). Toward a self-evaluation maintenance model of social behavior. In L. Berkowitz (Ed.), *Advances in experimental social psychology* (Vol. 21, pp. 181–227). New York: Academic Press.

Tesser, A., & Bau, J. J. (2002). Social psychology: Who we are and what we do. *Personality and Social Psychology Review, 6*, 72–85.

Tetlock, P. E., & Kim, J. I. (1987). Accountability and judgment processes in a personality prediction task. *Journal of Personality and Social Psychology, 52*, 700–709.

Tetlock, P. E., Peterson, R. S., McGuire, C., Chang, S., & Feld, P. (1992). Assessing political group dynamics: A test of the groupthink model. *Journal of Personality and Social Psychology, 63*, 403–425.

Tetlock, P. E., Skitka, L., & Boettger, R. (1989). Social and cognitive strategies for coping with accountability: Conformity, complexity, and bolstering. *Journal of Personality and Social Psychology, 57*, 632–640.

Tharp, R. G. (1994). Intergroup differences among Native Americans in socialization and child cognition: An ethnogenetic analysis. In P. M. Greenfield & R. R. Cocking (Eds.), *Cross-cultural roots of minority child development* (pp. 87–105). Hillsdale, NJ: Erlbaum.

Theodore, P. S., & Basow, S. A. (2000). Heterosexual masculinity and homophobia: A reaction to the self? *Journal of Homosexuality, 40*, 31–48.

Theron, W. H., Matthee, D. D., Steel, H. R., & Ramirez, J. M. (2000). Direct and indirect aggression in women: A comparison between South African and Spanish university students. In J. M. Ramirez & D. S. Richardson (Eds.), *Cross-cultural approaches to research on aggression and reconciliation* (pp. 99–109). Huntington, NY: Nova.

Thibaut, J. W., & Kelley, H. H. (1959). *The social psychology of groups.* New York: Wiley.

Thoits, P. A. (1982). Conceptual, methodological, and theoretical problems in studying social support as a buffer against life stress. *Journal of Health and Social Behavior, 23*, 145–159.

Thoman, E. B. (1999). Morningness and eveningness: Issues for study of the early ontogeny of these circadian rhythms. *Human Development, 42*, 206–212.

Thomas, Fletcher, G. J. O., & Lange, C. (1997). One-line empathic accuracy in marital interaction. *Journal of Personality and Social Psychology, 72*, 839–850.

Thomas, G., & Fletcher, G. J. O. (1997). Empathic accuracy in close relationships. In W. Ickes (Ed.), *Empathic accuracy* (pp. 194–218). New York: Guilford.

Thomas, G., & Fletcher, G. J. O. (2003). Mind-reading accuracy in intimate relationships: Assessing the roles of the relationship, the target, and the judge. *Journal of Personality and Social Psychology, 85*, 1079–1094.

Thomas, M. H., Horton, R. W., Lippincott, E. C., & Drabman, R. S. (1977). Desensitization to portrayals of real-life aggression as a function of exposure to television violence. *Journal of Personality and Social Psychology, 35*, 450–458.

Thorndike, E. L. (1911). *Animal intelligence: Experimental studies.* New York: Macmillan.

Thornton, B., & Maurice, J. (1997). Physique contrast effect: Adverse impact of idealized body images for women. *Sex Roles, 37*, 433–439.

Thornton, K. C. (2003). When the source of embarrassment is a close other. *Individual Differences Research, 1*, 189–200.

Thurstone, L. L. (1928). Attitudes can be measured. *American Journal of Sociology, 33*, 529–554.

Tice, D. M. (1991). Esteem protection or enhancement? Self-handicapping motives and attributions differ by trait self-esteem. *Journal of Personality and Social Psychology, 60*, 711–725.

Tice, D. M., & Baumeister, R. F. (1985). Masculinity inhibits helping in emergencies: Personality does predict the bystander effect. *Journal of Personality and Social Psychology, 49*, 420–428.

Tice, D. M., Bratslavsky, E., & Baumeister, R. F. (2001). Emotional distress regulation takes precedence over impulse control: If you feel bad, do it! *Journal of Personality and Social Psychology, 80,* 53–67.

Tice, D. M., Butler, J. L., Muraven, M. B., & Stillwell, A. M. (1995). When modesty prevails: Differential favorability of self-presentation to friends and strangers. *Journal of Personality and Social Psychology, 69,* 1120–1138.

Timmers, M., Fischer, A. H., & Manstead, A. S. R. (1998). Gender differences in motives for regulating emotions. *Personality and Social Psychology Bulletin, 24,* 974–985.

Tjaden, P., & Thoennes, N. (2000). *Extent, nature, and consequences of intimate partner violence.* Washington, DC: U.S. Department of Justice.

Tolnay, S. E., & Beck, E. M. (1995). *A festival of violence: An analysis of Southern lynchings, 1882–1930.* Urbana: University of Illinois Press.

Tolstedt, B. E., & Stokes, J. P. (1984). Self-disclosure, intimacy, and the depenetration process. *Journal of Personality and Social Psychology, 46,* 84–90.

Tormala, Z. L., & Petty, R. E. (2002). What doesn't kill me makes me stronger: The effects of resisting persuasion on attitude certainty. *Journal of Personality and Social Psychology, 83,* 1298–1313.

Tower, R. K., Kelly, C., & Richards, A. (1997). Individualism, collectivism and reward allocation: A cross-cultural study in Russia and Britain. *British Journal of Social Psychology, 36,* 331–345.

Townsend, J. M., & Levy, G. D. (1990). Effects of potential partners' physical attractiveness and socioeconomic status on sexuality and partner selection. *Archives of Sexual Behavior, 19,* 149–164.

Townsend, J. M., & Wasserman, T. (1997). The perception of sexual attractiveness: Sex differences in variability. *Archives of Sexual Behavior, 26,* 243–268.

Tracey, T. J. (1994). An examination of the complementarity of interpersonal behavior. *Journal of Personality and Social Psychology, 67,* 864–878.

Tracey, T. J. G. (2004). Levels of interpersonal complementarity: A simplex representation. *Personality and Social Psychology Bulletin, 30,* 1211–1225.

Trafimow, D., & Finlay, K. A. (1996). The importance of subjective norms for a minority of people: Between-subjects and within-subjects analyses. *Personality and Social Psychology Bulletin, 22,* 820–828.

Trafimow, D., Triandis, H. C., & Goto, S. G. (1991). Some tests of the distinction between the private self and the collective self. *Journal of Personality and Social Psychology, 60,* 649–655.

Trapnell, P. D., & Campbell, J. D. (1999). Private self-consciousness and the five-factor model of personality: Distinguishing rumination from reflection. *Journal of Personality and Social Psychology, 76,* 284–304.

Trappey, C. (1996). A meta-analysis of consumer choice and subliminal advertising. *Psychology and Marketing, 13,* 517–530.

Travis, C. B., McKenzie, B., Wiley, D. L., & Kahn, A. S. (1988). Sex and achievement domain: Cognitive patterns of success and failure. *Sex Roles, 19,* 509–525.

Travis, L. E. (1925). The effect of a small audience upon eye-hand coordination. *Journal of Abnormal and Social Psychology, 20,* 142–146.

Triandis, H. C. (1972). *The analysis of subjective culture.* New York: Wiley.

Triandis, H. C. (1989). The self and social behavior in differing cultural contexts. *Psychological Review, 96,* 506–520.

Triandis, H. C., Botempo, R., Villareal, M. J., Asai, M., & Lucca, N. (1988). Individualism and collectivism: Cross-cultural perspectives on self-ingroup relationships. *Journal of Personality and Social Psychology, 54,* 323–338.

Triplett, N. (1897). The dynamogenic factors in pace-making and competition. *American Journal of Psychology, 9,* 507–533.

Trivers, R. L. (1971). The evolution of reciprocal altruism. *Quarterly Review of Biology, 46,* 35–57.

Trivers, R. L. (1983). The evolution of cooperation. In D. L. Bridgeman (Ed.), *The nature of prosocial development.* New York: Academic Press.

Trope, Y. (1998). Dispositional bias in person perception: A hypothesis-testing perspective. In J. M. Darley & J. Cooper (Eds.), *Attribution and social interaction: The legacy of Edward E. Jones* (pp. 67–97). Washington, DC: American Psychological Association.

Trudeau, K. J., & Devlin, S. (1996). College students and community service: Who, with whom, and why? *Journal of Applied Social Psychology, 26,* 1867–1888.

Trzesniewski, K. H., Donnellan, M. B., & Robins, R. W. (2003). Stability of self-esteem across the life span. *Journal of Personality and Social Psychology, 84,* 205–220.

Tschann, J. M. (1988). Self-disclosure in adult friendship: Gender and marital status differences. *Journal of Social and Personal Relationships, 5,* 65–81.

Tulving, E. (1997). Human memory. In M. S. Gazzaniga (Ed.). *Conversations in the cognitive neurosciences.* Cambridge, MA: M.I.T. Press.

Turner, C. W., Layton, J. F., & Simons, L. S. (1975). Naturalistic studies of aggressive behavior: Aggressive stimuli, victim visibility, and horn honking. *Journal of Personality and Social Psychology, 31,* 1098–1107.

Turner, J. C. (1985). Social categorization and the self-concept: A social cognitive theory of group behavior. In E. J. Lawler (Ed.), *Advances in group processes* (Vol. 2, pp. 77–122). Greenwich, CT: JAI Press.

Turner, J. C. (1987). *Rediscovering the social group: A self-categorization theory.* Oxford, England: Basil Blackwell.

Turnley, W. H., & Bolino, M. C. (2001). Achieving desired images while avoiding undesired images: Exploring the role of self-monitoring in impression management. *Journal of Applied Psychology, 86,* 351–360.

Tuten, T. L., & Bosnjak, M. (2002). Need to evaluate and the big-five factor model. In S. P. Shohov (Ed.), *Advances in psychology research* (Vol. 15, pp. 111–120). Hauppauge, NY: Nova Science.

Tversky, A., & Kahneman, D. (1973). Availability: A heuristic for judging frequency and probability. *Cognitive Psychology, 5,* 207–232.

Tversky, A., & Kahneman, D. (1974). Judgment under uncertainty: Heuristics and biases. *Science, 185,* 1124–1131.

Twenge, J. M. (1997). Changes in masculine and feminine traits over time: A meta-analysis. *Sex Roles, 36,* 305–325.

Twenge, J. M., & Campbell, W. K. (2001). Age and birth cohort differences in self-esteem: A cross-temporal meta-analysis. *Personality and Social Psychology Review, 5,* 321–344.

Twenge, J. M., Catanese, K. R., & Baumeister, R. F. (2003). Social exclusion and the deconstructed state: Time perception, meaninglessness, lethargy, lack of emotion, and self-awareness. *Journal of Personality and Social Psychology, 85,* 409–423.

Tyler, T. R. (1997). The psychology of legitimacy: A relational perspective on voluntary deference to authorities. *Personality and Social Psychology Review, 1,* 323–345.

Tyler, T. R., & Blader, S. L. (2000). *Cooperation in groups: Procedural justice, social identity, and behavioral engagement.* Philadelphia: Psychology Press.

U.S. Bureau of the Census. (1998). *Statistical abstract of the United States* (118th ed.). Washington, DC: U.S. Government Printing Office.

U.S. Department of Commerce. (2002). *A nation online: How Americans are expanding their use of the Internet.* Washington, DC: U.S. Government Printing Office.

U.S. House of Representatives. (1994). *Climate change action plan and assessment: Hearing before the Committee on Science, Space, and Technology, 103rd Congress, First Session* (Publication No. 79-623). Washington, DC: U.S. Government Printing Office.

Uehara, E. S. (1995). Reciprocity reconsidered: Gouldner's "moral norm of reciprocity" and social support. *Journal of Social and Personal Relationships, 12,* 483–502.

Uhlmann, E., & Swanson, J. (2004). Exposure to violent video games increases automatic aggressiveness. *Journal of Adolescence, 27,* 41–52.

Uleman, J. S. (1999). Spontaneous versus intentional inferences in impression formation. In S. Chaiken & Y. Trope (Eds.), *Dual-process theories in social psychology* (pp. 141–160). New York: Guilford.

Unger, L. S. (1996). The potential for using humor in global advertising. *Humor: International Journal of Humor Research, 9,* 143–168.

Unger, L. S., & Thumuluri, L. K. (1997). Trait empathy and continuous helping: The case of voluntarism. *Journal of Social Behavior and Personality, 12,* 785–800.

Unger, R. K. (2002). Them and us: Hidden ideologies—Differences in degree or kind? *Analyses of Social Issues and Public Policy, 2,* 43–52.

United Nations. (1991). Special topic: International migration studies. In *United Nations demographic year book.* New York: Author.

Vaes, J., Paladino, M. P., Castelli, L., Leyens, J.-P., & Giovanazzi, A. (2003). On the behavioral consequences of infrahumanization: The implicit role of uniquely human emotions in intergroup relations. *Journal of Personality and Social Psychology, 85,* 1016–1034.

Vala, J., Lima, M. L., & Caetano, A. (1996). Mapping European social psychology: Co-word analysis of the communications at the

10th general meeting of the EAESP. *European Journal of Social Psychology, 26,* 845–850.

Valsiner, J. (2000). *Culture and human development.* Thousand Oaks, CA: Sage.

van Baaren, R. B., Holland, R. W., Kawakami, K., & van Knippenberg, A. (2004). Mimicry and prosocial behavior. *Psychological Science, 15,* 71–74.

van Baaren, R. B., Holland, R. W., Steenaert, B., & van Knippenberg, A. (2003a). Mimicry for money: Behavioral consequences of imitation. *Journal of Experimental Social Psychology, 39,* 393–398.

van Baaren, R. B., Maddux, W. W., Chartrand, T. L., de Bouter, C., & van Knippenberg, A. (2003b). It takes two to mimic: Behavioral consequences of self-construals. *Journal of Personality and Social Psychology, 84,* 1093–1102.

van de Kragt, A. J. C., Dawes, R. M., Orbell, J. M., Braver, S. R., & Wilson, L. A. (1986). Doing well and doing good as ways of resolving social dilemmas. In H. A. M. Wilke, D. M. Messick, & C. G. Rutte (Eds.), *Experimental social dilemmas* (pp. 177–204). Frankfurt: Verlag Peter Lang.

Van der Zee, K., Oldersma, F., Buunk, B. P., & Bos, D. (1998). Social comparison preferences among cancer patients as related to neuroticism and social comparison orientation. *Journal of Personality and Social Psychology, 75,* 801–810.

van Dick, R., Wagner, U., Pettigrew, T. F., Christ, O., Wolf, C., Petzel, T., Castro, V. S., & Jackson, J. S. (2004). Role of perceived importance in intergroup contact. *Journal of Personality and Social Psychology, 87,* 211–227.

Van Hooff, M. H., Voorhorst, F. J., Kaptein, M. B., Hirasing, R. A., Koppenaal C., Schoemaker J. (2000). Insulin, androgen, and gonadotropin concentration, body mass index, and waist-to-hip ratio in the first years after menarche in girls with regular menstrual cycle, irregular menstrual cycles, or oligomenorrhea. *Journal of Clinical Endocrinology and Metabolism, 85,* 1394–1400.

Van Lange, P. A. M. (1999). The pursuit of joint outcomes and equality in outcomes: An integrative model of social value orientation. *Journal of Personality and Social Psychology, 77,* 337–349.

Van Lange, P. A. M., Otten, W., De Bruin, E. M. N., & Joireman, J. A. (1997). Development of prosocial, individualistic, and competitive orientations: Theory and preliminary evidence. *Journal of Personality and Social Psychology, 73,* 733–746.

Van Overwalle, R., & Jordens, K. (2002). An adaptive connectionist model of cognitive dissonance. *Personality and Social Psychology Review, 6,* 204–231.

Van Overwalle, R., & Labiouse, C. (2004). A recurrent connectionist model of person impression formation. *Personality and Social Psychology Review, 8,* 28–61.

Van Overwalle, R., Drenth, T., & Marsman, G. (1999). Spontaneous trait inferences: Are they linked to the actor or to the action? *Personality and Social Psychology Bulletin, 25,* 450–462.

Van Vugt, M. (2001). Community identification moderating the impact of financial incentives in a natural social dilemma: Water conservation. *Personality and Social Psychology Bulletin, 27,* 1440–1449.

Van Vugt, M., & De Cremer, D. (1999). Leadership in social dilemmas: The effects of group identification on collective actions to provide public goods. *Journal of Personality and Social Psychology, 76,* 587–599.

Van Vugt, M., & Hart, C. M. (2004). Social identity as social glue: The origins of group loyalty. *Journal of Experimental Social Psychology, 86,* 585–598.

Vandereycken, W. (1994). Emergence of bulimia nervosa as a separate diagnostic entity: Review of the literature from 1960 to 1979. *International Journal of Eating Disorders, 16,* 105–116.

Vangelisti, A. L., Knapp, M. L., & Daly, J. A. (1990). Conversational narcissism. *Communication Monographs, 57,* 251–274.

Vassar, M. J., & Kizer, K. W. (1996). Hospitalizations for firearm-related injuries: A population-based study of 9,562 patients. *Journal of the American Medical Association, 275,* 1734–1739.

Vaughn, B. E., & Langlois, J. H. (1983). Physical attractiveness as a correlate of peer status and social competence in preschool children. *Developmental Psychology, 19,* 561–567.

Verkuyten, M., & Hagendoorn, L. (1998). Prejudice and self-categorization: The variable role of authoritarianism and in-group stereotypes. *Personality and Social Psychology Bulletin, 24,* 99–110.

Verkuyten, M., Drabbles, M., & van den Nieuwenhuijzen, K. (1999). Self-categorization and emotional reactions to ethnic minorities. *European Journal of Social Psychology, 29,* 605–619.

Verplanken, B., & Orbell, S. (2003). Reflections on past behavior: A self-report index of habit strength. *Journal of Applied Social Psychology, 33,* 1313–1330.

Vescio, T. K., Snyder, M., & Butz, D. A. (2003). Power in stereotypically masculine domains: A social influence strategy X stereotype match model. *Journal of Personality and Social Psychology, 85,* 1062–1078.

Viki, G. T., Abrams, D., & Hutchison, P. (2003). The "true" romantic: Benevolent sexism and paternalistic chivalry. *Sex Roles, 49,* 533–537.

Vingilis, E., Wade, T. J., & Adlaf, E. (1998). What factors predict student self-rated physical health? *Journal of Adolescence, 21,* 83–97.

Vinokur, A. D., & Vinokur-Kaplan, D. (1990). In sickness and in health: Patterns of social support and undermining in older married couples. *Journal of Aging and Health, 2,* 215–241.

Visser, P. S., & Krosnick, J. A. (1998). The development of attitude strength over the life cycle: Surge and decline. *Journal of Personality and Social Psychology, 75,* 1389–1410.

Visser, P. S., Krosnick, J. A., & Simmons, J. P (2003). Distinguishing the cognitive and behavioral consequences of attitude importance and certainty: A new approach to testing the common-factor hypothesis. *Journal of Experimental Social Psychology, 39,* 118–141.

Vittengl, J. R., & Holt, C. S. (2000). Getting acquainted: The relationship of self-disclosure and social attraction to positive affect. *Journal of Social and Personal Relationships, 17,* 53–66.

Vohra, N. (2000). Are you likely to ingratiate in a context you are unfamiliar with? *Journal of the Indian Academy of Applied Psychology, 26,* 103–107.

Vohs, K. D., & Heatherton, T. F. (2001). Self-esteem and threats to self: Implications for self-construals and interpersonal perceptions. *Journal of Personality and Social Psychology, 81,* 217–230.

Vohs, K. D., & Schmeichel, B. J. (2003). Self-regulation and the extended now: Controlling the self alters the subjective experience of time. *Journal of Personality and Social Psychology, 85,* 217–230.

Von Hippel, W., Hawkins, C., & Schooler, J. W. (2001). Stereotype distinctiveness: How counterstereotypic behavior shapes the self-concept. *Journal of Personality and Social Psychology, 81,* 193–205.

Von, J. M., Kilpatrick, D. G., Burgess, A. W., & Hartman, C. R. (1991). Rape and sexual assault. In M. L. Rosenberg & M. A. Fenley (Eds.), *Violence in America: A public health approach* (pp. 95–122). New York: Oxford University Press.

Vorauer, J. D., & Kumhyr, S. M. (2001). Is this about you or me? Self- versus other-directed judgments and feelings in response to intergroup interaction. *Personality and Social Psychology Bulletin, 27,* 706–719.

Vrij, A. (2000). *Detecting lies and deceit: The psychology of lying and the implications for professional practice.* Chichester, UK: Wiley.

Vrij, A., Edward, K., & Bull, R. (2001). Stereotypical verbal and nonverbal responses while deceiving others. *Personality and Social Psychology Bulletin, 77,* 899–909.

Wagner, J. A. (1995). Studies of individualism-collectivism: Effects on cooperation in groups. *Academy of Management Review, 38,* 152–172.

Wagner, U., van Dick, R., Pettigrew, T. F., & Christ, O. (2003). Ethnic prejudice in East and West Germany: The explanatory power of intergroup contact. *Group Processes and Intergroup Relations, 6,* 22–36.

Walkner-Haugrud, L. K., Gratch, L. V., & Magruder, B. (1997). Victimization and perpetration rates of violence in gay and lesbian relationships: Gender issues explored. *Violence and Victims, 12,* 173–184.

Waller, D., Loomis, J. M., Gollege, R. G., Beall, A. C. (2002). Place learning in humans: The role of distance and direction information. *Spatial Cognition and Computation, 2,* 333–354.

Walster [Hatfield], E., Walster, G. W., & Traupmann, J. (1978). Equity and premarital sex. *Journal of Personality, 36,* 82–92.

Wänke, M., Bless, H., & Biller, B. (1996). Subjective experience versus content of information in the construction of attitude judgments. *Personality and Social Psychology Bulletin, 22,* 1105–1113.

Wänke, M., Bless, H., & Igou, E. R. (2001). Next to a star: Paling, shining, or both? Turning interexemplar contrast into interexemplar assimilation. *Personality and Social Psychology Bulletin, 27,* 14–29.

Wann, D. L., & Branscombe, N. R. (1990). Die-hard and fair-weather fans: Effects of identification on BIRGing and CORFing tendencies. *Journal of Sport and Social Issues, 14,* 103–117.

Wann, D. L., Haynes, G., McLean, B., & Pullen, P. (2003). Sport team identification and willingness to consider anonymous acts of hostile aggression. *Aggressive Behavior, 29,* 406–413.

Wanshaffe, K. R. (2002). Social facilitation in young toddlers. *Psychological Reports, 90,* 349–350.

Ward, A., Lyubomirsky, S., Sousa, L., & Nolen-Hoeksema, S. (2003). Can't quite commit: Rumination and uncertainty. *Personality and Social Psychology Bulletin, 29,* 96–107.

Wartella, E., & Reeves, B. (1985). Historical trends in research on children and the media: 1900–1960. *Journal of Communication, 35,* 118–133.

Wason, P. C. (1960). On the failure to eliminate hypotheses in a conceptual task. *Quarterly Journal of Experimental Psychology, 12,* 129–140.

Wasti, S. A., & Cortina, L. M. (2002). Coping in context: Sociocultural determinants of responses to sexual harassment. *Journal of Personality and Social Psychology, 83,* 394–405.

Wasti, S. A., Bergman, M. E., Glomb, T. M., & Drasgow, F. (2000). Test of the cross-cultural generalizability of a model of sexual harassment. *Journal of Applied Psychology, 85,* 766–778.

Waterman, C. K., Dawson, L. J., & Bologna, M. J. (1989). Sexual coercion in gay male and lesbian relationships: Predictors and implications for support services. *Journal of Sex Research, 26,* 118–124.

Waters, E., Merrick, S., Treboux, D., Crowell, J., & Albersheim, L. (2000). Attachment security in infancy and early adulthood: A twenty-year longitudinal study. *Child Development, 71,* 684–689.

Watson, D., Suls, J., & Haig, J. (2002). Global self-esteem in relation to structural models of personality and affectivity. *Journal of Personality and Social Psychology,83,* 185–197.

Watson, W. E., Kumar, K., & Michaelsen, L. K. (1993). Cultural diversity's impact on interaction process and performance: Comparing homogeneous and diverse task groups. *Academy of Management Journal, 36,* 590–602.

Way, N., Cowal, K., Gingold, R., Pahl, K., & Bissessar, N. (2001). Friendship patterns among African American, Asian American, and Latino adolescents from low-income families. *Journal of Social and Personal Relationships, 18,* 29–53.

Webb, T. L., & Sheeran, P. (2003). Can implementation intentions help to overcome ego-depletion? *Journal of Experimental Social Psychology, 39,* 279–286.

Webb, T. T., Looby, E. J., & Fults-McMurtery, R. (2004). African American men's perceptions of body figure attractiveness: An acculturation study. *Journal of Black Studies, 34,* 370–385.

Weber, E. U., Bockenholt, U., Hilton, D. J., & Wallace, B. (1993). Determinants of diagnostic hypothesis generation: Effects of information, base rates, and experience. *Journal of Experimental Psychology: Learning, Memory, and Cognition, 19,* 1151–1164.

Weber, J. G. (1994). The nature of ethnocentric attribution bias: Ingroup protection or enhancement? *Journal of Experimental Social Psychology, 30,* 482–504.

Wechsler, H. Lee, J. E., Kuo, M., Seibring, M. Nelson, T. F., & Lee, H. (2002). Trends in college binge drinking during a period of increased prevention efforts: Findings from 4 Harvard School of Public Health college alcohol study surveys, 1993–2001. *Journal of American College Health, 50,* 203–217.

Wechsler, H., & Kuo, M. (2000). College students define heavy episodic drinking and estimate its prevalence: Results of a national survey. *Journal of American College Health, 49,* 59–64.

Wechsler, H., Lee, J. E., Kuo, M., & Lee, H. (2000). College binge drinking in the 1990s: A continuing problem. *Journal of American College Health, 48,* 199–210.

Wechsler, H., Lee, J. E., Kuo, M., Seibring, M., Nelson, T. F., & Lee, H. (2002). Trends in college binge drinking during a period of increased prevention efforts: Findings for 4 Harvard Public School of Public Health College Study Surveys: 1993–2001. *Journal of American College Health, 50,* 203–217.

Wedell, D. H., & Parducci, A.(2000). Social comparison: Lessons from basic research on judgment. In J. Suls & L. Wheeler (Eds.), *Handbook of social comparison: Theory and research* (pp. 223–252). New York: Kluwer Academic/Plenum.

Wedell, D. H., Parducci, A., & Geiselman, R. E. (1987). A formal analysis of ratings of physical attractiveness: Successive contrast and simultaneous association. *Journal of Experimental Social Psychology, 23,* 230–249.

Wegener, D. T., & Petty, R. E. (1994). Mood management across affective states: The hedonic contingency hypothesis. *Journal of Personality and Social Psychology, 66,* 1034–1048.

Wegener, D. T., & Petty, R. E. (1995). Effects of mood on persuasion processes: Enhancing, reducing, and biasing scrutiny of attitude-relevant information. In L. L. Martin & A. Tesser (Eds.), *Striving and feeling: Interactions between goals and affect.* Hillsdale, NJ: Erlbaum.

Wegener, D. T., Petty, R. E., & Smith, S. M. (1995). Positive mood can increase or decrease message scrutiny: The hedonic contingency view of mood and message processing. *Journal of Personality and Social Psychology, 69,* 5–15.

Wegener, D. T., Petty, R. E., Dove, N. L., & Fabrigar, L. R. (2004). Multiple routes to resisting attitude change. In E.S. Knowles & J.A. Linn (Eds.), *Resistance and persuasion* (pp. 13–38). Mahwah NJ: Erlbaum.

Wegner, D. M. (1994). Ironic processes of mental control. *Psychological Review, 101,* 34–52.

Wegner, D. M., & Schneider, D. J. (2003). The white bear story. *Psychological Inquiry, 14,* 326–329.

Wegner, D. M., Erber, R., & Raymond, P. (1991). Transactive memory in close relationships. *Journal of Personality and Social Psychology, 61,* 923–929.

Weick, K. E. (1985). Systematic observational methods. In G. Lindzey & E. Aronson (Eds.), *The handbook of social psychology* (3rd ed., Vol. 1, pp. 567–634). New York: Random House.

Weigel, R. H., Vernon, D. T., & Tognacci, L. S. (1974). Increasing attitude-behavior correspondence by broadening the scope of the behavioral measure. *Journal of Personality and Social Psychology, 30,* 724–728.

Weinberger, M. G., & Campbell, L. (1991). The use and impact of humor in radio advertising. *Journal of Advertising Research, 30,* 44–52.

Weiner, B. (1980). A cognitive (attribution)-emotion-action model of motivated behavior: An analysis of judgments of help-giving. *Journal of Personality and Social Psychology, 39,* 186–200.

Weiner, B. (1982). The emotional consequences of causal attributions. In M. S. Clark & S. T. Fiske (Eds.), *Affect and cognition: The 17th annual Carnegie symposium on cognition* (pp. 185–210). Hillsdale, NJ: Erlbaum.

Weiner, B. (1986). *An attribution theory of motivation and emotion.* New York: Springer-Verlag.

Weiner, B. (1995). *Judgments of responsibility: A theory of social conduct.* New York: Guilford.

Weiner, B., Frieze, I., Kukla, A., Reed, L., Rest, S., & Rosenbaum, R. M. (1972). Perceiving the causes of success and failure. In E. E. Jones, D. E. Kanouse, H. H. Kelley, R. E. Nisbett, S. Valins, & B. Weiner (Eds.), *Attribution: Perceiving the causes of behavior* (pp. 95–120). Morristown, NJ: General Learning Press.

Weinfield, N. S., Sroufe, L. A., & Egeland, B. (2000). Attachment from infancy to early adulthood in a high-risk sample: Continuity, discontinuity, and their correlates. *Child Development, 71,* 695–702.

Weinshenker, N., & Siegel, A. (2002). Bimodal classification of aggression: Affective defense and predatory attack. *Aggression and Violent Behavior, 7,* 237–250.

Weinstein, R. S. (2002). *Reaching higher: The power of expectations in schooling.* Cambridge, MA: Harvard University Press.

Weir, W. (1984, October 15). Another look at subliminal "facts." *Advertising Age,* p. 46.

Weisbuch, M., Mackie, D. M., & Garcia-Marques, T. (2003). Prior source exposure and persuasion: Further evidence for misattributional processes. *Personality and Social Psychology Bulletin, 29,* 691–700.

Weissman, D. H., Giesbrecht, B., Song, A. W., Mangun, G. R., & Woldorff, M. G. (2003). Conflict monitoring in the human anterior cingulate cortex during selective attention to global and local object features. *NeuroImage, 19,* 1361–1368.

Weitzman, E. R., Nelson, T. F., & Wechsler, H. (2003). Taking up binge drinking in college: The influences of person, social group, and environment. *Journal of Adolescent Health, 32,* 26–35.

Weldon, E., & Gargano, G. M. (1988). Cognitive loading: The effects of accountability and shared responsibility on cognitive effort. *Personality and Social Psychology Bulletin, 14,* 159–171.

Wells, G. L., & Petty, R. E. (1980). The effects of overt head movements on persuasion: Compatibility and incompatibility of responses. *Basic and Applied Social Psychology, 1,* 219–230.

Welzel, C., Inglehart, R., & Klingemann, H.-D. (2003). The theory of human development: A cross-cultural analysis. *European Journal of Political Research, 42,* 341–379.

Wenzlaff, R. M., & Luxton, D. D. (2003). The role of thought suppression in depressive rumination. *Cognitive Therapy and Research, 27,* 293–308.

Werking, K. (1997). *We're just good friends.* New York: Guilford.

Werner, C. M., Kagehiro, D. K., & Strube, M. J. (1982). Conviction proneness and the authoritarian juror: Inability to disregard information or attitudinal bias? *Journal of Applied Psychology, 67,* 629–636.

Werth, L., & Foerster, J. (2002). Implicit person theories influence memory judgments: The circumstances under which metacognitive knowledge is used. *European Journal of Social Psychology, 32,* 353–362.

West, J. O. (1988). *Mexican-American folklore.* Little Rock, AK: August House.

West, S. G., & Brown, T. J. (1975). Physical attractiveness, the severity of the emergency and helping: A field experiment and interpersonal simulation. *Journal of Experimental Social Psychology, 11,* 531–538.

Wheeler, L., & Kim, Y. (1997). What is beautiful is culturally good: The physical attractiveness stereotype has different content in collectivist cultures. *Personality and Social Psychology Bulletin, 23,* 795–800.

Wheeler, L., Koestner, R., & Diener, R. E. (1982). Related attributes in the choice of comparison others: It's there but it isn't all there is. *Journal of Experimental Social Psychology, 18,* 489–500.

Wheeler, L., Reis, H., & Nezlek, J. (1983). Loneliness, social interaction, and sex roles. *Journal of Personality and Social Psychology, 45,* 943–953.

Whitbeck, L. B., & Hoyt, D. R. (1994). Social prestige and assortive mating: A comparison of students from 1956 and 1988. *Journal of Social and Personal Relationships, 11,* 137–145.

White, G. L. (1980a). Inducing jealousy: A power perspective. *Personality and Social Psychology Bulletin, 6,* 222–227.

White, G. L. (1980b). Physical attractiveness and courtship progress. *Journal of Personality and Social Psychology, 39,* 660–668.

White, G. L., Fishbein, S., & Rutstein, J. (1981). Passionate love: The misattribution of arousal. *Journal of Personality and Social Psychology, 41,* 56–62.

White, M., & LeVine, R. A. (1986). What is an *Ii ko* (good child)? In H. Stevenson, H. Azuma, & K. Hakuta (Eds.), *Child development and education in Japan* (pp. 55–62). New York: Freeman.

Whiting, B. B., & Edwards, C. P. (1988). *Children of different worlds: The foundation of social behavior.* Cambridge, MA: Harvard University Press.

Whitley, B. E. (1999). Right-wing authoritarianism, social dominance orientation, and prejudice. *Journal of Personality and Social Psychology, 77,* 126–134.

Whyte, W. F. (1994). *Participant observer: An autobiography.* Ithaca, NY: ILR Press.

Wicker, A. W. (1969). Attitude versus actions: The relationship of verbal and overt behavioral responses to attitude objects. *Journal of Social Issues, 25,* 41–78.

Widom, C. S. (1989). Does violence beget violence? A critical examination of the literature. *Psychological Bulletin, 106,* 3–28.

Wigboldus, D. H. J., Dijksterhuis, A., & Knippenberg, A. V. (2003). When stereotypes get in the way: Stereotypes obstruct stereotype-inconsistent trait inferences. *Journal of Personality and Social Psychology, 84,* 470–484.

Wiggins, J. A., Dill, F., & Schwartz, R. D. (1965). On "status-liability." *Sociometry, 28,* 197–209.

Wilke, H. A. M. (1996). Status congruence in small groups. In E. Witte & J. Davis (Eds.), *Understanding group behavior: Vol. 2. Small group processes and interpersonal relations* (pp. 67–91). Hillsdale, NJ: Erlbaum.

Willan, V. J., & Pollard, P. (2003). Likelihood of acquaintance rape as a function of males' sexual expectations, disappointment, and adherence to rape-conducive attitudes. *Journal of Social and Personal Relationships, 20,* 637–661.

Williams, D. G. (1985). Gender, masculinity-femininity, and emotional intimacy in same-sex friendship. *Sex Roles, 12,* 587–600.

Williams, K. D. (2001). *Ostracism: The power of silence.* New York: Guilford.

Williams, K. D., & Sommer, K. L. (1997). Social ostracism by coworkers: Does rejection lead to loafing or compensation? *Personality and Social Psychology Bulletin, 23,* 693–706.

Williams, K. D., & Zadro, L. (2001). Ostracism: On being ignored, excluded, and rejected. In M. Leary (Ed.), *Interpersonal rejection* (pp. 21–53). New York: Oxford Press.

Williams, K. D., Cheung, D. K. T., & Choi, W. (2000). Cyberostracism: Effects of being ignored over the internet. *Journal of Personality and Social Psychology, 79,* 748–762.

Williams, K. D., Harkins, S., & Latané, B. (1981). Identifiability as a deterrent to social loafing: Two cheering experiments. *Journal of Personality and Social Psychology, 40,* 303–311.

Williams, K. D., Jackson, J. M., & Karau, S. J. (1995). Collective hedonism: A social loafing analysis of social dilemmas. In D. A. Schroeder (Ed.), *Social dilemmas: Perspectives on individuals and groups* (pp. 116–141). Westport, CT: Praeger.

Williams, W. L. (1992). The relationship between male-male friendship and male-female marriage. In P. M. Nardi (Ed.), *Men's friendships* (pp. 186–200). Newbury Park, CA: Sage.

Willingham, D. T., & Dunn, E. W. (2003). What neuroimaging and brain localization can do, cannot do, and should not do for social psychology. *Journal of Personality and Social Psychology, 85,* 662–671.

Wilson, B. J., Donnerstein, E., Linz, D., Kunkel, D., Potter, J., Smith, S. L., Blumenthal, E., & Gray, T. (1998). Content analysis of entertainment television: The importance of context. In J. T. Hamilton (Ed.), *Television violence and public policy* (pp. 13–53). Ann Arbor, MI: University of Michigan Press.

Wilson, D. W. (1981). Is helping a laughing matter? *Psychology, 18,* 6–9.

Wilson, E. O. (1996). *In search of nature.* Washington, DC: Island Press.

Wilson, M. S., & Liu, J. H. (2003). Social dominance orientation and gender: The moderating role of gender identity. *British Journal of Social Psychology, 42,* 187–198.

Wilson, T. D., Lindsey, S., & Schooler, T. Y. (2000). A model of dual attitudes. *Psychological Review, 107,* 101–126.

Wilson, T. D.(2002). *Strangers to ourselves: Discovering the adaptive unconscious.* Boston: Harvard University Press.

Windschild, P. D., & Wells, G. L. (1997). Behavioral consensus information affects people's inferences about population traits. *Personality and Social Psychology Bulletin, 23,* 148–156.

Winstead, B. A. (1986). Sex differences in same-sex friendships. In V. J. Derlega & B. A. Winstead (Eds.), *Friendship and social interaction* (pp. 81–100). New York: Springer-Verlag.

Wittenbaum, G. M. (1998). Information sampling in decision-making groups: The impact of members' task-relevant status. *Small Group Research, 29,* 57–84.

Wittenbaum, G. M., & Stasser, G. (1996). Management of information in small groups. In J. L. Nye & A. M. Brower (Eds.), *What's social about social cognition? Research on socially shared cognition in small groups* (pp. 3–28). Thousand Oaks, CA: Sage.

Wittenbaum, G. M., Hubbell, A. P., & Zuckerman, C. (1999). Mutual enhancement: Toward an understanding of the collective preference for shared information. *Journal of Personality and Social Psychology, 77,* 967–978.

Witvliet, C. V. O., Ludwig, T. E., & Vander Laan, K. L. (2001). Granting forgiveness or harboring grudges: Implications for emotion, physiology, and health. *Psychological Science, 12,* 117–123.

Woll, S. (2002). *Everyday thinking: Memory, reasoning, and, judgment in the real world.* Mahwah, NJ: Lawrence Erlbaum.

Wonderly, D. M. (1996). *The selfish gene pool: An evolutionarily stable system.* Lanham, MD: University Press of America.

Wood, J. N. (2004). Social cognitive neuroscience: The perspective shift in progress. *Behavioral and Brain Sciences, 27.*

Wood, J. V. (1996). What is social comparison and how should we study it? *Personality and Social Psychology Bulletin, 22,* 520–537.

Wood, J. V., Heimpel, S. A., & Michela, J. L. (2003). Savoring versus dampening: self-esteem differences in regulating positive affect. *Journal of Personality and Social Psychology, 85,* 566–580.

Wood, M. R., & Zurcher, Louis A. (1988) *The development of a postmodern self: A computer-assisted comparative analysis of personal documents.* New York: Greenwood Press.

Wood, W. L., Rhodes, N., & Biek, M. (1995). Working knowledge and attitude strength: An information-processing analysis. In R. E. Petty & J. A. Krosnick (Eds.), *Attitude strength: Antecedents and consequences* (pp. 283–313). Mahwah, NJ: Erlbaum.

Wood, W., & Kallgren, C. A. (1988). Communicator attributes and persuasion: Recipients' access to attitude-relevant information in memory. *Personality and Social Psychology Bulletin, 14,* 172–182.

Wood, W., Lundgren, S., Ouellette, J. A., Busceme, S., & Blackstone, T. (1994). Minority influence: A meta-analytic review of social influence processes. *Psychological Bulletin, 115,* 323–345.

Wood, W., Wong, F. Y., & Chachere, J. G. (1991). Effects of media violence on viewers' aggression in unconstrained social interaction. *Psychological Bulletin, 109,* 371–383.

Worchel, S., & Andreoli, V. M. (1978). Facilitation of social interaction through deindividuation of the target. *Journal of Personality and Social Psychology, 36,* 549–556.

Worringham, C. F., & Messick, D. M. (1983). Social facilitation of running: An unobtrusive study. *Journal of Social Psychology, 121,* 23–29.

Wosinska, W., Cialdini, R. B., Barrett, D. W., & Reykowski, J. (Eds.). (2001). *The practice of social influence in multiple cultures.* Mahwah, NJ: Erlbaum.

Wosinska, W., Dabul, A. J., Whetstone-Dion, R., & Cialdini, R. B. (1996). Self-presentational responses to success in the organization: The costs and benefits of modesty. *Basic and Applied Social Psychology, 18,* 229–242.

Wright, P. H. (1982). Men's friendships, women's friendships and the alleged inferiority of the latter. *Sex Roles, 8,* 1–20.

Wright, P. H., & Scanlon, M. B. (1991). Gender role orientations and friendship: Some attenuation, but gender differences abound. *Sex Roles, 24,* 551–566.

Wright, S. C., Aron, A., McLaughlin-Volpe, T., & Ropp, S. A. (1997). The extended contact effect: Knowledge of cross-group friendships and prejudice. *Journal of Personality and Social Psychology, 73,* 73–90.

Wrightsman, L. S., Kassin, S. M., & Willis, C. S. (1987). *In the jury box: Controversies in the courtroom.* Thousand Oaks, CA: Sage.

Wrosch, C., Scheier, M. F., Miller, G. E., Schulz, R., & Carver, C. S. (2003). Adaptive self-regulation of unattainable goals: Goal disengagement, goal reengagement, and subjective well-being. *Personality and Social Psychology Bulletin, 29,* 1494–1508.

Wyer, N. A., Sadler, M. S., & Judd, C. M. (2002). Contrast effects in stereotype formation and change: The role of comparative context. *Journal of Personality and Social Psychology, 38,* 443–458.

Wyland, C. L., Kelley, W. M., Macrae, C. N., Gordon, H. L., & Heatherton, T. F. (2003). Neural correlates of thought suppression. *Neuropsychologia, 41,* 1863–1867.

Xu, Y., & Burleson, B. R. (2001). Effects of sex, culture, and support type on perceptions of spousal social support: An assessment of the "support gap" hypothesis in early marriage. *Human Communication Research, 27,* 535–566.

Yamagishi, T. (1986). The provision of a sanctioning system as a public good. *Journal of Personality and Social Psychology, 51,* 110–116.

Yamagishi, T. (1988). Seriousness of social dilemmas and the provision of a sanctioning system. *Social Psychology Quarterly, 51,* 32–42.

Yamagishi, T., Tanida, S., Mashima, R., Shimona, E., & Kanazawa, S. (2003). You can judge a book by its cover: Evidence that cheaters may look different from cooperators. *Evolution and Human Behavior, 24,* 290–301.

Yancey, M. P., & Hummer, R. A. (2003). Fraternities and rape on campus. In M. Silberman (Ed.), *Violence and society: A reader* (pp. 215–222). Upper Saddle River, NJ: Prentice-Hall.

Yaniv, I. (in press). The benefits of additional opinions. *Current Directions in Psychological Science.*

Yost, J. H., & Weary, G. (1996). Depression and the correspondent inference bias: Evidence for more effortful cognitive processing. *Personality and Social Psychology Bulletin, 22,* 192–200.

Yousif, Y., & Korte, C. (1995). Urbanization, culture, and helpfulness: Cross-cultural studies in England and the Sudan. *Journal of Cross-Cultural Psychology, 26,* 474–489.

Yu, D. L., & Seligman, M. E. P. (2002). Preventing depressive symptoms in Chinese children. *Prevention & Treatment, 5,* n.p.

Yzerbyt, V. Y., Rocher, S., & Schadron, G. (1996). Stereotypes as explanations: A subjective essentialistic view of group perception. In R. Spears, P. J. Oakes, N. Ellemers, & S. A.

Haslam (Eds.), *The social psychology of stereotyping and group life.* Cambridge: Blackwell.

Zadro, L., Williams, K. D., & Richardson, R. (2004). How low can you go? Ostracism by a computer is sufficient to lower self-reported levels of belonging, control, self-esteem, and meaningful existence. *Journal of Experimental Social Psychology, 40,* 560–567.

Zahavi, A. (2003). Anniversary essay: Indirect selection and individual selection in sociobiology: My personal views on theories of social behavior. *Animal Behaviour, 65,* 859–863.

Zahn-Wexler, C., Robinson, J., & Emde, R. N. (1992). The development of empathy in twins. *Developmental Psychology, 28,* 1038–1047.

Zajonc, R. B. (1965). Social facilitation. *Science, 149,* 269–274.

Zajonc, R. B. (1968). Attitudinal effects of mere exposure. *Journal of Personality and Social Psychology Monograph Supplement, 9* (2, Part 2), 1–27.

Zajonc, R. B. (1984). On the primacy of affect. *American Psychologist, 39,* 117–123.

Zajonc, R. B. (1993). Brain temperature and subjective emotional experience. In M. Lewis & J. M. Haviland (Eds.), *Handbook of emotions* (pp. 209–220). New York: Guilford.

Zajonc, R. B., Murphy, S. T., & Inglehart, M. (1989). Feeling and facial efference: Implications of the vascular theory of emotion. *Psychological Review, 96,* 395–416.

Zanna, M. P., & Rempel, J. K. (1988). Attitudes: A new look at an old concept. In D. Bar-Tal & A. W. Kruglanski (Eds.), *The social psychology of knowledge* (pp. 315–334). New York: Cambridge University Press.

Zanna, M. P., Kiesler, C. A., & Pilkonis, P. A. (1970). Positive and negative attitudinal affect established by classical conditioning. *Journal of Personality and Social Psychology, 14,* 321–328.

Zanot, E. J., Pincus, J. D., & Lamp, E. J. (1983). Public perceptions of subliminal advertising. *Journal of Advertising, 12,* 37–45.

Zaragoza, M. S., & Mitchell, K. J. (1996). Repeated exposure to suggestion and the creation of false memories. *Psychological Science, 7,* 294–300.

Zárate, M. A., Garcia, B., Garza, A. A., & Hitlan, R. T. (2004). Cultural threat and perceived realistic group conflict as dual predictors of prejudice. *Journal of Experimental Social Psychology, 40,* 99–105.

Zdaniuk, B., & Levine, J. M. (2001). Group loyalty: Impact of members' identification and contributions. *Journal of Experimental Social Psychology, 37,* 502–509.

Zebrowitz, L. A. (1997). *Reading faces.* Boulder, CO: Westview.

Zebrowitz, L. A., & Montepare, J. M. (1992). Impressions of babyfaced individuals across the life span. *Developmental Psychology, 28,* 1143–1152.

Zebrowitz, L. A., Tenenbaum, D. R., & Goldstein, L. H. (1991). The impact of job applicants' facial maturity, sex, and academic achievement

on hiring recommendations. *Journal of Applied Social Psychology, 21,* 525–548.

Zebrowitz, L. A., Voinescu, L., & Collins, M. A. (1996). "Wide-eyed" and "crooked-faced": Determinants of perceived and real honesty across the life span. *Personality and Social Psychology Bulletin, 22,* 1258–1269.

Zhou, M. (2002). Between *us* and *them* in Chinese: Use of *lai* (come) and *qu* (go) in the construction of social identities. In A. Duszak (Ed.), *Us and others: Social identities across languages, discourses and cultures* (pp. 52–67). Amsterdam: John Benjamins Publishing.

Zillmann, D. (1983). Arousal and aggression. In R. G. Geen & E. I. Donnerstein (Eds.), *Aggression: Theoretical and empirical reviews: Vol. 1. Theoretical and methodological issues* (pp. 75–101). New York: Academic Press.

Zillmann, D. (1984). *Connections between sex and aggression.* Hillsdale, NJ: Erlbaum.

Zillmann, D. (1994). Cognition-excitation interdependencies in the escalation of anger and angry aggression. In M. Potegal & J. F. Knutson (Eds.), *The dynamics of aggression: Biological and social processes in dyads and groups* (pp. 45–71). Hillsdale, NJ: Erlbaum.

Zillmann, D., Katcher, A. H., & Milavsky, B. (1972). Excitation transfer from physical exercise to subsequent aggressive behavior. *Journal of Experimental Social Psychology, 8,* 247–259.

Zimbardo, P. (1969). The human choice: Individuation, reason, and order versus deindividuation, impulse, and chaos. In W. J. Arnold & D. Levine (Eds.), *Nebraska Symposium on Motivation, Vol. 17.* Lincoln: University of Nebraska Press.

Zimbardo, P. G. [Producer]. (1972). *The Stanford prison experiment.* [Slide/tape presentation].

Zlotnick, C., Kohn, R., Peterson, J., & Pearlstein, T. (1998). Partner physical victimization in a national sample of American families: Relationship to psychological functioning, psychosocial factors, and gender. *Journal of Interpersonal Violence, 13,* 156–166.

Zuckerman, E. W., & Jost, J. T. 92001). What makes you think you're so popular? Self-evaluation maintenance and the subjective side of the "friendship paradox." *Social Psychology Quarterly, 64,* 207–223.

Zuckerman, M., & Gerbasi, K. C. (1977). Belief in a just world and trust. *Journal of Research in Personality, 11,* 306–317.

Zuckerman, M., DePaulo, B. M., & Rosenthal, R. (1981). Verbal and nonverbal communication of deception. In L. Berkowitz (Ed.), *Advances in experimental social psychology* (Vol. 14, pp. 1–59). New York: Academic Press.

Zulawski, D. E., & Wicklander, D. E. (2002). *Practical aspects of interview and interrogation.* New York: CRC Press.

Zurcher, L. A. (1977). *The mutable self.* Beverly Hills, CA: Sage.

Zuwerink, J. R., Devine, P. G., Monteith, M. J., & Cook, D. A. (1996). Prejudice toward Blacks: With and without compunction? *Basic and Applied Social Psychology, 18,* 131–150.

TEXT AND LINE ART CREDITS

CHAPTER 2

Table 2.3: Reprinted with permission from H. Schuman, J. Scott, "Problems in the Use of Survey Questions to Measure Public Opinion," *Science* V. 236, p. 957–959, May 22, Copyright © 1987, AAAS. Used by permission of AAAS and the Institute for Social Research.

CHAPTER 3

Figure 3.3: Reprinted with permission from Miller, George A., Eugene Galanter, and Karl H. Pribram, *Plans and the Structure of Behavior,* 1960. Reprint. New York: Adams, Bannister, Cox, 1986. All rights reserved.

Figure 3.5: H.R. Markus, S. Kitayama, "Culture and the Self: Implications for Cognition, Emotion, and Motivation," *Psychological Review,* 98:224–253. Copyright © 1991 by the American Psychological Association. Reprinted with permission.

Table 3.3: A. Fenigstein, M.F. Scheier, A.H. Buss, "Public and Private Self-Consciousness: Assessment and Theory," *Journal of Consulting and Clinical Psychology,* 43:522–527. Copyright © 1975 by the American Psychological Association. Adapted with permission.

Table 3.5: From *Conceiving the Self,* by Morris Rosenberg, © 1979. Used by permission of The Morris Rosenberg Foundation, The University of Maryland.

CHAPTER 4

Table 4.2: K.M. Kelly, W.H. Jones, "Assessment of Dispositional Embarrassability," *Anxiety, Stress, and Coping,* 10:307–333. http://www.tandf.co.uk/journals Used by permission of Taylor & Francis Group.

Figure 4.3: L. Ross, T.M. Amabile, J. L. Steinmetz, "Social Roles, Social Control, and Biases in Social Perception Processes," in *Journal of Personality and Social Psychology* 35:485–494. Copyright © 1977 by the American Psychological Association. Adapted with permission.

Figure 4.5: M. D. Storms, "Videotape and the Attribution Process: Reversing Actors' and Observers' Points of View," *Journal of Personality and Social Psychology* 27:165–175. Copyright © 1973 by the American Psychological Association. Adapted with permission.

CHAPTER 5

Table 5.2: Z. Rubin, L.A. Peplau, "Just World Scale," in "Who Believes in a Just World," *Journal of Social Issues* 31:65–89, © 1975.

Used by permission of Blackwell Publishing Ltd.

Figure 5.3: N. Schwarz, H. Bless, F. Strack, G. Klumpp, Rittenauer-Schatka, A. Simon, "Ease of Retrieval as Information: Another Look at the Availability Heuristic," *Journal of Personality and Social Psychology,* 61:195–202. Copyright © 1991 by the American Psychological Association. Adapted with permission.

Figure 5.5: From *Pygmalion in the Classroom* 1st edition by Rosenthal. © 1968. Reprinted with permission of Wadsworth, a division of Thomson Learning: ww.thomsonrights.com. Fax 800 730–2215.

CHAPTER 6

Figure 6.2: S.H. Schwartz, "Are there universal aspects in the content and structure of values?" *Journal of Social Issues,* 50, 19–45, Copyright Blackwell Publishing Ltd. Used by permission.

Figure 6.9: D.E. Linder, J. Cooper, E.E. Jones, "Decision Freedome as a Determinant of the role of Incentive Magnitude in Attitude Change," *Journal of Personality and Social Psychology,* 6:245–254. Copyright © 1967 by the American Psychological Association. Adapted with permission.

Figure 6.10: E. Aronson, J. Mills, "The Effect of Severity of Initiation on Liking for a Group," *Journal of Abnormal and Social Psychology,* 59:177–181, © 1959.

Table 6.1: W.B.G. Jarvis, R.E. Petty, "The Need to Evaluate," *Journal of Personality and Social Psychology,* 70, 172–194. Copyright © 1996 by the American Psychological Association. Adapted with permission.

Table 6.5: R. Cialdini, M. Trost, J. Newson, "Preference for Consistency: The Development of a Valid Measure and the Discovery of Surprising Behavioral Implications," *Journal of Personality and Social Psychology,* 69:318–328. Copyright © 1995 by the American Psychological Association. Adapted with permission.

CHAPTER 7

Excerpt pp. 225–226: Richard I. Evans, *The Making of Social Psychology: Discussions with Creative Contributors,* © 1980. Used by permission of the author, Richard I. Evans, Distinguished Professor of Psychology, University of Houston.

Figure 7.4: M. Snyder, K.G. DeBono, "Appeals to Image and Claims About Quality: Understanding the Psychology of Advertising," *Journal of Personality and Social Psychology,* 49:586–597. Copyright © 1985

by the American Psychological Association. Adapted with permission.

Figure 7.5: R.E. Petty, Z.L. Tormala, D.D. Rucker, "Resisting persuasion by counterarguing: An attitude strength perspective," *Social Psychology: The Yin and Yang of scientific progress,* p. 37–51. Copyright © 2004 by the American Psychological Association. Reprinted with permission.

Figure 7.6: R.L. Miller, P. Brickman, D. Bolen, "Attribution versus Persuasion as a Means for Modifying Behavior," *Journal of Personality and Social Psychology,* 31:430–441. Copyright © 1975 by the American Psychological Association. Reprinted with permission.

Figure 7.7: Reprinted from E.J. Strahan, S.J. Spencer, M.P. Zanna, "Subliminal priming and persuasion: Striking while the iron is hot," *Journal of Experimental Social Psychology,* 38, 556–568, Copyright © 2002, with permission from Elsevier.

Table 7.2: J.T. Cacioppo, R.E. Petty, "The Need for Cognition," *Journal of Personality and Social Psychology,* 42:116–131. Copyright © 1982 by the American Psychological Association. Adapted with permission.

CHAPTER 8

Table 8.1: "Three Forms of Prejudice," from *Understanding Genocide: The Social Psychology of the Holocause,* edited by Leonard Newman and Ralph Erber. Copyright by Oxford University Press, Inc. Used by permission of Oxford University Press, Inc.

Figure 8.2: Reprinted from D.L. Hamilton, R.K. Clifford, "Illusory Correlation in Interpersonal Judgments," *Journal of Experimental Social Psychology,* 12:392–407, Copyright © 1976, with permission from Elsevier.

Figure 8.6: C.W. Perdue, J.F. Dovidio, M.B. Gurtman, R.B. Taylor, "Us and Them: Social Categorization and the Process of Intergroup Bias," *Journal of Personality and Social Psychology,* 59:475–486. Copyright © 1990 by the American Psychological Association. Reprinted with permission.

Table 8.3: I. Katz, R.G. Hass, "Racial Ambivalence and American Value Conflict: Correlation and Prime Studies of Dual Cognitive Structures," *Journal of Personality and Social Psychology,* 55:893–905. Copyright © 1988 by the American Psychological Association. Adapted with permission.

Table 8.4: Peter Glick, Susan T. Fiske, "Ambivalent Sexism Inventory: Differentiating Hostile and Benevolent Sexism," *Journal of Personality and Social Psychology,* 70:491–512. Copyright 1995 by Peter Glick and Susan T. Fiske. Used by permission.

PHOTO CREDITS

NAME INDEX

Clark, E. M., 433
Clark, K. B., 84, 266, 583
Clark, M., 266, 583
Clark, M. P., 84
Clark, M. S., 445, 453
Clark, R. D., III, 549
Clary, E. G., 237
Clore, G. L., 422
Coan, D., 350
Coats, S., 268
Codol, J. P., 378
Cogan, J. C., 415
Cohen, D., 482, 512
Cohen, G. L., 303
Cohen, R. H., 60
Cohen, R. L., 208
Cohn, E. G., 502
Coker, D. R., 70
Cole, M., 448
Collins, B. E., 325
Collins, M. A., 413
Collins, N. L., 453
Collins, P. F., 403
Collins, R. L., 87
Colombo, J., 47
Comer, D. R., 368
Compton, R. J., 179
Comstock, G., 510
Comte, I. A., 533
Conger, J. A., 383, 448
Conger, J. D., 431
Congregation for the Doctrine of the Faith, 258
Conner, M., 175, 193
Conner, R. C., 536
Conrath, D. W., 406
Conway, L. G., 20
Conway, M., 224
Cook, G. I., 112
Cook, H. B. K., 492
Cook, S. W., 297, 299, 479
Cook, T. D., 40
Cooley, C. H., 62
Coombs, F. S., 189
Cooper, H., 76
Cooper, H. H. A., 494
Cooper, J., 199
Copper, C., 358
Corby, N. H., 193
Corney, R., 565
Correll, J., 268
Correll, S. J., 360
Cortina, L. M., 292
Cossrow, N. H. F., 260
Cottrell, N. B., 366
Cowan, G., 513
Cowan, G. A., 259
Cowan, P. A., 507
Cox, M. G., 111
Coyne, J. C., 475
Cozby, P. C., 460
Craig, R. S., 575
Crandall, C. S., 260, 299, 324, 416
Crano, W. D., 190, 330
Crawford, M., 274
Crenshaw, M., 494
Crichlow, S., 381
Crisp, R. J., 275
Critelli, J. W., 519
Crocker, J., 13, 58, 76, 81, 83, 261, 270
Croizet, J-C., 271, 274, 577
Cromwell, R. L., 266
Crosby, F., 229, 561
Cross, S. E., 72, 73, 404, 443, 446
Cross, W. E., 84

Crowley, A. E., 224
Crowley, M., 533, 562
Culos-Reed, S. N., 61
Cummings, E. M., 446
Cummings, J. S., 446
Cunningham, M. R., 335, 417, 428, 554, 555
Cunningham, P. B., 503
Cunningham, W. A., 21, 172, 174, 255, 277
Curran, J. P., 436
Curtis, R. C., 429
Cutrona, C., 433
Cutrona, C. E., 475

D

Dabbs, J. M., 497
Dakof, G. A., 564
Dallager, C., 527
Dall'Ara, E., 292
Daly, J. A., 430
Daly, M., 482, 492, 496, 519
Damasio, A. R., 65
Dambrun, M., 281
Dana, E. R., 66
Dardenne, B., 156
Darley, J. M., 13, 160, 341, 537, 544, 545, 546, 547,
     548, 549, 550, 551, 566, 567, 568
Darwin, C., 20, 105
Das, E. H. H. J., 222
Dasgupta, A. N., 255
Davidson-Podgorney, G., 302
Davies, M., 514
Davies, M. F., 63
Davila, J., 450
Davis, D., 449
Davis, C. G., 154, 410
Davis, C. M., 513
Davis, J. H., 375, 394
Davis, J. L., 426
Davis, K. E., 12, 117, 118, 426, 450, 478, 579
Davis, M. H., 62, 64, 434, 474, 559, 560
Davis, T. L., 110
Davison, J., Jr., 240
Dawes, R. M., 391
Dawkins, R., 21
Dawson, E., 156
Dawson, R. E., 234
Dean, K. E., 519
Deaux, K., 84, 268
Debono, K., 234
DeBono, K. G., 233
De Cecco, J. P., 461
De Cremer, D., 390
De Dreu, C. K. W., 391
DeFleur, M. L., 247
Dehle, C., 475
De Houwer, J., 173
Deiger, M., 383
Delgado-Gaitan, C., 15
Dembroski, T. M., 219
Demetriou, C., 370
DeNeve, K. M., 76
DePaulo, B. M., 107, 109, 131, 132, 430
Dèpret, E., 269, 270
Dèpret, E. F., 269
Depue, R. A., 403
Derlega, V., 455
Derlega, V. J., 423, 456
Desforges, D. M., 298
DeSteno, D. A., 482
Deutsch, M., 312, 320
Deutsch, R., 14
Devine, P. G., 21, 269, 287, 295, 296, 297, 299
Devlin, P. K., 259

Devlin, S., 535
DeVos, G., 72
de Waal, F., 109, 403
DeWine, S., 565
de Wit, J. B. F., 222
Diamond, L. M., 468
DiBaise, R., 456
Diekmann, K., 157
Diener, E., 371, 372, 414, 446, 559
Dijker, A. J., 263
Dijksterhuis, A., 142, 194, 263, 316, 317
Dijkstra, P., 481, 482
Dill, J. C., 123, 129
Dill, K. E., 511
Dillehay, R. C., 393, 394
Dimberg, U., 332
Dindia, K., 454
Dion, K. C., 472
Dion, K. K., 412, 413, 462, 469, 472
Dion, K. L., 462, 469
Dionne, E. J., Jr., 537, 562
Dittmann-Kohli, F., 237
Ditto, P. H., 156
Dodge, K. L., 478
Dodgson, P. G., 205
Dodwell, P., 136
Dolderman, D., 474
Dollard, J., 12, 498
Donnerstein, E., 513, 514
Doob, A. N., 201
Doob, L., 498
Doosje, B., 262
Dordick, G. A., 98
Dorfman, D. D., 227, 407
Dorfman, J., 15
Dossett, D. L., 194
Doty, R. M., 283
Douthitt, E. A., 366
Dovidio, J. F., 142, 174, 263, 264, 285, 287, 288,
     297, 298, 304, 552, 553, 562
Downey, G., 430
Downey, K. T., 259
Downing, R. L., 372
Downs, A. C., 419
Drabman, R. S., 511
Drachman, D., 219
Drigotas, S. M., 473
Dryer, D. C., 426
Duan, C., 557
Dubé, L., 224
DuBois, D. L., 571
DuCharme, K. A., 194
Duck, S., 434, 454
Duckitt, J., 256, 277, 282, 283, 284
Duclos, S. E., 183
Duff, R. W., 31
Dunbar, R., 358
Dunbar, R. I. M., 55, 357, 358
Duncan, C. P., 222
Dunkel-Schetter, C., 564
Dunn, E. W., 21
Dunn, J., 524
Dunning, D., 11, 14, 79, 127
Duntley, J. D., 495
Durlak, J. A., 571
Dutton, D. G., 466
Dutton, K. A., 79
Duval, S., 13, 61
Duval, T. S., 13, 65, 126

E

Eagly, A. H., 13, 109, 171, 209, 219, 220, 326, 327,
     386, 413, 428, 491, 533, 562

Subject Index

A

Academic achievement, promotion of, 302–303
Acquaintance rape, 518–519, 527–528
Action, men's bodies as instruments of, 419, 420t
Actor-observer effect, 124–126, 444
Affiliation needs, 400–405
  factors influencing, 402–405
  group satisfaction of, 363–364
  social comparison and, 401
  social exchange and, 401–402
Age
  loneliness and, 433
  susceptibility to persuasion and, 234–239
Aggression, 487–529, 579–580
  alcohol consumption and, 504–505
  biology of, 495–497
  cognitive-neoassociationist model of, 500–504
  delegitimization of outgroups and, 494
  frustration-aggression hypothesis of, 498–500
  gender and, 491–492
  instrumental versus hostile, 489–491
  intensification by excitation transfer, 505–506
  as intentional harm, 488–489
  media and video violence fostering, 509–512
  personality and, 493
  reducing, 522–526
  rewards of, 507
  sexual. See Rape; Sexual aggression
  social learning theory of, 506–509
Aggressive cues, 502–504
Aggressive scripts, 509
Alcohol consumption, aggression and, 504–505
Altruism. See Prosocial behavior
Altruistic helping, 533
Ambivalent prejudice, 256
Ambivalent sexism, 289–290, 291t
Amygdala, 255
Anchoring and adjustment heuristic, 148–149
Anonymity, improvement in group performance by, 369
Anterior cingulate, 55, 60, 65, 139, 255
Antiaggression beliefs, internalizing, 524–525
Anticonformity, 326
Anxiety
  affiliation need and, 408–412
  intergroup, 299–300
  social. See Social anxiety
  speech, alleviation of, 435–436
Apologies to control aggression, 525
Applied research, 26
Archival research, 33
Arousal, misattribution of, 431
Arousal:cost-reward model, 552–553
Associative meaning, illusory correlations and, 264
Attachment, 446–451
  as inborn adaptive response, 446–447
  influence on adult relationships, 448–451
  styles of, 447–448
Attention, schemas and, 142–143
Attitudes, 169–209, 574
  accessibility of, 190–191
  behavior as cause of, 182–183
  certainty of, counterargument and, 241–242
  classical conditioning of, 179–181
  cognitive consistency and, 194–205
  cognitive dissonance and. See Cognitive dissonance
  determinants of, 192
  dual, 174

as evaluations of objects, 171–172
  facial expression, head movement, and body posture related to, 183–185
  factors determining relationship to behavior, 188–191
  group membership and assumed similarity of, 206
  toward groups. See Heterosexism; Prejudice; Racism; Sexism
  implicit, underlying explicit attitudes, 174–175
  labeling and, 242–245
  mere exposure and, 177–179
  need satisfaction by, 185–187
  need to evaluate and, 172–174
  operant conditioning of, 181
  political, reference groups and, 207–209
  toward self. See Self-esteem
  shaping of intentions by, 191–194
  social, reference groups and, 207–209
  strength of, attitude-behavior relationship and, 189–190
  values shaping, 175–177
Attraction. See Interpersonal attraction; Physical attractiveness
Attribution(s), 95, 115–121
  biases in, 121–129
  correspondent inferences and, 117–119
  covariation principle and, 119–121
  external (situation), 116
  internal (person), 115–116
  intimacy and, 444
  locus of causality and, 115–116
  stability and controllability of causality and, 116–117
Audience inhibition effect, 547–549
Audience mood, persuasion and, 230–231
Authoritarianism, hostility toward outgroups and, 281–284
Authoritarian personality, 282–284
Availability heuristic, 147–148

B

Balance theory, 424
Base-rate fallacy, 147
Basic research, 26
Beauty, women's bodies as objects of, 418–419
Behavior
  attitudes and. See Attitudes
  nonverbal. See Nonverbal behavior
  planned, theory of, 191–194
Behavior genetics, aggression and, 497
Beliefs, 171
  confirmation bias and, 155–156
  just-world, 159–160, 562
  social, stereotypes as, 262–263
Biases
  in attribution, 121–129
  confirmation, 155–156, 222
  correspondence, 573
  hindsight, 151–153
  ingroup, 127, 275
  negativity, 113
  observer, 32
  partner-enhancing, 473
  positivity, 113
  self-serving, 126–129, 155, 473
  social desirability, 36
Biculturalism, self-concept and, 74–76
Body esteem, 419

Body movements, communication by, 106–107
Body posture, attitudes and, 183–185
Brain
  affiliation needs and, 403
  anterior cingulate of, 55, 60, 65, 139, 255
  caudate nucleus of, 464
  cerebral cortex of, 55–56
  frontal lobes of, 55, 56
  mirror neurons in, 108
Brain-imaging techniques, 21, 44–45
Bystander intervention, 544–553
  audience inhibition effect and, 547–549
  diffusion of responsibility and, 549–551
  emotional arousal and cost-reward assessments and, 551–553
  imagining presence of others and, 566

C

Campus Acquaintance Rape Education (CARE), 528
Careers in social psychology, 582–584
Categories, 139–141
Catharsis, 498
Caudate nucleus, 464
Causality
  locus of, 115–116
  stability and controllability of, 116–117
Caution, group decision making and, 376–377
Central nervous system. See also Brain
  activity of, affiliation needs and, 403
Central route to persuasion, 214
Central traits, impression formation and, 111–112
Cerebral cortex, 55–56
Characterization-correction model, 128–129, 142
Choice, freedom of, insufficient, cognitive dissonance and, 198
Classical conditioning
  attitude formation through, 179–181
  subliminal, 181
Closed-ended questions, 34–35
Cognition
  dual-process models of, 14–15
  explicit, 137, 138
  implicit, 137, 138
  need for, susceptibility to persuasion and, 232–233
Cognitive associations, male, about women, sex, hostility, and power, 526–527
Cognitive consistency, 194–205
  challenges to theory of, 202–205
  cognitive dissonance and. See Cognitive dissonance
  weak of motivation for, 201–202
Cognitive dissonance, 195–201
  freedom of choice and, 198
  insufficient justification and, 195–198
  justification of effort and, 198–200
  postdecision, altered perceptions and, 200–201
Cognitive intervention, higher-order, in aggression, 501–502
Cognitive-neoassociationist model of aggression, 500–504
Cognitive-response approach to persuasion, 213–216
Collectivism, 15, 16–18, 19
  affiliation needs and, 404
  conformity and, 327–328
  nonverbal cues and, 109
  romantic love and, 461–462
  self-concept and, 72–73

self-disclosure and, 451–453
superficial, 451
Frontal lobes, 55, 56
Frustration-aggression hypothesis, 498–500
Functional approach to attitudes, 185–187
Functional magnetic resonance imaging
(fMRI), 21, 44
Fundamental attribution error, 121–124
cultural differences and, 123–124
predictability need and perceptual salience and,
122–123

G

Game stage in development of self, 57
Gender. *See also* Females; Males
affiliation needs and, 404
aggression and, 491–492
conformity and, 326–327
disappearance of differences between, in
homosexual friendships, 458–459
experience of love and, 469–471
heterosexual friendships and, 454–457
leadership style and, 385–386
loneliness and, 433
self-concept and, 73–74
Gender identity, 70
Gender schemas, 70–71, 141–142
Gender socialization, nonverbal cues and, 109–110
Generosity, mood and, 554
Genetics, behavior, aggression and, 497
Group(s), 355–375, 577–578. *See also* Intergroup
entries
affiliation needs satisfied by, 363–364
assumed attitude similarity among members
of, 206
attitudes toward. *See* Heterosexism; Prejudice;
Racism; Sexism
cooperation in, 390–391
decision making in. *See* Group decision making
deindividuation and loss of individual identity
and, 370–373
group versus individual interests and, 387–390
instrumental task accomplishment by, 363–364
leadership of. *See* Leadership
lowering of inhibitions induced by, 370–373
phases of membership in, 360–362
reference, social and political attitudes and,
207–209
social facilitation by, 364–367
social loafing and, 367–369
structure of, 359–360
Group cohesiveness, 357–359
conformity and, 324
group size and, 357–358
member similarity and diversity and, 358–359
Group decision making, 374–381
cautiousness of, 376–377
decision rules and, 376
group polarization and, 377–378
groupthink and, 379–381
in juries, 392–394
majority influence in, 375–376
stages of, 374–375
types of issues and, 375
Group identity, solving social dilemmas and, 390
Group polarization, 377–378
Group size
cohesiveness and, 357–358
conformity and, 323–324
Groupthink, 379–381
research on, 381
symptoms of, 380–381
Guilt, falsely accepting, 349

H

Habits, 194
Head movement, attitudes and, 183–185
Health care, social psychology and, 582–583
Heat hypothesis of aggression, 502
Helping behavior. *See* Prosocial behavior
Heterosexism, 258–259
Heterosexual masculinity, 259
Heterosexual relationships, romantic relationships
and, 460–461
Heuristics, 146–150
Hindsight bias, 151–153
Homosexual friendships, 458–459
Hormones, aggression and, 497
Hostile aggression, 489–491
Humor, persuasion and, 222–224
Hypotheses, 28

I

Identity(ies)
ethnic, 83–84
gender, 70
group, solving social dilemmas and, 390
oppositional, 170–174
social. *See* Social identities
Ideology, 15
Idiosyncrasy credits, 382
Illusory correlations as basis of stereotypes, 264–266
Implementation stage of group decision making,
374–375
Implicit Association Test (IAT), 82, 175
Implicit attitudes, 174–175
Implicit cognition, 137, 138
Implicit personality theory, 112–113
Implicit prejudice, 255
Implicit self-esteem, 81
Impressionable years hypothesis, 234–235
Impression formation, 95, 105–114
cultural and personality influences on, 109–111
nonverbal behavior and, 105–109
positivity bias and negativity effect in, 113
primacy and recency effects in, 113–114
traits in, 111–113
Impression involvement, persuasion and, 231–232
Incompatible responses, aggression and, 523–524
Independence, 312
Independent self, 72–73
Independent variable, 39
Individual differences
in empathic responding, 559–561
in monitoring nonverbal cues, 110–111
in susceptibility to persuasion, 232–239
Individualism, 15–16, 18, 19
affiliation needs and, 404
conformity and, 327–328
nonverbal cues and, 109
romantic love and, 461–462
self-concept and, 72–73
Inference, correspondent, 117–119
Inferential statistics, 30
Informational influence
conformity and, 321
in group decision making, 374–375
Information dependence, 321
Informed consent, 47
Ingratiation, 99
Ingroup(s), 84, 327
Ingroup bias, 127, 275
Inhibitions, group-induced lowering of, 370–373
Insecure attachment style, 447
Institutional discrimination, 254–255
Institutional review boards (IRBs), 29, 46–47

Instrumental aggression, 489, 490–491
Intellective issues in group decision making,
374–375
Interaction effect, 41
Interactionism, 14
Interdependent self, 72–73
Intergroup anxiety, 299–300
Intergroup competition, prejudice and, 276–280
Intergroup conflict
reduction in schools, 302–303
social conditions that can reduce, 297–300
Intergroup contact to reduce prejudice, 300–302
Intergroup cooperation, reducing intergroup conflict
through, 298
Interjudge reliability, 33
Internal attribution, 115–116
Internal validity, 40
Internet, research uses of, 43–44
Interobserver reliability, 32
Interpersonal attraction, 399–439, 578–579
affiliation needs and, 400–405
anxiety and, 408–412
complementarity and, 426–428
familiarity and, 406–407
liking and, 428–429
physical attractiveness and. *See* Physical
attractiveness
proximity and, 406
similarity and, 422–426
social isolation and, 430–434
Intimacy, 441–484, 579
friendship and, 451–459
including another in one's self-concept and,
443–446
jealousy and, 481–483
in male relationships, avoidance of,
456–457
parent-child attachment and, 446–451
in romantic relationships. *See* Romantic
relationships
Intimidation, 98
Investigation phase of group membership,
360–361
Ironic reversal, 139
Issue involvement, persuasion and, 231–232

J

Jealousy, 481–483
Jigsaw classroom, 302–303
Judgmental issues in group decision making,
374–375
Juries, decision making by, 392–394
Justification, insufficient, cognitive dissonance and,
195–198
Just-world belief
helping behavior and, 562
psychological adjustment and, 159–160

K

Kin selection, helping and, 536
Knowledge function of attitudes, 186

L

Labeling, attitudes and, 242–245
Laboratory experiments, 40–42
Leadership, 382–387
contingency model of, 383–385
leaders as influence agents and, 382
styles of, 384, 385–386
transformational leaders and, 382–383
Learned helplessness, 160–161